Routledge History of World Philosophies
Volume 2

Routledge History of
World Philosophies

Since the publication of the first volumes in 1993, the prestigious
Routledge History of Philosophy, edited by G. H. R. Parkinson and
S. G. Shanker, has established itself as the most comprehensive chronological survey of Western philosophy available. It discusses the most
important philosophical movements from the sixth century BC up to
the present day. All the major figures in Western philosophy are covered
in detail in these volumes. The philosophers are clearly situated within
the cultural and scientific context of their time.

Within the main corpus of the *Routledge History of Philosophy*,
the Jewish and Islamic traditions are discussed in the context of Western
philosophy, with which they are inextricably linked. The *History of
Islamic Philosophy* and the *History of Jewish Philosophy* are designed
to supplement the core volumes by dealing specifically with these two
philosophical traditions; they provide extensive analysis of the most
significant thinkers and concepts. In keeping with the rest of the series,
each volume has a comprehensive index and bibliographies, and includes
chapters by some of the most influential scholars in the field. They
form the first volumes of a new series, *Routledge History of World
Philosophies*.

Routledge History of World Philosophies
Volume 2

History of Jewish Philosophy

EDITED BY

Daniel H. Frank and Oliver Leaman

London and New York

First published 1997
by Routledge
11 New Fetter Lane, London EC4P 4EE

Simultaneously published in the USA and Canada
by Routledge
29 West 35th Street, New York, NY 10001

Phototypeset in Garamond by Intype London Ltd

Printed and bound in Great Britain by TJ Press (Padstow) Ltd, Padstow, Cornwall

British Library Cataloguing in Publication Data
A catalogue record for this book is available from the British Library

Library of Congress Cataloging in Publication Data
A catalogue record for this book has been requested

ISBN 0-415-08064-9

Contents

CONTENTS

Contributors

Haggai Ben-Shammai, Department of Arabic Language and Literature, Hebrew University of Jerusalem

Alexander Broadie, Department of Philosophy, University of Glasgow

Elisheva Carlebach, Department of History, Queens College, City University of New York

Shalom Carmy, Department of Judaic Studies, Yeshiva University

Richard A. Cohen, Department of Religious Studies, University of North Carolina at Charlotte

Idit Dobbs-Weinstein, Department of Philosophy, Vanderbilt University

Lois C. Dubin, Department of Religion and Biblical Literature, Smith College

David Ellenson, Hebrew Union College–Jewish Institute of Religion, Los Angeles, California

Seymour Feldman, Department of Philosophy, Rutgers University

Mordecai Finley, Hebrew Union College–Jewish Institute of Religion, Los Angeles, California

Daniel H. Frank, Department of Philosophy, University of Kentucky

Lenn E. Goodman, Department of Philosophy, Vanderbilt University

Kenneth Hart Green, Department for the Study of Religion, University of Toronto

Steven T. Katz, Center for Judaic Studies, Boston University

Howard Kreisel, Department of History, Ben-Gurion University of the Negev

Daniel J. Lasker, Department of History, Ben-Gurion University of the Negev

Oliver Leaman, Department of Philosophy, Liverpool John Moores University

Harry Lesser, Department of Philosophy, Victoria University of Manchester

Ze'ev Levy, Department of Jewish History and Thought, University of Haifa

Charles H. Manekin, Department of Philosophy, University of Maryland at College Park

Abraham Melamed, Department of Jewish History and Thought, University of Haifa

Michael L. Morgan, Department of Philosophy, Indiana University

David N. Myers, Department of History, University of California at Los Angeles

David Novak, Department for the Study of Religion, University of Toronto

Judith Plaskow, Department of Religious Studies, Manhattan College

Richard H. Popkin, Department of Philosophy, Washington University; Departments of History and Philosophy, University of California at Los Angeles

T. M. Rudavsky, Department of Philosophy, Ohio State University

Norbert M. Samuelson, Department of Religion, Temple University

Marc Saperstein, Department of History, Washington University

Kenneth Seeskin, Department of Philosophy, Northwestern University

David Shatz, Department of Philosophy, Yeshiva University

Hava Tirosh-Rothschild, Department of Religious Studies, Indiana University

Steven M. Wasserstrom, Department of Religion, Reed College

David Winston, Center for Jewish Studies, Graduate Theological Union, Berkeley, California

Elliot R. Wolfson, Skirball Department of Hebrew and Judaic Studies, New York University

Preface

This volume is planned as a companion to the Routledge *History of Islamic Philosophy*, and both take their place in the *Routledge History of World Philosophies*, a series designed to supplement and amplify the *Routledge History of Philosophy*. The idea of placing histories of Islamic and Jewish philosophy in such close proximity to a history of Western philosophy is in our view timely and important. Jewish and Islamic philosophy are often viewed as mere footnotes in general histories of Western philosophy. The reason for this is not hard to discover. The 'West' has historically been defined in exclusivist terms, in ways which make no reference to Judaism or Islam, by contrast to Greco-Roman, Christian, and Enlightenment culture. All these designations seem to bypass the traditions of Judaism and Islam. Of course, there are liminal cases, Spinoza perhaps being the prime example. But the example tends to prove the rule: Spinoza was excommunicated from the Jewish community.

But as scholarship proceeds apace, such cultural imperialism as supports an exclusivist understanding of the 'West' cannot stand. More and more we learn about Jewish Hellenism (no oxymoron), the Jewish roots of Christianity, and a Jewish Enlightenment, and what we learn is that Jews gave as much as they took. Such a dialectical interchange makes most timely the appearance of a history of Jewish philosophy which strives to present Jewish philosophy as part of the general history of Western philosophy. In this regard it is to be noted that our authors are not simply concerned with direct historical influences of Jewish thinkers upon non-Jewish thinkers, such as Maimonides upon Aquinas, but they are also concerned to show how the philosophical issues which concerned Greek, Latin, and German thinkers had parallel developments in Jewish thought. The philosophical influences move in both directions, and this is as it should be if one views the philosophical traditions in the West as inclusive of non-Christian philosophical traditions. Jewish philosophy is desegregated by seeing both how it influences and how it is influenced by extra-Jewish sources. There simply is no Jewish philosophy apart from general philosophy. In this way, then, we hope that this volume will begin to break down long-established barriers.

This project commenced in autumn 1991 and was completed in summer 1995. That such a large undertaking proceeded so expeditiously is in no small measure due to the seriousness and hard work of all involved. We thank our contributors and the staff at Routledge (London) for their assistance. We are very grateful to Nina Edwards for her work on the index.

The editors worked together very closely during all stages of the project, from the pleasant task of inviting contributors to the more onerous one of demanding and correcting for a common bibliographic style. The organization of sections I and II is Frank's and of sections III and IV Leaman's, but we have both worked through the entire text.

Apart from thanking again all individuals involved for their effort, we acknowledge the financial assistance of the British Academy for a timely fellowship which allowed us to work together in Liverpool in summer 1994 and to make substantial progress on the volume.

Lexington, Kentucky   *Daniel H. Frank*
Liverpool, England   *Oliver Leaman*

August 1995
Elul 5755

CHAPTER 1

What is Jewish philosophy?

Daniel H. Frank

In his introduction to the English translation of Julius Guttmann's monumental *Die Philosophie des Judentums* (first edition, 1933), Zwi Werblowsky writes:

> Philosophers and historians may be at variance on the question of the nature, or even of the very existence, of constant factors or structures making up an "essence" of Judaism. It is not only philosophies – including philosophies of Judaism – that may change, but also the historian's views on the nature and historical function of earlier philosophical expressions. Perhaps sometime in the near or more distant future, a new history of the philosophy of Judaism will have to be written.[1]

We believe the time has come, and not only because of advances in historical scholarship. There has also been a reconsideration of the nature of the (essentialist) foundations upon which histories such as Guttmann's are written. As Werblowsky already noted in the 1960s, there is debate among philosophers and historians about the "very existence" of an essence of Judaism. This foundational debate is ongoing and now includes discussion of the nature or essence of philosophy itself.[2] At present everything seems unsettled. Little wonder, then, that the question before us – what is Jewish philosophy? – appears particularly timely, indeed timely in two senses. One sense has to do with the obvious relevance of the question in current debates; the other, foreshadowing a point I shall later stress, is perhaps best hinted at by Werblowsky himself at the end of his introduction:

> Guttmann's work stands out, not only as a reliable study which condenses sound and subtle scholarship, and a unique survey of the history of Jewish scholarship; it also represents the fruit and the summing up of an important period in the history of

Jewish scholarship. As such, it will remain a lasting monument of a significant phase in the history of Jewish philosophy and its attempt to elucidate not only Judaism, but also itself.[3]

What Werblowsky, writing approximately thirty years after Guttmann, is here penning is an obituary, an obituary to the kind of historical scholarship which Guttmann represents, as well as the presuppositions upon which it is based. In this "terminal" sense, then, the question before us is a timely one, wearing its lineage on its sleeve, as it were. The questions of our forebears remain, relevant to current concerns and yet evocative of a bygone era in the annals of scholarship.

The question, what is Jewish philosophy? is not a perennial one, although in the way it has often been discussed it may appear to be so. Usually it is supposed that the question is a query into the essence of Jewish philosophy, a property or set of properties that Jewish philosophy has always possessed and that distinguishes it from all other branches of philosophy. The discussion of the issue demands that one should isolate common strands in the thought of Philo, Saadia, Maimonides, Crescas, (maybe) Spinoza, Mendelssohn, Cohen, Buber, Rosenzweig, Levinas, and others. This may or may not be possible to do, but it is important to realize at once that reflection on the nature of Jewish philosophy is of comparatively recent vintage. We are fooled into thinking that the question, what is Jewish philosophy? is a perennial one, because its subject matter, Jewish philosophy, extends far into the past in a unified and connected way. But so characterized, the subject matter is question-begging, for the supposition that all the thinkers we have listed are Jewish philosophers, in some non-trivial sense, and that they are together engaged in something called "Jewish philosophy" is a construct *we* impose upon the past by virtue of the very question we are asking. Such a construction may or may not be legitimate, indeed may or may not be inevitable, but we ought at least to be aware of what we are doing when we ask about the nature of Jewish philosophy.

Much the most important part of any answer we give to our initial query into the nature of Jewish philosophy is that Jewish philosophy is an academic discipline. It is an invention, for reasons important to ponder, of nineteenth-century historians, intent on bringing together certain thinkers, while simultaneously excluding others. Before the invention of Jewish philosophy as an academic discipline no one asked or wondered about the nature of Jewish philosophy, quite simply because the subject did not exist. Put another way: a certain Platonism holds us captive. In the particular case before us, we think that there is a certain essence "out there," namely Jewish philosophy, awaiting study and analysis by historians. But that is not the way to understand the relation which obtains between a subject and the study of it. The discipline itself "makes" the subject as much as it studies it. What counts as relevant and essential is not transparent. Liminal cases are important here and establish the point I am trying to make. In Jewish philosophy, Spinoza comes readily to mind as the paradigm of a figure who wrecks any attempt to derive a definition or essence of the subject. Try as one might, as Wolfson more than others did, Spinoza reveals himself as a protean person for all seasons, defying any attempt at a neat categorization. And what this shows is that Jewish philosophy and its study are much more intimately related to one another than a simple-minded Platonism would have it. And with the demise of such a Platonism we free ourselves to ask about the motivation of those engaged in the study of Jewish philosophy, the impetus which led to the development of the academic discipline.

No one in premodern, indeed in much of modern times understood Jewish philosophy as a subdiscipline of philosophy, as a way of philosophizing. No one felt the need to ascertain the essence of Jewish philosophy – "philosophy among the Jews" as it was invariably (and reductively) construed – distinguishing it from every other kind of philosophy or mode of theological interpretation. Note that the claim here about the relative lack of interest in earlier times in a category of Jewish philosophy is not a claim about the status of philosophy in premodern times, although it is important to remember that such demarcations as we make between philosophy, science, and theology were not always so. In the Islamic world, wherein one finds the efflorescence of medieval Jewish philosophy from the tenth century on, there existed a branch of wisdom called *falsafa*; presumably those engaged in it had an image of themselves as philosophers (*falāsifa*). Once again, the claim is not that the philosophers had no image of themselves as such, but rather that neither they nor anyone else had an awareness of them as *Jewish* (or *Muslim*) philosophers. Neither Maimonides nor Gersonides nor even Mendelssohn, in the modern period, thought of himself as a Jewish philosopher. To the extent that they thought of themselves as philosophers, they imaged themselves as providing an interpretation of the biblical and rabbinic tradition according to universal, philosophical categories.[4] For them, the Bible is a philosophical book, and they interpret it accordingly. But such an interpretation of the tradition hardly amounts to what we call "Jewish philosophy," if by the latter we mean to refer to an inquiry that is "by a Jew and for Jews,"[5] with no universal implications whatsoever. For the classical Jewish philosophers, there is a duty for those able to philosophize to do so. And so they do. They philosophize about Judaism, they interpret the tradition in philosophical terms, discussing such (general) issues

3

as divine language, creation, providence, and prophecy. But such a philosophical interpretation of the tradition is in essence not an enterprise specific to Judaism. Consider Philo, the first Jewish philosophical commentator on the Bible, and his influence upon the early Church Fathers. Wolfson considers Philo and his exegetical method as foundational for religious philosophy in all three monotheistic traditions.[6] Again, Maimonides was a Jew and a philosopher, but he did not engage in something called "Jewish philosophy," and the *Guide* is not, except in the most trivial sense, "a Jewish book."[7] Maimonides did not philosophize in a certain, Jewish, way; rather he speculated about his tradition in philosophical terms, about issues of general import embedded in the traditional texts. In essence Averroes did the same thing, and little is to be gained by distinguishing the Maimonidean project from the Averroean one.

What begins to emerge from all this is that not only do we err in thinking that Jewish philosophy is some sort of natural kind, but we are also misled by the surface grammar of the phrase. To the extent that Jewish philosophy has any relevance to the classical thinkers, and here I would include some modern thinkers like Hermann Cohen, it must be parsed as "philosophy of Judaism." Jewish philosophy is not a branch of philosophy, a subdiscipline. Rather, it is, as previously noted, a way, among others, of interpreting the tradition, the philosophical way. The detractors of the *Guide* were surely wrong in thinking that what Maimonides was up to was at variance with the tradition. On the contrary, it was part of it, a way of understanding the tradition – the philosophical way.[8] So construed, the understanding of a particular religious tradition becomes the vehicle for speculation about a host of general philosophical issues. The project is analogous to that of any creative thinker's use of the past for present purposes. One thinks of MacIntyre's use of Aristotle, Murdoch's of Plato, and Gauthier's of Hobbes. History of philosophy becomes philosophy. Similarly, textual exegesis subserves theoretical (and practical[9]) concerns.[10]

If Jewish philosophy, understood as requiring a self-consciousness of itself as an idiosyncratically Jewish enterprise, cannot be imposed upon premodern times, it seems, not surprisingly, that one ought to turn to the modern period to fix the genesis of our initial question. Only with emancipation in the eighteenth and nineteenth centuries does the (consequent) fear of assimilation and loss necessitate the need to forge an identity, an identity, in the present context, of subject matter. And so one sees the emergence in the nineteenth century in Germany and, to a much lesser extent, in France of the writing of the history of the nominal subject matter of this book, Jewish philosophy.

To ask, then, about the nature of Jewish philosophy is to position oneself in a certain historical framework, one in which there is the felt need to establish a boundary, a marker whereby the definiendum gains legitimacy. Again, to ask about the nature of Jewish philosophy is to accede to a certain characterization of thinkers, ideas, and texts. And this may, of course, be a false characterization, false in the sense that it is insufficiently attentive to the historical context in which the grouped thinkers and their ideas were originally nested. Indeed, if I am right, there was no Jewish philosophy and there were no Jewish philosophers before the nineteenth-century historians of Jewish philosophy invented the subject. Husik's famous and oft-quoted remark at the end of his influential *A History of Mediaeval Jewish Philosophy* (1916), "there are Jews now and there are philosophers, but there are no Jewish philosophers and there is no Jewish philosophy,"[11] seems to me just backwards. For now there are Jewish philosophers, or at least individuals who imagine that they are engaged in something called "Jewish philosophy," whereas before the modern period, before the nineteenth century, there was no one who had such a thought. Again, this is not to suggest that there were no philosophical influences upon Jews – of course, Plato and Aristotle influenced Halevi, Maimonides, Gersonides, and del Medigo, and Kant influenced Mendelssohn (and vice versa). Nor is it to suggest that we are wrong in understanding and even interpreting the medieval Jewish thinkers and their immediate successors as part of the philosophical tradition. Rather the point is that their being influenced by current philosophical trends and the plain fact of their being Jews writing from within the tradition does not mean that they were engaged in something called "Jewish philosophy" or that in some non-trivial sense they were themselves Jewish philosophers.

As noted, Jewish philosophy came into being as a disciplinary response of Jewish academics to a particular historical condition, one which threatened the very identity and being of Jewish culture. Jewish philosophy came into being as an attempt to delineate, along standard academic lines, a certain body of literature. Perforce Jewish philosophy quickly came to exclude those elements which did not fit the regnant academic model. Mysticism was excluded from the discipline because of its (supposed) arationality, even though we have come to learn of its *philosophical* (Neoplatonic) antecedents. Again, to gain a foothold of academic respectability, Jewish philosophy quickly began to parallel, even ape, current trends. It still does.

But there is no a priori reason why Jewish philosophy must parallel non-Jewish philosophy. Why does it? Is it part of an assimilationist ideology, to which Scholem more than anyone else drew our attention?[12] It was Scholem's general charge against the proponents of Wissenschaft des Judentums that they, historians of Judaism, whitewashed the past in the service of a liberal, assimilationist, ultimately anti-Zionist agenda. Ought the great historians of Jewish philosophy to stand accused of the same charge? Why really has the history of mysticism been so notably absent in histories of Jewish philosophy? To answer in a positivist way that its absence is due to its unphilosophical nature is, first, to be historically misinformed and, second and most importantly, to evince a way of doing the history of philosophy which is patently derivative, driven by current or recent trends.

Let us return to the initial question. At first it gave the appearance of an essentialist inquiry into the nature of the subject. Now I hope we see that such an inquiry is a non-starter and that in fact the question is ill-formed or, at least, admits of a radically different answer than it originally suggested. For now the simple answer to the question, what is Jewish philosophy? is: Jewish philosophy is an academic discipline invented in the nineteenth century by scholars intent on gaining a foothold of academic respectability. I pass no value judgement here whatever. I hope merely to provide a bit of genealogy. In this regard I stand with Nietzsche in attempting to "historicize" what too often is taken in an atemporal sense.

I have intimated at a great divide between premodern and modern times. But more important is a distinction, not quite identical to the temporal one alluded to, between history and tradition. A distinction there is, but it can be overdrawn. History, historical events can be appealed to in order to confirm tradition. Further, tradition is not monolithic and unchanging. Traditional Jews and Judaism are as multiform as are their varieties of self-understanding. Maimonides writes the *Guide* to help a co-religionist understand the tradition in a new (and better) way. Presumably such (self-)understanding constitutes in itself a transformation or change in the tradition; at least it constitutes a change in the life of a traditional Jew.

But while we must guard against an overdichotomization of the distinction between history and tradition, there is no doubt that at some point in the recent past such traditional bonds as held the community together began to fray. Prior to this, tradition (texts and norms) was the explicandum for all thoughtful Jews; even Spinoza presents his critique of the rabbinic tradition as congruent with the intentions of the foundational texts, as the best reading of the tradition. But with the advent of modernity, which I would place well into the nineteenth century, tradition came to be viewed as the antithesis to progress and progressive thinking. In the course of such re-evaluation of the tradition, Orthodoxy came into being in response to reform. So too, Jewish philosophy came into being in response to traditional biblical exegesis. And with this a new set of problems and questions began to emerge, about autonomy and community, the commensurability of reason and revelation, and, perhaps most significant, the historicization of tradition.

These are the problems of the modern philosopher. These are problems that arise at the end of the tradition, at a time when a certain distancing from the tradition has occurred. What we take to be the (obvious) dichotomy between reason and revelation did not arise before the modern separation of church and state. Averroes, Maimonides, and Aquinas never imagined that there was a problem about the commensurability of reason and revelation. Their respective projects were to understand and interpret revelation (the tradition) in the best way they knew how. Indeed, there was a divine injunction to do so. What to us seems like a problem of divided loyalties, to philosophy and to revealed truth, is to the classical thinkers a non-starter. Again, for them, the issue is one of interpretation, of understanding the tradition, not of questioning it, as a skeptic would. Further, as noted, the historicization of tradition takes on for us a rather different sense than in earlier times. For us, history gives the lie to tradition; by revealing the latter's genesis and temporality, it undercuts the authority of tradition. But, alternatively, history could in fact ground tradition. Indeed, medieval thinkers, some more than others, appealed to a variety of developmental schemes and historical successions to ground the tradition. The transition from the Noachide laws to the Mosaic laws, via the Patriarchal period, is appealed to in order to demonstrate divine beneficence and the necessity of the Mosaic revelation for the benefit of humankind. Far from standing in opposition to the law, history necessitates it. But for us moderns, history undermines the law.

I mention all of this because I wish to clarify the non-perennial nature of many of the standard problems of Jewish philosophy. And I wish to clarify the historical nature of the latter because I want to call into question the notion that there is something "out there" called "Jewish philosophy," of which we can write its (continuous) history. If, as suggested, Jewish philosophy emerged only with the writing of the history of Jewish philosophy, and for the self-serving reasons noted, then we can begin to disabuse ourselves of imposing upon the past our problems. We can begin to read the classical and modern thinkers in context, in their very different times and places; and, in so doing, we can begin to break down artificial, indeed recent, disciplinary and conceptual barriers.[13] This kind of Skinnerian enterprise[14] reaps enormous dividends, as it allows us to develop, as best we can, a degree of imaginative empathy too often lost in our positivist, "imperialistic," urges to read the present into the past. Such an approach also allows us to flex our historical and philological muscles in the service of accuracy and (historical) truth. The very last thing I would hope to be calling for when I urge a reconsideration of the "eternity" of the

7

questions we ask and the categories according to which we ask our questions is a Gadamerian relativism that imprisons us in our own historical epoch.[15] Of course we write from a point of view, a certain historical context, but this is simply to announce our starting point, from whence we use every scholarly tool at our disposal to try to understand the questions of our forebears. In sum, that Jewish philosophy is an artificial construct, a category imposing certain questions upon certain thinkers, should set us eagerly upon the (historical) task of trying to understand what precisely the problems and issues are which exercised earlier generations, and how dissimilar those problems are to those that we are inclined to pose.

To embark upon such a quest is not to attempt the impossible, namely, to resuscitate a tradition now irretrievably lost. What is past is past. To this extent such a historical quest is paradigmatically modern. To write the history of Jewish philosophy will not, cannot, pull together generations of thinkers or heal old wounds. But it can, if done sensitively, record the efforts of Jewish thinkers through the ages to make sense of the tradition(s) they inhabit.

When my co-editor and I commenced upon this project, we had many choices to make. Perhaps the most important concerned the division of the subject. We opted for a most conservative division, one according to canonical temporal demarcations: biblical and rabbinic, medieval, modern, contemporary. This presumes a single subject matter, Jewish philosophy, that is divisible by temporal categorization. But I have just denied the existence of something called "Jewish philosophy" before the writing of its history. Given this, I urge the reader to read the chapters in this volume from a critical (modern) vantage point, sensitive to the way problems emerge and the contexts in which they are nested. Ask yourself what is presupposed or taken for granted in the way questions are asked and problems posed. Immerse yourself in the historical framework – this is why we commissioned essays that present, at crucial junctures, the social and cultural context. Ideas have histories.

Our hope has been that by historicizing the subject, by embracing the modern propensity of rethinking old categories, we can begin to overcome a certain parochialism that has bedeviled the study of Jewish philosophy from the start and thereby begin to integrate it into the mainstream of philosophical and theological speculation. In becoming aware of the apologetic nature of much of Jewish philosophy, we can begin the task of its reconstruction.

❧ NOTES ❧

1 In Guttmann 1973 [1933], p. x.
2 Seeskin 1990, introduction (pp. 1–29).
3 In Guttmann 1973 [1933], p. x.
4 Feldman (1990) says of Maimonides that his "philosophical *magnum opus* should be more properly classified and understood as a book in biblical exegesis *more philosophico*" (p. 4); see also Feldman 1987 (pp. 213ff.), Twersky 1967 and 1980 (pp. 359–64), and, recently, Eisen 1995 (pp. 178–83) for a correlative point about the philosophical nature of (seemingly) non-philosophical texts, namely biblical commentaries and codes.
5 Strauss 1963, p. xiv.
6 Wolfson 1948, preface.
7 Strauss 1963, p. xiv.
8 See note 4.
9 See Yovel 1973 and Frank 1995a and 1995b for the practical dimension of biblical exegesis.
10 Two notable recent examples in the tradition of the classical commentators are Goodman 1991 and Halbertal and Margalit 1992. These two books are "by Jews," but not only "for Jews"; nor are they "Jewish books," even though they are grounded in Jewish sources. See also Burrell 1986 and 1993 to disabuse one of the notion that serious work on Jewish philosophical themes needs to be written by a Jew.
11 Husik 1976 [1916], p. 432.
12 See especially Scholem 1975 [1944–5]. The standard study on Scholem's intellectual position is Biale 1979 (rev. ed. 1982).
13 Barriers between religion and philosophy, philosophy and biblical commentary (see note 4), philosophy and law, and philosophy and mysticism; for the latter, see Idel 1991 and 1992.
14 Skinner 1969.
15 Gadamer 1979.

❧ BIBLIOGRAPHY ❧

Biale, D. (1979) *Gershom Scholem: Kabbalah and Counter-History* (Cambridge, MA: Harvard University Press (rev. ed. 1982)).

Burrell, D. (1986) *Knowing the Unknowable God: Ibn-Sina, Maimonides, Aquinas* (Notre Dame: University of Notre Dame Press).

—— (1993) *Freedom and Creation in Three Traditions* (Notre Dame: University of Notre Dame Press).

Eisen, R. (1995) *Gersonides on Providence, Covenant, and the Chosen People* (Albany: State University of New York Press).

Feldman, S. (tr.) (1987) Levi ben Gershom (Gersonides), *The Wars of the Lord*, vol. 2 (Philadelphia: Jewish Publication Society).

—— (1990) " 'In the Beginning God Created': A Philosophical Midrash," in *God and Creation: An Ecumenical Symposium*, edited by D. Burrell and B. McGinn (Notre Dame: University of Notre Dame Press), pp. 3–26.

Frank, D. (1995a) "Reason in Action: The 'Practicality' of Maimonides's *Guide*," in *Commandment and Community: New Essays in Jewish Legal and Political Philosophy*, edited by D. Frank (Albany: State University of New York Press), pp. 69–84.

—— (1995b) New Introduction, in Maimonides, *The Guide of the Perplexed*, edited by J. Guttmann and translated by C. Rabin (Indianapolis: Hackett (originally published in London, 1952)).

Gadamer, H.-G. (1979) "The Problem of Historical Consciousness," in *Interpretive Social Science*, edited by P. Rabinow and W. M. Sullivan (Berkeley: University of California Press), pp. 103–60.

Goodman, L. E. (1991) *On Justice: An Essay in Jewish Philosophy* (New Haven: Yale University Press).

Guttmann, J. (1973) [1933] *Philosophies of Judaism* (New York: Schocken Books (first edition published as *Die Philosophie des Judentums*)).

Halbertal, M. and A. Margalit (1992) *Idolatry* (Cambridge, MA: Harvard University Press).

Husik, I. (1976) [1916] *A History of Mediaeval Jewish Philosophy* (New York: Atheneum).

Idel, M. (1991) "Maimonides and Kabbalah," in *Studies in Maimonides*, edited by I. Twersky (Cambridge, MA: Harvard University Press), pp. 31–81.

—— (1992) "Jewish Kabbalah and Platonism in the Middle Ages and Renaissance," in *Neoplatonism and Jewish Thought*, edited by L. E. Goodman (Albany: State University of New York Press), pp. 319–51.

Scholem, G. (1975) [1944–5] "Reflections on the Science of Judaism" [Hebrew], in G. Scholem, *Devarim be-Go: Pirke Morashah u-Techiyah* (Tel Aviv: Am Oved), pp. 385–403.

Seeskin, K. (1990) *Jewish Philosophy in a Secular Age* (Albany: State University of New York Press).

Skinner, Q. (1969) "Meaning and Understanding in the History of Ideas," *History and Theory* 8: 3–53.

Strauss, L. (1963) "How to Begin to Study *The Guide of the Perplexed*," in Maimonides, *The Guide of the Perplexed*, translated by S. Pines (Chicago: University of Chicago Press), pp. xi–lvi.

Twersky, I. (1967) "Some Non-Halakic Aspects of the *Mishneh Torah*," in *Jewish Medieval and Renaissance Studies*, edited by A. Altmann (Cambridge, MA: Harvard University Press), pp. 95–118.

—— (1980) *Introduction to the Code of Maimonides (Mishneh Torah)* (New Haven: Yale University Press).

Wolfson, H. (1948) *Philo: Foundations of Religious Philosophy in Judaism, Christianity, and Islam*, 2 vols (Cambridge, MA: Harvard University Press).

Yovel, Y. (1973) "Bible Interpretation as Philosophical Praxis: A Study of Spinoza and Kant," *Journal of the History of Philosophy* 11: 189–212.

I

Foundations and first principles

CHAPTER 2

The Bible as a source for philosophical reflection

Shalom Carmy and David Shatz

INTRODUCTION: ISSUES OF METHODOLOGY

Is the Bible a source for Jewish philosophical reflection? A natural reaction is that it is. The Bible depicts the character of God, presents an account of creation, posits a metaphysics of divine providence and divine interventions, suggests a basis for morality, discusses many features of human nature, and frequently poses the notorious conundrum of how God can allow evil. Surely, then, it engages questions that lie at the very heart of Jewish philosophy, indeed of religious philosophy generally.

Yet this categorization of the Bible as philosophy must be qualified. For the Bible obviously deviates, in many features, from what philosophers (especially those trained in the analytic tradition) have come to regard as philosophy.

First, the Bible contains, at its very core, a great deal of material that is not necessarily philosophical: law, poetry, and narrative.

Second, we expect philosophical truth to be formulated in declarative sentences. The Bible yields few propositional nuggets of this kind.[1]

Third, philosophical works try to reach conclusions by means of logical argumentation. The Bible contains little sustained argument of a deductive, inductive, or practical nature, and attempts to impose the structure of rational argument on the biblical text yield meager profit.

Fourth, philosophers try to avoid contradicting themselves. When contradictions appear, they are either a source of embarrassment or a spur to developing a higher order dialectic to accommodate the tension between the theses. The Bible, by contrast, often juxtaposes contradictory ideas, without explanation or apology: Ecclesiastes is entirely constructed on this principle. The philosophically more sophisticated work of harmonizing the contradictions in the biblical text is left to the exegetical literature.[2]

Fifth, much of what the Bible has to say about subjects of manifest philosophical importance seems primitive to later philosophical sensibilities. For example, the biblical God ostensibly has human form and human emotions; he regrets his actions and changes his mind (e.g. Genesis 6:6; 1 Samuel 15:11). Miracles are commonplace, and natural events like earthquakes and winds are often identified as direct divine acts. If Jewish philosophy begins with the Bible, cynics might suggest, it can advance only by casting it behind.

This last problem is at the core of the concerns that Jewish philosophers have often felt about biblical material. Indeed, an acute awareness of the gap between the centrality of biblical teaching in Jewish thought and its apparent philosophical deficiency precipitated much of the subsequent history of Jewish philosophy. Many will derive from that history a pessimism about finding philosophy in the Bible. In particular, the most strenuous attempt ever to wed the Bible to philosophy – that of medieval thinkers – was of mixed value to biblical theology, as in many cases it arguably forced biblical texts into an artificial model.

Beginning with Philo and continuing on through medieval thinkers like Saadia Gaon and Maimonides, biblical hermeneutics often rested on the principle that the Bible conveys major philosophical and scientific truths. Biblical discourse, insist medieval rationalists, is not always to be taken literally. Although biblical portrayals of God and of events introduce the masses to basic truths – educating and elevating them – the proper understanding of these texts is available only to those who enter the realm of philosophy and science. Interpreting the text through the prism of reason reveals a philosophically impressive and compelling core. The books of the prophets thus reflect the philosophical acumen of their authors, though these individuals are philosophers of a special kind: not only do they perceive intellectual truths, but their faculty of "imagination" presents these truths in figurative terms and concrete images (Maimonides 1963, 1.36–7). The showcase example of prophet-as-philosopher is Ezekiel's detailed vision of the chariot (Ezekiel 1; 10), which Maimonides treats as a repository of Aristotelian metaphysics (*Guide of the Perplexed*, 3.1–3.8). Other examples abound. In their analyses of the book of Job, medieval philosophers sometimes take each character to be espousing a different philosophical position on the basis and scope of divine providence.[3] In the Garden of Eden story, man represents form, that is, intellect, the essence of a human; woman represents matter. Man sinned as a result of woman's promptings. Hence the story of Eden captures the human predicament – matter interferes with the proper exercise of intellect and with the realization of the human telos.[4]

A telling indicator of the close connection between philosophy and Bible in medieval times is that Maimonides' *Guide of the Perplexed*, the greatest of Jewish philosophical works, is in significant measure an exegesis of the Bible. Gersonides, renowned for his philosophical and scientific achievements, authored a biblical commentary, as did Saadia Gaon and Abraham ibn Ezra. An entire exegetical tradition, down to the end of Jewish life in Spain (Isaac Abravanel) and even beyond, resorted to medieval philosophy – or rebelled against it.

Opposition to the rationalist biblical interpretation came from two directions.[5] Some medieval Jews thought that the Bible must be read with absolute literalness and then taken on faith. If its doctrines, so understood, conflicted with those of philosophy, so much the worse for philosophy: philosophy would then have been exposed as heresy and falsehood. In early modern times, a different critical response emerged, one which in effect accused Maimonides and other medievals of a colossal anachronism. Spinoza put the charge especially sharply, proclaiming that any and all attributions of philosophical sophistication and truth to the Bible and the prophets were fictions (Spinoza 1951); his subversion of Maimonides' doctrines, however overstated, marked the eclipse of the medieval enterprise. Later efforts to read the Bible through the prism of Kantian or Romantic philosophy, whether of rabbinic or academic provenance (such as the commentaries of Rabbi Samson Raphael Hirsch or Yechezkel Kaufmann's theory of Israelite monotheism), could be and were subjected to a hermeneutic of suspicion.[6]

In light of the clear differences we have outlined between the Bible and works of philosophy – in style, method, and purpose – and in light of the checkered history of attempts to read good philosophy into the Bible, anyone proposing to portray the Bible as a source of philosophical reflection has to tread very carefully. And yet to claim that the religious and moral wisdom of the Bible is philosophically naive is grossly unfair – and not only to believers in divine revelation. An analogy to ancient philosophy is helpful. Recent work in ancient philosophy, including Presocratic philosophy, shows a remarkable alertness to contemporary problems along with perspicuous avenues for solution (see, for example, Barnes 1982); differences in terminology ought not blind us to the philosophical character of our predecessors' insights. Philosophy in general has been rediscovering its roots of late, leading to a greater appreciation of centuries past. Although the Bible serves first and foremost as a record of primary religious experience, study of the Bible, in its original context and trailing clouds of exegesis, evokes fruitful lines of theological reflection that repay philosophical attention even today.

In the remainder of this chapter we hope to illustrate the possibilities for a meaningful encounter between Bible and philosophy, one that will accord the Bible its place among the important sources of Jewish philosophy without exaggerating its analytical character and without blurring the lines between its formulations of certain problems or approaches and the formulations utilized by later philosophers. Needless to say, someone mining for philosophical ore is not likely to treat biblical texts in the same way that scholars in other fields would. Consequently, we have to gloss over and bracket a variety of linguistic, historical, and literary issues that could either complement or undermine our suggestions. "The Torah has seventy faces," but no one can display all of them at once.[7]

The purposes and scope of this volume dictate a focus on familiar biblical sources, texts whose place in the treatment of theological issues has been hallowed by time: the story of Job, the binding of Isaac, the Garden of Eden, and others. We do not seek to uncover neglected corners of the biblical canon with unexpected or oblique implications for Jewish philosophy.[8] We are forced to omit some significant matters that can, and often do, attract reflective philosophical attention, and we devote little room to philosophical issues implicit in the legal material that is so central to the Bible. All that having been said, our selection should amply demonstrate that narrative and poetry and law, no less than discursive writing, can express and stimulate philosophical thinking, a point that is surely abundantly evident to students of literature and Jewish law respectively.

～ DIVINE COMMANDS AND ～ HUMAN MORAL STANDARDS

"Is an action right because God commands it, or does God command it because it is right? Is an action wrong because God prohibits it, or does God prohibit it because it is wrong?"

These questions, modeled after one posed in Plato's *Euthyphro*, have long stood at the heart of religious reflections on morality. Like their Muslim and Christian counterparts, Jewish philosophers have differed sharply over whether there can be a valid morality independent of God's law.[9]

Biblical teaching on the subject confronts us with contradictions. When patriarchs and prophets ask how God could allow evil, they are judging God's conduct by human moral standards. In Genesis 18, Abraham remonstrates with God not to destroy the innocent of Sodom together with the guilty: "Will you destroy the righteous with the wicked. . . . Far be it from you! Will the judge of all the earth not exercise justice?" (Genesis 18:25). If God's will alone determined right and wrong, Abraham's plea and God's favorable response to it would be senseless. God is expected to be moral by human standards. Yet in chapter 22 the very same Abraham rises early in the morning to carry out God's command to sacrifice his beloved Isaac. No moral scruples are raised either about the seeming command to commit murder or about God's having reneged on his promise to Abraham, "through Isaac you will have seed" (Genesis 21:12). God later commands King Saul to kill all the Amalekites, "man and woman, infant and suckling, ox and sheep, camel and ass" (1 Samuel 15:3), and wrenches the kingship from Saul when he does not comply.[10] Midrashic and talmudic interpretations of this episode see Saul as questioning God on moral grounds and trying to be "more righteous than your creator" (*Ecclesiastes Rabbah* 7:16; B. *Yoma* 22b). The biblical evidence, then, is confusing and contradictory as to whether there is a standard of ethics outside God's will and command.[11]

One episode that none the less has assumed a pre-eminent place in explorations of this issue is the binding of Isaac (*Aqedah*). In Genesis 22:2 Abraham is commanded by God to "take your son, your only son, whom you love – Isaac – and go to the land of Moriah, and offer him up there as a burnt offering". In his brilliant "dialectical lyric" *Fear and Trembling*, the nineteenth-century Danish philosopher Søren Kierkegaard advanced a reading of the *Aqedah* that has dominated interpretations of the episode ever since. Abraham is the "knight of faith," whose greatness consists in obeying God even while he remains conscious of the moral imperative in its full Kantian force and majesty. Abraham was prepared to commit an act whose religious description is "sacrifice," though its ethical description is "murder". This paradoxical "teleological suspension of the ethical" characterizes the religious stage. Note that Kierkegaard's is not a "divine command" theory of morality in the pure sense; for Kierkegaard does not reduce moral prescriptions to divine commands (Seeskin 1990, chapter 5). However, Kierkegaard recognizes the possibility of conflict between divine commands and morality, and asserts the supremacy of religious faith in all such situations.[12]

The Kierkegaardian image of Abraham has affected not only depictions of religious morality but depictions of cognitive faith as well.[13] His interpretation has become so influential that some modern readers may be surprised to learn that in its time the reading was novel; until Kierkegaard the *Aqedah* was not explained in the manner he suggests (Green 1988, chapters 4, 5). Abraham's potential conflict need not be understood as one between obedience to God and adherence to morality. It could be – and was – readily analyzed as a potential conflict between morality, identified with obedience to God, and natural paternal love. The Rosh Hashanah musaf liturgy asks God to let his compassion conquer his anger, just as "[Abraham] conquered his compassion to do your will wholeheartedly." Natural feeling for his son, not rational morality, is what made the *Aqedah* difficult. Other readers had identified the challenge to Abraham as that of keeping faith that "through Isaac you will have seed," despite what God commanded. Some have rejected the very premise that obedience to God overrides conventional morality, in the *Aqedah*, on the grounds that God finally commands Abraham to refrain from the sacrifice (Steinberg 1960, p. 147; cf. Jacobs 1978, pp. 53–4). At the same time Rabbi Joseph B. Soloveitchik has pointed to kindred situations in the Bible where no angel appears to stay the upraised slaughtering knife (Soloveitchik 1994).

The problems raised by our brief discussion of *Fear and Trembling* illustrate the pitfalls in extrapolating a modern philosophical doctrine from an ancient and not explicitly philosophical text. One question is whether the modern philosophical theory indeed conforms to what the Bible would have said had it only employed modern formulations: in other words, would Abraham, or the narrator, have chosen the terminology "teleological suspension of the ethical" over the alternatives? Second, assuming that the philosophical theory is congenial to the spirit of the text, is it actually implied by the words of the narrative? Some contemporary approaches deny in toto the pertinence of these questions; we do not.[14]

Another well-known, though perhaps overshadowed, text for illuminating the problem of religion and morality is the Garden of Eden story. The first instance of a divine command to human beings is: "And from the tree of knowledge of good and evil, do not eat" (Genesis 2:17). Why did God enjoin Adam and Eve from partaking of this tree?

The serpent explains: "For God knows that on the day you eat from [the tree] your eyes will be opened and you will be like gods, knowing the difference between good and evil" (3:5). God, insinuates the serpent, is jealously guarding his own prerogatives of knowing the difference between good and evil. We may regard the serpent as an unreliable source of information, and therefore assume that his rationale is contrived and duplicitous. But the serpent's claim is partially confirmed later in the story: "and the Lord God said, now that man has become like one of us knowing the difference between good and evil, perhaps now he will stretch out his hand, eat also from the tree of life, and will live forever" (3:22).

Thus the serpent's words contain a large measure of truth. God prohibited the fruit so that humans will not become knowers of good and evil. What does this mean? If "knowledge of good and evil" is the capacity to make moral discriminations, why would God begrudge this to human beings? And in any case, if human beings would become "knowers of good and evil" only after eating the forbidden fruit, how could they sensibly have been issued a command to begin with? If "ought" implies "can," then by commanding humans to refrain from eating, was not God implying that they already had an understanding of good and evil (right and wrong)?

Most classical construals of "knowers of good and evil" – knowers of sexual passion, knowers of sensual temptation, knowers of conventional moral judgments as distinct from knowers of theoretical truths – face a challenge from Genesis 3:22.[15] The contemporary philosopher Michael Wyschogrod has offered a proposal that accounts for 3:22 and also sheds light on the issue of divine command morality. According to Wyschogrod, "knowers of good and evil" means: beings who make autonomous judgments of good and evil grounded in their own criteria of right and wrong (Wyschogrod 1986).[16] The turning point in human history was "and the woman saw that the tree was good for eating and that it was attractive to the eyes and desirable as a source of wisdom. She took from its fruit and ate; and she also gave it to her man with her and he ate" (Genesis 3:6). The words "and the woman saw that [it] was good" mark the first time that anyone other than God "saw that [it] was good," that is, made value judgments. That God had prohibited the fruit has no motivational impact on the woman; her decision to eat or not to eat was based upon her own criteria and standards. While the introduction of sensuality into her thinking is also a critical part of the verse, and has been duly stressed by classical exegetes, the main point for our purposes is that the woman has become an autonomous judger. Suppose Eve had decided to refrain from eating but did so because she found the fruit unattractive. This too would have been wrong, for she would have been just as unresponsive to God's command as she is when she decides to eat. The complete lack of rationalization in God's original directive alerts us to the heteronomous character of the command. God gives a command for which he supplies no reason. Humans should not question it but should obey without understanding why.

No wonder that later, when Adam and Eve cover themselves because their nakedness now embarrasses them, and Adam then explains to God that he hid because he was naked, God scolds Adam: "Who told you that you are naked? Did you eat from the tree from which I commanded you not to eat?" (Genesis 3:11). Eating from the tree means becoming an autonomous judger. If Adam judged that nakedness is shameful, he must have eaten the forbidden food.[17]

With this insight we can understand how a command could have been issued to beings who supposedly could not differentiate right from wrong. Adam and Eve always had the capacity to obey or disobey God's commands. Free choice was theirs, along with recognition of what was right (obedience) and what was wrong (disobedience). And it is the wrong exercise of freedom that constitutes their sin. Yet, in another sense, namely, appraising autonomously the content of God's commands, they still did not "know good and evil." Eating from the tree did not cause them to become knowers; rather it *represented* their becoming knowers, that is, judgers of good and evil.

Wyschogrod's explanation of the sin dovetails with a general motif in Genesis: the drawing and preserving of boundaries (Sykes 1985). In the ordered sequence of chapter 1, where, until the sixth day, God is alone in the world, as it were, the boundaries between created things are clear and distinct. In chapter 2, where the human world and not the natural cosmos becomes the focus, the lines between the days and between parts of creation are obliterated in the narration, anticipating the crossing of lines that will take place in the next chapter. Before sin, only God categorizes the created universe and only God originates value judgments of a non-heteronomous nature. When humans sin by producing their own judgments, God fears that they will now strive to become immortal as well, usurping another prerogative of the divine. The human being is therefore banished from Eden.

If we were to stop here, we would leave with the impression that Genesis does not want humans to make autonomous judgments. But the continuation of the Adam narrative complicates our response and suggests an addendum to Wyschogrod's analysis. In chapter 4, Cain kills Abel. As in the case of Adam and Eve, God seeks out the sinner. This time, too, he holds the sinner accountable (Genesis 4:10 ff.). But this time the sinner is not accused of disobeying a command – the text mentions no explicit prohibition of murder.[18] Rather, he is held accountable for *not* "knowing," for evading the responsibility of applying his judgment correctly. Cain tries to disclaim responsibility: "I do not know! Am I my brother's keeper?" To which God retorts, "What have you done? Your brother's blood cries out to me from the earth!" (Genesis 4:10). In the post-expulsion world, God expects humans to make moral judgments of their own; concomitantly, they cannot avoid accountability for the judgments they make. Within several generations the world is destroyed because of human oppression: as Nachmanides observes, the sinfulness of social corruption can be grasped independent of revealed divine injunction.[19] The transfer of power to human beings continues in augmented form after the deluge. When the world is recreated by the family of Noah after the flood,[20] human beings are given even more prerogatives than before. They may now eat animals and may now institute capital punishment for the sin of murder

(Genesis 9:6). Steadily, their moral prerogatives grow. (For further development, see Steinmetz 1994.)

True to this expanding autonomy and responsibility, characters in Genesis who evaluate their own or others' actions apply their independent moral reflection. The sons of Jacob kill the Shechemites because they had treated as a harlot their sister Dinah (Genesis 34:31); the same brothers blame themselves for their callous disregard of Joseph's pain when they cast him into a pit (42:41); covenants are made and kept, reflecting the judgment that they are binding. Societies in Genesis are built not on prescriptions imposed from without but on moral thinking. Only at Sinai does God issue a lengthy set of commands (Exodus 19), and questions about how to act will no longer be typically answered by giving human beings autonomy to judge. Yet even after Sinai, God responds to moral give-and-take. For example, when the daughters of Tzelofechad argue that their father's estate ought not to pass from the family simply because he left no sons, God ratifies their claim and permits daughters to inherit in such circumstances (Numbers 27:1–11).

Is there then a final biblical position on the basis of morality? No single position is reflected in every portion. Before the sin, human beings are expected to hearken to God's command and not initiate autonomous moral reflection. That expectation is altered after the sin and as a result of the sin. Sinai represents the heteronomous imposition of conduct. But even after Sinai, God is responsive to moral dialectic.

❦ THEODICY ❦

"Is God willing to prevent evil, but not able? Then he is not omnipotent. Is he able, but not willing? Then he is malevolent. Is he able and willing, but ignorant of evil's existence? Then he is not omniscient." The Bible does not enunciate the problem of evil with the analytical precision familiar to readers of Hume (*Dialogues Concerning Natural Religion* 10), but it does not shrink from seeking to understand and even challenge the ways of God in the face of apparent injustice. Consternation over evil is a familiar theme in Psalms (13:2; 37; 73), in the prophetic books of Jeremiah (12:1–2), Isaiah (62–3), and Habakkuk, in Lamentations, in Ecclesiastes, and of course in the book of Job.

That the prophets frequently raise the problem of evil has important ramifications. First, it is evident that challenging the justice of God's ways is not blasphemous – if it were, the prophets would not have allowed themselves to engage in it. Abraham even elicits a positive response from God when he argues that to destroy the innocent of Sodom with its wicked, as God seemed ready to do, would be unjust ("Will the judge of all the earth not do justice?", Genesis 18). Second, despite Isaiah's famous dictum, "My thoughts are not your thoughts, nor my ways your ways" (Isaiah 55:8) (which played an important role in Maimonides' doctrine of attributes, *Guide* 3.20), the problem of evil is not dismissed with the glib assertion that "good" as applied to God does not mean the same as "good" when applied to humans. If such a resolution were valid, authoritative figures in the Bible would not persist in raising the question and leaving it unanswered (see Gellman 1977). Finally, the repeated discussions of the problem throughout the Bible invite another insight, namely, that the biblical writers did not consider the problem of evil as an analytic conundrum, to be solved once and for all, but rather as a mystery perennially tugging at the sensitive theological conscience.[21]

Because the Bible's "problem of evil" is situated within a set of theological presuppositions and a fund of experience, it diverges from articulations of the problem that are promulgated by philosophers. In philosophy, the question of evil is usually posed as, "why is there evil?" The biblical formulation, however, starts with certain background beliefs: that suffering is usually punishment for sin; that God loves Israel. In the Bible, therefore, the problem's formulation is usually narrower: Why do the righteous suffer while the wicked prosper? or: How could God allow Israel to suffer and the Temple be destroyed? In short, why do such-and-such evils befall these people or groups? Another difference between biblical and philosophical formulations is that in the philosophical literature evil is often thought to disconfirm the *existence* of God, while the Bible does not come remotely near considering that position. The biblical writers are instead concerned about the threat that evil poses to belief in God's *goodness* or steadfastness.

The most elaborate biblical treatment of evil is, of course, the book of Job. A common approach to biblical theodicy attempts to derive a conclusion from this book as a whole. Leaving aside some stubborn obstacles – most notably that God's wager with the Satan in the narrative prologue (chapters 1–2) is not alluded to in the denouement, and the sudden appearance, and disappearance, of Elihu – let us focus on some key points.

The first is negative. At the end of the work, God chastises the friends "because you did not speak properly to me as did my servant Job" (42:7). In other words, God rejects, in whole or in part, their position. Whatever the differences among the three friends, and whatever development occurs in their respective positions in the course of the dialogue, they are finally united in the conviction that Job deserves his bad fortune. Whatever the fine points of temperament and argument, they were determined to uphold the traditional theodicy of justified retribution at all cost. Job, by contrast, had stridently and consistently complained that he was a good man, and that his actions do not warrant his fate. He had come close to blasphemy. Yet it is Job who must pray on behalf of his friends before *they* can be forgiven. A stronger indictment of the retributivist theodicy could hardly be imagined.

Rabbinic literature was to go beyond the denial of the simple formula that all suffering is punishment for sin by offering a range of explicit alternative explanations of evil.[22] But does the book of Job provide us with any such alternative? Or is its sole conclusion the negative one we have outlined?

If Job contains a positive theodicy, it is presumably to be found in God's two speeches (38–41) which lead Job to humility and reconciliation. Alas, the precise philosophical point of these speeches is elusive. Do they contain an argument from the perfect design of the universe as proposed by Gersonides in his commentary to these chapters? Or is it the dysteleological features of creation that enable us to perceive the numinousness of the divine other, as was influentially asserted by Rudolf Otto (Otto 1950, pp. 77–81)? Are we intended to identify a discursive solution, or is the resolution the theophany itself ("I had heard of you by ear, now my eye has seen you") (42:5), when God accedes to Job's existential plea for his tormentor not to hide his face but to respond to his creature's anguish (see, for example, Glatzer 1969)?

The idea that Job's *experience* of God is the key to his reconciliation suggests the primacy of the human drama in Job, and this insight leads us to a distinct philosophical appropriation of the book; we discover in Job's ordeal a "theodicy of soulmaking". Take the problem of God's wager with the Satan. God's rationale is theologically problematic, to say the least. Can God justifiably make Job a pawn in order to prove a point? If Job is, at bottom, an exploration of what people make of suffering, then the dispute between God and the Satan becomes less capricious. The Satan holds that suffering inexorably corrupts; faithfulness is a luxury only the prosperous can afford. God says that suffering can ennoble; faithfulness can be forged in the crucible of anguish.

Who is right? Ultimately God's prediction – and Job himself – will be vindicated by the process of suffering. For the voice of God and its aftermath are signs of two things: Job's heightened spiritual perception and his heightened sense of interpersonal responsibility. Perceiving God out of the whirlwind is a climactic achievement; "and *now* my eye has seen you" (note however 5:17). The end result of Job's suffering is that he has the ability to perceive that which previously he could not perceive. And whereas in the prologue Job brought sacrifices for his family alone, he has now broadened his concern to include others – he brings sacrifices for the friends as well (Soloveitchik 1965, pp. 37–8). Job has grown through crisis. Hence God was right, the Satan was wrong.[23]

The philosophically reflective student of Job, like the reader of other biblical texts, would be remiss in abandoning the rich detail of the text to philologists and literary scholars. We must not create a false dichotomy between philosophical and literary or psychological readings. Although, as we noted earlier, exegetes such as Maimonides and Gersonides assign specific philosophical positions to the participants in the dialogue, it is surely in keeping with the atmosphere of the debate to emphasize the psychological stance of Job and the other characters. The book of Job is a veritable phenomenology of faith in a state of challenge. It spans moments of commitment (13:15), doubt (23:5), self-pity (19:21), self-confidence (13:18?), and defiance (9:22–3) (Seeskin 1990, p. 173). The friends' rhetoric may evolve – and their temper may degenerate – but their faith, in contrast to Job's, is throughout simple and simplistic.

By selecting a single passage we can highlight the lively interaction between philosophical and psychological issues and the suggestiveness of the exegetical tradition, even when the commentators respond to the text in categories alien to its original intellectual setting.

In Job's first answer to Bildad, he addresses God, crying out: "Is it good that you oppress, that you despise the work of your hands, and shine upon wicked thoughts? Are your eyes of flesh? Do you see like man?" (10:3–4). For Nachmanides, Job is accusing God of an obsessive concern with man's inner thoughts: Is God like a jealous lover who must constantly probe the recesses of the creature's mind and provoke his potential for rebellion? Gersonides, who denied divine foreknowledge of contingents, ascribes his own doctrine to Job: God does not know as man does, that is, he does not know particulars, hence he cannot be held responsible for Job's troubles. The Gersonidean Job proclaims his innocence without expressing resentment: the angry tone is not Job's, but rather describes the foul mood which the friends, who have not understood Gersonides, mistakenly attribute to him. Rabbi Meir Leibush Malbim, the nineteenth-century exegete, adopts the more conventional teaching on foreknowledge. On his reading Job here advances the classic medieval problem of foreknowledge and freedom: because God is omniscient, and not limited as man's knowledge is, his knowledge determines man's actions, and Job cannot be held responsible for the sins he may have committed.

The philosophical interpretations of Gersonides and Malbim violate our expectations not only because they are based on anachronistic theories but also because they presume a pursuit of metaphysical argument at odds with the existential situation of Job on his dung heap. What happens, however, when we take Job's psychological state in full seriousness? Remember the context: at the point where we join Job's meditation, his view of the situation has undergone several changes. From the "patient Job" of the prologue, he has moved to the initial curse of chapter 3, a curse that avoids addressing God by focusing instead on his unlucky birthday. In the response to Eliphaz (6–7) Job saw himself as a persecuted figure, misunderstood by his friends and hounded by God. By chapter 9, the logic of the discourse has led Job to see himself as a self divided against itself. His very attempt to exculpate himself becomes a gesture of rebellion that makes him appear all the more guilty: "If I wash with snow water, and purify my hands with lye, then shall you immerse me in the muddy pit, and my very clothes shall detest me" (9:30–1). In short, he is helpless not only because his adversary is powerful but because his adversary condemns him from within, as it were.

Against this background, the argument at the beginning of chapter 10 reflects precisely Job's psychological situation. It is not only that Job's insistence on his innocence does not belong to him, fueling instead the fires of his antagonists who undermine his claim to innocence. Now, he realizes, his very being is not his: he is the handiwork of the same God against whom he must strive. And Job goes on to portray eloquently the experience of creatureliness. All this is reminiscent of Malbim's interpretation, but stripped of the formal philosophical theorizing. The nineteenth-century attempt to read a medieval conundrum into an ancient text helps us, paradoxically, to capture the existential import of the original, the moment we learn to avoid being captured by the formal anachronism.

We have proposed taking Job's religious growth as the kernel of a compelling explanation of evil, suggesting a perspective that lives through the various stages of the poetic portion and emerges at the other side after God has spoken. However that might be, the text does not seem preoccupied with preaching this or any other insight as a "solution" to a philosophical problem; God, after all, never tells Job the true genesis of his tribulations.[24] Phenomenology more than theodicy occupies center stage.

❧ FREE WILL AND DIVINE PROVIDENCE ❧

Philosophers have devoted enormous energy to resolving the seeming contradiction between divine foreknowledge and human free choice. If God knows at a certain time that persons will later do particular acts, how can those persons be said to act freely? And if they cannot act freely, how can they be morally responsible for their deeds?

As noted in the previous section, this difficulty is not explicitly encountered in the Bible; indeed the very notion of foreknowledge is sometimes conspicuously missing. Thus the Bible speaks of God "regretting" that he had made man, as if he had not foreseen the corruption that brought about the deluge (Genesis 6:6);[25] he tests Abraham and the angel proclaims "*now* I know that you are God-fearing" (Genesis 22:12; emphasis added), as if his heart would otherwise have been hidden from its creator.[26] Obvious conflicts between divine providence and human free choice are left unarticulated. God hardens the heart of Pharaoh and of the Amorite king Sihon (Exodus 9:12; 10:20; 11:10; 14: 4, 8, 17; Deuteronomy 2:30), without concern that owing to this divine interference these individuals ought not to be held responsible for their acts of rebellion. Again, God declares that he will harden Pharaoh's heart "in order to multiply my signs and wonders in the land of Egypt" (Exodus 10:1; 12:9; see also 7:3). Anyone who deems free will a value might well be struck by the invocation of God's greater glory as a reason for depriving someone of free choice. And we must not ignore the implications of legal texts. Thus God is assigned causal agency in cases of unintentional homicide (Exodus 21:13);[27] the commandment to build a guard rail around one's rooftop "lest someone fall" (Deuteronomy 22:8) implies that, despite divine foreknowlege, the victim would not have fallen had proper caution been exercised.[28] Exegetes grapple with the implications of these texts, and their proposals may be judged plausible or strained. What is important for us, however, is that the Bible itself does not address the issues.

At the same time, there is a particular type of tension between divine providence and human choice, carrying broad implications for the theology of history, that is often aroused by common reflection on biblical texts and articulates dilemmas that are often more momentous existentially than the classical ones.[29] God determines the course of history. He elects certain outcomes. Hence he stage-manages history so as to bring about these results. What responsibility do human beings bear for their actions if the outcome is inevitable? What freedom do they exercise if they are instruments in a divine plan? And does the fact that God wants the result justify the means chosen by humans to achieve it?

These questions come to the surface in the Joseph stories (Genesis 37–50). The brothers of Joseph, jealous of the special treatment he receives from his father Jacob, conspire to throw him into a pit. He is then taken by merchants, who sell him as a slave to Egyptians. Soon he is thrown into an Egyptian dungeon and incarcerated for two years on a trumped-up charge. By a remarkable sequence of events, Joseph eventually becomes the viceroy of Egypt. His brothers come to Egypt to procure food during a famine. Joseph recognizes them, they do not recognize him; Joseph proceeds to perpetrate a hoax on them. At last he reveals his identity.

Interestingly, of all the characters in the story, only one seeks to absolve the brothers of guilt – Joseph himself. He does so three times. "And now, be not saddened or angry that you sold me here [or: caused me to be sold]. For God sent me before you for sustenance" (Genesis 45:5). "You did not send me here; rather God did" (Genesis 45:8). "You thought ill for me; God thought it for good" (Genesis 50:20). Is Joseph's orientation as correct as it is generous?

It is hard to tell; the text plants the question in our minds, but leaves us to our own conclusions. To be sure, a quiet critique of Joseph inheres in the narrative. When Joseph asserts that the purpose of his being brought to Egypt was to save his brothers from the famine, he is being short-sighted and somewhat self-involved. Actually, he has been sent there because Jacob's descendants are destined to be enslaved "in a land not theirs" (Genesis 15:13). Joseph, the great prognosticator, sees into the future, but his lens does not reach far enough. Absorbed with his own place in the here-and-now, he seems oblivious to the persecution that awaits his family. His father Jacob realizes the bitter truth, and does not want to join Joseph in Egypt until God reassures him that he will return to Canaan with Jacob, that is, with his descendants (Genesis 46:3–4).[30] So the text at least mildly suggests the shortcoming of Joseph's reasoning concerning his brother's actions (by suggesting that he misperceives his place in history). But would Joseph's reasoning have been correct had he focused on the impending enslavement rather than on famine relief? Since the texts we have cited do not resolve *that* query, our original question returns: if the sequence of events in the Joseph narrative is necessary for the realization of God's plan and God *desires* the Jews to wind up in Egypt, would *this* mitigate the brothers' culpability, in spite of their keenly experienced and painfully expressed sense of guilt (42:21; 50:15)?

Joseph's exoneration of his brothers is indeed logically strained.[31] First, their *motive* was plainly nefarious. Second, as commentators note, even if their motivation were to fulfill a divine plan for history, "God has many agents." A divine plan can be realized in several different ways.[32] Hence the ends justify the means only if the means too are the direct act of God. These considerations render Joseph's assessment open to question.

Nevertheless, Nachmanides, contrary to the position just cited, affirms that if God has foreordained a certain end, then human beings who act to realize this divine end act rightly. So, for example, Nachmanides explains why Joseph prolonged his father's grief for over twenty years by failing to communicate with him: the fulfillment of his dreams required that *all* the brothers should bow down to him, and this could not be accomplished until Benjamin would be brought to Egypt through Joseph's subterfuge (commentary to 42:6). Likewise Nachmanides maintains that the nations that oppressed Israel in the Bible (such as Egypt, Assyria, Babylonia) would have been without culpability – even commended – had they sought thereby to implement divine prophecies and had they not persecuted the Jews more than the prophecies required.[33] Nachmanides' view would of course not vindicate Joseph for exonerating his brothers – Nachmanides requires an agent to be conscious of the divine plan and be motivated by this knowledge. Nevertheless, his thesis is intriguing, even if unconfirmed by biblical material.

The phenomenon of events that are integral to the divine plan but are dependent on human initiative – and sometimes on acts that leave room for moral questioning – appears frequently in the Bible. Rebekah and Jacob deceive Isaac by dressing Jacob as Esau and tricking Isaac into bestowing Esau's apparent blessing upon Jacob. What justified Rebekah in devising the hoax? Perhaps it was the oracle she heard before her twin sons were born: "And the elder [Esau] shall serve the younger [Jacob]" (Genesis 29:29).[34] Her actions sought to bring the prediction to fulfilment. Let us assume this interpretation and inquire how hers and Jacob's behavior is viewed by the narrative.

Often the Bible neither condones nor approves behavior explicitly. It lets the reader draw his or her own conclusions by subtle literary suggestions. We have already seen how the text imparts a partial censure of Joseph. The Bible also suggests that Jacob suffered in later life measure-for-measure. His uncle Laban substitutes an older sister (Leah) for the younger sister whom Jacob planned to marry (Rachel), defending his behavior with the cutting words, "in our place, such is not done, to give the younger before the elder" (Genesis 29:26). And the deception perpetrated on him by his sons, including both that of Joseph's brothers and that of Joseph himself, leads him to sum up his years as "few and bad" (Genesis 47:9). As for Rebekah, she sends Jacob away to live with her brother Laban "for a few days," while Esau's fury over the theft cools (Genesis 27:44), but Jacob is forced to remain with Laban for over twenty years and Rebekah never sees her son again.[35] Divine plan or no divine plan, deception is spiritually costly.[36]

In these episodes, the Jacob and Joseph stories, God is rarely acknowledged as the cause of events. From the time that Joseph is incarcerated by Potiphar, the Tetragrammaton, which generally signifies direct divine intervention, is absent; only *Elohim*, indicating God's general providence, appears. Furthermore, *Elohim* is depicted as the initiator of events only by the characters, not by the biblical narration itself. In the book of Esther, which takes place in exile and during a period when the light of prophecy has become obscured, God absconds completely from the narrative.[37] And yet the light of the events' author shines through the cracks and crevices of the naturalistic causal network.[38]

Traditional philosophical theories have sought to impose on the Bible a unified theological doctrine, true for all books and circumstances. Our approach recognizes that the biblical metaphysic is as complex as it is enigmatic. Such concepts as providence, history, and responsibility are grasped by human beings in a variety of contexts. Sometimes God is depicted in total control of events; sometimes he appears to relinquish the initiative.

❧ THE ORIGINS OF THE UNIVERSE ❧

We began by asking whether, and in what ways, the Bible can be fruitfully studied as a source of philosophical reflection. Some treatments of the creation story confront us in especially sharp form with the methodological pitfall of taking a book to be something it isn't intended to be; at the same time they enable us to see why the Bible's *philosophical* trajectory might be of special importance.

Traditionally Jewish schoolchildren have gained their first insight into the purpose of the Bible (or more specifically the Torah) from the very first comment of Rabbi Shlomo Yitzhaki (Rashi):

> R. Yitzhak said: the Torah should have begun from "this month is for you the first of the months" [Exodus 12:2], for that[39] is the first precept commanded to Israel. And why did it begin with "In the beginning"? Because "he has related the power of his deeds to his people, to give them the inheritance of the nations" [Psalms 111:5]. For if the nations of the worlds say to Israel, "you are thieves for having conquered the land of the seven [Canaanite nations]", Israel will say: all the earth is God's – he created it and gave it to whomever he saw fit.

A striking assumption underlies Rabbi Yitzhak's question in the quoted midrash, namely, that cosmogonical and historical narratives are altogether irrelevant to the Torah's purposes; only the laws are pertinent.[40] Although the answer attributed to Rabbi Yitzhak shows that he later modifies this startling assumption[41] – the Torah does more than inculcate laws, it also validates Israel's claim to the land of Israel – Rashi's approach none the less tends to minimize the value of any hermeneutic of the Bible that is not centered on its laws. It thereby broaches the possibility that the Bible is not terribly interested in providing accurate cosmogony for its own sake.[42]

Consider next the comment of Nachmanides:

One may question [Rabbi Yitzhak's view as cited by Rashi]. For there is a great necessity to begin the Torah with "In the beginning God created." It is the root of faith; and one who does not believe in it [creation ex nihilo] and thinks the world is eternal denies the essential principle [of Judaism] and has no Torah! The answer is that the story of creation is a deep mystery not to be understood from the verses. ... It is for this reason that Rabbi Yitzhak said that it was not necessary for the Torah to begin with the chapter of "In the beginning God created" – what was created on the first day, what was done on the second and other days, as well as an extended account of the creation of Adam and Eve, their sin and punishment, and the story of the Garden of Eden and the expulsion of Adam from it – because all this cannot be understood completely from the verses. All the more, it was not necessary for the story of the generations of the flood and of the dispersion to be written, for there is no great need of these narratives, and for people who believe in the Torah, it would suffice without these verses.[43]

For Nachmanides, unlike Rashi, the inclusion of cosmogony is not puzzling per se, as the Bible aims to convey *'iqqarei emunah*, fundamentals of faith. Still, the extensive elaboration of these fundamentals – what was created on each day – is seemingly otiose, and the Torah's narrative is in any case too meager to furnish genuine understanding.[44] Nor is there need for the detailed history of the patriarchs that follows. Nachmanides explains the necessity for the ostensibly otiose narrative sections by pointing out the moral lesson they convey to Israel. The stories of Eden, the flood, and the dispersion teach that "it is proper that when a people continues to sin it should lose its place and another people should come and inherit the land" (Nachmanides 1971, p. 19). Like Rashi, Nachmanides adopts a restricted view of the aims of the Torah.

Needless to say, neither Rashi nor Nachmanides questions the historicity of the biblical narrative. On the contrary, to infer the lesson each gleans from the Bible's inclusion of the narrative – the absolute right of the Jews to the land of Israel (Rashi), the dependence of the Jews' right to the land upon their deeds (Nachmanides) – the narratives must be *true*. For Rashi's lesson to be learned, God must have created the world and granted Israel a particular land; for Nachmanides' to be inferred, there must have been a previous *factual* pattern of sin and expulsion. Nevertheless, approaches like those of Rashi and Nachmanides tend to deter the kind of emphasis on historical and scientific accuracy that would obscure the Torah's larger purposes.

This issue has become particularly acute and sensitive with the emergence of modern cosmology, anthropology, biology, and history. In the twentieth century, Rabbi Abraham Isaac Kook, the first Ashkenazic chief rabbi of Palestine and a major theologian of the century, addressed the clash between evolution and creation along with the contradiction between the scientific assessments of the age of the earth and the biblical chronology which makes the universe less than six thousand years old. He wrote:

> It makes no difference for us if in truth there was in the world an actual Garden of Eden, during which man delighted in an abundance of physical and spiritual good, or if actual existence began from the bottom upward, from the lowest level of being toward its highest. . . . We only have to know that there is a real possibility that even if man has risen to a high level, and has been deserving of all honors and pleasures, if he corrupts his ways, he can lose all that he has, and bring harm to himself and to his descendants for many generations.[45]

Surely this is not meant to imply that biblical religion, or a theology sensitive to it, is indifferent to matters of historical and scientific fact. The centrality of the creation motif and the history of the Jewish people in the Bible are enough to belie any such notion. Of course not everyone will draw the line in the same place: thus, for example, there are those who insist that observance of the Sabbath makes sense only on the basis of a literal six-day creation. It should not be difficult, however, to agree on the significance of the Bible's perspective on the fundamental questions of the examined life. Our own attempt in these pages to map a coherent biblical view of morality, of evil, and of human responsibility points to some of the possibilities.

❧ CONCLUSION ❧

Judaism is of course not identical with the Bible. Jewish philosophy must carry on a conversation with Talmud and Midrash, kabbalah, and Jewish philosophy from all ages. This quest for integration is often based on the assumption that there is an underlying continuity to Judaism; it also recognizes that unmediated access to the Bible, abstracted from its canonical form and exegetical history, is an unattainable chimera (see Carmy 1996). The examination of biblical ideas requires the thinker to perceive the continuities between the various biblical statements and the other chambers in the mansion of Torah, even while taking careful note of the ruptures.

The Bible is the primary source for Jewish philosophical reflection. It indeed warrants philosophical attention, as it supplies rich resources for philosophical analysis and exegesis. Paradoxically, however, the Bible can be appreciated properly by the philosopher only when he or she liberates the Bible from the vocabulary and preoccupations of some subsequent philosophical school – escaping a relentless rationalism and avoiding the anachronistic identification of a particular theory with the living data it seeks to capture. As we have seen, "literary" and "philosophical" dimensions of the text are not hermetically sealed off from each other. All ventures at exegesis are condemned to the endless process of trial and error in the effort to situate the work in its own context and grasp it in its own terms. Only by meeting the Bible on its own ground, in terms of its actual contents – as a compendium of divine law, as a narrative of God's rendezvous with humankind and with a singular people, as the drama of humanity's yearning for the creator and God's revelation to humanity – can we acquire the power to interpret the text in the light of later generations' intellectual framework and existential concerns.[46]

∾ NOTES ∾

1 A single example demonstrates the impossibility of limiting philosophy to conventionally formulated sentences. The book of Jonah concludes on a long rhetorical question: "You were concerned for the gourd on which you did not labor. . . . Shall I not be concerned for Nineveh . . .?" There is no way of turning this interrogation into the indicative mood; yet if this verse is not philosophy, then nothing in the Bible is philosophy!

2 Even those modern scholars who would account for contradictions by assigning the conflicting materials to distinct traditions and sources are not blind to the fact that the Bible has generally been understood as a unified document in Jewish tradition.

3 See Maimonides (1963, 3.22–3) and Gersonides' commentary to the book.

4 See *Guide* 1.1 – 1.2; Berman 1980; Klein-Braslavy 1986.

5 We also should mention a third negative reaction, that of kabbalists. Like the philosophers, and unlike either of the two views we will describe, kabbalists posited a deeper, esoteric level of meaning to the biblical text. However, they rejected the particular contents that rationalists claimed were found in those esoteric layers and replaced them with a different set of meanings.

6 See Hirsch 1982; Kaufmann 1960; cf. Halbertal and Margalit 1992, pp. 68–73.

7 Our failure to address diachronic questions within the Bible should not be taken to gainsay or even downplay their importance for theology and for elucidating the intellectual history of many concepts in biblical literature.

8 For example, David's consecutive inquiries about Saul's intentions and about the subsequent behavior of the men of Keilah in the event that Saul goes there (1 Samuel 23:10–12) suggested to later philosophers the problem of whether middle knowledge is possible (that is, knowledge of how a free creature would

act in all possible situations, including purely hypothetical ones). (See Adams 1987.) But such questions are distant from the Bible's agenda.

9 For Christian responses, see Idziak 1979.

10 Biblical interpreters have sometimes defined the episode differently, seeing it as a clash between king and prophet over whether the prophet is the sole arbiter of the divine intent.

11 See Jacobs 1978, Leiman 1978, and Lichtenstein 1978 for further analysis of the sources.

12 Kierkegaard is generally taken to define the ethical stage in a Kantian manner. (See most recently Green 1992). Gellman 1994 opts for a Hegelian provenance of the ethical. More radically, he construes obedience to God as a label for authentic individual self-expression. For a creative reading of the story as *favoring* Abraham's making independent moral judgments, see Bodoff 1993.

13 See for example Leibowitz 1987, p. 16. This despite Leibowitz's distaste for Kierkegaard's "Christian bellyaching" (Leibowitz 1987).

14 Compare the discussion of Phyllis Trible's analysis of Genesis 22 in Carmy (1996); see also Jacobs 1981.

15 Cf. Maimonides 1963, 1.2; Nachmanides, commentary to Genesis 2:9; other sources quoted in Leibowitz 1981, pp. 17–37.

16 For an assortment of Jewish and Christian discussions of this chapter, including a similar analysis of good and evil by Karl Barth, see Morris and Sawyer 1992.

17 Wyschogrod does not directly explain *why* they were now embarrassed by nakedness; precisely at this point, his approach should be combined with the traditional exegesis that relates the "knowledge of good and evil" to sexual arousal. But we shall not seek to develop such a synthesis here.

18 The rabbis (*Sanhedrin* 56b) derived an Adamic prohibition of murder from Genesis 2:16–17.

19 See his comment to Genesis 6:2.

20 On the theme of recreation, see Fishbane 1979.

21 See Albo 1929–30, 4.14, 15.

22 See Urbach 1987, pp. 420–61; Elman 1990 and 1990–1; Goldenberg 1982.

23 Some also see the soulmaking theodicy in remarks of Elihu (33:16–20).

24 See Saadia Gaon 1988, chapter 38.

25 Rashi, following the rabbis in the Midrash, holds that the divine pathos, like the human, adopts, as it were, the emotions appropriate to the present tense: when a child is born, one rejoices, though knowing too well that the road from birth leads to death. See also R. Chayyim ibn Atar's *Or ha-Chayyim*.

26 This verse is, in fact, cited by Gersonides to support his limitation of divine foreknowledge; see his commentary to Genesis 22. Also see Albo 1929–30, 5.13; Leibowitz 1981, pp. 188–93; Feldman 1985; Cohen 1985.

27 See Rashi, who takes this to imply that God "arranges" the accident to punish both the victim and the perpetrator for previous offenses.

28 See ibn Ezra, ad loc.

29 See also Alter 1981, pp. 33–5.

30 Joseph's later request for the Israelites to take his remains with them when they finally leave Egypt (Genesis 50:24) reflects Jacob's eventual influence upon him (note Jacob's request at 47:29).

31 According to some readings of Amos 2:6, the prophet there condemned the brothers' actions.

32 See for example Isaac Abravanel's comment to Genesis 37:1; see also Maimonides, *Mishneh Torah*, Laws of Repentance, 6.5; Rabinovitch 1977.

33 See commentary to Genesis 15:14 and *Or ha-Chayyim* ad loc. Note Nachmanides' exploitation of typology as a tool of exegesis in Genesis (see 12:7, inter alia).

34 A different interpretation would highlight the ambiguity of the Hebrew: either "elder" or "younger" could be taken as the subject and the other phrase as the object; see Cassuto 1961, pp. 86–7.

35 Kenneth Waxman pointed this out to us.

36 See Leibowitz 1981, pp. 264–79, on Jacob's deception. Late medieval thinkers such as R. Isaac Arama (*Aqedat Yitzhak* 1.28) rejected Nachmanides' approach to the Joseph story because they objected to the implication that the divine end justifies unacceptable human means. Wurzburger 1969 developed the view that Joseph subscribed to Nachmanides' thesis, but was wrong to do so.

37 Scholars have noted numerous literary parallels between the Joseph and Esther narratives. There may be other explanations of why the divine name is absent from these stories, but finding a common reason seems to us methodologically preferable in light of the other parallels between the stories.

38 One other issue that these episodes raise is the contingency of Jewish history. We are accustomed to think that Jewish history would not be Jewish history had, say, the theft of the blessing, or Joseph's sojourn in Egypt, never occurred. But if, pace Nachmanides, we impute blame even to people who try to fulfill the divine plan, this may imply that only certain end results are ordained, not the means; agents are culpable because they did not have to be the ones to bring the ordained result about. Hence Jewish history does carry an element of contingency. Rabbi Joseph Soloveitchik's lectures on the Bible frequently dramatize the question of alternative outcomes: what if certain meritorious acts had not been performed and what if certain temptations had been resisted? (see especially Soloveitchik 1992). He thus combines Nachmanides' consciousness of the large-scale repercussions of acts recorded in the Bible with an existentialist emphasis on the burden of individual choice.

39 The rabbis of the Talmud regard Exodus 12:2 as the commandment to sanctify each new moon.

40 Levenson 1985 has emphasized that the classic Christian works on Old Testament theology, such as those of Eichrodt and von Rad, are virtually oblivious to the centrality of law in the Bible.

41 Rashi's supercommentaries, for example, those of R. Eliyahu Mizrachi and Maharal, offer detailed analysis of the difference between the implied position of the question and that of the conclusion.

42 Rashi's grandson, Rashbam, goes even farther. In his view the story of creation is included in order to establish the seven-day week culminating in the Sabbath (see Kamin 1986). Remarkably, the sectarian pseudepigraphic book of Jubilees, dated to the second century BCE, opens with Moses on Sinai, and reviews creation as a backdrop to the revelation of the law, thus providing, as it were, an alternative version of the Torah that comes close to the spirit behind R. Yitzhak's question.

43 Commentary to Genesis 1:1. We have followed closely the translation of C. B. Chavel in Nachmanides 1971.
44 One way to put Nachmanides' thesis is this: the Bible conveys metaphysical *truth*, but is not devoted to metaphysical *enlightenment*. The enlightenment is esoteric, accessible only to kabbalists; for the ordinary reader of the Bible, the fundamentals of faith suffice.
45 Kook, letters, 1, no. 134 (in Feldman 1986, p. 12); also Rabbi Kook's additional reference to talmudic remarks on 'confused dates' in prophetic texts (cited in Carmy 1996). A zesty formulation of the point is found in Hertz 1941, 1: 195: "And fully to grasp the eternal power and infinite beauty of these words – 'And God created man in his own image' – we need but compare them with the genealogy of man, condensed from the pages of one of the leading biologists of the age (Haeckel): 'Monera begat Amoeba, Amoeba begat Synamoebae, Synamoebae begat Ciliated Larva. . . .' Let anyone who is disturbed by the fact that Scripture does not include the latest scientific doctrine, try to imagine such information proved in a Biblical chapter." A contemporary philosopher, Peter van Inwagen (1993), a committed Christian, has likewise emphasized in a colorful way the moral and spiritual value of the creation stories and the relative unimportance of its scientific implications.
46 We thank David Berger, Devorah Steinmetz, and Kenneth Waxman for their comments and suggestions.

❧ BIBLIOGRAPHY ❧

Texts

Albo, J. (1929–30) *The Book of Roots (Sefer ha-Ikkarim)*, translated by I. Husik, 5 vols (Philadelphia: Jewish Publication Society).
Hertz, J. H. (1941) *The Pentateuch and Haftorahs: Hebrew Text, English Translation, and Commentary*, 2 vols (New York: Metzudah).
Hirsch, S. R. (1982) *The Pentateuch: Translated and Explained by Samson Raphael Hirsch*, 2nd ed., translated by I. Levy (Gateshead: Judaica Press).
Maimonides (1963) *Guide of the Perplexed*, translated by S. Pines, 2 vols (Chicago: University of Chicago Press).
Nachmanides (1971) *Commentary on the Torah*, translated and annotated by C. D. Chavel (New York: Shilo).
Saadia Gaon (1988) *The Book of Theodicy* (Commentary on the Book of Job), translated and annotated by L. E. Goodman (New Haven: Yale University Press).
Spinoza (1951) *Theological-Political Treatise*, translated by R. H. M. Elwes (New York: Dover).

Studies

Adams, R. M. (1987) "Middle Knowledge and the Problem of Evil," in *The Virtue of Faith* (New York: Oxford University Press), pp. 77–93.

Alter, R. (1981) *The Art of Biblical Narrative* (New York: Basic Books).

Barnes, J. (1982) *The Pre-Socratic Philosophers* (London: Routledge & Kegan Paul).

Berman, L. (1980) "Maimonides on the Fall of Man," *AJS Review* 5: 1–15.

Bodoff, L. (1993) "The Real Test of the *Akedah*: Blind Obedience vs. Moral Choice," *Judaism* 42: 71–92.

Carmy, S. (1996) "A Room with a View, But a Room of Our Own," in *Modern Scholarship in the Study of Torah: Contributions and Limitations*, edited by S. Carmy (Northvale: Jason Aronson).

Cassuto, U. (1961) *The Documentary Hypothesis and the Composition of the Pentateuch: Eight Lectures*, translated by I. Abrahams (Jerusalem: Magnes).

Cohen, J. (1985) "Philosophical Exegesis in Historical Perspective: The Case of the Binding of Isaac," in *Divine Omniscience and Omnipotence in Medieval Philosophy*, edited by T. Rudavsky (Dordrecht: Reidel), pp. 135–42.

Elman, Y. (1990) "The Suffering of the Righteous in Palestinian and Babylonian Sources," *Jewish Quarterly Review* 80: 315–39.

—— (1990–1) "Righteousness as its Own Reward: An Inquiry into the Theologies of the Stam," *Proceedings of the American Academy for Jewish Research* 57: 35–68.

Feldman, S. (1985) "The Binding of Isaac: A Test Case of Divine Foreknowledge," in *Divine Omniscience and Omnipotence in Medieval Philosophy*, edited by T. Rudavsky (Dordrecht: Reidel), pp. 105–33.

Feldman, T. (1986) *Rav A. Y. Kook: Selected Letters*, translated and annotated by T. Feldman (Ma'aleh Adumim, Israel: Ma'aliot Publications).

Fishbane, M. (1979) *Text and Texture* (New York: Schocken).

Gellman, J. (1977) "The Meta-philosophy of Religious Language," *Nous* 11: 151–61.

—— (1994) *The Fear, the Trembling and the Fire* (Washington, DC: University Press of America).

Glatzer, N. (ed.) (1969) *The Dimensions of Job* (New York: Schocken).

Goldenberg, R. (1982) "Early Rabbinic Explanations of the Destruction of Jerusalem," *Journal of Jewish Studies* 33: 517–25.

Green, R. (1988) *Religion and Moral Reason* (New York: Oxford University Press).

—— (1992) *Kierkegaard and Kant* (Albany: State University of New York Press).

Halbertal, M. and A. Margalit (1992) *Idolatry*, translated by N. Goldblum (Cambridge, MA: Harvard University Press).

Idziak, J. M. (ed.) (1979) *Divine Command Morality* (Toronto: Edwin Mellen).

Jacobs, L. (1978) "The Relationship Between Religion and Ethics in Jewish Thought," in *Contemporary Jewish Ethics*, edited by M. Kellner (New York: Hebrew Publishing), pp. 41–57.

—— (1981) "The Problem of the *Akedah* in Jewish Thought," in *Kierkegaard's Fear and Trembling: Critical Appraisals*, edited by R. L. Perkins (Birmingham: University of Alabama Press), pp. 1–9.

Kamin, S. (1986) "Rashbam's Conception of the Creation in Light of the Intellectual Currents of his Time," *Scripta Hierosolymitana* 31: *Studies in Bible*, edited by S. Japhet, pp. 91–132.

Kaufmann, Y. (1960) *The Religion of Israel: From its Beginnings to the Babylonian Exile*, translated by M. Greenberg (Chicago: University of Chicago Press).

Klein-Braslavy, S. (1986) *Perush ha-Rambam la-Sippurim al Adam be-Parashat Bereshit* (Jerusalem: Reuben Mass).

Leibowitz, I. (1987) *Al Olam u-Meloo* (Jerusalem: Keter).

Leibowitz, N. (1981) *Studies in Bereshit (Genesis) in the Context of Ancient and Modern Jewish Bible Commentary*, 4th ed., translated by A. Newman (Jerusalem: World Zionist Organization).

Leiman, S. (1978) "Critique of Louis Jacobs," in *Contemporary Jewish Ethics*, edited by M. Kellner (New York: Hebrew Publishing), pp. 58–60.

Levenson, J. D. (1985) *Sinai and Zion: An Entry into the Jewish Bible* (New York: Harper & Row).

Lichtenstein, A. (1978) "Does Jewish Tradition Recognize an Ethic Independent of Halakha?," in *Contemporary Jewish Ethics*, edited by M. Kellner (New York: Hebrew Publishing), pp. 102–23.

Morris, P. and D. Sawyer (eds) (1992) *A Walk in the Garden: Biblical, Iconographical, and Literary Images of Eden* (Ithaca: Cornell University Press).

Otto, R. (1950) *The Idea of the Holy*, translated by J. W. Harvey (Oxford and New York: Oxford University Press).

Rabinovitch, N. (1977) "The One and The Many: Early Stochastic Reasoning in Philosophy," *Annals of Science* 34.4: 331–44.

Seeskin, K. (1990) *Jewish Philosophy in a Secular Age* (Albany: State University of New York Press).

Soloveitchik, J. B. (1965) "Lonely Man of Faith," *Tradition* 7.2: 5–67.

—— (1992) *Divrei Hashkafah*, translated by M. Krone (Jerusalem: World Zionist Organization).

—— (1994) "Ha-yehudi Mashul Le-Sefer Torah" [Hebrew], translated from Yiddish by S. Carmy, *Beit Yosef Shaul* 4, edited by E. A. Adler, pp. 68–100.

Steinberg, M. (1960) *Anatomy of Faith* (New York: Harcourt Brace Jovanovich).

Steinmetz, D. (1994) "The Vineyard, Farm, and Garden: The Drunkenness of Noah in the Context of the Primeval History," *Journal of Biblical Literature* 113.2: 193–207.

Sykes, D. (1985) *Patterns in Genesis*. Ph.D. dissertation, Yeshiva University.

Urbach, E. (1987) *The Sages: Their Concepts and Beliefs*, translated by I. Abrahams (Cambridge, MA: Harvard University Press).

van Inwagen, P. (1993) "Genesis and Evolution," in *Reasoned Faith*, edited by E. Stump (Ithaca: Cornell University Press), pp. 93–127.

Wurzburger, W. (1969) "Yavneh Studies in Vayechi," in *Yavneh Studies in Parashat ha-Shavua: Bereshit*, edited by J. B. Wolowelsky (Yavneh: The Religious Jewish Students Association), pp. 40–42.

Wyschogrod, M. (1986) "Sin and Atonement in Judaism," in *The Human Condition in the Jewish and Christian Traditions*, edited by F. Greenspahn (New York: Ktav), pp. 103–26.

CHAPTER 3
Hellenistic Jewish philosophy
David Winston

◆◆ INTRODUCTION ◆◆

Early Greek references to the Jews included the notion that they were a race of philosophers or descendants of the philosophers of India, and it is even argued that Moses had arrived at his non-anthropomorphic conception of God through astrophysical speculation.[1] Moreover, the Greek inclination to idealize Eastern wisdom led to the assertion that Pythagoras was dependent on the doctrines of the Jews and Thracians, and is exemplified by the anecdote that Aristotle learned more from a certain Jew of Coele-Syria, who had sought him out while he was in Asia Minor, than the latter had learned from him.[2] A reflection of this Greek tendency is found in various Hellenistic Jewish writings and culminates in Philo's statements that pagan lawgivers borrowed from Moses, and that Heraclitus and Zeno also derived some of their teachings from the great Jewish prophet.[3] The reality, of course, was just the reverse. It was the Greek philosophical tradition that inseminated the Jewish mind in an encounter that largely took place in the Diaspora, since the sages of the land of Israel were essentially indifferent to philosophical speculation, though in a general way even they were not completely untouched by it.

The initial penetration of Greek philosophical thought seems to have occurred in the writings of the Jewish wisdom tradition, inasmuch as the wisdom schools had international connections and its members were frequently recruited for foreign service, some even serving in the courts of foreign kings (Isaiah 22:15). It has been demonstrated, for example, that Proverbs 22:17–23:12 is dependent on the Egyptian *Instruction of Amenemope*, while the 'Sayings of Agur' (Proverbs 30:1–14) and the 'Sayings of Lemuel' (Proverbs 31:1–9) "appear to be borrowed from Transjordanian, probably Aramaic, wisdom collections."[4] We shall accordingly begin our account of Hellenistic Jewish

38

philosophy with the biblical text of Qohelet, and the extra-canonical Wisdom of Ben Sira, and Wisdom of Solomon.

❧ QOHELET ❧

The first glimmer of Jewish contact with the philosophical genius of the Greek mind appears to involve an interaction that is largely context-ual and reflects a broad level of Greek conceptuality and mood rather than specific schools of thought or technical doctrines. Qohelet is concerned above all with the individual, and his basic approach is rooted in personal experience and observation, self-consciously described and emphasized by the frequent redundant first-person pronoun and the twelvefold reference to his heart in 1:12–2:26.[5] Fox has noted that the importance Qohelet gives to the validation of his thought is unique in Jewish wisdom literature, since the wisdom teachers do not offer their experience as a source of new knowledge and rarely invoke experi-ential arguments. When they do, it is for the most part a rhetorical strategy, used to engage the pupil's attention.[6] Moreover, Qohelet's highly introspective reporting, which constantly draws attention to his personal reactions to various situations in an apparent effort to persuade by empathy (2:2,17; 7:26), has no close parallels in other wisdom litera-ture, and is clearly reminiscent of Socratic dialogue. Indeed, Socrates' relentless probing, which in Plato's early dialogues invariably ends in utter perplexity and puzzlement, is closely analogous to Qohelet's end-less questioning and his firm conviction that the true nature of the divine plan for humanity constitutes an impenetrable mystery (3:11; 7:23–4; 8:17).[7]

It has been observed that Qohelet has a strong preference for the word *kol*, 'all', which is exhibited in his frequent attempts to character-ize and evaluate various physical and psychological manifestations, and that this form of expression is not found elsewhere in Scripture, though it is very common in Greek philosophical literature.[8] Qohelet indeed opens with just such an evaluation, declaring that all is *hevel*, a word that is variously translated as "vanity," "futility," or "absurdity." Levy and Amir have noted the resemblance between this recurrent judgment of Qohelet and the aphorism attributed to the Cynic Monimus of Syracuse (fourth century BCE) declaring all human supposition to be illusion (*typhos*, literally "smoke").[9]

Hengel cites a series of Greek texts that reflect popular Greek philosophy and provide close parallels to Qohelet. The problems raised by the doctrine of divine retribution,[10] which inform Qohelet's running critique, are similarly taken up by a Greek contemporary, Cercidas of Megalopolis (c. 290–220 BCE), a politician and poet influenced by the

Cynics. "Is the eye of justice," he writes, "as blind as a mole? . . . Does a mist dim the eye of Themis the bright?" In Babrius' fable 127, the old view that Zeus records human actions is satirized with the remark that he orders Hermes to write down their misdeeds severally on shards and piles them up in a chest close by himself, but since the shards lie heaped up one upon another awaiting the time he can examine them, some are late to fall into his hands (cf. Qohelet 8:10–14). Somewhat analogously, according to Rabba, the famed third-generation Babylonian Amora, Job blasphemed by saying to God, "Perhaps a tempest has passed before you, and caused you to confuse *Iyyov* [Job] and *Oyav* [enemy]" (B. *Bava Batra* 16a). Qohelet's obsession with the incalculability of death, which renders us like animals trapped in a snare (9:12), is paralleled in a Greek epitaph from the third century BCE: "Truly the gods take no account of mortals; no, like animals we are pulled hither and thither by chance [*automato*; cf. Qohelet's use of *miqreh* in 3:19], in life as in death." Finally, Qohelet's advice to "seize the day" (9:7–10), paralleled in the Babylonian epic of Gilgamesh and the Egyptian Song of the Harper, is also a popular theme in Greek tradition: "Remembering that the same end awaits all mortals, enjoy life as long as you live . . . . For know this well: once you have descended to the drink of Lethe, you will see no more of those things that are above." Similar advice is given in the Greek graffiti from the tomb of Jason in Jerusalem, dating from the time of Alexander Jannaeus (first century BCE). Hengel concludes that the crisis in religion reflected in the above citations, which reached its climax about the third century BCE, "presumably did not fail to make a mark on the thought of Qohelet, and was apparently communicated to him by Ptolemaic officials, merchants and soldiers, who were not lacking even in Jerusalem."[11]

Fox (1989, p. 47) correctly remarks that "underlying Qohelet's *hevel* judgments is an assumption that the system should be rational, i.e. that actions should invariably produce appropriate consequences." The injustices that God allows to mar his creation render it for Qohelet contradictory and absurd, and this offends the inviolable criterion that anchors his entire intellectual existence, casting a pall over his life's work. This demand for rationality constitutes the heart of the mainstream tradition in Greek philosophy. For a philosopher like Nietzsche, "the fanaticism with which all Greek reflection throws itself upon rationality betrays a desperate situation," and is "pathologically conditioned."[12] In any case, it is this fundamental drive for rationality that prevents Qohelet from ignoring the ineluctable absurdity that characterizes the human enterprise as a whole and thus sharply distinguishes his approach from that of the Jewish wisdom tradition.

❧ THE WISDOM OF BEN SIRA ❧

There can be little doubt that Ben Sira's opus (c. 180 BCE) is marked by a consistent effort to effect a new synthesis of ideas. In an age when Hellenistic wisdom dominated the civilized world, he did his best to broaden the bounds of the Mosaic law so that it would encompass universal wisdom. As Collins has remarked, Ben Sira's so-called nationalization of wisdom constituted in reality the universalization of the Torah.[13] The Torah is refracted for Ben Sira through the lens of wisdom, and the case for its legitimacy is made in wisdom's terms: "The whole of wisdom is fear of the Lord; complete wisdom is the fulfillment of the Law."[14]

It is especially, however, in his confrontation with the problem of evil that Ben Sira moves beyond the earlier wisdom tradition and is actively engaged in adapting Stoic arguments for the formulation of his main solution to this puzzling paradox, namely, that nature is to be seen as a harmony of opposites. Although Platonism did not arrive in Alexandria before the first century BCE, some knowledge of Stoic philosophy does appear to have penetrated the Alexandrian intellectual scene already in the third century BCE, for we are told that when Cleanthes, scholarch of the Stoic school from 263 to 232, refused the invitation of Ptolemy Philadelphus, he sent his pupil Sphaerus there instead.[15] The visit of an isolated Stoic philosopher does not constitute a major presence and it is therefore unlikely that in the absence of a flourishing Stoic center such as those found in Rhodes and in Tarsus, Ben Sira would have possessed a detailed and technical knowledge of the Stoic philosophy. But its broad outlines were probably well known to him. Although he does not speak explicitly of the harmony of the universal order, his words clearly imply it. In 33:7–14, he seeks to reconcile the unity of creation with a divine plan that consistently discriminates between pairs of opposites: good and evil, life and death, the sinner and the godly. In his effort to explicate the dietary laws, pseudo-Aristeas had likewise noted the paradox that, in spite of the fact that creation was one, some things are regarded by the Torah as unclean for food, and in the course of his explanation of this surprising fact he noted that although all things are to the natural reason similarly constituted, being all administered by a single power, in every case there is a profound logic for our abstinence from some and our use of others (129, 143). Ben Sira similarly indicates that although every day has its light from the sun, certain days were by the Lord's decision distinguished and made holy, and though all humans were created out of the earth, some, in God's great wisdom, were hallowed and brought near to him, while others were cursed and removed from their place: "See now all the works of the Most High: they come in pairs, the one the opposite of the other" (33:15). All this evidently implies that the universe consists of a harmony of opposites in accordance with a mysterious divine design.[16]

The Stoics taught a similar doctrine. First, like Ben Sira, they declared that divine providence is "chiefly directed and concentrated upon three objects: to secure for the world the structure best suited for survival, absolute completeness, and above all consummate beauty and embellishment of every kind."[17] Then, too, like Ben Sira, they taught that this is the best possible world that could be produced, and that, notwithstanding apparent imperfections here and there, Nature so organized each part that harmony is present in the whole.[18] As for the evil of natural disasters, "it has a rationale peculiar to itself . . . and is not without usefulness in relation to the whole, for without it there could be no good."[19] Ben Sira's attitude is similar: "No cause then to say: What is the purpose of this? Everything is chosen to satisfy a need" (39:21). Indeed, the very elements that are good for the godfearing turn to evil for sinners (39:28–31; cf. Wisdom 16:24).

Another aspect of the theodicy issue in regard to which Ben Sira seems to have followed the Stoic lead is in his formulation of the paradox of freedom and determinism. The older wisdom literature did not feel this contradiction too keenly, and was content to assert that all was determined by the gods in advance, and yet at the same time to insist that success and failure, punishment and reward, were conditioned by human behavior. In the Egyptian *Instruction of Ptahhotep* (Old Kingdom period) we read: "His guilt was fated in the womb; he whom they guide cannot go wrong, whom they make boatless cannot cross."[20]

It has been pointed out that the demotic wisdom instruction known as *Papyrus Insinger* was the first such Egyptian writing to deal consciously and explicitly with the freedom/determinism dilemma. What we find here is very much like the paradoxical Stoic formulation that all is in accord with *heimarmene* (fate), yet our actions are in our power. In light of the many Hellenistic elements in *Papyrus Insinger*, Lichtheim has concluded that it is very likely that in this case too we are dealing with such an influence. In view of the striking similarities between *Papyrus Insinger* and Ben Sira, it is reasonable to assume that their similar formulations of the freedom/determinism paradox were the result of their common use of Stoic sources (Lichtheim 1983, pp. 107–96). Although a palpably determinist strain does run through the book of Proverbs, it nevertheless lacks an explicit and conscious expression of the paradox under discussion. Thus the author of Proverbs teaches that the sage will acquire wisdom, while the fool will hold it in contempt, thereby implying that their life courses are fixed in advance (Proverbs 14:6; 9:7; 13:19; 20:12). There is even a verse that asserts that God has created all, including the fool, for a special purpose (16:4). Nowhere, however, does the book of Proverbs declare unequivocally, as does Ben Sira, that God has determined the human character even before birth (Sirach 1:14–15), or that humans were fashioned by God as clay in the power of the potter, so that, in accordance with an eternal cosmic plan, the godly or blessed stand over against the sinner or the cursed (Sirach 33:10–15). Moreover, Ben Sira includes, along with his starkly predestinarian passages, emphatic statements concerning one's freedom to choose one's life-path accompanied by an explicit warning against blaming God for causing human sin (see Winston 1989a; 1979, pp. 46–58).

❧ WISDOM OF SOLOMON ❧

In the Wisdom of Solomon, the Hellenistic Jewish wisdom tradition so palpably verges on the philosophical that we can readily identify this book's Middle Platonist affinities and its considerable use of Greek philosophical terminology (Winston 1979, pp. 13 and 16n.14). An exhortatory discourse featuring a highly enthusiastic and eulogistic invocation of Wisdom, it was written in Greek by a profoundly hellenized Jew of Alexandria, after that city's conquest by Rome in 30 BCE, when the earlier optimism of the Alexandrian Jewish community for a rapprochement with the Greeks and for social and cultural acceptance by them had been replaced by a mounting sense of disillusionment and disappointment. The centrality of its Platonic teaching of the immortality of the soul represents a new emphasis in Jewish tradition, while its concept of the pre-existent soul (8:19), although it is only hinted at, may be the earliest attestation of this notion in Jewish literature. Even more significant, however, is the fact that Plato's doctrine of the adverse influence of body on soul (*Phaedo* 66b; *Republic* 611c; *Timaeus* 43b-c) and the superior state of soul pregnancy over its bodily form (*Symposium* 208e) is faithfully echoed in Wisdom 4:1, where it is said that it is better to be childless, provided one is virtuous, and in 9:15, where, in a verse replete with Platonic phraseology, the author speaks of "a perishable body weighing down the soul and a tent of clay encumbering a mind full of cares" (cf. *Phaedo* 81c; *Phaedrus* 247b).

In sketching his own spiritual odyssey, the author confesses to a passion for Woman Wisdom (*Sophia*) that had gripped him from early youth and had led him to cast his lot with her for ever. This unbridled love for Wisdom is vividly reflected in his magnificent fivefold description of her, in which she is conceived as an eternal emanation of God's power and glory (7:25–6, 29–30), a Neopythagorean notion that even the more philosophically ambitious Philo was reluctant to express explicitly, preferring instead to use locutions that only implied it (Winston 1979, pp. 38, 185–6). Unlike Ben Sira (1:4; 24:9), who asserts that God has created Wisdom, he says not a word about her creation, describing her instead in the present tense as a divine effulgence, of which one would have to say more precisely that she is "ever being produced and in a state of having been produced," to use a formulation later employed by the fifth-century Neoplatonist Proclus (1967: 2:141). As for the creation of the world, he adopts the Platonic notion that it was created "out of formless matter" (11:17), a view not inconsonant with that of the rabbis (Winston 1979, p. 38; 1971; 1986).

In 7:22–4 the author describes Wisdom by a series of twenty-one epithets (such as intelligent, subtle, agile, unsullied, unhindered, steadfast), borrowed largely from Greek philosophy, especially that of the Stoa. Posidonius, for example, had defined God as "intelligent breath [*pneuma noeron*] pervading the whole of substance" (F100, Edelstein and Kidd 1972), and Stoics had defined the soul as a "subtle [*leptomeres*], self-moving body" (von Arnim 1903–24: 2:780). Moreover, according to Chrysippus, "since the universal nature extends to all things, everything that comes about in anyway whatever in the whole universe ... will necessarily have come about conformably with that nature and its reason in due and unimpeded [*akoloutos*] sequence" (von Arnim 1903–24: 2:137). What characterizes the Stoic *pneuma* above all, however, is that it pervades (*diekei*) and permeates (*chorei*) all things (von Arnim 1903–24: 2:416, 1021, 1033). According to Stoic cosmology, an active principle, the divine logos, totally pervaded a passive principle, qualityless matter, as the passage of body through body. The *pneuma*'s extension through matter is described as tensional motion (*tonike kinesis*), characterized as a form of oscillation, a simultaneous motion in opposite directions (Todd 1976, pp. 34–7). This scientific theory appealed so strongly to both Philo and the author of Wisdom that they were willing to take up this stark corporealism and adapt it to their own Platonist way of thinking, no doubt made possible by their transposing the materialist Stoic terminology into literary metaphor.

In a fine ode to Wisdom's saving power in history (10:1–21), the author assimilates the old covenantal salvation history with its miraculous and sudden divine irruptions to the immanent divine ordering of human events as mediated by the continuous activity of Wisdom. It is her generation-by-generation election of holy servants (7:27) that structures the life of Israel. As the divine mind immanent within the universe and guiding and controlling all its dynamic operations, Wisdom represents the entire range of the natural sciences (7:17–21), is the teacher of all human arts and crafts, skilled in ontology, logic, and rhetoric, and the source of all moral knowledge (8:7 enumerates the four cardinal virtues, emphasized by Plato, Aristotle, and the Stoics).

It is undoubtedly significant that the author, unlike Ben Sira, nowhere explicitly identifies Wisdom with Torah. His statement that "love of Wisdom means the keeping of her laws" (6:18) is ambiguous, and probably refers to the statutes of natural law. All we have from him in this regard is but a passing allusion to Israel's mission of bringing the imperishable light of the law to the world (18:4). Very likely he believed with Philo that the teachings of the Torah were tokens of the divine wisdom, and that they were in harmony with the law of the universe and as such implant all the virtues in the human psyche (Winston 1979, pp. 42–3).

❧ THE FOURTH BOOK OF MACCABEES ❧

In 4 Maccabees (probably first century CE) we have an overtly philo-sophical discourse on the theme of the mastery of religious reason over the emotions, illustrated, in what constitutes the major portion of the text, by a panegyric of the martyrs (Eleazar, the seven brethren, and their mother), which the author, a skilled rhetorician, binds to the discourse (the first three chapters) by repeated references to his main thesis.[21] The essential component in the book's argument is that the Torah, the divine *nomos*, is consistent with the world order. In the confrontation between Antiochus and Eleazar, the king claims that the Jewish ban on eating pork shows that Judaism does not accord with nature (5:8–9). In his response, Eleazar, identified both as a philo-sopher and an expert in the law (5:4), argues, in spite of the king's mockery of the Jewish philosophy and his assertion that it is contrary to reason, that in fact it inculcates in its followers the virtues of temper-ance, courage, justice, and piety (5:22–5). His reasoning is couched in the language of Greek natural law theory: "For believing that the law has been established from God, we know that the creator of the world, in laying down the law, feels for us [*hemin sympathei*] in accordance with [our] nature [*kata physin*] and commands us to eat whatever is well suited to our soul" (5:25–6, my translation). The thrust of Eleazar's statement is that *nomos* and *physis*, deriving as they do from one creator, cannot be mutually antagonistic. The law is perfectly rational, and the term *logismos*, reasoning, as Redditt has noted, occurs character-istically seventy-three times, for the most part in the context of the author's recurring theme that human reason is sovereign over the emotions.[22]

Gutman (1949) and Hadas (1953, pp. 115–18) think that Eleazar's position is modelled on that of Socrates in Plato's *Gorgias*, where, in answer to Callicles' objection that the tyrant can subject his victim to torture, Socrates insists that "any injustice against me and mine is both worse and more shameful for the man who does the injustice than for me who suffers it" (508e, trans. Irwin). Moreover, at the final judgment, says Socrates, relating an ancient tale as the word of truth, the soul, stripped of its body, will be subjected to the ultimate scrutiny of justice. Similarly, the author of 4 Maccabees justifies the fate of the martyrs by emphasizing the immortality of the soul and its future vindication. Victory in their contest, he says, was "incorruption in long-lasting life," and "they now stand beside the divine throne and live the life of the age of blessing, for Moses says (Deuteronomy 33:3), 'All the holy ones are under your hands' " (17:12–19, cf. 18:23, and Wisdom 3:1).

Although there are clear echoes of Stoic teaching in the book, this may merely indicate that the author's philosophical orientation is that of the highly stoicized Middle Platonism of the age. The well-known Stoic definition of wisdom as "knowledge of things divine and human and of their causes" (von Arnim 1903–24: 2:35) is reproduced in 1:15–17, where wisdom is identified with the education given by the law; the famous Stoic paradox that the sage is not merely free but also a king (Cicero, *Academica* 2.136) is echoed in 2:23, 7:23, and 14:2; and the martyrs are said to behave with true Stoic apathy (9:17; 11:25; 15:11, 14). Wolfson (1948, 2:270–1) argued that "by the time of Philo, the question whether virtue means the extirpation of the emotions or only their control seems to have been a subject of discussion among Hellenistic Jews. Guided by Jewish tradition, the author of 4 Maccabees comes out in opposition to the Stoics." Renehan has correctly pointed out, however, that the platonizing Middle Stoic Posidonius had also maintained that the passions cannot be eradicated.[23] But the Middle Platonists generally followed the Middle Stoa in this matter, so once again the author's philosophical orientation points in the direction of Middle Platonism.[24]

PSEUDO-ARISTEAS

It was the Greek Bible that ultimately provided the occasion for a large-scale penetration of Greek philosophy into Hellenistic Jewish thought. Although the *Letter of Aristeas* (second century BCE) purports to be the eye-witness account by a courtier of Ptolemy II (283–247 BCE) of the events connected with the Greek translation of the Pentateuch, scholars are agreed that the book is a literary fiction, and that the author is in reality an Alexandrian Jew seeking to demonstrate the superiority of the Jewish faith and the possibility for mutual respect and peaceful coexistence between Jews and Greeks. In a letter to the high priest Eleazar, Ptolemy announces his resolve to have the Hebrew Bible translated into Greek so that it could find its rightful place in the great library at Alexandria (34–40). Aristeas refers to the high priest as *kalos kagathos*, the "true gentleman," and makes him use the same expression in his description of the seventy-two elders chosen to execute the translation (46). Not only did the latter have a thorough knowledge of the literature of the Jews, but they possessed equal mastery of Greek literature as well, "zealously cultivating the quality of the mean [*to meson*] and eschewing any uncouth and uncultivated attitude of mind" (121–2, Charlesworth 1985, 2:21).

Interrupting the narrative of the translator's departure from Jerusalem is an important digression consisting of the high priest's rationale of the law (128–72). In view of the fact that creation is one, asks the Greek delegation, why is it that some things are regarded by Scripture as unclean? To this the high priest replies that the lawgiver has enclosed his people with unbreakable palisades to prevent them from mingling with other nations and to keep them pure in body and spirit. Like Aristobulus, pseudo-Aristeas asserts that "nothing has been set down in Scripture heedlessly or in the spirit of myth but only with the intent that we practice justice towards all people and be mindful of God's sovereignty" (168). The dietary rules are meant to promote holy contemplation and perfection of character, for the permitted animals are gentle and clean, whereas those forbidden are wild and carnivorous. By way of allegory, the "parting of the hoof" and the "cloven foot" that characterize the permitted animals symbolize discrimination in our actions with a view to what is right. "Chewing the cud," on the other hand, signifies memory, admonishing us to remember, "what great and marvelous things the Lord thy God did in thee" (Deuteronomy 10:21), that is, the marvelous construction of the human body and the acuity and infinite scope of the intellect. Furthermore, the character of "the weasel and the mouse and the rest of the forbidden animals is one that is prone to evil." Weasels, for example, conceive through the ears and give birth through the mouth, and this is taken to symbolize the maleficent actions of informers, who hear rumors and give body to them by word of mouth. This bit of physiological folklore was widespread in the ancient world, and an analogous symbolic interpretation of it can be found in Plutarch, where it is said to portray the creation of speech.[25] This kind of allegorizing by pseudo-Aristeas may owe something to the influence of the Pythagoreans, who also possessed unusual dietary rules, which they later sought to justify philosophically.[26] Although there is considerable similarity here with Philo's allegorization of the dietary regulations, there is as yet nothing remotely resembling the Philonic "allegory of the soul." On the other hand, in insisting that these strange food laws have been legislated "with a view to truth and as a token of right reason" (161), he anticipates Philo's firm conviction that the Mosaic law is no arbitrary set of decrees handed down from on high, but rather the truest reflection of the logos.

The section of the seven banquets (187–294), in which the king's seventy-two questions are answered, one each, by the Jewish envoys, forms the largest single unit of the book, and its special significance is indicated by the author's emphasis on the king's bedazzled admiration for every answer and the incessant applause at the end of each banquet. Indeed it is part of the author's strategy to provide his reader with a list of distinguished gentile "witnesses" attesting to the excellence and "philosophic purity" of the divine lawbooks of the Jews. In addition to the Egyptian priests who have dubbed the Jews "men of God" (reproducing the Egyptian expression *rmt ntr*) as distinguished from "men of food, drink, and raiment" (140), the list of witnesses includes Demetrius of Phalerum, Hecataeus of Abdera, and the philosopher Menedemus of Eretria (10, 31, 200–1). The king himself is perhaps the strongest witness, filling the Jerusalem Temple with sumptuous gifts (51–82), calling the translators "God-fearing" (179), acknowledging that the highest God (that is, the God of Israel) has preserved his kingdom in peace and honor (37), bowing down seven times before the Torah scrolls, his eyes suffused with tears of joy (177–8), and confessing at the conclusion of the banquet that he had been given "a lesson in kingship" (294). As Boccaccini has perceptively remarked, pseudo-Aristeas is not even concerned to make Greek *paideia* dependent on the greater antiquity of Jewish *paideia*, a path well trodden by many oriental and Hellenistic Jewish authors, including the redoubtable Philo. The road to salvation is fully open to the gentiles, for it is rooted in the "love of learning" (*philomatheia*), "the supreme human quality, through which a pure disposition of mind is acquired, by seizing upon what is noblest" (2).[27]

Tcherikover (1958) has observed that the remarkable thing about the seventy-two answers of the Jewish sages is the absence in them of any trace of Jewish particularism. The Torah, Moses, Sinai, the Jewish nation, Palestine – none of these appears. The one strikingly Jewish feature that characterizes every answer is the reference of all things to God, and even when that reference degenerates into a mere "tag," the impact of this emphasis on God as the ultimate source and standard of right remains undiminished, and it is just this "making God the starting-point of their reasoning" that wins the king's approval and is seconded by the philosopher Menedemus of Eretria, a member of the Megarian school, known for its skill in dialectics and its assertion that the good is a unity, though called by many names, and that God, too, was but another name for the goodness that was knowledge (Diogenes Laertius 2.106).

The God-centeredness aside, much of the conceptuality of the seventy-two answers is essentially Greek.[28] Typically Greek, for example, are the statements that persuasion (*to peisai*) is the object of discourse (266), that a clear conscience gives freedom from fear (243), that one should not be carried away by impulses but moderate one's emotions (the Peripatetic ideal of *metriopatheia* (256; cf. 223), and that one should not covet the unattainable (*anephikton*; cf. Philo, *Allegorical Interpretation* 1.75; *Confusion of Tongues* 7; *Special Laws* 1.44). It is especially noteworthy that, in making mercy a key divine attribute, the term used repeatedly by pseudo-Aristeas is not *eleemon* (which occurs only in 208; cf. LXX Exodus 34:6), but *epieikes* (192, 207, 211), which means "equitable" or "fair," thus avoiding (at least from the vantage point of the modified position of the Middle and Late Stoa) the embarrassment occasioned by the former term for one who is aware of the Stoic philosophical objection to its irrational character. This is especially striking, since even the author of the Wisdom of Solomon and Philo frequently speak of God's *eleos*. Equally striking is pseudo-Aristeas' unusually strong emphasis on divine grace, which includes the notion that all effective moral action is wholly dependent on God (231, 236–8). The same conception is found in Wisdom 8:21–9:6 (cf. Proverbs 2:6), in Plato's *Laws* 715e, and in the pseudo-Platonic *Epinomis* 989d. Philo, in particular, never tires of insisting that, without God's bounteous help, a human being could accomplish nothing, and that those who ascribe anything to their own powers are godless villains (*Posterity of Cain* 136; *The Worse Attacks the Better* 60; *Cherubim* 127–8; cf. M. *Avot* 3.7).

The door opened by pseudo-Aristeas very likely contributed greatly to the formation of an entire school of Jewish philosophical exegetes of Scripture, and, though the major part of its output has virtually disappeared, its single most outstanding and sparkling representative has largely survived the wholesale shipwreck. It is to this lone survivor and one of his precursors that we now turn.

❧ ARISTOBULUS: PRECURSOR OF PHILO ❧

The elaborate biblical commentaries of Philo were undoubtedly part of a flourishing Jewish Alexandrian scholastic tradition of biblical interpretation, as can readily be inferred from his frequent allusions to earlier and contemporary fellow exegetes (Hay 1979–80). Unfortunately, only one such predecessor is known to us by name. Aristobulus (second century BCE), descended from the high-priestly line, inaugurates an interpretative philosophical approach to Scripture that dimly prefigures that of Philo.[29] Like the latter, his aim is to establish that the Torah's teaching is in accord with philosophical truth. To this end, he takes great pains to interpret anthropomorphic descriptions of God allegorically. He thus maintains that the biblical expression "hand of God" signifies the divine power, the "standing of God" (Genesis 28:13; Exodus 17:6) refers to the immutability of God's creation, and the "voice of God" to the establishment of things, for, as Moses continually says in his description of creation, "And God spoke and it came to pass." As for God's resting on the seventh day, this does not signify the end of his work but only that "after he had finished ordering all things, he so orders them for all time" (cf. Philo, *Allegorical Interpretation* 1.6), and the "work of the six days" refers only to the establishment of the course of time and the hierarchical structure of the universe.[30]

Although Aristobulus wishes the reader to understand the Torah philosophically (*physikos*) and "not slip into the mythological mode," and chides those who cling to the letter for their lack of insight and for providing a reading of the Torah in the light of which Moses fails to appear to be proclaiming great things,[31] there is no evidence that the biblical text as a whole ever became for him an allegory in the Philonic manner. Aristobulus further asserts that, if anything unreasonable remains in the biblical text, the cause is to be imputed not to Moses but to himself. This seems to indicate his awareness of using a relatively new exegetical method and that he could not rely on a well-established tradition (Walter 1964, pp. 124–9).

⚬ PHILO OF ALEXANDRIA ⚬

Hellenistic Jewish philosophy reaches its climax in the subtle synthesis produced by Philo (c.20 BCE to c.50 CE) through his elaborate philosophical commentary on Scripture. Scion of a wealthy Jewish family and possibly of priestly descent like his forerunner Aristobulus, he played an important public role by heading a Jewish embassy to Gaius Caligula in 39–40 CE. His atticized Greek displays a wide variety of rhetorical figures and styles, including a special fondness for the diatribe, the popular moral invective so characteristic of the Greco-Roman age. Although fully acquainted with the Greek philosophical texts at first hand, Philo is not to be regarded as an original philosopher, nor did he claim that distinction for himself. He saw his task more modestly as that of the great reconciler who would bridge two disparate traditions that were both close to his heart. Although there is still no consensus, it is likely that the apparent eclecticism of his thought is in fact representative of Middle Platonism, a philosophical tradition marked by stoicizing and pythagorizing tendencies, including a strong dose of number symbolism.

The vast Philonic corpus may be divided into three divisions: exegetical, historical/apologetic, and philosophical. The exegetical writings, which constitute the main body of Philo's work, can be subdivided into three Pentateuchal commentaries: first, the so-called *Allegory of the Law*, a series of treatises that provide verse-by-verse commentary on biblical texts taken from Genesis 2: 1–41:24, but constantly incorporating related texts that are in turn investigated at length; second, the so-called *Exposition of the Law*, constituted by a series of treatises organized around biblical themes or figures, generally following the chronology of the Pentateuch; and, third, *Questions and Answers on Genesis and Exodus* (surviving only in Armenian and some Greek fragments).

The fundamental goal of his great biblical commentary was to uncover the hidden meaning of the Mosaic text, using allegorical interpretation, the "method dear to men with their eyes opened" (*Noah as Planter* 36). Greek allegorism had its start towards the end of the sixth century BCE in the writings of Theagenes of Rhegium, who, in an apparent effort to defend Homer against his detractors, interpreted his description of the internecine battle of the gods as the antagonism of three pairs of opposites: dry/wet, hot/cold, light/heavy. Philo was especially indebted to Stoic allegorizing of the last two centuries BCE, such as that of Crates of Mallos, who found in Homer's description of the shield of Agamemnon (*Iliad* 11.32–7) an image of the cosmos. A characteristic feature of the Stoic exegetical technique, of which Philo was particularly fond, was the etymologizing of names, a direct outgrowth of the school's linguistic theory, according to which names exist by nature, "the first articulate sounds being imitations of things."[32] Philo was thus heir to an exuberant allegorizing tradition, which served him well in his heroic task of defending his ancestral heritage. It should be noted, however, that Stoic and Middle Platonic allegoresis did not include the recognition of different levels of interpretation, and Philo is the earliest extant example of a writer who tries to maintain the validity of both the literal and the allegorical levels.

Logos and psychic ascent

Since Philo's mystical theology bars a direct approach to God's essence, we must seek it out through the oblique traces disclosed by its noetic aspect, the divine mind or logos. Thus in Philo's hierarchical construction of reality the essence of God, though utterly concealed in its primary being, is nevertheless made manifest on two secondary levels, the intelligible universe constituting the logos, which is God's image, and the sensible universe, an image of that image.[33] Philo further delineates the dynamics of the logos' activity by defining its two constitutive polar principles, goodness or the creative power, and sovereignty or the ruling power, which are clearly reminiscent of the principles of unlimit and limit in Plato's *Philebus* (23c–31a), and reappear in Plotinus' two logical moments in the emergence of Intellect, where we find unlimited intelligible matter proceeding from the One and then turning back to its source for definition (*Enneads* 2.4.5; 5.4.2).[34]

Although the human soul, as a fragment of the logos, might be thought to have a natural claim on immortality, the latter can be forfeited if the soul is not properly assimilated to its divine source. From Philo's Platonist perspective, the body is a corpse entombing the soul, which at its death returns to its own proper life (*Allegorical Interpretation* 1.107–8).[35] Alternatively, its sojourn in the body may be taken to be a period of exile (*Questions on Genesis* 3.10), a theme undoubtedly familiar to Philo from Middle Platonic exegesis of Homer's *Odyssey*, according to which Odysseus' arduous homeward journey symbolizes the soul's labors in its attempt to return to its original home (Plutarch, *Moral Essays* 745–6). The gradual removal of the psyche from the sensible realm and its ascent to a life of perfection in God is represented for Philo by two triads of biblical figures, the first (Enosh, Enoch, Noah) symbolizing the initial stages of the striving for perfection, the second (Abraham, Isaac, Jacob) its culmination (*Abraham* 7–59; *Rewards and Punishments* 10–66). The Abraham of Philo is a mystical philosopher who, after having mastered the general studies (symbolized by Hagar), in which stage all he could produce was Ishmael or sophistry, has abandoned the realm of sense (symbolized by his parting with Lot) for the intelligible world and, despite his initial flirtation with Chaldean (that is, Stoic) pantheism, has attained to the highest vision of deity, resulting in his transformation into a perfect embodiment of natural law.[36]

God and creation

Philo defines two paths leading to a knowledge of God's existence. The first involves an apprehension of God through his works by those who are not yet initiated into the highest mysteries and are thus constrained to advance upward by a sort of heavenly ladder and conjecture his existence through plausible inference. The genuine worshipers and true friends of God, however, are "those who apprehend him through himself without the cooperation of reasoned inference, as light is seen by light" (*Praem.* 41). This formula is precisely that used later by Plotinus, when he speaks of "touching that light and seeing it by itself, not by another light, but by the light which is also its means of seeing"

(*Enneads* 5.3.17:34–7: p. 135 (Armstrong)).[37] Although there is no consensus concerning the precise meaning of Philo's second and superior path to God, some arguing that it results from a special grace of God, whose illumination flashes into the human psyche from without, it is, in my opinion, very likely based on the notion of a direct and continuous access of the human mind to God from within and may perhaps be viewed as an early form of the ontological argument, as it had already been formulated by the Stoics (Winston 1985, pp. 43–7).

Whether or not Philo's overpowering conviction of God's existence owes something to the Stoic ontological argument or perhaps to a Middle Platonist version of it, his doctrine of creation clearly echoes the Stoic way of formulating that issue. Having attained philosophy's summit, Moses, according to Philo, recognized that there are two fundamental principles of being, the one active, the other passive (von Arnim 1903–24: 2:300, 312), the former an absolutely pure universal mind, beyond virtue and knowledge, the latter lifeless and motionless (*Creation* 7–9). God thus created the universe by means of his "all-incising logos" (*logos tomeus*), out of a qualityless primordial matter, containing in itself nothing lovely and so utterly passive as to be virtually non-existent. All things were created simultaneously, and the sequential creation account in Genesis is meant only to indicate the logical order in God's design. As to whether the act of creation is understood by Philo as having a temporal beginning or as an eternal process, this continues to be a highly controversial issue, though a very substantial case can, I think, be made for the latter view (Winston 1992a, pp. 222–7; 1986).

Mysticism

Dodds (1965, pp. 70–2) has correctly noted that the ecstatic form of prophecy as defined by Philo is not a description of mystical union but a state of temporary possession. Philo, however, speaks also of another form of prophecy, which may be designated "hermeneutical" or "noetic" and is mediated not through ecstatic possession but through the divine voice. Whereas in the state of possession the prophet's mind is entirely pre-empted, it is clear from Philo's analysis of the giving of the Decalogue, the paradigm of divine-voice prophecy, that in the latter the inspired mind is extraordinarily quickened. Since ecstatic possession is employed by Philo for the explanation of predictive prophecy alone, whereas the core of the Mosaic prophecy, the particular laws, are delivered by him in his role of hermeneutical or noetic prophet, it is in this form of prophecy that we must locate Philo's conception of mystical union. In his allegorical interpretation of the divine voice as the projection of a special "rational soul full of clearness and distinctness" making unmediated contact with the inspired mind that "makes the first advance," one can readily discern a reference to the activation of the human intellect (*Decalogue* 33–5). In Philo's noetic prophecy, then, we may detect the union of the human mind with the divine mind, or, in Dodds' terms, a psychic ascent rather than a supernatural descent (Winston 1989b).

A series of Philonic passages contain most of the characteristic earmarks of mystical experience: knowledge of God as one's supreme bliss and separation from him as the greatest of evils; the soul's intense yearning for the divine; its recognition of its nothingness and of its need to go out of itself; attachment to God; the realization that it is God alone who acts; a preference for wordless contemplative prayer; a timeless union with the All and its resulting serenity; the suddenness with which the mystical vision occurs; the experience of sober intoxication; and, finally, the ebb and flow of the mystical experience. These passages go well beyond a merely spirited religiosity, revealing instead what constitutes at the very least an intellectual or theoretical form of mysticism, but may well represent a genuine inner experience that envelops Philo's psyche and fills it with God's nearness (Winston 1981, pp. 164–74). Whether we can go further and attribute to him mystical happenings involving union with the deity as such must remain uncertain in view of the absence of anything more than vague descriptions of psychic states that at most represent only a mystical experience of the deity qua logos.[38]

❧ NOTES ❧

1 Theophrastus, Megasthenes, Clearchus of Soli, Hecataeus of Abdera (Stern 1976: 1:10, 46, 50, 28). Cf. Herodotus, *History* 1.131; Strabo, *Geography* 16.35.

2 Hermippus of Smyrna, Clearchus of Soli (Stern 1976: 1:50, 95); Origen, *Against Celsus* 1.15. The high point of this admiration for Eastern wisdom is reached in the well-known statement of the Neopythagorean Numenius of Apamea (second century CE), "What is Plato, but Moses speaking Attic Greek?" (Stern 1976: 2:209).

3 *Special Laws* 4.61; *Questions on Genesis* 3.5; 4.152, 167; *Allegorical Interpretation* 1.108; *Every Good Man is Free* 57; *On God* 6–7: Moses spoke of the "designing fire" (*pyr technikon*) that informs the world long before the Stoics did, and much more clearly (Siegert 1988, pp. 27–8). Significantly, Philo leaves the question of dependence open with regard to Socrates (*Questions on Genesis* 2.6: "whether taught by Moses or moved by the things themselves") and never mentions it with regard to his revered Plato, whom he characterizes as "most holy" and "great" (*Every Good Man is Free* 13; *Eternity of the World* 52). In *On Providence* 1.22, he merely states that Moses had anticipated Plato in saying

that there was water, darkness, and chaos before the world came into existence, just as in *Eternity of the World* 17 he similarly states that Moses had anticipated Hesiod in saying that the world was created and imperishable. (Citation of Philo's works follows Colson and Whittaker's English titles somewhat abbreviated.) Cf. Aristobulus, who asserts that Plato, Pythagoras, and Socrates, as well as Orpheus, Linus, Hesiod, Homer, and even Aratus, borrowed from Moses, whose books had been translated into Greek long before the Septuagint (frs. 2 and 4, Charlesworth 1985, 2:839–41). Eupolemus (first century BCE), by claiming that Moses was the first wise man, contends that wisdom originated among the Jews, and thus implies that Greek philosophy is ultimately dependent on Moses.

4 Lemaire 1990, p. 173. See also Lichtheim 1983.

5 Plato defined thought as "a silent inner conversation of the soul with itself" (*Sophist* 263e).

6 See Fox 1989, pp. 86–100. Fox notes that, unlike the other wisdom teachers, Qohelet's favorite verb of perception is "seeing," not "hearing" (p. 98). This too is characteristically Greek and is a notion that is highly prominent in Philo's writings (*Abraham* 57; *Unchangeableness of God* 45; *Special Laws* 4.60–1; cf. Heraclitus, Diels and Kranz 1956, 1:173, fr. 101a). Fox also points out that, although Qohelet is painfully aware that human knowledge is severely limited by God, it is none the less his view that "through wisdom we may rise above our helplessness, look at the world and at God from a certain distance, and judge both" (p. 119). "My father related to me," writes R. Joseph B. Soloveitchik (1983, pp. 73–4), "that when the fear of death would seize hold of R. Chayyim [Joseph's grandfather, founder of the Brisker method of conceptual analysis of talmudic law], he would throw himself, with his entire heart and mind, into the study of the law of tents and corpse defilement.... When halakhic man fears death, his sole method wherewith to fight this terrible dread is the eternal law of the Halakhah.... It is through cognition that he 'acquires' the object that strikes such alarm into him."

7 See von Loewenclau 1986. She notes that Spinoza designates Qohelet as *philosophus* in his *Tractatus* 6 (1925, p. 95, line 19). She also compares Qohelet 12:11, "The sayings of the wise are like goads, like nails fixed in prodding sticks," with Plato, *Apology* 30e, where Socrates describes himself as one who attaches himself to the city "as a gadfly to a horse which is sluggish on account of his size and needs to be aroused by stinging." "Qohelet and his circle have a new goal: The sage's task is not only to give counsel, but to rouse people from their certainties. Such an accentuation fits the Hellenistic period with its multifaceted intellectual and political upheavals." Significantly, Qohelet describes his activity not as teaching but as "studying and probing" (1:13; 7:25). Of the 227 verses of Qohelet, we find only twenty-seven to be admonitory. Socrates similarly says, "I was never any one's teacher" (*Apology* 33a), and "I know that I do not know" (*Apology* 21d; cf. *Charmides* 165b). Finally, she draws a parallel between the complaint that Socrates "keeps repeating the same thing" (*Gorgias* 490e) and the fact that Qohelet's mind is similarly fixed on one basic theme, *hevel*, a word that recurs no fewer than thirty-two times, in addition to the recurrence of other key words to which he is addicted, such as *miqreh, amal, pitron* and *at*.

8 See Amir 1964–5, pp. 36–8. Ben Sira has a similar predilection for the abstract concept of the "all" (*hakkol*).

9 Diogenes Laertius 6.83; Sextus Empiricus, *Against the Logicians* 1961: 1:88 (Bury): "Anaxarchus and Monimus [abolished the criterion] because they likened existing things to a scene-painting [*skenographia*; cf. Wisdom 15: 4 and my comment ad loc (Winston 1979)] and supposed them to resemble the impressions experienced in sleep or madness"; M. Aurelius, *Meditations* 2.15. See Levy 1912, p. 12; Amir 1964–5, pp. 38–9; Braun 1973, pp. 45–6.

10 Hengel (1974: 1:121) speaks of the "break" with the doctrine of retribution, but Fox (1989, p. 121) has argued convincingly that "Qohelet both affirms divine justice and complains of the injustices that God allows. The contradiction is most blatant in 8:10–14, where Qohelet says that the righteous live long and the wicked die young, *and* that the opposite sometimes occurs. Qohelet recognizes it, bemoans it, but does not resolve it" (1989, p. 121). "The book concludes with the affirmation of the certainty of divine judgment (12:14). Whether written by an editor or the author, it does not conflict with anything in the body of the book. The difference between the epilogue and the rest of the book is that the epilogue emphasizes God's judgment without raising the problem of the delay in judgment" (p. 128).

11 Hengel 1974: 1:115–28. For texts and translations of the above citations, see Cercidas 1953, p. 197 (translation cited is that found in Hengel); Babrius 1965, p. 165; Peek 1960: nos. 308 and 371; Benoit 1967; Lifshitz 1966.

12 *The Twilight of the Idols.* The Problem of Socrates 10: 478 (Kaufmann 1954).

13 Collins 1977, p. 53. See also Winston 1979, p. 36.

14 Sirach 19:20; cf. 1:27. See von Rad 1972, pp. 245–7. All translations from Sirach are from Skehan and di Lella 1987.

15 Diogenes Laertius 7.185. See Fraser 1972, 1:481; 2:695 n. 17; Pautrel 1963.

16 Cf. Qohelet 7:14; *Test. Naftali* 2.7; *Test. Asher* 1.4–5; Philo, *Creation* 33.

17 Cicero, *Nature of the Gods* 2.58 (Rackham). Cf. Sirach 41:17, 22–4; 43:1, 9, 11; Philo, *Special Laws* 3.189; von Arnim 1903–24: 2:1009; Xenophon, *Education of Cyrus* 8.7.22; Cicero, *Nature of the Gods* 2.93.

18 Cicero, *Nature of the Gods* 2.87; Epictetus, *Discourses* 1.12.16; Seneca, *Natural Questions* 7.27.4. See Hengel 1974: 1:147–9, and Gutman 1958: 1:171–85.

19 Chrysippus, in Plutarch, *On Common Conceptions* 1065b (Cherniss); cf. M. Aurelius, *Meditations* 10.6.

20 See Lichtheim 1973, 1:67; Morenz 1973, pp. 66–8.

21 Lebram 1974 identifies the genre of the narrative on the martyrs with that of the *epitaphios logos*, or funeral oration.

22 Redditt 1983. Moreover, six times reason is modified by the adjective *eusebes*, "religious," and, as Redditt has correctly remarked, "the three terms *nomos*, *logismos*, and *eusebeia* form a circle of interrelated concepts."

23 Edelstein and Kidd 1972, p. 143, F161 and F187; Long and Sedley 1987: 1: 413–17. See Renehan 1972. Panaetius, too, seems to have taken the same position (Cicero, *On Duties* 1.102).

24 Interestingly, in this case, Philo does not follow the Middle Platonic view but considers *apatheia* the higher ideal (*Allegorical Interpretation* 3.129, 134), although he does on one occasion attribute *metriopatheia* to the sage Abraham (*Abraham* 257; cf., however, *Questions on Genesis* 4.73, Greek fragment, Marcus

2.220, where he says that Abraham experienced on the death of his wife Sarah not a *pathos* but a *propatheia*. See Winston 1992b, p. 41 n. 51, and Lilla 1971, pp. 99–103).

25 Plutarch, *Isis and Osiris* 381a; cf. Aristotle, *Generation of Animals* 756b30; Antoninus Liberalis, *Collection of Metamorphoses* 29.

26 Diogenes Laertius 8.18, 24, 34; Porphyry, *Life of Pythagoras* 42; Aristotle 1984, 2.2442, F195 and F197. See Heinemann 1932, pp. 498–500. Interestingly, as in Philo, the ethical interpretations stand side by side with the literal. According to Heinemann, the Pythagoreans had the same prohibition of the weasel and gave the same justification for it that pseudo-Aristeas provides. Cf. Philo, *Every Good Man is Free* 2: "Now we are told that the saintly company of the Pythagoreans teaches among other excellent doctrines this also, 'walk not on the highways' [Diogenes Laertius 8.17]. This does not mean that we should climb steep hills – the school was not prescribing foot-weariness – but it indicates by this figure that in our words and deeds we should not follow popular and beaten tracks." For the Pythagorean symbolism of salt, see Philo, *Special Laws* 1.175, and Diogenes Laertius 8.35.

27 See the excellent discussion in Boccaccini 1991, pp. 161–85, esp. 177–9.

28 Some few answers, however, as Zuntz (1959, p. 23) has pointed out, "are entirely rooted in Jewish tradition. Ptolemy's fifth question (193), 'how to be invincible in war,' elicits the answer, 'if he did not place his trust in unlimited power but throughout invoked God to give success to his enterprises'. Never was an answer like this given by a Greek adviser to a Greek king. It is in the spirit of Ps. 20:8."

29 See 2 Maccabees 1:10 and Goldstein 1983, p. 168 and Gutman 1958: 1:187.

30 Fragments 2, 4 and 5, in Charlesworth 1985, 2:837–42.

31 Cf. B. *Qiddushin* 49a: "R. Judah said, If one translates a verse literally, he is a liar."

32 Von Arnim 1903–24: 2:146. A good example of Crates' playful manipulations of words in the manner of Stoic etymologizing (similar to the rabbinic *al tikrei*) is his interpretation of *Odyssey* 12.62–3, where the pigeons (*peleiai*), which are said to carry ambrosia to Zeus, are converted into the Pleiades (*Pleiades*), since it is beneath Zeus' dignity to imagine that the birds bring him ambrosia (Athenaeus, *The Sophists at Dinner* 11.490b-e).

33 *Dreams* 1.239; *Confusion of Tongues* 147–8; *Creation* 25.

34 Philo, *Cherubim* 27–8; *Sacrifices of Abel and Cain* 59; *Who is the Heir* 166; *Abraham* 124–5.

35 Cf. M. Aurelius, *Meditations* 4.41; Plato, *Republic* 585b; *Timaeus* 96b; *Sophist* 228–9; *Gorgias* 493a.

36 *Abraham* 68–71, 119–32; *Migration of Abraham* 1–12, 176–95; *Dreams* 1.41–60; *Giants* 62–4. See Sandmel 1956, pp. 96–211.

37 In *Allegorical Interpretation* 1.38, Philo writes: "For how could the soul have conceived of God had he not infused it and taken hold of it as far as was possible?" Cf. Nicholson 1963, p. 50: "This is what [the Caliph] 'Ali meant when he was asked, 'Do you see God?' and replied: 'How should we worship One whom we do not see?' The light of intuitive certainty (*yaqin*) by which the heart sees God is a beam of God's own light cast therein by Himself; else no vision of Him were possible. 'Tis the sun's self that lets the sun be seen."

See also Spinoza, *Short Treatise* 1.1.10: p. 65 (Curley): "But God, the first Cause of all things, and also the cause of himself, makes himself known through himself."

38 See *Migration of Abraham* 34–5; *Cherubim* 27; *Allegorical Interpretation* 2.32, 85; *Dreams* 2.252.

❧ BIBLIOGRAPHY ❧

Texts

Aulus Gellius (1968) *The Attic Nights*, vol. 2, translated by J. C. Rolfe (Cambridge, MA: Harvard University Press) (Loeb Classical Library).

Aristotle (1984) *The Complete Works of Aristotle*, edited by J. Barnes, 2 vols (Princeton: Princeton University Press).

Babrius (1965) *Aesopic Fables in Iambic Verse*, edited and translated by B. E. Perry (Cambridge, MA: Harvard University Press) (Loeb Classical Library).

Cercidas (1953) *Meliambs, Fragments, and Cercidea*, edited and translated by A. D. Knox (Cambridge, MA: Harvard University Press) (Loeb Classical Library).

Charlesworth, J. H. (1985) *The Old Testament Pseudepigrapha*, 2 vols (Garden City: Doubleday).

Cicero (1951) *De Natura Deorum*, translated by H. Rackham (Cambridge, MA: Harvard University Press) (Loeb Classical Library).

Curley, E. (trans.) (1985) *The Collected Works of Spinoza*, vol. 1 (Princeton: Princeton University Press).

Diels, H. and W. Kranz (eds) (1956) *Die Fragmente der Vorsokratiker*, 8th ed., 3 vols (Berlin: Weidmannsche Verlagsbuchhandlung).

Diogenes Laertius (1931–50) *Lives of the Eminent Philosophers*, translated by R. D. Hicks (Cambridge, MA: Harvard University Press) (Loeb Classical Library).

Edelstein, L. and I. G. Kidd (ed. and tr.) (1972) *Posidonius. Volume I: The Fragments* (Cambridge: Cambridge University Press).

Goldstein, J. A. (1983) *II Maccabees* (Garden City: Doubleday (Anchor Bible 41a)).

Hadas, M. (1953) *The Third and Fourth Books of Maccabees* (New York: Harper & Brothers).

Kaufmann, W. (1954) *The Portable Nietzsche* (New York: Viking).

Lichtheim, M. (1973) *Ancient Egyptian Literature*, 3 vols (Berkeley: University of California Press).

Long, A. A. and D. N. Sedley (eds and trans.) (1987) *The Hellenistic Philosophers*, 2 vols (Cambridge: Cambridge University Press).

Philo of Alexandria (1956–62) *Philo*, translated by F. H. Colson and G. H. Whittaker, 10 vols; and 2 supplementary vols translated by R. Marcus (Cambridge, MA: Harvard University Press) (Loeb Classical Library).

Plato (1979) *Gorgias*, translated by T. Irwin (Oxford: Clarendon Press).

Plotinus (1966–88) *Enneads*, translated by A. H. Armstrong, 7 vols (Cambridge, MA: Harvard University Press (Loeb Classical Library).

Plutarch (1976) *Moralia*, vol. 13.2, translated by H. Cherniss (Cambridge, MA: Harvard University Press) (Loeb Classical Library).

Proclus (1967) *Commentaire sur le Timée*, vol. 2, translated by A. J. Festugière (Paris: Vrin).

Sextus Empiricus (1961) *Against the Logicians*, translated by R. G. Bury (Cambridge, MA: Harvard University Press) (Loeb Classical Library).

Siegert, F. (1988) *Philon von Alexandrien: Über die Gottesbezeichnung "wohltätig verzehrendes Feuer" (De Deo). Text, Translation and Commentary* (Tübingen: Mohr).

Skehan, P. W. and A. di Lella (trans.) (1987) *The Wisdom of Ben Sira* (New York: Doubleday).

Spinoza (1925) *Tractatus Theologico-Politicus*, in *Opera*, edited by C. Gebhardt, vol. 3 (Heidelberg: Winter).

Stern, M. (1976) *Greek and Latin Authors on Jews and Judaism*, 3 vols (Jerusalem: Israel Academy of Sciences and Humanities).

von Arnim, H. F. A. (1903–24) *Stoicorum Veterum Fragmenta*, 4 vols (Leipzig: Teubner).

Winston, D. (1979) *The Wisdom of Solomon* (Garden City: Doubleday (Anchor Bible 43)).

—— (1981) *Philo of Alexandria: The Contemplative Life, the Giants, and Selections* (New York: Paulist Press).

Studies

Amir, Y. (1964–5) "On the Question of the Relationship Between Qohelet and Greek Wisdom" [Hebrew], *Beit Miqra* 22.1: 36–42.

Benoit, P. (1967) "L'Inscription grecque du tombeau de Jason," *Israel Exploration Journal* 17.2: 112–13.

Boccaccini, G. (1991) *Middle Judaism: Jewish Thought 300 BCE to 200 CE* (Minneapolis: Fortress).

Braun, R. (1973) *Kohelet und die frühhellenistische Popularphilosophie* (Berlin: De Gruyter).

Collins, J. J. (1977) "The Biblical Precedent for Natural Theology," *Journal of the American Academy of Religion* 45.1 Supplement, B: 35–67.

Dodds, E. R. (1965) *Pagan and Christian in an Age of Anxiety* (Cambridge: Cambridge University Press).

Fox, M. V. (1989) *Qohelet and His Contradictions* (Decatur: Almond).

Fraser, P. M. (1972) *Ptolemaic Alexandria*, 3 vols (Oxford: Clarendon Press).

Gutman, Y. (1958) *The Beginnings of Jewish Hellenistic Literature*, 2 vols [Hebrew] (Jerusalem: Mossad Bialik).

—— (1949) "The Mother and her Sons in the Aggadah and in II and IV Maccabees [Hebrew], in *Commentationes Iudaico-Hellenisticae in Memoriam Iohannis Lewy*, edited by M. Schwabe and J. Gutman (Jerusalem: Magnes), pp. 25–37.

Hay, D. M. (1979–80) "Philo's References to Other Allegorists," *Studia Philonica* 6: 41–75.

Heinemann, I. (1932) *Philons griechische und jüdische Bildung* (Breslau: M. & H. Marcus).

Hengel, M. (1974) *Judaism and Hellenism*, translated by J. Bowden, 2 vols (Philadelphia: Fortress).

Lebram, J. C. H. (1974) "Die literarische Form des Vierten Makkabäerbuchs," *Vigiliae Christianae* 28: 81–96.

Lemaire, A. (1990) "The Sage in School and Temple," in *The Sage in Israel and the Ancient East*, edited by J. G. Gammie and L. G. Perdue (Winona Lake: Eisenbrauns), pp. 165–81.

Levy, L. (1912) *Das Buch Qohelet* (Leipzig: Hinrichs).

Lichtheim, M. (1983) *Late Egyptian Wisdom Literature in the International Context* (Freiburg: Universitätsverlag; Göttingen: Vandenhoeck & Ruprecht).

Lifshitz, B. (1966) "Notes d'Épigraphie Palestinienne," *Revue Biblique* 73: 248–55.

Lilla, S. R. C. (1971) *Clement of Alexandria* (Oxford: Oxford University Press).

Morenz, S. (1973) *Egyptian Religion*, translated by A. E. Keep (London: Methuen).

Nicholson, R. A. (1963) *The Mystics of Islam* (London: Routledge & Kegan Paul).

Pautrel, R. (1963) "Ben Sira et le Stoicisme," *Recherches de Science Religieuse* 51: 535–49.

Peek, W. (1960) *Griechische Grabgedichte* (Berlin: Akademie).

Redditt, P. L. (1983) "The Conception of Nomos in Fourth Maccabees," *Catholic Biblical Quarterly* 45: 249–70.

Renehan, R. (1972) "The Greek Philosophical Background of Fourth Maccabees," *Rheinisches Museum für Philologie* 115: 223–38.

Sandmel, S. (1956) *Philo's Place in Judaism* (Cincinnati: Hebrew Union College Press).

Soloveitchik, J. B. (1983) *Halakhic Man* (Philadelphia: Jewish Publication Society).

Tcherikover, V. (1958) "The Ideology of the Letter of Aristeas," *Harvard Theological Review* 51: 59–85.

Todd, R. B. (1976) *Alexander of Aphrodisias on Stoic Physics* (Leiden: Brill).

von Loewenclau, I. (1986) "Kohelet und Sokrates," *Zeitschrift für die Alttestamentliche Wissenschaft* 98: 327–38.

von Rad, G. (1972) *Wisdom in Israel*, translated by J. D. Martin (Nashville: Abingdon).

Walter, N. (1964) *Der Thoraausleger Aristobulos* (Berlin: Akademie).

Winston, D. (1971) "The Book of Wisdom's Theory of Cosmogony," *History of Religions* 11.2: 185–202.

—— (1985) *Logos and Mystical Theology in Philo of Alexandria* (Cincinnati: Hebrew Union College Press).

—— (1986) "Creation Ex Nihilo Revisited: A Reply to Jonathan Goldstein," *Journal of Jewish Studies* 37.1: 88–91.

—— (1989a) "Theodicy in Ben Sira and Stoic Philosophy," in *Of Scholars, Savants and their Texts*, edited by R. Link-Salinger (New York: Lang), pp. 239–49.

—— (1989b) "Two Types of Mosaic Prophecy According to Philo of Alexandria," *Journal for the Study of the Pseudepigrapha* 4: 49–67.

—— (1991) "Philo's Linguistic Theory," *Studia Philonica Annual* 3: 109–25.

—— (1992a) "Review of D. T. Runia, *Philo of Alexandria and the Timaeus of Plato*," *Ancient Philosophy* 12: 222–7.

—— (1992b) "Philo's Conception of the Divine Nature," in *Neoplatonism and*

Jewish Thought, edited by L. E. Goodman (Albany: State University of New York Press), pp. 21–42.

Wolfson, H. A. (1948) *Philo: Foundations of Religious Philosophy in Judaism, Christianity and Islam*, 2 vols (Cambridge, MA: Harvard University Press).

Zuntz, G. (1959) "Aristeas Studies I: The Seven Banquets," *Journal of Semitic Studies* 4: 21–36.

CHAPTER 4

The Talmud as a source for philosophical reflection

David Novak

TALMUD AND PHILOSOPHY

The first methodological question any philosophical reflection must deal with is: What am I reflecting on? The second is: Why am I to reflect on it? The third is: How can I reflect on it?

Among the ancient Greeks, who were the first to designate their intellectual discipline as "philosophy" and themselves as its practitioners – philosophers – the proper object of the philosopher's reflection is nature (*physis*), which is the unchanging and perpetual order underlying the changing and ephemeral things of human experience. This order is to be the object of philosophical reflection because it alone can be understood as what is beyond the reach of anyone's change, control, or invention (*techne*). As such, it is the general object that is alone truly worthy of human respect. It is seen as the final standard to which everything and everyone is ultimately referred. The highest norm is to become "like nature" (*kata physin*). Philosophical reflection, then, is the study of nature, not at the level of its appearances (*phainomena*) inasmuch as their changeability does not command respect, but rather at the level of its most basic components, its "first things" (*archai*). They alone are sufficiently transcendent so that no one can ever conceive of changing, controlling, or inventing them. They themselves are unchangeable, uncontrollable, uncreated. They are eternal being. They are truth itself by which anything beneath them is true only by partici-pation. Consequently, the only proper medium of philosophical reflec-tion on nature is reason (*nous*). It alone is considered to be the most distinguishing capacity of humans, namely, the capacity to separate the true from the false. And reason consistently separates humans who exercise it from the animals. Human reason is what is truly attracted by nature per se and thus perpetually interested in it.

But what happens when there are attempts to practice philosophy within a tradition in which the primary datum for consideration is not nature per se but the word of God? Is it possible to practice philosophy in this kind of context? Does revelation lend itself as an object (*noema*) to the same kind of rational inquiry that characterized philosophy as a meditation on the first things of nature in its original Greek habitat? Can there be a science of revelation as there is a science of nature?

Some students of either philosophy or religion or both have denied the possibility of there being anything like a *religious* philosophy precisely because the data of revelation seem to call for obedience, whereas the data of nature seem to call for wonder and rational consideration. In the case of Judaism, especially, as the original religion of revelation, they have argued that the Bible is a decidedly non-philosophical – even anti-philosophical – work.

But other students of religion and philosophy have argued that, although the Bible is not a philosophical book itself, its message is so coherent and its concerns so profound that it can be the object of philosophical reflection. In other words, like nature it both transcends philosophical reflection as an object transcends a subject interested in it, and yet it attracts that subject with whom it has something (but not everything) in common. That "something in common" is "wisdom" (*chokhmah*), which the Bible predicates of both God (Psalms 104:24) and humans, especially those humans who are properly related to God (Deuteronomy 4:6). Without this assumption, the Bible is only the expression of a totally inscrutable divine will, a will that calls for a similarly inscrutable response on the part of its human addressees.

The view that emphasizes the primacy of divine wisdom in revelation, however, is further buttressed by the teaching that the same divine wisdom that created the world is that by which the Torah is written (Proverbs 8:22). Thus philosophy can be the love of wisdom, whether that wisdom is natural (*sophia*) or revealed (*chokhmah*). That wisdom can, to a certain extent, be the subject of human speech; thus the Hebrew *davar* easily translated into the Greek *logos* (see LXX on Isaiah 2:3). Indeed, both nature and revelation are characterized by the wisdom inherent in them, wisdom that is discoverable by those who are wise. Hence nature is relevant for the understanding of the Torah, and the Torah is relevant for the understanding of nature. For both the ancient Greeks and the ancient Hebrews, then, the wisdom that philosophers love and seek, although never of their own making, nevertheless still gives some of itself to them (see B. *Berakhot* 58a). Accordingly, there can be Jewish philosophers as much as there can be Greek philosophers, despite great differences between them as to where philosophical attention should be primarily directed.

In the Hellenistic Jewish tradition, there were certainly philosophers of the Bible; the name of Philo need only come to mind. But that tradition was one that came into direct contact with Greek philosophy; Philo read and confronted Plato and some of the Stoics. He and some others like him had the benefit of the intellectual legacies of both Jerusalem and Athens. But what about the other biblically based Jewish tradition, that of the rabbis? There is no evidence that they had any real intellectual contact with Greek philosophy, much less that they were actually influenced by it. Can they be considered philosophers of the Bible in the same way that Philo was? Can any philosophy be discerned in their greatest and most comprehensive work, the Talmud? (By "the Talmud" I mean both the larger and better known *Babylonian Talmud* – the *Bavli* (hereafter "B") – and the smaller and lesser-known *Palestinian Talmud* – the *Yerushalmi* (herafter "Y")).

At first glance, the answer to this question would seem to be no. Unlike Philo, who approached the Bible in a recognizably philosophical way by seeing it as *the* datum of universal truth, the rabbis seem to have approached the Bible (and the rest of Jewish tradition) as jurists and homilists of a decidedly particularistic bent. The main thrust of their legal discussions (*halakhah*) are concerned with how biblical and traditional rules are to be applied to the life of the Jewish people at various points in its history. The main thrust of their speculative discussions (*aggadah*) is to expand biblical and traditional narratives imaginatively and to draw various moral exhortations from them. Although Jewish philosophers of later periods did use talmudic materials in their own recognizably philosophic discussions, this use was highly selective. Thus, unlike the Bible which the tradition took to be the work of the one, coherent, totally consistent divine mind, the Talmud clearly presents itself as the edited transcript of discussions among a variety of human minds, who often disagreed with each other more than they agreed (see B. *Sanhedrin* 88b). Not only is the Talmud, like the Bible, not a philosophical work, but, unlike the Bible, it does not even seem to lend itself to ever becoming the object of philosophical meditation. How then can anyone make a philosophical connection with it?

❧ COMMANDMENTS AND THEIR ❧ REASONS

In order to pursue this necessary question, one must now make a further philosophical distinction; one must distinguish between theoretical reason and practical reason. Heretofore in our discussion of philosophy, we have seen it as theoretical reason. Its concern is the truth and knowledge for its own sake. As systematic rational inquiry, there seems to be very little of this type of philosophy in the Talmud. However, what about practical philosophy, whose concern is the good and knowledge for the sake of action? Is there systematic discussion of that in the Talmud? If so, where is it to be located, and how is it to be understood as influencing more recognizably philosophical reflection by Jewish thinkers who came after the rabbis and who looked to them as authorities?

The way to locate this inquiry into practical philosophy in the Talmud, and as a source for further philosophical reflection by Jews, is by carefully analyzing the use and development of the term *ta'am*, which in later rabbinic Hebrew came to mean "reason," as in "*ta'amei ha-mitzvot*" – "the reasons of the commandments". Here we will see how philosophy grew up within the Jewish tradition itself even before it came into real intellectual contact with the philosophical tradition of the Greeks. Accordingly, Jewish philosophy cannot be regarded as the result of a synthesis with aspects of another tradition, however much there have been similarities and cross-influences between these traditions (the Jewish and the Greek) that did subsequently come about.

The word *ta'am* is found in later biblical Hebrew and in biblical Aramaic. It means a "decree," as for example, "Everything that is by the decree [*min ta'am*] of the God of heaven is to be done diligently" (Ezra 7:23). In the Talmud, however, its meaning developed. It now came to mean the *reason* of a decree. Thus one of the most frequently asked questions in the Talmud is "what is the reason" ("*m'ai ta'ama*") of this decree? Yet this question itself is not a philosophical one. For most frequently, it is an inquiry into the authoritative basis for a decree confronted by someone in the present. That is, it is an inquiry for a past cause of a presently normative rule. It is, then, mostly a question of *where* the source of the rule is located in older and more authoritative texts, and *how* the present rule was actually derived from the designated source (see, for example, B. *Qiddushin* 68b on Deuteronomy 21:13). Thus, in a well-known talmudic legend (*Menachot* 29b), Moses is portrayed as being disturbed that he could not understand the intricate legal interpretations of Rabbi Aqibah, into whose second-century CE academy he had been miraculously transported incognito. But, as the legend continues, he felt better after Rabbi Aqibah answered a student's question – "Rabbi, what is your source?" – by saying, "It is a traditional law [*halakhah*] from Moses at Sinai." Nevertheless, as this text indicates, the student's question was, in fact, "where is the authority of this law?" not "why – for what reason or purpose – was it so decreed?". Only this latter question, which was not asked here, could be taken to be philosophical.

∼∼ THE AQIBAN AND ISHMAELIAN ∼∼
SCHOOLS

The answer of Rabbi Aqibah is especially illuminating precisely because it is quite atypical of him. For the answer is a direct reference to an authoritative source, albeit not a written one but one from the oral tradition ("*torah she-b'al peh*"). In this case, then, the student had to trust Rabbi Aqibah's reliability as an accurate transmitter of a tradition that the student himself could not verify by referring to a written work. Much more often, however, Rabbi Aqibah's answer to such a question would be the result of a highly intricate exegesis of a biblical passage. In this process, the connection between the authoritative source (the biblical, usually pentateuchal, text) and the actual normative ruling would be quite indirect. In fact, his exegesis was at times so intricate that it frequently appeared contrived to many of his colleagues (see, for example, B. *Pesachim* 66a), who could see no real connection at all between his conclusions and the biblical text upon which he claimed it was really based.

At this point, it would seem that the exegetical methodology of Rabbi Aqibah is counter-philosophical. For if philosophy is seen as the attempt to discern simple order underlying complex chaos, then the methodology of Rabbi Aqibah, appearing more intricate than the biblical text it was dealing with, would seem to be diametrically opposed to philosophy. Nevertheless, a careful examination of the assumptions underlying Rabbi Aqibah's exegesis will show how by theological means it laid the groundwork for indigenous philosophical reflection within the rabbinic tradition itself, and this was long before rabbinic thinkers actually studied the books of the Greek philosophers. Furthermore, it should be emphasized here that Rabbi Aqibah was undoubtedly the single most important and influential thinker in the rabbinic tradition in its formative period (see B. *Qiddushin* 66b; B. *Eruvin* 46b).

Since the rabbinic tradition is so highly dialectical in substance and style, Rabbi Aqibah's exegetical theology is best understood when seen in contrast with that of his most consistent intellectual opponent, Rabbi Ishmael. The most important assumptions of Rabbi Ishmael's exegetical theology are summed up in two of his dicta: first, "the Torah speaks by means of the language [*ke-lashon*] of humans" (B. *Sanhedrin* 64b; cf. Y. *Sotah* 8.1/22b); second, "the general principles [*kelalot*] of the Torah were spoken at Sinai, but the specifics [*peratot*] were spoken in the Tent of Meeting" (*Zevachim* 115b; cf. B. *Eruvin* 54b). Both of these assumptions are seen by the editors of the Talmud as being contrary to the views of Rabbi Aqibah. Careful examination of these fundamental theological differences will show that the theology of Rabbi Aqibah, rather than that of Rabbi Ishmael, lays the foundation for a philosophical approach to the Torah.

By "the language of humans" Rabbi Ishmael means that one cannot press the verses of the Torah for any meanings that would ignore its ordinary stylistic features, especially the repetition of words that are easily seen as being put there in order to add emphasis to the point being made in that overall context. But since the Torah's ordinary sense does not seem to deal with the abstract issues of theory and practice that one associates with philosophical reflection, it would seem that these issues are therefore precluded from any authentic theological interpretation of the Torah. In Rabbi Ishmael's disputes with Rabbi Aqibah, he often objects to Rabbi Aqibah's interpretations of Scripture that seem to read more into the biblical text than out of it (for example, B. *Sanhedrin* 51b).

For Rabbi Aqibah, however, the Torah is not comparable to a human text. As such, each of its words – even each of its letters – must be seen as having its own unique function. There are no words just for added effect, or for purposes of illustration. Like nature, the object of philosophical reflection, nothing in the Torah is seen as being superfluous or of arbitrary significance. The Torah is wholly and consistently intelligible (*ratio per se*), even if that intelligibility is only partially grasped by finite human intelligences (*ratio quoad nos*). Therefore, the underlying meaning of the text must be worked out speculatively. The ostensive meaning of the text is only its appearance; the deeper reality of the text is what is gained by refusing to be bound by the surface of the text with all its seeming limitations (and contradictions).

This point is even more philosophically significant in the second major theological dispute between Rabbi Aqibah and Rabbi Ishmael. For Rabbi Ishmael, the general principles of the Torah are clearly of greater importance than the specifics. That is why they are given as the foundational revelation of Sinai, whereas the specifics are worked out in the Tent of Meeting. In Rabbi Ishmael's exegesis, specific statements are subordinate to general statements, whereas in Rabbi Aqibah's exegesis no such distinction is made. For him, there is no subordination but interaction between words of equal value (see B. *Shevuot* 26a). Therefore, in the theology of Rabbi Ishmael, there is no more generality to the Torah than the ostensive text of the Torah itself gives. But in the theology of Rabbi Aqibah, questions of generality are, in effect, meta-questions, that is, they are models developed to recontextualize the text rather than actual data located within the words of the text itself. Consequently, there is much more latitude for the type of increasingly abstract conceptualization that characterizes philosophical reflection. Indeed, following this line of thought, it is evident why the whole process of the structure of the Mishnah, which recontextualizes Jewish law according to conceptual categories rather than following the seemingly random order of biblical verses (*midrash*), is considered to have been the primary achievement of Rabbi Aqibah (see *Avot de-Rabbi Nathan*, chapter 18; Y. *Sheqalim* 5.1/48c; cf. B. *Pesachim* 105b).

❧ RABBINIC ANTI-TELEOLOGY ❧

If the beginnings of philosophical reflection by the rabbis are seen more in the area of practical reason than that of theoretical reason, then one must look not only at the increasingly abstract methods of conceptualization begun by Rabbi Aqibah but especially at efforts to develop a teleological conceptuality by the rabbis. For practical reason is primarily concerned with the ends or purposes (*tele*) of human action. Philosophical reflection on human action, as both Plato and Aristotle consistently emphasized, is primarily a concern with what are the goods that human beings seek by their actions when they are fully aware of what they are doing and why.

For the Ishmaelian school of thought and those akin to it, there would seem to be little prospect for developing a teleology of the commandments, inasmuch as the Torah text itself rarely presents specific reasons for observing any of the commandments. The Torah usually only presents two general reasons for observing any of the commandments: the authority of God and the benevolence of God. Thus when God offers the Torah to Israel at Sinai, the people accept it on his authority alone: "Everything that the Lord has spoken, we shall do" (Exodus 19:8). And when Moses reiterates the Torah to the people of Israel forty years later on the plains of Moab, he emphasizes that it is "for our good" (Deuteronomy 6:24; see B. *Berakhot* 5a on Proverbs 4:2). However, the text there seems to mean that the good result of observing the commandments of the Torah overall will be a benevolence brought about by God as a reward. The use of the term "good" there does not seem to be an argument for the inherent good of the respective commandments themselves. As such, in this view, one cannot evaluate the commandments of the Torah in relation to each other because one does not know what the final rewards will really be (Mishnah (hereafter "M."): *Avot* 2.1; see *Chullin* 142a).

Indeed, one passage in the Talmud argues against the effort to find reason for the commandments as follows:

Rabbi Isaac asked why the reasons of the Torah (*ta'amei torah*)

68

were not [usually] revealed. [He answered by saying that this is] because there are two commandments whose reasons are revealed, and the greatest man in the world was misled by them. [As for the first of them], it states [regarding the king], "He shall not take for himself many wives [lest they turn his heart away]" [Deuteronomy 17:17]. Solomon said, "But I shall take many and I shall not be turned away [*ve-lo asur*] [from God]." Yet Scripture writes, "And at the time of Solomon's old age his wives turned [*hitu*] his heart" (1 Kings 11:4).

B. *Sanhedrin* 21b

This rabbinic argument builds upon the text of 1 Kings itself, where the prohibition of Deuteronomy that Solomon so arrogantly violated is paraphrased (1 Kings 11:2). So, in other words, the search for the reasons of the commandments is seen as being motivated by a desire to escape the observance of the commandments by discovering what their ends are and then devising other means to fulfill them that are more personally attractive. The very use of reason, according to this view, seems to be based on the desire (whether conscious or unconscious) to escape the authority and benevolence of God and to constitute the relationship with God on one's own human terms. According to this view, then, God's commandments very likely have no other reason than to test human will by the greater will of God (see, for example, M. *Avot* 2.4; *Bereshit Rabbah* 4.1; *Bemidbar Rabbah* 19.1).

❧ THE BEGINNINGS OF RABBINIC ❧ TELEOLOGY

The prohibition of the king taking many wives, for which the Torah atypically does give a reason, is used to make the anti-philosophical point about the religious danger of giving reasons for the commandments altogether. Yet there is another rabbinic discussion of this biblical text that can be seen as making an important pro-philosophical – or perhaps pre-philosophical – point. Careful analysis of this text might show just how the theology of the Aqiban school of thought does lay the groundwork for a Jewish philosophy. Such a philosophy, as we have already seen, must primarily be a philosophical meditation on the practices mandated by the Bible.

The Mishnah states:

[When Scripture prescribes] "He shall not take for himself many wives" [Deuteronomy 17:17], that means no more than eighteen. Rabbi Judah says he may take as many [as he desires] provided (*bilvad*) they do not turn his heart away [from God]. Rabbi Simeon says that he should not marry even one were she to turn his heart away. [But Rabbi Simeon was queried] if so, then why does Scripture say, "He shall not take for himself many wives"? [He replied] even if many wives were like Abigail.

M. *Sanhedrin* 2.4

In the Mishnah, which is the early rabbinic text upon which the subsequent discussions in the Gemarah are based (thus the Mishnah and the Gemarah make up the Talmud), there are three opinions. In the opinion of the first, anonymous, authority (*tanna*), the number of wives, not their character, is the issue. Hence "many wives" means more than eighteen. Here the meaning of an unclear general statement in the Bible is simply stipulated (cf. B. *Yoma* 80a), although the Gemarah does attempt to find some biblical basis for the insistence on this number (B. *Sanhedrin* 21a). In the opinion of Rabbi Judah, the character of the wives and their number is the issue. Up to eighteen wives may be taken by the king regardless of their character, but after these eighteen, character is the criterion for addition. Finally, in the opinion of Rabbi Simeon, the point of the biblical proscription pertains to the preclusion of unsuitable wives for the king (cf. B. *Qiddushin* 68b on Deuteronomy 7:4) among the eighteen he may take. And no more may be taken even if they are like Abigail, the wife of King David, whose great virtue is praised by Scripture (1 Samuel 25:3).

The discussion of this mishnaic text in the Gemarah (B. *Sanhedrin* 21a) concentrates on the difference of opinion between Rabbi Judah and Rabbi Simeon. The point of difference between them is located at the question of how one interprets the reasons given in the Bible itself ("*ta'ma de-qra*") for the restriction of the king's marriages.

Rabbi Judah is seen as holding that the reason explicitly given in the biblical text, itself an unusual procedure, should be interpreted literally because such an unusual addition is in the text for a definite function. That is an opinion with strong affinities to the Ishmaelian school of thought (see B. *Sotah* 3a). The function of the reason added to the biblical text is to qualify teleologically the rule concerning the number of wives the king may marry. Since the reason for the proscription of a limitless number of royal wives is that they will very likely turn the king's heart away from God (as did the wives of King Solomon), the explicit mention of the reason overrides the numerical limitation of eighteen *if* it can be shown that the additional wives are indeed of good character and, *therefore*, they will not turn the king's heart away. (Such, of course, was not the case with the women whom Solomon married, inasmuch as his interest in them seems to have been lust or for the purpose of cementing relations with foreign powers by dynastic means, as the text in 1 Kings 11:1 implies; see Y. *Sanhedrin* 2.6/20c.)

But Rabbi Simeon is seen as holding that this reason could have been inferred without any explicit mention of it in the biblical text. Therefore, the "reason" given in the text is not a reason at all for we could already infer the reason ourselves (see, for example, B. *Pesachim* 18b for a similar premise and its exception). What ostensibly appears to be a reason is really an additional rule instead. That additional rule is that even one extra wife, one even as virtuous as Abigail, will in effect turn the king's heart away. The implication is that it is not the character of the wives that is at issue but their number; too many wives will be too distracting to the king as the moral leader of the people (see Deuteronomy 17:18–20). As for the first eighteen wives being morally suitable, that is hardly a requirement only for kings (cf. B. *Qiddushin* 70a). In the view of Rabbi Simeon, the Bible does not have to waste its words by giving reasons for commandments; rather it leaves that task to the human intellect of its interpreters. Not encumbered by a reason already given, the human intellect of the interpreter has wider range to speculate. This wider range for speculation can certainly be seen as a precondition for philosophical meditation, which in the area of practical reason is teleological. For within the biblical text itself, there is very little teleology given for the specific commandments themselves. Outside the biblical text, however, much teleology can be proposed. And to make this process applicable throughout the interpretation of Scripture, even the little teleology within the biblical text has to be reinterpreted deontologically precisely so that teleological interpretation will not be confined to these exceptional cases alone (cf. B. *Qiddushin* 24a). All this is conceptually akin to the thought of the Aqiban school. Furthermore, it should be noted that Rabbi Simeon [ben Yochai] was one of Rabbi Aqibah's closest disciples (see B. *Pesachim* 112a).

AQIBAN ONTOLOGY

The discernment of the reason for a commandment cannot be the means for its elimination. That would only be the case if we were absolutely sure that the reason we have discerned is in truth the original intent of the divine lawgiver. However, the Talmud indicates that all interpretation of the commandments is secondary to the normative status of the commandments themselves (see B. *Berakhot* 19b on Proverbs 21:30). Human wisdom cannot usurp divine wisdom.

On the surface, this might seem to be a dogmatic limitation placed on human reason and thus anti-philosophical. Yet, when seen in the light of the theological premises of the Aqiban school of thought, it has considerable philosophical value. In the Aqiban point of view, the words of the Torah are to be taken as data rather than dicta. In other words, precisely because the Torah does *not* speak by means of human language, its words must be seen as one would see the entities of nature. Being given rather than devised, the entities of nature can only be explained by humanly devised theories, theories that are always only *about* them, never *above* them. Therefore, they cannot be eliminated by these theories and replaced by something else in their stead. Such would only be the case in humanly devised projects in which means are subordinate to ends and thus contingent upon them for their very existence. In other words, in the Aqiban way of understanding the nature of the Torah, the words – even at times the letters – of the Torah have an ontological status that they do not have in the Ishmaelian way of understanding.

The Ishmaelian view strikes one as being somewhat akin to the type of ordinary language analysis so prevalent in Anglo-American analytical philosophy since the later work of Wittgenstein. Conversely, the Aqiban ontology of the Torah and its connection to human action have some intriguing similarities to Plato's constitution of a bilateral relation between theoretical reason and practical reason, that is, that practical reason has theoretical intent and theoretical reason has practical application. As such, it is dissimilar to Aristotle's constitution of the ultimate transcendence of ethics by metaphysics.

In the Aqiban view, the Torah is a perfect harmony with nothing lacking and nothing superfluous in it. This comes out in the following interpretation of a younger contemporary of Rabbi Aqibah, Rabbi Eleazar ben Azariah, of the verse "The sayings of the wise are like goads, like nails [*u-khe-masmerot*] planted in prodding sticks. They were given by one shepherd" (Ecclesiastes 12:11): "They are like nails that are planted, which are neither too little nor too much" (Tosefta on *Sotah* 7.11). But then this rabbinic interpretation emphasizes the word "planted" (*netu'im*) in the biblical text: "Just as what is planted is fruitful and multiplies, so are the words of the Torah fruitful and multiplying" (cf. B. *Chagigah* 3b). By "multiplying" he does not mean that the original text of the Torah is subsequently augmented; rather he means that the words of the Torah are intelligible and thus they stimulate humans to devise continually new and satisfying interpretations and applications of them. This emphasis on expanding interpretation was the hallmark of Rabbi Aqibah and his disciples. With this theological stimulus to intellectual speculation, it is not surprising that the historical preconditions for the emergence of philosophy were being simultaneously prepared.

❧ NORMATIVE TELEOLOGY ❧

Throughout the Talmud one finds numerous examples of the rabbis' speculating on what the reason for a commandment is (see, for example, *Niddah* 32b). Nevertheless, these interpretations can usually be seen as functioning ex post facto, namely, they are subsequent, imaginative, speculations on the value of the commandments. But as such, they do not play any real constitutive role in the normative interpretation of the commandments themselves. In other words, they do not function as essences that determine the structure and application of the specific commandments at hand. They are "reasons" in the sense of the other etymology of the word *ta'am* that means "taste" (see Job 34:3). Just as taste is not part of the essential nutritional function of food but only attracts us to eat it, so are these "reasons" given only to attract us to the commandments. In other words, they are like homilies (*aggadah*) that are attractive to the masses (see B. *Shabbat* 87a), but which themselves do not function normatively (see Y. *Pe'ah* 2.4/17a). Therefore, it is difficult to see these interpretations as having import for a philosophy of Jewish practice.

Occasionally, however, one does find interpretations of the reasons of the commandments that do have a determinative function in the legal reality of the commandments themselves. Thus they can be taken as examples of philosophy *of* law and not just surmisals *about* the law. This comes out in the following later rabbinic text:

> Mar Zutra and Rav Adda Sabba the sons of Rav Mari bar Isur were dividing his estate among themselves. They came before Rav Ashi and said to him that the Torah prescribes "by the testimony of two witnesses" [*yaqum davar* – "a legal matter shall be established"] [Deuteronomy 19:15]. Does this apply only to cases where one person wants to back out of a legal agreement he made with another person, and he may not do so [because the witnesses will testify to the original agreement]? [If that is the reason], then we would not do so. Or, perhaps, no legal matter whatsoever is valid without the presence of witnesses. Rav Ashi answered them that witnesses are selected only when there is concern about the parties denying [an agreement].

> B. *Qiddushin* 65b

The sons of Rav Mari bar Isur are asking a fundamental question about the purpose of the law requiring witnesses at a contractual proceeding. Are the witnesses only a requirement *if* there is the likelihood that there will be contesting claims by the two parties involved in an agreement, or are the witnesses a requirement for there to be any legally valid agreement *at all*, irrespective of the likelihood or unlikelihood of contesting claims? Rav Ashi's answer, then, is his judgment about the purpose of the biblical commandment requiring witnesses, at least as regards commercial proceedings. This judgment of the *why* of this commandment determines *how* it is to be applied and *how* it is not to be applied. And following Rav Ashi's conclusion here (for the great authority of Rav Ashi in talmudic jurisprudence, see B. *Bava Metzia* 86a), the important twelfth-century Franco-German authority Rabbenu Tam made the general conclusion that commercial proceedings have no inherent requirement for the presence of two witnesses, although such presence is customarily the case (Tosafot on B. *Qiddushin* 65b, s.v. *"la ibru sahaday"*).

The question raised in this talmudic case is of philosophical import since it ultimately involves the larger question of the relationship of the individual to society. (Certainly since the sixteenth century, this has been the central question of political philosophy in the West.) In this particular context the question is about what the role of witnesses, being the agents of society itself, is to be in the private agreements, between individuals. If, on the one hand, individual persons are essentially defined as being the constituents of society, then it would seem that society in the person of witnesses should be present in any agreement made between two parties. After all, both the status of the persons agreeing and the very value of the commodities that are the subject of the agreement are themselves socially determined. But, on the other hand, if persons are essentially defined as individuals even before they have any relationship with society (what Hobbes, Locke, and Rousseau called "the state of nature"), then the role of society is only that of a mediator in the case of disputes between the parties themselves. For these persons are *in* society but not *of* it. So, if they can mutually agree among themselves, then the presence of society in the person of witnesses is unwarranted. And, furthermore, unlike many social contract thinkers who see the usual relationship of individuals among themselves to be a predatory one (*homo homini lupus*), this talmudic text seems to regard the usual social situation to be one of mutual cooperation and trust (cf. M. *Avot* 3.2).

Following this type of philosophical analysis, it would seem that the opinion of Rav Ashi as to the essential function of witnesses is basically in accord with the view that restricts the role of society to that of adjudication in the event or the likely event of disputes. At least in the realm of commercial activities, individuals are not to be burdened with unnecessary social interference (see B. *Sanhedrin* 32a). Society itself must trust the basic integrity of its citizens. Indeed, without such trust, ultimately the only remaining options are either anarchy or tyranny, that is, society has to become either absent or ubiquitous. On the other hand, though, when it comes to marital covenants the same talmudic text we have just looked at insists upon the presence of witnesses in a foundational capacity. There the Talmud distinguishes between marital relationships that have greater meaning for the rest of society and commercial transactions that have less meaning for it. This, of course, reflects the view that the family is a more basic component of society than individuals as property holders and traders; indeed that persons themselves are more *interested* in familial relationships than they are in commercial transactions. The society that the Talmud deals with and intends to preserve and enhance is more concerned with status than with contract.

❧ LAW AND SOCIETY ❧

The question we have been examining about the role of society in human disputes also comes out in an early rabbinic debate about the legitimacy of arbitration in lieu of formal legal litigation. Here again, the philosophical import of the debate concerns the fundamental purposes of civil law.

> Rabbi Eliezer the son of Rabbi Yose the Galilean said that it is forbidden to arbitrate ... but let the law [*ha-din*] pierce the mountain, as Scripture says, "for the judgment [*ha-mishpat*] is God's" [Deuteronomy 1:17] ... Rabbi Joshua ben Korhah said that it is meritorious [*mitzvah*] to arbitrate as Scripture says, "a true and harmonious judgment [*u-mishpat shalom*] you shall judge in your gates" [Zechariah 8:16]. But is it not so that where there is justice [*mishpat*] there is no harmony [*shalom*] and where there is harmony there is no justice? So, what kind of justice contains harmony? That is arbitration [*bitz'ua*].
>
> B. *Sanhedrin* 6b

The philosophical point being debated here seems to concern the relation of law and society. Is society for the sake of the law, or is law for the sake of the society? The answer seems to depend on what one sees the essential function of society to be. If society is simply to reflect a higher order and implement it on earth, then one will agree with Rabbi Eliezer in the above debate. However, if society is to be a communion of persons, a covenantal entity not just implementing divine authority but participating in the harmony of divine care for the universe, then one will agree with Rabbi Joshua ben Korhah in the debate. Moreover, it is clear that arbitration involves more independent human reasoning than formal adjudication based on written law (see Y. *Sanhedrin* 1.1/18b). The tendency of the later Jewish legal tradition was to follow this latter view of the relation of law and society. And that tendency has some important philosophical affinities to Aristotle's insistence on the priority of friendship (*philia*) over strict justice in the truly human community (*koinonia*), although the theological component in the rabbinic view makes for essential differences from Aristotle's view. This affinity helps explain why Aristotelian ethical and political concepts became so attractive to a number of medieval Jewish philosophers who were rooted in the rabbinic tradition before they approached the work of Aristotle and the Aristotelians.

❦ THE LATER EMPHASIS ON ❦
HUMAN LAW

In the early rabbinic sources, there is no real distinction made between divine law and human law. The Torah is the divine law that is given to be interpreted by humans. It is *from* God, but not *in* heaven, that is, its meaning is determined by exegesis and learned consensus, not by any further oracular revelation (see B. *Bava Metzia* 59b on Deuteronomy 30:12). This proved to work out quite well as long as the rabbis were convinced that any new problem that arose could be related to the authority of the Torah by exegetical means. The exegetical bridge between the Torah and the human situations it is to judge was constituted through a number of hermeneutical principles.

In the earlier rabbinic sources, it seems that conclusions derived by means of these principles are logically compelling, especially the principle called "*qal va-chomer*," which is an inference a fortiori. Yet already in these sources there are questions that suggest that even this type of reasoning is more analogical than deductive, hence not totally compelling after all (see, for example, M. *Bava Qamma* 2.5; M. *Yevamot* 8.3). By the time of the later rabbinic sources, the logical weakness of even *qal va-chomer* reasoning had been further exposed (see B. *Qiddushin* 4b).

What growing dissatisfaction with the complete sufficiency of formal exegetical reasoning accomplished was to make room in the realm of rabbinic normative discourse for more teleological reasoning. As we have already seen, that opens the door for practical philosophy. The rabbinic authority who did more in this area than anyone else is the fourth-century Babylonian sage Rava.

By the time of Rava, the distinction between the divine law of the Torah (*d'oraita*) and the human law of the rabbis (*de-rabbanan*) was already in place. The human law of the rabbis is not seen as independent of the divine law of the Torah; rather it is seen as being mandated by that law (B. *Shabbat* 23a on Deuteronomy 17:11). In this theological view of the nature of the Torah, the rabbis are given authority by the Torah itself not only to interpret its law and adjudicate cases based on their interpretation, but also to augment the law of the Torah with their own legislation. The formal distinction between these two kinds of law, however, was constantly emphasized in the later rabbinic texts to distinguish between direct revelation and human wisdom (albeit seen as inspired), and to give normative priority to divine law over human law (see B. *Berakhot* 19b; B. *Betzah* 3b).

What, then, is the essential difference between the earlier and the later rabbinic views of the relation between the divine and the human in the realm of law? The difference seems to be as follows. In the earlier view, all law is seen as coming *from* God, however tenuous the exegetically constituted relation between divine ground and normative consequent in fact is. But in the later view, there is a considerable body of Jewish law that is not seen as specifically coming from God, but only the *general authority* to make it is seen as coming from God. Instead, its essential methodology is that it is made *for the sake of* God. Its function, then, is to enhance the quality of human life, the pinnacle of which is the covenantal relationship with God (see M. *Makkot* 3.16 on Isaiah 42:21; B. *Bava Qamma* 6b). Thus its very nature is teleological.

How does one know what is for the sake of God? In the narrower sense, of course, that was discovered by justifying human legislation as an enhancement of specific laws of the Torah so that the usual careless violation of the law would more likely be violation of the humanly constructed "fence around it," rather than the divinely given core within that fence (M. *Avot* 1.1; M. *Berakhot* 1.1; M. *Betzah* 5.2). But this explains only the function of restrictive rabbinic decrees (*gezerot*). When it comes to the more innovative rabbinic enactments (*taqqanot*), where the rabbis devised new legal institutions, then what is for the sake of God involves a philosophical reflection on what are the more general overall ends of the Torah itself.

It is in the area of these positive rabbinic enactments that the legal philosophy of Rava is most evident. For example, the rabbis were interested in what is the actual scriptural warrant for including the book of Esther in the canon. Prima facie, the story told in this book is a secular one. In fact, the name of God is not mentioned anywhere in the book. Nevertheless, the book had long been accepted by the Jews as Scripture, and it became the basis for the popular holiday of Purim. Earlier rabbis had tried to find a specific scriptural text *from* which to deduce a warrant for the inclusion of this book in the biblical canon and thus justify the religious celebration of Purim. After reviewing various early attempts to locate such a specific scriptural warrant, the second-century Babylonian authority Mar Samuel stated, "Had I been there, I would have been able to give a much better interpretation than any of them [of what it] says [about the introduction of Purim] in the book of Esther [9:27], 'They upheld it and accepted it', [namely,] they upheld in heaven what had already been accepted on earth" (B. *Megillah* 7a). Rava then states that all of the earlier interpretations could be refuted, but that the interpretation of Samuel is irrefutable. The reason is that Samuel's interpretation is not derived *from* a biblical verse at all. Instead, it takes a biblical verse as a description of a human enactment that is *for the sake of* God because it celebrates an event perceived to be especially providential. The reasoning described in the verse is teleological. The divine approval it receives is not ab initio but ex post facto (cf. B. *Shabbat* 87a). In order for such approval to be won, the enactment itself had to be based on a consideration of the purposes of the Torah in general. These purposes are explicated by a process of philosophical reflection.

Rava's emphasis on teleology appears in numerous of his opinions recorded in the Talmud. In one text, he explicitly rejects earlier exegetical reasoning and insists that the reasoning involved in the interpretation of a rabbinic law be conducted according to "the canons of reason" (*"be-torat ta'ama"*), that is, by teleological rather than by deductive logic (B. *Berakhot* 23b). In another text, he accepts one earlier rabbinic legal opinion over a rival opinion because the first opinion is more rational (*mistabra*), even though the biblical exegesis used in the second opinion is sounder (*Arakhin* 5b). The rationality of the first opinion consists of its better grasp of the original purpose of the law under discussion. Thus even though Rava did not himself develop what we would call a "systematic" philosophy of Jewish practice, he did lay the groundwork for a teleological approach to the Jewish tradition. Without his achievement, teleological analysis by Jewish thinkers who came after him could be attributed to their exposure to Greek, especially Aristotelian, philosophy. The truth is, however, that by the time these Jewish thinkers were exposed to Greek philosophy they were already prepared for teleological thinking by the Talmud. Hence they could not only appreciate the insights of Greek philosophy but critically evaluate them as well.

Rava's achievement was possible because of the later talmudic recognition that large portions of Jewish law were really rabbinic decrees and enactments. In fact, in a number of these later texts, even laws supposedly based on biblical exegesis are judged to be rabbinic laws in essence and only biblical by subsequent association (*asmakhta* – see, for example, *Chullin* 64a-b). That being the case, teleological analysis of rabbinic laws is at a considerable advantage over similar analysis of biblical laws. The advantage is that in the case of biblical laws the reasons of the divine lawgiver for prescribing or proscribing as he did are more often than not unknown. The assumption is "My thoughts are not your thoughts" (Isaiah 55:8). Therefore, teleological analysis here can only be speculative, although, as we have seen, it can sometimes have normative effect. In the case of rabbinic law, conversely, the reasons for the humanly made law are almost always explictly stated (see B. *Gittin* 14a); and, in fact, when they are absent, subsequent commentators were quick to surmise what they are. Human minds are much more able to understand the reasons of other human minds than they are able to understand the reasons of the divine mind. As such, the more law that is considered rabbinic the more room there is for the teleological analysis that characterizes practical reason. Thus rabbinic law, at least in principle although rarely in practice, was subject to repeal, unlike biblical law for which the suggestion of overt repeal would be considered blasphemous (see M. *Eduyot* 1.5; B. *Avodah Zarah* 36a-b; cf. B. *Sotah* 47b).

All this might well be why the Mishnah designates Jewish civil law as the discipline one should engage in if one "wants to become wise" (*she-yahkim* – M. *Bava Batra* 10.8). For even in early rabbinic times, Jewish civil law was already based on a minimum of biblical verses and a maximum of rabbinic decrees and enactments (see, for example, M. *Gittin* 4.3 and the extensive discussion thereof in both Talmuds; also B. *Yevamot* 89b on Ezra 10:8).

Rava's emphasis on the importance of human reason in the religious life itself is most succinctly expressed in his statement that, when a person is brought before the throne of divine justice after one's life is over, one will be asked (among other things), "Did you reason wisely ["*pilpalta be-chokhmah*"]? Did you infer [*hevanta*] one thing from out of another?" (B. *Shabbat* 31a). It seems that Maimonides, the most important Jewish philosopher to emerge out of the rabbinic tradition, basing himself on this text and another in the Talmud (B. *Qiddushin* 30a), located an actual religious *duty* to philosophize (*Mishneh Torah*: Talmud Torah, 1.11) – of course, for those both able and inclined to do so.

❧ BIBLIOGRAPHY ❧

Texts

Babylonian Talmud (1935–48), translated by I. Epstein (London: Soncino).
Mishnah (1933), translated by H. Danby (Oxford: Clarendon Press).
Montefiore, C. G. and H. Loewe (eds) (1963) *A Rabbinic Anthology* (New York: Meridian).

Studies

Halivni, D. W. (1986) *Mishnah, Midrash, and Gemara: The Jewish Predilection for Justified Law* (Cambridge, MA: Harvard University Press).

—— (1991) *Peshat and Derash: Plain and Applied Meaning in Rabbinic Exegesis* (New York: Oxford University Press).

Lieberman, S. (1962) *Hellenism in Jewish Palestine*, 2nd ed. (New York: Jewish Theological Seminary of America).

Schechter, S. (1936) *Some Aspects of Rabbinic Theology* (New York: Behrman).

Urbach, E. E. (1971) *The Sages: Their Concepts and Beliefs*, translated by I. Abrahams, 2 vols (Jerusalem: Magnes).

Wolfson, H. A. (1929) *Crescas' Critique of Aristotle* (Cambridge, MA: Harvard University Press), esp. pp. 24–9.

II

Medieval Jewish philosophy

CHAPTER 5

The nature of medieval Jewish philosophy

Alexander Broadie

What is medieval Jewish philosophy? Perhaps the most obvious answer is that it is philosophy written by a Jew during the Middle Ages. But even if obvious, it is also false. In this chapter its falsity will be demonstrated, and thereafter a more satisfactory answer to the opening question will be developed.

Faced with an unattributed text, is it possible, without looking further, to identify it as a piece of medieval Jewish philosophy? It might be said that we can at least determine by consideration of the linguistic evidence that the author is a medieval Jew, for the Hebrew or Judeo-Arabic of the text will contain sufficient evidence for that. But linguistic evidence is not always sufficient to establish that the author is a medieval Jew, for some medieval Jewish philosophy was written in Latin, and there is almost certainly no evidence of a purely linguistic nature supporting the fact that the Latin was written by Jews, even if the Latin points, as it does in each case, to a specifically medieval authorship. And on the other hand there are medieval Hebrew translations of Muslim philosophical writings, and indeed some of Averroes' writings are known to us now only in their Hebrew versions. Of course translating them was not a way of making the philosophy Jewish.

However, even if the linguistic data permitted the conclusion that a text was by a medieval Jew, what features would permit the conclusion that the text was a piece of medieval Jewish philosophy? Are there positions defended or arguments deployed in medieval Jewish philosophy that are not to be found in medieval Christian or Islamic philosophy? If so, what are these positions or arguments? If there are none such, then is there nothing philosophically distinctive about medieval Jewish philosophy? And if so then should we perhaps settle

83

for saying that medieval Jewish philosophy is, after all, simply philosophy written by Jews during the Middle Ages?

If we are forced to this conclusion it might turn out that by the same set of arguments it can be shown that medieval Christian philosophy and medieval Islamic philosophy do not have distinctive voices either, with the result that all that can be said is that philosophy was written in the Middle Ages by members of the three faith communities, and that the philosophical content, if not the linguistic style, did not vary from one community to another. We might settle for this position on the grounds that philosophy makes its appeal on the basis of reason, not faith, and an appeal to reason, if well founded, will receive an affirmative response from a reasonable audience of no matter what faith community. In that sense the universalism of philosophy would be presented as being in contrast to the particularism of each of the three religions. However, we have some distance to cover before being able to decide whether we must settle for this conclusion. It is necessary first to set out the conflicting arguments and to weigh them up.

Let us take as our starting point the terms in the phrase "medieval Jewish philosophy." It will quickly emerge that they are all problematic, and that, though some of the problems are trivial, others go to the heart of things, and should be of interest to anyone with an interest in Jewish philosophical speculation.

First the term "medieval." There are difficulties here, some trivial and some which constitute an obstacle to a proper understanding not only of medieval Jewish philosophy but of the history of Jewish culture. "Medieval" means "pertaining to the Middle Ages." This is to define an age negatively, in terms not of itself but of the ages which flank it, the ages which it mediates. But what ages are at issue when we speak about the ages which flank the *medium aevum*, the age in the middle? It should first be noted that the Middle Ages do not need to be seen as lying in the past in relation to the person who calls them "Middle Ages." That towering figure from the late Roman period, Augustine, who had a deeper insight into the nature of time than most people do, said that he was living in the Middle Ages, meaning thereby that he was living in the period between the first coming and the second. But when modern historians use the phrase they are likely to be referring to the time between the Dark Ages and the Renaissance. That period cannot be dated with great precision, perhaps cannot even be pinned down to within a century or two, but no doubt that does not matter greatly. Let us suppose that it signifies the period from the beginning of the tenth century to the end of the fourteenth, or perhaps a period within that, or overlapping it, though not by much, on one side or the other.

However, it is not the precise dating of the Middle Ages that concerns us here but the cultural background which is presupposed. In relation to what culture were those centuries the Middle Ages? The answer is obvious; it is the European, and particularly the West European, culture. West Europe lived through a Dark Age, lasting for a few centuries from the collapse of the Roman Empire in the West, and then, after an intermediate period, the Middle Ages, it enjoyed the Renaissance, which lasted for a few centuries until the Enlightenment. But we are not to suppose that these descriptive phrases, used as large historical categories by modern historians, make much sense, or any at all, when applied to the cultural experience of peoples in other regions during the period 900–1400 CE.

In particular the Maghreb and the Middle East, that is, countries occupying a swathe of territory under Muslim control from north-west Africa to at least as far east as Baghdad, were enjoying a rich cultural life during the period that European historians call the Dark Ages. The phrase "Dark Ages" is employed as a convenient way of expressing simultaneously two distinct concepts, those of, first, being an age backward in civilized accomplishment, and, second, being an age about which we know little – though no doubt our ignorance is due in substantial measure to the paucity of literary skills during the period in question. But very extensive written records provide ample testimony to the flourishing arts and sciences in Baghdad, Cairo, and other great centers of the Middle East; indeed, the initiators of the medieval Jewish philosophical tradition, Saadia Gaon (882–942), who lived in Baghdad, Aleppo, and Sura, and his contemporary Isaac Israeli (b. 850), who lived for a time in Khartoum, did not come at the end of a Jewish cultural dark age. Far from it.

The point is not a quibble. To apply these Western cultural categories to these distant cultures is to impose an alien categorial framework upon them, and this could lead the unwary to have a false understanding of those cultures. This is of immediate concern to our topic since in the main the major works of Jewish philosophy written in what we in the West call the "Middle Ages," were not written in the Middle Ages in relation to the cultural environment of those works. And this is true even of those Jewish philosophical works written in Spain, for it is Moorish Spain that is at issue here and Moorish Spain was culturally at least as closely linked to the Middle East as to Western Christendom. However, the phrase "medieval Jewish philosophy" is no doubt too well entrenched now to be shifted. But I hope I have made clear my reasons for thinking that the word "medieval" is in its own way working on behalf of a Western cultural imperialism against which we should be on our guard. It would of course be preferable to employ cultural categories that are dictated by the Jewish historical experience, rather than categories imposed upon it by an alien culture seeking to dictate the terms of the discussion.

The term "Jewish" is more problematic than the term "medieval". What makes a work of medieval Jewish philosophy Jewish? The obvious answer is that it was written by a Jew, but I shall argue that although obvious it is also incorrect. A distinction has to be made between the philosopher and the philosophy. The former could be Jewish without the latter being so, and that is how it would be unless something of the Jewishness of the person affects the philosophy, enabling us, without knowing the author, to identify the work, from the evidence of the ideas themselves, as a piece of Jewish philosophy. I think that, unless it is possible to identify a philosophy as Jewish in the way just described, the concept of Jewish philosophy is of no practical or theoretical value.

It should be clear that what is at issue here is not merely the philosophical ideas in so far as the writer provides support for them in the form of citations of authoritative texts. It is common, normal, for the medieval Jewish philosophers to quote extensively not only from the Hebrew Bible but also from rabbinic literature and especially, of course, from the sages of the Talmud. And equally they do not, except in extremely rare cases, quote from the New Testament or the Church Fathers – Maimonides no more invokes Augustine than Thomas Aquinas invokes the sages of the Talmud. Consequently, it is not in general difficult to recognize that the author of a given work of medieval philosophy is Jewish or Christian. Or, put otherwise, the *auctoritates* can be sufficient to stamp a philosophical work as a Jewish book or as a Christian one. And in so far as a philosophy book is a Jewish work, we could reasonably be said to be dealing with a work of Jewish philosophy. The *auctoritates*, so to say, appropriate the work for the faith community whose culture is most particularly expressed in the book.

But the mere citation of rabbinic authorities in support of a philosophical position does not by itself imply that the philosophical position could not equally be adopted by Christian or Muslim philosophers. They would no doubt wish to cite different authorities but citing different authorities does not affect the content of the idea that is being thus supported. Our question is whether there are philosophical ideas which are recognizably Jewish in the sense that even in the absence of clues provided by the *auctoritates* the provenance of the ideas is recognizably Jewish, with the result that a Christian or Muslim thinker would have to reject those ideas as being incompatible with his or her faith. There are no doubt several senses that might be ascribed to the phrase "medieval Jewish philosophy," but the one I am outlining is probably the strongest of them.

Certainly there are writings, commonly described as works of medieval Jewish philosophy, which the above account does not fit. What for example should be said of the *Meqor Chayyim* of ibn Gabirol? During a period of six centuries most of those who knew the book knew of it as the *Fons Vitae* by the Muslim scholar Avicebron or Avicebrol, and some, on the contrary, thought that the author of the *Fons Vitae* was a Christian. Very few indeed knew that a Jew had written it.[1] I shall leave aside the puzzling point that during that lengthy period scholars were not alerted to what seem to us the obvious implications of the fact that the title of Avicebron's book is a phrase from Psalms 36:10, and I shall attend instead to the fact that the general failure to realize that the book was by a Jew prompts a question regarding the sense, if any, in which the *Meqor Chayyim* counts as a work of Jewish philosophy. Now that we know who wrote it, we assign it to the tradition of medieval Jewish Neoplatonism. Some Jews, for example Isaac Israeli, Bachya ibn Paquda (second half of eleventh century), and Abraham ibn Ezra (1089–1164), did write philosophy which could fairly be described as Neoplatonic, and here is yet another work of that kind, and some now say that they see that it is a specifically Jewish work and are puzzled that it took centuries for the truth to become generally known. It does not much matter whether we are suspicious of these apparent examples of clarity of hindsight. The important point is the conceptual one, that, whatever our decision about the proper classification of the *Meqor Chayyim*, whether or not it is to be classified as a work of Jewish philosophy should be determined by whether its content is Jewish, not by the fact that its author was.

People do not philosophize within a cultural vacuum. In particular, if philosophers are members of a faith community, we should expect their faith to be reflected in their philosophy, and certainly we cannot suppose that people who know God to exist would approach philosophical problems about the nature of existence, whether the existence of God or of created things, as if they did not have that knowledge. If the philosophers are Jews and their Judaism sets the agenda for their philosophizing, prompting them to ask about the mode of existence of the God of Israel or about the metaphysical and moral relations between God and his creatures, or about the nature of the insight of the biblical prophets, then the resultant philosophy can be called a "Jewish" philosophy, though the sense is weaker than that outlined earlier. It is weaker because the agenda just given, even if it were spelled out in much more detail, might also be the agenda for works of Christian or Muslim philosophy. Hence, on this account the agenda of a Jewish philosophy may not be peculiarly Jewish. Of course the philosophers' Judaism might also be providing them with a distinctively Jewish perspective upon traditional philosophical problems, in which case, again, it would be appropriate to speak about their philosophy as Jewish, though of course it would be necessary to say what constitutes a distinctively Jewish perspective. All this is a far cry from the simplistic, and false, view that a philosophy is Jewish if the philosopher is, and it should be plain that it is also a much more persuasive view than the simplistic one that I have rejected.

Some might object that "medieval Jewish philosophy" is a misnomer, basing their proof upon the fact that books surveying the field[2] tend to employ two grand classificatory concepts, Aristotelian and Neoplatonic. Most Jewish philosophers from the eleventh century, that is from the century after Saadia (who was heavily influenced by the Muslim school of kalām philosophy – itself owing a great deal to Greek atomism), are classed as one or the other, or even both, though a few, of whom Halevi is perhaps the most conspicuous, cannot readily be fitted into this schema. But how Jewish can a philosophy be if it is Aristotelian? Should we not say that to see Judaism in Aristotelian terms, letting Aristotle set the agenda for a Jewish investigation of the basis of Judaism, is already to have sold the pass to an alien culture? Is that not to permit the imposition upon Judaism of a categorial framework alien, not indigenous, to it, in which case how can the resultant philosophy be classified as Jewish?

But, as just stated, those medieval Jewish philosophers did not philosophize in a cultural vacuum. As well as the biblical and rabbinic literature which they inherited, they lived in an environment which had a rich philosophical tradition, and which was even then alive with philosophical activity. Many things that the non-Jewish philosophers said, on the basis of their reading of Aristotle, of the Neoplatonists, and of the Muslim kalām philosophers, were supported by persuasive arguments, and Jews could not ignore those arguments, especially as many of the subjects at issue were of immediate concern to Judaism. Among those subjects are the existence of God and the nature of his oneness, where the crucial questions are whether his existence can be proved and whether his existence is identical with his essence. If they are identical then this would imply that God is, in a profound metaphysical sense, one. The question of the eternity or otherwise of the world was also a matter of central concern. So also was the possibility of providence, and the related question of the compatibility of human free will with divine foreknowledge of every human act. The whole question of the proper way for human beings to conduct themselves was also of course the subject of extensive discussion among ancient writers, and questions such as the relation between, on the one hand, Aristotle's doctrine of the ethical mean and, on the other hand, the halakhah were bound to attract the attention of Jewish philosophers once they alighted upon the *Nicomachean Ethics*. To what extent could a life lived in accordance with halakhic requirements also conform with Aristotelian ethical values? And finally, in this abbreviated list, there was the overarching question of the appropriate way to interpret terms when predicated of God: are they to be understood literally, or perhaps negatively? And the ancient logicians discuss several other uses of terms also, for example, analogical and amphibolous, uses duly appropriated by medieval Jewish thinkers in their attempts to make sense of terms used of God.

Plainly the non-Jewish philosophers, even pagan philosophers, could not be ignored by Jews. If conclusions of the philosophers were correct then it had to be demonstrated that Judaism did not contradict them, and if Judaism did contradict them then the errors of the philosophers had to be exposed. And since there were many philosophies, it was necessary to determine which of these was most congenial to Judaism, or at least to Judaism as understood by the particular Jewish philosophers at issue. And here it is necessary to note that Judaism is of course no more a monolith than philosophy is, and that the content of a person's concept of Judaism might be deeply influenced by what was learned from philosophers, even pagan philosophers. Apart from the point that Judaism might become intellectually impoverished if it did not seek to respond to current philosophical ideas, there was also a danger, to which some were alert, that the faith of the philosophically minded among the faithful might be set at risk, if it were not demonstrated that the fundamentals of their faith were compatible with highly plausible theses of non-Jewish philosophers. There were therefore pressures from several directions forcing Jews to engage very positively with the surrounding philosophical culture. The point is that there were powerful arguments for plausible theses, and whatever their origins, pagan or not, it was necessary, for intellectual and pastoral reasons, for Jews to respond.

This is not to deny that there were in the Middle Ages pressures in the opposite direction also. It is noteworthy that in his *Sefer Emunot ve-De'ot (Book of Beliefs and Opinions)* Saadia attempts to counter the charge that speculation of the kind to be found in that book leads to unbelief and is conducive to heresy, a charge that is apparently supported by a famous talmudic saying: "Whoever speculates about the following four matters would have been better off had he not been born; namely, what is below and what is above, what was before and what will be behind?"[3] However, it is Saadia's view, for which he finds support in Isaiah (40:21) and Job (34:4), that this rabbinic warning is aimed at those who lay aside the books of the prophets and, as Saadia puts it, "accept any private notion that might occur to an individual about the beginning of place and time." In short it is not philosophical speculation as such that is at issue, but such speculation which is not guided by Scripture.[4] And in the centuries following Saadia, the centuries I shall classify for practical purposes as medieval, Jews, guided by Scripture, produced an immense and rich literature of philosophical speculation.

In the light of the foregoing remarks it is possible to draw some tentative conclusions concerning how a piece of Jewish philosophy is to be identified as Jewish. In almost all cases the writings which we classify as medieval Jewish philosophy are richly imbued with Aristotelian, Neoplatonic, or kalāmist philosophical ideas, ideas which are present as presuppositions, or which are there as theses to be defended, or there as targets of attack. Plotinus and Proclus were particularly important as informing the thought of Jewish philosophers from the time of Isaac Israeli in the mid-ninth century. And as regards Aristotle, it is necessary to keep sight of the fact that, just as it was only within the context of the commentaries of Alexander of Aphrodisias, Themistius, Philoponus, and others that Aristotle's writings penetrated the Islamic philosophical schools, so also it was only within the context of the commentaries of those ancient writers and also of the commentaries of Muslim thinkers such as al-Fārābī, Avicenna, ibn Bājja, and Averroes that Aristotle's writings penetrated Jewish philosophical circles.

It is in virtue of the fact that certain Jewish writings are sustained, rational reflections upon Aristotelianism, Neoplatonism, and the atomist philosophy of the kalām that those writings have to be classified as philosophy. It is not a matter for dispute that the Jewish philosophers of the Enlightenment or of the post-Enlightenment periods do not stand in anything like the same relation to Aristotelianism, Neoplatonism, and the kalām. As regards those later periods, classifications such as neo-Kantian or existentialist are more appropriate and more common. And in these later periods, as with the earlier ones, it is the philosophical schools of the wider philosophical community which provide the principles of classification that enable us to place contributions to specifically Jewish philosophy.

A tentative articulation of the concept of medieval Jewish philosophy has now been provided. Maimonides' *Guide of the Perplexed* played a special role in fixing that concept, for it was treated as a paradigm or exemplar – if the *Guide* is not, in some plausible sense, a piece of medieval Jewish philosophy, then nothing at all is. In addition it determined the agenda for almost all subsequent Jewish philosophizing in the Middle Ages. No account of medieval Jewish philosophy can be taken seriously that does not give pride of place to the *Guide*.

In recent work on medieval Jewish philosophy there is no topic which has been more vigorously disputed than the extent of Maimonides' Aristotelianism.[5] But no one has sought to deny that he is a follower of Aristotle, even if perhaps, as some have maintained, a follower of a highly judaicized Aristotle. A glance at the chapters in the *Guide* on the doctrine of creation should make the point. Whether he is attacking Aristotle, as when discussing belief in the eternity of the world, or defending him, as when denying that Aristotle thought he had demonstrated the eternity of the world, or arguing in what seems non-Aristotelian territory, as when investigating the presuppositions of the law of Moses, he shows himself to be aware of Aristotle's presence. The influence that Aristotle, overwhelmingly and at all times, exerts on Maimonides stamps him as a philosopher of what we are accustomed to call the "Middle Ages". By the same token the way in which Saadia brings the kalām philosophy to bear upon Jewish themes, and the way Halevi brings his Neoplatonism to bear upon Jewish themes, mark both out as major contributors to the tradition of medieval Jewish philosophy.

❧ NOTES ❧

1 For a sketch of the history of its transmission, see Loewe 1989, pp. 39–43.
2 For example, Husik 1916; Guttmann 1973; Sirat 1985.
3 Babylonian Talmud, *Chagigah* 11b.
4 Saadia Gaon 1948, pp. 26ff.
5 See for example Strauss 1952, pp. 38–94; 1988, pp. 30–58; 1963, pp. xi–lvi.

❧ BIBLIOGRAPHY ❧

Guttmann, J. (1973) *Philosophies of Judaism*, translated by D. Silverman (New York: Schocken).

Husik, I. (1916) *A History of Mediaeval Jewish Philosophy* (New York: Macmillan).

Loewe, R. (1989) *Ibn Gabirol* (London: Grove).

Saadia Gaon (1948) *The Book of Beliefs and Opinions*, translated by S. Rosenblatt (New Haven: Yale University Press).

Sirat, C. (1985) *A History of Jewish Philosophy in the Middle Ages* (Cambridge: Cambridge University Press).

Strauss, L. (1952) "The Literary Character of the *Guide for the Perplexed*," in *Persecution and the Art of Writing* (Glencoe: Free Press), pp. 38–94. (Reprinted with changes in J. A. Buijs (ed.) *Maimonides: A Collection of Critical Essays* (Notre Dame: University of Notre Dame Press, 1988), pp. 30–58.

—— (1963) "How to Begin to Study *The Guide of the Perplexed*," in Maimonides,

The Guide of the Perplexed, translated by S. Pines, 2 vols (Chicago: University of Chicago Press), 1: xi–lvi.

CHAPTER 6

The Islamic social and cultural context

Steven M. Wasserstrom

•~ *STATUS QUAESTIONIS* ~•

Philosophy by most measures played a rather minor role in the history of medieval Judaism.[1] Thus, in recently published standard reference works on Jewish and Islamic history, philosophy plays next to no role.[2] One reason for this lacuna is that medieval Jews wrote little "pure" philosophy. Salo Baron thus was correct to observe that only two Jewish philosophers of this period, Isaac Israeli (tenth century) and ibn Gabirol (d. 1058), wrote works of philosophy which were not conceived explicitly as philosophical defences of Judaism. Ibn Gabirol's *Fons Vitae*, notes Baron, was "(next to the early and less significant attempt by Israeli) a singular example of philosophic detachedness in medieval Jewish letters."[3] As he continues:

> Even in the countries of Islam, the Jewish people were prone to disregard all the more objective scientific endeavors, and to cherish only those which restated the old tenets of Judaism in a fashion plausible to the new generation. They cast aside Israeli's and Ibn Gabirol's philosophic works, because these contained no direct defense of Judaism.[4]

Jewish philosophy in this period, in short, would seem to conform to the generalization made current by Harry Wolfson, that the Jewish philosophical tradition running from Philo to Spinoza was near-universally one of "religious philosophy," that is, philosophy in the defence of revelation, and not pure philosophy as such.[5] Julius Guttmann similarly generalized that Judaism never developed an autonomous philosophical orientation, but rather is characterized by its reactive mode:

93

> The Jewish people did not begin to philosophize because of an irresistible urge to do so. They received philosophy from outside sources, and the history of Jewish philosophy is a history of the successive absorptions of foreign ideas which were then transformed and adapted according to specific Jewish points of view.[6]

On the other hand, Sabra properly cautions against drawing the inference that Islamicate science – under which rubric Jewish philosophy may be included – should be understood as being a secondary epiphenomenon contingent upon a primary phenomenon, as a reactive episode in the "history of Western science," or as a passive reception of a more ancient discourse. Rather, he contends that a model which accentuates appropriation over reception more properly reflects the truly autonomous and active development of this philosophical tradition.[7] The same caution should be applied when considering the relative scale and autonomy of Jewish philosophy.

And, indeed, in spite of its small scale and derivative character, Jewish-Muslim philosophy has commonly been seen as the pre-eminent intellectual endproduct of the so-called Jewish-Muslim "creative symbiosis".[8] For historians of the period tend to agree that the period of and the content of "creative symbiosis" coincide with the most productive flourishings of philosophy among Muslims and Jews. Characterizations of this era also tend to emphasize, for example, the efflorescence of freethinking and of interreligious tolerance. S. D. Goitein set (or reflected) the dominant tone:

> We are also able to confirm [Werner] Jaeger's assumption that a truly international fellowship of science existed in the days of the Intermediate civilization. Both literary sources . . . and documentary sources . . . prove that in general a spirit of tolerance and mutual esteem prevailed between the students of Greek sciences of different races and religions.[9]

According to this understanding then, the time, content, and setting of the "symbiosis" coincided with that of the "rise and fall" of medieval Jewish-Muslim philosophy.

Goitein was a social historian, and, as such, was keenly aware that his "spirit of tolerance and mutual esteem" emerged from the needs of a new bourgeoisie.[10] Shlomo Pines, perhaps the greatest student of Jewish-Muslim philosophy in this century, joined Goitein in locating the newly critical Jewish thinkers in their social setting:

> In the ninth and tenth centuries, after a very long hiatus, systematic philosophy and ideology reappeared among Jews, a phenomenon indicative of their accession to Islamic civilization.

There is undoubtedly a correlation between this rebirth of philosophy and theology and the social trends of that period, which produced Jewish financiers – some of whom were patrons of learning and who, in fact, although perhaps not in theory, were members of the ruling class of the Islamic state – and Jewish physicians who associated on equal terms with Muslim and Christian intellectuals.[11]

In addition to the needs of commerce to cross cultural barriers, other factors have been adduced to account for the rise of a Jewish-Muslim philosophy. Another reason for common cause on the part of Jewish and Muslim philosophers was their joint monotheistic opposition to a common pagan adversary. The ostensible impetus of this joint counterforce remains a leitmotif of scholarship on Jewish-Muslim symbiosis. In her overview of Judeo-Arabic culture, Hava Lazarus-Yafeh thus reminds the readers of the *Encyclopedia Judaica* that there was

a profound religious-cultural alliance among these three positive religions in their common confrontation with the pagan cultural legacy, which, in its philosophical Arabic guise, threatened equally the existence of the three revelational religions. The extent and depth of their spiritual collaboration is highly astonishing and probably has no parallel in any other period of human history.[12]

Scholarship on this "spiritual collaboration" has additionally tended to emphasize a marked sympathy of Jews for Arabic philosophy. Already in 1922, Etienne Gilson could express this sympathy in vigorous terms. "Sans aller jusqu'à soutenir avec Renan que la philosophie arabe n'a réellement été prise bien au sérieux que par les Juifs, on doit accorder que la culture musulmane a poussé dans la culture juive du moyen âge un rejeton extrêmement vivace et presque aussi vigoureux que la souche dont il sortait."[13] This influential formulation readily found repetition. In fact, it is reflected, in various intensities, throughout the standard textbook and encyclopedia entries on this subject. No less a successor than Pines would come to make an analogous point.

Approximately from the ninth to the thirteenth centuries, Jewish philosophical and theological thought participated in the evolution of Islamic philosophy and theology and manifested only in a limited sense a continuity of its own. Jewish philosophers showed no particular preference for philosophic texts written by Jewish authors over those composed by Muslims, and in many cases the significant works of Jewish thinkers constitute a reply or reaction to the ideas of a non-

Jewish predecessor. Arabic was the language of Jewish philosophic and scientific writings.[14]

The history of Jewish philosophy has thus depicted the Jewish-Muslim "alliance" as a truly collective effort in the cultivation of philosophy, but one in which Jews were drawn to the dominant discourse controlled by the Muslim majority.

Consistent with this interpretation, the thirteenth-century "decline" of the Jewish-Muslim social contract in turn foreclosed its philosophical mortgage. On this reading, the end of the symbiosis concluded a joint philosophical tradition, one at least as much Jewish as Muslim.

> The famous altarpiece by Francesco Traini, in St. Catarina at Pisa, and many similar paintings depict the triumph of Thomas over Averroës, who lies prostrate before the Christian philosopher. Characteristically enough, Averroës wears the Jewish badge upon each shoulder. There is poetic truth in his presentation as a Jew, seeing that Jewish commentators and translators had a large share in making Averroës known to Latin Christianity. As has been pointed out by Steinschneider, the preservation of Averroës's *Commentaries on Aristotle* is due almost entirely to Jewish activity.[15]

Indeed, some of the sweetest fruits of Islamic philosophy – al-Fārābī (870–950), ibn Bājja (d.1138), ibn Ṭufayl (d.1185) – were preserved, translated, transmitted, and reverently studied by Jews.[16] The work of the Spanish philosopher ibn al-Sīd al-Baṭalyūsī (1052–1127) was preserved overwhelmingly within Jewish philosophical circles.[17] In conclusion, there is little dissent from the general agreement that Jewish philosophy from the tenth to the thirteenth centuries functioned in a social and cultural context which was thoroughly arabicized, if not islamicized. Of the eighteen philosophers listed in Husik's *A History of Mediaeval Jewish Philosophy*, thirteen lived in the Islamicate world; while the proportions are slightly different in Sirat's *A History of Jewish Philosophy in the Middle Ages*, the Islamicate character of medieval Jewish philosophy remains beyond dispute.[18]

❧ ORIGINS: POLEMIC, ❧ HERESIOGRAPHY, AND COMPARISON

> They foregather all, in search of a solution, they circle and tremble like angels of intoxication, and to the last one states one thing, while a second tells the opposite.[19]

After Philo of Alexandria at the dawn of the Common Era, the first Jewish philosophers, Saadia Gaon (882–942), Dāwūd al-Muqammiṣ (fl. c. 900) and al-Qirqisānī (d. 930), emerged at the end of the ninth century, in the context of Muslim defensive apologetics known as kalām.[20] By the late ninth century Arabic had become the lingua franca of the Islamicate empire, within which domain the overwhelming bulk of world Jewry resided. Among many other philosophical and religious works of antiquity, Aristotle and the Bible were being translated and annotated in Arabic. By this time, moreover, Jewish and Muslim theologies, both written in Arabic, had dovetailed to a substantial extent. Hodgson uses the term "Islamicate" to refer to this common culture, which was not restricted to the religion of Islam but which encompassed arabophone Jews and Christians as well.[21] In short, Jews and Muslims were speaking a common language, at once linguistic, exegetical, theological, and comparativist.

Inter-religious comparisons could be tested in live performances. Rival claims were sporadically adjudicated in salons, at court, and in private homes.[22] Already from the beginning of the career of the Prophet Muḥammad, Muslims had been in continual contact with Jews. But the disputation constituted a form of contact which seems to have climaxed in the ninth to tenth centuries. What might be termed "official" and "unofficial" interdenominational disputations both flourished at that time. As for "official" disputations, Jewish and Muslim leaders of their respective religious communities are depicted as officially representing their constituencies in public disputations.[23] In the early ninth century, to take just one of many such examples, the Shī'ite imām al-Riḍa (765–818) neatly confutes a Jewish exilarch at some considerable length: much of their discussion concerns the precise truth or falsity of specific biblical verses.[24] Likewise, another unnamed Jewish leader debated under the auspices of the caliph al-Ma'mūn (reigned 813–33), a detailed record of which is preserved as well.[25] Indeed, most of the Umayyad and early 'Abbāsid caliphs (the great Sunnī monarchs), as well as all of the early Shī'ite imāms, are depicted as sponsoring or participating in such forums.

But "official" leaders defending their religions in public was not the only form inter-religious meetings took. For not all pioneer philosophers were official leaders. Some were, at times, radical freethinkers held in suspicion even by their own leaders. Here one may consider the Jews Dāwūd al-Muqammiṣ and Ḥīwī al-Balkhī (ninth century) and the Muslims ibn al-Rāwandī (ninth century), Abū 'Īsā al-Warrāq (d. 909), and Muḥammad Abū Bakr al-Rāzī (d. 932) to form a certain interlinked cohort.[26] We know precious little with regard to the biographies of these philosophical radicals, though it has been assumed that they met together privately, presumably in their own homes. Nemoy suggested that Dāwūd al-Muqammiṣ, the first Jewish theologian to write in Arabic, and sole Jewish scholar of comparative religion in this era, may have been "a Jewish member of the fairly small contemporary group of 'liberal' thinkers who felt an equal regard for all monotheistic religions as in their basic essence mere variants of the same divine faith."[27] If this was the case, then these inter-religiously liminal intellectuals may be said to have shared a common cause. Not surprisingly, their precise allegiances remain a mystery. This oblivion can be only partially blamed on the typical fate of outsiders, whose writings magnetically attract suppression. Jointly espousing an approach perceived to be threatening, they were all derogated as being "deviant."

In the case of both Judaism and Islam, in fact, religious leaders sometimes condoned if not encouraged the cultivation of philosophy, and were often sensitive to its usefulness – for their purposes.[28] The success of this domestication of philosophy in the interests of defensive apologetics, as much as any other factor, kept "pure philosophy" from gaining a foothold from the start. The figure generally considered to be the first Jewish philosopher under Islam, Dāwūd al-Muqammiṣ, still operated within a framework not yet extricated from its apologetic background.[29] Saadia Gaon, likewise, absorbed current approaches which allowed him to negotiate the legitimacy of Judaism in terms of a Mu'tazilism shared, *mutatis mutandis*, by his contemporaries in the leadership of the Christian, Ismā'īlī, Twelver, and Sunnī communities.[30] But this defensive apologetics was not yet philosophy (*falsafa*) as such. Lenn Goodman describes the crucial Avicennan shift from an essentially doxographic discourse to one freed of the restricting limitations of ideas necessarily linked to identifiable parties. While al-Fārābī "regularly cloaks his own intentions in a descriptive and abstract mode, writing about languages, cultures and religions, prophets, philosophers and theologians, statesmen and the credos necessary to diverse types of polity . . . [ibn Sīnā] made good his transition to more original work, aimed at more universal intellectual purposes."[31] This shift rarely could be affected by Jewish philosophers, even when, as in the case of Saadia, the "diverse types of polity" were not mentioned by name.

❧ INTELLECTUAL SUBCULTURES ❧

The notion of a "symbiosis" between Muslim and Jew has been utilized consistently in scholarship on this subject ever since Goitein gave currency to the term.[32] The Islamicate society which gave rise to Jewish philosophy under Islam was urban and multicultural, and more than occasionally allowed a certain freedom of interfaith contact and cooperation.[33] Leaving aside the economic means and political freedom necessary for the pursuit of philosophy (addressed in the two following sections), this pursuit can also be understood in terms of interconfessional *subcultures* which jointly cultivated it.

The Islamicate philosopher may be understood, first of all, in the context of the sciences, and, more specifically, in the context of the health sciences.[34] If there was any one *déformation professionnelle* which distinctively shaped the careers of Jewish philosophers, it was that of the physician-scientist. Speaking of "cooperation between adherents of different religions belonging to the same class or group of occupations," Goitein succinctly noted that, in addition to "the prominence of a merchant class ... which brought remote countries, classes and religions near to one another, physicians and druggists [as representatives of Greek science] were to a large extent Jewish and Christian, which again was a most important factor promoting interconfessional contacts."[35] Jewish and Muslim physician-philosophers thus met with and learned from each other. Their occasional friendships could develop such intensity that ibn al-Qifṭī (d. 1248) and ibn ʿAqnīn (d. early thirteenth century) were said to have vowed "that whoever preceded the other in death would have to send reports from eternity to the survivor."[36] Both formal and informal friendships between Muslim and Jew are well known from a variety of sources.[37] Correspondence survives, for example, between the influential Muslim philosopher ibn Bājja and his friend, the logician and converted Jew, Yūsuf ibn Chasdai, the great-grandson of the famous Spanish Jewish dignitary Chasdai ibn Shaprut.[38] Jewish and Muslim philosophically oriented physicians, then, could become friends who both met together and corresponded with one another.

From the Jewish confessional standpoint, however, these contacts were fraught with dangers, as indeed the high incidence of conversion itself indicates. At the end of the period of flourishing Jewish philosophy, yet more Jewish thinkers apparently converted to Islam in the pursuit of philosophy, though we lack sufficient biographical data to say much with certainty concerning their precise motives for doing so. These figures of the twelfth and thirteenth centuries – Abu'l Barakāt al-Baghdādī, ibn Kammūna, Samauʾal al-Maghribī, Abū Sayyīd al-Isrāʾīlī, Saʿīd ibn Ḥasan, and Isaac ibn Ezra – seem to have formed a kind of subculture, the sociological characteristics of which unfortunately remain obscure.[39]

Of all such subcultures in which Jews and Muslims interacted as intellectual peers, perhaps none was as fully reciprocal as that which produced the Avicennan philosophical mysticism associated with the idea of "illumination" (*ishrāq*). Three Muslim philosophers were particularly implicated in the social context of *ishrāqī* thought, to which Jewish (or Jewish-convert) philosophers also seem markedly to have been drawn. These Muslim philosophers, Suhrawardī (d. 1192), ibn Ṭufayl (d. 1185), and ibn Sabʿīn (d. 1270), explicitly were beholden to the still mysterious *ḥikma al-mashriqīya* of Avicenna. Suhrawardī capitalized (in the words of Fakhry) "to the utmost on the anti-Peripatetic sentiments of ibn Sīnā and the mystical and experiential aspirations which he and kindred spirits had sought to satisfy"; ibn Ṭufayl explicitly enjoined that "whoever wishes to learn the Pure Truth should consult [*ḥikma al-mashriqīya*]"; while ibn Sabʿīn similarly asserted that *ḥikma al-mashriqīya* was "closer to the truth than all the rest."[40] For the purpose at hand, their subculture also may be said to have been significantly interconfessional in at least four senses. First, the curriculum, so to speak, of these thinkers was one distinctively (though not exclusively) cultivated over several centuries in Jewish-Muslim circles. Second, some of these Muslim philosophers both met with Jewish philosophers and initiated Jewish students: their circles were intertwined with those of contemporaneous Jewish philosophers in certain fundamental respects. Third, they occasionally studied and sometimes even taught Jewish works. Fourth, a number of their works were popular among Jewish philosophers for several centuries.

This combination of factors, taken as a whole, serves to highlight a significant and still little-studied intercultural context for Jewish philosophy, which therefore deserves to be treated in more detail. The first of these factors, that of a certain shared curriculum, may be discerned, for example, in the interconfessional reception-history of such Neoplatonic classics as the *Theology of Aristotle* and the *Liber de Causis*. The *Theology of Aristotle*, particularly in the so-called "Longer Version," seems to have emerged into Islamicate philosophical discourse out of a context at once Ismāʿīlī and Jewish.[41] The text-history of the *Liber de Causis* seems particularly striking in this regard. Its primary readers were al-ʿĀmirī, an exponent of pseudo-Empedoclean traditions heavily favored by Andalusian Jewish philosophers; Moses ibn Ezra, whose son became a "philosophical convert"; ʿAbd al-Laṭīf al-Baghdādī, who studied the *Guide of the Perplexed*; and ibn Sabʿīn, who also studied Maimonides' masterwork.[42]

Second, the philosophers associated with *ishrāq* met and taught Jews, Jewish converts, and judaicizing Muslims. The martyred mystical philosopher Suhrawardī initiated (with the *khirqa*) one Najm al-Dīn ibn Isrāʾīl, who taught, along with an appropriately Muslim confessional doxology, non-Muslim confessions as well.[43] A commentator on Suhrawardī, Quṭb al-Dīn Shīrāzī, gave the *ijāza* to Abū Bakr Muḥammad ibn Muḥammad al-Tabrīzī in 701/1301–2; this would appear to be the same al-Tabrīzī who wrote a celebrated gloss on sections of the *Guide of the Perplexed*.[44] As for ibn Sabʿīn, he not only explicitly cited the *Guide* in his *Risāla al-Nūriyya*, and displayed further knowledge of

Maimonidean thought in his correspondence with the Emperor Frederick II, but he also produced disciples like ibn Hūd, who taught the *Guide* to Muslims and Jews alike.[45] Ibn Sab'īn was also followed by a leading disciple in Damascus, 'Alī al-Ḥarrālī, whose father was a Jewish convert.[46] Ibn Ṭufayl's biography is extremely scanty, but he could have met Moses Maimonides at the court in Fez, where ibn Ṭufayl served as vizier, precisely at the time when Maimonides was passing through on the road to Cairo. Fellow Aristotelians strongly influenced by ibn Bājja, these fellow Spanish exiles would have had much to discuss.[47]

The third aspect to the interconfessional context of "illuminationism" which deserves mention is the Muslim study and teaching of Jewish philosophical works. The converted Jew Abu'l Barakāt al-Baghdādī influenced certain conceptions of Suhrawardī.[48] One leading commentator on Suhrawardī, ibn Kammūna, was a Jewish convert, if indeed he ever converted.[49] Ibn Sab'īn, as noted above, was familiar with the work of Maimonides. So too was 'Abd al-Laṭīf al-Baghdādī, like ibn Sab'īn, a philosopher with interest in hermeticism.[50] Two works of Maimonides have been said to bear some relation to the *Ḥayy ibn Yaqẓān* of ibn Ṭufayl. Although this likelihood has been suggested for many years, a systematic investigation of the relationship between the *Guide* and *Ḥayy* has not been undertaken.[51] The other text has not been proved conclusively to belong in the Maimonidean oeuvre. But, this work, the *Peraqim be-Hatzlachah (Chapters on Beatitude)* cites *Ḥayy ibn Yaqẓān* and emerges from this milieu, if not from the hand of Maimonides himself.[52] It should be noted that ibn Ṭufayl explicitly identifies himself with the "*ishrāq*" tradition in his epistolary introduction to *Ḥayy ibn Yaqẓān* (which provides the rhetorical framework for the book, just as an epistolary introduction frames the *Guide*).[53] None the less, clarifying the relation between the two must proceed on the basis of internal evidence, inasmuch as neither one cites or even alludes to the other. Thus Urvoy is accurate in his recent observation that, for Maimonides, "the Almohad background constituted a framework... he comes close to the Avicennism of ibn Ṭufayl in juxtaposing a strictly deductive method in the details of the analysis with the concept of metaphysical knowledge known as illumination, but without revealing the link between the two."[54]

Finally, works by Muslim philosophers which emerged from this interconfessional context were studied and annotated by Jews. Suhrawardī emphatically influenced R. David b. Joshua Maimonides, the "last of the Maimonidean Negidim."[55] And ibn Ṭufayl enjoyed an impact on Jewish philosophers from Moshe Narboni and Yochanan Alemanno to Spinoza and Ernst Bloch.[56]

The paucity of attention paid to this subculture on the part of historians of philosophy may be attributed in part to its liminal position between mythos and logos. Peter Heath has recently investigated this liminality in the case of Avicenna's allegories, and has illuminated its programmatic defiance of categorization.[57] Beyond its effective lurking on the boundaries of the sciences, this subculture flourished liminally in another sense of that term. That is, it operated at the intersection of two of the most controversial subjects in the history of philosophy in this period, the work of Maimonides and the project of *ishrāq*. Scholarship in both these areas remains intractably inconclusive on the issue of the fundamentally esoteric character of these philosophies.[58]

❧ POLITICAL SETTINGS, POLITICAL ❧ CONSTRAINTS, POLITICAL PHILOSOPHY

Three observations may be made concerning the political context of Jewish-Islamic philosophy. These respectively concern questions of political setting, political constraints, and political philosophy. First, it may be observed that dynastic variations naturally produced developmental variations in Jewish philosophical thought under these respective dynasties. Joel Kraemer, for example, has amply portrayed the situation under the Buyids. Kraemer has shown that "intellectual Shīʿism . . . which held the political reins while Shīʿī theology and jurisprudence were being formulated, was largely responsible for the intensive cultural activity which the Renaissance of Islam witnessed."[59] While this may be true for the early stages of Jewish philosophy – Isaac Israeli and Saadia Gaon emerge from a Shīʿī milieu – intellectual Shīʿism was not the only Islamicate setting in which Jewish philosophy emerged. It has been observed that the early Ayyūbid period, for example, was particularly rich in interconfessional cross fertilization, in both personal and intellectual terms.[60] Even the Almohad debacle, while socially catastrophic, likewise stimulated a surprisingly fertile philosophical interconfessionalism.[61]

The so-called "Golden Age" of the Jews of Spain, across the Mediterranean, was not distinguished by the flourishing of pure philosophy. Of its two greatest minds, Judah Halevi wrote an *anti*-philosophical classic, while Moses Maimonides wrote his masterpiece of philosophy at the other end of the Mediterranean Sea. One could argue that, despite the presence of indisputably important philosophers, the Andalusian contribution was distinctively theological and mystical, and not distinctively philosophical. Rather, such works of piety as the religious hymns of ibn Gabirol, the major expressions of Hebrew poetry, the *Kuzari*, and the kabbalah constitute the pre-eminent cultural productions of Jewish Spain.[62] That being said, the philosophical tradition of Jewish Spain comprised perhaps the most distinguished and consistently developed philosophical subculture of any medieval Jewish society. Even alongside their fellow Muslims, they were innovators in this area. Urvoy thus notes that the "first true 'philosophical system' to be developed in al-Andalus" was that of ibn Gabirol.[63]

With regard to political constraints, it may be legitimate to speak of the *vizierial* function of philosophy. That is, Muslim philosophers, and to a lesser extent Jewish philosophers, functioned at the behest of rulers, and served regimes in the capacity of adviser at court and minister of state.[64] While this function was necessarily attenuated in the case of Jewish philosophers, who rarely served directly as vizier, the contingent if not vulnerable posture of dependency remained in force for Jewish as well as for Muslim philosophers. Moreover, the vizierial function of Islamicate philosophy stimulated a "political philosophy" as such. The current usage of "political philosophy," coined by Leo Strauss, has been elaborated by his successors, including those trained and influenced by Muhsin Mahdi.[65] This approach, however, is almost entirely ahistorical, inasmuch as it neglects inquiry into social and cultural context.[66] In addition to the opacity generated by a general lack of social inquiry, understanding the political coloration of Jewish philosophy is further clouded by the esotericism of Islamicate philosophy in general. Leo Strauss influentially argued that Jewish and Muslim philosophers, Maimonides pre-eminent among them, wrote in an esoteric mode owing to persistent conditions of persecution.[67] However, even if one grants the obvious fact that most philosophers in this period practiced the esoteric "art of writing," the precise sociological relation between Islamicate "political philosophy" and the political circumstances of the philosophers – the social and cultural context of such secrecy – remains little explored.

MATERIAL CONSTRAINTS

If the Jewish philosopher was acutely dependent on the beneficence of his local ruler, he was chronically vulnerable to the flow of manuscripts, or the interruption thereof. Jews had no access to the great madrasa libraries, once these spread through the Muslim world starting in the eleventh century.[68] Lack of public access to libraries was one reason for the growth of extensive personal libraries on the part of cultured Jews.

The primary material constraint on the pursuit of philosophy, then, may have been the sheer difficulty of access to information. This difficulty took the form of obstacles in locating texts and securing teachers to teach those texts. Costly in itself, and dependent on local hospitality, travel in pursuit of knowledge (*talab al-'ilm*) was nevertheless celebrated in theory and actively pursued in practice.[69] Other material constraints included the costs of transmission. This meant buying writing materials and paying scribes, as well as incidental expenses, including transportation. We possess a considerable amount of information on these problems from the Cairo Geniza.[70] Yet another constraint was the difficulty of storage. An apocryphal account of the death of the great Muslim polymath littérateur al-Jāḥiẓ claims that he died by being crushed under the weight of his books piled around him.[71] On the other hand, wealth brought leisure and bought means to construct capacious libraries, pay reliable scribes, and patronize authoritative scholars. Perhaps the best-known such example is the Fāṭimid vizier and converted Jew ibn Killis, who lavishly supported such enterprises.[72]

CONCLUSION: "EFFLORESCENCE" AND "DECLINE"

Schemes of periodization which derive from a Eurocentric perspective tend to portray intellectual currents flowing into Islamicate civilization as tributaries feeding the mainstream of universal thought. Thus, Goitein termed the period of Islamic civilization under consideration here "the Intermediate civilization," that is, intermediate "between Hellenism and Renaissance."[73] Earlier, Adam Mez had already popularized such terms in his widely read *The Renaissance of Islam*.[74] And such terminology has been adopted in the more recent work of Joel Kraemer.[75] Inasmuch as historians of Jewish philosophy in this period agree that the respective histories of Jewish and Muslim philosophy are inextricably intertwined, Jewish philosophy likewise has tended to be characterized in light of such a scheme.

In his succinct overview of standard works on Jewish-Muslim history, R. Stephen Humphreys raises a concern with such periodization. He properly wonders "whether the familiar categories of tolerance/intolerance and efflorescence/decline are the most useful ones to apply to this subject."[76] Certainly these categories were consistently utilized by Goitein, who, even in one of his last works, still concluded that the "thirteenth century witnessed the definite turn for the worst. With the fourteenth, the night of the Middle Ages had become total."[77] That the thirteenth century constituted a kind of peak cultural moment has long been asserted by medievalists more generally.[78] But such an assertion, however venerable, remains unsupported by – or at least uncorrelated with – the data of social life and economic realities. Most pressingly, the imputation of a post-thirteenth-century "decline" must now be correlated with the evidence for the existence of "the Thirteenth

Century World System," which apparently found its global impetus at that time.[79] In other words, the standard periodization of Islamicate philosophy in metaphors of "rise and fall" may now be tested against studies of this period framed in larger (and perhaps more neutral) economic and political perspectives.

By whatever gauge one uses, the social context of Jewish-Muslim philosophy can be understood as one of enormous consequence. Alfred North Whitehead succinctly articulated this point:

> The record of the Middle Ages, during the brilliant period of Mahometan ascendency, affords evidence of joint association of Mahometan and Jewish activity in the promotion of civilization. *The culmination of the Middle Ages was largely dependent on that association.... The association of Jews with the Mahometan world is one of the great facts of history from which modern civilization is derived.*[80]

Still, today, despite continuing recognition of its dramatic impact, much remains intractably obscure concerning the actors in the intercultural context of Jewish-Muslim philosophy. We are left to speculate on an epochal drama performed by players whose actual personalities largely remain hidden from our view.

❧ NOTES ❧

1 The intention of this chapter is to consider historiographic problems in understanding the Islamicate context for the development of Jewish philosophy. See the appropriate caveat of Sabra concerning the application of the notion of "context": Sabra 1987, p. 224.

It is not the intention here to collate facts as such, but rather to summarize and to critique salient issues in the critical study of this subject. The historical sociology of Judeo-Islamic philosophy, as is the case with most of the areas of medieval Jewish-Islamic studies, remains in its infancy. The present chapter therefore eschews reiteration of a metanarrative concerning this period in the history of thought. Such an unproblematic story cannot yet be told confidently, if for no other reason than that we lack sources for doing so. See the following exchange, published in 1975: J. van Ess: "Well, we have about two million Arabic or Persian manuscripts in the world. There are more than 500,000 in Istanbul alone. Only a small percentage of the texts – perhaps six or seven per cent – are known and printed." R. Rashed: "Things are better for you than for us in the history of Islamic science" (van Ess 1975, p. 111). See also Sabra 1987 for a more recent such lament.

2 For example, no entry of any length concerning philosophy can be found in the indexes of Humphreys 1991, Lewis 1984, or Gil 1992.

3 Baron 1958, p. 135.

4 Baron 1958, p. 137.

5 Wolfson 1965.

6 Guttmann in Schweid 1990, p. 172. The same has been said of Islam. E. I. J. Rosenthal thus observed that "neither Islamic nor Jewish medieval philosophy is pure philosophy" (Rosenthal 1961, p. 95).

7 Sabra 1987, pp. 223–9 ("Appropriation versus Reception").

8 Goitein 1955 coins the usage "creative symbiosis" with reference to Jewish-Muslim interaction. However, he also argued there that the "most perfect expression of Jewish-Arab symbiosis is not found in the *Arabic* literature of the Jews, but in the *Hebrew* poetry created in Muslim countries" (p. 155).

9 Goitein 1963, p. 230.

10 Goitein 1957, pp. 583–604.

11 Pines 1967, 4:262–3.

12 Lazarus-Yafeh 1979, p. 102.

13 Gilson 1922, 1: 368. While I accept Gilson's characterization, I reject his explanation: "Ce phénomène s'explique non seulement par le contact intime et prolongé des civilisations juives et arabes, mais encore, et peut-être surtout, par leur étroit parenté de race et la similitude de leur génies."

14 Pines 1967, 4: 262–3.

15 Altmann 1949, p. 86.

16 Urvoy agrees that ibn Rushd's "work only survived thanks to his influence on a certain Jewish bourgeoisie": Urvoy 1991, p. 109.

17 Altmann 1969, pp. 41–73.

18 Husik 1969; Sirat 1985. Cf. Wasserstrom 1995, pp. 226–7.

19 The anonymous author of "Bible Difficulties," cited in Baron 1958, p. 305.

20 Wolfson 1967; Wolfson 1979; Vajda 1973; Sirat 1985, pp. 15–56 (Chapter 2, "The Mutakallimūn and other Jewish Thinkers inspired by Muslim Theological Movements").

21 Hodgson 1974.

22 Lewis 1984, pp. 3–66. See the presentation of evidence in Kraemer 1986a.

23 Zayyāt 1937.

24 Ibn Babuya 1967, pp. 427–41. Concerning such meetings, Lazarus-Yafeh 1992 notes that the "literary discussion must echo, at least in part, the many personal encounters between followers of different religions and sects, in which ideas were exchanged orally" (p. 133). See all of Lazarus-Yafeh's excellent discussion of these meetings in 1992, pp. 132–5. See also Holmberg 1989–90, pp. 45–53.

25 Ibn 'Abd Rabbihi 1956, pp. 384–7.

26 Kraemer argues that the "counter-tradition" in Islam was represented by the *falāsifa*, which constituted a discourse "radically other" than that posed by these "revolutionary saints": Kraemer 1984, pp. 160–1.

27 Nemoy 1974, p. 703. For this author, see now the definitive work of Stroumsa 1989.

28 Davidson 1974; and Endress 1990.

29 Stroumsa 1989.

30 Goodman 1988.

31 Goodman 1992.

32 Wasserstrom 1990.

33 Goitein 1967–88.

34 Hamarneh 1983.

35 Goitein 1973, p. 26. For Maimonides as a physician, see now Cohen 1993.

36 Kaufmann 1981, p. 225.

37 Goitein 1971.

38 Dunlop 1955, pp. 111–12; Pines 1964, p. 444. See also Pines 1955, esp. p. 134 n. 107, for more on early philosophical contacts across denominational lines.

39 Stroumsa 1991 and Cohen 1991, pp. 228–9. Fischel spoke of "a wave of conversions which swept over the intellectual strata of Babylonian-Persian Jewry in the second part of the 13th century": Fischel 1969, p. xx n. 26. See also Kraemer 1992.

40 Fakhry 1983, p. 294; Cruz Hernández 1981, p. 308; and Cruz Hernández 1992, p. 789 and p. 798.

41 Fenton 1986.

42 Taylor 1992, pp. 11–12.

43 Pouzet 1988, p. 220.

44 For the *ijāza*, see Walbridge 1992, p. 174 n. 14. For the gloss on the *Guide*, see Wolfson 1929, pp. 19–23; and Mohaghegh 1981.

45 For the citation of the *Guide of the Perplexed* in the *Risāla al-Nūriyya*, see ibn Sab'īn 1965, p. 157. For the Maimonidean questions which Frederick II posed to ibn Sab'īn in their correspondence, see Munk 1988, pp. 144–5 n.2; and Kaufmann 1981, p. 232. For ibn Hūd, see Pouzet 1986; Pouzet 1988, pp. 218–19; and especially Kraemer 1992. Massignon went so far as to argue that ibn Sab'īn had an "interconfessional plan": Massignon 1962, p. 671.

46 Pouzet 1988, pp. 218–19; Addas 1989, pp. 229, 230, 294, 302; Dermenghem 1981, pp. 276–88. Al-Ḥarrālī exerted a strong influence on al-Biqā'ī, one of the only medieval Muslim authors known to have studied a written (Arabic) text of the Torah. He also worked with a Jewish translator; see Lazarus-Yafeh 1992, p. 128 n. 62.

47 Heschel, for one, raises the possibility of a meeting in Fez: Heschel 1982, p. 20.

48 Pines 1980, p. 356 n. 120, and p. 358; Pines 1979, pp. 254–5, 336, and "Addenda et Corrigenda" to nn. 95, 202; Ziai 1990; Corbin 1960, s.v "Abu'l Barakāt"; and Corbin 1964, pp. 248, 250.

49 For a comprehensive review of the problem of ibn Kammūna's Jewishness, see now Bacha 1984, pp. xxv–xxxv. He relies on but supersedes the classic study of Baneth 1925.

50 See the discussion in Fenton 1981, p. 65 n. 100, on the famous report by ibn Abī Uṣaybī'a. See also Stern 1962, pp. 60–1, on 'Abd al-Laṭīf's familiarity with ibn Sham'ūn, the pupil for whom Maimonides wrote his *Guide*.

51 Though Goodman has made an important start; see Goodman 1976, p. 186; Goodman 1988, pp. 70–1; Goodman 1989, p. 21 n. 50, and p. 22 n. 69.

52 Baneth and Davidovitz 1939, p. 33, line 21. In his recent English translation, Rosner reviews the considerable consensus that this work is a pseudepigraphon: Rosner 1991, pp. 12–13. None the less, this work was written by some other (roughly contemporaneous) Jewish philosopher familiar with ibn Ṭufayl's work.

53 Ibn Ṭufayl 1936, p. 17. For a discussion of ibn Ṭufayl in light of *ishrāq* and other philosophical currents, see now Radtke forthcoming. I thank Professor Radtke for sharing a preprint of this article with me.

54 Urvoy 1991, p. 123.
55 Originally misidentified in an otherwise superb study, Rosenthal 1940. The work has now been translated and annotated closely, with special reference to the influence of Suhrawardī, in Fenton 1987.
56 Hayoun 1986; Hayoun 1988; Idel 1990, p. 167 and 187 n.10; Bloch 1952, pp. 25–30.
57 Heath 1992, p. 9: "From the perspective of the sociology of knowledge, the commitment of philosophers to logos as their preferred form of narrative discourse constitutes a fundamental element in what ibn Khaldun (d. 808/1406) would call their 'aṣabiyya or 'feeling of group solidarity'.... Not surprisingly, this philosophical 'aṣabiyya has tended to make experts in other fields nervous and defensive."
58 See Kraemer 1992 for some allusive suggestions concerning these circles.
59 Kraemer 1986a, p. 288. Netton also cites these conclusions, in Netton 1992, p. 28.
60 Goitein 1986, p. 404 and Cahen 1983, p. 211.
61 Urvoy specifically stresses the impact of "Almohadism" on Maimonides, ibn Ṭufayl, and Averroes: Urvoy 1990 and 1991; see also the still standard work of Corcos-Abulafia 1967.
62 Goitein saw the Hebrew poetry of Spain as the "acme" of the "creative symbiosis": Goitein 1955, pp. 155–67.
63 Urvoy 1991, p. 5.
64 Fischel 1969.
65 Udoff 1991, Butterworth 1992.
66 Mahdi's early study of ibn Khaldūn is a vital exception to this stultifying rule: Mahdi 1971.
67 Strauss 1952. While this observation may not be inaccurate, it has been seen by some scholars as itself masking a tendentious defence of philosophical elitism; see Burnyeat 1985.
68 Green 1988. For the culture of Islamic books more generally, see Pedersen 1984.
69 Eickelman and Piscatori 1990; Netton 1993. For knowledge of geography among Jews in this period, see Golb 1983.
70 Goitein 1988 and Sokolow 1988.
71 Pellat 1969, p. 9.
72 Fischel 1969, pp. 45–68; and Cohen and Somekh 1990.
73 Goitein 1963.
74 Mez 1937.
75 Kraemer 1986a and Kraemer 1986b.
76 Humphreys 1991, p. 265.
77 Goitein 1986, p. 404.
78 Taylor 1911, 2:419: "one might say that the student of the year 1250 stood to his intellectual ancestor of the year 1150 as a man in full possession of the Encyclopedia Britannica would stand toward his father who had saved up the purchase money for the same." Compare now Burns 1990: "The thirteenth century was remarkable for its glories, to the degree that some have too exuberantly claimed for it the title 'the greatest of centuries' " (p. 5, with examples).
79 Abu-Lughod 1989 and Frank 1990.

80 Whitehead 1948, p. 79 (my emphasis). The sobriquet "Mahometan" is of course now an archaism, and the citation of it was chosen for historical and not programmatic purposes.

BIBLIOGRAPHY

Texts

Bacha, H. (ed.) (1984) *Hawāshī (Notes) d'ibn al-Maḥrūma sur le "Tanqīḥ" d'ibn Kammūna* (Jouníeh and Rome: Patrimoine Arabe Chrétien).

Baneth, D. H. (tr.) and H. S. Davidowitz (ed.) (1939) *The Chapters on Beatitude Ascribed to R. Moses Maimonides* [Hebrew] (Jerusalem: Mekitze Nirdamim).

Fenton, P. B. (1981) *The Treatise of the Pool* (London: Octagon).

—— (1987) *Deux traités de mystique juive* (Paris: Verdier).

Hayoun, M. R. (1988) "Le Commentaire de Moïse de Narbonne (1300–1362) sur le *Ḥayy ibn Yaqẓān* d'ibn Ṭufayl (mort en 1185)," *Archives d'Histoire et Littéraire du Moyen Age* 60: 23–98.

ibn 'Abd Rabbihi (1956) *Kitāb al-'iqd al-Farīd*, vol. 2 (Cairo).

ibn Babuya, Abū Ja'far Muḥammad al-Qummī (1967) *Kitāb al-Tauḥīd* (Tehran).

ibn Sab'īn (1965) *Rasā'il ibn Sab'īn*, edited by A. A. Badawi (Cairo).

ibn Ṭufayl (1936) *Ḥayy ibn Yaqdhān, roman philosophique d'ibn Thofail*, 2nd ed., edited and translated by L. Gauthier (Beirut).

Mohaghegh, M. (1981) *Tabrīzī's Commentary on the Twenty-Five Premises from The Guide of the Perplexed by M. Maimonides*, translated into Persian by S. J. Sajjadi (Tehran: Tehran University).

Rosner, F. (1991) *Six Treatises Attributed to Maimonides*, translated and annotated (Northvale, NJ: Aronson).

Stroumsa, S. (1989) *Dāwūd ibn Marwān al-Muqammiṣ's Twenty Chapters ('Ishrūn Maqāla)* (Leiden and New York: Brill).

Studies

Abu-Lughod, J. (1989) *Before European Hegemony: The World System A.D. 1250–1350* (New York: Oxford University Press).

Addas, C. (1989) *Ibn 'Arabi ou la quête du soufre rouge* (Paris: Gallimard).

Altmann, A. (1949) "Judaism and World Philosophy: From Philo to Spinoza," in *The Jews: Their Role in Civilization*, edited by L. Finkelstein (New York: Schocken), pp. 65–116.

—— (1969) "The Ladder of Ascension," in A. Altmann, *Studies in Religious Philosophy and Mysticism* (Ithaca: Cornell University Press), pp. 41–73.

Baneth, D. H. (1925) "Ibn Kammūna," *Monatsschrift für Geschichte und Wissenschaft des Judentums* 69: 295–311.

Baron, S. W. (1958) *A Social and Religious History of the Jews*, vol. 8 (Philadelphia: Columbia University Press and Jewish Publication Society).

Bloch, E. (1952) *Avicenna und die Aristotelische Linke* (Berlin: Rütten Loening).

Burns, R. I. (1990) *Stupor Mundi*: Alfonso X of Castile, the Learned," in *Emperor of Culture: Alfonso X the Learned of Castile and his Thirteenth Century Renaissance*, edited by R. I. Burns (Philadelphia: University of Pennsylvania Press), pp. 1–14.

Burnyeat, M. F. (1985) "Sphinx Without a Secret," *New York Review of Books* (30 May): 30–6.

Butterworth, C. E. (ed.) (1992) *The Political Aspects of Islamic Philosophy: Essays in Honor of Muhsin S. Mahdi* (Cambridge, MA: Harvard University Press).

Cahen, C. (1983) *Orient et Occident au temps des Croisades* (Paris: Aubier Montaigne).

Cohen, G. D. (1991) "The Soteriology of R. Abraham Maimuni," in *Studies in the Variety of Rabbinic Cultures* (Philadelphia and New York: Jewish Publication Society), pp. 209–42.

Cohen, M. R. "The Burdensome Life of a Jewish Physician and Communal Leader: A Geniza Fragment from the Alliance Israélite Universelle Collection," *Jerusalem Studies in Arabic and Islam* 16: 125–37.

Cohen, M. R. and S. Somekh (1990) "In the Court of Yaʿqūb ibn Killis: A Fragment from the Cairo Genizah," *Jewish Quarterly Review* 80: 283–314.

Corbin, H. (1960) *Avicenna and the Visionary Recital*, translated by W. R. Trask (Princeton: Princeton University Press).

—— (1964) *Histoire de la philosophie islamique* (Paris: Gallimard).

Corcos-Abulafia, D. (1967) "The Attitude of the Almohadic Rulers Towards the Jews" [Hebrew], *Zion* 32: 137–60.

Cruz Hernández, M. (1981) *Historia de pensiamiento en el mundo islámico 2: Desde el islam andalusi hasta el socialismo árabe* (Madrid: Alianza).

—— (1992) "Islamic Thought in the Iberian Peninsula," in *The Legacy of Muslim Spain*, edited by Salma Khadra Jayyusi (Leiden: Brill), pp. 777–803.

Davidson, H. A. (1974) "The Study of Philosophy as a Religious Obligation," in *Religion in a Religious Age*, edited by S. D. Goitein (Cambridge, MA: Ktav), pp. 53–69.

Dermenghem, E. (1981) *Vies des saints musulmans* (Paris: Sindbad).

Dunlop, D. M. (1955) "Philosophical Predecessors and Contemporaries of Ibn Bājjah," *Islamic Quarterly* 2: 100–16.

Eickelman, D. F. and J. Piscatori (1990) *Muslim Travellers: Pilgrimage, Migration, and the Religious Imagination* (Berkeley and Los Angeles: University of California Press).

Endress, G. (1990) "The Defense of Reason: The Plea for Philosophy in the Religious Community," *Zeitschrift für Geschichte der Arabisch-Islamischen Wissenschaften* 6: 1–49.

Fakhry, M. (1983) *A History of Islamic Philosophy*, 2nd ed. (New York: Columbia University Press).

Fenton, P. B. (1986) "The Arabic and Hebrew Versions of the *Theology of Aristotle*," in *Pseudo-Aristotle in the Middle Ages: The Theology and other Texts*, edited by J. Kraye, W. F. Ryan, and C. B. Schmitt (London: Warburg Institute), pp. 241–64.

Fischel, W. J. (1969) "The Court Jew in the Islamic World," in *Jews in the Economic and Political Life of Mediaeval Islam* (New York: Ktav), pp. ix-xxii.

Frank, A. (1990) "The Thirteenth-Century World System: A Review Essay," *Journal of World History* 1: 249–56.

Gil, M. (1992) *A History of Palestine 634–1099*, translated by E. Broido (Cambridge: Cambridge University Press).

Gilson, E. (1922) *La philosophie au moyen âge*, 2 vols (Paris: Payot).

Goitein, S. D. (1955) *Jews and Arabs: Their Contacts Through the Ages* (New York: Schocken).

—— (1957) "The Rise of the Near-Eastern Bourgeoisie in Early Islamic Times," *Journal of World History* 3: 583–604.

—— (1963) "Between Hellenism and Renaissance – Islam, the Intermediate Civilization," *Islamic Studies* 2: 215–33.

—— (1966) "A Turning Point in the History of the Muslim State," in *Studies in Islamic History and Institutions* (Leiden: Brill), pp. 149–68.

—— (1971) "Formal Friendship in the Medieval Near East," *Proceedings of the American Philosophical Society* 115.6: 484–9.

—— (1973) "Interfaith Relations in Medieval Islam," The Yaacov Herzog Memorial Lecture, delivered at Columbia University, 22 October.

—— (1967–88) *A Mediterranean Society: The Jewish Communities of the Arab World as Portrayed in the Documents of the Cairo Geniza*, 5 vols (Berkeley and Los Angeles: University of California Press).

—— (1986) "The Maimonides-Ibn Sanā' al-Mulk Circle (A Deathbed Declaration from March 1182)," in *Studies in Islamic History and Civilization in Honour of Professor David Ayalon*, edited by M. Sharon (Leiden and Jerusalem: Brill), pp. 399–405.

—— (1988) "Books: Migrant and Stationary: A Geniza Study," in *Occident and Orient: A Tribute to the Memory of A. Scheiber*, edited by R. Dan (Budapest and Leiden: Akademiai Kiado and Brill), pp. 174–98.

Golb, N. (1983) "Aspects of Geographical Knowledge among the Jews of the Earlier Middle Ages," in *Popoli e paesi nella cultura alto medievale* (Spoleto: Settimane di Studio del Centro Italiano di Studi Sull'Alto Medioevo), 1: 175–202.

Goldziher, I. (1915) "Stellung der alten islamischen Orthodoxie zu den antiken Wissenschaften," *Abhandlungen der Königlich Preussischen Akademie der Wissenschaften* (Berlin), 8: 3–46 [English translation in Swartz 1981, pp. 185–216].

Goodman, L. E. (1976) *Rambam* (New York: Viking).

—— (1988) "Maimonides' Responses to Sa'adya Gaon's Theodicy and their Islamic Backgrounds," in *Studies in Islamic and Judaic Traditions*, vol. 2, edited by W. M. Brinner and S. Ricks (Atlanta: Scholars Press), 2: 3–22.

—— (1989) "Ordinary and Extraordinary Language in Medieval Jewish and Islamic Philosophy," *Manuscrito* 2: 57–83.

—— (1992) *Avicenna* (London and New York: Routledge).

Green, A. H. (1988) "The History of Libraries in the Arab World: A Diffusionist Model," *Libraries and Cultures* 23: 454–74.

Hamarneh, S. (1983) *Health Sciences in Early Islam: Collected Papers of Sami K. Hamarneh*, edited by M. A. Anees (San Antonio: Noor Health Foundation).

Hayoun, M. R. (1986) *Moshe Narboni* (Tübingen: Mohr (Paul Siebeck)).

Heath, P. (1992) *Allegory and Philosophy in Avicenna (Ibn Sīnā): With a Translation of the Book of the Prophet Muhammad's Ascent to Heaven* (Philadelphia: University of Pennsylvania Press).

Heschel, A. J. (1982) *Maimonides: A Biography*, translated by J. Neugroschel (New York: Farrar, Strauss, Giroux).

Hodgson, M. G. S. (1974) *The Venture of Islam*, 3 vols (Chicago: University of Chicago Press).

Holmberg, B. (1989–90) "The Public Debate as a Literary Genre in Arabic Literature," *Orientalia Suecana* 37–9: 45–53.

Humphreys, R. S. (1991) *Islamic History: A Framework for Inquiry*, rev. ed. (Princeton: Princeton University Press).

Husik, I. (1969) [1916] *A History of Mediaeval Jewish Philosophy* (New York: Athenaeum).

Idel, M. (1990) *Golem: Jewish Magical and Mystical Traditions on the Artificial Anthropoid* (Albany: State University of New York Press).

Kaufmann, D. (1981) "Maimonides's *Guide* in World Literature," in *Studies in Jewish Thought: An Anthology of German Jewish Scholarship*, edited by A. Jospe (Detroit: Wayne State University Press), pp. 220–47.

Kraemer, J. L. (1984) "Humanism in the Renaissance of Islam: A Preliminary Study," *Journal of the American Oriental Society* 104: 135–65.

—— (1986a) *Humanism in the Renaissance of Islam: The Cultural Revival during the Buyid Age* (Leiden: Brill).

—— (1986b) *Philosophy in the Renaissance of Islam: Abu Sulayman al-Sijistani and his Circle* (Leiden: Brill).

—— (1987) "The *Jihād* of the *Falāsifa*," *Jerusalem Studies in Arabic and Islam* 10: 288–325.

—— (1992) "The Andalusian Mystic Ibn Hūd and the Conversion of the Jews," *Israel Oriental Studies* 12: 59–73.

Lazarus-Yafeh, H. (1979) "Judeo-Arabic Culture," *Encyclopedia Judaica Yearbook 1977/1978* (Jerusalem: Keter), pp. 101–10.

—— (1992) *Intertwined Worlds: Medieval Islam and Bible Criticism* (Princeton: Princeton University Press).

Lewis, B. (1984) *The Jews of Islam* (Princeton: Princeton University Press).

Mahdi, M. (1971) *Ibn Khaldūn's Philosophy of History*, 2nd ed. (Chicago: University of Chicago Press), pp. 17–62.

Massignon, L. (1962) "Ibn Sab'īn et la 'conspiration hallagienne' en Andalousie, et en Orient au XIIIᵉ siècle," in *Études d'orientalisme dédiées à la Mémoire de Lévi-Provençal* (Paris: Maisonneuve et Larose), 2: 661–81.

Mez, A. (1937) *The Renaissance of Islam*, translated by S. K. Bukhsh and D. S. Margoliouth (Patna: Jubilee Printing and Publishing House).

Munk, S. (1988) [1855–65] *Mélanges de philosophie juive et arabe* (Paris: Vrin).

Nemoy, L. (1974) "The Attitude of the Early Karaites towards Christianity," in *Salo Wittmayer Baron Jubilee Volume on the Occasion of his Eightieth Birthday*, edited by S. Lieberman and A. Hyman (Jerusalem and New York: Columbia University Press) 2: 697–715.

Netton, I. R. (1992) *Al-Fārābī and his School* (London and New York: Routledge).

—— (ed.) (1993) *Golden Roads: Migration, Pilgrimage and Travel in Mediaeval and Modern Islam* (Richmond: Curzon).

Pedersen, J. (1984) *The Arabic Book*, translated by G. French (Princeton: Princeton University Press).

Pellat, C. (1969) *The Life and Works of Jāḥiẓ* (Berkeley and Los Angeles: University of California Press).

Pines, S. (1955) "A Tenth Century Philosophical Correspondence," *Proceedings of the American Academy for Jewish Research* 24: 103–34.

—— (1964) "La Dynamique d'Ibn Bājja," in *L'Aventure de la science: Mélanges Alexandre Koyré* (Paris: Hermann), 1: 442–68.

—— (1967) "Jewish Philosophy," in *The Encyclopedia of Philosophy*, edited by P. Edwards (New York: Macmillan), 4: 261–77.

—— (1979) *Collected Works*, vol. 1 (Jerusalem and Leiden: Magnes and Brill).

—— (1980) "Le *Sefer ha-Tamar* et les *Maggidim* des Kabbalistes," in *Hommage à Georges Vajda*, edited by G. Nahon and C. Touati (Louvain: Peeters), pp. 333–63.

Plessner, M. (1971) "Heresy and Rationalism in the First Centuries of Islam," [Hebrew] in *The Ulama and Problems of Religion in the Muslim World: Studies in Memory of Professor Uriel Heyd*, edited by G. Baer (Jerusalem: Magnes), pp. 3–10.

—— (1979) "The Natural Sciences and Medicine," in *The Legacy of Islam*, 2nd ed., edited by J. Schacht and C. E. Bosworth (New York and Oxford: Oxford University Press), pp. 425–61.

Pouzet, L. (1986) "De Murcie à Damas: le chef des Sab'īniens Badr ad-Dīn al-Ḥasan Ibn Hūd," in *Actes du XIᵉ Congrès de l'Union Européenne des arabisants et islamologues*, edited by A. Sidarus (Evora: University of Evora), pp. 317–30.

—— (1988) *Damas au VIIᵉ/XIIIᵉ siècle: Vie et structures religieuses d'une métropole islamique* (Beirut: Dar el-Machreq).

Radtke, B. (forthcoming) "How Can Man Reach the Mystical Union? Ibn Ṭufayl and the Divine Spark."

Rosenthal, E. I. J. (1961) *Judaism and Islam* (London and New York: Yoseloff).

Rosenthal, F. (1940) "A Judaeo-Arabic work under Sufic Influence," *Hebrew Union College Annual* 15: 433–87.

Sabra, A. I. (1987) "The Appropriation and Subsequent Naturalization of Greek Science in Medieval Islam: A Preliminary Statement," *History of Science* 25: 223–43.

Schweid, E. (1990) "Religion and Philosophy: The Scholarly-Theological Debate Between Julius Guttmann and Leo Strauss," *Maimonidean Studies* 1: 163–97.

Sirat, C. (1985) *A History of Jewish Philosophy in the Middle Ages* (Cambridge: Cambridge University Press).

Sokolow, M. (1988) "Arabic Books in Jewish Libraries: The Evidence of Genizah Booklists," in *The Medieval Mediterranean: Cross-Cultural Contacts*, edited by M. J. Chiat and K. L. Reyerson (St. Cloud, Minnesota: Medieval Studies at Minnesota).

Stern, S. M. (1962) "A Collection of Treatises by 'Abd al-Laṭīf al-Baghdādī," *Islamic Studies* 1: 53–70.

Strauss, L. (1952) "Persecution and the Art of Writing," in *Persecution and the Art of Writing* (Glencoe: Free Press), pp. 22–37.

Stroumsa, S. (1991) "On Apostate Jewish Intellectuals in the Early Middle Ages under the Rule of Islam" [Hebrew], *Pe'amim* 42: 61–76.

Swartz, M. (ed. and tr.) (1981) *Studies on Islam* (New York and Oxford: Oxford University Press).

Taylor, H. O. (1911) *The Medieval Mind*, 2 vols (New York: Macmillan).

Taylor, R. C. (1992) "A Critical Analysis of the Structure of the *Kalām fī mahd al-khair (Liber de causis)*," in *Neoplatonism and Islamic Thought*, edited by P. Morewedge (Albany: State University of New York Press), pp. 11–41.

Udoff, A. (ed.) (1991) *Leo Strauss's Thought: Toward a Critical Engagement* (Boulder and London: Lynne Rienner).

Urvoy, D. (1990) *Penseurs d'Al-Andalus: La vie intellectuelle à Cordoue et Seville au temps des empires Berberes (fin xiᵉ siècle-début xiiiᵉ siècle)* (Paris: Editions du CNRS and Presses Universitaires du Mirail).

—— (1991) *Ibn Rushd (Averroes)* (London and New York: Routledge).

Vajda, G. (1973) "Le 'kalām' dans la pensée religieuse juive du Moyen Age," *Revue de l'Histoire des Religions* 183: 143–60.

van Ess, J. (1975) "The Beginnings of Islamic Theology," in *The Cultural Context of Medieval Learning*, edited by J. E. Murdoch and E. D. Sylla (Dordrecht: Reidel), pp. 87–111.

Walbridge, J. (1992) *The Science of Mystic Lights: Qutb al-Dīn Shīrāzī and the Illuminationist Tradition in Islamic Philosophy* (Cambridge, MA: Harvard University Press).

Wasserstrom, S. M. (1990) "Recent Works on the 'Creative Symbiosis' of Judaism and Islam," *Religious Studies Review* 16: 43–7.

—— (1995) *Between Muslim and Jew: The Problem of Symbiosis under Early Islam* (Princeton: Princeton University Press).

Whitehead, A. N. (1948) "An Appeal to Sanity," in *Science and Philosophy* (New York: Philosophical Library), pp. 61–85.

Wolfson, H. A. (1929) *Crescas' Critique of Aristotle* (Cambridge, MA: Harvard University Press).

—— (1965) *Religious Philosophy: A Group of Essays* (New York: Atheneum).

—— (1967) "The Jewish Kalām," in *The Seventy-Fifth Anniversary Volume of the Jewish Quarterly Review*, edited by A. A. Neuman and S. Zeitlin (Philadelphia: Jewish Quarterly Review), pp. 554–73.

—— (1979) *Repercussions of the Kalām in Jewish Philosophy* (Cambridge, MA: Harvard University Press).

Zayyāt, H. (1937) "Sects, Innovation and the Salons of the Kalāmists" [Arabic], *al-Machriq* 35: 37–40.

Ziai, H. (1990) *Knowledge and Illumination: A Study of Suhrawardī's "Hikmat al-Ishrāq"* (Atlanta: Scholars Press).

CHAPTER 7
Kalām in medieval Jewish philosophy
Haggai Ben-Shammai

GENERAL OUTLINE OF THE HISTORY AND DEVELOPMENT OF KALĀM

Kalām is the common name of medieval Islamic, mostly rationalist, sometimes apologetic (or polemic), religious philosophy.[1] The literal meaning of the Arabic word is speaking, speech, things said, discussion.[2] In the context of religious thought it seems that around the middle of the eighth century kalām came to denote a method of discussing matters relating to religious doctrines, or to politico-religious questions, and of deciding them by means of rational argument rather than by the authority of tradition supported by political or military force. Those engaged in such arguments, or debates, and in reflection and speculation of them, were called *mutakallimūn*. For them, the attainment of knowledge was not an end in itself, but rather a means in the service of religious doctrine and practice. The mutakallimūn must be distinguished from thinkers (Muslims as well as Christians) who considered themselves committed to the legacy of Greek philosophy, mainly a Neoplatonic interpretation of Aristotelianism. These were the *falāsifa*, and their systems and methods *falsafa*.[3] The falāsifa, who were, with few exceptions, observant members of their respective religious communities (Muslims, Christians, Jews), professed the attainment of true knowledge for its own sake, as the actual realization of perfection.

The following is a very general outline of the development of kalām during its first three centuries, until the middle of the eleventh century, which is the period during which a significant number of Jewish thinkers may be described as followers of kalām, or perhaps even as participants in its development.

A number of factors contributed to the formation of kalām. First,

115

early historiographical and heresiographical sources indicate close ties between political propagandists of the 'Abbāsid political opposition to the regime of the Umayyads (towards the middle of the eighth century) and persons who were interested in what may be called, in modern terms, the ethical as well as the theoretical aspects of religious practice, often in a polemical or sectarian context. Second, the Arabic translations of Greek philosophical and scientific works (directly from Greek or from Syriac versions), the first of which may have appeared already before the middle of the eighth century, and later on in ever increasing numbers,[4] made the Greek philosophical tradition accessible to the Muslims. Third, constant contacts between the Muslims and Christian clergymen and thinkers, some of whom quite early became Arabic-speaking, resulted in the Muslims becoming acquainted with important elements of Christian thought of the period – the tradition of Greek learning in which many clergymen had been brought up and the apologetic literature, in both Greek and Syriac, which aimed at accommodating Christian theology with classical philosophy, with its peculiar style of an imagined dialogue composed of long series of questions and answers.[5] Fourth, the Muslim rulers encountered in their newly created empire members of various religions and faiths whom they wanted to convert to Islam and who, in their turn (and often numerical superiority), posed a political and intellectual challenge to Islam. In the provinces which were taken from the Byzantine Empire the challenge came mainly from transmitters of the classical legacy of philosophy and science, while in the eastern provinces the challenge came mainly from dualistic religions or movements. The intellectual challenge had to be answered in kind, but very often the nascent, though politically ascendant, Islam lacked the adequate means. The quite rapid spread of the use of the Arabic language as a vehicle for theoretical discourse, by followers of different origins and of various religious and philosophical persuasions, facilitated the flow of ideas between the various groups, but, at the same time, underlined the need of the Arabic-speaking Muslims to defend their religion, to answer the challenge for the sake of those who had already embraced Islam, and to create the tools to convince and convert larger numbers to their religion. The polemical/apologetic aspect of kalām has always been emphasized by both supporters and opponents (mainly the falāsifa) of the system.

From an early stage of the encounter between Islam and the classical heritage, mainly the Peripatetic school as well as certain Neoplatonic currents of thought, the Muslims seem to have felt that their faith was threatened. This feeling may have resulted from differences on major questions, such as the relationship between God and the universe or the validity of revelation as a source of knowledge and authority of laws. They may have shared this feeling with the Christians. However, whereas classical philosophy was for the Christians part of their culture,[6] it was not such for the Muslims. This difference may account for the fact that Greek thinkers are very rarely mentioned or quoted in kalām works, even in cases where the modern researcher can easily discern the Greek (often Stoic) source of kalām doctrines or methods.[7] This is an important difference, though more a methodological than a strictly philosophical one between the mutakallimūn[8] on the one hand, and the falāsifa, starting at the latest with al-Kindī (d. c. 870), on the other. The same difference is found also between Jewish followers of kalām and their co-religionists who preferred the path of the falāsifa.

❧ SCHOOLS OF KALĀM ❧

All these factors enhanced the evolution of a somewhat hybrid doctrinal system, which rather rapidly developed into a variety of sophisticated parallel, or rival, systems of religious philosophy which came to be known by the common name of kalām. They developed their characteristic sets of logic, philosophical concepts, and terminology that made them distinct from falsafa, the systems of the followers of classical philosophy, mostly (but not exclusively) Neoplatonic-flavored Aristotelianism. The most famous among the early kalām groups is the Mu'tazila.[9] They are said to have been active already under the Umayyads (toward the middle of the eighth century). It is certain, however, that their doctrines became recognized as the official theology of the realm under the 'Abbāsid caliph al-Ma'mūn (813–33) and also under his successors al-Mu'taṣim and al-Wāthiq, as well as al-Mutawakkil during the first years of his reign, until c.850. Opposition to the Mu'tazilite rationalistic theology came both from the Traditionists, who rejected in principle the Mu'tazilite system and method, in fact any form of rationalistic reasoning applied to religious doctrines, and also from various theologians who objected to certain major Mu'tazilite positions, but accepted in principle the method of rationalistic reasoning, and came to be known from the beginning of the tenth century by the name of Ash'ariyya. Since the Mu'tazila is the most relevant system to the history of Jewish philosophy, the following is a survey of that system; at the end of this survey the main different positions of the Ash'ariyya are described.

❧ MU'TAZILITES ❧

Only a few of the early Mu'tazilite works have survived.[10] These were mainly short monographs (styled as epistles[11] or responsa (*rasā'il, masā'il*)), refutations, or heresiographies.[12] Much of the information concerning the positions of early Mu'tazilite thinkers comes from polemical, hostile sources (mainly Ash'arite authors[13]) or later Mu'tazilite authors who wrote comprehensive compendia of the school's system, among whom 'Abd al-Jabbār (d. 1025) figures prominently.

At a quite early stage (not later than early ninth century), with a growing tendency to define membership of the faith in dogmatic rather than practical terms, the Mu'tazila formulated their theological system in a concise list of five principles: first, unity of God (*tawḥīd*); second, divine justice (*'adl*); third, reward and punishment (*al-wa'd wa-'l-wa'īd*, lit.: promise and threat); fourth, classification of all human actions, according to ethico-religious criteria, as belief and disbelief, good and evil, praise and blame (*al-asmā' wa-'l-aḥkām*); and fifth, enjoining good and preventing evil (cf. e.g. Qur'ān 3:104).[14] These principles constitute a scheme according to which many kalām compendia, mainly Mu'tazilite ones, are structured.

The first two principles became hallmarks of the Mu'tazila, who were widely known as "the people of justice and unity" (*ahl al-'adl wa-'l-tawḥīd*). In Mu'tazili thought the principle of unity involves a very rigid concept of the incorporeality of God, who cannot be perceived by the senses, and a distinction between attributes of God's essence (knowing, living), which cannot be negated, and those of his actions (such as hearing, seeing, speaking, willing, creating), which represent the relationship between him and his creations. The fact that God's essence is referred to through multiple attributes does not indicate any multiplicity, but is rather due to the shortcoming of human language, which is the vehicle that conveys God's message to humankind. Thus, the theory of attributes is ultimately based on linguistic and exegetical considerations rather than on metaphysical ones.[15] The same very strict concept of God's incorporeality would seem in conflict with the literal meaning of many scriptural descriptions of God, ascribing to him bodily organs or postures or motions or human emotions.[16] The Mu'tazila resolved this conflict by various exegetical techniques, such as metaphorical interpretations or supplementing explicative nouns or verbs. These techniques are based on the premise that Scripture and reason cannot contradict each other, but rather complement and confirm each other. On this point the Mu'tazila were in permanent conflict with the literalists and Traditionists who considered any rejection of the literal meaning of such anthropomorphic statements as heresy.

According to the doctrine of God's incorporeality, he is invisible. On the other hand, according to the Mu'tazilite epistemology, the most immediate and certain knowledge is that perceived by the senses.[17] Consequently, in order to attain certain and proper knowledge of God, one may or rather should perceive him by the senses, but only indirectly by means of his creations. His creations constitute the empirical proofs (or rather "indicators"[18]) for his existence as the sole creator, who created the world from nothing at a certain point of time. The method by which this is established as a valid proof is termed "inference of the imperceptible/invisible by means of the perceptible/visible."[19] Accordingly, the discussion of the proofs for the createdness of the world is arranged in many kalām works (notably the compendia) at the beginning of the sections on divine unity.

The large majority of the mutakallimūn tied the proofs for the createdness of the world ex nihilo to a rather complex atomistic theory, which they may have derived from both ancient Greek and Indian philosophies.[20] According to this theory all bodies are composed of identical atoms of substance, which do not have any essential characteristics, and which have been understood by many modern researchers to have no spatial dimensions. Upon these atoms reside the atoms of the qualities or characteristics that are defined as accidents, including both physical (for example, composition and separation, motion and rest, colors) and abstract or mental properties (for example, life, knowledge, will, capacity).[21] In many kalām compendia the exposition of this theory constitutes the basis for the discussion of the createdness of the world. This theory differs from any other atomistic theory on one important point of principle: the universe is not governed by chance; instead, the existence or the extinction of every single individual atom, of substance or accident, is a creation of God, whose absolute omnipotence is thus emphatically underlined. The same applies also to any aggregation or separation of atoms by which bodies are formed or dissolved. Causality is thus denied; what appear to be laws of nature or a causal sequence are rather a "customary" recurrence of isolated, unrelated events which result from God's unlimited will and power. Some Mu'tazilites, mainly from the Baghdad school, did not accept the atomistic theory, and established a theory that recognized essential properties of species and individuals, a certain mode of causality and the laws of nature.[22]

The principle of divine justice involves the absolute self-sufficiency of God, and hence his absolute benevolence (Arabic aṣlaḥ; some Mu'tazilites had certain reservations with respect to the totality of the latter doctrine) and the freedom of choice. All humans are fully responsible for their actions, and are rewarded or punished according to their deeds. In order to enable one to practice freedom of choice God has endowed the human being with reason, thus providing adequate tools to attain accurate knowledge of God's will as to the actions commanded or prohibited by him. God also endowed humans with the ability to act. However, the Mu'tazilites were divided as to whether this ability (which in their atomistic world view they considered an accident) is a durable property, or whether God creates it (as he does all accidents) individually and momentarily for each action. They were also divided as to whether the responsibility of an agent extends to the generated effects or consequences of his action, or whether those effects are not due to the agent's action.[23]

In principle human beings can know God's will, at least the ethical norms or social laws which are to govern the life of the human individual and society, by means of reason alone. However, in reality this does not always work, and even when it does, one is not capable of knowing unaided the details of many social laws, certainly not the ritual ones. Those are revealed by God to the prophets, who then convey them to humans. The purpose of revelation is thus to inform humans of positive legislation; to inform those whose minds are too weak to discover by themselves even the basic ethical laws; to justify (or to increase) the reward given for performing the laws, which would not have been deserved if performed solely on the basis of one's own cognition. Revelation is an evident manifestation of God's justice, through which he carries out, as it were, his obligation to inform humans, in advance and in clear comprehensible terms, of their duties and of the reward or punishment to which they are eligible or liable respectively if they carry out those duties or fail to do so.[24] Praise and blame, or reward and punishment, are the only effective means to make one perform God's commands, but they are not known in their details by reason. Revelation may also constitute divine grace, assistance and guidance (lutf), by making the laws known in a shorter and quicker way, which also assures the correctness of laws.

The truthfulness of the divine message as conveyed by the prophets, and which is embodied in Scripture, is proven by miracles. Miracles are a special creation by God in breach of the customary or conventional recurrence of events[25] at the particular time and place where revelation actually takes place.[26] According to the Mu'tazila, God cannot be described as speaking, since this is an action of human beings performed with bodily speech organs;[27] revelation then is a sequence of utterances created by God specifically in the given circumstances.

The prophet has no part in the formulation of the prophetic message; he is merely a vehicle for the transmission of the text as it is given to him. Similarly the prophet is not endowed with any extraordinary powers that would enable him to perform miracles that are beyond the capability of any normal human being. Here too he is merely a vehicle through which God carries out miracles. The moral order of the prophet's person should be high, and he is impeccable. Had he been a potential sinner, he would not have been reliable in the faithful transmission of the message. The actual prophet that the Muslim mutakallimūn had in mind in this context was Muḥammad alone, the "Seal of the Prophets," who brought the message that superseded or abrogated any previous one.

In the context of their discussion of the laws, the Mu'tazila developed the important distinction between immediately reasonable (or rational) knowledge and reasonable (or rational) laws (sharā'i' 'aqliyya, 'aqliyyāt) on the one hand and revealed knowledge and laws (sharā'i' sam'iyya, sam'iyyāt) on the other. The former is immediate in the sense that God has "planted" (in the Mu'tazilite terminology) such rational knowledge in the human mind, so that once it is uncovered it is attained without any effort of learning and does not have to be rationally demonstrated; it is self-evident. The name of the latter class indicates that this revealed knowledge (or law) is acquired through hearing or audition, which is the customary way by which revelation is received by its addressees. This distinction has both ethical and epistemological implications. It involves an essential Mu'tazilite doctrine, namely, that of the immediate knowledge of ethical principles,[28] that is, the self-evident distinction between true and false, between good and evil, which are objective and absolute concepts binding equally on God and humanity. On the epistemological level this belongs to a more elaborate structure. The Mu'tazila discussed it in two contexts.

First, in the context of divine justice, it is God's duty to furnish the tools (that is, reason) to attain knowledge of the laws and to convey that knowledge; and correlatively, it is human duty to use reason for that purpose. Second, from their early days the Mu'tazila claimed to be able to defend and interpret their religion by means of human reason, and even to make revelation subject to the critique of reason. For both aims knowledge ('ilm) and rationalistic speculation (naẓar,[29] or inquiry/search, baḥth) have become in Mu'tazilite ideology religious duties, in fact the first duty imposed on the true believers.[30] Full observance of this duty is obligatory only on those who are capable of it, the "chosen" learned ones (khāṣṣa), while the masses ('āmma) can do with the knowledge of generalities.[31] Notwithstanding, unlike the falāsifa, most early mutakallimūn seem to have believed that initially all human individuals of sound mind and body were equally capable of comprehending all true knowledge.

Consequently the processes through which knowledge is attained and the correct methods of reasoning had to be defined. Chapters on these subjects are often found in Mu'tazilite works, both in introductory sections and in sections dealing with various aspects of divine justice. Classification of knowledge into immediate (both perceptible and rational) on the one hand, and acquired, or inferred, on the other, and the means of verification or ascertaining of true knowledge, are major themes in such chapters. Immediate knowledge is termed in Arabic *ḍarūrī*, which may be translated literally as "necessary." However, it is not necessary in the Aristotelian sense, as a consequence of logical demonstration, but in the sense that it is self-evident and cannot be refuted. When applied to perceptible objects, their perception by a healthy human being, and their very physical existence, must lead to the most certain knowledge. When applied to theoretical knowledge, mostly mathematical axioms or generally accepted ethical principles are meant. These are planted in the human mind from birth. The criterion by which the veracity of such knowledge is tested is the mental disposition described as "peace of mind" (*sukūn al-nafs*).[32]

The typical logical procedure in kalām[33] commences with a disjunctive syllogism (*qisma, taqsīm*). However, the elimination of all invalid possible propositions (one or several, depending on the kind of syllogism applied), with only one proposition established as valid, is not the result of a formal demonstration (along Aristotelian lines), but rather the result of a very basic (or primitive) inference (*istidlāl*) from some "immediate" (concrete or abstract) data that serve as "indicator" (*dalīl*).[34] The validity of a proposition that conveys immediate data to serve as "indicator" is established by a cause (*'illa*), that is, a characterstic property shared by the indicator and the object "indicated at". If the cause is shown to be relevant to the case under discussion, the proof is valid.[35] This procedure is used both to establish positive doctrines and to refute an adversary's doctrine or view.[36] The dominant style of most kalām works during the first centuries is the conventional dialogue between the author (or his side, "we") and a supposedly imagined interlocutor or adversary.[37] The author's aim is either to convince the latter or to refute him and invalidate his doctrines.

On the level of general principles kalām can accommodate any faith that is based on the belief in one (according to the Mu'tazila, absolutely just) creator who reveals his will to humanity through prophets, and notwithstanding the central place that reason occupies in the Mu'tazilite system, it should be emphasized that this system is to a large extent scripto-centric with exclusive reference to the Qur'ān.[38] Although most of the Mu'tazila thought that Scripture can be truly verified and correctly interpreted only by reason, the validity of the authority and veracity of Scripture seems to be a dogma, even though the Mu'tazilite theologians manage to present it as being as valid as immediate knowledge perceived by the senses, since the miracles which testify to its veracity are perceived by the senses. The Mu'tazila accepted also the authority of tradition as a source of religious legislation and guidance, provided that it complied with certain, rather rigorous, conditions concerning its transmission and its rational admissibility.

⚛ ASH'ARITES ⚛

The Ash'ariyya are named after Abu'l-Ḥasan al-Ash'arī (d. 935), a disciple of the Mu'tazilite master Abu 'Alī al-Jubbā'ī. Ash'ari abandoned the Mu'tazilite school in favor of what may be described in very general terms as more orthodox positions. His views attracted circles of theologians who already held similar views, and developed over a few centuries to become the most important Islamic rationalist school of theology, achieving an official or semi-official status in various Islamic states in the Middle Ages.[39] Ash'arī's own views were closer to those of the Traditionists than those of many later Ash'arites, and seem less sophisticated. The following survey of the main differences with the Mu'tazila relates mainly to the later Ash'arites.

Ash'arite kalām gradually gained acceptance and following in the Islamic East from the end of the tenth century onwards, especially among members of the Ḥanafi school of Islamic law. With the decline of the Mu'tazila, and as a result of the activity of al-Ghazālī (d. 1111), it came to enjoy the status of a semi-official theology in most Islamic countries of the East. Nevertheless, ardent followers of the exclusive authority of the Qur'ān and Tradition continued to attack the Ash'ariyya and polemicize against it. In the Islamic West kalām was rejected for a long time by the dominant Mālikī scholars, and only under the regime of the Muwaḥḥidūn (Almohads, mid-twelfth century) was it officially recognized (and vigorously disputed by ibn Rushd).[40]

For the Ash'arites, although it is important to apply reason in studying questions of faith, none the less revelation, prophetic tradition, and general consensus are superior to reason. Therefore there is no a priori obligation to know the truth of revelation by means of reason. Such an obligation can be valid only on the basis of an explicit injunction in revelation.[41] If the plain meaning of scriptural language seems incompatible with the common usage as judged by human reason, then the qualifications of human reason have to be abandoned and the language of Scripture and the canonical tradition have to be accepted in the "plain" meaning without qualification (bi-lā kayf, lit. "without [asking] how"). Ash'arite thinkers from the late eleventh century onwards tended to become increasingly associated with the tradition of falsafa on the conceptual level. Nevertheless, they continued to adhere strictly to the basic tenets of the school and tended to use dialectic in a very formal way for the purpose of defense and the demonstrative interpretation of the dogmas.

With respect to divine attributes, the Ash'arites held that God has essential attributes,[42] which are neither identical with himself nor other than him, but are nevertheless distinct from him in a way which cannot be adequately captured by human language or reason (*bi-lā kayf*). Among these attributes is also the capacity for speech.[43] His creations are the attributes of his action.[44] On the question of God's corporeality and visibility, with respect to anthropomorphisms in Qur'ān and Tradition (Ḥadīth), certainly al-Ash'arī but also many of his followers tended to explain those away by avoiding qualification (*bi-lā kayf*) and by accepting the possibility of seeing God at the last judgment, or the hereafter.

The Ash'arites held that God is not bound by any objective ethical values, since the latter do not exist. Good and evil correspond to God's commands and prohibitions. God is the sole creator of any substance (atoms composing a body) or accident (event, action, property). Ash'arite atomism is total and pervasive, thus preserving the doctrine of God's absolute omnipotence. God creates within an agent the ability to perform an action. This ability is created in that part of the agent's body by which, or in which, the action takes place simultaneously with the performance. This formulation appears to abet determinism. In order to avoid this, the Ash'ariyya, following Ash'arī and his predecessors, argued that, as a result of God's creating the capacity for action in an agent, combined with the fact that God makes the action take place in a certain part of the agent's body, these two constitute *kasb* (literally doing, performing, or acquiring). As a result, the agent is responsible for the action, hence subject to reward and punishment. It goes without saying that the Ash'ariyya, being rigid atomists, did not ascribe any responsibility to an agent for the generated effects of personal actions; those are created by God individually and independently of any previous action that had been completed.

❧ JEWISH KALĀM – GENERAL SURVEY ❧

The earliest known Jewish philosopher in the Middle Ages, Dāwūd b. Marwān al-Muqammiṣ (early ninth century), was a mutakallim. It goes without saying that the adoption or absorption of any system of religious philosophy in the lands of Islam[45] was the result of the adoption of the Arabic language and Arab civilization, which was becoming the common denominator of all inhabitants of those areas, regardless of their religious affiliation. Naturally, the first Jewish followers of kalām came from such segments of the Jewish population that already in the early ninth century had been integrated into the general culture. It should be noted, however, that Jewish kalām was connected from its very beginning with biblical exegesis, and for some chapters in the history of Jewish kalām, notably Karaite kalām of the tenth century, the main available source material is exegetical works. Two of the most prominent representatives of this genre are al-Qirqisānī (active in Iraq in the 930s)[46] and Yefet b. 'Eli (in Jerusalem, second half of the tenth century). In other cases the format of responsa served for monographic discussions of theological questions, by Rabbanites and Karaites alike. Beginning in the early tenth century kalām attracted several leading figures in the Jewish communities in the eastern parts of Islam. The most prominent of them in the Rabbanite camp was Saadia Gaon (d. 942). It should be emphasized that it was the Mu'tazilite brand of kalām that attracted Jewish thinkers; it may be said with all probability that there is no positive evidence of Jewish Ash'arites.[47] However kalām did not dominate the scene exclusively. On the one hand there were those who, like their counterparts among the Muslims, opposed the study of, or the engagement in, anything other than the canonized texts – the Bible only for Karaites and the talmudic tradition (and for some perhaps also certain mystical texts) for Rabbanites. They are said to have feared that such occupations would lead to heresy.[48] On the other hand there is enough evidence from the tenth century about Jews of various social origins who were interested in a Neoplatonized Aristotelian philosophy, both in the East[49] and in the West.[50]

From the end of the tenth century through the eleventh, there developed in the East a school of Jewish kalām that followed very closely, almost to the point of imitation, the Baṣran school of the Mu'tazila. Among the Rabbanites the prominent representative of this tendency is Samuel b. Chofni, the head of the Yeshiva of Sura, and among the Karaites one finds such figures as Yūsuf al-Baṣīr and Yeshu'a b. Judah.

In the Islamic West, Jewish kalām is found from the early eleventh century in partial acceptance of certain doctrines of Jewish kalām of the Geonim in the East or Eastern Karaites, or in reaction to kalām on the part of conservative leaders, such as R. Nissim of Qayrawan (mid-eleventh century), or later philosophers (most notably Maimonides).

❧ BEGINNINGS OF JEWISH KALĀM ❧

The earliest Jewish mutakallim is Dāwūd b. Marwān al-Muqammiṣ (early ninth century).[51] Al-Muqammiṣ, a Jewish convert to Christianity who, after receiving good philosophical training, reverted to Judaism, probably did not belong to the Jewish establishment or leadership. Yet his works are quoted by various later authors, such as Qirqisānī,

Bachya, and Judah b. Barzilai. His system is typical of early Jewish kalām, including Saadia, insofar as he is not committed to a certain school of kalām; inspired by the tradition of his Christian teachers[52] he shows familiarity with basic concepts of the Aristotelian system (such as the theory of causation and the ten categories), which he freely integrates into his thought. Yet his style, techniques of argumentation, logical methodology, and philosophical terminology make him a mutakallim. The structure of his work is the precursor of the scheme that has become most typical for kalām works and is thus one of the earliest documents of *Arabic* kalām, in which the links of kalām to Christian sources are still clearly discernible.

The basic concepts of al-Muqammiṣ' cosmology are substance and accident, not matter and form. He employs these concepts to prove that the world is not eternal, and is thus the earliest Jewish author to use what was to become the "standard proof of kalām," but not in an atomistic context. From the createdness of the world the existence of a unique creator is inferred, the latter attribute of unity indicating the essence of God. Al-Muqammiṣ discusses both God's unity and the divine attributes in highly polemical terms, aimed mainly against Christianity. Consequently he seems to profess a negative view on the divine attributes;[53] however, by referring to a number of attributes as being "due to [or: by means/because of] his essence," al-Muqammiṣ at least alludes to the distinction between essential attributes and those of action.[54] On the questions related to divine justice al-Muqammiṣ' views are in agreement with current Muʿtazilite views about good and evil as absolute concepts binding on God and humanity, God's absolute benevolence, freedom of choice and action, and the central role of prophecy in conveying God's message and law, in its particular Jewish sense of the Hebrew Scripture.[55] In this context al-Muqammiṣ is the earliest Jewish or other mutakallim to polemicize against the rejection of prophecy (its epistemological validity and mainly its legislative authority) by the Barāhima (Indian Brahmans or Buddhists).

Another representative of early Jewish kalām is an exposition of theological principles found in a Hebrew epistle (or sermon) ascribed to Daniel al-Qūmisī (around 900).[56] The exposition has a distinct Muʿtazili tendency and the Hebrew phraseology clearly reflects the Arabic terminology. If the ascription is correct,[57] it has a number of important implications. First, this is the earliest kalām exposition in Hebrew. Second, one should assume several decades for the process of absorbing Muʿtazilite theology into Karaite thought before presenting it as genuinely Jewish in contradistinction to other, "foreign," ideologies.[58] The beginning of such a process would thus coincide with the period of al-Muqammiṣ' activity. Third, this is the earliest extant attempt in Judaism to formulate a set of normative doctrines, or dogmas, or articles of faith.[59] Very typically each statement is supported by one scriptural proof-text at least. The exposition revolves around the two main traditional Muʿtazili foci, divine unity and justice, and a number of particular Jewish themes, such as the exclusiveness of the Mosaic law. The following are the main points.[60]

First, there is a religious duty to use reason. God created the world from nothing. This is proved by the fact that all things are limited (in size and space) and are liable to the occurrence of accidents. Human reason (self-cognition) indicates[61] that there is the One who creates humans and who will call them to account.[62] God is one alone, the sole creator. Second, human beings are different from all other creations of God in possessing reason, choice, and speech. By themselves these indicate that God will pass judgment on humankind. There are in this world exemplary punishments which indicate that there is an ultimate comprehensive retribution in the hereafter. Ultimate reward and punishment in the hereafter will be applied to both body and soul. There will be bodily resurrection. Third, God gave his law to the nation of Israel; Moses wrote it at God's behest and command, and only the written law is binding. Miracles are created directly by God, not by angels or human beings.

These principles are presented as particularly Karaite, as opposed to the Rabbanite or other non-Karaite, principles. Karaite authors generally tend to extend their differences with the Rabbanites from legal questions to include also theological ones. A typical accusation made by Karaites in this context is that the Rabbanites are anthropomorphists. These accusations may have been true with respect to popular beliefs in all camps, and possibly to some authorities, but there is very little evidence of an official Rabbanite position of the kind claimed by the Karaites.

❧ TENTH CENTURY – SAADIA AND ❧ KARAITE CONTEMPORARIES

Saadia ben Joseph al-Fayyūmī (882–942), the most prominent figure in Jewish public life and in the rabbinic establishment in his time, a most creative figure in Jewish intellectual activity, artistic as well as scholarly, and an outstanding systematizer of knowledge, was also the thinker and author who made it his task to rephrase and reconstruct, in language (Arabic) and contents, the rabbinic interpretation of the Hebrew Scripture according to those achievements of scientific and rationalist thinking of his day which he considered both most appropriate and most advanced. His activity should nevertheless be seen against the background of increasing numbers of Jewish intellectuals being attracted to the general culture to the degree of challenging the authority of the faith of their ancestors and even turning against it. In the field of religious thought this resulted in works written in two genres: first, systematic works, notably the *Commentary on the Book of Creation (Sefer Yetzirah)* and the definitive *summa*, the *Book of Beliefs and Convictions (al-Amānāt wa-'l-I'tiqādāt)*; second, exegetical works, including monographic introductions to books of the Bible. All these are interwoven with theological expositions related to his systematic works. The latter contain many important discussions on exegetical matters.[63] The connection between theology and exegesis played an important role in Jewish kalām in general, not only by Saadia. He established the rationalist trend in the interpretation of Scripture. Although Saadia was not the first medieval Jewish philosopher, in light of his public standing, the scope of his philosophical oeuvre, and the influence it had on subsequent generations, he can be considered the founding father of medieval Jewish philosophy.

The structure of Saadia's main work, the *Book of Beliefs and Convictions*,[64] is typical of kalām compendia. The main sections are, first, vindication of rationalist theology and theory of epistemology (introduction); second, creation and creator; God's unity and attributes (discourses 1–2); third, divine justice, free will; good and evil actions; reward and punishment (4–5, 9). Between the second and third sections there is a discussion of the law and prophecy, and into the third section are interwoven, with respect to the general theme of retribution, discussions of Israel's redemption (8) and resurrection from a particularistic Jewish angle (7). The latter is introduced by a theoretical discourse (6) on the soul. The whole structure is concluded by a discourse (10) on practical ethics, commending the mean in all areas of human activity. It may be that this discourse represents in Saadia's system the fifth principle of the Mu'tazila (enjoining good and preventing evil).

An important parallel to this work is a list of ten articles of faith[65] found in Saadia's commentary on 2 Samuel 22:2–3, which is part of his *Commentary on the Ten Songs*.[66] This is a more advanced attempt than al-Qūmisī's to lay down a set of normative beliefs for those who are not capable of reaching the level of rationalist religious convictions. This is the "dogmatic" aspect of Saadia's chief theological work. Each article in the list is accompanied by proof-texts that add the particular Jewish dimension even to the most general principles. The articles are: (1) God is eternal; (2) he comprehends all things; they all exist in/by him; (3) he creates everything and brings it forth; (4) he is the believer's God who has imposed a religion or law on him; the believer has to act according to God's rational or revealed commandments and refrain from his rational or revealed prohibitions; (5) reliance on God and contentment with his decrees; (6) the duty to act in accordance with

God's law transmitted by means of his messengers; (7) God will redeem his nation in the messianic age; (8) he will defend them against the wars of Gog and other nations; (9) eternal reward for the righteous in the world to come; (10) he has a harsh punishment for those who do not believe in him and disobey him.[67]

Saadia's logical methodology, philosophical terminology, and conceptual vocabulary are in the main those typical for kalām. It is true that Saadia is in some respects eclectic, that he is well aware of various philosophical theories which are rarely mentioned in kalām works,[68] and that he does not share with most mutakallimūn their atomistic theories.[69] But the decision on the question whether Saadia should be considered a mutakallim or not does not depend on his position on particular points but rather on his methodological and logical principles and the general outline of his world view, and those point very clearly in the direction of kalām. It may be added that in some instances Muʿtazilite terminology penetrated Saadia's thought even in minute, yet typical and important, details. Thus Saadia uses the Muʿtazilite terminology of the "intermediate status" in his classification of the sinners.[70]

Generally the epistemology and logic adopted by Saadia is the one found in the early Muʿtazila.[71] In Jewish kalām from Saadia onwards sense perception is the first and foremost source of any knowledge by human beings. In this respect Jewish kalām corresponds to an early stage in the development of Muslim kalām, unlike later Muslim kalām as presented by Maimonides.[72] Together with immediate rational knowledge it forms the basis for the next level of knowledge, for which Saadia, like a typical mutakallim, uses inference by analogy.[73] This is in fact what he calls "inferential knowledge;" for example, one has to accept the existence of the soul as a concrete being because it is possible to see its manifest activity, movement at will, which one cannot deny.[74] The "indicator" is of course a basic concept in this system. Another important element in this system which is also shared by Rabbanites and Karaites is the "authentic transmission" (or, veridically transmitted knowledge). It includes of course any knowledge gained indirectly, through a process of transmission, instruction, etc. For the Rabbanites it covers the transmission of the scriptural text, but mainly rabbinic tradition, while for the Karaites it applies exclusively to the former.[75] Qirqisānī's discussions of logic are in the main an exposition of Karaite rationalist hermeneutics of the legal portions of the Bible (still, a serious endeavor to form a systematic epistemological theory)[76] and a manual for dialectic.[77]

Saadia introduced into Jewish religious thought the important distinction, which occupied a central place in the Muʿtazilite thinking, between immediately reasonable (or rational) knowledge and reasonable (or rational) laws[78] (*sharā'i' 'aqliyya, 'aqliyyāt*) on the one hand, and revealed knowledge and laws (*sharā'i' sam'iyya, sam'iyyāt*) on the other,[79] with all its epistemological and ethical implications, with respect to human beings and also to God who is equally bound by the absolute concepts of good and evil.

Saadia formulated in much clearer terms than his predecessors the religious obligation of rational speculation on religious doctrines. This position was shared by all Jewish mutakallimūn, in fact all medieval Jewish philosophers.[80] The knowledge attained as a result of such speculation is the actualization[81] of the potential knowledge received from the prophets. However, for those who are not able to engage in theoretical contemplation, passive acceptance of the prophets' message may suffice. This position may be parallel to the Mu'tazilite distinction between the obligation of detailed knowledge of religious doctrines and their theoretical basis, which is binding on the "chosen" (*khāṣṣa*), and the knowledge of generalities, formulated as propositions (*jumal*), which is sufficient for the masses (*'āmma*). In Saadia's terminology such propositions are the "beliefs" (*amānāt*; in the sing. *amāna*).[82] In fact they constitute dogmas or confessions. After the *amāna* undergoes a speculative process and is rationally established in the believer's mind, it assumes the status of conviction (*i'tiqād*).[83]

With respect to his physical views Saadia and his contemporaries continued and established the line of al-Muqammiṣ regarding the dichotomy of substance and accidents, rejecting Aristotle's dichotomy of matter and form. This is an important factor in classifying Saadia as a follower of kalām.[84] At the same time he rejected the kalām atomistic theory. As is known so far[85] all Jewish philosophers, except the Karaites, rejected atomism. Atomism was discussed mainly in the context of creation, but had implications also in other contexts. Saadia seems to have believed that things have a specific or particular nature, which is normally permanent, and may change only as a result of miraculous divine intervention.[86]

On the question of creation, the Jewish mutakallimūn of the tenth century, on Saadia's authority, established the doctrine of creation ex nihilo as the exclusive doctrine of authentic Judiasm.[87] By the tenth century this doctrine not only had long been established as an exclusive one in Islamic kalām, but it also carried with it a certain set of proofs derived from those of John Philoponus (sixth century). It is important to note that the proofs found in Jewish kalām, notably in Saadia, are among the earliest attestations in Arabic, and made a deep impact on medieval Jewish thinkers, even those who are not classified as followers of kalām.

Saadia offers four proofs for the creation of the world. First, "from finitude": the bodies of heaven and earth are limited, therefore their power is limited; and since the power that maintains them ceases, they necessarily have a beginning and an end.[88] Second, "from composition": the fact that all bodies are composed of parts and segments shows signs of generation and art of an artisan.[89] The latter part of the proof refers not only to the question of creation but also to the existence of a creator. Third, "from accidents": bodies cannot be void of accidents (i.e. properties, characteristics, events), which are evidently changing continuously, therefore limited in time, and therefore generated. What cannot be void of the generated is itself generated. This is the "standard proof of kalām," and is reported to have been known in kalām from the time of the Mu'tazilite Abu'l-Hudhayl (early ninth century).[90] Fourth, "from time": if the world had been eternal, it would have taken an infinite number of generations (spans of time) in the past to reach the present; since this is impossible, the world must have a beginning.[91]

All four proofs are mentioned or alluded to in Qirqisānī's commentaries, and from Yefet b. 'Eli's commentaries it is clear that he is well aware of the first three. Both emphasize that the proofs for creation are actually established in all existent beings.[92] It seems that, unlike Saadia, both authors were inclined to accept some form of atomism, which also influenced their interpretation of miracles.[93] In addition to these proofs, the proof from the design is often mentioned in their works, including the one from the self-cognition of human beings that is related to Job 19:26 and the notion of microcosm.[94]

All Jewish mutakallimūn accepted the distinction between attributes of the essence of God and attributes of his actions, which was typical of most mutakallimūn, especially the Basran school. From the beginning, since al-Muqammis, the foundation point was that the multiplicity of attributes (especially of the essential ones) has no ontological status. As in Mu'tazilite theory since the end of the ninth century, the question thus turns into a linguistic-exegetical one rather than an ontological one, namely, that the (apparent) multiplicity of God's nature is due to the shortcomings of human language. In this context Saadia discusses the issue on two levels: with respect to its logical principles, for which he uses Aristotle's categorial theory, and with respect to biblical anthropomorphisms, which have to be interpreted appropriately.[95] It is evident that the Jewish mutakallimūn were taking sides in a controversy that was not necessarily limited to the Jewish arena. Like al-Muqammis before him, Saadia very clearly states that his position on the matter is aimed against the Christians: it is inadmissible that God should contain, include, or possess any property (concrete or abstract) or bodily organ.[96] Yet the way in which Jewish mutakallimūn formulate their position is very close to the one used by their Mu'tazilite counterparts for the same purpose. The formulation of the Muslim Mu'tazilites was aimed mainly at the Ash'ariyya, that is, at the Ash'arite view that the attributes have an independent ontological status.[97] If one does not accept that the Jewish mutakallimūn take sides in an internal Muslim controversy, then one may have to assume that there were Jewish Ash'ariyya, or that the Jewish mutakallimūn saw in rabbinic views of God a resemblance of Ash'ariyya, in addition to their polemic against Christianity.

Divine justice is not restricted to the doctrine of free will, but features also in Saadia's position on the commandments, and the linkage between ritual (or works) and reward.[98] However, the matter has also an ethical aspect: one is not allowed to rely absolutely (*tawakkul*) on God's providence, but has to fend for one's sustenance and has to do works to deserve reward, even though God could have given the bliss of Paradise without imposing the performance of ritual duties, in fact without being brought into existence in this world.[99]

❧ GEONIM AND KARAITES FROM THE ❧ END OF THE TENTH CENTURY ONWARDS

The impact of Saadia's work was immediate, and is discernible in works of Geonim that were composed already in his lifetime, such as Aaron b. Sarjado.[100] The most prominent follower of kalām among the Geonim after Saadia was Samuel b. Chofni (d. 1013). He expounded his doctrinal views in a number of works, among them a theological compendium, entitled *Kitāb al-Hidāya* (*The Book of Guidance*),[101] and biblical commentaries. These have mostly been preserved in a fragmentary form.[102] Unlike Saadia, Samuel b. Chofni followed closely a specific kalām school, namely, the Baṣran school as it developed during the second half of the tenth century. The terminology he uses, the questions discussed, the positions he takes, are all typical of that school.[103] Samuel b. Chofni, as well as his Karaite younger contemporaries, shared with the Mu'tazila another important characteristic, namely, the close relationship, to the point of overlap, between doctrines of the faith and principles of legal philosophy.[104] The concept of *taklīf* (literally, commanding, assignment, imposition), which focuses the relationship between God and humanity on the roles of lawgiver and obedient performer of the law, and had become pivotal in the Mu'tazilite theories of late tenth century, became central also in Samuel b. Chofni's theory.[105]

Other issues discussed by Samuel b. Chofni, similarly typical of the Baṣran Mu'tazilite school are: the obligation to know God, which can be fulfilled only through rational inference;[106] the brief exposition of the principal Mu'tazilite version of the "standard proof for creation" (the terminology used there[107] apparently makes sense only in an atomistic context);[108] the divine attributes (on which Samuel b. Chofni is said to have written a separate treatise);[109] the impeccability of the prophets;[110] the revealed commandments as divine benevolent assistance.[111] Some questions are discussed in a polemical context which is aimed against the Muslims in a very explicit manner, such as the Muslim claim of the abrogation of the Mosaic law or the question of the universality and particularity of the revealed laws.[112] In such contexts Samuel b. Chofni not only uses the typical Mu'tazilite nomenclature, but even mentions names of Muslim Mu'tazilites in a manner that indicates that his knowledge of them was based on a reading of their writings and not merely on oral information. Another Gaon who showed interest and acquaintance with kalām was Samuel b. Chofni's son-in-law, Hai Gaon (d. 1038). He left his indelible imprint on the halakhic oeuvre of the Geonim in the form of important compendia and numerous responsa. In some responsa[113] he dealt also with theological problems in typical kalām style, terminology, and argumentation. A famous and representative example is his responsum on the predetermined span of life (ajal), a classical topic in Islamic kalām, which is discussed in connection with the problem of whether God's foreknowledge is mere knowledge or whether it determines the fate of the individual, and conversely whether one's destiny can be changed through one's behavior. The Ash'ariyya, who believed in some form of predestination, did not believe that man could change anything about it. Hai Gaon, who does not decide the matter in clear terms but shows a distinct inclination to the Mu'tazila, argues that there probably is a connection between human behavior and human destiny, and yet one is unable to know it. God alone knows in advance future happenings, and the relationship between one's action and fate. In his responsum Hai mentions explicitly the position of the Muslim mutakallimūn on the question, which testifies to his interest in, and his access to, Islamic kalām sources.[114] It seems that kalām continued to have a following among the rabbinic leadership in the East, mainly in Babylonia (Iraq).

Yūsuf al-Baṣīr was a younger Karaite contemporary of Samuel b. Chofni. The latter may have been a source of inspiration for al-Baṣīr in his endeavor to create a Jewish version of the Baṣran brand of the Mu'tazila. The importance of al-Baṣīr for the history of Jewish kalām is that his teachings, with the additions and refinements of Yeshu'a b. Judah, became the recognized theology of Karaism for centuries to come. Many of al-Baṣīr's works (all in Judeo-Arabic[115]) have survived, some in complete form, others in fragments. He wrote two theological compendia, several theological and halakhic monographs and numerous epistles and responsa.[116] Many of his and Yeshu'a's works were translated into Hebrew by Byzantine Karaites, and copies of the Arabic original texts of these works reached as far as Spain. Al-Baṣīr's system follows closely, both in style and content, the Baṣran school. He explicitly states his reliance on 'Abd al-Jabbār. The arrangement of his compendia follows exactly his Islamic models. His metaphysics are centered on the notion of "being" as the only necessary accident of all existing beings. He follows (as does his pupil Yeshu'a) the atomistic views of the Baṣrans, which is the basis for their version of the "standard proof for creation".[117] The same applies to his theory of God's unity, divine attributes and actions, the self-sufficiency of God, and divine justice. The Jewish element in many chapters of the theological works is minimal. Al-Baṣīr and Yeshu'a polemicize at length against the Muslims, mainly on the question of the abrogation of the Mosaic law. However, in many instances they take sides in disputes that are of interest chiefly for Muslim theologians, such as the chapters in al-Muḥtawī against the Bakriyya and 'Abbād,[118] or the chapter on human actions which has long discussions of positions that are not attested in Jewish sources.[119] Another typical example is his polemic against the belief in transmigration of souls, in which he argues along lines known from Muslim sources,[120] in complete disregard of earlier Rabbanite and Karaite discussions.[121] Through the Hebrew translations of his works, as well as those of his pupil Yeshu'a, al-Baṣīr's system had a determining influence on the development of Karaite thought in those centers where Hebrew became the main means of communication. It is found in works which were quite popular, such as Judah Hadassi's *Eshkol ha-Kofer* (1148–9),[122] and in works that were accepted as definitive, notably Aaron b. Elijah's (d. 1369) theological summa entitled *Etz Chayyim*.[123]

⚬ JEWISH KALĀM IN THE ISLAMIC WEST ⚬

Jews of the western Islamic countries apparently first learned of kalām theories from Jewish sources. Saadia's theological and exegetical works reached North Africa and Spain quite soon after their completion. So, for example, Dunash b. Tamim (Qayrawan, d. after 955/6) composed his commentary[124] on *Sefer Yetzirah* as a response to Saadia's shortly after the latter was written; Spanish exegetes of the middle of the eleventh century were familiar with works by Saadia and Samuel b. Chofni; for Bachya b. Paquda, the extant works on theology were those by al-Muqammiṣ, Saadia, and Samuel b. Chofni.[125] At that time Karaite Bible commentaries and theological works were probably brought to Spain by ibn al-Taras and others, as is reported by Abraham ibn Daud (middle of twelfth century) and borne out by numerous quotations from Karaite sources by twelfth-century Spanish authors.[126] It would seem that by that time kalām (which was just being welcomed by the regime of the Muwaḥḥidūn) was identified by some Spanish Jewish thinkers with Karaism. Thus Joseph ibn Tzaddik knows the kalām mainly from Karaite sources, as is indicated by the fact that he mentions al-Baṣīr's compendium *al-Manṣūrī* three times as a source for the views of the mutakallimūn: twice in the course of his discussion of the divine attributes and in the third a whole chapter is quoted from al-Baṣīr on the possibility of compensation to children and animals for their sufferings.[127] Also Judah Halevi, when he introduces the system of kalām (*Kuzari* 5:15), seems to ascribe it exclusively to the Karaites. These facts may be at the background of Maimonides' attitude towards kalām.[128]

These observations notwithstanding, important elements of the old kalām theories from Geonic works are present in Jewish philosophical works from Spain, none of which are classified as kalām.[129] Bachya recognizes the Saadianic distinction between rational and revealed laws.[130] The religious duty to know and to work religious doctrines through a speculative process in order to turn them into convictions is discussed at length by Bachya more than once,[131] and he is followed in this by ibn Tzaddik.[132] Bachya adopts the second and the fourth of Saadia's proofs for the creation of the world.[133] Ibn Tzaddik also adopts the "standard kalām proof" for the creation of the world, namely, "from accidents."[134]

Judah Halevi has a somewhat ambivalent attitude towards kalām. On the one hand, he gives the impression that kalām can be identified with Karaism; this in itself may reflect a deliberate attempt to stigmatize kalām, since Halevi could have easily known, and probably did, that kalām had been followed also by prominent Geonim. On the other hand, he has the Khazar king ask the Jewish sage for the doctrines of kalām. The rabbi responds by stating that although kalām is inferior to simple belief based on immediate and personal experience, it still can sometimes (but not necessarily!) help in establishing religious truths in the souls of its disciples, and it may serve as an effective means in the defense of the faith against adversaries and skeptics.[135] Saadia's relationship between simple belief and the rational-dialectic foundations of faith is thus squarely turned upside down. According to Halevi, kalām may be preferable to falsafa, which occupies the lowest degree in Halevi's epistemological hierarchy. Interestingly, Halevi used for the exposition of kalām doctrines (*Kuzari* 5:18) a ready-made epitome from al-Ghazālī.[136]

A further turn in the attitude toward kalām was brought about by Maimonides, who undertook a sweeping criticism of a number of the main doctrines of kalām as philosophically feeble and inadequate.[137] It may well be that Maimonides took up a line that had been started before him in Spain by ibn Tzaddik. At the same time, it may also be that Maimonides' criticism in the *Guide*, which was written in the East, reflects the different situation there, where kalām was still a much more established and accepted option as a religious philosophy than in Spain. And yet, it was in Spain that kalām entered a new phase in its history in Jewish philosophy, owing to the Hebrew translations not only of the Jewish mutakallimūn and other thinkers and philosophers, but also of Muslim falāsifa and mutakallimūn, notably al-Ghazālī.

✵ NOTES ✵

1 "Religious philosophy" is used here in a broad sense of the term "philosophy," and mainly for the sake of brevity. Other terms might be equally justified, such as "theology," "philosophical/rationalistic theology," "apologetics," but these seem to be less general; and cf. R. M. Frank 1992. On the meaning of theology (and kalām in particular) in Islam and Judiasm as compared to Christianity, see Vajda 1973. The following are encyclopedic summations (with extensive bibliographical lists) of kalām in general and the Mu'tazila in particular: Anawati 1987; van Ess 1987; Gimaret 1993. For surveys on the Ash'ariyya, see below, note 39.

2 On the history of the meaning of the term and its synonyms, see Frank 1992. Frank discusses mainly Ash'arite kalām. On the possibility that the term in an earlier stage is related to Greek *dialexis*, see van Ess 1970, p. 24.

3 In this sense these terms will be used henceforth.

4 In the first half of the ninth century under the auspices of the 'Abbāsid government.

5 See Cook 1980.

6 A philosopher like John Philoponus could be sharply opposed to certain views of Aristotle and at the same time, or perhaps because of that, write commentaries on Aristotle's works.

7 See especially with respect to logic, but also to other areas, van Ess 1970.

8 To be sure, later mutakallimūn, starting with al-Ghazālī (d. 1111), were less reserved in naming Aristotle and other Greek philosophers or their Muslim followers, whether to reject or to adopt their views (the earlier Jāḥiẓ is the odd exception in the ninth century). They were also more aware of the concepts and systems of the falāsifa; see Frank 1992, and, with respect to logic, van Ess 1970, pp. 47–9.

9 They were not the earliest, though. On the early stages of the Mu'tazila, see van Ess 1991–3, 2: 233–342 (pp. 335–42 on their name).

10 See for instance Gimaret 1976, pp. 277–9.

11 A common format in Islam for theological or philosophical essays or monographs; see *"Risāla"* in *Encyclopedia of Islam*.

12 Also creeds, mainly by Ash'arites or their 'precursors'; see Wensinck 1932.

13 To be sure, heresiographic works even when written by authors hostile to the Mu'tazila, e.g. al-Ash'arī's *Maqālāt al-Islāmiyyīn*, are mostly quite reliable, and still constitute an important source on the early history of Mu'tazilite thought.

14 According to later Muslim historiographic sources, the fourth and the fifth principles were chronologically the first ones that had evolved in the politico-theological debates or disputes of the early eighth century. The initial formu-

lation of the fourth principle had been "the intermediate status," and was said to have been important at that period of time, as a compromise in the controversy between rigorous believers like the Khawārij (who taught that only those who strictly observe the ritual, civil, and ethical practices enjoined by the Qur'ān are considered believers, while others who profess Islam only verbally are actually disbelievers and therefore should be the object of holy war (*jihād*)) and the Umayyad rulers and their associates (some of whom are said to have been lax in the observance of the laws, ritual or otherwise, and still considered themselves full members of the community). Jewish followers of kalām occasionally make use of the characteristic Mu'tazilite terminology used with respect to the fourth principle. The fifth principle was the main framework for the discussion of the political leadership (*imāma, khilāfa*) of the Islamic community in all theological schools and movements, in both the Sunnī and the Shī'i camps, and therefore is of little relevance to the present discussion. It may still be related to some sections of Saadia's positive ethical code.

15 This is generally the position of the Baṣran branch of the Mu'tazila at the beginning of the tenth century, which was upheld also by some later authorities of the school. Earlier formulations of the relationship between God and his attributes (linked mainly to the name of Abu'l-Hudhayl, early ninth century) presented the (essential) attributes as aspects of the divine essence that are identical with it. Other developments or refinements of the theory, which are associated mainly with the name of Abu Hāshim al-Jubbā'ī (d. 933), are not relevant to the discussion here; see Wolfson 1976, pp. 167–205.

16 Such scriptural statements may be considered the initial cause of the problem of the attributes.

17 This position was upheld by the Mu'tazila down to a rather late period. It was abandoned by later Ash'arite thinkers, who held that sense perception is liable to be misled by imagination or the weakness of the organs of the senses; their position is described by Maimonides, in *Guide* 1.73. Jewish followers of kalām followed the position of the early Mu'tazila.

18 See below on the logical procedures in kalām; on the relationship between the "indicator" and its referent (i.e. God), see van Ess 1970, pp. 27, 34.

19 Arabic *al-istidlāl bi-'l-shāhid 'alā 'l-ghā'ib*; see van Ess 1970, p. 34; Frank 1992, p. 31.

20 Pines 1936 is still a classic discussion of this theory; see also Wolfson 1976, pp. 466–517; Daiber 1975, pp. 283–337. Dhanani (1994) has recently re-examined the findings of Pines in the light of many primary kalām sources (some rather late, though), as well as Epicurean and similar sources that had not been available to Pines. Dhanani showed that the Indian element in kalām atomism is rather questionable, but because of textual evidence cannot be entirely ruled out, and can therefore be explained as a result of Persian mediation. Dhanani also argued that kalām atomism is in fact a continuation of the minimal parts doctrines of ancient atomism, and that it may be better understood in the light of classical geometrical theories. Dhanani has contested the understanding of the atoms of the mutakallimūn as unextended particles.

21 On the relationship between this theory and human capability and freedom of choice, see below.

22 Wolfson 1976, pp. 559–78; van Ess 1991–3, 3: 309–42; and cf. Schwarz 1991, pp. 162–9.

23 Such effects are termed in Arabic *mutawalladāt*; see Wolfson 1976, pp. 644–55; Gimaret 1980, pp. 25–49, 85–7. The possibility that an act can generate effects that are beyond the agent's power or control is conditioned by some recognition of causality.

24 Initially God carries out this obligation by endowing man with reason.

25 Not of laws of nature (see above on the atomistic theory).

26 In the Qur'ān there are no records of miracles performed by Muḥammad. A number of them are recorded in Islamic tradition, and a whole genre developed of collections of such records. At the same time a theory was developed about the miraculous nature of the Qur'ān (*i'jāz al-qur'ān*) as a whole, which is usually translated "the inimitability of the Qur'ān." Muslim theologians as well as literary critics were divided on the question whether this characteristic of the Qur'ān applies only to its language or also to its contents; see *Encyclopedia of Islam*, s.v. "I'djāz al-Ḳur'ān"; Audebert 1982, esp. pp. 57–111.

27 This issue is related to the problem of God's attributes and the anthropomorphisms found in Scripture and in other sacred texts; on the subject in general (and on many other questions related to Mu'tazilite kalām), see Peters 1976, esp. pp. 278–402.

28 A still valuable contribution on this topic is Hourani 1971. Hourani tends to use the terms "immediate" and "intuitive" interchangeably; it seems that intuition does not belong to the Mu'tazilite world view; cf. also Hourani 1985, pp. 67–97.

29 On this term see Frank 1992, p. 10 n. 5, with references to previous publications.

30 This religious obligation is found already in the earliest Patristic sources. On Origen and Tertullian, see Wolfson 1970, pp. 109ff.

31 For this purpose, abridged expositions of the Mu'tazilite theology, or creeds, were written; see Gimaret 1979.

32 On the process of speculation (*naẓar*) leading to knowledge (*'ilm*) that is validated by "peace of mind," see Vajda 1967, pp. 145–54.

33 Kalām does not recognize logic (*manṭiq*) as a theoretical discipline of any status, only dialectic (*jadal*) as a technique of debate or dispute; the term *qiyās* (often translated as "analogy") also frequently serves to describe speculative procedure; see van Ess 1970, p. 38, where the logic of kalām is referred to as "propositional logic."

34 For a survey of this topic see van Ess 1970.

35 For details see van Ess 1970.

36 The latter technique is known by the term *ilzām*, i.e., forcing the adversary to accept the inadmissibility of his doctrine or argument by itself, or by the results that "necessarily" follow from it (*lāzim*).

37 An example for the change of this format in later stages is 'Abd al-Jabbār's *al-Muḥīṭ*. Fragments of the original version survived only in a Judeo-Arabic Karaite copy. This version still retains the dialogue format. In the version current among Muslims, which is a revision made two generations later by ibn Mattawayh (d. 1076), most "dialogue" elements were dropped; see Ben-Shammai 1974 and the remarks of Gimaret in ibn Mattawayh 1981, 2: 26–30.

38 Islam does not recognize Scriptures of other monotheistic religions as valid

records of God's message; they were abrogated or superseded by the Qur'ān. Some Mu'tazilite thinkers also wrote commentaries on the Qur'ān; about the Jubbā'īs, see Gimaret 1976, pp. 284–5, 289, 312.

39 See Frank 1987, 1992; Gimaret 1990.

40 On the vicissitudes of Jewish kalām in Spain, see below.

41 See Frank 1988.

42 Between al-Ash'arī himself and his followers, they vary between seven and ten.

43 This was a specially sensitive matter. The Mu'tazila insisted that God's speech is created, since he cannot be described as speaking. The Ash'ariyya taught that his speech was uncreated (=eternal). However many of them qualified this statement by arguing that it applied only to the content of revelation and not to its actual material manifestations.

44 On the Ash'arī position on attributes, see Frank 1992. In twelfth-century Ash'arite works the divine attributes are sometimes presented in a way that may seem to resemble the position of the Baṣran Mu'tazila, namely, as aspects of God's essence.

45 The term "Islam" or "Islamic countries" is used here to denote the political framework in which Arabic culture developed and was predominant.

46 Qirqisānī is said, according to his own testimony, to have written a systematic theological work entitled *Kitāb al-Tawḥīd (The Book of Unity)*; see *Encyclopedia Judaica*, 10: cols. 1047–8. So far nothing of that work has been recovered.

47 On the historical statements of Maimonides and Judah Halevi regarding the preference of Jews for the Mu'tazila, or the sectarian identity of the Jewish followers of kalām, see Wolfson 1976, pp. 82–91.

48 For Saadia's evidence, see *Amānāt*, introd.: 6, pp. 23–4 (Kafih); pp. 26–7 (Rosenblatt). Qirqisānī reports that certain Karaite authorites expressed their opposition in terms of religious prohibition; see Hirschfeld 1918, pp. 14–15 (Qirqisānī alludes to Karaite authorities, not "to the warnings of the Rabbis"; cf. Ben-Shammai 1977, 1: 8–11).

49 See Kraemer 1986, pp. 83–4 (with references to primary sources and previous publications of Goldziher, Goitein, F. Rosenthal, and Pines), and, on the historical circumstances of a Neoplatonic popular work from late tenth century, Ben-Shammai 1989; and on polemics against such trends see Ben-Shammai 1977, 1: 315–17.

50 On Isaac Israeli and Dunash b. Tamim, see the bibliography in Sirat 1985, p. 422.

51 Most chapters of the major philosophical work of al-Muqammiṣ (written in Judeo-Arabic) were published, with an extended introduction and richly documented annotations, by Stroumsa in 1989. The following discussion is based on this work, especially the introduction, pp. 15–33. On his exegetical works, see p. 20.

52 On instances where the Christian education of al-Muqammiṣ is reflected in his work, see Stroumsa 1989, pp. 28, 32.

53 Notwithstanding, al-Muqammiṣ explicitly dissociates himself from what seems to him the position of the philosophers, especially Aristotle, namely, the doctrine of negative attributes; positive statements can also be true, and in this case the meaning is that God has "neither diversity nor variety" (Stroumsa 1989, p. 201).

54 See Stroumsa 1989, pp. 28–9, 196–201.

55 In this context biblical verses are quoted in Arabic translation only; see Stroumsa 1989, index of biblical references.

56 For an English translation of the entire work, the text itself, and an extensive introduction, see Nemoy 1976; the theological sections are on pp. 55–60, 88–90. About fragments of Arabic theological works by early Karaites (perhaps also al-Qūmisī) see Zucker 1959, pp. 175–82, 480–5.

57 Nemoy, while doubting the authorship of Daniel al-Qūmisī, fully accepts that it "belongs to a very early period of Karaite history" (1976, p. 50).

58 On a similar feature in tenth-century Karaite sources, see Ben-Shammai 1977, I: 318–23.

59 This is the common theme of the entire document: normative practices and beliefs according to the sectarian position of the author. To be sure, the style is somewhat loose and lacks the form of an orderly list.

60 The order of the points has been somewhat changed here.

61 The Hebrew of the document contains several Arabisms, one of which is the technical term *dalīl*. The author (or translator) was not sure that the Hebrew term *moreh* can convey the meaning of the Arabic term and therefore appended everywhere the Arabic as well.

62 This principle is supported by Job 19:26, and is the earliest attestation to the introduction of the "Delphic Maxim" into medieval Jewish philosophy in the form of that verse; see Altmann 1963.

63 On Saadia's philosophical oeuvre there is considerable secondary literature; see Sirat 1985, pp. 417–18; for more recent publications, especially with relation to biblical exegesis, see Goodman 1988, pp. 3–27; a brief and vivid historian's survey of Saadia's activity, with his philosophy as a climax, is found in Goitein 1988, 5: 379–90.

64 Arabic *al-Amānāt wa-'l-I'tiqādāt*. For the important editions and translations, see Sirat 1985, pp. 416–17.

65 The number is the same as that of the discourses of *al-Amānāt*.

66 On the work see Ben-Shammai 1986–7; on the list see ibid., pp. 322–3; Ben-Shammai 1996 (including discussion of parallel lists in Saadia's works).

67 Principles 1–3, 9–10 are qualified by the verb "to believe"; 4, 7–8 by the verb "to entertain a conviction" (*ya'taqid*); and 5–6 describe mental dispositions. Note the absence of resurrection from this list.

68 Many philosophical or theological theories with which Saadia was acquainted are explicitly mentioned by him, mainly on occasions of listing different opinions, beliefs, or doctrines on a given topic, such as the creation or the origin of the world (*Amānāt* 1: 3; introduction to *Commentary of Sefer Yetzira*, for which see Wolfson 1979, pp. 124–62); the essence of the human soul (*Amānāt* 6: 1, for which see Davidson 1967); and various other theories and opinions which certainly have their origin in written or oral philosophical and scientific non-Jewish sources. Saadia does not specify any of these sources by name (only occasionally by collective terms, such as philosophers, dualists, materialists, Christians), and it seems that he does so intentionally, since his interest is mainly in rejecting those doctrines rather than enlightening his audience about

their origin. It is therefore difficult, sometimes impossible, to identify his sources.

69 See Ben-Shammai 1985, pp. 243, 260 n. 83; Saadia was even acquainted with the theory of the Mu'tazilite opponent of atomism, al-Naẓẓām (d. 845), about the "leap," which makes possible the actual traversal of a distance that may be divided into an infinite number of particles, although he does not mention his name; see Wolfson 1979, pp. 165–6; Davidson 1987, p. 118.

70 In his *Commentary on Job*: p. 17 (Kafih); p. 128 (Goodman) (on p. 142 (Goodman), n. 49 should be corrected: the terminology and the concepts employed there by Saadia are Mu'tazilite not Kharijite); and also *Amānāt* 5: 4, p. 181 (Kafih); pp. 218–19 (Rosenblatt).

71 See Vajda 1967.

72 See for now Schwarz 1991, pp. 159–61. A conservative mutakallim like R. Nissim of Qayrawan argues even later, perhaps against Samuel b. Chofni, that while demonstrative or analogical speculation (*ṭarīq al-istidlāl*) is subject to mistakes, sense perception is certain (Abramson 1965, p. 344).

73 Arabic *istidlāl bi–'l-shāhid 'alā 'l-ghā'ib*; see above note 19.

74 *Amānāt*, introd.: 5: p. 14 (Kafih); p. 36 (Altmann). Saadia's definition is "that which immediate knowledge leads to" or even "obliges to"; contrary to n. 5 (Altmann) and p. 16 (Rosenblatt), it is not related to "logical necessity". A large section of that chapter (pp. 17–22 (Kafih); pp. 19–26 (Rosenblatt); pp. 38–42 (Altmann)) is devoted to a thorough discussion of the procedures of inference. Saadia devises a hierarchy of natural phenomena by which true knowledge may be attained. If there is an apparent contradiction between such phenomena the "more important" prevails. With respect to van Ess' remark (1970, p. 33) regarding the difference between "commemorative sign" and "indicative sign," it should be noted that the "commemorative sign" is mostly present in the kalām inferences, even if the terminological distinction is not explicitly spelled out. This is also true regarding Saadia (who mentions the same example of smoke, for whose Stoic origin see van Ess 1970, p. 27), not only in the case of proving God's existence but also in the proofs for the existence of the soul and the intellect. In both cases the commemorative sign must be evoked; otherwise the proofs make no sense.

75 See *Amānāt*, pp. 15–16 (Kafih); pp. 18–19 (Rosenblatt); p. 37 (Altmann) (cf. *Amānāt* 7: 1: pp. 219–20 (Kafih); pp. 265–7 (Rosenblatt)); Ben-Shammai 1977, 1: 89–100.

76 French translation and discussion in Vajda 1946–7.

77 Vadja 1963.

78 It should be emphasized that the rationality of this knowledge or these laws refers to their epistemological status, namely, how, or by means of which source, they are known, and does not refer to their justification or explanation.

79 See Sklare 1992, pp. 220–1 on the attitude of other Jewish thinkers toward the concept.

80 See Davidson 1974. About Qirqisānī and Yefet b. 'Eli, see Ben-Shammai 1977, 1: 8–35.

81 Note that Saadia emphasizes that this actualization is only one aim of rational speculation on religion. The other aim is apologetic, to defend the faith against its adversaries.

82 This term is otherwise unknown in this sense in the Arabic terminology of Muslim religious thinkers or their Jewish counterparts. It may be an arabicized form of a parallel term in mishnaic Hebrew with a somewhat similar sense; see the reference in note 66 above.

83 *Amānāt*, introd.: 6: pp. 24–8 (Kafih); pp. 27–32 (Rosenblatt). When investigation or speculation is conducted improperly it may result in a false conviction. On the relationship between true conviction and knowledge in Saadia's system, and its parallels in Baṣran Muʿtazila, see Vajda 1967, pp. 140–5; on the connection between these notions and the Arabic translation of Aristotle's *De Interpretatione*, see Vajda 1948–9, pp. 85–91.

84 For an explicit rejection of the Aristotelian world view, see Wolfson 1979, pp. 145–59; see also below, note 89.

85 See above, note 69. An important exception may be Samuel b. Chofni, who followed the Baṣran school of the Muʿtazila more closely than any other Rabbanite thinker.

86 *Amānāt* 3: 4: pp. 124–5 (Kafih); pp. 147–8 (Rosenblatt).

87 In rabbinic tradition this doctrine was not at all unanimously or exclusively accepted; see Altmann 1969.

88 *Amānāt* 1: 1: pp. 35–7 (Kafih); pp. 41–2 (Rosenblatt); Davidson 1987, pp. 99–101, 409–11. According to Davidson, this is a simplified form of the same argument in John Philoponus (1987, pp. 89–92). It seems that Saadia is almost the only mutakallim to have taken up this proof (on remnants of it in al-Kindī's thought, see ibid., pp. 114–15). It is found (in a crude form) as one of two proofs mentioned by Qūmisī.

89 *Amānāt* 1: 1: p. 37 (Kafih); pp. 42–3 (Rosenblatt); Davidson 1987, pp. 101–2. According to Davidson, this is taken from an "auxiliary argument from composition" that John Philoponus used to support his proof from the principle that a finite body can contain only finite power (ibid., p. 92). However in Saadia the composition is not of matter and form, as in Philoponus, but of parts, which shows that Saadia received and accepted it from a kalām source that did not agree with the Aristotelian dichotomy between matter and form (ibid., p. 103 n. 88). This proof too did not have much following in kalām. It is interesting that the evidence for this proof in Arabic philosophical or theological texts before Saadia, in addition to al-Kindī, is only in Christian sources (Davidson 1987, pp. 146–53).

90 *Amānāt*, 1: 1: p. 38 (Kafih); pp. 43–4 (Rosenblatt); Davidson 1987, pp. 103–6, 134–43. It is found as one of two proofs mentioned by Qūmisī. According to Davidson, this is a reflection of the "auxiliary argument" of Philoponus from the succession of forms over matter, by which he supports his proof from the principle that a finite body can contain only finite power (ibid., p. 92).

91 *Amānāt* 1: 1: pp. 38–9 (Kafih); pp. 44–5 (Rosenblatt); Davidson 1987, pp. 95–7, 117–20. It is actually a slightly transformed version of the first proof of Philoponus that the infinite is not traversible.

92 Ben-Shammai 1977, pp. 174–80. The division line between proofs for creation and proofs for a creator is not very well defined in the works of these authors. Qirqisānī has a peculiar version of the fourth proof: time is an independent being, not one that measures the duration of other beings; the units of time prove that there is no eternal time; therefore, the world cannot be eternal or infinite.

93 See Ben-Shammai 1985, pp. 245–54.

94 Ben-Shammai 1977, pp. 180–8; see above, note 62; Davidson 1987, pp. 213–36.

95 *Amānāt*, 2: 9–12: pp. 97–111 (Kafih); pp. 112–30 (Rosenblatt).

96 *Amānāt*, 2: 5–7: pp. 90–5 (Kafih); pp. 103–12 (Rosenblatt).

97 It is not impossible that the Mu'tazilite-Ash'arite controversy itself has to be seen as belonging to the context of the Muslim-Christian debate.

98 These are discussed at length in *Amānāt* discourse 3, on a theological level.

99 *Amānāt* 10: 15: pp. 316–17 (Kafih); pp. 395–7 (Rosenblatt); the latter part of the argument is a repetition of *Amānāt* 3: exordium: pp. 116–17 (Kafih); pp. 137–8 (Rosenblatt). This argument should not be confused with another argument (raised by Saadia, *Amānāt* 4: 5: p. 159 (Kafih); p. 192 (Rosenblatt)) that one of the reasons for the revelation of the rational laws is to make their performer deserve reward, because voluntary performance deserves less reward than performance that is in obedience to a commandment; for a similar statement by Samuel b. Chofni, quoted by R. Nissim, see Abramson 1965, pp. 343–4, with reference to Talmud, *Qiddushin* 31a; and cf. Zucker 1984, pp. 23–4.

100 See Sirat 1985, p. 418.

101 See Sklare 1992, pp. 45–6, 93.

102 For a comprehensive survey of this Gaon and his works, a detailed discussion of some of the most basic concepts of his theories, and a selection of hitherto unedited texts, see Sklare 1992, pp. 145–210, on "The Jewish High Culture Outside the Yeshivot."

103 Sklare 1992, pp. 85–97.

104 Sklare 1992, chapter 5.

105 This is the first topic discussed in *al-Hidāya*; see Sklare 1992, 3: 123–4, and the discussion in 1: 219–26.

106 A fragmentary text of the discussion in *Kitāb al-Hidāya* is found in Sklare 1992, 3: 142–5; it is quoted by R. Nissim in a polemical context; see Abramson 1965, pp. 192–3, and see above, note 72.

107 Of the type discussed in Davidson 1987, pp. 140–3.

108 This exposition is found in fragments of *Kitāb al-Hidāya*; see Sklare 1992, 3: 135–6.

109 Sklare 1992, p. 44; for fragments of the discussion in *al-Hidāya* (according to the partial list of contents, in Sklare 1992, 3: 119, it occupied at least twelve chapters) see Sklare 1992, 3: 138–42.

110 Arabic *'iṣma*; on the Islamic term see *Encyclopedia of Islam*, s.v., and on Samuel b. Chofni see Zucker 1965–6.

111 Arabic *lutf*; Sklare 1992, pp. 88–9, 222–5; see *"Lutf"* in *Encyclopedia of Islam*; Vajda 1985, pp. 502–17, 525–45.

112 Sklare 1992, 1: 47–9, 226–34.

113 On this format of theological discussions, see above, note 11.

114 Hai's responsum has survived in a verbal quotation in a Judeo-Arabic commen-

tary on Isaiah by Judah ibn Bal'am (Spain, eleventh century); part of the text was published in Derenbourg 1891. The responsum was also published with notes and comments by Weil (1953b); for further discussion and comparison to Saadia's position (*Amānāt*, pp. 209–10 (Kafih); pp. 253–5 (Rosenblatt)), see Weil 1953a, pp. 33–7.

115 Many were translated into Hebrew already in the eleventh century.

116 Bibliographic references and indices can be found in Vajda 1985, with many references to, quotations from, and discussions of the Hebrew translations, paraphrases, and compendia made by Byzantine Karaites from the eleventh century onwards; and see the review article by Ben-Shammai (1988–9).

117 See Ben-Shammai 1985, pp. 254–73; Davidson 1987, pp. 141–3.

118 See the Arabic text in Vajda 1985, pp. 722–4; annotated translation, pp. 339–45; and commentary, with reference to an abundance of medieval Jewish and Muslim materials, pp. 346–86.

119 Vajda 1985, pp. 727–30 (Arabic); pp. 404–13 (translation); pp. 460–501 (discussion).

120 Vajda 1985, pp. 388–96.

121 See Ben-Shammai 1991.

122 See *Encyclopedia Judaica* 7: cols. 1046–7; Lasker 1988. Hadassi includes in his discussion typically Islamic chapters from Karaite Arabic works.

123 On this work see Frank 1991.

124 This is not a kalām work; see above, note 50.

125 Bachya ibn Paquda, *Kitāb al-Hidāya ilā Farā'iḍ al-Qulūb (Duties of the Heart)*, p. 18 (Kafih).

126 Abraham ibn Daud, *The Book of Tradition*, pp. xlvi–xlix (Cohen).

127 Joseph ibn Tzaddik, *'Olam Qatan*, pp. 44, 47, 72 (Horovitz); elsewhere, on p. 34, ibn Tzaddik criticizes certain mutakallimūn for their theory that the soul is an accident (a theory refuted by Saadia, *Amānāt*, pp. 194–5 (Kafih); pp. 236–7 (Rosenblatt); pp. 142–3 (Altmann)) without naming al-Baṣīr; and see Vajda 1982, pp. 467–77.

128 See above, note 126.

129 This is another proof, if any is needed, that this kind of material does not always lend itself to traditional criteria of classification.

130 Bachya, p. 16 (Kafih).

131 Bachya, introduction, pp. 25–8 (Kafih); 1: 1–3, pp. 44–51 (Kafih).

132 Joseph ibn Tzaddik, *'Olam Qatan*, pp. 43–4 (Horovitz).

133 Davidson 1987, pp. 120, 152–3.

134 Davidson 1987, p. 141.

135 See the English translation by I. Heinemann in Heinemann 1976, p. 125.

136 See Baneth 1942, p. 317. The source which Halevi used is probably the section "Qawā'id al-'aqā'id" in *Iḥyā' 'ulūm al-dīn* (Cairo, AH 1316), pp. 91–2.

137 See Pines 1963, pp. cxxiv–cxxxi.

❧ BIBLIOGRAPHY ❧

Texts

Bachya ibn Paquda (1973) *Kitāb al-Hidāya ilā Farā'iḍ al-Qulūb*, edited by J. Kafih (Jerusalem) [English translation: *Duties of the Heart*, translated by M. Hyamson (Jerusalem Boys Town, 1962)].

Goodman, L. E. (tr.) (1988) *The Book of Theodicy: Translation and Commentary on the Book of Job by Saadiah ben Joseph al-Fayyumi* (New Haven: Yale University Press).

Heinemann, I. (tr.) (1976) Jehuda Halevi: *Kuzari*, in *Three Jewish Philosophers* (New York: Atheneum).

ibn Daud, Abraham (1967) *The Book of Tradition (Sefer ha-Qabbalah)*, edited and translated by G. D. Cohen (Philadelphia: Jewish Publication Society).

ibn Mattawayh (1981) *al-Majmu' fi l-Muḥīt bi-l-Taklīf*, vol. 2, edited by J. J. Houben (Beirut).

ibn Tzaddik, Joseph (1903) *'Olam Qatan*, edited by S. Horovitz (Breslau: Shatzky).

Nemoy, L. (tr.) (1976) "The Pseudo-Qumisian Sermon to the Karaites," *Proceedings of the American Academy for Jewish Research* 43: 49–105.

Pines, S. (tr.) (1963) Maimonides: *The Guide of the Perplexed* (Chicago: University of Chicago Press).

Saadia (1970) *Kitāb al-Amānāt wa-' l-I'tiqādāt*, edited with Hebrew translation by J. Kafih (Jerusalem, 1970) [English translation: *The Book of Beliefs and Opinions*, translated by S. Rosenblatt (New Haven: Yale University Press, 1948); abridged English translation: *Book of Doctrines and Beliefs*, translated by A. Altmann, in *Three Jewish Philosophers* (New York: Atheneum, 1967)].

—— (1973) *Commentary on the Book of Job*, edited with Hebrew translation by J. Kafih (Jerusalem) [English translation and commentary: see above, Goodman 1988].

Stroumsa, S. (ed. and tr.) (1989) *Dāwūd ibn Marwān al-Muqammiṣ's Twenty Chapters* (Leiden: Brill).

Vajda, G. (ed. and tr.) (1985) *Al Kitāb al-Muḥtawī par Yūsuf al-Baṣīr* (Leiden: Brill).

Zucker, M. (ed.) (1984) *Saadya's Commentary on Genesis* (New York: Jewish Theological Seminary of America).

Studies

Abramson, S. (1965) *R. Nissim Gaon* (Jerusalem: Mekitze Nirdamim).

Altmann, A. (1963) "The Delphic Maxim in Medieval Islam and Judaism," in *Biblical and Other Studies*, edited by A. Altmann (Cambridge, MA: Harvard University Press), pp. 196–232.

—— (1969) "A Note on the Rabbinic Doctrine of Creation," in *Studies in Religious Philosophy and Mysticism* (Ithaca: Cornell University Press), pp. 128–39.

Anawati, G. C. (1987) "Kalām," in *Encyclopedia of Religion*, edited by M. Eliade (New York: Macmillan), 8: 231–42.

Audebert, C.-F. (1982) *al-Ḥaṭṭābī et l'inimitabilité du Coran* (Damascus: Institut Français de Damas).

Baneth, D. Z. (1942) "R. Judah ha-Levi and al-Ghazālī" [Hebrew], *Kennesset le-Zekher Bialik* 7: 311–28.

Ben-Shammai, H. (1974) "A Note on Some Karaite Copies of Muʿtazilite Writings," *Bulletin of the School of Oriental and African Studies* 37: 295–304.

—— (1977) *The Doctrines of Religious Thought of Abu Yūsuf Yaʿqūb al-Qirqisānī and Yefet Ben ʿEli* [Hebrew]. Ph.D dissertation, Hebrew University of Jerusalem.

—— (1985) "Studies in Karaite Atomism," *Jerusalem Studies in Arabic and Islam* 6: 243–98.

—— (1986–7) "New Findings in a Forgotten Manuscript: Samuel b. Hofni's Commentary on Ha'azinu and Saadya's 'Commentary on the Ten Songs' " [Hebrew], *Kiryat Sefer* 61: 313–32.

—— (1988–9) Review of Vajda 1985 [Hebrew], *Kiryat Sefer* 62: 407–26.

—— (1989) "A Philosophical Study Group in Tenth Century Mosul – A Document for the Socio-Cultural History of a Jewish Community in a Muslim Country" [Hebrew], *Peʿamim* 41: 21–31.

—— (1991) "Transmigration of Souls in Tenth Century Jewish Thought in the Orient" [Hebrew], *Sefunot* 20: 117–36.

—— (1996) "Saadya Gaon's Ten Articles of Faith" [Hebrew], *Daʿat* 37: 11–26.

Cook, M. (1980) "The Origins of Kalām," *Bulletin of the School of Oriental and African Studies* 43: 32–43.

Daiber, H. (1975) *Das theologisch-philosophische System des Muʿammar ibn ʿAbbād al-Sulamī* (Beirut: Orient-Institut).

Davidson, H. A. (1967) "Saadia's List of Theories of the Soul," in *Jewish Medieval and Renaissance Studies*, edited by A. Altmann (Cambridge, MA: Harvard University Press), pp. 75–94.

—— (1974) "The Study of Philosophy as a Religious Obligation," in *Religion in a Religious Age*, edited by S. D. Goitein (Cambridge, MA: Association for Jewish Studies), pp. 53–68.

—— (1987) *Proofs for Eternity, Creation and the Existence of God in Medieval Islamic and Jewish Philosophy* (New York: Oxford University Press).

Derenbourg, J. (1891) "Gloses d'Abou Zakariya ben Bilam sur Isaïe," *Revue des Études Juives* 22: 202–6.

Dhanani, A. (1994) *The Physical Theory of Kalam* (Leiden: Brill).

Frank, D. (1991) *The Religious Philosophy of the Karaite Aaron ben Elijah: The Problem of Divine Attributes*. Ph.D. dissertation, Harvard University.

Frank, R. M. (1987) "Ashʿarī," "Ashʿariyah," in *Encyclopedia of Religion*, edited by M. Eliade (New York: Macmillan), 1: 445–55.

—— (1988) "Al-Ashʿarī's 'Kitāb al-Ḥaththth ʿalā alʿ Baḥth'," *Mélanges d'Institut Dominicain d'Études Orientales* 18: 83–152.

—— (1992) "The Science of Kalām," *Arabic Science and Philosophy* 2: 7–37.

Gimaret, D. (1976) "Matériaux pour une Bibliographie des Gubbā'ī," *Journal Asiatique* 264: 277–332.

—— (1979) "Les *Uṣūl al-Hamsa* du Qadi ʿAbd al-Jabbār et leur Commentaires," *Annales Islamologiques* 15: 47–96.

—— (1980) *Théories de l'acte humain en théologie musulmane* (Paris: Vrin).

—— (1990) *La Doctrine d'al-Ashʿarī* (Paris: Vrin).

—— (1993) "Muʿtazila," in *Encyclopedia of Islam*, 2nd ed. (Leiden: Brill), 7: 783–93.

Goitein, S. D. (1988) *A Mediterranean Society*, vol. 5 (Berkeley and Los Angeles: University of California Press).

Hirschfeld, H. (1918) *Qirqisānī Studies* (London: Jews' College Publications, no. 6).

Hourani, G. F. (1971) *Islamic Rationalism: The Ethics of ʿAbd al-Jabbār* (Oxford: Clarendon).

—— (1985) "Islamic and non-Islamic Origins of Muʿtazilite Ethical Rationalism," in *Reason and Tradition in Islamic Ethics* (Cambridge: Cambridge University Press), pp. 67–97.

Kraemer, J. L. (1986) *Humanism in the Renaissance of Islam* (Leiden: Brill).

Lasker, D. (1988) "The Philosophy of Judah Hadassi the Karaite" [Hebrew], *Jerusalem Studies in Jewish Thought* 8: 477–92.

Peters, J. R. T. M. (1976) *God's Created Speech* (Leiden: Brill).

Pines, S. (1936) *Beiträge zur islamischen Atomenlehre* (Berlin: Heine).

Schwarz, M. (1991) "Who were Maimonides' Mutakallimūn?" *Maimonidean Studies* 2: 159–209.

Sirat, C. (1985) *A History of Jewish Philosophy in the Middle Ages* (Cambridge: Cambridge University Press).

Sklare, D. E. (1992) *The Religious and Legal Thought of Samuel ben Hofni Gaon: Texts and Studies in Cultural History*. Ph.D dissertation, Harvard University.

Vajda, G. (1946–7) "Études sur Qirqisānī," *Revue des Études Juives* 107: 52–98.

—— (1948–9) "Études sur Saâdia," *Revue des Études Juives* 109: 69–102.

—— (1963) "Études sur Qirqisānī," *Revue des Études Juives* 122: 7–74.

—— (1967) "Autour de la théorie de la connaissance chez Saadya," *Revue des Études Juives* 126: 135–89, 375–97.

—— (1973) "Le 'Kalām' dans la pensée religieuse juive du moyen âge," *Revue de l'Histoire des Religions* 183: 143–60.

—— (1982) "La philosophie et la théologie de Joseph ibn Çaddiq," in *Mélanges Georges Vajda*, edited by G. E. Weil (Hildesheim: Gerstenberg).

van Ess, J. (1970) "The Logical Structure of Islamic Theology," in *Logic in Classical Islamic Culture*, edited by G. E. von Grunebaum (Wiesbaden: Harrassowitz), pp. 21–50.

—— (1987) "Muʿtazilah," in *Encyclopedia of Religion*, edited by M. Eliade (New York: Macmillan), 10: 220–9.

—— (1991–3) *Theologie und Gesellschaft im 2. und 3. Jahrhundert Hidschra*, vols 1–3, 5 (Berlin and New York: de Gruyter).

Weil, G. (1953a) *Maimonides über die Lebensdauer* (Basle: Karger).

—— (1953b) "The Responsum of R. Hai Gaon on the Predetermined Span of Life" [Hebrew], in *Sefer Assaf* (Jerusalem: Mossad ha-Rav Kook), pp. 261–79.

Wensinck, A. J. (1932) *The Muslim Creed* (Cambridge: Cambridge University Press).

Wolfson, H. A. (1970) *The Philosophy of the Church Fathers*, 3rd ed. (Cambridge, MA: Harvard University Press).

—— (1976) *The Philosophy of the Kalam* (Cambridge, MA: Harvard University Press).

—— (1979) *Repercussions of the Kalam in Jewish Philosophy* (Cambridge, MA: Harvard University Press).

Zucker, M. (ed. and tr.) (1959) *Rav Saadya Gaon's Translation of the Torah* (New York: Feldheim).

—— (1965–6) "The Problem of 'Iṣma – Prophetic Immunity to Sin and Error in Islamic and Jewish Literature," *Tarbitz* 35: 149–73.

CHAPTER 8

Medieval Jewish Neoplatonism

T. M. Rudavsky

INTRODUCTION

Textual transmission

Medieval Neoplatonism, which was largely based on the writings of Plotinus and Proclus, dates from the ninth century. It provided the philosophical context for the thought of many cultivated Jews of the eleventh and twelfth centuries, and during the Arabic period it was more or less complemented by elements stemming from Islamic religious traditions and some Aristotelian ideas. Serious Jewish thinkers had to deal with Jewish Neoplatonism if only because they saw in the speculations of certain Neoplatonist philosophies the epistemological and metaphysical notions that were quite compatible with their own attempts to characterize the nature of God and his nature and relation to humans. Although not all Jewish thinkers supported Neoplatonism, it was extremely influential on the formation of Jewish thought during the late Hellenistic, Roman, and medieval periods.[1]

The Islamic school of Neoplatonism most clearly influenced medieval Jewish writers. The work of Plotinus was transmitted in a variety of ways, most notably through the *Theology of Aristotle* (a paraphrase of books 4, 5, and 6 of the *Enneads*), and through doxographies, collections of sayings of Plotinus which were circulated among religious communities. The *Theology of Aristotle* exists in two versions. The shorter (vulgate) version, belonging to a later period and found in many manuscripts, was the version first published by Dieterici. The second, longer version exists in three fragmentary manuscripts in Hebrew script, discovered by Borisov in St. Petersburg.[2] Underlying the longer version of the *Theology of Aristotle* is an additional pseudographical work discovered by Stern, which he calls *Ibn Chasdai's Neoplatonist*. In an important article Stern has argued that the independent treatise *Ibn Chasdai's Neoplatonist* was incorporated into the long version of the *Theology of Aristotle*, that it strongly influenced Isaac Israeli's philosophy, and that it was preserved almost in its entirety in a Hebrew translation incorporated into ibn Chasdai's work *Ben ha-Melekh ve-ha-Nazir (The Prince and the Ascetic)*.[3]

Two other influential works are worthy of note. Proclus' *Elements of Theology* was transmitted to Jewish thinkers in the period between the early ninth and late tenth centuries through an Arabic translation, *Kalām fī mahd al-khair*. Known to Latin thinkers as the *Liber de Causis*, it was translated in the twelfth century from Arabic into Latin most likely by Gerard of Cremona and was generally attributed by medieval philosophers to Aristotle.[4] And finally, the *Book of Five Substances* attributed to Empedocles was originally written in the ninth century in Arabic and translated into Hebrew in the fourteenth to fifteenth centuries. Published by David Kaufmann in 1899, this pseudo-Empedoclean work represents a variant of ibn Chasdai's Neoplatonism and was highly influential upon the work of ibn Gabirol, especially in its placement of "spiritual matter" as the first of the five substances.[5]

Neoplatonist themes

To define Neoplatonism thematically would require a chapter in itself. Recent articles, for example, have questioned even whether Plotinus himself is a Neoplatonist.[6] Following Sweeney and Katz, let us suggest that Neoplatonism is a monism which incorporates minimally these three traits. First, it posits as the primal reality an existent who is the One/Good; who transcends all becoming, being, knowledge, and description; and who actually exists. Second, it grants that there are existents other than the One, but that inasmuch as any reality they have is congruent with the One, they are at bottom identical with the One. Third, it finds operative two sorts of causality: (1) the emanation of effects from the perfection of the One to the imperfection of existents (termed "hypostases"); (2) a return of imperfect effects for the perfection of the One which commences with contemplation and culminates in full identification with the One.[7]

That these traits are all to some extent reflected in Jewish Neoplatonist writings will become evident in this chapter. But one other trait must be mentioned as well, namely, the problem inherent in the very process of philosophical analysis. As pointed out by Katz,[8] Neoplatonism generally, and especially Jewish Neoplatonism, presents a familiar yet profound problem. According to its declared premises, verbal descriptions of the ultimate realities are not possible: language operates upon and within a given categorical structure and is of limited applicability to those entities that lie outside its domain. Plotinus, for example, suggests that, inasmuch as the One must be without form and is thereby not a substance, it transcends being and language. By the Middle Ages, the ineffability of the One was taken as an indisputable axiom by both mystics and Neoplatonic philosophers.[9] One way, Katz notes, that medieval Neoplatonists used to interpret this axiom was to emphasize the utter ineffability of God's true nature. Strictly speaking, when we deny the possibility of linguistic expression, nothing more should be said. On this line of argument, it becomes impossible to say which linguistic forms are appropriate to the One, because all language is equally inappropriate. One problem with this approach, however, is that negative predicates become more appropriate for describing God than positive ones. Metaphysical attributes are no more attributable than their opposites. Katz is right to note that the Neoplatonists never really overcome this difficulty. For as we shall see in our ensuing discussion, Jewish Neoplatonists speak of the One in ways that carry content, even if only implicitly and connotatively, by reference to the larger conceptual context that informs everything they say.

◄◄ ISAAC ISRAELI ►►

Introduction and works

Isaac Israeli (c. 855–c. 955), a physician and philosopher, is considered to be the first Jewish Neoplatonist. Although it has been said of him that he is not an original philosopher,[10] Israeli is considered one of the great physicians of the Middle Ages. He was born in Egypt and began his career as an oculist.[11] At about the age of fifty, he emigrated to Tunisia to study medicine under the Muslim Isḥāq ibn Imrān. Later, he was appointed court physician by 'Ubayd-Allāh al-Mahdi, the founder of the Fāṭimid dynasty. His works were widely circulated and translated into Arabic, Latin, and Hebrew. They were translated (or adapted) from the Arabic into Latin by Constantine the African (1087) and were thus introduced to Europe and included in the Salerno school.[12]

Of his many surviving works, the *Book of Definitions* and the *Book of Substances* are the main sources of his philosophical ideas. His best known work, the *Book of Definitions*, is influenced by al-Kindī and ibn Chasdai, and deals with definitions of philosophical, logical, and other terms.[13] The *Book of Substances* has survived only in incomplete fragments of the original Arabic.[14] It appears to be a general treatise on philosophy aimed at a general audience rather than being a specifically Jewish work. The *Book on Spirit and Soul*, the only work to refer to the Bible, appears to have been written for a Jewish public.[15] In both these works Israeli develops his doctrine of emanation which is derived from ibn Chasdai.

The *Book on the Elements* is the most substantial, in bulk, of his extant philosophical writings.[16] The text is essentially an exposition of the Aristotelian doctrine of the elements, which the author identifies with that of Hippocrates and Galen, together with a criticism of differing conceptions regarding the idea of elements. As Altmann notes, the course of the argument is continually interrupted by naive insertions of medical, logical, and metaphysical investigations. Finally, the *Chapter on the Elements* (the *Mantua Text*) exists only in manuscript, at Mantua.[17] From this text we learn that Israeli based his view of creation and the series of emanations on *Ibn Chasdai's Neoplatonist*, alluded to above.[18]

The emanation of beings in Israeli's cosmology

The extant Israeli texts do not give a significant explanation of the concept of God or his existence. As a result, concepts of God and creation must be pieced together from isolated discussions. God is described as a perpetually active creator who created the universe ex nihilo and in time, "and in acting is in no need of things outside Him."[19] He created the "first substance" and the "truly first genus" without mediator.[20] They came into being by his "power"[21] or by his "power and will."[22] The simple substances and the sphere are generated from the power and will of the creator, whereas the bodies are made by nature.[23] Israeli treats "power" and "will" as aspects of God, identical with his essence or being – they are not hypostases as they are in the *Long Theology* and later Neoplatonists such as ibn Gabirol and Judah Halevi. He does not incorporate Plotinus' paradoxical formulation of freedom and necessity, nor do any of his extant writings present a negative theology of divine attributes.

In general, the philosophical doctrine of Israeli describes the various stages of being as a series of emanations, or hypostases, from the Intellect; the Intellect itself is constituted by the union of first matter and first form, which are "created" by the power and will of God. Israeli thus upholds the notion of creation ex nihilo in the case of the first three hypostases, while adopting the Plotinian concept of emanation for the rest. Israeli distinguishes three cosmological processes. The first, creation ex nihilo, is used only for Intellect which is created from matter and form, and is due to an act of power and will. The second process, emanation, is the logical and necessary order through which spiritual substances emanate. The third process accords with the causality of nature, or creation from something already existent, and reflects the way corporeal substances are caused.[24] Hence, the more perfect substances are created without the mediation of intervening stages – nothing stands between them and the creator. Only Intellect is completely unmediated. Compared to the material world, the spiritual world is also unmediated.

Israeli presents two schemes of emanation. In the *Mantua Text*, he describes emanation as a series of ever-diminishing radiances, using metaphors of sun and water, similar to standard images in Plotinus. But, unlike Plotinus, in the *Book of Definitions* each hypostasis acquires more shadows and darkness, out of which the next hypostasis emanates. The shadow accounts for its loss of strength. In the *Book of Substances*, he tries to combine both metaphors by claiming that the shadow is the new substance; the essence or light is not what emanates. Unfortunately, Israeli is seemingly unaware of the contradiction in maintaining that emanation is both the passing of the essence and the passing of a shadow.[25]

Israeli shares the Neoplatonic view that there is a common substratum or matter (absolute body which underlies the four elements).[26] The four elements come into being from the motion of the sphere.[27] They are simple, but this does not mean that Israeli rejects the view that they are composed of matter and form – spiritual substances, too, are simple, yet they are composed of matter and form.[28] Prime matter is the lowest grade of spiritual substance, both ontologically and morally. There is no ambiguity over the status of matter. The demonic function of matter is taken over by the force of darkness and shells which obscure human intellect. On this scheme shells represent the corporeal aspect of images.[29]

Whereas Plotinus describes Intellect as emanating directly from the One, Israeli, following his pseudo-Aristotelian source, interposes two simple substances – first matter and first form or wisdom – between the Creator and Intellect as representing the first hypostasis.[30] First matter is described as "the first substance which subsists in itself and is the substratum of diversity,"[31] whereas first form or substantial form is described as "impregnating first matter," and is identified with "the perfect wisdom, the pure radiance, and clear splendour!"[32] Like first matter, first form is created "by the action, without mediation, of the power and the will [of God]."[33]

Israeli's discussion of Intellect as "the specificality [naw'iyya] of things" is derived from that of al-Kindī.[34] Intellect represents the second hypostasis and is divided into three kinds. The first is active intellect, "the intellect which is always in actuality; this is the intellect about which we were saying above that the specificity of things was present with it forever." The second, potential intellect, is found in the soul. And the third intellect, which refers to the actualization in the soul of the potential intellect by perception, is termed by Israeli "second intellect." This latter intellect refers to the actualization in the soul of the potential intellect by way of sense-perception and is distinct from the intuitive knowledge of intellect.[35]

It is not entirely clear how Israeli distinguishes between wisdom and Intellect. However, interposing first matter and form or wisdom between God and the Intellect is a characteristic feature of Israeli's metaphysical doctrine which Altmann claims can be traced back to his pseudo-Aristotelian source. This interposition sets Israeli's doctrine apart from the variant of Neoplatonism based on the pseudo-Empedoclean *Book of Five Substances*, where matter alone is interposed between God and Intellect.[36] This introduction of a hypostasis of matter and form prior to Intellect, foreign to the *Theology of Aristotle* and Plotinus, may have been motivated by theological considerations and a desire to allow for creation in time within the framework of Neoplatonic metaphysics.

Soul follows Intellect in this triad of hypostases and is divided into a higher phase and a lower one, which Israeli calls "nature".[37] The *Book of Substances* describes the three souls (rational, animal, vegetative) as the forms (specificalities) of the three stages of living beings (humans, animals, plants).[38] The sphere, or heaven, is the last of the "simple substances" and is an addition to the three souls. It holds an intermediate position, acting as a bridge between the spiritual and corporeal worlds. It has a lasting existence, but is not purely spiritual because its light is the least in brightness and it has matter in it. Its function is equated with that of nature. Composed of the fifth element, it is "unaffected by growth and decrease, coming to be and passing away," and has a "lasting existence."[39]

Philosophy and the ascent to God

The three stages of ascent described in Israeli's texts are taken from Proclus' *in Alcibiadem I*.[40] The first, purification, is a turning away from passions of the lower soul. The human soul now contains little of darkness and shells. Israeli lists the virtues which result from this process of purification. The second stage, illumination, corresponds to wisdom. The soul acquires true knowledge of external things. And finally, in union, the soul becomes spiritual and intellectual as the rational soul is raised to the level of Intellect. This is a final union not with God but with wisdom. The term *devequt* (attachment) is also used and reflects a Jewish influence. According to Israeli, this stage can be achieved even when the soul is still in the body. Hell is the counterpart to ascent – an evil soul is weighted down and unable to pass through the spheres.[41]

Israeli's theory of purification and the soul corresponds to his conception of philosophy. Philosophy is essentially a drawing near to God, as far as is possible for human beings. This ideal of imitatio Dei, which goes back to Plato's *Theaetetus* and which was used for the definition of philosophy in the Neoplatonic commentaries on Aristotle, was in fact also a presence in biblical and talmudic thought.[42]

Section two of the *Book of Definitions* describes philosophy in three ways.[43] The name "philosopher," from the Greek *philia*, love, and *sophia*, wisdom, provides the view of the philosopher as " 'the lover of wisdom,' and if 'philosopher' means the 'lover of wisdom,' 'philosophy' must mean 'love of wisdom.' "[44] Philosophy is also described as "the assimilation to the works of the Creator, may He be exalted, according to human capacity."[45] Finally, philosophy is described from its effect as "man's knowledge of himself."[46]

Intimately connected to the philosopher is the prophet. Israeli's discussion of prophecy occurs mainly in the second chapter of the *Book on the Elements* and parts of the *Book of Definitions*.[47] It is not as elaborate as that of later medieval Jewish philosophers and he does not clearly distinguish between the roles of prophet and philosopher. God reveals the "intellectual precepts" to the elect among his creatures – prophets and messengers and the true teachers (philosophers), whose task it is to "guide His creatures towards the truth and to prescribe justice and equity."[48]

In his conception of prophecy Israeli distinguishes between three forms: that of a created voice (*qol*); of spirit (*ruach*), including vision (*chazon*); and of speech (*dibbur*), which designates union with the supernal light and represents the highest rank. It is identical to ecstatic experience, which can come in degrees. The paradigm of Moses' prophetic achievement is described in terms of this highest stage:

> The creator, exalted and blessed be He, therefore chose from among his creatures one qualified in this manner to be his messenger, caused him to prophesy, and showed through him His veridical signs and miracles. He made him the messenger and intermediary between Himself and His creatures, and caused His book of Truth to descend through him.[49]

The function of prophecy is, however, also conceived in terms of spiritual guidance of the multitude of people, for which reason the divine truths must be couched in imaginative, allegorical form. There is no sharp dividing line between prophet and philosopher in that both share in the common task of guiding humankind towards the same goal: both are concerned with the ascent of the soul, its liberation from the bondage of matter, and its eventual union with the supernal light.[50]

❧ SOLOMON IBN GABIROL ❧

Introduction

Representing the flourishing of Jewish intellectual life in Andalusia under the enlightened reign of the Umayyad caliphate, ibn Gabirol was one of the first Jewish philosophers in Spain to benefit from the intellectual ferment of this Golden Age. Although ibn Gabirol lived barely forty years, he is known primarily for his metaphysical writings: his major philosophical work *Meqor Chayyim* is a purely metaphysical treatise which presents a rigorously defined Neoplatonic cosmology. Of ibn Gabirol's life we know very little. He was born in Malaga, Spain, in 1021/2, spent the majority of his life in Saragossa, and died in Valencia probably in 1057/8 at the age of thirty-five to thirty-eight. Living during the height of the Arabic reign in southern Spain, ibn Gabirol is a product of the rich Judeo-Arabic interaction which colored Spanish intellectual life during the eleventh century. Much of his work was written in Arabic, and many of his ideas and poetic styles reflect Arab intellectual and stylistic components. Ibn Gabirol himself boasted of having written over twenty books, but only two works are now extant: *Meqor Chayyim* and *Tiqqun Middot ha-Nefesh*.[51]

Ibn Gabirol's major literary contribution comprises what we may term his "wisdom poetry." Clearly spanning the interface between poetry and philosophy, these poems reflect ibn Gabirol's obsession with the search for knowledge, the ascent and rediscovery of wisdom. The underlying motif of these poems, reflected in his philosophical works as well, is that our sojourn on this earth is but temporary. Ibn Gabirol depicts himself as devoting his life to knowledge in order to transcend the void and worthlessness of bodily existence. The mystical undercurrents are much akin to Sufi poetry, as well as to themes in earlier kabbalistic literature. The best-known and most elegant example of this philosophical poetry is ibn Gabirol's masterpiece *Keter Malkhut*, which to this day forms the text for the Yom Kippur service.

Ibn Gabirol's major contribution to ethics is his work *Tiqqun Middot ha-Nefesh*.[52] In *Tiqqun Middot ha-Nefesh*, which is primarily a treatise on practical morality, the qualities and defects of the soul are described, with particular emphasis upon the doctrine of the Aristotelian mean. This mean is supported by biblical references, as well as by quotations from Greek philosophers and Arab poets. Ibn Gabirol describes humans as representing the pinnacle of creation; inasmuch as the final purpose of human existence is perfection, they must overcome their passions and detach themselves from this base existence in order to attain to felicity of the soul.

Many of these standard elements can be readily found within classical Jewish Neoplatonism. However, as Schlanger has pointed out, ibn Gabirol does introduce an original element, namely the connection between the moral and physiological make-up of the human. That is, each of twenty personal traits is correlated to one of the five senses. Hence, the body as well as the soul must participate in the person's aspirations toward felicity: "In the actions of the senses as well as in the moral actions, one must reside in the mean and not fall into excess or defect."[53] In effect, ibn Gabirol has delineated a complete parallel between the microcosm, as represented by the human being, and the macrocosm which is the universe.

Philosophical strands within Meqor Chayyim

This contrast between the microcosm and the macrocosm finds its fullest expression in ibn Gabirol's most comprehensive philosophical work, *Meqor Chayyim (Fountain of Life)*.[54] The form of *Meqor Chayyim*, a dialogue between a teacher and his disciple, reflects a style popular in Arabic philosophical literature of the period. It comprises five books of unequal length, the third book of which is the most comprehensive (over three hundred pages in the Latin edition). A succinct summary of the work is given by ibn Gabirol himself in his introduction:

> Inasmuch as we propose to study universal matter and universal form, we must explain that whatsoever is composed of matter and form comprises two elements: composed corporeal substance and simple spiritual substance. The former further subdivides into two: corporeal matter which underlies the form of qualities; and spiritual matter which underlies corporeal form. . . . And so in the first treatise we shall treat universal matter and universal form; in the second we shall treat spiritual matter. This will necessitate subsequent treatises as well. In the third we shall treat the reality of simple substances; in the fourth, the search for knowledge of matter and form of simple substances; and in the fifth, universal matter and form in and of themselves.[55]

In classical Neoplatonic fashion, ibn Gabirol adduces several basic themes. First, ibn Gabirol is clear that science or knowledge is the ultimate aim of human life.[56] Second, knowledge of oneself (the microcosm) contains the science of everything (the macrocosm).[57] Further, the world was created by and is dependent upon divine will. The human soul was placed in this world of nature, a base and degrading existence; in order to return to the world of spirit, the soul must purify itself from the pollutions of this base world. Finally, the purpose of human existence overall is the knowledge of being: being comprises matter and form, God, and will.[58]

Without characterizing the many details of ibn Gabirol's Neoplatonic cosmology, let us concentrate upon several of his own specific modifications. Ibn Gabirol's most creative contribution centers on his hylomorphic conception of matter. All substances in the world, both spiritual and corporeal, are composed of matter and form. Types of matter are ordered in a hierarchy which corresponds to a criterion of simplicity: general spiritual matter, general corporeal matter, general celestial matter, general natural matter, and particular natural matter. Particular matter is associated with prime matter, which lies at the periphery of the hierarchy, thus epitomizing the very limits of being.[59]

How are form and matter interrelated? Ibn Gabirol is ambivalent toward this question and presents two alternatives. On the one hand, he argues that form and matter are mutually interdefined and are differentiated only according to our perspective of them at a particular time; accordingly both are aspects of simple substance. On the other hand, he emphasizes the complete opposition between matter and form, suggesting that each possesses mutually exclusive properties which render a reduction of one to the other an impossibility.[60]

The importance of these discrepancies is reflected in ibn Gabirol's discussion of creation. When describing the yearnings of matter, ibn Gabirol argues that, inasmuch as matter was created bereft of form, it now yearns for fulfillment.[61] However, in other contexts, he asserts that matter subsists not even for an instant without form.[62] In this latter case, matter is and always was united with form. Additionally, ibn Gabirol offers two accounts of the actual process of creation. According to *Meqor* 5.42, universal matter comes from the essence of God, and form from the divine will, whereas other texts suggest that both were created by the divine will.[63]

The status of divine will is suitably ambiguous. The will is clearly one of the hypostases inserted between God and universal form and matter. But whether will is identical with wisdom is not clear. In *Meqor Chayyim* will and wisdom are construed as identical. But in *Keter Malkhut* a distinction is made between the two. As Hyman has pointed out, ibn Gabirol speaks of creation by will in several places, suggesting that creation took place through a volitional act. Yet he also uses models for creation like water flowing from a fountain, the reflection of light in a mirror, and the issuing of human speech, suggesting that creation should be understood as necessary emanation. In both cases, however, it is clear that divine will is posited as an intermediary between God and intellect in order to explain how multiplicity can come to be from a unitary being.[64] The ultimate metaphysical principle in ibn Gabirol's system is not intellect but will; this voluntarism becomes an important motif in later kabbalistic thought.

From this brief synopsis of *Meqor Chayyim* several points may be made with respect to ibn Gabirol's sources. First, as Sirat has pointed out, ibn Gabirol's cosmology differs from standard Muslim Neoplatonism in two important respects: in his concept of form and matter, and in his view of divine will.[65] In his conception of matter, ibn Gabirol has incorporated both Aristotelian and Stoic elements, the latter possibly from having read Galen. It has been suggested that the notion of spiritual matter may have been influenced by Proclus' *Elements of Theology*, a Neoplatonic work which was translated into Arabic. Unlike ibn Gabirol, however, Proclus does not maintain that universal form and matter are the first simple substances after God and will. It is more likely that on this point ibn Gabirol was influenced by both pseudo-Empedocles and Isaac Israeli, both of whose views on matter and form are very similar to those of ibn Gabirol.[66]

As mentioned earlier, ibn Gabirol's influence upon Jewish philosophy was limited. *Meqor Chayyim* was not translated into Hebrew during his lifetime, and the original Arabic text was soon lost. Possibly because ibn Gabirol does not discuss issues so close to the heart of the thirteenth century, such as faith and reason, Jewish philosophers steeped in Aristotelianism had little interest in his work. *Meqor Chayyim* did, however, influence several Neoplatonists such as ibn Tzaddik and Moses ibn Ezra, as well as important kabbalistic figures such as ibn Latif.[67]

❧ BACHYA BEN JOSEPH IBN PAQUDA ❧

Introduction

Bachya ben Joseph ibn Paquda was the immediate successor of ibn Gabirol. He lived during the second half of the eleventh century, most likely at Saragossa. Little is known of his life other than that he had the office of judge of the Jewish community in Spain. His major philosophical work *Book of Guidance to the Duties of the Heart* (*Kitāb al-Hidāya ilā Farā'iḍ al-Qulūb*) was first translated into Hebrew by Judah ibn Tibbon around 1160. This work cites both Arabic and Jewish philosophers, in particular Saadia Gaon, and contains many quotations from Arabic literature. Many have pointed to the considerable similarities between his general philosophical orientation and that of the Arabic school of encyclopedists known as the Brethren of Purity (Ikhwān al-Ṣafā').⁶⁸ It has also been suggested that Bachya fell under the influence of the Sufi mystics of Islam, chiefly because of his emphasis on the cultivation of self-renunciation and indifference to the goods of the world in the last three books of *Duties of the Heart*.⁶⁹

In part because his book is devotional rather than metaphysical Bachya is considered a Neoplatonist in a qualified sense. In the introduction to his work Bachya distinguishes three types of wisdom: science of created things, of ancillary things, and of theology. The science of created things deals with the essential and accidental properties of material bodies; that of ancillary things deals with arithmetic, geometry, astronomy, and music; and the science of theology deals with the knowledge of God.⁷⁰ This latter, according to Bachya, is the highest duty.

Bachya then distinguishes two parts of the science of Torah: practical duties pertaining to external conduct and "duties of the heart" pertaining to "the science of the inward life."⁷¹ Practical duties can be either rational or revelatory. Duties of the heart, on the other hand, are all rooted in rational principles and they comprise both positive and negative duties. This distinction between duties of the heart and duties of the limb, or external duties, was first made by Islamic theologians who distinguished between duties to humans and those to God.⁷² Bachya's distinction, however, is slightly different, corresponding more to a distinction between intention and act. Duties of the heart are all rational and not visible to others: they are judged by God alone. Duties of the limb comprise rituals and other forms of visible worship which are incomplete if not accompanied by the will of the heart: "I am certain that even the practical duties can not be efficiently performed without willingness of the heart and desire of the soul to do them."⁷³ In short, Bachya sees his purpose in writing as reintroducing the duties of the heart and purifying religion by introducing sincerity and devotion into actions.

Philosophical underpinnings to these duties

Because theoretical knowledge is a prerequisite to the religious life – there can be no relationship to God without knowledge of God – Bachya begins his discussion of duties with an intellectual examination of God and his attributes. The first principle articulated as a "duty of the heart" is God's absolute unity. But in order to initiate its acceptance Bachya first must demonstrate the existence of God. Bachya's proofs that there must exist a creator of the universe are borrowed from kalām sources and are based on the premise that a series of composite things requires a first cause.[74] For Bachya, as for the kalām philosophers, this series is teleological in nature. First, three principles are assumed, each of which is proved in turn: (1) nothing can create itself; (2) since principles are finite in number, there must be a first principle in order to avoid an infinite regress; and (3) no composite thing existed from eternity.[75] His proof is as follows. The world is synthetic and composite, as evidenced by the fact that all of its parts demonstrate composition. Since "the universe as a whole and in each of its parts exhibits throughout combination and synthesis,"[76] it is composed of primal elements. But these elements could not "coalesce of themselves ... or combine through their essential character."[77] Thus Bachya concludes that a Being must have coalesced these elements. Hence, the world must have had a beginning in time. This beginning must have had to be created by a first principle which created the world ex nihilo. This principle is the creator. "This being so, and as a thing cannot make itself, it necessarily follows that this Universe had a Maker to whom it owes its beginnings and its existence."[78] Bachya dismisses as absurd the notion that the world could have come about by accident, arguing that the harmony and purpose in nature refute such a suggestion.[79]

He next proves the unity and uniqueness of God in accordance with kalām thought. This leads to the motif, common to Neoplatonic thought, that God is the absolute unity which precedes all things. Only the attributes of unity, being, and eternity are essential to God. However, even they cannot be attributed directly to God.[80] That the creator (God) is one, is demonstrated as follows. Since causes are fewer than their effects, we can move from infinite individuals to finite species to the ten highest genera to matter and form to the will of God, which must be one. God's unity is seen in the unity of plan and wisdom in the universe – there is a uniformity in all its parts. Since unity precedes plurality, it would follow that one creator created the universe. It is ridiculous to believe that there is more than one creator, for one must have been created by the other. Since plurality is an accidental property, it cannot be attributed to God. If there is more than one creator, one would have been superfluous anyway.[81]

Bachya must show that God's attributes do not conflict with his unity. God's attributes are either essential or active. We ascribe the essential attributes, existence, unity, and eternity, in order to indicate God's being and to call attention to his glory.[82] However, they do not imply change in his essence but only a denial of their contradictories. Further, each of the attributes implies necessarily the other two.[83] Active attributes are ascribed with reference to God's works and are of two kinds, those that indicate form and bodily likeness, God's image (for example, "by the mouth of the Lord"), and those that indicate bodily movement and action (for example, "God smote," "God remembered"). These, Bachya reminds us, should be understood in the metaphorical sense of allowing us to formulate a concept of God, to come to a knowledge of him.

From here, much of the text represents an exhortation to the spiritual life and obedience to God's will. Teaching a modified asceticism, Bachya advocates purification of the soul and detachment from this worldly existence.[84] But how is this to be achieved if the soul is already determined to act in certain ways, and to desire worldly goods? In a famous passage of dialogue between the Soul and Intellect (*ha-Sekhel*), the Soul states its confusion over contradictory utterances in the Bible pertaining to freedom and compulsion. The Intellect, speaking on Bachya's behalf, notes that we notice through experience that our actions are both free and not free (sometimes they accord with our purposes and sometimes they do not). According to the Intellect, some scholars have argued, all human actions follow from one's free choice. Thus God's will is simply denied. Others have claimed that every action is predestined and God is just, committing no wrong.[85] But this solution ignores the problem of justice. Bachya adopts a pragmatic position and says that we must act as if both positions are true, as if we were free, but we must nevertheless trust God's all-knowing guidance: "The proper course to follow is to act on the principle of one who believes that actions are left to a human being's free will. ... At the same time we ought to trust in God, fully convinced that all things and movements, together with their advantageous and injurious results, happen by the decree of the Eternal."[86] So Bachya's formula binds his faith in divine justice with his dependence on God, without recognizing the inherent contradictions in such a view.

Ultimately, as argued by Vajda, the soul is sustained both by religious law and by reason.[87] Law communicates with the soul by means of revelation. Reason communicates with the soul by means of inspiration. Inspiration reaches those who have achieved a plenitude of intellectual capacity and a release from mundane matters. If one realizes one has not achieved this level of inspiration, one undergoes an interior struggle. The sick soul is tied to the body, tied to vices of society, and is unable to achieve reunion with God. It can only be cured by removing the cause – superfluity in this material existence.

❧❧ "PSEUDO-BACHYA" ❧❧

Introduction

For many years the short treatise *On the Essence of the Soul* (*Kitāb Ma'ānī al-Nafs*) was attributed to Bachya ibn Paquda. It was most likely written between the middle of the eleventh and middle of the twelfth centuries.[88] The Arabic manuscript was published by Broyde in 1896, and ascribed to Bachya. In 1907, however, the original Arabic text was published by I. Goldziher. He determined that the treatise was not by Bachya on the grounds that, first, no mention of this treatise is made in any of Bachya's other works, and, second, it is purely Neoplatonic in scope, whereas Bachya often followed kalām doctrines.[89] In the text Neoplatonism is presented in a loose fashion and is identified with biblical teachings. In fact, often biblical quotations are used to support philosophical positions.

The structure of the universe

According to our author, the world is divided into simple and composite parts. Simple parts are spiritual, pure, and good, and are close to their source. They comprise the first ten elements in creation. Composite parts are further away from their source, and depicted as corporeal and bad.[90] All the created levels emanate from God, but in different ways. The first emanation is God's essence, his actual presence, identified with the *shekhinah*. But it differs from Saadia's conception of *shekhinah* as a created being. It is an apparition that God created so that people might feel his presence.[91] From this first level emanates the universal soul, *ha-nefesh ha-klallit*, which moves the spheres through a natural force, in the same way that the individual soul moves the bodies with the power of nature.[92] Nature is the third emanation in the hierarchy. These first three emanations are eternal and totally spiritual.

In contrast, the fourth emanation, matter (*chomer ha-olam*), is created in time and space and introduces corporeality into the universe. It had no activity or life at first, only the power to receive. It is associated with the darkness mentioned in Genesis 1:2.[93] From matter the other simple bodies emanate. *Galgal* is already a complex substance, the agent of motion. The sixth emanation comprises the separate stars in the sphere (*gufot ha-kokhavim*), which were created before time and place; that is, they are co-eternal with God. Emanations seven to ten are the four elements, which came into existence along with time.[94]

Humans comprise the last of the emanations and bear the traces of all ten previous elements, but in inverted order; therefore, the human soul is a divine emanation, related to universal soul and intellect. Reminiscent of the gnostic motif of descent, the soul passes through every sphere, becoming progressively more impure. Much of the book is devoted to this journey of the soul back to the Intellect. All individual differences between souls are due to these spherical impressions. The Hebrew term *roshem* is used for this imprinting upon the soul.[95] Our anonymous author argues against the naturalists who argued that the soul is an accident of the body and dies along with it, and Avicenna's notion that the soul is created with the body but is imperishable. Rather he adheres to those theologians (*ba'alei ha-elohut*) who believe that the soul is a spiritual substance independent of the body.[96] Thus the human being is composed of independent soul and corporeal body.

In chapter 21 the soul is compared to a piece of clothing which, when dipped in water, will remain pure if it was pure to begin with. But if the water is dirty it will become dirty.[97] One must honor the soul which is a gift from God. Upon entering the body, the soul forgets its original knowledge and succumbs to sensuality; only through virtue can purification be achieved. The purpose of the soul is twofold: to purify the animal and vegetative souls and to realize the value of its original world in comparison with this one. Since the soul originates in the suprasensible world, immortality is a return to its origins. Souls are graded according to their measure of knowledge and the value of their conduct: those which have regained their original intellectual and moral perfection can return to their origin, while those which have not attained knowledge must learn more first. The wicked must wander around under the heavens.[98] Our author paints a graphic description of the various afflictions which await the ignorant and wicked soul, reinforcing the importance of knowledge acquisition and perfection.

❧ BAR CHIYYA ❧

Introduction

Born in Soria, Spain in 1065, Bar Chiyya lived in Barcelona in the first half of the twelfth century and died sometime after 1136. He bore the title *nasi* ("prince"), denoting a judiciary function within the Jewish community. Bar Chiyya was the first philosophic author to write in Hebrew. Known primarily as an astronomer and mathematician, Bar Chiyya co-operated with the Christian Plato of Tivoli in translating scientific works from Arabic into Latin. His astronomical works introduced Hebrew speakers to the works of Ptolemy for the first time. His philosophical thinking is presented in two books: *Megillat ha-Megalleh* (*Scroll of the Revealer*) and *Hegyon ha-Nefesh ha-Atzuvah* (*The Meditation of the Sad Soul*). *Hegyon ha-Nefesh* is a book on morality and is thought by some to have been designed to be read during the ten days of penitence between Rosh Hashanah and Yom Kippur.[99] In this work, Bar Chiyya follows a combination of Neoplatonic and Aristotelian patterns.[100] He posits the universe as a graded process of cosmic existences emanating from God's light. Emanation is purposeful activity guided by wisdom, and the world is characterized by purpose. However, since only the corporeal world is a composite of form and matter, one must distinguish between the suprasensible essences and the corporeal world. He implicitly assumes the existence and unity of God, as well as God's omniscience, omnipotence, and omnipresence.

Cosmogony

Unlike Plotinus, Bar Chiyya assumes creation ex nihilo: God first created things to exist potentially. Substance is composed of matter and form, both of which correspond to the biblical account of creation. After the two kinds of matter and form, motion is created through the spheres (the light emanates on the spheres and causes them to move). Creation constitutes the act of actualizing the potential matter by endowing it with form – thus he draws a compromise between Aristotelian arguments for the eternity of matter and the rabbinic espousal of creation ex nihilo. Time comes into being together with motion, so that neither the world nor time is eternal.[101] A doctrine of emanation in the strict sense is lacking.[102]

Body has width, depth, and length; it is divided into form and matter, each of which is independent of the other. Just as matter must be joined by form, so too form must clothe matter. Each can be subdivided into two parts. Matter can be divided into pure and clean matter, which enters into the composition of the heavens, and impure matter or dregs, which forms the substratum of terrestrial bodies. So too form is divided into closed and sealed form, which is too pure to attach to matter, and hollow, open form, which can attach to matter.[103]

In this cosmogony light is a definite metaphysical principle. The upper intelligible world is divided into five worlds of light which correspond to the five times in Genesis 1 where light is mentioned: world of wonderful light (*ha-or ha-niflah*, throne of glory); divine light, or world of dominion; world of intellect (wisdom and Torah); world of soul (divine spirit in each person); and world of nature.[104]

The world of wonderful light is the purest form and illuminates lesser forms. Bar Chiyya thus introduces what we may call a modified form of creation in postulating stages of creation. In the first stage, creation is caused by the emanation of light from the closed form which is near to God. In the second stage, a splendor emanates from the closed form and shines on an open form so that it may combine with matter; the hollow, open form then subdivides into two. One part joins pure matter to make the firmament while the other part joins impure matter to form world bodies (that is, the four elements). In the third stage, light emanates from the sealed form and it spreads from point to point, causing the form to move and change its place; thus stars are created. In the fourth stage, a splendor emanates from the stars which forms the three types of living beings – water, air, and terrestrial beings.[105]

Bar Chiyya finds corresponding terms in Genesis to represent this emanation scheme: *tohu* is equivalent to matter in that both lack form and shape; *vohu* represents form in that both are in matter; and *mayyim* is that form from which all others are derived.[106] Three types of form result from this discussion: the pure self-subsistent form which never combines with matter, corresponding to the light created on the first day; the second form which is inseparably united with matter and is the firmament created on the second day; and the form which is temporarily united with matter, corresponding to the creatures created on the third day. These latter two depict the form which cannot exist apart from matter.[107] To these Bar Chiyya adds a fourth, soul, which can exist both with and without a body.

Psychology: the soul

Human beings represent the summit of creation; it is the duty of humans to find out why they are in control of other animals – thus leading to an investigation into the origins of all things. Humans are distinguished from other creatures in three ways: humans alone were created directly by God, they contain the divine spirit within them, and were given dominion over other creatures.

The human soul has three faculties: vegetative, animal, and rational. Bar Chiyya elucidates three properties or faculties of the soul: generation, locomotion/motion, and discrimination between good and evil.[108] There is a constant struggle between rational and animal faculties. The rational faculty represents the potentiality to receive all forms and must be able to subdue the animal faculties.[109]

Turning to Bar Chiyya's eschatology, the saint emerges as the highest type of soul who has health and life. Bar Chiyya distinguishes five types of people: the completely righteous saint; one who must fight to subdue all his inclinations; one who repents and doesn't sin again; one who repents but relapses into sin; and one who sins and never repents. Representing the highest group of true believers, the saint is separated from the world and devotes himself to the next world. His life, devoted fully to God, is described as a perpetual Sabbath. The second group of true believers, called by Bar Chiyya "the separate community," is the community which busies itself with this world but also observes all divine commandments. Finally, there is the third group, termed "the separate nation," which has to be on guard against outsiders.[110]

In his emphasis on a philosophy of history, Bar Chiyya is furthest away from medieval Neoplatonism, for whom existence is timeless. In his messianic treatise *Scroll of the Revealer*, he tries to determine the exact date of the messiah by finding a relevant explanation for each event in history. This, Guttmann has suggested, is the first Jewish concern with a philosophy of history.[111]

❧ JOSEPH BEN JACOB IBN TZADDIK ❧

Introduction

Of ibn Tzaddik's life we know very little. He seems to have been a well-known poet. From 1138 he exercised the functions of a *dayyan* (rabbinical judge) at Cordoba and he died in 1149.[112] He was clearly influenced by both Isaac Israeli and ibn Gabirol. His major work, written originally in Arabic, has survived in an anonymous Hebrew translation called *Ha-Olam ha-Qatan* (*The Microcosm*). The text is divided into four parts: physics, principles, and constitution of the corporeal world; anthropology and psychology; existence, unity, and other attributes of God; and theodicy, freedom of will, and reward and punishment. Influenced by Saadia, Bachya, ibn Gabirol, and Islamic kalām philosophy, ibn Tzaddik expounds familiar Neoplatonic themes along with Aristotelian influences.

Why one engages in self-study

Two requisites are necessary for the knowledge of philosophical terms: knowledge of God and performance of his will. But in order to acquire this one must have a knowledge of everything else as well. Therefore, ibn Tzaddik shows how one can know oneself – for knowledge of self, according to ibn Tzaddik, leads to knowledge of all. Human beings are microcosms because they have in themselves all elements of the universe.[113] Part one of the text thus starts with knowledge of the physical world.

Through the process of knowledge, humans perceive things in two ways, through sense (*ha-regesh*) and through intellect (*ha-sekhel*). The five senses yield knowledge of accidental qualities, whereas reason penetrates through to the essence of a thing. Knowledge can be classified as either necessary (immediate) or demonstrated (mediate).

Correspondingly, there are four kinds of objects of knowledge: percepts of sense (*murgashot*); self-evident truths (*mefursamot*); tradition (*mequbalot*); and first principles/axioms (*musqalot*). According to ibn Tzaddik, each of these can be traced back to either rational or sensory knowledge.[114] The former is superior for it distinguishes us from animals.

The second section of this part treats of matter, form, substance, and accident, and it displays the influence of ibn Gabirol. Matter is the foundation (*ha-yesod*) and principle of all things. The common matter of the four elements is prime matter which is endowed with the form of corporeality (*etzem gishmi*). Matter and form are relative to each other. Spiritual things are also composed of matter and form. In spiritual things, we may compare genus to matter, species to form, specific difference to efficient cause, and individual to final cause.[115] Everything exists either in itself (*omed be'atzmo*) or in something else (*omed be'zulatto*). Matter exists in itself, whereas form exists in matter. After matter assumes a form, matter becomes an actual substance. However, matter and form can only be separated in thought, not in reality. Substance is then defined as that which bears opposite and changing qualities. A substance can be the opposite of another only through its accidents. Absolute substance is pure and spiritual (*ha-etzem ha-muchlat*). It is what remains of a corporeal substance when we take everything away, and is similar to ibn Gabirol's substance which supports the categories.[116]

In the third section ibn Tzaddik turns to the corporeal world (*ha-olam ha-gishmi*), namely, the spheres, the four elements, and the three natures. The sphere (*galgal*) differs from other bodies in matter, form, and qualities. It is not cold, warm, wet, dry, light, or heavy (like other bodies). The sphere moves in a circle, the most perfect of motions, and has no beginning or end. It is more perfect than other bodies and has a knowledge of God. The four elements – fire, air, water, earth – are simple bodies and have no qualities. They can change into each other. The basis of the elements is a substance filling place as a result of its assuming the form of corporeality. The three natures – plant, animal, and mineral – are composed of the four elements. The general process of the sublunar world is genesis and dissolution. Thus, the world is not permanent, for the basis of its processes is change.[117]

In the fourth section ibn Tzaddik turns to the human body. The human body corresponds to the corporeal world in that it too is subject to genesis and decay. It is composed of elements and has powers of growth and sustenance like plants. In true Neoplatonic fashion, ibn Tzaddik claims that humans are superior to all other beings in that they comprise all of them.[118]

The function of the soul

Part two of *ha-Olam* deals with the different types of soul. Clearly combining Platonic and Aristotelian themes in an uncritical fashion, ibn Tzaddik distinguishes three types of soul: the vegetative, the animal, and the rational soul. The faculty of the plant soul is appetition and its seat is in the liver. All of its powers derive from universal powers in the upper world. The animal soul is seated in the heart and is borne in the blood. Its functions are motion and sensation. Motion can be active (heart) and passive (emotions). Life is the effect of the animal soul, while death is characterized as the separation of rational soul (*ha-nefesh ha-chokhmah*) from the body. Death results from an imbalance in the heart of the four humors (blood, yellow and black gall, and phlegm), or by disease or injury to the brain. The rational soul is incorporeal and not in the body.[119] The soul is a substance, not an accident, for it is permanent, that is, reason is essential to man. Moreover, soul is superior to body, so it must be a spiritual substance. All three souls are spiritual powers. Both the rational soul and intellect have a common matter. When the soul is perfected it becomes intellect; the only difference between them is one of degree and excellence, inasmuch as the intellect comes straight from God without any intermediary.[120] The function of the rational soul is knowledge, exploring the unknown. If one studies, a person's rational soul is destined for the spiritual world. In order to study, a person must first deaden the animal impulses. One then comes to know first the corporeal world, then the spiritual world, and finally the creator. Knowledge of God is the highest kind of knowledge and the cause of human perfection. Those who have no such knowledge are doomed to error. The existence of many individual souls shows there must be a universal or world soul. The universal soul is received into all the bodies, just as objects receive the sun's light. The splitting of the world soul into many souls is due to the plurality of bodies which absorbs it.

The unity of God

How do we achieve knowledge of God? To know a thing, we must investigate its four causes, but with God we can only know whether he is.[121] Ibn Tzaddik offers a rudimentary proof for the existence of God as follows. If substance and accident are not eternal, something must have brought them into being. This something is God. Further, he argues that since the cause of the many must be the one, God is one. Ibn Tzaddik then shows, by means of kalām arguments, that there cannot be two eternal beings.[122]

The troubling question, of course, is why God created the universe at all. Clearly this is not because God experienced a lack, because, inasmuch as God is complete, he needs nothing and is dependent upon nothing. Ibn Tzaddik argues that God's will is eternal and not created by God. But what is the relation of will to God? As Guttmann points out, ibn Tzaddik's answer is ambiguous. Divine will is identical with divine essence, yet ibn Tzaddik does not explain or amplify this identification further. More specifically, he does not explain how will and essence correlate with God's immutability. According to ibn Tzaddik, God is beyond space and time, and when we say that the will of God created the world, neither the statement that creation is taking place nor the statement that creation took place at a definite time corresponds to the truth of the matter.[123] Hence ibn Tzaddik simply concludes that God created the world ex nihilo and it is perfect. When ibn Tzaddik speaks of creation as a secret, he suggests that not everyone can understand the secrets of philosophy; thus only an indication of these matters should be given, and the intelligent individual will comprehend of his own accord.[124]

With respect to God's attributes, he claims that they are different from all other attributes, in that they are all accidental to his essence. God's attributes, however, can only be applied figuratively. Divine attributes are either of action or of essence, both of which are two aspects of the same attribute. Divine attributes become models of moral action. We derive our knowledge of God from his effects, but ultimately we can really only apply them negatively.[125]

Theodicy

Ibn Tzaddik's distinction between rational and traditional commandments is similar to that of Bachya and Saadia.[126] The commandments are for our own good, so that we may be happy in the next life. Ibn Tzaddik's discussion of the four virtues (wisdom, courage, temperance, and justice) is clearly influenced by Plato's four virtues.[127] For ibn Tzaddik, as for many of his contemporaries, knowledge of a suprasensible world is a prerequisite for eternal happiness. As Sirat points out the identification of prophecy and philosophy causes problems because philosophy includes a number of sciences hard to envisage as having been revealed at Sinai.[128] Ibn Tzaddik attempts to resolve this problem by affirming that, at the time of the giving of the Torah, God bestowed prophecy on the whole people, for such was his will; but since at the present time no one can attain philosophy, that is, prophecy, except via the intermediary of science, all must successively acquire the various degrees of science. Science and the desire urging man toward God are common to all, but the aptitude for science depends essentially on climatic conditions.[129] The good (knowledgeable) soul continues its existence in the upper world. The bad soul loses its spirituality and revolves for ever with the spheres in the world of fire. When the messiah comes, the saints will be brought back to life and never die again; the wicked souls will be rejoined to their bodies and burnt.

❧ CONCLUSIONS ❧

Ending our chapter with ibn Tzaddik is somewhat arbitrary, for the history of Jewish Neoplatonism includes many other figures as well. For example, we might have included Abraham ibn Ezra who, born in Tudela in 1089, was a poet, grammarian, biblical exegete, philosopher, astronomer, astrologer, and physician. He lived in Spain until 1140, where he was a friend of ibn Tzaddik, ibn Daud, Moses ibn Ezra, and Judah Halevi. Most of his works were composed between 1140 and 1146. He died in 1164 in either Rome or Palestine.[130] Best known for his biblical commentaries, he also wrote many short treatises on grammar, astrology, and number. Although ibn Ezra did not write any specifically philosophical works, he was strongly influenced by ibn Gabirol. For example, he accepts ibn Gabirol's doctrine that intelligible substances are composed of matter and form, and he uses ibn Gabirol's descriptions of God as the source from which everything flows. Ibn Ezra's theory of soul reflects Neoplatonic motifs as well. The source of the rational soul is the universal soul. Immortality is understood as reunification of rational soul with world soul.

Neoplatonism continues as an influential doctrine throughout late medieval thought, culminating in the seventeenth century. Neoplatonic influences can be traced in the works of Maimonides, Gersonides, and Crescas.[131] Equally striking Neoplatonic motifs can be found in the works of medieval kabbalists.[132] In the sixteenth century Leone Ebreo incorporated many Neoplatonic ideas, most notably the notion of the journey of the soul, into his celebrated Renaissance work *Dialoghi d'Amore*. Although primarily a secular philosophical work, this text is steeped in Jewish Neoplatonic motifs.[133] And in the works of Spinoza, particularly in his conception of God, the doctrine of emanation plays an important role.[134]

Of the numerous themes developed by our authors, let us close by emphasizing the importance of the soul in the overall scheme of emanation. This scheme places matter at one end of the hierarchy, God at the other, and the human soul as engaged on a quest away from the material world back to God. We have seen that in Plotinus matter is identified with the principle of evil, non-being, and lack of existence, residing as it does at the lowest pole of the emanation hierarchy. Ibn Gabirol introduced a new element into Neoplatonic thinking by suggesting that matter is a principle of generality which occurs on all levels: even incorporeal substances have matter as their base. Distinguishing between corporeal and spiritual matter, he argues that matter as such is incorporeal and must unite with the form of materiality. Ibn Tzaddik reflects the influence of ibn Gabirol in claiming that the common matter of the four elements is endowed with the form of corporeality, and that spiritual entities also contain matter and form.

Although the doctrine of emanation, with its insistence upon the debasement of matter, is a basic ingredient in the majority of Neoplatonic texts, it is tempered by the biblical insistence upon creation ex nihilo. Our authors have all grappled with the underlying ontological question, "How can the many be generated from the One?" and have offered a variety of responses. According to ibn Gabirol, for example, creation is dynamic and occurs outside of time. In his emanation scheme, the emphasis is upon the relation of form to matter, rather than on just a "flow" from the deity. Both Bar Chiyya and ibn Tzaddik assume that God has created the world ex nihilo. Bar Chiyya has no strict emanation scheme, but rather employs a system in which open and closed form works on matter.

These creation doctrines give rise to the related issue of God's will: does God create freely? In Plotinus the question is framed in terms of whether the One has free will. On some readings of the *Enneads*, the One, Will, and Nature are seen as identical, since the One can only will itself. The *Long Theology* incorporates the notion of *kālima* (word), suggesting an intermediary between God and Intellect. But it is not clear whether *kālima* is identical to will. In our pseudo-Empedocles text, will represents God's infinity, while Israeli identifies power and will with God's essence. Ibn Gabirol posits divine will as a divine force which binds to matter and form. He distinguishes two moments of will: as pure being it is identified with God, and as it begins to act it becomes a hypostasis and is finite. Thus will is part essence, part hypostasis. We have seen as well that in *Meqor Chayyim* ibn Gabirol identifies will and wisdom, while in *Keter Malkhut* a distinction is made between the two.

And finally, the human soul represents within itself all levels of created existence: functioning as a microcosmic prism, it incorporates elements of matter, form, intellect, and will. The soul is engaged in a perennial journey back to its source, the success of which is wholly dependent upon its moral character. The fate of the soul has been eloquently described by the author of *Ibn Chasdai's Neoplatonist*, who contrasts the fates of the rational and sinful soul respectively. The sinful soul, which has not cleansed itself from the defilements of this world, deserves its exile:

> It [the sinful soul] remains sad and despondent, ... hungering and thirsting to find a way so as to go home to its country and return to its native place. It resembles a man who travelled away from his house, brothers, children and wife, relatives and family, and stayed abroad for a long time. When finally he was on his way back and approached his country and the goal of his desires ... and was filled with the strongest desire to reach his home and rest in his house – obstacles were put in his way and the gates were shut and he was prevented from passing through. He called, but it was of no avail. ... He wandered about perplexed to find a refuge, weeping bitterly and sorrowfully bewailing the great good which he has lost and the evil which had befallen him.[135]

The rational soul, on the other hand, acts according to truth, purifies itself from the corporeal defilement of the material world, and thus receives its reward:

> If the rational soul is righteous ... it is then worthy of receiving its reward and goes to the world of intellect and reaches the light which is created from the Power, its pure brilliance and unmixed splendour and perfect wisdom, from where it had been derived; it is then delighted by its understanding and knowledge. This delight is not one of eating, drinking and other bodily delights, but the joy of the soul in what it sees and hears, a delight which has nothing in common with other delights except the name.[136]

This reward, in the world of medieval Jewish Neoplatonism, is the ultimate aim of human existence.[137]

❧ NOTES ❧

1 Harris 1992, p. xi.

2 For further discussion of the relation between these two versions see the discussions in Pines 1954. Altmann and Stern (1958, p. 80) argue, along with Pines, that the shorter version is the original and the longer is the result of editorial refashioning of the text. Detailed discussion of recent editions and translations of the *Theology of Aristotle* can be found in Taylor 1992, p. 26 n.5. Fenton (1992, pp. 27–39) has recently discovered that Shem Tov ibn Falaquera translated quotations directly from the original "vulgate" Arabic version of the *Theology*

into his own work *Sefer ha-Maʿalot*, making ibn Falaquera the only medieval Jewish author to have done so.

3 Stern 1961 traces the history and influence of this treatise, offering a reconstruction of the text. Ibn Chasdai's treatise *Ben ha-Melekh ve-ha-Nazir* is a Hebrew adaptation of the Arabic book *Bilawhar wa-Yūdāsaf*, which goes back to the legend of the Buddha. A complete translation of ibn Chasdai's work can be found in Stern 1961, pp. 102ff.

4 For the extensive history of this work, see Taylor 1992, pp. 11ff. Fenton traces influences upon Jewish philosophers in Fenton 1976.

5 For a critical examination of this work, see Kaufmann 1962.

6 See for example Blumenthal 1981, where he outlines four major areas of disagreement between Plotinus and other Neoplatonists; see also Sweeney 1983.

7 For a fuller exposition of these three traits, see Sweeney 1983, p. 191.

8 Katz 1992.

9 Among Jewish Neoplatonists, it was a premise in Zoharic and post-Zoharic kabbalah as well as in the philosophy of ibn Gabirol and ibn Paquda and even Maimonides, who says that we cannot grasp God's essence as it truly is; see Katz 1992, p. 281.

10 Guttmann for example calls him "an eclectic compiler" (1964, p. 84).

11 Altmann (1972) dates this from the period 875–904.

12 Ibid. Among Israeli's medical and quasi-medical writings are books on urine, fevers, the pulse, drugs, and the *Treatise on Spirit and Soul* in a half-medical and half-philosophical treatise, probably part of a commentary on Genesis.

13 The entire treatise exists in Hebrew and Latin translations; only a portion survives in the original Arabic. It opens with an account of Aristotle's four types of inquiry (whether, which, what, why) and an elaboration of al-Kindī's definitions of philosophy.

14 Discovered by A. Borisov and edited by S. M. Stern, this work seems to have been written in Arabic characters, though the extant manuscripts are in Hebrew script; see Altmann and Stern 1958, p. 80.

15 Preserved in Hebrew translation (except for a small fragment in Arabic), this treatise may have formed part of a larger work (possibly an exegetical treatise on "Let the waters bring forth abundantly"); for further discussion see Sirat 1985, p. 59.

16 The Arabic original is lost, but it exists in two Hebrew translations, one of which was made by Abraham ibn Chasdai at the request of David Kimchi and the second which exists in a Hebrew closer to that of the Tibbonids. The Latin translation is by Gerard of Cremona.

17 Attributed to Israeli by Altmann and Stern, this text is a commentary on a work by Aristotle. The *explicit* says that the aim of the text is to explain the words of the philosopher by way of arguments and proofs; see Altmann and Stern 1958, p. 118.

18 Ibid., p. 119.

19 Isaac Israeli, *BSubst.* 5.12v: p. 91 [Altmann and Stern]. As Altmann points out, Israeli appears to believe in creation ex nihilo and creation in time. This latter notion ill accords with the doctrine that God is "acting perpetually". The passages relating to this view bear striking witness to Israeli's Neoplatonic background. The image behind them is that of emanation, of an eternal flow

from the divine source which is never exhausted and gives itself ungrudgingly. It also explains the motive of creation as stated by Israeli. Israeli does not solve this conflict; for further discussion, see Altmann and Stern 1958, p. 153.

20 Isaac Israeli, *BDef.*, s. 2, ll. 107–8; s. 3, ll. 10–11: pp. 27, 32 [Altmann and Stern].

21 Ibid.

22 Isaac Israeli, *BSubst.* 4.5r: p. 85 [Altmann and Stern].

23 Isaac Israeli, *BSubst.* 5.12v: p. 91 [Altmann and Stern]. See Altmann and Stern 1958, p. 152.

24 This tripartite distinction is found in the *Theology of Aristotle* and ibn Chasdai as well.

25 As in Plotinus, emanation does not imply change; the source remains unaffected. Plotinus used this fact to explain how multiplicity arises from unity; however, because Israeli introduces a notion of creation, he cannot do the same. Instead he tries to harmonize the two motifs. Hence Israeli ignores Plotinus' important distinction of the two moments in emanation: the pure uninformed moment, and the turning back to the source in contemplation.

26 Description of the origin of the elements in *Mantua* s. 2 is based on Aristotle, *On Generation and Corruption* 2.4; see Altmann and Stern 1958, p. 183.

27 They owe their existence to the process of generation caused by the motion of the sphere.

28 The natural qualities are said by him to be only "natural accidents" inherent in the substance of the elements because they do not constitute their essence. Heat, for example, does not constitute the essence of fire because there are hot things which are not fire. The statement "fire is hot" cannot be reversed. Fire is, however, properly defined as "a subtle, light, luminous body, tending to rise upward"; see Altmann and Stern 1958, p. 183.

29 This identification of matter with the demonic can be traced back to *Republic* 10, 611d. See Altmann and Stern 1958, p. 184.

30 Altmann and Stern 1958, p. 159.

31 Isaac Israeli, *Mant.*, s. 1: p. 119 [Altmann and Stern].

32 Isaac Israeli, *Mant.*, s. 1: p. 119 [Altmann and Stern]; Altmann and Stern 1958, p. 159.

33 Isaac Israeli, *BSubst.* 4.5r: p. 85 [Altmann and Stern]. The *Book of Substances* says it is "the perfect wisdom, pure science and unmixed knowledge" [ibid.]. Paraphrasing the Neoplatonic source, Israeli refers to it as "the absolute brilliance, i.e. the perfect wisdom," *Book on Spirit and Soul* s. 9: p. 111 [Altmann and Stern], while the *Book of Definitions* (s. 2, l. 59: p. 25 [Altmann and Stern]) refers to "the beauty and splendor of wisdom" as something distinct from "the light of intellect." "The light created by the power of God without mediator," mentioned in *BDef.* (s. 2: p. 27 [Altmann and Stern 1958, pp. 61–2]), is identical with wisdom [ibid., p. 159]).

34 Isaac Israeli, *BDef.*, s. 3: p. 37 [Altmann and Stern].

35 Israeli's discussion occurs in *BDef.*, s. 4, ll. 33–54: p. 36 [Altmann and Stern]. It is not entirely clear how Israeli distinguishes between wisdom and Intellect. Intellect contains the totality of forms and knows them by an act of intuitive self-knowledge, so it does not seem possible for there to be a level of knowledge superior to it. It comes to be from the conjunction of first matter and form, as it is composed of them. The *BSubst.*, however, suggests that matter and form

or wisdom have no existence except in Intellect. See Altmann and Stern 1958, pp. 37–9 for further discussion of this point.

36 Ibid., p. 162.

37 Other Neoplatonic sources also equate the sphere with nature. There is no warrant for this in Plotinus – he only identifies nature with the vegetative soul. Following his pseudo-Aristotelian source, Israeli transfers Aristotle's divisions of the individual soul (rational, animal, vegetative) to the universal soul, giving us three hypostases of soul, to which he adds as a final quasi-spiritual substance the "sphere" or heaven, representing the Plotinian hypostasis of nature. Altmann and Stern 1958 cite many examples of how this scheme can be seen in his writings; it also occurs in ibn Chasdai and the *Long Theology*.

38 Isaac Israeli, *BSubst.* 5.12r: p. 91 [Altmann and Stern]. They are analogous to intellect which is the "specificality of all things," the "intelligibilia of the Creator" [ibid., 12v], the archetypes, as it were, of all living souls which must be assumed to draw their life from them. Strangely enough, Israeli does not shed much light on the nature of the three universal souls beyond making them mere replicas, on a macrocosmic scale, of the tripartite division of the particular souls familiar from Aristotle's *De Anima*; for further discussion, see Altmann and Stern 1958, p. 165.

39 Altmann and Stern 1958, pp. 166–7. This simple, perfect, circular movement also appears in the *Mantua Text* and *Book of Substances*.

40 Like al-Kindī and the Ikhwān al-Ṣafā', Israeli adopts Proclus' theory of the three stages of purification, illumination, and union. The bliss of the highest stage is, in Israeli's view, tantamount to the bliss of paradise. In this way, he links traditional Jewish eschatology with Neoplatonic mysticism. He interprets the notion of Hell in terms of the impure soul's inability to penetrate beyond the sphere; it is doomed to remain beneath the sphere and to be consumed.

41 Altmann and Stern 1958, p. 193.

42 For a history of this notion of "love of God" in Jewish philosophy, see Vajda 1957.

43 These three descriptions are borrowed from al-Kindī and derive, with the exception of the last one, from the traditional list of definitions of philosophy contained in the Alexandrian commentaries on the *Isagoge*. The Neoplatonic background of Israeli's concept of philosophy is equally pronounced in the case of the third description which can be shown to reflect the influence of Proclus, and was probably included in some lost Alexandrian commentary which served as al-Kindī's immediate source. All three descriptions assign to philosophy a role intimately connected with the "upward way" or "return" of the soul; see Altmann and Stern 1958, p. 31.

44 Isaac Israeli, *BDef.*, s. 2, ll. 7–13: p. 24 [Altmann and Stern].

45 By the words "assimilation to the works of the Creator" is meant the understanding of the truth of things, namely, acquiring true knowledge of them and doing what corresponds to the truth; by the words "understanding the truth of things" is meant understanding them from their four natural causes, which are the material, formal, efficient, and final causes.

46 Israeli claims that, "This also is a description of great profundity and elevated intelligence, for the following reason. Man, if he acquires a true knowledge of himself, viz. of his own spirituality and corporeality, comprises the knowledge

of everything, viz. of the spiritual and corporeal substance, as in man are joined substance and accident. . . . This being so, it is clear that man, if he knows himself in both his spirituality and corporeality, comprises the knowledge of all, and knows both the spiritual and corporeal substance, and also knows the first substance which is created from the power of the Creator without mediator, which is appropriated to serve as substratum for diversity; as well as the first generic accident, which is divided into quantity, quality, and relation, together with the remaining six compound accidents which derive from the composition of substance with the three accidents. If man comprises all these, he comprises the knowledge of everything and is worthy to be called a philosopher." (Isaac Israeli, *BDef.*, s. 2, ll. 91–113: p. 27 [Altmann and Stern]).

47 As Altmann points out, the doctrine of prophecy which emerges from the sources at our disposal has a decidedly Neoplatonic flavor. It belongs to the same climate of opinion as the references to prophecy in the *Epistles* of the Ikhwān. It is characteristic of Israeli as well as of the Ikhwān that the prophets and philosophers are as a rule bracketed together. Thus Israeli says of the "intellectual precepts" that God reveals them to "the elect among his creatures, meaning thereby the prophets and messengers and the true teachers" – the latter obviously denoting the philosophers (see ibid., ll. 75–7: p. 27 [Altmann and Stern]). In another passage he describes the rank of the rational soul as "spiritual," "near to perfection," and "resembling the spirituality of the angels," and then adds "like the souls of the prophets, peace be upon them, and the teachers guided aright." (Isaac Israeli, *BSubst.* 7. 15v: p. 93 [Altmann and Stern]; see also *Mant.*, s. 6: pp. 124–5 [Altmann and Stern]).

48 Isaac Israeli, *BDef.*, s. 2, ll. 75–7: p. 26 [Altmann and Stern].

49 Altmann and Stern 1958, p. 139.

50 Altmann 1972.

51 Several other works have been attributed to him over the years, but with little evidence. For example, the treatise *Mibchar Peninim (Choice of Pearls)* is a collection of practical moralisms composed of 610 proverbs, maxims, and parables; there is not sufficient evidence to determine whether ibn Gabirol actually composed the work. Two other philosophical treatises which ibn Gabirol mentions in *Meqor Chayyim* are not extant, and it is not clear whether these works ever really existed. Ibn Gabirol did, however, write hundreds of poems. These poems have been scattered throughout the Jewish liturgical and literary corpus and have not yet been fully collected.

52 This work was written in 1045 in Saragossa, and is available in the original Arabic, as well as in a Hebrew translation of Judah ibn Tibbon dated 1167. This latter Hebrew edition has been reprinted in many versions.

53 Schlanger 1968, p. 18.

54 This text has had a checkered history. The original work was written in Arabic, and has come down to us in a Latin translation of the twelfth century made by John of Spain, in collaboration with Dominicus Gundissalinus. Hebrew extracts were compiled in the thirteenth century by Shem Tov ben Joseph ibn Falaquera, and then subsequently translated into Latin under the author's name of "Avicebrol" or "Avicebron." Latin scholastics reading the *Fons Vitae*, as it had become known by the thirteenth century, had no idea that this work was written by a Spanish Jew. In 1857, a French scholar named S. Munk edited and

translated the Hebrew extracts once again. It was while comparing the various editions that Munk noted that the appellations "Avicebron," "Avencebrol," "Avicebrol" in fact referred to the great Jewish poet Solomon ibn Gabirol. He did this by comparing passages in the Hebrew translation by Falaquera with certain other quotations in Albertus Magnus. Before Munk's discovery, it had been assumed that ibn Gabirol and Avicebron were different writers. Perhaps one reason for the obscurity of the text lies in its form. As Pines pointed out (1948), *Meqor Chayyim* is unique among Jewish medieval works in that it contains virtually no references to any other Jewish texts, ideas, or sources: it is wholly lacking in Jewish content. Inasmuch as nothing in the work belies the Jewish predilections of its author, later readers had no reason to suspect that the author was in fact ibn Gabirol, a noted Jewish poet.

55 Ibn Gabirol, *Meqor Chayyim*, 1.1 [Blübstein].
56 Ibid., 1.2.
57 Ibid., 1.4.
58 Ibid., 1.3.
59 Ibid., 5.4.
60 Ibid., 4.2.
61 Ibid., 5.32.
62 Ibid., 5.42.
63 See ibid., 5.42 and 5.36–8 for examples of these two depictions.
64 For further discussion, see Hyman 1992, pp. 119ff.
65 Sirat 1985, p. 69.
66 For further discussion of the influences of Isaac Israeli and pseudo-Empedocles upon ibn Gabirol, see Kaufmann 1962.
67 With respect to the Christian world, the story is quite different. Upon the translation of *Meqor Chayyim* into Latin in the twelfth century, many Scholastics, Thomas Aquinas included, read and were affected by ibn Gabirol's conception of matter. While Aquinas subjected ibn Gabirol's theory of spiritual matter to virulent critique, others, most notably Franciscans such as Bonaventure and Scotus, accepted a number of his views. It might be argued that the Franciscan notion of universal matter is directly indebted to ibn Gabirol's hylomorphism, for this notion of universal matter provided a way of explaining the difference between creatures and God by introducing the ontological distinction of spiritual matter. For further discussion of ibn Gabirol's conception of matter, see Rudavsky 1978 and Brunner 1980a.
68 See for example the discussion in Vajda 1972; see also Pines 1954, pp. 76ff.
69 See the discussion in Lazaroff 1970, p. 25, for possible Sufi sources which may have influenced Bachya.
70 Bachya, *Duties*, p. 15 [Hyamson].
71 Ibid., p. 17.
72 Guttmann 1964, p. 107.
73 See Bachya, *Duties*, p. 21 [Hyamson].
74 For a more extensive discussion of the kalām arguments for God's existence, see Davidson 1987.
75 Bachya's statement of these principles is found in *Duties*, p. 71 [Hyamson].
76 Ibid., p. 75.
77 Ibid., p. 77.

78 Ibid., p. 77.
79 In this respect Bachya's proof falls squarely into the class of cosmological arguments so common in medieval philosophy; see Davidson 1987 for further discussion of these arguments in medieval Jewish and Islamic thought.
80 Guttmann 1964, p. 106.
81 See *Duties*, pp. 81–9 [Hyamson], for a variety of arguments offered by Bachya.
82 Ibid., p. 99.
83 Ibid., p. 101.
84 A detailed exhortation toward renunciation of physical pleasures is found in ibid., pp. 235ff. Lazaroff 1970 traces the rabbinic and Islamic roots of Bachya's asceticism, as drawn against his Neoplatonic proclivities.
85 These two positions correspond to the views of Mu'tazilites and Ash'arites respectively.
86 Bachya, *Duties*, p. 261 [Hyamson].
87 For a more extensive discussion, see Vajda 1937.
88 See Guttmann 1964, p. 110.
89 Husik 1946, p. 106.
90 Pseudo-Bachya, *Sefer Torat ha-Nefesh*, chapter 16, p. 70 [Broyde].
91 Ibid., chapter 16, p. 17.
92 Ibid.
93 Ibid., chapter 16, p. 72.
94 Our author notes that the term *bara* or "creation" is used only for the first emanation. The term *hamtza'ah* is used only for those emanations which result through God's will independently of time and place. After the "creation" of the earth, we have only instances of composition (*yetzirah*); see pseudo-Bachya, *Sefer Torat ha-Nefesh*, chapter 16, p. 73 [Broyde].
95 Ibid., chapter 16, p. 74.
96 Ibid., chapter 1, pp. 3–4.
97 Ibid., chapter 21, p. 85.
98 See ibid., chapter 21, pp. 88ff. for a rich description of the tortures of the damned.
99 See Sirat 1985, pp. 97–8 for further biographical discussion.
100 Stitskin (1961, p. 79) goes so far as to suggest that Bar Chiyya was "the first philosopher to take on all three basic challenges to Judaism created by an Aristotelianism overgrown with neoplatonic views, and attempt to bring them into harmony with the Hebraic spirit."
101 Bar Chiyya, *Hegyon ha-Nefesh*, part 1, p. 14 [Wigoder].
102 Husik 1946, p. 115.
103 Bar Chiyya, *Hegyon ha-Nefesh*, part 1, p. 14 [Wigoder].
104 Ibid., part 1, pp. 14–15. Vajda (1946) points out that the first two come from Arabic doctrine, the last three from Neoplatonism. In pseudo-Empedocles, first matter is a divine light, intelligible, as opposed to material. Many Arabic texts place this light at the intelligible level; but none place it as high up as Bar Chiyya. But Bar Chiyya criticizes systems which place intelligible matter at the top of emanation. Perhaps, Vajda suggests, Bar Chiyya meant for the first two worlds to correspond to primary intelligible matter, which is however transformed in a theological sense.
105 As Wigoder (in Bar Chiyya, 1971, p. 10) points out, Bar Chiyya's treatment

differs from that of Plotinus and ibn Gabirol; in certain respects he has an affinity to the Ikhwān. The Aristotelian aspects of this system include the distinction between potentiality and actuality, that form and matter are not emanations but creations, and that creation takes place in time, whereas for Plotinus it is timeless. Jewish elements include that the doctrine of creation stems from Genesis, and the doctrine of divine attributes.

106 See Bar Chiyya, *Hegyon ha-Nefesh* part 1, pp. 42ff. [Wigoder]. Husik (1946, p. 118) suggests that Bar Chiyya modified Neoplatonic doctrine in order to agree with Genesis. Thus originally form and lights would correspond to the Intellect, Soul, and Nature of Neoplatonism.

107 See Bar Chiyya, *Hegyon ha-Nefesh*, part 1, pp. 44ff. [Wigoder].

108 This classification is significant for two reasons. First, it stresses faculties and not separate souls. Second, it follows the Aristotelian classification into vegetative, animal, and rational soul. In this regard Bar Chiyya deviates from ibn Gabirol; see Bar Chiyya, *Hegyon ha-Nefesh*, part 2, pp. 55ff. [Wigoder].

109 See Stitskin 1961, pp. 109ff., for further discussion of Bar Chiyya's philosophical psychology.

110 These groups are described in Bar Chiyya, *Hegyon ha-Nefesh*, part 3, pp. 88ff. [Wigoder].

111 See Guttmann 1964, pp. 128–9 and Wigoder in Bar Chiyya 1971, pp. 23ff. for further discussion of this point.

112 Sirat 1985, p. 86.

113 Hence ibn Tzaddik follows Israeli's definition of philosophy as man's knowledge of himself.

114 Ibn Tzaddik, *ha-Olam*, pp. 5–8 [Horovitz].

115 Ibid., pp. 9–10. It is here that ibn Gabirol's influence is most evident.

116 Ibid., p. 11.

117 Ibid., p. 15.

118 Ibid., p. 21.

119 Ibid., p. 35.

120 Ibid., p. 43. This is one of the few touches of Neoplatonism in this discussion.

121 Ibid., pp. 45–50.

122 Ibid., pp. 51–3. For further discussion of the kalām roots for these arguments, see Davidson 1987, pp. 213ff.

123 Sirat 1985, pp. 86–7.

124 Ibid., p. 87.

125 Ibn Tzaddik, *ha-Olam*, pp. 59–61 [Horovitz].

126 Ibid.

127 See Plato's discussion in *Republic* 4, 427c–434d.

128 Sirat 1985, p. 87.

129 Ibid.

130 See Sirat 1985, p. 104, for further discussion.

131 For recent discussions of Neoplatonic influences upon these and other medieval Jewish philosophers, see the collection of essays in Goodman 1992, in particular, the essays by Ivry and by Feldman. Attention should be paid as well to the many astrological authors delineated by Sirat. In her estimation these writers propagated Neoplatonic doctrines and transmitted themes and ideas to later Jewish philosophers; see Sirat 1985, pp. 93–112.

132 For a brief discussion of these influences, see Idel 1992.

133 See Leone Ebreo 1924. Dethier 1992 addresses some of these motifs.

134 Spinoza, *Ethics* 1. Wolfson (1959b) discusses the importance of Spinoza's appropriation of the doctrine of emanation.

135 Stern 1961, p. 120.

136 Ibid., p. 119.

137 I would like to thank my graduate assistant Mr. Joseph Casella for his invaluable work and feedback on this paper.

❧ BIBLIOGRAPHY ❧

Texts

Bar Chiyya, Abraham (1860) *Hegyon ha-Nefesh, o Sefer ha-Musar*, edited by I. Freimann (Leipzig: Vollrath).

—— (1924) *Megillat ha-Megalleh*, edited by A. S. Poznanski (Berlin: Mekitze Nirdamim).

—— (1969) *The Meditation of the Sad Soul*, translated by G. Wigoder (New York: Schocken).

—— (1971) *Hegyon ha-Nefesh ha-Atzuvah*, edited by G. Wigoder (Jerusalem: Bialik Institute).

ibn Ezra, Abraham (1834) *Sefer ha-Shem*, edited by H. Lippmann (Fürth: Zurndorff).

—— (1927) *The Astrological Works of Abraham Ibn Ezra: A Literary and Linguistic Study with special Reference to the old French Translation of Hagin*, edited and translated by R. Levy (Baltimore and Paris: Johns Hopkins University Press).

—— (1931) *Yesod Morah v'Sod Torah*, edited by S. Waxman (Jerusalem: Hokhmat Yisrael).

—— (1939) *The Beginning of Wisdom, an Astrological Treatise by Abraham Ibn Ezra*, edited and translated by F. Cantera (Baltimore: Johns Hopkins University Press).

—— (1976) *Commentary on the Torah*, edited by A. Wieser (Jerusalem: Mossad ha-Rav Kook).

ibn Gabirol, Solomon (1859) *Liqqutim min ha-Sefer Mekor Hayyim*, collected by R. Shem Tov ibn Falaquera and edited by S. Munk (Paris: Franck).

—— (1892) *Avencebrolis Fons Vitae ex Arabico in Latinum translatus ab Iohanne Hispano et Domenico Gundissalino*, edited by C. Bäumker. *Beiträge zur Geschichte der Philosophie des Mittelalters*, 1.2–4 (Münster: Aschendorf).

—— (1902) *The Improvement of Moral Qualities*, translated by S. Wise (New York: Columbia University Press).

—— (1926) *Mekor Hayyim*, translated by J. Blübstein (Tel Aviv: Mossad ha-Rav Kook).

—— (1961) *The Kingly Crown*, translated by B. Lewis (London: Vallentine, Mitchell).

—— (1967) *Tikkun Middot ha-Nefesh* (Jerusalem: Mossad ha-Rav Kook).

ibn Paquda, Bachya (1489) *Sefer Hovot ha-Levavot* (Naples).

—— 1970 (repr. 1986) *Duties of the Heart*, edited and translated by M. Hyamson, 2 vols. (Jerusalem: Feldheim).

ibn Tzaddik, Joseph ben Jacob (1854) *Ha Olam ha-Qatan*, edited by A. Jellinck (Leipzig: Fishel).

—— (1903) *Sefer ha-Olam ha-Qatan*, edited by S. Horovitz (Breslau: Shatzky) (repr. Jerusalem).

—— (1954) *The Microcosm*, translated with notes and introduction by J. Haberman. Ph.D. dissertation, Columbia University.

Israeli, Isaac (1900) *Sefer ha-Yesodot*, edited by S. Fried (Drohobycz: Zupnik).

Leone Ebreo (1924) *Dialoghi d'Amore, poesie hebraiche*, ristampati con introduzione di C. Gebhardt (Heidelberg: Winter; London: Oxford University Press).

Plotinus (1951) *Opera*, edited by P. Henry and H. R. Schwyzer (Paris: Desclée de Brower).

—— (1966–88) *Enneads*, translated by A. H. Armstrong, 7 vols. (Cambridge, MA: Harvard University Press) (Loeb Classical Library).

Proclus (1963) *Elements of Theology*, edited and translated by E. R. Dodds (Oxford: Clarendon Press).

—— (1965) *Alcibiades I*, translated and edited by W. O'Neill (The Hague: Nijhoff).

pseudo-Bachya (1896) *Sefer Torat ha-Nefesh*, edited by D. Broyde (Paris: Levinsohn-Kilemnik).

Studies

Altmann, A. (1956) "Isaac Israeli's Chapter on the Elements," *Journal of Jewish Studies* 7: 31–57.

—— (1958) "Problems of Research in Jewish Neoplatonism," *Tarbitz* 27: 501–7.

—— (1972) "Isaac Israeli," in *Encyclopedia Judaica* (Jerusalem: Keter), 9: 1063–5.

—— (1981) "Creation and Emanation in Isaac Israeli, a Reappraisal," in *Essays in Jewish Intellectual History*, edited by A. Altmann (Hanover: University Press of New England), pp. 1–15.

Altmann, A. and S. M. Stern (1958) *Isaac Israeli: A Neoplatonic Philosopher of the Early Tenth Century* (Oxford: Clarendon).

Armstrong, A. H. (1967a) *The Architecture of the Intelligible Universe in the Philosophy of Plotinus* (Amsterdam: Hakkert).

—— (1967b) *The Cambridge History of Later Greek and Early Medieval Philosophy* (London: Cambridge University Press).

Baneth, D. H. (1980) "Jehuda Hallewi und Gazali," in *Jewish Neoplatonism*, edited by S. T. Katz (New York: Arno).

Blau, J. (1974) "On the Supposedly Aristotelian Character of Ibn Gabirol's *Keter Malkhut*," in *Salo Baron Jubilee Volume*, edited by S. Lieberman and A. Hyman (Jerusalem: American Academy for Jewish Research), 1: 219–28.

Blumenthal, H. J. (1981) "Plotinus in Later Platonism," in *Neoplatonism and Early Christian Thought: Essays in Honour of A. H. Armstrong*, edited by H. J. Blumenthal and R. A. Markus (London: Variorum), pp. 212–22.

Bréhier, E. (1958) *The Philosophy of Plotinus*, translated by J. Thomas (Chicago: University of Chicago Press).

Brunner, F. (1952) "Sur le *Fons Vitae* d'Avicebron (Ibn Gabirol), Livre III," *Studia Philosophica* 12: 171–83.

—— (1965) *Platonisme et aristotelisme – la critique d'Ibn Gabirol par St. Thomas d'Aquin* (Louvain: Beatrice-Nauwelaerts).

—— (1969) "Sur la philosophie d'Ibn Gabirol," *Revue des Études Juives* 128: 317–37.

—— (1980a) "La Doctrine de la Matière chez Avicebron," in *Jewish Neoplatonism*, edited by S. T. Katz (New York: Arno).

—— (1980b) "Sur l'Hylémorphisme d'Ibn Gabirol," in *Jewish Neoplatonism*, edited by S. T. Katz (New York: Arno).

Cantarino, V. (1967) "Ibn Gabirol's Metaphysic of Light," *Studia Islamica* 26: 49–71.

Davidson, H. (1987) *Proofs for Eternity, Creation and the Existence of God in Medieval Islamic and Jewish Philosophy* (New York: Oxford University Press).

Dethier, H. (1992) "Love and Intellect in Leone Ebreo: The Joys and Pains of Human Passion," in *Neoplatonism and Jewish Thought*, edited by L. E. Goodman (Albany: State University of New York Press), pp. 353–386.

Dillon, J. (1977) *The Middle Platonists* (London: Duckworth).

—— (1992) "Solomon ibn Gabirol's Doctrine of Intelligible Matter," in *Neoplatonism in Jewish Thought*, edited by L. E. Goodman (Albany: State University of New York Press), pp. 43–59.

Efros, I. (1926 and 1929) "Studies in Pre-Tibbonian Philosophical Terminology," *Jewish Quarterly Review* 17: 129–64, 323–68; 20: 113–31.

Eisenberg, Y. (1981) "Reason and Emotion in 'Duties of the Heart'," *Da'at* 7: 5–35.

Feldman, S. (1992) "Platonic Themes in Gersonides' Doctrine of the Active Intellect," in *Neoplatonism and Jewish Thought*, edited by L. E. Goodman (Albany: State University of New York Press), pp. 255–77.

Fenton, P. (1976) "Gleanings from Moses ibn Ezra's *Maqalat al-Ḥadiqa*," *Sefarad* 36: 285–98.

—— (1992) "Shem Tov ibn Falaquera and the Theology of Aristotle," *Da'at* 29: 27–39.

Fleischer, E. (1990) *The Proverbs of Sa'id ben Babshad* [Hebrew], (Jerusalem: Ben Tzvi Institute).

Friedländer, M. (1964) *Essays on the Writing of Abraham ibn Ezra* (London: Trubner).

Gil, C. R. (1980a) "Bahya ibn Paquda: El puro Amor Divino," in *Medieval Jewish Philosophy*, edited by S. T. Katz (New York: Arno).

—— (1980b) "La Demostracion de la existencia divina en Bahya ibn Paquda," in *Medieval Jewish Philosophy*, edited by S. T. Katz (New York: Arno).

—— (1980c) "La Patria de Bahya Ibn Paquda," in *Medieval Jewish Philosophy*, edited by S. T. Katz (New York: Arno).

Goldziher, I. (1906) "Mélanges judéo-arabes," *Revue des Études Juives* 52: 187–90.

—— (1980) "Mélanges Judéo-Arabes: Le Amr Ilâhi (hâ–inyân hâ–élôhi) chez Juda Halévi," in *Jewish Neoplatonism*, edited by S. T. Katz (New York: Arno).

Goodman, L. E. (ed.) (1992) *Neoplatonism and Jewish Thought* (Albany: State University of New York Press).

Greive, H. (1973) *Studien zum jüdischen Neoplatonismus: Die Religionsphilosophie des Abraham ibn Ezra*, Studia Judaica 7 (Berlin and New York: de Gruyter).

Guttmann, J. (1903) "Über Abraham bar Cijjas 'Buch der Enthüllung'," *Monatsschrift für Geschichte und Wissenschaft des Judentums* 47: 446–68, 545–69.

—— (1956) *Dat U-Maddah* (Jerusalem: Magnes).

—— (1964) *Philosophies of Judaism*, translated by D. Silverman (New York: Holt, Rinehart & Winston).

Harris, R. B. (1992) "Preface," in *Neoplatonism and Jewish Thought*, edited by L. E. Goodman (Albany: State University of New York Press), pp. ix–xiii.

Heschel, A. J. (1980a) "Das Wesen der Dinge nach der Lehre Gabirols," in *Jewish Neoplatonism*, edited by S. T. Katz (New York: Arno).

—— (1980b) "Der Begriff des Seins in der Philosophie Gabirols," in *Jewish Neoplatonism*, edited by S. T. Katz (New York: Arno).

—— (1980c) "Der Begriff der Einheit in der Philosophie Gabirols," in *Jewish Neoplatonism*, edited by S. T. Katz (New York: Arno).

Husik, I. (1946) *A History of Mediaeval Jewish Philosophy* (Philadelphia: Jewish Publication Society).

Hyman, A. (1992) "From What is One and Simple only What is One and Simple Can Come to Be," in *Neoplatonism and Jewish Thought*, edited by L. E. Goodman (Albany: State University of New York Press), pp. 111–35.

Idel, M. (1992) "Jewish Kabbalah and Platonism in the Middle Ages and Renaissance," in *Neoplatonism and Jewish Thought*, edited by L. E. Goodman (Albany: State University of New York Press), pp. 319–52.

Inge, W. R. (1929) *The Philosophy of Plotinus* (The Gifford Lectures at St. Andrews, 1917–1918) [3rd ed.] (London: Longman, Green).

Ivry, A. L. (1992) "Maimonides and Neoplatonism: Challenge and Response," in *Neoplatonism and Jewish Thought*, edited by L. E. Goodman (Albany: State University of New York Press), pp. 137–56.

Katz, S. T. (ed.) (1980a) *Jewish Neoplatonism* (New York: Arno).

—— (ed.) (1980b) *Medieval Jewish Philosophy* (New York: Arno).

—— (1992) "Utterance and Ineffability in Jewish Neoplatonism," in *Neoplatonism and Jewish Thought*, edited by L. E. Goodman (Albany: State University of New York Press), pp. 279–98.

Kaufmann, D. (1877) *Geschichte der Attributenlehre in der Jüdischen Religionsphilosophie des Mittelalters von Saadja bis Maimuni* (Gotha: Perthes).

—— (1899) *Studien über Salomon ibn Gabirol* (Budapest: Gregg).

—— (1962) "The Pseudo-Empedocles as a Source of Salomon Ibn Gabirol," *Mehqarim be-sifrut ha'ivrit shel yemei ha-binayim*, edited by D. Kaufmann (Jerusalem: Mossad ha-Rav Kook), pp. 78–165.

Kokowzoff, P. (1980) "The Date of Life of Bahya ibn Paqoda," in *Medieval Jewish Philosophy*, edited by S. T. Katz (New York: Arno).

Kreisel, H. (1990) "The Place of Man in the Hierarchy of Existence in the Philosophy of Ibn Gabirol and Maimonides" [Hebrew], in *Alei Shefer: Studies in the Literature of Jewish Thought*, edited by M. Hallamish (Ramat Gan: Bar Ilan University Press) pp. 95–108.

—— (1994) "On the Term *Kol* in Abraham Ibn Ezra: A Reappraisal," *Revue des Études Juives* 153: 29–66.

Lazaroff, A. (1970) "Bahya's Asceticism against its Rabbinic and Islamic Background," *Journal of Jewish Studies* 21: 11–38.

Levin, I. (1992) " 'He'achezi Be'sullam Hokhma' ['Hold to the Ladder of Wisdom']"

[Hebrew], in *Studies in the Works of Abraham ibn Ezra*, edited by I. Levin (Tel Aviv), pp. 41–86.

Liebes, Y. (1987) "Rabbi Solomon ibn Gabirol's Use of the *Sefer Yetzira* and a Commentary on the Poem 'I Love Thee'" [Hebrew], in *The Beginnings of Jewish Mysticism in Medieval Europe* [= *Jerusalem Studies in Jewish Thought* 6], edited by J. Dan (Jerusalem), pp. 73–123.

Lipchitz, A. (1979) "The Theory of Creation of Rabbi Abraham ibn Ezra," *Sinaï* 84: 105–25.

Loewe, R. (1967) "Ibn Gabirol's Treatment of Sources in the *Keter Malkhut*," in *Jewish Medieval and Renaissance Studies*, edited by A. Altmann (Cambridge, MA: Harvard University Press), pp. 183–94.

McGinn, B. (1992) "Ibn Gabirol: The Sage among the Schoolmen," in *Neoplatonism and Jewish Thought*, edited by L. E. Goodman (Albany: State University of New York Press), pp. 77–109.

Mathis, C. K. (1992) "Parallel Structures in the Metaphysics of Iamblichus and Ibn Gabirol," in *Neoplatonism and Jewish Thought*, edited by L. E. Goodman, (Albany: State University of New York Press), pp. 61–76.

Merlan, P. (1953) *From Platonism to Neoplatonism* (The Hague: Nijhoff).

Morewedge, P. (ed.) (1992) *Neoplatonism and Islamic Thought*, Studies in Neoplatonism: Ancient and Modern 5 (Albany: State University of New York Press).

Munk, S. (1859) *Mélanges de philosophie juive et arabe* (Paris: Franck).

Netton, I. R. (1982) *Muslim Neoplatonists: An Introduction to the Thought of the Brethren of Purity* (London: Allen & Unwin).

Orschansky, G. (1900) *Abraham ibn Ezra als Philosoph* (Breslau: Schatzky).

Pines, S. (1948) "Sefer arugat ha-bosem, haqetaïm, mi-tokh Sefer Meqor Hayyim," *Tarbitz* 27: 218–33.

—— (1954) "La Longue Récension de la théologie d'Aristote dans ses rapports avec la doctrine ismaélienne," *Revue des Études Islamiques* 22: 7–20.

—— (1964) *Toldot ha-Filosofia ha-Yehudit, me-Philon ad ha-Rambam* (Jerusalem: Hebrew University).

—— (1980a) " 'And He called out to nothingness and it was split:' A Note on a Passage in ibn Gabirol's *Keter Malkhut*," *Tarbitz Anniversary Volume* 3: 183–94.

—— (1980b) "Shī'ite Terms and Conceptions in Judah Halevi's *Kuzari*," *Jerusalem Studies in Arabic and Islam* 2: 165–251.

Plessner, M. (1973) "The Meaning of Kitāb Ma'ānī al-nafs . . . ," *Kiryat Sefer* 48: 491–8.

Rist, J. M. (1962) "The Indefinite Dyad and Intelligible Matter in Plotinus," *Classical Quarterly* 12: 99–107.

—— (1964) *Eros and Psyche: Studies in Plato, Plotinus and Origen* (Toronto: University of Toronto Press).

—— (1967) *Plotinus: The Road to Reality* (Cambridge: Cambridge University Press).

—— (1981) "Plotinus on Matter and Evil," *Phronesis* 6: 154–66.

Rosin, D. (1890) "Die Zahlensymbolik des Abraham ibn Ezra," in *Jubelschrift für Israel Hildesheimer* (Berlin: Engel), pp. 99–106.

—— (1891) "The Ethics of Solomon ibn Gabirol," *Jewish Quarterly Review* 3: 159–81.

—— (1898–9) "Die Religionsphilosophie Abraham ibn Ezra," *Monatsschrift für*

Geschichte und Wissenschaft des Judentums 42: 17–33, 58–73, 108–15, 154–61, 200–14, 241–52, 305–15, 345–62, 394–407, 444–52; 43: 22–31, 75–91, 125–33, 168–84, 231–240.

Rudavsky, T. (1978) "Conflicting Motifs in ibn Gabirol's Discussion of Matter and Evil," *The New Scholasticism* 52: 54–71.

Schlanger, J. (1968) *La Philosophie de Salomon ibn Gabirol: Étude d'un néoplatonisme* (Leiden: Brill).

Scholem, G. (1931) "Reste neuplatonischer Spekulation in der Mystik der deutschen Chassidim und ihre Vermittlung durch Abraham bar Chijja," *Monatsschrift für Geschichte und Wissenschaft des Judentums* 75: 172–91.

—— (1980) "Reste neuplatonischer Spekulation in der Mystik der deutschen Chassidim und ihre Vermittlung durch Abraham bar Chijja," in *Jewish Neoplatonism*, edited by S. T. Katz (New York: Arno).

Simon, H. (1978) "Lost Treatises of Ibn Gabirol?" *Proceedings of the Second International Conference on Studies on Cultures of the Western Mediterranean*, pp. 264–8.

Sirat, C. (1985) *A History of Jewish Philosophy in the Middle Ages* (Cambridge: Cambridge University Press).

Sister, M. (1980a) "Bachja-Studien (Bahya Studies)," in *Medieval Jewish Philosophy*, edited by S. T. Katz (New York: Arno).

—— (1980b) "Einige Bemerkungen über Bachjas Stil im *Kitab al-Hidaja 'Illa Fara'id al-Qulub* und dessen Übersetzung durch J. ibn Tibbon," in *Medieval Jewish Philosophy*, edited by S. T. Katz (New York: Arno).

Stern, S. M. (1956) "Isaac Israeli and Moses Ibn Ezra," *Journal of Jewish Studies* 7: 83–9.

—— (1961) "*Ibn Ḥasdāy's Neoplatonist* – A Neoplatonic Treatise and its Influence on Isaac Israeli and the Longer Version of the *Theology of Aristotle*," *Oriens* 13–14: 58–120.

Stitskin, L. D. (1961) *Judaism as a Philosophy: The Philosophy of Abraham bar Hiyya* (New York: Bloch).

Sweeney, L. (1983) "Are Plotinus and Albertus Magnus Neoplatonists?" in *Graceful Reason: Essays in Ancient and Medieval Philosophy Presented to Joseph Owens, CSSR*, edited by L. P. Gerson (Toronto: Pontifical Institute of Medieval Studies), pp. 177–202.

Taylor, R. C. (1992) "A Critical Analysis of the Structure of the *Kalām fī mahd al-Khaïr (Liber de Causis)*," in *Neoplatonism and Islamic Thought*, edited by P. Morewedge (Albany: State University of New York Press), pp 11–31.

Vajda, G. (1937) "Le Dialogue de l'âme et de la raison dans les *Devoirs des Coeurs* de Bahya ibn Paquda," *Revue des Études Juives* 102: 93–104.

—— (1938) "Abraham Bar Hiyya et al-Farabi," *Revue des Études Juives* 104: 113–19.

—— (1939) "Quelques notes sur le commentaire kairouanais du Sefer Yesira," *Revue des Études Juives* 105: 132–40.

—— (1946) "Les Idées théologiques et philosophiques d'Abraham bar Hiyya," *Archives d'Histoire Doctrinale et Littéraire du Moyen Age* 15: 191–223.

—— (1947a) *Introduction à la pensée juive du moyen âge* (Paris: Vrin).

—— (1947b) *La Théologie ascetique de Bahya ibn Paquda* (Paris: Cahiers de la Société Asiatique).

—— (1949) "La Philosophie et la théologie de Joseph ibn Zaddiq," *Archives d'Histoire Doctrinale et Littéraire du Moyen Age* 24: 93–181.

—— (1957) *L'Amour de Dieu dans la théologie juive du moyen âge* (Paris: Vrin).

—— (1961) "Notes sur divers manuscrits hébraïques," *Revue des Études Juives* 119: 159–61.

—— (1962) "Le système des sciences exposé par Abraham Bar Hiyya et une page de Juda ben Barzilai," *Sefarad* 22: 60–8.

—— (1971) "Le Néoplatonisme dans la pensée juive du moyen âge," *Atti della Accademia Nazionale dei Lincei 368* 26 (8 séries): 309–24.

—— (1972) "Bachya ibn Paquda," in *Encyclopedia Judaica* (Jerusalem: Keter), 4: 105–8.

Wallis, R. T. (1972) *Neoplatonism* (New York: Scribner).

Weinsberg, L. (1980) "Der Mikrokosmos: Ein Angeblich im 12. Jahrhundert von dem Cordubenser Josef ibn Zaddik verfasstes philosophisches System," in *Jewish Neoplatonism*, edited by S. T. Katz (New York: Arno).

Whittaker, T. (1961) *The Neoplatonists: A Study in the History of Hellenism* (Hildesheim: Olms).

Wijnhoven, J. H. A. (1965) "The Mysticism of Solomon Ibn Gabirol," *Journal of Religion* 45: 137–52.

Wittmann, M. (1980) "Die Stellung des Hl. Thomas von Aquin zu Avencebrol (ibn Gabirol)," in *Jewish Neoplatonism*, edited by S. T. Katz (New York: Arno).

Wolfson, E. (1990) "God, the Demiurge and the Intellect: On the Usage of the Word *Kol* in Abraham Ibn Ezra," *Revue des Études Juives* 149: 77–111.

Wolfson, H. A. (1959a) "The Meaning of Ex Nihilo in Isaac Israeli," *Jewish Quarterly Review* 50: 1–12.

—— (1959b) *The Philosophy of Spinoza*, 2 vols. (New York: Schocken).

—— (1961) "Notes on Isaac Israeli's Internal Senses," *Jewish Quarterly Review* 51: 275–87.

—— (1965) "Joseph ibn Saddik on Divine Attributes," *Jewish Quarterly Review* 55: 277–98.

CHAPTER 9

Judah Halevi
Lenn E. Goodman

Born around 1075 into a cultured Jewish family of Muslim Toledo,[1] capital of the ancient Visigothic kingdom, a home to Spanish Jews since Roman times, Judah Halevi was broadly educated in Arabic as well as Hebrew letters and sciences. Jews had lived and struggled under Islam from its inception, often at great human and communal cost, but also with cultural profit, as participants and beneficiaries in the intellectual progress that accompanied the elaboration of Islam from the horizon-sweeping faith of a small tribal society into the religion that would goad and shape an immense cosmopolitan civilization. Classics of Jewish thought like Saadia's biblical commentary, his *Book of Critically Chosen Beliefs and Convictions* and ibn Gabirol's *Fons Vitae* and *On the Improvement of the Moral Qualities* had been written in Arabic. Philosophy, medicine, mathematics, and astronomy were studied in Arabic texts and Arabic translations of the ancient Greek classics. As if by induction, the brilliant Islamicate culture fostered by the Umayyad dynasty of Cordoba (756–1031) had produced a Mozarab, or arabized, subculture among sophisticated Iberian Christians.

Arabic song and rhetoric were part of the allure. The rhyme and meter of the new Hebrew poetry of Halevi's youth were artfully adapted from the Arabic. Halevi joined in the art. He would become one of the great poets of the Hebrew language, perhaps the greatest since the Psalms, turning the themes and cadences of biblical Hebrew to the rhyme and measure of Arabic prosody. But, like most Andalusian Hebrew poets and like many of their Arab predecessors and Christian successors in the Middle Ages, he was a critical and somewhat ambivalent secular artist.[2] He criticized the very practice that underwrote his art and grumbled not just at the achievements of others but, more tellingly, at his own.[3]

Where the pre-Islamic ode or *qaṣīdah* traditionally opened with the reminiscence of lost love, brought to mind by the sight of an abandoned tribal encampment, and then shifted to boastful celebration of the poet's manliness, his horse, his battle days or hunts, and reflections on his fate, Halevi transformed the ruined campsite into the ruins of the Temple in Jerusalem, elevating the *qaṣīdah*'s elegiac tones to a loftier use. In medicine, as in poetry, he took part with learning and vigor. But he also found the received medical tradition somehow wanting, both technically and spiritually.[4] In philosophy, which he understood profoundly and worked at willingly and incisively,[5] he again found grave limitations in the dominant tradition and deep rifts between the ideals of theory and sadly disappointing practice.

At the time of Halevi's birth, Alfonso VI of Castile was doing battle for Iberia against the Muslim states that succeeded the Umayyad hegemony. He captured Toledo in 1085 and levied tribute from many Muslim princes. Drawn by the rich cultural resources of Islamic Spain and unexcited by the possibilities open in the Christian North, the young Halevi was sent south to Andalusia, to study in Lucena, at the academy of Isaac Alfasi (1013–1103), whose elegy he would later write. Like many a student, he found pleasures in al-Andalus beyond the law books. Of his eight hundred surviving poems, some eighty speak of love of a gazelle, celebrating the pleasures and pains of courtship or offered as epithalamia for friends. Some of Halevi's poems are witty jeux d'esprit. Others tell of wine, or gardens, friendship, and, in time, the death of friends. Still others speak of spiritual quest, devotion, and the joyous love of God.[6]

Nearly half of Halevi's poetic works are *piyyutim*, liturgical meditations, many mourning the exile of Israel. Few medieval Jews took the fact of exile as a mere abstraction. But in the dialectic of Halevi's poetic disputations, exile becomes more than a tragic fact. It will loom in his consciousness, darken, intensify, and activate his vision, and block his natural sense of delight, as the poet comes to see that exile will forever frustrate his love of life and that of his people, until somehow it is brought to an end.

Like many of his contemporaries, Halevi was more in search of fame than fortune. In a letter written in highly decorous and decorated rhymed prose, humbly addressed to Moses ibn Ezra (c. 1055 – c. 1138), himself an alumnus of Lucena but already a well-established poet, talmudist, and scholar of Greek philosophy, who, like ibn Gabirol, had pioneered the use of Arabic rhyme and meter in Hebrew, Halevi paints a vivid picture of a small triumph of his own that he says took place at Cordoba soon after his arrival in al-Andalus. At a gathering of poets, as Halevi tells the story, he was pressed to compete in producing a worthy imitation of a Hebrew poem based on an Arabic love song in the popular *muwashshaḥ* form. At first modestly declining, rather like the bashful-seeming youth in al-Hamadhānī's "Poesy Encounter,"[7] Halevi improvised a brilliant poem, which he subjoins for the senior poet's approval. Moses ibn Ezra responded to this performance, whether literal or imagined, by hailing the young Halevi in a poem of his own, welcoming him into his friendship and the literary circles of Granada.

The seeming security of Andalusian Jewry was shattered by the invasion of the Almoravids. This militant Islamic dynasty, the leaders of an Islamic revival and protest movement, was invited into Iberia by the romantic but ill-starred al-Mu'tamid, the 'Abbāsid ruler of Seville and Cordoba, in a fatal attempt to protect his realm from Alfonso and his sometime paladin El Cid, the freebooter Rodrigo Diaz de Bivar. The Almoravids (*al-Murābiṭūn*) had arisen among the Berbers of North Africa and had nurtured a sense of grievance and a bitter demand for theocratic power while exiled in a fortress abbey (*ribāṭ*) in upper Senegal. Spreading through the Sudan and building a power base in Morocco, centered in their newly founded capital of Marrakesh, they conquered southern Spain between 1086 and 1110.

Granada, long a Jewish settlement in the foothills of the Sierra Nevada, was built up as a citadel overseeing the fertile plain below by the Zīrids, also a Berber dynasty from North Africa. It had been defended by the celebrated Jewish *wazīr* Samuel ibn Naghrela (d. 1056, known as Shmuel ha-Nagid, himself a poetic as well as a political and military virtuoso) and his son Joseph (d. 1066). In 1090 the city fell to the Almoravid invaders. Ibn Ezra's brothers went into exile. But Moses stayed on after the sack of Granada, only later leaving behind its beloved gardens for forty years of wanderings and hardships. Halevi's elegy to their friendship transposed his grief at their parting into the counsel not to try to spar with time or fate: was not every union only for the sake of parting? How would the earth have been settled, had not the sons of men parted long ago?[8] Yet Halevi was whistling in the dark when he tried to cheer up his mentor with a humorous midrashic overlay on his counsels of Stoic acceptance. There was little choice but brave acceptance, if one was not to succumb to weeping. Ibn Ezra would never return to the city where once, as he put it, his friends had awaited his words like dew. In time he would make a virtue of isolation, as his poetry grew more spiritual. But his writings never renounced the slender thread of poetry that had once sustained the world he had loved and now was all that remained of it.

Halevi's words of comfort touched himself as well as his friend. For he too was set adrift, travelling from one city to the next, not in desperate need but reliant on contacts like Joseph ibn Migash in Lucena or the *wazīr* Meir ibn Kamniel in Seville. Among his closest friends in his years of wandering was his younger contemporary Abraham ibn Ezra (c. 1089/92–1164/7), the brilliant but impoverished poet, exegete, grammarian, astronomer, mathematician, and champion of rational mysticism. Halevi roamed with his friend as far as North Africa and clearly talked with him about everything. Ibn Ezra's philosophical work is deeply influenced by ibn Gabirol's; his pithy and witty Bible commentaries often cite Halevi. A champion of the close reading of the Bible for its plain sense, he complained of Saadia's penchant for reading external ideas into the text. Those who desired secular knowledge, he urged, should learn it first hand, from the sources. These attitudes may reflect Halevi's as well. For he used and valued the science and the methods of Greco-Arabic philosophy, but objected to its naive imposition as a censor or a sieve to the ideas and practices of his ancestral tradition.

Returning to Toledo, Halevi married and established a thriving and demanding medical practice. His patron at the court, the powerful Jewish *wazīr* Joseph ibn Ferrizuel, known as Cidellus, was Alfonso's physician. Halevi's poetry praised him as a bulwark of the Jews scattered between the hammer of the Reconquista and anvil of the Almoravid invasion. Yet, although Toledo was a refuge, it no longer seemed a home. In his poetry Halevi called Andalusia the East and Christian Spain the West.[9] But in time his poetic geography would locate the East further off, in the land of Israel, and his longing for it, fusing spiritual yearning and estrangement with a powerful sense of place and particularity, would become the great theme of his life as well as his art. Beside it, even medicine seemed a vanity; the Christian rulers of northern Spain, inhuman taskmasters; the Jews, their ministering slaves: "we heal Babel, but it will not be healed."[10] When Joseph's nephew Solomon ibn Ferrizuel, a diplomat in the service of the King, was murdered by Christian mercenaries en route home from a mission to Aragon in 1108, Halevi poured out his heart in anger and grief.

Leaving Castile for the South, the scene of his first triumphs and the heartland of what already seemed a lost Golden Age, Halevi settled in Cordoba with his wife and their one beloved daughter. But in his poetry he pined for a more distant homeland, which he had never known. Traversing Spain he had seen the streams of Jewish refugees who fled the Almoravids and the Christian plundering and destruction of whole Jewish towns. He knew of the danger and destruction visited upon his fellow Jews beyond Spain, as the spirit of the Reconquista, of the Almoravid response, and of the First Crusade, preached by Pope Urban II in 1095, took hold. "How can I savor my food, how find it sweet? ... when Zion is in Christian chains, and I in the shackle of Islam?"[11]

Baer, who wrote his history during the Holocaust, frankly lays out the parallels between the destruction his generation witnessed and that seen by Halevi. Halevi's vision of devastation, "tender maidens exiled from their homes, from soft beds and gentle havens, scattered among a people devoid of understanding, babbling in strange tongues," made him in Baer's words "the seer of a decisive period in history – a prophet for his contemporaries and for the coming generations."[12] The burden of the prophecy that historians like Baer and Baron see in Halevi's vision was the untenability of Jewish life in Iberia and in the diaspora at large, where the Jewish populace lay at the mercy of Christian mobs and Muslim armies, dependent for a fragile moment on the favor that a few brilliant courtier-physicians could win from a monarch often himself dangerously alien to his own subjects.[13] The vision was no dark similitude but the smoldering scene of a medieval Guernica that broad daylight laid out before the poet's eyes:

> Between the hosts of Seir and Kedar
> My host is lost.
> They wage their wars, and when they fall we fall . . . .
> This time the angel, razing houses, did not
> Pass over the homes of Israel's sons.
> From God the decree came forth
> To destroy a metropolis of Israel . . . .
> And on the day the city was taken,
> Vengeance was wreaked upon Israel by the sons of Seir,
> And their streets were filled with the slain.
> Philistines retreat and Edomites plunder,
> Some in cars and some on horse . . .
> The foes do battle like savage beasts,
> The princes of Eliphaz
> Against the Chieftains of Nebaioth—
> In terror between them, the young lambs.[14]

Kedar and Nebaioth here are the Muslim Arabs; the Philistines are the Berber Almoravids; Seir, Eliphaz, and Edom, the Christians, taking vengeance on the Jews for their presumed betrayal of the city to the siege. It was this vision that made Halevi a proto-Zionist, this vision capping countless earlier experiences – the boundless joy of the chance to repair the old Toledo synagogue, when the asperities and enthusiasms of the Reconquista had made even so simple a project problematic, or the drafting of letters seeking to ransom a Jewish woman, held captive by a Spanish queen, beseeching her temporary release on bond, so that she might celebrate the Jewish festivals and Sabbaths, while her fee was gathered, the third part of a hundred gold dinars.[15]

Halevi moved between Christian and Muslim Spain, not so much freely as dependently on the Jewish courtiers whose learning and admiration for his poetic and medical skills seemed always able to offer him safe passage and a warm haven. Like many a prosperous physician, he invested in business ventures. Some of his correspondence survives in the Cairo Geniza, including letters to and from the merchant Chalfon ben Netanel, a kinsman of Halevi's son-in-law and in some ways Halevi's Atticus. Chalfon was based in Egypt but traveled often to Spain and as far away as India, South Arabia, and East Africa.[16] One letter tells of his sending 150 gold pieces to Halevi, perhaps his share in the profits of a voyage. But neither Halevi's relative affluence nor the welcome he won in the increasingly threatened principalities of Iberia allayed his recognition that without independence there was no security for the hard-pressed people of Israel, let alone spiritual growth: "The hand of redeemers is too weak to redeem me.... For the son who but yesterday was a prince is now enslaved, and his abode is in the hands of every foe."[17]

Restless and troubled with what seemed the false position of the Jews of Spain, Halevi was drawn to the spiritual. In one poem he asked himself:

Will you still pursue youth after fifty,
With your days already girded for flight?

His conscience urged him to stop fleeing God's service for the sake of servitude to mere men.[18]

But the spirituality that would hold him was not that of convention. He refused to sublimate his longings or mute them in the common mold.[19] Shalom Spiegel hears tones of triumph in Halevi's liturgical prelude to the call to worship of the *Borchu*. He writes:

The heart of the Jewish service is the *Shema*, the Jew's acceptance of the Kingship of Heaven. It begins with a summons to the worshippers: "Bless ye (*bareku*) the Lord!" It is here, before the call is sounded, that the medieval poet asks "leave" (*reshut*) to intersperse the hallowed prayers with his own effort . . . For in the holy tongue, God's name is Truth (Jeremiah 10:10), and in the view of the Rabbis, His seal is truth. These are also the last words of the *Shema*: "I am the Lord your God – Truth . . . . The beginning and the end of the *Shema* set the theme of one of the magnificent preludes by Judah Ha-Levi:

With all my heart, O Truth, with all my might
I love Thee; in transparency or night,
Thy Name is with me; how then walk alone?
He is my Love; how shall I sit alone?
He is my Brightness; what can choke my flame?
While He holds fast my hand, shall I be lame?

> Let folk despise me: they have never known
> My shame for Thy sake is my glorious crown.
> O Source of Life, let my life tell Thy praise,
> My song to Thee be sung in all my days!

> When promptly thereafter the congregation is summoned
> to praise or bless the Lord, the familiar *bareku* of the
> prayer book seems now immeasurably widened in meaning,
> or perhaps restored to its real meaning. For what is
> required cannot be the mere mouthing of pious words, but
> the truth of a whole life given in service to the Truth that
> is God. Given? Gained is the better word, for what speaks
> here is not renunciation, nor even resentment of the
> world's scorn and hate, but the glad surrender of the failing
> self to the "source of life" wherefrom every breath is
> borrowed and all our strength supplied.[20]

But in the same poem, a more recent reader catches hints of a more minor key. Raymond Scheindlin renders:

> With all my heart – O truth – and all my might
> I love You, with my limbs and with my mind
> Your name is with me: Can I walk alone?
> With it for lover, how can I be lorn?
> With it for lamp, how can my light go dim?
> How can I slip with it the stick
> By which I stand?

> They mock who do not understand: The shame
> I bear because I bear Your name is pride to me.

> Source of my life, I bless You while I live;
> My Song, I sing to You while yet I breathe.

Glossing, Scheindlin writes:

> The "I" is extraordinarily prominent ... the Biblical "heart" and
> "might" are paired chiastically with words meaning literally,
> "my public self ... my inner self." These words reflect such
> terms of Islamic pietistic literature as *ẓāhir* and *bāṭin*, to which
> they are roughly equivalent in meaning. They also recall the
> complementary pair "duties of the limbs" and "duties of
> the heart," characteristic of that literature, the source of both
> theme and title of Baḥya Ibn Paquda's Jewish classic. As a
> commentary on "all your heart ... and all your might," they
> point away from the nation and toward the individual ... The
> speaker declares it as a given that God is with him .... The
> words "Your name is with me" seem to confirm this idea, for

they recall the verse of Psalms (16:8) so beloved of Jewish pietists, "I have set the Lord before me always"; the poet does not say "I set God's name before me," but "God's name *is* before me." The verbal allusion to the verse underscores the difference between the *Shema*, which demands that man take the spiritual initiative, and the poem, with its satisfaction in God's having already taken it.

Yet comparison with the poem's source, the *Shema*, shows that the speaker has also replaced the authoritarian voice of Deuteronomy with a vulnerable one that expresses itself in rhetorical questions. "How can I walk alone" are words one might say to oneself precisely when one *feels* alone. This sense of whistling in the dark is only intensified by the use of pronouns referring not to God Himself but to God's name. The effect is one of distancing: for a moment God is not "You" but "he" or "it."[21]

Halevi's I is the spiritual I of prayer and the lyrical I of the poet. It is also the predecessor of the Renaissance I, quizzical, skeptical, half-alienated but groping and grasping for solidity. And it is the I of the physician and the statesman, who hold that understanding should bring control and who refuse spiritual consolations for physical sufferings, insistent on a redemption that is visible in the here and now, integrating rather than isolating the spirit and the body, the nation and soul. Can redemption be deferred to a future that recedes indefinitely in time? What would become of the sincerity of the poet who abandoned his people by retreating into the spiritual, questing for the vision of God for himself alone?[22] Israel's need is immediate and present. But redemption has not come. The houses of Israel are not passed over. What is needed is not a spiritual promise alone but a present fact, clear as the revelation that still spoke so lucidly to all Israel out of the past. In wishful calculations Halevi seemed to see the date: 1130, by our common reckoning. But the year passed without his dream's fulfillment. Israel still languished in the West.

The East was clearly more than Zion when Halevi wrote his famous lines, "My heart is in the East, but I am in the farthest West."[23] But how could the East be less than Zion? And how, he asked, could a Jew fill his mouth with lamentations for the lost Jerusalem and prayers for its restoration, yet make no move to travel there? How could a poet give voice to the ancient longings of his people, enshrined in all their prayers, without feeling – and not merely feeling but acting decisively on the demand which the tearful words of those prayers had spoken?[24] Could a poet who sharply felt the hurt and hope voiced by his fellow poets in the past not call upon all who were still moved by the stir of their common language to take up the promise so often repeated in the comforting prophecies those prayers always cited?

Halevi's friends could urge him to reconcile himself to what was, in many ways, a life of comfort. Unlike the masses of his people, he would clearly never be far from princely courts. But, as his vision of the historic situation deepened and darkened, he could answer only that his friends seemed drunk. Casting them in the stock role of the "Reproacher" of Arabic love lyrics, he turned on them for their seeming dismissal of the object of his desire: "How can one be happy in the service of kings, if it is like idolatry in his eyes? Is it good for a pure and honest man to be led about like a captive bird in the hands of children?"[25] It was the tension of such questions that Halevi sought to resolve in his *Kuzari*, an Arabic philosophical dialogue, which Herder once compared to the dialogues of Plato. Its full title is *Kitāb al-Radd wa-'l-Dalīl fī 'l-Dīn al-Dhalīl*, that is, *A Defense and an Argument on behalf of the Abased Religion.*[26]

ᴥ THE *KUZARI* ᴥ

Written between 1130 and 1140, the *Kuzari* takes its setting from a striking episode of Jewish history. King Bulan (reigned 786–809), monarch of the Finno-Ugrian Khazar people of the Volga basin, along with some four thousand of his nobles, had adopted Judaism. His choice was guided in part by geopolitical considerations. The Khazars had conquered the Volga Bulgars and held sway over the Crimea, always under pressure from the Byzantines to the West and the Muslims to the South and East. The king had sought a monotheistic alternative to the pagan faith of his Turkic ancestors, but one that would not compromise his own equipoise between the Muslim and Christian powers that hemmed him in. The Khazar state levied tribute from Eastern Slavs, Bulgars, and Georgians, when it did not actually rule them. It was a major force in trade. Its dominions spread from the northern shores of the Black Sea and the Caspian to the Ural Mountains, and westward as far as Kiev. Khazar military power was of strategic weight all the way to the Oxus and was critical in restraining the Muslim advance into Europe.

The Khazar monarchy maintained religious freedom for its subjects; most, it seems, never became Jews. By the tenth century Khazaria was a Byzantine buffer state. Its power was shaken by Sviatoslav the Duke of Kiev in 965 and broken by Archduke Jaroslav in 1083. But until the Khazars were swept away in the Tatar invasion of 1237, Judaism was the state religion. Chasdai ibn Shaprut, the learned and committed Jewish *wazīr* of the Umayyad caliph 'Abdu'l-Raḥmān III

of Cordoba, thrilled at the reports of a powerful and independent
Jewish state in the East. He wrote to the Khazar monarch around 960,
and after some delay a reply was received from the Khazar King Joseph
telling of the conversion of the Khazars and describing their realm.[27]

The conversion had taken place after a debate among Christian,
Jewish, and Muslim spokesmen. Now Halevi fictively constructed the
conversation that might have led a king to adopt "the abased religion".
In the tale Halevi uses to frame his dialogue, the Khazar king has had
a dream informing him "that his intentions were pleasing to God, but
his practices were not. While he still slept, he was commanded to seek
a way of life pleasing to God." For this reason he asked a philosopher
to expound his convictions.[28] But the response, a recital of the generic
intellectualism of a Neoplatonic Aristotelian, proves disappointing to
the king. The philosopher speaks of God as above favor or displeasure,
above intentions or even knowledge of mutable individuals, let alone
governance of their destinies. "If philosophers say that God created
you, that is metaphorical, of course. For He is the Cause of all the
causes that conspire in the creation of all things – but not in the sense
that this was the outcome intended from the beginning."[29]

The argument of the philosopher runs smoothly, with many
"therefores" and an equally seamless stream of disembodied intellects
and secondary causes, through which God's act, but not his will, spreads
forth upon the world. "God never created man. For the world is
eternal. Human beings have always arisen one from another, their forms
compounded and their characters formed from those of their fathers
and mothers, and their environment – airs, lands, foods, and waters –
along with the influences of the spheres, the constellations, and the
signs of the Zodiac."[30] The human goal is to purify the soul. For
the perfect, at least, may reunite with the nearest of the intellectual
hypostases through which the world is given form, the active intellect,
which the perfect human, in fact, ignoring mere limbs and organs,
already is. Religion is a valued moral conditioner for the people,
especially the ordinary mass of humanity. But once its function is
grasped, it may be molded and fashioned at will.

> "Your argument is impressive," the king said, "but it does not
> meet my needs. I know on my own that my soul is pure. I am
> ready to devote my actions to my Lord's pleasure. But the
> answer I get is that my present actions are not pleasing to Him,
> even though my intentions are. Surely there is some way of life
> that is genuinely acceptable in itself, and not just as a matter
> of opinion. Otherwise, why do the Christian and the Muslim,
> who divide the world between them, constantly do battle with
> one another? Clearly both have sincere intentions, wholly

devoted to God – monastically, ascetically, in fasting and in prayer – earnestly bent on one another's murder in the sincere belief that this is the pathway to paradise and the road to heaven. Yet reason shows that both cannot be right."

The philosopher replied: "In the faith of the Philosophers there is no such killing, since we foster the mind."[31]

The exchange is a telling indictment of academic philosophy and the entire neoplatonizing project that engulfs much of medieval mysticism. The king's irony charges the philosophical school with an implicit relativism: surely, not all sects can be right, when they so diligently set about sacrificing themselves and one another. Yet philosophy seems to wish to stand above the fray, deeming all God-seeking monotheists alike adherents of the truth, regardless of their actions. All are seeking heaven. But, as with Pascal's wager, surely some critical differentiation of the purported paths to heaven is called for before commitments of life and death are made.

The sharp contrast of action with intention in the king's dream marks for criticism not only scholastic philosophers but also spiritualizing pietists like Bachya ibn Paquda, whose *Kitāb al-Hidāya ilā Farā'iḍ al-Qulūb* or *Book of Guidance to the Duties of the Heart* (1080) re-emphasized the moral, intellectual, and intentional aspects of piety, lest ritual observances become a mere empty shell. Extreme but all too real cases of religious zeal and spiritually inspired violence had shown that the highest intentions do not differentiate martyrs from fanatics, the slayers from the slain, acts of heroism from atrocities, noble works of self-denial from obscene follies of scrupulosity or self-destruction. These are matters not merely of intention but of ethos, culture, the customary way of life of an individual or a community. Vivid experience is ample proof of their underdetermination by an abstract ideology.

Halevi's indictment does not spare critics of the Greco-Arabic philosophical tradition like al-Ghazālī, who had called all monotheists, philosophers and non-philosophers alike, adherents of the truth (*muḥaqqiqūn*), at least in their intention. Al-Ghazālī's magisterial *Revival of the Religious Sciences* integrated Sufi mysticism and pietism into the heart of orthodox Islam, and the Muslim theologian's sharp attack on the Islamic philosophical school in *The Incoherence of the Philosophers* is a resource whose arguments Halevi knows well and uses judiciously. But, by the time Halevi wrote, al-Ghazālī's monistic theology, itself grounded in a revised Neoplatonic metaphysics, had already inspired the leaders of the Almohads (*al-Muwaḥḥidūn*, that is Monists, affirmers of God's absolute unity), who would lead a new wave of Berber militants out of North Africa into Spain, finding the Almoravids too soft, too tolerant, too decadent. The Almohad conquest of Andalusia (1145–50) would make the Almoravid invasion pale by comparison. Halevi did not live to witness the event. But he clearly saw and condemned the moral vacuity of a too purely intellectual and spiritual way of thought that somehow seemed as open to the likes of the Almohads as to the most saintly – and that indeed offered no criterion for differentiating one from the other.

Halevi has no quarrel with Bachya's theme that sincerity of intention, spiritually, morally, and intellectually, is necessary to genuine piety. But spirituality alone is insufficient. Not that Halevi hopes simply to redress the balance by re-emphasizing the behavioral side of ritual observance. Piety, he insists, is not a matter of half-closed eyes and devout postures. The rocking motion of the body in prayer stems from the ancient practice of sharing books and has no particular spiritual meaning.[32] What does concern Halevi is *khalāṣ*. *Khalāṣ* might be translated as "sincerity" or "devotion," if we bear in mind that sincerity in the pietist tradition implies not just meaning what one says but dedication to the true ideals, and that devotion is not just a matter of intention but of action.

When Plato sought to make sense of Socrates' paradoxical claim that to know the good is to do the good, he could do so only by enriching and intensifying the idea of knowledge, ultimately to include the rational intuition of the Forms, and to exclude anything less. He had to assume as well that knowledge, as intended by Socrates, was no mere matter of theory but an awareness so intense that no question could arise as to the through-put from thought to action. Socratic knowledge entailed commitment, and commitment entailed performance. It is this weld that Halevi's analytic torch severs when he makes it the gravamen of the Khazar king's dream that God is pleased with his intentions but not with his actions. For intentions do not imply the corresponding actions. To translate intentions into actions, one needs the virtue of *khalāṣ*, engagement. This is the great virtue that Halevi's poetry and philosophy have in common. For in Halevi the dialogue form and the discourse of poetry are not, as they so often are in other writers, devices for establishing aesthetic or intellectual distance. On the contrary, they only increase the directness and intensity of commitment. As Ross Brann writes, Halevi's piety "was neither reflexive nor conventional but lyrical."[33]

Yet commitment must be guided. The right intentions and the best character are not enough. For character must be refined and intentions trained and directed. The deep problem with an intellectualism like that of the Neoplatonists is not that it is merely intellectual but that it is too general, too generic to name an ethos, to differentiate one culture or historic pathway from another. The allied traditions of spirituality and pietism fare no better. Aristotelians may claim to corner rationality; Sufis and their Christian and Jewish counterparts may claim to corner spirituality. But, like our contemporary Alasdair MacIntyre, Halevi has ample reason to ask, "Whose rationality? Which piety?" For all such notions are mere abstractions if they underdetermine the realm of practice, which is perforce a realm of particularity and embeddedness of a kind that philosophy characteristically glosses over in the seeming interest of universality, and that pietism too often takes for granted, whether because it assumes its homilies are cosmopolitan or because it really has not reckoned with the embodiment of an ethos – or, to put the matter still more pointedly, because it has ignored the crucial, delicate, and dangerous nexus between ethos and ethnicity.

Halevi's problem with philosophy is not so much that he thinks it is misguided or incorrect but that he thinks it pays too little mind to history. He will engage skillfully in natural theology and sculpt the overly baroque ontology of his Neoplatonist predecessors with strokes that treat its ontic epicycles as so many cobwebs. But philosophy as an enterprise, as practiced in his time, is problematic for him most deeply not because it is wrong in its conclusions or even in its methods, but because it does not say enough. It leaves the most important issues open, undecided, up for grabs. Thus the pointed reference to the carnage which philosophy so obviously disclaims.

If it is true that some higher gnosis renders the mind proof against what Plotinus called "this blood-drenched life," what value has that for the innocents who are slain? And if actions are needed to give effect to intentions, what point is there in appealing to the sincerity of intentions? Seizing on the manifestly apologetic character of the *Kuzari*, some readers have argued that the basic question Halevi intends to answer, especially in the welter of credal violence that he and his contemporaries face, is "Why remain a Jew?" But this is only the smallest question Halevi raises here, and only the most defensive way of stating what he sets out as a salient against the dominant faiths and as a challenge to the philosophy that prides itself on rising above their particularisms but seems to Halevi to sink to the level of their generic type, the locus of their lowest common denominator.

If Christianity and Islam are no more than poetic presentations of a philosophic ideology that stands aloof and alone above the particularities of their credos, the ethically and philosophically sensitive must ask not only why one metaphor or symbol system is preferable to another, but also how one is to live by a mere symbol system, acknowledged to be no more than that. If one is not to descend into the sheer relativism of simply acknowledging that all (monotheistic) faiths are different avenues to the same end, one must ask whether sincerity, in the formal sense of moral consistency or in the richer classic sense of seeking the highest and noblest, is sufficient. Surely those knights of faith who sacrifice themselves, their limbs and organs, their passions and desires, and their fellow humans on the altar of their divine ideal, whether as monks or as warriors, cannot *all* be right, even when they slay one another in what Islam is pleased to call the Path of God. Here Halevi must ask: can carnage be sincere service of the all-perfect; can the quest for perfection in God bring one to a plateau where the bloodshed, in effect, becomes invisible? To say so is not to choose a way of life but to choose a way *from* life.

The philosopher has not merely failed to choose among rival ways of life. He has provided a generic cosmology, metaphysics, and epistemology that will, in the hands of a Ghazālī or a Bachya, create the illusion that one has somehow left behind the realm where human suffering matters, and that will none the less continue to serve as a philosophic rationale for any number of rival creeds, whose followers will carry on their pillage and destruction, not despite their creeds but in their name, and, as they imagine, on their behalf. Christians and Muslims may believe that they are battling on the road to heaven. And if heaven is their intended destination, all of them kill with only the highest intentions. Yet only half of them, at most, can be right about where the road they fight on leads. At least half must be wrong. And, witnessing the carnage, Halevi cannot help but sense that all of them are wrong, and that the philosophy which proudly claims to know nothing of such slaying is wrong too.

Can it be that God does not care – that the slaughter of innocents goes on unknown to him? If so (we can almost hear Halevi asking himself), what meaning can there be in all ibn Gabirol's subtle glosses that locate the repository of the human immortal souls in the storage space beneath God's throne? What manner of throne is it, if from it God reigns but does not rule? Here we see the sense of Halevi's dramatic irony in allowing the philosopher in the dialogue to explain that God transcends intention or desire and that his pleasure means no more than the union in the active intellect of the philosophic rational soul with those of Hermes, Asclepios, Socrates, Plato, and Aristotle. As Aryeh Motzkin notes, the Jewish spokesman begins his conversation with the Khazar king by saying, "I believe," specifically, "I believe in the God of Abraham." The spokesman for the established philosophical tradition opens with the words, "There is not," specifically, "There is not any pleasure or displeasure in God."[34]

If it is true that philosophers are in intimate contact with so supernal a hypostasis as the active intellect of their description, the king asks, why are so few of them prophets? Why do so few perform miracles? Prophets teach that the world is created. Philosophers deny it. But that puts them on all fours with any doctrinal sect. They too hold views about cosmology, views which they do not sustain empirically. The king's curiosity is piqued about Christians and Muslims: "Surely one of these two ways of life [*'amalayn*] is the pleasing one. For in the case of the Jews, their obvious abasement, small numbers, and universal detestation suffice to show that theirs is not."[35]

The Christian spokesman appeals to the divinity of Christ; the Muslim, to the inimitable language of the Qur'ān. The king's responses tellingly signal Halevi's method and its goal: he advises the Christian that a little philosophy would not hurt his case, which is on the face of it so alien to experience and logic:

> There is no logical inference here. Logic, in fact, would tend to reject most of this account. If experience vouched for it, so that it won the heart's consent, that would be another matter. But unless imagination vouches for an idea, it takes logic to make it plausible. Otherwise it seems farfetched. Thus, when naturalists discover some exotic phenomenon that they would have denied had they heard of it before seeing it, they try to make it credible, since they have seen it, by assigning to it some cause – astral or spiritual. They do not reject firsthand experience.[36]

The king, for his part, does not find himself too well disposed to such an effort. "Not having grown up in these beliefs," he does not feel the need to find a way of making them believable.

The exchange is a telling exposition of Halevi's response to the epistemologies of philosophers like Saadia. He does not miss the opportunity to look askance at the philosophical naturalists' characteristic appeal to ad hoc astrological and spiritual hypotheses. But his epistemological point goes deeper: logic will seek explanations for what is observed, since direct experience compels credence. The heart is the locus of such commitments. But experience, not reason, must be the epistemic anchor point. Firsthand experience can create an existential commitment, winning over the heart. Halevi's words echo those of al-Ghazālī and other pietist authors. Once there is such a commitment, logic will serve belief, constructing a theory to accommodate the evidence. But without such a commitment, logic can just as readily be skeptical. Notice the order of march. First comes experience, not faith. Then comes commitment, grounded in experience. This commitment is what is commonly called faith and what Pascal, who has access to the pietist tradition in which Halevi and al-Ghazālī work, calls "the reasons of the heart." The task of logic is to accommodate the givens that experience presents. Its work is synthetic, not merely analytic or dialectical. But the springs of its motivation lie in the heart, that is, an individual's sense of identity and worth, the grounding for our appraisal and appropriation of the primary givens of experience.

The Muslim speaker takes a different tack. Like Muḥammad, he avoids resting his case on miracles, except for the miraculous Qur'ān, whose every verse Muslims call a portent. Again the Khazar king answers in existential terms, which again betray a hint of disparagement:

> If someone aspires to guidance from God's Word and hopes to be convinced, against his own skepticism, that God does speak to mortals, things ought to be manifest and incontrovertible. Even then one would hardly credit that God spoke to a man. But, if your book is miraculous, being written in Arabic its uniqueness and inimitability are indiscernible to a non-Arab like me. When read to me, it sounds like any other Arabic book.[37]

Both the Christian and the Muslim, however, appeal to Jewish history. For the Christian claims that Jesus came not to destroy but to fulfill the laws of Moses, and the Muslim presents Muḥammad as the seal of the prophets, culminating God's revelation to Israel. So theology gives way to history, and the king must summon a Jew to speak with him after all. The discussion with the Christian and the Muslim has prepared the ground for the line of argument Halevi will use: unabashedly historical and particularistic, not cosmological and universal.

The rabbi, who now appears, and who is consistently described as a *chaver* or fellow of a talmudical academy, does not open with a cosmological credo. His opening reference to God not as the creator but as the God of Abraham, Isaac, and Jacob establishes an intimacy and directness that contrasts sharply with the intellectualism of the philosopher. He does not base his claims on appeals to speculative proofs like the argument from design. For, as he argues, "If you were told that the ruler of India was a virtuous man whom you should hold in awe and whose name you should revere, but his works were described to you in reports of the justice, good character, and fair ways of the people of his land, would that bind you to him?" "How could it?" the king answers, "when the question remains whether the people of India act justly of their own accord and have no king at all, whether they do so on account of their king, or whether both are true."[38] Cosmological arguments do not settle the question whether the order and design of nature are the work of God, as Scripture would have it; or intrinsic to nature, as naturalists like Democritus would have it; or some combination of the two, as in the view of the Neoplatonic Aristotelians, who saw the natural order as imparted by God but resident in the God-given natures of things.

"But if a messenger came to you from that king," the rabbi argues, "with Indic gifts, that you were certain could be had only in India, and only in the palace of a king, and he brought you a written attestation that these came from the king, and enclosed medicines to treat your illnesses and preserve your health . . . would this not bind you to his allegiance?"[39] In the same way, the chaver explains, God was introduced to Pharaoh (Exodus 5:1) not as the cosmic creator but as the ancestral Help of the Hebrews; and to the Israelites assembled at Sinai (Exodus 20:2) not as their creator but as the one who had saved them from Egypt. For what mattered at that moment was not what God had done for the universe but what God had done for them.

Only Israel, the rabbi argues, has a true and continuous tradition regarding the divine. India may be ancient, but its people have no coherent system of ideas, and they are polytheists. Greek philosophy is derivative of ancient Israelite tradition; but, without Israel's tradition to stabilize and orient it, Greek philosophical thinking lacks guidance. As Halevi put it in a late poem to a friend, "Greek wisdom . . . bears no fruit but only flowers." Aristotle and the other leaders of Greek philosophy must be forgiven, for they worked alone; their slips are the understandable result of their lack of sound historical traditions.[40] Greek philosophical originality, then, may be a tour de force, but it shows the unsteady gait of solecism and deracination. Aristotle has nothing to keep him from going overboard, as, for example, when he ascribes intelligence to nature at large.

What distinguishes the religion of Israel, Halevi argues, through the chaver, is its combination of publicity and intimacy: the intimacy of God's unique historical relationship with Israel, the publicity of the entire nation's experience of God's act and receipt of his gifts and their written attestation, passed down through the generations in an undisrupted tradition, so that subsequent generations lose nothing of the certitude that accompanied God's self-revelation to their forebears. The true religion, the rabbi urges, did not evolve over time, as artificial religions do, but, like the creation itself, was completed in a moment, when six hundred thousand Israelites experienced their own redemption, and, after wandering in the desert, heard God's words, each individual directly and personally inspired.[41]

Reacting to the palpable chauvinism (ta'aṣṣub) of the chaver's claims, the king asks if the sin of the Golden Calf does not diminish the rabbi's pride, which he warns borders on the insufferable. But every nation, the chaver replies, was full of idolators at the time. Any philosophers among them who could prove that God was one would still have rationalized pagan worship, finding concrete symbols indispensable in mediating the divine presence to the masses. The Israelites' backsliding was grievous principally because the sin was theirs. True, the people sinned. But they were also forgiven. What matters is that they were chosen. Israel had preserved the pristine perfection of Adam, God's direct work. Even the women of Israel prophesied. The land they were given was perfect in climate and would prepare its inhabitants to live by God's word and will.[42]

Why, the king asks, was God's revelation confined to the Hebrew language, depriving the people of Sind, Khazaria, and India of direct access to it? Why was it not shared with all people? Why not with animals? the rabbi snorts, again at risk of seeming insufferable. Has Halevi forgotten his own arch remarks about the Islamic doctrine of the inimitable beauties of the Qur'ān? The rabbi does not rest the Torah's authority on the claim that its style is divine but on the historicity of its revelation. But if publicity and the ability of any human being to judge a revelation are important standards, as he claimed, why does he suppose that the Torah is somehow more universal in its appeal than the Qur'ān? And does it not seem arbitrary that other nations must rely on Israel for access to the word of God? Beyond the shock therapy that seeks to undo the injuries to Jewish pride wrought by centuries of Christian and Muslim disparagement, it is the need to answer that question that prompts Halevi to press the particularism of the chaver's claims.

Prophecy, the rabbi argues, was God's special gift to Israel, which he promised would never depart from them. Israel's great gift is not the specious reward of a sensuous afterlife, or even a spiritual afterlife, which no one really wants, but the abiding presence of the divine, with them in this life. Philosophers imagine that only supernal intellects are immortal. Muslims and Christians compound such exclusivity with the superstitious notion that a spoken word somehow confers it. But Jews believe that God rewards the righteous of all nations. They are far from exclusivist in their soteriology. Nor are Jews distinguished by a belief in their own uniqueness, or even superiority. Rather, what distinguishes them is the nature of the gift to which they lay claim.

Halevi spells this out more fully later in the dialogue, when the Khazar king asks the rabbi why Jewish prayers say so little of the hereafter. The chaver answers with a characteristic parable:

> A man presented himself to the ruler, who welcomed him lavishly and gave him leave to enter his presence whenever he liked. He grew so close to the monarch that he could invite him to his home and table, and the king would come and send his most distinguished ministers. He treated this man as he treated no one else. When the man was guilty of some omission or infraction and so was barred from the court, the king would only entreat him to return to his former ways, so as to lift the disability. He did not even bar any of his ministers from visiting him.
>
> All the other people of that land called upon the king only

when they were traveling, begging him to send someone along with them on the road, to protect them from brigands, beasts, and other dangers. They were sure that he would help them in this way and look after them on their journey, even though he had never done so before they left. Each used to boast to the others that the king cared for him more than anyone else, reckoning that he had glorified the king more than the rest.

But the stranger rarely spoke of his journey and did not ask for a guard. When the time came for his journey, the people of that land told him he was sure to perish in that treacherous passage, since he had no one to protect him. "Who gave you your protectors?" he asked. They answered, "The king, whose aid and intercession we have been entreating as long as we have been in this city. But we never see you doing so." "Lunatics!" cried the stranger. "Can't one who called on him in time of safety all the more hope for his help in time of danger, even without saying a word? Doesn't one whom he answered in time of comfort have all the more grounds to expect a favorable response in time of need? You all think yourselves entitled to his aid because you make much of him. But which of you has honored him and cleaved to him as I have? Which of you has borne the hardships I have, for the sake of holding fast to his commands, or as faithfully kept his fame unsullied, or as reverently upheld his name and code. All that I have done has been at his command and instruction. You glorify him calculatedly, in your own interest. Yet he has never failed you. How then will he abandon me on my journey, just because I did not bring up the matter as you did but trusted to his justice."[43]

What Halevi is saying here is not just that Israel's intimacy with God and faithful service to his commands are the best assurance of the hereafter. He is also saying that the afterlife is less central to us than the manner of our life in the present. As the Khazar king remarks, no one seems so eager for the hereafter that he would not gladly delay the moment of access to it.[44] What is distinctive in the Jewish idea of the aim of life, sharply distinguishing it from other monotheistic ideals, is its rootedness in this world. We achieve intimacy with God by living a life devoted to his commands. Christian and Muslim expectations, despite, or perhaps because of, their professed otherworldliness, seem to the Khazar rather gross (asman) by comparison. As the rabbi remarks, the rival faiths seem to put off everything until after death, as though there were nothing of the transcendent in this life nor even anything that points toward it.[45]

Convinced that Judaism must be the way of life his dream told him to seek, the king and his *wazīr* embrace Judaism and gradually win over many of their nation. They study the Torah and win great worldly success, honoring the Israelites among their people as the first and most fully Jewish of their countrymen. Only after extensive study of the Torah does the king begin to inquire speculatively into its theology. Halevi's point, of course, is that theology needs the guidance of culture, tradition, and commitment, that the existential is prior to the speculative, a point that the ancient rabbis made by saying that ethics (*derekh eretz*) is prior to Torah and that Maimonides would later make by treating moral virtue as a prerequisite for sound speculation. But many readers, both medieval anti-rationalists and modern Romantics who seek a culture hero in Halevi, neglect the fact that Halevi does intend, in the remaining four parts of his five-part work, to make a positive contribution to natural theology, guided by tradition as he understands it, but not slavishly, unquestioningly, or uninquiringly directed by thoughtless repetition of its unexamined dicta.

The inquiry begins with the vexed question of how we are to talk about God, if God is utterly transcendent. Halevi proposes, through the medium of the dialogue, that God is described, first, in terms of negative attributes, indicative of his perfection, that is, his transcendence of deficiency, as when we say "the living God," to distinguish him from the dead, that is, false gods of idolaters; second, in terms of relative attributes, which express human attitudes toward God, as when we call him "blessed" and "exalted"; and, third, in terms of creative attributes, which speak of his acts in so far as these emanate from him by way of some natural medium or agency, as when we say, "making poor and rich". When Scripture speaks of God's immediate creative agency, it always links the attribution to the tetragrammaton, as when it says, "To Him who alone doeth great wonders" (Psalms 136:4).

The agency of God in nature is his will. It is this that is the motive force behind all natural and supernatural events. God's will is also the source of the created glory that manifests God's grace to Israel in their own land, the favored place for its appearance, at least when it is properly cultivated. When Israel is dwelling on its soil in peace and justice, prophecy becomes possible among the pious. For the pious of Israel are the true bearers of prophecy, just as naturally sound intellects have the potential to become philosophers. All true prophecy took place either in or on behalf of the land of Israel. It is the center of the globe, the reference point of day and night, east and west, the point of origin of the weekly cycle, which has spread from Israel to the nations of the world. The very air of the land imparts wisdom. So the sages were not misled when they said that one who walks four cubits there is assured of happiness in the world to come. For, as Halevi implies, such a person already tastes transcendence in the here and now.

But if so, the Khazar king objects, the rabbi is himself remiss in not returning to that land. For even if the *shekhinah*, God's immanence, is no longer present there, one should surely seek to purify the soul in such a holy place, as people resort to the shrines of holy men, if only because the *shekhinah* once was there. The rabbi accepts the reproach, answering only that Israel's return to its land has always depended on the willingness of the people to return, for "God's Word grants a man no more than he is capable of receiving."[46]

Having addressed attribute theory, God's mode of action, and the cause and cure of Israel's continued exile, the rabbi and his royal pupil consider the sacrificial cult. This was the nominal focus of rabbinic grief when Israel was first exiled. But in the *Kuzari* it becomes quite secondary to the attainment of a life of intimacy with God. God, the chaver argues, does not need sacrifices; he requires no food. But the fires of sacrifice establish an order and dignity, as a king's panoply might do. And the divine inspiration that must nourish the people of Israel depends upon the establishment of that order and dignity. God is to the nation as reason is to the body; and, just as the body is sustained by the food proper to it, so the nation is sustained by the sacrifices. They are not, then, propitiations; still less, an end in themselves, or in any way pleasing to God, except in so far as they prepare his people to receive his word.

Israel today, the rabbi explains, is no longer a body but only dry bones. Yet these bones once had life and still preserve a trace of life, which can return to them, if the Temple which animated them, and made them vulnerable, is restored.[47] Platonists like al-Fārābī make the philosopher the natural recipient of prophecy – since philosophers have the mind and the access to the active intellect that will convey the conceptual content of revelation. They need only the gift of imagination to clothe the relevant concepts in the concretely apprehensible garb of poetry, ritual, and institutions. Working to the same pattern, Halevi makes the pious of Israel the natural prototypes of prophets. He completes the thought by applying to Israelites the same critical apology that Plato used for philosophers: Israel is the heart among the nations, at once the most vital and strong and the most delicate and vulnerable, the most sensitive to corruption – the most sick and the most healthy.[48]

> You have learned that the elements emerged so that minerals
> might arise from them, then plants, then animals, then man,
> and finally the cream of Adam [the Jews]. Thus all evolved for
> the sake of that purest assay, so that the Divine Word might
> touch it; and that assay, for the still further one, such persons
> as prophets and saints.[49]

But prophets and saints, the chaver explains, are not the same as hermits and ascetics. Mere renunciation does not achieve the intimacy with God that makes a nation the true seedbed of prophecy and saintliness. Justice, not humility or spirituality, is the natural, rational, necessary foundation of a nation's life. It can be neither forgotten nor neglected if a nation is to live. Indeed (as Plato taught) even a band of thieves will not survive long without justice among its members. "The divine law cannot be fulfilled until the civil and rational laws are perfected."[50] This means that Israel can no more survive and fulfill God's commandments and their own destiny as a soul without a body than they can as a body without a soul. Not withdrawal and asceticism are demanded but the full life of an economy and a state – of feasts, social interactions, and development – the tithes, fallow years, and the harvest festivals. It is as much a divine commandment to labor and cultivate the soil as it is to keep the Sabbath. For both celebrate God's act of creation and his liberation of Israel from Egypt. And the Sabbath brings us nearer to God, through the love and joy and affirmation it shines into our lives, than does any act of monasticism or self-denial.[51]

Strange as it may seem to the Khazar king and to many since Halevi's time, God can be honored or dishonored by human actions. God, Halevi insists, is glorified by the joyous and fulfilled life of his people no less than by the light of the sun. The comparison is in fact proposed by Psalm 19, when it strikingly parallels the sun's universal influence on nature with the similarly salubrious influence upon Israel of the commandments of the Torah.[52] Piety is not best shown by upturned eyes, fine words, meditative postures and gestures, and talk that intends no action, but by genuine commitment and sincere intentions (al-niyyāt al-khalāṣa), that is, intentions that manifest themselves in demanding actions performed with zeal and dedication.[53]

The good life

What Halevi calls for here is not simply a return to Zion; still less, mere spiritual longing, or the presence in Zion of some merely mystical or contemplative community. He is calling for reconstitution of the full, robust life of Israel in its land, under its laws – political, moral, social, economic, intellectual, and spiritual rebirth. The members of the Sanhedrin, he argues, were responsible for knowledge of every science – veritable, conventional, or fanciful – from botany and zoology to hygiene, medicine, astronomy, and music, the profession of the Levites. They needed the authentic sciences to fulfill the intentions of the law and to look after the health and welfare of the people; the conventional sciences, to perfect their use of language; and the specious sciences, evidently to understand superstitions regarding magic and the like.[54]

These sciences, whose relics still distinguish Jews, must be restored, along with the Hebrew language, which has fallen into a decline since the days of the psalmists, and has become the toy of lackeys and misfits.[55]

Israel's aim, the chaver urges, is not the otherworldliness so common among the spiritually inclined. We love life and all its goods. True, one who reaches moral perfection, as did Enoch or Elijah, will grow uncomfortable in the world and will feel no isolation in solitude. Philosophers, similarly, seek the company of their disciples. For students stimulate the mind, but the common crowd is a distraction. Yet today, when there is no clear vision, the good man (al-khayr) must be the guardian of his country.[56] He must give all his powers their due, preparing them to serve when called on. The king is surprised at so political an answer to a question about personal goodness. "I asked about the good man," he says, "not about a prince." But the rabbi answers that human goodness is political, for Plato's reason, that it rests on command over one's powers: "He who ruleth his spirit is better than one who taketh a city" (Proverbs 16:32). The good man here stands in the place of Plato's philosopher-king as the rightful ruler, who must train his forces, marshal his faculties and await his day: "The good man is the prince, obeyed by his senses, and by his spiritual and physical powers . . . . It is he who is fit to rule. For if he led a state, he would apply the same justice in it as he does in governing his own body and soul."[57]

The good man holds before his eyes the service of the Temple, the epiphany of Sinai, the binding of Isaac, the desert Tabernacle – all the scenes the Torah sets before us, not as icons, mandalas, or sacraments, but as dramatic re-enactments of the great moments in a history of spiritual enlightenment.[58] These scenes, pictured in thought, refresh the good man's soul, purge his mind of doubts, restore the harmony of his powers, and guide him to array his limbs like a soldier standing at attention to hear the orders of his commander. It is in this posture, not prostrate before his God, that he prays. Prayer becomes the fruit of his day, not an onerous charge or a meaningless routine, empty as the chatter of a parrot or a starling, but a nourishment for the soul, taken three times each day, just as nourishment is given to the body.[59]

Civilly, socially, and politically, human rationality regulates the good man's life. But God adds further requirements to refine the life of Israel, rendering specific the generic obligations of reason, and instituting the visible symbolisms without which such notions as that of a covenant between God and all the descendants of Abraham would be mere abstractions. The ritual without the idea is meaningless; but the idea without the enactment is empty.[60] Even kings have not the perfect rest of Israel's Sabbath. But good Israelites, who live in the thought that God is ever-present to them, view the world not as a piece of work that the artisan has finished or abandoned but as an ongoing creation, in which even their own words and the songs that spring from their mouths at God's behest, typically issue forth without the least knowledge on their part of how it is that the God-given powers of the body and creativity of the mind spring to their service.[61]

Prophecy is the fitting outcome of such a life, which regards all good things as God's blessings, a life in daily converse with God's will. Obedience, not zeal, is God's desire. Moderation, not excess, is the basis of God's plan. Just as only God, and no mere alchemist, knows the proportions of matter needed to compound a living body, so no mere tinkerer can compound the principles of a law of life. Personal insight alone cannot possibly replace the careful and systemic modulation that will produce not only life but the good life. Halevi's analogy of the individualist with the alchemist aims pointedly at the Karaites, whose rejection of the oral law – that is, the Talmud and the ongoing authority of rabbinic tradition to amend and adjust the understanding of that law – seemed, if taken at face value, to leave each reader of the Torah, like a fundamentalist preacher, to read and understand the text in isolation. How would the literalist or fundamentalist who reads Scripture individualistically, as though untutored reason were a sufficient key to unlock the hermeneutic circle, even know that the Torah does not command retaliation but requires acceptance of appropriate compensation in the case of torts? Without an oral tradition, Halevi laughs, we would not even know how to vocalize the Hebrew text, or parse it, let alone how to govern by it.[62]

> Just as I told you [says the chaver, when the king remarks on the originality (*ijtihād*) of the Karaites], that is characteristic of the work of reason and personal judgment. Those who strive to work out ideas of their own about how to worship God are much more original [*akthar ijtihādan*] than those who simply do God's will as He commanded. For the latter are at ease with their traditionalism [*taqlīd*]. Their spirits are calm and confident, like those of town dwellers who fear no attack. But the former are like a foot soldier in no man's land. He has no idea what might happen, so he goes armed and ready for battle, trained and practiced in warfare. So you should not be surprised at seeing these people girded up, or dismayed at the seeming laxity of those who follow tradition, the Rabbanites. For the others are searching for a stronghold they can fortify, but these couch secure in their own beds in an ancient and well fortified city.[63]

Clearly, the king replies, if the Karaites won the day there would be as many codes as opinions; how, then, could all Israel follow the single law that the Torah enjoins (Exodus 12:49)? Once again Halevi's standard is not only biblical, but public and political. Personal religion and private spirituality, no matter how ingenious – and Halevi concedes the intelligence and sophistication of the Karaites – can never become a unified and coherent system of law. Modern history, not least in the French and Soviet revolutions, affords the seeming exceptions that prove the rule. For as Michael Oakeshott, Eric Voegelin, Friedrich von Hayek, and others have argued in the twentieth century, and as Edmund Burke argued at the end of the eighteenth, a private vision can be made public, but only with great violence. Even then it cannot endure, if it has not grown from the soil of a tradition of civil culture and public virtue, which is the secular counterpart of the sort of tradition that Halevi speaks for. God is the radical origin, but Israel is the material vehicle of the law's unfolding.

The oral law is stricter than the law of Moses, in view of the general intent of making a margin (*seyag*) around the Torah. But for that very reason, the rabbis can qualify and mitigate their rulings, which are constantly guided by God's still present word. Even the aggadah or narrative of rabbinic tradition is not to be despised. True, it may seem silly at times; it can be marred by the inclusion of the less elevated and edifying remarks of the sages, which their disciples set in the canon more out of zeal than out of poor judgment. Yet the rigor of the sages in matters of practice (halakhah) is ample evidence that their flights of aggadic fancy are no mere daydreams but careful and methodical devices for eliciting important themes, treating the verses of Scripture as springboards, hallmarks, and touchstones of tradition, rather than as strict grounds of proof alone.[64]

Elohim, the common biblical term for God, originally meant "a ruling power." Its plural form reflects the ancients' ascription of differentiated spheres of action to diverse deities. Originally it was a collective noun; then, a generic descriptor of the divine. But the tetragrammaton names God properly, not generically. It reflects the personal contact of prophets with God as an individual and the historic experience of Israel with God's self-revelation and redemption. For conceptually we know the divine only by inference from its effects in nature;[65] and such reasoning is inherently open to ambiguity, leading to such errors as eternalism, dualism, fire-worship, sun-worship – or, at best perhaps, the doctrine of the philosophers that God is too exalted to know or care about his creatures. Fortunately, we are not confined to the flickering light of reason, but can know God through our intercourse with him and the long history of our growing awareness, traceable in a tradition that Scripture reports, all the way back to Adam.

Metaphysics

God's will is executed in nature without intermediaries, the chaver argues. Here Halevi takes aim at the elaborate ontology which clogs the Neoplatonic cosmos with disembodied intelligences and mediating hypostases. The system was devised to address what Neoplatonists called the problem of the many and the One – to answer the question why God did not remain in supernal isolation but permitted, even promoted, a world of multifarious things, no one of which, nor even the whole of which, could pretend to God's own absolute unity and perfection. Emanation, the intellectual causation that is the core idea of Neoplatonism, seemed indispensable in explaining how God, the One or the First in Neoplatonic parlance, related to the world – how he knew it and governed it. In the version developed by such thinkers as al-Fārābī and ibn Sīnā (Avicenna), the self-reflection of the One projects a diversity out of the merely notional distinction of the divine as subject from the divine as object. This diversity allows or rather entails the emergence of a pure Intellect from the One, which remains in itself undifferentiated and undiminished. The universal intelligence of this first dependent hypostasis contemplates both itself and its source and so gives rise to a second Intellect and a far more solid concrescence, the outermost sphere of the heavens. This mechanism seemed to the Muslim and Jewish followers of ibn Sīnā capable of explaining the whole sequence of intelligences (the realities behind the poetic notion of angels) and spheres (the transparent, simplex, and indestructible vehicles of the motion of the stars and planets), down to the lowest of the supernal disembodied minds, the active intellect, and the nethermost of the celestical spheres, that of the moon.

God's knowledge is of himself. His thought is of himself. His pleasure, life, and wisdom, like his creativity, are all identical with his self-knowledge. Thus God knows and governs the world obliquely, through the universal ideas which are the archetypes of all things in nature and the content of the thinking of the supernal intelligences. For these disembodied minds are neither wholly separate nor wholly identical with God's own. This means that God knows particulars by way of the universals which in a Neoplatonic scheme are both their causes and their ultimate reality. I say reality in the singular, since all real universals resolve into diversifications and specifications of God's own absolute unity and goodness. God governs through the active intellect's projection of these ideal archetypes onto matter. For the active intellect is the source of form in things, and of inspiration in the minds of philosophers, scientists, and prophets – although not, of course, their ultimate source.

Halevi has little patience with the scheme. Like other critics, including ibn Gabirol and al-Ghazālī, he finds the idea that emanation is the truth behind the scriptural idea of creation reductionistic and unsatisfactory, in part because it treats God's creativity too much as a mechanism, an automatism, or a necessity of logic. He finds the account of God's knowledge too remote, placing God himself at a remove from nature and setting the ideas of things between God and his creatures, as though God, like some absolutely theoretical scientist, knew only the general ideas, and cared not at all for the fate of vulnerable individuals. Halevi expresses his distaste for mediated emanation when, like ibn Gabirol, he makes a prominent issue of the primacy of God's will, the attribute that ibn Gabirol and al-Ghazālī found to be dissolved away in the philosophies of al-Fārābī and ibn Sīnā.

But Judaism has no categories of "heresy" or "innovation," like those which al-Ghazālī applied to twenty dicta of the Islamic philosophers. So, unlike al-Ghazālī, Halevi does not seek to isolate the theses on which the philosophers, Neoplatonic Aristotelians of the stamp of al-Fārābī and ibn Sīnā, can be deemed at fault. Like al-Ghazālī, Halevi wants to salvage some of the cosmology and metaphysics of these philosophers. But, unlike al-Ghazālī, he does not choose their own scholastic method as his chief means of filtering off what he finds most valuable. Rather, since he knows his battle is with intellectual authority, and since his quarrel is (as Erasmus' will be) at least as much with the spirit and method of the philosophers as with their doctrine, he resorts to reductio ad absurdum and to the poet's device of satire, even ridicule, maintaining the skeptic's external stance to the very enterprise of philosophy, at least as conceived by its most prominent practitioners in his day:

> The philosophers aver that from one can issue only one. So they posit an angel close to the First, from whom, they would have it that it emanates. Then they propose that this angel has two attributes [violating their own principle that the simple gives rise only to the simple]: its knowledge of its existence through itself, and its knowledge that it has a cause. [But why should it have any attributes; and if it has, why should they be cognitive? And have the philosophers not contradicted themselves in making this "angel" aware both of its self-sufficiency and of its dependence on the First?] This entails [!] the emergence of two more things from it: an angel and the sphere of the fixed stars. [Has this sphere, with its countless stars, Maimonides will ask, preserved the simplicity called for in the first premise?] This too, in so far as it is intellectually aware of the First entails the issuance from it of another angel, and in so far as it is intellectually aware of itself entails the issuance from it of the

sphere of Saturn. And so on, down to the moon, and thence, to the active intellect.

People have accepted this and been so taken in by it that they thought it was a proof. For it was ascribed to Greek philosophers. But it is sheer supposition without a shred of cogency, and it lies open to objection from several different directions. One, why did this emanation cease? Through some insufficiency in the First? . . . How do we know that intellectual self-knowledge entails the issuance from oneself of a celestial sphere? Or that intellectual knowledge of the First entails the emergence of an angel? When Aristotle claimed to know himself intellectually, one ought to expect a sphere to emanate from him; and if he claims to know the First intellectually, an angel!

I mention these principles to you so that you will not be overawed by the philosophers and assume that if you follow them your spirit will come to rest in soothing proof. But in fact, all their principles are as illogical and as impossible for reason to swallow as these.[66]

Dispensing with the whole elaborate apparatus of disembodied intellects, "star-souls" or sphere-angels, Halevi makes God's knowledge and governance of the world direct. Only his word, the direct manifestation of his will and wisdom, intervenes in nature. Yet this commanding word still has the double-edged efficacy of its ancient Philonic counterpart: it is immanent in nature without compromising God's absoluteness, but what it expresses is in no way separate from God. It is his will. The 'amr or divine word of command is still, in a way, an emanation. For it does convey the divine plan and idea and impress it upon the world, Zion, and the prophets, who are recipients of inspiration. It is this fact that David Neumark has in mind when he identifies Halevi as a philosopher "of the Ibn Gabirol type."[67] But the emergence of the word from God in Halevi, like the initial differentiation of the first essence in ibn Gabirol,[68] is now volitional. The work of emanation is no longer conceived through a mystification of logic that makes entailment somehow a source or vehicle of creation and makes thought of self or of the First a means of projecting angels, intelligences, or spheres.[69]

Direct governance and volitional emanation have precedents not only in ibn Gabirol's spirited volitional recasting of Neoplatonic ontology but also in Saadia's adaptation of the idea of God's created glory and his immanentist remarks about God's rejoicing in his creatures. For the impact of the approach is to make immanent divine volition, much as classical Neoplatonism made immanent the archetypal logos. The approach has a long afterlife: in Maimonides' theory of angels as forms and forces, in the kabbalistic developments pioneered by Nachmanides, in Spinoza's idea of the conatus, Bergson's élan vital, Whitehead's conception of creativity, and beyond.

In dismissing intellectualist emanation, Halevi has not rejected logic or philosophy. He has rejected the specific product that prominent practitioners of philosophy ascribed to logic. He holds that in fact only tradition can account for the assumption of these philosophers that there is any cogency at all in arguments so suppositious and speculative as those by which they projected the hierarchy of celestial intellects. The tradition of late Neoplatonism, in this case, conceived its problematic so narrowly that solutions whose alternatives were invisible to the philosophers seemed risible to their adversaries.[70] Al-Ghazālī, in another case, rightly asks the Neoplatonists to produce the middle term that would arm their argument, if they have one, or to explain, if their claims are indeed proferred as self-evident, why it is that not everyone agrees. Similarly, Halevi thinks that what is a matter of demonstration should not seem ridiculous to an outsider.

Thus he faults the philosophers not for their logic but for their want of logic. He rejects their conclusions because their reasoning fails by the standards of rationality. By the same token, he has not wholly rejected philosophy. For the critique of arguments that fail in cogency is of the essence in philosophy. Indeed, the naturalism to which Halevi appeals in rejecting the idea that mere self-reflection or contemplation of the divine can entail spheres or angels into being is of a piece with philosophic speculation – although it is corrosive to the intellectualist assumptions of a school which treated the name "philosopher" as their patent.

God acts in the world, Halevi urges, as the soul acts in the body. His name bespeaks his absoluteness, and he remains unseen in all his roles, as the soul does in the body. As a king may appear now as a warrior, now as a civil magistrate, God remains one in all his acts and guises – for the senses never perceive the inner essences of things. What prophets saw, they saw with the inner eye of the mind, "forms shaped to accommodate their own natures and wont, which they described in terms of the corporeal attributes they experienced. Their descriptions were true on the level of sense, imagination, and projection [al-wahm], but not in terms of the God's real identity, as an object of reason."[71]

Even a squint-eyed and myopic person may aid one who is clear sighted, if the latter knows how to discount for the distortions of the other's vision. It is in this sense, Halevi suggests, that prophets of varying sensibilities corroborate one another's visions. Some portray God in human form, to highlight God's relevance to our concerns. The divine glory that prophets see is either some specially created object or some part of God's retinue, known only to the pure, or nature itself viewed as an epiphany, as when Isaiah says (6:6), "The whole earth is full of His glory."[72] All such visions, even the extreme ones that seem to treat the divine far too corporeally, have the poetic power of immediacy, cutting through the necessary resort of the conceptual to discursive language: "The human soul feels terror in the presence of what is frightening, not when told about it. We feel desire for a fair form that is present and seen, not one that we have only heard about."[73]

Philosophers may say that love of God follows from knowledge of his omnipotence, but such inferences are too abstract to command the heart. With love, as with generation, mere entailment does not do the job. Thus, with all their most impressive arguments, the philosophers find no following among the common people – not because the people are too crude, as the philosophers suppose, but because the philosophers are too far removed from life.[74] What is needed, if people are to be moved, is not even the sheer will or creativity that may create a world, but symbols. Human beings need language to communicate. They need images, even rituals. "Do not believe the would-be reasoner who claims that his thought has reached such a stage of intimacy and order that he has grasped all the ideas requisite in the study of divinity by sheer reason, without any sensory prop or experiential canon."[75] Ordinary philosophers seem to want to study the divine as they might seek to study the earth. But such methods give them no real access to God's will or actions. Thus Socrates wisely said, "I have only human wisdom."[76] We Israelites, the rabbi confesses freely, rely on our clear-sighted prophets, who have (to borrow Plato's image) looked at the sun. Choosing those times of day and seasons of the year when God's light seems less blinding, we seek to join our seers in their vision, prepared by what they have related, not to be blinded or confused by what we see.[77]

Having acquired the basics of Halevi's historicist and traditionalist views, which make direct encounter with God the foundation of religious knowledge and which treat life in God's law as the foundation of religious fulfillment, Halevi's Khazar king is ready to confront theology (kalām). The purpose of doing so is the traditional one, of learning to refute foolish and dangerous alternatives to the truth. But Halevi reserves a dramatic irony here as the chaver leads the king through a typical cosmology.

The Khazar learns that bodies are as we perceive them in quality and quantity, but that they possess an underlying substrate, their materiality, whose very nature is imperfection, otherness, and sheer virtuality. Matter, as Aristotle put it, seems ashamed to appear naked. It is, perhaps, the "water" of Genesis 1:2; and the spirit that brooded over that water would be the divine will, which permeates all matter, giving it form. The suggestion that the *tohu ve-vohu* of the same verse is unformed matter betrays to the alert reader that this system of theology is anything but standard kalām creationist fare. For it introduces the idea that matter, as a sheer virtuality, is uncreated and that the act of creation is the imparting of form upon the receptivity that Plato called "the receptacle." God's creative intellect bestows the forms which the elements interchange when they are radically altered, and it follows that God can give any form to any matter – the thesis that was the basis of al-Ghazālī's naturalization of the possibility of miracles in particular and divine governance in general.

Of course vines grow from seeds, and seeds germinate with the turning of the spheres, the rabbi says. But it is God, the Khazar chimes in, who turns the spheres. And new species cannot simply arise, or old ones perish, adds the rabbi, in deference to the naturalism enshrined canonically in Aristotle's essentialism. The teleology of (pseudo-)Aristotle's *The Utility of the Species of Animals* and Galen's *On the Usefulness of the Organs* refutes Epicurus' view that the world arose by accident and without design. The presence of a soul is shown by the animation of living things, which grow, respond to stimuli, and think, not because of their materiality but because of an entelechy that perfects them as exemplars of their kind, that is, a soul, which is no mere product of the combination of elements but a nature and thus a substance in its own right.

Again the alert reader might be troubled. Why is Halevi's earlier polemical tone on behalf of creatio ex nihilo here dropped in favor of a tacit acceptance of formatio mundi? Why the acceptance of the substantial soul, when al-Ghazālī has already rejected spiritual immortality as a pale shadow and insufficient surrogate of resurrection, and when rabbinic immortality is founded on the conjoint responsibility of the soul and body that make up a moral personality only when united? Why the acceptance of the immutability of species, when that implies their eternity and the eternity of the world? And above all, in view of Halevi's thematic, why is matter suddenly relegated to the Platonic position of mere otherness and virtuality, when the great theme of Halevi's theology has been the localization and particularization of the divine presence and the great theme of his ethical and religious instruction has been the need to re-embody the disembodied spirituality of his people Israel?

The chaver traces the Aristotelian psychology of ibn Sīnā from the vegetative soul to the sacred intellect, which rises above mere discursive reasoning and becomes the vehicle of revelation, repeating ibn Sīnā's arguments for the immortality of the rational soul and its conjoining after death with the active intellect. He then pulls up short his royal disciple with the warning that the whole attractive picture is delusory. Philosophers do not need their four elements as building blocks of nature, since their world is eternal. Nor do we, since ours is the immediate work of God. Ashes are not earth, and plants do not contain fire; nor is their sap water – for it may be poison. The idea of purely spiritual immortality cannot (as al-Ghazālī warned) successfully differentiate the disembodied souls it posits, and ibn Sīnā's notion that rational thought is independent of the body and even of the aging process takes insufficient account of the clinical facts of senility and depression. We cannot blame the philosophers for their errors, for their intentions were good, their morals followed the laws of reason, and they led virtuous lives. But they lacked authentic tradition to guide them. Reason alone was insufficient, and the tradition they evolved, quite unselfconsciously, which they mistook for the pure work of reason, led them into many errors.[78]

What we need to know in the realm of theology is that the world is created, as are motion and rest, that it has a cause in God, who is eternal and unconditioned, incorporeal, omniscient and omnipotent, living and willing eternally. Finally, the human will, like God's, is free. Volition is delegated to human beings, just as natural dispositions are imparted to all animate and inanimate things. For, to mention only the most revealing of Halevi's dialectical arguments, if an external determinism is true, then "a man's speaking would be compulsory, like his pulse, which our immediate experience shows that it is not." The immediate experience here is very particular and personal. For who would know better than the physician-poet Halevi how the pulse will beat, or how freely a man may speak or keep silent?[79]

Drawing his teaching to a close, the chaver returns to thoughts of Zion, which has never been far from the aim of his argument. For it is in Zion that God's immanence is made most manifest, and only there that Israel lives the full life of God's commandments. Halevi's central goal is not the formulation of broad theological dicta but the recognition that these two are one: that is, that the life of Israel in her land and the will of God are one and the same. This theme rises closer and closer to the surface as the rabbi repeatedly cites the yearning for Zion expressed in Israel's prayers. He dismisses the pious notion that Israel's sins debar it from its land, taking the confessional lines from the liturgy ("and for our sins were we exiled from our land") as hortatory and admonitory, not explanatory, nor expressive of any norm or law. The Psalm (102: 14–15) prayerfully holds out the vivid hope: "Thou wilt arise and take pity on Zion, for the time to favor her is here, the time is come – since Thy servants delight in her stones and cherish her dust." This means that Jerusalem *will* be rebuilt when Israel so yearns for it that the people cherish its very stones and dust. No verse could better sum up the hearty, and indeed physical, rootedness that Halevi counterpoises to Neoplatonic intellectualism, and the lively optimism that he finds in the heart of his people's spirituality. Responding to the chaver's words, the king offers a courtly opportunity for his teacher to take his leave: "If this be so, it would be culpable to detain you."

Halevi himself acted on the conclusion he had reached. In 1140, he left Spain and made his way eastward. His wife was dead. Leaving behind his daughter and the land of "his fathers' graves," he traveled with Isaac, apparently his son-in-law, the son of his old friend Abraham ibn Ezra. Arriving in Alexandria on 8 September, he apparently tried without success, after recovering from this journey, to make his way further but was detained by the difficulty of coastal travel as the winter set in. By Chanukkah, he was brought up to Cairo and warmly welcomed by his old friend Chalfon. As he waited out the winter, he came to fear – between the hardships of travel, the unsettled times, the impositions of the Muslim authorities, and the sociability of the many friends and acquaintances who flocked to meet the famous and still prolific poet – that he might not reach his goal. For his friends urged him to remain in Egypt rather than risk the journey to the Crusader kingdom. When he finally took ship in the spring, unfavorable winds turned him back. He might indeed have died in Egypt, but seems in fact to have set sail.

The journey was not the one Halevi's heart had most ached for. The historical Khazar kingdom, after all, was not a utopian realm beyond the legendary Sabbath-keeping river Sambatyon, but a flesh and blood realm that faced real social and economic, military and political problems. And, in the same way, Halevi was not the pious rabbi of the *Kuzari* but a man of flesh and blood, who longed for the East when he was in the furthest West, and who voiced his delight, even in old age, at the forms of the girls on the banks of the Nile, whose slender arms, laden with bracelets, enchanted the heart and made the old poet forgetful of his age. His journey, delayed not only by weather but by his very celebrity, was not the long-dreamed-of return of Israel to its land, pictured in one illuminated hagaddah with charming little figures in medieval garb joyously bearing their great menorah back to its place on Mount Zion. It was the weary return of one elderly doctor, whose one hope in life had diminished and focused to a sharp, burning point, the urgent desire to lay his bones near those of his forebears. It was a journey of return not to life but to death, and not for a nation but for a soul that had now grown nearly as lonely, in a throng of friends, patrons, and admirers, as Moses ibn Ezra had grown in his exile.

If Halevi's last journey had meaning, it was only by the direction that it pointed. But the significance of that pointing itself was encoded not by the poet's life but by his work, above all by the *Kuzari* and its intellectually serious demand for the reintegration of Israel, body and spirit, law and lore, mind and practice, land, language, and logos, the freely imparted direction of God's eternal idea. Only a fiction draws the point to the arrow of Halevi's trajectory: legend has it that he lived to kiss the ground outside Jerusalem, where, as he spoke the words of his famous ode to Zion,[80] he was ridden down by an Arab horseman and killed.

In an important comparative essay, David Baneth, who devoted much of his life to establishing the critical text of the *Kuzari*, compares Halevi's work with that of his Muslim elder contemporary al-Ghazālī. He marks Halevi's rejection of the four-element scheme, which is not precedented in al-Ghazālī. He contrasts al-Ghazālī's theory that God acts in all things with Halevi's idea of the variable receptivity of created beings to the delegated power of God. Above all, he notes Halevi's optimism and openness:

> Ghazali's doctrine points toward asceticism, detachment from the world. His writings are pervaded by a stern and not infrequently gloomy strain.... Judah Halevi, on the other hand, unaffected by the influence of the cultural trends around him, perceives religious joy as the essential ingredient of Jewish piety. He lists the fear of God, the love of God, and rejoicing in God as the cardinal religious virtues, as it were, of Judaism, and he considers the rejoicing on festival days, as long as it is grounded in religious devotion, to be no less important than repentance and contrition on fast days. Rejoicing is an emanation of love, from which in turn flows a sense of gratitude to God.[81]

Complementing and spelling out this optimism is Halevi's happy confidence in his people and their underlying critical, moral, and spiritual sense.

> Ghazali's piety, like religiosity based on asceticism and mysticism, is the piety of the individual.... For Ghazali, there is a wide gap between the piety of the few God-seekers and the piety of the masses, who know only the literal text of the credo and the externalities of ceremonial practice. Not so Judah Halevi. His theory of the special religious faculty granted to Israel already places the entire Jewish people on essentially the same level. The religious acts he stresses serve to unite the nation; intellectual differences remain insignificant.[82]

❧ NOTES ❧

1 An ambiguous Bodleian manuscript reading suggests that Halevi may have been born in Tudela; see Schirmann 1937–8, 10: 237–9; 1979. Baer argues (1971, 1:

391 n. 48), "it is not very important whether Halevi was born in Toledo or Tudela, since the fact of his residence in Toledo and his close association with the Jewish courtiers of the Castilian court is well attested." Baron similarly notes (1952–83, 4: 248) that Moses ibn Ezra hails Halevi as coming from Seir, an apparent reference to Toledo. For Tudela "remained in Muslim hands for thirty years longer" than Toledo. "Moreover, Tudela was incorporated in 1115 in Navarre, not Castile," so Halevi's epithet "the Castilian" seems to refer to Toledo.

2 For the ambivalences of the Andalusian Hebrew poets, see Brann 1991, esp. pp. 19–22, 44–7, 59, 66, 93–6.

3 In a little work on prosody written in 1138, Halevi commends eleven Arabic meters as gratifying, and a twelfth (*ramal*) as suitable for short poems. "It is an ugly thing," he urges, to force Arabic vocalic discreteness on to Hebrew poesy. Halevi objects to quantitative prosody altogether, since elemental Hebrew semantics calls for stress accents, and the subtleties of Hebrew diction rest on phonetic patterns not found in Arabic. In practice Halevi used more meters than the essay favors. He experimented with syllabic meters but continued to use the Arabic quantitative measures to the end of his life. Clearly his ear gave him greater liberties than his canon countenanced. But he was not simply allowing his practice to outrun some casually adopted or arbitrarily overwrought formal theory. He makes the same points about Hebrew phonetics and semantics in the *Kuzari* (2.69–78). In both works he argues that the greatest Hebrew poetry needs no meter and wants none; for meters interfere with Hebrew linguistic values, which he hopes will be restored, and with the musical flexibility of Hebrew, which is syntactical at its core. For, as Halevi sees, melody is no more bound to meter than poetry is. Here Halevi seems to view his own practical poetics as a compromise with the *Sitz im Leben*. In the *Kuzari* he even argues that the acknowledged aesthetic gratifications of Arabic prosody are a detriment to the spiritual aims of Hebrew poetry at its ideal, as represented for Halevi by the chaste *semantical* rhythms of the Psalms, the compositions of the Levites, those ancestors whose heritage Halevi followed but never dreamed he could fulfill. For Halevi's critique of prosody, see Schirmann 1945; Halevi 1930a; Stern 1949, p. 62; Allony 1951, p. 161; Brann 1991, pp. 96–118; Baron 1952–83, 7: 200–1. For the Arabic distinction between poetry and verse, see Goodman 1992, pp. 221–6.

4 See *Kuzari* 2.64. The critical edition of the Arabic text was prepared by David H. Baneth. The English translation by Hartwig Hirschfeld is imprecise and misleading on almost every page; his *editio princeps* is also marred by numerous errors. Barry Kogan is preparing a new translation for the Yale Judaica Series based on Baneth's text and on a draft begun by the late Lawrence Berman. Translations in the present essay are my own. See also Halevi's letters edited by Ratzhaby 1953, pp. 268–72, and by Brody in *Dīwān Jehuda Halevi* 1: 224, letter 6 (Halevi 1930b).

5 As an antidote to the widely repeated view that Halevi's thought is antiphilosophical, see Strauss 1952 and Motzkin 1980.

6 For the themes of Golden Age poetry, see Scheindlin 1986 and 1991.

7 The topos is revisited by Hamadhānī's Jewish imitator al-Charīzī; the young man's posture resonates with that of the young Elihu in the book of Job 32.

8 Halevi 1930a, 1: 18, no. 14.

9 See Baer 1971, 1: 68.

10 Ibid.

11 "*Libbi be Mizrach*," tr. after Carmi.

12 Baer 1971, 1: 69–70.

13 See Baer 1971, 1: 70 and 27–8; Baron 1952–83, 7: 154.

14 Halevi 1930a, 4: 131–4, nos. 58–9; tr. after Baer 1971, 1: 70.

15 See Goitein 1967–88, 5: 457. Goitein identifies the "wicked queen" of Halevi's letter with Doña Urraca (reigned 1109–26), who was known for her cruelty.

16 See Goitein 1967–88, 5: 453–4. Chalfon was the dedicatee of the essay on meters; see Brann 1991, pp. 96–7.

17 Baer 1971, pp. 1–72.

18 The poem is printed in Hebrew and English in Halevi 1974, pp. 10–13.

19 Compare al-Ghazālī's decision, in the fateful year 1095, to abandon the false public position in which he found himself – but for the life of a Sufi.

20 Spiegel 1976, pp. 189–90.

21 Scheindlin 1991, pp. 130–4.

22 Halevi had longed for such visions; see Scheindlin 1991, pp. 198–200.

23 Halevi 1974, p. 2.

24 See *Kuzari* 2.24.

25 Baer 1971, 1: 73.

26 The traditional title, the *Kuzari*, derives from the popular pronunciation of the title used for the Hebrew translation by ibn Tibbon. But Halevi himself informally called the work *Al-Khazarī* in a letter written while he was at work on the book.

27 See Dunlop 1954.

28 *Kuzari* 1.1: p. 6 (Baneth).

29 Ibid., pp. 3–4.

30 Ibid. Halevi echoes the language of Hippocrates' famous title *Airs, Waters, and Places*.

31 *Kuzari* 1.3: p. 6 (Baneth). To call the philosopher's arguments "impressive" is a backhanded compliment, as Motzkin 1980 notes (p. 114). The suggestion is that the level of argumentation is only persuasive rather than demonstrative. Such a put-down was characteristic of Aristotelian philosophers when evaluating the arguments of "theologians." Maimonides will similarly turn the tables in the *Guide of the Perplexed* (2.15), holding that, if Aristotle had had any apodeictic proof of the world's eternity, he would not have resorted to persuasive language; for it was Aristotle himself who taught humankind the conditions of rigorous demonstration.

32 *Kuzari* 2.56, 79–80: pp. 73–4, 83 (Baneth). One pious gloss assigns such rocking a spiritual significance: the worshipper draws near to the light of God's word and then draws back from the intensity of its heat. Halevi thinks such glosses trivialize – not God's word, to be sure, but the idea we may have of how to fulfill it, as though standing and rocking in place were an adequate response to the words of the living God.

33 Brann 1991, p. 86.

34 See Motzkin 1980, p. 112.

35 *Kuzari* 1.4: p. 6 (Baneth).

36 Ibid., 1.5: p. 8.
37 Ibid., 1.6: pp. 8–9.
38 Ibid., 1.19–20: p. 11.
39 Ibid., 1.21: p.11.
40 See *Kuzari* 1.65.
41 Ibid., 1.81–91.
42 Ibid., 1.92–7.
43 Ibid., 3.21: pp. 110–11 (Baneth).
44 Ibid., 1.106; cf. Goodman 1991, chapter 6.
45 *Kuzari* 1.105: p. 35 (Baneth).
46 Ibid., 2.24: p. 58 (Baneth). "God's word," here and throughout the *Kuzari*, is *al–'amr al-Ilāhī*, a favorite expression of Halevi's for the divine agency in nature. The expression stems ultimately from the Philonic idea of the logos, mediated by the Islamic expression *'amr*, which construes as an imperative the word that is an archetype, hypostasis, and divine attribute; see Baljon 1958, pp. 7–18 and Pines 1960, 1: 29–30, s.v. *'amr*. The connotative force of *al–'amr al-Ilāhī* is "the commanding word of God." The Arabic redactor of the Plotinian collection known as the *Theology of Aristotle* saw the affinity of the Neoplatonic version of Philo's logos to the Qur'ānic divine command, perhaps aided by familiarity with the Gospel's reliance on the logos. So *'amr* quite naturally and appropriately becomes the counterpart of the Greek logos. It is a mistranslation to render *al–'amr al-Ilāhī* "the divine thing," as is regrettably done in David Neumark's otherwise important essay in Neumark 1971, p. 224. It is misdirection to render the expression transparently or euphemistically as "God's influence," "God's power," or the like. The word of God in Halevi is an immanent hypostasis. Its presence is crucial to the special role Halevi ascribes to the people of Israel in the world, and to the special role he assigns to prophetic poetry in the life of the people of Israel; see also Altmann 1969 and Pines 1980.
47 *Kuzari* 2.30.
48 Ibid., 2.36–42. Cf. Plato, *Republic* 6.495: "the very qualities that make up the philosophical nature do in fact become, when the environment and nurture are bad, in some way the cause of its backsliding."
49 *Kuzari* 2.44: pp. 67–8 (Baneth). Halevi's evolutionism seems to echo that of the Ikhwān al-Ṣafā' of Baṣra, whose popularity is alluded to by the oblique reference: "You have learned." As I emphasized in introducing their *Case of the Animals vs Man* (Ikhwān al-Ṣafā' 1978), theirs is a Neoplatonic evolutionism; it does not proceed by natural selection. In Halevi it is clearly temporal, as biblical creationism suggests it should be; it is also teleological, in the Stoic, anthropocentric, not the Neoplatonic, universalist sense that Maimonides will later accept.
50 *Kuzari* 2.48: p. 69 (Baneth).
51 Ibid., 2.50.
52 Ibid., 2.50–5.
53 Ibid., 2.56: pp. 73–4 (Baneth).
54 Ibid., 2.64; cf. Maimonides, *Guide* 3.29, 37, 49.
55 *Kuzari* 2.64–5, 68.
56 The *democratic* orientation implicit in Halevi's nationalism is striking: the good person here replaces Plato's Guardian.

57 *Kuzari* 3.1–5: pp. 90–2 (Baneth). Unlike the Muslim philosopher ibn Bājja (d. 1138), who was, after all, a *wazīr*, Halevi did not carry his alienation to the point of urging spiritual withdrawal from political engagement. He did urge Jewish withdrawal from dispersion among the nations, but for the sake of re-integrating the political and the spiritual. He did not accept the view that the two were incompatible but held fast to the political Platonism of al-Fārābī in a new recension of his own; cf. Melamed forthcoming, pp. 24–6.

58 Nachmanides relies on Halevi's thinking here for his theory that the festivals and celebrations of Jewish law enable all Israel continuously to relive the unique moments of their spiritual history; see Novak 1992, pp. 103–4.

59 *Kuzari* 3.5: pp. 93–4 (Baneth).

60 Ibid., 3.7–8, where circumcision is the paradigm case.

61 Ibid., 3.11.

62 Ibid., 3.35, 47. An autograph letter of Halevi's preserved in the Cairo Geniza reveals that the *Kuzari* began as an occasional piece, a "trifle." The initial irritant was Halevi's questioning by a visiting Karaite philosopher from Christian Spain; see Goitein 1967–88, 5: 456.

63 *Kuzari* 3.37; cf. 49. *Ijtihād* is originality, thinking for oneself; *taqlīd* is tradition-alism, even dogmatism. Halevi here reverses the fields of the familiar valuation of creativity. Hirschfeld mangles the passage by taking *ijtihād* to mean zeal, a sense for which there is no lexical foundation. It does not help much that Hirschfeld takes Halevi's foot soldier to be a straggler, since the point of Halevi's simile is the preparedness of the Karaites, a reference to their well-known achievements in scientific hermeneutics.

64 *Kuzari* 3.73.

65 Cf. Plato, *Apology* 27b: "Is there anyone in the world, Meletus, who believes in human activities and not in human beings?"

66 *Kuzari* 4.25: p. 183 (Baneth). Halevi here plays on the title of ibn Sīnā's philosophical magnum opus, the *Shifā'* or *Healing*, and on the ancient idea that proof gives intellectual repose to the questioning mind. The Skeptics claimed that such repose is reached by learning that certain questions are best dropped.

67 See Neumark 1971, pp. 219–300; cf. Davidson 1972 and Hamori 1985.

68 For the role of will in ibn Gabirol's philosophy, see McGinn 1992.

69 Halevi seems to enjoy the rhyme of *malak* and *falak*, angel and sphere. The clanging syllables and repeated issuance of intellects and spheres, like the slamming doors in a bedroom farce, heighten the comedy of the very idea of sheer thought entailing into existence something so real as a Platonic intelligence or so solid as a celestial sphere.

70 See *Kuzari* 5.14.

71 Ibid., 4.3: p. 155 (Baneth); p. 208 (Hirschfeld). Halevi here seems to stand midway between Saadia's theory of God's created glory and Maimonides' thesis that prophetic visions are vivid subjective apprehensions.

72 *Kuzari* 4.3: pp. 158–9 (Baneth); p. 212 (Hirschfeld).

73 Ibid., 4.5: pp. 159–60 (Baneth); p. 213 (Hirschfeld).

74 Ibid., 4.17–19.

75 Ibid., 4.6: p. 60 (Baneth).

76 Ibid., 4.13; 5.14.

77 Ibid., 4.7.

78 Ibid., 5.14.
79 Ibid., 5.20: p. 218 (Baneth).
80 In Halevi 1974, no. 2, pp. 3–7.
81 Baneth 1981, p. 197.
82 Baneth 1981, pp. 197–8.

⚬ BIBLIOGRAPHY ⚬

Texts

Halevi, Judah (1930a) *Dīwān*, edited by H. Brody, as *Jehuda Ha Levi, Die Schönen Versmasse* (Berlin: Mekitze Nirdamim); and in H. Brody (ed. and tr.) *Selected Poems of Jehudah Halevi* (Philadelphia: Jewish Publication Society, 1974).

—— (1930b) Letter to David Narboni, in Halevi 1930a, *Dīwān Jehuda Halevi* 1: 224, letter 6.

—— (1953) "A Letter from R. Judah Halevi to R. Ḥaviv" [Hebrew], edited by H. Ratzhaby, *Gilyonot* 28: 268–72. [Cf. S. Abramson in *Kiryat Sefer* 29 (1953): 133–44.]

—— (1977) *Kitāb al-Radd wa-'l-Dalīl fī 'l-Dīn al-Dhalīl* [known as *The Kuzari*], edited by D. Baneth and H. Ben-Shammai (Jerusalem: Magnes); translated by H. Hirschfeld (London: Routledge, 1905; reprinted New York: Schocken, 1974).

Ikhwān al-Ṣafā' (1978) *The Case of the Animals vs Man*, translated by L. E. Goodman (Boston: Twayne).

Maimonides (1856–66) *Le Guide des Egarés* [*The Guide of the Perplexed*], edited by S. Munk, 3 vols. (Paris; reprinted Osnabrück: Zeller, 1964).

Studies

Allony, N. (1951) *Torat ha-Mishkalim – The Scansion of Medieval Hebrew Poetry: Dunash, Jehuda Halevi, and Abraham ibn Ezra* [Hebrew] (Jerusalem: Mossad ha-Rav Kook).

Altmann, A. (1969) "Ibn Bajjah on Man's Ultimate Felicity," in *Studies in Religious Philosophy and Mysticism* (Ithaca: Cornell University Press), pp. 73–107.

Baer, Y. (1971) *A History of the Jews in Christian Spain*, translated by L. Schoffman, 2 vols. (Philadelphia: Jewish Publication Society).

Baljon, J. M. S. (1958) "The *'amr* of God in the Koran," *Acta Orientalia* 23: 7–18.

Baneth, D. H. (1981) "Judah Halevi and al-Ghazali," in *Studies in Jewish Thought: An Anthology of German Jewish Scholarship*, edited by A. Jospe (Detroit: Wayne State University Press), pp. 181–99.

Baron, S. (1952–83) *A Social and Religious History of the Jews*, 16 vols. (Philadelphia: Jewish Publication Society).

Brann, R. (1991) *The Compunctious Poet: Cultural Ambiguity and Hebrew Poetry in Muslim Spain* (Baltimore: Johns Hopkins University Press).

Davidson, H. (1972) "The Active Intellect in the Cuzari and Hallevi's Theory of Causality," *Revue des Études Juives* 131: 351–96.

Dunlop, D. N. (1954) *The History of the Jewish Khazars* (Princeton: Princeton University Press).

Goitein, S. D. (1967–88) *A Mediterranean Society*, 5 vols. (Berkeley: University of California Press).

Goodman, L. E. (1991) *On Justice* (New Haven: Yale University Press).

—— (1992) *Avicenna* (London: Routledge).

Hamori, A. (1985) "Lights in the Heart of the Sea: Some Images of Judah Halevi's," *Journal of Semitic Studies* 30: 75–93.

McGinn, B. (1992) "Ibn Gabirol: The Sage among the Schoolmen," in *Neoplatonism and Jewish Thought*, edited by L. E. Goodman (Albany: State University of New York Press) pp. 77–109.

Melamed, A. (forthcoming) *The Philosopher King in Medieval and Renaissance Jewish Political Thought* (Atlanta: Scholars Press).

Motzkin, A. (1980) "On Halevi's *Kuzari* as a Platonic Dialogue," *Interpretation* 9: 111–24.

Neumark, D. (1971) [1929] "Jehuda Hallevi's Philosophy," in *Essays in Jewish Philosophy*, edited by S. Cohon (Amsterdam: Philo), pp. 219–300.

Novak, D. (1992) *The Theology of Nahmanides Systematically Presented* (Atlanta: Scholars Press).

Pines, S. (1960) "*'Amr,*" in *Encyclopedia of Islam* (London: Luzac) 1:29–30.

—— (1980) "Shi'ite Terms and Conceptions in Judah Halevi's *Kuzari*," *Jerusalem Studies in Arabic and Islam* 2: 165–251.

Scheindlin, R. (1986) *Wine, Women, and Death: Medieval Hebrew Poems on the Good Life* (Philadelphia: Jewish Publication Society).

—— (1991) *The Gazelle: Medieval Hebrew Poems on God, Israel and the Soul* (Philadelphia: Jewish Publication Society).

Schirmann, H. (1937–8) "The Life of Yehudah Halevi," *Tarbitz* 9: 36ff., 219ff.; 10: 237–9.

—— (1979) "Where was Judah Halevi Born?" in *Studies in the History of Hebrew Poetry and Drama* (Jerusalem: Mossad Bialik), 1: 247–9.

—— (1945) "Halevi's Treatise on Meters" [Hebrew], *Studies of the Research Institute for Hebrew Poetry* 6: 319–22.

Silman, Y. (1995) *Philosopher and Prophet: Judah Halevi, the Kuzari, and the Evolution of His Thought* (Albany: State University of New York Press).

Spiegel, S. (1976) "On Medieval Hebrew Poetry," in *The Jewish Expression*, edited by J. Goldin (New Haven: Yale University Press), pp. 174–216.

Stern, S. (1949) "Notes on the Text of Yehudah Halevi's Article on Poetic Meters" [Hebrew], *Tarbitz* 21: 62.

Strauss, L. (1952) "The Law of Reason in the *Kuzari*," in *Persecution and the Art of Writing* (New York: Free Press), pp. 95–141.

CHAPTER 10

Medieval Jewish Aristotelianism: an introduction

Norbert M. Samuelson

►► INTELLECTUAL SOURCES ◄◄

The philosophic activity of the ancient Greek world culminated in three basic ways of viewing all of reality. One is atomism, another is associated with Plato, and the third with Aristotle. By atomism I mean a tradition of Greek and Roman science that begins with the Presocratic thinkers,[1] and continues with both atomists proper[2] and Stoics.[3] For our purposes, this tradition culminates in the form of science and theology, kalām, which dominated Muslim intellectual life from the eighth to the tenth centuries CE. The mutakallimūn (exponents of kalām) include the two Mu'tazilite dominant sects of Muslim apologists,[4] the Ash'ariyya, and such notable Muslim theologians as al-Rāzī (d. c.925) and al-Ghazālī (1058–1111). It is this form of philosophy that I shall subsequently refer to as "the old science."

Platonism is to be found in the known corpus of the works attributed to Plato (428–347 BCE) as these works were interpreted in a chain of commentaries that begins with the students in Plato's Academy[5] and continues with Latin translations and commentaries on those works by Christian theologians in the Roman Empire, culminating in Neoplatonism.[6] However, Platonism encompasses more than Neoplatonism. It also includes interpretations of all of Plato's works in the Muslim world, most notably of Plato's *Republic* and his *Timaeus*, by scholars such as al-Kindī (c. 801–c. 866).

It would be a mistake to treat Platonism simply as the ideas of Plato. His works are the origin of this philosophic tradition, but they do not function as a kind of Scripture, that is, as texts whose words must be true when properly understood. A better way to interpret the Platonists would be as follows. They are a group of independent thinkers committed to knowing the truth. In pursuing this goal they had great respect for the method, language, and results of Plato as they understood him. They paid great attention to his recorded words, but they did not do so because they were committed to his defense – on the contrary, most of these philosophers were quite prepared to criticize Plato if and when they concluded that what he said was wrong.

Aristotelianism is similar in this respect to Platonism. It is to be found in the known corpus of works attributed to Aristotle (384–322 BCE) as these works were interpreted in a chain of commentaries that begins with the students in Aristotle's Lyceum,[7] and continues with Arabic and Judeo-Arabic translations and commentaries on those works by Muslim and Jewish theologians in the Muslim world, culminating in Hebrew translations and commentaries in late medieval Europe.[8] It is this form of philosophy that I shall subsequently refer to as "the new science."

As in the case of the Platonists, so here too it would be a mistake to treat all of the works of these Aristotelians simply as the ideas of Aristotle. Again, his works function as the *origin* of a philosophic and scientific tradition whose primary concern was to discover truth.

These, then, are the primary intellectual influences in the story that will follow of medieval Jewish Aristotelianism.

❧ HISTORICAL CONTEXT ❧

In about 750 CE the 'Abbāsid dynasty supplanted the Ummayad dynasty and moved its capital from Damascus to Baghdad. Less than forty years later, the regions of the Muslim world west of Egypt, choosing to preserve the Ummayad caliphate, asserted their independence from the 'Abbāsids. For our purposes the significance of this political split in the Muslim world is that it was paralleled by a split in the intellectual world. The east continued the old (kalām) science while the west generated a new (Aristotelian) science.

The ninth century was the critical period during which the scientific, mathematical, and philosophic legacy of Hellenism was translated into Arabic. This work occurred primarily in the 'Abbāsid east, centered in royal houses of learning in Baghdad. It was here that kalām dominated the intellectual life of both Muslims and Jews. The dominance of the old science over both Platonism and Aristotelianism was a reasonable reflection of the course of scientific theory in Hellenism, where the atomists in science and the Stoics in popular philosophy became the dominant influences. Particularly in the case of Aristotelianism, the old science would have clearly been seen by those who knew the history of Greco-Roman science to be the more "progressive" alternative. Critical to the old science was the judgment that the apparent dynamism of the universe could be accounted for by quantitative models, and the progress in mathematical sophistication in Baghdad would have reinforced this faith in a mathematical (anti-Aristotelian) model for doing science. In other words, given the history of science and mathematics prior to the Muslim conquest of the Mediterranean world, it was reasonable that Muslims educated in the learning of both Christian Byzantium and Hindu India would have ignored Aristotelianism.

Whether or not a lack of such knowledge can account for the distinctive rise of Aristotelianism in every area of knowledge in the Ummayad west is a matter of pure speculation. Certainly the new science had a great deal to recommend itself. Not the least of its advantages over both atomism and Platonism is its empiricism, namely, that it presented a view of the universe in which what seems through our senses to be the case is in fact the case. What our external senses tell us is that the things that exist in the world are objects like minerals, fish, animals, and humans, and that humans in particular have real choices about their fate and destiny in this world. Both atomism and Platonism, contrarily, denied the reality of the sensible realm. For the atomists, the universe ultimately consists of discrete, imperceptible quantities which are what they are by sheer chance; nothing that exists has purpose or reason. Similarly for the Platonists, the universe consists of pure, equally imperceptible forms which are what they are necessarily; everything that exists is mathematically determined. From this vantage point the sensible realm is suspect. As a result, Aristotelian empiricism is appealing, but, whatever was the common sense appeal of the new science over its two alternative ways of viewing the universe, it had many, seemingly insurmountable problems.

From a scientific perspective, the critical terms in Aristotelianism lacked the precision of technical terms in both atomism and Platonism, and judgments were at best equivocal, significantly lacking in the precision possible if the universe can in fact be mathematically constructed. From a religious perspective, the situation was even worse. The new science made claims about the universe which prima facie were far more difficult to reconcile with the claims of revealed tradition – be it rabbinic commentary (midrash) on the Hebrew Scriptures or Muslim *ijmāʿ* and interpretations of the Qurʾān and sunnah. In terms of Platonism, the dogma of creation is a good example. Clearly, the text of Plato's *Timaeus* is more readily compatible with the text of Genesis 1 than the biblical text could possibly be with the Aristotelian view that the universe consists of substances composed of form and matter whose proximate causes ad infinitum are similar composite substances. In other words, the new science posits an eternal universe that prima facie contradicts the claims of both Platonism and Scripture that the universe was created.

In terms of atomism, the belief in miracles is a good example of the inherent problems in the new science. Prima facie a miracle is a contingent event which cannot be accounted for by any impersonal laws that determine what is independent of divine will. To the extent that what is occurs by chance, to that extent miracles are reasonable, that is, logically possible and rationally conceivable. However, to the extent that what is is causally necessary, there is no room for miracles. Aristotelian astronomy and physics presented their Muslim and (more importantly for our purposes) Jewish advocates with a world in which much (if not all) of what occurs occurs through formal and material causes. To the extent that what is true is caused, it is necessary; to the extent that it is necessary, miracles are neither logically possible nor rationally conceivable. Furthermore, the Aristotelian account of causation also contradicts what Jews as Jews accepted about divine and human power. To the extent that any event is causally determined, it is not subject to intervention by any will, be it human or divine. Hence, to the extent that events are determined, divine and human power in the universe is restricted. This means that God is not omnipotent, and humans have limited responsibility for what they do. This last consequence is particularly troublesome. To the extent that what humans do is determined by causes, to that extent humans cannot be held responsible for their actions. However, Scripture teaches that we are responsible. Hence, if the Aristotelian account of causation is correct, then divine commandments (*mitzvot*) are futile and divine reward or punishment for obedience or disobedience to God's commandments is unjust.

Given the foregoing, it may seem surprising that Aristotelianism arose and dominated Andalusia and North Africa in the eleventh to fifteenth centuries. But it did. That it did, and the problems that dominance created, determine the themes that occupied the writings of the Jewish Aristotelians.

The history of Jewish Aristotelianism falls into two distinct periods. The first and earlier stage occurs when Jews were culturally part of the western Muslim world. The second occurs when Jewish intellectual life had moved into the European empire of the Roman Catholic Church.[9] The first stage begins in Andalusia with Abraham ibn Daud (Rabad) (1110–1180) and concludes with Moses ben Maimon (Maimonides) (1135–1204). The second stage includes a number of individuals who lived either in southern Spain,[10] French Provence,[11] or Italy.[12] Of these Jewish philosophers, the most important were Levi ben Gershom (Gersonides) (1288–1344) and Chasdai Crescas (c. 1340–1411).

Subsequent chapters will deal with Maimonides, Gersonides, and Crescas. The focus in the remainder of this chapter will be on the origin of the new science in ibn Daud's *Exalted Faith*.[13]

The *Exalted Faith* is the first systematic effort to apply the diverse elements of the new science to a religious philosophy of rabbinic Judaism. Its importance for intellectual history is that it begins Jewish Aristotelianism, which itself is the most important development in medieval Jewish philosophy. The Jewish new science absorbs all of the attempts to formulate Jewish belief that preceded it, from the earliest forms of biblical commentary in midrash through the old scientific systems of Jewish philosophy,[14] and develops what are until this day the most comprehensive, sophisticated, and authoritative statements of traditional Jewish belief. In this respect, Jewish Aristotelianism functions for Jewish belief as the Babylonian Talmud functions for Jewish praxis, that is, as the foundation and most critical body of literature for any contemporary discussion of the nature or character of Judaism.

Again, it is ibn Daud's *Exalted Faith* that initiates this new, what will prove to be definitive, direction in rabbinic theology. Clearly ibn Daud's arguments and statements are not as developed as those of Gersonides, but that would be an unfair comparison. Those who initiate a line of thought necessarily cannot have worked out the thought as well as later figures who extend the line. However, Gersonides is not as comprehensive as is ibn Daud. No Jewish Aristotelian is as comprehensive as ibn Daud. Furthermore, in many respects his treatment of topics is more thorough or philosophically sophisticated than that of Maimonides.[15] In fact I would say that the relationship between the Jewish Aristotelians ibn Daud, Maimonides, and Gersonides is comparable to that between the British Empiricists Locke, Berkeley, and Hume. Locke is not as rigorous as Berkeley and Hume, but that is because the latter have the former as a foundation for their speculation.

IBN DAUD'S *EXALTED FAITH*: A SUMMARY

From the tenth century on there are Jews in Muslim civilization who are Aristotelians. However, none of them attempted to reconcile their religious beliefs with their scientific commitments until ibn Daud published his major work in Jewish philosophy, *The Exalted Faith*. It is divided into three books. In the first he explains the presuppositions of Aristotelianism to his intended audience of cultured Jews who know of, but little about, this new science. In the second book ibn Daud determines a list of six basic principles of Judaism and explains them in the light of the new science. In the third book he applies the listed presuppositions and principles to ethics.[16]

The first book, on the presuppositions of Aristotelianism, contains eight chapters. The first three define the key technical terms in the new science, namely, substance, accident, and the ten categories (chapter 1), form and matter (chapter 2), and motion (chapter 3). The second unit of the first book contains two chapters on physics. Here ibn Daud explains the claims that material bodies possess neither actual nor potential infinity (chapter 4), that all motion comes from a mover and that there exists a first mover (chapter 5). The third unit contains two chapters on rational psychology. Here ibn Daud describes the nature and powers of the soul (chapter 6), and defends the claim that the rational power is immaterial (chapter 7). Finally, the fourth unit (chapter 8) deals with astronomy. Here ibn Daud argues for the critical claim that the heavens are rational, living organisms that possess intentional motion.

The second book uses the topics of the first to explain what ibn Daud judged to be the basic principles of the faith and religious law of the Jewish people. The first four principles deal with the existence and nature of God. The second unit, which consists solely of the fifth principle, deals with the claim that rabbinic tradition is an authoritative source of truth in religious law. The third and final unit of the second book, concerning the sixth principle, deals with an issue ibn Daud identified in the introductory abstract to the work as a whole, namely, the problem of free will and determinism.

The first two principles are that God is a necessary being (principle one), and, as a consequence, he is one (principle two). This second principle is developed in three chapters in which ibn Daud argues that only a necessary being can be truly one (chapter 1), that God's unity admits to no plurality of any kind (chapter 2), and that this unity is an essential, rather than an accidental, attribute of God.

The third principle states that all affirmative attributions to God, including the claims that he is necessary and one, are equivocal. What they express is either a negation or a relation.[17]

The fourth principle deals with divine actions. They turn out not to be statements about God at all. Rather, they are fundamental claims about angels. This principle is explained in three chapters. In general, God orders the universe by means of what Scripture calls "angels," whom ibn Daud identifies with the separate intellects of Aristotelian astronomy. The first two chapters of this principle are proofs of their existence. Chapter 1 is based on rational psychology. Here the existence of angels is inferred from claims in epistemology, specifically, in connection with the general causal powers of the soul. Chapter 2 is based on physics and astronomy. Finally, chapter 3 is a hierarchical ordering of the kinds of entities in the universe in relation to the different kinds of angels or separate intellects who govern them on behalf of God.

The fifth principle moves away from the subject of God to the topic of the Torah. It asserts that rabbinic tradition, that is, the Hebrew Scriptures as interpreted by the rabbis,[18] is an authoritative source of truth in religious law. It consists of an introductory essay or abstract followed by two chapters. The abstract argues for the general claim that authentic traditions make veridical claims, while the subsequent chapters are intended to prove that rabbinic Judaism is an authentic tradition. The first chapter deals with the nature of the prophecy recorded in the Scriptures. It presents a general discussion of the nature of prophecy and its different degrees, which provides the grounding for ibn Daud's more specific argument that the prophecy of Moses, as recorded in the Torah, is an unimpeachable witness to the word of God. In other words, the origin of rabbinic tradition, namely, Mosaic prophecy, is true.

Chapter 2 argues that the transmission of Moses' initial report through the *tannaim* and *amoraim* has been faithful to Moses' original testimony, so that statements in rabbinic tradition are veridical.[19] In other words, statements in the Hebrew Scriptures, interpreted on the authority of rabbinic commentaries, have the same epistemic status in an argument as either direct reports of sense experience or reliable traditions about such reports.

The sixth and final principle deals with the possibility of human choice in the context of both divine and natural necessity. As ibn Daud puts it, the problem is the following: If God rules over everything in the universe, then no human would have any real choice. But this is not possible, since God commands and punishes disobedience, and no one can be either punished or commanded about something over which they have no choice. On the other hand, if people do have choice, then to that extent God does not rule over the universe. But it is not possible for there to be anything over which God does not have dominion. This philosophical/theological dilemma is reinforced in the words of Scripture, where some texts seem to say that God determines everything while others assert that human beings have choice. The problem is discussed in two chapters. The first grounds ibn Daud's solution in his earlier discussion of divine attributes. Since all terms predicated of God are equivocal, no statements about divine power ought to be understood literally. The second chapter presents his answer. In a word, he affirms both, namely, that everything is determined by God *and* human beings have choice, and claims that when both statements are properly understood they are not incoherent.

In summary, ibn Daud's list of fundamental principles of rabbinic Judaism are that, first, God necessarily exists and is one, which entails that no literal, positive statements can be about who or what he is, for, when properly interpreted, they express how he is related to the world, which is through the mediation of angels; second, the Torah is the word of God to Moses through the highest epistemic level of prophecy, whose meaning has been passed down through a thoroughly reliable tradition of rabbinic interpretations, so that rabbinic interpretations of Scripture provide us with a rationally indubitable source of truth claims; third, everything is determined by God through his ordering of the universe, but this ordering gives human beings the power to choose, so that people are morally responsible for what they do and, as such, are subject to divine providence.[20]

All of ibn Daud's theses are important both as philosophy and as intellectual history. While everything that ibn Daud says is rooted in his inherited tradition of rabbinic thought, what he says is original as well. Furthermore, all of his theses, when carefully examined,[21] are prescient of the issues that will dominate the entire history of Jewish Aristotelianism. However, there is not sufficient space here to discuss all of them. Instead I will limit my final discussion in this chapter to the one issue that ibn Daud himself stated is the most important – how determinism (*ha-hekhreach*) and choice (*ha-bechirah*) are related.

❧ DETERMINISM AND CHOICE ❧

Ibn Daud's presentation of the problem is confined to the two extreme answers to this question, that is, the one that says that everything is determined, so that nothing can be subject to human choice, and the other that says that there are instances of choice that are absolutely free, so that they can in no way be subject to determinism. It seems to ibn Daud from the very beginning that both views are not simply incoherent; they are wrong. The correct understanding of their relation must lie somewhere in between, so that all actions are to some extent determined and some determined actions are subject to human choice.

The issue does not apply to everything. Clearly things happen that are independent of actors making choices. For example, when a rock falls, the rock does not choose to fall. Rather, the issue is confined to a single set of actions, namely those in which human beings may or may not sin.

The problem is both religious and scientific. In terms of science, if the categories of formal necessity and material chance exhaust all the possibilities of schematizing (that is, making intelligible) an event, then moral responsibility makes no sense. One becomes responsible for doing neither what could not have been done otherwise nor what merely happened to happen. For there to be moral culpability – that is, for an action to be subject to evaluative judgment – it must be in some respect neither necessary nor by chance, that is, these two categories cannot exhaust all of the options for interpretation.

Ibn Daud does not present this issue in philosophic terms. Rather, he does it in more specifically religious terms. Rabbinic Judaism is a faith that is rooted in a text, the Hebrew Scriptures; that text is claimed to be revealed, and what, for the most part, it communicates are positive and negative commandments that are associated with rewards for obedience and punishments for disobedience. Now, if human beings fail to fulfill a commandment, either because it was impossible for them to do otherwise than they did or because what they did was merely accidental, then it is not (morally) just for punishment to be associated with the action. However, human beings are commanded and punished. This is utterly unintelligible in terms of the new science, where all events occur through either formal necessity or material accidence. Hence, acts are commanded if and only if they are neither determined nor accidental.

This is one side of the problem, the one that deals with the nature of causation. But there is a second side as well, one that deals with the nature of God. If human beings have choice, then what they do may or may not occur. In other words, before they choose, what they will do is in principle unknown. This would be the case for any strict Aristotelian. Every concrete event is subject to material conditions, and to that extent it is indeterminate. Hence, it can be known only after the fact. But this position becomes problematic when we introduce a consideration about God. If there are human choices, then God cannot know before they are made what they will be. However, if God lacks this knowledge, then he is not perfect. However, if he is not perfect, then why should we be obligated to obey his commands? In other words, it makes no sense for God to issue commands.

So far the argument has been purely "philosophical." Now ibn Daud introduces a specific textual dimension to the issue. The question of the relationship between determinism and choice is as problematic when we look at the words of Scripture as it is when we look at science. On the one hand, the most obvious interpretation of some of the texts of Scripture suggests that God makes commands and punishes disobedience even when he has determined the actor to disobey. For example, God commands Pharaoh to let the children of Israel leave, and punishes him when he refuses, even though God "hardened his heart," the most obvious meaning of which is that God necessitated Pharaoh's will to disobey. On the other hand, there are many texts that explicitly say that people have choice, how they choose has life and death consequences, and these consequences are understood to be rewards and punishments for obedience and disobedience.

Ibn Daud's proposed method for solving the textual problem parallels his method for solving the scientific/philosophic problem. The starting point for all scientific thought is direct empirical observation. But mere observation is not knowledge. Data do not contain their own interpretation. It is the job of the scientist to interpret, that is, to provide a schema through which the data becomes intelligible, coherent, and consistent. To the extent that the proposed intellectual schema fails to do that, it must be revised or be replaced. Similarly, the starting point for all religious thought is an inherited tradition of texts about God's revelation to his prophets. But texts in themselves are not knowledge, since they do not contain their own interpretation. It is the job of the theologian to interpret, to provide a schema through which the words in the texts become intelligible. Here "intelligibility" does not only involve making the written words coherent. Since these are words of revelation, and not fiction, their interpretation must also cohere with what is known through science, that is, what we know from the data of experience to be true. Now, in this case it is clear that not every statement in Scripture can be understood literally, since consistent literal interpretation of every statement of Scripture would be unintelligible, that is, many statements in Scripture would be incoherent with other statements in Scripture or with what we know to be true from experience.

Ibn Daud's method for reading Scripture in this context is simple. Where the most literal meaning of Scripture would make what Scripture says false, interpret it non-literally. The issue is not, how do we interpret Scripture to agree with science. For ibn Daud, religion is no more the slave of science than science is the slave of religion. Rather, the issue is this: Given that God is perfect, then what God reveals must be true; God has revealed to Israel the Hebrew Scriptures; hence, what those Scriptures mean must be true. The problem is, how can we know what they mean? Ibn Daud's answer is that the correct interpretation of any text within the corpus of divine revelation rests on its coherence with the entire corpus. If the literal meaning of the text is incoherent, then that meaning is not the true one.

In this context, ibn Daud asks, why is it that so many of the words in Scripture are not to be understood literally? In other words, why is God cunning and devious? Why doesn't he say what he means to say as literally and as clearly as possible? Ibn Daud here succinctly gives an answer that Maimonides will elaborate on in his *Guide of the Perplexed*.[22] The answer is contained in what the rabbis meant when they said, "The Torah speaks in the language of human beings."[23] In brief, this means that the Bible is not a secret document intended solely for an elite. Rather, God intended the Torah to speak to each of the children of Israel, irrespective of their intellectual abilities or accomplishments. To do so, God had to speak at many different levels at the same time, with at least one level appropriate to every level of intellectual competence. However, the greater their conceptual excellence, the greater the ability of the readers to approximate Scripture's true interpretation, that is, the meaning that is true.

It is important to note that the rabbis who succeeded ibn Daud recognized that there are many different levels at which it is proper to interpret Scripture. The most succinct statement of these different approaches was given by Nachmanides. Every rabbinic commentator on the Hebrew Scriptures sought to explain the biblical text in any or all of the following ways. He explained its simple or its hidden meaning. The former dealt primarily with linguistic questions: semantics and grammar. The latter was homiletic, philosophical, or mystical. All four kinds of interpretation are important to understand how the rabbis understood Scripture. Often these different approaches produce contrary explanations, and most commentators recognized the contradictions. However, for most rabbis this diversity of meaning was not problematic. God expresses his truth in multiple ways in his written word. While one kind of hidden meaning may not seem to agree with another kind, the conflict is not real. The difference lies only in the mode of expression. A homiletic and a philosophical statement, for example, may seem from their language to be dealing with the same question and reaching different conclusions, when in fact each kind of statement is dealing with a different question, and for that very reason there need not be any conflict between them. This is not to say that the rabbis advocated any kind of double truth theory. Without exception the rabbis believed that the one God of the universe is the source of only one truth. However, this epistemological unity has diverse expressions. Consequently, within each kind of commentary there is a need to determine coherence and consistency, in keeping with the logical rules of that language. Hence, two philosophical interpretations that violate the law of the excluded middle cannot both be true. However, to give a reason is not the same thing as to give a homily, and what the language of a text explicitly says or what that explicit statement logically entails need not be consistent with what the text alludes to or how the text is used in a homily. Allusions or hints are subject to their own distinct kind of grammar.

For ibn Daud and the Jewish Aristotelians he spawned, from Maimonides through Gersonides, there is no such thing as religious truth *and* scientific truth. There is only truth. If religion has any real value, then it, no less than science, makes truth claims, and, if its claims have value, then they must be true. Furthermore, because there is only one truth, true religion and true science must be coherent. If they are incoherent, then either or both may be false, but both cannot be true.

Furthermore, a faith like Judaism cannot be confined to only part of one's life; it must include everything. Hence, Judaism includes, and is not separate from, true science. Consequently, no understanding of Judaism that excludes the insights of science can be called (in the language of contemporary Orthodox religious thinkers) "Torah true."

In general terms, this is ibn Daud's understanding of the relationship between science and religion. It provided him with a model to incorporate the new science of Aristotelianism into the dogmatic system of rabbinic Judaism. This model set the agenda for all subsequent classical Jewish philosophers, from Maimonides through Gersonides to its eventual overthrow by Crescas and Spinoza when Aristotelianism was itself again surpassed by a new form of atomism, Newtonian physics.

❧ NOTES ❧

1 Such as Thales, Anaximander, and Anaximenes, all of Miletus in Asia Minor.
2 Such as Leucippus of Miletus, Democritus of Abdera, Epicurus of Samos, and Lucretius.
3 Such as Zeno of Citium, Chrysippus of Soli, and Posidonius of Apamea.
4 Namely, the Qadariyya and the Jabariyya.
5 Notably, Eudoxus of Cnidus and Callipus.
6 Notably, Plotinus, Porphyry, Proclus, and Boethius.
7 Notably, Theophrastus.
8 With specific reference to the Jewish Aristotelians, the most influential Muslim theologians were al-Fārābī (c. 870–950), ibn Bājja (d. 1138), and ibn Sīnā (Avicenna) (980–1037). Of the commentators, the most notable influences for Jewish intellectual life in the Muslim world were Alexander of Aphrodisias (third century CE), Themistius (c. 317–88 CE), and John Philoponus (c. 490–c. 580 CE). After the twelfth century, when the center of Jewish intellectual activity moved to Christian southern Europe, the single most important influence on reading Aristotle was the commentaries of ibn Rushd (Averroes) (1126–98).
9 Jews left the Muslim empires for the Holy Roman Empire because the former was in decline and the latter was in ascension. That Christians were successful only in moving into the western extremes rather than the eastern, and that the Jews who entered Christian Europe came from the west rather than from the east, has considerable (as yet unrecognized) importance for the history of science, mathematics, and philosophy. Because Christian intellectual contact was limited largely to the west, what they took over as new science and philosophy was Aristotelian. This Muslim new science was the foundation of Christian Scholasticism in the thirteenth to fifteenth centuries. It was not until this new science was fully assimilated into their universities and finally examined critically that the Muslim old science of atomism gained an audience in Christian Europe. In my judgment it is the beginnings of atomism in Christian European sciences

that is a major hallmark of the Renaissance. If the above analysis is correct, then, had the Europeans been successful militarily in the eastern extremes of the Muslim world, it is most likely that what we call "modern science," Newtonian atomism, would have arisen in Europe at least three hundred years earlier than it did. The same would be even more applicable to Europe's final discovery of the advances that Hindu Indians and Persian Muslims made in all branches of mathematics.

10 Notably, Judah ha-Cohen (b. c. 1215), Isaac ben Abraham ibn Latif (c. 1210–80), Abraham ben Samuel Abulafia (1240–1291), Simeon ben Zemach Duran (1361–1444), Joseph Albo (d. 1444), Joseph ben Shem Tov ibn Shem Tov (1400–60), Abraham ben Shem Tov Bibago (d. c. 1489), Isaac Arama (c. 1420–94), Abraham ben Isaac Shalom (d. 1492), and Isaac Abravanel (1437–1509).

11 Notably, Samuel ben Judah ibn Tibbon (d. c. 1232), David ben Joseph Kimchi (c. 1160–1235), Shem Tov ben Joseph Falaquera (c. 1225–c.1295), Isaac Albalag (second half of thirteenth century), Yedaiah ben Abraham Bedersi ha-Penini (c. 1270–1340), Nissim ben Moses of Marseilles (c. 1325), Joseph ben Abba Mari ben Joseph ben Jacob Kaspi (b. 1279), and Moses ben Joshua Narboni (d. c. 1362).

12 Notably, Zerachiah ben Shealtiel Gracian of Barcelona (lived in Rome between 1277 and 1291), Hillel ben Samuel of Verona (lived c. 1220–95), Judah ben Moses ben Daniel Romano (c. 1280–c. 1325), and Immanuel ben Solomon of Rome (c. 1261–1328).

13 *Al-Aqidah al-Rafi'ah*. It was composed in Judeo-Arabic in 1160. It survived through two Hebrew translations – one by Samuel Motot, entitled *Ha-Emunah ha-Nisa'ah*, and a second, better known translation by Solomon ibn Labi, entitled *Ha-Emunah ha-Ramah*.

14 Notably, the theologies and/or commentaries of Saadia ben Joseph al-Fayyumi (882–942), Solomon ibn Gabirol (1021–58), Bachya ibn Paquda (c. 1090–1156), Abraham Bar Chiyya (d. 1136), Joseph ibn Tzaddik (d. 1149), and Judah Halevi (c. 1075–1141).

15 For example, ibn Daud's topology of kinds of soul is far clearer than anything Maimonides presents in either the *Guide* or his *Shemonah Peraqim*. For example, ibn Daud explains, while Maimonides does not, what is meant in claiming that, while souls have multiple functions (such as nutrition, reproduction, and locomotion), there are not multiple souls in each individual and that a particular function of the soul of one kind of entity is not the same as a particular function of the soul of another kind of entity, even though those functions have the same name.

16 The status of this third book (entitled "The Healing of the Soul") within the whole is problematic. Ibn Daud tells us that his goal in composing this work was to solve the so-called problem of free will and determinism. That question is dealt with directly in the final chapter of the second book. Given his stated intention, this is where the *Exalted Faith* ought to end. In fact, everything discussed prior to this chapter (2.6.2) can be seen as material whose purpose is to justify his presuppositions here. Furthermore, the internal structure of all of the material presented in every known manuscript of this third book is incoherent. For example, it is supposed to consist of two chapters, but all existing manuscripts contain only a first chapter that deals with a potpourri of issues

in ethics. At best book 3 is only an addendum to the treatise. For these reasons the following summary is limited to the first two books.

17 The critical difference between Rambam and Rabad on divine attributes has to do with relations. Rabad admits them and Rambam does not, which forces the latter to make the kind of extreme claims about negative theology that are most characteristic of his discussion of God. Ibn Daud also affirms negative theology, but in a form that saves him from the kinds of logical attacks Maimonides' theology received in the writings of those Christian and Jewish Aristotelians who followed him, notably Aquinas and Gersonides.

18 In opposition to the Karaites, the Muslims, and the Christians.

19 Ibn Daud's *Sefer ha-Qabbalah* should be understood not as a work in history, but as his detailed theological defense of the claim presented in this chapter. The evidence for his failure to defend his claim of the absolute authenticity of rabbinic tradition is apparent in the ways he was forced to alter his account of Jewish history. In this respect it is interesting to note that neither Maimonides nor any of the subsequent Jewish Aristotelians used rabbinic statements as initial premises for arguments about truth claims in the way that ibn Daud and his Jewish philosophical predecessors did.

20 It is interesting to note that ibn Daud does not list creation as a fundamental principle of rabbinic Judaism, despite the fact that his predecessor, Saadia, made creation the corner-stone of all Jewish belief. I suspect that Rabad omitted creation because he found it to be the one central belief in Judaism that could not be explained or defended from the conceptual orientation of the new Aristotelian science. This apparent incoherence between Aristotle's posited eternal universe and Scripture's claim about creation becomes a central theme in the Jewish philosophies of both Maimonides and Gersonides.

21 Which they must be, because his form of expression is curt. His intention is to summarize what others have said, but in fact much that he says is original. In other words, his statements only have the external form of summaries. In reality they are often subtle expressions of sophisticated reasoning rooted in the logic of both his religious and scientific traditions.

22 In particular, in 1.26, 2.47, and 3.29.

23 B. *Yevamot* 71a; *Bava Metzia* 31b.

❧ BIBLIOGRAPHY ❧

Texts

Crescas (1962–3) *Sefer Or Adonai* (Tel Aviv: Esther).

Gersonides (1560) *The Wars of the Lord* (Riva di Trento); (Leipzig: Lorck, 1866). Book 1 translated by S. Feldman (Philadelphia: Jewish Publication Society, 1985); Book 3 translated by N. Samuelson, *Gersonides on God's Knowledge* (Toronto: Pontifical Institute of Mediaeval Studies, 1977); Book 4 translated by J. D. Bleich, *Providence in the Philosophy of Gersonides* (New York: Yeshiva University Press, 1973); critical edition with translation and commentary by B. Goldstein, *The Astronomy of Levi ben Gerson* (New York: Springer, 1985).

Gersonides (1946) *Commentary on the Book of Job*, translated by A. I. Lassen (New York: Bloch).

Grant, E. (1974) *A Source Book in Medieval Science* (Cambridge, MA: Harvard University Press).

ibn Daud, A. (1986) *The Exalted Faith*, edited by N. Samuelson and G. Weiss and translated by N. Samuelson (Cranbury, NJ: Associated University Presses).

Maimonides (1963) *The Guide of the Perplexed*, translated by S. Pines, 2 vols. (Chicago: University Of Chicago Press).

—— (1966) *The Eight Chapters of Maimonides on Ethics*, edited by J. Gorfinkle (New York: AMS).

Staub, J. (1986) *The Creation of the World According to Gersonides* (Chicago: Scholars Press).

Studies

Davidson, H. (1972) "Alfarabi and Avicenna on the Active Intellect," *Viator* 3: 109–78.

—— (1979) "Maimonides' Secret Position on Creation," in *Studies in Medieval Jewish History and Literature*, edited by I. Twersky (Cambridge, MA: Harvard University Press), 1: 16–40.

Diesendruck, Z. (1935) "The Philosophy of Maimonides," *Central Conference of American Rabbis Yearbook* 65: 355–68.

Efros, I. (1974) *Studies in Medieval Jewish Philosophy* (New York: Columbia University Press).

Fakhry, M. (1953) "The Antinomy of the Eternity of the World in Averroes, Maimonides and Aquinas," *Muséon* 66: 139–55.

—— (1970) *A History of Islamic Philosophy* (New York: Columbia University Press).

Feldman, S. (1967) "Gersonides' Proof for the Creation of the Universe," *Proceedings of the American Academy for Jewish Research* 35: 113–37.

—— (1974) "Platonic Themes in Gersonides' Cosmology," in *Salo W. Baron Jubilee Volume*, edited by S. Lieberman and A. Hyman (Jerusalem: American Academy for Jewish Research), pp. 383–405.

—— (1980) "The Doctrine of Eternal Creation in Hasdai Crescas and Some of His Predecessors," *Viator* 11: 289–320.

Fontaine, T. (1990) *In Defense of Judaism: Abraham Ibn Daud: Sources and Structures of Emunah Ramah* (Assen: Van Gorcum).

Gilson, E. (1955) *History of Christian Philosophy in the Middles Ages* (New York: Random House).

Goldstein, B. (1969) "Preliminary Remarks on Levi Ben Gerson's Contributions to Astronomy," *Proceedings of the Israel Academy of Sciences and Humanities* 3 (9).

—— (1980) "The Status of Models in Ancient and Medieval Astronomy," *Centaurus* 24: 132–47.

—— (1984) "The Origins of the Doctrine of Creation Ex Nihilo," *Journal of Jewish Studies* 35: 127–35.

—— (1985) *Theory and Observation in Ancient and Medieval Astronomy* (London: Variorum).

—— (1991) "Levi ben Gerson: On the Relationship between Physics and Astronomy," in *Physics, Cosmology, and Astronomy, 1300–1700: Tension and Accommodation*, edited by S. Unguru (Dordrecht: Kluwer), pp. 75–82.

Henry, D. (1972) *Medieval Logic and Metaphysics: A Modern Introduction* (London: Hutchinson).

Husik, I. (1958) *A History of Mediaeval Jewish Philosophy* (Philadelphia: Jewish Publication Society).

Kogan, B. (1981) "Averroes and the Theory of Emanation," *Mediaeval Studies* 43: 384–404.

—— (1984) "Eternity and Origination: Averroes' Discourse on the Manner of the World's Existence," in *Islamic Theology and Philosophy*, edited by M. E. Marmura (Albany: State University of New York Press), pp. 203–35.

—— (1985) *Averroes and the Metaphysics of Causation* (Albany: State University of New York Press).

Manekin, C. (1985) "Preliminary Observations on Gersonides' Logical Writings," *Proceedings of the American Academy for Jewish Research* 52: 85–113.

Novak, D. and N. Samuelson (eds) (1986) *Creation and the End of Days: Judaism and Scientific Cosmology* (Lanham, New York, and London: University Press of America).

Samuelson, N. (1969a) "On Knowing God: Maimonides, Gersonides and the Philosophy of Religion," *Judaism* 18: 64–77.

—— (1969b) "Philosophic and Religious Authority in the Thought of Maimonides and Gersonides," *Central Conference of American Rabbis Journal* 16: 31–43.

—— (1970) "The Problem of Free Will in Maimonides, Gersonides and Aquinas," *Central Conference of American Rabbis Journal* 17: 2–20.

—— (1971a) "Comments on Maimonides' Concept of Mosaic Prophecy," *Central Conference of American Rabbis Journal* 18: 9–25.

—— (1971b) "Saadia and the Logic of Religious Authority," *Judaism* 20: 460–6.

—— (1976) "The Problem of Future Contingents in Medieval Jewish Philosophy," *Studies in Medieval Culture* 6: 71–82.

—— (1977) "Ibn Daud's Conception of Prophecy," *Journal of the American Academy of Religion* 45: 883–900.

—— (1979) "Causation and Choice in the Philosophy of Ibn Daud," in *The Solomon Goldman Lectures* (Chicago: Spertus College of Judaica Press), 2: 81–90.

—— (1982) "Ibn Daud and Franz Rosenzweig on Other Religions: A Contrast Between Medieval and Modern Jewish Philosophy," in *Proceedings of the Eighth World Congress of Jewish Studies, Division C: Talmud and Midrash, Philosophy and Mysticism, Hebrew and Yiddish Literature* (Jerusalem: World Union of Jewish Studies), pp. 75–80.

—— (1984) "Medieval Jewish Philosophy," in *Back to the Sources: Reading the Classic Jewish Texts*, edited by B. Holtz (New York: Simon & Schuster), pp. 261–303.

—— (1990) "Gersonides' Place in the History of Philosophy," in *The Solomon Goldman Lectures*, edited by B. L. Sherwin and M. Carasik (Chicago: Spertus College of Judaica Press), 5: 105–18.

—— (1991a) "The Role of Elements and Matter in Gersonides' Cosmogony," in

Gersonide en son temps, edited by G. Dahan (Louvain and Paris: Peeters), pp. 199–233.

—— (1991b) "Maimonides' Doctrine of Creation," *Harvard Theological Review* 84.3: 249–71.

Sirat, C. (1985) *A History of Jewish Philosophy in the Middle Ages* (Cambridge: Cambridge University Press).

Waxman, M. (1966) *The Philosophy of Don Hasdai Crescas* (New York: AMS).

Wolfson, H. (1929) *Crescas' Critique of Aristotle: Problems of Aristotle's Physics in Jewish and Arabic Philosophy* (Cambridge, MA: Harvard University Press).

—— (1948) "The Meaning of Ex Nihilo in the Church Fathers, Arabic and Hebrew Philosophy and St. Thomas," in *Medieval Studies in Honor of J. D. M. Ford* (Cambridge, MA: Harvard University Press), pp. 355–67.

—— (1973a) "Halevi and Maimonides on Design, Chance and Necessity," in *Studies in the History of Philosophy and Religion* (Cambridge, MA: Harvard University Press) 2: 1–59.

—— (1973b) "The Platonic, Aristotelian and Stoic Theories of Creation in Halevi and Maimonides," in *Studies in the History of Philosophy and Religion* (Cambridge, MA: Harvard University Press), 1: 234–49.

—— (1976) *The Philosophy of the Kalam* (Cambridge, MA: Harvard University Press).

—— (1979) *Repercussions of the Kalam in Jewish Philosophy* (Cambridge, MA: Harvard University Press).

CHAPTER 11

Moses Maimonides

Howard Kreisel

➳ INTRODUCTION ➳

"From Moses (the prophet) to Moses (Maimonides), none arose like Moses (Maimonides)." This well-known epigram conveys the unique position in Jewish history attained by Maimonides (1135?-1204). His achievements rapidly assumed mythic proportions. Maimonides' legal code, the *Mishneh Torah*, was a pioneering work that revolutionized the study of Jewish law. Its significance has not waned with the passing of the centuries, and it remains one of the most thoroughly studied works in rabbinic literature. His *Guide of the Perplexed* is the single most important Jewish philosophical work ever written. It has left a sharp impress on diverse currents in Jewish thought from his own time to the present. Maimonides was a prolific writer. In addition to these two compositions, he wrote a commentary on the Mishnah, an enumeration of the commandments of the Torah (*Book of the Commandments*), numerous legal responsa and letters, and a series of medical treatises. He also lived a busy public life. He was appointed as one of the royal physicians in the court of the vizier in Egypt, and also served as the head of the Jewish community. His prominence as a Jewish legal authority spread well beyond the borders of Egypt within his own lifetime. Queries were addressed to him by Jews from around the world.

Maimonides' life embraced seemingly conflicting characteristics. He was the consummate scholar desiring solitude in order to study. At the same time, he was the political leader of the Jewish community, actively engaged even in its mundane affairs. He was the Jewish legal authority who mastered the entire library of rabbinic literature, and who was totally engrossed in even the relatively minor points of law. Yet he was also the philosopher, primarily concerned with the gamut of the sciences culminating in metaphysics, and whose avowed teachers were Aristotle and his ancient and Islamic disciples. Maimonides' wholehearted commitment both to Jewish law and to philosophical study posed a particularly vexing problem to many. In the eyes of staunch Jewish traditionalists, Aristotelian philosophy is synonymous with heresy. It rejects the creation of the world and the personal God of history, who knows and rewards each individual in accordance with his or her deeds. How then could a person so totally at home in the world of rabbinics engage in the study of such thought, let alone openly embrace it on several issues? Many Jewish rationalists, on the other hand, viewed Jewish legal studies as at best secondary to the philosophic pursuit, upon which depended one's true felicity. Was this not also Maimonides' view as it emerges from several of his writings? Why then would he devote most of his literary efforts to the law, painstakingly studying and codifying even those laws which had no practical relevance in his own day? Maimonides' dual commitment has also contributed to an unusual historical phenomenon. Through the ages, many diverse and sharply antagonistic groups within Judaism looked to Maimonides as their spiritual hero, and interpreted his life and works in accordance with their own ideological predilections.

A harmonistic picture of Maimonides' literary and social activity emerges when one views it from the perspective of his political philosophy. Politics, in its ideal manifestation, is the rule by one who has attained intellectual perfection, and whose aim is to mold a well-ordered society devoted to the pursuit of perfection. It represents the highest human vocation. In a short philosophic treatise written by Maimonides, the *Treatise on Logic*, he concludes with a description of the practical philosophy of politics:

> As for the governance of the city, it is a science that provides
> its inhabitants with knowledge of true happiness and the way
> of striving to attain it ... and with training their moral qualities
> to abandon things that are presumed to be happiness ... It
> likewise prescribes for them rules of justice by means of which
> their associations are well ordered. The learned men of bygone
> nations used to posit directives and rules in accordance with the
> perfection of each individual among them, by means of which
> their kings governed subjects. They called them nomoi .... The
> philosophers have many books concerning all these things which
> have been translated into Arabic .... But in these times all this
> has been dispensed with it, I mean, the regimes and the nomoi,
> for people are governed by the divine commands.[1]

Maimonides' subsequent discussion of the law of Moses (*Guide* 3.27–8) elaborates upon these notions. He maintains that the divine law aims at the well-being of the body and the well-being of the soul. The former goal lies in the attainment of social harmony by means of laws preventing people from harming each other, and by training them in the moral virtues. The latter, and more noble, goal lies in inculcating correct opinions to all members of society, each in accordance with his or her respective capacity. Maimonides regards society as necessary for the preservation of the human species and for the human being's attainment of ultimate perfection – intellectual apprehension of all that exists culminating in knowledge of God. Moses attained the highest possible level of perfection in Maimonides' view. This resulted in his reception/ legislation of an ideal law, designed to create a society in which its members achieve the highest perfection of which they are capable. Since the law was given to society at large, it does not enter into all the details of correct opinions – for example, the existence of God – but communicates them in a summary manner. It imposes a legal obligation upon all its adherents to pursue knowledge of them, in effect commanding the study of the theoretical sciences by which knowledge of God is attained. Many correct opinions are presented in a veiled manner by means of parables. These are the opinions that may prove harmful to the multitude, who are incapable of the proper understanding and appreciation of them. A number of opinions presented by the law are politically necessary – for example, that God is angry with those who disobey.

Maimonides views the law of Moses as eternal, each of the individual commandments being irrevocable. Nevertheless, he recognizes that changes in historical circumstances demand modifications in the law. The law itself provides the mechanisms for such changes by granting subsequent legal authorities the right to interpret laws, temporarily suspend them when the need arises, and issue additional decrees. It also limits the circumstances under which many of the historically relative laws are to be practised – for example, the laws of sacrifice that are performed only in the Holy Temple – though these laws remain formally valid. Moses, in Maimonides' thought, assumes the role of Plato's philosopher-king, whom al-Fārābī had already transformed into the supreme prophet-legislator. Unlike his philosophical mentors, Maimonides limits this role to Moses alone. He thereby attempts to safeguard belief in the continuous validity of Jewish law in the face of the manifold challenges, while allowing for its adaptation to changing historical circumstances. The prophets and sages are also philosopher-rulers according to Maimonides. They play the role al-Fārābī assigned to the "princes" of the law. These are individuals sufficiently well versed in the law and its purpose to adapt it to their own times. Owing to their inferior level of perfection in comparison to the ideal lawgiver, however, they lack authority to introduce a new legislation. Already in his earliest writings, Maimonides attempted to show that a deeper understanding of the prophetic parables and rabbinic midrashim reveals that they are figurative representations of philosophical truths. The prophets and sages employed the parable as a pedagogical tool for educating all the strata of society, each in accordance with its intellectual level.

The renewal of this historical chain, interrupted after the close of the Talmud, was the task to which Maimonides dedicated his life's work. A study of Aristotelian philosophy, together with Plato's political thought as adapted by al-Fārābī, opened Maimonides' eyes to what he regarded as the proper understanding of the divine law. In composing the *Mishneh Torah*, Maimonides took for his model the law of Moses, in accordance with his interpretation of the purpose of the law. He incorporated into his code the entire body of law, including those laws with no practical relevance in his own time, to underscore the inviolability of all the parts of Mosaic legislation. His innovative rational organization of Jewish law made knowledge of the law far more easily accessible to its adherents. Yet he adopted for the most part a conservative stance, anchored firmly in his rabbinic sources, in the legal rulings contained in the code. Significantly, Maimonides' most novel and far-reaching legal decisions come at the very beginning of his code, though he masterfully rooted them in the classic Jewish texts. He opens with a section, *Laws of the Principles of the Torah*, that treats theoretical knowledge of God as the ultimate legal obligation. Maimonides depicts God as Aristotle's first cause and self-intellecting intellect, devoid of all corporeal traits, or any positive attribute in addition to God's essence. Absent from this description is the personal, corporeal, creator-God found in the traditional texts. He provides a general outline of the knowledge that it is incumbent to pursue in order to fulfill the commandments to love and to fear God. The outline is essentially a brief synopsis of Aristotelian metaphysics and physics. In the following section, *Laws of Character Traits*, he adapts Aristotelian ethics to Jewish society at large. Maimonides maintains that one thereby fulfills the obligation of walking in God's ways. These two sections lay the foundation for the twin goals of the law presented in Maimonides' other writings. Maimonides sought to direct the adherents of the law to the understanding and pursuit of true human perfection. From this perspective, Maimonides' code was his crowning achievement, the practical adaptation of theoretical political philosophy to Jewish law.

GUIDE OF THE PERPLEXED: AN OVERVIEW

While Maimonides' philosophical views emerge from a number of writings, the *Guide of the Perplexed* contains the most mature and detailed expression of his philosophy. Unlike the *Mishneh Torah*, it is a work attempting to guide people to true beliefs by means of rational discourse, rather than through the medium of legal obligations. If the latter approach is linked by Maimonides to Moses, the former is linked to Abraham (*Guide* 3.29). Abraham discovered God through rational speculation, and attempted to direct others to this belief by means of various arguments. Maimonides addressed the *Guide* to one of his students, and those like him, whose soul yearned for knowledge of divine matters. When such students turn to the study of philosophy, Maimonides indicates, they are overwhelmed by the numerous dilemmas that result from the comparison between its teachings and those of traditional Judaism. They feel they must choose between intellect and religious faith. The *Guide* aims at mitigating the perplexity that accompanies the attempt to maintain the dual commitment characterizing Maimonides' own life.

Maimonides divides the *Guide* into three parts. He devotes most of the first part to a discussion of the individual terms denoting God's corporeality appearing in the Bible, showing that these terms must be interpreted figuratively. In addition, he deals with several topics relating to his conception of God – epistemology and metaphysics (chapters 31–5), divine attributes (50–60), divine names (61–4), divine essence (68), and God's relation to the totality of existence (69, 72). The first part concludes with a discussion of the demonstrations of the Islamic theologians, the kalām, for the existence, unity, and incorporeality of God (71, 73–6). The second part opens with the Aristotelian philosophical demonstrations for the existence, unity, and incorporeality of God (introduction–1). Maimonides then turns to the topics of God's governance of the world by means of "angels" (2–12), whether the world is eternal or created (13–31), and prophecy (32–48). The concluding part is devoted to an esoteric explication of the *Account of the Chariot* (introduction–7), the problem of evil and divine providence and knowledge (8–24), the reasons for the commandments (25–50), and human perfection (51–4). Throughout the treatise, Maimonides explicates various biblical verses and rabbinic midrashim, alluding to the philosophical truths they mask.

It is important to stress that Maimonides did not regard the *Guide* as a "philosophical" work in the technical sense of the term – a work dealing with one of the sciences following the procedures laid down by the Aristotelian tradition. He explicitly indicates that his work was not designed to replace the philosophical literature necessary to one's understanding of existence. The *Guide* was written as a Jewish work covering those topics wherein lie the apparent contradictions between Judaism and philosophy. It treats philosophical topics only to the extent necessary to accomplish this end. The thrust of Maimonides' argument is that many of the apparent contradictions between Judaism and philosophy disappear when one appreciates the fact that the esoteric teachings of the Bible correspond to philosophical truths. The masses understand the teachings literally in accordance with their capacity, while the astute penetrate the inner meaning. In regard to some of the apparent contradictions, however, Maimonides appears to be of the opinion that they result from the false conclusions of the philosophers in those areas in which they were incapable of arriving at demonstrative truths. In this chapter, I will focus on some of the major issues involved in interpreting the *Guide*, and then briefly discuss several of its central topics. Particular attention will be paid to the problems which emerge from Maimonides' presentation.

❧ INTERPRETING THE *GUIDE* ❧

The *Guide* was written to mitigate perplexity in the area of religion and philosophy, but it has left its readers more than a little perplexed in their attempt to understand its teachings. The literary character of this treatise has made it an exceptionally difficult work to decipher. Maimonides indicates in the introduction to the *Guide* that he will not reveal many of his views in a straightforward manner. He points to a number of techniques that he employs to hide them from all but the philosophically astute reader – for example, mentioning certain views in passing, and not in their proper context, in order to illuminate topics discussed elsewhere in the work; and introducing deliberate contradictions. He assures his readers that every word in the *Guide* is carefully chosen (Maimonides wrote his treatise in Arabic) and every contradiction is introduced deliberately. In this manner, Maimonides seeks to overcome the dilemma of revealing physical and metaphysical truths without violating the rabbinic prohibition to conceal them from the unworthy, whose faith may otherwise be undermined. The list of the subjects involving the "secrets of the Torah" to be concealed from the masses is enumerated by Maimonides:

> attributes and the way they should be negated in regard to Him, the meaning of attributes that may be ascribed to Him, the discussion of His creation of that which He created, the character of His governance of the world, the "how" of His providence with respect to what is other than He, the notion of His will, His apprehension, and His knowledge of all that He knows, the notion of prophecy and the "how" of its various degrees, and the notion of His names.

> *Guide* 1.35: 80[2]

Maimonides' techniques laid the foundation for sharply different interpretations of his views on a range of subjects. How one understands Maimonides very much depends on one's approach. As seen from Maimonides' exhortation in the introduction, it is insufficient to look only at the currents existing on the surface of his thought. One must also attempt to see if there is an even more significant undercurrent. The presentation of a "simple" summary of Maimonides' views on some of the topics with which he deals thus fails to convey the rich texture of his presentation. The reader, however, continuously faces the problem of whether "hints" to a concealed doctrine are not figments of his or her own imaginative reading, and whether all the contradictions which are detected are in fact real or intended. Even when one decides that a certain contradiction is purposefully introduced, it is not always clear what conclusion one should draw.

Two general approaches mark both medieval and modern interpretations of the *Guide*. The first views Maimonides as an Aristotelian philosopher in Jewish garb. God is the first cause of an eternal world. God does not intervene in the order of nature, nor is there any immediate point of contact between God and human beings in history. God is not the immediate agent of the divine law, nor does God directly will the "miraculous" phenomena recorded in the Bible. There is also no direct correlation between observance of the commandments and ultimate felicity. If there is an "afterlife," it lies in the eternal existence of the perfected intellect that has apprehended the existents divorced from matter. In summary, Maimonides regards the world view of the philosophers as being the true view of the law, hidden from the eyes of the masses for its potentially devastating effects on their commitment to Judaism. This approach relies heavily on the esoteric/exoteric distinction in interpreting Maimonides' views. It sees in the views of Maimonides' Islamic Aristotelian predecessors the proper frame of reference for understanding Maimonides' philosophy. Disagreements exist among the adherents of this approach concerning specific issues, but this is the basic thrust of their interpretation. Perhaps the most brilliant exponent of this approach in the Middle Ages was Moses Narboni. Its best-known exponent in modern times is Leo Strauss.[3]

The alternative approach is to view Maimonides as adopting an independent position, differing both from that of the Islamic Aristotelians and from traditional views. Maimonides severely limits the realm of God's voluntaristic activity outside the workings of the natural order. He views the order as the principal means of God's governance, and the primary expression of divine wisdom. Nevertheless, he does not completely eliminate God's voluntaristic activity. Maimonides differs from the Aristotelians by maintaining that the world was created ex nihilo, thereby laying the foundation for belief also in the personal

God of history. While Maimonides makes sparing use of this approach to God, it plays an integral role in his philosophy. God is treated by him as the immediate author of the law. The biblical miracles are seen as voluntaristic acts on the part of God, though Maimonides constricts their numbers and the extent of their deviation from nature. Maimonides also believes that God knows all individuals and exercises providence in accordance with one's actions. The adherents of this approach tend to limit the significance of the esoteric/exoteric distinction in interpreting Maimonides' views. They rely primarily on Maimonides' explicit statements on the topics with which he deals. Many, if not the majority, of Maimonides' medieval and modern commentators have adopted a version of this approach. It is the view of, for example, Julius Guttmann. In general, the approaches the interpreters adopted in understanding Maimonides' philosophy, and the conclusions to which they arrived, may be more indicative of their own thought than that of Maimonides. Certainly Leo Strauss' and Julius Guttmann's far different views of Maimonides in no small part stem from the differences in their own philosophical views. What is true of these outstanding scholars is even more true of the towering intellectuals, such as Asher Ginzberg (Achad Ha'am) and Yeshayahu Leibowitz, who have read many of their own thoughts into Maimonides.

❦ GOD, THE DIVINE ATTRIBUTES, AND ❦ THE PROOFS FOR EXISTENCE (*GUIDE* 1.50–2.1)

Several basic philosophic notions underlie Maimonides' approach to God. The first is the Neoplatonic notion of the absolute unity and unfathomability of the divine essence. This notion leads Maimonides to repudiate ascribing to God not only all the Aristotelian categories pertaining to corporeal entities – for example, quality, quantity, relation – but any affirmative attribute. All the divine attributes are to be treated as attributes of action or "negative" attributes. The traditional reference to God as merciful does not mean that God possesses the trait of mercy. It should be construed as imputing to God activities that in a human context we normally associate with the emotion of mercy. The same is true of the other emotions, such as anger or graciousness. While multiple traits entail multiplicity in the essence, multiple actions do not. "Negative" attributes are attributes whose opposites are to be negated of God, in order that the trait in question should not be imputed to God. To say that God possesses life, for example, is to negate the trait of death. Thus knowledge of God is attained by apprehending the divine actions – the manner in which God governs the existents – or by intellectually grasping all the attributes to be negated of God. This approach predominates in Maimonides' formal discussion of the topic.

At the same time, Maimonides continues to accept the Aristotelian notion identifying God as self-intellecting intellect (*Guide* 1.68). Nor does he wish to surrender the conception of a living, powerful, willing, and knowing deity (1.53). Despite Maimonides' negation of attributes of relation, he regards God as the final and formal cause of the world, in addition to the efficient cause, who continuously endows the world with its existence (1.69). God is related to the world as the intellect is to the human organism (1.72). There is an obvious tension between some of these conceptions, only partially reconciled by Maimonides. He treats the essential attributes of life, will, power, and knowledge as identical with God's essence and as forming a single notion, so as not to violate the principle of divine unity. Moreover, Maimonides considers these attributes as equivocal, having absolutely no relation between their meanings when applied to God and when applied to others. He bases his view of the difference between God's essence and those of all others on the Avicennian notion of necessary existence. All other existents, whether generated or eternal, have only possible existence in themselves, in so far as they owe their existence to an external cause. For them, existence is a notion superadded to their essence. Only in the case of God is existence identical with essence (1.56–7). Maimonides' view of the equivocality of these attributes has left many interpreters wondering what sense they convey when applied to God. He appears to want to have it both ways – ascribing and negating these notions in reference to God – ultimately "solving" all problems by pointing to the complete "otherness" of the divine essence. He attempts to avoid the problems raised by the analogy of the relation between the intellect and the human organism by insisting that God nevertheless remains completely separate from the world. Maimonides may well have harbored an esoteric doctrine underlying his discussion of God. On the other hand, the tensions one encounters may have resulted from Maimonides' difficulty in integrating the diverse philosophical conceptions accepted by him into a harmonious whole.

The proof for the existence and absolute unity of God follows the discussion of the divine attributes. The Islamic theologians based their proof of God's existence on their proof for the creation of the world. The philosophers proved the existence of God based on the eternity a parte ante of the world. Maimonides proceeds to argue that the theologians have failed to provide demonstrative proof for the world's creation, entailing their failure to demonstratively prove God's existence. The philosophers' proofs for God's existence suffer a similar shortcoming, for they fail to demonstrate the eternity of the world.

From the dialectical proofs of the theologians and the philosophers, Maimonides constructs what he regards as a demonstrative proof. At the heart of the proof lies the disjunctive proposition that either the world is created or it is eternal. No third possibility exists. If it is created, the existence of God inevitably follows. If it is eternal, God's existence and unity is proven by the philosophers. Maimonides concludes the first section of the *Guide* with a discussion of the Islamic theologians' proofs for the creation of the world, and the unity and incorporeality of God, together with the premises upon which they build their proofs. He opens the second section with a discussion of the premises of Aristotelian philosophy, and the proofs for the existence, unity, and incorporeality of God based on them.

Maimonides' discussion underlines the conclusions shared in common by the theologians and the philosophers in regard to God's unity and incorporeality. Given the fact that the kalāmic and philosophic proofs ostensibly belong to the same topic, it is puzzling why Maimonides should locate the discussion of them in two different sections of his treatise. The order of Maimonides' discussion, and the manner in which he divides his treatise, should be taken into consideration in the interpretation of his views. Maimonides leaves little doubt that he regards the philosophers' approach as much more intellectually rigorous. All the philosophical premises are regarded by him as demonstrative, except for the eternity of motion. On the other hand, he is highly critical of many of the kalāmic premises and proofs. His discussion appears to skirt the implications of the fact that the profound differences in their conceptions of God emerge directly from their proofs. The God proved by the philosophers is the unmoved mover, first cause, and necessary existent. The Islamic theologians certainly do not reject this conception, but the God proved by them is the willing God of creation. Maimonides ultimately comes to the defense of the latter conception of God. Significantly, however, his discussion of divine governance follows immediately on the heels of the former conception.

❧ DIVINE GOVERNANCE (*GUIDE* 2.2–12) ❧

The issue of divine governance belongs to Maimonides' list of esoteric topics. Yet his discussion surprisingly reveals the extent to which he explicitly agrees with the Aristotelian world view, a view summarized by him at the beginning of the section. Maimonides maintains that God governs by means of the order of separate intellects, which exist completely divorced from matter, and the celestial spheres, responsible for the natural forces found in the sublunar world. He adopts the Aristotelian explanation for the nature of the spheres, and the reason for their fixed, uninterrupted circular motion. More significantly, he accepts the Neoplatonic doctrine of emanation as developed by al-Fārābī. Al-Fārābī adapted this doctrine to an astronomic model of the structure of the world. From God's intellection emanates the separate intellects in linear order, each one being the immediate source of the one below it in rank. From each separate intellect emanates one of the celestial spheres, beginning with the diurnal sphere and culminating with the sphere of the moon (2.4, 11). Each sphere moves out of a desire to imitate its separate intellect, which is the beloved object of its representation. Each separate intellect thus serves as the immediate efficient cause of one of the spheres, and the immediate final cause of its motion. Maimonides treats the active intellect, the last of the separate intellects, as the immediate source of all the essences or "forms" of the sublunar world, including the human intellect. Matter always attains the emanating "form" that it is naturally prepared to receive. The motion of the spheres produces the changes in matter responsible for its casting off one form and attaining another. The activity of all the existents above the sublunar world remains constant throughout eternity, undergoing no change. God is the remote efficient and final cause of all that exists, but is the immediate cause only of the first of the separate intellects.

Maimonides adopts al-Fārābī's view that God is not the immediate cause even of the diurnal sphere and its motion, in order to preserve the notion of God's unity. God cannot be endowed with two separately conceivable things – that represented by the act of causing bodies to move, which it shares in common with the separate intellects, and that by which it is distinct from each of the separate intellects. This conception of divine unity is also based on an Aristotelian proof (2.1). Maimonides makes no attempt to reconcile this conception with the Aristotelian notion of God as the prime mover, whose existence is demonstrated from the motion of the sphere. The tension between these two conceptions does not appear to signal an esoteric doctrine in Maimonides' thought. Rather it serves as a further example of the problems arising from the attempt to fuse in a coherent manner the different notions regarding the deity in the Neoplatonic-Aristotelian tradition. Maimonides' acceptance of the doctrine of emanation in this context, however, poses a more difficult dilemma to the interpreter of his thought. As we shall presently see, Maimonides criticizes this doctrine in his subsequent discussion. Such a blatant apparent contradiction could hardly be considered a mere oversight on Maimonides' part.

The separate intellects, together with the celestial spheres and the natural existents and forces of the sublunar world, are the "angels" spoken of in the Bible and in rabbinic literature according to

Maimonides. The only existents not considered by him to be angels are the "angels" as they are literally depicted. Such creatures do not exist in his ontology. Maimonides considers the biblical and rabbinic descriptions of the angels to be imaginative representations, predominantly of the separate intellects. He illustrates how certain midrashim should be interpreted from this philosophical perspective. He polemicizes against those who adopt a supernaturalistic approach to divine governance. How great is their ignorance in his view. God's wisdom and power are expressed precisely by the natural workings of the order (2.6). The angels – the separate intellects – are immaterial and do not accomplish their actions by any form of physical contact. Nor does God issue "commands" to the angels by means of speech consisting of letters and sounds. All these views, Maimonides concludes, "follow the imagination, which is also in true reality the *evil impulse*. For every deficiency of reason or character is due to the action of the imagination or consequent upon its action" (2.12: 280). The only issue upon which Maimonides indicates that he parts with the philosophers is that of creation.

✎ CREATION, ETERNITY, AND THE ✎ *ACCOUNT OF THE BEGINNING (GUIDE 2.13–31)*

Much more emphasis is placed on the belief in the creation ex nihilo of the world in the *Guide* than in his legal writings. Maimonides labels this belief a principle of the law, following that of the unity of God (2.13). In his previous lists of principles in the *Commentary on the Mishnah: Introduction to Pereq Cheleq* and in the *Mishneh Torah: Laws of the Principles of the Torah; Laws of Repentance*, belief in creation is conspicuous by its absence. Only after having written the *Guide* does Maimonides revise his list of principles in the *Commentary on the Mishnah* to include creation explicitly (within the fourth principle dealing with the primordiality of God). His earlier approach in his legal writings was meant to instill in the Jewish people a more philosophically refined view of God. Maimonides consciously chose to develop his approach in a manner that was in harmony with the Aristotelian doctrine of eternity. In the *Guide*, he takes pains to qualify this approach. He is well aware of the stakes involved in this issue. "With a belief in the creation of the world in time, all the miracles become possible and the Law becomes possible" (2.25: 329). Belief in the law, in other words, depends upon belief in God's ability to act directly in history. For all of Maimonides' stress on God's governance of the world through the natural order, he realizes that belief in this other aspect of divine governance is indispensable to religion. The question that has engaged Maimonides' medieval and modern commentators is whether he emphasized belief in creation since it was a necessary belief for Judaism, with the added virtue of being also true, or whether it was a politically necessary, though false, belief. While the thrust of his discussion supports the former conclusion, certain undercurrents in his discussion suggest the latter.

Maimonides opens his discussion with a presentation of three different opinions concerning the creation of the world. The first is the opinion of the law asserting that the world as a whole was created ex nihilo. Time too was created. Time is an accident of motion, which in turn is an accident of corporeal bodies. The second is the philosophical opinion that the world was created from primordial matter and will pass away into matter. The main exponent of this opinion is Plato. The final opinion is that of Aristotle who maintains the eternity of the world, both a parte ante and a parte post. The whole higher and lower order were always in existence and will always be in existence. No innovation can ever take place in the world that is not according to nature. In laying down the three opinions, Maimonides treats the problem of whether matter can be generated from absolute non-existence as the primary philosophical issue upon which the opinion of the law differs from the other two opinions. The exponents of the latter two opinions regard this as an absolute impossibility, comparable to the negation of the law of contradiction. Even God cannot perform what is absolutely impossible. In the opinion of the law, on the other hand, this is not an absolute impossibility, and we in fact are required to believe that God performed such an act in creating the world. While Maimonides outlines a number of salient differences between the Platonic and Aristotelian positions, he equates the two in positing the existence of something eternal existing simultaneously with God. He maintains that the falseness of the Epicurean position, asserting that the world came about by chance, has already been demonstrated by the philosophers, so he sees no need to discuss it further. The remainder of his discussion is devoted to a rebuttal of the Aristotelian position.[4]

The following chapter contains an outline of the Aristotelian proofs for the eternity of the world. Afterwards, Maimonides turns to a discussion of these proofs, arguing that they are non-demonstrative. He divides the Aristotelian proofs into two categories: those derived from the laws of nature operative in the world, and those derived from the nature of God. An example of a proof belonging to the former category is one based on the notion that motion has no beginning or end, hence the world is eternal. For if a motion is generated, the argument runs, it must be preceded by another motion belonging to all generated things – namely, its actualization after being non-existent. Consequently, motion already must exist for a motion to be generated. An infinite regress results unless one posits that motion is without beginning. The proofs based on the nature of God approach the problem of creation from the perspective that God is unchanging, and cannot be subject to any external cause. There is no potentiality in God. The creation of the world, however, entails a change from a potential creator to an actual creator, and hence a cause that was responsible for this change. Moreover, just as God's will and wisdom are permanent, so must be the actions that result from them – namely, giving existence to the world. Maimonides dismisses the first category of proofs by arguing that the laws of nature hold for the world as it now exists. We cannot infer from this state of affairs that these laws were also applicable to the situation before the world's existence. God implanted these laws into the world at creation. Maimonides next grapples with the proofs based on the nature of God, which cannot be dismissed quite as easily. He argues that only corporeal beings pass from potentiality to actuality when they act after not having acted. This is not true of incorporeal existents. Furthermore, the nature of the will is to will and not to will. An existent is said to undergo change only when an external cause acts upon its will. No such cause operates on the divine will and activity, thus no change in God's essence occurs when willing after not willing. The eternity of divine wisdom also does not entail an eternal world, for we cannot fathom the rules of God's wisdom in deciding to create the world in the manner it was created, or when it was created.

Maimonides' arguments up to this point are not designed to prove the doctrine of creation, only that there are no demonstrative proofs for the doctrine of eternity. He concedes that he possesses no demonstrative proof for creation. He continues his discussion by presenting what he considers to be the strongest dialectical proof for creation, a philosophically rigorous version of the kalāmic argument based on the notion of particularization (2.19; cf. 1.74, fifth method). Maimonides accepts the Aristotelian naturalistic explanation for all the particularities of the sublunar world. The particulars of the celestial realm are a different matter. The order of the celestial spheres is certainly not fortuitous. Yet the lack of uniformity in regard to the size of the spheres, their direction of motion, and velocity cannot be accounted for by natural necessity. Only the notion of purposeful action can account for the particularities of the celestial realm. This notion, in turn, entails that it was brought into existence in this manner after its non-existence.

Many of the Islamic philosophers did not regard the notions of purposeful activity and the eternity a parte ante of the world as mutually exclusive. They posited the doctrine of eternal creation. Maimonides is aware of this position and responds that it is based on semantic gymnastics. The eternity of the world entails its necessity, no matter what expressions are employed to remove the sting from this notion.

Only the doctrine of the creation of the world after its non-existence leaves room for divine will and purpose. Maimonides goes on to show many of the incongruities entailed by the doctrine of emanation. He concludes that far graver philosophical objections can be raised against the doctrine of eternity than against that of creation, hence the latter should be maintained even on the basis of philosophical considerations.

Ultimately, however, the religious considerations are those that determine the issue. The doctrine of eternity is harmful to the belief that should be maintained in regard to God. Furthermore, the doctrine of creation was taught by the two foremost prophets – Abraham and Moses (2.23). Maimonides indicates that a desire to follow the literal interpretation of Scripture is not the primary consideration governing his approach. A figurative interpretation is certainly possible if philosophic demonstration warrants it. In the case of creation, however, no figurative interpretation is required. The doctrine of eternity has not been demonstrated. Far more crucial to Maimonides is the point that belief in eternity, by not allowing for even the smallest change in nature, negates all the miracles, the promises of rewards and punishments, and in short, "destroys the Law in its principle" (2.25: 328).

While Maimonides ostensibly differs with the philosophers on the issue of the creation of the world, he accepts their position in regard to its eternity a parte post. He adopts this position despite the Aristotelian principle that everything that is generated is corrupted. Maimonides goes to great lengths to show that all the prophecies regarding the end of the world are figurative descriptions of historical events. He regards the order in the world as being immutable, the world being a perfect creation requiring no changes. For this reason he even partially "naturalizes" the phenomenon of miracles. He cites, with apparent approval, the rabbinic dictum that, in the creation of the various elements, God implanted the miracles destined to occur (2.29). Maimonides then presents an exegesis of the first two chapters of Genesis dealing with the creation of the world and the story of Adam and Eve in the Garden of Eden (2.30). He concludes his discussion of this topic of creation by underscoring the importance of the Sabbath. Observance of the Sabbath serves to strengthen belief in the principle that the world was created, in addition to providing for the well-being of the body.

Maimonides' discussion of creation can be read in a straightforward manner, without reference to an underlying esoteric doctrine. His philosophic argument for creation based on the doctrine of particularization has been seen by many as highly persuasive. The same is true of his counter-arguments to the Aristotelian proofs of the world's eternity. A number of the medieval interpreters, on the other hand, were less persuaded by Maimonides' arguments and felt that he had not seriously answered the Aristotelian proofs. The weakness of Maimonides' arguments, some concluded, may in itself be a subtle way of signaling his agreement with the Aristotelian position. Though most of the interpreters viewed Maimonides as adopting either the doctrine of creation ex nihilo or the Aristotelian doctrine of the eternity of the world (or the eternal creation of the world as presented by the Islamic Aristotelians), two alternative views have also been advanced. One is the view that Maimonides accepted the Platonic doctrine of creation from primordial matter. The other is that Maimonides adopted a skeptical stance, suspending his judgment as to what is the true doctrine. Acceptance of belief in creation, everyone realized, is necessary for insuring the masses' obedience to the law. From this perspective, it is clear why Maimonides went to such lengths to defend it. Each of the views rejecting Maimonides' explicit statements on this issue is based on a subtle, and at times ingenious, reading of his discussion. A few examples of the "hints" discerned pointing to an esoteric view convey how subtle some of these readings are.

Maimonides' attitude to Plato is inconsistent. In presenting the Platonic position in *Guide* 2.13, Maimonides equates it with the Aristotelian position. Both posit something other than God as existing contemporaneously with God. For this reason, Maimonides indicates, he dispenses with a discussion of the proofs of this doctrine. His subsequent brief mention of the Platonic doctrine is surprising in light of this stance:

> If, however, one believed in eternity according to the second opinion [Platonic] . . . this opinion would not destroy the foundations of the Law and would be followed not by the lie being given to miracles, but by their becoming admissible. It would also be possible to interpret figuratively the texts in accordance with this opinion. And many obscure passages can be found in the texts of the Torah and others with which this opinion could be connected or rather by means of which it could be proved.
>
> (2.25: 328)

In the following chapter, Maimonides ascribes this position to one of the greatest of the talmudic sages, Rabbi Eliezer ben Hyrcanus. His dual attitude to the Platonic position can certainly be interpreted as signaling an esoteric view.

The view that Maimonides accepted the Aristotelian position relies on a greater range of arguments involving even subtler readings of the text. As indicated above, the very weakness of several of Maimonides' arguments against the Aristotelian position suggested to some his agreement with it. Maimonides' view that God can will after not willing without experiencing a change of essence appears to be an exceptionally disingenuous argument given the identity between essence and will accepted by Maimonides. His example of the active intellect as an entity that undergoes no change, though it acts at times and does not act at others in accordance with the preparedness of matter, is hardly applicable to the case of God, as Maimonides himself is aware. From a philosophical perspective, Maimonides' defense of creation is rooted in the view that the structure of the heavenly order can result only from purposeful activity, and this type of activity presupposes the creation of the world. Maimonides, it is important to stress, does not prove creation from God's ability to differentiate between two possibilities that are completely equal from the standpoint of wisdom, such as the direction of motion of the spheres. This is the argument advanced, for example, by al-Ghazālī in his *Incoherence of the Philosophers*, and was undoubtedly known to Maimonides. Maimonides' argument is based on the lack of uniformity in the heavenly order, but he maintains that all the particulars are the product of divine wisdom rather than arbitrary acts of will. The philosophers too ascribe the eternal existence of the world to an intellectual principle, perfectly ordering all of its parts. There appears to be no difference between Maimonides and the philosophers on this fundamental point. His contention that the doctrine of eternity cannot be harmonized with the notion of purposeful activity, but signifies instead the necessary existence of the world, may be read as an ingenious or disingenuous argument in defense of creation, depending upon one's point of view. His etymological discussion of the verb *bara'* (create) has also been seen as signaling an esoteric doctrine. His apparently inconsistent stance in regard to the doctrine of emanation is certainly puzzling, strengthening the view that there is an esoteric level to his discussion.

One of the strongest reasons I have found for favoring an esoteric approach to Maimonides' discussion of this issue lies in the non-philosophical reasons adduced by him for believing in creation. Maimonides indicates that he could interpret the Torah figuratively to agree with the doctrine of eternity if the doctrine were proved. The two reasons he presents for not taking this route raise a number of questions in their wake. The first is that the Torah should not be figuratively interpreted in order to uphold an opinion whose contrary (creation) can be defended by various arguments. This suggests that Maimonides maintains a literal reading of the Torah whenever no demonstration against it can be adduced. Yet a careful reading of the *Guide* reveals that this is hardly the case. Maimonides adopts figurative interpretations in relation to a number of issues – for example, prophecy and miracles – even though he is not compelled to do so by demonstrative argumentation. The second reason advanced by Maimonides is even more problematic: "Know that with a belief in the creation of the world in time, all the miracles become possible and the Law becomes possible, and all questions that may be asked on this subject vanish" (2.25: 329). Maimonides proceeds to raise a number of questions involving prophecy and the law that he maintains can be answered only with recourse to the doctrine of creation. Just as God particularized the world in the manner he did, in accordance with his unfathomable wisdom, so too in these matters. In subsequent discussions in the *Guide*, however, he answers some of these questions, either explicitly or implicitly, in a manner that is in complete harmony with the philosophers' naturalistic approach – for example, why God gave prophetic revelation to one and not another, or what the divine aim was in giving the law. This suggests that the argument advanced here is only for the benefit of the masses. The philosophically astute reader can discern that the law remains valid even if the world is deemed to be eternal.

Many additional 'hints' to an esoteric doctrine can be detected, some of them found in the course of other discussions. One of them will be mentioned in the next section, dealing with Maimonides' approach to prophecy. The intellectual vigor displayed by Maimonides in defending the doctrine of creation on one hand, yet the subtle allusions to his possible agreement with either Aristotle or Plato on the other, may ultimately be construed as signaling a skeptical stance as to what is the true doctrine. In any event, it is easy to see how Maimonides' discussion lent itself to such diametrically opposed interpretations.

❦ PROPHECY (*GUIDE* 2.32–48) ❦

Maimonides opens his formal discussion of prophecy by delineating three fundamental approaches to this phenomenon. The first denies any necessary conditions for the attainment of prophecy, treating its bestowal upon the individual as completely dependent upon the divine will. The second is the Aristotelian approach that regards prophecy as a natural perfection, inevitably attained by one who is perfect in the rational and moral virtues and who possesses a perfect imagination. God plays no immediate role in the bestowal of prophecy. The third view is labeled by Maimonides as that of the law. It agrees with the Aristotelian view that rational and moral perfection is a necessary condition for prophecy. Maimonides considers this point a fundamental principle. It differs from Aristotle, however, in not viewing the attainment of perfection as a sufficient condition. God can intervene and deny prophecy from one who is otherwise worthy. This is similar to the case of miracles in general. In this manner, Maimonides preserves the notion of God's exercise of free will in a world that operates primarily in conformity with the order of nature.

Two further phenomena associated with prophecy are treated in a manner suggesting that a miraculous element is involved in their occurrence, namely, Mosaic prophecy and the revelation at Sinai. Both these phenomena are excluded by Maimonides from his discussion of prophecy proper. He treats them as sui generis, though he attempts to show that they do not violate the principle of the conditions necessary for the attainment of prophecy. It is not a coincidence that Maimonides singles out precisely those two phenomena that serve as the basis for the acceptance of the law. This allows him to maintain an essentially naturalistic approach to the attainment of prophecy, while safeguarding belief in the uniqueness and inviolability of the law.

The writings of the Islamic Aristotelians, particularly al-Fārābī, provided Maimonides with two naturalistic models from which to draw in understanding prophecy.[5] The first model views prophecy as the perfect intellect's conjunction (*ittiṣāl*) with the active intellect and the attainment of revelation (*waḥy*) in divine matters. Prophecy is seen as involving primarily metaphysical apprehension beyond that attained by means of discursive reasoning. This results in the permanent transformation of the individual's intellect. In the view of al-Fārābī, such an individual also serves as the ideal ruler. No explicit role is ascribed to the imaginative faculty in the description of the state of conjunction. The other model, also found in the writings of al-Fārābī, treats prophecy as an emanation specifically upon the imagination. It results in the figurative representation of theoretical knowledge or knowledge of the future.

Maimonides' approach to prophecy in the range of his writings reflects his attempts to integrate these two models. At times his description underscores the former, treating prophecy primarily as a phenomenon involving the intellect (*Mishneh Torah: Laws of the Principles of the Torah* 7.1; *Introduction to Pereq Cheleq*, sixth principle; *Guide* 3.51). In the present context, Maimonides makes more extensive use of the latter. Not only is a perfect imagination a necessary condition for the attainment of prophecy, but the emanation upon the imagination is part of the definition of this phenomenon: "Know that the true reality and quiddity of prophecy consist in its being an overflow flowing from God through the intermediation of the Active Intellect, toward the rational faculty in the first place and thereafter toward the imaginative faculty" (2.36: 369).

Maimonides treats veridical dreams as a phenomenon similar to prophecy in being the product of the activity of the imagination while the rest of the senses lie dormant. He implicitly rejects the approach that views the entities reportedly "seen" by the prophets as having real corporeal existence. They exist only within the prophet's own soul, and are not beheld by the external senses. Non-Mosaic prophecy is divided into two basic levels: dreams and visions (2.41). Both levels are directly related to the activity of the imagination. The latter occurs while the prophet is awake, and the senses cease to function due to the strength of the activity of the imaginative faculty. In 2.45 Maimonides brings his most detailed enumeration of the levels of prophecy. He subdivides dream prophecy into five different levels: seeing parables in a dream, hearing speech, seeing a man speaking, seeing an angel speaking, and seeing God speaking. Vision prophecy is subdivided into four levels, stopping short of being able to see God speaking in a vision. Maimonides offers also an alternative view that there is only one level of vision prophecy – seeing parables. Only in the case of Moses' prophecy does the imagination play no role in the reception of the emanation, according to Maimonides. Preceding all these levels are two sub-prophetic levels: first, the feeling of being driven to perform some great and noble action; second, an overpowering force resulting in the utterance of exceptional speech – for example, words of wisdom or praise. Both these levels are identified with the Holy Spirit. The model that treats prophecy as a phenomenon primarily involving the intellect is certainly not absent from Maimonides' discussion. Maimonides maintains that just as the prophets are able to attain information not available to others by simple divination, they are able to grasp speculative matters that others are incapable of grasping by means of speculation alone (2.38).

In the course of his discussion of prophecy, Maimonides treats the intellectual emanation flowing from the active intellect to the prophet as conveying knowledge in three different areas: theoretical philosophy (physics and metaphysics), governance, and divination. This intellectual emanation, according to Maimonides, is not received by the prophets alone but by other groups as well. The philosophers receive the emanation only by their rational faculty, owing to paucity of the overflow or a defect in their imagination. Rulers and diviners, on the other hand, receive the emanation only by their imagination, owing to a defect in their rational faculty (2.37). This view suggests that the emanation to the prophet's rational faculty is immediately responsible for his knowledge in physics and metaphysics. The continuation of the emanation to the imagination is responsible for his knowledge of governance and divination. In addition, it results in the figurative representation of theoretical knowledge that serves an important pedagogical function in the prophet's role as educator. Yet it is clear that, for Maimonides, precisely the combination of intellect and imagination in the reception of the emanation allows the prophet to govern and divine far better than those possessing only a perfect imagination. The prophet is able

to govern in accordance with his knowledge of the true end of humankind. His superior knowledge of reality guards against errors entering
into his prognostications. Maimonides may also have been of the
opinion that the imagination plays a role in enabling the prophet to
rise to heights in theoretical matters beyond what is attained by those
receiving the emanation by their rational faculty alone. He does not,
however, elucidate this point.

The precise role of the imagination in prophecy is complicated by
the fact that Maimonides excludes the use of imagination in Moses'
reception of prophecy. This position is hardly supported by a literal
reading of the descriptions of Moses' visions in the Torah. One is
tempted to conclude that other considerations play a dominant role in
Maimonides' thought. Maimonides emphasizes the role of the imagination in prophecy precisely in order to present a criterion by which
Moses' prophecy can be distinguished from all others. The superiority
and uniqueness of Mosaic prophecy has obvious ramifications for Maimonides' approach to the law. Yet Maimonides deliberately refrains
from entering into detail on these matters. He hints in other discussions
that Moses progressed in the level of his prophecy, initially attaining
prophecy through the mediation of his imaginative faculty. Maimonides'
description of the final perfection of Moses, in which his imagination
was no longer involved in the prophetic experience, suggests that he
attained nearly complete conjunction with the active intellect. His intellect divorced itself from the remaining vestiges of matter. The "voice"
heard by Moses represents the purely intellectual emanation upon
Moses' intellect resulting from this state of conjunction. It has been
suggested, however, that Maimonides' doctrine that the imagination did
not enter into Mosaic prophecy is an exoteric doctrine serving religious
purposes. By means of his alternative view of the levels of prophecy,
Maimonides perhaps hints that Moses attained the level of hearing
speech in a vision of prophecy. Some commentators have interpreted
Maimonides' view that Moses did not attain prophecy via the mediation
of an angel to signify that Moses received his prophecy directly from
God, the "angel" being a reference to the active intellect. This position
accords a supernatural status to Mosaic prophecy, but is difficult to
sustain in light of Maimonides' view of the hierarchy of separate intellects. Only the first of the separate intellects receives an emanation
directly from God. Maimonides may have wished to signify that Moses
joined the realm of the separate intellects, a realm which stands in
immediate relation to God.

The precise nature of the prophetic "emanation" from the active
intellect is yet another subject that remains obscure in the context
of Maimonides' approach. Does the "emanation" consist of specific
information bestowed by God via the active intellect, or does it repre-

sent the special power by which the human intellect and imagination function and arrive at the knowledge they attain? Maimonides' discussion suggests the latter conclusion. Not only then are the human faculties responsible for the specific form the prophecy assumes, but its specific content as well.

While the dominant distinction between the prophets in Maimonides' discussion revolves around the activity of the imagination (dream prophecy versus vision prophecy), other criteria for distinguishing between the prophets are also presented. One of these criteria sheds much light on Maimonides' view of human perfection. Maimonides distinguishes between public and private prophecy. Public prophecy results from the strength of the emanation, causing its recipient to try to bestow his or her perfection upon others. A similar phenomenon occurs also among the philosophers. Some are content in attaining knowledge for themselves, while others feel the need also to educate others. Entailed by Maimonides' approach is the view that the prophetic "mission" should be understood as the internal compulsion experienced by the prophet causing him to act, and does not result from a specific communication issued by God. It is the outcome of the emanation that forces the prophet to take an active role in leading others, and is an integral part of his perfection. For this reason Maimonides maintains that the faculty of courage is exceptionally strong among the prophets. In this manner prophecy, though a natural perfection, also serves as the extension of God's providence over humankind.

No issue is more central to the problem of the extent to which Maimonides adopts a naturalistic approach to prophecy than that of God's relation to the law. Though Maimonides draws a relation between the uniqueness of Mosaic prophecy and his reception of the Torah, he is careful to obfuscate the precise nature of this relation. In his legal writings Maimonides treats the belief that every word of the Torah was dictated by God to Moses as a principle of the faith. Moses' unique perfection made him the one suitable individual to be singled out for the reception of the law, but God is regarded as the immediate author of the entire contents of the law. The law then represents the most important instance of God's governance independent of the natural order. There is no shortage of passages in the *Guide* that supports this view. Yet there is also a strong undercurrent in Maimonides' discussion suggesting a far different conclusion. Maimonides explains the divinity of the law in terms of its final cause. Only the law that aims at intellectual perfection, and not only social well-being, is considered divine (2.40). Maimonides also points to the moderation exhibited by the law in its commands as a sign of its perfection. He may have wished to signal to his readers that it is not God's immediate authorship of the law that establishes its divinity. God serves only as the remote efficient cause of the divine law, as is the case in fact with all legislation. The perfection of the law is the reason for its being considered "divine." Only a perfect individual can lay down a perfect law, by translating knowledge of physics and metaphysics into a regimen governing society. This individual was Moses, the law being the product of the emanation characterizing his prophetic experience. Those not attaining intellectual-ethical perfection may attempt to imitate the divine law, but are incapable of producing a perfect legislation. If this interpretation is correct, the legislation of the divine law should be understood in light of the naturalistic workings of the order, even though Maimonides regards it is a unique phenomenon. He certainly could not reveal this view except in the most veiled manner, for the allegiance of the vast majority of the adherents of the law is based on their belief in God as the immediate author.

Maimonides lays the foundation for a supernaturalistic approach to prophecy by maintaining in the initial chapter of his discussion that God can withhold prophecy from one who is worthy. On the surface, he thereby leaves room for God's exercise of free will directly in history. The continuation of his discussion, however, raises questions whether Maimonides in fact held this view. He illustrates God's withholding of prophecy with the example of Jeremiah's assistant, Baruch ben Neriah, who did not attain prophecy despite his being worthy. He immediately proceeds to disqualify this example by suggesting that Baruch wasn't prepared for prophecy. Maimonides also disqualifies another apparent example of God's withholding of prophecy, "Yea her prophets find no vision from the Lord" (Lamentations 2:9). He explains that this is due to their being in exile. Subsequently, he presents a naturalistic approach for understanding the relation between exile and the failure to attain prophecy, namely, the sorrow produced by the state of exile upsetting the emotional equilibrium necessary for the attainment of prophecy. No further allusion is made to God's withholding of prophecy. Maimonides concludes his discussion of prophecy by treating the divine will as the remote efficient cause of all that happens in the world but not the proximate cause. The proximate causes are natural, voluntary, or accidental. In this manner he explains the biblical terms "command," "say," "speak," "send," and "call" when used in reference to God. Maimonides thereby hints that even in reference to the prophetic experience God never operates in a direct manner. His "command" simply refers to his role as the remote cause of the experience and its contents.

The topic of prophecy comes on the heels of Maimonides' discussion of the problem of creation. A literary convention strengthens the relation between the two in that Maimonides opens both discussions with a presentation of three opinions. Lest the point be lost upon his readers, Maimonides begins by remarking, "the opinions of people concerning prophecy are like their opinions concerning the eternity of the world or creation in time" (2.32: 360). Not lost upon Maimonides' medieval and modern commentators is the fact that there is a blatant lack of correspondence between the opinions ascribed by Maimonides to the law – creation ex nihilo and prophecy requiring perfection with God capable of withholding it from the worthy. The view of creation ex nihilo corresponds most closely to the view that God bestows prophecy upon whomever he chooses, with no constraints fettering his will. Maimonides' strong rejection of this position may be construed as a further hint that he does not accept the traditional view of creation. His explicit view of prophecy appears to correspond most closely to Plato's view of creation. Further complicating the picture is Maimonides' disqualification of the examples suggesting instances of God's intervention. This may be construed as Maimonides signaling his complete agreement not only with the Aristotelian position regarding prophecy but also regarding the eternity of the world and miracles.

THE PROBLEM OF EVIL AND DIVINE PROVIDENCE (*GUIDE* 3.8–24)

Maimonides discusses the problem of evil with two objectives in mind. The first is to negate the view that God is the agent of evil. The second is to inculcate in his readers an appreciation of what is truly good and evil in reference to humankind. Maimonides opens his discussion by dealing with the nature of sublunar entities. All of them are subject to generation and corruption because of matter. Matter continuously divests itself of form and receives form. Neither can exist without the other in the sublunar world. Maimonides treats all physical and moral evils confronting human beings as consequent upon matter, while all the virtues are consequent upon the human form, the intellect. The intellect is granted the power to subjugate matter. He posits as the goal of human existence the apprehension of the intelligibles, culminating in knowledge of the deity, the separate intellects, and divine governance. Maimonides also refers to one's conjunction with the active intellect in consequence of intellectual attainment. He hints that this state results in the individual's immortality, a position reflecting al-Fārābī's earlier view. This position can already be found in Maimonides' legal writings – for example, in *Laws of the Principles of the Torah* – as well as in other discussions in the *Guide*.[6] Maimonides counsels his readers that individuals striving for perfection should distance themselves as much as possible from corporeal desires. One is to admit only that which is indispensable for physical existence, while focusing one's life-endeavors on the attainment of intelligibles (3.8). He attempts to impress upon his readers the view that the greatest evil in reference to human existence is the failure to pursue and attain intellectual perfection. Natural evils are comparatively rare and far fewer than those perpetrated by human beings on each other. Most numerous are the evils individuals perpetrate upon themselves in their pursuit of imaginary goods (3.12).

The various evils are treated by Maimonides as privations, rather than existent things. Blindness, for example, is not the contrary of sight but the absence of sight. Ignorance is the privation of knowledge, and death the privation of form. In this manner, Maimonides proves that God cannot produce evil. All of God's acts involve the production of being, while evil has no being. This formal solution to the problem of evil only defers the obvious rejoinder. Why did God create a world characterized by privation? Would it not have been better to create a world characterized only by perfection without privation? Maimonides answers this problem only in part. God brought into existence sublunar matter, whose nature is to be a concomitant of privation. While this nature entails death and all other evils that befall sublunar existents, sublunar matter in itself is good. It allows for the perpetuity of generation and the permanence of the sublunar world. Maimonides may be interpreted as offering a version of the doctrine of plenitude. A world containing the three basic types of existents beneath God (forms divorced of matter – the separate intellects; forms joined to matter and not experiencing corruption – the spheres and stars; and forms joined to matter and continuously undergoing generation and corruption – the existents of the sublunar world) is more whole, or full of existence (= good) than a world in which one of the levels of existence is missing.

Human beings occupy an intermediate position in this hierarchy of existence. For this reason, Maimonides polemicizes against anthropocentric views that treat humankind as the goal of creation, and evaluate all existence in reference to the evils confronting human beings. Nevertheless, Maimonides also treats humans in an exceptional manner. While they share the corporeal nature characterizing all sublunar existents, the intellect apprehends its final end as being the attainment of the non-corporeal existence characterizing the separate intellects. This dual nature of human beings is the key to understanding Maimonides' approach to divine providence.

The major consideration leading the philosophers to deny individual providence, according to Maimonides, is the apparent lack of justice in the circumstances surrounding individuals. An additional consideration is also mentioned: God's knowledge of anything that undergoes change would entail a change in God's essence. This latter consideration, however, is treated as secondary. It would not have posed an obstacle to positing individual providence if it were not for the former consideration. This observation forms the prelude to Maimonides' formal discussion of providence.

Maimonides begins by listing five different views on the subject (3.17). The first is the view of Epicurus, denying any form of providence. This view was demonstratively negated by Aristotle, who viewed providence as extending only to that which is eternal. The separate intellects, spheres, and stars experience individual providence, while providence in the sublunar world belongs to individuals only qua members of a species. The circumstances of any given individual, whether an ant or human being, belong to the realm of chance. Aristotle, in Maimonides' opinion, was driven to this view by empirical considerations. A third view, that of the Islamic theological school the Ash'ariyya, agrees with Aristotle that no distinction should be drawn between any of the individuals of the sublunar world, but posits instead a radical form of determinism. God is the immediate cause of all events. In this manner, it thereby preserves the notion of God's absolute omnipotence and omniscience. The older theological school, the Mu'tazila, ascribes a limited freedom to human beings. It thereby preserves the notion of divine wisdom in issuing commandments, and divine justice in rewarding and punishing in accordance with one's deeds. The infirmities suffered by infants and the death of the righteous are also traced to God's wisdom. They occur in order to increase the sufferer's reward in the next world. Even animals will attain compensation in the next world for their suffering.

The list of approaches is completed with that of the Torah. Human freedom and a radical form of individual providence are the twin pillars upon which this approach is based. All that befalls individuals, no matter how minor the event, is in strict accordance with the principle of merit. Maimonides continues by dismissing the view of some of the sages, identical to the Mu'tazilite view, that God increases the individual's suffering in order to increase reward. The view that God compensates the animals for their suffering also undergoes attack. Maimonides concludes with a presentation of his own opinion that individual providence watches over only human beings from among the sublunar existents. In regard to the other species, Maimonides adopts an Aristotelian view. The basis for this distinction is the intellect. Divine providence is consequent upon the divine intellectual emanation, by virtue of which human beings are endowed with intellect. The actions of all those with whom the intellectual emanation is united are appraised from the standpoint of reward and punishment. The capsizing of a ship may be due to chance, but the presence of those particular passengers on board was in accordance with divine judgment. The degree of providence one experiences is in proportion to the level of human perfection one attains.

Much of the continuation of Maimonides' discussion focuses on the issue of divine knowledge. If God possesses no knowledge of individuals, as the philosophers claim, God can certainly not exercise individual providence. But the positing of God's foreknowledge of all individuals through the eternity of time entails a number of serious problems. God would then know what is non-existent, which cannot be an object of knowledge. Furthermore, God's knowledge would embrace a multiplicity of things, thereby negating God's unity. Divine knowledge would necessarily embrace the infinite, and undergo change as the circumstances of individuals change. Divine foreknowledge would also negate the "possible," for everything would necessarily be actualized in accordance with God's knowledge. Ultimately, Maimonides "solves" all these problems by arguing the complete non-similarity between human and divine knowledge. God can know the infinite, changing circumstances of individuals with a single, unchanging knowledge that does not negate the nature of the "possible." Moreover, God's knowledge of everything does not come from the objects themselves but is identical with the divine essence. Thus God's knowledge is not dependent on any external cause. Divine knowledge is like the knowledge possessed by the creator of his creation. The creation follows and conforms to the knowledge, rather than vice versa.

An exegesis of the book of Job, and a discussion of the biblical notion of "trial," are the topics that conclude Maimonides' treatment of providence. The book of Job is regarded as a philosophic parable. This is certainly true of the story of Satan and God that opens the book. Job and his friends each represent one of the different opinions concerning providence.

The main issue underlying Maimonides' discussion is whether God should be conceived as the personal God of history, a conception which is inherent in Jewish tradition. Or does God confine his activity to sustaining the impersonal order of nature, with providence being integrated into the order? On the surface, Maimonides continues to uphold the former position, though moderating it by connecting providence wholly to the level of one's naturally attained perfection. As is the case with some of the previous topics discussed, however, a strong undercurrent in his discussion suggests an esoteric doctrine essentially conforming to the approach of the philosophers. His exegesis of the book of Job leaves little doubt that this is the case. The five opinions Maimonides mentions in connection with the book of Job are not identical with those outlined by him at the beginning of his discussion of providence. Gone is the opinion of Epicurus, and a clear distinction is made between the opinion of the law (represented by Eliphaz, and treated as a false opinion) and Maimonides' own opinion (represented by Elihu). Elihu's speech shows that providence is integrated into the natural order. The intellect enables a person to avoid impending catastrophes, though death must ultimately overcome him as it does all corporeal creatures. More important, Job comes to realize that all the afflictions he suffered involved the corporeal aspect of his being, which is essentially insignificant. He learned that the only thing that truly matters is the perfection of his intellectual form. Maimonides' message is that there is individual providence, but it is not "personal" in the traditional sense. As one rises on the ladder of perfection, one is capable of seeing the oncoming corporeal evils, and of adopting steps to avoid them. Moreover, as one gradually frees oneself from preoccupation with the corporeal and becomes a "separate intellect," one no longer suffers from the corporeal afflictions that occur. Satan represents the matter of the sublunar world, characterized by privation. This is the meaning of God's decree that Satan may do as he wishes with Job but may not touch the "soul," the perfect intellect *in actu* which is not subject to the privations of matter. The person who continues to live a life focused upon the corporeal "merits" all the sufferings that such a life brings in its wake. The story of Job thus is the story of the human condition, with Job representing the individual who ultimately attains enlightenment about the nature of existence and divine providence.

❧ REASONS FOR THE COMMANDMENTS ❧ (*GUIDE* 3.25–50)

The cardinal principle underlying Maimonides' discussion of the commandments is that each has a purpose, none of them being arbitrary products of the divine will. Every action performed by God aims at a noble end and furthers the attainment of the end. Moreover, none of the commandments contributes anything to God, but is legislated solely for the benefit of the adherents. The commandments come to further two ends. The first is physical perfection, which requires the creation of a well-organized, moral society. Maimonides adopts the Aristotelian view that human beings are social animals, requiring society for their survival and corporeal well-being. The second, and more noble, end is intellectual perfection. The divine law creates the social milieu enabling one to pursue this perfection, and it provides the true beliefs that point the seeker of perfection in the proper direction for achieving this quest. The attainment of knowledge of physics and metaphysics is even made into a legal obligation.

Maimonides divides the commandments into fourteen different categories. Interestingly, they are not completely identical to the fourteen categories he presents in the *Mishneh Torah*. The differences should be viewed in light of the differences in Maimonides' intended audience and objectives. In the *Guide*, Maimonides also adopts an historical-anthropological approach to the numerous commandments that has no obvious purpose. Given the negative ramifications of this approach for the observance of the masses, he refrains from presenting it in his legal composition. Maimonides appreciated the fact that at times silence is the better part of wisdom, while at other times revealing the truths one has discovered is the course one is compelled to take. All of Maimonides' compositions reflect the balance between these two principles. Maimonides believed he found the key to understanding many of the commandments from books purporting to report the beliefs and practices of the ancient idolaters known as the Sabians, particularly the book, *The Nabatean Agriculture*. Idolatry, in Maimonides' view, poses the main obstacle to the attainment of true knowledge of God. For this reason, the Torah goes to such lengths in combatting it. The commandments whose purpose is obscure were meant to eliminate the practices, and by extension the beliefs, of these idolaters, who dominated the ancient world. The very obscurity of the reasons for the commandments, such as the laws forbidding mingling wool and linen or shaving a corner of the beard, attest to the singular victory of the divine law in ridding the world of the Sabian religion. The practices forbidden by the law were precisely those prevalent among the ancient idolaters, and were believed to bring about fertility.

The Torah, however, does not attempt to eliminate all the practices of the idolaters. Maimonides regards the commandments involving sacrifice as a form of historical compromise. Prayer is a more preferable way of worshipping God than is sacrifice, while intellectual meditation is the ideal manner in which God is to be served. But people cannot be forced to abandon overnight the practices to which they had become accustomed. They would sooner abandon the divine law and return to their idolatrous practices if they were forbidden to offer sacrifices. God thus leaves the sacrifices in place, replacing the planets as their sole recipient. Practices that beforehand came to reinforce belief in many corporeal gods now come to reinforce belief in the one God beyond the celestial bodies. The Torah also changes all the salient details of these practices, for example, the types of animals that may be sacrificed – in order to distance itself from the idolatrous religions. Furthermore, it attempts to wean the people gradually away from their customary behavior, by severely limiting the circumstances under which sacrifices are to be performed. The same restrictions, on the other hand, do not apply to prayer, which helps promote perfection in a more direct manner. While Maimonides views all the commandments as instrumental in molding an ideal society, their effectiveness nevertheless depends on taking historical conditions under consideration. Often, the longer, roundabout route is the only viable route for reaching the ultimate destination.

✥ HUMAN PERFECTION (*GUIDE* 3.51–4) ✥

A parable of a king in his palace opens 3.51. Various groups of people in the polis (and outside of it) attempt to approach the king, but only a few gain entrance to the inner chamber. In order that the meaning of the parable should not be lost on his readers, Maimonides identifies the various groups. The masses of law-abiding Jews remain far from the palace and do not even see its walls. Even the rabbinical authorities remain outside, searching for the entrance. Only those who apply themselves to the apprehension of the principles of the religion, and who study the natural sciences, gain entrance to the antechambers. Those who grasp the science of metaphysics enter the inner chamber. Finally, those who attain perfection in this science and proceed to devote themselves wholly to the apprehension of God and his governance are present in the king's council. These are the prophets.

Maimonides advocates a form of asceticism for those pursuing perfection. A similar stance can be discerned in several other discussions in the *Guide* (see 2.36; 3.8). He stresses the importance of social isolation, and strongly disparages the activities associated with the sense of touch. Implicit in his approach is the view that those closer to perfection must engage in a more severe regimen than that entailed by the doctrine of the mean, a doctrine generally presented by him as the ethical ideal. Maimonides incorporates the performance of the commandments into this regimen in an interesting manner. Engaging in commandments affords one an opportunity to meditate upon God. Preoccupation with corporeal matters is reserved for the other times of the day. By means of such training, one may attain a state in which one continuously contemplates God even while engaging in corporeal activities. Intellectual isolation is maintained while actively interacting with others. This is the state of the Patriarchs. These individuals in effect maintain a dual identity – that of a "separate" intellect, in addition to that of a corporeal creature whose soul is integrally tied to the body.

Maimonides concludes this chapter with a mystical motif – the physical death of the individual due to the strength of contemplation. This state of intense contemplation is labeled by him one of "passionate love" (*chesheq*). Maimonides interprets the rabbinic discussion of the death of Moses, Aaron, and Miriam by means of God's "kiss" as a reference to this state. The individual experiencing this type of death in truth achieves "salvation from death. . . . After having reached this condition of enduring permanence, that intellect remains in one and the same state ... and will remain permanently in that state of intense pleasure, which does not belong to the genus of bodily pleasures" (3.51: 628).

The final chapter of the *Guide* essentially reiterates the same approach to perfection. Intellectual perfection is the true perfection of humankind, belonging to the individual qua individual. Most of the commandments aim at ethical perfection, which is regarded as a means rather than the final end. The attainment of possessions, and bodily perfection, are dismissed by Maimonides as imaginary perfections, though the masses place great value upon them. Given this approach to perfection, Maimonides ends the *Guide* on a note that has perplexed many of his interpreters. After showing that Jeremiah stressed the perfection of the intellect as the final end ("But let him that glories glory in this, that he understands and knows Me," Jeremiah 9:23), Maimonides continues by citing the rest of the verse, "that I am the Lord who exercises loving-kindness, judgment, and righteousness in the earth, for in these things I delight, says the Lord." Maimonides explains that our goal should be the knowledge and imitation of God's actions after having attained apprehension of him. The way of life of such an individual will always have in view loving-kindness, righteousness, and judgment.

At first glance, it appears that Maimonides posits the ethical ideal, previously treated as a means, as the final end. Intellectual perfection, on the other hand, is no longer regarded as the end but a means. This has lead some interpreters to distinguish between two different ethical ideals – one preceding the attainment of intellectual perfection and one following it. More likely, Maimonides sees the imitation of God's actions as complementing intellectual perfection, rather than supplanting it as the final end. The ideal he has in mind is the emanating perfection of the prophets, particularly Moses, who actively engage in the bestowal of their perfection upon others by means of governance. These are the individuals who attempt to live on the intellectual and corporeal planes simultaneously. The dilemma faced by Plato in his famous allegory of the cave is solved by Maimonides by means of his view of emanating perfection. The return to the cave by the individual who has beheld the direct light of the sun results from one's internal feeling of compulsion to perfect others. Moreover, one does not entirely sacrifice one's perfection in the descent back into the darkness of corporeal affairs, for the intellect may continue to enjoy the direct light of the sun. The perfect individual extends divine providence to humankind by imitating divine governance, while continuing to experience the passionate love resulting from the contemplation of God and the world.

✎ OTHER WORKS ✎

Maimonides incorporated many of his philosophical views in his legal works. His commentary on the Mishnah deals with a range of philosophical-theological issues. He outlines his views of the final end of humankind in the introduction to the commentary. His views on eschatology and perfection are treated in the introduction to the tenth chapter of the tractate *Sanhedrin (Pereq Cheleq)*. Maimonides also presents there his thirteen principles of Judaism, acceptance of which is incumbent upon every Jew. These principles touch upon God, prophecy, and eschatology. The introduction to the tractate *Avot, Eight Chapters*, contains Maimonides' ethical philosophy, as well as a discussion of the problem of human free will in the face of divine omnipotence and omniscience. Many of the same topics are dealt with in the *Mishneh Torah*, particularly in the opening part, the *Book of Knowledge*. Maimonides presents philosophical views also in some of his epistles and shorter treatises. Reference has already been made to Maimonides' only strictly philosophical work, *Treatise on Logic*. The letter on astrology, addressed to the rabbis of Provence, contains Maimonides' views on the relation between astronomy and astrology, and touches upon such issues as determinism and free will. In his *Treatise on Resurrection*, a work written after the *Guide*, Maimonides presents his approach to miracles and the natural order.

None of these works, all of them addressed to Jewish society at large, are as important as the *Guide* for an appreciation of Maimonides' philosophy. None the less, they cast further light on his thought. One can detect in the range of Maimonides' writings a remarkable consistency in the outline of his thought. At the same time, Maimonides modified his views, or at least the manner in which he formulated them, on a number of specific issues. Maimonides seldom engages in these works in discussions as detailed as those in the *Guide*, a notable exception being in the area of ethics. His presentations appear to be more straightforward, with no explicit allusions to an esoteric level. Significantly, at times Maimonides even more openly adopts an Aristotelian stance in his legal writings than in the *Guide*, a fact that is only partially veiled by the brevity of his remarks. This is true, for example, of the first four chapters of the *Laws of the Principles of the Torah*.

There has hardly been unanimity among scholars, however, in their interpretation of Maimonides' views as they emerge from these writings. Nor have they agreed in their approach on the relation between these writings and the *Guide* for an understanding of his philosophy. Some scholars have gone so far as to dismiss the importance of these writings in this area, given their popular nature. Others have argued that some of these writings too – for example, *Eight Chapters* and the *Treatise on Resurrection* – contain an esoteric level.

❦ MAIMONIDEAN SCHOLARSHIP ❦

Much of contemporary scholarship on the *Guide* focuses on the core topics which stand in the forefront of Maimonides' philosophy – the deity and the problem of attributes, divine knowledge and will, creation, prophecy, providence and the problem of evil, free will, possibility and determinism, the commandments, ethics and human perfection. New problems, perspectives, and insights are continuously being adduced, while old arguments are discarded or modified and strengthened, in the presentation of Maimonides' views in these areas. The relation between Maimonides' philosophy in the *Guide* and his positions in his other writings is still another topic that continues to occupy the attention of scholars.

In developing his approach to Maimonides' *Guide*, Leo Strauss paid particular attention to methodological issues.[7] His remarks provided the starting point for much of the subsequent scholarship in this area, whether defending the esoteric approach or challenging it. Some scholars devoted themselves to the application of new methodologies to the study of Maimonides' treatise. Exceptionally noteworthy is the methodological approach developed by Abraham Nuriel, an approach that reinforces an esoteric interpretation of the *Guide*. Nuriel maintains that one way of unlocking the secrets in the *Guide* is to pay very close attention to the Arabic terminology. In so far as Maimonides notes that he carefully selected every word in the treatise, his choice between different possible terms for conveying a certain concept may signal his latent views regarding the issue. Based on a careful study of all the occurrences of Maimonides' terms for the divine will (*irāda*, *mashī'a*) and for the creator (*bāri'*), Nuriel attempted to show that an esoteric message underlies Maimonides' discussion, signaling his essential agreement with the philosophers' view in these areas.[8]

The problem of Maimonides' sources has long preoccupied students of his thought, both medieval and modern. A good number of studies have traced the sources underlying Maimonides' discussion of different topics. Harry Wolfson's studies have been singularly important for their contributions in this area.[9] The most comprehensive study of this topic was undertaken by Shlomo Pines in the introduction to his English translation of the *Guide*.[10] The study is based upon those thinkers cited in the *Guide*, or mentioned by Maimonides in a letter to his Hebrew translator, Samuel ibn Tibbon. Maimonides assigns pride of place to Aristotle, and strongly recommends the commentaries of

Alexander of Aphrodisias, Themistius, and Averroes. The latter commentator apparently was studied by Maimonides only after the completion of the *Guide*. Plato is also cited by Maimonides, though treated as far inferior to Aristotle. Nevertheless, his views influenced several of Maimonides' discussions, at times directly but more often through the writings of al-Fārābī. From among the Islamic philosophers, Maimonides held the highest regard for al-Fārābī, followed by ibn Bājja and to a lesser extent Avicenna. All these philosophers maintained a Neoplatonized version of Aristotelianism that left a strong impress upon Maimonides' thought. Pines does not ignore the non-Aristotelian sources cited by Maimonides. He deals with them too, though to a lesser extent. Maimonides' bibliography, as summarized and discussed by Pines, provides an important key for interpreting his views. Much work continues to be done in delineating the influence of the Aristotelian thinkers, particularly the Islamic ones. At the same time, greater strides have been made in tracing the influence exercised by medieval non-Aristotelian thinkers, both Jewish and Islamic, in order to present a more balanced picture of the currents that enter into the formation of Maimonides' philosophy.

Recent scholarship has made inroads in exploring topics that have not received sufficient attention in the past. For example, much effort is being made in exploring Maimonides' exegetical approach to the Bible, and showing the centrality of this topic for understanding his treatise. Of particular note are the works of Sara Klein-Braslavy in this area.[11] Maimonides' scientific views, and their sources, are also attracting increased scholarly attention.

❧ NOTES ❧

1 This translation is based on that found in Kraemer 1991, pp. 95–6. Efros 1938, pp. 34–65, is a complete English translation of the *Treatise*.

2 All English citations are from Pines' translation of *The Guide of the Perplexed* (Maimonides 1963).

3 For an historical survey of esoteric approaches to the *Guide*, see Ravitzky 1990.

4 An excellent background for the study of this topic is presented in Davidson 1987.

5 See Macy 1986.

6 For Maimonides' approach to the intellect and to immortality, see Altmann 1987.

7 See his introductory essay "How to Begin to Study *The Guide of the Perplexed*," in Maimonides 1963.

8 Nuriel 1964 and 1970.

9 Many of his studies are collected in Wolfson 1973 and 1977.

10 Pines 1963.

11 Klein-Braslavy 1986 and 1987.

❧ BIBLIOGRAPHY ❧

Texts

Efros, I. (ed. and tr.) (1938) *Maimonides' Treatise on Logic* (New York: American Academy for Jewish Research); rev. ed. 1966: "Maimonides' Arabic Treatise on Logic," *Proceedings of the American Academy for Jewish Research* 34: 155ff.

Maimonides (1963) *The Guide of the Perplexed*, translated by S. Pines, 2 vols. (Chicago: University of Chicago Press).

—— (1995) [1952] *The Guide of the Perplexed*, abridged edition with introduction and commentary by J. Guttmann; translated by C. Rabin; new introduction by D. Frank (Indianapolis and Cambridge, MA: Hackett).

Twersky, I. (ed.) (1972) *A Maimonides Reader* (New York: Behrman House).

Weiss, R. L. and C. E. Butterworth (ed. and tr.) (1975) *The Ethical Writings of Maimonides* (New York: New York University Press).

Studies

Altmann, A. (1987) "Maimonides on the Intellect and the Scope of Metaphysics," in *Von der Mittelalterlichen zur Modernen Aufklärung: Studien zur jüdischen Geistesgeschichte* (Tübingen: Mohr (Paul Siebeck)), pp. 60–127.

Ben-Shammai, B. (1991) "Maimonidean Studies 1965–90: Hebrew Bibliography" [Hebrew], *Maimonidean Studies* 2: 17–42.

Davidson, H. (1987) *Proofs for Eternity, Creation and the Existence of God in Medieval Islamic and Jewish Philosophy* (New York and Oxford: Oxford University Press).

Diesendruck, Z. (1927) "Maimonides' Lehre von der Prophetie," in *Jewish Studies in Memory of Israel Abrahams* (New York: Jewish Institute of Religion), pp. 74–134.

—— (1928) "Die Teleologie bei Maimonides," *Hebrew Union College Annual* 5: 415–534.

Fox, M. (1990) *Interpreting Maimonides: Studies in Methodology, Metaphysics, and Moral Philosophy* (Chicago: University of Chicago Press).

Guttmann, J. (1964) [1933] *Philosophies of Judaism* (New York: Holt, Rinehart & Winston), pp. 172–207.

Husik, I. (1916) *A History of Mediaeval Jewish Philosophy* (New York: Macmillan), pp. 236–311.

Hyman, A. (1972) "Maimonides," in *Encyclopedia Judaica* (Jerusalem: Keter) 11: 768–77.

—— (ed.) (1990–) *Maimonidean Studies*, vols. 1– [an annual publication devoted exclusively to Maimonides, though not confined to his philosophy].

Klein-Braslavy, S. (1986) *Maimonides' Interpretation of the Adam Stories in Genesis* [Hebrew] (Jerusalem: Reuben Mass).

—— (1987) *Maimonides' Interpretation of the Story of Creation* [Hebrew] (Jerusalem: Reuben Mass).

Kraemer, J. L. (1991) "Maimonides on the Philosophic Sciences in his *Treatise on the Art of Logic*," in *Perspectives on Maimonides: Philosophical and Historical Studies*, edited by J. L. Kraemer (Oxford: Oxford University Press), pp. 77–104.

Lachterman, D. R. (1990) "Maimonidean Studies 1950–86: A Bibliography," *Maimonidean Studies* 1: 197–216 [a bibliography of books and articles in English, French, German, Italian, Spanish, and Portuguese].

Macy, J. (1986) "Prophecy in al-Farabi and Maimonides: The Imaginative and Rational Faculties," in *Maimonides and Philosophy*, edited by S. Pines and Y. Yovel (Dordrecht: Nijhoff), pp. 185–201.

Nuriel, A. (1964) "The Question of a Created or Primordial World in the Philosophy of Maimonides" [Hebrew], *Tarbitz* 33: 372–87.

—— (1970) "The Divine Will in *Moreh Nevukhim*" [Hebrew], *Tarbitz* 39: 39–61.

Pines, S. (1963) "The Philosophic Sources of *The Guide of the Perplexed*," in Maimonides 1963, pp. lvii–cxxxiv.

Ravitzky, A. (1990) "The Secrets of the *Guide of the Perplexed*: Between the Thirteenth and the Twentieth Centuries," in *Studies in Maimonides*, edited by I. Twersky (Cambridge, MA: Harvard University Press), pp. 159–207.

Rawidowicz, S. (1935a) "The Problem of the Structure of the *Guide of the Perplexed*" [Hebrew], *Tarbitz* 6: 285–333.

—— (1935b) "Philosophy as a Duty," in *Moses Maimonides*, edited by I. Epstein (London: Soncino), pp. 177–88.

Strauss, L. (1963) "How to Begin to Study *The Guide of the Perplexed*," in Maimonides 1963, pp. xi–lvi.

Twersky, I. (1980) *Introduction to the Code of Maimonides (Mishneh Torah)* (New Haven: Yale University Press) [revised and updated bibliography in Hebrew translation of the book: (Jerusalem: Magnes) 1991].

Wolfson, H. A. (1973 and 1977) *Studies in the History of Philosophy and Religion*, edited by I. Twersky and G. Williams, 2 vols. (Cambridge, MA: Harvard University Press).

CHAPTER 12

Maimonides and Aquinas

Alexander Broadie

Comparison of Aquinas (1224/5–1274) with Maimonides (1135/8–1204) is for two reasons, one historical and the other doctrinal, an obvious exercise to undertake. As regards the first reason, through the centuries the two thinkers have been overwhelmingly influential within their own faith communities, and are uniquely entitled to be regarded as their spokesmen within the fields of both philosophy and theology. Furthermore both faced bitter opposition within their communities; and the public incineration of part of Maimonides' *Mishneh Torah* by Provençal Jews[1] is comparable with the condemnations in Paris and Oxford in the 1270s of propositions defended by Aquinas.[2] As regards the second reason, that concerning doctrine, it has often been noted that there are close similarities between the teachings of the two, and that some of the similarities concern matters at the heart of the belief systems of Jews and Christians. It is upon such central matters that I shall focus here.

The question of the precise causal relation between Maimonides and Aquinas will not be at issue here. Whether Aquinas adopted certain ideas because he found Maimonides' arguments for them compelling, or whether a mode of expression used by Maimonides attracted Aquinas' attention and caused him to modify his position – these are interesting historical questions which are extraordinarily difficult to answer, and no attempt will be made here to answer them. For present purposes it is sufficient to note that whatever the answers might be to these questions, there is greater significance in the sheer closeness of the positions of the two men on key philosophical and theological matters, and it is to that philosophical and theological closeness that we shall be attending in this chapter. Nevertheless it is necessary to bear in mind that Aquinas was familiar with a Latin version of the *Guide of the Perplexed*, and that he refers to it rather often, sometimes with acknowledgment to "Rabbi Moyses" and to his book the *Doctor Dubiorum*. The *Guide* was translated from Judeo-Arabic into Hebrew by Samuel ibn Tibbon in 1204, and not long after that a less accurate translation into Hebrew was made by Judah al-Charīzī. It was al-Charīzī's translation that formed the basis of the Latin version, made in the 1220s, which Aquinas read.[3]

In order to indicate the closeness of Maimonides and Aquinas I shall attend to four topics that loom large in their writings; first, the question of the proper way to interpret the "names of God," that is, terms predicated in the Bible of God; second, the question of whether the world is eternal or had a beginning in time; third, the objects of God's knowledge; and fourth, the problem of the apparent incompatibility of the claims that human acts are free and that God foreknows all future human acts.

Despite the range and depth of the similarities, Aquinas is at certain points strongly critical of Maimonides, indeed sees him as the person he has to oppose. A striking example of such disagreement is to be found in the famous discussion in the *Summa Theologiae* on the names of God. It can however be demonstrated that the disagreement is not as deep as Aquinas thinks it is. Both philosophers accept that certain terms predicated affirmatively of God in the Bible do not in that context have their customary signification but are being used metaphorically. All terms implying that God is corporeal fall into this category. Are there however any terms which do have their customary signification when predicated affirmatively of God in the Bible? We read that God is just, merciful, wise, powerful, and so on. Are these predications to be taken literally? Maimonides says not, on the grounds that to say otherwise would be to fall into the error of denying the principle of God's oneness. Understood literally, the terms signify attributes. Hence to say that God is just, merciful, wise, and powerful would be to imply that there are in God many attributes, which would imply that God is a many-in-one, and therefore not one in the required sense.

Maimonides' solution, that affirmative predications are to be understood negatively, is an effective fence round the principle of God's oneness, since to deny that God has a given attribute is not to attribute anything to him. Hence if we accede to the demand to deny, and never to affirm, things of God, we would not predicate things of him in such a way as to imply that he has any attributes, and in that case we would not be ascribing to God the complexity that is possessed by any substance in virtue of its having attributes.

Aquinas writes as follows: "Some have said that though all these terms are said affirmatively of God, they are used to deny, rather than to affirm, things of him. Thus they say that when we say that God is alive we signify that God does not exist in the way that inanimate things do, and likewise with other such terms. Rabbi Moyses said this in the book *Doctor Dubiorum*."[4] But this position does not satisfy Aquinas. Let us agree with Maimonides in holding that God's being alive is no more (or less) than God's not being inanimate. In that case, adds Aquinas, we could say that God is a body, for to say that he is a body is to deny that he is mere potency like prime matter.

It can however be shown that Aquinas' argument against Maimonides is itself open to criticism. One criticism is this: If to predicate body affirmatively of something is no more than to deny mere potency of it, then it could indeed be said that God is a body, for God is not in mere potency. But to be a body is not simply not to be in mere potency. The pure intelligences are not in mere potency and yet neither Maimonides nor Aquinas thought that they were bodies. Hence the fact that God is not in mere potency does not, after all, imply that he is a body.

A second criticism is based firmly upon a position that is presented several times in the *Guide*. Maimonides writes:

> One has ascribed to Him, may He be exalted, everything that in our opinion is a perfection in order to indicate that He is perfect in every manner of perfection and that no deficiency whatever mars Him. Thus none of the things apprehended by the multitude as a deficiency or a privation are predicated of Him ... On the other hand, everything that the multitude consider a perfection is predicated of Him, even if it is only a perfection in relation to ourselves – for in relation to Him, may He be exalted, all things that we consider perfections are the very extreme of deficiency. However, if people imagined that this human perfection was lacking in Him, may He be exalted, this would constitute in their opinion, a deficiency in Him.[5]

Thus the crucial point that Aquinas is missing is that on Maimonides' agenda there is not only philosophy but also pastoral care. Maimonides does indeed think that, literally understood, "alive" and "wise" are no more truly predicable of God than "inanimate" and "foolish" are – to attribute "wisdom" to God, understanding the term as we ordinarily understand it, would be to attribute to God what would, in relation to God, be "the very extreme of deficiency". But Maimonides recognizes that if the ordinary people were told that terms signifying what from their point of view are perfections were not truly predicable of God, they would think him deficient and would cease to obey his commandments. Since there is a special significance in such obedience, even when grounded on ignorance about a fundamental truth about religious language, the Bible predicates of God terms which ordinary people are bound to misinterpret. Better to be wrong about theology than to disobey divine law.

Aquinas gives a second reason for rejecting Maimonides' *via negativa*, namely: "It is contrary to what people have in mind when they speak about God. For when they say that God is alive what they mean is something other than that he is different from inanimate bodies."[6] However, Maimonides has prepared the ground for a reply to this criticism by distinguishing between the philosophically sophisticated and the multitude. He would grant Aquinas' premise that "It is contrary to what people have in mind," but Maimonides would deny that the multitude's rejection of a sophisticated philosophical doctrine is proof, even weak proof, that the doctrine is incorrect. If people misunderstand a doctrine, then their rejection of it carries no implication concerning the doctrine's correctness. Indeed Aquinas' criticism is a risky one for him to put forward since his own account of the proper way to interpret terms when they are predicated affirmatively of God may be no more kindly received by the multitude than Maimonides' account would be.

Aquinas' account, that terms predicated of God and of creatures are to be understood not negatively but analogically, is based upon the insight, accepted also by Maimonides, that human language is an inadequate instrument for representing God. Maimonides holds however that we cannot form a concept of God, and that therefore our language is a totally inadequate instrument, whereas Aquinas holds that we can form a concept of God, though one that represents him imperfectly, and hence we can use our language to speak about him, but to do so imperfectly. We are bound to understand terms in a creaturely way, which is of course an inappropriate way when they are predicated of God, but, as Aquinas insists, the terms are truly predicated of God, even though our understanding of them in that context is imperfect, and indeed the terms for the perfections are more properly predicated of God than of ourselves. It is in virtue of our imperfect grasp of those terms that Aquinas holds that they are applied analogically, not univocally, to God.

The contrast between Maimonides and Aquinas is not however as clear cut as at first sight it seems to be. Both philosophers stress the concept of the absolute oneness of God, and they describe this oneness in very similar terms. In particular God is not to be conceived as a substance in which attributes inhere. Both hold that though we can, with biblical warrant, say that God has many perfections, these perfections, as existing in God, do not differ from each other nor differ from God. It is plain that both men believe it more appropriate to say that God is, than that he has, goodness, and that he is, rather than has, wisdom, and so on for all perfections. Futhermore, all those perfections are identical in God and with God. Maimonides encapsulates these points in his doctrine of negative predication and Aquinas encapsulates them in his doctrine of analogy. Most especially, Aquinas' doctrine of analogy must be read in the light of the introduction to his discussion of divine simplicity.[7] He writes: "Since we can know what God is not but not what he is, we can consider in what way God does not exist but not in what way he does." On the basis of these related considerations, therefore, I should wish to defend the thesis that conspicuous differences of formulation conceal an identity of substance. Later I shall provide further support for the thesis.

It was of course impossible for Maimonides and Aquinas to discuss the creation of the world without looking over their shoulders at Aristotle. The rabbi and the priest, profoundly affected by the system of Aristotle, knew the strength of his doctrine that the world is eternal a parte ante and a parte post. Yet they were also heirs to a tradition that the world had a beginning in time. Athens appeared to be contradicting Jerusalem. Maimonides showed how the contradiction should be dealt with, and Aquinas, accepting his solution, took the matter further. The influence of Maimonides upon Aquinas in this matter is generally recognized in respect both of Maimonides' grand strategy and of his detailed argumentation.

In the course of his discussion of the eternity of the world Maimonides affirms: "I shall pay no attention to anyone who besides Aristotle has engaged in speculative discourse, for it is his opinions that ought to be considered,"[8] and indeed the discussion focuses almost entirely on Aristotle's conclusions and on his route to them. Consideration of those arguments is of special importance, for of course if Aristotle has succeeded in providing a scientific demonstration of the doctrine that the world is eternal, then that demonstration has to be accepted. To reject a scientific demonstration is to abandon the very standards of rationality in terms of which the debate is being conducted. Maimonides' tactic therefore is to argue that none of Aristotle's arguments for the eternity of the world is a scientific demonstration, and that they are, instead, probable arguments only. Granted that we cannot rule out on scientific grounds the possibility that the world is not eternal, a question can then be raised as to whether there are arguments supporting the doctrine that the world had a beginning in time. Maimonides finds probable, though not demonstrative, arguments for the doctrine and concludes that it is reasonable to turn to the Torah for guidance. And the Torah teaches that the world did have a beginning in time.

A distinction, equally crucial for Maimonides and Aquinas, has to be drawn here between the world coming into being ex nihilo and its having a beginning in time. We learn from the Torah that the world is a product of the divine will. The world thus has the metaphysical status of absolute dependency; it is absolutely dependent upon God's will for its existence. For Maimonides, as also later for Aquinas, it is this status of absolute dependency for its existence upon something other than the world itself that is expressed by the phrase "ex nihilo". Thus, that the world was created ex nihilo implies not that it had a beginning in time but that its existence is absolutely dependent upon the divine will, whether it had a beginning in time or not. Hence proof that the world was eternal would not by itself undermine the claim that the world was created ex nihilo. Maimonides, like Aquinas, believes that he has demonstrated that the world is created ex nihilo. What he accepts on faith is that it had a beginning in time. This, then, is Maimonides' strategic response to Aristotle, and Aquinas' response to Aristotle is identical.

But what are the arguments for the eternity of the world? One that Maimonides offers as due to Aristotle's "later followers" is this: If we say that the world was produced in time, then before it was produced the fact that it was going to be produced could not have been necessary (for otherwise it would never not have existed) nor have been impossible (for otherwise it would never have existed), and therefore its future existence was merely possible. But every possibility has a substratum; that is, to say that there is a possibility is to say that there is something which has the possibility. Hence, to say that the world was produced in time presupposes that something existed prior to the world's production, which is tantamount to saying that the world existed before it was produced. Therefore, it was not produced in time.[9] This argument is reproduced by Aquinas as the first of his arguments for the thesis that the world never began but always existed. He writes:

> Regarding whatever has begun to exist, before it existed its existence was possible, otherwise it was impossible that it would exist. If therefore the world began to exist, then before it began its existence was possible. Now that which is able to exist is matter, which is in potency to existence which comes through a form, and to non-existence which is through the absence of form. If therefore the world began to exist, then matter existed prior to the world. But matter cannot exist without form, and the world's matter plus form is the world. Therefore the world existed before it began to exist, which is impossible.[10]

Against this Aquinas sets out his own position, that God's will is the cause of things, and that since there was no need for God to will anything but himself, there was no need for God to will an everlasting world. Rather, Aquinas adds: "The world exists just as long as God wills that it exist, since the existence of the world depends on his will as its cause. Therefore it is not necessary that the world always exist, and hence that it is necessary cannot be demonstrated."[11]

This leaves Aquinas having to deal with the objection based on the insight that before the world existed it must have been possible that it would exist. But Aquinas is not impressed with the insight, for it ignores the fact that there is more than one way of being possible. His response, very Maimonidean, is that to say that before the world existed its existence was possible is to refer not to the passive power of matter, its power to receive form, but to the active power of God, that is, the power of his will. And taking "possible" in this way, the objection under discussion does not work. Aquinas proceeds immediately to a discussion of the question: *utrum mundum incoepisse sit articulus fidei* – whether it is an article of faith that the world began,[12] and his reply is based on the consideration just stressed, that the existence of the world is due to an act of divine will. Since we cannot on the basis of a reading of nature rule out either that the world did have a beginning in time or that it did not, we are left having to read God's will, that is, Scripture, which affirms that the world had a beginning in time. Our acceptance of that affirmation is an act of faith. Aquinas could hardly sound more like Maimonides.

The nature of God's knowledge is explored by Maimonides and Aquinas, and their conclusions are sufficiently close to warrant at least a second look at the claim that Aquinas' *via analogica* is based upon a rejection of Maimonides' *via negativa*. If the two philosophers really have very different ideas as to the significance of terms predicated of God, why do they say almost exactly the same thing when discussing the term "know" as predicated of God? The problem both men face is this: Though we have some idea what it is for human beings to know things, it does not follow that we have any insight into what divine knowing is like, for our knowing is constrained by the conditions of creatureliness under which we live. We are infinitely restricted in our knowing by the fact that we look out upon the world from a spatial point, our here, and from a temporal point, our now, and we draw conclusions by using our fallible reasoning about a world we know from our infinitely restricted perspective. God is not constrained in these ways. Maimonides and Aquinas take his unconstrainedness as their starting point. They investigate what it is like to be a divine knower, and recognize that the investigation requires us to attend first to human knowledge and then to undertake the psychological, or conceptual, experiment of thinking away the conditions of creatureliness which constrain such knowledge.

Significantly Maimonides' account of divine knowledge is imbedded in his discussion of divine providence, for he has to reply to some philosophers who have claimed that since God does not reward the virtuous and punish the wicked, this must be because he does not know the world. In a word, absence of divine providential acts implies divine ignorance of his world. Maimonides' reply is that God cannot be the creator and not know his world. No doubt his knowledge is very different from ours but we cannot deny that he has knowledge and also maintain that he is the creator. How different is his knowledge? Maimonides lists several differences and we find them listed also by Aquinas. I shall mention three in particular.

Things exist now which previously did not exist. We now know them but previously we could not have done since they were not there to be known. But there cannot be things that God now knows that he previously did not. Do we say, therefore, that since he had not known certain things, for they did not exist, he now does not know them? Maimonides and Aquinas draw the opposite conclusion. Since there is nothing in God's world with which he is unacquainted, it follows that he must know non-existent things, and know them as fully as existent ones. That is, there are things which do not exist today but will tomorrow, and God does not now know them the less for their presently not existing. Both philosophers say this, but there is a difference. Maimonides holds that "that which is never brought into existence is, with reference to His knowledge, an absolutely nonexistent thing, which is not an object for His knowledge, as that which is nonexistent for us is not an object for our knowledge."[13] Aquinas on the other hand distinguishes between "knowledge of vision" (*scientia visionis*) and "knowledge of simple understanding" (*scientia simplicis intelligentiae*).[14] By *scientia visionis*, God knows things which do not exist though they have existed or will exist. By *scientia simplicis intelligentiae*, God knows those things which it is within the power of God or of creatures to produce but which in fact neither do, nor will, nor did exist.

This appears to be a substantive difference between the two philosophers. They agree that God sees in a timeless instant whatever was, is, and will be, and that in consequence whatever was, is, and will be are all simultaneously present to God. Hence, they agree that a thing that now does not exist but did or will exist is not less present to God than what exists now is present to us. However, what is to be said of, for example, a painting of which a painter forms a concept although the painter never realizes it in pigment on canvas? Does God know that painting? Maimonides would no doubt argue that knowledge of the painting is impossible for there is no such thing as "the painting," and that what Aquinas would call "knowing the painting" would better be described as knowing the concept. Aquinas would surely reply that though the painting does not exist *in actu* it does *in potentia*, and existence *in potentia* is existence of a sort, and certainly sufficient for God to know the painting itself.

A further area discussed by both philosophers is God's knowledge of the infinite, though their stated positions on this matter, while close, are not identical. Maimonides tells us that, unlike our knowledge, God's "may embrace the infinite"[15] and that "it may have as its object something that is infinite,"[16] while Aquinas affirms that "God knows infinite things even by *scientia visionis*."[17] Maimonides' repeated use of the modal auxiliary "may" contrasts with Aquinas' formulation. Aquinas is thinking of things (in a broad sense of "things") in the created world, and declares these to be infinite, and it is possible that Maimonides prefers not to commit himself on the question of whether they are infinite. Aquinas is explicit on this matter. "God knows the thoughts and affections of our hearts, which will be multiplied to infinity for rational creatures will always exist."[18] Here Aquinas is speaking as a theologian basing himself on the authority of Scripture, rather than as a philosopher, and I speculate that Maimonides was speaking as a philosopher rather than a theologian. Had he based himself on Scripture he would no doubt have omitted the modal auxiliaries.

Finally in this section we should note the agreement between the two philosophers on the question of whether God is immutable if he knows the changing world. The argument with which both have to deal is simply stated: knowing a changing world implies knowing first one thing and then another; hence, the knower is changing and therefore not immutable. Both reject this argument. Maimonides' statement on the matter represents the position of Aquinas also:

> No new knowledge comes to Him in any way. For, seeing that
> He knows that a certain man is now nonexistent, but will exist
> at a certain time, will go on existing for such and such a duration,
> and will then again become nonexistent, there will be for Him
> no additional knowledge when that individual comes into
> existence as He had known beforehand. Nothing was produced
> thereby that was unknown to Him.[19]

Here Maimonides is deploying the concept of *scientia visionis*, for what he is maintaining is that everything that was, is, or will be is present instantaneously to God. God sees things which have a temporal ordering, knows the temporal ordering, but knowing these temporally successive events is not a temporally successive act of God's. Aquinas' formulation of the underlying metaphysical reality would have been accepted in full by Maimonides: "Since God's knowledge is his substance, just as his substance is entirely immutable so his knowledge must be entirely invariable."[20]

There is no doubt that on certain matters regarding God's knowledge Maimonides and Aquinas are not in agreement. But there is also no doubt that across the whole range of issues in that area the positions of the two philosophers are strikingly similar. Some of the evidence for this has just been presented. And this similarity surely provides support for the thesis that there is no significant philosophical difference between the *via negativa* and the *via analogica*. The difference cannot be great if their application to terms predicated of God results in closely similar analyses.

The issue of the apparent incompatibility of the doctrines of divine foreknowledge and of human freedom is still a major one. Both Maimonides and Aquinas deal with it, and it is appropriate to comment here, if briefly, on the relation between the two philosophers on this matter.

Maimonides raises the question of whether a future contingent event is any the less contingent for God's knowing the event. He writes:

> One of the things that has become clear to me by the texts of the Torah is that His knowledge, may He be exalted, that a certain possible thing will come into existence, does not in any way make that possible thing quit the nature of the possible. On the contrary, the nature of the possible remains with it; and knowledge concerning what possible things will be produced does not entail one of the two possibilities becoming necessary ... The whole of religious legislation, the commandments, and the prohibitions goes back to this principle: namely, that His knowledge concerning what will happen does not make this possible thing quit its nature.[21]

On the one hand therefore there is God's cognitive relation to the future event, and on the other there is the metaphysical status of the event itself. The event is known by God, and therefore it must occur, for otherwise God could not know it. But what is necessary is not the occurrence of the event but the truth of "If God knows the future event, then it will occur." The event remains contingent despite God's foreknowledge of it. Here we need to recall Maimonides' discussion of God's knowledge of the created world as being an instantaneous knowledge of all events past, present, and future. Since future events are present to him, he knows them now, as we now know what is present to us. And just as our seeing a contingent event unfold before our eyes does not affect the contingency of the event, so also God's seeing the event now does not affect its contingency. It follows that God's foreknowledge is not foreknowledge in relation to him, for the event, though future in relation to us, is present to, or in the presence of, God.

Whether this is a coherent story is a matter of current debate, and indeed Maimonides himself stresses the difficulty of understanding how God can have the kind of knowledge of future events that the story requires. He is not however tempted to retreat from the account; instead he notes that the underlying problem for us is the fact that the term "know" is used equivocally when predicated of God. In the present context however my chief concern is to point out that Aquinas' solution to our problem concerning the apparent incompatibility of human freedom with divine foreknowledge is substantially the same as Maimonides'.

Aquinas gives us a famous metaphor: a man who is walking along a road does not see those who are walking along it behind him, but the person who is high up and sees the whole road sees all the wayfarers simultaneously.[22] Likewise God sees all past, present, and future events simultaneously. What is future to us is known infallibly by God because it is present to him, that is, is in his presence. But according to Aquinas this does not affect the contingent character of events future in relation to us, for a distinction has to be made between, on the one hand, the certainty of the event, a certainty which God has because the event is unfolding before his gaze, and, on the other hand, the contingent nature of the event, for the knowledge is not itself the cause of the event: it has causes in nature, and so long as there is a contingent cause among its causes, the effect also has the character of the contingent. There is room for uncertainty about the precise relation between Maimonides' solution to the problem under discussion and Aquinas' solution. But there can be no doubt that they take lines which are at least very similar in response to the difficulty.

It has not been the aim of this chapter to argue that right across the board there is a deep agreement between Maimonides and Aquinas; there manifestly is no such across-the-board agreement, as becomes clear if one seeks a well-worked-out theory of natural law in Maimonides' writings corresponding to the very detailed theory that Aquinas developed. Nevertheless, it has been demonstrated in this chapter that there is a close correspondence between the two philosophers on a number of philosophical matters, including the creation of the world, the nature of divine knowledge, and the relation between divine foreknowledge and human freedom. On any account these are matters of central philosophical importance.

❧ NOTES ❧

1 Silver 1965.
2 Weisheipl 1974, chapter 7.
3 The most readily accessible medieval Latin version is *Dux seu Director Dubitantium aut Perplexorum*, edited by Augustinus Justinianus (Paris, 1520) (reprinted Minerva GmbH: Frankfurt am Main, 1964).
4 *Summa Theologiae* part 1, question 13, article 2 body (= *corpus*) of text, hereinafter 1.13.2c.
5 *The Guide of the Perplexed*, translated by S. Pines (Chicago: University of Chicago Press, 1963) part 1, chapter 26, p. 56, hereinafter *Guide* 1.26: p. 56.
6 *Summa Theologiae* 1.13.2c.
7 Ibid. 1.3.
8 *Guide* 2.14: p. 285.
9 Ibid. 2.14: p. 287.
10 *Summa Theologiae* 1.46.1.1.
11 Ibid. 1.46.1c.
12 Ibid. 1.46.2.
13 *Guide* 3.20: p. 481.
14 *Summa Theologiae* 1.14.9c.
15 *Guide* 3.20: p. 481.
16 Ibid. 3.20: p. 483.
17 *Summa Theologiae* 1.14.12c.
18 Ibid.
19 *Guide* 3.20: pp. 480–1.
20 *Summa Theologiae* 1.14.15c.
21 *Guide* 3.20: p. 482.
22 *Summa Theologiae* 1. 14.13 ad 3.

❧ BIBLIOGRAPHY ❧

Broadie, A. (1973–4) "Maimonides on Negative Attribution," *Transactions of the Glasgow University Oriental Society* 25: 1–11.
—— (1987) "Maimonides and Aquinas on the Names of God," *Religious Studies* 23: 157–70.
—— (1994) "Maimonides on the Great Tautology *Exodus 3,14*," *Scottish Journal of Theology* 47: 173–88.
Burrell, D. (1983) "Aquinas and Maimonides: A Conversation about Proper Speech," *Immanuel* 16: 70–85.
—— (1986) *Knowing the Unknowable God: Ibn Sina, Maimonides, and Aquinas* (Notre Dame: University of Notre Dame Press).
—— (1987) "Aquinas's Debt to Maimonides," in *A Straight Path: Studies in Medieval Philosophy and Culture*, edited by R. Link-Salinger (Washington, DC: Catholic University of America Press), pp. 37–48.
Dienstag J. I. (ed.) (1975) *Studies in Maimonides and St Thomas Aquinas* (New York: Ktav).

Fakhry, M. (1953) "The Antinomy of the Eternity of the World in Averroes, Maimonides and Aquinas," *Muséon* 66: 139–55.

Harvey, W. (1988) "Maimonides and Aquinas on Interpreting the Bible," *Proceedings of the American Academy for Jewish Research* 55: 59–77.

Maurer, A. (1987) "Maimonides and Aquinas on the Study of Metaphysics," in *A Straight Path: Studies in Medieval Philosophy and Culture*, edited by R. Link-Salinger (Washington, DC: Catholic University of America Press), pp. 206–15.

Silver D. J. (1965) *Maimonidean Criticism and the Maimonidean Controversy 1180–1240* (Leiden: Brill).

Tirosh-Rothschild, H. (1986) "Maimonides and Aquinas: The Interplay of Two Masters in Medieval Jewish Philosophy," *Conservative Judaism* 39: 54–66.

Weisheipl, J. (1974) *Friar Thomas d'Aquino: His Life, Thought, and Work* (Oxford: Blackwell).

Wohlman, A. (1988) *Thomas d'Aquin et Maimonide: Un Dialogue Exemplaire* (Paris: Cerf).

CHAPTER 13

The social and cultural context: thirteenth to fifteenth centuries

Marc Saperstein

The study of Jewish philosophy[1] in Christian Europe during the period from the late twelfth to the fifteenth century (or, to use a more internal framework, from the Almohad invasion ending Jewish life in Muslim Spain to the expulsion ending Jewish life on the Iberian peninsula) has followed several well-worn paths.

The first continues the approach used for Jewish philosophy in its classical, Islamic period. It is essentially a history of ideas, based on a rigorous philological and conceptual analysis of philosophical texts.[2] The great philosophical problems of the medieval tradition – the existence, unity, and incorporeality of God, the creation of the world and the order of being within it, the nature of the human soul, the meaning of revelation and prophecy, freedom of the will, and so forth – are traced in the works of Jewish thinkers to detect their sources and determine where innovation may be found. The impact of Maimonides and the influence of Arabic philosophers, especially al-Fārābī, Avicenna, and Averroes, are demonstrated and assessed. Evidence for the influence of Christian scholasticism is duly noted.

This approach to Jewish philosophy generally focuses on the texts of those judged by modern scholars to be the most powerful minds, the most original thinkers. Gersonides and Crescas are the two giants, perhaps a dozen lesser figures are included, usually with an apologetic concession that, while not really belonging to the major league, they are the best the period can offer. Influence is traced from one writer to a colleague in the following generation, not from a profound thinker to the society in which he or his children lived. This is therefore a study of the thinking of a tiny sub-section of the Jewish community, an analysis of disembodied texts and ideas in isolation from their historical and social milieu. In this perspective, the philosophy of the fifteenth century may well appear, as it did to Julius Guttmann, to contain nothing "productive" or "original," without a trace of "boldness," in short, not particularly interesting.[3]

This decision to focus on a limited number of the deepest thinkers might appear to be justified by the ideology of the philosophers themselves. Many of them – most famously Maimonides – presented their own enterprise in elitist terms, emphasizing that their work was intended not for the masses of ordinary Jews but rather for the happy few who were capable, in intellectual endowment, temperament, and preparation, of comprehending the esoteric doctrine of the prophets and sages. But this common perception of Jewish philosophy as "the privileged possession of an intellectual elite"[4] becomes increasingly inaccurate during our period, when a sustained effort by philosophers to communicate with wider circles of the Jewish population can be documented. Gersonides wrote on three different levels: technical supercommentaries on Averroes, an independent theological treatise, and biblical commentaries intended for broad readership, and there is little question about the coherence and interrelatedness of the full corpus of his work.[5] The decision to "go public" by making accessible to the community of educated Jews what was hitherto concealed from all but a tiny elite is an important theme in the work of many central figures,[6] and it suggests an approach to Jewish philosophy that takes seriously its social context and function.

The historian Yitzhak Baer has indeed emphasized the social consequences of philosophy. Following the lead of several medieval writers[7] and reacting against the positive assessment of medieval Jewish philosophy by nineteenth-century German Jewish historians, Baer presented the enterprise of Jewish philosophy during our period in an extremely negative light.[8] He argued that philosophy, serving as the ideology of the courtier class, was fostered primarily by Jews whose loyalties to Judaism became increasingly attenuated as they rose to positions of influence in the power structure of Christian society. "Averroism," which taught a universal truth transcending the particularistic doctrines of specific religions, corroded the foundations of traditional Judaism and sapped the willingness to sacrifice, suffer, and even die for one's faith. In times of crisis, the philosophers converted en masse, while the unsophisticated Jews who never opened a philosophical text were prepared to die as martyrs.[9] Trenchant critiques of this thesis[10] have not succeeded in undermining its enduring influence.

A similar analysis has been given to the thirteenth- and early fourteenth-century conflicts over the proper role of philosophy in Jewish culture. It was widely assumed (though rarely demonstrated) that the upper classes were more positively disposed to philosophy than those beneath them in socio-economic status. Attempts to restrict or ban the study of philosophical works were therefore explained as the efforts by the representatives of the Jewish population as a whole and its traditional rabbinic leadership to throw off the oppressive rule of an oligarchy with values diverging from the tradition.[11]

During the past generation, scholars have attempted a more sophisticated assessment of the evidence for the role of philosophy in Jewish society and culture. Isadore Twersky, noting that "Provence had no entrenched courtier class and yet became the seat of rationalism," succinctly suggested that the relationship between socio-economic status and cultural-ideological positions was considerably more complex than Baer had posited. More recently, Joseph Shatzmiller has devoted considerable effort probing archival collections to investigate the social position of individuals involved in the philosophical enterprise, focusing particularly on physicians.[12]

Examination of the influence of philosophy within Jewish society as a whole has led to a broader definition of the philosophical canon, including figures less original and profound but certainly more representative than the best-known and encompassing the process of popularization by which philosophical assumptions, ideas, categories, and modes of reasoning penetrated widening circles of the Jewish population. This agenda requires that the net be cast beyond the classical philosophical texts to include encyclopedias, biblical and aggadic commentaries, sermons, moralistic tracts. For these purposes the introductions and colophons to the manuscripts of translators or super-commentators are often more important than the technical arguments over creation or freedom of the will.[13]

ECONOMIC BASES

Like every cultural enterprise, medieval Jewish philosophy in Christian Europe had an economic foundation. Unlike contemporary Christian philosophers – predominantly celibate friars pledged to poverty whose basic needs were provided within the framework of the mendicant orders[14] – Jewish philosophers, even those who reached radically ascetic and world-renouncing conclusions in their speculative thought, had to provide for themselves and for the sustenance and education of their families. Unless they were independently wealthy or supported by a patron, they had to be able to derive income from their philosophical writing or from other work, sometimes related to philosophy (medicine), sometimes not (money-lending).[15] Furthermore, their intellectual work required access to books. These books had to be purchased, or copies of existing books commissioned from scribes. Since many crucial texts were available only in languages not intelligible to most European Jews, there was a need for translation: first from Arabic, later from Latin. Teachers were needed to help those not yet expert to master the demanding material. All of this required funding. Yet we know relatively little about the economics of the philosophical enterprise.

In the middle of the thirteenth century, philosophical texts – original books written by Jews, translations, and copies of existing works – began to proliferate in the Jewish communities of southern Europe. Writing in the first years of the fourteenth century, Abba Mari of Lunel complained that "Aristotle and Plato succeeded in filling every nook and cranny with their books,"[16] a hyperbolic formulation in a polemical context, to be sure, but a reaction nevertheless to a significant cultural shift. As Harry Wolfson pointed out, the large number of extant Hebrew manuscripts of Averroean commentaries on Aristotle demonstrates a significant interest in, and demand for, such texts.[17] In the early fourteenth century, a Jewish philosopher writing his own supercommentary on Averroes' epitome of the *Physics* had enough manuscripts accessible to be able to do textual comparisons of a problematic passage, writing "This is the reading you find in a few manuscripts, but it is not what you find in most."[18]

Immanuel of Rome describes an encounter with a Jew who had spent seven years in Toledo and brought back to Italy a collection of some one hundred and eighty Hebrew and Arabic manuscripts. He left these manuscripts in sealed barrels, making the local Jews promise not to touch them while he traveled to Rome. As soon as the owner departed, Immanuel, his curiosity stimulated by the list of titles he had been shown, convinced his friends to break the seal and copy ten of the manuscripts. A month later, the owner returned and protested, causing Immanuel to defend his behavior.

The identity of the texts becomes clear from the argument of Immanuel's brief. By showing the list of titles, the owner had aroused an overpowering desire "to free them from their prison, and to show people their beauty and their splendor." "Our arid souls thirsted for the voice of the new learning," Immanuel continues; "our thoughts cried out, 'who will sate our hunger from the texts of the translations of Rabbi Moses ibn Tibbon?' " Therefore, he continues, "if I have copied the *Physics*, that is my nature."[19] We see here the dynamics of cultural diffusion: the philosophical works, recently translated into Hebrew, were known in Immanuel's community but not readily available. Manuscripts purchased by a traveler to Spain, brought into this new environment, are jealously guarded. And the desire for access to the "new learning" becomes a cultural *force majeure* justifying the violation of an explicit pledge. These texts, Immanuel tries to persuade us, are too important to be reserved for the few individuals wealthy enough to purchase them; they should be copied and made accessible to others.

This process, which forms the cultural background to the conflict over the study and dissemination of philosophy in the early years of the fourteenth century,[20] involves several categories of participants: translators, scribes, patrons, and "consumers." The extraordinary achievement of thirteenth-century Jewish translators in recasting the literature of Greco-Arabic philosophy into Hebrew (and in some cases into Latin) has been extensively researched from a bibliographical perspective. The economic bases and cultural implications are less well understood.

In the Christian world, translation into Latin was situated in the institutional context of cathedral schools and royal or imperial courts.[21] Translation into Hebrew, by contrast, seems to have been considerably less structured. The classics of Jewish philosophy written in Arabic were translated by Joseph Kimchi and Judah and Samuel ibn Tibbon in southern France during the twelfth century, an undertaking endorsed and apparently subsidized by some of the pillars of Provençal Jewish society, especially Meshullam ben Jacob of Lunel and Jonathan ha-Kohen of Lunel.[22] This apparently whetted the desire for access to texts written by non-Jews, but the mechanisms of patronage are less well known.

The first translation of an Aristotelian text is the *Meteora*, completed by Samuel ibn Tibbon in 1210 at the request of Joseph ben Israel of Toledo, described as "desirous of wisdom and enlightened in it." Presumably this difficult work was not done merely as a favor for a friend, but no details of any financial arrangement are recorded.[23] The earliest completed translation of an Averroean commentary on Aristotle is Jacob Anatoli's translation of the middle commentary on the *Organon*, dated 1232. In his introduction, Anatoli speaks of two motivations: the need to make the discipline of logic accessible to his fellow Jews so that they will be able to respond to the sophisticated arguments of their religious rivals, and the urging of friends among the scholars and leaders of Narbonne and Beziers to undertake the task. Apparently, the interest in this text justified the translator's expectations, as there are some forty manuscripts extant, and many supercommentaries on the Hebrew text of Averroes were written.[24]

After this initial effort, the floodgates opened. Within two generations, virtually all of Aristotle in his Arabic garb was available in Hebrew, along with many other scientific and philosophical works. By the early fourteenth century, a greater proportion of scientific thought was accessible in the Hebrew language than at any other time in history; Levi ben Gershom (Gersonides) could be at the cutting edge of contemporary scientific disciplines and Jewish physicians could pass the most rigorous official exams, without reading any other language.[25] Who subsidized the enormous investment in labor that these translations required?[26] Some Jewish translators worked in royal courts,[27] but the bulk of the Hebrew translations were not produced in this environment. Nor were there well-known Jewish patrons, such as Meshullam ben Joseph. Some individuals apparently sought out texts to translate simply out of intellectual curiosity or a commitment to further the knowledge of fellow Jews.[28] But could Moses ibn Tibbon have devoted so many years to translation without deriving any income from it? There is, as yet, no satisfactory answer to this question.

Also in the thirteenth century we see the beginning of translation from Latin into Hebrew. Accustomed to believe that the most sophisticated expressions of secular culture were to be found in Arabic texts, it took a while for Jews to recognize that their Christian neighbors were producing philosophical and scientific work of significance. In the early fourteenth century, Judah Romano translated selections from the writings of "the distinguished Dominican Friar" Giles of Rome, Albertus Magnus, Thomas Aquinas, and others in order "to demonstrate their wisdom" to those Jews who arrogantly thought that "truth and insight are absent from the Gentile nations, especially from the Christians."[29] Later in that century, however, such an assumption had become clearly untenable. Leon Joseph of Carcassonne studied Latin and translated Latin medical books by Christian authors because he knew that, without access to such works, Jewish physicians simply could not compete with their Christian colleagues.[30]

Once the works were translated, they had to be copied. The many aspects of this enterprise have only recently begun to be studied. Who were the scribes and copyists involved? Did they specialize in philosophical and scientific texts or did the same men work on rabbinic material as well? Did they have a special interest in the subject matter or was it merely a technical task to be performed, perhaps without even understanding what they were copying? How long did it take to copy a text of, say, a hundred folios? Who commissioned and paid them for their work, and how much could they expect to earn?[31] Scattered through the Hebrew manuscripts of philosophical texts is abundant information pertinent to these questions that needs to be systematically gathered and analyzed.

Here too, the passage cited from the *Machberot* of Immanuel is significant. It informs us that ten philosophical works were copied in Immanuel's community within a month, including a commentary by Averroes on Aristotle's *Physics*.[32] This sounds like a prodigious feat that would have required intensive work by a team of copyists, probably including amateurs. The anger of the owner is not explained, but it might have been caused by the realization that the unauthorized copying had diminished the value of his manuscripts in Italy, or that he had expected to charge a fee for permission to copy them. Such an arrangement is reflected in an early fourteenth-century contract whereby the owner of an important book charged a considerable fee for granting to a Jewish physician the right to keep the book for a year and copy it, stipulating that he would not allow anyone else to copy it and would limit the circulation of the copy.[33]

There is other evidence of the problems involved in copying texts. Samuel ben Judah of Marseilles, a fourteenth-century Provençal scholar, traveled with his brother from Aix to Trinquitailles to find an Arabic text of ibn Aflaḥ's epitome of the *Almagest*. The two of them worked feverishly for two days copying as much as they could – less than one eighth of the text – before they had to return it to its owner. He then found a copy of the translation by Jacob ben Machir and arranged with the owner for permission to copy it. Finally he gained access once again to the Arabic manuscript and corrected errors in the translation by comparing it with the original.[34]

Here too the cultural dynamics and the economics of the enterprise need to be investigated. In some cases, such as that of Samuel ben Judah, the individual seems to be copying a text primarily for his own use.[35] The contract published by Shatzmiller requires that the text be limited to the private use of the physician who was permitted to copy it.[36] On the other hand, manuscript colophons are filled with information about individuals for whom the texts were copied: sometimes the scribe's teacher,[37] but more frequently a patron or employer who seems to have commissioned the task.[38] Identification of the scribes known from the colophons of extant manuscripts and the persons for whom the manuscripts were written has begun, but a systematic study of this material as a resource for social and cultural history of the diffusion of philosophical materials is greatly to be desired.

Given the difficulties and cost of translating and copying philosophical texts,[39] it is rather impressive that Jews collected them into significant holdings. Medieval Christian Europe had its monastic, royal, and university libraries;[40] by contrast, we know nothing of communal or institutional Jewish collections of philosophical manuscripts. Individual initiative was paramount. Judah ibn Tibbon's celebrated description of the library he made available to his son Samuel is short on details, telling us only that the books were in Hebrew and in Arabic.[41] But several book lists from the fourteenth and fifteenth centuries provide a good indication of the kind of collection a reasonably wealthy Jewish intellectual could amass.

The picture emerging from the lists of Leon Mosconi, a fourteenth-century Majorcan physician, Astruc of Sestiers, a fifteenth-century physician from Aix-en-Provence, and the great Jewish scientist and philosopher Levi ben Gershom is fairly consistent. The three libraries are of the same order of magnitude: between 147 and 179 books. And they are all remarkably diverse. Each contains philosophical and scientific works by Greek and Arabic writers in Hebrew translations. But they also contain numerous manuscripts of biblical texts and commentaries (Mosconi had a special affinity for Joseph ibn Kaspi, while Astruc collected work by David Kimchi) and of rabbinic literature, including Talmud and Midrash.[42] These libraries belie any facile generalization that a commitment to philosophical study in the fourteenth and fifteenth centuries indicated a weakening attachment to Jewish tradition.

If the translation and copying of philosophical texts are two components of the diffusion of philosophy that necessarily had a financial component, a third was teaching. While it was theoretically possible for people to educate themselves in philosophy simply by reading texts, it was more common for a teacher to guide the student through the curriculum. In an environment where even teachers of traditional Jewish learning were becoming professionalized,[43] it is not surprising that many philosophical teachers expected to be paid.

For some it was a matter of economic necessity. In late thirteenth-century southern France, Levi ben Abraham, author of popular philosophical works that aroused the ire of conservative opponents, was described as being so poor he had to teach Arabic to whoever would hire him, whether old or young. Yedaiah Bedersi, defending the culture of southern France against the accusation that children were taught philosophical material for which they were not prepared, conceded that in the past some men, competent in the discipline of logic, "had fallen upon bad times and were forced to sell their expertise and reveal their views publicly."[44]

In the fifteenth century, Spanish opponents to the influence of philosophy complained that young men would pay to be taught secular sciences, while slighting those who taught Torah for nothing.[45] A similar complaint from contemporary Italy makes it clear that Jews were studying philosophy with Christian scholars. But here the economics were reversed: the Jews prefer to study "wisdom" with Christian scholars, who charge low fees (presumably because they have stipends from patrons), rather than hire rabbinic scholars who charge more.[46] The economics of higher education are revealed in this same source, as the writer complains: "If I had said these things in distant academies in the Middle East, where the students truly desire Torah and love Talmud, they would give me at least 10 ducats.... But these rabbis in our region do not value such things at all."[47]

The one way in which philosophical knowledge could be widely disseminated without cost was through the pulpit. Beginning in the thirteenth century, if not before, the sermon became a vehicle through which philosophical ideas were readily popularized: simplified, integrated with traditional texts, and communicated to an audience composed of Jews at various social levels, including those without the means to purchase books or the inclination to study them. The preachers ranged from men like Jacob Anatoli, himself competent in the most technical philosophical material, to some who were accused of knowing their philosophy only at second or third hand. Many were appalled at the intrusion of what they considered to be radical, even heretical, ideas into the sermons. They protested vociferously and attempted – unsuccessfully – to exert control over what could be said from the pulpit.[48]

By the fifteenth century, there is abundant evidence of philosophical material as an integral part of the sermons delivered in Spain. This included not only some rather technical discussions but also the use of philosophical modes of reasoning – the syllogism and the scholastic disputed question – which gave new forms to Jewish homiletics.[49] While the sermon was not an instrument conducive to philosophical originality or profundity, there can be no question that it served to spread many of the basic elements of philosophical thought considerably beyond the circle of serious students.

∼ INSTITUTIONAL STRUCTURES ∼

A second set of questions relates to the institutional context for philosophical study among Jews. In the contemporary Christian community, the flourishing of philosophical study was intimately bound up with the emergence of the universities, which supplanted the monasteries and the cathedral schools as the centers of intellectual activity. These universities provided a standardized curriculum, a process for evaluation of progress and certification of mastery over a field, and a set of social rewards for excellence. Eventually, they acquired an identity transcending the individuals who happened to be teaching at a particular time. The very name by which this enterprise is commonly known – scholasticism – reveals its rootedness in the new institutional context of the university.[50]

In the Jewish community, there is little evidence for anything even remotely analogous as a framework for philosophical study. The educational institutions of the Jewish community were devoted almost exclusively to the study of traditional Jewish texts, primarily Bible and Talmud. Recently it has been questioned whether in northern Europe there existed an organized system of community-sponsored elementary education, or of academies for higher scholarship that were recognized as stable public institutions transcending a particularly noted individual.[51] But even in southern France and Christian Spain, where the evidence for the existence of recognized academies is considerably stronger, these do not appear to be the context in which philosophy was studied or philosophical writings produced.[52]

Philosophical learning among Jews seems to have been transmitted predominantly through private instruction: fathers teaching their children or providing teachers for them, mature students seeking experts from whom they could learn. Judah ibn Tibbon describes the need to travel far to bring back a suitable teacher in the secular sciences for his son.[53] This son, the distinguished translator Samuel, in turn became the philosophical mentor of his own son-in-law, Jacob Anatoli.[54] Moses Narboni was studying the *Guide of the Perplexed* with his father when he was thirteen years old.[55] Autobiographical accounts written by an anonymous disciple of Abraham Abulafia, Joseph ibn Kaspi, and Kalonymus ben Kalonymus describe a pattern of travelling to find a satisfactory teacher of philosophical texts – the Jewish equivalent of the medieval *peregrinatio academica*.[56]

We also hear of individual teachers. Zerachiah ben Shealtiel Gracian of Barcelona had a considerable reputation as a teacher of philosophy in Rome, although he did not seem to have an academy of his own.[57] Sen Astruc de Noves, not particularly famous as a philosopher or scientist in his own right, served as the mentor in Salon of several Jews who went on to successful careers, including Kalonymus ben Kalonymus and Samuel ben Judah of Marseilles.[58] Levi ben Abraham was invited by the wealthy and pious patron Samuel Sulami to live in his home and instruct him in philosophy.[59] The extensive literature pertaining to the conflict over philosophical study in the early fourteenth century makes no mention of formal schools; the bans promulgated by R. Solomon Adret (Rashba) in 1305 seem to be directed at individuals studying with other individuals.[60]

A number of books are described as having been written for the educational needs of a particular individual. Judah ibn Tibbon speaks of the books he has made for his son "on all the sciences," possibly compendia intended for his son's use.[61] Joseph ibn Kaspi says he has made a digest of Aristotle's *Ethics* (*Terumat Kesef*) for his son, and hopes to do the same for the *Organon* (*Tzeror ha-Kesef*).[62] Shem Tov Falaquera describes his works *Reshit Chokhmah*, *Sefer ha-Ma'alot*, and *De'ot ha-Pilosofim* as intended to guide a certain Jew with no background in philosophy or knowledge of Arabic through the philosophical curriculum.[63] This may have been a topos, exemplified in Maimonides' *Guide* and rooted in the rabbinic tradition, that certain philosophical doctrines are not to be taught to more than one at a time.[64] But it suggests the absence of established schools to which those who wanted a systematic training in philosophy could turn. All of this indicates a pattern of philosophical study described by Colette Sirat: there was "no organized teaching of the sciences, no school, but only a transmission from master to pupil."[65]

Yet there are tantalizing hints of a different picture. One text is so suggestive that it deserves to be cited at length. It appears in *Tagmulei ha-Nefesh*, by Hillel of Verona:[66]

> Therefore I say that this statement of Aristotle [implying that the intellect is not immortal] does not represent his own position or his own thought, but rather the position of his predecessors that he had previously been reporting. This is what I said in my youth in the *beit ha-midrash*, when I was studying in Spain with the master [*ha-rav*] who taught me physical science, and my fellow students [*benei ha-yeshivah*] argued against me for a long time, and my master also would not agree with me. He disputed with me extensively, for from the commentaries of ibn Rushd [Averroes] no solution was to be found to this problem.
>
> Finally it pleased God that our master found an old text, written in an ancient hand, of a commentary by Themistius, who wrote commentaries on all the works of Aristotle. In it was written that Themistius interpreted this statement to mean that Aristotle was reporting the position of Plato and his colleagues, not his own view. Thus Themistius writes that when Aristotle said this in that chapter of the first book of *De Anima*, he was still undertaking his account of the position of his predecessors, and had not yet begun a refutation of those who hold that there is no difference between intellect and sense. Throughout the entire chapter he speaks of the intellect as he does of the senses . . . .
>
> This is what the master found in the commentaries of Themistius. Then he was pacified, and he accepted my position. I was delighted and thankful to God that my position agreed with that of Themistius, for he is one of the greatest of the commentators on the works of Aristotle, and all the masters rely on his commentaries as they do on the commentaries of ibn Rushd, or even more.

The substance of the debate need not concern us here. What is crucial for our purpose is the setting. The author describes youthful philosophical studies in Spain, probably in the 1240s or 1250s. According to the passage, these studies occurred in the context of a school, referred to by the Hebrew terms *beit midrash* and *yeshivah*. Instruction was led by a master, called *rav*,[67] and a number of students were present.

The subject matter included physics and psychology, investigated through the works of Aristotle with the commentaries of Averroes. Finally, the commentaries of Themistius, specifically to *De Anima*, but to other works of Aristotle as well, are described as particularly influential among "the masters" (*ha-rabbanim*).

Were the texts studied in Hebrew or in Arabic? Hebrew translations of Averroes' commentaries on *De Anima* were being produced in precisely this period, but no Hebrew translation is known of Themistius' commentary on *De Anima*.[68] Since the Themistius text is described as old and quite rare, it is most unlikely that it could refer to an unknown thirteenth-century Hebrew translation of the text. The conclusion, therefore, is that the philosophical texts described must have been in Arabic.

If this passage is to be believed,[69] there was at least one school in Spain in the mid-thirteenth century where philosophy was being taught on a rather high level. If this was indeed a Jewish school, we are impelled to look for other confirming evidence of a Jewish institutional structure for philosophical study.[70] For example, Isaac ben Yedaiah's description of the academy of R. Meshullam ben Moses in Beziers, probably referring to the 1230s, mentions "learned scholars with reputations in every discipline and branch of knowledge," and notes that students came there to learn not only the "disputations of Abaye and Rava" but also "the work of the chariot and the wheel of the wagon." This suggests that something more than talmudic dialectic was being studied. As Meshullam was an opponent of the early kabbalah in Provence, it stands to reason that the "work of the chariot" here is to be understood in its Maimonidean sense, referring to philosophy.[71]

Other material pertains to the late fourteenth and fifteenth centuries. Harry Wolfson believed that Jewish philosophy in Spain was indeed taught in a formal institutional structure. He wrote that Crescas' *Or ha-Shem* "had its origin in class-room lectures and discussions. We know of other instances where Hebrew philosophic works were the result of class-room lectures."[72] Elsewhere he maintained that the commentaries of Averroes were intensively studied "by individual scholars as well as by organized classes in schools,"[73] and he describes Isaac ibn Shem Tov as "a teacher actively engaged in expounding the text of the *Physics* to successive classes of students."[74] The evidence for these statements, however, is meager and circumstantial at best, applying just as readily to individual instruction as to formal class lectures.

In the final generation of Jewish life in Spain, Isaac Arama complained bitterly that "many are the teachers of alien disciplines, antagonistic to our Torah and our faith, and it is a trivial matter in their judgment to teach these disciplines in their own language"; philosophy has become the "foundation of our yeshivas, which have become devoid of Torah and Talmud."[75] This sounds like the hyperbolic rhetoric of a polemicist. Yet given the interest in philosophy on the part of leading rabbinic scholars such as Isaac Conponton and Isaac Aboab, it is not inconceivable that philosophy found its way into the curriculum as an adjunct to talmudic studies. There are references to philosophical work done in the academy of Abraham Bibago at Saragossa.[76] In the first years of the sixteenth century, Joseph Garçon complains about those who "wear themselves out beating a path to the academy [yeshivah] of external disciplines," yet another tantalizingly ambiguous reference to what may or may not be a Jewish institution for philosophical study.[77]

The most detailed information of a Jewish institutional base for philosophical study comes from Italy. Judah Messer Leon writes about his academy (yeshivah) in Mantua, in which he gave daily instructions in the *Posterior Analytics* (on which Judah had written a supercommentary) to a "David the Spaniard," who in turn taught Judah's students for pay al-Ghazālī's simpler text *Principal Purposes of the Philosophers*. While it is unclear whether any rabbinic study took place at this "academy," it does describe a school which, though probably centered on one primary scholar, included students at different levels and instruction by different individuals.[78]

The alternative possibility is that the passage should be understood as referring to Hillel's studies at a Christian institution. This does not at first seem likely, for the terminology used by Hillel, "*beit ha-midrash*," "*yeshivah*," "*rav*," has specifically Jewish connotations. Yet Jewish writers did use such terms to describe Christian or Muslim institutions for which there was no distinctive Hebrew equivalent.[79] Is it conceivable that a Jew from Italy could have studied philosophy from Arabic texts in mid-thirteenth-century Spain in a Christian institution of higher learning? The Hillel of Verona passage opens up a possibility that needs further investigation.

ᴥ SOCIAL STATUS ᴥ

What is known about the social status of those who participated in the philosophical enterprise? Do available data substantiate the thesis that philosophy was primarily the preoccupation of the upper class? There are several problems in addressing this issue. One is a problem of definition: who is to be included in the category of "philosophers"? For our purposes, it will not be sufficient to limit the investigation to a few outstanding names. In order to understand the social dimensions of Jewish philosophy, it is necessary to include the less original figures, the translators, popularizers, and purveyors of philosophy, alongside the intellectual giants.[80] Those who devoted a significant portion of their energy to philosophical work are as much a part of the subject as those who made a lasting contribution to the history of Jewish thought. So are those who might be termed the "consumers": the patrons of philosophical writers, those who commissioned translations, those who purchased scientific texts. Unfortunately, in many cases little is known about certain figures beyond the texts they wrote, which contain meager biographical information.[81] Nevertheless, enough material can be gathered to justify some preliminary conclusions.

Let us begin with the most profound and original figure among the Jewish philosophers and scientists of this era, Levi ben Gershom (Gersonides). Recent archival research by Joseph Shatzmiller and others has elucidated the position of Ralbag (Gersonides) and his family in the community of Orange.[82] Despite medieval traditions that he was a descendant of Nachmanides or Levi ben Abraham, little is definitely known about his lineage. Notarial records indicate that his family was thoroughly integrated in the life of the community, though not among its official leaders (parnasim: the equivalent, as Shatzmiller informs us, of the Latin consules). Like many contemporary Jews, Ralbag engaged in money-lending. His brother Samuel was a physician, and Ralbag may have been as well.

Shatzmiller has documented the considerable interest shown by contemporary Christian intellectuals in Ralbag's work. His reputation gave him access to the papal court in Avignon; indeed, his last piece of writing, never finished, was an astrological prediction requested by the Pope. He may have used his access to the court and prestige on behalf of his fellow Jews, although there is no evidence of specific intervention. Ralbag thus provides an example of philosophical achievements combined with court connections, but in a model quite different from that posited by Baer. He is not a wealthy, aristocratic Jewish courtier who used philosophy to rationalize his abandonment of Jewish commitments and assimilation into the society of the court, but rather a Jew whose Jewish commitments are beyond reproach, who came to the attention of the Christian elite precisely because of his achievements in philosophy and science.

A figure comparable in cultural profile though certainly not of similar world-class stature is Yedaiah Bedersi. Like Ralbag, he wrote in a number of different genres; all of his work is suffused with the philosophical ethos, though the philosophy is presented on varying levels of difficulty. There were extremely technical works, including commentaries on Averroes' epitome of the *Physics* and Avicenna's *Canon* and independent treatises that reveal the influence both of Islamic and Scholastic philosophy.[83] He wrote a commentary on traditional Jewish material – selected passages from the Midrashim – in which he incorporates specific references to a variety of technical philosophical texts.[84] And he wrote more popular literary works in which the philosophical commitment is fused with a more traditional piety.

Yedaiah's father, Abraham, was apparently from a wealthy, well-bred family; his financial activities made him economically independent to the point where he could support other poets. In a polemical context, he expresses contempt for the low origins of his opponent. He was apparently related to courtiers in Beziers. At some point, however, he experienced a financial reversal; forced to flee from Perpignan, he became dependent upon the sale of poems to patrons.[85] Yedaiah was apparently educated as a prodigy in Perpignan within a context of affluence. Yet his was not an aristocratic family; in the introduction to "Ohev Nashim," written at the age of eighteen, he describes the two sons of Don Salomon de les Infants of Arles as above him in social prestige.[86] The economic reversals seem to have left their mark. His most popular work, *Bechinat Olam*, reveals a deep suspicion of wealth.[87] Like Ralbag, he confirms the conclusion that Jewish philosophy could flourish without any direct connections to a courtier class, and without undermining Jewish loyalties and commitments.

A different category is composed of those intimately involved in philosophy, though not original philosophers themselves. To this category belongs the ibn Tibbon family, crucial in the process of transplanting Jewish philosophy from the Islamic to the Christian context through their ongoing project of translation. The "ethical will" of Judah ibn Tibbon provides considerable information about his social and economic status. In addition to his scholarly activities, he was a merchant. He refers to an incident in Marseilles in which his son Samuel took the initiative for an unfortunate investment on behalf of the family. He traveled extensively. He took pride in the library he acquired at great expense. He was respected and honored by the community, by Christians as well as Jews.[88]

Yet the text indicates that he was not an extremely wealthy man. While he paid thirty gold dinars a year to a teacher, he had to pledge books and borrow from friends to provide for the marriage of his two daughters. He feels impelled to remind his son that he did not arrange a marriage with an otherwise undesirable daughter of a wealthy man "as others richer than I have done with their sons." Samuel's wife is described as having been brought up in a good family, but having simple tastes, without a servant.[89] This is clearly a description of the middle class, not of the Jewish aristocracy.

Little is known of the social position of the other Tibbonids. A recent scholar describes them all as physicians, but concedes that "aside from their translations we know nothing of their medical activities."[90] Judah Alfakhar, scion of an aristocratic family and one of the leaders of Toledan Jewry, refers to Samuel ibn Tibbon with little respect.[91]

Moses ibn Tibbon produced such a prodigious number of translations between 1240 and 1283 that this must have been virtually a full-time occupation, yet it remains unclear how this work was subsidized.[92]

Connected with the ibn Tibbon family by marriage was Jacob Anatoli.[93] While not an original philosopher, his importance as a translator and a popularizer of philosophical ideas in a homiletical context has already been noted. Anatoli refers to friends among the most learned Jews in Narbonne and Beziers, who encouraged him to translate Averroes' commentary on Aristotle's *Organon*. But he also indicates that powerful forces in the Jewish community rebuked him for his study of logic in Arabic and forced him to discontinue his weekly Sabbath preaching.[94] This is someone who had a base of supporters, but certainly not someone who wielded power in the Jewish community or outside it.

Jacob ben Machir was part of the same distinguished family. In the first years of the fourteenth century, he led the Jews in Montpellier who opposed Abba Mari's efforts to restrict the study of philosophy. An astronomer and mathematician of some consequence, he and several Jewish colleagues had considerable interaction with Christian scholars in the University of Montpellier. It is clear, however, that this did not put him in the power elite either of the Jewish community or of Christian society.[95] The ibn Tibbon family thus serves as an example of an ongoing philosophical commitment, sustained for at least four generations, without any links to a courtier class or any indication of an erosion of Jewish loyalties.[96]

A third category is composed of those who did not produce philosophy at all, either by writing independent texts or by translating, but rather spread or popularized the philosophical work of others in their own writings. A good representative is David Kimchi (Radak), significant because of his incorporation of philosophical ideas in popular biblical commentaries and because of his role as a defender of Maimonides in the 1232 conflict. He was apparently a teacher by profession, noting that "most of my time has been spent teaching boys Talmud." This was not a position that guaranteed particularly high status in medieval Jewish society.[97] Even at the end of his career, during his 1232 campaign to Spain in defense of Maimonides, he was treated rather roughly by his opponents, informed that he was not welcome in Burgos, and addressed with what seems to be an air of condescension by Alfakhar.[98] His own writings express sympathies for the poor, and he attacks opponents for living in the lap of opulence.[99] Clearly, Kimchi's commitment to philosophy was not connected with a social status that could be described in any way as aristocratic.

Another figure in this category is Joseph ibn Kaspi. Like Kimchi, he produced no significant philosophical work of his own, devoting his energy rather to exegesis in the spirit of philosophy.[100] Ibn Kaspi's ethical will indicates that he spent considerable time traveling in pursuit of knowledge, noting without undue modesty that "wherever I go, wealth and honor are with me."[101] In the famous description of his "family feast," he reveals that a servant woman was in the kitchen, and that not only invited guests but "the poor" were in attendance.[102] At the same time, he disparages wealth as unworthy of one's efforts, recommending rather attention to the insights of the traditional moralistic literature.[103] The picture seems to be of one whose economic success had given him the independence and leisure to follow his intellectual pursuits, not one whose social status predisposed him to find a philosophical rationale for assimilation to an elite circle.[104]

To be sure, courtiers and wealthy Jews were associated with philosophy.[105] But this review of the social status of representative figures bearing various relations to the broad enterprise of Jewish philosophy does not substantiate any decisive relationship with a courtier class. Nor should it be forgotten that some of the most influential Jewish courtiers were anything but enamored of philosophy, and in some cases they actively opposed it. R. Meir Halevi Abulafia (Ramah), who challenged Maimonides over what he thought was an overly rationalistic eschatology, was from one of the aristocratic families of Castilian Jewry; he was financially independent and may have had connections with the royal court.[106] Judah Alfakhar, a physician who despite his philosophical study strongly defended an anti-Maimonidean position against David Kimchi, was from one of the most illustrious and influential families in Toledo.[107]

At the end of the thirteenth century, R. Todros ben Joseph Halevi Abulafia was from yet another aristocratic family of Toledo. He was wealthy, with access to the Castilian court; other Jewish courtiers were part of his circle. Yet he was an ascetic and a mystic, one of the leaders of the "Gnostic school" of kabbalah, with little use for philosphy.[108] Kalonymus ben Todros, the *nasi* (head) in Narbonne, became a leader in the anti-philosophy camp of Abba Mari, and his role appears to have been decisive in preparing the groundwork for Rashba's ban.[109] Chasdai Crescas, the great critic of Aristotelian philosophy (though a profound master of the philosophical tradition), was one of the most influential Jews in Aragon because of his access to the court.[110] And of course the paradigmatic Jewish courtier at the end of our period, Don Isaac Abravanel, was a trenchant critic of Jewish rationalism and its representatives.[111]

This leaves us with a final category: the "extremist" philosophers, the "Averroists," whose self-serving ideology was supposedly so devastating to traditional Jewish loyalties. The evidence adduced in the writings of contemporaries comprises complaints about excessive allegorization of Bible and aggadah, claims that philosophical ideas such as *ta'amei mitzvot* were used to rationalize neglect of the commandments, accusations that philosophers did not pray and had contempt for the sages.[112]

Several points need emphasis here. First, extreme care must be taken when judging views based on the presentation of those views in the polemical attacks of opponents. There is a natural tendency in polemical literature to take a position out of context and present it in its most radical form. Where the actual writings of the attacked individuals can be examined, they usually appear far more moderate and reasonable than what is described by their enemies.[113] Consider, for example, a passage in one of the texts of Rashba's ban from 1305:

> One of them [the extreme philosophers being attacked] said when preaching publicly in the synagogue as though in surprise: "What reason did Moses have to prohibit pork? If it is because of its poor quality, the scientists have not found its quality so bad." And one of them said, "The purpose of the commandment of the phylacteries is not to place them actually on the head and the arm – God has no delight in this – but only that a man should understand and remember the Lord."[114]

The implication in this passage is that the philosophers no longer observe the prohibition of pork and no longer put on phylacteries because of their rational approach to the commandments. But, assuming that these are accurate quotes, the antinomian conclusion is by no means a necessary consequence.

The rhetorical question about pork could have been asked by a traditionalist opposed to any attempt to find reasons for the command- ments, a kabbalist repudiating rational reasons in favor of mystical ones, or a rationalist rejecting Maimonides' connection of dietary restrictions with hygienic considerations in favor of a different rational explanation – for example, that pork is prohibited not because it is bad for health but as a reminder that we should avoid disgraceful and filthy personal qualities.[115] In all three cases the meat remains forbidden. As for the second statement about the phylacteries, it could mean that God does not want the Jew to place them on head and arm, but it also could mean that God has no delight in a mechanical performance unless it is accompanied by the intellectual and emotional awareness of God represented by the heart and the brain – a purpose for the command- ment quite similar to what Rashba himself wrote at the beginning of his commentary on the aggadot.[116] We have no evidence from their own words of even the most philosophy-intoxicated Jews at this time arguing that the performance of the commandments may be abandoned so long as their purpose is fulfilled. What we frequently find is the statement that, without an inner awareness of the purpose, the mechanical unthinking act has no value in God's sight, and it might as well not be done. It is not difficult to imagine the opponents of philosophy transforming this rhetorical assertion into a more extreme rationalization for abandoning the act.[117]

Second, the adherents of extreme philosophical positions are almost invariably presented without detailed information about their identity or their social status. They are a shadowy, anonymous group, the members of which cannot be identified with individuals whose work we know. Those philosophers whom we do know, even those who themselves were criticized by conservatives, often present their position as a moderate middle ground and attack extremists (usually called *ha-mitpalsefim*) whom they reject because they misuse philosophy.[118] Descriptions of these extremists do not regularly characterize them as upper class; in some cases it is the opposite. The preachers who incorporated extreme allegorical interpretations in their sermons, so frequently attacked during the controversy of the early 1300s, are described as itinerants on the peripheries of Jewish society, using philosophy not to escape the Jewish community but to assert some influence within it.[119] According to Moses Narboni, the philosopher Abner of Burgos was driven to apostasy out of despair stemming from impoverishment.[120]

Third, we must be careful of assuming that every reference to skepticism or ritual laxness in the medieval Jewish community is the result of the influence of philosophy. The term "Averroist" is often used quite loosely, referring not to those whose philosophical views were deeply influenced by the writings of ibn Rushd,[121] or even to those who held a "double truth" theory,[122] but rather as a general synonym for those "heretical" in beliefs and "licentious" and "immoral" in behavior.[123] For example, Baer describes a certain Moses Faquim as a "confirmed Averroist," who "blasphemed against all religions." But the document providing information about Faquim says nothing about philosophical study as the motivation for his behavior.[124] "Averroism" is posited, or rather defined, as the culprit, even where no historical connection is in evidence.

Even when a correlation between philosophical study, upper-class status, and a weakening of traditional Jewish loyalties can be established, it does not follow that philosophy was the cause. The attenuation of characteristically Jewish behavior and beliefs perceived by conservatives may be caused by large social forces; philosophy may have served to rationalize the continuation of Jewish identity as much as the abandonment of it. It is striking how many philosophical works during our period are justified by their authors as necessary for the dignity of the Jewish people, faced with the charge that Jews, ignorant of philosophy and the sciences, possessed a culture inferior to that of their Christian neighbors.[125]

In the final generation of Jewish life on the Iberian peninsula, there is little evidence to justify the conclusion that an infatuation with extreme rationalism had undermined the Jewish loyalties of the leadership class and thereby demoralized the masses. There is, by contrast, abundant evidence that a moderate rationalism based on a familiarity with philosophical works written originally in Greek, Arabic, or Latin permeated the cultural life of Spanish Jewry, suffusing its sermons and biblical commentaries, sharpening its polemical literature, influencing even its talmudic scholarship. Philosophical notions, terminology, and modes of thinking are apparent even in writers like Isaac Arama and Isaac Abravanel who were ultimately suspicious of its impact. While it is impossible to determine how the experience of these communities would have differed if the attempts to ban philosophical study had succeeded, it is plausible to argue that without the capacity to articulate Judaism in a frame of reference intelligible to the surrounding society, and without a cadre of Jews whose scientific training rendered them useful to their Christian neighbors,[126] disaster might have befallen even earlier.[127]

❧ NOTES ❧

1 The term "philosophy" is more encompassing in its medieval context than it is today, and I therefore include the natural sciences. Although attempts were made to distinguish between the status of, say, medicine and metaphysics, most recognized the existence of a comprehensive philosophical curriculum in which many disciplines were included. See Wolfson 1973, pp. 493–550, and the succinct statement by H. Davidson in Freudenthal 1992, p. 195: Gersonides "recognized no dividing line between the natural sciences and speculative philosophy."

2 See, for example, Harry Wolfson's classic definition of what he called the "hypothetico-deductive method of text interpretation" as applied to philosophical works (Wolfson 1957, pp. 24–8).

3 Guttmann 1964, p. 275. Cf. the even more extreme statement by Isaac Barzilay 1967: "There is indeed but little original and innovating intellectual creativity in medieval Judaism after Halevi and Maimonides" (p. 16).

4 Barzilay 1967, p. 12.

5 A recognition of the interconnectedness of his work underlies Touati (1973) and Herbert Davidson's study "Gersonides on the Material and Active Intellects," in Freudenthal 1992, pp. 195–265. See also Kellner 1991, p. 93 on Gersonides' rejection of esotericism, and p. 104 for his thesis that Gersonides "was continuing the Tibbonian project of spreading philosophic erudition and sophistication among the Jews."

6 See, for example, Ravitzky 1981a, p. 115, citing Samuel ibn Tibbon and Moses

Narboni on the legitimation of transcending Maimonides' esotericism (and a similar statement by ibn Kaspi in Dinur 1972, p. 242); Harvey 1987, p. ix, on a "philosopher's attempt to interest the multitude in philosophy"; Jospe 1988, p. 1 and Fenton 1992, p. 27 on Falaquera's efforts at "spreading philosophical learning among the Jewish people." The decision to produce encyclopedic works that would make the doctrines of the various scientific disciplines accessible without the arduous task of mastering each one reflects a similar sense of mission. See, for example, the introduction to "Battei ha-Nefesh ve-ha-Lach-ashim," in Davidson 1939, p. 86, where Levi ben Abraham expresses his purpose in terms strikingly analogous to Maimonides' explanation of the need for his *Mishneh Torah*, and a similar statement by Gershon ben Solomon in his introduction to "Sha'ar ha-Shamayim" (Dinur 1972, p. 184). Views expressing contempt toward the masses as incapable of understanding philosophy were, however, still expressed in this period.

7 Best known are Solomon Alami, Isaac Arama, and Joseph Yabetz.

8 Baer 1961, 1: 3: The external forces of political and religious oppression "were assisted from within by a rationalism and scepticism which undermined tradition." For other references, see Schachter 1992, pp. 180–2. Cf. also Barzilay 1967, p. 11: Rationalism, "by its very nature, tended to weaken and undermine" the foundations of Judaism in the Diaspora, evoking "centrifugal tendencies of social dissolution and religious decline."

9 On philosophy and the courtiers, see especially Baer 1961, 1: 240–2, 263. On the links between philosophical commitments (usually called "Averroism") and apostasy, see Baer 1961, 2: 137–8, 144, 148, 224, 274, and elsewhere.

10 Twersky 1968, p. 189 n. 15; Ben-Sasson 1984, pp. 232–8.

11 See for example, Ben-Sasson 1976, p. 543, speaking about the conflict in the early fourteenth century: "The social tension between the middle and lower classes, which gathered round the *halakhic* scholars and the mystics, steadily increased at the sight of the opulent and, according to the moralists, dissolute way of life of the upper classes, most of whose members were inclined towards Maimonides and rationalism." A more subtle attempt to link sociopolitical tensions in Jewish society with the conflict of the 1230s is in Septimus 1973 and 1979; cf. Saperstein 1980, p. 263 n. 25.

12 Twersky 1968, p. 189 (cf. however, Iancu-Agou 1987, p. 11). Shatzmiller: see works in bibliography.

13 See bibliography for the work of Ravitzky (especially his programmatic statement in 1981b), Sirat, Talmage, Iancu-Agou, and my own statement in Saperstein 1980, pp. 205–6, 209–10, and Saperstein 1996, pp. 75–87. A striking illustration of the shift in approach is the contrast in the treatment of the thirteenth to fifteenth centuries in the surveys by Husik (1940), Guttmann (1964), and Sirat (1985). Husik devotes a few pages to the influence of Maimonides and one chapter each to Hillel of Verona, Gersonides, the Karaite Aaron ben Elijah, Crescas, and Albo. Guttmann expands the canon a bit; in addition to lengthy treatments of Gersonides and Crescas, he discusses a dozen others (the translators, Hillel of Verona, Albalag, Abner of Burgos, Pollegar, Narboni, Duran, Albo, Abravanel, Judah Messer Leon, del Medigo). Sirat treats several dozen writers from the same period. Valuable source material for a social and cultural

history of Jewish philosophy in Christian Europe was made accessible by Dinur (1972, pp. 173–257).

14 See, for example, Southern 1970, pp. 292–9.

15 Jewish philosophers were not insensitive to economic constraints. Jacob Anatoli states that he was too "burdened by worldly matters" to write any of his sermons; it was apparently only after his position in the court of Frederick II made his life more secure (below, note 24) that he had the opportunity to write (Anatoli 1866, introduction). In the introduction to his astronomical tables, Jacob ben Machir, writing in early 1301, asserts that the study of astronomy has been relatively neglected by Jews because its practitioners, unlike scholars of medicine and law, cannot derive income from their knowledge; the discipline has therefore been left to those who have independent economic security (Renan 1877, pp. 616–17). If this economic consideration was true for astronomy, how much more would it have been true for logic or metaphysics. Solomon Bonafed gives an economic explanation for the superiority of Christian scholars over Jews in the various disciplines: "They imbibe the abundance of the seas [Deuteronomy 33:19]; they do not need to provide sustenance for their students or to hunt and bring game as we do today: our economic base is too small for comfort [cf. Isaiah 28:20], and we have no true scholars among us" (Gross 1993, p. 36).

16 Abba Mari 1838, p. 31; repeated by Adret 1958, p. 52. Abba Mari complains in particular about Jewish preachers using books written by Gentile authors: 1838, p. 3.

17 Wolfson 1973, p. 431.

18 Saperstein 1980, p. 272 n. 9, citing Parma Hebrew MS 1399 fol. 159v. There are many similar passages, making this work a valuable resource for the textual criticism of philosophical manuscripts. The same approach characterizes Yedaiah's commentary on ibn Sīnā's *Canon*, for example: "This reading is extremely corrupt, and I found it this way in all the manuscripts, and we probed after the Arabic manuscripts and it was the same. . . . In my search to remove this confusion, I found in the Baghdad recension. . . . This is the correct reading; apparently an error crept into the Arabic text from which our translation was made" (Escorial Hebrew MS G.III,9, fols. 102v–103r).

19 Immanuel 1957, 1: 161–5. Cf. Ben-Sasson 1976, pp. 524–5, where the content of the manuscripts is not revealed.

20 While the conflicts of 1232 and 1302–5 are often lumped together as "Maimonidean controversies," the purview had clearly changed. Rashba's ban applies not to Maimonides but to the philosophical works by "the Greeks" that had been translated into Hebrew. Even in the earlier conflict, Samuel ibn Tibbon was attacked for having made Maimonides' *Guide* accessible through his translation and having "revealed what Maimonides concealed" – perhaps in his *Ma'amar Yiqqavu ha-Mayim*. See "Iggerot Qena'ot" 1859, p. 3b; "Qevutzat Mikhtavim" 1975, pp. 100 and 36 (where al-Charīzī is criticized more than ibn Tibbon).

21 On the translation project in Toledo under the patronage of the Archbishop Raimundo, see Kritzeck 1964, pp. 52–4; Gilson 1954, pp. 235–6. In the thirteenth century, the arena for translation shifted to royal courts; the most important figures were the Emperor Frederick II, Alfonso X "the Wise," and Robert d'Anjou.

22 Twersky 1968, pp. 196–202; cf. Abba Mari 1838, p. 85.

23 Steinschneider 1893, pp. 132–3; Dinur 1972, p. 200. On this translation and the influence of the work, see Ravitzky 1990.

24 Steinschneider 1893, pp. 58–60, 65–94. At the conclusion of the text, Anatoli expresses gratitude to Frederick II, "lover of wisdom and those who seek it," who has "generously provided me nourishment and sustenance" (Anatoli 1969, p. viii). Clearly Frederick was motivated by goals different from those described in Anatoli's introduction.

25 There remains some question about Ralbag's reading knowledge of other languages, but Touati reports that he cites only Hebrew works (Touati 1973, p. 39), and the inventory of his private library lists only books in Hebrew (Freudenthal 1992, p. xv).

26 Cf. Shatzmiller 1980, pp. 468–9: he is the only scholar I know to address (in passing) the question of "the economic aspect of this wave of translation."

27 Anatoli (above, note 24). For Kalonymus ben Kalonymus translating in the service of Robert of Anjou, see Immanuel 1957, 2: 426–8; Renan 1893, p. 441; Steinschneider 1893, p. 330. Judah Romano worked as a translator in the same court (see below, note 29). For Jewish translators in the court of Alfonso X, see Roth 1985.

28 Samuel ben Judah in Berman 1967, pp. 307–20; Leon Joseph of Carcassonne in Renan 1893, pp. 772–4.

29 Neubauer 1886, pp. 497–8. On Romano as translator, see Steinschneider 1893, pp. 263–4; Sirat 1985, pp. 271–2; Sermoneta 1990, p. 106 n. 34. Just as the philosophical material translated from Arabic soon found its way into Hebrew biblical commentaries, so did that translated from Latin: see Sermoneta 1984, pp. 352–6. Immanuel of Rome praises Romano for these translations, which gather the insights of wisdom from their dispersion (among the Christians) and restore them to the Jews: Immanuel 1957, 1: 222.

30 Renan 1893, p. 772; cf. Dinur 1972, pp. 177 and 214 no. 13, the latter explaining the translation of Latin medical works as a way to encourage Jews to seek out Jewish physicians rather than Christians, who give them non-kosher medicines. See also the introduction by Meir Alguades to his early fifteenth-century translation from the Latin of Aristotle's *Nicomachean Ethics*, explaining that he has access to expert Christian scholars and a fine Latin commentary on the *Ethics*: Berman 1988, pp. 157–8. In 1472, Eli ben Joseph Habillo justified his translation of Joannes Versor's "questions" on Aristotle's *Physics* by arguing that Christian scholars, unlike their Jewish counterparts, had studied Greek philosophy in a manner consistent with religious faith, concluding that "whoever wants to become learned in these disciplines should study carefully these [Latin] books": Margoliouth 1965, 3: 185. For an example of a Jewish preacher using a newly completed translation of Aquinas, see Saperstein 1996, p. 79.

31 For some general comments pertaining to the earlier (Islamic) period, see Baron 1952–83, 7: 137.

32 Immanuel 1957, 1: 162.

33 Shatzmiller 1980, pp. 466–7; cf. Sirat 1991, p. 332. Shatzmiller suggests that this might have been an unusual arrangement, in which the owner was related to the translator. But there is no reason why an owner of a rare and valuable

manuscript would not have wanted compensation for access to it, especially if he had traveled to procure it or commissioned its copying.

34 Berman 1967, pp. 315–16. Samuel says he has heard of a translation by Moses ibn Tibbon but was unable to find a copy; cf. Steinschneider 1893, p. 544.

35 Cf. also the text described by Sirat 1991, pp. 328–30.

36 Shatzmiller 1980.

37 For example, Wolfson 1977, p. 480: "The work [Isaac ben Shem Tov's commentary on the *Physics*] was completed by me, Abraham ibn Adret, here at Aguilar di Campaha, while I was studying this discipline from the inexhaustible fountain, the consummate scholar, Rabbi Isaac ibn Shem Tov." Cf. also Margoliouth 1965, 3: 212.

38 For example, Asher ben Samuel of Marseilles copying a logical text by ibn Rushd for a Spanish Jew (Berman 1967, p. 301). Abraham Farissol was employed copying manuscripts by the Norsas, prominent bankers of Mantua, a position characteristic of his career as a scribe (Ruderman 1981, p. 12). Less information is available about the economics of scribes on the open market: see, for example, the text in Dinur 1972, p. 420 (from 1315): "There is no scribe in the world who will copy this for less than six small gulden, not counting the cost of the parchment".

39 The cost of manuscripts can be determined through the study of owners' inscriptions and notarial records. For example, a text of Maimonides' *Guide* completed in 1283 and bound together with Samuel ibn Tibbon's *Yiqqavu ha-Mayim* and some other texts was sold in 1378 for 50 gold florins, then resold together with a *Machzor* in 1461 for 100 Florentine florins (Margoliouth 1965, 3: 212). A Hebrew copy of an unspecified medical book brought 25 florins in 1434 (Iancu-Agou 1987, p. 17); cf. Shatzmiller 1980, pp. 466–7, and see also Zunz 1845, pp. 211–13. The cost was determined not only by the length of the text, the aesthetic character of the writing, the quality of parchment or paper, but by other factors as well. In the late fourteenth century, Leon Joseph of Carcassonne reported that for twelve years he tried in vain to acquire two new Latin medical books, as the Christians of Montpellier had banned their sale to non-Christians. He finally succeeded, paying "twice their value," explaining that "I bought them to benefit myself by reading them, and to benefit other [Jews] by translating them" (Renan 1893, p. 774). The library of the wealthy Samuel Sulami must have been a powerful inducement for the impoverished Levi ben Abraham to remain in his home (Abba Mari 1838, p. 47).

40 According to Weil 1991, p. 59, the royal library of Charles V in 1373 contained 843 volumes; the pontifical library in Avignon had some two thousand; the library of the convent of San Domenico of Bologna had 472.

41 Judah ibn Tibbon in Abrahams 1926, 1: 57, 80–2.

42 Levi 1899; Steinschneider 1900; Iancu-Agou 1975; Weil 1991. In Gersonides' collection, there were 37 biblical works, 71 rabbinic texts, and 60 manuscripts of a scientific nature (Weil 1991, pp. 45–6).

43 On the arguments relating to financial subsidy for Torah teaching, see Septimus 1984 and Kanarfogel 1992, chapter 3.

44 Abba Mari 1838, p. 48; Yedaiah Bedersi in Adret 1958, 1: 168a.

45 Hacker 1987, p. 116; 1983, pp. 55–6. Solomon Bonafed wrote (without

complaining) that he paid "much money" to the Christian who taught him logic in Latin for a year (Gross 1993, p. 36).

46 Assaf 1928–43, 2: 99ff.; Tirosh-Rothschild 1991, pp. 43–4.

47 Assaf 1928–43, 2: 102.

48 Menachem ha-Me'iri, in Saperstein 1989, p. 383. For complaints about the use of philosophy in sermons at the beginning of the fourteenth century and attempts to regulate this through the use of the ban, see Saperstein 1989, pp. 381–3.

49 For a fourteenth-century example of a Jew admiring the scholastic disputed question, see Leon Joseph of Carcassonne in Renan 1893, p. 773. For use of this form in sermons, see Saperstein 1989, pp. 395–6; Saperstein 1996, pp. 84–6, 200–7.

50 On monasteries and cathedral schools as centers of learning, see Leclercq 1961, esp. pp. 76–151; Smalley 1952, esp. pp. 37–84. On universities: Leff 1968.

51 Kanarfogel 1992, pp. 17–19, 55–7.

52 There are, to be sure, many curricula that incorporate the sciences alongside Bible and rabbinic texts (the most famous of which from Christian Europe is probably that of Joseph ibn Kaspi: see Abrahams 1926: 1: 144–6). But these are curricula for individual study, not for an established institution. Abraham Neuman stated it succinctly: "One looks in vain for any institutions where these elaborate curricula could have been taught" (Neuman 1942, 2: 73). Perhaps the reason was connected with the rabbinic tradition against the *public* teaching of philosophy, on which see Harvey 1987, pp. x–xi. In a text dated 1402, Leon Joseph of Carcassonne states that Jews "were not permitted to expound [philosophic] wisdom in the marketplaces or the public squares . . . or to establish an academy [yeshivah] in public" (Renan 1893, p. 772), referring apparently to opposition within the Jewish community.

53 Abrahams 1926, 1: 57.

54 Anatoli 1866, introduction.

55 Narboni 1852, pp. 1a (introduction), 11b (on *Guide* 1.63). Cf. the statement by Solomon Bonafed that a Christian scholar taught him logic for a year after he had previously studied that discipline with his father (Gross 1993, p. 36).

56 Abulafia's disciple wrote, "I returned to my native land and God brought me together with a Jewish philosopher with whom I studied some of Maimonides' *Guide of the Perplexed*" (Scholem 1941, p. 148). Ibn Kaspi wrote his ethical will before setting off in search of a teacher, companion, or disciple for his studies (Abrahams 1926, 1: 130–1; cf. Mesch 1975, p. 46). Kalonymus complains of his inability to find an appropriate teacher in southern France and is satisfied only in Barcelona. While many of the teachers he described were talmudists, the chief attraction in Barcelona is the ibn Chisdai brothers, "learned in every branch of science and medicine"; see Kalonymus ben Kalonymus 1966, pp. 49–50, 21. For a discussion of this theme of wandering scholars in search of the best education as it pertains primarily to yeshivah learning in the context of medieval Christian Europe, see Breuer 1989.

57 Sirat 1985, pp. 267–8; Ravitzky 1977, p. 71: "I have already taught this book, namely the *Guide for the Perplexed*, many times to others."

58 Berman 1967, pp. 291, 313; Renan 1893, pp. 548–52, 419.

59 Abba Mari 1838, pp. 47–8.

60 Adret 1958, 1: 151a: "No one from our community shall teach a single Jew these disciplines until they are 25 years old." In his defense of the culture of southern France, Yedaiah Bedersi conceded that some men had taught logic to children (see above, note 44) and suggests that this may have occurred in schools, for he states that "the children returned to the houses of their mothers" without having been harmed by this exposure (in Adret 1958, 1: 168a). The situation is described, however, as an anomaly.

61 Abrahams 1926, 1: 57.

62 Abrahams 1926, 1: 144; cf. Mesch 1975, pp. 7, 46, 51. Cf. also Judah ibn Tibbon in Abrahams 1926, 1: 68.

63 Harvey 1987, pp. 51, 79, 97.

64 M. *Chagigah* 2:1; see Maimonides' reference to this in the introduction to the *Guide*.

65 Sirat 1985, p. 243. Cf. Neuman 1942, 2: 74: the "amazing accomplishments [of the Jews] in the domains of science and philosophy were attained by private study rather than through a system of formal instruction." Joseph Shatzmiller has shown that the same pattern applies to medical studies in southern France: no formal schools (Christian or Jewish) but rather study with a master, who was paid for his instruction, and then submitting to official examinations; see Shatzmiller 1980, pp. 464–5. His insistence (1992) that there is no evidence for Jews in the medical school of Montpellier before the last quarter of the fourteenth century does not, however, consider the text in Dinur 1972, p. 221, which indicates a Jewish presence there in the first half of the century.

66 Hillel of Verona 1981, pp. 133–4.

67 An obvious question is how this relates to Hillel's statement in his letter to "Isaac the Physician" that "I lived in Barcelona for three years and I studied before my teacher, Rabbi Jonah" ("Iggerot Qena'ot" 1859, p. 14c). Clearly, Jonah Gerondi could not have been the "rabbi" in the above-cited passage; Hillel describes Jonah teaching halakhah with reference to the *Mishneh Torah*, and in the same letter he refers to a different mentor in philosophical studies. It is not impossible that Hillel spent periods of time in Spain devoted to halakhah and to philosophy; the details of his early life are almost completely unknown.

68 Moses ibn Tibbon's translation of Averroes' middle commentary was dated 1261; another translation, by Shem Tov ben Isaac of Tortosa, may have been completed slightly earlier. The translation of the compendium of *De Anima* was finished by Moses ibn Tibbon in 1244. (There is some question whether any Hebrew translation from the Arabic of the long commentary ever existed.) See Steinschneider 1893, pp. 147–50. For the Arabic translation of Themistius on *De Anima*, see Peters 1968, p. 42.

69 In his scientific edition of the text, Joseph Sermoneta maintained that the entire story of Hillel's interpretation confirmed by his teacher's discovery of an old Themistius manuscript is a fraud (Hillel of Verona 1981, p. 134). Hillel actually got the idea from a work by Thomas Aquinas that was written in 1270, and invented the story to take credit for the idea. According to this view, the passage tells us nothing about the realities of philosophical study in Spain, only about the fertile imagination of Hillel. There are several reasons why I believe that the passage should not be so quickly dismissed: first, Hillel refers to his

philosophy mentor in a totally different text (see note 67); second, Hillel's passage is more detailed than the Aquinas passage on which Sermoneta maintains it was based; third, there is no reason why such a fabrication should have been introduced in this one place to take credit for one interpretation of an Aristotelian crux; and, fourth, a person who wants to be believed about a substantive issue usually does not make up a story in which the entire setting has no correspondence to reality. Space does not permit elaboration of these arguments, which I hope to pursue in a different context. (After writing this, I discovered that Warren Harvey had questioned Sermoneta's dismissal of this passage; see Harvey 1983, p. 535.)

70 Assaf apparently assumes that the text is reliable and does refer to a Jewish school: see Assaf 1928–43, 2: 48. Dinur reproduces the passage without comment on its meaning or relevance to the history of Jewish education (1972, p. 243).

71 Saperstein 1980, p. 179; text in Neubauer 1890, pp. 245–8; Assaf 1928–43, 2: 34. In a highly rhetorical encomium of Beziers, the poet Abraham Bedersi seems to be saying that "external disciplines" are studied in its *beit midrash*: Vienna Hebrew MS 111, fol. 228v.

72 Wolfson 1957, pp. 29–31. Abraham Neuman (1942, 2: 80) states that Crescas "discussed philosophical problems at his academy," giving as his source for this the introduction to *Or ha-Shem*. I can find no such evidence in this text, except for the statement that the author has investigated philosophical problems "with the most distinguished colleagues" ("*im chashuvei ha-chaverim*").

73 Wolfson 1973, p. 431.

74 Wolfson 1977, pp. 488, 481.

75 Arama 1884, chapter 12, p. 24a; Assaf 1928–43, 2: 91.

76 Lazaroff 1981, p. 1 and p. 52 n. 7; scribe's colophon to Alguades' translation of the *Ethics*, San Francisco Sutro MS 162 (Jerusalem Microfilm Institute reel 34658). As neither Abraham Bibago nor Shem Tov ibn Shem Tov was known to be a halakhist with a talmudic academy of his own, there is some question about precisely what kind of institution is mentioned in these texts.

77 Hacker 1983, p. 55, and Hacker's uncertainties about the phrase there. Note Hacker's conclusion, based on the same source, that kabbalah was taught in some fifteenth-century Spanish yeshivahs (1983, pp. 52, 54, 25–26 n. 29).

78 Messer Leon 1983, pp. xxvii–xlii, esp. xxxvi–xxxvii, xl–xli.

79 For example, Neubauer 1886, p. 869: "*ha-moreh ha-gadol sar ha-yeshivah,*" referring to the rector of the studium in Bologna, Nicola de Fava; cf. Shatzmiller 1992, pp. 244, 247. Renan 1893, p. 773: "*va-eshev bi-yshivotehem u-veit iyyunam,*" referring to Christian institutions of higher learning. Solomon Bonafed: "*u-sheqedat midrashehem,*" referring to Christian philosophical study in *scholae* (Gross 1993, p. 36). Ibn Kaspi in Abrahams 1926, 1: 154: "*kav'u sham midrashot,*" referring to Islamic schools where Maimonides' *Guide* was studied.

80 There is also a problem in classifying those who did important philosophical or scientific work, yet criticized fundamental principles of philosophy or its influence in Jewish life. Crescas is the primary example in our period, as Judah Halevi was in the previous one. Members of the ibn Chisdai family in Barcelona signed Rashba's ban on philosophical study, yet were identified by Kalonymus as scientists: Kalonymus 1966, pp. 21–2, 49–50. Kalonymus himself sided with Abba Mari and Rashba, yet produced important translations of Arabic philo-

sophical works (ibid., pp. 16–17). Hillel ben Samuel of Verona is generally considered a philosopher, but he is classified by one scholar as "the first anti-rationalist of Italian Jewry" (Barzilay 1967, pp. 14, 42).

81 Indeed, it is something of a topos for a scholar beginning a study of a philosopher's thought to start by noting how little is known about his life; for example: Isaac Albalag (Vajda 1960, p. 1), Nissim of Marseilles (Sirat 1990, p. 53), Abraham Bibago (Lazaroff 1981, p. 1), Abraham Shalom (Davidson 1964, p. 1).

82 Shatzmiller 1972, 1975, 1991; Feldman in Levi ben Gershom 1984, pp. 1–5.

83 Pines 1977, pp. 180–2, 223–53, 263–76.

84 Saperstein 1979 and 1984 on Yedaiah's Midrash commentary; 1979, pp. 32–3 for references to philosophical works.

85 Schirmann 1960a, 4: 468; Saperstein 1980, pp. 166–7; Schirmann 1960b, p. 163.

86 Bedersi 1884, Hebrew section, p. 1; German section, pp. 138–9.

87 See Schirmann 1960a, 4: 497 lines 7–9 and frequently elsewhere in the work.

88 Judah ibn Tibbon, "Musar Av," in Abrahams 1926, 1: 71–2, 57, 66–7.

89 Ibid., pp. 66, 78.

90 Romano 1977, p. 369.

91 For example, "Iggerot Qena'ot" 1859, p. 3b; contrast the reference by David Kimchi, ibid., p. 4a top.

92 He also wrote independent works in Hebrew: a supercommentary on ibn Ezra, a commentary on Song of Songs, and an interpretation of the aggadot of the Talmud. On the last work, see Sirat 1985, pp. 229–31.

93 Anatoli speaks of having studied logic in Arabic with his father-in-law Samuel ibn Tibbon (Anatoli 1866, introduction); yet, in his commentary on the Song of Songs, Moses refers to Anatoli as "my lord my uncle". Thus Colette Sirat identifies him as son-in-law of Samuel and uncle of Moses (1985, pp. 226, 228); for both of these to be true, Moses would have had to be Samuel's grandson.

94 See Anatoli 1866, introduction; also p. 6b: "I exposed myself to their reproaches and their vilifications;" cf. also pp. 121b, 159a.

95 In *Minchat Qena'ot* (Abba Mari 1838, p. 62), he is identified merely as "one of the scholars," a relative of Judah ben Moses ibn Tibbon. On his career as a scientist and his contacts with Christian academics, see Shatzmiller 1992, pp. 243–4.

96 In this same category of those who produced philosophical works without necessarily adding much original thought we include Shem Tov Falaquera, Kalonymus ben Kalonymus, Samuel ben Judah of Marseilles, and Joseph, Isaac, and Shem Tov ibn Shem Tov. Falaquera was indeed from an aristocratic family in Tudela (Jospe 1988, p. 2), and his "Book of the Seeker" provides a strong statement of the ideology of the wealthy, which is, however, subjected to a withering critique (cf. Baer 1961, 1: 203–4). On his abilities as a philosopher, see Jospe 1988 and Fenton 1992, pp. 27–39. Kalonymus also apparently came from an aristocratic family, as both he and his father are referred to with the title *nasi* (Renan 1893, pp. 417, 426; Kalonymus 1966, p. 14). However, he describes himself as "pursued by sorrows" (ibid., p. 35) and his writings also attack those who are overly concerned with the amassing of wealth (ibid., p. 31) or who boast of their lineage (Schirmann 1960a, 4: 508–10). The translator Samuel ben Judah of Marseilles presents a similar pattern: scion of an aristocratic

and wealthy family (Berman 1967, pp. 290–1, 293), he refers to "continuous calamities" that came upon him (ibid., p. 314). While Joseph ibn Shem Tov might be described as a courtier, he apparently suffered an extreme reversal of fortune, as he describes himself in the introduction to his major work as an impoverished vagrant (Saperstein 1989, p. 167). His brother Isaac and his son Shem Tov had no known connection with court life or an aristocratic ethos.

97 Talmage 1975, p. 14. Talmage's statement that "teaching was a career which bore considerable esteem in his times" (p. 14) is too general. While scholars who taught Talmud on a high level to advanced students were indeed esteemed, those who introduced the subject to younger students were often treated with a notable lack of respect. See Kanarfogel 1992, pp. 25–30 for contemporary Ashkenaz. Epstein 1968, 1: 65: "The teachers seemed to have been very poor" (citing Adret's *Responsa* 5, 166); Baron 1942, 2: 184: "even Spain and Italy record complaints about the inferior status of Jewish teachers."

98 Talmage 1975, p. 34; "Iggerot Qena'ot" 1859, p. 2c top.

99 Talmage 1975, p. 20.

100 Twersky 1979, p. 232. Ibn Kaspi wrote an epitome of the translation by Samuel ben Judah of Averroes' commentary on Aristotle's *Ethics* and *Politics* (Steinschneider 1893, pp. 225–7), but these were intended as popularizations of the works, perhaps for his son.

101 Ibn Kaspi, "Sefer Musar," in Abrahams 1926, 1: 130–1; Mesch 1975, p. 47, asserts, "it appears that he had a good deal of money."

102 Abrahams 1926, pp. 151–2.

103 Ibid., p. 145: "Pay no regard to money, for true wealth consists only of a sufficiency of bread to eat and raiment to wear. Why worry thyself to gain great riches?"

104 Other examples in this category would include Isaac ben Yedaiah (see Saperstein 1980, especially p. 174); Levi ben Abraham (as noted above, extremely poor and dependent upon patrons), Immanuel of Rome (described by Cecil Roth as "wandering from place to place to earn his living, presumably as a house-tutor for the children of the wealthy Jewish loan-bankers," 1959, p. 90; see Immanuel's references to his reversals in 1957, 1: 179, 233).

105 An example is Sheshet Benveniste, courtier in Aragon, who took a leading role in defense of Maimonides during the earliest conflict (see Baer 1961, 1: 91, 100; Septimus 1982, pp. 46–8). Solomon of Lunel, a leader of the opponents to Abba Mari in 1305, was a royal tax collector and an extremely wealthy man. As is clear from the discussion in part 1, the philosophical enterprise required financial backing. Meir Alguades, translator from Latin of the *Nicomachean Ethics*, describes himself as "frequenting the courts of the kings of Castile" (Berman 1988, p. 157, cf. p. 149), and writes that his work was undertaken at the request of Don Benveniste ibn Lavi of Saragossa (p. 158; cf. Baer 1961, 2: 211).

106 Septimus 1982, pp. 5, 11, 16–17.

107 Septimus 1982, pp. 17–18; cf. p. 66: the supporters of Maimonides were opposed by "the aristocratic leadership of Castile."

108 Baer 1961, 1: 119; Schirmann 1960a, 3: 164–5; Scholem 1974, p. 55; Baer describes him as "the very antithesis of the current tendency among Jewish

courtiers to assimilate the ways of the Christian knighthood and the licentious-ness of the royal courts" (Baer 1961, 1: 119).

109 Abba Mari 1838, pp. 120–1, 134–7, 141.

110 Baer 1961, 2: 84–5, 126–30.

111 See, for example, Abravanel's comment on Joshua 10, and the extensive and incisive critique of sciences and philosophy in his comment on 1 Kings 3:6ff.

112 Accusations against extreme philosophers are rampant during the entire period (and see below, note 118), but especially in the literature of the conflicts of 1232 and 1305.

113 Levi ben Abraham is an example: see Halkin 1966, concluding, "a grave injustice has been done to Levi ben Abraham ben Hayyim in branding him a heretic, a seducer and a subverter" (p. 76). And cf. Schwartz 1989, p. 150 and Schwartz 1992, p. 42.

114 Adret 1958, 1: 153b; cited in Ben-Sasson 1976, p. 544. I have corrected the translation of "*ha-chakhamim*" in the first internal quote from "the sages" to "the scientists" based on Abba Mari 1838, p. 152, which reads "the physicians." In the second internal quote, I have substituted a better rendering of "*she-ein ha-chefetz ba-zeh*" than the translation "which serves no useful purpose."

115 For an example, see the passage from Me'iri quoted in Saperstein 1980, pp. 138–9.

116 Adret 1966, pp. 5–6. Cf. Levi ben Abraham in Renan 1877, p. 642.

117 Anatoli 1866, pp. 148b-149a: the phylactery is placed upon the head "so that one will turn his eyes to God and not turn aside to follow what one sees.... If one forgets all this, and adorns himself with his phylacteries in order to lord it over his neighbors, what value does this commandment have for him? It would be better for him if he left his phylacteries in their bag" (cf. Saperstein 1989, p. 126). It is all but inconceivable that anyone who identified with Judaism enough to preach in the synagogue would have argued that phylac-teries are *unnecessary* so long as one directs one's heart to God. For a rare example of repudiating halakhic practice (as opposed to the performance of a *mitzvah*) on philosophical grounds, see Saperstein 1980, pp. 141–2.

The confusion over the "antinomianism" of Jewish philosophers continues in contemporary scholarly literature. For example, Dov Schwartz has published striking allegorical interpretations of commandments such as the sending away of the mother bird (Deuteronomy 22:6) by the fourteenth-century philosopher Solomon Alconstantin (Schwartz 1991, p. 108). Based on this passage, Michael Glatzer recently wrote, "Only a small step from such an allegoristic approach is liable to bring one to the claim that after the internalization of the lesson of the commandment, he no longer needs to observe it in actuality.... On the basis of this example, Baer's thesis can be substantiated" (Glatzer 1993, p. 105). But what may seem like a "small step" to a modern scholar may have been a gigantic step to a medieval writer. The passage in Alconstantin remains in the category of philosophical *ta'amei mitzvot*, not antinomianism, and cannot serve to substantiate Baer's thesis.

118 Cf. Twersky 1968, p. 205. For examples: Anatoli in Saperstein 1989, pp. 115, 118, 122 and in many of his other sermons; Moses ibn Tibbon in Sirat 1985, p. 230; Hillel ben Samuel 1981, p. 182; ibn Kaspi in Abrahams 1926, 1: 146–8

and Mesch 1975, p. 66; Kalonymus ben Kalonymus 1936, p. 107; del Medigo 1984, pp. 33–5.

119 Me'iri, "Choshen Mishpat," in Saperstein 1989, p. 383.

120 Baer 1961, 1: 332. These points are illustrated in an oft-cited passage from Moses de Leon's *Sefer ha-Rimmon* (see Scholem 1941, pp. 397–8), accusing the "disciples of the books of the Greeks" of abandoning traditional Jewish study, casting behind them the words of Torah and the commandments, considering the sages to have spoken lies. On Sukkot, they appear in the synagogues with no palm branch or citron in their hands; on other days they have no phylacteries upon their heads. When asked why, they explain their behavior by appealing to the purpose of the commandments (rejoicing on the festival, remembering God), which they claim to observe. Daniel Matt cites this passage as proof that "rationalism became the vogue among the Jewish upper class. Many of these wealthy, assimilated Jews embraced a rationalistic ideology not for the pursuit of truth but in order to justify their neglect of tradition" (Matt 1983, p. 6). But the passage itself says nothing that connects the objects of de Leon's attack with the upper class, or with "assimilation"; it certainly does not allow us to pass judgment on the motivation for their commitment to philosophical study, and it is suspect as a description of their practice.

121 Wolfson 1957, p. 31: Isaac, Joseph, and Shem Tov ibn Shem Tov were "strict partisans of Averroes"; cf. Schwartzmann 1991: Isaac ibn Shem Tov "dedicated his life to the interpretation of ibn Rushd's commentaries," but "it is impossible to call him an Averroist, even though he tends to accept the positions of Averroes" (pp. 43, 59). Cf. also Ivry 1983.

122 On the "double truth theory" among Jewish thinkers, see Vajda 1960; Ivry 1983; del Medigo 1984. Virtually nothing is known about the family or social status of Albalag, but there is absolutely no indication that he was connected with the courtier upper class. Del Medigo came from a respected family in Crete, and his scholarship provided a certain influence among Christian intellectuals in Italy, but he was dependent on the financial support of patrons such as Pico della Mirandola. He himself attacked more extreme "philosophizers" among the Jews; see del Medigo 1984, pp. 33–5.

123 For example, Baer 1961, especially 2: 253–7.

124 Baer 1961, 2: 52. The underlying document is in Baer 1929, 1: 644–7.

125 Anatoli 1969, p. 1; Leon Joseph of Carcassone in Renan 1893, p. 733; Bibago in Steinschneider 1893, p. 140. Cf. also the cultural defense of translation by Shem Tov Falaquera: "it is better that we study them [the branches of philosophy] in our own language than that we study them in the language of another people" (Dinur 1972, p. 186). Cf. also above, note 30.

126 Cf. Leon Joseph of Carcassone: "No one from among our nation is esteemed in their eyes except for the physician who can cure them" (Renan 1893, p. 773).

127 A year after submitting this article, I received from the author an offprint of a monumental study, Freudenthal 1993, which covers much of the material I treat here, although from the perspective of the history of science rather than cultural and social history. Reference to this article could be included in virtually every note above.

❧ BIBLIOGRAPHY ❧

Texts

Abba Mari of Lunel (1838) *Minchat Qena'ot* (Pressburg: Schmid; reprinted Jerusalem, 1968).

Abrahams, I. (1926) *Hebrew Ethical Wills*, 2 vols. (Philadelphia: Jewish Publication Society).

Adret, S. (1958) *She'elot u-Teshuvot ha-Rashba*, 5 vols. (Benei Beraq: Sifriyati).

—— (1966) *Chiddushei ha-Rashba al-Aggadot ha-Shas* (Tel Aviv: Friedman).

Anatoli, J. (1866) *Malmad ha-Talmidim* (Lyck: Mekitze Nirdamim); reprinted Jerusalem: Mekitze Nirdamim, 1968.

—— (1969) *Ha-Be'ur ha-Emtza'i shel ibn Rushd al Sefer ha-Mavo le-Porfirius ve-Sefer ha-Ma'amarot le-Aristoteles*, edited by Herbert Davidson (Cambridge, MA: Mediaevel Academy of America).

Arama, I. (1884) *Chazut Qashah* (Warsaw: Shuldberg).

Assaf, S. (1928–43) *Meqorot le-Toledot ha-Chinnukh be-Yisra'el* (Tel Aviv: Dvir).

Bedersi, Y. (1884) "Ohev Nashim," edited by A. Neubauer, in *Tiferet Seiva: Jubelschrift zum neunzigsten Geburtstag des Dr. L. Zunz* (Berlin: L. Gerschel).

del Medigo, E. (1984) *Sefer Bechinat ha-Dat*, edited by J. J. Ross (Tel Aviv: Chaim Rosenberg School of Jewish Studies).

Harvey, S. (1987) *Falaquera's Epistle of the Debate* (Cambridge, MA: Harvard University Press).

Hillel ben Samuel of Verona (1981) *Sefer Tagmulei ha-Nefesh le-Hillel ben Shmu'el mi-Verona*, edited by J. Sermoneta (Jerusalem: Magnes).

"Iggerot Qena'ot" (1859) *Qovetz Teshuvot ha-Rambam ve-Iggerotav*, edited by A. L. Lichtenberg (Leipzig: Schnauss), 3: 1–24.

Immanuel of Rome (1957) *Machberot*, edited by D. Yarden, 2 vols. (Jerusalem: Mossad Bialik).

Jospe, R. (1988) *Torah and Sophia: The Life and Thought of Shem Tov ibn Falaquera* (Cincinnati: Hebrew Union College Press).

Kalonymus ben Kalonymus (1936) "Iggeret Musar le-Kalonymus ben Kalonymus," edited by I. Sonne, *Qovetz al Yad* 1 (11): 93–110.

—— (1966) "Megillat Hitnatzlut ha-Qatan," edited by J. Shatzmiller, *Sefunot* 10: 7–52.

Levi ben Gershom (1984) *The Wars of the Lord: Book One*, translated by S. Feldman (Philadelphia: Jewish Publication Society).

Margoliouth, G. (1965) *Catalogue of the Hebrew and Samaritan Manuscripts in the British Museum*, 4 vols. (London: British Museum).

Matt, D. (1983). *The Zohar: The Book of Enlightenment*, translation and introduction by D. Matt (New York: Paulist Press).

Messer Leon, J. (1983) *The Book of the Honeycomb's Flow*, edited and translated by I. Rabinowitz (Ithaca: Cornell University Press).

Narboni, M. (1852) *Be'ur le-Sefer Moreh Nevukhim* (Vienna: K. K. Hof- und Staatsdruckerei).

Neubauer, A. (1886) *Catalogue of Hebrew Manuscripts in the Bodleian Library* (Oxford: Clarendon).

"Qevutzat Mikhtavim" (1975) *Qevutzat Mikhtavim be-Inyenei ha-Machloqet al devar Sefer ha-Moreh ve-ha-Mada*, edited by S. Halberstam, *Jeschurun* (Kobak) 8.

Saperstein, M. (1989) *Jewish Preaching 1200–1800* (New Haven: Yale University Press).

Schirmann, J. (1960a) *Ha-Shirah ha-Ivrit bi-Sefarad u-vi-Provens*, 4 vols. (Jerusalem: Mossad Bialik; Tel Aviv: Dvir).

Studies

Baer F. (1929) *Die Juden im Christlichen Spanien*, 2 vols. (Berlin: Akademie).

—— (1961) *A History of the Jews in Christian Spain*, 2 vols. (Philadelphia: Jewish Publication Society).

Baldwin, J. (1971) *The Scholastic Culture of the Middle Ages 1000–1300* (Lexington: Heath).

Baron, S. W. (1942) *The Jewish Community*, 3 vols. (Philadelphia: Jewish Publication Society).

—— (1952–83) *A Social and Religious History of the Jews*, 18 vols. (Philadelphia: Jewish Publication Society).

Barzilay, I. (1967) *Between Faith and Reason: Anti-Rationalism in Italian Jewish Thought, 1250–1650* (The Hague: Mouton).

Ben-Sasson, H. (1976) *A History of the Jewish People* (Cambridge, MA: Harvard University Press).

—— (1984) *Retzef u-Temurah* (Tel Aviv: Am Oved).

Berman, L. (1967) "Greek into Hebrew: Samuel ben Judah of Marseilles, Fourteenth-Century Philosopher and Translator," in *Jewish Medieval and Renaissance Studies*, edited by A. Altmann (Cambridge, MA: Harvard University Press), pp. 289–320.

—— (1988) "Ha-Tirgum ha-Ivri min ha-Latinit shel 'Sefer ha-Middot' le-Aristo al Shem Nichomachos," in *Sefer ha-Yovel le-Shelomo Pines*, edited by M. Idel, E. Schweid, and W. Z. Harvey (Jerusalem: Daf Noy), 1: 147–68.

Breuer, M. (1989) "Nedudei Talmidim ve-Chakhamim – Aqdamut le-Fereq be-Toledot ha-Yeshivot," in *Tarbut ve-Chevrah be-Toledot Yisrael bi-Ymei ha-Beinayim*, edited by R. Bonfil, M. Ben-Sasson, and J. Hacker (Jerusalem: Merkaz Zalman Shazar), pp. 445–68.

Davidson, H. (1964) *The Philosophy of Abraham Shalom* (Berkeley and Los Angeles: University of California Press).

Davidson, I. (1939) "L'Introduction de Lévi ben Abraham à son encyclopédie poétique," *Revue des Études Juives* 105: 80–94.

Dinur, B. (1972) *Yisra'el ba-Golah*, (Tel Aviv: Dvir; Jerusalem: Mossad Bialik) vol. 2, book 6.

Epstein, I. (1968) *Studies in the Communal Life of the Jews in Spain*, 2 vols. in 1 (New York: Hermon).

Fenton, P. (1992) "Shem Tov Falaquera ve-ha-Theologiyah shel Aristo," *Da'at* 29: 27–39.

Freimann, A. (1950) "Jewish Scribes in Medieval Italy," in *Alexander Marx Jubilee Volume* (New York: Jewish Theological Seminary of America), pp. 231–42.

Freudenthal, G. (ed.) (1992) *Studies on Gersonides* (Leiden: Brill).

—— (1993) "Les Sciences dans les communautés juives médiévales de Provence: leur appropriation, leur rôle," *Revue des Études Juives* 152: 29–136.

Gilson, E. (1954) *History of Christian Philosophy in the Middle Ages* (New York: Random House).

Glatzer, M. (1993) "Bein-Yehoshua ha-Lorqi le-Shelomoh ha-Levi," *Pe'amim* 54: 103–16.

Gross, A. (1993) "Ha-Meshorer Shelomoh Bonafed u-Me'ora'ot Doro," in *The Frank Talmage Memorial Volume I*, edited by B. Walfish (Haifa: Haifa University Press), pp. 35–61.

Guttmann, J. (1964) [1933] *Philosophies of Judaism* (Garden City: Doubleday).

Hacker, J. (1983) "Li-Demutam ha-Ruchanit shel Yehudei Sefarad be-Sof ha-Me'ah ha-Chamesh Esreh," *Sefunot* 2. 17: 21–95.

—— (1987) "The Intellectual Activity of the Jews of the Ottoman Empire During the Sixteenth and Seventeenth Centuries," in *Jewish Thought in the Seventeenth Century*, edited by I. Twersky and B. Septimus (Cambridge, MA: Harvard University Press), pp. 95–135.

Halkin, A. (1966) "Why Was Levi ben Hayyim Hounded?" *Proceedings of the American Academy for Jewish Research* 34: 65–76.

Harvey, W. (1983) "Mahadurah shel *Sefer Tagmulei ha-Nefesh*," *Tarbitz* 52: 529–37.

Hillgarth, J. (1991) "Majorcan Jews and *Conversos* as Owners and Artisans of Books," in *Exile and Diaspora: Studies in the History of the Jewish People Presented to Professor Haim Beinart*, edited by A. Mirsky, A. Grossman, and Y. Kaplan (Jerusalem: Ben-Zvi Institute), pp. 125–30.

Husik, I. (1940) [1916] *A History of Mediaeval Jewish Philosophy* (Philadelphia: Jewish Publication Society).

Iancu-Agou, D. (1975) "L'Inventaire de la bibliothèque et du mobilier d'un médecin juif d'Aix-en Provence au milieu du xve siècle," *Revue des Études Juives* 134: 47–80.

—— (1987) "Une vente de livres hébreux à Arles en 1434," *Revue des Études Juives* 146: 5–62.

Ivry, A. (1983) "Remnants of Jewish Averroism in the Renaissance," in *Jewish Thought in the Sixteenth Century*, edited by B. Cooperman (Cambridge, MA: Harvard University Press), pp. 243–65.

Kanarfogel, E. (1992) *Jewish Education and Society in the High Middle Ages* (Detroit: Wayne State University Press).

Kellner, M. (1991) "Gersonides' Commentary on Song of Songs: For Whom Was It Written and Why?" in *Gersonide en son temps*, edited by G. Dahan (Louvain: Peeters), pp. 81–107.

Kritzeck, J. (1964) *Peter the Venerable and Islam* (Princeton: Princeton University Press).

Lazaroff, A. (1981) *The Theology of Abraham Bibago* (University, AL: University of Alabama Press).

Leclercq, J. (1961) *The Love of Learning and the Desire for God* (New York: Fordham University Press).

Leff, G. (1968) *Paris and Oxford Universities in the Thirteenth and Fourteenth Centuries* (New York: Wiley).

Levi, I. (1899) "L'Inventaire du mobilier et de la bibliothèque d'un médecin juif de Majorque aux xive siècle," *Revue des Études Juives* 39: 242–9.

Mesch, B. (1975) *Studies in Joseph ibn Caspi* (Leiden: Brill).

Neubauer, A. (1890) "Yedaya de Beziers," *Revue des Études Juives* 20: 245–8.

Neuman, A. (1942) *The Jews in Spain*, 2: *A Social-Cultural Study* (Philadelphia: Jewish Publication Society).

Peters, F. (1968) *Aristoteles Arabus* (Leiden: Brill).

Pines, S. (1977) *Bein Machshevet Yisra'el le-Machshevet ha-Amim* (Jerusalem: Mossad Bialik).

Ravitzky, A. (1977) *Mishnato shel R. Zerachiah ben Yitzhaq ben Shealtiel Hen ve-ha-Hagut ha-Maimunit-Tibbonit ba-Me'ah ha-Shelosh-Esreh*. Ph.D. dissertation, Hebrew University of Jerusalem.

—— (1981a) "Samuel ibn Tibbon and the Esoteric Character of the *Guide for the Perplexed*," *AJS Review* 6: 87–123.

—— (1981b) "Al Derekh Chaqiratah shel ha-Pilosofiyah ha-Yehudit bi-Ymei ha-Beinayim," *Mechqerei Yerushalayim be-Machshevet Yisra'el* 1: 7–22.

—— (1990) "Sefer ha-Meterologica le-Aristo ve-Darkhei ha-Parshanut ha-Maimunit le-Ma'aseh Bereshit," *Mechqerei Yerushalayim be-Machshevet Yisra'el* 9: 225–50.

Renan, E. (1877) "Les Rabbins français du commencement du xive siècle," in *Histoire littéraire de la France* (Paris: Imprimerie Nationale), 27: 431–734.

—— (1893) "Les Écrivains juifs français du xive siècle," in *Histoire littéraire de la France* (Paris: Imprimerie Nationale), 31: 351–789.

Romano, D. (1977) "La transmission des sciences arabes par les Juifs en Languedoc," in *Juifs et judaïsme de Languedoc* (Toulouse: Privat).

Roth, C. (1959) *The Jews in the Renaissance* (Philadelphia: Jewish Publication Society).

Roth, N. (1985) "Jewish Translators at the Court of Alfonso X," *Thought* 60: 439–55.

Ruderman, D. (1981) *The World of a Renaissance Jew: The Life and Thought of Abraham ben Mordecai Farissol* (Cincinnati: Hebrew Union College Press).

Saperstein, M. (1979) "R. Isaac b. Yeda'ya: A Forgotten Commentator on the Aggada," *Revue des Études Juives* 138: 17–45.

—— (1980) *Decoding the Rabbis: A Thirteenth-Century Commentary on the Aggadah* (Cambridge, MA: Harvard University Press).

—— (1984) "Selected Passages from Yedaiah Bedersi's Commentary on the Midrashim," in *Studies in Medieval Jewish History and Literature*, edited by I. Twersky, (Cambridge, MA: Harvard University Press), 2: 423–40.

—— (1986) "The Conflict over the Rashba's Herem on Philosophical Study: A Political Perspective," *Jewish History* 1: 27–38.

—— (1996) *"Your Voice like a Ram's Horn:" Themes and Texts in Traditional Jewish Preaching* (Cincinnati: Hebrew Union College Press).

Schachter, J. (1992) "Echoes of the Spanish Expulsion in Eighteenth Century Germany: The Baer Thesis Revisited," *Judaism* 162: 180–9.

Schirmann, J. (1960b) "Iyyunim ba-Qovetz ha-Shirim ve-ha-Melitzot shel Avraham Bedersi," in *Sefer Yovel le-Yitzhaq Baer*, edited by S. Ettinger, S. Baron, B. Dinur, and Y. Hailperin (Jerusalem: Israel Historical Society), pp. 154–73.

Scholem, G. (1941) *Major Trends in Jewish Mysticism* (New York: Schocken).

—— (1974) *Kabbalah* (Jerusalem: Keter).

Schwartz, D. (1989) " 'Chokhmah Yevanit' – Bechinah Mechudeshet bi-Tequfat ha-Pulmos al Limmud ha-Pilosofiyah," *Sinai* 104: 148–53.

—— (1991) "Ha-Yeridah ha-Ruchanit-Datit shel ha-Qehillah ha-Yehudit bi-Sefarad be-Sof ha-Me'ah ha-Yod-Daled," *Pe'amim* 46–7: 92–114.

—— (1992) "Maga'im bein Filosofiyah le-Mistiqah Yehudit be-Reshit ha-Me'ah ha-Tet-Vav," *Da'at* 29: 41–67.

Schwartzmann, J. (1991) "Isaac ibn Shem Tob's Commentary on *The Guide of The Perplexed*," *Da'at* 26: 43–60.

Septimus, B. (1973) "Ma'avaq al Shilton Tzibburi be-Vartzelonah bi-Tequfat ha-Pulmus al Sifrei ha-Rambam," *Tarbitz* 42: 389–97.

—— (1979) "Piety and Power in Thirteenth-Century Catalonia," in *Studies in Medieval Jewish History and Literature*, edited by I. Twersky (Cambridge, MA: Harvard University Press), 1: 197–230.

—— (1982) *Hispano-Jewish Culture in Transition: The Career and Controversies of Ramah* (Cambridge, MA: Harvard University Press).

—— (1984) " 'Kings, Angels or Beggars': Tax Law and Spirituality in a Hispano-Jewish *Responsum*," in *Studies in Medieval Jewish History and Literature*, edited by I. Twersky (Cambridge, MA: Harvard University Press), 2: 309–35.

Sermoneta, G. (1984) "Prophecy in the Writings of Yehuda Romano," in *Studies in Medieval Jewish History and Literature*, edited by I. Twersky (Cambridge, MA: Harvard University Press), 2: 337–74.

—— (1990) " 'Le-Reach Shemanekha Tovim' – R. Yehudah Romano ve-Shitat 'Ha-Yetzirah ha-Petuchah'," *Mechqerei Yerushalayim be-Machshevet Yisra'el* 9: 77–113.

Shatzmiller, J. (1972) "Ha-Ralbag u-Qehillot Orange bi-Ymei Chayyav," *Mechqa-rim be-Toledot Am Yisra'el ve-Eretz Yisra'el* 2: 111–26.

—— (1975) "Od al ha-Ralbag u-Qehillot Orange bi-Ymei Chayyav," *Mechqarim be-Toledot Am Yisra'el ve-Eretz Yisra'el* 3: 139–43.

—— (1980) "Livres médicaux et éducation médicale: à propos d'un contrat de Marseille en 1316," *Mediaeval Studies* 42: 463–70.

—— (1991) "Gersonide et la société juive de son temps," in *Gersonide en son temps*, edited by G. Dahan (Louvain and Paris: Peeters), pp. 33–43.

—— (1992) "Étudiants juifs à la faculté de médecine de Montpellier, dernier quart du XIVe siècle," *Jewish History* 6: 243–55.

Sirat, C. (1985) *A History of Jewish Philosophy in the Middle Ages* (Cambridge: Cambridge University Press).

—— (1990) "Raayanot Politiyim shel Nissim ben Mosheh mi-Marseilles," *Mechqerei Yerushalayim be-Machshevet Yisra'el* 9: 53–76.

—— (1991) "Le Livre hébreu au moyen âge," *Michael* 12: 299–336.

Smalley, B. (1952) *The Study of the Bible in the Middle Ages* (New York: Philo-sophical Library).

Southern, R. (1970) *Western Society and the Church in the Middle Ages* (Harmondsworth: Penguin).

Steinschneider, M. (1893) *Die Hebräischen Übersetzungen des Mittelalters und die Juden als Dolmetscher* (Berlin: Kommisionsverlag des Bibliographischen Bureaus).

—— (1900) "La Bibliothèque de Leon Mosconi," *Revue des Études Juives* 40: 60–73.

Talmage, F. (1968) "David Kimhi and the Rationalist Tradition," *Hebrew Union College Annual* 38: 213–35.

—— (1972) "David Kimhi and the Rationalist Tradition II: Literary Sources," in *Studies in Jewish Bibliography, History and Literature in Honor of I. Edward Kiev*, edited by C. Berlin (New York: Ktav), pp. 453–78.

—— (1975) *David Kimhi. The Man and the Commentaries* (Cambridge, MA: Harvard University Press).

—— (1989) "Apples of Gold: The Inner Meaning of Sacred Texts in Medieval Judaism," in *Jewish Spirituality*, edited by A. Green (New York: Crossroad), 1: 313–55.

Tirosh-Rothschild, H. (1991) *Between Worlds: The Life and Thought of Rabbi David ben Judah Messer Leon* (Albany: State University of New York Press).

Touati, C. (1973) *La Pensée philosophique et théologique de Gersonide* (Paris: Minuit).

Twersky, I. (1968) "Aspects of the Social and Cultural History of Provençal Jewry," *Journal of World History* 11: 185–207.

—— (1979) "Joseph ibn Kaspi: Portrait of a Medieval Jewish Intellectual," in *Studies in Medieval Jewish History and Literature*, edited by I. Twersky (Cambridge, MA: Harvard University Press), 1: 231–57.

Vajda, G. (1960) *Isaac Albalag – Averroiste, juif, traducteur et commentateur d'Al-Ghazali* (Paris: Vrin).

Weil, A.-M. (1991) "Levi ben Gershom et sa bibliothèque privée," in *Gersonide en son temps*, edited by G. Dahan (Louvain and Paris: Peeters), pp. 45–59.

Wolfson, H. (1957) *Crescas' Critique of Aristotle* (Cambridge, MA: Harvard University Press).

—— (1973, 1977) *Studies in the History of Philosophy and Religion*, edited by I. Twersky and G. H. Williams, 2 vols. (Cambridge, MA: Harvard University Press).

Zunz, L. (1845) *Zur Geschichte und Literatur* (Berlin: Veit).

CHAPTER 14

The Maimonidean controversy

Idit Dobbs-Weinstein

Moses Maimonides, the most respected and best-known medieval Jewish philosopher, died on 8 December 1204. Less than thirty years later, in 1232, his philosophical work the *Guide of the Perplexed* and one of his halakhic works, the *Book of Knowledge*, were banned and burnt. The controversies[1] generated by his work, which began with their publication during his lifetime and which are still evident in contemporary scholarship, albeit in a less vitriolic manner, have caused a rift in the Jewish community of a severity and magnitude such that it threatened its survival from within and from without. Ironically, despite Maimonides' tremendous influence, whether good or bad, upon subsequent Jewish halakhic and philosophical thought, many precise details of the events remain unknown and many of the early anti-Maimonideans lacked direct knowledge of Maimonides' actual works. That the controversy is rife with irony is not surprising if we take into account the facts that both the Maimonideans and numerous anti-Maimonideans professed to follow and defend the master, and that many of the protagonists were either ignorant or incapable of understanding Maimonides' philosophical works.

The present chapter will, first, briefly outline the history of the events leading to the first ban and burning; second, it will trace the nature and significance of the most controversial view attributed to Maimonides; and, third, it will examine the development of Maimonides' teachings by early Maimonideans in order to show (1) the respective degrees to which they rely upon and depart from Maimonides and (2) the extent to which the anti-Maimonidean controversies arise from their radicalizing appropriation of Maimonides' thought as much as from Maimonides' specific doctrines.

At the outset, we cannot over-emphasize the tentative nature of our knowledge of significant details of the events leading to the condemnations, banning, and burning, especially since much of the evidence originates in the highly polemical writings of the various interested parties. There exists conflicting evidence about the date and place of the burning, and the identity of the actual informer(s) to the Church authorities is unknown, although many allegations had been leveled against various anti-Maimonideans.[2] The terminus a quo for the burning is provided by the dated document of the Saragossa counterban in July-August 1232, whereas the terminus ad quem can be seen as January 1235, the date when Maimonides' son, Abraham, was informed of the burning. Silver's surmise that "the burning can be placed no earlier than, say, December of 1232 or early 1233" is probably as accurate a date as can be deduced from the evidence (Silver 1965, p. 148 n. 3). Whereas David Kimchi (c. 1160–1235) places the denunciation of the *Guide* and the incitement to its burning in Montpellier (Maimonides 1858, 3.4), Hillel of Verona (c. 1220–1295), whose knowledge of the events is less reliable because it is less direct, places the burning in Paris (Maimonides 1858, 3.14), probably confusing it with the burning of the Talmud (Silver 1965, p. 148 n. 4).

Prior to the inflamed and inflaming controversy in the early 1230s, some criticisms were raised against the *Mishneh Torah*, especially against its uncompromisingly strict regulation of all practice which ignored custom or refused to admit the de facto differences among diverse Jewish communities (ibid., pp. 69ff.); but these were relatively peaceful. In addition to the halakhic criticism, a more serious and acrimonious opposition to the *Mishneh Torah* was raised by Meir Abulafia of Toledo and Abraham ben David of Posquières in the late 1190s. Both men accused Maimonides of rejecting the resurrection of the dead, and both called for a ban on the study of the text, but without success. Although Meir Abulafia did not explicitly identify Maimonides' philosophical interpretation of the Bible and tradition as the source of his alleged heterodoxy as did Abraham ben David, his vehement opposition to Maimonides' emphasis upon the immortality of the soul as the true human end amounts to a rejection of a philosophical approach to the Torah and manifests the same distrust of philosophy as the one explicitly voiced by Abraham. Despite their lack of immediate success, however, both men can be understood to have paved the way for the later bitter controversy.

At some time in the first decades of the thirteenth century, probably subsequent to the Hebrew translation of the *Guide* and the appearance of Samuel ibn Tibbon's *Ma'amar Yiqqavu ha-Mayim* and the *Commentary on Ecclesiastes*, both of which are devoted to philosophical interpretations of the Bible, the leading opponent of Maimonides, Solomon ben Abraham of Montpellier, and his two major disciples, David ben Saul and Jonah ben Abraham Gerondi, became concerned about philosophically inclined Jewish thinkers who interpreted the Bible and the Talmud allegorically, citing Maimonides as their authority. Solomon maintained that these interpretations undermined the validity of the Torah and the tradition (Silver 1965, p. 151). Ironically, Solomon and his disciples sought two mutually exclusive goals. On the one hand, they sought a ban on the study of the *Guide* and the *Book of Knowledge* in order to render void the authoritative status of Maimonides and, on the other, they deferred to his authority and claimed to preserve Maimonides' reputation, maintaining that, in so far as his followers translated Maimonides' works, they popularized them and, thus, violated explicitly stated Maimonidean principles. Clearly, by deferring to Maimonides' authority, those who sought a ban upon the study of the *Guide* and the *Book of Knowledge* inadvertently assured its continued authoritative status.[3]

Unlike their anti-Maimonidean predecessors, the explicit aim of Solomon and his disciples was a ban not only on the study of Maimonides' works but on the study of philosophy simpliciter. But when Jonah ben Abraham was sent to Provence in order to enlist support for the proposed ban, the result was both a counterban *in support of* philosophical pursuit and the countermission by David Kimchi to Aragon and Castile. Whereas most of the Aragon communities joined the counterban, many Castilians supported the ban.[4] Notwithstanding their initial failure, the anti-Maimonideans continued to seek support for the ban from community and spiritual leaders whom they believed to be sympathetic to their goal, in particular from Nachmanides of Gerona (1194–1270). Since there are no "ifs" in history, it would be idle to speculate what would have happened had the missions and countermissions, bans and counterbans, taken their own course rather than being violently interrupted by the burning. In the light of Nachmanides' later interventions in an attempt to calm the after-effects of the burning, however, it is reasonable to surmise that the various protagonists would have been willing to effect some compromise so as to avoid a radical split in the Jewish community of a kind that would render it more vulnerable to the Christian authorities. Speculation aside, shortly after the ban and counterban, the *Guide* and the *Book of Knowledge* were burned in Montpellier.

"Of the burning itself little is known that is certain except that it occurred" (Silver 1965, p. 153). What is known is derived from the testimony of the Maimonidean David Kimchi and Maimonides' son, Abraham, neither of whom had direct evidence concerning the event; the former was sick in Avila at that time and the latter had no knowledge of the burning until a much later date. Whereas David Kimchi lays blame for the burning directly upon Solomon ben Abraham, accusing him of being the actual informant to the Franciscans, Dominicans, and the Cardinal of Montpellier, Abraham does not. Rather, in *Milchamot Adonai*, he discusses the substantial questions underlying the controversies and attempts to refute the anti-Maimonideans by exhibiting their errors.

Since, as we have already pointed out, we have no direct evidence of the actual events, no immediately *direct* blame can be laid upon any one person. None the less, regardless of their "good intentions" and the outstanding testimonies concerning their reputations (Silver 1965, pp. 153ff.), there is little doubt that Solomon ben Abraham and his disciples were responsible for the burning of Maimonides' works, as well as for rendering possible subsequent attacks by the Christian authorities upon authoritative Jewish works, including the Talmud.[5] In addition, despite Nachmanides' valiant attempts at breaching the antagonism (Maimonides 1858, 3.4ff., 8ff.), the numerous subsequent revivals of strong anti-Maimonidean agitations and the progressive anti-rationalist direction of later Jewish thought[6] clearly exhibit the fact that Abraham and his disciples succeeded to a much greater extent than they lived to witness.

Prior to proceeding to address our central concern here, namely, the central philosophical questions constitutive of the controversy, it is important to note the other factors which inform it to an equal degree and which are necessary for a full appreciation of its extent and gravity.[7] Broadly speaking, the controversy can be divided into three historical phases and three distinct problems. Historically, it should be divided into, first, the criticism during Maimonides' lifetime; second, the criticism directly succeeding Maimonides' death and leading to the ban, counterban, and burning; and, third, the attempts at reconciliation following the burning, and their ultimate failure. Substantially, it should be understood to consist of, first, the question of authority internal to Judaism; second, the question of the relation between the Jewish community and Christian political power; and, third and last, but far from least, the question of the alleged notorious conflict between belief and reason, or Torah and logos. Needless to say, this latter tripartite division is too neat, since the position taken on the relation (if any) between belief and reason directly affects the stand adopted in relation to authority and indirectly affects one's understanding of the mode of cohesion necessary for the preservation of a community in relation to external powers.[8]

It should also be noted that during Maimonides' lifetime the various criticisms leveled at his teachings ostensibly concerned halakhic, legal questions, but that he was able to respond to most of them and that, with the exception of the *Treatise on Resurrection*, Maimonides' responses were less vitriolic or more conciliatory than those of his disciples.[9] And for him, every discussion on halakhic matters is informed by philosophical reflection concerning the human end or good.

Upon reading Maimonides' responses to disputed questions concerning halakhic interpretation, especially when his tone becomes less conciliatory and more acerbic, it becomes clear that, for him, halakhic interpretation, the interpretation of the practice of Jewish daily life, is essentially philosophical. Thus, when he compassionately responds to questions concerning the status of covert Jewish practice after forced conversion in the "Epistle on Martyrdom" and the "Epistle to Yemen," Maimonides' most vehement criticism against the strict legalists, regardless of their rabbinic, authoritative stature, consists of an attack on their intellectual ability. In particular, Maimonides accuses those whom the *Guide* names "jurists" of the inability to distinguish between appearance and reality, between imagination and understanding, between compelled and free action and, most important, of reducing the true human good to a corporeal one. Again, regardless of authority and standing, that is, of their *apparent* theoretical or intellectual stature, Maimonides goes so far as to accuse some of the jurists of idolatry.

Ironically, Maimonides is simultaneously accused of the desire to usurp for himself halakhic authority and for the *Mishneh Torah* the place of the Talmud, *and* of being an elitist so disdainful of the common people and common practice as to render him an apostate and one who deliberately separates himself from the community.[10] It is also ironic that it is Maimonides' most "exoteric" text, the *Mishneh Torah*, written in Hebrew, whose deliberate aim is to safeguard the salvation of the "vulgar," that occasions both types of criticism. And, whereas many of the religious leaders viewed Maimonides as a danger to religious cohesion, their views attest to the growing popularity of the *Mishneh Torah* as well as to the increasing respect that Maimonides gained as a halakhic authority.

Although in a few instances the real reasons motivating the criticisms were the desire for power, fear of loss of authority, and even financial advantage (Silver 1965, pp. 49–68), it would be misleading to doubt the motives or sincerity of the anti-Maimonideans. On the other hand, in many instances their intellectual abilities and their direct familiarity with Maimonides' writings may be questioned (as Maimonides does in his responses), since on many of the disputed questions familiarity with, or understanding of, Maimonides' concerns would have eliminated the difficulties. At stake between Maimonides and the Maimonideans, on the one hand, and the jurists and Jewish mutakallimūn, on the other, are two fundamentally opposed, essentially ethical, world views, namely, the nature of the highest human good and the best means to achieve it. In this respect, for Maimonides, there is little or no difference between the jurists and the mutakallimūn. For him, the mutakallimūn were at least as dangerous to the community as the anti-philosophical jurists, since their subordination of philosophy to the literal interpretation of the Torah violates the principles and purposes of both, and, thereby, renders impossible intellectual (true) human perfection. In fact, the mutakallimūn may be understood as more harmful, since their methods may lead to perplexity concerning the Torah in one capable of intellectual perfection (*Guide* 1, prefatory letter: 4).

The most serious charge leveled against Maimonides and the one which remained the central focus of vehement criticism for the longest period of time was the denial of bodily resurrection, despite the fact that he enumerated it among the principles of Judaism in *Pereq Cheleq*. Ironically, it was Maimonides' response to the charge, the *Treatise on Resurrection* itself, that established the credibility as well as importance of that very principle, since the response was soon (c. 1202) translated into Hebrew (Silver 1965, p. 37). As a brief analysis of the *Treatise* will make evident, the charge of heterodoxy results from a failure to understand Maimonides' teachings, lack of familiarity with his work, and the failure to distinguish between the two human ends, bodily and intellectual.

As a result of the denial of resurrection by some scholars in Damascus and Yemen, purportedly on the basis of the *Mishneh Torah*, and after Maimonides' response to queries concerning resurrection from the Yemen community was shown to Samuel ben 'Alī, the Baghdad Gaon, the latter proceeded to publish an attack on Maimonides, charging him with a denial of resurrection. In response to the accusation, Maimonides wrote a letter to Joseph ibn Gabir of Baghdad (Maimonides 1858, 2.15b) as well as the *Treatise* in which he accuses Samuel of false accusation, and of misunderstanding him, the Torah, and philosophy. Maimonides' strong condemnation of Samuel is quite striking:

> Whoever wishes and chooses to malign me and to attribute to me opinions which I do not hold – like one who suspects the pious of sin – and to invent the most farfetched explanations of what I have written, so that he can prove me guilty, will surely be punished for it, and will be treated like anyone who suspects the innocent.
>
> Halkin 1985, p. 221

That is, Maimonides' strongest accusation against Samuel is of *deliberately* maligning him by bearing false witness. In fact, Maimonides is charging the Baghdad Gaon with a transgression of the commandments. Failure of understanding or ignorance may be pitiful, but it is not blameworthy, although a Gaon ought not to speak nor write on that of which he is ignorant,[11] whereas deliberately bearing false witness is both blameworthy and excludes one from the "world to come" (*Book of Knowledge* 3, no. 6).

Maimonides' substantial response to the accusation focuses upon two major failures at drawing proper distinctions, first, the failure to distinguish between "the messianic age" or "End of Days" and the "world to come," and, second, the failure to distinguish between natural and rational possibility. The first failure, with which he deals very briefly since he has discussed it at length in many other contexts, simply repeats previous conclusions concerning the distinction between corporeal and intellectual perfection, between the soul as the natural, perishable form of the body and the immortal, acquired intellect. (*Shemonah Peraqim* 1). This failure, which is common to the "vulgar," who believe that "the more they endow something with corporeality, the more they secure its existence" (Halkin 1985, p. 221), is dangerous only if it leads to or entails the belief in divine corporeality, since this belief, for Maimonides, is tantamount to idolatry. What is most striking about the brief discussion is Maimonides' explicit attribution to the Baghdad Gaon of a vulgar opinion and his characterization of the Gaon as a mutakallim who confuses kalām with philosophy and whose claim to philosophical understanding is misleading and, hence, potentially endangers both himself and the community of believers (ibid., p. 218).[12]

Maimonides' discussion of the second failure is lengthier, not surprisingly in light of the fact that the only prior discussion devoted to the failure to draw the distinction between the necessary, possible, and impossible occurs in the *Guide* in the context of the discussion of creation and, hence, is less likely to be commonly known, let alone understood.[13] As in the *Guide*, so in the *Treatise*, Maimonides identifies this failure with the methods of the mutakallimūn. But precisely from the perspective of the *Guide*, the numerous references to such a distinction in the context of a popular discussion are surprising. Not only is the general reading audience incapable of understanding the *Guide*, but also Maimonides is transgressing his own principles. The audience of the *Treatise* must be both capable of reading Arabic and philosophically trained or at least in possession of some rudimentary philosophical knowledge, for the distinction between necessity, possibility, and impossibility requires an understanding of Aristotle's *Categories* and *De Interpretatione* or of Maimonides' *Treatise on Logic*. Moreover, since the relevance of the logical distinction in the discussion of resurrection also requires an understanding of the distinction between natural and rational possibility, the reader(s) must have undergone propaedeutic training in Aristotelian physics. The precise audience of the *Treatise on Resurrection* then must be Samuel and others like him, namely, Jewish mutakallimūn whose prior philosophical training achieved no more than a mimetic ability, a techne which they confuse with philosophical understanding. These individuals are dangerous not so much because they confuse kalām with philosophy but because they profess to be able to teach others. And, as the *Treatise* makes amply evident, the failure to draw distinctions is as evident in their interpretations of the Bible and the tradition as it is in philosophy. According to Maimonides, these individuals are not even able to distinguish between the plain text and parabolic speech. Biblical interpretation of prophetic discourse requires philosophical understanding.

Maimonides claims that, although Samuel has falsely attributed to him the metaphorical interpretation of resurrection, whether resurrection is interpreted plainly or metaphorically is entirely irrelevant to its veracity. Since resurrection means that (sui generis) revival which signifies "the return of the soul to the body" (Halkin 1985, p. 222), it cannot refer to anything else nor can it be used amphibolously or equivocally. In so far as possibility and impossibility can refer either to rational or to natural possibility, and in so far as rational possibility is derived by abstraction from the existing natural universe, it does not extend to unique singular events that exceed the experience, either preceding the existing universe or succeeding it. But whereas past events are necessary in so far as they have occurred, future events are only possible and their natural and rational possibility is determined by the existing universe. Precisely for this reason, neither unique past events nor unique future events can be inferred; rather, both types of events are known to be possible only through authoritative report.

Since no actual resurrection has ever been experienced, it can neither be known nor rationally inferred. Having neither a natural nor rational referent, the affirmation or denial of resurrection is an affirmation of belief in the veracity of prophetic utterances and the rabbinic tradition. Notwithstanding, the fact that resurrection is unknown and, as yet, unknowable does not render it, in principle, naturally impossible and unbelievable.

Since Maimonides' discussion of miracles perplexed both his followers and his opponents, and since it constituted the ground of all the subsequent controversies, one must ask whether (or not) he is deliberately contradicting himself when he simultaneously states, "I shun as best I can changes in the physical order" (Halkin 1985, p. 224), and "with miracles the understanding of what is told is neither hidden nor difficult" (ibid., p. 225). In the light of the foregoing brief discussion, the charge of dissimulation seems to be unwarranted. The key to understanding the non-contradictory nature of the two statements is the distinction between the order of nature and the order of reason and language. The first statement above concerns an order known through experience about which any statement has an external referent and is thus verifiable. The second statement, which refers to an unknown event (seemingly) contradictory to the experienced natural order, is verifiable or falsifiable only if and when it comes to pass. Since no experience confirms resurrection, none can falsify it. The credibility of resurrection then depends upon the cognitive as well as moral status of the speaker. Like all first principles, especially principles of nature, resurrection cannot be inferred. But, while knowledge of the resurrection is not necessary for inference with respect to the existing universe as it is, an understanding of the origin of the universe, whether it is created or eternal, is. Whereas on the basis of the existing universe creation can be shown to be possible, resurrection cannot. That is why, for Maimonides, resurrection is believable, if and only if one first accepts creation.[14]

Rather than violate his own rationalism, it is precisely his rationalism that forbids Maimonides to violate the rule of nature or of reason. To do so would amount to being a mutakallim who does not know the difference between contradiction and contrariety, nor understands the relation between nature and reason, nor that between discursive ratiocination and immediate understanding and, most important for the discussion of miracles, does not even understand the difference between reason and imagination. As Maimonides points out throughout the *Guide* when he criticizes the mutakallimūn, to attempt to demonstrate or verify a miracle amounts to the desire to conform the nature of that which exists to the imagination, rather than conform imagination and reason to that which exists.

In contrast to the mutakallimūn and the vulgar who "like nothing better and, in their silliness, enjoy nothing more than to set the Law and reason at opposite ends," Maimonides announces his intentions to

> try to reconcile the Law and reason, and wherever possible consider all things as of the natural order. Only when something is explicitly identified as a miracle, and reinterpretation of it cannot be accommodated, only then I feel forced to grant that it is a miracle.
>
> Halkin 1985, p. 223

Reiterating time and again that resurrection (in contrast to the immortality of the soul) is an indemonstrable, extra-natural miracle and that, precisely for that reason, he has previously refrained from speaking about it at length, Maimonides proceeds reluctantly[15] to clarify the distinction between naturally possible and impossible miracles.

One of three conditions must obtain in order that the class of naturally possible events be miracles: first, the possible event is predicted by a prophet, for example, the promise of rain; second, the possible event is singular in kind and hence beyond imaginative or conceptual representation, for example, the locust and other plagues;

third, the possible event is of great duration and persistence, for example, the blessings and the maledictions (ibid., p. 232). While the inclusion of a repeatedly occurring event in the class of miracles may seem strange, Maimonides claims that it is precisely its persistence that qualifies an event of this kind as miraculous. The repetition and duration of an event that interrupts the regularity of the ordinary course of nature is precisely what excludes the possibility of explaining the interruption as a chance incident.

When he turns to the explanation of the naturally impossible miraculous event, Maimonides is, again, remarkably reticent. What characterizes such a miracle is its singular non-enduring nature. Unlike the naturally possible singular event which can both endure and recur, the naturally impossible event cannot. Whereas the former is unimaginable and even unthinkable prior to the first occurrence only, the latter is absolutely unimaginable and unthinkable. Consequently, naturally possible events can be understood and, hence, discussed after they have occurred, whereas naturally impossible events can occur only once and hence can only be believed and affirmed. In a striking conclusion, Maimonides characterizes the enduring naturally possible miracles as "wondrous," the naturally impossible ones as "unknowable." That is, the former class of miracles arouses wonder or the desire for understanding, whereas the latter underscores the limits of human understanding. It is no wonder then that Maimonides considers the former "wonder-ful" since they pave the way for that understanding which is true human perfection.

In the light of the foregoing discussion and despite its tragic irony, there can be little doubt that Maimonides is partly responsible for the controversy surrounding resurrection. Although his violent critique of the Jewish mutakallimūn may seem distasteful and, at times, ad hominem, and although it may have inadvertently led to the exile of philosophy from subsequent Jewish thought, Maimonides' battle with pseudo-philosophy was impersonal and impartial. Imprudent as it may have been, Maimonides was fighting for what he understood to be the ultimate well-being of the Jewish community, namely, intellectual perfection. Conversely, the mutakallimūn, who presented themselves as defenders and teachers of the Torah, hindered the possibility of attaining true perfection, both in so far as they failed to distinguish between the two human perfections, bodily and intellectual, and in so far as they presented bodily resurrection as the true end of the Torah. Ironically, it is the natural possibility of intellectual perfection, of which the exemplary instance is Mosaic prophecy, that renders the prediction of resurrection believable. Were intellectual perfection not the true end of the Torah, Mosaic prophecy would not manifest the highest human perfection and Mosaic law would not have its absolutely binding status.

For Maimonides, failure of understanding the Torah entails failure of acting in accordance with its precepts. Ultimately, the battle against pseudo-philosophy is a battle against apostasy and disbelief. If Maimonides is guilty of any charge, then it is of the insistence that philosophical understanding is a necessary condition for true obedience to the Torah's precepts.

The tragic irony of many subsequent charges against Maimonides is that both his adherents and his better-informed, intellectually astute critics, for example, Nachmanides, shared his intellectual elitism, albeit in different ways. For the kabbalists, like the Maimonideans, insisted that true understanding of the Torah is reserved for the few who are capable of apprehending its secrets. The greatest irony, though, is that Maimonides' defenders not only radicalized his thought, perhaps to such an extent as to undermine the status of the Torah, but also did not believe that his affirmation of naturally impossible miracles was sincere. The more philosophically astute Maimonides' followers were, the less willing they were to accept any limitations to human knowledge and the more willing they were to embrace a "Latin Averroist"[16] (double truth) approach to truth. The remaining part of the chapter will be devoted to a discussion of two of Maimonides' followers who exemplify the radical appropriation of his thought, namely, Samuel ibn Tibbon (d. c. 1232) and Joseph ibn Kaspi (1279–c. 1332).

Despite the fact that Samuel ibn Tibbon did not take part in the controversy itself, his translation of the *Guide* into Hebrew with his appended philosophical lexicon as well as his translation of *Pereq Cheleq* and the *Shemonah Peraqim* were the explicit targets of Solomon ben Abraham's and other anti-Maimonideans' attacks. Nor, as will become evident, was ibn Tibbon unaware of his responsibility in generating and even exacerbating anti-Maimonidean sentiments. He was associated with the scholars of Lunel, who were involved in the controversy with Meir Abulafia as early as 1203,[17] and he explicitly discusses the controversies between the Maimonidean few and the anti-Maimonidean majority dividing the Jewish communities in his *Commentary on Ecclesiastes*.[18] In fact, ibn Tibbon claims that the true Maimonideans are fewer than those who profess to follow Maimonides, many of whom would have despised him had they truly understood his esoteric writings. Ibn Tibbon also points out that, were Maimonides to be understood by the many, he would be equally despised. Thus, whereas Maimonides' primary concern with the well-being of the perplexed few, who are capable of true perfection, did not preclude a concern for the many, whom he believed would derive some benefit even from the "esoteric" *Guide* (*Guide*, introduction: 16), ibn Tibbon denies any benefit for the many either from the *Guide* or from his own work.

Since ibn Tibbon is aware of the dangers inherent in public expositions on the "secrets of the Torah" and equally aware of the danger of being perceived as an innovator and contradicting commonly held beliefs, how are we to understand the charge by Solomon ben Abraham that ibn Tibbon's guilt consists of revealing what Maimonides had concealed and of public pronouncements that the entire Torah, including some commandments, is allegorical? Was ibn Tibbon simply an inept Maimonidean, unable to compose properly esoteric works? This question is pressing not simply because of ibn Tibbon's own claims concerning his unique understanding of the *Guide*'s intentions, but also because of Abraham Maimoni's testimony that Maimonides held ibn Tibbon in high esteem as one who understood the secrets of the *Guide* (Ravitzky 1981, p. 91). In the light of this testimony, we are justified in raising questions concerning Solomon ben Abraham's intention. More precisely, since upon reading ibn Tibbon's highly esoteric writings it is rather difficult to view him as a popularizer, what seems to have infuriated Solomon and other anti-Maimonideans is quite simply the *explicit* claim concerning the esoteric teaching of the Bible, the Talmud, and Maimonides' writings. For if this claim were true, if philosophical acuity were necessary for understanding these texts, it would follow that the majority of the Jewish community has no share in (true) human perfection. The opposition to ibn Tibbon then is an opposition to philosophy as the key to salvation.

Although ibn Tibbon may have extended the range of esoteric texts further than Maimonides, there can be little doubt about the Maimonidean origin of his claims. The most radical tendency of his thought, then, is not the claim to an esoteric layer of meaning in traditional texts, but rather the nature of that esotericism in relation to the revealed or exoteric layer of the various texts.

Since for Maimonides the key to understanding the Bible as well as to belief is the "miracle" of creation, since the possibility of creation is prior to that of resurrection, and since, as one of the profound secrets of the Torah, a discussion of creation must be esoteric, we must turn briefly to ibn Tibbon's interpretation of the "Account of the Beginning." Even a brief examination of *Ma'amar Yiqqavu ha-Mayim* and the *Commentary on Ecclesiastes* will reveal the extent of ibn Tibbon's radical appropriation of Maimonides.

What is most striking about ibn Tibbon's discussion of creation is his reticence. Although his *Ma'amar Yiqqavu ha-Mayim* is purportedly devoted to the first verses of Genesis, he does not address the question of the origin of the universe directly, as that question arises precisely out of the conflict between the religious belief in creation and the philosophical belief in eternity. The reticence is especially glaring in the light both of ibn Tibbon's lengthy treatment of providence and of his explicit disagreement with some of Maimonides' explicit statements about it, and in the light of his interpretation of resurrection as an allegory whose true meaning is intellectual immortality. As Ravitzky points out concerning the question of creation,

> [i]t is difficult to give an unequivocal answer to this question [of creation] since it depends on our interpretation of Ibn Tibbon himself and of his own esoteric writing; there is also the difficulty of distinguishing between the views which he attributed to Maimonides and those he considered as having developed himself.

> Ravitzky 1981, p. 118

However, given the fact that, whenever he is explicit about "miracles" or events contrary to nature, ibn Tibbon provides a naturalistic interpretation, even at the expense of contradicting Maimonides,[19] given statements in *Ma'amar Yiqqavu ha-Mayim* about the philosophical futility of asking questions about origin (p. 5), given his claim that questions concerning origin arise from the imagination (ibid.), and given his identification of the divine will with the order of nature (ibid., p. 119), it seems reasonable to conclude that ibn Tibbon subscribed to "eternal creation" or emanation.[20]

The obvious question arising from this conclusion is whether or not anti-Maimonideans such as Solomon ben Abraham understood ibn Tibbon to a sufficient extent such that they could charge him with heterodoxy. It may be doubted. Contrarily, ibn Tibbon's "elitist" esotericism, which involves the historicizing of the *written* texts in a manner that voids particular actual events and particular figures of real significance, transforming (allegorizing) them into ahistorical, universal notions (for example, Adam stands for the human intellect),[21] *is* readily evident and, hence, is more likely to have elicited a vitriolic response. As will become clear in the brief concluding discussion of ibn Kaspi, it is neither historicism nor esotericism per se that provoked the ire of the anti-Maimonideans, else the kabbalists would have met with the same response; rather, it is philosophical esotericism, precisely in so far as it is philosophical or inaccessible to the many.

Joseph ibn Kaspi, whose work was written after the 1305 Spanish ban against the study of philosophy by anyone under the age of twenty-five and the subsequent Provençal counterban,[22] is a more radical Maimonidean than ibn Tibbon, at least with respect to the status of the written biblical texts and his contempt for the multitude. At the same time, and likely owing to historical hindsight, his commentaries on biblical texts and reflections upon their central questions are more cautious than those of ibn Tibbon. Despite his caution, however, and owing to his philosophical radicalism, his biblical commentaries "have for the most part elicited a negative response from their readers" (Mesch 1975, p. 33). In fact, properly understood, ibn Kaspi's caution reflects his radicalism.

Although he described himself as a Maimonidean, ibn Kaspi does not hesitate to criticize Maimonides and the Maimonideans either with respect to biblical interpretation, where he adopts a striking and sui generis approach, or with respect to metaphysics, where he follows Averroes on one of the two most profound mysteries of the Torah, namely, "the Account of the Chariot."[23] For ibn Kaspi, proper biblical interpretation requires a thorough knowledge of logic and grammar, and a subtle appreciation of historical perspective. Unique among the Maimonideans or rationalist philosophers, ibn Kaspi insists upon a literal, minimalist biblical interpretation, criticizes the use of allegory in interpretation, and severely restricts its use to the moral education of the multitude. His criticism and restriction of allegorical interpretation is especially striking, in so far as this seemingly methodological difference manifests a substantive one as well. For the claim that allegory is an appropriate method of teaching the multitude *only* is simultaneously a claim that it is philosophically both useless and errant.[24] It is especially ironic, then, that the first written criticism of ibn Kaspi's work, the "Teshuvah" of Kalonymus ben Kalonymus, reproaches him for violating Maimonides' dicta on esotericism and for revealing hidden truth that could lead to perplexity. As Pines (1963) and Sirat (1985) point out, in this as well as in a number of other respects ibn Kaspi can be seen as Spinoza's predecessor.

Whereas ibn Tibbon's historicism reflects a belief in progressive human intellectual perfection of a kind that requires a philosophical or allegorical interpretation of particular biblical events and figures, ibn Kaspi's reflects a conviction that proper historical understanding entails the recognition that the Bible is simply an historical narrative of real events and persons presented in a manner that reflects their popular language, customs, and beliefs. Consequently, he denies the perfect intellectual or philosophical status of biblical figures, dismisses the understanding of their statements and deeds as instances of philosophical instruction,[25] and, most important for the present discussion, denies the claim that miracles belong to a class of naturally impossible events. Properly understood, ibn Kaspi's rejection of allegorical interpretation is simultaneously a rejection of miracles.

Rather than reflecting a radical relativism, ibn Kaspi's historicism is perspectival. Indeed, the understanding of events and deeds depends upon the status of the knower; but, precisely for this reason, we are forced to admit that what is miraculous to an individual ignorant of natural science is possible for one who understands nature (*Tirat Kesef*, pp. 12–13). Unlike the historicism of the progressive Enlightenment, historical perspectivism assumes that differences exist naturally both in customs and language and in intellectual capacity, at all times and in all places. Although ibn Kaspi does not deny resurrection outright, he restricts its possibility to one of the three natural possibilities enumerated by Maimonides in the *Treatise on Resurrection*. More precisely, in enumerating the classes of miracle he does not mention a separate class of possible miraculous events that are contrary to nature. Finally, ibn Kaspi adds that true perfection or immortality refers to the soul and that strictly speaking human life refers to "the life of the soul remaining after death" (*Tirat Kesef*, p. 18).

The greatest, final irony in the Maimonidean controversy is manifested most clearly by the differences between two of Maimonides' most committed followers, Samuel ibn Tibbon and Joseph ibn Kaspi. For the implications of ibn Kaspi's philosophical, literal interpretations of the Bible are far more radical than are Maimonides' or ibn Tibbon's allegorical ones. Thus, despite the charges of the anti-Maimonideans that allegorical interpretations undermine the status of the Bible and the tradition, (philosophical) literalism blurs the difference between sacred and profane history. The conflict between the Maimonideans and the anti-Maimonideans is quite simply a conflict between a popular and a philosophical adherence to the Torah.[26]

❧ NOTES ❧

1 Properly speaking, there were a number of concurrent as well as consecutive controversies surrounding Maimonides' thought. Consequently, the term "controversy" will be used strictly in reference to, first, the entire context of the debates and, second, a set of particular issues which can and should be grouped under a single category.

2 The two most thorough studies of the history of the controversies are Sarachek 1935 and Silver 1965; see also Jospe 1980.

3 Whether or not Solomon, his disciples, and their other supporters were aware of their contradictory goals, whether or not the deference to Maimonides was an acknowledgement of his already established status, and whether or not they were simply dissimulators who refrained from alienating Maimonidean halakhic authorities is impossible to determine. What is clear, though, is that henceforth Maimonides' authority could not be ignored, so that all Jewish thought, be it kabbalist, mystical, or philosophical, was determined by Maimonides. See Dan 1989, passim.

4 For the political motives exerting influence upon these decisions, see Silver 1965, pp. 152ff.

5 Even Silver (1965), who is clearly sympathetic to the anti-Maimonideans and who repeatedly attempts to minimize their guilt by underlining the tenuous

political position of the Provençal Jewish communities during the anti-Albigensian crusade, is forced to admit Solomon's responsibility.

6 Barzilay's (1967) study of anti-rationalism between 1250 and 1650 is an exemplary study of this tendency.

7 For a more comprehensive examination of other significant aspects of the controversy, see Sarachek 1935 and Silver 1965. Although, as will become evident below, I believe that the central problem leading to, and further inflaming, the debates is that of the relation between religion and philosophy, it is equally possible to argue, for example, from a Marxist perspective, that the social and political issues are of greater significance. The only justification that can be provided for the strictly "philosophical" bias is that *de principiis non disputandum est*.

8 A comparison of the attitude adopted by the Spanish and French communities with that of the Italian is exemplary of this claim. Whereas the Spanish and French anti-Maimonideans viewed the external threat as such that it required a strict ideological unity and, hence, were willing to "sacrifice" Maimonides for the greater well-being of the community, the Italians neither viewed the threat as great, quite the contrary, nor banned Maimonides' works. In fact, as Jacob Anatoli's *Malmad ha-Talmidim* makes evident, the real threat to the community was not internal disagreement but rather assimilation of Christian beliefs and attitudes. Ironically, whereas the French attempt at "appeasement" failed, as can be seen from the subsequent burning of the Talmud and the intensification of the inquisition, the Italian Jewish communities did not suffer a similar fate.

9 Even on halakhic matters and even during his lifetime Maimonides' students were less prudent than their teacher; see Silver 1965, passim.

10 In the *Book of Knowledge* Maimonides numbers the individuals who separate themselves from the community among those who have no share in the world to come; see "Repentance," treatise 5, 3, no. 6.

11 "My writings are in circulation; let them be perused, and let someone show where I say this" (Halkin 1985, p. 219).

12 Maimonides also ridicules Samuel's interpretation, depicting it as a rehearsal of "homilies and curious tales, of the sort that women [sic] tell one another in their condolence calls" (Halkin 1985, pp. 217–18). It should also be noted that the very failure to draw proper distinctions is a philosophical failure.

13 Since the *Guide* was written in Judeo-Arabic, even if it had been circulating at the time of the debate (it was completed in 1190 and the *Treatise* was written in 1191), both its language and its deliberate philosophical subtlety would have rendered it inaccessible to the wider community. Although the *Treatise* is a popular treatment of a philosophical difficulty, it is none the less written in Judeo-Arabic. Still, the lack of philosophical prudence evident in rendering more accessible a subject which exceeds popular understanding seems to violate Maimonides' own principles. None the less, such imprudence cannot be understood simply as an attempt to vindicate his name, but rather should be viewed as an attempt to avoid harm to others who have misunderstood his writings. See the advice to Joseph in the introduction to the *Guide* (Pines, in Maimonides 1963, p. 15).

14 For a discussion of the status of principles of nature and their epistemic status, see Klein-Braslavy 1987, Fackenheim 1946–7, and Dobbs-Weinstein 1992.

15 Maimonides' reluctance to discuss miracles is expressed throughout the *Treatise*, and is not surprising in the light of the fact that resurrection is unknowable. When he turns to the distinction between natural possibility and impossibility he points out that he must discuss it "although it is too important for this essay" (Halkin 1985, p. 231).

16 While a discussion of the difference between Averroes and "Latin Averroism" is clearly beyond the confines of the present chapter, the distinction should, at least, be noted.

17 See above pp. 332–3.

18 Ravitzky's excellent study (1981) of ibn Tibbon's relation to Maimonides includes a clear and succinct discussion of ibn Tibbon's place in the controversy.

19 See the discussion of providence in *Ma'amar Yiqqavu ha-Mayim*, pp. 61–121, and the "Epistle on Providence" (Diesendruck 1936, pp. 341–66).

20 Ibn Tibbon's discussion of the intermediary role of the separate intellects in the ordering of the course of natural sublunar events, as well as his references to ibn Ezra and Avicenna, further substantiate this conclusion; see Sirat 1985 and Ravitzky 1981, passim.

21 For a discussion of ibn Tibbon's "historical approach" to traditional written texts, see Ravitzky 1981, pp. 111–16.

22 Gross (1899) has even suggested that ibn Kaspi's emigration from Argentière to Arles in 1306 was a result of the controversy.

23 Although our concern here is not with metaphysics, it is noteworthy that ibn Kaspi follows Averroes on the relation between the agent intellect and the sphere of the moon, and implicitly claims that, had Maimonides read Averroes' commentary on Aristotle's *Metaphysics*, he would have followed Averroes rather than al-Fārābī and Avicenna; see *Menorat Kesef* 2.80.

24 In the context of the controversy, it is important to note that ibn Kaspi rejects Maimonides' and the Maimonidean interpretation of biblical references to female and male as signifying matter and form.

25 See *Tirat Kesef* 31, where ibn Kaspi points out that many perplexities come about from the attempt to interpret biblical figures "as if they were Aristotle."

26 I wish to dedicate this chapter to my late teacher, Frank Talmage.

❧ BIBILIOGRAPHY ❧

Texts

Anatoli, J. (1866) *Malmad ha-Talmidim*, edited by S. Z. H. Halberstam (Lyck: Siebert).

Halkin, A. (tr.) (1985) *Crisis and Leadership: Epistles of Maimonides* (Philadelphia: Jewish Publication Society).

ibn Kaspi, J. (1893) *Menorat Kesef*, in *Les Écrivains juifs français du XIVe siècle*, edited by E. Renan (Paris: Imprimerie Nationale).

—— (1905) *Tirat Kesef*, in *Zwei Schriften des Josef ibn Kaspi*, edited by I. Last, vol. 1 (Pressburg: Alkalay).

ibn Tibbon, S. *Commentary on Ecclesiastes*, MS Parma 2182.

—— (1837) *Ma'amar Yiqqavu ha-Mayim* (Pressburg: Bisliches).

Kalonymus ben Kalonymus (1913) [1879] *Sendschreiben an Josef Kaspi (Ha-Teshuvah)*, edited by J. Perles (Munich); reprinted in I. Last (ed.), *Tam Ha-Kesef* (London: Narodiczky).

Kobak, J. I. (ed.) (1868–78) *Sefer Ginze Nistarot* (Bamberg: Selbstverlag des Herausgebers).

Maimoni, A. (1937) *Teshuvot Rabbenu Avraham ben ha-Rambam*, edited by A. Friedman (Jerusalem: Mekitze Nirdamim).

—— (1952–3) *Milchamot Adonai*, edited by R. Margaliyot (Jerusalem: Mossad ha-Rav Kook).

Maimonides, M. (1858) *Qovetz Teshuvot ha-Rambam ve-Iggerotav*, 3 parts, edited by A. L. Lichtenberg (Leipzig: Schnauss).

—— (1958) *Mishneh Torah: Sefer ha-Madda'*, edited by M. D. Rabinowitz (Jerusalem: Mossad ha-Rav Kook).

—— (1960) *Moreh Nevukhim*, translated by Samuel ibn Tibbon (Jerusalem: Mossad ha-Rav Kook).

—— (1963) *The Guide of The Perplexed*, translated by S. Pines, 2 vols. (Chicago: Chicago University Press).

—— (1964a) [1855–66] *Dalālat al-Ḥā'irīn*, edited by S. Munk (Paris; reprinted in 3 vols. Osnabrück: Zeller).

—— (1964b) *Perush ha-Mishnah: Nezikin*, edited by J. D. Kafih (Jerusalem: Mossad ha-Rav Kook).

—— (1965) *Mishneh Torah: The Book of Knowledge*, edited and translated by M. Hyamson (Jerusalem: Boys Town).

—— (1975) *The Eight Chapters*, in *Ethical Writings of Maimonides*, translated by R. L. Weiss and C. E. Butterworth (New York: New York University Press).

Studies

Barzilay, I. E. (1967) *Between Reason and Faith: Anti-Rationalism in Italian Jewish Thought 1250–1650* (The Hague: Mouton).

Dan, J. (1989) "Jewish Thought in the 13th Century: An Introduction," in *Studies in Jewish Thought*, edited by S. O. Heller Wilensky and M. Idel (Jerusalem: Magnes).

Diesendruck, Z. (1936) "Samuel and Moses ibn Tibbon on Maimonides' Theory of Providence," *Hebrew Union College Annual* 11: 341–66.

Dobbs-Weinstein, I. (1992) "Matter as Creature and Matter as the Source of Evil: Maimonides and Aquinas," in *Neoplatonism and Jewish Thought*, edited by L. E. Goodman (Albany: State University of New York Press), pp. 217–35.

Fackenheim, E. (1946–7) "The Possibility of the Universe in Alfarabi, ibn Sina and Maimonides," *Proceedings of the American Academy for Jewish Research* 16: 39–70.

Gross, H. (1899) *Gallia Judaica*, translated by M. Bloch (Paris: Cerf).

Jospe, R. (1980) "Faith and Reason: The Controversy over Philosophy in Judaism," in *Great Schisms in Jewish History*, edited by R. Jospe and S. Wagner (New York: Ktav), pp. 73–117.

Klein-Braslavy, S. (1987) *Maimonides' Interpretation of the Story of Creation* [Hebrew] (Jerusalem: Reuben Mass).

Mesch, B. (1975) *Studies in Joseph ibn Caspi: Fourteenth-Century Philosopher and Exegete* (Leiden: Brill).

Pines, S. (1963) "Histabrut ha-Tequmah me-Hadash shel Medinah Yehudit le-fi Yosef Ibn Kaspi u-le-fi Spinoza," *Iyyun* 16: 298–317.

Ravitzky, A. (1981) "Samuel ibn Tibbon and the Esoteric Character of the *Guide of the Perplexed*," *AJS Review* 6: 87–123.

Sarachek, J. (1935) *Faith and Reason: The Conflict Over the Rationalism of Maimonides* (Willamsport, PA: Bayard).

Silver, D. J. (1965) *Maimonidean Criticism and the Maimonidean Controversy, 1180–1240* (Leiden: Brill).

Sirat, C. (1985) *A History of Jewish Philosophy in the Middle Ages* (Cambridge: Cambridge University Press).

CHAPTER 15

Hebrew philosophy in the fourteenth and fifteenth centuries: an overview

Charles H. Manekin

➳ INTRODUCTION ➳

The golden age of Hebrew philosophy began in 1204 with the first translation of Maimonides' *Guide of the Perplexed* into Hebrew, and it lasted for approximately three centuries until the expulsion of the Jews from Spain in 1492.[1] For the first and only time in Jewish history, philosophers and scientists writing in Hebrew played a central role in the intellectual and cultural life of the Jewish communities of France, Spain, Italy, and the Near East. Especially in the south of France, Italy, and, at a later date, Spain, there arose a "class" of translators, commentators, and students of the Greek scientific and philosophical corpus as it had been preserved and interpreted by the Arabs. What was hitherto an esoteric activity reserved for the elite and well-to-do was now a dominant intellectual force within the Jewish community at large, with philosophers playing a prominent role.[2]

Some of these philosophers devoted their energies to what might be called "philosophical Judaism," that is, the philosophical interpretation of the doctrines of classical Judaism. Philosophical Judaism had originated several centuries earlier among the Jews of Muslim lands, and the writings of its main exponents, Saadia Gaon, Bachya ibn Paquda, and Judah Halevi, were translated from Judeo-Arabic into Hebrew already in the second half of the twelfth century. As time passed, the canon of philosophical Judaism was enriched with new treatises, philosophical commentaries, and sermons, now composed in Hebrew by Jews who knew little, if any, Arabic.

What sets this period apart from the previous one, then, is the creation of an indigenous Hebrew philosophical culture, which alters the scope and direction of Jewish philosophy, as well as the attitudes of Jewish philosophers to their work. One might say with only a little exaggeration that philosophy "entered the covenant of Abraham" in the thirteenth and fourteenth centuries. In the earlier period Jews in Muslim countries had availed themselves of Arab philosophical works without viewing themselves as counterparts to the Muslim falāsifa (philosophers). Maimonides himself never wrote a treatise or commentary on a purely philosophical topic, with the exception of a short work on logic. True, his treatment of the encounter between philosophy and religion in the *Guide of the Perplexed* remained the main frame of reference for Jewish philosophers throughout the medieval period, and the Arab Aristotelians remained their main authorities, even after scholastic philosophy had made inroads. But the development of a philosophical discourse, spurred on by the tremendous translation activity from Arabic into Hebrew in the thirteenth and fourteenth centuries, ensured that the scope of Hebrew philosophy would exceed that of philosophical Judaism.

The philosophical curriculum of the typical student of the period consisted mainly of the works of Aristotle as presented by Averroes, some works of al-Fārābī and al-Ghazālī, and a few by Avicenna. The commentaries of Averroes on Aristotle, especially his condensations and paraphrases, were especially popular, and they were the subjects of commentaries and compendia by Jewish authors. Although Jewish philosophers occasionally wrote treatises on a particular topic of general philosophy or theology, the preferred mode of expression was commentary, either of a philosophical work or of classics like the *Guide of the Perplexed* by Maimonides or the *Commentary on the Bible* by Abraham ibn Ezra; one should also note the popularity of philosophical sermons. In time, European Jewish thinkers become increasingly familiar with the writings of their Christian neighbors, either in Latin or in Hebrew translation. This process begins in Italy in the thirteenth century, followed by Spain in the fourteenth and fifteenth, and Provence in the fifteenth.

It is difficult to say how much scholastic influence is found in Jewish philosophy of the fourteenth and fifteenth centuries.[3] One major problem is that Jewish philosophers rarely mention Christian authors by name; the earliest Hebrew translations of Latin works appear without attribution, or with vague references to "the Gentile sages," etc. Thus, in Hillel of Verona's *Retributions of the Soul* (1291) one finds passages from the Latin Avicenna and Averroes woven with passages of Dominico Gundisalvo (Gundissalinus) and Thomas Aquinas in a less than coherent whole. An anonymous Hebrew translator of the *Tractatus* of Peter of Spain (later Pope John XXI) attributes the work to Aristotle! By the first quarter of the fourteenth century, however, the Italian philosopher Judah Romano has translated, with proper attribution, Gundisalvo, Giles of Rome, Albertus Magnus, Alexander of Alessandri (d. 1314), Angelo of Camerino (late thirteenth century), and Thomas Aquinas. In the fifteenth century the Iberian peninsula becomes a major center of translation activity, thanks to the labors of Elijah Habillo (late fifteenth century), Abraham Shalom (d. 1492), Meir Alguades (d. 1410), and Azariah ben Joseph (late fifteenth century), who render works by Aristotle, Boethius, Albertus Magnus, Aquinas, Ockham (d. 1347/9), and Marsilius of Inghen (d. 1396). Though important in their own right, the impact of these translations on most Jewish philosophers appears to be marginal; they are rarely extant in more than one or two manuscripts.

Equally difficult to determine is the extent to which Jewish philosophers of our period were familiar with developments in scholastic philosophy, and the channels through which they received their information. This is actually part of a larger question of the nature and degree of Christian influence on Jewish thought of the fourteenth and fifteenth centuries. The answer depends, needless to say, on the geographical region, the period, and the particular circumstances of the individual thinker. In general, the major Jewish philosophers of northern Spain and Provence in the fourteenth century – Gersonides (d. 1344), Isaac Pollegar (d. c. 1330), Joseph ibn Kaspi (d. 1340), and Moses Narboni (d. c. 1362) – show little signs, if any, of scholastic influence. They appear to fit squarely within the Arabic-Hebrew tradition, and, with the notable exception of Gersonides, they tend to follow Averroes in philosophical matters. In religious doctrines they usually adopt the untraditional and, in some instances, radical interpretations associated with Averroism. By contrast, the Spanish Jewish philosophers who flourish in the late fourteenth and fifteenth centuries – Profiat Duran (d. c. 1414), Chasdai Crescas (d. 1411), Simeon Duran (d. 1444), Joseph Albo (d. 1444), Abraham Bibago (d. c. 1489), Isaac Arama (d. 1494), Abraham Shalom (d. 1492), and Isaac Abravanel (d. 1509) – are much more conservative, partly as a response to the spiritual crisis in the Spanish Jewish community, which left them battling Christian conversionary attempts on the one hand, and Jewish Averroist tendencies on the other.

Unlike their French and Spanish co-religionists, Italian Jewish philosophers were well-integrated into their host culture, which enabled them to keep abreast of intellectual developments. At the beginning of the fifteenth century the University of Padua opened its doors to Jews, who contributed to the Paduan revival of Averroes during the Renaissance. Because fifteenth-century Italy is a center of diverse intellectual trends, the Italian Jewish philosophers are hard to classify;

philosophical eclecticism and syncretism are the order of the day. Many of them may be called "Averroists," but the name is no longer automatically identified with theological unorthodoxy. Thus, traditional Italian Jewish philosophers like Judah Messer Leon (d. 1498) and Moses ibn Habib (d. late fifteenth century) may be called "orthodox Averroists" because of their loyalty to Averroes' commentaries, if not to his radical doctrines.

Most Hebrew philosophy of the fourteenth and fifteenth centuries is extant only in manuscript or poorly edited printed editions;[4] this is especially true of the commentaries and compendia in the more technical areas of logic, psychology, physics, and metaphysics. Still, the major works of philosophical Judaism have been published, and these contain much material of philosophical interest. Rather than summarize their contents, I will focus on four issues that were much discussed by the Jewish philosophers of our period: the relationship between *emunah* (belief/faith) and rational knowledge, the question of divine attributes, the interpretation of the world's creation, and the antinomy of free choice and determinism. Aside from their intrinsic importance, these issues highlight the shift in philosophical currents from fourteenth-century rationalism to late fourteenth- and early fifteenth-century conservatism, as well as the growing influence of Christian thought on Jewish philosophy.

❧ *EMUNAH* – BELIEF OR FAITH? ❧

The shifting philosophical climate of this period can be seen in the various interpretations given to the word *emunah*. In biblical and rabbinic thought, the root of this word carried the connotation of "trust," "reliance," and "acceptance." But owing to the lack of technical philosophical terms in Hebrew, the twelfth-century Hebrew translators chose *emunah* to render the Arabic term *i'tiqād*, "belief" or "conviction." This "cognitive" sense of *emunah*, based on the Arabic philosophical tradition, dominates Jewish discussions until the late fourteenth century, when scholasticism begins to penetrate Jewish circles. Then *emunah* takes on the additional meaning of "faith" (*fides*), as in the contrast between faith and reason. By the end of the fifteenth century, a concept as fundamental as "*emunah* in the creator" can mean "trust in the creator" or "belief in the existence of the creator," or "faith in the creator," depending upon the philosophical context.[5]

The cognitive interpretation was well known to Jewish philosophers of our period from Maimonides' definition of *emunah* (Arabic *i'tiqād*) as "the notion that is conceived in the soul when it has been affirmed of it that it is in fact just as it has been represented."[6] To believe something about *x* involves, first, a mental conception of *x* and, second, an affirmation that this conception corresponds to an extramental existent. By defining belief with reference to conception and affirmation, two ideas that were central in Arabic logic and epistemology, Maimonides wished to stress that *emunot* are *truth-bearers*.[7] They can be either true or false, dubious or certain, rational or traditional. As for certain belief, Maimonides argued that it arises only from rational proof, the only warrant for the belief that something is necessarily the case and cannot be otherwise. He excluded all beliefs that are accepted by virtue of traditional authority from the realm of certainty. Thus, non-philosophers may possess true beliefs about God, but not certain ones. Still, despite his clear preference for certain beliefs over traditional ones, Maimonides allowed the latter some cognitive value. Theological beliefs that are accepted on traditional authority provide the non-philosophers with a true, albeit indistinct, conception of God, a necessary condition for the immortality of the soul.[8]

Under the influence of Averroes, however, the Jewish philosophers in Provence generally replaced Maimonides' distinction between rational and traditional beliefs with Aristotle's distinction between knowledge (*yedi'ah*) and true opinion (*machshavah amitit*).[9] They argued that to know *x* is to understand why *x* is what it is, and how it cannot be otherwise. Anything less than this, although it may be true opinion, is not knowledge ("knowledge" here refers to theoretical knowledge or science). Now such strict conditions for knowledge, along with other philosophical assumptions, yield difficult conclusions for traditional religion. For example, if, as these philosophers held, the possession of theoretical knowledge about the world is a prerequisite for individual providence and immortality, then the uneducated multitude are unable to share in these matters, even if they possess true beliefs about God and the world.[10] Moreover, if knowledge about *x* must include the *rational explanation* for why *x* must be so, then most prophecy and foreknowledge is, strictly speaking, not knowledge at all. This conclusion is reached by Gersonides, who holds that people who foresee what will occur, yet do not possess any rational explanation for what will occur, do not possess fore*knowledge*. With respect to knowledge, the prophet can claim no superiority over the philosopher.[11] So committed is Gersonides to the strict Aristotelian conditions for theoretical knowledge that when he considers the phenomenon of receiving theoretical knowledge in dreams – a phenomenon which he claims to have experienced – he is forced to say that either the dreamer receives the rational explanation, or the information follows from premises learned while awake.[12] Gersonides, and after him Narboni, make the possession of theoretical knowledge a sufficient condition for human felicity and the immortality of the soul; for Gersonides, the human soul achieves a certain conjunction with the supernal agent intellect, the giver of sublunar forms, while at the same time retaining its particularity;[13] for Narboni, the soul upon death merges itself entirely with the agent intellect.[14]

Partly because of these extreme implications, the Spanish Jewish philosophers of the fourteenth and fifteenth centuries developed alternative approaches to *emunah*, of which we shall examine three: a cognitive approach that sees *emunah* as non-volitional, and accordingly devalues its religious significance; a quasi-cognitive approach that views *emunah* as superior to rational knowledge, yet still non-volitional; and a quasi-cognitive approach that sees *emunah* as volitional, and, hence, of great religious significance. In Spain one also notes several attempts to systematize Jewish beliefs,[15] as well as efforts to reinterpret the relationship of these beliefs to Jewish observance. If the fourteenth-century Jewish Aristotelians viewed the commandments merely as instruments whereby one acquires good moral habits, thereby facilitating the acquisition of rational knowledge, their fifteenth-century successors consider them as ends in themselves.[16]

ᴥ *EMUNAH* AS NON-VOLITIONAL ᴥ

The view that *emunot* are non-volitional arose, in part, as a response to Maimonides' legal position that Jews are commanded to believe that God exists.[17] According to Chasdai Crescas, not only are Jews not commanded to believe that God exists, they are not *commanded* to believe anything because assent or denial is not subject to choice or will.[18] Believing is not a volitional act, and, since reward and punishment are appropriate only for volitional acts, the possession of beliefs per se is neither praiseworthy nor blameworthy. On behalf of this position Crescas offers three arguments. First, the idea that one can "will to believe" two contradictory propositions, one after the other, is absurd. Second, where assent is compelled by the evidence, then willing to believe is otiose; where assent is underdetermined, then willing does not make the putative belief any more certain. Third, belief is defined as the affirmation that the extramental existent conforms to the idea we have of it – and the will has no power over the extramental existent.[19]

Now clearly Crescas does not wish to do away with the idea that certain beliefs are obligatory; on the contrary, because he still adheres to the cognitive approach of *emunah*, he requires Jews to be instructed in the dogmas of their religion, as a result of which they will possess true beliefs of necessity. What bothers him is the significance accorded to the possession of true beliefs by the Jewish Aristotelians. Crescas rejects the idea that possession of true beliefs is its own reward, because this would bring him dangerously close to the view of "some of our sages" (apparently, Gersonides and Narboni) articulated above, that possession of knowledge is a sufficient condition for immortality of the soul. On the other hand, it seems odd that a just God rewards and punishes someone for his or her beliefs, given their non-volitional nature. Crescas' solution involves arguing that the will plays a role in the attitude of joy and pleasure one takes toward one's beliefs, as well as in the diligence one displays in confirming their truth. Crescas is not always clear in his formulations here; he does not say that one wills to be joyful towards one's beliefs, but rather that will has something to do with that joy.[20] As we shall see, Crescas did not believe in the freedom of the will, but he did believe that the same will can effect different alternatives, given different motivating causes. So the mere fact that one can take varying attitudes towards the beliefs that one necessarily holds implies that there is a volitional aspect to these attitudes, and this can be rewarded or punished, even though it is not free.

∾ *EMUNAH* AS DISTINGUISHED FROM ∾ RATIONAL BELIEF

Other Spanish Jewish philosophers move beyond the old Arab-inspired cognitive approach to *emunah* in order to distinguish it from rational belief. Whereas *emunah* was once a generic term that encompassed different types of belief, it now refers specifically to faith. Thus, Albo defines *emunah* as "a firm conception of the thing in the mind, so that the latter cannot in any way imagine its opposite, *even though it may not be able to prove it.*"[21] This definition collapses Maimonides' distinction between true and certain *emunot*; all *emunot* are ipso facto certain, and certainty no longer need be attained through rational proof. Albo extends this to traditional beliefs such as the revelation at Sinai. According to Simeon Duran, *emunot* are accepted as true by virtue of miracles, or by virtue of a reliable tradition of the miraculous that lodges them firmly in the soul.[22] A similar idea appears in Abravanel, who argues that *emunot*, while true and certain, are distinct from knowledge and opinion.[23] These philosophers understand *emunah* as, first, a strong conviction that is true and certain, but, second, whose truth and certainty do not derive from demonstration, or from any other Aristotelian guarantor of knowledge. They also share the opinion that the Aristotelian approach is inadequate to understand the biblical conception of *emunah*, and that rational knowledge is inferior to *emunah*.

The ultimate devaluation of rational knowledge in favor of *emunah* comes at the hands of Isaac Arama, who views the latter not only as superior but as often contrary to reason. True wisdom is attained when one assents to the dictates of the Torah that are *opposed* to speculation. The patriarch Abraham knew God initially as a philosopher, that is, through rational speculation; his test of *emunah* was his willingness to obey God's *irrational* command to sacrifice Isaac, just as the sign of his covenant was circumcision, "which clearly transcends logical reasoning."[24] The devaluation of philosophical knowledge in favor of traditional knowledge (revelation) had its origins in Judah Halevi's *Kuzari*, a twelfth-century Judeo-Arabic work that enjoyed renewed popularity in the fifteenth century.[25] But the language of *emunah* that dominates the discussions of the Spanish philosophers is most probably influenced by Christian treatments of *fides*.

Scholastic influence, especially Aquinas, is found in Abraham Bibago's exhaustive treatment of *emunah* in his *The Way of Emunah*. Unlike Arama, Bibago is not stridently anti-philosophical. On the contrary, in order to make *emunah* epistemologically respectable, Bibago argues that knowledge can be achieved either through rational inquiry (the way of investigation) or by accepting propositions on faith (the way of *emunah*). That is because the manner of achieving knowledge is irrelevant to its content. Two people can have the exact same knowledge of a city, even though only one of them actually saw it. In fact the second is in a better position because he or she accepted the testimony of the first on faith, thereby saving himself or herself the inconvenience of the first. Similarly, one who knows through faith is better off than the one who knows through rational investigation, because Jewish doctrines are based on a reliable tradition that stretches back to Moses, whereas many philosophical doctrines are subject to endless debate. Moreover, knowledge based on faith is superior to philosophical knowledge, in that it is accessible to all, not merely to the wise.[26]

While this analysis makes the concept of faith palatable from an epistemological standpoint, it still does not demonstrate the essential superiority of faith over rational belief. For, as Bibago himself admits, if what counts with respect to knowledge is the conclusions and not the method of achieving them, then what real advantage does the faithful have over the philosopher? The question is particularly troublesome because, on standard Aristotelian principles, there is an identity between the knower and the known, and therefore the philosopher and the faithful who believe the same thing, albeit on different grounds, are virtually identical. Bibago's first reply is that rational knowledge is not as true or as certain as is knowledge acquired from faith; hence the mind (and the ultimate felicity) of the faithful is superior to that of the philosopher. But his second reply suggests that *emunah* is fundamentally different from rational knowledge, for *emunah* is the "assent to unseen things," whereas knowledge is of revealed things. Divine science – theology and metaphysics – can be attained only through *emunah*/faith.[27]

<small>➤➤</small> *EMUNAH* AS VOLITIONAL <small>➤➤</small>

For Bibago, the superiority of *emunah* over rational knowledge lies in its volitional character. Whereas a rational argument compels assent, *emunah* is willed by the faithful. For this reason alone *emunah* possesses religious significance.[28] Bibago is, to my knowledge, the only medieval Jewish thinker who overtly interprets *emunah* as volitional, and at first glance he seems to be in direct conflict with Crescas. That the conflict is only apparent is due, in the main, to the ambiguity of the term *emunah*. In one passage Bibago refers approvingly to the sages who hold that *emunot* (beliefs) are compelled by the intellect, and then he claims that *emunah* (faith) is voluntary.[29] His point is that Crescas was right with respect to rational beliefs, but that the basis of Judaism lies in the acceptance of divine truths that may be rationally underdetermined. Yet he does not consistently maintain this opinion because he also holds that these truths are backed by a reliable tradition, which is more in keeping with the Maimonidean view of the reasonableness of possessing traditional beliefs.

Bibago's theory of the volitional character of belief is therefore opaque and not as developed as volitional theories found in scholastic philosophers.[30] He does not give up the reasonableness of traditional doctrines, yet he wishes to foster a religious attitude in which accepting these doctrines as an act of the will is the ideal. True to his Jewish roots, he links faith with the observance of the law. One wills to believe traditional doctrines in order not to neglect the performance of the laws, and one acquires *emunah* only through the performance of the laws.[31] Here Bibago tries to reconcile the instrumentalist approach to the law found in Maimonides with the new emphasis on the performance of the law as a necessary condition for human felicity; while all humans can possess *emunot*, only Jews can possess *emunah*.[32]

<small>➤➤</small> DIVINE ATTRIBUTES AND THE <small>➤➤</small>
KNOWABILITY OF GOD

Maimonides' influence in fourteenth- and fifteenth-century Jewish philosophy is ubiquitous, but it is most clearly seen in the various treatments of the problem of divine attributes. Although Jewish philosophers before Maimonides had also considered the problem, he was the first to analyze in detail its logical and epistemological dimensions. The logical dimension deals with the questions of how to describe God and how to form a concept of God. Given the standard Aristotelian theory of predication, argued Maimonides, one cannot say anything about God which relates to his essence. This is so because the logic of predication presupposes an ontology that cannot be applied to God without damaging his unity and uniqueness. Since the Bible does describe God, and since our worship of God presupposes that we have a concept of him, we must reinterpret the function and signification of religious language in such a way as to preserve divine uniqueness while providing us with a real concept of God. Maimonides allowed predication of actional attributes (attributes that relate to divine activity), because different effects can be produced by a sole agent. But attributes that purport to describe the divine essence must be understood negatively, as signifying what God is not; for example, "God is wise" should be taken as denying ignorance of God. Philosophy purifies our concept of God, for it teaches us what predicates are incompatible with his perfection. As students progress, their concept of God refers with greater precision to that entity which is God.[33]

While the main thrust of the problem is logical, the epistemological dimension cannot be ignored, for in his discussion of divine knowledge Maimonides links the problem of attributes with the question of the knowability of God. Thus he claims that the terms "knowledge," "purpose," and "providence" are entirely equivocal in meaning when applied to God and to others because we cannot know the nature of his knowledge, purpose, and providence.[34] This is different from his earlier point that "knowledge," "power," "will," and "life" are to be taken as equivocal terms in relation to God and to others because otherwise they would damage divine unity. Understood in this manner, the problem of divine attributes concerns less the limitations of human language than the limitations of human knowledge. And this latter problem, if unresolved, raises serious questions for the project of philosophical theology.[35]

The first to point this out was Gersonides. It is noteworthy that his critique of Maimonides centers almost entirely on the latter's analysis of divine knowledge; when he refers to Maimonides' general analysis of divine attributes he is a bit more approving.[36] Gersonides argues that terms predicated of God cannot be absolutely equivocal because we do affirm things of God, such as that he is intellect-in-act. If the phrase "intellect-in-act" means something entirely different with reference to God than with reference to others, then we have no warrant to make the predication. Moreover, we cannot deny imperfections of God such as corporeality, because how are we to know what the equivocal term "corporeal" means when referring to God? As a fourteenth-century

Aristotelian, Gersonides did not seriously consider the possibility, advanced by modern readers, that Maimonides doubted man's ability to know God.[37] He simply felt that Maimonides was forced into a corner by his inability to reconcile biblical claims over divine knowledge with Aristotelian philosophical principles.

Gersonides solves the logical aspect of the problem in the following manner. To preserve divine uniqueness he argues that attributes are predicated of God "by priority" and of other creatures "by posteriority." While the sense of the attribute is analogous in both predications, no relation between God and his creatures is thereby implied. Maimonides had argued that if the sense is analogous, then the two entities described must fall under a common genus; this is denied by Gersonides. To preserve divine unity Gersonides argues that not all propositions of a subject-predicate form imply a real dualism of substance and attribute. There are logical subjects that do not refer to substances, and there are logical predicates that do not refer to attributes separate from their subjects.[38] This "nominalist" reading of attributes was not original to Gersonides,[39] although he was apparently the first to introduce it in Jewish philosophy.

❧ CRESCAS AND ESSENTIAL ❧ ATTRIBUTES

Although Crescas discusses Maimonides' theory under the rubric of divine unity, he is almost entirely concerned with the epistemological dimension of the knowability of God. Crescas reads Maimonides as claiming that negative attributes provide the believer with knowledge of God. This seems to him to be pointless: since any beginner in philosophy knows that the divine essence cannot be apprehended, and that affirmative attributes cannot be predicated without entailing multiplicity, of what advantage is the *via negativa* for knowing God? Maimonides' answer – that the more imperfections one denies of God, the clearer one's conception – is judged to be inadequate. If the general proposition that all predicates are to be denied of God is demonstrable, then what is gained by demonstrating the particular proposition for each attribute?[40] Moreover, as Crescas famously argues, to deny an imperfection of God implies, or presupposes, that we are tacitly affirming the corresponding perfection: if God is not ignorant, then we are implying, or presupposing, that he is knowing, which means that we are claiming to know something about God.[41]

Crescas' arguments show that in the early fifteenth century the question of attributes had shifted away from the logical issue of the signification of divine attributes, with its rich semantical implications, to the epistemological issue of knowledge of God and his attributes. Or to put this differently, the question was no longer how does our language refer to, or pick out, God, but how do we know the unknowable God? As a result, he attributes to Maimonides positions that the latter would never have taken. For example, Crescas criticizes Maimonides for denying that there is any relation between God and his creatures, or, to put this technically, that they do not fall under the same genus. Since God can be properly described as cause, then the relation of cause and effect must obtain between God and his creatures. But Maimonides himself affirms that God is the efficient, formal, and final cause of the world,[42] and he also calls him by such names as "creator," "intellect," "prime being," etc., which imply some sort of relation between God and the world. The real question that exercises Maimonides is: how should these terms be taken so as not to impugn divine unity and uniqueness? Crescas does not seem seriously perturbed by this question, but rather with the ability to make knowledge-claims about the divine essence.

Unwilling to claim that we really do know the divine essence, Crescas distinguishes between knowledge of essence (which remains impossible) and knowledge of essential attributes, for example, existing, one, knowing, willing. Since we are able to distinguish these attributes conceptually, it is impossible to identify them with the divine essence, but they are none the less, first, essential and, second, predicated affirmatively.[43] (There is some confusion in Crescas between "positive attributes," that is, attributes whose signification is positive, and "attributes predicated affirmatively." The attribute "eternal," for example, is an essential attribute predicated affirmatively of God, and yet it signifies "that which is ungenerated." Crescas regularly attaches negative signification to essential attributes, which makes his theory look closer to that of Maimonides than one would think.)

Crescas' distinction between essence and essential attributes drew strong critiques from Maimonideans such as Abraham Shalom[44] and Isaac Abravanel,[45] who thought the distinction incoherent. Crescas himself criticized a similar move taken by Christian theologians who distinguished between the divine essence and the persons of the Trinity.[46] Yet it is not difficult to see what Crescas wished to gain with his theory. As we have seen, Maimonides' theory, on Crescas' interpretation, undermines the basis for theology. A God who is indescribable is, it is claimed, unknowable. But Scripture and philosophy provide us with certain knowledge about God, so we must construct a theory of divine attributes which will sanction this knowledge, while at the same time answer the logical problems about divine unity. If God is knowable, argues Crescas, then he must have essential attributes. That Crescas holds out for the unknowability of the divine essence is a tribute to the influence of Maimonides, as well as to the influence of the Jewish philosophical arguments against the Trinity of which he approves.

Later philosophical treatments of divine attributes read like attempts to improve on Maimonides' treatment in light of the objections of Gersonides and Crescas. Thus Abraham Shalom suggests that negative attributes provide us with some positive knowledge about God: what we apprehend is that God is not ignorant of anything, but we do not know *how* God knows; the same is true of *how* he wills, etc.[47] Albo rejects the idea of essential attributes, but uses the negative signification of attributes to provide a positive content to our idea of God. He points out that not all attributes are negated in the same manner; although it is true that all negations are predicable of God, still no one "can negate any attribute unless he knows how the positive attribute applies to the thing characterized by it, and understands the aspect of perfection, as well as of defect which the attribute contains."[48] The meaning of "God is not living" is that he is not living in the same way that others are living.

With Albo we have come back full circle to Maimonides, who held that the problem is not so much our lack of knowledge about God as it is our incapacity to frame a conception of him without running into logical problems. Thus after Albo demonstrates that God is "an existent who is necessarily existent through Himself, having no cause, nor any one similar to Him . . . , the cause of all existents; their existence being preserved through Him, but His existence not being dependent upon theirs, or on anything else," he says that this does not constitute a definition or even a description about God, but rather a "conceptual understanding" (*havanah tziyyurit*) of Him.[49] Albo clearly wants to have philosophical knowledge of God, while avoiding the problems pointed out by Maimonides. He goes so far as to posit ad hoc a principle of divine perfection that allows him to predicate attributes, positively or negatively, in so far as those predications do not imply anything defective about God. While this move is suspect from a logical point of view, it shows to what lengths Albo will go to justify philosophical knowledge about God.

❧ CREATION VERSUS ETERNITY OF ❧ THE WORLD

Jewish philosophers of the fourteenth and fifteenth centuries were familiar with three major positions on the origin of the world: temporal creation of the world ex nihilo (Maimonides, al-Ghazālī); eternal emanation of the world out of God (al-Fārābī, Avicenna); and eternal production of the world by God (Averroes). From Maimonides and

Averroes they learned of the Aristotelian theory of the eternity of the universe, as well as the Platonic theory of creation from pre-existent matter. These positions were subjected to critical examination, which, in the case of Crescas, included a reassessment of fundamental concepts of Aristotelian physics. As a result, the discussions concerning creation contain some of the most interesting treatments of time, matter, motion, and infinity that are to be found in medieval Jewish philosophy.

The creation issue had important theological implications, because a philosopher's position on the origin of the world was directly related to his views on the relationship of God to the world. Maimonides, for example, found it difficult to square the hypothesis of an eternal world with the concept of an omnipotent and willing God. Yet he also felt that the Aristotelian arguments for the world's eternity were irrefutable, since he considered Aristotle's physical principles to constitute the best scientific explanation of the world. His way out of this dilemma was to claim that Aristotle's arguments fail as conclusive proofs because they are valid for the world only as it exists in its present state; they are inapplicable in its nascent state. He argued that the creation/eternity antinomy cannot be settled on the basis of physical theory, but only through an appeal to the nature of God: unless the world was created ex nihilo as the result of divine will, God does not possess complete mastery over natural laws, thereby rendering miracles impossible – which is patently opposed to any reasonable interpretation of Scripture. In order to make this move philosophically plausible Maimonides found evidence for God's inscrutable will in anomalies of nature, such as the differing movements of the heavens, and the differences in the stellar configurations, which are inexplicable on Aristotle's principles. One might say that, according to Maimonides, God created ex nihilo an Aristotelian world with just enough traces of divine will within the heavens to convince us of its createdness.[50]

Owing to Maimonides' authority and prestige, the belief in the temporal creation of the world ex nihilo eventually became a fundamental doctrine of philosophical Judaism; versions can be found in Albo,[51] Arama,[52] Abravanel,[53] and others. But this was not the case for most of the fourteenth and early fifteenth centuries. Radical Aristotelians like Albalag and Narboni followed their master Averroes in arguing that the world was eternally produced by God as first cause. According to Albalag, the Aristotelian belief in the eternity of the world is nothing more than the belief that its production is eternal, and that there is no time in which it is not produced.[54] Narboni argues that the eternity of God is linked to the eternity of the world, for the one produces at all times the other.[55] Both Albalag and Narboni provided exegeses of Genesis conducive to their claims.

Gersonides disagreed with Maimonides' claims, both that the

creation of the world was indemonstrable and that the world was created ex nihilo. In arguing against the first claim he appealed to some of the very phenomena that Maimonides used to support his thesis. For example, as we saw above, Maimonides considers the differing motions of the stars and celestial bodies as anomalies in nature that can be "explained" only by reference to God's impenetrable will. Gersonides uses similar phenomena as evidence of design, but he provides teleological explanations for what Maimonides considered inexplicable. His major argument for the creation of the world is teleological. That every thing has a purpose is taken as evidence for existence of a supreme intellect who brings into being the world according to a supreme plan.[56] Gersonides' deep conviction that all phenomena, celestial and sublunar, have discoverable ends is a leitmotif that runs throughout his writings.[57]

Gersonides finds fault both with the Maimonidean view that the world was created out of nothing and the Platonic view that the world was formed out of chaos. Steering a middle course, he posits a "preexistent"[58] body that is devoid of all forms, upon which God, in the sole act of creation, imprints two forms: a lower form, which transforms the inferior part of the body into a potential for receiving the four elemental forms, and a higher form, which transforms the superior part into the "quintessence," the matter of the celestial bodies. (The remnant of this primordial body, also called "the body that does not preserve its shape,"[59] serves as a buffer between the celestial spheres to prevent one from transmitting motion to the other.) After this solitary divine act, which is consequent upon the divine will, the world operates according to the divine plan through the instrument of nature.[60]

Of course, Gersonides had to refute the Aristotelian arguments for the eternity of the world, and he uses the same general strategy proposed by Maimonides, namely, to claim that principles that plausibly apply to partial generation within the world do not necessarily apply to the absolute generation of the world. But, unlike Maimonides and Crescas, Gersonides does not use this argument to foster an attitude of total skepticism with respect to the origin of the universe. He wishes rather to hold fast to *some* Aristotelian principles that will apply to absolute generation as well as to partial generations, such as the necessity of positing something corporeal to serve as the substratum for generation.[61] Gersonides' willingness to allow exceptions weakens his general refutation, and so it is not surprising that he undertakes to refute each Aristotelian argument on its own merits.[62] As is often the case in Gersonides' writings, these arguments show no fundamental break with Aristotelian physics; on the contrary, they tend to leave the reader with the impression that a correct, or more precisely a corrected, version of Aristotelian principles entails the createdness of the heavenly bodies, time, and motion.

By contrast, Crescas' arguments against Aristotle are much more destructive of Aristotelian concepts than are Gersonides'. For example, Aristotle had used his principle of the impossibility of a vacuum to argue for the eternity of matter; he reasoned that for matter to be generated out of nothing, its place would previously have been occupied (absurdly) by a vacuum. Gersonides accepts this line of reasoning and uses it to support his hypothesis of the pre-existent body that is devoid of all forms.[63] Crescas, on the other hand, rejects it by arguing that *nothing* exists before creation since dimensions are created by God. Now this argument, which is used by Aquinas[64] and Abravanel,[65] says nothing about the principle of the impossibility of the vacuum, only that this principle cannot be used as an argument against creation out of nothing. But Crescas goes further by arguing for the necessity of a vacuum, which he understands as an incorporeal extension or magnitude;[66] in fact, the world is created within a vacuum, understood in the sense of *space* free of bodies.[67]

❧ ETERNAL CREATION ❧

Crescas' own theory of creation sees the world as eternally emanated from God by virtue of the eternal divine will. What creation out of nothing means is that everything that exists – whether material or formal – proceeds from God.[68] Creation is an eternal process because otherwise there would have to be a moment in which the world's existence is emanated, and another moment in which its continued existence is emanated. Because each moment is an equal candidate for the world being created at it, the world is created at all moments. Moreover, God's will and his intellect coincide, so that in eternally thinking the world he eternally wills it into being, *will* being defined as "nothing but the love of the willer for that which he wills."[69] This is an important point, not only because this notion of will is new to the Jewish tradition, but also because of its emphasis on divine love as a metaphysical principle.

Although Crescas generally advocates an eternal creation theory, he attempts to reconcile this with the traditional view that the world is generated at a definite instant.[70] His attempt amounts to the suggestion that this world could have been preceded by other worlds, and that other worlds may succeed it. Scholars have been puzzled by this apparent about-face, but it contains no fatal blow to the theory of eternal creation, provided that one views the successive creation of worlds as one eternal act of continual creation. In any event, there is no evidence that Crescas seriously rejected eternal creation. After all, Crescas goes to some length to refute Gersonides' argument against continual creation, and his points are at least consistent with his dominant position. His medieval successors, all of whom reverted to a Maimonidean theory of creation, understood him to adhere to a position of eternal creation.

❧ CHOICE, WILL, AND MORAL ❧ RESPONSIBILITY

Aristotelian doctrine and traditional Jewish teaching differed on many things, but they agreed on the fundamental incompatability of involuntariness and moral responsibility. If human actions are involuntary, if they are not "up to us," then praise or blame is inappropriate (Aristotle), as is divine reward and punishment (Maimonides). In this Jewish philosophers were influenced not only by the Jewish legal tradition but also by the discussion of the Islamic theologians and philosophers.[71]

Until the fourteenth century, most Jewish philosophers appeared to be uninterested in or unaware of the metaphysical dimensions of human action, especially with the problem of "freedom of the will." In fact, the phrase is inappropriate for thirteenth-century Jewish philosophy for at least three reasons: first, it conjures up the un-Aristotelian notion of a faculty of the will distinct from the intellect; second, the will's alleged freedom is often taken to imply the very mysterious idea that human choice leading to action is uncaused; and third, *bechira* ("choice") and *efshar* ("contingency"), rather than *ratzon* ("will") and *chofshi* ("free"), are the Hebrew terms used most frequently in these discussions. All of these reasons were due to the influence of Aristotle. Maimonides, for example, asserts strongly the contingency of human actions, while holding at the same time that choices are caused.[72] For him the greatest threat to the contingency of human action is not the fact that our choices are caused, but rather that they are fated or predestined by the movements of the heavenly bodies. Jewish philosophers like Maimonides find the necessary condition of moral responsibility not to be freedom of will but rather real choice and the voluntariness of actions.

❧ THE FOURTEENTH-CENTURY ❧ DEBATE OVER DETERMINISM

The first Jewish philosopher to challenge the prevailing Aristotelian picture was Abner of Burgos, who assumed the name of Alfonso de Valladolid when he converted to Christianity. Combining a strict determinism with a belief in the primacy of the will over the intellect, Abner defined a voluntary agent as one who can, by his nature, equally perform one of two alternatives, that is, one who is not constrained by his nature, or by virtue of himself, to perform just one alternative. But that agent has no control over what he does or refrains from doing. What causes him to pursue one alternative and not the other is a combination of the motivating stimulus (sense image, cognition, or "intelligible imagination"), which stretches back in a causal chain to the movement of the spheres, and the imaginative faculty; this conjuction yields a new assent which Abner calls the "complete will." So actions are voluntary in so far as they are the product of a will, but completely determined in so far as the will is part of a rigid causal chain. If there are various outcomes, it is only because the will can be determined in various ways.[73]

Although it appears that our deliberations are "up to us" and undetermined, this is merely an illusion, planted within us by God in order that we should continue to act. It was part of the deity's providential design that humans should be ignorant of the causes that operate on them, and of what lies in store for them. Abner does not deny that human deliberation is efficacious; on the contrary, it is efficacious precisely because it forms an intermediate link in a causal change. But he does reject the Aristotelian idea that our deliberations are not predestined. These two propositions – that everything is predestined, and yet effort is not thereby rendered otiose – form the gist of Abner's contribution to the debate.

The Aristotelian side was defended by Isaac Pollegar and Moses Narboni. Pollegar, a former friend and a disputant of Abner, advances his arguments in the form of a dialogue between an astrologer and a sage. This is in itself worthy of note; Pollegar, like others in the Judeo-Arabic philosophical tradition, saw the question of determinism mainly within the context of the claims of astrology. Yet Abner's determinism seems to be motivated as much by theological considerations, such as divine omnipotence and omniscience, as by astrology. In fact, the apostate Abner portrays himself as the defender of the faith against the heresies of the Aristotelians; he maintains that Pollegar's arguments, if correct, would refute not only astral determinism but divine knowledge of particulars and accidents.[74] Although the theological aspect of the debate over determinism had a long history, and could have been known to Jewish philosophers from the writings of al-Ghazālī, it is likely that Abner was more aware of scholastic discussions, which provided the framework for his approach, than was Isaac. Thus, the debate between Abner and Isaac is not merely a debate between apostate and Jew, or even between a determinist and a libertarian, but also between the new scholastic-influenced framework of Jewish philosophy and the older Islamic one. The question merits further study.

Pollegar marshals many of the familiar arguments against astrology, but he also brings some general arguments against determinism. Thus, to Abner's notion that the contingency of choice is only epistemic, he replies that "all things visible deny this; it is simply incredible that all my acts are necessarily determined and decided in advance without my thought, my reflection, or my deliberation having a real input in their production."[75] This point, made also by Narboni,[76] does not constitute a conclusive refutation of the determinist. After all, Abner is as aware as Pollegar that we believe ourselves to be in control of our actions, yet he argues that this belief is an illusion. One best interprets Pollegar as following a general Aristotelian strategy of argumentation in which one is not required to answer the skeptic with an irrefutable argument. Rather, one need only answer him or her with an argument that one sincerely believes to be true.[77] Pollegar takes the experience of being in control of one's actions as fundamental, and feels no theological constraint to explain it away as illusory.

Both Pollegar and Narboni argue that Abner's determinism collapses fundamental metaphysical distinctions between the necessary and the possible,[78] and between the natural and the accidental.[79] Abner's response, as related by Pollegar, is to distinguish between things that are necessary by their very nature and those that are possible by nature, yet necessitated by their cause. This distinction has roots in Aristotle's logical distinction between absolute and hypothetical necessity, and in Avicenna's metaphysical distinction between existence that is necessary per se, and that which is possible per se but necessary with respect to its cause. Yet Abner refers to possible particulars, claiming that they are necessitated to exist at a certain time but possible in their nature. He cites the example of a lump of wax, whose shape at every instant is determined, but which retains the possibility to receive shapes. So, too, prime matter possesses an eternal possibility because of its eternal existence, even though the particular state-of-affairs at t is necessitated by its cause. With this he wishes to uphold the eternal contingency of future particulars, while maintaining at the same time that they are temporally necessitated, and hence foreknown, by God. We shall examine the problem of contingency and foreknowledge presently; here it is sufficient to note that Pollegar limits what Abner calls "eternal contingency" to prime matter, and argues that all contingency is removed from a particular once it has become actual. Something that is determined to exist in a certain way cannot be called "possible."[80] This position is held by other Jewish philosophers of the period such as Gersonides, Narboni, and ibn Kaspi, and it is a legacy of Islamic

Aristotelianism; so is the view that connects possibility (contingency) with potentiality and gives to both a temporal interpretation.

∾ DIVINE OMNISCIENCE AND ∾ CONTINGENCY

The contingency of human choice and action has implications for divine omniscience, especially if it is claimed that God foreknows events that are connected with such choice. The conundrum was familiar from ancient times: if God knows what Dinah will do tomorrow, and God is infallible, then is Dinah able to do otherwise? If she is not, then does this mean that she is determined now to do what she will do tomorrow? And how, then, can she be held responsibile for her actions? On the other hand, if she is able to do otherwise, then how can God's putative knowledge be considered genuine? The conundrum belongs to a group of problems that arose from assuming that God knows particulars, a natural assumption for religious thinkers, and so it is not surprising that virtually every medieval Jewish philosopher had something to say on the subject. Maimonides had argued that we are obliged to believe both in divine omniscience, including knowledge of future events, and in the contingency of human action, despite our inability to provide a philosophical explanation that will reconcile the two. In effect, he argued that the conundrum is a pseudo-problem that arises from an insufficient appreciation of the radical uniqueness of divine knowledge.[81] His immediate Jewish successors, however, saw the conundrum as real; since they were committed both to upholding divine omniscience and human contingency, they were forced to reinterpret those concepts in such a way as to reconcile them.

Averroists like Albalag and Narboni interpreted divine knowledge in such a way as to exclude God's knowledge of particulars. In so far as events are considered particulars, this implies that God lacks historical knowledge. Albalag and Narboni argued that God knows himself, and through this self-knowledge knows the world in a way that is vastly different from how we know it. It is the knowledge that the agent has of its action, and, in the case of God, it is through this knowledge that the world exists. Accordingly, since everything that exists is from God, everything is known by God.[82] So far, these formulations are general enough to be embraced by more theologically conservative thinkers such as Maimonides. Yet they mask an epistemic and metaphysical bias against the particular that is a hallmark of medieval Aristotelianism, especially in its Averroist version. For most Aristotelians, genuine knowledge is of the universal, the necessary, and the permanent in nature, and not of the concrete particular, the possible, or the transient.

A knowledge that includes particulars would be inferior to one that does not, and so it is inconceivable that God knows particulars. It should be pointed out that this conclusion is not made explicitly by Albalag or Narboni. They prefer the positive formulation that God, in knowing himself, knows everything that exists.

Gersonides proposes a less radical theory than his Aristotelian contemporaries in Provence: God knows both universals and particulars, the latter, however, not qua particulars but "from their universal aspect," as instantiations of rules.[83] Though not explicit, the argument for God's knowing particulars in this manner can be pieced together from several of his statements: God, in knowing himself, knows the intelligible order of reality, which includes all the rules by which the universe operates. Now on Aristotelian principles, if there is a rule that describes a permanent class of individuals, then that rule must be instantiated; in the case of God, whose knowledge is productive, God can justifiably be said to know not only the rules that apply to the world (universals), but also the instantiations of the rules (particulars in their universal aspect).

One can raise several objections to this account. First, it appears that Gersonides' argument is insufficient to prove that God knows the instantiations of rules; at best he knows only *that* these rules are instantiated. Gersonides would reply, "If by 'knowing' you mean something like 'being acquainted with,' then you are correct; God cannot be acquainted with individuals in this manner because he lacks perceptual apparatus. But true knowing is more like 'understanding' than 'being acquainted with'; one understands Dinah by understanding what makes her tick, which are the rules under which she operates. These rules utterly exhaust what is knowable about her." For Gersonides:

S knows $x =_{df.}$ *S* understands the rule(s) that explain x

This is not a characteristic solely of divine knowledge, but of knowledge in general. If I know every rule that applies to an arbitrary individual of a certain type, and I then become (perceptually) acquainted with one such individual, I have not added to my knowledge about that individual. One might wish to claim that I now know that I can apply my knowledge to this particular individual. But, for reasons that go beyond the scope of this chapter, Gersonides would reject this as well.

The second objection to Gersonides' account is that much of human activity does not appear to be governed by rules, at least rules governing the species as a whole. Thus, the occurrence of speaking or writing within the human species can be explained with reference to human rationality, but not the occurrence of bouncing a basketball or that of striking one's neighbor. Aristotelians could write off these activities as non-essential, hence, not strictly human, and unworthy of divine knowledge. But it seems counter-intuitive to exclude so much of what humans do from the scope of divine science. Moreover, there is an incredible variety of these seemingly non-essential activities, which, to believe the Aristotelians, amount to nothing at all.

Gersonides attempts to solve this problem by claiming that:

> Accidents (transient occurences, events, properties) are explicable, hence knowable

– the explanations making reference to astrological rules. Thus, a particular evil befalls Peter at time t because that time was not propitious for people like Peter. One might say that the sort of astral configuration instantiated at t adversely influences members of Peter's nativity-class. Peter's misfortune is explicable, hence knowable, by any good astrologer, a fortiori by God. This significant move enables Gersonides to expand the scope of knowledge to include *all* of human activity, non-essential as well as essential.[84] Virtually everything that happens to humans is, in principle, explicable with reference to either the laws of nature (physics) or the laws of astrology. In effect, Gersonides divides the human species into subgroups, each with its own "nativity-rule." Astral causality operates identically on individuals with the same nativity, influencing their dispositions, temperaments, and even thoughts. In most cases astral causality is sufficient to determine human actions.

Does it follow that all human activity is determined? This would be an odd conclusion, if only because of Gersonides' reputation as the libertarian par excellence of the fourteenth century. He is generally understood to hold that while most human actions are determined by astral causality, occasionally one freely chooses to leave this causal nexus. All that God knows is what action someone will probably take, yet his knowledge is incomplete because one could choose otherwise. If this interpretation were correct, then Gersonides would be open to Crescas' criticism that God has no foreknowledge of the people Israel, because their history can be traced back to the free choice of Jacob to dwell in Egypt.[85] But, in fact, the interpretation is incorrect on two grounds: it makes particular events into putative objects of knowledge, which is explicitly rejected by Gersonides, and, more importantly, it fails to recognize that rational choice is not "free" in the sense of "uncaused." All human actions are caused, and all human actions are explicable. But humans, because they are rational animals, can act according to their native temperament (astral causality) or according to intellect (rational causality). In cases of conflict, the stronger causal force will produce the result. Gersonides is indeed an indeterminist, not because he believes in random or uncaused events but because he holds that there is no (second-order) rule that determines how individuals of a certain nativity-group will choose in certain situations. It is up to humans, with the aid of the divine law, to control their base impulses, and to choose according to reason. This power is given to humans by virtue of their being rational.

Despite their differences, Albalag, Narboni, and Gersonides all denied that God knows particulars qua particulars. Since they did not resolve the omniscience/choice conundrum in a way that preserves the commonsense notion of foreknowledge – prior knowledge of particular events – their solutions were condemned by the theologically conservative philosophers of fifteenth-century Spain. Gersonides' treatment in particular aroused the ire of Crescas, Arama, Abravanel, and, in Italy, Judah Messer Leon, who attempted to have Gersonides' *Commentary on the Pentateuch* banned on account of it.[86] These later thinkers affirmed divine knowledge of particulars, and so, in order to solve the conundrum, they argued either that foreknowledge does not remove possibility or that divine knowledge is radically different from human knowledge. This conservative approach can be seen as a dialectical reaction to radical Aristotelianism or as a theological entrenchment because of the precarious political and religious position of the Jews within Christian Spain. But it may also be the result of the scholastic milieu, in which the doctrine of divine knowledge of particulars qua particulars was taken for granted by the fourteenth century.

CRESCAS' DETERMINISM AND ITS DETRACTORS

No consideration of determinism and choice would be complete without mentioning the views of medieval Jewry's most famous determinist, Chasdai Crescas. It is often said that Crescas' determinism stems from his need to provide a coherent philosophical explanation for divine foreknowledge of particulars. But he argues that foreknowledge of particulars implies nothing more than logical determinism: since God foreknows future possibilities, including how one will choose, that choice is necessitated, but only in the sense that, if God knows it, then it must be true. In other words, the necessity is conditional on God's knowledge. But this does not remove the intrinsic possibility of choice, no more than knowledge of the present negates the possibility of choice. So, causal determinism is not a necessary condition for divine foreknowledge.[87]

Nevertheless, Crescas is a causal determinist, and his determinism represents a return to the determinism of Abner of Burgos, who influenced him greatly.[88] Like Abner, he argues that all actions and events are part of a rigid chain of cause and effect, and yet this does not negate the possibility of choice. Like Abner, he sees commandments and prohibitions as motivating causes of the Jew's actions, and reward and punishment as the necessary consequences. Like Abner, he argues that humans are ignorant of the causes that necessitate their choice. And, finally, like Abner, he suggests that these ideas should not be disseminated to the multitude, who may use them as excuses for inaction and lazy behavior. But there are at least two important differences between the fourteenth-century apostate and the fifteenth-century champion of orthodox Judaism: first, Crescas is much less willing than Abner to consider an action voluntary if one is coerced into doing it. Abner's position implies that a person who assents under torture to performing an action does so voluntarily, despite the obvious coercion. And second, Crescas stresses that the reward for performing a commandment depends upon the quality and nature of the inner assent to perform it, just as the punishment for a transgression depends upon the mental attitude surrounding it. These inner assents and attitudes are themselves causally determined, and they, in turn, determine the degree of reward and punishment.[89]

Crescas' determinism, like his theory of eternal creation, brought forth strong denunciations by Arama[90] and Abravanel.[91] The incompatibilism of determinism with moral responsibility was too ingrained within Jewish tradition for Crescas' interpretation to attract adherents. Not surprisingly, his fifteenth-century successors returned to a more traditional Maimonidean attitude that defended the contingency of choice, while at the same time upholding divine knowledge of particulars.[92]

❧ NOTES ❧

1 By "Hebrew philosophy" I mean philosophy that was written in, or translated into, Hebrew. There is actually an unbroken tradition of Hebrew philosophy from the Middle Ages until the present, but after the expulsion from Spain its size and influence wanes.

2 Sirat 1985, pp. 431–56, lists over a hundred Jewish philosophers from the thirteenth to fifteenth centuries.

3 See Pines 1977, for the classic statement on behalf of scholastic influence.

4 See Steinschneider 1956.

5 See Rosenberg 1984.

6 Maimonides, *Guide* 1.50: p. 111 (Pines, with modifications).

7 In his commentary to *Guide* 1.50 Moses Narboni relates an incident in which, as a youth, he heard a preacher criticized for claiming that there can be false *emunot*. This is an important indication that as late as the early fourteenth century in Perpignan the notion of *emunot* as truth-bearers was controversial. See Rosenberg 1984, p. 273.

8 See Manekin 1990, pp. 131–2.

9 Rosenberg 1984, p. 277.

10 Philosophers like Narboni and ibn Kaspi read Maimonides in the same light. For the medieval esoteric reading of Maimonides, see Ravitzky 1981, pp. 87–123.

11 Gersonides, *Wars of the Lord*, introduction: pp. 94–5 (Feldman).

12 Gersonides, *Wars of the Lord* 2.4: pp. 44–5 (Feldman).

13 Gersonides, *Wars of the Lord* 1.12–13: pp. 218–25 (Feldman).

14 Narboni, *Commentary of Ḥayy ibn Yāqẓān* fol. 57b, cited in Hayoun 1989, pp. 212–13.

15 See Kellner 1986, pp. 83–195.

16 According to Abravanel (*Peirush ʿal ha-Torah* to Exodus 25.10: 252b), all Jews should spend their days in meditating on the law, "either through reading it or through observing its commandments, for through [the law] they acquire their perfection and happiness." Similar statements can be found in Albo, *ʿIqqarim* 3.28: pp. 260–8 (Husik) and Arama, for which see Heller Wilensky 1956, p. 146. For Bibago, see below, p. 358.

17 So Maimonides' *Book of Commandments*, written in Arabic (the term uses the same root as *iʿtiqād*); in the *Mishneh Torah*, written in Hebrew, the commandment is phrased *ledaʿ*, "to know."

18 Crescas, *Or ha-Shem*, preface: p. 10 (Fisher).

19 Ibid., 2.5.5: pp. 219–20.

20 Ibid., 2.5.5: pp. 222–23. An entirely satisfactory account of Crescas' views on this issue has yet to be worked out; see the analysis of Ravitzky 1988, pp. 34–61, esp. 38.

21 Albo, *ʿIqqarim* 1.19: p. 65 (Husik); emphasis added.

22 Duran, *Magen Avot*, introduction, fol. 2.

23 Abravanel, *C. Guide* 1.50, in Maimonides 1960, pp. 69–70.

24 Arama, *Chazut Qashah* 2 (n.p.). Cf. Heller Wilensky 1956, pp. 63–7.

25 Sirat 1985, p. 398.

26 Bibago, *Derekh Emunah* 2.4: pp. 212–15 (Fränkel-Goldschmidt).

27 Ibid., 2.7: pp. 244–55. The editor points out that the view of *emunah* as assent to hidden things is similar to Aquinas' definition of *fides* in *De Veritate* 14.2.

28 Bibago, *Derekh Emunah* 2.5: pp. 222–7 (Fränkel-Goldschmidt).

29 Ibid., 2.5: pp. 222–3.

30 See Korolec 1982, pp. 636–9.

31 Bibago, *Derekh Emunah* 2.5: pp. 227–33 (Fränkel-Goldschmidt).

32 Ibid., 3.7: p. 286.

33 Maimonides, *Guide of the Perplexed* 1.50–60: pp. 111–47 (Pines).

34 Ibid., 3.20: pp. 480–4.

35 Maimonides' claim that the divine essence cannot be apprehended (*Guide* 1.58) straddles the boundary between logic and epistemology. The claim is often confused with the more sweeping thesis of the unknowability of God, a claim that Maimonides does not make in the section on attributes.

36 Gersonides, *Wars of the Lord* 3.3: p. 112 (Feldman), although here, too, he demurs. Gersonides' treatment of the logical dimension of the question of attributes is taken up in the next paragraph.

37 Pines 1979, pp. 99–100.

38 Gersonides, *Wars of the Lord* 3.5: pp. 112–15 (Feldman).

39 Wolfson 1977a, pp. 241–3.

40 Crescas, *Or ha-Shem* 1.3.3: p. 103 (Fisher).
41 Ibid., 1.3.3: p. 111.
42 Maimonides, *Guide to the Perplexed* 1.69: p. 168 (Pines).
43 Crescas, *Or ha-Shem* 1.3.3: pp. 112–13 (Fisher).
44 *Neveh Shalom* 12.1.3, cited in Wolfson 1977b, p. 323.
45 Abravanel, C. *Guide* 1.50, in Maimonides 1960, p. 72.
46 Crescas, *Sefer Bittul 'Iqqarei ha-Notzrim* 3: pp. 58–9.
47 Davidson 1964, pp. 38–9.
48 Albo, *'Iqqarim* 2.30: p. 200 (Husik).
49 Ibid., 2.1: pp. 35–6.
50 Maimonides, *Guide* 2.13–2.25: pp. 281–330 (Pines).
51 Albo, *'Iqqarim* 1.12: p. 117 (Husik).
52 Arama, *Aqedat Yitzhak* 1: pp. 8b–9a.
53 Abravanel, *Mif'alot Elohim* 1.3: pp. 15–27 (Genut-Dror); cf. Abravanel, *Principles of Faith*, pp. 34–6.
54 Albalag, *Tikkun ha-De'ot* 30: pp. 30–1 (Vajda).
55 Hayoun 1989, p. 139.
56 Gersonides, *Milchamot* 6.1.8–9: pp. 52ab–54ab (Riva di Trento).
57 This conviction is quite evident in Gersonides' treatment of the divine commandments in his commentary on the Pentateuch. He often gives teleological explanations to the *details* of the commandments, once again in contradistinction to Maimonides. See Touati 1973, p. 495.
58 "Pre-existent" cannot refer to temporal priority since time is created at the first instant. See Davidson 1987, pp. 42–3.
59 See Freudenthal 1986.
60 Gersonides, *Milchamot* 6.1.17: pp. 59ba–60ba (Riva di Trento).
61 Ibid., 6.1.4: p. 50ba.
62 For these arguments, see Touati 1973, pp. 208–42.
63 Gersonides, *Milchamot ha-Shem* 6.1.17: p. 60aa (Riva di Trento).
64 Aquinas, *Summa Theologica* 1.46 ad 4.
65 Abravanel, *Mif'alot Elohim* 4.3: p. 89 (Ganut-Daror).
66 Wolfson 1929, p. 62.
67 Crescas, *Or ha-Shem* 3.1.5: p. 314 (Fisher).
68 Ibid., 3.1.5: p 310.
69 Ibid., 3.1.5: p. 311.
70 Ibid., 3.1.5: p. 315.
71 For background, see Altmann 1981, pp. 35–64. As Altmann points out, Aristotle also frames the question of choice within a legal framework.
72 *Guide of the Perplexed* 1.48: pp. 409–13 (Pines). Both Pines 1960, p. 198, and Altmann 1981, p. 56, focus on a phrase which Pines translates "[the Deity] . . . has necessitated this particular free choice in the rational animal [i.e., man]," which leads them to refer to a deterministic strain within Maimonides. (Actually, Altmann speaks paradoxically of the "deterministic character of Maimonides' notion of *free* choice" (p. 57) because, following Pines, he translates *ikhtiyār/bechira* as "free choice".) Altmann points out that Maimonides appears to be no more "deterministic" than other Aristotelians.
73 Baer 1940, pp. 191–2.
74 Ibid., p. 191.

75 Pollegar, *Ezer ha-Dat* 3: p. 120 (Levinger).
76 Hayoun 1982, pp. 146 and 151.
77 See Lear 1988, pp. 94–5.
78 In the present context "possible" means "that which is neither necessary nor impossible," that is, "contingent."
79 Pollegar, *Ezer ha-Dat* 3: pp. 133–4 (Levinger); Hayoun 1982, p. 146.
80 Pollegar, *Ezer ha-Dat* 3: pp. 137–8 (Levinger).
81 Maimonides, *Guide* 3.21: pp. 484–5 (Pines).
82 Albalag, *Tikkun ha-De'ot* 42: pp. 64–9 (Vajda); Hayoun 1982, pp. 148–9 [Hebrew]; 159–64 [French].
83 The word used by Gersonides is *siddurim* ("patterns"). Precedents for this view have been found in ibn Ezra, Abraham ibn Daud, and Avicenna.
84 Although the accidental is knowable, it may not be that the random is knowable.
85 Crescas, *Or ha-Shem* 2.1.3: p. 138 (Fisher).
86 See Touati 1973, pp. 545–50 for these and other reactions.
87 Crescas, *Or ha-Shem* 2.1.4: p. 148 (Fisher).
88 See Baer 1940, pp. 204–6; cf. Ravitzsky 1988, pp. 169–175 for differences between the *Light of the Lord* and the *Sermon on the Passover*.
89 Crescas, *Or ha-Shem* 2.5.5: p. 226 (Fisher).
90 Arama, *Aqedat Yitzhak* 19, cited in Heller Wilensky 1956, p. 160.
91 Abravanel, *Nachalat Avot*, p. 179, cited in Ravitzsky 1988, p. 47; cf. C. *Genesis*, p. 241b.
92 See Bibago, *Derekh Emunah* 1.2: pp. 101–3 (Fränkel-Goldschmidt); Albo, *'Iqqarim* 4.3: pp. 12–24 (Husik); Arama, *Aqedat Yitzhak* 15: p. 115a; 19: p. 136a; Abravanel, *Peirush 'al ha-Torah* to Genesis 18:20: p. 241a.

❦ BIBLIOGRAPHY ❦

Texts

Abravanel, I. (1964) *Peirush 'al ha-Torah (Commentary on Pentateuch)* (Jerusalem: Arabel).
—— (1982) *Principles of Faith (Rosh Amanah)*, translated with an introduction and notes by M. M. Kellner (Rutherford: Associated University Presses).
—— (1988) *Mif'alot Elohim (Works of God)*, edited by B. Genut-Dror (Jerusalem: Reuben Mass).
Albalag, I. (1973) *Tikkun ha-De'ot (Improvement of the Opinions)*, edited by G. Vajda (Jerusalem: Israel Academy of Sciences and Humanities).
Albo, J. (1946) *Sefer ha-'Iqqarim: Book of Roots*, edited and translated by I. Husik, 5 vols. (Philadelphia: Jewish Publication Society).
Arama, I. (1849a) *Aqedat Yitzhak (The Binding of Isaac)* (Pressburg); Jerusalem rept.
—— (1849b) *Chazut Qashah (Stern Visage)* (Pressburg); Jerusalem rept.
Bibago, A. (1978) *Derekh Emunah (The Way of Faith)*, edited by C. Fränkel-Goldschmidt (Jerusalem: Bialik Institute).

Crescas (1990a) *Or ha-Shem (Light of the Lord)*, edited by S. Fisher (Jerusalem: Sifrei Ramot).

—— (1990b) *Sefer Bittul 'Iqqarei ha-Notzrim: The Book of the Refutation of the Principles of the Christians*, edited by D. J. Lasker (Ramat Gan and Beer Sheva: Bar Ilan University Press and Ben Gurion University Press).

Duran, S. (1785) *Magen Avot (Shield of the Fathers)* (Livorno); Jerusalem rept.

Gersonides (1560) *Milchamot ha-Shem (The Wars of the Lord)* (Riva di Trento); Jerusalem rept.

—— (1987) *The Wars of the Lord*, vol. 2, translated by S. Feldman (Philadephia: Jewish Publication Society).

Maimonides (1960) [1904] *Moreh Nevukhim (The Guide of the Perplexed)*, with commentaries of Efodi, Shem Tov ben Shem Tov, Asher Crescas, and Abravanel (Vilna); Jerusalem rept.

—— (1963) *The Guide of the Perplexed*, translated by S. Pines, 2 vols. (Chicago: University of Chicago Press).

Pollegar, I. (1984) *Ezer ha-Dat*, edited by J. Levinger (Tel Aviv: Tel Aviv University).

Studies

Altmann, A. (1981) "Free Will and Predestination in Saadia, Baḥya, and Maimonides," in *Essays in Jewish Intellectual History* (Hanover and London: University Press of New England), pp. 35–64.

Baer, I. (1940) *"Minchat Qenaot* and its Influence on Hasdai Crescas," *Tarbitz* 11: 188–206.

Davidson, H. A. (1964) *The Philosophy of Abraham Shalom: A Fifteenth-Century Exposition and Defense of Maimonides* (Berkeley: University of California Press).

—— (1987) *Proofs for Eternity, Creation and Existence of God in Medieval Islamic and Jewish Philosophy* (New York and Oxford: Oxford University Press).

Feldman, S. (1980) "The Theory of Eternal Creation in Hasdai Crescas and Some of His Predecessors," *Viator* 11: 289–320.

Freudenthal, G. (1986) "Cosmogonie et physique chez Gersonides," *Revue des Études Juives* 145: 295–314.

Hayoun, M. (1982) "L'Epitre du libre-arbitre de Moïse de Narbonne," *Revue des Études Juives* 141: 139–67.

—— (1989) *La Philosophie et la théologie de Moïse de Narbonne (1300–1362)* (Tübingen: Mohr (Paul Siebeck)).

Heller Wilensky, S. (1956) *The Philosophy of Isaac Arama* [Hebrew] (Jerusalem and Tel Aviv: Bialik Institute and Dvir).

Kellner, M. (1986) *Dogma in Medieval Jewish Thought* (Oxford: Oxford University Press).

Korolec, J. (1982) "Free Will and Free Choice," in *The Cambridge History of Later Medieval Philosophy*, edited by N. Kretzmann, A. Kenny, J. Pinborg, and E. Stump (Cambridge: Cambridge University Press), pp. 629–41.

Lear, J. (1988) *Aristotle: The Desire to Understand* (Cambridge: Cambridge University Press).

Manekin, C. (1990) "Belief, Certainty, and Divine Attributes in the *Guide of the Perplexed*," *Maimonidean Studies* 1: 117–41.

Pines, S. (1960) "Studies in Abu'l-Barakāt al-Bagdādī's Physics and Metaphysics," *Scripta Hierosolymitana* 6: 195–8.

—— (1977) "Scholasticism after Thomas Aquinas and the Teachings of Hasdai Crescas and his Predecessors," *Proceedings of the Israel Academy of Sciences and Humanities* 1 (10): 1–101.

—— (1979) "The Limitations of Human Knowledge According to Al-Fārābī, Ibn Bājja, and Maimonides," in *Studies in Medieval Jewish History and Literature*, edited by I. Twersky (Cambridge, MA: Harvard University Press), 1: 82–109.

Ravitzky, A. (1981) "Samuel ibn Tibbon and the Esoteric Character of the *Guide of the Perplexed*," *AJS Review* 6: 87–123.

—— (1988) *Crescas' Sermon on the Passover and Studies in his Philosophy* [Hebrew] (Jerusalem: Israel Academy of Sciences and Humanities).

Rosenberg, S. (1984) "The Concept of *Emunah* in Post-Maimonidean Jewish Philosophy," in *Studies in Medieval Jewish History and Literature*, edited by I. Twersky (Cambridge, MA: Harvard University Press), 2: 273–309.

Sirat, C. (1985) *A History of Jewish Philosophy in the Middle Ages* (Cambridge: Cambridge University Press).

Sorabji, R. (1983) *Time, Creation, and the Continuum* (Ithaca: Cornell University Press).

Steinschneider, M. (1956) [1893] *Die Hebräischen Übersetzungen des Mittelalters und die Juden als Dolmetscher* (Graz: Akademische Druck- u. Verlagsanstalt).

Touati, C. (1973) *La Pensée philosophique et théologique de Gersonide* (Paris: Minuit).

Wolfson, H. (1929) *Crescas' Critique of Aristotle* (Cambridge, MA: Harvard University Press).

—— (1977a) "Maimonides and Gersonides on Divine Attributes as Ambiguous Terms," in *Studies in the History of Philosophy and Religion*, edited by I. Twersky and G. Williams (Cambridge, MA: Harvard University Press), 2: 231–46.

—— (1977b) "Crescas on the Problem of Divine Attributes," in *Studies in the History of Philosophy and Religion*, edited by I. Twersky and G. Williams (Cambridge, MA: Harvard University Press), 2: 247–337.

CHAPTER 16

Levi ben Gershom (Gersonides)

Seymour Feldman

➤ LIFE AND TIMES ➤

We do not know much concerning the life of Levi ben Gershom (Gersonides), about which he was reticent. Born in 1288 in the Provence, where he lived all his life, he was a member of a prominent family; his father was a rabbinic scholar and one of his brothers was a physician. Perhaps Gersonides himself was also a physician; he may also have been a money-lender. His renown as an astronomer and mathematician brought him into contact with high-ranking Christian scholars and clerics connected with the Avignon papal court, perhaps even the Pope himself. Several of his scientific writings were commissioned by these scholars and others were translated into Latin for their use. On occasion Gersonides was able to use these connections with the Church to the benefit of his coreligionists. Among his local Jewish contemporaries he was highly respected for his biblical and rabbinic learning. He died in 1344. Whether he had any children is unknown.[1]

Probably the most prolific and versatile medieval Jewish scholar, Gersonides' writings encompass virtually the whole range of medieval secular and Jewish religious learning, with one exception, halakhah. Although his Torah commentary shows deep talmudic learning and sophistication, which earned him a good reputation among local Jewish scholars, Gersonides rarely wrote on talmudic matters as such. His main contributions to Jewish learning were his biblical commentaries – he wrote commentaries on all the books of the Bible except the later Prophets, Psalms, and Lamentations; a commentary of Isaiah is referred to by Gersonides (*Commentary on the Torah* 197c, 227b), but is not extant – and his philosophical-theological magnum opus, the *Wars of the Lord.* In pure philosophy, he commented upon many of Averroes' commentaries on Aristotle and wrote an independent treatise on logic. Finally, he wrote a number of mathematical and astronomical treatises, some of which were originally included in the *Wars* but now survive in separate manuscripts. Gersonides' astronomical contributions were quite significant, and have been studied recently by Bernard Goldstein[2] and others. But for the Jewish world and the history of Jewish philosophy, it is Gersonides' *Wars of the Lord* that is his most important legacy. It is here where his philosophy in general and his philosophy of Judaism in particular are found.

Gersonides' philosophical bibliography looks slight: Aristotle, Averroes, and Maimonides were his sole, philosophical primary sources. In fact, his knowledge of Aristotle was obtained primarily through Hebrew translations of Averroes' commentaries, as was much of his acquaintance with al-Fārābī and Avicenna, whom he cites but probably did not read first-hand. His references to the late Greek philosophers such as Alexander of Aphrodisias, Themistius, and John Philoponus were also via Averroes' commentaries. Nevertheless, since these commentaries were so comprehensive, Gersonides was familiar with and well-versed in almost all of the important issues in ancient and medieval philosophy as it was developed in the Arabic-Hebrew philosophical tradition. It is unlikely that he knew Latin: he refers to no Latin text or philosopher writing in Latin. His philosophical world is really the world of medieval Muslim Spain, despite the fact that he lived his whole life in southern France and could not read philosophical Arabic.

At the end of the thirteenth century, Jewish philosophical circles were faced with a twofold dilemma: first, the anti-philosophical, more specifically the anti-Maimonidean, reaction was beginning to be felt, especially in Spain and the Provence; second, the hebraization of Averroes' writings had forced Jewish thinkers to rethink the status of philosophy in general and the philosophy of Maimonides in particular. Although Gersonides rarely makes any specific references to the former problem, his major philosophical work, the *Wars of the Lord*, is in a sense a comprehensive and critical appreciation of the philosophies of both Averroes and Maimonides. Throughout this book Gersonides is engaged in a running debate with his two mentors, sometimes agreeing with one against the other, sometimes rejecting both. Averroes represents for Gersonides the Aristotelian tradition despite some individual differences among its advocates; Maimonides is the spokesman for those whose first allegiance is to the Torah but who use philosophy to defend it against the criticisms of the Aristotelians. In short, for Gersonides, Maimonides was primarily a theologian, a Jewish specimen of kalām, and Averroes was a *failasūf*, a disciple of Aristotle. Since Maimonides was acquainted only with some of Averroes' writings, and it would seem at the end of his life, a critical Jewish appreciation of Averroes was a desideratum. Gersonides accepted this challenge.

❧ CREATION ❧

Although the question of creation is discussed in the sixth and last book of the *Wars of the Lord*, it was probably the earliest philosophical issue that caught Gersonides' attention. It is quite clear from the number of pages that he devotes to this subject that it is the dominant theme in his philosophy. (Almost forty per cent of the *Wars* deals with creation.) Why was this problem so important for him? In the first place, like many of his predecessors, Gersonides believed that creation of the universe was not only a fundamental dogma of Judaism but a principle with which other key philosophical and theological ideas were linked. The belief in creation makes credible a number of other important principles, especially those more intimately concerned with the Jewish religion, such as the Torah and the End of Days. Second, in Gersonides' eyes this fundamental question had not been adequately answered, either by Averroes or by Maimonides. Averroes had concluded, agreeing with Aristotle, that the universe is eternal; Maimonides had claimed that although philosophy could not resolve this question, the Torah teaches creation ex nihilo, and this is what a Jew must accept. Gersonides rejected all these claims: neither eternity of the universe nor creation ex nihilo is true; nor is it the case that philosophy is unable to decide this issue. For Gersonides, one cosmological theory is true – creation out of eternal matter – and this theory can be philosophically proved. His strategy is as follows: first, he proves that the universe is created, that the eternity thesis is absurd; second, he proves that creation ex nihilo is false and that Plato's theory of creation and of eternal matter, suitably revised, is correct. Finally, he argues against the whole Aristotelian tradition that, although the universe had a beginning, it has no end. (Maimonides too believed this thesis, but did not provide any detailed philosophical discussion of it.) In short, Aristotle, Averroes, and Maimonides are wrong, although in different ways.

Given the large number of arguments Gersonides provides for creation, one would think that he did not believe he had proved it. But numbers can be deceiving. He firmly believed that the creation of the universe was provable and that he had proved it. It is possible to subsume his many arguments under three types: first, those that infer creation from some teleological facts about the universe; second, those that infer creation from some contingent facts about the world; and, third, those that conclude that creation is true because the theory of eternity implies an absurdity, namely, an actual infinite.

The first type is in an important sense a philosophical justification of the biblical verse, "the heavens proclaim the handiwork of the Lord" (Psalms 19:2). Gersonides claims that, first, heavenly bodies, which for Aristotle are eternal, exhibit teleological properties; and that, second, such properties imply that these bodies have been created. A teleological property in this context is a feature of a thing that is goal-directed; in particular, it is a property that expresses itself most explicitly in its activity or influences upon some other thing. Gersonides claims that the heavenly bodies exhibit teleological properties that prove they are literally "creatures." This is most evident in the case of the sun: its activities are most beneficial for terrestrial life. If it is objected that these benefits are just sheer accidents or chance phenomena, Gersonides quickly replies that Aristotle himself precludes such a reply, since he claimed that in the celestial domain there is no chance (Aristotle, *Physics* 2.8). Aristotle himself admits, indeed emphasizes, the teleological character of nature throughout his scientific writings. Now, Gersonides argues, either we say that these teleological features are due to chance, which we cannot in this case, or we admit that they *have been made on purpose*. Or, to use Gersonides' term, they are the products of the "activity of an agent" (*Wars* 6.1.7 and 9).

This line of argumentation is reinforced if we look at another sort of fact about the heavenly bodies: they exhibit properties that are not features necessitated by their essence. If we put our finger in the flame and get burned, we are not surprised since we expect, indeed know, that fire is *essentially* hot, and thus burns. Now, fire has other properties that are not essential, for example, its colors or smells. But these "accidental" features are not problematic in the case of fire because we can explain them in terms of its chemical constitution, its elements. But when we look at the heavenly bodies, we find ourselves at a loss to explain some of their properties. Consider the differences in illumination in Mars and in Venus: Venus emits a bluish light, but Mars a reddish light. Why is this so, if, as Aristotle insists, both planets have the same nature? Or, why does Saturn have rings (a fact not known to Gersonides or any other astronomer before Galileo) and Mars not? Aristotle's failed attempt to account for these astronomical anomalies had already been noted by Maimonides (*Guide* 2.24). But whereas for him these "irregularities" were only inductive evidence against Aristotle's doctrine of eternity, for Gersonides they amount to a decisive proof for creation (*Wars* 6.1.8). Aristotle's own teleological framework and strong commitment to a thoroughgoing causal account of nature require there to be no inexplicable facts, especially in the heavenly domain.

But there are such facts; thus, they *prove* that the world has been created.

Gersonides' third type of argument focuses upon the nature of the infinite, a topic that interested him as a mathematician as well as philosopher. He claims that the thesis of the eternity of the world entails the existence of an actual infinite or infinites of different sizes, neither consequence admissible within Aristotle's philosophy. Although this kind of proof has been rendered obsolete by modern mathematics, it is successful as an ad hoc argument against Aristotle, who claimed that, first, there is no actual infinite and that, second, the admissible, or potential, infinite magnitudes, such as time, motion, and divisibility, are all "equal," that is, no infinite is larger or smaller than another. Gersonides takes Aristotle at his word, but shows that, if he is right about the infinite, then he is wrong about the eternity of the universe.

Using an argument originally invented by Philoponus and developed in kalām, Gersonides tries to expose the absurdities inherent in the notion of infinite past time (*Wars* 6.1.11–12). Among his many arguments of this type there is one that is perhaps original with him; it is certainly the most interesting of them. Suppose, as Aristotle believes, that time is infinite in the past. Now this infinite interval is not empty: it is filled up with all kinds of events, especially motions, since, for Aristotle, time is an accident of motion. But each such event is *real*: it is a fact about the world that in a sense never goes away. To be sure, dinosaurs no longer exist, but they did. More important, some events of the past have or leave effects, not just traces. The destruction of the Second Temple by the Romans in 70 CE caused significant changes in the Jewish polity and religion, some of which are still present today. Although we like to think of the past as gone, nevertheless, it is present in so far as at least some of the events of the past affect us now. At any rate, the whole history of past time is filled up by, or saturated with, facts, all of which are real, and hence actual. But this means that if time were infinite in the past, then past time would be an *actual infinite*, whose possibility Aristotle denies. Aristotle's thesis of the eternity of the world turns out then to be inconsistent with his own physics! (*Wars* 6.1.10)[3]

More important than his affirmation of the provability of creation is Gersonides' negation of the traditional, almost orthodox, doctrine of ex nihilo creation, and his defense of a modified version of the Platonic cosmological model of creation from matter. Again, Maimonides' discussion set the stage for the debate. He had claimed that (1) the Torah view of creation is creation ex nihilo, and that (2) Platonic creation is compatible with the dogmatic content of the Torah, especially with the belief in miracles, but that (3) the Platonic theory has not been proved (*Guide* 2.25). Gersonides accepts (2), but rejects (1) and (3). He first proceeds to demonstrate that ex nihilo creation is false, indeed absurd; then he revises the Platonic theory by removing from it the errors that Aristotle had noted; and, finally, he shows how the Torah itself teaches creation out of matter.

Ironically, in this context Gersonides relies heavily upon Aristotle. Not only is creation ex nihilo counter-intuitive – after all, who has ever seen anything come into being literally out of nothing? – but this doctrine violates some of the more fundamental theorems of Aristotle's natural philosophy, taken here by Gersonides to be true. Consider carefully what ex nihilo creation commits one to. The picture is this: first there was absolutely nothing; then suddenly a material world exists, created by an incorporeal agent. Besides having to explain *how* an incorporeal agent can make a corporeal system from no pre-existing matter, the defender of this doctrine is faced with the problem of the vacuum, which in Aristotle's physics is impossible. A vacuum is, according to Aristotle, that which is empty of body (*Physics* 4.7). Accordingly, when the world was created, it was created *in* this empty space, which acts as a kind of "receptacle" for it. But not only was there an antecedent vacuum prior to creation, there still is one outside the world, since for Aristotle, and most medievals, the physical world is only finitely large. Indeed, since some of the defenders of creation ex nihilo admit that God could have made the universe larger or smaller than it actually is, they are implicitly assuming the existence of a vacuum in which this larger or smaller world "resides." But why stop? Since no region in this vacuum is more fitting to be the locus of the world than any other region, the world should be infinite, which it not only is not but cannot be. Thus, the doctrine of ex nihilo creation is committed not only to the existence of a vacuum prior to and after creation but to the existence of an actually infinite body, both unacceptable doctrines within Aristotelian natural philosophy (*Wars* 6.1.17). Maimonides then was wrong and Plato right, at least for the most part.

But if creation out of matter is the correct theory, we still need to know something about this matter. Gersonides claims that this original matter occupies the lowest level in the "chain of being." It is so formless that it "doesn't keep its shape." It cannot even be said strictly to have irregular motion, as Plato mentioned; for only formed bodies are capable of motion. The "divine craftsman," to use Plato's language, used this shapeless body to make this world. Some of it was made into heavenly bodies; some of it became the terrestrial domain. Indeed, some of it still remains in its pristine shapelessness between the heavenly bodies, facilitating their motions. In Genesis it says that God made the firmament, which for Gersonides is the domain of the heavenly bodies, "in the midst of the *waters*." Moreover, the Torah never says that the waters were created. If anything, Genesis 1:2 suggests that the waters were with God from eternity. So far from teaching creation ex nihilo, the Torah actually teaches that God created the physical universe out of some shapeless body, to which it refers by the term *vohu* (Genesis 1:2). Moreover, Gersonides claims that the miracles reported in Scripture are all described as a creation *from something*; Moses' *staff* became a snake, the gnats came from the *dust*, etc. To believe then in miracles does not require us to believe in creation ex nihilo. Just the contrary, not only is creation from matter consistent with Aristotle's physics, it is in addition compatible with the plain meaning of the biblical text.

A concluding point: this created world is everlasting. Again, Gersonides harkens back to Plato, who in the *Timaeus* makes the heavenly bodies generated but everlasting (*Timaeus* 41a-b). Actually, Gersonides goes further than Plato: whereas for Plato the heavenly bodies are everlasting because of divine will, for Gersonides they are literally incorruptible. After all, they are perfect and simple, possessing no internal compositeness or contrariety, and thus not liable to decay or disintegration. Moreover, why would God want to destroy them? Being perfect, they cannot be improved upon; being perfect, God also cannot improve upon the original creative act. So they endure ad infinitum. The world then for Gersonides had a beginning, but will have no end (*Wars* 6.1.16 and 27).[4]

❧ DIVINE NATURE AND HUMAN ❧ FREEDOM

Gersonides' strong defense of the doctrine of creation is at the same time a proof of the existence of God. This is why, unlike Maimonides or Aquinas, he gives no separate treatment of the question of God's existence. Although there is in Gersonides a proof for God's existence, it is almost an afterthought. Moreover, it is not the favored proof among many medieval thinkers, namely, Aristotle's argument from motion to the existence of an incorporeal unmoved mover. In fact, Gersonides explicitly rejects this argument, since he rejects its main premise – everything in motion is moved by another (*Wars* 5.3.6). Departing from Aristotle's physics in this regard, Gersonides favors the teleological argument found both in the Bible and in Plato: "the heavens proclaim the handiwork of the Lord" (Psalms 19:2; cf. Plato, *Laws* 10, 889–93). As we have seen, teleology serves as one of the proofs for creation. So Gersonides does not need an independent proof for God's existence. That the universe is created is *the* proof of God's existence.

Nevertheless, there is in Gersonides a "theology," a doctrine about God, especially about the divine attributes, one of the standard topics in medieval metaphysics. By the time Gersonides entered the debate, two different questions had been distinguished: first, how are we to understand the semantics and logic of divine attributes? and, second, which attributes in particular are most appropriately ascribable to God? Maimonides had given a radical answer to the first and more important of these questions: all divine attributes are best formulated and understood as negative attributes (*Guide* 1.51–60). Whenever we say in our prayers "God is one," we are to understand this formula as equivalent to "God is not non-one." Gersonides rejects this view. He discusses these issues in two separate books of the *Wars*: in book 3.3, which is devoted to the question of divine knowledge, he criticizes Maimonides' doctrine of negative attributes; in book 5.3.12, he discusses the specific attributes that are to be ascribed to God. The first of these questions is the more interesting and important one, for not only does he reject Maimonides' doctrine, but he proposes an alternative account of the logic of divine attributes.

Since Maimonides' solution to the dilemma concerning divine omniscience and human freedom presupposes his doctrine of negative attributes, Gersonides discusses this doctrine before he develops his own solution to the dilemma. In short, he wants to argue that the verb "knows" in "God knows that . . ." is not absolutely equivocal, as Maimonides claimed (*Guide* 3.16, 20–1). Suppose this were true; consider then the statement, "God has an outstretched arm." If Maimonides were to accuse the asserter of this statement of heresy, since taken literally it attributes corporeality to God, the would-be heretic could say that "arm" here does not mean the arm that humans have, but a *totally different* kind of limb. He would not be guilty of "corporealizing" God, since he makes it clear that the divine arm is *unique*. In general, Gersonides claims, *any* predicate could be asserted of God, if the predicate is understood to be asserted equivocally. If so, there would be no principle of exclusion in our theology: *any* attribute could be ascribed to God as long as it is indicated that we are speaking equivocally. Moreover, in negating a predicate of some subject, one must understand this predicate in the identical way as one understands it when affirmed of the subject; when one says, "this flower is not red," the term "red" has the same meaning as it has when someone says "this flower is red." Otherwise, we have a fallacy of equivocation, and the negation would not be a denial of the original affirmation. So, if "God is one" really means, as Maimonides claims, "God is not non-one," the term "one" in both sentences has to have the same meaning in order for the latter to be semantically equivalent to the former. Thus, "one" cannot be predicated equivocally in sentences about God. Besides being contrary to our customary religious language, especially in liturgy,

Maimonides' negative theology is logically defective, according to Gersonides.

Recognizing that he cannot fall back upon the opposite view, that attributes predicated of God have exactly the same meaning as when they are predicated of humans, Gersonides proposes a "middle view." Divine attributes are predicated according to the relation of priority and posteriority: when one says, "God exists," the term "exists" is neither univocal nor absolutely equivocal; rather, it is said of God in a prior sense, while it is said of Moses in a posterior sense. This relation has two aspects: first, it implies, at least for Gersonides, that God is in some sense the cause of Moses' existing; second, it connotes the more eminent or perfect character of the attribute in God. So in the original case of knowledge, when one says, "God knows..." and "Moses knows..." one is not using the term "knows" equivocally; rather, one is asserting that, although both God and Moses have different cognitive capacities and techniques, there is some feature common to their respective cognitive acts; otherwise, there would be no point in uttering these statements. To be sure, Moses did not know *all* that God knows; nor, in cases in which he did know what God knows, did he know it in the same way as God knows it. Yet, there must be something similar in their respective cognitive acts: for both Moses and God, $1474 \div 22 = 67$ is true, although Moses has to use a calculator, while God just "sees it" (*Wars* 3.3).[5]

Having disposed of Maimonides' general theory of divine attributes, Gersonides turns to the attribute of knowledge in particular. Does God have knowledge of what Abraham will choose to do on Mount Moriah *before* Abraham actually ascends it? For most medieval theologians, including Maimonides, the answer is yes, although they differ in their explanations of how this divine foreknowledge is compatible with Abraham's free will. The Aristotelian philosophers, however, deny that anyone, including God, has foreknowledge of free actions. After all, if God did know what Abraham would choose to do, why did he bother to "test" him? In trying to resolve the dilemma, Gersonides, unlike most of his predecessors and successors, assumes the dilemma to be genuine: there is a real incompatibility in claiming both that God knows what I am going to choose to eat tomorrow at 8 a.m. and that what I shall choose to eat tomorrow at 8 a.m. is a free choice. Gersonides accepts the logical force of the Aristotelian arguments against the compatibility of divine foreknowledge and free will. This means that, for him, God did not know what Abraham would choose to do when he commanded him to ascend Mount Moriah. It was truly an "open question." If God did know that Abraham was going to choose to sacrifice Isaac, then Abraham's choice was preordained and not free, and thus not meritorious. What makes the story so poignant and powerful is that Abraham *chooses* to kill his beloved son. If this choice were known in advance, it would have been necessitated; no real choice would have been involved.[6]

So if God does not have foreknowledge of future contingent events, is there any sense to the traditional concept of divine omniscience? There is, for Gersonides: God knows *whatever* is knowable. Future contingent events, actions done as a result of choice, are not knowable, for to know them is to annul their contingency. If these events are genuinely contingent, they are unknowable, even to God. Yet this does not make God ignorant; for God knows the general laws governing the world, including the laws true of human behavior. So, God knows that *in general* humans will not choose to sacrifice their (only) child; in addition, God knows it is possible, albeit extremely remote, that some father may choose to sacrifice his (only) child. But God has no knowledge of any particular person's choice. This latter does not fall within the domain of what can be known. Accordingly, the testing of Abraham was a *genuine* test.

DIVINE PROVIDENCE AND IMMORTALITY

For many medieval thinkers, the problem of divine providence was closely connected with that of divine omniscience. If God does know individuals as individuals, then there does not seem to be a problem about individual providence: those who deserve it will merit divine notice and care. But for some medieval philosophers, the problem was more complicated. Maimonides wondered whether every *individual* falls within the range of divine providence. And his answer is that it is only individuals in the *human* species who warrant divine providence. But, for Gersonides, the problem was aggravated by his own thesis that God does *not* know individuals as individuals. Does this imply that there is no individual human providence at all? Is divine providence entirely general, even for the human species as well? To advocate such a thesis would have committed Gersonides to a form of Aristotelianism that he was not prepared to accept. So some sort of reconciliation had to be found between his radical view about divine omniscience and his more conservative commitment to the biblical doctrine of individual human providence.

Gersonides' full treatment of this question is found both in the *Wars of the Lord* (book 4) and in his *Commentary on Job*. Like Maimonides, he recognized the philosophical dimensions of the book of Job and read it as a philosophical dialogue in which competing views concerning providence are advanced by its characters. He also agreed with Maimonides that individual providence extends *only* to human beings; for all other living species, providence is general: the natural order, especially the heavenly bodies, as created by God, guarantees the survival of each species in the animal and plant worlds. Particular members of such species are not "covered" by providence. Although he works within this Maimonidean framework, Gersonides' treatment of this topic is more detailed and systematic; in addition, his answer to the correlative question of theodicy – why do the righteous suffer? – has a particular flavor that is non-Maimonidean, perhaps even anti-Maimonidean.

Gersonides accepted the Maimonidean thesis that it is only the person who has attained both moral and intellectual perfection who merits providential concern. This follows from a simple syllogism:

1 Individual providence consists in a link between the individual and God.
2 The link between God and a human being is the intellect.

Therefore,

3 Individual providence is a function of intellectual achievement.

Although this doctrine does have an "elitist" aspect, it does capture the biblical and rabbinic idea that the saint is "dear to God" (Psalms 116: 15) and that only a wise man can be a saint (*Avot* 2:6). It also expresses the traditional Jewish emphasis upon learning and its appreciation of intellectual prowess and proficiency. But what about the obvious fact of human suffering, even of scholars? After all, Rabbi Aqibah died a martyr's terrible death. And what about innocents who are incapable of intellectual perfection? Should little children suffer and die because (ex hypothesi) they have not mastered Maimonides' *Guide*? There seems to be something wrong with this doctrine.

Gersonides is aware of these problems; indeed, he accuses Job's three friends of not being sufficiently empirical in their simple-minded replies to Job's complaints. Gersonides' response involves several distinctions. First, we have to recognize that not all goods and evils are *genuine* goods and evils. Gersonides discounts the wealth and pleasures of the haughty rich and the poverty and deprivations of the humble poor. All of these are material goods and evils, and as such do not matter. The only things that count are spiritual goods and evils. So one hour of intellectual enjoyment is superior to a life of sensual pleasure. Indeed, the rabbis recognized this when they said both that only the righteous enjoy "the splendor of the divine presence" and that there is no reward in this world for doing the commandments (*Qiddushin* 39b). True human happiness is to be sought and enjoyed when we are no longer tied to our mundane material existence, that is, after death.[7]

This traditional answer to the question – why do the righteous suffer while the evil prosper? – may satisfy the sage; but does it pacify the complaints of the parents of a child suffering from a painful and terminal disease? The innocent child seems to be abandoned, even by God. Is there any divine justice here at all? At this point, Gersonides provides an answer that is unavailable to the rabbinic and Maimonidean theodicies. The answer is found in his cosmology.

It will be recalled that, for Gersonides, the universe was created by God from formless matter, which is of "utmost imperfection." All natural evils, such as earthquakes and diseases, not only derive from this matter but are necessary consequences of it. Gersonides refers to this as the "necessity of matter": natural evils are ineliminable elements within the natural order. No matter how orderly and purposeful God made our universe, there is an irremediable residue of imperfection that surfaces in natural catastrophes and disease. God can no more eliminate such imperfection than square the circle or undo the past. Just as the latter are impossible, so is the former. Accordingly, the parents of the dying child should not doubt or curse God. God is not to blame, for there is nothing to be done. "The Rock! – His deeds are perfect; yea, all His ways are just" (Deuteronomy 32:4).

Gersonides' theory of providence already hints at his doctrine of immortality. Again, he is indebted to his predecessors in the Islamic-Jewish philosophical tradition, especially Averroes, but not slavishly. Indeed, he rejects much of Averroes' theory, but he works within a conceptual and linguistic framework that had been initially formulated by Alexander of Aphrodisias and elaborated upon by al-Fārābī, Avicenna, and Averroes. The major theme is that human immortality consists of the conjunction of unification of the human intellect with a supernal, immaterial intellect, the agent (or active) intellect. Its function, according to Aristotle, was to stimulate human thought; but in the hands of Avicenna and others the agent intellect assumed the additional roles of proffering to humans both secular knowledge and prophecy as well as being the efficient cause of natural generation. The "intellectualist" bias of this doctrine is patent, commensurate with the doctrine that individual providence is a function of intellectual perfection. The highest form of such providence is of course immortality, and this is reserved for those who are "attached to" and have become unified with the agent intellect. Although Maimonides is silent about the question of conjunction with the agent intellect, his doctrine of immortality is clearly intellectualist: it is the perfected intellect that becomes immortal, not the corporeal aspects of our personality, and certainly not our bodies.

Gersonides is highly critical of this doctrine of conjunction in virtually all of its forms, although he retains its intellectualist thrust.

Unlike Avicenna and others, he rejects the view that the human intellect is a substance, a subsistent entity that is capable of immortality. Like Alexander of Aphrodisias, he considers the human intellect to be a disposition, or capacity, of the human body to acquire knowledge. For many, this capacity is barely or never realized; for some, only partially. But, for a small group, it is actualized by means of their own cognitive abilities as well as by the assistance of the agent intellect. A cognitively perfected human intellect becomes the "acquired intellect." This alone is immortal, since the cognitions it consists of are themselves grounded in the agent intellect, which everlastingly exemplifies the rational order for the terrestrial domain. Since this plan is immutable and permanent, knowledge of it "participates" in its everlastingness. Our immortality then is identified with our intellectual capital.

But Gersonides steadfastly denies that this involves conjunction or unification with the agent intellect itself; although the agent intellect is the necessary condition for human cognition, one can never aspire to be "attached to" it, such that one becomes unified with it. Gersonides offers several different arguments against this thesis, but one point is especially noteworthy. If one could become unified with the agent intellect, there would be no longer any difference between Einstein and a high-school teacher of physics. In the agent intellect all become one. How then could immortality be individuated? Indeed, is there any justice in a theory of immortality that obliterates individuality? Here Gersonides takes a conservative stand and defends the traditional doctrine of *individual* immortality, although he formulates it within the medieval Aristotelian theory of the intellect.[8]

❧ PROPHECY AND MIRACLES ❧

So far Gersonides' philosophy seems to be religiously neutral. With the exception of the book on providence and the second part of book 6, the *Wars of the Lord* does not have a decidedly Jewish character. But Gersonides was not just a philosopher and scientist. Much of his intellectual career was devoted to biblical exegesis, which he pursued while he was writing the *Wars* as well as after he finished it. In his biblical commentaries one clearly sees not only Gersonides' Jewishness but a valiant attempt to discover his philosophical conclusions in the text of the Torah. Far from preaching any form of a double-truth doctrine or distinguishing between esoteric and exoteric levels of truth, Gersonides' commentaries on the Bible have the same philosophical content as does the *Wars*. The radical conclusions about divine cognition advanced in the *Wars* are found in his exegesis of the Binding of Isaac; the doctrine of creation from matter is present in his account of creation. Unlike Maimonides, he seemed to have a more optimistic attitude towards his audience. Yet, the Torah is the basis for Judaism, and it is not surprising to find in his commentary a more Jewish Gersonides, one who comments in detail on certain specifically religious concerns of Judaism.

One of these issues was the status and character of Mosaic prophecy, which for Jews is not only authoritative but unique as well, a thesis denied by both Christian and Muslim. Maimonides was at such pains to elevate Moses' level of prophetic achievement that Moses became almost a "son of God," an angel (*Commentary on the Mishnah, Pereq Cheleq*, principle 7). Gersonides, however, was not as obsessed with Moses as was Maimonides. Although he certainly believed in the uniqueness of Mosaic prophecy, which he understands and describes within the vocabulary of Maimonidean prophetology, Gersonides' account of prophecy in general and Moses' prophecy in particular have a somewhat different agenda. Consider first the location of his treatment of prophecy in the *Wars*: it is discussed along with the phenomena of dreams and divination. For Gersonides, prophecy is one among several types of extra-sensory perception. His main concern in book 2 of the *Wars* is to distinguish prophecy from divination, not Mosaic prophecy from ordinary prophecy. For Maimonides, on the other hand, divination was a form of idolatry; it had no relevance to prophecy. Moreover, prophecy for Gersonides was not primarily, as it was for Maimonides, a cognitive medium, especially for the transmission of truths that are allegedly inaccessible to human reason. To be sure, the prophet may receive theoretical knowledge in prophecy, but that is not the main purpose of prophecy; if the prophet does receive such knowledge, his understanding and formulation of it is no better than that of the philosopher, who also possesses the same knowledge. Indeed, it may even be *less* clear and precise. What is primary in prophecy is the predictive and, in Moses' case, the legislative functions. Now no one denied these roles, but Maimonides tended to de-emphasize them in his exaltation of the cognitive function, especially in Moses. For Gersonides, the uniqueness of Moses consists in his legislation: not only is he *the* lawgiver but the law he gave is everlasting, and it is everlasting because it is perfect and completely rational. It should therefore be expected that when he comes to the legal portions of the Pentateuch Gersonides will provide a detailed analysis of the laws, showing their internal logic and essential intelligibility. Indeed, it is the legislative side of Moses that for Gersonides distinguishes him from the messiah; the latter will have a wider audience than Moses and will perform a miracle that transcends all of those performed by Moses – the resurrection of the dead. Yet, because of the permanence of the Torah, Moses' status is unique; indeed, the uniqueness of Moses is itself a miracle.[9]

But what about miracles themselves? A biblical religionist must believe in them; otherwise, Maimonides claims, the Torah itself "falls." Yet, the belief in miracles is not philosophically respectable; after all, they violate the laws of nature. So what does a Jewish philosopher do with miracles, especially one who is an outstanding astronomer as well? Already in Maimonides one can detect an attempt to deflate the miraculous. Although he states that Judaism stands or falls with the belief in miracles, he does not want to give them undue attention or emphasis. Indeed, as some scholars have noted, Maimonides' attitude toward miracles is ambiguous and ambivalent. One thing does seem clear: Maimonides is not comfortable with the idea of a sudden ad hoc rupture of nature's laws. This is not the way God works. For Maimonides, miracles are somehow part of the laws of nature; they are programmed ab initio within the original plan of nature. In this way the immutability of God's will and nature's course is preserved.

Although this is a concern for Gersonides, he first addresses several other questions (*Wars* 6.2.9–12). Is the domain of miracles wide open? Can miracles occur anywhere? Who actually is the "agent" of miracles: God, an angel, or the prophet? Many religious people believe not only that God is the agent of miracles, but that he can do *anything*. After all, doesn't God stop the sun and the moon from moving for Joshua and the Israelites? Gersonides rejects both that God can do anything and that God is the direct agent of miracles. Miracles fall within the range of that which is possible in itself, although impossible relative to the standard laws of nature (*Commentary on the Torah* 69a, 74d). This immediately rules out situations such as undoing the past or an immaterial substance becoming a body. Such occurrences are impossible, since by definition the past is over and irreversible and the very essence of an immaterial substance is to be immutable. So far Gersonides' definition of the scope of miracles is not unique: Maimonides and others would have agreed; even the conservative Muslim theologian al-Ghazālī maintained that miracles cannot violate the laws of logic. But Gersonides further narrows the range of the miraculous when he claims that miracles cannot occur within the celestial domain (*Wars* 6.2.12). This means that the miracle of the sun's stopping for Joshua needs to be reinterpreted. The sun did not stop moving at all. It looked as if it did stop, at least to those who did not know any astronomy; for at high noon, when the battle took place, the sun *ordinarily appears* to halt since it is at its highest point in the sky. The miracle consisted in the victory being accomplished during the brief interval when the sun appears to be standing still.

In general, Gersonides "naturalizes" the miraculous, an orientation one already detects in Maimonides. Gersonides emphasizes the fact that the Torah describes miracles as being brought about through natural phenomena; for example, the splitting of the Sea of Reeds was caused by a "strong east wind." Indeed, as a general policy, miracles are effected in "the least strange way possible" (*Commentary on the Torah* 206, 68a, 69a-70b, 215b). In one passage Gersonides suggests that a miracle such as the transformation of Moses' staff into a snake is just the speeding-up of a natural process: eventually the wood decomposes and ultimately is transformed into the elements out of which a snake is generated. Nor are miracles sudden and unique eruptions into and contraventions of the laws of nature. There is a "law and order" to miracles, especially since they are providential and, for Gersonides, providence itself is lawful. But miracles are not entirely natural; otherwise they would not be miracles. They manifest a volitional character, like creation itself. But this does not mean that each miracle is individually willed into being at the time of its occurrence or at any time earlier. Just as the laws of nature were "programmed" in the physical system at creation, so too was the law of miracles "preset" at creation. Yet, unlike the view of some of the rabbis and perhaps also of Maimonides, this does not mean that miracles are individually predetermined to occur when they do occur. If this were true, then human freedom would be annulled. The law of miracles, like the law of nature, is general and has a conditional clause built into it: the splitting of the Sea of Reeds will take place if and only if certain conditions obtain, one of which (perhaps the most important) is that Pharaoh *chooses* to pursue the Israelites. Just as the laws of natural, or general, providence governed by the heavenly bodies can be contravened by human choices, so too the law of miracles is conditional. Miracles are lawful, and thus natural, but they are also contingent, and hence volitional.

But now we must ask, who is the real "agent" of miracles? God, an angel, or the prophet? Since the miracle occurs within the general system of nature, its agent must be someone who knows this entire system. No human then can be the cause of miracles, although one can be the instrument through which it is brought about. The agent of miracles must be either God or the agent intellect, for they alone have the requisite knowledge of the providential plan and order of this earthly domain. Although most people would be inclined to say that God is the agent of miracles, Gersonides refuses to go this route. The agent intellect is *the* cause of miracles. After all, it is the agent and cause of subhuman generation and development; and it is in addition the proximate cause of prophecy wherein many miracles are predicted. In short, the agent intellect is in charge of terrestrial providence (*Wars* 5.3). So it is no wonder that it is the proximate cause of miracles, which are in effect providential occurrences in the earthly domain.

One should, however, not think that the agent intellect is capable of momentary volitions, whereby it wills and performs the miracle at a particular moment for a specific person. Just as in prophecy so here, the occurrence of a miracle, like prophecy, is "impersonal." *Whoever* is qualified and worthy of receiving it receives it. The recipients of a miracle are those who are worthy of having the providential plan concretized or manifested through them. The agent intellect does not really do anything particular or temporal. That is why we do not pray to it to perform miracles. When miracles occur in response to a prayer, it is only because the individual (for example, Moses) exemplifies the *kind* of person for whom miracles are performed in certain conditions. Or, the law of miracles is instantiated in Moses' case because his actions, including his prayers, are the kinds of events that trigger or set into operation the laws of individual providence. In this sense the miracle is ordered and determined, although it comes about only because of the free acts of individuals.

TORAH AND COMMANDMENTS

The giving of the Torah through Moses was for Gersonides the greatest of all miracles, for the Torah is no ordinary book. Again, like Maimonides, Gersonides conceives of the Torah in Platonic terms as the perfect law, one that reveals the path to human happiness. Indeed, unlike human legal codes, which are frequently felt to be burdens and bonds, the Torah attracts followers by its very perfection. It is not an imposition but a gift, whose inner "sweetness" entices, not compels, its adherents (*Wars* 6.2.1). The Torah not only does not burden us with false beliefs, it also does not encumber us with senseless commandments (*Commentary on the Torah, Parshat Yitro* 75a). Indeed, one who lives by it not only attains the moral and intellectual perfection requisite for human immortality, but is in this life deserving of individual providence.[10]

Gersonides' deep appreciation of the Torah is most evident in his discussions of the Mosaic legislation. Although he did not contribute much to the standard halakhic literature, his detailed analyses of the legal norms in the Pentateuch are both halakhically well informed and philosophically fecund. Perhaps more so than Maimonides he takes seriously the idea that every commandment has a purpose and reason. This is most apparent in his treatment of ritual, precisely that part of the law that seems most remote from reason. Take, for example, dietary laws. In commentating upon the prohibition against eating certain kinds of insects and reptiles (Leviticus 11: 41–5), Gersonides focuses upon the passage "You shall not make your souls [*nafshotekhem*] unclean . . . , for I am the Lord your God: you shall sanctify yourselves and be holy, for I am holy" (11: 43–4). The eating of these animals, he maintains, is one of many ways whereby we infect and contaminate our souls, specifically our intellects, whose "light" is "extinguished" by the coarse matter of these creatures. Observance of this commandment, as well as the other dietary laws, is part of a system of holiness, whose ultimate reason is emancipation from our materiality. Just as God is pure intellect, so we become truly like God, that is, incorporeal, to the extent that we follow these commandments. Holiness is for Gersonides synonymous with separation from matter and perfection of the intellect. This is the main theme and underlying purpose of the entire Torah (*Commentary on the Torah, Parshat Shemini* 137bc).

CONCLUSION

Gersonides' position in the world of traditional Judaism has been ambiguous. On the one hand, his biblical commentaries have been continually studied and some of them have been incorporated into the canonical editions of the rabbinic bibles. On the other hand, the *Wars of the Lord* has been more the subject of criticism or neglect than praise or study, although his critics did recognize his enormous learning, both secular and religious. Gersonides himself was most sincere in his beliefs that, first, he was a defender of the faith and "fighting God's battles" and that, second, true philosophy is identical with the teachings of the Torah properly understood. This true philosophy is not identical with Aristotle's teachings, as Averroes had believed; nor is it unavailable through human reason, as Maimonides had maintained. What makes us human is our intellect; it cannot then be the case that the link between us and God is intrinsically imperfect. With the guidance provided by the Torah, we can attain intellectual perfection through the use of reason. It is not an easy undertaking; the pitfalls are many and various. Nevertheless, as Spinoza (who refers to Gersonides' biblical commentaries) was to remark, although the way to true happiness is indeed difficult, what is ultimately gained is excellent.

NOTES

1 Shatzmiller 1972; Touati 1973, pp. 34–48; Dahan 1991.
2 Goldstein 1969.
3 Feldman 1967.
4 Feldman 1975.
5 Wolfson 1953.
6 Rudavsky 1983.
7 Bleich 1973, introduction.

8 Feldman 1978.
9 Kellner 1977.
10 Kellner 1980.

❧ BIBLIOGRAPHY ❧

Texts

Gersonides (Levi ben Gershom) (1480) *Perush ha-Ralbag al ha-Torah* (*Commentary of Gersonides on the Pentateuch*) (Mantua); reprint Israel 1967.
—— (1866) *Milhamoth Hashem* (*The Wars of the Lord*) (Leipzig: Lorck).
—— (1946) *Commentary of Levi ben Gershom on the Book of Job*, translated by A. Lassen (New York: Bloch).
—— (1984 and 1987) *The Wars of the Lord*, translated by S. Feldman, 2 vols. (books 1–4) (Philadelphia: Jewish Publication Society).
Goldstein, B. (1985) *The Astronomy of Levi ben Gershom (1288–1344)* (New York: Springer).
Touati, C. (1968) *Les Guerres du Seigneur: Livres III et IV* (Paris: Mouton).

Studies

Bleich, J. D. (1973) *Providence in the Philosophy of Gersonides* (New York: Yeshiva University Press).
Dahan, G. (1991) "Les Traductions latines médiévales des oeuvres de Gersonide," in *Gersonide en son temps*, edited by G. Dahan (Louvain and Paris: Peeters), pp. 329–68.
Feldman, S. (1967) "Gersonides' Proofs for Creation of the Universe," *Proceedings of the American Academy for Jewish Research* 35: 113–37.
—— (1975) "Platonic Themes in Gersonides' Cosmology," in *Salo W. Baron Jubilee Volume*, edited by S. Lieberman and A. Hyman (Jerusalem: American Academy for Jewish Research), 1: 383–406.
—— (1978) "Gersonides on the Possibility of Conjunction with the Agent Intellect," *AJS Review* 3: 99–120.
Goldstein, B. (1969) "Preliminary Remarks on Levi ben Gershom's Contributions to Astronomy," *Proceedings of the Israel Academy of Sciences and Humanities* 3(9): 239–54.
Kellner, M. (1977) "Maimonides and Gersonides on Mosaic Prophecy," *Speculum* 52: 62–79.
—— (1980) "Gersonides on Miracles, the Messiah and Resurrection," *Da'at* 4: 5–34.
Manekin, C. (1991) "Logic and its Application in the Philosophy of Gersonides," in *Gersonide en son temps*, edited by G. Dahan (Louvain and Paris: Peeters), pp. 133–49.
Rudavsky, T. (1983) "Divine Omniscience and Future Contingents in Gersonides," *Journal of the History of Philosophy* 21: 513–36.

MEDIEVAL JEWISH PHILOSOPHY

Samuelson, N. (1972) "Gersonides' Account of God's Knowledge of Particulars," *Journal of the History of Philosophy* 10: 399–416.

Shatzmiller, J. (1972) "Gersonides and the Community of Orange in the Middle Ages" [Hebrew], in *Studies in the History of the Jewish People and the Land of Israel* 2: 111–26.

—— (1991) "Gersonide et la société juive de son temps," in *Gersonide en son temps*, edited by G. Dahan (Louvain and Paris: Peeters), pp. 33–43.

Touati, C. (1973) *La Pensée philosophique et théologique de Gersonide* (Paris: Minuit).

Wolfson, H. (1953) "Maimonides and Gersonides on Divine Attributes," in *Mordecai M. Kaplan Jubilee Volume*, edited by M. Davis (New York: Jewish Theological Seminary of America), pp. 515–30.

CHAPTER 17

Chasdai Crescas

Daniel J. Lasker

Chasdai ben Judah Crescas (c. 1340–1410/11) is generally considered to be the last outstanding original Jewish philosopher of the Middle Ages. His trenchant philosophical criticism of the rationalistic thought of his important Aristotelian predecessors, Maimonides (1138–1204) and Gersonides (1288–1344), gives evidence of a fertile mind struggling to replace the accepted scientific verities of the day with traditionally religious, non-philosophical beliefs. Yet there is more to Crescas' thought than a conservative reaction to perceived rationalistic excesses, since Crescas himself often chose an untraditional opinion if he felt that such a position was warranted. The result of Crescas' argumentation was a philosophical system which could compete with Aristotelianism on its own terms. Crescas' unique argumentation and conclusions, however, won few adherents among his contemporaries and successors in the late Middle Ages, even though moderns often point to Crescas' achievements as a highlight of medieval Jewish thought.

Crescas was born in Barcelona, where he studied under the outstanding Iberian rabbinic personality of the day, Rabbenu Nissim Gerondi (known by the acronym Ran, c. 1310–75). Crescas later moved to Saragossa, the capital of Aragon, where he was chief rabbi and an important courtier. In the wake of the riots of 1391, in which his only son was killed, Crescas took upon himself the responsibility of rehabilitating the Jewish community of Aragon. Crescas' inner circle consisted of young scholars, a number of whom eventually became prominent in their own right. They frequently disagreed with their master, whom they often had trouble understanding because of the extreme terseness of both his written and oral styles (Baer 1971, p. 523 (index, s.v. Hasdai Crescas)).

Though Crescas was an original and imaginative author, his actual literary output is quite meager. Only three treatises have survived (the existence of a fourth one is known, but it is not extant), and, of these three treatises, only one is a major literary production. The three treatises consist of an anti-Christian polemical composition (*Refutation of the Christian Principles*, c. 1398), a philosophical/halakhic sermon (*Sermon on the Passover*, date unknown), and a full-scale philosophical treatise (*Light of the Lord*, completed 1410). In addition, Crescas' student Abraham ben Judah composed a philosophical treatise while studying with Crescas in Barcelona (in 1378), and the views expressed there may very well be those of the teacher more than of the student (Rosenberg 1983–4, pp. 525–621).

Given this paucity of Crescas' literary output, it is of interest that one of the central questions addressed by scholars today concerns the development of Crescas' thought. The medievals perceived contradictions between Crescas' positions in his different works; recent research has provided evidence that Crescas produced his oeuvre over a period of years in which he changed his mind and re-edited already completed sections of his treatises. It is perhaps this constant editorial activity (the result of indecision or perfectionism?) which prevented Crescas from achieving his major goal, a halakhic critique of Maimonides' *Mishneh Torah*. An analysis of Crescas' thought, therefore, requires an evaluation of his three extant works and their interrelationship.

❧ REFUTATION OF THE CHRISTIAN ❧ PRINCIPLES

Crescas' anti-Christian polemical work is known as *Bittul 'Iqqarei ha-Notzrim* (*Refutation of the Christian Principles*). Originally written in a vernacular language, it survives only in a Hebrew translation executed by Joseph ibn Shem Tov (c. 1400–60) in 1451. The purpose of the work is to demonstrate that the principal doctrines of Christianity are contradicted by reason and, hence, are not to be accepted. A second vernacular anti-Christian polemical work, consisting of exegetical arguments from the Prophets, was not translated into Hebrew and has not survived.[1]

According to Crescas, there are ten principal beliefs of Christianity, namely: the punishment for original sin; the redemption from original sin; the Trinity; incarnation; the virgin birth; transubstantiation; baptism; the coming of the messiah; the new Torah; and demons.[2] In his discussion of each of these principles Crescas first lays out the premises upon which the principles are based and then distinguishes between those premises acceptable to both Jews and Christians and those premises acceptable to Christians alone. Thus, concerning the first principle, the punishment for Adam's sin, Crescas determined that there are three common premises: "(1) the punishment was just; (2) the punishment was corporeal and spiritual; (3) the corporeal punishment was not removed and is still in force." One premise, however, was the subject of disagreement: "The Christians believe and maintain that the spiritual punishment was the withholding of the grace of paradise from all souls who come after Adam. The Jew maintains and believes that the spiritual punishment pertains solely to the soul of Adam and punishment did not pass on to any other soul" (Lasker 1992, p. 24). Throughout the *Refutation*, Crescas attempts to demonstrate that, where there is a disagreement between Jewish premises and Christian ones, the Jewish premises are reasonable while the Christian premises are either self-contradictory or inconsistent with other premises.

While Crescas' arguments in the *Refutation* are incisive and display a wide-ranging knowledge of Christianity, the real interest in the book lies in what it might or might not tell us about Crescas' philosophical views and intellectual development. In the decades after Crescas' death, a number of contradictions were pointed out between this polemical work and Crescas' philosophical treatise, *Light of the Lord*. Thus, in the *Refutation* Crescas argues against positive divine attributes in the form of persons of the Trinity, but in *Light of the Lord* he argues in favor of positive attributes, in opposition to Maimonides' negative theology. Joseph ibn Shem Tov recorded that his contemporaries upbraided Crescas for this apparent contradiction, but Joseph defended Crescas and said that the issues were different and should not be confused. What might have misled the critics, averred Joseph, is the fact that the same Hebrew term (*to'ar*) was used for both attribute and person of the Trinity (Lasker 1992, pp. 46–7).[3]

Perhaps the most interesting contradiction between the *Refutation* and *Light of the Lord* concerns the question of eternal creation. In the polemical work, Crescas employed Gersonides' arguments against eternal creation, in order to refute the Christian belief in the eternal generation of the Son by the Father. In the philosophical work, however, Crescas accepted the concept of eternal creation and specifically refuted Gersonides' arguments. The translator of the *Refutation*, Joseph ibn Shem Tov, explained this contradiction by claiming that Crescas changed his mind after having written *Light of the Lord* and that his definitive view is that expressed in the *Refutation*, namely, that eternal creation is impossible (Lasker 1992, pp. 38–43).

Modern scholarship has renewed the question of the contradictions, and a number of researchers have tried to draw conclusions about Crescas' views and development based on material in the *Refutation*. Some have agreed with Joseph ibn Shem Tov that Crescas changed his mind between the writing of *Light of the Lord* and the writing of the

Refutation. According to this view, although *Light of the Lord* was edited in its final form only a number of years after the composition of the *Refutation*, many parts of it predate the polemic (Ophir 1993, pp. 137–9). The discussion of eternal creation would be such a part. Others have argued that the opposite is true, namely that the *Refutation* was written first and Crescas changed his mind when he composed *Light of the Lord* (Rosenberg 1983–4, p. 527). Crescas' refutation of Gersonides' arguments and his innovative adoption of the possibility of eternal creation were, hence, the product of his mature thought.

It is very possible, though, that no philosophical conclusions should be drawn from the *Refutation* for two reasons. First, the *Refutation* is a polemic and polemicists are notorious for using arguments with which they themselves do not agree.[4] Second, Joseph ibn Shem Tov's translation is often only a paraphrase of the lost original and thus should not be relied upon overly much.[5] Hence, while an endeavor to reconstruct Crescas' intellectual development from a comparison between his polemical and philosophical treatises is tempting, it is unclear how productive such an enterprise would be.

SERMON ON THE PASSOVER

A similar situation confronts the scholar in the case of Crescas' *Derashat ha-Pesach (Sermon on the Passover)*,[6] which went unrecognized as part of his oeuvre until comparatively recently (Ravitzky 1988). As is the case in the *Refutation*, there are prima facie contradictions between the *Sermon* and *Light of the Lord*. Since, however, the Sermon is not dated, it is impossible to know for certain whether or not it preceded *Light of the Lord*.[7]

The *Sermon* deals with two philosophical issues which are also present in *Light of the Lord*, namely, human choice versus determinism and who is the facilitator of miracles.[8] The discussion of choice in the *Sermon* is very similar to that found in *Light of the Lord* 2.5.5–6 and recognizes the place of human will in determining human actions. In *Light of the Lord*, however, these passages are preceded by arguments in favor of strict determinism, arguments which were taken from the works of the Jewish apostate Abner of Burgos (Alfonso de Valladolid, 1270–1348). In the *Sermon*, miracles are effected by the prophet; in the philosophical work, God alone is the author of the miracles.

As in the case of the *Refutation*, scholars are divided on the question as to which treatise contains Crescas' definitive views. One opinion maintains that the *Sermon* is a preliminary study to *Light of the Lord* (in which case its conclusions are superseded by those of the philosophical work). Another view, however, holds that the *Sermon* is a summary produced after the completion of the philosophical work, containing, therefore, Crescas' mature deliberations concerning choice and miracles.[9] As in the case of the relationship between the *Refutation* and *Light of the Lord*, there is as yet no definitive conclusion as to which view of the *Sermon* is correct.[10]

❧ *LIGHT OF THE LORD* ❧

Crescas' main contribution to Jewish philosophy is his book *Or Adonai* (*Light of the Lord*).[11] Originally conceived as a philosophical critique of Maimonides, prefacing a halakhic critique of Maimonides, the book now stands alone since the second part was never realized. Maimonides was the central figure of Jewish philosophy, and even though he had aroused opposition both within and outside of philosophical circles, no one had previously attempted to overturn his Aristotelian philosophy completely by using philosophical tools. This was Crescas' goal in *Light of the Lord*.[12]

The question has been raised as to Crescas' motivation in his critique of Maimonides. Was it simply an intellectual disagreement in which Crescas believed that Maimonides had made fundamental mistakes? Or were there other factors involved, such as a perception that Maimonidean/Aristotelian rationalism was undermining Jewish loyalty at a time of crisis brought about by the riots of 1391 and the waves of Jewish conversion to Christianity?[13] Whereas Crescas was undoubtedly motivated by a desire to preserve Jewish loyalty, his *Refutation* demonstrates that he believed that an Aristotelian viewpoint does not necessarily lead to Christianity; indeed, Aristotelian rationalism is employed in that work to demonstrate that Christianity is a false religion. Thus, the roots of Crescas' dissatisfaction with Aristotelianism, which is subjected to a withering criticism in *Light of the Lord*, must run deeper than just a reaction to the wholesale conversions in the wake of the riots of 1391. Nevertheless, Crescas' perception that rationalism weakened Jewish resolve must have played a part in his refutation of Maimonidean presuppositions. He may also have felt, along with a number of contemporaries, that Jews who were most enamoured of philosophical rationalism were specifically those who were most likely to undergo conversion during times of stress.[14]

An important aspect of Crescas' critique of Maimonideanism is his rejection of Maimonides' thirteen principles of Judaism.[15] This rejection is both formal and material, in that Crescas averred not only that Maimonides' dogmatic enterprise was misplaced, but also that the specific principles or dogmas chosen by Maimonides were incorrect. For

Crescas, as for Ran his teacher (Klein-Braslavy 1980b), dogmas should be chosen on an *inductive* basis, that is, what the beliefs are without which Judaism as a religion would collapse. Maimonides had offered a *deductive* reading of the dogmas – that is, which beliefs in Judaism have actually been ordained by the Torah – without distinguishing between more fundamental and less fundamental dogmas.

As a result of Crescas' view that the principal beliefs of Judaism are those without which there could be no revealed religion in general or Judaism in particular, he divided the various doctrines into four categories: first, "roots" (*shorashim*) or "first principles" (*hatchalot*), without which one cannot even imagine revelation of a divine law; second, "corner-stones" (*pinnot*), ideas the acceptance of which makes belief in revelation in general possible; third, "true doctrines" (*de'ot amitiot*) or "true beliefs" (*emunot amitiot*), namely, doctrines actually taught by the Torah; and fourth, "doctrines and theories" (*de'ot u-sevarot*), about which the Torah gives no definitive teaching. This division of dogmas is unique in the history of Jewish thought and made little or no impact on later discussions of the principles of Judaism. It did, however, serve as the framework for Crescas' philosophical discussions and can serve the same purpose here (Kellner 1986, pp. 108–39).

Roots

Crescas argued that any revelation presupposes the existence of God, his unity, and his incorporeality, and, as a result, these root beliefs cannot be commanded by revelation. They must be accepted as true before one assumes the possibility of any particular divine religion. Maimonides, for his part, had ruled that belief in God's existence is a revealed commandment, and yet he presented proofs of God's existence, unity, and incorporeality which were based upon Aristotelian physics. After first organizing the whole corpus of Aristotelian physics into twenty-six propositions, Maimonides proceeded to use those propositions to establish the fundamental beliefs of Judaism concerning the deity (Maimonides, *Guide* 2, introduction–1: 235–52 (Pines)). Thus, according to Maimonides, in order for Jews to hold correct beliefs about God, they must first adhere to Aristotelian principles.

Crescas objected to the Maimonidean approach, arguing that Aristotelian physics is scientifically inaccurate. God's existence, unity, and incorporeality cannot be dependent upon philosophical proofs, if those proofs employ false propositions. Crescas, therefore, first provided the arguments for the Aristotelian propositions (something which Maimonides himself had failed to do), and then proceeded to show the weaknesses inherent in them. Crescas challenged some of the most basic premises of Aristotelian thought, such as the impossibility of a vacuum or of an actual infinite, the definition of space as the limit of a particular body, and the definition of time as the measure of motion (Crescas 1990a, pp. 13–55; 61–88). Although Crescas' critique of Aristotle hints at later scientific developments which overthrew medieval physics, it is hard to determine the extent of Crescas' contribution to this development.[16]

With the overthrow of Aristotelian physics, Crescas is able to discredit Maimonides' proofs of the existence, unity, and incorporeality of God. If, for instance, an actual infinite, such as an infinite causal chain, can exist, there is no reason to assume that one of the causes in the chain is a "first cause." Furthermore, if infinite space outside this world were possible, then there could be many worlds and more than one God.

Crescas was not satisfied simply with demonstrating the weaknesses of Aristotle's physics as the basis for the root beliefs of Judaism, or with refuting the Maimonidean proofs of those beliefs as based on Aristotelian principles. He demonstrates those beliefs using other means. Yet, his proof of God's existence is very similar to one offered by Maimonides, namely, that in order for possible existents in a causal chain (finite or infinite) actually to exist, there must be one cause whose existence is necessary and who is the ultimate cause of the causal chain. That cause is God.

Despite his philosophical proof of God's existence, Crescas believes that God's unity is not amenable to rational demonstration, since any argument against two gods can be refuted by the assumption of one god who is active and another god who is non-active. Only reliance on revelation ("Hear O Israel, the Lord our God, the Lord is One," Deuteronomy 6:4) can guarantee the truth of the belief in one God. Similarly, God's incorporeality is attested by Scripture (despite its use of anthropomorphisms) and by the sages, as well as being in consonance with reason (Crescas 1990a, pp. 55–61, 88–122).

If Crescas had confined his criticism of Maimonides' theology to epistemological issues (that is, how do we know that God exists, is one, and is incorporeal?), his view of God would ultimately have been similar to that of Maimonides. Crescas, however, went beyond epistemological questions in order to attack the heart of Maimonidean theology, namely, the theory of negative attributes (Maimonides, *Guide* 1.50–60: 111–47 (Pines)). Maimonides had argued that anything positive said about God would impinge on his absolute unity, and, therefore, one may say only that which God is not. The result of this theory is a totally transcendent God, one who cannot be said to have a relationship to this world. Crescas objected to such a conception of God, arguing instead that positive terms can be attributed to God, if they are understood as essential attributes of God. This means that such attributes are neither identical to God's essence (in which case there would be no room for multiple attributes) nor superadded to God's essence (in which case God's absolute unity would be compromised). Specifically denying any connection between his own theory and trinitarianism, Crescas employed an image from the mystical *Book of Creation (Sefer Yetzirah)*, "a flame connected to a burning coal," to demonstrate how multiplicity does not impinge on absolute unity (Crescas 1990a, pp. 99–115; Wolfson 1977a).

Corner-stones

Crescas listed six beliefs as intrinsic to the notion of a divine revelation. The six are: (1) God's knowledge of particulars (without which he could not reveal himself to a particular people); (2) providence (the giving of the Torah is an act of providence);[17] (3) divine power (without which he would be incapable of fulfilling the promises made in revelation); (4) prophecy (without which humans would be incapable of receiving the divine revelation); (5) free will (without which there could be no purpose to commanding humans to do particular actions); and (6) purposefulness of revelation (without which there would be no point to revelation). Each belief is analyzed in order to determine what Crescas held to be the proper meaning of these doctrines in light of both religion and reason.

If there is one common thread in Crescas' discussion of these corner-stones of Judaism, it is a rejection of the Aristotelian 'intellectualist' view of the relation between God and humanity. That view can be summarized as follows (using the rubric of Crescas' six corner-stones): (1) Divine knowledge: God cannot know individuals because that would require multiplicity in his essence (knowledge of many individuals), change (as he learns more about each individual), and dependence upon the creations (who would complete his knowledge by *their* existence and actions). (2) Divine providence: since God cannot know individuals, he cannot exercise providence over them; at most, humans can aspire to an intellectualist providence in which the intellectually adept can aspire to a sort of divine protection dependent upon their intellectual achievements. (3) Divine power: God's power is limited by the laws of nature; the biblical miracles are not to be understood literally. (4) Prophecy: prophecy is a natural phenomenon which requires intellectual preparation on the part of the prophet and is independent of divine will; the prophets cannot learn intelligibles through prophecy, since they must already have been cognizant of them. (5) Free will: human free will is a possibility since God has no foreknowledge of how individuals will choose to act. (6) Purposefulness of revelation: the purpose of the Torah is to allow gifted individuals to perfect their intellects, thereby achieving immortality; observance of the commandments plays no role in ultimate human happiness.

Crescas rejected this intellectualist approach to God's relation to the world, replacing it with the concept that God acts toward the world through his goodness, love, and grace. As creator of the world, God knows individuals and exercises providence over them. In fact, there is special providence for the people of Israel because of the commandment of circumcision (which mitigates the effect of original sin) and because of Abraham's willingness to sacrifice his only son Isaac,[18] as well as an extra portion of providence for the land of Israel and during certain periods of the year. God's power is infinite not only in duration (with which Aristotle would agree, since he believed in the eternity of motion), but also in intensity (as creation ex nihilo demonstrates). The biblical miracles (such as Balaam's talking ass) are to be taken literally and not figuratively as the rationalists believed. Prophecy is a function not of intellectual perfection but of the prophets' love for God as expressed through their cleaving to God's commandments. Prophecy is an emanation from God which reaches the human intellect, either with or without an intermediary, imparting knowledge for the purpose of guiding either the prophets or the people (Crescas 1990a, pp. 123–205).

Crescas' discussions of free will and the purpose of the Torah are the occasion of some of the most interesting aspects of his thought. Gersonides had been able to account for human free will by denying God's knowledge of individuals qua individuals. If God knew in advance how people would choose to act, this would lead to their choices and actions being determined; as far as Gersonides was concerned, God did not know how people would choose to act.[19] Crescas, though, upheld God's absolute knowledge of particulars, and, therefore, Crescas was incapable of allowing free will. He held that human choices and actions are determined by a chain of causes and effects which makes those choices and actions determined.

Crescas was aware that a deterministic view of human choice and action may be thought incompatible with the religious belief that each individual is responsible for his or her own actions and is rewarded or punished accordingly. Crescas offered an analogy; just as paper burns when in contact with fire through its nature and not as a consequence of the paper's intentional action, so, too, sinners will naturally be punished whether or not they were predetermined to sin, and the righteous will be rewarded for their actions no matter what the causes of those actions are. This analogy, however, hardly solves the problem, since one expects divine reward or punishment on account of choices one has made. Therefore, Crescas attempts to lighten the impact of his deterministic views by asserting that reward and punishment are a consequence of the feeling of pleasure or discomfort which accompanies human actions. One who feels pain at the sin which is committed under compulsion will not be punished for such a sin (Crescas 1990a, pp. 205–25; Feldman 1982).[20]

According to Crescas, the purpose of the Torah is to bring the worshipper to eternal life through love of God. The Aristotelians claimed that the soul can achieve immortality only by transforming the material intellect with which each person is born into an "acquired intellect." This is done by intellectual activity, not by the observance of particular religious commandments. Crescas argued against this view on both religious and philosophical grounds. If the theory of the acquired intellect means that immortality is achieved by the apprehension of any intelligible whatsoever, then anyone who learns even one principle of Euclid's geometry, for instance, is guaranteed life after death. If, however, a human being must apprehend truths about God and the angels in order to gain immortality, then immortality is impossible since God and the angels are ultimately unknowable. Instead, Crescas argued, the worshipper achieves ultimate happiness and eternal life through the love of God as expressed in observance of the commandments. It is for this purpose that the Torah was revealed (Crescas 1990a, pp. 225–72; Harvey 1973).

True beliefs

Whereas roots and corner-stones provide the necessary presuppositions of divine law in general, that divine law which is of interest to Crescas, the Mosaic Torah, contains a number of specific beliefs which are independent of the roots and corner-stones. These beliefs are: creation ex nihilo; immortality; reward and punishment; resurrection; eternity of the Torah; the superiority of Mosaic prophecy; the use of the *urim* and *tummim* (oracles) to learn the future; and the messiah.[21] Without these beliefs, the Torah would still exist, yet it would be a different Torah. Thus, for instance, the Torah did not have to teach that there would be a messiah, but, in fact, it did teach such a belief. Hence, the denier of this belief is a denier of the whole Torah.

Crescas' discussion of creation ex nihilo is of particular interest, since he argued that creation is not a corner-stone of a revealed religion; one could believe in revelation, even if the world were eternal. This contention opposes the assertion of Maimonides (*Guide* 2.25: 327–30 (Pines)) that the doctrine of creation is necessary to uphold religion. Crescas' view is also in opposition to the conviction of many other

Jewish dogmatists concerning the centrality of the doctrine of creation, yet it may have its origin in the teachings of Ran (Kellner 1986, pp. 213–17; Klein-Braslavy 1980b).

Furthermore, whereas Crescas held that creation ex nihilo is a belief actually taught by the Torah, he contended that this doctrine is best understood as eternal emanation of the world. Gersonides had argued that eternal emanation is impossible, contending that there must have been creation at a discrete moment, even if that creation were from a kind of prime matter. As noted above, Crescas adopted Gersonides' proofs for his own refutation of the Christian doctrine of eternal generation of the second person of the Trinity (the Son). In *Light of the Lord*, however, Crescas rejected such argumentation, asserting instead that the doctrine of creation ex nihilo means solely that the world is a possible existent which depends on God for its existence. There did not have to be creation after absolute nothingness. This explanation of ex nihilo has a number of philosophical precedents, for instance, in the works of Aquinas (Crescas 1990a, pp. 273–318; Wolfson 1977b).

Crescas' discussions of the other true beliefs merely reinforce the impression he gives of himself as a conservative theologian. Building upon his refutation of the Aristotelian doctrine of the acquired intellect, Crescas argues that immortality of the soul is a function of the love of God as expressed through observance of the Torah. Resurrection is accepted literally as the return of some souls to their bodies soon after the coming of the messiah. The Torah is eternal because of its perfection; Moses' superior prophecy is expressed through the miracles he wrought which were significantly different from those of other prophets. The *urim* and *tummim* on the high priest's breast plate were an accurate source of information concerning future events. The messiah's delay in coming should not lead to despair; the length of the present exile is not to be compared to that of the Babylonian exile, because the Second Temple period was not one of true redemption, since many Jews did not return to the land of Israel (Crescas 1990a, pp. 318–72).

Doctrines and theories

Crescas' *Light of the Lord* concludes with short discussions of various topics which exercised medieval philosophers and theologians. Though Crescas was willing to offer his opinion on these subjects, he did not make agreement with his position mandatory. Indeed, he was willing to accept a view with which he might otherwise have disagreed, if it were reliable tradition.[22]

The topics discussed in this section are the future eternity of the world (a parte post); the possible existence of other worlds; whether the heavenly spheres are intelligent, living beings; whether the movements of the heavenly bodies influence human affairs; the efficacy of amulets and charms; demons; reincarnation; the immortality of infants; paradise and hell;[23] whether the "Account of the Beginning" refers to physics and the "Account of the Chariot" refers to metaphysics;[24] if the intellect, the activity of intellection and the object of intellection are all one thing; the prime mover; and the impossibility of apprehending God's essence (Crescas 1990a, pp. 383–414).

In his discussions of these questions, Crescas generally took a conservative stance, arguing against the rationalist (Aristotelian) view. Thus, for instance, he accepted the existence of demons (contrary to most of his philosophical predecessors such as Maimonides and Gersonides), at the same time arguing against the Christian view that demons are fallen angels.[25] As opposed to the Aristotelians, Crescas allowed the possibility of the existence of multiple worlds and expressed strong doubts concerning the life and intelligence of the spheres. Maimonides' view that the "Account of the Beginning" and the "Account of the Chariot" refer to physics and to metaphysics is denied out of hand.

CONCLUSION

In the words of one scholar, Crescas' "teachings were formulated both too late and too early" (Ravitzky 1988, p. v). On the one hand, Crescas was too late, because his unconventional views and his terseness of expression were not appreciated by a community ravaged by persecution and incapable of a new radical departure in Jewish thought. On the other hand, he was too early in his daring critique of Aristotelianism, since "modern physics" was still in the future. Today, however, readers can appreciate Crescas' innovativeness. While Crescas' style presents as much of a challenge for the moderns as it did for the medievals, and his parsimony of expression is still the cause of exegetical disputes among readers, his philosophical contribution is undeniable.

NOTES

1 Joseph ibn Shem Tov's Hebrew translation of the extant polemic can be found in Crescas 1990b. An English translation is provided in Lasker 1992. There is no way of knowing what the original title of the book was; the title *Refutation of the Christian Principles* is found in only two manuscripts. (Since one of those manuscripts was used by the editor of the first edition, that name has become accepted.) Whether the original language of the two polemical works was Catalan or Aragonese is unknown.

Crescas' lost treatise is known solely because of a comment by Joseph ibn Shem Tov, who refrained from translating it into Hebrew because it was based on exegetical arguments, of which "there are very many of this kind in our nation" (Lasker 1992, p. 84).

2 It is of interest that whereas Crescas innovated a multi-layered view of Jewish principles (see below; and Kellner 1986, pp. 108–39), he did not introduce any of his insights concerning dogmatics into his discussion of Christian principles.

3 Another contradiction is evident in Crescas' rejection of the Christian doctrine of original sin in the *Refutation* and his acceptance of a form of original sin in his *Light of the Lord* (Lasker 1988).

4 This stricture is applicable in general when employing polemical literature for purposes of intellectual history. Thus, Nachmanides' statement in the disputation of Barcelona (1263) that he did not accept the authority of every midrash has been the source of much (perhaps needless) speculation as to the extent of the author's sincerity; for recent discussions, see Fox 1989; Wolfson 1989, pp. 172–8; Chazan 1992, pp. 142–57.

5 The view that not much can be learned about Crescas' own views from the *Refutation* is the one which I have taken in my introduction to the text and English translation; see Lasker 1992, pp. 12–15. It should be noted, in addition, that there are quite a number of points of contact between the philosophical and polemical works, indicating that certain themes remained constant in Crescas' thought; see ibid., p. 13.

6 This is the name given by its recent editor, Aviezer Ravitzky; it is possible that Crescas referred to the work as *Derash Or le-Yod-Dalet (Sermon for the Eve of the Fourteenth [of Nisan])* or *Ma'amar Or le-Yod-Dalet (Treatise for the Eve of the Fourteenth [of Nisan])*; see Harvey 1989, p. 532.

7 The *Refutation* is not dated either, but a reference to the papal schism allows us to locate it with some certainty to 1398; see Lasker 1992, p. 4. On the date of *Light of the Lord*, see Ophir 1993, pp. 11–24.

8 The third subject of the *Sermon*, the division of legal duties connected with the Passover festival, is missing in *Light of the Lord*, but undoubtedly would have been incorporated into the longer, unwritten, halakhic treatise.

9 The editor of the *Sermon*, Aviezer Ravitzky, is of the opinion that the *Sermon* was a preliminary study (Ravitzky 1988). Warren (Zev) Harvey and Natan Ophir have argued that the *Sermon* is the later of the two works (Harvey 1989 (and in an unpublished lecture); Ophir 1993).

10 No matter what chronology we give for Crescas' three extant treatises, it seems clear that he was greatly influenced by Christian thought and by the traumatic events of 1391. He must have studied or researched some Church theology in the period preceding the composition of his anti-Christian polemics, which themselves were occasioned by the increased pressure on the Jewish community in the 1390s. This decade, during which the Jewish communities were decimated and Crescas wrote his *Refutation*, was undoubtedly a watershed period in Crescas' thought; see Ophir 1993; Lasker forthcoming. Christian influence on Crescas' thought is discussed as well by Baer 1939–40; Pines 1967; Harvey 1985–6; and Ravitzky 1988.

11 The first editions of *Light of the Lord* (generally known in Hebrew as *Or ha-Shem* for pietistic reasons) are almost unusable because of printer's errors and

other mistakes. Recently, Shlomo Fisher published a vocalized text which takes manuscript readings into account, but it is not a critical edition (Crescas 1990a). Warren (Zev) Harvey has been working for a number of years on a critical edition of this text, the publication of which will greatly enhance Crescas studies.

12 Judah Halevi (c. 1075–1141) criticized Aristotelianism but did not offer a fully developed competing view of the world. Nachmanides (1194–1270) criticized Maimonidean rationalism, mostly from the point of view of nascent kabbalah. Both authors had a great impact on Crescas' thought. Perhaps the closest model to Crescas' critique of Aristotelianism is found in the works of the Muslim al-Ghazālī (1058–1111), but it is unclear to what extent Crescas was familiar with his works; see Wolfson 1929, pp. 16–18.

13 This is the view expressed in Harvey 1973, pp. 12–27. Ophir (1993) is of the opinion that Crescas' turn from philosophy was a direct result of the 1391 riots, as a consequence of which there are contradictions between early and late sections of *Light of the Lord.*

14 Yitzhak Baer has been the most enthusiastic exponent of this fifteenth-century accusation; see the sources in Baer 1971, 2: 162–6, 232–43, 253–9.

15 Maimonides had posited thirteen doctrines or principles, belief in which defined one as a Jew, in the introduction to the commentary on *Pereq Cheleq* in his *Commentary on the Mishnah*; for a discussion, see Kellner 1986, pp. 10–65.

16 The essential discussion of these issues is found in Wolfson 1929.

17 Crescas did not explain the exact relationship between providence and revelation; see Kellner 1986, p. 123.

18 The centrality of circumcision is apparently a by-product of the Jewish-Christian debate (see Lasker 1988), whereas the importance of the Binding of Isaac may very well reflect Crescas' loss of his only son in the riots of 1391.

19 Maimonides (*Guide* 3.16–24: 461–502 (Pines)) argues that there is no contradiction between God's knowledge and providence, on the one hand, and God's knowledge and free will, on the other. Gersonides and Crescas, who took Maimonides at face value, as opposed to certain Maimonidean exegetes, were obviously unimpressed with his solution to this traditional conundrum.

20 This development of Crescas' strict determinism is found in *Light of the Lord,* 2.5.5–6, and the arguments therein are influenced by Scotism. The unelaborated discussion of determinism (2.5.1–4) takes most of its argumentation from Abner of Burgos (Baer 1939–40). As noted above, the arguments of 2.5.5–6 are found as well in the *Sermon on the Passover,* where the passages from Abner are missing. Harvey and Ophir, who believe that the *Sermon* was written after *Light of the Lord,* argue that Crescas elaborated his earlier deterministic position in light of the events of 1391 and that the *Sermon* represents Crescas' final position on the subject. See also Harvey, 1984–5.

21 As a sub-category of true beliefs, Crescas added a group of "beliefs dependent upon commandments," namely, that God answers prayers and the priestly blessing; that repentance is efficacious; and that the Day of Atonement and the four divisions of the year arouse us to worship God.

22 Crescas 1990a, p. 405: "*ve-im qabbalah neqabbel be-sever panim yafot.*" The word "tradition" (*qabbalah*) was also the accepted term for Jewish mysticism,

raising the issue of Crescas' attitude toward Jewish esoteric lore; for a discussion of this question, see Harvey 1982–3.

23 See Klein-Braslavy 1980a.

24 *Ma'aseh Bereshit* and *Ma'aseh Merkavah* are terms referring to discussions based on the creation narratives of Genesis and the description of the divine chariot by the prophet Ezekiel. The Mishnah, *Chagigah* 2:1, prohibits the public discussion of these topics.

25 Cf. his treatment in the *Refutation* and Joseph ibn Shem Tov's comments thereon (Lasker 1992, pp. 79–83).

❧ BIBLIOGRAPHY ❧

Texts

Crescas (1990a) *Sefer Or ha-Shem*, edited by S. Fisher (Jerusalem: Sifrei Ramot).
—— (1990b) *Bittul 'Iqqarei ha-Notzrim*, edited by D. J. Lasker (Ramat Gan and Beer Sheva: Bar Ilan and Ben Gurion University Presses).
Lasker, D. J. (1992) *The Refutation of the Christian Principles by Hasdai Crescas* (Albany: State University of New York Press).
Maimonides (1963) *The Guide of the Perplexed*, translated by S. Pines, 2 vols (Chicago: University of Chicago Press).

Studies

Baer, Y. (1939–40) "Sefer Minchat Qena'ot shel Avner mi-Burgos ve-Hashpa'ato 'al Hasdai Crescas," *Tarbitz* 11: 188–206.
—— (1971) *A History of the Jews of Christian Spain*, 2 vols (Philadelphia: Jewish Publication Society).
Chazan, R. (1992) *Barcelona and Beyond: The Disputation of 1263 and Its Aftermath* (Berkeley: University of California Press).
Feldman, S. (1982) "Crescas' Theological Determinism," *Da'at* 9: 3–28.
Fox, M. (1989) "Nahmanides on the Status of Aggadot: Perspectives on the Disputation at Barcelona, 1263," *Journal of Jewish Studies* 40: 95–109.
Harvey, W. Z. (1973) *Hasdai Crescas' Critique of the Theory of the Acquired Intellect*. Ph.D. dissertation, Columbia University.
—— (1982–3) "Kabbalistic Elements in Crescas' *Light of the Lord*" [Hebrew], *Jerusalem Studies in Jewish Thought* 2: 75–109.
—— (1984–5) "The Expression 'Feeling of Compulsion' in Crescas" [Hebrew], *Jerusalem Studies in Jewish Thought* 4: 275–80.
—— (1985–6) "R. Hasdai Crescas and Bernat Netge on the Soul" [Hebrew], *Jerusalem Studies in Jewish Thought* 5: 141–54.
—— (1989) "Hotza'ah Rishonah shel Derasha le-R. Hasdai Crescas," *Tarbitz* 58: 531–5.
Kellner, M. (1986) *Dogma in Medieval Jewish Thought* (Oxford: Oxford University Press).

Klein-Braslavy, S. (1980a) "*Gan Eden* et *Gehinnom* dans le système de Hasdaï Crescas," in *Hommage à Georges Vajda*, edited by G. Nahon and C. Touati (Louvain: Peeters), pp. 263–78.

—— (1980b) "Terumato shel R. Nissim Gerondi le-Itzuvan shel Torot ha-'Iqqarim shel Hasdai Crescas ve-shel Yosef Albo," *Eshel Beer Sheva* 2: 177–97.

Lasker, D. J. (1988) "Original Sin and its Atonement According to Hasdai Crescas" [Hebrew], *Da'at*: 127–35.

—— (forthcoming) "The Impact of Christianity on Late Iberian Jewish Philosophy," in *Iberia and Beyond: Hispanic Jews Between Two Cultures*, edited by B. Cooperman and A. Seeff (Newark: University of Delaware Press).

Ophir, N. (1993) *R. Hasdai Crescas as Philosophic Exegete of Rabbinic Sources in Light of the Changes in his Writings.* Ph.D dissertation, Hebrew University of Jerusalem.

Pines, S. (1967) "Scholasticism after Thomas Aquinas and the Teachings of Hasdai Crescas and his Predecessors," *Proceedings of the Israel Academy of Sciences and Humanities* 1(10): 1–101. Jerusalem.

Ravitzky, A. (1988) *Crescas' Sermon on the Passover and Studies in his Philosophy* [Hebrew] (Jerusalem: Israel Academy of Sciences and Humanities).

Rosenberg, S. (1983–4) "The *Arba'ah Turim* of Rabbi Abraham bar Judah, Disciple of Don Hasdai Crescas" [Hebrew], *Jerusalem Studies in Jewish Thought* 3: 525–621.

Wolfson, H. A. (1929) *Crescas' Critique of Aristotle* (Cambridge, MA: Harvard University Press).

—— (1977a) "Crescas on the Problem of Divine Attributes," in *Studies in the History of Philosophy and Religion*, edited by I. Twersky and G. Williams (Cambridge, MA: Harvard University Press), 2: 247–337.

—— (1977b) "Emanation and Creation *Ex Nihilo* in Crescas" [Hebrew], in *Studies in the History of Philosophy and Religion*, edited by I. Twersky and G. Williams (Cambridge, MA: Harvard University Press), 2: 623–9.

Wolfson, E. (1989) "By Way of Truth: Aspects of Nahmanides' Kabbalistic Hermeneutic," *AJS Review* 14: 103–78.

CHAPTER 18

Medieval and Renaissance Jewish political philosophy
Abraham Melamed

The question of how to define Jewish political philosophy is no less complicated and subject to disagreement than the question of what Jewish philosophy in general is, and in many respects the first question is a direct derivation from the second.[1] This state of affairs is well characterized by the fact that Jewish political philosophy can be defined in at least four different ways, from the minimalist to the maximalist: first, as political ideas developed by Jews, which have no necessary thematic or ideological common denominator, and which are not necessarily Jewish in their context – these may even include ideas which reject the basic political premises of rabbinic Judaism, such as Spinoza's; second, as a reservoir of theories and terms, derived from both Jewish and general sources, which were employed in order to describe Jewish political institutions, such as communal government (*kahal*), or political theories which originated in Judaism and acquired a Platonic or Aristotelian garb, as in Philo of Alexandria and Maimonides; third, as a defined and continuous tradition of political thought, which has different expressions and underwent internal changes during the ages, as it is expressed in the Bible, the Mishnah, the Talmud, the halakhic literature, and in Hellenistic, medieval, and modern Jewish philosophy; fourth, as a system of halakhic thought, religiously fundamentalist in its extreme, which is characterized by a great measure of thematic unity and ideological consistency.

My discussion is mainly based on the third formulation.

The sources of political thought, both Jewish and general, may be classified as follows: first, as a defined, detailed, and organized body of political thinking; second, as political ideas which are scattered in various (not essentially political) literary, exegetical, and philosophic sources; third, as historical documents, such as constitutions and legal proceedings; fourth, as patterns of communal organization and modes of behavior which shed light on the values of a given political culture and the principles of its political organization.

Of these sources, the first kind is completely absent from Jewish political philosophy. This state of affairs stands in sharp contrast to Christian political philosophy, which is mainly expressed in writings of the first kind, such as Dante's *De Monarchia*, Machiavelli's *The Prince*, or Hobbes' *Leviathan*.

This situation has given rise to the fairly widespread assumption that Jewish sources devoted very little space to political issues. The main justification for this assumption was that since Jews did not enjoy an independent political existence through most of their history, they were not interested in political issues.

This explanation can be rejected in two ways. First, even in the absence of an independent political existence, it is possible to deal with theoretical political questions, such as the nature of the future Jewish state. The debate on this question is clearly manifested in the rationalistic current of the messianic literature, as in Maimonides. Second, even in the absence of an independent state, it is possible to develop and maintain an active political life, in the framework of an autonomous Jewish communal life. Many of the political issues which are dealt with in a sovereign state, and are a topic of discussion for political philosophers, did in fact arise in this framework.

The main problem here, however, is not with the explanation for Jewish lack of interest in political philosophy, but rather with the basic assumption itself. The presumed absence of any notable body of Jewish political philosophy is erroneous and is based upon a projection of characteristics unique to the framework of *Christian* political philosophy. Further, this false presumption is exacerbated when one approaches medieval texts from a modern secular perspective, which takes, for example, Locke's *Two Treatises on Government* as paradigmatic. From this vantage point, it is difficult to identify any political context in the seemingly obscure, theology-laden medieval texts at all.[2]

This is the main reason why until recently there was so little research in the history of Jewish political philosophy. It is still quite negligible in comparison to other branches of Jewish philosophy, on the one hand, and the amount of research into the history of Christian (and even Muslim) political philosophy, on the other. There are already quite a few general histories of Christian political philosophy of the Middle Ages and other periods, but nothing of this sort exists for the Jewish counterpart. Only when scholars such as Leo Strauss, Harry Wolfson, Erwin Rosenthal, Ralph Lerner, Shlomo Pines, Lawrence Berman, and a few younger scholars who followed their lead, started to approach Jewish political philosophy from its own theo-political vantage point, and not from a Christian or a modern secular perspective, was the rich heritage of Jewish political philosophy exposed.[3]

In order to understand the difference between the Jewish and Christian political starting points, it would be profitable to employ a distinction between political philosophy and political theology. Political philosophy deals with the principles and essence of every human society, wherever it may be. It was originally formulated in the writings of Plato and Aristotle. Political theology, on the other hand, deals with the particular political meaning of the revelation of each faith as expressed in their holy scriptures.[4] All three monotheistic cultures shared the basic premise of Greek political philosophy. The difference among them lay in political theology. Here we find a good measure of agreement between Judaism and Islam. The case of Christianity, however, is qualitatively different.

Judaism and Islam were both fashioned in the desert, a place where law was absent. It was vital for them to present their revelations as law – an exclusive, divine law. Christianity, on the other hand, developed within an existing civilization. It did not manifest itself as law, but as *religio*. In order to survive, it had to recognize the legitimacy of other laws, and conceded the sphere of law to the temporal authority. Christianity consciously confined itself to the area of beliefs and opinions. Thus, in Judaism and Islam there is no distinction between law and faith, while in Christianity such a distinction is vital.

Christianity conceived of revelation as a source of religious dogma. It followed the theory of the two swords, which sharply separated temporal from spiritual authority, the former being influenced by Roman law. Medieval Christianity tended to see the political sphere as separate and independent, engaged in inquiring into laws and temporal rule, which was by and large isolated from divine law and the affairs of spiritual authority, which were deemed non-political or supra-political in essence. With the advent of the Renaissance and the Enlightenment, this initial separation between spiritual and temporal issues, between Church and State, was crystallized and made possible the appearance of the great secular political writings of early modern times, those of Machiavelli, Hobbes, and Locke.

By contrast, Judaism and Islam, as Leo Strauss so forcefully pointed out, laid special stress on the *political* quality of revelation, which is divine law given through a prophet who is also a lawgiver and political leader. For this reason, the basic issues of religious thought, such as the nature of revelation, the purpose of the Torah, the nature and purpose of prophecy, and the nature of human perfection all become political issues. And if one considers belief in creation ex nihilo to be a political myth, a kind of Platonic "noble lie," then even creation becomes a political issue. In sum, Judaism did not develop a systematic division between the "powers" as Christianity did. The Jewish theory of the Three Crowns is quite a different matter.[5]

This lack of systematic division is well illustrated by the medieval Hebrew meaning of the term *dat*. While in modern Hebrew *dat* signifies religion in the broad meaning of the term, its medieval meaning was much more limited, signifying law in particular. Thus, it is misleading to translate Isaac Pollegar's *Ezer ha-Dat* or Elijah del Medigo's *Bechinat ha-Dat*, for instance, into *The Defence of Religion* and *The Examination of Religion* respectively, as some modern scholars and translators erroneously do. *Dat* should be properly translated "(divine) law." Moreover, the terms *dat* and *torah* do not necessarily signify divine law, but law in general, which could (then) be sub-classified into divine law (*dat elohit, torah elohit*) or human (*dat enoshit, torah enoshit*). In this last meaning it completely corresponds to the Greek *nomos*. The narrow legal meaning ascribed to the terms *dat* and *torah* in medieval Hebrew terminology only proves again the essential political context of revelation in medieval Judaism (and Islam).

This essential theological difference between Judaism and Islam, on the one hand, and Christianity, on the other, can explain both their employment of different kinds of literary forms, and their usage of different sources of classical political philosophy.

Since Christian theology differentiated between the two realms, that is, between the temporal and the spiritual aspects of human existence, it could understand political philosophy in separation from philosophy and theology as a whole. Consequently, it could produce writings which were specifically devoted to politics, such as Aquinas' *De Regimine Principum*, Dante's *De Monarchia*, or Marsilius of Padua's *Defensor Pacis*. There are also political discussions in general theological writings, in Aquinas' great *summas*, for example. However, it is not accidental that most of the Christian medieval political discussions are contained in independent treatises.

Both medieval Jewish and Muslim political philosophies, however, were based upon a holistic perception of reality and human existence, in which the law, whether it is the Torah or the Sharī'a, is inclusive of every aspect of human existence. This nature of the Jewish and Muslim world view almost prevented the development of a distinct body of political literature. Such literature is generally contained within various halakhic systems, such as Maimonides' *Code* and his three introductions to the *Commentary on the Mishnah*, and within theological and philosophical discussions, such as Philo's *Life of Moses*, Saadia Gaon's *Book of Beliefs and Opinions*, Judah Halevi's *Kuzari*, Maimonides' *Guide of the Perplexed*, Joseph Albo's *Book of Roots*, Isaac Abravanel's *Commentary on the Bible*, Spinoza's *Theological-Political Treatise*, and Moses Mendelssohn's *Jerusalem*.

The difference between the world view of Christianity and that of Judaism and Islam also explains why they based themselves upon different sources of classical political philosophy.

Medieval Christian philosophy based its political thinking upon Aristotle's *Politics* from the time this work was translated into Latin in the mid-thirteenth century. Muslim and Jewish political philosophies, however, were squarely based upon Plato's *Republic* and *Laws*, with modifications from Aristotle's *Nicomachean Ethics* and Neoplatonic writings. Rosenthal rightly entitled the second part of his magnum opus on Muslim political thought, "The Platonic Legacy."[6] The *Republic*, however, was unheard of in the Christian West until the early Italian Renaissance. Even Klibansky, who emphasized the continuity of the Platonic tradition in medieval Christian culture, stresses that this influence was exerted through dialogues such as *Timaeus* and *Parmenides*. There is no trace of the *Republic* in medieval Christian sources in the West.[7] Thus, Barker, who completely ignored the Muslim and Jewish traditions, and dealt with the Christian only, could state bluntly: "Compared with the *Politics*, the *Republic* has no history. For a thousand years it simply disappeared."[8]

In Muslim and Jewish political thought the situation was completely the opposite. What disappeared was Aristotle's *Politics*. Muslims and Jews were acquainted with most of Aristotle's extant writings, and were markedly influenced by the Aristotelian tradition. They did not, however, possess a copy of the *Politics*, although they knew about the existence of the text. While in most areas of philosophy the Muslim and Jewish traditions were firmly based upon the Aristotelian tradition, this is not true of their political philosophy. The *Nicomachean Ethics* strongly influenced Muslim and Jewish medieval thought, as opposed to the *Politics*. The first direct – and very short – quotation from the *Politics* in a Jewish text is found in Albo's *Book of Roots*, at the end of the Middle Ages, and this reference was mediated by the influence of Latin-Christian culture.[9]

This bias might have been the result of pure chance, in that the *Politics* simply did not reach Jewish and Muslim scholars. Perhaps, as Richard Walzer supposed, it proves that late Hellenistic philosophy preferred the *Republic* to the *Politics* as a basic textbook on politics. The fact is that we do not have any commentary on the *Politics* dating from this time.[10]

Muslim political philosophy proceeded accordingly, since it inherited those works prominent in the late Hellenistic period, and adapted them to its own theological world view. It also continued the accepted practice in late Hellenistic philosophy of integrating Plato's different texts, especially the *Republic* and the *Laws*, and blurring the differences between them.

Although the history of textual transmission exerted a considerable influence, it would be erroneous to attribute the emphasis on Plato's political philosophy to that alone. In their great translation enterprise, between the eighth and the tenth centuries, the Muslims sought and commissioned the translation of a great body of Greek texts into Arabic, including most of the Aristotelian corpus. Why did they not get hold of the *Politics*, which was available in the libraries of Byzantium? Was this only accidental? For that matter, one could also query why Christian scholars of the Latin West who brought a Greek manuscript of the *Politics* from Byzantium did not seek a copy of Plato's *Republic*. And when they translated so many texts from the Arabic and the Hebrew into Latin from the thirteenth century on, why did they not make the effort to translate Averroes' *Commentary on Plato's Republic*?

More important than the history of textual transmission is the basic difference between the political theology of the great monotheistic cultures. This dictated which text they chose to adapt. The difference in the textual traditions reflects the difference between the political theology of Judaism and Islam, on the one hand, and Christianity, on the other.

When Albertus Magnus commissioned the translation of the *Politics* into Latin in the thirteenth century, it was because of the "appropriateness" of the Aristotelian text to the political context of Christian theology. Likewise, when al-Fārābī and Averroes used the *Republic* as their basic political textbook, and Maimonides followed suit, it was precisely because they all believed the Platonic text to be especially relevant to the political context of Muslim and Jewish theology.

In all three religious cultures, theology preceded the appearance of the particular text and its concomitant influence. The text, whether it simply chanced to find its way into their hands or was deliberately selected, was used solely for the purpose of commentary on and ongoing development of theological tenets.

The basic assumptions of Plato's *Republic* well suited the theological world view of Muslim and Jewish medieval thinkers. The principles and raison d'être of the Platonic philosophical state could be easily translated into the theological terminology of the Muslim (ideal) imamite state, or the Mosaic constitution. Not so, Aristotle's *Politics*. Plato's political point of departure was essentially philosophical. It considered the ideal state an integral part of a holistic metaphysical *Weltanschauung*. This suited the all-inclusive nature of Muslim and Jewish political theologies. Aristotle, however, at least in the *Politics*, considered the political sphere as a political scientist rather than as a philosopher, and tended to separate the political discussion *per se* from any metaphysical discussion. This is why the *Politics* appealed to medieval Christian thought, which tended to separate the temporal from the spiritual realm. The spirit of the *Nicomachean Ethics*, however, is much more "Platonic" in nature, grounding politics in a philosophical anthropology and offering a "theory"–oriented interpretation of the human good. This is why it had such a successful career in medieval Muslim and Jewish thought, in stark contrast to that of the *Politics*.[11]

Platonic political philosophy, which so emphasized the "spiritual" content of political existence, and hence identified the philosopher as the perfect political leader, was extremely relevant for Muslim and Jewish political thinking. The prophet-lawgiver of the Jewish and Muslim traditions could easily be identified with the Platonic philosopher-king. Plato's emphasis on the political duties of the philosopher correlated with the halakhic emphasis on the leadership responsibilities of the sage. The monarchic nature of the Platonic theory of government was also more appropriate to the halakhic position than the more ambivalent Aristotelian position, which tended to support a kind of limited democracy.

Christianity, however, generally identified its founder as one who had wholly detached himself from the life of political action. Moses and Muḥammad may be depicted as Platonic philosopher-kings, while for understanding the apolitical Jesus, the model of the Platonic philosopher-king was quite irrelevant.

Following Augustine's *Civitas Dei*, medieval Christian political thought did not consider the possibility of actualizing the ideal community here and now. It was a matter for the world to come. In this world Christianity sought no more than the existence of a political community that was attainable. In this sense the *Politics*, which set only "worldly" political goals, suited it better. Judaism and Islam, however, did pursue the existence of the ideal community in this world. For both, the *civitas temporalis*, too, could and must be a perfect community. The Jewish state that would arise after the coming of the messiah, like the ideal Platonic state, was supposed to be such a perfect state.[12]

Thus, the difference between the political theology of Judaism and Islam, on the one hand, and of Christianity, on the other, caused them to produce different genres of political literature and employ different classical political texts. It is important to emphasize, however, that in their political philosophy the three medieval religious traditions held the same *philosophical* position, influenced by the same classical writings, chiefly those of the "other" Aristotle, the Aristotle of the *Nicomachean Ethics* and the *Metaphysics*. All concurred that the supreme purpose of human existence was not the attainment of *practical* intelligence, but rather of *theoretical* intelligence – recognizing the intelligible God and loving him.[13]

In this respect, Leo Strauss' attempt to interpret the whole body of medieval Muslim and Jewish thought as Platonic political philosophy disguised in monotheistic theological garb is rather excessive. As Julius Guttmann correctly cautioned, for the medieval mind, as for its Greek predecessors, political philosophy is no queen of the sciences but a by-product of the basic premises of ethics, metaphysics, and theology.[14] As the fifteenth-century Italian Jewish scholar Moses of Rieti put it, political philosophy is only "wisdom's little sister."[15] Al-Fārābī and Maimonides, however, following Platonic teachings, translated the limited theoretical knowledge of God available to humans, namely, the knowledge of his attributes of action, into a political imitation of divine activities by the philosopher-king. Thus, even this originally Aristotelian definition of the final end of human existence underwent a Platonic metamorphosis, from a God who is known to a God whose attributes of action are imitated, from the sphere of theory to the sphere of praxis.[16] Strauss' view, then, although somewhat excessive, was nevertheless not so far from the truth.

Like other branches of Jewish philosophy, political philosophy origin-ated with Philo of Alexandria, the first scholar to try and create a synthesis between the Torah and the teachings of the Greek philo-sophers. Philo portrayed Moses in the image of the philosopher-king and explained the nature of the Mosaic constitution on the basis of Greek legal theory.[17] This initial effort was not renewed until the second great encounter between Judaism and the dominant general culture. As with other branches of medieval Jewish philosophy, political philosophy was a direct outcome of the encounter between Jewish political theology and Greek political philosophy in Arabic translation. Medieval Muslim philosophy flourished as a result of the great translation enter-prise of Greek texts into Arabic from the eighth to the tenth centuries. Arabic translations, paraphrases, and commentaries on Plato's *Republic* and the *Laws* and on Aristotle's *Nicomachean Ethics* strongly influenced the political thinking of Muslim philosophers, from al-Fārābī's *The Virtuous State* to Averroes' *Commentary on Plato's Republic*.[18]

Jewish scholars who were active in the Muslim environment from Baghdad to Cordoba, between the tenth and the late twelfth centuries, from Saadia Gaon to Maimonides, were well acquainted with the trans-lated Greek texts and their Arabic paraphrases and commentaries. This is well documented in the comments Maimonides made in the last chapter of his *Treatise on Logic* concerning the classification of the practical sciences: "In all these matters [i.e. politics], the philosophers [i.e. Greeks] have written many books which were already translated into Arabic. Those books which have not been translated yet, however, are even more numerous."[19] There is an awareness here that, although many of the Greek philosophical writings on politics were not as yet translated into Arabic (Aristotle's *Politics*, for instance), many others were already translated. Maimonides obviously refers here to the Platonic political works and to Aristotle's *Nicomachean Ethics* and *Rhetoric* and the pseudo-Aristotelian *Economics*.

In the writings of Maimonides and other Jewish authors of this period, there is much evidence of the influence of these Greek political texts in Arabic translation, with the exception of the *Politics*, of course. There is also a great deal of influence of Muslim political philosophy itself, like al-Fārābī's *The Virtuous State, On the Attainment of Happiness, On Political Governance, The Philosophy of Plato*, and *Aphorisms of the Statesman*, ibn Bājja's (Avempace's) exceptional *The Governance of the Solitary*, Averroes' *Commentary on Plato's Republic*, and others.[20]

As has already been noted, Platonic political theology also suited the basic premise of Jewish political theology, which in turn enabled Jewish authors to make extensive use of these writings and interpret the Torah accordingly. The fact that the Muslim falāsifa refrained from phrasing their Platonic political teachings in a concrete Muslim context and preferred a more general philosophical approach[21] made it easier for Jewish authors to adapt their teachings to Jewish political theology.

The first examples of a political discussion in medieval Jewish philosophy can be found in Saadia Gaon's *Book of Beliefs and Opinions* (*Emunot ve-De'ot*) and Halevi's *Kuzari*. Saadia based his discussion of the purpose of the commandments (*ta'amei ha-mitzvot*) in the third chapter of *Beliefs* on the assumption that divine law corresponds to the law of reason, which he phrased in a language very reminiscent of classical Stoic natural law.[22] Saadia's book ends with a detailed discussion of the thirteen "loves" the perfect individual must possess, with great emphasis on one's need for a proper social and political framework in order to achieve the final end of human existence. It is no coincidence that the perfect individual is identified by Saadia as a king. In this, he presented, for the first time since Philo, the Platonic philosopher-king.

Halevi's *Kuzari* can be well described as a Platonic political dialogue, in which the Khazar king is portrayed as a righteous king, possessed of sound intentions and seeking right action. The work may be seen as part of the literary genre devoted to the education of rulers, a genre present in the Platonic political tradition and later developed in the Islamic and Christian political literature of the "mirror of princes" (*speculum principum*). The *Kuzari* represents one of the two alternatives presented by Plato for the generation and maintenance of the ideal state, namely, that the existing rulers would become philosophers through being well educated. The Khazar king went to the philosopher and then to religious sages in search of the right path, until he found the ideal teacher in the Jewish scholar. He approached each potential master not simply as a private individual seeking the way of truth, but as a *ruler* in search of the true path for his community. He was looking not for correct opinions proper for apolitical philosophers only, but for action-guiding opinions relevant to a leader. He rejected the words of the philosopher as irrelevant, because the philosopher, following ibn Bājja, argued for the withdrawal of the perfect man from human society, and rejected the Platonic connection between intellectual perfection and public commitment. The Jewish scholar was preferred in part because he laid more emphasis than the rest on right action.

The Jewish scholar, who convinces the Khazar king of the truth and justice of Judaism and teaches him its practical beliefs and commandments, transforms him not only with respect to his own individual perfection but also with respect to his political capacities. Halevi's pious ruler is portrayed as being superior to the Platonic philosopher-king in that his rule is not based on perfection of the human intellect alone, but also on revelation.[23]

As in other branches of medieval Jewish philosophy, in political philosophy as well, Maimonides constitutes the apex; he created the terms of reference for subsequent Jewish thinkers up to the early modern period. While there is already some treatment of political issues in the Jewish-Aristotelian tradition prior to Maimonides, most notably in the last chapter of Abraham ibn Daud's *Book of the Exalted Faith (Sefer ha-Emunah ha-Ramah)*,[24] Maimonides, in the more philosophical sections of his halakhic writings, but mainly in the *Guide of the Perplexed (Moreh Nevukim)*, brought Jewish political philosophizing to fruition.

Maimonides' point of departure is the Aristotelian assertion (in *Nicomachean Ethics* 1.7, not the *Politics*!) that the human being is a political animal (*zoon politikon*) by nature (*Guide* 2.40, 3.27). One can only survive and provide for one's essential material needs in an organized social framework, where labor and products of labor are distributed according to the common good. One also can only fulfill emotional and spiritual needs and reach moral and intellectual perfection in the perfect political order. This is so, first of all, since without fulfilling basic material needs, one would not be able to reach spiritual perfection, but also because the intellectual process itself is social in nature, and provides for Maimonides a Socratic-like spiritual cooperation among students and rabbis.

Many animals exist in a social framework, but most of them could survive and fulfill the purpose of their creation, sheer survival, without social cooperation. Only for human beings is social cooperation indispensable, on account of their being the highest and therefore also the most complex organism in the hierarchy of all living things. One's many essential needs, and the great differences among the individuals of the species, a negative aspect of human superiority, make organized social existence mandatory (*Guide* 1.72, 2.40). However, by insisting that many animals are also social creatures, Maimonides points out that human uniqueness is not in one's political nature but rather in intellectual capacity.[25]

This emphasis on the political nature of humanity, however, contradicts the basic theological premise that Adam was brought into being in a divine, secluded condition in Eden. His original nature was essentially non-political. He fulfilled perfectly all his material and spiritual needs without effort, and consequently without the need for social cooperation.

This description of the original state of humanity completely contradicts the premises of Greek political philosophy, which viewed politics as an essential means to elevate humanity from its primeval bestial state. Theology and philosophy are at odds. Theology views political life as an expression of humanity's deterioration from its original perfect state. However, for Plato and Aristotle, political life is an expression of humanity's elevation from the original bestial state. Such opposing views regarding the natural human condition necessarily created opposing views of the value of political life.

Maimonides, and most subsequent Jewish thinkers, tried to solve this contradiction by viewing the political nature of humanity not as its original nature, but rather as an acquired nature, adapted as a result of the fall. After Adam was reduced into an almost bestial state (*Guide* 1.2), only proper political organization could provide for his essential needs and elevate him again toward intellectual perfection.[26] Only Abravanel diverged from this compromise, and urged a theocratic-utopian quest for the prepolitical, paradisic condition of man.[27]

In order to create and maintain the proper political organization, law is needed, and authority to implement and enforce it. One of the unique features in Maimonides' presentation of the Mosaic prophecy is Moses' role as first lawgiver, who conveyed the revealed Torah to the people of Israel (*Guide* 2.39). The superiority of the Torah over any other (human) law is manifest both in its origin and its scope. Its divine origin entails that the Torah would always offer sound guidance for avoiding evil and doing good. Human law, however, is capable at best only of approximating it. Further, while the scope of divine law is all-inclusive and covers the material and spiritual aspects of human existence, human law has reference only to the (inferior) material sphere (*Guide* 2.40, 3.27–8).

In his classification of the law, Maimonides followed the traditional twofold distinction between human and divine law. Although he was extremely critical of Saadia's assertion that most of the commandments are rational, and insisted that social laws are essentially *nomoi* based upon "generally accepted opinions" (*mefursamot*), never-theless, Maimonides came close to Saadia's position. Although Saadia, Halevi, and Maimonides all adopted the distinction between human law and divine law, their theory of the law hints at the idea of natural law. This is manifest in their assertion that one has an instinctive comprehension that only by social cooperation and the rule of law can one survive and provide for material as well as spiritual needs. The idea of natural law, however, would fully penetrate Jewish political philosophy only with Albo, in the fifteenth century.[28]

If the Torah is a revealed divine law, then the prophet, whether as lawgiver (Moses) or one who exhorts the people and their rulers to obey the law (all other prophets), becomes a political leader. The pro-phet is, first of all, a philosopher, who knows God's attributes of action, the only divine attributes which are humanly knowable. Such knowledge of the attributes of action, which are the most remote from God's unknowable essence, is not only a manifestation of human epistemological limitations but is also related to his political function.

By divine grace which cares for the well-being of all created things, the philosopher-prophet is able to have knowledge of those attributes most relevant for the fulfillment of his political duties. He who has knowledge of the attributes of action must also practice what he has learned, by attempting to imitate God through leadership of human society. Thus the governance of the state becomes a microcosmic reflection of the way God rules the universe by loving-kindness, judg-ment, and righteousness (*Guide* 1.54, 3.53–4). When the whole cosmos is described in political terms as "the city of God" (*civitas Dei*), to borrow Augustine's phrasing, then the earthly city should become its microscopic reflection (*Guide* 3.51). This is why the word "God" in Hebrew (*Elohim*) is presented by Maimonides as a paronymous term, which primarily refers to every kind of ruler, king, and judge, and secondarily denotes God (*Guide* 1.2). This is also why Maimonides, like Halevi before him, uses so many parables of kings in order to describe the relationship between humans and God (*Kuzari* 1.19–24, 109; *Guide* 1.46, 3.51, etc.).[29]

Thus Maimonides' prophet, in contrast to the philosopher, must also have a well-developed imaginative capacity. This is necessary not only in order to be able to experience prophetic visions, but also to be able to lead the masses, who are ruled by the imaginative soul. It is not incidental that imagination is the common denominator between the prophet and the king. With his developed rational and imaginative soul, the prophet combines the functions of the philosopher, who has a developed rational soul only, and the king, who has a developed imaginative soul only (*Guide* 2.37).

Social existence, albeit limited, is a personal need of the philosopher himself. Without it he would not be able to fulfill his own material, emotional, and intellectual needs.[30] It is mainly his educational mission, however, which obligates him to engage in politics.

While the Aristotelian tradition emphasized the *theoretical* knowledge of God, the Platonic-Farabian and Jewish traditions emphasized *practical* imitation of divine attributes. Maimonides oscillates between the philosopher's urge, as a private person, to isolate himself in his intellectual activities, and his duty, as a "public prophet," to fulfill all his educational and political missions. Like (the Socratic) Jeremiah, with whom he so identifies, Maimonides struggles as a philosopher and communal leader between ibn Bājja's inclination toward the governance of the solitary, and the Platonic-Farabian – and very Jewish – emphasis on political involvement (*Guide* 3.51, 54).

In the end, Maimonides opted for political involvement. While the *Guide* commences with the theoretical knowledge of God (1.1), it ends with, and is climaxed by, the 'practical' *imitatio Dei* (3.54). Likewise, Maimonides' *Code* starts with theoretical knowledge, in *Hilkhot Yesodei ha-Torah*, and ends with praxis, in *Hilkhot Melakhim*. Dialectically, precisely the one who has reached the state where he is able to exist in complete intellectual isolation is obligated to engage in political life. In Platonic terms, he who sees the light of the sun is required to return to the darkness of the cave. In Maimonidean terms, he who reaches the uppermost rungs of the ladder available to humanity, is compelled to descend "with a view to governing and teaching the people of the land" (*Guide* 1.15). The Patriarchs who reached the highest possible degree of the knowledge of God were nevertheless engaged in material activities in order "to bring into being a religious community that would know and worship God" (*Guide* 3.51). Likewise, Moses ascended Sinai only to descend "and communicate to the people what he had heard" (*Guide* 3.22).[31]

The person charged with the daily operation of the state in the Maimonidean system is the king. Although, like most other Jewish thinkers, Maimonides' attitude toward monarchy was ambivalent, from the halakhic as well as the philosophical point of view, Maimonides did accept monarchy as the preferred regime. However, he severely limited its powers by the binding legal authority of the Torah, and the moral authority of the prophets.[32]

Maimonides' messianic views are markedly naturalistic, political, and restorative. The perfect political community, established by Moses, and reaching its climax with the reign of Solomon, would be re-established with the coming of the king-messiah, son of David, who would again create a perfect, Platonic-like state in the land of Israel.[33]

Maimonides' political philosophy, the issues it raised and the opinions he offered, became the point of departure for all subsequent

Jewish thinkers. The debate about the political functions of the philosopher-prophet became a bone of contention in future generations. Thinkers like Jacob Anatoli, Isaac Pollegar, and Yochanan Alemanno continued the Platonic-Farabian-Maimonidean emphasis on the prophet's political mission, while others, like Samuel ibn Tibbon, Moses Narboni, and Joseph ibn Shem Tov, insisted upon his intellectual isolation.[34] While most Jewish thinkers, albeit hesitantly, accepted limited monarchy as the perfect regime, Abravanel stood in almost isolated opposition, insisting upon the inequities of monarchy and advocating a republican theocracy. Likewise in sharp contrast to the Maimonidean system, Abravanel also described humanity's original state, and correspondingly the messianic era, in starkly anti-political terms.[35]

From the second half of the twelfth century, the cultural centers of medieval Judaism gradually shifted from a Muslim to a Christian-Latin environment, especially in Christian Spain, Provence, and Italy. The great philosophical and theological works of the Muslim period were now translated into Hebrew, serving the needs of a new reading public which did not know Arabic. Jewish émigrés from Muslim Spain, such as the Tibbonids and the Kimchis, brought with them to the new flourishing communities of southern Europe their expertise in Arabic and in Muslim philosophy and science. No less valuable, they also carried with them the manuscripts of the great works of Jewish and Muslim philosophers.

A great translation enterprise arose which covered all areas of philosophy, including politics. To begin with, the great Jewish works, such as those of Saadia Gaon, Bachya ibn Paquda, Halevi, and Maimonides were translated by Judah ibn Tibbon and his son Samuel. In the second stage, works written by Muslim philosophers, including their major political writings, were also translated. This was the first time texts of political philosophy had been translated into Hebrew. Whole sections of al-Fārābī's *The Virtuous State* were translated – twice – into Hebrew, paraphrased, and commented upon by Isaac ibn Laṭīf and Shem Tov ibn Falaquera in the first half of the thirteenth century. Major parts of ibn Laṭīf's *Gate of Heaven (Sha'ar ha-Shamayim)* and Falaquera's *Book of Degrees (Sefer ha-Ma'alot)* were translated, almost verbatim, from al-Fārābī's major political work. Falaquera also included in his *The Beginning of Wisdom (Reshit Hokhmah)* long paraphrases of al-Fārābī's *On the Attainment of Happiness* and his *Philosophy of Plato*. Moses ibn Tibbon translated al-Fārābī's *On Political Governance (Sefer ha-Hatchalot)*. There is also an anonymous translation of al-Fārābī's *Aphorisms of the Statesman*. Moses Narboni translated and commented upon ibn Ṭufayl's *Ḥayy ibn Yaqẓān* and ibn Bājja's *Governance of the Solitary*. Averroes' major political works, the *Com-*

mentary on Plato's Republic and the *Middle Commentary on the Nicomachean Ethics*, were translated in the early fourteenth century by Samuel ben Judah of Marseilles, while his *Middle Commentary on the Rhetoric* was translated, about the same time, by Todros Todrosi. The translation of Averroes' commentary on the *Republic* is of major importance, since the Arabic original is lost, and the Hebrew translation is all that is left of Averroes' most important political writing. The Hebrew translation was recopied and paraphrased quite a few times in the late Middle Ages, and during the Renaissance it was translated twice into Latin and exerted great influence.[36]

This translation enterprise created a philosophic and scientific Hebrew terminology. It also created, for the first time, Hebrew terms of political philosophy. In their translations from the politico-philosophical writings of Maimonides and al-Fārābī, Samuel ibn Tibbon and his son Moses created terms such as *medini* ("political") to describe human political nature, *kibbutz medini* for "state," and Hebrew terms for the various kinds of regimes, as transmitted from the Platonic original by al-Fārābī, such as *medinah mekubbetzet* or *kibbutzit*, literally "an associated state," or *kibbutz ha-cherut*, literally "the association of the free," both of which stand for democracy.[37]

A typical case is the history of the term *nimus*, which can stand for law in general, or human law in particular, depending on the context. This term was transferred to the Hebrew from the Arabic *namus*, which is a transliteration of the Greek *nomos*. *Nimus* now joined older Hebrew terms for law, such as *torah*, *choq*, and *dat*.[38]

Subsequent Jewish translators, such as Samuel ben Judah of Marseilles and Todros Todrosi, coined variants of these terms and others, and gradually created a full Hebrew dictionary of political philosophy.[39]

These translations, and the new Hebrew political terminology originated by them, created a framework in which Jewish thinkers in southern Europe from the thirteenth century on gradually developed a body of Jewish political thought in Hebrew. Main examples of this enterprise in the general theologico-philosophical literature can be found in Falaquera's *Book of Degrees*, Isaac Pollegar's *Defense of the Law (Ezer ha-Dat)*, Joseph Albo's *Book of Roots*, Abraham Shalom's *Abode of Peace (Sefer Neveh Shalom)*, Joseph ibn Shem Tov's *The Dignity of God (Kevod Elohim)*, and Yochanan Alemanno's *Eternal Life (Chai ha-Olamim)*. In the literature of philosophical homilies, such political discussions can be found in Jacob Anatoli's *Goad of the Students (Malmad ha-Talmidim)*, Nissim of Gerona's *Twelve Sermons (Sheteim Asar Derashot)*, Shem Tov ben Joseph ibn Shem Tov's *Sermons on the Torah (Derashot al ha-Torah)*, and Isaac Arama's *The Binding of Isaac (Aqedat Isaac)*.[40]

Philosophical commentaries on the Bible were an especially fertile ground for political discussion. The biblical text gave an abundance of opportunities to dwell on political issues. Major, but by no means isolated, examples are the story of Eden and the description of the development of humankind (Genesis 2–11), Jethro's advice to Moses (Exodus 18, Deuteronomy 1), and the laws of monarchy (Deuteronomy 17 and 1 Samuel 8). Some of the commentators eagerly pursued this opportunity and did not hesitate to interpret the biblical text according to the most up-to-date philosophical currents and political developments. Typical examples can be found in the commentaries of Joseph ibn Kaspi, Immanuel of Rome, and primarily Isaac Abravanel, who enthusiastically carried forth this tendency, almost ad absurdum.[41]

All these scholars based their political thinking on texts carried over from the Muslim milieu, which were based on a Platonic world view, and adapted to religious language by al-Fārābī, Averroes, and Maimonides. They continued in this manner for centuries after the centers of Jewish scholarship had moved to the Christian-Latin milieu.

Jewish scholars were quite knowledgeable about contemporary cultural trends in the Christian-Latin world. The emerging scholastic philosophy had a growing impact upon Jewish thought, at least from the late thirteenth century; not so, however, in the field of political philosophy. There were major developments in Christian political philosophy from the thirteenth century on, mainly as a result of the revolutionary impact of the translation of Aristotle's *Politics* into Latin (c. 1260). These developments, however, barely touched Jewish political thought.[42]

Various influences of scholastic political thought can be detected in the writings of late medieval Jewish thinkers. Such influences should not be overlooked, although they are still largely uninvestigated. Albo, and others following him, insinuated into Jewish thought the scholastic classification of the law and the term "natural law" (*lex natura, dat tivi'it*). By this they revolutionized legal theory in medieval Jewish philosophy, which was until then based upon a dual classification of the law into divine and human.[43]

Abravanel was somewhat acquainted with the writings of Aquinas and other scholastic writers. He did not hesitate to quote them directly in his biblical commentary, and sometimes even preferred their opinions over those of Jewish sages. His distinction between human government (*hanhagah enoshit*) and divine government (*hanhagah elohit*) seems to be influenced by the Christian distinction between temporal and spiritual authorities.[44]

There are a few translations into Hebrew of scholastic political texts, from Aquinas' *Summa* and others. A notable example is Giles of Rome's influential *De Regimine Principum*, which was anonymously translated into Hebrew in the fifteenth century under the title *Sefer Hanhagat ha-Melakhim*. The very fact that the anonymous Jewish scholar made the effort to translate such a long text demonstrates a well-grounded interest in scholastic political philosophy (at least on his part). There is, however, in our present knowledge, no detectable influence of this translation upon Jewish political philosophy. The fact that only the original manuscript survived, and we do not know about any copies made in subsequent generations, only reinforces this conclusion.[45]

The lack of reference to Aristotle's *Politics* in late medieval Jewish political philosophy well illustrates this state of affairs. The influence of the *Politics* penetrated Christian thought exactly at the time when the transition of Jewish culture from a Muslim to a Christian-Latin cultural milieu was in process. It could have been expected that now, at least, Jewish scholars would also be touched by the powerful influence of the *Politics*. This, however, did not happen. Samuel ben Judah of Marseilles, and, following him, Joseph ibn Kaspi in the fourteenth century, despite their knowledge of contemporary cultural trends, still translated and summarized the Averroist versions of Plato's *Republic* and Aristotle's *Ethics* and, following their Muslim masters, still assumed that the text of the *Politics* was not yet available in the West.[46]

Meir Alguades of Castille in the early fifteenth century was the first Jewish scholar to inform us that he "saw" a copy of the *Politics*. He still refrained, however, from translating the text, since Moerbeke's (literal) translation was quite incomprehensible to him, and he did not have a proper commentary on the text. There were already in existence quite a few Latin commentaries by Albertus Magnus, Aquinas, and others, but Alguades apparently did not have access to them. He thus continued in the traditional path by yet again translating the *Ethics*, this time from the Latin. From what Alguades informs us, however, it is clear that he had at least some knowledge of Aristotle's political philosophy. He was definitely aware of the great influence the *Politics* exerted upon Christian political philosophy.[47]

No late medieval or Renaissance Jewish scholar ever made the attempt to translate the *Politics* or any of its many commentaries into Hebrew, and very few even used the text. When Albo in the fifteenth century and Simone Luzzatto in the seventeenth century made use of the text, they mainly referred to Aristotle's critique of the Platonic system in the second book of the *Politics*. They preferred Aristotle's inductive and empirical approach over the deductive and idealistic approach of Plato's *Republic*. Both scholars, however, still used the *Politics* more as a critique of the Platonic system than as an independent system of politics. Their terms of reference were still essentially Platonic.[48]

Even Abravanel, who purportedly made massive use of the third book of the *Politics* in his famous commentary on 1 Samuel 8, did not use the text directly at all. He was influenced by some scholastic commentators who interpreted the text in accordance with their own political leanings. Thus, Abravanel mistakenly attributed to Aristotle's *Politics* a monarchic position which he himself opposed. Had he been better informed, he would have surely noticed that he himself, a professed "republican," was not so far from Aristotle's real position. Like most other Jewish scholars of the late Middle Ages, Abravanel knew the Aristotle of the *Ethics* and the *Metaphysics* well. His knowledge of the *Politics*, however, was still largely indirect and inaccurate, covered with a thick layer of scholastic misinterpretation. On the other hand, he was very familiar with Plato's *Republic* in its Farabian and Averroist interpretations, and the Platonic political tradition strongly influenced various aspects of his political philosophy.[49]

So strong was the power of cultural traditions and theological constraints that Jewish political thought continued to be attached to the *Republic* and the *Nicomachean Ethics* for a few hundred years after it had moved away from the sphere of the Muslim cultural milieu and into the orbit of Christian-Latin culture. Despite the enormous impact of the *Politics* upon late medieval Christian political philosophy, only faint echoes penetrated Jewish thought. It continued to be dependent upon the Platonic tradition up to the beginning of modern times. Al-Fārābī and Averroes, not Aquinas, continued to dominate Jewish political thought.

The full influence of scholastic thought upon Jewish political philosophy should still be investigated. However, even in this early stage of our knowledge, it can be assumed with a fairly high degree of certainty that it was quite marginal. This assessment becomes even stronger when we compare the marginal influence of scholastic political thought to the continuing influence of the Platonic-Muslim tradition, on the one hand, and the influence of scholastic philosophy upon other areas of Jewish philosophy, on the other.

In this respect, we cannot accept the theory presented some years ago by Ralph Lerner and Muhsin Mahdi, who distinguished between two branches of medieval Jewish political philosophy, one which was influenced by the Platonic-Muslim tradition and another which was influenced by the Christian-Latin tradition.[50] Our conclusion is that there was but one tradition, the Platonic-Muslim one. This tradition continued to dominate up to the beginning of modern times. The influence of Christian-Latin thought was quite marginal.

This state of affairs continued into the Renaissance. Jewish scholars contributed their medieval heritage to the humanist milieu. The Platonic tradition reappeared now in Renaissance Italy, after the Greek text of the *Republic* was brought from Byzantium and translated into Latin in the early fifteenth century. After that the *Republic* exerted a strong influence upon Renaissance political philosophy, culminating with Ficino's translation and commentary in the 1480s.[51] This situation created among Christian scholars an interest in the Hebrew translation of the Averroist paraphrase of the *Republic*. The text was retranslated – twice – into Latin by Jewish scholars for the consumption of a Christian audience. The first translation, in the mid-1480s, by Elijah del Medigo, was commissioned by Pico della Mirandola, while the second translation was made by Jacob Mantinus in the early sixteenth century, and was republished a few times during that century.[52]

Correspondingly, the Averroist text continued to dominate Jewish political thought. Now, however, it was well coordinated with the new dominant trend in Christian political philosophy. Long sections of the Hebrew text, dealing with the virtues of the philosopher-king, were inserted, almost verbatim, by Yochanan Alemanno into his eclectic *Eternal Life*.[53] This influence is also evident in del Medigo's rationalistic and anti-kabbalist treatise *The Examination of the Law (Bechinat ha-Dat)*,[54] and in Abravanel's later commentaries on the Bible, written in Italy in the last decade of the fifteenth century and at the beginning of the sixteenth century. Likewise, the Mantovan rabbi Judah Messer Leon inserted long paragraphs from Todrosi's Hebrew translation of Averroes' paraphrase on Aristotle's *Rhetoric*, dealing with the subject matters of politics and the classification of regimes, into his *Honeycomb's Flow (Nofet Tzufim)*, a rhetorical treatise which attempts to integrate the medieval rhetorical tradition with the Ciceronian trends of humanism.[55]

With the advent of the sixteenth century, influences of early modern political philosophy begin slowly to penetrate Jewish thought. The myth of the perfect Venetian constitution, which exerted enormous influence on early modern political philosophy, is manifest already in Isaac Abravanel's commentary on Exodus 19, where he interprets the Mosaic constitution, created by Jethronian advice, as the archetype of the Venetian *repubblica perfeta*. This Venetian influence culminated with Luzzatto's *Discorso* in the 1630s.[56]

Even some influence of Machiavelli started to penetrate, albeit slowly and hesitantly. Machiavelli was a very difficult influence to absorb. His assumed secularity, and his sharp separation of politics from spiritual issues, which he insisted upon, made it extremely difficult for Jewish scholars to graft it on to their theological, still medievally anchored, foundations. Still, Abraham Portaleone, in the late sixteenth century, kept a copy of Machiavelli's *Art of War (Arte della Guerra)* in his library. In the military discussion in his encyclopedic *Shields of the Mighty (Shiltei ha-Gibborim)*, where the ancient Israelite army is described as a popular militia, clear Machiavellian influence can be detected.[57] The Machiavellian influence is manifest in Luzzatto's *Discorso* and *Socrate*, written in the mid-seventeenth century. Here the term *ragione di stato* ("reason of state") appears for the first time in Jewish writing, and is employed in order to analyze biblical history and the Mosaic constitution.

Answering anti-Jewish propaganda, and basing himself upon Tacitus' *History*, which was very popular at the time, Luzzatto insists that Moses applied the principles of reason of state in the most perfect manner in order to solve political and military problems. If Tacitus, the wise politician, would not have been hindered by his own anti-semitism, he would have understood Moses' reasoning and admired his political acumen. Luzzatto here employs Tacitean political ideas in order to combat Tacitean anti-semitism. The whole tradition of the *ragione di stato* was heavy with Tacitean influence, which, like Machiavelli, was republican in essence, and approached politics from a secular and utilitarian angle.

The Machiavellian and Tacitean influences forced Luzzatto to deal with biblical history in a purely political context, devoid of any religious overtones or moral considerations. This is well illustrated by the way he chillingly describes Absalom's rebellion against his father, David, as a legitimate tactic in the struggle to acquire political power, where all means are justified by the successful outcome. Moreover, he also came close to the radical Machiavellian approach, which considered religion (merely) as a tool to serve temporal political ends. In this way Luzzatto explained to the gentile Taciteans the political raison d'être of such mitzvot as the prohibition to eat pork, celebrating the Sabbath, and the sabbatical year.

Along with his Machiavellianism and Taciteanism, Luzzatto was also heavily influenced by the myth of (the "perfect") Venice, noted above, and by economic proto-capitalist, mercantile ideas, common in the political thought of his day. He also employed the most up-to-date scientific theories in physics, astronomy, and medicine in order to analyze political phenomena.[58]

Luzzatto was the most "modern" Jewish political thinker we have encountered thus far. Still, he can also be called the last of the medievals. For all the influence of contemporary political thought upon him and others, they all still worked within an essentially theological and medieval framework. No traditional Jew, however much influenced by contemporary intellectual trends, could ever have rejected the revealed nature of the Mosaic constitution. In this respect, prior to the onset of the Enlightenment, Jewish political philosophy, like Jewish philosophy at large, was still essentially medieval, and only flavored with Renaissance ideas, not revolutionized by them.

It was Spinoza, following Luzzatto's ambivalent beginnings, who, in his *Theological-Political Treatise*, took Jewish political philosophy out of the medieval framework. He no longer presented the Torah as the eternal divine law, encompassing both temporal and spiritual aspects of human life, but rather as a humanly established law, contingent in nature, and aiming at solving the temporal problems of a particular people, at a particular juncture of their development.

Likewise, for Spinoza, Moses is described no longer as a divinely motivated prophet-lawgiver, a theological analogue of the Platonic philosopher-king, but rather as a shrewd Machiavellian politician who consciously exploited the mob's superstitions and their fear of God, in order to advance his own temporal political goals. By developing the myth of his divinely established mission and law, Moses secured the cooperation and obedience of the multitude in that difficult period in the formation of the nation. In this way, Spinoza completely secularized Jewish political philosophy; indeed, his *Political Treatise* has hardly any Jewish content at all.[59]

With Mendelssohn's *Jerusalem* and Nachman Krochmal's *Guide of the Perplexed of the Time (Moreh Nevukei ha-Zeman)*, written in the nineteenth century, there would be new attempts to create again a synthesis of Jewish political theology with contemporary political philosophy. On the other hand, however, modern Zionist literature, following Spinoza's lead, attempted to complete the process of "secularizing" Jewish political philosophy.[60]

❦ NOTES ❦

1 Jospe 1988b.
2 Lerner and Mahdi 1967, introduction; Susser and Don Yihyeh 1981; Susser 1981.
3 Lerner and Mahdi 1967, introduction. For the relevant publications of these scholars, see below and in the bibliography.
4 Lerner and Mahdi 1967, introduction.
5 Cohen 1984.
6 Rosenthal 1968.
7 Klibansky 1981, pp. 14–18, 39–41.
8 Barker 1964, p. 525.
9 Albo, *Roots* 1.9 (Husik). For knowledge of the *Politics* in Muslim philosophy, see Pines 1975; in Jewish philosophy, see Melamed 1992a, 1992b.
10 Walzer 1963a, pp. 41–2; 1963b, pp. 244–5.
11 Lerner and Mahdi 1967, introduction; Berman 1978; Melamed 1992a.
12 Walzer 1963a, p. 44; 1963b, pp. 244–5.
13 Lerner and Mahdi 1967, introduction.
14 Guttmann 1975; Strauss 1987.
15 Moses Rieti, *Miqdash Me'at* 22.

16 Berman 1961, 1974, 1981.

17 Wolfson 1962, p. 13.

18 For Muslim political philosophy in general, see Galston 1979, 1990; Marmura 1979; Lambton 1954, 1981; Leaman 1980; Pines 1957; Rosenthal 1940, 1948, 1968; Walzer 1963a.

19 Maimonides, *Millot ha-Higgayon* 14.7: p. 112 (Roth).

20 See in general note 18 above. For al-Fārābī, see al-Fārābī 1849, 1961, 1969, 1985; Berman 1961, 1974; Galston 1990; Kraemer 1979; Mahdi 1969; Strauss 1936, 1945, 1959, 1987. For Averroes, see Averroes 1842, 1969, 1974, 1992; Butterworth 1986; Daiber 1986; Mahdi 1978; Pines 1957. For ibn Bājja, see ibn Bājja 1896; Hayoun 1989, 1990; Leaman 1980; Shiffman 1991.

21 Berman 1974, p. 162; Kraemer 1987; Lambton 1981, p. 317; Walzer 1963b, p. 246.

22 Saadia Gaon, *Beliefs* 3.1–3: 137–47 (Rosenblatt); Altmann 1944; Fox 1975; Melamed 1986.

23 Motzkin 1980; Melamed forthcoming a, 3.1.

24 Ibn Daud, *Exalted Faith* 1852, pp. 98–101.

25 On Maimonides' political philosophy in general, see Altmann 1972; Berman 1959, 1961, 1974, 1987; Blidstein 1983; Davidson 1963; Epstein 1935; Frank 1985; Galston 1978, 1978–9; Goldman 1968, 1987; Hartman 1976, 1985; Harvey 1991; Harvey 1980; Kellner 1990, 1991; Kraemer 1979, 1986; Kreisel 1986, 1988, 1992; Lerner 1969, 1991; Levinger 1989; Loberbaum 1993; Macy 1982, 1986; Melamed 1985a, forthcoming a, 3.2; Pines 1963, 1979; Rosenthal 1935; Rotter 1979; Schwarzschild 1977; Strauss 1936, 1987; Wolfson 1936. On the debate about man's political versus solitary existence in Maimonides' thought, see Blumberg 1976; Kreisel 1992; Lerner 1991; Melamed 1994.

26 Berman 1980; Klein-Braslavy 1986.

27 Baer 1937; Netanyahu 1972, 2.3; Strauss 1937; Urbach 1937.

28 For Saadia's theory of law, see above, note 22. For Halevi's, see Strauss 1952a; for Albo, see Lerner 1964; Melamed 1985b, 1986, 1989. For the problem of natural law in Judaism in general, see Bleich 1982; Husik 1925; Novak 1988. There is considerable debate concerning Maimonides' view about natural law; see Dienstag 1987; Faur 1969; Fox 1972; Goodman 1978; Hyman 1980; Kasher 1985; Levine 1986; Melamed 1986; Schwarzschild 1962–3.

29 Berman 1959, 1961, 1974, 1981; Galston 1978; Goldman 1968; Melamed 1985a, forthcoming a, 3.2; Pines 1979; Strauss 1936, 1987.

30 Maimonides, *Commentary on the Mishnah: Introduction to Sefer Zeraim* (Rosner); *Guide* 3.51, 54 (Pines); Melamed 1994 and forthcoming a, 3.2.

31 For the political duties of the philosopher-prophet, see note 29 above. For ibn Bājja's influence upon Maimonides, see Berman 1959. For the parable of Jacob's dream, see Klein-Braslavy 1988.

32 For Maimonides' attitude towards monarchy, see Blidstein 1983. On the attitude toward monarchy in general, see Blidstein 1982–3; Melamed forthcoming a, 1.3; Polish 1971, 1989, 1991; Rosenthal 1958.

33 Blidstein 1983; Funkenstein 1977; Hartman 1978; Kraemer 1984; Ravitzky 1991.

34 For ibn Tibbon, see Kellner forthcoming; Ravitzky 1981. For Anatoli, see Melamed 1988a. For Alemanno, see Melamed 1988b. For Narboni, see Hayoun

1989, 1990. For Gersonides and Crescas, see Harvey 1990; Rosenthal 1980; and see in general, Melamed forthcoming a, 3.3.

35 Baer 1937; Netanyahu 1972, 2.3–4; Smoler and Auerbach 1972; Strauss 1937; Urbach 1937.

36 For ibn Latif, see Heller Wilensky 1967. For Falaquera, see *Book of Degrees* 16–17, *The Beginning of Wisdom* 70–1; Efros 1934–5; Jospe 1986, 1988a, 3.5; Plessner 1956; Shiffman 1991. For both, see Melamed 1992c, forthcoming a, 5. For the Hebrew translation of al-Fārābī's *Aphorisms of the Statesman*, see the introduction in al-Fārābī 1961. For Narboni and ibn Bājja, see Hayoun 1989, 1990; Rosenthal 1980. For Averroes, see *Averroes' Commentary on Plato's Republic* (trans. Rosenthal 1969), *Averroes on Plato's Republic* (trans. Lerner 1974), and Berman 1967, 1968–9. For the manuscripts of the Hebrew translation, see Averroes 1969, introduction; Teicher 1960. For the Latin translations, see note 52 below. For the translation of the *Nicomachean Ethics*, see Berman 1978, 1988. For the *Rhetoric*, see Averroes 1842; Lesley 1984; and see Chiesa 1986.

37 Efros 1924; Klatzkin 1928; Melamed 1976, 2:1–60; 1993a.

38 See note 37 above and Kraemer 1986.

39 See note 37 above and Averroes 1969, pp. 306–32; 1974, pp. 167–70.

40 All these texts except Alemanno's have been published already. For Falaquera's political thought, see note 36 above. For Pollegar, see Belasco 1905; Melamed forthcoming a, 7; Pines 1986. For Shalom, see Melamed forthcoming a, 7 and Tirosh-Rothschild 1990. For Joseph ibn Shem Tov, see Gutwirth 1988; Melamed forthcoming a, 3.3. For Alemanno, see Melamed 1976, 1982b, forthcoming a, 6; Rosenthal 1979. For Anatoli, see Melamed 1988a; forthcoming a, 4. For Nissim of Gerona, see Loberbaum 1993; Melamed forthcoming d; Ravitzky 1990. For Arama, see Heller Wilensky 1956; Melamed forthcoming d. There is no research as yet on the sermons of Shem Tov ben Joseph ibn Shem Tov.

41 Melamed 1982a, 1985a, 1990a, 1993b; Segal 1938; Smoler and Auerbach 1972.

42 For scholastic influences upon Jewish philosophy, see Pines 1977a. For scholastic political philosophy, see Ullmann 1956; Aquinas 1970. For the influence of the *Politics* on Christian political philosophy, see Dunabin 1982.

43 See note 28 above.

44 Melamed 1990a; Netanyahu 1972, 2.3.

45 Melamed 1992a, forthcoming c.

46 Berman 1967; Melamed 1992a.

47 Berman 1988; Melamed 1992a.

48 Melamed 1992a.

49 Baer 1937; Melamed 1988a, 1992a, 1992b; Netanyahu 1972, 2.3; Strauss 1937.

50 Lerner and Mahdi 1967, introduction; Melamed 1992a.

51 On the Platonic tradition, see Hankins 1991; on Renaissance political philosophy in general, see Skinner 1988.

52 Averroes 1992, introduction; Melamed 1995.

53 Melamed 1982b, 1988b, forthcoming a, 6; Rosenthal 1979.

54 Melamed 1995.

55 Melamed 1976, 1978.

56 Melamed 1976, 1983, 1987, 1990a; Netanyahu 1972, 2.3.

57 Melamed 1976. For the treatment of the ancient Hebrew leaders by Machiavelli,

see Melamed 1990b, forthcoming a, 8; also Robinson 1975. On Machiavelli in general, see Winiarski 1969.

58 Backi 1946; Melamed 1976, 1984; Ravid 1978; Septimus 1987.

59 Guttmann 1979; Harvey 1978, 1981; Lazaroff 1982; McShea 1968; Motzkin 1990; Pines 1977b, 1986; Rava 1931; Septimus 1987; Strauss 1952b; Wolfson 1969; Yerushalmi 1983.

60 For Mendelssohn's political thought, see Altmann 1980; Berney 1950; Fox 1976; Guttmann 1979; Lazaroff 1982; Rotenstreich 1953. For Krochmal, see Harris 1991. On Zionism, see Avineri 1982.

❧ BIBLIOGRAPHY ❧

Texts

Abravanel, I. (1956) *Commentary on the Early Prophets* (Jerusalem: Torah ve-Da'at).

—— (1957) *Commentary on the Later Prophets* (Jerusalem: Torah ve-Da'at).

Albo, J. (1929) *Book of Roots*, edited and translated by I. Husik, 5 vols. (Philadelphia: Jewish Publication Society).

Al-Fārābī (1849) *Sefer ha-Hatchalot*, translated by Samuel ibn Tibbon, in *Sefer ha-Asif*, edited by Z. Filipowsky (Leipzig: Köhler; reprinted Jerusalem, 1970), pp. 1–64.

—— (1961) *Aphorisms of the Statesman*, translated by D. M. Dunlop (Cambridge: Cambridge University Press).

—— (1969) *Alfarabi's Philosophy of Plato and Aristotle*, translated by M. Madhi (Ithaca: Cornell University Press).

—— (1985) *On the Perfect State*, translated by R. Walzer (Oxford: Oxford University Press).

Anatoli, J. (1866) *Malmad ha-Talmidim* (Lyck: Mekitze Nirdamim).

Aquinas (1970) *Selected Political Writings*, edited by A. P. D'Entreves and translated by J. G. Dawson (Oxford: Blackwell).

Aristotle (1967) *The Politics*, translated by T. A. Sinclair (Harmondsworth: Penguin).

—— (1969) *Ethics*, translated by J. A. K. Thomson (Harmondsworth: Penguin).

Averroes (1842) *Biur Sefer ha-Halazah le-Aristo be-Ha'atakat Todros Todrosi*, edited by I. Goldenthal (Leipzig).

—— (1969) *Averroes' Commentary on Plato's Republic*, translated by E. I. J. Rosenthal (Cambridge: Cambridge University Press).

—— (1974) *Averroes on Plato's Republic*, translated by R. Lerner (Ithaca and London: Cornell University Press).

—— (1992) *Parafrasi della "Republica" nella traduzione latina di Elia del Medigo*, edited by A. Coviello and P. E. Fornaciari (Florence: Olschki).

Halevi, J. (1968) *The Kuzari*, translated by H. Hirschfeld (New York: Schocken).

Hartman, D. (ed.) (1985) *Crisis and Leadership: Epistles of Maimonides* (Philadelphia: Jewish Publication Society).

ibn Bājja (1896) "Beur Kavanat le-Abu Baker Al-Zaig be-Hanhagar ha-Mitboded," *Kovetz Al Yad* 6: 3–33.

ibn Daud, A. (1852) *Ha-Emunah ha-Ramah* (Frankfurt am Main; reprinted Jerusalem, 1967).

ibn Falaquera, S. (1902) *Reshit Hokma*, in *Ketavim*, vol. 2 (Berlin; reprinted Jerusalem, 1970).

—— (1894) *Sefer ha-Ma'alot*, in *Ketavim*, vol. 2 (Berlin; reprinted Jerusalem, 1970).

ibn Kaspi, J. (1903) *Mishneh Kesef*, in *Ketavim*, vol. 1 (Pressburg: Alkalay).

ibn Tibbon, S. (1837) *Ma'amar Yiqqavu ha-Mayim* (Pressburg: Schmid).

Immanuel of Rome (1487) *Commentary on the Book of Proverbs* (Naples; reprinted with an introduction by D. Goldstein, Jerusalem, 1981).

Krochmal, N. (1863) *More Neboche ha-Seman* [Hebrew] (Leopoli: Michaelis F. Poremba).

Lerner, R. and M. Mahdi (eds.) (1967) *Medieval Political Philosophy: A Sourcebook* (New York: Free Press).

Luzzatto, S. (1638) *Discorso circa il stato degli ebrei in Venezia* (Venice; reprinted Bologna, 1976).

—— (1651) *Socrate overo del humano sapere* (Venice).

—— (1951) *Ma'amar al Yehudei Venezia*, translated by D. Lates (Jerusalem: Bialik Institute).

Machiavelli, N. (1940) *The Prince and the Discourses*, translated by M. Lerner (New York: Modern Library).

Maimonides (1963a) *The Guide of the Perplexed*, translated by S. Pines, 2 vols. (Chicago: University of Chicago Press).

—— (1963b) *The Code of Maimonides, Book 14: Book of Judges*, translated by A. M. Hershman (New Haven and London: Yale University Press).

—— (1965a) *Millot ha-Higgayon*, translated by Moses ibn Tibbon and edited by L. Roth (Jerusalem: Magnes).

—— (1965b) *The Book of Knowledge*, translated by M. Hyamson (Jerusalem: Boys Town).

—— (1968) *The Commentary to Mishnah Avot*, translated by A. David (New York: Bloch).

—— (1975a) *Ethical Works of Maimonides* translated by R. L. Weiss and C. E. Butterworth (New York: New York University Press).

—— (1975b) *Commentary to the Mishnah: Introduction to Sefer Zeraim*, translated by F. Rosner (New York: Feldheim).

—— (1987) *Iggrot ha-Rambam*, edited by I. Shilat, 2 vols. (Jerusalem: Ma'aliot).

Mendelssohn, M. (1983) *Jerusalem*, translated by A. Arkush (Hanover and London: University Press of New England).

Messer Leon, J. (1983) *The Book of the Honeycomb's Flow*, edited and translated by I. Rabinowitz (Ithaca: Cornell University Press).

Nissim of Gerona (1973) *Shneim Asar Derashot le-ha-Ran*, edited by L. A. Feldman (Jerusalem: Institute Shalom).

Philo (1957) *On the Life of Moses,* in *Works*, translated by F. H. Colson, vol. 6 (Cambridge, MA: Harvard University Press).

Plato (1937) *The Dialogues of Plato*, translated by B. Jowett (New York: Random House).

—— (1967) *The Republic*, translated by F. M. Cornford (New York and London: Oxford University Press).

Pollegar, I. (1984) *Ezer ha-Dat*, edited by J. Levinger (Tel Aviv: Tel Aviv University Press).

Rieti, M. (1851) *Miqdash Me'at*, edited by J. Goldenthal (Vienna).

Saadia Gaon (1967) *The Book of Beliefs and Opinions*, translated by S. Rosenblatt (New Haven: Yale University Press).

Shalom, A. (1575) *Sefer Neveh Shalom*, 2 vols. (Venice; reprinted Jerusalem, 1967).

Shem Tov, J. (1556) *Kevod Elohim* (Ferarra).

Shem Tov, ben J. (1507) *Derashot al ha-Torah* (Venice; reprinted Jerusalem, 1974).

Spinoza, B. (1951) *The Chief Works of Spinoza*, vol. 1: *Theologico-Political Treatise* and *Political Treatise*, translated by R. H. M. Elwes (New York: Dover).

Studies

Altmann, A. (1944) "Sa'adia's Conception of the Law," *Bulletin of the John Rylands Library* 27: 320–39.

—— (1972) "Maimonides' Four Perfections," *Israel Oriental Studies* 2: 15–24.

—— (1980) "The Quest for Liberty in Moses Mendelssohn's Political Philosophy" [Hebrew], *Da'at* 5: 13–24.

Avineri, S. (1982) *The Making of Modern Zionism: The Intellectual Origins of the Jewish State* (London: Weidenfeld & Nicolson).

Backi, R. (1946) "La dottrina sulla dinamica della città – secondo Giobanni Botero e secondo Simone Luzzatto," *Atti della Accademia Nazionale dei Lincei* 8: 369–78.

Baer, I. (1937) "Don Isaac Abravanel on the Problems of History and State" [Hebrew], *Tarbitz* 8: 241–58.

Barker, E. (1964) *The Political Thought of Plato and Aristotle* (New York: Dover).

Belasco, G. (1905) "Isaac Polgar's *Support of Religion*," *Jewish Quarterly Review* 27: 26–56.

Berman, L. V. (1959) *Ibn Bājja and Maimonides: A Chapter in the History of Political Philosophy* [Hebrew]. Ph.D. dissertation, Hebrew University of Jerusalem.

—— (1961) "The Political Interpretation of the Maxim: The Purpose of Philosophy is the Imitation of God," *Studia Islamica* 15: 53–61.

—— (1967) " 'Greek into Hebrew': Samuel ben Judah of Marseilles, Fourteenth Century Philosopher and Translator," in *Jewish Medieval and Renaissance Studies*, edited by A. Altmann (Cambridge, MA: Harvard University Press), pp. 289–320.

—— (1968–9) "Review of E. I. J. Rosenthal's *Averroes' Commentary on Plato's Republic*," *Oriens* 21–2: 436–9.

—— (1969) "A Re-examination of Maimonides' Statement on Political Science," *Journal of the American Oriental Society* 89: 106–11.

—— (1974) "Maimonides, The Disciple of Alfarabi," *Israel Oriental Studies* 4: 154–78.

—— (1978) "Ibn Rushd's Middle Commentary on the *Nicomachean Ethics* in Medieval Hebrew Literature," in *Multiple Averroes*, edited by J. Jolivet (Paris: Belles Lettres), pp. 287–301.

—— (1980) "Maimonides on the Fall of Man," *AJS Review* 5: 1–15.

—— (1981) "Maimonides on Political Leadership," in *Kinship and Consent*, edited by D. J. Elazar (Philadelphia: Turtledove), pp. 13–25.

—— (1987) "The Ideal State of the Philosophers and the Prophetic Laws," in *A Straight Path: Studies in Medieval Philosophy and Culture in Honor of A. Hyman*, edited by R. Link-Salinger (Washington, DC: Catholic University of America Press), pp. 10–22.

—— (1988) "The Latin to Hebrew Translation of the *Nicomachean Ethics*" [Hebrew], in *Shlomo Pines Jubilee Volume*, edited by M. Idel, E. Schweid, and W. Z. Harvey (Jerusalem: Daf Noy), 1: 147–68.

—— (1991) "The Ethical Views of Maimonides within the Context of Islamicate Civilization," in *Perspectives on Maimonides*, edited by J. L. Kraemer (Oxford: Oxford University Press), pp. 13–32.

Berney, A. (1950) "Moses Mendelssohn's Historical and Political Outlook" [Hebrew], *Zion* 5: 99–111, 248–70.

Bleich, J. D. (1982) "Judaism and Natural Law," in *Proceedings of the Eighth World Congress of Jewish Studies* (Jerusalem: World Union of Jewish Studies), 3: 7–11.

Blidstein, G. J. (1980) "On Political Structure," *Jewish Journal of Sociology* 22: 47–58.

—— (1982–3) "The Monarchic Imperative in Rabbinic Perspective," *AJS Review* 8–9: 15–39.

—— (1983) *Political Concepts in Maimonidean Halacha* [Hebrew] (Ramat Gan: Bar Ilan University Press).

Blumberg, Z. (1976) "Al Farabi, Ibn Bajja and Maimonides on the Governance of the Solitary" [Hebrew], *Sinai* 78: 35–45.

Butterworth, C. E. (1986) *Philosophy, Ethics and Virtuous Rule: A Study of Averroes' Commentary on Plato's Republic* [Cairo Papers in Social Sciences 9].

Chiesa, B. (1986) "Note su al-Farabi, Averroè ibn Bagga (Avempace) in traduzione ebraica," *Henoch* 8: 79–86.

Cohen, S. A. (1984) "The Concept of the Three Ketarim: Its Place in Jewish Political Thought and its Implications for a Study of Jewish Constitutional History," *AJS Review* 9: 27–54.

Daiber, H. (1986) "The Ruler as Philosopher: A New Interpretation of Al-Fārābī's View," in *Mededelingen der Koninklijke Nederlandse Akademie van Wetenschappen* (Amsterdam: North Holland), pp. 133–49.

Davidson, H. A. (1963) "Maimonides' *Shemonah Perakim* and al-Fārābī's *Fuṣūl al-Madanī*," *Proceedings of the American Academy for Jewish Research* 31: 33–50.

Dienstag, J. I. (1987) "Natural Law in Maimonidean Thought and Scholarship," *The Jewish Law Annual* 6: 65–77.

Dunabin, J. (1982) "The Reception and Interpretation of Aristotle's Politics," in *The Cambridge History of Later Medieval Philosophy*, edited by N. Kretzmann, A. Kenny, and J. Pinborg (Cambridge: Cambridge University Press), pp. 723–37.

Efros, I. (1924) *Philosophical Terms in the Moreh Nebukhim* (New York: Columbia University Press).

—— (1934–5) "Palquera's *Reshit Hokmah* and Alfarabi's *Ihṣa' al-'ulūm*," *Jewish Quarterly Review* 25: 227–35.

Epstein, I. (1935) "Maimonides' Conception of the Law and the Ethical Trend of His Halachah," in *Moses Maimonides*, edited by I. Epstein (London: Soncino), pp. 61–86.

Faur, J. (1969) "The Source of the Obligation of the Law According to Maimonides" [Hebrew], *Tarbitz* 38: 43–53.

Fox, M. (1972) "Maimonides and Aquinas on Natural Law," *Dine Israel* 3: 5–36.

—— (1975) "The Rational Commandments in Sa'adia's Philosophy: A Re-examination," in *Modern Jewish Ethics*, edited by M. Fox (Columbus: Ohio State University Press), pp. 174–87.

—— (1976) "Law and Ethics in Modern Jewish Philosophy: The Case of Moses Mendelssohn," *Proceedings of the American Academy for Jewish Research* 43: 1–13.

—— (1987) "Law and Morality in the Thought of Maimonides," in *Maimonides as Codifier of Jewish Law*, edited by N. Rakover (Jerusalem: Library of Jewish Law), pp. 105–20.

Frank, D. H. (1985) "The End of the *Guide*: Maimonides on the Best Life for Man," *Judaism* 34: 485–95.

Funkenstein, A. (1977) "Maimonides: Political Theory and Realistic Messianism," *Miscellanea Medievalia* 11: 81–103.

—— (1991) "The Image of the Ruler in Late Medieval Jewish Thought" [Hebrew], in *Perceptions of Jewish History from the Antiquity to the Present* (Tel Aviv: Am Oved), pp. 180–8.

Galston, M. (1978) "Philosopher King vs. Prophet," *Israel Oriental Studies* 8: 204–18.

—— (1978–9) "The Purpose of the Law According to Maimonides," *Jewish Quarterly Review* 69: 27–51.

—— (1979) "Realism and Idealism in Avicenna's Political Philosophy," *The Review of Politics* 41: 561–77.

—— (1990) *Politics and Excellence: The Political Philosophy of Alfarabi* (Princeton: Princeton University Press).

Goitein, S. D. (1968) "Attitude Towards Government in Islam and Judaism," in *Studies in Islamic History and Institutions*, edited by S. D. Goitein (Leiden: Brill), pp. 197–213.

Goldman, E. (1968) "The Worship as Practiced by One who Has Apprehended the True Realities Peculiar Only to Him: A Commentary on the *Guide* 3, 51–54" [Hebrew], *Sefer Bar Ilan* 6: 287–313.

—— (1987) "Political and Legal Philosophy in the *Guide of the Perplexed*," in *Maimonides as Codifier of Jewish Law*, edited by N. Rakover (Jerusalem: Library of Jewish Law), pp. 155–64.

Goodman, L. E. (1978) "Maimonides' Philosophy of Law," *Jewish Law Annual* 1: 72–107.

Guttmann, J. (1975) "Philosophy of Religion or Philosophy of Law" [Hebrew], *Proceedings of the Israel Academy of Sciences and the Humanities* 5: 188–207.

—— (1979) "Mendelssohn's *Jerusalem* and Spinoza's *Tractatus Theologico-Politicus*" [Hebrew], in *Religion and Knowledge* (Jerusalem: Magnes), pp. 192–217.

Gutwirth, E. (1988) "El governador judio ideal: acerca de un sermo inédito de Yosef ibn Shem Tob," in *Congresso internacional encuentre tres culturas* (Toledo), 3: 67–75.

—— (1989) "Duran on Ahitofel: The Practice of Jewish History in Late Medieval Spain," *Jewish History* 4: 59–74.

Hankins, J. (1991) *Plato in the Italian Renaissance* (Leiden: Brill).

Harris, J. (1991) *Nachman Krochmal: Guiding the Perplexed of the Modern Age* (New York: New York University Press).

Hartman, D. (1976) *Maimonides: Torah and Philosophic Quest* (Philadelphia: Jewish Publication Society).

—— (1978) "Maimonides's Approach to Messianism and its Contemporary Implications," *Da'at* 1: 5–33.

Harvey, S. (1991) "Maimonides in the Sultan's Palace," in *Perspectives on Maimonides*, edited by J. K. Kraemer (Oxford: Oxford University Press), pp. 47–75.

Harvey, W. Z. (1978) "Maimonides and Spinoza on the Knowledge of Good and Evil" [Hebrew], *Iyyun* 28: 165–85.

—— (1980) "Between Political Philosophy and Halakha in Maimonides' Thought" [Hebrew], *Iyyun* 29: 198–212.

—— (1981) "Spinoza vs. the Prophets on the Problem of the Critique of Government" [Hebrew], *Kivunim* 12: 83–90.

—— (1990) "The Philosopher and Politics: Gersonides and Crescas," in *Scholars and Scholarship: The Interaction Between Judaism and Other Cultures*, edited by L. Landman (New York: Yeshiva University Press), pp. 53–65.

Hayoun, M. R. (1989) "Moses Narboni and ibn Bajja" [Hebrew], *Da'at* 18: 27–44.

—— (1990) "Ibn Bajja and Moses Narboni: *Iggeret ha-Petirah*" [Hebrew], *Da'at* 25: 93–125.

Heller Wilensky, S. O. (1956) *Isaac Arama and his Philosophical System* [Hebrew] (Jerusalem and Tel Aviv: Bialik Institute).

—— (1967) "Isaac ibn Latif: Philosopher or Kabbalist?" in *Jewish Medieval and Renaissance Studies*, edited by A. Altmann (Cambridge, MA: Harvard University Press), pp. 185–223.

Husik, I. (1925) "The Law of Nature, Hugo Grotius and the Bible," *Hebrew Union College Annual* 2: 382–93.

Hyman, A. (1980) "A Note on Maimonides' Classification of Law," *Proceedings of the Jewish Academy for Jewish Research* 46–7: 323–43.

Jospe, R. (1986) "Rejecting Moral Virtue as the Ultimate End," in *Studies in Islamic and Judaic Traditions*, edited by W. Brinner and S. D. Ricks (Denver: Scholars Press), pp. 185–204.

—— (1988a) *Torah and Sophia: The Life and Thought of Shem Tov Ibn Falaquera* (Cincinnati: Hebrew Union College Press).

—— (1988b) *What is Jewish Philosophy?* (Tel Aviv: Open University Press).

Kasher, H. (1985) "Maimonides' Attitude Towards the Classification of the Laws into Rational and Revealed" [Hebrew], *Hebrew Union College Annual* 56: 1–7.

Kellner, M. (1990) *Maimonides on Human Perfection* (Atlanta: Scholars Press).

—— (1991) "Reading Rambam: Approaches to the Interpretation of Maimonides," *Jewish History* 5: 73–93.

—— (1994) "Politics and Perfection: Gersonides vs. Maimonides," *Jewish Political Studies Review* 6: 49–82.

—— (forthcoming) "Maimonides and Samuel ibn Tibbon on Jeremiah 9:22–23 and Human Perfection," in *Festschrift for E. Rackman*.

Klatzkin, J. A. C. (1928) *Thesaurus Philosophicus Linguae Hebraicae et Veteris et Recentioris*, 3 vols. (Berlin: Eschkol).

Klein-Braslavy, S. (1986) *Maimonides' Interpretation of the Adam Stories in Genesis: A Study of Maimonides' Anthropology* [Hebrew] (Jerusalem: Reuben Mass).

—— (1988) "Maimonides' Interpretation of Jacob's Dream of the Ladder" [Hebrew], *Sefer Bar Ilan* 23: 329–49.

Klibansky, R. (1981) *The Continuity of the Platonic Tradition During the Middle Ages* (London: Warburg Institute).

Kraemer, J. L. (1979) "Al Farabi's *Opinions of the Virtuous State* and Maimonides' *Foundation of the Law*," in *Studia Orientalia Memoriae D. H. Baneth Dedicata*, edited by J. Blau, M. Kister, S. Pines, and S. Shaked (Jerusalem: Magnes), pp. 107–53.

—— (1984) "On Maimonides' Messianic Posture," in *Studies in Medieval Jewish History and Literature*, edited by I. Twersky (Cambridge, MA: Harvard University Press), 1: 109–42.

—— (1986) "*Namus* and *Sharia* in Maimonides' Thought" [Hebrew], *Teudah* 4: 183–202.

—— (1987) "The *Jihad* of the *Falasifa*," *Jerusalem Studies in Arabic and Islam* 10: 289–324.

Kreisel, H. (1986) "Wise Man and Prophet in Maimonides' Thought and His Circle" [Hebrew], *Eshel Beer Sheva* 3: 149–69.

—— (1988) "The Practical Intellect in the Philosophy of Maimonides," *Hebrew Union College Annual* 59: 189–215.

—— (1992) "Individual Perfection vs. Communal Welfare and the Problem of Contradictions in Maimonides' Approach to Ethics," *Proceedings of the American Academy for Jewish Research* 58: 107–41.

Lambton, A. K. S. (1954) "The Theory of Kingship in the *Nasihat al-muluk* of Ghazali," *Islamic Quarterly* 1: 47–55.

—— (1981) *State and Government in Medieval Islam* (Oxford: Oxford University Press).

Lazaroff, A. (1982) "The Concept of Judaism as Revealed Law in Spinoza's *Tractatus Theologico-Politicus* and Mendelssohn's *Jerusalem*," *Proceedings of the Eighth World Congress of Jewish Studies* (Jerusalem: World Union of Jewish Studies), 3: 81–6.

Leaman, O. (1980) "Ibn Bājja on Society and Philosophy," *Der Islam* 57: 109–19.

Lerner, R. (1964) "Natural Law in Albo's *Book of Roots*," in *Ancients and Moderns*, edited by J. Cropsey (New York: Basic Books), pp. 132–47.

—— (1969) "Maimonides," in *History of Political Philosophy*, edited by L. Strauss and J. Cropsey (Chicago: Rand McNally), pp. 181–200.

—— (1991) "Maimonides' Governance of the Solitary," in *Perspectives on Maimonides*, edited by J. L. Kraemer (Oxford: Oxford University Press), pp. 33–46.

Lesley, A. M. (1984) "A Survey of Medieval Hebrew Rhetoric," in *Approaches to Judaism in Medieval Times*, vol. 1, edited by D. R. Blumenthal (Chico: Scholars Press), pp. 107–33.

Levey, G. B. (1987) "Judaism and the Obligation to Die for the State," *AJS Review* 12: 175–203.

Levine, M. P. (1986) "The Role of Reason in the Ethics of Maimonides: or Why

Maimonides Could Have Had a Doctrine of Natural Law Even If He Did Not," *Journal of Religious Ethics* 14: 279–95.

Levinger, J. (1989) *Maimonides as Philosopher and Codifier* [Hebrew] (Jerusalem: Bialik Institute).

Loberbaum, M. (1993) *Politics and the Limits of Law in Jewish Medieval Thought: Maimonides and Nissim Gerundi* [Hebrew]. Ph.D. dissertation, Hebrew University of Jerusalem.

McShea, R. J. (1968) *The Political Philosophy of Spinoza* (New York: Columbia University Press).

Macy, J. (1982) *Maimonides' Shemonah Peraqim and Al-Fārābī's Fuṣūl al Madanī: A Study in Medieval Jewish and Arabic Political Philosophy* [Hebrew]. Ph.D dissertation, Hebrew University of Jerusalem.

—— (1986) "The Rule of Law and the Rule of Wisdom in Plato, al-Farabi and Maimonides," in *Studies in Islamic and Judaic Traditions*, edited by W. Brinner and S. D. Ricks (Atlanta: Scholars Press), pp. 205–21.

Mahdi, M. (1969) "Al Farabi," in *History of Political Philosophy*, edited by L. Strauss and J. Cropsey (Chicago: Rand McNally), pp. 160–80.

—— (1978) "Al-Farabi et Averroes: remarques sur le commentaire d'Averroes sur la *République* de Platon," in *Multiple Averroes*, edited by J. Jolivet (Paris: Belles Lettres), pp. 91–101.

Malter, H. (1910) "Shem Tov ben Joseph Palquera," *Jewish Quarterly Review*, n.s. 2: 151–81.

Marmura, M. E. (1979) "The Philosopher and Society: Some Medieval Arabic Discussions," *Arab Studies Quarterly* 1: 309–23.

Melamed, A. (1976) *The Political Thought of Jewish Thinkers in the Italian Renaissance*, 2 vols. [Hebrew]. Ph.D. dissertation, Tel Aviv University.

—— (1978) "Rhetoric and Philosophy in Judah Messer Leon's *Nofet Zufim*" [Hebrew], *Italia* 1: 7–38.

—— (1982a) "The Dignity of Man in late Medieval and Renaissance Jewish Thought in Spain and Italy" [Hebrew], *Italia* 3: 39–88.

—— (1982b) "Yohanan Alemanno on the Development of Human Society" [Hebrew], *Proceedings of the Eighth World Congress of Jewish Studies* (Jerusalem: World Union of Jewish Studies), 3: 85–93.

—— (1983) "The Myth of Venice in Italian Renaissance Jewish Thought," *Italia Judaica* 1: 401–13.

—— (1984) "Simone Luzzatto on Tacitus: Apologetica and Ragione di Stato," in *Studies in Medieval Jewish History and Literature*, edited by I. Twersky (Cambridge, MA: Harvard University Press), 2: 143–70.

—— (1985a) "Philosophical Commentaries on Jeremiah 9: 22–23 in Medieval and Renaissance Jewish Thought" [Hebrew], *Jerusalem Studies in Jewish Thought* 4: 31–82.

—— (1985b) "Natural, Human, Divine: Classification of the Law among Some Fifteenth and Sixteenth Century Italian Jewish Thinkers," *Italia* 4: 59–93.

—— (1986) "The Law of Nature in Medieval and Renaissance Jewish Thought" [Hebrew], *Da'at* 17: 49–66.

—— (1987) "English Travellers and Venetian Jewish Scholars: The Case of Simone Luzzatto and James Harrington," in *Gli ebrei in Venezia*, edited by G. Cozzi (Venice: Edizioni Comunita), pp. 507–25.

—— (1988a) "The Political Discussion in Anatoli's *Malmad ha-Talmidim*" [Hebrew], *Da'at* 20: 91–115.

—— (1988b) "The Hebrew *Laudatio* of Yohanan Alemanno: In Praise of Lorenzo il Magnifico and the Florentine Constitution," in *Jews in Italy: Studies Dedicated to the Memory of U. Cassuto*, edited by H. Beinart (Jerusalem: Magnes), pp. 1–34.

—— (1989) "Did ibn Wakar Precede Albo in the Classification of the Law?" [Hebrew], in *Tura: Studies in Jewish Political Thought*, edited by M. Ayali (Tel Aviv: Ha-Kibbutz Hameuchad), 1: 270–84.

—— (1990a) "Jethro's Advice in Medieval and Early Modern Jewish and Christian Political Thought," *Jewish Political Studies Review* 2: 3–41.

—— (1990b) "Machiavelli on the Fathers of the Hebrew Nation: A Prototype for Political Leadership" [Hebrew], in *Proceedings of the Eleventh World Congress of Jewish Studies* (Jerusalem: World Union of Jewish Studies), 2: 338–44.

—— (1992a) "Aristotle's *Politics* in Medieval and Renaissance Jewish Thought" [Hebrew], *Pe'amim* 51: 27–69.

—— (1992b) "Abravanel and Aristotle's *Politics*: A Drama of Errors" [Hebrew], *Da'at* 29: 69–82.

—— (1992c) "Ibn Latif and Falaquera on the Virtues of the Philospher-King" [Hebrew], in *Tura: Studies in Jewish Thought* (Tel Aviv: Ha-Kibbutz Hameuchad), 2: 162–77.

—— (1993a) "The Attitude Towards Democracy in Medieval Jewish Thought," *Jewish Political Studies Review* 5: 33–56 (reprinted in *Commandment and Community: New Essays in Jewish Legal and Political Philosophy*, edited by D. H. Frank (Albany: State University of New York Press, 1995), pp. 173–94).

—— (1993b) " 'For the transgression of a land many are the princes thereof' (Proverbs 28:2): Political Commentaries on a Biblical Verse" [Hebrew], *Beit Miqrah* 38: 265–77.

—— (1994) "Maimonides on the Political Nature of Man: Needs and Responsibilities" [Hebrew], in *Tribute to Sara: Studies in Jewish Philosophy and Kabbala Presented to Prof. Sara O. Heller Wilensky*, edited by M. Idel, D. Dimant, and S. Rosenberg (Jerusalem: Magnes), pp. 292–323.

—— (1995) "Elia del Medigo and the Platonic Political Tradition in the Renaissance" [Hebrew], *Italia* 11: 57–76.

—— (forthcoming a) *The Philosopher King in Medieval and Renaissance Jewish Political Thought* (Atlanta: Scholars Press).

—— (forthcoming b) "Medieval Jewish Political Philosophy: Between Plato and Aristotle," in *Proceedings of the Ninth International Congress of Medieval Philosophy*.

—— (forthcoming c) "The Anonymous Hebrew Translation of Aegidius Romanus' *De Regimine Principum*: An Unknown Chapter in Medieval Jewish Political Philosophy," *Aegidiana*.

—— (forthcoming d) " 'Prophecy rests only on he who is wise and strong and rich': Philosophical Commentaries on the Sages' Dictum in Medieval Jewish Thought," *Maimonidean Studies*.

Motzkin, A. L. (1980) "On Halevi's *Kuzari* as a Platonic Dialogue," *Interpretation* 9: 111–24.

—— (1990) "Maimonides and Spinoza on Good and Evil," *Da'at* 24: 5–23.

Netanyahu, B. (1972) *Don Isaac Abravanel: Statesman and Philosopher* (Philadelphia: Jewish Publication Society).

Novak, D. (1988) "Natural Law, Halakhah and the Covenant," *Jewish Law Annual* 7: 45–67.

Pines, S. (1957) "On Averroes' Political Philosophy" [Hebrew], *Iyyun* 8: 65–83.

—— (1963) "The Philosophic Sources of the *Guide of the Perplexed*," in Maimonides, *The Guide of the Perplexed*, translated by S. Pines (Chicago: University of Chicago Press), 1: lviii–cxxxiv.

—— (1970) "Ibn Khaldun and Maimonides: A Comparison Between Two Texts," *Studia Islamica* 32: 265–74.

—— (1971) "The Societies Providing for the Bare Necessities of Life According to Ibn Khaldun and the Philosophers," *Studia Islamica* 34: 125–38.

—— (1975) "Aristotle's *Politics* in Arabic Philosophy," *Israel Oriental Studies* 5: 150–60.

—— (1977a) "Scholasticism After Thomas Aquinas and the Philosophy of Hasdai Crescas and his Predecessors" [Hebrew], in *Studies in the History of Jewish Philosophy: The Transmission of Texts and Ideas* (Jerusalem: Bialik Institute), pp. 277–305.

—— (1977b) "Spinoza's *Tractatus Theologico-Politicus*, Maimonides and Kant" [Hebrew], in *Studies in the History of Jewish Philosophy: The Transmission of Texts and Ideas* (Jerusalem: Bialik Institute), pp. 306–49.

—— (1979) "The Limitations of Human Knowledge According to Al-Fārābī, Ibn Bājja and Maimonides," in *Studies in Medieval Jewish History and Literature*, edited by I. Twersky (Cambridge, MA: Harvard University Press), 1: 82–109.

—— (1986) "On Some Issues Included in Polkar's *Ezer ha-Dat* and Their Equivalences in Spinoza" [Hebrew], in *Studies in Philosophy, Mysticism, and Ethical Literature Presented to Isaiah Tishby on his Seventy-fifth Birthday*, edited by J. Dan and J. Hacker (Jerusalem: Magnes), pp. 405–44.

Plessner, M. (1956) "The Importance of Shemtov ibn Falaquera for the History of Philosophy," in *Homenaje a Millas Vallicorosa* (Barcelona: Consejo Superior de Investigaciones Científicas), 2: 161–84.

Polish, D. (1971) "Some Medieval Thinkers on the Jewish King," *Judaism* 20: 323–9.

—— (1989) *Give Us a King: Legal-Religious Sources of Jewish Sovereignty* (Hoboken: Ktav).

—— (1991) "Rabbinic Views on Kingship – A Study in Jewish Sovereignty," *Jewish Political Studies Review* 3: 67–90.

Rava, A. (1931) "Spinoza e Machiavelli," *Studi filosofico-giuridici* 2: 299–313.

Ravid, B. C. I. (1978) *Economics and Toleration in Seventeenth Century Venice: The Background and Context of the Discorso of Simone Luzzatto* [American Academy for Jewish Research Monograph Series, 2] (Jerusalem: Central Press).

Ravitzky, A. (1981) "Samuel ibn Tibbon and the Esoteric Character of the *Guide of the Perplexed*," *AJS Review* 6: 87–123.

—— (1990) "Kings and Laws in Late Medieval Jewish Thought (Nissim of Gerona vs. Isaac Abravanel)," in *Scholars and Scholarship: The Interaction Between Judaism and Other Cultures*, edited by L. Landman (New York: Yeshiva University Press), pp. 67–90.

—— (1991) "To the Utmost of Human Capacity: Maimonides on the Days of the Messiah," in *Perspectives on Maimonides*, edited by J. L. Kraemer (Oxford: Oxford University Press), pp. 221–56.

Robinson, S. B. (1975) "The Biblical Jewish State as the Ideal State in the Writings of Political Thinkers of the Sixteenth-Eighteenth Century" [Hebrew], in *Education Between Continuity and Openness* (Jerusalem: Hebrew University), pp. 13–69.

Rosen, S. (1969) "Spinoza," in *History of Political Philosophy*, edited by L. Strauss and J. Cropsey (Chicago: Rand McNally), pp. 413–32.

Rosenthal, E. I. J. (1935) "Maimonides' Conception of State and Society," in *Moses Maimonides*, edited by I. Epstein (London: Soncino), pp. 191–206.

—— (1940) "On the Knowledge of Plato's Philosophy in the Islamic World," *Islamic Culture* 14: 387–422.

—— (1948) "Some Aspects of Islamic Political Thought," *Islamic Culture* 22: 1–17.

—— (1958) "Some Aspects of the Hebrew Monarchy," *Journal of Jewish Studies* 9: 1–17.

—— (1966) "*Torah* and *Nomos* in Medieval Jewish Philosophy," in *Studies in Rationalism, Judaism and Universalism in Memory of L. Roth*, edited by R. Loewe (London: Routledge & Kegan Paul), pp. 215–30.

—— (1968) *Political Thought in Medieval Islam* (Cambridge: Cambridge University Press).

—— (1979) "Some Observations on Yohanan Alemanno's Political Ideas," in *Studies in Jewish Religious and Intellectual History*, edited by S. Stern and R. Loewe (University, AL: University of Alabama Press), pp. 249–61.

—— (1980) "Political Ideas in Moshe Narboni's Commentary on Ibn Ṭufail's *Ḥayy Ben Yaqẓān*," in *Hommage à G. Vajda*, edited by G. Nahon and C. Touati (Louvain: Peeters), pp. 227–34.

Rotenstreich, N. (1953) "Mendelssohn and Political Thought" [Hebrew], in *Mordecai Kaplan Jubilee Volume*, edited by M. Davis (New York: Jewish Theological Seminary of America), pp. 237–47.

Rotter, I. (1979) "The Islamic Sources of Maimonides' Political Philosophy," *Gesher* 7: 182–204.

Schwarzschild, S. S. (1962–3) "Do Noachites Have to Believe in Revelation?" *Jewish Quarterly Review* 52: 297–308.

—— (1977) "Moral Radicalism and 'Middlingness' in the Ethics of Maimonides," *Studies in Medieval Culture* 11: 65–93.

Segal, I. (1938) "Abravanel as a Commentator of the Bible" [Hebrew], *Tarbitz* 8: 266–99.

Septimus, B. (1987) "Biblical Religion and Political Rationality in Simone Luzzatto, Maimonides and Spinoza," in *Jewish Thought in the Seventeenth Century*, edited by I. Twersky (Cambridge, MA: Harvard University Press), pp. 399–435.

Shiffman, Y. (1991) "Ibn Bajja as a Source for Falaquera's Commentary on the *Guide* 3:51, 54" [Hebrew], *Tarbitz* 60: 224–35.

Sirat, C. (1990) "Political Ideas of Nissim ben Moses of Marseille" [Hebrew], in *Shlomo Pines Jubilee Volume*, edited by M. Idel, E. Schweid, and W. Z. Harvey (Jerusalem: Daf Noy), 2: 53–76.

Skinner, Q. (1988) "Political Philosophy," in *The Cambridge History of Renaissance Philosophy*, edited by C. B. Schmitt, Q. Skinner, E. Kessler, and J. Kraye (Cambridge: Cambridge University Press), pp. 389–452.

Smoler, L. and M. Auerbach (1972) "Kingship in Abrabanel's Thought" [Hebrew], in *Hebrew Scholarship in America* (Tel Aviv: Yavneh), 2: 134–57.

Strauss, L. (1936) "Quelques remarques sur la science politique de Maimonide et de Farabi," *Revue des etudes Juives* 100: 1–37.

—— (1937) "On Abravanel's Philosophical Tendency and Political Teaching," in *Isaac Abravanel, Six Lectures*, edited by J. B. Trends and H. Loewe (Cambridge: Cambridge University Press), pp. 95–129.

—— (1945) "Farabi's Plato," in *Louis Ginzberg Jubilee Volume* (New York: American Academy for Jewish Research), pp. 357–93.

—— (1952a) "The Law of Reason in the *Kuzari*," in *Persecution and the Art of Writing* (Glencoe: Free Press), pp. 95–141.

—— (1952b) "How to Study Spinoza's *Theologico-Political Treatise*," in *Persecution and the Art of Writing* (Glencoe: Free Press), pp. 142–201.

—— (1953) "Maimonides' Statement on Political Science," *Proceedings of the American Academy for Jewish Research* 22: 115–30.

—— (1959) "How Farabi Read Plato's *Laws*," in *What is Political Philosophy?* (New York: Free Press), pp. 7–63.

—— (1987) *Philosophy and Law*, translated by F. Baumann, with a foreword by R. Lerner (Philadelphia: Jewish Publication Society).

Susser, B. (1981) "On the Reconstruction of Jewish Political Theory," in *Comparative Jewish Politics: Public Life in Israel and the Diaspora*, edited by S. N. Lehman and B. Susser (Ramat Gan: Bar Ilan University Press), pp. 13–22.

Susser, B. and E. Don Yihyeh (1981) "Prolegomena to Jewish Political Theory," in *Kinship and Consent: The Jewish Political Tradition and its Contemporary Uses*, edited by D. J. Elazar (Philadelphia: Turtledove), pp. 91–111.

Teicher, J. L. (1960) "Review of E. I. J. Rosenthal's *Averroes' Commentary on Plato's Republic*," *Journal of Semitic Studies* 5: 176–95.

Tirosh-Rothschild, H. (1990) "The Political Philosophy of Abraham Shalom: The Platonic Tradition" [Hebrew], in *Shlomo Pines Jubilee Volume*, edited by M. Idel, E. Schweid, and W. Z. Harvey (Jerusalem: Daf Noy), 2: 403–40.

Ullmann, W. (1956) *A History of Political Thought: The Middle Ages* (Harmondsworth: Penguin).

Urbach, E. E. (1937) "Die Staatsauffassung des Don Isaac Abravanel," *Monatsschrift für Geschichte und Wissenschaft des Judentums* 81: 257–70.

Walzer, R. (1945) "Arabic Transmission of Greek Thought to Medieval Europe," *Bulletin of the John Rylands Library* 29: 165–83.

—— (1963a) "Aspects of Islamic Political Thought: al-Farabi and ibn Kaldun," *Oriens* 16: 40–60.

—— (1963b) *Greek into Arabic* (Oxford: Oxford University Press).

Winiarksi, W. (1969) "Machiavelli," in *History of Political Philosophy*, edited by L. Strauss and J. Crospey (Chicago: Rand McNally), pp. 247–76.

Wolfson, H. A. (1925) "The Classification of Sciences in Medieval Jewish Philosophy," *Hebrew Union College Jubilee Volume*, pp. 263–315.

—— (1936) "Note on Maimonides' Classification of the Sciences," *Jewish Quarterly Review* 26: 369–77.

—— (1962) *Philo: Foundations of Religious Philosophy in Judaism, Christianity and Islam* (Cambridge, MA: Harvard University Press).

—— (1969) *The Philosophy of Spinoza* (New York: Schocken).

Yerushalmi, Y. H. (1983) "Spinoza on the Existence of the Jewish People," *Proceedings of the Israel Academy of Sciences and the Humanities* 6. 10 (Jerusalem).

CHAPTER 19

Jewish mysticism: a philosophical overview

Elliot R. Wolfson

MYSTICISM AS A RELIGIOUS PHENOMENON

In the current state of scholarly research on Jewish mysticism no general theory regarding the nature of this phenomenon has emerged. Indeed, the term "mysticism" itself is one that has not been defined in a uniform way by historians of religion. Notwithstanding the lack of definition, the two most salient approaches to the academic study of Jewish mysticism have been the historical and the phenomenological. The former approach sets as its primary concern the charting of the evolution of Jewish mysticism within an historical framework. What is of interest to the historian, therefore, is how Jewish mystics have had an impact on the intellectual, social, and religious history of Jews at different periods of time. The other dominant orientation, that of the phenomenologist, seeks in the first instance to uncover the structures of religious experience that have informed the beliefs and practices enunciated in mystical texts. In the final analysis, these two approaches must be welded together for the phenomenological orientation must itself take into account the historical context wherein the particular expression of the mystical phenomenon takes shape and unfolds. My argument is predicated on the assumption that there is an irreducible aspect to the religious experience. The multifarious nature of the religious phenomenon must be illuminated by a variety of methodological approaches including anthropology, psychology, sociology, political theory, economics, feminist studies, literary criticism, the history of music and art, performance studies, and so on. The adoption of multiple disciplines does not imply, however, that the religious experience can be reduced to any or all of them. In my view, the phenomenon of Jewish mysticism must be treated in the same way.

I will cite here one example that underscores the methodological issue at stake: a recurrent theme in Jewish mystical literature is the ontic transformation of human beings into angels. Literary attestations to the phenomenon of angelification can be found in many sources, including apocalyptic and ancient Jewish throne mysticism, medieval Jewish philosophy and religious poetry (influenced in part by the older mystical sources), German Pietism, ecstatic and theosophic kabbalah. If one identifies mysticism primarily from the historical vantage point, then the expressions of this phenomenon in philosophical or poetic literature may fall outside the scope of inquiry. That is, one might argue that, historically speaking, the description of the high priest being transformed into an angel in a particular poem should not be considered as part of the history of Jewish mysticism, in so far as the relevant poet did not belong to a circle of individuals whose activity has been labeled by modern research as representative of a major trend of Jewish mysticism. The phenomenological orientation, by contrast, would identify the phenomenon of angelification as the primary and critical factor and would thus include any expression of that phenomenon within the parameters of Jewish mysticism. Needless to say, the particular expressions of this phenomenon will vary from author to author, reflecting the larger intellectual milieu of the cultural context of each thinker. But beyond these differences one can discern a pattern of experience, which may be singled out as the essential feature that justifies the use of the term "mysticism."

The approach that I have taken to the relationship of mysticism and history may be fruitfully compared to a position articulated by Alexander Altmann in the lecture "Jewish Mysticism" delivered in June 1935. Without denying the need for the "scientific comprehension" that helps one "ascertain the different centers of origin and the different influences" in the history of Jewish mysticism, Altmann insists that it is equally important for the scholar "to see the constant elements in this process of becoming, or better, the continuity in this becoming."[1] This continuity, according to Altmann, is "an orientation toward the Bible," that is, the mystical phenomenon "always seeks to comprehend itself from a starting position in the Bible and to legitimize itself exegetically. The source of mysticism is ... the piety of the believing individual to whom revelation was granted but for whom this gift has now become the object of constant contemplation."[2] In this brief phenomenological sketch of Jewish mysticism, Altmann stressed the practical over the theoretical; the contemplative ideal is intrinsically connected to a life of piety. Consequently, the essential thing for the mystic is not that God is but that he lives. "Only mysticism," concludes

Altmann, "is ultimately and radically serious about positing God as actual."[3] This actuality of God, the intention-meaning of religious experience, is realized through ritual performance, the true source of mystical inspiration. Moreover, as Altmann astutely observes, in some fundamental sense the Jewish mystics are exegetes who strive to legitimate their own unique experience in terms of biblical precedents.[4]

What is essential to point out in Altmann's analysis is the distinction that he draws between the two approaches, which may be called the scientific–historical and the theological–phenomenological. Although it would be difficult to accept Altmann's characterization in an unqualified way, I do think that his call for the need to recognize continuity linking the various historical manifestations of mysticism in Judaism is well taken. Such an orientation shifts the primary emphasis away from historical criteria to an appreciation of the religious phenomenon. This is not to say that historical context is not vital for a proper understanding of mysticism. It is merely to argue, as I stated above, that mysticism ought to be treated as a religious phenomenon that occurs in history, rather than as an historical phenomenon with a religious dimension.

❧ RELATIONSHIP OF PHILOSOPHY AND ❧ MYSTICISM

Of the many contributions that Gershom Scholem's prolific research has made to the field of Judaica, one of the most significant is the broadening of the parameters of the intellectual history of the Jews from late antiquity to the modern period. This expansion of intellectual horizons is perhaps nowhere more apparent than in the study of medieval Jewish culture, the richest period of mystical creativity in Jewish history. Together with the more traditionally studied forms of philosophical expression, reflecting in particular the Aristotelian and Neoplatonic legacies transmitted to the Jews through the Arabic translations of Greek and Syriac works, Scholem introduced a canon of texts that approached many of the same problems in metaphysics, epistemology, psychology, and cosmology as did the works of classical philosophy.

Despite the fact that Scholem was keenly aware of the textual, philological, and historical influence of philosophical authors on Jewish mystics in the Middle Ages, he dichotomized the intellectual currents of mysticism and philosophy in too simplistic a fashion.[5] In part this has to be seen as Scholem's reaction to his intellectual predecessors, the nineteenth-century German scholars of Wissenschaft des Judentums, who viewed the medieval philosophical sources as the apex of cultural creativity, whereas the mystical texts were derisively considered to be an affront to the reified ethical monotheism of Judaism. Responding to such an attitude, Scholem argued repeatedly that the mystical sources, and not the philosophical, tapped the deepest recesses of religious consciousnesss by reviving what he considered to be the long-suppressed mythical dimension of Judaism. To cite one representative example of this: "the old God whom Kabbalistic gnosis opposed to the God of the philosophers proves, when experienced in all His living richness, to be an even older and archaic one."[6] The bifurcation of mysticism and philosophy led Scholem to such distinctions as symbol versus allegory that break down under the weight of textual detail.[7] Ironically, in his attempt to legitimate the mystical vitality of Judaism, Scholem reiterates the overly simplistic distinction between rationalistic philosophy and pietistic mysticism in the Jewish Middle Ages. As an alternative to Scholem a number of scholars, including, most significantly, Georges Vajda and Alexander Altmann,[8] presented a far more complex picture of the relationship of philosophy and mysticism by demonstrating in a number of motif studies that the philosophers and mystics utilized similar images and were influenced by the same sources. More recent scholarship has gone beyond the comparativist framework of Vajda and Altmann by arguing that in the lived situation of the medieval philosophers the influence of mystical speculation is clearly discernible.[9] That is, it is not simply that medieval philosophers and mystics used the same language, but that the religious context of the philosophers was one that was saturated with mystical traditions. Even Scholem's schematization of the two major currents that influenced the history of kabbalah as Gnosticism and Neoplatonism must be qualified inasmuch as these two strands were intertwined in the very channels that may have transmitted gnostic myth and philosophic speculation to the kabbalists in medieval Europe. In the telling phrase of a kabbalist active in the last decades of the thirteenth century, Moses ben Simeon of Burgos, the mystic stands on the head of the philosopher. The import of this statement is not only that the mystical tradition exceeds the bounds of philosophical discourse, but that the former is unimaginable without the latter. There is a great deal of truth in this comment, as it is impossible to disentangle the threads of philosophy and mysticism when examining the texture of medieval Jewish mysticism in any of its major expressions. This entanglement is both historical and ideational.

❧ ESOTERICISM AND ECSTASY: ❧ THE PHENOMENOLOGICAL POLES OF JEWISH MYSTICISM

It is possible to isolate two distinct concerns running through all the major texts that scholars include in the corpus of Jewish mysticism. On the one hand, there is the claim to an esoteric knowledge (whose content will naturally vary from one period to another) that is not readily available to the masses through the more common avenues of religious worship, ritual, or study. This knowledge, moreover, is not attained through ordinary rational or sentient means, but is transmitted orally from master to disciple or is the result of some divine or angelic revelation. To be sure, those enlightened in either of these ways can then find the truths and secret meanings hidden within the traditional textual canons of Judaism. The former assumption regarding oral transmission provided the key term used to designate different forms of Jewish esotericism in the Middle Ages, namely, kabbalah, which means "tradition" or "that which is received." Frequently, the esoteric knowledge conveys truths about the inner workings of the divine world and is therefore theosophical in its orientation.

The second major element identifiable in Jewish mystical literature is the emphasis placed on intense religious experience. The particular form of this experience varies, but it usually includes one or more of the following: heavenly ascent, vision of the divine form, angelification, or mystical union. What also distinguishes the ecstatic experience is the claim that special techniques of a meditative sort were required to induce the desired frame of mind. It is on account of these techniques – especially those that involve recitation and/or combination of the letters of divine names – that an important strand of Jewish mysticism bears a strong resemblance to magical practices. Indeed, in some cases it is extremely hard to draw the line between mysticism and magic within Jewish sources. Those texts that are of an almost purely magical sort are referred to in the traditional literature itself as practical kabbalah (*qabbalah ma'asit*), to be distinguished from the more theosophical or speculative kabbalah (*qabbalah 'iyyunit*). It must be noted, however, that important theosophical elements are often found in these more practical texts, the study of which has been grossly neglected by scholars. Even a cursory glance at magical charms, amulets, incantations, exorcisms, and formulae reveals to what extent this genre of literature is indebted to various forms of doctrinal information regarding, for example, the nature and names of angels and demons, attributes of God, the nature of the soul, the fate of the heavenly bodies, and so on, which are essential elements in Jewish mystical texts as well. One may legitimately distinguish mysticism from magic on the basis of the stated goals of a given source, but one must at the same time recognize the conceptual underpinning shared by both enterprises.

The word "mysticism" will be used here to refer to those trends of thought in Judaism that lay claim to either an esoteric knowledge of the Godhead (theosophy) or to an intense religious experience of a visionary or unitive sort (ecstasy), though I do not think these two can always be separated in a clear and distinct manner. In the remainder of this chapter I will present a phenomenological sketch of the major currents of Jewish mysticism from the classical period to the Middle Ages. I have accepted the historical framework of Scholem even though I would reverse the relationship of history and phenomenology. I presume that, in spite of the significant differences from one period to another, there are some basic themes, motifs, and religious practices that recur in continuous lines of tradition. It may be unwarranted to define Jewish mysticism, but it is certainly justifiable to delineate critical aspects that are at the center of the religious world of the Jewish mystics through the ages. One must avoid reductionism on all fronts: ignoring any manner of historical change is no better than discarding any possibility of historical continuity.

❧ MERKAVAH MYSTICISM ❧

The first major expression of mysticism within post-biblical Judaism can be found in the writings that make up the so-called Merkavah (chariot) or Hekhalot (palace) corpus. These terms are used to designate those texts, composed and redacted over a period of several centuries, that describe in detail the ascent of an individual through the heavenly realms, culminating with an ecstatic vision of the luminous form on the throne located in the seventh palace of the seventh heaven. The details of the vision of the divine chariot were first recorded in the book of Ezekiel, a prophet living in Babylonia in the sixth century BCE. The first use of the technical term *merkavah* to refer to Ezekiel's vision of the enthroned glory is found in the apocryphal book of Ben Sira 49:8. While many of the themes in the biblical prophecy served as the exegetical basis for the visionary experiences elaborated in the Merkavah corpus, the essential difference beween the prophetic theophany and mystical vision is evident. Closer to the spirit of the Merkavah praxis are remnants of heavenly ascents recorded in Jewish and Christian apocalyptic literature from the second century BCE to roughly the third century CE.[10] It is has been argued by some scholars that Merkavah mysticism is an outgrowth of Jewish apocalypticism, though some important differences are found as well.[11] Another important link in this chain is the so-called *Angelic Liturgy* of the Qumran sectarians, the *Songs of the Sabbath Sacrifice*, as well as other liturgical fragments found in the Qumran collection.[12] While there is some uncertainty regarding the appropriateness of the term "mystical" to refer to the poetic descriptions of the angelic realm and the throne contained in these documents,[13] there can be little doubt that the motifs discussed in these sources bear a striking resemblance to the main concerns of the Hekhalot literature.[14]

More difficult to ascertain is the relationship between the Merkavah mysticism and the esoteric discipline mentioned by the rabbis in the Mishnah, *ma'aseh merkavah* (account of the chariot). It may be assumed that this discipline, as the other ones specified by the rabbis, *ma'aseh bereshit* (account of the creation) and *'arayot* (illicit sexual relationships), was exegetical in nature. Indeed, recent scholarship has argued that *ma'aseh merkavah*, as understood by the Palestinian rabbis of the first centuries, referred to explication of the literary account of Ezekiel's prophetic vision, involving no ecstatic experience or mystical practice.[15] A striking example of this exegetical-homiletical genre of *ma'aseh merkavah* can be found in the treatise known as *Re'uyot Yechezqel*.[16]

Awareness on the part of the rabbis of the distinction between esoteric study and mystical praxis is evident from the following comment: "Many have expounded the *merkavah* without ever seeing it" (Tosefta on Megillah 3[4]:28).[17] Still, it must be said that from some of the legendary accounts of rabbinic authorities engaged in homiletic speculation on the *merkavah*, especially Yochanan ben Zakkai and his disciples,[18] it is evident that this form of exegesis was capable of producing paranormal states of consciousness related particularly to the reliving of the theophany at Sinai.[19] A clear thematic connection links the Sinaitic revelation and Ezekiel's chariot theophany in rabbinic homiletical literature.[20] The exposition of the scriptural account of the chariot, as midrashic activity more generally,[21] must be viewed as a means to re-experience the seeing of God at the historical moment of Sinai; that is, interpretation is an effort to reconstitute the original experience of revelation. Nevertheless, these experiences do not yet amount to a mystical praxis, at least not as defined as the ascent to the chariot. Whatever pneumatic powers the study of Ezekiel's chariot vision could impute to the exegete, this study did not constitute a vision of the chariot itself. On the other hand, given the literary and conceptual continuity linking apocalyptic and the Hekhalot sources, it is difficult to maintain that the rabbis who lived in the period of the Mishnah were not cognizant of heavenly ascensions to the throne when they spoke of expounding the chariot.

Although it is certainly valid to distinguish the "exegetical mysticism" of the rabbis and the "experiential mysticism" of the anonymous

Hekhalot mystics, it is far too simplistic to say that the crucial turning point in the development of Merkavah mysticism occurs "when active mystical ascent to the divine world replaced passive homiletical specu-lation in the midrashic manner concerning the chariot envisioned by Ezekiel."[22] The characterization of rabbinic exegesis of the chariot vision of Ezekiel as "passive homiletical speculation in the midrashic manner" completely misses the mark. It is true that the rabbinic *ma'aseh merka-vah*, technically speaking, did not involve heavenly ascent to the throne, but that criterion alone is not sufficient to remove all forms of ecstasy and mysticism from the rabbinic figures who cultivated an interest in the chariot. On the other hand, it would be equally misleading to suggest that exegesis of Scripture did not play a significant role for the mystic visionaries described in the Hekhalot sources. One may assume that vision of the *merkavah* was, at least in part, occasioned by reflec-tion on the relevant scriptural (and perhaps apocalyptic) passages. An appreciation of the mystical nature of exegesis in general, and exegesis on the chariot vision of Ezekiel in particular, should narrow the gap separating exegetical and experiential forms of mystical speculation connected to the *merkavah*.

It is not known precisely when and where the interest in heavenly ascent reflected in the main Hekhalot compositions occurred, but it is likely that this mystical praxis was cultivated in Babylonia sometime in the Amoraic period (fourth to fifth centuries).[23] The five most important texts that provide descriptions of the mystical ascent or the celestial throne-world are *Hekhalot Zutarti*,[24] *Hekhalot Rabbati*,[25] *Sefer Hekhalot*, also known as 3 *Enoch*,[26] the treatise published by Scholem with the title *Ma'aseh Merkavah*,[27] a fragment from the Geniza referred to by the scribe as *Chotam ha-Merkavah* and called by scholars the Ozhayah text,[28] and *Massekhet Hekhalot*.[29] The protagonists of these ascent texts are Ishmael, Aqibah, and Nechuniah ben ha-Qanah. While we may say with relative certainty that the use of these rabbinic figures is a mere literary device to transmit the mystical teachings in the name of established authorities, the precise historical and social context of the authors who produced these works is not at all clear.[30] It may be assumed that the texts in the form in which they have been preserved were redacted sometime between the seventh and twelfth centuries. Not only do the first explicit references to Hekhalot compositions occur in Geonic material, but the first account of mystical techniques employed for ascent is found in Hai ben Sherira Gaon (939–1038).[31] Additionally, there is substantial textual evidence from this period to show that interest in the mystical and magical traditions (especially connected with divine names) continued to have a decisive impact.[32] There has been a tendency in some current scholarship to reclaim the view expressed by several nineteenth-century scholars concerning the influence of Islamic mysticism on Jewish mystics in general and on the Merkavah mystics in particular.[33] In addition to the possible impact of specific Sufi techniques, the combination of ancient gnostic and philosophic ideas characteristic of various forms of Islamic esotericism (especially Ismāʿīlī sources) may prove important in future research on the evolution of Jewish mysticism from late antiquity to the Middle Ages.[34] It must be pointed out, however, that another important milieu for understanding the cultivation and transmission of Hekhalot texts and traditions was southern Italy, as a number of scholars have noted.[35] The presence of this material in the Islamic and Byzantine–Christian context underscores the centrality of speculation on the throne in the religious history of the Jews and it is likely that a common source for both currents lies in Palestine.

The study of the literary nature of the Hekhalot corpus has been greatly enhanced by the publication of the main writings in the *Synopse zur Hekhalot-Literatur* and the *Geniza Fragmente zur Hekhalot-Literatur* by Peter Schäfer and his colleagues. The most important result of the presentation of the material in synoptic form is the undermining of the view that this corpus is made up of distinct and clearly defined textual units. The comparison of the manuscripts shows that there are enough substantial differences with regard to organization of material as well as textual units included in a specific work to render it virtually impossible to establish, restore, or demarcate an urtext of any given composition within this corpus. The attempt to reconstruct individual works of Hekhalot literature is a false presupposition since the redactional identity of any given work varies in accord with the manuscripts that were written at different times and places. There are discrete "texts" in the corpus, but the manuscript evidence indicates that the boundaries of the texts are fluid and have been crystallized over time in what Schäfer calls "macroforms."

These macroforms are superimposed literary units that were arranged into clearly defined works or texts at a certain stage in the redactional process. Within the larger macroforms are also discernible smaller literary units, "microforms," that may indeed comprise autonomous traditions that were woven into the fabric of the macroforms and thence became part of a literary tradition of a distinct textual unit.[36] It may be the case that these units were in a fluid state as late as the period in which they were being copied either in the Orient (attested by the Geniza fragments) or in the Occident (mainly in the German manuscripts or Italian copies of the former). Here it is particularly significant to note the role of the medieval German Pietists who may have had a great hand at shaping these texts.[37]

It is possible, as various scholars have noted, to distinguish two central elements in the Hekhalot texts, the mystical ascent culminating in a visionary experience and the adjuration of angels achieved through various magical techniques, as, for example, the technique of putting on or clothing oneself with the divine name.[38] The adjuration of angels in the Hekhalot literature is aimed at the understanding of the secrets and treasures of Torah through magical study that does not require the ordinary effort of study. This aim is related especially in a section appended to *Hekhalot Rabbati* known as *Sar-Torah* as well as in other fragments in the Hekhalot corpus that reflect a similar praxis and orientation.[39] Of the two elements enumerated above, it may be said that the former is centered on the heavenly ascension, whereas the latter constitutes, in the words of Peter Schäfer, a "reverse heavenly journey,"[40] that is, an effort to bring the angel down to earth by means of adjurations that consist of mentioning the divine names and displaying the magical seals that likewise are composed of divine names. While it is valid to distinguish the mystical and magical aims present in this corpus, it must be noted that magical or theurgical means are employed in the heavenly ascent as well.[41] It is virtually impossible to separate entirely mysticism and magic, either conceptually or textually, in these compositions: the mystical component embraces in a fundamental way magical techniques and the magical component is frequently linked to an experience of a mystical nature.[42] From a redactional standpoint, there is little justification employing the terms "mysticism" and "magic" to refer to absolutely distinct phenomena, nor is there sufficient reason to ascribe priority to the one over the other. Certainly the medieval authors, who received and in some instances help to shape these sources, made no discernible attempt to isolate the mystical and magical elements.

In spite of the recent critique of various scholars,[43] it seems to me that Scholem's insight regarding the centrality of the visionary experience as a major element in the mystical-magical praxis of these texts is an entirely defensible position.[44] That is, even if one were to bracket the question of the "originary" or "primary" status of the vision in relation to other aspects such as liturgical participation with the angels, the fact remains that the seeing of the divine is upheld in several macroforms as the distinctive quality of the mystical adept. The culmination of the ascent is a direct vision of the divine glory (*kavod*) or power (*gevurah*) referred to by several technical terms including most prominently, on the basis of Isaiah 33:17, beholding the king in his beauty.[45] Although the vision of God is stressed time and again in these texts, one finds as well the opposing claim that God cannot be seen. Scholem noted this tension when he observed that for the Merkavah visionaries the enthroned glory is "at once visible and yet, by virtue of His transcendent nature, incapable of being visualized."[46] Hekhalot literature thus incorporates the tension, rooted in the biblical tradition, between a visible, corporeal form of God, on the one hand, and the prohibition of seeing God, on the other.[47] Moreover, as I have suggested elsewhere, the paradox of seeing the invisible glory in the Hekhalot texts could be understood in terms of a sexual dynamic.[48] That is, the moment of enthronement is presented in some of these literary units as an intense erotic drama, the glory assuming masculine characteristics and the throne, feminine. Indeed, in *Hekhalot Rabbati* we explicitly read that the throne is compared to a bride and the glory to a bridegroom. What the mystic beholds, therefore, is the erotic drama that unfolds in the celestial realm when the glory occupies the throne. Enthronement is a form of *hieros gamos* and the vision of the enthroned glory imparted to the mystic facilitates his participation in this sacred union.

According to the terminology employed in some of the principal texts in this corpus, the approach to the throne is called *yeridah la-merkavah*, literally, the "descent to the chariot," and the mystics who approach it are designated *yorede merkavah*, the "descenders to the chariot." Most scholars, following Scholem, consider this a paradoxical expression that refers to the act of ascending.[49] I have argued, however, that a careful examination of the texts where this terminology appears indicates that *yeridah la-merkavah* denotes entry to the throne.[50] The heavenly journey involved an ascent through the seven heavens and the first six palaces of the seventh heaven, followed by entry into the seventh palace wherein the throne was located. At the time of this entry the mystic stands before the enthroned glory and utters the appropriate praises together with the angels; he is then placed on the throne of glory or on a throne alongside of or facing the throne of glory and he has a vision of the luminous divine form. The *yeridah la-merkavah*, therefore, results in a deifying vision. To be sure, as Scholem already observed, there is no unio mystica in these texts, for the ontic distinction between God and human is never fully overcome.[51] On the other hand, there is ample evidence to show that the enthronement of the mystic was a central part of this ascent experience, an enthronement that involved a form of quasi-deification. To see God requires that one be made like God, that is, that one be substantially transformed into a spiritual (angelic) being. The classic example of the apotheosis of a human occurs in 3 *Enoch* where the biblical Enoch (here understood to represent the prototype of the Merkavah mystic) is translated into the heavenly realm and transformed into the angelic Metatron who occupies a throne alongside of the divine glory. While this last step is not explicitly taken in the other major texts from this corpus, it is nevertheless clear that the enthronement of the mystic signifies his elevation to the status of the highest angel in the celestial retinue. It is in virtue of this enthronement that the mystic can see that which is ordinarily hidden from human perception. Interestingly, the process of angelification is also well attested in the *Sar-Torah* material. The adjuration of an angel requires that the adjurer himself become angelic, a process that is achieved through specific rituals of mortification and purification.[52] The ontic transformation of a human into an angel is thus a common denominator of the heavenly journey and the magical adjuration in Hekhalot literature.

The most detailed description of the visualized form of God is given in the cluster of texts known as *Shi'ur Qomah*. These texts should be considered distinct textual units that were grafted on to the Hekhalot macroforms at some stage in the redactional process. The attitude of a variety of scholars that the *Shi'ur Qomah* fragments belong to the same stream of tradition as the Hekhalot texts is based on the fact that in some manuscript witnesses of these sources the two are found together. This impression, however, is due mainly to the medieval Ashkenazi scribes who interpolated *Shi'ur Qomah* material into Hekhalot macroforms, as we find for instance in the case of one passage of *Hekhalot Rabbati* or more fully in *Merkavah Rabbah*.[53] From a redactional standpoint one can continue to speak of *Shi'ur Qomah* traditions that have been incorporated into Hekhalot literature,[54] but phenomenologically and conceptually it is necessary to isolate these two currents.

In the *Shi'ur Qomah* texts the reader is provided with graphic details of the various limbs of the body of the enthroned divine figure, the *yotzer bereshit* (that is, the demiurge or creator), in terms of both unpronounceable names and unfathomable dimensions.[55] The secret knowledge is said to be revealed to the mystic, represented by the rabbinic figures Aqibah and Ishmael,[56] by Metatron, designated as the "great angel" or the "angel of the divine countenance."[57] Some scholars have conjectured that the core theosophic speculation underlying the *Shi'ur Qomah* tradition distinguished between the supreme Godhead and the secondary demiurgic power (identified as Metatron) who was subject to corporeal measurement.[58] In the texts that are extant no such distinction is immediately evident.[59] On the contrary, it is the angelic Metatron who reveals the measurements and names of the demiurge and he is thus called the "great angel of testimony,"[60] for he is like a witness that provides information. Yet, there are allusions in the *Shi'ur Qomah* material to the demiurgic status of Metatron. There is, for instance, the description of Metatron's stature filling the entire universe and of his being inscribed with the letter by which heaven and earth were created.[61] Moreover, this demiurgic status probably underlies the claim in some versions of the *Shi'ur Qomah* text that the name of Metatron "is like his Master's," which is linked exegetically to the verse, "My name is in him" (Exodus 23:21).[62] It is likely that this reference is related to the tradition explicitly mentioned in 3 *Enoch* and alluded to in B. *Sanhedrin* 38b to the effect that Metatron is the "Lesser Tetragrammaton," *yhwh ha-qatan*.[63] It is likely that this tradition was based on a demiurgic conception of Metatron.

There is evidence for such an interpretation of the *Shi'ur Qomah* traditions from medieval philosophical,[64] pietistic, and kabbalistic sources.[65] Thus, for example, in a fragment of Abraham ben David of Posquières reported by his grandson, Asher ben David, we find the following interpretation of the talmudic statement that God wears phylacteries (B. *Berakhot* 6a):

> This refers to the Prince of the Countenance [i.e., Metatron] ....
> And it is he who appeared to Moses at the bush, and to Ezekiel "in the semblance of a human from above" (Ezekiel 1:26). ...
> And this is the secret of the account of creation: "whoever knows the measurement of the Creator can be assured of his portion in the world-to-come,"[66] and this is [the subject of the verse] "Let us make man in our image" (Genesis 1:26).[67]

A similar approach is attested in the following statement of Isaac of Acre: "I have received a true tradition concerning the fact that this measurement applies only to the created Metatron for he is the supernal Adam,[68] but above him the prophet said, 'To whom, then, can you liken God, etc.' (Isaiah 40:18). The one who says something contrary to this has not seen the light."[69] Given the alternative approach found in medieval kabbalistic literature, to apply the *Shi'ur Qomah* to the *sefirotic* edifice (see below), it seems to me that the tradition of applying the measurements to the angelic Metatron is an older Jewish esoteric doctrine that the kabbalists did not innovate but rather received as oral lore. Some scholars have also maintained that the *Shi'ur Qomah* is a mystical reading of the description of the lover in the Song of Songs.[70] According to more normative rabbinic modes of exegesis, the Song of Songs was read as an allegorical depiction of God's love for Israel.[71] Given this reading of the text, it would stand to reason that the description of the physical body of the lover (especially in the fifth chapter) should be applied to God and would therefore suggest the corporeal measurements enumerated in the mystical tradition. Other scholars, however, have rejected or questioned the proposed connection between the *Shi'ur Qomah* and the Song of Songs.[72]

The measurements of the limbs are quite extraordinary, indeed impossible to imagine from a normal human perspective. While the dimensions of the divine body differ according to the different textual traditions, one of the standard measures of the height of the creator, and that which was most frequently cited by later authors, is 236,000 parasangs,[73] or according to other texts 2,360,000,000 parasangs.[74] This number is exegetically related in the Aqiban text to the expression *we-*

rav koach, "full of power," in Psalms 147:5, whose numerical equivalence is 236.[75] Similarly, in the sections of the text attributed to Ishmael and to his student, Nathan, the holy names of God, which appear to the modern reader to be a list of meaningless Hebrew consonants, are linked to the different limbs.[76] It has been suggested that the astronomical size of the limbs together with the incomprehensibility of the names indicates that the anthropomorphism of this text should be construed as a *reductio ad absurdum* of the very notion of applying corporeal characteristics to God.[77] It is also possible, and in my opinion preferable, to interpret the bizarre names and incomprehensible measurements as an indication of the fundamental paradox of the mystical experience presupposed by this work: the measurable God is immeasurable and the visible God invisible.[78] In any event, it is clear that the convergence of letter symbolism and anthropomorphism is one of the characteristic features of Jewish theosophic speculation through the ages: one of the primary ways that Jewish mystics iconically imagined the corporeal form of God was through linguistic means, that is, the limbs of God are constituted by the Hebrew letters.

❧ *SEFER YETZIRAH:* LINGUISTIC ❧ MYSTICISM AND COSMOLOGICAL SPECULATION

Another important treatise in the history of Jewish mystical speculation is the *Sefer Yetzirah*, which is dated anywhere from the third to ninth centuries.[79] Properly speaking, the work should not be described as a single composition but rather as a composite of distinct literary strands that have been woven together through a complicated redactional process whose stages are not clearly discernible. Most scholarship on *Sefer Yetzirah* has been marred by a decided lack of attention to redactional issues.[80] Thematic descriptions of the text as well as attempts to date it chronologically and to place it geographically have labored under the assumption that the book is of one piece. It is inaccurate, in my opinion, to speak of a date of composition of this work nor is it particularly helpful to speak of an author. It is better to think of the textual issues in terms of critical periods of redaction when isolated and autonomous tradition-complexes were welded together to take the shape of a literary source.[81] A more sophisticated redactional analysis may support the claim that some of the material contained in *Sefer Yetzirah* reflects a relatively early date but it seems likely that the final redaction occurred within a ninth-century Islamic milieu.[82] The relatively unstable nature of the text is evident from the words of Saadia Gaon (882–942) near the end of the introduction to his commentary on *Sefer Yetzirah*: "I will begin with the version of the book. I wanted to establish each and every tradition[83] in its completeness, and afterward I will translate it, because the book is not found a lot and not many people preserved it so that there would be no change or deviation in it."[84] Saadia's remark is very significant for it attests to the fluid nature of the text as late as 931, the year that he composed his commentary. Thus Saadia saw as one of his major tasks the need to stabilize the text, for it was not a work widely disseminated and people did not take care to preserve the text in a rigorous way.

The primary interest in *Sefer Yetzirah* is not on a mystical ascent culminating with a vision of God or even magical adjuration of the angels. *Sefer Yetzirah* is principally concerned with cosmology and cosmogony, and therefore belongs to the other esoteric tradition known from rabbinic literature, *ma'aseh bereshit*.[85] However, even though most of the text stands apart from the rest of the Hekhalot corpus, some parts of it belong to the environment of Merkavah mysticism.[86] The text is extant in three different redactions: the long version, the short version, and that which is incorporated in Saadia's commentary on it.[87] All versions share the view that the means of divine creativity are the thirty-two paths of wisdom that comprise ten primordial ciphers (*sefirot*) and the twenty-two Hebrew letters. It is possible that originally these were distinct modes of Jewish speculation on divine creativity that were brought together fairly early in the redactional process.

It is generally assumed that the term *sefirot* in the first part of *Sefer Yetzirah* is to be understood as "numbers," but it must be noted the *sefirot* exemplify traits hardly befitting numbers in any ordinary way. Indeed, from a redactional standpoint it appears that three different explanations of the *sefirot* are found in the first part of *Sefer Yetzirah*. In the first unit the *sefirot* are understood theosophically as the attributes of the divine.[88] Thus, the initial passage in this unit depicts the *sefirot* in anthropomorphic terms: "Ten *sefirot belimah*: The number of the ten fingers, five corresponding to five. The covenant of unity is set in the middle, in the circumcision of the tongue and mouth and in the circumcision of the foreskin." As I have suggested elsewhere, the anthropomorphic imagery here relates to the divine form, which is constituted by the ten *sefirotic* potencies.[89] The locus of this form is in the imagination of the mystic. The imaginative visualization is described in the continuation of *Sefer Yetzirah*: "Know, contemplate, and imagine, establish the matter clearly, and set the Creator in His place. Their measure is ten without end." By imagining the anthropomorphic shape of the deity, related to the ten *sefirot* that are immeasurable, one sets God in his place, which may be a reference to the divine throne.[90] In another passage the *sefirot* are said to bow down before God's throne.

Obviously, the *sefirot* are characterized as the celestial beasts who bear the throne.[91] Some scholars have argued that the author simply wanted to describe the *sefirot* in these terms for a pure literary effect, but it seems to me that implied here is the more daring claim that the *sefirot* are dynamic potencies that collectively make up the habitation of the divine.[92] This confirms the reading I suggested above of the intent of the imaginative visualization: by forming an image of the divine anthropos one sets God upon his throne.

There are two other explanations of the *sefirot* preserved in the first part of *Sefer Yetzirah*. The first of these is extant in one passage, which appears to be a fragment of an older cosmological speculation. In this text the ten *sefirot* are explained as the ten depths, which consist of the beginning, the end, goodness, evil, height, depth, east, west, north, and south.[93] The *sefirot* are thus interpreted in a cosmological vein as referring to the depths of the created world. These depths embrace a temporal, spatial, and moral character. The second of the three explanations of the *sefirot* also has a cosmological application, but in this case the *sefirot* are correlated with the fundamental elements of being. The ten *sefirot* are delineated as follows: the spirit of the living God (or the holy spirit that is said to comprise three elements, voice, spirit, and speech), the spirit from the spirit, water, fire, height, depth, east, west, north, and south.[94] I suggest that in this case two traditions have been conflated, one that deals with four spiritual elements and the other with the six cosmic dimensions. The autonomous nature of the latter tradition is evident in one passage that describes God's sealing each of these six dimensions with a permutation of the three-letter name, YHW.[95] These two traditions were combined in an attempt to explain the nature of the enigmatic ten *sefirot*. What is crucial to emphasize is that there is no uniform explanation of the *sefirot* in *Sefer Yetzirah*. On the contrary, one must appreciate the redactional complexity of this document, and the claim that the *sefirot* has a primary signification of ciphers is not substantiated by a close reading of the text.

The letter symbolism in the second part of *Sefer Yetzirah* is meant to convey a different idea that has also had a profound impact on Jewish mystics through the ages. The letters, divided into three groups (three mothers, seven doubles, and twelve simples), are not merely the tools of divine creativity, a notion found in more normative rabbinic sources; they are treated in *Sefer Yetzirah* as the material stuff of reality.[96] That is, a given thing is brought into life by means of a process of letter-combination, for the appropriate letters inform us of that thing's most basic structure. Each of the letters is said to have an impact on three ontological planes: space (*'olam*, literally, "cosmos"), time (*shanah*, literally, "year"), and the microcosm (*nefesh*, literally, "life" or "soul"). Just as other forms of reality are composed of the letters, so too the human body. The correlation between letter-combination (by means of 231 gates of permutation) and limbs of the human body in *Sefer Yetzirah* parallels the correlation between letters and the anthropomorphic figure (whose standard measure, as I indicated above, equals 236 thousand myriad parasangs) of the divine described in *Shi'ur Qomah*.[97] While no explicit connection between the two modes of speculation is made in the earlier sources, it is of interest to note that the two are brought together in subsequent kabbalistic speculation, including, for example, in the Zoharic tradition[98] as well as other sources, which in turn influenced the version of Lurianic kabbalah expounded in the latter part of the sixteenth century by Israel Sarug.[99] The central role played by letter symbolism is evident in all the main branches of medieval Jewish mysticism, including German Pietism, the ecstatic kabbalah of Abraham Abulafia (1240–c.1292), and the theosophic kabbalah.

❧ MYSTICAL THEOSOPHY OF THE ❧ GERMAN PIETISTS

Merkavah traditions were transported from their Babylonian milieu to the Jewish communities of Europe, most likely through Italy, in the eighth and ninth centuries.[100] But the most important source for the preservation and transmission of these documents were the German Pietists who were active in the Rhineland in the twelfth and thirteenth centuries.[101] The main circle of Pietists was led by Judah ben Samuel ben Kalonymus of Regensburg (d. 1217) and his disciple, Eleazar ben Judah ben Kalonymus of Worms (d. 1240). In addition to preserving the older Merkavah texts, the Pietists developed their own theosophy, which combined Hekhalot mysticism and magic, the philosophy of Saadia Gaon, the writings of Shabbetai Donnolo (b. 913) and Judah ben Barzilai (eleventh to twelfth century), and Jewish Neoplatonism, especially that of Abraham ibn Ezra (c. 1092–1167).[102] At the center of the Pietistic theosophy is the doctrine of the divine glory (*kavod*), which is largely based on some of the sources mentioned above.[103] The discussions reflected in the Pietistic writings concerning the nature of the glory are not merely theoretical in nature but related to the problem of directing human prayer to a supposedly incorporeal deity. It is not an exaggeration to say that the primary issue that occupied the Pietistic authors was the problem of visualizing an incorporeal deity, an act that in some sense traditional prayer demands.[104] Three distinct approaches related to the ontic status of the glory and its phenomenal accessibility to the human being can be identified: the glory is a created light extrinsic to God (Saadia); the glory is emanated from God and therefore attached to the deity (Shabbetai Donnolo and Abraham ibn Ezra); the visible form of the glory is an image within the mind of the prophet or mystic and not an entity outside the mind (Hai Gaon (939–1038)) as transmitted by Chananel ben Chushiel (d. 1055/6). For the most part, the Pietists seem to reject the first opinion and waver between the second and third.[105] Following the view expressed by Nathan ben Yechiel of Rome (1035–c. 1110), itself based on earlier sources, the Pietists, as may be gathered from the writings of Eleazar of Worms, distinguished between an upper and lower glory. The former is an amorphous light, called the "presence" (shekhinah) or "great splendor" (hod ha-gaddol), while the latter is the aspect that assumes different forms within the prophetic or mystical imagination. Yet, as the Pietists insist, the creator is simultaneously outside and inside the image.[106] One can therefore pray to the visible glory, which is an image, for God is present in that very image.[107]

The forms that the lower glory assumes are multiple in nature, changing in accordance with God's will and the particular capacity of the given visionary. The most important of these images is the anthropomorphic shape suggested already by biblical theophanies including the chariot-vision of Ezekiel. In one passage in Sefer ha-Shem, Eleazar even goes so far as to say that one should conjure an image in one's heart of the supernal God sitting on a throne so that he could bow down and worship him, and "he will remember the One."[108] The realization of divine oneness is here connected to the enthronement of God, which is actualized only through the imaginative visualization, since the One is not a body that occupies a throne. The point is underscored in a second passage from this work: "The One has no limit [ha-yichud 'ein lo sof] for He is everything, and if not for the fact that 'through the prophets [God] was imaged' (Hosea 12:11) as a king sitting upon a throne, they would not have known to whom to pray. . . . This is what is said in Sefer Yetzirah (1:8) 'and set the Creator on His place.' "[109] The imaginative visualization of God, which provides the iconic representation necessary for prayer, is expressed particularly in terms of the structure of enthronement, a motif to which I shall return below.

Furthermore, Eleazar appropriates the anthropomorphism of the ancient Shi'ur Qomah by applying the corporeal measurements not to the creator (as the text explicitly states) but to the form that is constituted within the imagination.[110] Eleazar has thus reinterpreted the earlier mystical tradition that ascribed corporeal dimensions to the divine form. From the vantage point of the Pietistic theology, at least in its exoteric formulation, there is no divine form – God is not a body and therefore can possess no form or shape – but only that which is apprehended in the mind of the visionary. The measurements specified in the ancient esoteric work therefore are not attributable to the creator or even to the glory as it is in and of itself; they represent rather the proportions of the glory as it is visualized through the imagined forms within the prophetic or mystic consciousness. By contrast, according to the writings of a distinct group of Pietists, the *Chug ha-Keruv ha-Meyuchad*,[111] the measurable enthroned figure is the being designated as the Special Cherub, the anthropomorphic representation of the invisible, incorporeal, divine glory.[112]

It must be noted, however, that alongside the exoteric doctrine of the glory, the main circle of the Kalonymide Pietists preserved and developed an esoteric tradition that applied in a more veridical way the measurements of the *Shi'ur Qomah* to the glory. Thus, for example, in a text attributed by Joseph Dan to Judah the Pious, it is stated explicitly that the measurement of the *Shi'ur Qomah* is applied "to that which cleaves," an allusion to the glory that emanates from the One to which it is attached.[113] Similarly, in one context Eleazar writes:

> The essence of the glory is seen above, and a fire of radiance which is unfathomable was opposite the throne. Within [that radiance] the glory is seen in accordance with the will of the Creator, at times like an elder and at times like a youth.[114] The measure of the stature is 2,360,000,000 parasangs, as it is written, "Great is our Lord and full of power" (Psalms 147:5), "full of power" (*we-rav koach*) numerically equals 236.... The stature of the visible glory is 2,360,000,000 parasangs.[115]

Two of the main tenets of the esoteric tradition cultivated by the Rhineland Pietists include the identification of the glory with the Tetragrammaton[116] and the possibility of imaging the letters of this divine name as an anthropos.[117] While this esoteric tradition is alluded to in various Pietistic writings, it is stated most explicitly in *Sefer ha-Navon*: "The name [YHWH] appears in its letters to the angels and prophets in several forms and radiance and it appears in the image of the appearance of an anthropos ... it appears 'in the semblance of a human form' (Ezekiel 1:26), this refers to the *Shekhinah* and the angel of the glory (*mal'akh ha-kavod*), which is the Tetragrammaton."[118] This text reflects one of the oldest ideas in Jewish esotericism: the identification, or blurring of the distinction, between the glory, on the one hand, and the angelic being, on the other, which is the anthropomorphic manifestation of the divine.[119] Eleazar himself alludes to this matter when he writes that "the glory is symbolized by the angel that changes to many forms," including most importantly the form of an anthropos.[120]

One may also discern from the Pietistic writings that study of the chariot was understood as speculation on the divine names, especially the Tetragrammaton.[121] This speculation, moreover, involved a contemplative vision of the name. Knowledge of the chariot encompassed a mystical praxis of meditation on the divine name by means of which the Pietist ascended.[122] Eleazar thus specifies a series of rituals of purification as a prelude to both the study of the chariot[123] and the activity of mentioning the divine name.[124] It is hardly a coincidence that virtually the same procedure is outlined in these two contexts. It is also evident from Eleazar, as well as other contemporary Ashkenazi material, that the German Pietists cultivated the technique of recitation of divine or angelic names (itself rooted in the older Hekhalot literature) in order to induce a state of religious ecstasy akin to prophecy. The technique of recitation of the names and that of letter–combination transmitted in Eleazar had a decisive influence on both theosophic and ecstatic kabbalists active in Spain in the latter part of the thirteenth century.[125]

Another part of the esoteric tradition of the German Pietists involves the use of sexual imagery to characterize processes within the divine sphere. The use of feminine imagery to describe events in the throne-world is present in a cluster of texts that describe the chariot in terms of the structure of a nut. Alexander Altmann was the first scholar to present a systematic account of this material,[126] but it was Joseph Dan who suggested that these texts preserved an ancient esoteric reading of Song of Songs 6:1, "I went down to the garden of nuts," which formed part of the chariot mystical speculation that originated in Babylonia.[127] With respect to the masculine and feminine element of the nut, Dan proposed that these were innovated by the Pietists, but he categorically denied that the idea of sexual dualism in the divine sphere had any other influence on Pietistic theosophy. He therefore rejects any attempt to see a connection between kabbalistic speculation, which is predicated on a male–female polarity within the Godhead (see below), and German Pietistic theology.[128] More recently, Asi Farber has thoroughly reinvestigated the development of the secret of the nut tradition in the Pietistic corpus. Like Dan, Farber maintains that this represents an older tradition that the Pietists received, but she takes issue with Dan's conjecture that the Pietists themselves added the sexual images. On the contrary, these images were part of the "original" texts, which the Pietists attempted to minimize or even obscure, in some cases by altering the texts. Yet, a careful reading of their own writings shows that there are veiled allusions to the bisexual nature of the divine realm. According to Farber, then, one must distinguish between the "exoteric" side of the Pietistic theology, which attempted to attenuate or supress sexual images, and the "esoteric" side that described aspects of the divine in precisely such terms. The esoteric aspect was not fully committed to writing but was transmitted orally.[129]

The feminine quality of the glory is especially evident in the proto-kabbalistic text included in Eleazar's *Sefer ha-Chokhmah*, the commentary on the forty-two-letter name of God attributed to Hai Gaon.[130] In that text the *shekhinah* is identified as the crown (*'atarah*), prayer (*tefillah* or the Aramaic *tzelota'*), the divine voice (*bat qol*), the king's daughter (*bat melekh*), the bride (*kalah*) who sits to the left of the groom, God, the tenth kingship (*malkhut 'asirit*) or the tenth *sefirah*. Dan has argued that this text in all probability was not written by Eleazar as it employs terminology and concepts not known from his voluminous writings.[131] It must be pointed out, however, as Scholem himself noted,[132] that from a phenomenological point of view the glory does receive in the teachings of the Pietists a dynamic character that is very close to the description of the tenth emanation in the divine pleroma according to kabbalistic sources. Furthermore, Moshe Idel has shown that the elevation of the crown, understood hypostatically, in German Pietistic texts has a decidedly theurgical connotation that bears a close likeness to older midrashic as well as kabbalistic motifs.[133] In a separate study I have argued that an even more pronounced theurgy is evident in the Pietistic treatment of the commandments.[134] The lower glory, identified as the cherub or the image of Jacob engraved on the throne, is equated with the union of two cherubim, which (on the basis of older traditions) correspond to the divine names, YHWH and Adonai, or the two attributes of God, mercy and judgment. Through a complicated numerological exegesis the two names are said to comprise the 613 commandments or the Torah in its totality, the same numerological equivalence of the expression *yhwh 'elohe yisra'el*, which is one of the proper names of the enthroned glory. The Pietists draw the obvious theurgical implications: by performing the 613 traditional commandments one unites the two names of God or the glory. In an essential way, therefore, the secret theosophy cultivated by the German Pietists bears a striking similarity to the emerging kabbalistic doctrines of Provence and northern Spain. This similarity is not a coincidence, but reveals a common heritage that informed both the Pietists and kabbalists.

THEOSOPHIC KABBALAH AS A VISIONARY GNOSIS

During this same period that German Pietism became an active social and religious force, theosophic kabbalah began to take root in Provence and northern Spain. The precise origins of kabbalistic speculation remain somewhat obscure, though it is generally assumed that fragments of older documents made their way to central Europe from the East. Rabbinic writings themselves (aggadic statements contained in the Palestinian and Babylonian Talmuds or in independent collections of scriptural exegeses known as *midrashim*) may be viewed as a repository of ancient Jewish theosophic theologoumena that have been preserved in a very fragmentary form. These fragments were elaborated into a comprehensive and systematic doctrine by the medieval kabbalists.[135] It is also likely that there was a prehistory to some kabbalistic ideas that were transmitted orally in a subterranean fashion. One of the crucial problems in the historical development of theosophic kabbalah is the relationship between Gnosticism, an ancient syncretistic religious movement that flourished in the Mediterranean countries in the first centuries of the Common Era, and Jewish esotericism. Some scholars maintain that the similarities between these two are purely phenomenological in nature, whereas others insist on an historical connection as well.[136]

Whatever the relationship between Gnosticism and kabbalah, it is evident that in the twelfth century a theosophic conception of God begins to crystallize in Jewish writings. The main elements of this theosophy include the imaging of God in terms of a male–female polarity and the theurgical understanding of normative religious practice such that fulfillment of the traditional precepts increases the stature of the divine structure and, conversely, failure to do so weakens it. Both of these elements are present in the first text dedicated fully to a theosophical–theurgical conception of God, *Sefer ha-Bahir*, which presumably surfaced in twelfth-century Provence, though the text obviously contains earlier literary strata.[137] Standard biblical and rabbinic images are here transformed into symbols for the dynamic life of divinity. The presentation of the theosophy is not systematic in the case of the *Bahir*, which is, in fact, structured like a traditional midrash.[138] On the contrary, it is clear that comprised within the Bahiric texts are multiple tradition-complexes and clusters of theosophic exegeses that have been fused together in the process of redaction. In one section, however, we can discern a fairly cohesive textual unit according to which the ten powers that make up the divine pleroma are called *ma'amarot* (sayings), a reference to the traditional rabbinic notion of the ten logoi by means of which the world was created.[139] The authors of the *Bahir* opted for mythical ways to describe these divine grades, referring to them parabolically in such images as crowns, trees, gardens, and the like. The potencies are on one occasion called *sefirot*,[140] the term employed in *Sefer Yetzirah*, as we have seen. It was this term that eventually emerged as the predominant denotation of the divine potencies in the kabbalistic literature of the following centuries.

The *Bahir* supplied two important ways of pictorially depicting these potencies: either as a tree[141] or as an anthropomorphic figure.[142] Both of these images had an important influence on subsequent kabbalistic thought, but it is the second that goes to the heart of kabbalah, providing as it does the background for both the theosophical and theurgical axes of the kabbalistic Weltanschauung. The *Bahir* interprets the notion of humanity being created in God's image (Genesis 1:26) in terms of the divine body; that is, the limbs of the human correspond to the upper divine limbs (seven[143] or eight[144] are specified and not ten) and as such can influence them through proper or improper action. In virtue of this anthropomorphism, one can see continuity between the ancient Jewish mystical speculation and the theosophy expressed in the *Bahir*. The position assumed by the enthroned demiurgical being is now taken by the divine gradations that are visualized in the shape of an anthropos.[145] This cornerstone of kabbalistic thought is well articulated by the anonymous author of *Ma'arekhet ha-'Elohut*, a work composed in the late thirteenth or early fourteenth century:

> Know that a person's physical form is made in the [likeness of the] supernal image [*demut 'elyon*], and the supernal image is the [*sefirotic*] edifice, whose essence is *Tif'eret* [the sixth *sefirah*], which is called the anthropos in the chariot.... Now that you know the structure of the human form you can comprehend if you have received orally the truth of the prophetic vision seen by the prophets. The rabbis, blessed be their memory, called this vision the measure of the stature (*shi'ur qomah*).[146]

It is on the basis of this correspondence between human limbs and those of the divine that the kabbalists assign a central role to the normative life of traditional Judaism.[147] That is, by fulfilling the commandments one strengthens the corresponding limb above in the divine edifice, while neglecting to do so or doing what is prohibited causes a blemish above. Joseph of Hamadan, a kabbalist writing at the end of the thirteenth or beginning of the fourteenth century, put the matter as follows:

> You already know that man was created in the form of the supernal chariot [i.e., the *sefirotic* realm].... Each and every limb of man exists from the sparks that originate in the chariot from that very limb, eye from the eye, and so on with respect to all the other limbs.... Thus the [sages], blessed be their memory, said, "a limb strengthens a limb." When a person fulfills a commandment he sustains the upper limb and the lower limb ... but if a person sins with the eye and in a commandment

connected to it, he creates, as it were, a blemish in the supernal eye.[148]

The import of kabbalistic theurgy, therefore, can only be understood against the background of the anthropomorphic conception of God, for the impact that one can have upon the divine is predicated on the morphological resemblance between God and human. Consider, for example, the following text:

> This is one of the great traditions pertaining to the matter of kabbalah. Know that a person is made in the image of the supernal *sefirot*, as it says, "Let us make man in our image, after our likeness" (Genesis 1:26), for there are supernal potencies [*koach 'elyonim*] called hand, foot, eye, and head. . . . Similarly in man there is an eye, foot, and [other] limbs. This is the import of the dictum of the rabbis, blessed be their memory, "The Torah speaks in the language of man" [cf. Babylonian Talmud, *Berakhot* 31b, and parallels]. In any event these [*sefirot*] are potencies [*kochot*] and not limbs [*'evarim*]. The limbs of man are called in accordance with these potencies. . . . Thus you find in many places that many kabbalists call the *sefirot* the supernal Adam [*'adam ha-'elyon*], and the lower man [*'adam ha-tachton*] is sanctified through his limbs . . . and then his limbs will be bound and joined to the limbs of the supernal Adam, and he himself will be called holy. . . . If, God forbid, a person . . . follows the obstinacy of his heart and defiles his limbs, all of them or some of them, it is considered as if, God forbid, he blemishes the limbs of the supernal Adam.[149]

This anthropomorphism is further accentuated by the kabbalistic identification of the Torah in its mystical essence with the divine edifice (*binyan 'elohi*), a term employed by Ezra of Gerona, or the "holy and pure supernal form" ("*tzurah ha-'elyonah ha-qedoshah we-ha-tehorah*") – according to the locution of Joseph of Hamadan.[150] The Torah is the shape or image of God, which is construed anthropomorphically by various kabbalists. That is to say, each of the laws corresponds to, or derives from, a particular limb in the supernal Adamic form, which is, at the same time, the Torah. The connection between kabbalistic theurgy and the anthropomorphic conception of Torah as the divine form is brought out in the following passage of Joseph of Hamadan:

> The Torah is the shadow of the Holy One, blessed be He. Happy is he, and blessed is his lot, who knows how to direct the limb corresponding to a [supernal] limb, and a form that corresponds to a [supernal] form in the holy and pure chain,

473

blessed be His name. In so far as the Torah is His form [*tzurato*], blessed be He, He commanded us to study Torah in order to know the pattern of the supernal form [*dugmato shel tzurah ha-'elyonah*].[151]

The view of Hamadan is expressed in slightly different terms by Menachem Recanati, an Italian kabbalist writing in the first part of the fourteenth century: "The commandments are one entity, and they depend upon the supernal chariot [i.e., the *sefirotic* realm] . . . each and every commandment depends on one part of the chariot. It follows that God is not something extrinsic to the Torah, nor is the Torah outside of God. . . . Thus the kabbalists say that the Holy One, blessed be He, is the Torah."[152]

At this juncture it must be noted that many of the kabbalists living in the high Middle Ages could not speak unqualifiedly of God as possessing a form or body, let alone masculine and feminine traits. Thus, we frequently find in kabbalistic literature the ascription of anthropomorphic characteristics to the *sefirotic* realm followed by the caveat that this anthropomorphism should not be taken in any literal sense to imply a belief in God's corporeality. A typical account of the kabbalists' reluctance to accept the anthropomorphic implications of their own thinking may be found in the following passage from Recanati, which is based, in turn, on Joseph Gikatilla:[153]

The true essence of the Creator, may He be elevated and blessed, is not comprehended by anyone but Him. . . . If so we must contemplate the [corporeal] attributes found in Scripture and in the words of the rabbis, blessed be their memory, e.g. hand, foot, ear, eye, and the like. . . . Do not think that the eye is in the form of a [physical] eye, or the hand in the form of a [physical] hand. Rather these things are inner matters in the truth of the reality of God, blessed be He, from which is the source and the flow that goes out to all created things. There is no similarity between God and us from the vantage point of substance or form . . . for He has no image in the created things. The intention [of these anthropomorphic expressions] rather is that the form of our limbs become symbols [*dimyon simanim*] for the supernal, hidden matters that the mind cannot grasp.[154] . . . Since God, may He be elevated and blessed, wanted to benefit us, He created in the human body certain wonderful and hidden limbs that are in the form of symbols for the [divine] chariot. If a person merits to purify one of his limbs, that limb will be like a throne for the inner supernal limb that is called by the name eye, hand, and the like.[155]

To speak of divine limbs, accordingly, means only to refer to the divine powers (*sefirot*) in the terms with which we describe the human body. These terms are symbols (*simanim*) for the divine reality that we cannot know in any essential manner. This approach is very close to Scholem's presentation of kabbalistic symbols as "an expressible representation of something which lies beyond the sphere of expression and communication."[156] The description of God's body or the mating of male and female does not tell us anything about God's true essence, for the latter is unknowable. While there is ample support for such an understanding of the function of religious symbols in kabbalistic texts such as the one cited above, I suggest that this is a reflection of the historical period in which kabbalah emerged as a literary force, and not indicative of its "originary" doctrine.[157] Underlying the ideational matrix of theosophic kabbalah is the mythological belief in the divine body that was expressed in earlier Jewish mysticism as well, producing the visionary element of the Hekhalot literature and the seemingly bizarre speculations of the *Shi'ur Qomah* tradition. In spite of repeated qualifications found in medieval kabbalistic texts, some of the more esoteric elements of kabbalah are intensely anthropomorphic in nature. This includes the literary units of the *Zohar*, which present the most recondite teachings about the Godhead, the *Idra Rabba* (Great Gathering) and *Idra Zuta* (Small Gathering), as well as the mythic theosophy promulgated in the sixteenth century in Safed by Isaac Luria and his disciples, largely based on the doctrine of the divine countenances (*partzufim*) elaborated upon in the *Idrot* sections of the *Zohar*. Epistemologically, the mythical representation of God is linked to the imaginative faculty.[158] That is, the imagination assumes a central role in kabbalistic literature for it is the means that allows for the corporeal depiction of the spiritual realities that are incorporeal. The point is particularly well emphasized in the following kabbalistic text:

> All the time that the rational soul is in the body it is given permission to form by the corporeal imagination the countenances of emanation [*partzufim de-'atzilut*], even though they are spiritual, pure and holy, to the Infinite. Thus R. Simeon bar Yochai conducted himself (as well as the *Tannaim*, especially in the *Idra*), for all his words involved the image of the body, the head, hairs of the beard, forehead, eyes, nose, mouth, throat, etc., masculine and feminine. There is no objection to this because we find it in the *Torah*, *Prophets*, and *Writings*. Therefore, do not wonder that the rabbi, the Ari, blessed be his memory, wrote in the *yichudim*, "you should imagine in your thoughts as if you saw with your eyes Arikh Anpin as an elderly being, as Daniel said, 'the Ancient of Days was sitting'

(Daniel 7:9)," for the intellect necessarily follows the imagination when one can find no rational means to discern the truth. . . . The intellect follows the physical sense in accord with what everyone sees, hears, smells, and feels, and the intellect follows the imagination. Since the object of the intellect is truth, and the intellect can comprehend things as they are and not as they are imagined, permission has been given to us to form images of the divinity, which is the beginning of the intellect's knowledge of truth as is required, for we know by definitive proofs that above there is no face and no back, no right and no left, no drinking and no eating, no standing and no sitting, no eye, no mouth, and no physical limb that is accidental. This is confirmed by the sages of the Talmud, and one must be careful not to believe otherwise. On account of this it is said at the beginning of the *Idra* [*Zohar* 3:127b-128a], "R. Simeon said, 'Cursed be anyone who makes a sculptured or molten image [abhorred by the Lord, a craftsman's handiwork] and sets it up in secret' (Deuteronomy 27:15)," in the secret of the world, so that one should not imagine in his mind that what one sees in one's imaginings is not an image but the truth. Through this you will comprehend the matter of prophecy, for it is evident that prophecy is not by the faculty of the intellect but by the faculty of the imagination.[159]

The author of this text affirms that the way of intellect is superior to the imagination because the intellect can discern the truth of the spiritual entities as they are themselves. Yet, in order for the embodied intellect to gain access to the divine realm, it is necessary for the intellect to acquiesce to the imagination, which imagines the incorporeal *sefirot* in corporeal images of a tangible and sensible nature. In that respect, kabbalistic gnosis is on a par with prophecy, which is also linked in an essential way with the imaginative process.

The literature of theosophic kabbalah spans an extensive period and incorporates many different aspects of Jewish esotericism. One may, however, legitimately isolate speculation on the ten *sefirot* as the distinctive doctrine of this tradition. These *sefirot* are characterized in various ways, but perhaps the most central characterization is that of light. According to one of the accepted etymologies in thirteenth-century kabbalah, the word "*sefirot*" is said to derive from the word "*sappir*," which means "sapphire," conveying therefore the notion of luminosity.[160] The centrality of the light symbolism is attested in any number of sources, deriving from either a gnostic–mythological background or a Neoplatonic one.[161] The former is evident in *Sefer ha-Bahir* and in other kabbalists whose thought can be said to emerge out of the ground of midrashic and Hekhalot literature. The latter influence is felt particularly in the systematic account of the emanation of the ten spiritual lights out of the *Ein-Sof*, the ineffable Infinite, which is first articulated in the Provençal kabbalah, especially as it appears in Isaac the Blind, and his disciples, Asher ben David, Ezra ben Solomon, and Azriel ben Menachem of Gerona. One of the distinctive features of the Zoharic literature (which had a critical impact on subsequent kabbalistic theosophy) is that it combines the mythic and more philosophical approach.

The *Ein-Sof* and the *sefirot* represent two aspects of the one God: the former is the nameless, boundless ground of being that assumes personality in the dynamic *sefirotic* structure. Though multiple, the *sefirot* form one organic unity and are said to be connected to the Infinite "like the flame bound to the coal," utilizing the language of *Sefer Yetzirah*. Another expression employed by kabbalists from the same source to depict the unity of the *sefirot* is "their end is fixed in their beginning and their beginning in their end." For the most part classical kabbalah depicts the process of emanation of the *sefirot* as issuing forth out of the Infinite like rays of light from the sun. However, there is also evidence for another important motif concerning the primordial withdrawal or contraction (*tzimtzum*) of light before the process of emanation could unfold. Allusions to this idea are found in some thirteenth-century kabbalistic sources,[162] but it was expanded into a systematic doctrine in the sixteenth-century kabbalah of Moses Cordovero (1522–70)[163] and Isaac Luria (1534–72).[164] Kabbalists also differed with respect to the question of the ontological status of the *sefirot* vis-à-vis the Infinite, with some maintaining that the *sefirot* are the essence (*'atzmut*) of God and others asserting that they are instruments or vessels (*kelim*) into which God infuses his infinite light.[165] The opposition between the essentialist and instrumentalist views was dialectically resolved in various ways by sixteenth-century kabbalists, such as Solomon Alkabetz (1505–76) and his student, Moses Cordovero,[166] who suggested that the *sefirot* were both God's essence and his vessels.

Finally, it should be mentioned that another essential doctrine in kabbalistic thought concerns the realm of unholy or demonic forces that structurally parallel the holy realm of *sefirot*.[167] While there is some speculation concerning an attribute of evil (personified as Satan) within the divine realm in the *Bahir* as well as some other evidence that early kabbalists had a tradition about demonic forces (both Isaac the Blind[168] and Nachmanides[169]), it was in the kabbalah developed in Castile in the second half of the thirteenth century that such speculation was elaborated as an explicit doctrine and assumed a position of supreme importance.[170] The teaching regarding the unholy forces in the writings of the

Castilian kabbalists, such as Isaac ben Jacob ha-Kohen, Moses ben Simeon of Burgos, and Todros ben Joseph Abulafia, had a decisive influence on the *Zohar*, which abounds with different accounts of the struggle between the holy and the unholy.[171] In the *Zohar* itself one can discern two distinct tendencies: on the one hand, there is clear evidence of a more dualistic posture according to which the forces of light are pitted against the forces of darkness (called the *Sitra Achra*, that is, the Other Side), whereas, on the other, there is a more monistic strain in *Zohar* that sees all of the forces as related in a cosmological chain and the ultimate religious ideal is containment rather than separation.[172] This tension is evident in subsequent stages of Jewish mystical thought as well. The more mythological descriptions of the destruction of the primordial forces of evil (unbalanced forces of judgment) or the elimination of impurity from the divine thought[173] had a decisive influence on later kabbalah, especially the teaching of Isaac Luria concerning the triadic myth within the Godhead consisting of, first, contraction (*tzimtzum*), second, the breaking of the vessels (*shevirat ha-kelim*) and the consequent formation of the shells (*qelippot*) and the fall of the sparks (*nitzotzot*), and third, restoration (*tiqqun*) or liberation of the fallen and entrapped sparks.[174]

While the main interest of kabbalists was clearly to speculate on and develop the metaphysical intricacies of their doctrine, underlying these theosophic speculations is a deeply experiential component. Recent scholarship has paid far greater attention to the experiential side of kabbalistic thought, including specific meditative or contemplative techniques intended to induce religious ecstasy, mystical union, and visionary experiences.[175] I should here like to emphasize that the study of the *sefirot* itself as viewed from within the tradition was considered to be an exercise in visualization. The emphasis on visualization is related to one of the most popular terms that kabbalists used to refer to themselves, *maskilim*, based ultimately on Daniel 12:3. This terminus technicus conveys the idea that the kabbalists are mystic visionaries, and what marks their path as distinct is the contemplative vision of the divine form that is at the center of their religious world view. The most important means for the enlightened mystic to visualize the divine form is clearly the study of Torah. By exegetically disclosing the secrets contained in Scripture, the kabbalist uncovers the lights hidden within the text, which is the divine image. From that vantage point it may be said that scriptural interpretation is itself a revelatory mode, that is, when one meditates on the text one is effectively contemplating the divine form. One of the boldest expressions of this is found in Joseph of Hamadan: "Therefore the Torah is called by this name, for it elucidates the pattern of the Holy One, blessed be He ... the Torah, as it were, is the shadow of the Holy One, blessed be He ... inasmuch as the Torah is the form of God, He commanded us to study it so that we may know the pattern of the upper form."[176]

The correlation of divine light and the letters of Scripture is substantiated by kabbalists by means of the numerical equivalence between *raz*, "secret," and *'or*, "light."[177] To comprehend the mystical meaning of Scripture is to behold the light of the divine gradations. A fairly typical account is given by Cordovero: "The mysteries of Torah are verily the splendor of the firmament, and when a person is occupied with the secret of the mysteries of Torah, he opens the supernal sources in the secret of their unity by means of the voices of Torah."[178] In slightly different words Abraham Azulai elaborates on the same point: "There are great lights in the Torah and they are its secrets, and there are several secrets that are still concealed, for they have not yet been revealed in the world; therefore the Torah is hidden and its light has not been disseminated. When the people below in this world bring to light secrets of the Torah, they cause that very matter above, which is hinted at in the secret of the Torah, to be revealed and to be disseminated."[179] The virtual identification of Torah with the divine, on the one hand, and the further specification of the luminous nature of the letters of Torah, on the other, provides us with one of the most frequently recurring themes in the kabbalistic literature. In eighteenth-century Chasidism this developed into a technical meditative technique centered on the cleaving of one's thought to the infinite light contained in the letters of the Torah as well as those of the traditional prayers.[180]

There is sufficient evidence to show, moreover, that kabbalists developed and propagated relatively simple mystical techniques in order to induce visions of the divine light or colors. In the case of some kabbalists, such as David ben Yehudah he-Chasid and other members of his school, the technique of visualizing colors within the imagination was part of the mystical intention of prayer. The imagined colors were not to be confused with the *sefirot* themselves, the visualization of which was forbidden, but were viewed rather as the electrum (*chashmal*) or cover (*levush*)[181] of the particular *sefirah* and therefore capable of being visualized. According to another tradition closely connected with the previous method of spiritual visualization, one is instructed to imagine the letters of the Tetragrammaton vocalized in a specific way and contained within a circle of a particular color corresponding to the appropriate *sefirah*.[182] The *Zohar* abounds in light imagery in its different characterizations of the divine emanations, influenced especially by the writings of a group of mystics known as the *Chug ha-'Iyyun*;[183] two specific, rather simple, techniques are mentioned in order to induce visual experiences. The first involves the rolling of the closed eyes, which produces three colors within the mind that correspond either to the three central *sefirot* in and of themselves or as reflected in the last of the *sefirot*, the *shekhinah*. The second technique, which is rooted in an ancient Jewish procedure to induce prophetic vision, involves placing a dish of water in sunlight so that one may watch the shadows cast upon a wall. This visualization results in a state of mystical comprehension or meditation upon the *sefirot*.[184]

✦ ECSTATIC KABBALAH ✦

In the latter part of the thirteenth century, at the time when theosophic kabbalah was flourishing, there emerged as well an alternative kabbalistic tradition with a different focus. The main exponent of this tradition was Abraham Abulafia.[185] Whereas the theosophic kabbalists focused their attention on the hypostatic potencies that made up the divine realm, Abulafia turned his attention to cultivating a mystical system that could assist one in achieving a state of unio mystica, which he identified as prophecy. He thus called his system "prophetic kabbalah" (*qabbalah nevu'it*), though modern scholars have referred to it as ecstatic kabbalah in so far as it is aimed at producing a state of mystical ecstasy wherein the boundaries separating the self from God are overcome. Prophetic kabbalah, according to Abulafia, embraces two parts, *qabbalat ha-sefirot* and *qabbalat ha-shemot*; the former is primary in time, but the latter is primary in importance. Abulafia is harshly critical of the theosophic kabbalists who interpret the *sefirot* as potencies that make up the divine. By contrast, according to him, the *sefirot* represent the separate intellects in the cosmological chain. Contemplation of the *sefirot* results in the intellectual overflow that facilitates the attainment of prophetic consciousness, which is essentially characterized as comprehension of the divine name. The process of intellection thus enables the mystic to unite with the divine.[186] In so far as this process facilitates the union of the self with its divine source, Abulafia on occasion describes the *sefirotic* entities as internalized psychological states. There is a perfect symmetry between the external cosmological axis and the internal psychical one.

Abulafia adopted the understanding of prophecy found in the philosophical writings of Moses Maimonides (1135–1204), who in turn was influenced by Islamic thinkers such as al-Fārābī and ibn Sīnā, to the effect that the prophet receives an overflow from, and thereby attains a state of conjunction with, the active intellect, the last of the ten separate intellects in the cosmological chain. For Abulafia, too, prophecy can be attained only when one is in a state of intellectual conjunction, a state that can come about only when the soul is freed from the bonds of the body. Thus, for example, he writes in his treatise *'Or ha-Sekhel*: "The connection of human existence with the divine existence during intellection – which is identical with the intellect in [its] existence – until he and He become one [entity]."[187] The union between human and divine intellects is so complete that in this state the individual can utter with respect to God, "He is I and I am He."[188]

One of the things that distinguishes Abulafia's mystical system from the more rationalist approach of Maimonides is that he introduced special techniques in order to bring about this state of conjunction or union (*devequt*). The main techniques consisted of letter-combination (in three stages: written, oral, and mental) and recitation of the divine names, which involved as well special breathing exercises and bodily postures.[189] Abulafia referred to his "science of letter-combination" (*chokhmat ha-tzeruf*), also identified as the "path of names" (*derekh ha-shemot*), as the true account of the chariot (the term "*merkavah*" deriving from the root "*rkb*," which can mean in one of its conjugational forms, "*leharkiv*," "to combine").[190] Idel has attempted to locate the Abulafian technique of recitation of names as an ecstatic exercise in the history of Jewish mysticism, beginning with the Merkavah texts of late antiquity and culminating in some of the writings of the German Pietists. Moreover, Idel has drawn our attention to some striking parallels between Abulafia's system of letter-combination and Eleazar of Worms, whose works Abulafia himself on occasion mentions by name.[191]

Although Abulafia gives preference to the auditory mode over the visual, accusing the theosophic kabbalists of focusing primarily on the latter,[192] in his own system visionary experience plays a critical role. For Abulafia, not only is the esoteric wisdom of the divine chariot brought about by knowledge of the various combinations and permutations of the names of God, but vision of the chariot itself consists of the very letters that are constitutive elements of the names. The ecstatic vision of the letters is not simply the means to achieve union with God; it is, to an extent, the end of the process.[193] The culminating stage in the via mystica is a vision of the letters of the divine names, especially the Tetragrammaton, originating in the intellectual and imaginative powers. These letters are visualized simultaneously as an anthropos. Gazing upon the divine name is akin to beholding the divine form as constituted within one's imagination. This vision results from the conjunction of the human intellect with the divine, but, like all prophecy, following the view of Maimonides and his Islamic predecessors, there must be an imaginative component. The latter is described either as the form of the letters or that of an anthropos. Both of these are figurative depictions of the active intellect who, in Abulafia's writings, is also personified as Metatron. In some sense, as is pointed out most emphatically in the anonymous *Sha'are Tzedeq*, written by a disciple of Abulafia, the image is a reflection of the individual prophet or mystic, an externalization of his inner self to the point of identification of the human intellect and the active intellect, personified as an anthropomorphic shape or the letters of the name.[194] With respect to the possibility of envisioning the letters as an anthropos, there is again an interesting parallel between Abulafia and the German Pietists as discussed above. The corporealization of the letters of the name in the shape of an anthropos represents, in my estimation, one of the cornerstones of kabbalistic thought, which has its roots in ancient Jewish esotericism. While it lies beyond the confines of this summary to substantiate my claim in detail, let me underline the essential point that the letters assume an anthropomorphic form. This renders problematic Scholem's general claim that Christian and kabbalistic doctrines of (visual) meditation should be distinguished on grounds that "in Christian mysticism a pictorial and concrete subject, such as the suffering of Christ and all that pertains to it, is given to the meditator, while in Kabbalah, the subject given is abstract and cannot be visualized, such as the Tetragrammaton and its combinations."[195] Scholem's point concerning the centrality of the Passion for mystical visions in Christianity is well taken, but his characterization of the subject of visual meditation in kabbalah as always being abstract needs to be qualified. The visualization of the letters of the name as an anthropos in German Pietism, in Abulafia, and in theosophic kabbalists indicates that in the Jewish mystical tradition as well the abstract can be rendered in a pictorial concrete image in the contemplative vision.

The ecstatic kabbalah had an important influence on the history of Jewish mysticism. In the last decade of the thirteenth century a circle of Abulafian kabbalah was established in northern Palestine.[196] From this circle, which combined Abulafian mysticism with Sufic ideas, there derived several works, including *Liqqute ha-Ran* (the teachings of Rabbi Nathan) and the anonymous *Sha'are Tzedeq*.[197] It is likely, moreover, that two important theosophic kabbalists, Isaac of Acre and Shem Tov ibn Gaon, were influenced by this circle, and thus assimilated ecstatic kabbalah within their respective theosophical traditions.[198] In the sixteenth century Abulafian kabbalah began to have a pronounced effect on some of the major kabbalists in Safed, such as Solomon Alkabetz, Moses Cordovero, Elijah de Vidas, and Chayyim Vital, and at the same time on kabbalists in Jerusalem, such as Judah Albotini and Joseph ibn Zaiah.[199] The influence of Abulafian kabbalah is also quite evident in eighteenth-century Chasidic literature, deriving directly from Abulafian manuscripts or indirectly through the writings of Cordovero and Vital.[200]

❧ CONCLUSION ❧

Jewish mysticism is not a monolith that can easily be defined or characterized. On the contrary, a plethora of different intellectual currents have converged to give shape to mystical trends within Judaism. While I do not think that we can speak of an "essence" of Jewish mysticism in some abstract and general manner, it is still possible to isolate certain "core" phenomena that have informed the religious mentality of Jewish mystics through the ages. We can thus establish the specific phenomenological contours that set Jewish mysticism apart from Islamic, Christian, Buddhist, or Hindu mysticism. This is not to deny that in given historical periods there may have been an influence of an external system of belief upon Jewish mystics. The point I am making is rather that discernible within the large corpus of texts identified by scholars as belonging to Jewish mysticism is a set of distinctive experiences, practices, and doctrines that are uniquely part of the Jewish esoteric tradition. Moreover, it has become increasingly clear that the distinction between the speculative–theosophical and the ecstatic–experiential orientation in Jewish mystical sources is not adequate. Theosophy is not simply a matter of study or exegesis, but serves as a means for the communion, or perhaps even union, of the mystic with the Godhead.

❧ NOTES ❧

1 Altmann 1991, p. 71.
2 Ibid., pp. 71–2.
3 Ibid., p. 72.
4 See Wolfson 1994c where I have articulated a similar position. Unfortunately, in that work I did not take into account the view of Altmann articulated in this lecture.
5 Scholem 1956, pp. 23–32; for a critical assessment of this issue, see Schweid 1985, pp. 41–5, 117–32.
6 Scholem 1969, p. 119.
7 See Talmage 1986.
8 See Vajda 1954 and 1957; Altmann 1969.
9 As representative studies see Idel 1986; Liebes 1987; Wolfson 1991.
10 The classic study on the motif of heavenly journey remains Bousset 1901. For recent surveys see Segal 1980; Smith 1981; Tabor 1986, pp. 57–111. A useful bibliography on matters pertaining to apocalyptic literature can be found in Hellholm 1989, pp. 795–825.
11 See Scholem 1956, p. 43; Gruenwald 1980; Himmelfarb 1988.
12 See Strugnell 1959; Scholem 1965, p. 128; Schiffman 1982; Newsom 1985, 1987, 1990; Halperin 1988, pp. 49–55; Baumgarten 1988; Nitzan 1992, 1994a, 1994b.
13 See Wolfson 1994c.

14 See the recent review of the issue in Schiffman 1994, pp. 351–60.

15 See Urbach 1967; Halperin 1980; 1988, pp. 11–37.

16 The text was published in Gruenwald 1972.

17 For a study of this passage, see Van Uchelen 1987.

18 See Neusner 1971; Séd 1973; Halperin 1980, pp. 107–40.

19 See Urbach 1967.

20 See Chernus 1982a; Halperin 1988, pp. 17–23, 141–9, 289–322.

21 For an extreme formulation of such a position, see Boyarin 1990a, pp. 532–50; 1990b, pp. 110, 118–22.

22 Dan 1986d, p. 292.

23 For an earlier dating see Scholem 1965; Smith 1963, pp. 155–60.

24 A critical edition of the text was published in Elior 1984. See also Schäfer 1982, §§ 335–74, 407–26, 496–7.

25 Schäfer 1982, §§ 81–306.

26 Odeberg 1973; Schäfer 1982, §§ 1–80. An English translation by P. S. Alexander is included in Charlesworth 1983, 1: 223–315.

27 Scholem 1965, pp. 103–17; Schäfer 1982, §§ 544–96. Prior to Scholem (though he neglects to mention it) fragments of this text were published in Altmann 1946. Two English translations are now available: Janowitz 1989; Swartz 1992.

28 The text was first published in Gruenwald 1968–9. See also Schäfer 1984, pp. 103–5.

29 A synoptic edition, translation, and study of this text has been published in Herrmann 1994.

30 See the recent summary given by Schäfer 1992, p. 160. While it is true that Scholem located the origins of the major Hekhalot texts in Palestine, he nevertheless readily admitted that many of the manuscripts that preserved these materials were redacted in Babylonia and from there were transmitted to Italy and Germany; see Scholem 1956, p. 47.

31 See Scholem 1956, p. 49; Fenton 1992.

32 See Graetz 1859; Hildesheimer 1931.

33 See Ariel 1985. For possible later reflections of Merkavah traditions in Islamic sources, see Halperin 1988, pp. 467–90.

34 The possible influence of Ismā'īlī sources on various aspects of the kabbalistic tradition have been noted by several scholars, although a full-length study is still a desideratum. See Goldreich 1987; Idel 1988e, p. 167 and references given on p. 244 n. 24; 1992b, pp. 343–4; Liebes 1993, pp. 152–3 n. 3. The significance of the Islamic context for the study of early kabbalah, including most importantly Sefer ha-Bahir, has been analyzed as well by Steven Wasserstrom in an unpublished paper that he has shared with me.

35 See Wolfson 1992, pp. 282–6, and other scholarly references discussed there.

36 See Schäfer 1988, pp. 8–16. In the same volume see also pp. 17–49, 50–62, 63–74, 154–233; Schäfer 1987. For a critical evaluation of Schäfer's methodology, see Gruenwald 1988, pp. 175–89.

37 See Gruenwald 1980, pp. 210 and 214 n. 9; Ta-Shema 1985, p. 309; Farber 1986, pp. 13, 88, 204 n. 9, 479–83 n. 132; Schäfer 1989, pp. xxxiii–xxxiv; 1992, p. 161; 1993a.

38 See Scholem 1956, pp. 77–8; 1965, pp. 12–13. Concerning the ritual of being clothed in the name, see also Scholem 1969, pp. 136–7. On the relationship of

the ecstatic heavenly journey and the magical-theurgic adjuration in Hekhalot literature, see Halperin 1988, pp. 376–87, 427–46, 450; Schäfer 1992, pp. 150–7.

39 For recent discussion of the *Sar-Torah* material see Swartz 1994b.

40 Schäfer 1988, p. 282.

41 As Scholem himself noted; see 1956, p. 50. See also Scholem 1965, pp. 75–83.

42 For a review of this problem, see Schäfer 1993b. On the relationship of magical texts and the Hekhalot corpus, see also Schiffman and Swartz 1992, pp. 24–6; Naveh and Shaked 1993, pp. 17–22.

43 See Schäfer 1988, pp. 285–9; 1992, pp. 164–5; Halperin 1988, pp. 370–5.

44 See Chernus 1982b, pp. 123–46; Gruenwald 1988, p. 184.

45 See Leiter 1973–4, pp. 143–5; Elior 1989, pp. 101, 106–8.

46 Scholem 1956, p. 66.

47 See Elior 1989, pp. 108–10.

48 See Wolfson 1994c, pp. 85–105.

49 See Scholem 1965, p. 20 n. 1; 1956, p. 47; Gruenwald 1988, pp. 170–3; Chernus 1987, p. 5; Kuyt 1990. For some other views regarding this expression, *yeridah la-merkavah*, see Bloch 1893, p. 25; Gruenwald 1980, p. 145 n. 15; Dan 1984, p. 34 n. 29; Halperin 1988, pp. 226–7.

50 Wolfson 1993b.

51 See Scholem 1956, pp. 5, 55–6.

52 For a recent treatment of this topic, see Swartz 1994b.

53 See Schäfer 1992, pp. 16 n. 19, 60, 99, 102–3, 106, 141.

54 Ibid., p. 162.

55 See Cohen 1983, pp. 99–109.

56 In the extant *Shi'ur Qomah* texts a third rabbi, Nathan, who was a student of R. Ishmael, is mentioned, but in this case Metatron is not the one who directly transmits the esoteric knowledge to the mystic. See Cohen 1983, pp. 86–7.

57 Cohen 1983, pp. 124–8.

58 See Scholem 1956, pp. 65–6; Stroumsa 1983, pp. 269–88.

59 On the actual roles played by Metatron in the extant *Shi'ur Qomah* texts, see Cohen 1983, pp. 124–37.

60 See Cohen 1983, pp. 125–6.

61 Cohen 1983, pp. 125, 230–1.

62 Schäfer 1982, §§ 396, 733, 960; 1984; Cohen 1983, pp. 126, 259.

63 Cohen 1983, pp. 132–3.

64 See Wolfson 1990.

65 See Wolfson 1994c, pp. 223–6.

66 This statement is found in the fragments of *Shi'ur Qomah*; cf. Schäfer 1982, §§ 711, 953.

67 The Hebrew text was published in *'Otzar Nechmad* 4 (1863), p. 37; and see Scholem 1987, pp. 212–15.

68 Concerning the traditions that link Enoch-Metatron and Adam, see Idel 1987.

69 Isaac of Acre, *Sefer Me'irat 'Einayim*, ed. A. Goldreich (Jerusalem: Akadamon, 1981), p. 40. The text is cited in Menachem Tziyyoni, *Perush 'al ha-Torah* (Jerusalem, 1964), 9a, and from there in Isaiah Horowitz, *Shene Luchot ha-Berit* (Warsaw, 1862), part 2, Torah shebikhtav, 46d.

70 See Jellinek 1967, 6: xxxxii; Scholem 1956, p. 63; 1965, pp. 38–40; and Lieberman 1965. See also Scholem 1974, p. 17.

71 See Urbach 1971. Boyarin 1990b, pp. 105–16, calls for the need to contrast the rabbinic reading as *mashal* and the allegorical exegesis prevalent in Christian authors such as Origen. For a shift from the allegorical to the metaphorical-symbolical to characterize rabbinic exegesis of the Songs of Songs, see Gottlieb 1992. I have argued that the rabbinic approach is based on a theosophic conception of the divine, related specifically to traditions about the divine phallus. See Wolfson 1993a, pp. 49–50 n. 68.

72 See Gaster 1928, 2: 1333; Cohen 1983, pp. 19–20, 22–3, 27–8, 31, 111–12.

73 See Cohen 1985, pp. 31–2; Nemoy 1930, p. 350.

74 See Cohen 1983, pp. 155–6 n. 80; 1985, p. 27. See also *Midrash 'Otiyyot de-Rabbi 'Akiva'*, in Wertheimer 1980, 2:370, where the measure of the body of the divine Presence (*gufo shel shekhinah*) is given as 2,360,000,000 parasangs.

75 See Scholem 1956, p. 365 n. 86; Cohen 1983, pp. 104, 107.

76 See Cohen 1983, p. 103.

77 See Scholem 1956, p. 64; 1991, pp. 24–5; Dan 1979.

78 See Elior 1989, pp. 108–10; Schäfer 1992, pp. 148–50, 162–3.

79 For a review of different scholarly opinions regarding the date of this work, see Allony 1981.

80 The lack of any concern for redactional issues pertaining to *Sefer Yetzirah* is epitomized in two relatively recent studies published by Israeli scholars. Dan 1993 distinguishes three periods in the history of *Sefer Yetzirah*: the first consists of the period from the time of its composition (which Dan acknowledges is uncertain) to the beginning of its influence in the tenth century; the second consists of the influence of this work on philosophical thinkers from the tenth to the twelfth centuries; and the third consists of the adoption of this text by various mystics from the twelfth century. This neat historical schematization takes no account of the fact that the redactional shaping of the text continued for quite a long period, probably until the ninth or tenth century. Y. Liebes 1992 argues for an early dating of *Sefer Yetzirah* on the basis of parallels of the second part of the text to Greek grammatical works. Assuming for the sake of argument that Liebes' conjecture is correct, it still would not justify any conclusion regarding the whole of *Sefer Yetzirah*, a work that is made up of various redactional layers.

81 An attempt to reconstruct the "original" version and demarcate later redactional accretions may be found in Weinstock 1972.

82 This view, espoused by such Islamicists as P. Krauss, L. Massignon, and H. Corbin, has been recently re-examined in Wasserstrom 1993. For a relatively early dating see Scholem 1956, p. 75; Pines 1989; Liebes 1990, pp. 101–3; Idel 1990, pp. 9–26.

83 The word that I have translated as "tradition" is *halakhah*, which appears in the original Arabic. Saadia's use of this word to refer to each section of the different chapters reflects his view that *Sefer Yetzirah* is a tannaitic work. According to Saadia, the text of *Sefer Yetzirah* was committed to writing in the time of the Mishnah by Judah the Prince. Moreover, in Saadia's mind, the mishnaic quality of *Sefer Yetzirah* is linked to the fact that it was transmitted orally for many years before it was communicated in a written form. See *Sefer Yetzirah (Kitāb al-Mabādi) 'im Perush R. Se'adyah bar Yosef Fayyumi*, ed. J. Kafih (Jerusalem, 1970), p. 33.

84 Ibid., p. 34.

85 Another important text of this genre, also transmitted as part of the Hekhalot corpus, is the *Seder Rabba di-Bereshit* (cf. Schäfer 1982, §§ 428–67, 518–40, 714–27, 743–820). This text will not be discussed here. For an extensive analysis, see Séd 1981.

86 See Hayman 1987.

87 See Gruenwald 1971, pp. 133–4.

88 According to Gruenwald 1971, pp. 141–3, §§ 3–7, 8.

89 Wolfson 1994c, pp. 70–3.

90 See Idel 1990, pp. 14–15.

91 See Scholem 1956, p. 76; Gruenwald 1973, p. 495; Hayman 1984, p. 171.

92 This interpretation is enhanced by the thematic connection of *Sefer Yetzirah* with the pseudo-Clementine homilies noted by several scholars. See Graetz 1846, pp. 110–15; Scholem 1969, pp. 172–3; Pines 1989.

93 Gruenwald 1971, p. 143, § 7.

94 Ibid., pp. 144–6, §§ 10–16.

95 Ibid., p. 146, § 15.

96 See Scholem 1972, pp. 71–6.

97 See Idel 1990, pp. 12–14.

98 See Wolfson 1989.

99 See Idel 1990, pp. 150–4.

100 See Klar 1974, p. 12; Dan 1968, pp. 16–20; Scholem 1974, p. 33.

101 For recent analysis of the relationship of the Rhineland Jewish Pietists and Hekhalot literature, see Kuyt 1993.

102 See Dan 1968, pp. 20–9, 39–40, 114–16. The influence of another Jewish Neoplatonist, Abraham bar Chiyya, is especially evident in the texts of the *Chug ha-Keruv ha-Meyuchad*. See Scholem 1931, pp. 172–91; Dan 1968, pp. 157, 204–5.

103 See Scholem 1956, pp. 111–16; Dan 1968, pp. 104–70. For an English summary see Dan 1986b, pp. 48–57.

104 See Dan 1968, pp. 165–6, 182–3; Marcus 1986, pp. 362–3; Wolfson 1994c, pp. 197–203.

105 See Dan 1968, pp. 129–43.

106 Cf. text attributed to Judah published in Dan 1975, p. 83; Eleazar of Worms, *Sefer ha-Shem*, MS London, British Museum 737, fol. 320b; *Sha'are ha-Sod ha-Yichud we-ha-'Emunah*, ed. J. Dan, *Temirin* 1 (Jerusalem, 1972), p. 155. For further discussion of this motif, see Wolfson 1994c, pp. 195–203.

107 The Pietists did not only come up with a theological response to the theoretical problem of prayer but developed a unique exegetical approach to the liturgy that may have had mystical implications; see Dan 1982.

108 MS London, British Museum 737, fol. 280a.

109 Ibid., fol. 288b.

110 *Sefer ha-Shem*, MS British Museum 737, fol. 373b.

111 Dan 1968, pp. 50–3; 1975, pp. 89–111.

112 Dan 1968, pp. 156–64.

113 Dan 1975, p. 154.

114 This is based on the earlier rabbinic tradition concerning the main theophanous

forms assumed by God at the splitting of the Red Sea and the revelation at Sinai; see Segal 1977, pp. 33–57.

115 *Sode Razaya*, ed. I. Kamelhar (Bilgoraj, 1936), p. 31.
116 See Dan 1968, pp. 135–6.
117 See Dan 1975, pp. 153–4, 169.
118 Ibid., pp. 119–20; and see Dan 1968, p. 135 n. 20.
119 See Wolfson 1994c, pp. 255–63.
120 *Sha'are ha-Sod*, pp. 151–2.
121 Cf. *Sefer ha-Shem*, MS London, British Museum 737, fol. 201a; Wolfson 1994c, pp. 234–47. On the especially esoteric nature of meditation upon (or indeed magical use of) the names in the writings of the German Pietists, see Dan 1968, pp. 19, 28, 74.
122 Cf. *Perush ha-Merkavah*, MS Paris, Bibliothèque Nationale héb. 850, fol. 49b.
123 Ibid., fols. 57a-58b. In another context Eleazar specifies similar techniques of purification (i.e., ritual immersion and the donning of white clothes) as a prelude to the study of *Sefer Yetzirah*. In this case the matter of purification is connected to the potential use of the ancient Jewish esoteric work for the purposes of creating a golem, an artificial anthropoid. See Scholem 1969, pp. 184–5; Dan 1968, pp. 53, 63, 214; Idel 1990, pp. 56–7.
124 *Sefer ha-Shem*, MS London, British Museum 737, fol. 166a. See Scholem 1969, p. 136; Dan 1968, pp. 74–6.
125 See Idel 1988a, pp. 98–103; 1988c, pp. 16–17, 22–3.
126 Altmann 1960. Scholem 1956, p. 239, briefly mentions the symbol of the nut in Eleazar.
127 Dan 1967.
128 Ibid., p. 77. The position articulated by Dan in his early work has been steadfastly maintained over the years; see 1987, pp. 137–8.
129 Farber 1986, pp. 101–23.
130 The text has been published and discussed by several scholars: Scholem 1987, pp. 184–7; Dan 1968, pp. 118–28; 1982, pp. 113–15; Farber 1986, pp. 231–44; Idel 1988a, p. 195.
131 See references to Dan in preceding note. Another important consideration raised by Dan is the fact that pseudepigraphy is not a feature generally employed by the main circle of Pietists.
132 Scholem 1987, pp. 186–7, 213.
133 Idel 1988a, pp. 160–1.
134 Wolfson 1994a.
135 See Idel 1988a, pp. 128–36, 156–72.
136 Ibid., pp. 30–2.
137 Scholem 1987, pp. 49–198.
138 Dan 1986d.
139 *Sefer ha-Bahir*, ed. R. Margaliot (Jerusalem, 1978), §§ 141–70. See also §§ 118, 138.
140 Cf. ibid., §§ 124–5.
141 Cf. ibid., §§ 95, 119.
142 Cf. ibid., §§ 82, 168, 172.
143 Ibid., §§ 82, 172.
144 Ibid., § 168. It should be pointed out, however, that, even in this case where

eight limbs or bodily parts are specified, there is an effort to collapse the eight into seven, for the torso (*guf*) and phallus (*berit*) are considered as one.

145 See Altmann 1969, pp. 189–94.

146 *Ma'arekhet ha–'Elohut* (Jerusalem, 1963), chapter 10, pp. 137b, 142b-144a.

147 See Altmann 1969, pp. 14–16.

148 Meier 1974, p. 428. See the parallel texts from the anonymous *Sefer ha-Yichud*, also composed at the end of thirteenth century by an author who had great affinity with Joseph of Hamadan, discussed in Idel 1988a, pp. 184–5.

149 MS Oxford 1943, fol. 28b. Regarding this text, see Scholem 1933–4, p. 512 n. 127.

150 Scholem 1969, pp. 44–6; Idel 1981; Tishby 1989, pp. 1080–1.

151 Meier 1974, p. 58.

152 Menachem Recanati, *Sefer Ta'ame ha-Mitzwot ha-Shalem*, ed. S. Lieberman (London, 1962), 2a-b. See Idel 1988a, pp. 189–90.

153 Cf. Joseph Gikatilla, *Sha'are 'Orah*, ed. J. Ben-Shlomo (Jerusalem, 1981), 1: 49–50.

154 See reference to Gikatilla in preceding note. Cf. the anonymous text in MS JTSA Mic. 1804, fol. 75a. On the use of the word *"siman"* in this technical way, see also *Sefer ha-Yichud*, MS Paris, Bibliothèque Nationale héb. 825, fol. 206a.

155 Menachem Recanati, *Perush 'al ha-Torah* (Jerusalem, 1961), 37b-c.

156 Scholem 1956, p. 27. See also Tishby 1982, p. 13; Dan 1986a, pp. 9–12. For a criticism of Scholem's emphasis on the "inexpressibility" of the *sefirotic* realm as being essential to kabbalistic symbolism, see Idel 1988a, pp. 231–2.

157 Scholem 1987, p. 211, considers anthropomorphism in the case of the kabbalists to be of an apologetic tone. The kabbalists too, Scholem insists, "undoubtedly maintained the absolute spirituality of the First Cause," but, on account of their "gnostic convictions," they became "the advocates of popular religion and of the faith of the common man," which involved an anthropomorphic conception of the deity.

158 See Wolfson 1994c.

159 The text, attributed to Solomon Alkabetz, is printed as an appendix to Menachem Azariah of Fano, *Ma'amar Shivre Luchot* (Safed, 1864).

160 Scholem 1974, pp. 99–100; 1987, p. 81.

161 See Tishby 1989, pp. 290–2.

162 See Scholem 1956, pp. 260 and 410 n. 42; Idel 1992a.

163 See Ben-Shlomo 1965, pp. 98–9; Zak 1989–90.

164 Scholem 1956, pp. 260–4; 1974, pp. 129–35.

165 See Scholem 1974, pp. 101–2; Gottlieb 1976, pp. 223–31; Idel 1988a, pp. 136–44.

166 See Ben-Shlomo 1965, pp. 100–15; Zak 1977, pp. 15–62.

167 For a discussion of the doctrine of evil in kabbalah, see Scholem 1991, pp. 56–87.

168 See Scholem 1987, pp. 289–99; Gavarin 1987.

169 R. Moses of Burgos attributed traditions regarding the demonic power to Nachmanides and his teacher, Judah ben Yaqar; see Scholem 1932, pp. 276–7, 279–80. See also the statement of R. Isaac of Acre in his *Sefer Me'irat 'Einayim*, ed. A. Goldreich (Jerusalem, 1981), p. 190: "I have heard from the pious one, R. David Cohen, may God protect him, that R. Todros ha-Levi, may his

memory be blessed, used to say to him that there is a great matter on the side of the *sefirot*, surrounding [them] from the outside, which is not perceived by those kabbalists who are enlightened with respect to the ten *sefirot*. He did not want to explain his words to him. Afterwards he said to him: 'Know that, in truth, R. Moses ben Nachman, may his memory be blessed, alluded to this in [his commentary on] the section *Naso'* in the matter of the *sotah* [i.e., a woman suspected of infidelity].' After he told me these things I investigated the matter and found that he was referring to Samael and his faction."

170 See Scholem 1927, pp. 193–7; see also the reference to Scholem given above, note 167. See Dan 1980; Oron 1987.

171 See Tishby 1989, pp. 447–546.

172 See Wolfson 1986; 1988a.

173 See Idel 1980.

174 See Tishby 1952; 1955.

175 Idel 1988a, pp. 59–73, 74–111; Wolfson 1994c.

176 Meier 1974, p. 58.

177 See Scholem 1969, p. 63; for other references, including earlier sources for this numerology, see Wolfson 1988b, p. 337 n. 61.

178 *Tiqqune Zohar 'im Perush 'Or Yaqar* (Jerusalem, 1972), 1: 82.

179 *Chesed le–'Avraham* (Bene-Beraq, 1986), 12b.

180 See Weiss 1985, pp. 56–68.

181 The precise connection between electrum (*chashmal*) and cover (*levush*) is not clear, although it may be suggested that underlying this association is the numerological equivalence found in other kabbalistic sources between the words "*chashmal*" and "*malbush*" (also meaning "cover" or "garment").

182 See Idel 1988b.

183 See Scholem 1987, pp. 309–64; Verman 1992.

184 See Wolfson 1994c, pp. 380–3.

185 For an exposition of Abulafia's system, see Scholem 1956, pp. 119–55; Idel 1988c; 1988d; 1989.

186 For a recent discussion of the role of *sefirot* in Abulafia's prophetic kabbalah, see Wolfson 1995–6.

187 Translated in Idel 1988d, p. 67 (I have slightly modified the translation).

188 See Idel 1988c, p. 127.

189 See Idel 1988c, pp. 13–54.

190 See Scholem 1956, p. 143; Idel 1988c, p. 21; 1989, pp. 50–2.

191 See Idel 1988a, pp. 97–103; 1988c, pp. 14–24.

192 See Idel 1988c, pp. 77–8.

193 Idel 1988c, pp. 30–7, 100–5.

194 A major portion of the text dealing with the ecstatic techniques is rendered in Scholem 1956, pp. 146–55.

195 Scholem 1974, p. 371.

196 See Idel 1988d, pp. 91–101.

197 Ibid., pp. 73–89.

198 Ibid., pp. 112–22.

199 Ibid., pp. 95–6; see also Scholem 1956, pp. 124, 378 n. 14.

200 See Idel 1988a, pp. 62–73. The influence of Abulafia on Chasidism is discussed in more detail in Idel 1995.

❦ BIBLIOGRAPHY ❦

Allony, N. (1981) "The Time of Composition of *Sefer Yetzirah*" [Hebrew], in *Temirin: Texts and Studies in Kabbala and Hasidism*, edited by I. Weinstock (Jerusalem: Mossad ha-Rav Kook), 2: 41–50.

Altmann, A. (1946) "Liturgical Poems in the Ancient Hekhalot Literature" [Hebrew], *Melilah* 2: 1–24.

——(1960) "Eleazar of Worms' *Hokhmath ha-Egoz*," *Journal of Jewish Studies* 11: 101–12.

——(1969) *Studies in Religious Philosophy and Mysticism* (Ithaca: Cornell University Press).

——(1991) *The Meaning of Jewish Existence: Theological Essays 1930–1939*, edited by A. Ivry with introduction by P. Mendes-Flohr (Hanover and London: University Press of New England).

Ariel, D. S. (1985) " 'The Eastern Dawn of Wisdom': The Problem of the Relation Between Islamic and Jewish Mysticism," in *Approaches to Judaism in Medieval Times*, edited by D. R. Blumenthal (Chico: Scholars Press), 2: 149–62.

Baumgarten, J. (1988) "The Qumran Sabbath Shirot and Rabbinic Merkabah Traditions," *Revue Qumran* 13: 199–214.

Ben-Shlomo, J. (1965) *The Mystical Theology of Moses Cordovero* [Hebrew], (Jerusalem: Mossad Bialik).

Bloch, P. (1893) "Die *Yorede Merkavah*, die Mystiker der Gaonenzeit, und ihr Einfluss auf die Liturgie," *Monatsschrift für Geschichte und Wissenschaft des Judentums* 37: 18–25, 69–74, 257–66, 305–11.

Bousset, W. (1901) "Die Himmelsreise der Seele," *Archiv für Religionswissenschaft* 4: 136–69, 229–73.

Boyarin, D. (1990a) "The Eye in the Torah: Ocular Desire in the Midrashic Hermeneutic," *Critical Inquiry* 16: 532–50.

——(1990b) *Intertextuality and the Reading of Midrash* (Bloomington: Indiana University Press).

Charlesworth, J. (ed.) (1983) *The Old Testament Pseudepigrapha* (New York: Doubleday).

Chernus, I. (1982a) *Mysticism in Rabbinic Literature* (Berlin: de Gruyter).

——(1982b) "Visions of God in Merkabah Literature," *Journal for the Study of Judaism* 13: 123–46.

——(1987) "The Pilgrimage to the Merkavah: An Interpretation of Early Jewish Mysticism," *Jerusalem Studies in Jewish Thought* 6.1–2: 1–36 (English section).

Cohen, M. S. (1983) *The Shi'ur Qomah: Liturgy and Theurgy in Pre-Kabbalistic Jewish Mysticism* (Lanham: University Press of America).

——(1985) *The Shi'ur Qomah: Texts and Recensions* (Tübingen: Mohr).

Dan, J. (1967) "*Hokhmath ha-'Egoz*, its Origin and Development," *Journal of Jewish Studies* 17: 73–83.

——(1968) *The Esoteric Theology of the German Pietists* [Hebrew], (Jerusalem: Bialik Institute).

——(1975) *Studies in Ashkenazi Hasidic Literature* [Hebrew], (Ramat Gan: Masadah).

——(1979) "The Concept of Knowledge in the *Shi'ur Qomah*," in *Studies in*

Jewish Religious and Intellectual History Presented to Alexander Altmann on the Occasion of His Seventieth Birthday, edited by S. Stein and R. Loewe (University, AL: University of Alabama Press), pp. 69–73.

—— (1980) "Samael, Lilith and the Concept of Evil in Early Kabbalah," *AJS Review* 5: 17–41.

—— (1982) "The Emergence of Mystical Prayer," in *Studies in Jewish Mysticism,* edited by J. Dan and F. Talmage (Cambridge, MA: Association for Jewish Studies), pp. 85–120.

—— (1984) "Three Types of Ancient Jewish Mysticism," *The Seventh Annual Rabbi Louis Feinberg Memorial Lecture in Judaic Studies* (Cincinnati: University of Cincinnati Press).

—— (1986a) *The Early Kabbalah* (New York: Paulist Press).

—— (1986b) *Jewish Mysticism and Jewish Ethics* (Seattle: University of Washington Press).

—— (1986c) "Midrash and the Dawn of Kabbalah," in *Midrash and Literature,* edited by G. Hartman and S. Budick (New Haven: Yale University Press), pp. 127–39.

—— (1986d) "The Religious Experience of the Merkavah," in *Jewish Spirituality from the Bible through the Middle Ages,* edited by A. Green (New York: Crossroad), pp. 289–307.

—— (1987) "A Re-evaluation of the 'Ashkenazi Kabbalah' " [Hebrew], *Jerusalem Studies in Jewish Thought* 6.3–4: 125–39.

—— (1993) "The Religious Meaning of *Sefer Yetzira*" [Hebrew], *Jerusalem Studies in Jewish Thought* 11: 1–35.

Elior, R. (1984) "Hekhalot Zuṭarti," *Jerusalem Studies in Jewish Thought,* Supplement 1.

—— (1989) "The Concept of God in Hekhalot Literature," in *Binah: Studies in Jewish Thought,* edited by J. Dan (New York: Praeger), 2: 97–120.

Farber, A. (1986) *The Concept of the Merkabah in Thirteenth-Century Jewish Esotericism: Sod ha-'Egoz and Its Development* [Hebrew]. Ph.D. dissertation, Hebrew University of Jerusalem.

Fenton, P. (1992) "La 'Tête entre les genoux': contribution à l'étude d'une posture méditative dans la mystique juive et islamique," *Revue d'Histoire et de Philosophie Religieuses* 72: 413–26.

Gaster, M. (1928) *Studies and Texts in Folklore, Magic, Mediaeval Romance, Hebrew Apocrypha and Samaritan Archaeology,* 3 vols (London: Maggs).

Gavarin, M. (1987) "The Problem of Evil in the Thought of R. Isaac the Blind and his Disciples" [Hebrew], *Da'at* 22: 29–50.

Goldreich, A. (1987) "The Theology of the *Iyyun* Circle and a Possible Source of the Term '*Achdut Shava*' " [Hebrew], *Jerusalem Studies in Jewish Thought* 6.3–4: 141–56.

Gottlieb, E. (1976) *Studies in the Kabbala Literature* [Hebrew], (Tel Aviv: Tel Aviv University Press).

Gottlieb, I. B. (1992) "The Jewish Allegory of Love: Change and Constancy," *The Journal of Jewish Thought and Philosophy* 2: 1–17.

Graetz, H. (1846) *Gnostizismus und Judentum* (Krotoschin: Monasch).

—— (1859) "Die mystische Literatur in der gaonäischen Epoche," *Monatsschrift für Geschichte und Wissenschaft des Judentums* 8: 67–78, 103–18, 140–52.

Gruenwald, I. (1968–9) "New Fragments from the Hekhalot Literature" [Hebrew], *Tarbitz* 38: 356–64.

—— (1971) "A Preliminary Critical Edition of *Sefer Yetzira*," *Israel Oriental Studies* 1: 132–77.

—— (1972) "Re'uyot Yechezqel" [Hebrew], in *Temirin: Text and Studies in Kabbala and Hasidism*, edited by I. Weinstock (Jerusalem: Mossad ha-Rav Kook), 1: 101–40.

—— (1973) "Some Critical Notes on the First Part of *Sefer Yetzira*," *Revue des Études Juives* 132: 475–512.

—— (1980) *Apocalyptic and Merkavah Mysticism* (Leiden: Brill).

—— (1988) *From Apocalypticism to Gnosticism* (New York: Lang).

Halperin, D. (1980) *The Merkabah in Rabbinic Literature* (New Haven: American Oriental Society).

—— (1988) *The Faces of the Chariot: Early Jewish Responses to Ezekiel's Chariot* (Tübingen: Mohr).

Hayman, A. P. (1984) "Some Observations on Sefer Yetzira: (1) Its Use of Scripture," *Journal of Jewish Studies* 35: 168–84.

—— (1987) "Sefer Yetzirah and the Hekhalot Literature," *Jerusalem Studies in Jewish Thought* 6.1–2: 71–85 (English section).

Hellholm, D. (ed.) (1989) *Apocalypticism in the Mediterranean World and the Near East* (Tübingen: Mohr).

Herrmann, K. (1994) *Massekhet Hekhalot Traktat von den himmlischen Palästen: Edition, Übersetzung und Kommentar* (Tübingen: Mohr).

Hildesheimer, E. E. (1931) "Mystik und Agada im Urteile der Gaonen R. Scherira und R. Hai," in *Festschrift für Jacob Rosenheim* (Frankfurt am Main), pp. 259–86.

Himmelfarb, M. (1988) "Heavenly Ascent and the Relationship of the Apocalypses and the *Hekhalot* Literature," *Hebrew Union College Annual* 59: 73–100.

Idel, M. (1980) "The Evil Thought of the Deity" [Hebrew], *Tarbitz* 49: 356–64.

—— (1981) "The Concept of the Torah in Hekhalot Literature and its Metamorphoses in Kabbalah" [Hebrew], *Jerusalem Studies in Jewish Thought* 1: 58–84.

—— (1986) "The World of Angels in Human Form" [Hebrew], in *Studies in Philosophy, Mysticism, and Ethical Literature Presented to Isaiah Tishby on his Seventy-Fifth Birthday*, edited by J. Dan and J. Hacker (Jerusalem: Magnes), pp. 1–66.

—— (1987) "Enoch is Metatron" [Hebrew], *Jerusalem Studies in Jewish Thought*, 6.1–2: 151–70. [English translation in *Immanuel* 1990, vol. 24–5 (*The New Testament and Christian-Jewish Dialogue: Studies in Honor of David Flusser*, edited by M. Lowe), pp. 220–40.]

—— (1988a) *Kabbalah: New Perspectives* (New Haven: Yale University Press).

—— (1988b) "Kabbalistic Prayer and Colors," in *Approaches to Judaism in Medieval Times*, edited by D. R. Blumenthal (Atlanta: Scholars Press), pp. 17–27.

—— (1988c) *The Mystical Experience in Abraham Abulafia* (Albany: State University of New York Press).

—— (1988d) *Studies in Ecstatic Kabbalah* (Albany: State University of New York Press).

—— (1988e) "Franz Rosenzweig and the Kabbalah," in *The Philosophy of Franz Rosenzweig*, edited by P. Mendes-Flohr (Hanover and London: University Press of New England), pp. 162–71.

—— (1989) *Language, Torah, and Hermeneutics in Abraham Abulafia* (Albany: State University of New York Press).

—— (1990) *Golem: Jewish Magical and Mystical Traditions on the Artificial Anthropoid* (Albany: State University of New York Press).

—— (1992a) "On the Concept of Tzimtzum in Kabbalah and its Research" [Hebrew], *Jerusalem Studies in Jewish Thought* 10: 59–112.

—— (1992b) "Jewish Kabbalah and Platonism in the Middle Ages and Renaissance," in *Neoplatonism and Jewish Thought*, edited by L. E. Goodman (Albany: State University of New York Press), pp. 319–51.

—— (1995) *Hasidism Between Ecstasy and Magic* (Albany: State University of New York Press).

Janowitz, N. (1989) *The Poetics of Ascent* (Albany: State University of New York Press).

Jellinek, A. (1967) *Bet ha-Midrash*, 3rd ed. (Jerusalem: Wahrmann).

Klar, B. (ed.) (1974) *The Chronicle of Ahimaaz* (Jerusalem: Sifre Tarshish).

Kuyt, A. (1990) "Once Again: Yarad in Hekhalot Literature," *Frankfurter Judaistische Beiträge* 18: 45–69.

—— (1993) "Traces of a Mutual Influence of the Haside Ashkenaz and the Hekhalot Literature," in *From Narbonne to Regensburg: Studies in Medieval Hebrew Texts*, edited by N. A. Van Uchelen and I. E. Zwiep (Amsterdam: Juda Palacha Institute), pp. 62–86.

Leiter, S. (1973–4) "Worthiness, Acclamation and Appointment: Some Rabbinic Terms," *Proceedings of the American Academy for Jewish Research* 41–2: 137–68.

Lieberman, S. (1965) "Mishnath Shir ha-Shirim," Appendix D in G. Scholem, *Jewish Gnosticism, Merkabah Mysticism and Talmudic Tradition* (New York: Jewish Theological Seminary of America), pp. 118–26.

Liebes, Y. (1987) "Rabbi Solomon ibn Gabirol's Use of the *Sefer Yetzira* and the Commentary on the Poem 'I Love Thee' " [Hebrew], *Jerusalem Studies in Jewish Thought* 6.3–4: 73–123.

—— (1990) *The Sin of Elisha, The Four Who Entered Paradise and the Nature of Talmudic Mysticism*, 2nd ed. [Hebrew], (Jerusalem: Akadamon).

—— (1992) "The Seven Double Letters *BGD KFRT*: On the Double *Reish* and the Background of *Sefer Yetzira*" [Hebrew], *Tarbitz* 61: 237–47.

—— (1993) *Studies in Jewish Myth and Jewish Messianism* (Albany: State University of New York Press).

Marcus, I. (1986) "The Devotional Ideals of Ashkenazic Pietism," in *Jewish Spirituality from the Bible through the Middle Ages*, edited by A. Green (New York: Crossroad), pp. 289–307.

Meier, M. (1974) *A Critical Edition of the Sefer Ta'amey ha-Mizwoth ("Book of Reasons of the Commandments") Attributed to Isaac ibn Farhi: Section I – Positive Commandments*. Ph.D. dissertation, Brandeis University.

Naveh, J. and S. Shaked (1993) *Magic Spells and Formulae: Aramaic Incantations of Late Antiquity* (Jerusalem: Magnes).

Nemoy, L. (1930) "Al-Qirqisānī's Account of the Jewish Sects and Christianity," *Hebrew Union College Annual* 7: 317–97.

Neusner, J. (1971) "The Development of the *Merkavah* Tradition," *Journal for the Study of Judaism* 2: 149–60.

Newsom, C. (1985) *Songs of the Sabbath Sacrifice: A Critical Edition*, Harvard Semitic Studies 27 (Atlanta: Scholars Press).

—— (1987) "Merkabah Exegesis in the Qumran Shabbat Shirot," *Journal of Jewish Studies* 38: 11–30.

—— (1990) " 'He Has Established for Himself Priests': Human and Angelic Priesthood in the Qumran Sabbath Shirot," in *Archaeology and History in the Dead Sea Scrolls: The New York University Conference in Memory of Yigael Yadin*, edited by L. H. Schiffman (Sheffield: JSOT), pp. 101–20.

Nitzan, B. (1992) "Hymns from Qumran – 4Q510–4Q511," in *The Dead Sea Scrolls: Forty Years of Research*, edited by D. Dimant and U. Rappaport (Leiden and Jerusalem: Brill; Magnes; Yad Itzhak Ben-Zvi), pp. 53–62.

—— (1994a) *Qumran Prayer and Religious Poetry* (Leiden: Brill).

—— (1994b) "Harmonic and Mystic Characteristics in Poetic and Liturgical Writings from Qumran," in *The Dead Sea Scrolls: Proceedings of a Conference at the Center for Judaic Studies of the University of Pennsylvania* (JQR Supplement) (Philadelphia: Center for Judaic Studies), pp. 163–83.

Odeberg, H. (1973) *3 Enoch or the Hebrew Book of Enoch*, (reprint) (New York: Ktav).

Oron, M. (1987) "Was the Kabbalah in Castile a Continuation or a Revolution? – A Study of the Concept of Evil in Castilian Kabbalah," *Jerusalem Studies in Jewish Thought* 6: 383–92.

Pines, S. (1989) "Points of Similarity between the Exposition of the Doctrine of the Sefirot in the *Sefer Yetzira* and a Text of the Pseudo-Clementine Homilies," *Proceedings of the Israeli Academy of Sciences and Humanities* 7: 63–242.

Schäfer, P. (1982) *Synopse zur Hekhalot-Literatur* (Tübingen: Mohr).

—— (1984) *Geniza Fragmente zur Hekhalot-Literatur* (Tübingen: Mohr).

—— (1987) "The Problem of the Redactionist Identity of 'Hekhalot Rabbati' " [Hebrew], *Jerusalem Studies in Jewish Thought* 6.1–2: 1–12.

—— (1988) *Hekhalot-Studien* (Tübingen: Mohr).

—— (1989) *Übersetzung der Hekhalot-Literatur*, vol. 3 (Tübingen: Mohr).

—— (1992) *The Hidden and Manifest God: Some Major Themes in Early Jewish Mysticism* (Albany: State University of New York Press).

—— (1993a) "Research on Hekhalot Literature: Where Do We Stand Now?" in *Rashi 1040–1990: Hommage à Ephraïm E. Urbach*, edited by G. Sed-Rajna (Paris: Cerf), pp. 229–35.

—— (1993b) "Merkavah Mysticism and Magic," in *Gershom Scholem's Major Trends in Jewish Mysticism 50 Years After: Proceedings of the Sixth International Conference on the History of Jewish Mysticism*, edited by P. Schäfer and J. Dan (Tübingen: Mohr), pp. 59–78.

Schiffman, L. H. (1982) "Merkavah Speculation at Qumran: the 4Q Serekh Shirot 'Olat ha-Shabbat," in *Mystics, Philosophers and Politicians: Essays in Jewish Intellectual History in Honor of Alexander Altmann*, edited by J. Reinharz, D. Swetschinski, and in collaboration with K. Bland (Durham, NC: Duke University Press), pp. 15–47.

—— (1994) *Reclaiming the Dead Sea Scrolls: The History of Judaism, the Background of Christianity, the Lost Library of Qumran* (Philadelphia and Jerusalem: Jewish Publication Society).

Schiffman, L. and M. Swartz (1992) *Hebrew and Aramaic Incantation Texts From* the Cairo Genizah: Selected Texts From Taylor-Schechter Box K1 (Sheffield: JSOT).

Scholem, G. (1927) "The Traditions of R. Jacob and R. Isaac, sons of R. Jacob ha-Kohen" [Hebrew], Madda'e ha-Yahadut 2: 165–293.

—— (1931) "Reste neuplatonischer Spekulation in der Mystik der deutschen Chassidim und ihre Vermittlung durch Abraham bar Chija," Monatsschrift für Geschichte und Wissenschaft des Judentums 75: 172–91.

—— (1932) "R. Moses of Burgos, the Student of R. Isaac" [Hebrew], Tarbitz 3: 258–86.

—— (1933–4) "Index to the Commentaries on the Ten Sefirot" [Hebrew], Kiryat Sefer 10: 498–515.

—— (1956) Major Trends in Jewish Mysticism (New York: Schocken).

—— (1965) Jewish Gnosticism, Merkabah Mysticism and the Talmudic Tradition, 2nd ed. (New York: Jewish Theological Seminary of America).

—— (1969) On the Kabbalah and Its Symbolism, translated by R. Manheim (New York: Schocken).

—— (1972) "The Name of God and the Linguistic Theory of the Kabbala," Diogenes 79: 59–80; 80: 164–94.

—— (1974) Kabbalah (Jerusalem: Keter).

—— (1987) Origins of the Kabbalah, edited by R. J. Z. Werblowsky and translated by A. Arkush (Princeton: Princeton University Press).

—— (1991) On the Mystical Shape of the Godhead: Basic Concepts in the Kabbalah (New York: Schocken).

Schweid, E. (1985) Judaism and Mysticism According to Gershom Scholem: A Critical Analysis and Programmatic Discussion, translated by D. A. Weiner (Atlanta: Scholars Press).

Séd, N. (1973) "Les Traditions secrètes et les disciples de Rabbanan Yohanan ben Zakkai," Revue de l'Histoire des Religions 184: 49–66.

—— (1981) La Mystique cosmologique juive (Paris: École des Hautes Études en Sciences Sociales).

Segal, A. F. (1977) Two Powers in Heaven: Early Rabbinic Reports about Christianity and Gnosticism (Leiden: Brill).

—— (1980) "Heavenly Ascent in Hellenistic Judaism, Early Christianity and their Environment," in Aufsteig und Niedergang der Römischen Welt, Principat II, 23: 1333–94.

Smith, M. (1963) "Observations on Hekhalot Rabbati," in Biblical and Other Studies, edited by A. Altmann (Cambridge, MA: Harvard University Press), pp. 142–60.

—— (1981) "Ascent to the Heavens and the Beginning of Christianity," Eranos-jahrbuch 50: 403–29.

Stroumsa, G. G. (1983) "Form(s) of God: Some Notes on Metatron and Christ," Harvard Theological Review 76: 269–88.

Strugnell, J. (1959) "The Angelic Liturgy at Qumran-4Q Serek Sīrot 'Ōlat Hassabbat," Supplements to Vetus Testamentum 7: 318–45.

Swartz, M. (1992) Mystical Prayer in Ancient Judaism: An Analysis of Ma'aseh Merkavah (Tübingen: Mohr).

—— (1994a) "Book and Tradition in Hekhalot and Magical Literatures," The Journal of Jewish Thought and Philosophy 3: 189–230.

—— (1994b) " 'Like the Ministering Angels': Ritual and Purity in Hekhalot and Magical Literatures," *AJS Review* 19: 135–67.

Tabor, J. D. (1986) *Things Unutterable: Paul's Ascent to Paradise in its Greco-Roman, Judaic, and Early Christian Contexts* (Lanham: University Press of America).

Talmage, F. (1986) "Apples of Gold: The Inner Meaning of Sacred Texts in Medieval Judaism," in *Jewish Spirituality From the Bible Through the Middle Ages*, edited by A. Green (New York: Crossroad), pp. 313–55.

Ta-Shema, I. (1985) "The Library of the Ashkenazi Sages in the Eleventh and Twelfth Centuries" [Hebrew], *Tarbitz* 40: 298–309.

Tishby, I. (1952) *The Doctrine of Evil and the Kelippah in Lurianic Kabbalism* [Hebrew], (Jerusalem: Magnes).

—— (1955) "Gnostic Doctrines in Sixteenth-Century Jewish Mysticism," *Journal of Jewish Studies* 6: 146–52.

—— (1982) *Paths of Faith and Heresy* [Hebrew], (Jerusalem: Magnes).

—— (1989) *The Wisdom of the Zohar*, translated by D. Goldstein (Oxford: Oxford University Press).

Urbach, E. E. (1967) "The Traditions about Merkabah Mysticism in the Tannaitic Period" [Hebrew], in *Studies in Mysticism and Religion presented to Gershom G. Scholem*, edited by E. E. Urbach, R. J. Z. Werblowsky, and C. Wirszubski (Jerusalem: Magnes), pp. 1–28.

—— (1971) "The Homiletical Interpretations of the Sages and the Expositions of Origen on Canticles, and the Jewish-Christian Disputation," *Scripta Hierosolymitana* 22: 247–75.

Vajda, G. (1954) *Juda ben Nissim ibn Malka: Philosophe Juif Marocain* (Paris: Institut des Hautes Études Marocaines).

—— (1957) *L'Amour de Dieu dans la théologie juive du moyen âge* (Paris: Vrin).

Van Uchelen, N. A. (1987) "Tosephta Megillah III, 28: A Tannaitic Text with a Mystic?" *Jerusalem Studies in Jewish Thought* 6.1–2: 87–94 (English section).

Verman, M. (1992) *The Books of Contemplation: Medieval Jewish Mystical Sources* (Albany: State University of New York Press).

Wasserstrom, S. (1993) "*Sefer Yeṣira* and Early Islam: A Reappraisal," *The Journal of Jewish Thought and Philosophy* 3: 1–30.

Weinstock, I. (1972) "A Clarification of the Version of *Sefer Yetzirah*" [Hebrew], in *Temirin: Texts and Studies in Kabbala and Hasidism*, edited by I. Weinstock (Jerusalem: Mossad ha-Rav Kook), 1: 9–57.

Weiss, J. (1985) *Studies in Eastern European Jewish Mysticism* (Oxford: Oxford University Press).

Wertheimer, S. (1980) *Batte Midrashot*, 2 vols. (Jerusalem: Ktav va-Sepher).

Wolfson, E. R. (1986) "Left Contained in the Right: A Study in Zoharic Hermeneutics," *AJS Review* 11: 27–52.

—— (1988a) "Light Through Darkness: The Ideal of Human Perfection in the *Zohar*," *Harvard Theological Review* 81: 73–95.

—— (1988b) "The Hermeneutics of Visionary Experience: Revelation and Interpretation in the *Zohar*," *Religion* 18: 311–45.

—— (1989) "Anthropomorphic Imagery and Letter-Symbolism in the *Zohar*" [Hebrew], *Jerusalem Studies in Jewish Thought* 8: 147–81.

—— (1990) "God, the Demiurge, and the Intellect: On the Usage of the Word *Kol* in Abraham ibn Ezra," *Revue des Études Juives* 149: 77–111.

—— (1991) "Merkavah Traditions in Philosophical Garb: Judah Halevi Reconsidered," *Proceedings of the American Academy for Jewish Research* 57: 179–242.

—— (1992) "The Theosophy of Shabbetai Donnolo, with Special Emphasis on the Doctrine of *Sefirot* in *Sefer Ḥakhmoni*," *Jewish History* 6: 281–316.

—— (1993a) "The Tree That Is All: Jewish-Christian Roots of a Kabbalistic Symbol in *Sefer ha-Bahir*," *The Journal of Jewish Thought and Philosophy* 3: 31–76.

—— (1993b) "*Yeridah la-Merkavah*: Typology of Ecstasy and Enthronement in Ancient Jewish Mysticism," in *Mystics of the Book: Themes, Topics, and Typologies*, edited by R. A. Herrera (New York: Lang), pp. 13–44.

—— (1994a) "The Image of Jacob Engraved Upon the Throne: Further Speculation on the Esoteric Doctrine of the German Pietists" [Hebrew], in *Massu'ot Studies in Kabbalistic Literature and Jewish Philosophy in Memory of Prof. Ephraim Gottlieb*, edited by M. Oron and A. Goldreich (Jerusalem: Mossad Bialik), pp. 131–85.

—— (1994b) "Mysticism and the Poetic-Liturgical Compositions from Qumran," in *The Dead Sea Scrolls: Proceedings of a Conference at the Center for Judaic Studies of the University of Pennsylvania (JQR* Supplement) (Philadelphia: Center for Judaic Studies), pp. 187–204.

—— (1994c) *Through A Speculum That Shines: Vision and Imagination in Medieval Jewish Mysticism* (Princeton: Princeton University Press).

—— (1995–6) "The Doctrine of Sefirot in the Prophetic Kabbalah of Abraham Abulafia," *Jewish Studies Quarterly* 2.4: 336–71; 3.1: 47–84.

Zak, B. (1977) *The Mystical Theology of Solomon Alkabez* [Hebrew]. Ph.D. dissertation, Brandeis University.

—— (1989–90) "The Doctrine of Tzimtzum in R. Moshe Cordovero" [Hebrew], *Tarbitz* 58: 207–37.

CHAPTER 20

Jewish philosophy on the eve of modernity[1]

Hava Tirosh-Rothschild

The period from 1400 to 1600 constitutes the transition from the medieval to the modern epoch in the history of Jewish philosophy.[2] During this time of continuity and change, the learned elite of Mediterranean Jewries continued to study philosophy and its related liberal arts and natural sciences, but the content and orientation of Jewish philosophy underwent significant changes.[3] Though most Jewish philosophers still theorized within the conceptual framework of medieval Jewish Aristotelianism, the discipline of Jewish philosophy became diverse and eclectic, dominated by theology and hermeneutics, engaged in polemics either against Christianity or against the Jewish critics of philosophy, and receptive to the mystical and mythical outlook of kabbalah. These changes paved the way for the rise of kabbalah as an alternative mode of thought to Maimonideanism, leading Jewish intellectuals to seek the harmonization of philosophy and kabbalah.

Though philosophy aspires for knowledge of universal truths, the study of philosophy is an intellectual activity that is carried out by people who respond to particular, historical circumstances. This chapter explains the transformation of Jewish philosophy in three major regions, Iberia, Italy, and the Ottoman Empire,[4] illustrates general trends by focusing on representative thinkers, problems, or discourses, and highlights the interaction between Jewish philosophy and contemporaneous intellectual currents in Europe.[5]

❧ THE ARISTOTELIAN TRADITION IN ❧ IBERIA

Between Maimonides and Crescas

The last chapter of medieval Jewish philosophy began with the crisis of Iberian Jewry.[6] In 1391, the Jews of Spain were unexpectedly attacked by the riots of the populace that turned into mass massacres of entire Jewish communities throughout Castile and Aragon. Many Jews were forcibly led to the baptismal font; others converted voluntarily, some of them with the hope of later returning to their mother religion; and many others fled the country. A new social class emerged in Spain – the *conversos* – leaving professing Jews to contend with scores of legal, economic, political, and spiritual problems. Before Spanish Jewry had time to recuperate, it faced forced preaching, anti-Jewish legislation, and the staged debate in Tortosa (1413–14). Christianity, and particularly Christian scholasticism, emerged triumphant while Judaism seemed helpless and hopeless.

These traumatic events compelled Jewish intellectuals in Spain to ponder their own conduct and cultural orientation. How could this have happened? According to the premises of traditional Jewish theodicy, this could not have been a manifestation of God's providential care for his people, Israel. It had to be interpreted as a punishment for Jewish transgressions and religious disobedience. But who was to blame? Since the study of philosophy and its related sciences characterized Judeo-Hispanic culture, any self-examination had to yield a debate on the status of the so-called "foreign wisdoms" (*chokhmot chitzoniyot*). Once again Maimonideanism and the *paideia* of the philosophers were put on the defensive as the cause of Jews' failure to uphold their faith.

The accusations that philosophy was the catalyst for the moral and spiritual bankruptcy of Spanish Jewry came from rabbinic orators, such as Shlomo Al'ami in Portugal,[7] who had but a limited exposure to philosophic literature, as well as from people who were themselves steeped in the Maimonidean tradition but who forsook philosophy to embrace kabbalah, such as Shem Tov ibn Shem Tov.[8] Though kabbalah would emerge as a credible alternative to Maimonideanism over a century later, ibn Shem Tov's response to the crisis of 1391 anticipated that shift.[9] The most scathing attack on Maimonideanism came from Chasdai Crescas, the rabbi of Saragossa, who had lost his only son in the riots. An erudite halakhist and a communal leader with close ties to the royal court of Aragon, Crescas was determined to rebuild Iberian Jewry.[10] Viewing Maimonides' intellectualism as the direct cause of Iberian Jewry's spiritual breakdown, Crescas set out to liberate rabbinic Judaism from the clutches of Aristotelian philosophy. He was inspired by a similar attempt of Judah Halevi during the twelfth century and by kabbalah.[11]

In his *Or ha-Shem* (*Light of the Lord*, 1410), Crescas mounted a two-pronged attack on philosophy. First, he attempted to undermine the validity of Aristotelian philosophy by disproving Aristotle's physics. Crescas rejected Aristotle's picture of the universe as a self-contained hierarchy of beings in which each entity tends toward its own natural place.[12] In contrast to Aristotle, who ruled out an actual infinite series of causes, Crescas argued that such a series is logically possible. Infinite time, infinite space, and an infinite series of causes was Crescas' central intuition. The infinite universe is held together by the abundance of infinite, divine love which regulates both the cosmic order and human affairs. Like Judah Halevi before him, Crescas insisted that God, rather than a series of incorporeal intermediaries, is the causal explanation of the universe.

Second, Crescas refuted Maimonides' political theory and especially his conception of ultimate human felicity.[13] Crescas ascribed to Maimonides a radical intellectualism according to which human felicity resides in one activity only – contemplation of God by the acquired intellect (*sekhel niqneh*). Crescas charged that this notion is unacceptable on religious and philosophic grounds. Religiously this ideal was subversive to Judaism because it denied personal immortality and ignored the intrinsic value accorded by the rabbinic tradition to performance of the commandments. Philosophically it was unsound because the doctrine of the acquired intellect was self-contradictory.[14]

Crescas agreed with Maimonides that the ultimate end of human life requires the attainment of certain perfections: perfection of the body, perfection of moral qualities, and perfection of opinions.[15] Crescas further conceded that these perfections are hierarchically ordered so that bodily and moral perfections are subordinated to perfection of opinions. However, Crescas sharply disagreed with Maimonides and with the Jewish Aristotelians in regard to perfection of opinions. Whereas they held that cognition of intelligibles constitutes life after death, Crescas severed the connection between cognition of universal truths and personal immortality. Instead, Crescas claimed that the ultimate end of human life consists in the union of the incorporeal, eternal soul with God in the afterlife. Such union is predicated on the human love of God which manifests itself in the freedom of the human will, rather than the perfection of the human intellect.[16] Human love of God is expressed in the actual performance of the Torah's commandments, the manifestation of God's infinite will and infinite love for Israel.

According to Crescas, the Torah does not merely establish the political order in which the intellectually gifted few can attain perfection, as Maimonides had maintained. Rather, the Torah defines the very activities which enable the soul to retain its essential incorporeality, that is, its holiness. By highlighting the importance of actual performance of *mitzvot*, Crescas obliterated the hierarchy between the philosophers and the multitude which was posited by Maimonides and his followers. Performance of the commandments is obligatory for all Jews, regardless of whether they hold perfect opinions or not. Crescas' emphasis on actual performance of the commandments also had a clear anti-Christian message: the road to personal immortality lies not in holding certain views but in the performance of specific acts which Israel alone is commanded to do. Therefore, only those who observed the divine commandments, that is, Israel, can be saved. Crescas spelled out his rational critique of Christianity in a systematic treatise.[17]

Crescas' bold critique and original alternative to Maimonides compelled Jewish thinkers to choose between two interpretations of Judaism. The choice was difficult because at stake was not only the legitimacy of philosophy as an intellectual discipline, but the survival of the whole medieval conceptual framework and educational system. Most Sephardi philosophers, including some of Crescas' own students, such as Joseph Albo, Zerachya Halevi, and Profiat Duran, were not ready to accept Crescas' refutation of Aristotelianism or his innovative views on free will and determinism, the primacy of the human will, and the compulsory dimension of faith.[18] Because his critique was derived from the theoretical analysis of Aristotle's own premises and employed the tools of Aristotelian logic, they viewed Crescas' philosophy as an "in house" debate within the Aristotelian tradition rather than a dismantling of the Aristotelian world view. Moreover, Crescas did not (and could not) offer a full-fledged cosmology in lieu of the Aristotelian one he had debunked. He did not have new scientific data to back up his theoretical claims against Aristotle, data that would become available only at the end of the sixteenth century. Not surprisingly, a loyal Aristotelian scholar such as Isaac ibn Shem Tov dismissed Crescas' critique of Aristotelian philosophy as evidence of misunderstanding based on lack of philosophic proficiency.[19] In this sense, Ravitzky is right to state that Crescas "came too late in one respect and too early in another respect."[20]

By the same token, most Jewish philosophers were unprepared to endorse Crescas' assault on Maimonides. Maimonides epitomized the very cultural identity and leadership claims of the Jewish elite in Iberia. To renounce Maimonides would mean to undermine one's sociocultural status. Therefore, throughout the period under consideration Sephardic philosophers continued to defend Maimonides against his critics even though they were increasingly receptive to Crescas' critique and even adopted several of Crescas' insights into their interpretation of Maimonides. To some extent, the history of Jewish philosophy in the period under consideration could be viewed as dialogue between two alternative approaches to Judaism, Maimonides' and Crescas'.

The impact of Christian scholasticism

By the 1430s the political situation in Spain stabilized and the Jewish community could focus its energies on cultural rebuilding. From the testimony of Joseph Garçon we learn that philosophy and its related arts and sciences enjoyed considerable popularity among Jewish youth in the second half of the fifteenth century.[21] Jewish students would travel long distances to study in academies that offered advanced studies in philosophy (*yeshivat ha-chokhmot ha-chitzoniyot*), and private tutors in philosophy were in high demand for their expertise. Indeed, even though the class of Jewish courtiers lost much of its previous luster and political power, it still produced diplomats, financiers, administrators, and physicians whose social status required the mastery of philosophico-scientific knowledge no less than personal wealth and business contacts.

Furthermore, the very renewal of halakhic studies in Spain was predicated on the incorporation of Aristotelian logic into the interpretation of the authoritative talmudic text.[22] The method was launched by Isaac Conponton and elaborated by his disciples, Isaac Aboab, Isaac de Leon, and Samuel Valensi, in an attempt to understand God's word with scientific precision. The talmudic scholar would thus actualize his rational potential and gradually progress toward intellectual perfection and ultimately a union of his perfected intellect with God. It is very plausible that the penetration of philosophy into the very heart of rabbinic training prompted the demonization of philosophy by a group of anonymous kabbalists in Castile who produced *Sefer ha-Meshiv* (*The Book of the Answering Angel*).[23] Philosophy was perceived not only as alien to Judaism but as inherently evil, associated with the mythic realm of evil (*sitra achra*). Such strong anti-philosophical sentiment makes sense only in a setting where philosophy is still a formidable cultural force.

In continuity with medieval patterns, the study of philosophy in fifteenth-century Iberia consisted first and foremost in mastering Aristotle's works with the authoritative commentaries of Averroes, all available in Hebrew.[24] Sephardi scholars such as Joseph ibn Shem Tov, Isaac ben Shem Tov ibn Shem Tov, Shem Tov ben Joseph ibn Shem Tov, Abraham Bibago, Abraham ben Isaac Shalom, and Baruch ibn Ya'ish composed new commentaries and supercommentaries on the Aristotelian-Averroean corpus.[25] The purpose of these commentaries was not to display the originality of the author but to ensure the perpetuation of the authoritative Judeo-Arabic philosophic tradition. Along with Aristotle and Averroes, the Jewish student of philosophy also consulted the writings of Avicenna, al-Ghazālī, ibn Bājja, and ibn Ṭufayl, as well as the works of Jewish Aristotelians, chief among them Levi ben Gershom (Gersonides) and Moses Narboni.

Aristotle's philosophy, however, was studied not for its own sake, but as the first step toward a systematic reflection about Judaism. Maimonides' *Guide of the Perplexed* served as the point of departure for all such reflections. Iberian scholars including Profiat Duran, Simeon ben Tzemach Duran, Asher Crescas, Joseph ben Shem Tov ibn Shem Tov, Isaac ben Shem Tov ibn Shem Tov, Shem Tov ben Joseph ibn Shem Tov, and Isaac Abravanel all wrote commentaries on the *Guide* or on certain problematic chapters of the book.[26] Through their interpretation of Maimonides, these thinkers pondered the major themes of medieval Jewish philosophy: the essence and existence of God, the origins and structure of the universe, providence, divine revelation, and the ultimate end of human life. In their systematic treatises Jewish philosophers frequently cited Maimonides, defended him against his critics, and even when they articulated a viewpoint which markedly differed from Maimonides', they still found it necessary to ascribe it to the revered master.[27] In this regard it is justifiable to view fifteenth-century philosophy as but "footnotes" to Maimonides.

The continued loyalty to Judeo-Arabic philosophy may create the impression that fifteenth-century Jewish philosophy lost its creative edge and suffered from intellectual stagnation.[28] This judgment is not without merit, but it does not capture the entire story. What distinguishes fifteenth-century Jewish philosophers in Iberia from their predecessors is the grafting of Christian scholasticism onto the Judeo-Arabic philosophic tradition. Paradoxically, Christian triumphalism itself compelled Jewish philosophers to become familiar with the scholastic tradition in order to address the challenge of Christianity.[29] After the mass apostasy of Jews and the debacle in Tortosa, the Jewish philosopher could no longer dismiss Christianity as an intellectually inferior religion. Indeed, Isaac Arama praised Christian clergymen for employing philosophy in order to enhance the Christian faith and conceded that Jews enjoyed listening to Christian preachers because of their rhetorical excellence.[30] Thus, it was the recognition that the surrounding Christian culture is a formidable intellectual challenge to Judaism that led Jewish scholars to study scholastic philosophy for the sake of rationalizing their continued allegiance to Judaism.

Christian scholasticism influenced the style and content of Jewish philosophical writings. While the commentary on authoritative texts (both philosophical or religious) remained the dominant literary genre, Jewish scholars increasingly adopted the scholastic method of argumentation in their theological treatises. As the works of Isaac Abravanel attest, Jewish thinkers organized their discourse thematically as a set of disputed questions, each of which includes a summary of arguments for and against the author's position and a rebuttal of the objections. Beyond literary style, Iberian scholars such as Judah ben Samuel Shalom, Abraham ben Isaac Shalom, Eli ben Joseph Chavilio, Abraham Nachmias ben Joseph, and Baruch ibn Ya'ish translated scholastic texts into Hebrew, thus expanding the corpus of philosophical texts in Hebrew.[31] According to Solomon Bonafed, Jewish scholars such as Isaac Arondi hired private Christian tutors to teach them scholastic logic which they held to be superior to Arabic logic.[32] Likewise, Joseph ibn Shem Tov expressed his admiration for the Christian scholastic commentaries on Aristotle's *Nicomachean Ethics* that informed courtly debates in ethics and political theory.[33]

The most extensive employment of scholastic philosophy is evident in the works of Abraham Bibago, who cited Dominican and Franciscan authors such as Alexander of Hales, Thomas Aquinas, Duns Scotus, Johannes Versoris, Francis of Mairone, Nicholas Bonet, Geraldus Odonis, and Petrus Aurioli.[34] And equally at home in scholastic literature was Bibago's contemporary Isaac Abravanel, the Jewish financier and statesman who reserved a special admiration for Thomas Aquinas.[35] Though quantitatively the reliance of Jewish scholars on scholastic philosophy was relatively small in comparison to the Judeo-Arabic philosophic sources, the impact of scholasticism was very significant. It accounted for the emergence of a new synthesis of reason and faith which differed from the strict intellectualism of Maimonides.

A new fusion of reason and faith

Following Maimonides, Jewish philosophers in the thirteenth and fourteenth centuries (for example, Joseph ibn Kaspi, Levi ben Gershom, and Moses Narboni) identified theology with metaphysics, depersonalized the Jewish conception of God, and posited the intellect as the essence of man. By the same token, they viewed prophecy as a natural phenomenon to be analyzed by the same epistemological theories that apply to all cognitive acts. With Maimonides, these Jewish rationalists interpreted Mosaic prophecy as the highest form of philosophical knowledge ever attained by a human being and, therefore, regarded the Torah as an esoteric, philosophical text. The figurative language of the Torah expresses the truths of Aristotelian physics and metaphysics and the laws of the Torah establish the most perfect social order in which the philosophic elite can attain perfection and reach the ultimate end of human life, knowledge of God.

The intensification of the Jewish-Christian polemics and the grow-ing influence of scholasticism led to a new synthesis of reason and faith. It was based on a marked distinction between "the path of investigation" (*derekh ha-chaqirah*) and "the path of tradition and faith" (*derekh ha-qabbalah ve-ha-emunah*).[36] This distinction parallels Aqui-nas' distinction between philosophy (or natural theology) and theology (or sacred doctrine), respectively. Philosophy and theology differ from each other in terms of origin, scope, and aim. Whereas philosophy consists of truths that natural human reason can demonstrate without divine assistance, theology contains true propositions that exceed the ken of natural human reason. Whereas philosophy proceeds from knowledge of the effect (*alul*) to knowledge of its cause (*'illah*), theology proceeds from knowledge of the cause to knowledge of the effects. Whereas philosophy encompasses knowledge extracted from sensible, created things, theology contains revealed knowledge about the supernatural realm of divine things. Whereas philosophy is prone to errors, mistakes, and uncertainty, theology is certain, reliable, and complete. Whereas philosophical wisdom is a cognitive activity of the intellect, theology involves the assent of the will through faith. Whereas philosophy alone falls short of securing personal immortality and can at best guarantee earthly happiness, the sacred doctrines of theology are salvific; they assure transcendent happiness in the world to come.

Philosophy and theology, however, do not genuinely contradict each other. In regard to some propositions – for example, that God exists, that God is one, and that God knows particulars – there is an overlap between philosophy and theology. Natural human reason can discover these truths (which are taught as well by divine revelation) without a special divine assistance. Yet the inherent imperfections of philosophy dictate that philosophy cannot ensure ultimate felicity. Only knowledge that comes from God, that is, revealed knowledge, is salvific. Out of his abundant grace (*chesed*) the perfectly good God revealed to Israel those truths necessary for individual salvation and personal immortality, truths which exceed the ken of natural human reason.[37] Divine revelation, therefore, is not the outcome of natural perfections, as Maimonides and the previous Jewish Aristotelians held, but is rather the volitional act of God to single out Israel and reveal to her supra-rational and supernatural truths. Though Jewish philosophers continued to interpret prophecy as an intellectual activity, they highlighted the mystical overtones of Averroist epistemology and portrayed the contact between the prophet's intellect and God in unitive terms.[38]

A similar reinterpretation of Maimonides took place in regard to the meaning of Torah. While all fifteenth-century Jewish theologians endorsed the assumption that the Torah is an esoteric, philosophic text, they did not identify the hidden meaning of the Torah with the propositions of Aristotelian physics and metaphysics, but rather with the ideal order of the universe which pre-exists in the divine mind in a supereminent way. As the wisdom of God, the esoteric Torah (*nistar*) is the eternal, ideal exemplar of the universe that serves as the blueprint of creation (*defus ha-nimtza'ot*).[39] It follows that there is a structural affinity between the created universe and the revealed text, and the more one studies the Torah, the closer one gets to understanding nature and God. And since the Torah contains not only true beliefs but also prescriptions for good conduct, the laws of the Torah have an intrinsic and not only an instrumental value, precisely as Crescas and the kabbalists maintained. The very performance of the divine law creates the perfect social order in which the individual attains perfection of body and soul, resulting in the immortality of the rational soul. In the afterlife the perfected soul enjoys the delight (*ta'anug*) of everlasting union with God.

The emphasis on the salvific nature of Torah led to yet another transformation of the Maimonidean legacy. Fifteenth-century theologians placed faith (*emunah*) in God, the giver of the Torah, as a necessary condition for individual salvation. For Maimonides, faith was a belief that "what has been represented is outside the mind just as it has been represented in the mind." As Rosenberg has shown, Maimonides' definition of faith (a belief *that p*) can be interpreted both objectively and subjectively.[40] The objective interpretation highlights the correspondence between belief and the extra-mental reality. To believe *that p* is equivalent to thinking *that p is true*. The subjective interpretation emphasizes the element of internal conviction in the act of believing, regardless of the correspondence between the content of the belief and the extra-mental reality. Maimonides followed Aristotle and al-Fārābī in contrasting true opinion, known on the basis of accepted tradition (*taqlīd*), with knowledge attained through rational demonstration. Tradition and demonstrable knowledge teach the same truths in different manners to different individuals or groups in accordance with their level of intellectual capacity.

In the fifteenth century faith was generally understood subjectively. It expressed the love of the believer for God, resulting not only in the endorsement of certain propositions – the articles of the Jewish faith – but also in the firm commitment of the believer to observe the revealed law. The highest expression of the believer's love of God is the willingness to sanctify one's life for the sake of God, a task that Iberian Jews were increasingly called upon to do as the century came to a close. By virtue of faith in God and the commitment to the life of Torah, each and every Jew (and not only the philosophic elite) could attain the supernatural end of human life – the immortality of the individual soul.

The hierarchical relationship between "the path of investigation" and "the path of faith" paralleled the distinction between the natural and supernatural orders of reality. This notion permeates the writings of Isaac Abravanel and was shared by his contemporaries, Abraham Bibago, Abraham Shalom, and Isaac Arama.[41] According to these thinkers, Israel (both collectively and individually) belongs simultaneously to the natural and supernatural orders. As created human beings, the affairs of Israel fall under the laws of nature (teva'), whose regularity and stability manifest God's wisdom and general providential care for the created universe. On this level, all events can be known scientifically, especially by employing the science of astrology, which was at the time an integral part of natural philosophy.[42] Yet, Israel also benefits from a special, direct, particular providence which transcends natural determinism and is not transparent to human reason. God's revelation at Sinai was a miraculous event, expressing God's free will and divine intervention in nature. As such, the revelation from God was not predicated on perfection of the natural human intellect and, therefore, encompassed all of Israel, regardless of their degree of intellectual perfection. With the giving of the Torah, Israel was governed directly by the will of God. Israel's affairs, therefore, manifested the believers' faith in God and willingness to observe the Torah's commandments.

Isaac Abravanel made this notion of faith the cornerstone of his philosophy of history.[43] Familiar with the writings of the Church Fathers, especially Augustine, as well as with the humanist revival of Stoic philosophy, Abravanel formulated a philosophy of history which emphasized the notion of human choice.[44] For Abravanel, the doctrine of the chosenness of Israel means neither that God elected Israel for a special task, as traditional Judaism teaches, nor that Israel possesses a natural, biologically transmitted propensity to encounter God directly, as Judah Halevi taught. Rather, echoing the humanist preoccupation with the freedom of the will, Abravanel understood the doctrine of chosenness to mean that Israel chooses God to the exclusion of everything else. In his *Commentary on the Pentateuch* Abravanel presents the Fall as a paradigm for human choice that propels history. Unlike Maimonides, who interpreted the Fall as a decline from philosophical perfection to moral deliberations about matters of good and evil, Abravanel understood the Fall as an alienation from God. The first sin expressed the human preference for productive life, based on scientific knowledge, over spiritual intimacy with God. In response, God punished humanity by limiting his direct providential care and enslaving humanity to the governance of intermediary natural forces, the astral powers, and natural causality. The human rebellion against God reached a new climax in the generation of the Tower of Babel, causing a further removal of divine providential care and increasing strife and misery. Only those who freely chose God, namely, Noah, Shem, Eber, and especially Abraham, benefited from God's direct providence. To the descendants of Abraham, God revealed his will in the Torah, thereby enabling the community of believers to transcend nature. The sacred, supernatural history of Israel is thus propelled by the exercise of human free will: because Israel rejected God, it was exiled from God's land and enslaved to the gentile nations; if Israel chooses God, it will be redeemed and enjoy blissful intimacy with God in the land of Israel. To explain the connection between human free will, faith in God, and redemption, Abravanel composed his messianic trilogy.[45] Abravanel's eschatological treatises manifest not only the acute messianism after the expulsions from Iberia, but also the shift from Maimonidean intellectualism to a humanist sensibility which accords to the will a central place in the divine-human nexus. Following Abravanel, Sephardi thinkers in the sixteenth century continue to reflect on the interplay between the intellect and the will in the pursuit of human perfection.

Jewish dogmatics

The emphasis on faith in fifteenth-century Jewish philosophy, however, did not entail radical fideism.[46] Throughout the fifteenth century Iberian Jewish scholars argued that Judaism is superior to Christianity precisely because the former is rational and the latter is not. In contrast to contemporary Christian theologians of the Ockhamist school who highlighted the absolute omnipotence of God and the irrationality of faith, Jewish scholars claimed that the beliefs of Judaism cannot be irrational because God cannot do what is logically impossible. The limits on God's omnipotence are not a deficiency but a perfection which manifests the perfect wisdom of God which God revealed in his Torah. The task of the Jewish theologian (*ha-chakham ha-datiyi*) was thus twofold: to provide a rational refutation of Christian dogmas, on the one hand, and to prove the rationality of Judaism, on the other. The efflorescence of anti-Christian philosophical polemics[47] and the preoccupation with Jewish dogmatics[48] were two aspects of the same endeavor.

Sephardi theologians generally agreed that Judaism has a specific set of dogmas whose affirmation is necessary for individual salvation, but they disagreed about their definition and number. For some, the dogmas were the axioms of Jewish theology from which all other propositions could be logically derived and arranged in a hierarchical order. For others, the dogmas of Judaism constituted the minimal number of beliefs whose affirmation defines one as a Jew and denial renders one a heretic. And for still others, the dogmas were the "foundations of the Torah" in the sense that they were logically prior to the belief in divine revelation and without them the entire Jewish religion and its numerous rituals would collapse. Once again, Maimonides' list of thirteen principles was the point of departure for reflection on the dogmas of Judaism. By analyzing Maimonides' criterion of selection and structure of the list of dogmas, or by proposing their alternative lists of cardinal beliefs, Jewish theologians formulated their own philosophies of Judaism.

For example, Joseph Albo followed Crescas in arranging the dogmas of Judaism hierarchically. Drawing upon the works of Simeon ben Tzemach Duran, Albo posited three "roots" (*'iqqarim*) for the Torah: God's existence, Torah from heaven, and retribution. From these he derived eight *shorashim*, or secondary principles: God's unity, God's incorporeality, God's atemporality, God's perfection, God's knowledge, prophecy, verification of God's messengers, and individual providence. Like Crescas, Albo held that there are additional beliefs which are taught by the Torah of Moses, but that these are logically and structurally independent of preceding principles. These included the belief in creation, Mosaic prophecy, eternity of the Torah, the attainment of perfection through the fulfillment of even one commandment, resurrection, and the messiah.

Most Sephardi theologians, however, differed from Albo and Crescas and considered creation ex nihilo to be *the* foundation of the Torah. Thus Abraham Shalom derived from the belief in creation a list of "principles" of the Torah: God's necessary existence, retribution, providence, God's omnipotence, revelation, prophecy, messiah, God's omniscience and human freedom, and resurrection. For Abraham Bibago, creation and miracles together were the foundational beliefs of the Torah from which all other principles of Judaism, as Maimonides defined them, are derived. And Isaac Arama also considered creation to be the foundation of the Torah, while stating that six beliefs are cardinal in Judaism: creation, God's power, prophecy and revelation, providence, repentance, and life after death. His distinct contribution to Jewish dogmatics was the association of each of these beliefs with a particular ritual of the Jewish tradition.

Conceivably, these different sets of "catechisms" meant that one could be considered a Jew according to one list of dogmas and a heretic according to another. But in reality (whether or not the theologians admitted it) Jewish dogmatics was an academic exercise with but limited political and practical import. Although in theory Jews could be excommunicated for holding heretical views, Jewish communities were too localized and fragmented to make excommunication effective. Therefore, the historical significance of Jewish dogmatism lies not in the battle against heresy, but rather in the clarification of what Judaism meant for its adherents.

The expulsion of the Jews from Spain and its dominions (1492) and later from Portugal (1497) intensified the Sephardi preoccupation with dogmatics. In his *Rosh Amanah* Isaac Abravanel – the most distinguished Jewish philosopher among the Iberian exiles – articulated a new approach to Jewish dogmatics.[49] With Maimonides, Abravanel regarded the affirmation of doctrine as a necessary condition for inclusion in the people of Israel and for salvation, and as grounds for deeming a non-affirmant as a heretic. But Abravanel opposed the notion that Judaism has a specific number of dogmas. Abravanel asserted instead that each and every teaching of the Torah is a necessary dogma which every believer must affirm in order to be saved. Abravanel's approach to the biblical text reflects the influence of kabbalah on philosophy.

The kabbalists objected to the dogmatic enterprise on the ground that the Torah is a unity which does not allow internal division between primary and secondary teachings. Each and every teaching of the Torah, indeed each word and even each letter, has a religious significance; each directs the believer to a specific locus in the Godhead. Like the kabbalists, Abravanel believed that acceptance of the Torah as a whole is necessary for human salvation. So while paying lip service to Maimonides that Judaism has dogmas, Abravanel rejected the dogmas proposed by Crescas, Albo, and those who followed them, and opposed the view that Judaism has axioms without which the entire faith would collapse. Abravanel, however, did recognize the pedagogical importance of dogmatic speculation. As a renowned courtier in three royal courts and an immensely learned scholar, Abravanel was no less an elitist than Maimonides. They both recognized the need to inculcate correct beliefs in the unlearned multitudes. So Abravanel defended Maimonides' principles as heuristic devices for the education of the masses, and for that purpose alone conceded that a Jew must hold one belief in particular – creation. Creation is the cardinal dogma of Judaism because it facilitates belief in miracles. For Abravanel, messianic redemption is the most important miracle. To console his people and strengthen belief in the coming redemption, Abravanel posited the belief in creation as the prime dogma of Judaism.

The expulsion of the Jews from Iberia was undoubtedly a traumatic event, but it did not exterminate Sephardi Jewry and did not demolish Sephardi culture. In fact, the forced release from Christian persecution proved especially good for the Sephardi Jews who settled in the multi-ethnic and multi-religious society of the Ottoman Empire. Islamic law granted them more freedom and protection, and furthermore they felt themselves culturally superior to the local Turks. In the Ottoman Empire the Sephardi exiles could focus on the preservation and development of their own heritage – a continued conversation with their beloved homeland without fear of Christian backlash. Thus, within two decades after the expulsions, Iberian Jewish philosophy experienced a renaissance of sorts in the Ottoman Empire. Indeed, it was the very encounter of Sephardi intellectuals with Renaissance culture outside of Iberia which partially explains the efflorescence of Jewish philosophy in the sixteenth century, both in Italy and in the Ottoman Empire. To understand the impact of Renaissance culture on the history of Jewish philosophy we now turn to Italy.

JEWISH PHILOSOPHY IN RENAISSANCE ITALY

By the dawn of the fifteenth century the Jewish rationalist tradition was already well entrenched among native Italian Jews. After the persecution of the early 1290s native Italian Jews migrated to northern and central-northern provinces, where they would encounter waves of Jewish immigrants from France and Germany.[50] Money-lending and pawnbroking provided the livelihood of these settlements. The specific needs of the Italian economy, the constant warfare among the Italian city-states, and the growing stratification of Italian society all fostered a benign tolerance of Jewish money-lending by Italian popes, secular princes, and republican governments. Individual Jewish money-lenders received short-term residential and business permits (*condotte*) in areas from which Jews had been previously expelled or in which they were never allowed to settle. Despite their marginal and precarious status, the Jewish money-lenders accumulated considerable wealth and consciously modeled their lifestyle after the norms of the Italian patriciate. In their attempt to cultivate a Jewish version of the refined Renaissance gentleman, the bankers established personal libraries of considerable size for their own use and became patrons of rabbinic scholars, philosophers, and poets. The education of upper-class Jewish youth combined the study of Torah and halakhah, the scholastic curriculum of the trivium and the quadrivium, and the humanist emphasis on eloquent speech in Latin and Italian.[51] Forever conscious of their religious and national "otherness," Italian Jews selectively adapted the aesthetic and educational norms of Renaissance culture in order to express their Jewishness and assert their spiritual superiority over their neighbors.[52]

The Aristotelian tradition

Medieval rationalism penetrated Judeo-Italian culture from Spain and Provence in the late twelfth century about the same time that scholastic

Aristotelianism was introduced into Italy from France.[53] Jewish philosophers – most notably, Jacob Anatoli, Zerachia ben Chen Shealtiel, Moses of Salerno, and Shemariah of Crete – were instrumental in the dissemination of scholasticism in Italy in the thirteenth and early fourteenth centuries.[54] They translated the works of Aristotle and the commentaries of Averroes from Hebrew and Arabic into Latin and cooperated with Christian scholars on the Latin translation of Maimonides' *Guide of the Perplexed*. This interaction made Jewish scholars in Italy more open to the influences of scholasticism than their coreligionists in Spain. For example, already in the early 1290s Hillel ben Samuel of Verona absorbed Aquinas' synthesis of reason and faith and applied it to his interpretation of Maimonides, and during the first decades of the fourteenth century Judah ben Moses Romano translated select works of Aquinas and Giles of Rome into Hebrew.[55] Jewish scholars were also quick to adapt the novelties of Italian vernacular poetry when Judah's cousin, Immanuel of Rome, translated Dante's poetry into Hebrew.[56] From the very start of its dissemination in Italy, Jewish philosophy fused Judeo-Arabic philosophy with Christian scholasticism. The influence of scholasticism deepened during the fifteenth and sixteenth centuries when Jews were admitted to the faculties of medicine and philosophy in Italian universities.[57]

The first extant philosophical text from the fifteenth century exemplifies both continuity with the medieval past and openness toward contemporary cultural trends. In 1416 Moses ben Isaac da Rieti – the physician of Pope Pius II Piccolomini, a logician, a polemicist, and a rabbi of the Jewish community in Rome – composed *Miqdash Me'at* (*A Lesser Sanctuary*).[58] Modeled after the *dolce stil novo* of Dante's *Divine Comedy*, this philosophical poem expressed in tercets the Neoplatonized version of medieval Jewish Aristotelianism, while summarizing and popularizing the various branches of philosophy.

Rieti conceptualized the universe as a hierarchical chain of beings in which each existent occupies its natural place and aspires to reach its ultimate end. Beginning with God, the great "chain of being" descends through the orders of spiritual substances (the angels and souls), the heavenly bodies and elementary spheres, the various species of animals, plants, and minerals, down to shapeless matter. The multiple levels of the universe are held together by a dynamic unity of forces and affinities which exist in miniature form within the human, the microcosm. Combining a common topos of medieval Hebrew poetry, namely, that poetic inspiration was akin to prophecy,[59] with the philosophic conception of prophecy, Rieti's poem depicts an ecstatic-prophetic experience. By virtue of acquiring moral and intellectual perfection, the poet's soul is released from its embodied condition and ascends to the heavenly realm where it encounters the immortal souls of Jewish saints – biblical heroes, rabbinic sages, Geonim, medieval philosophers and poets – enjoying the bliss of eternal life. The moral of Rieti's didactic poem was quite clear: paradise is for Jews only, notwithstanding Dante's eloquent claims to the contrary.

The more common method for the dissemination of philosophy among Italian Jews was the philosophical biblical commentary and public preaching. Moses ben Joab, who preached in the Jewish community of Florence during the 1450s, illustrates the dissemination of Maimonidean philosophical hermeneutics, which was introduced to Italy by Jacob Anatoli.[60] Moses ben Joab accepted the Maimonidean premise that the esoteric meaning of the Torah contains the truths of philosophy. As Melamed has shown, he departed from Maimonides and followed Joseph Albo, who was the first to discuss the Torah in light of Aquinas' fourfold division of law (eternal, divine, natural, and human).[61] Both Albo and Moses ben Joab, however, denied that natural law plays a role in the moral perfection of humans and transferred the functions which Aquinas assigned to natural law to either human or divine laws. According to Moses ben Joab, though human law "removes the base and promotes the noble," it cannot alone ensure the attainment of the supernatural end of human life. Therefore, a divinely revealed law which reflects the eternal law in the divine mind must complete and perfect human law. In his commentary on the legal portion of the Torah – *Etz Chayyim* (*The Tree of Life*) – he attempts to prove that the laws of the Torah are indeed divine because they ensure that those who live by them attain perfection in this life and immortal life after death.

The Maimonidean tradition in Italy was invigorated in the second half of the fifteenth century with the revival of Aristotelianism in Italian universities, due to the discovery of Aristotle's Greek texts, new translations into Latin, and the invention of printing.[62] The person most responsible for the revival of Aristotelianism among Italian Jews was Judah ben Yechiel Messer Leon.[63] Trained in the universities of Bologna and Padua, he was awarded a doctorate in philosophy and medicine from the Conte Palatino and was knighted by the Emperor Frederick III. His titles accorded him not only the customary privileges of *dignitas* and *nobilitas*, but also the unusual privileges of conferring doctorates in philosophy and medicine on Jewish students and treating non-Jewish patients. By virtue of his outstanding accomplishments and his familial ties with the wealthiest banking family in Italy – the da Pisa – Judah Messer Leon regarded himself as the official leader of Italian Jewry. He refers to himself, and was referred to by others, as *"rosh ha-golah"* ("the light of the exile") and felt empowered to mold the cultural orientation of Italian Jewry.

Judah Messer Leon's major contribution to the history of Jewish philosophy was in the field of logic.[64] Messer Leon was convinced that the key to the proper harmonization of religion and philosophy lies in the art of logic. He regarded scholastic logic – culled primarily from the works of Walter Burley and Paul of Venice – to be superior to conventional Arabic logic as taught by al-Fārābī and Averroes. His supercommentaries on Averroes' logical works and his massive encyclopedia of logic (*Mikhlal Yofi*) were a concerted effort to shift Jewish philosophical education from the Judeo-Arabic logical tradition to scholastic logic. To do so he painstakingly correlated the traditional commentaries of Averroes in the Judeo-Muslim tradition to those of Christian commentators. Because of his expressed preference for the latter, Messer Leon chided the Provençal Jewish logicians, Levi ben Gershom (Gersonides) and Moses Narboni, for following the Muslim philosophers too slavishly and for leading Jewish believers astray. Judah Messer Leon dismissed a certain Sephardi teacher of philosophy from his academy for advocating the unacceptable views of Narboni, and placed the recently printed biblical commentary of Gersonides under a ban. To ensure the dissemination of an "official" Jewish philosophy, Messer Leon commented on Yedaiah Bedersi's *Bechinat Olam* (*The Examination of the Universe*) and on Maimonides' *Guide of the Perplexed*.[65]

Judah Messer Leon was only partially successful in his attempt to determine the orientation of Jewish intellectual life in Italy. Though his logical encyclopedia became a very popular textbook for the study of logic among Italian Jews, he failed to curb the influence of Gersonides in Italy (most likely because of the influx of Spanish and Provençal immigrants), or to ensure that Jewish philosophers would devote their energies to logic. With the possible exception of Abraham Farissol,[66] Messer Leon's most outstanding students (for example, his son David, Yochanan Alemanno, and Abraham de Balmes) were not interested so much in Aristotelian logic as in the Platonism which had been recently revived by the humanists of Florence, who were also interested in kabbalah. Whereas Judah Messer Leon considered Neoplatonism an inferior philosophy to Aristotelianism and held kabbalah in contempt as second-rate Platonism, his own students taught themselves kabbalah, regarded it as an authoritative interpretation of Judaism, and attempted to reconcile kabbalah with Aristotelianism.

Judah Messer Leon's effort to place Aristotelian philosophy on a sound basis was further enhanced by Elijah del Medigo, a Jewish philosopher from Crete who sojourned in Italy from 1480 to 1490.[67] His outstanding command of the Aristotelian-Averroean corpus in Hebrew and Arabic made him a very popular teacher among Italian academics, clergymen, and humanists (for example, Girolamo Donato, Domenico Grimani, Antonio Pizammano of Venice, and Pico della Mirandola), who hired him to teach them Aristotle and Averroes and to translate their works from Hebrew and Arabic into Latin. Del Medigo published five of his Latin translations in a volume of John of Jandun's work which he himself edited.[68] For his Jewish readers, del Medigo translated into Hebrew several of Averroes' works and commented on those texts that were of the greatest interest to Jewish intellectuals, namely, those about Averroes' theory of knowledge, a topic that stood at the center of intellectual debates about the nature of human happiness.[69]

It appears that del Medigo's philosophical activity displeased some of his Ashkenazi coreligionists in Padua. Even though the study of philosophy was not unknown among Ashkenazi Jews,[70] the Ashkenazi leaders of Padua made it difficult for del Medigo to remain in Italy. He returned in 1490 to his native Crete, where the environment was more hospitable to Aristotelian philosophy,[71] and there composed his systematic theological treatise, *Bechinat ha-Dat* (*The Examination of Religion*). This subtle text was apparently written to express del Medigo's displeasure with the growing popularity of Platonism and Neoplatonism among Renaissance intellectuals, Jews and non-Jews alike. Even though del Medigo did not mention Yochanan Alemanno by name, it seems that *Bechinat ha-Dat* was written to discredit Alemanno's approach to Judaism. In 1488, Alemanno displaced del Medigo as Pico's teacher and introduced his young Christian prodigy to medieval Jewish and Muslim Neoplatonic sources, as well as to magic, alchemy, astrology, and kabbalah.[72] Pico also hired the notorious apostate Flavius Mithridates, who not only translated kabbalistic texts into Latin but also fabricated texts in which he dressed kabbalah up in christological garb.[73] In del Medigo's eyes, Alemanno and those who followed him (Jews and apostates) were "pseudo-intellectuals" (*mitchakmim*), who misinterpreted the tradition ("kabbalah" broadly defined) because they strayed from Aristotelianism to Neoplatonism.[74] Most vehemently, del Medigo opposed Alemanno's magical interpretation of kabbalah, which presupposed that the Torah is a manual to be used in magical and theurgic practices. We shall return to this point below. For now, suffice it to say that while del Medigo supplied Pico with kabbalistic texts, the Cretan philosopher opposed any attempt either to christianize kabbalah or to use kabbalah for magical purposes.

Del Medigo's own rational examination of revealed religion was in accord with the views of his older contemporaries in Spain, Joseph ibn Shem Tov and Abraham Bibago, and with the views of Moses ben Joab and Judah Messer Leon in Italy. Del Medigo was a loyal Aristotelian who was acutely aware of the inherent limitations of human reason. There are truths which can be known only through a revelation by God, the most perfect intellect, and it is that knowledge which assures the immortality of the human soul. According to del Medigo, a truly divine religion cannot contradict the truths of philosophy; in fact, the mark of a true religion is its rationality. Judaism alone, rather than Christianity, fits this description, because the doctrines of Christianity are so patently full of logical contradictions and inconsistencies.[75] A rational examination of the true divine religion – that is, the authentic kabbalah – proves that it is commensurate with the true philosophy, Aristotelianism. Precisely because Judaism is a rational religion, its truths have to be couched in figurative speech in order to become accessible to the many. The various members of the religious community thus grasp the truths of religion on a variety of levels, in accord with their degree of intellectual capacity. Apparent conflicts between religion and philosophy emerge only when pseudo-philosophers (such as Alemanno and his followers) stray from the path of the true religion and the true philosophy.

Del Medigo's departure from Italy did not halt the involvement of Jews in the revival of Aristotelianism or in the scholarly collaboration between themselves and Christians. In fact, the demand for the printed editions of Aristotle and Averroes created a brisk market in which Jewish scholars and recent apostates (most of whom were physicians in the service of popes and clergymen) were actively involved.[76] For example, in 1521 Jacob Mantino translated from Hebrew into Latin Averroes' epitome of the *Partibus Animalium* and the *De Generatione Animalium*, which he dedicated to Pope Leo X, and in 1524 Mantino published a Latin translation from the Hebrew of the epitome of the *Metaphysics*, which he dedicated to the cardinal, Hercules Gonzaga. Likewise, Abraham de Balmes translated a number of logical works of Aristotle and the *Rhetoric* into Latin in 1523, dedicating them to Cardinal Grimani, the patron of Averroist publications. De Balmes defended the quality of Averroes' rendering of Aristotle's text against the humanist tendency to prefer the Greek original. And Kalo Kalonymus translated Averroes' *Destruction of the Destruction* from Hebrew into Latin, which was included in the *editio princeps* of Averroes' *Opera Omnia* in 1550–2.

Aristotelianism remains the dominant philosophical school among Jewish intellectuals in Italy throughout the sixteenth century. Jewish Aristotelians (among them David ben Judah Messer Leon, Obadiah Sforno, Yechiel Nissim da Pisa, Joseph ibn Yachya, and Moses Provencallo) continued to reflect on the desired relationship between reason and faith and to prove that Judaism is superior to both pagan philosophy and other religions purporting to be divinely revealed. Standing within an authoritative tradition, the Jewish Aristotelians did not seek to break new philosophic ground but to resolve the subtle differences among the various interpreters of Aristotle, be they ancient or medieval, Jews or non-Jews, and to harmonize Aristotelianism with Renaissance Platonism.[77]

Obadiah Sforno's *Or Amim* (*Light of the Gentiles*) is a typical example of Jewish Aristotelianism in the first half of the sixteenth century in Italy. Sforno, as Bonfil has shown, was intimately familiar with the heated debates among Italian intellectuals about the nature of the human soul and the ultimate end of human life.[78] He based his systematic discussion of psychology and epistemology upon the commentaries of Agustino Nifo on Aristotle, and attempted to make an original philosophical contribution to the debate on the basis of the Jewish religious tradition. The thrust of Sforno's position was the claim that the human soul is by nature a divine substance and that its perfection is twofold: intellectual and practical. Departing from Maimonides to embrace the insights of Crescas, Sforno argued that praxis is superior to theoria and that the ultimate perfection of the soul in this life is expressed through action in the moral-social sphere. Accordingly, knowledge of God consists not in unification of the human intellect with the semi-divine active intellect (whose existence Sforno disproved, thus departing from the Judeo-Arabic tradition), but rather in the (voluntary) performance of God's will as revealed in the divine law. Voluntary acts of loving-kindness and justice toward other human beings, rather than contemplation of intelligibles, is the path to immortality of the soul, exactly as Crescas had argued. The philosophical debate on the nature of the soul thus amounted to a polemical defense of Judaism: only the doctrines of the divinely revealed Judaism and the actual performance of its laws lead to the salvation of the individual soul. Fully aware of the polemical import of his work, Sforno translated it into Latin and had it published in 1548.

From 1550 onward Jewish political status in Italy deteriorated significantly. The tolerance of the Church and the secular authorities turned into a harsh new policy of segregation, restrictions on Jewish economic activities, repression of Jewish culture, growing involvement of the Inquisition in Jewish affairs, and a series of local expulsions.[79] As Jewish physical insecurity increased, so did the polemical orientation of Jewish philosophy in Italy. In the second half of the sixteenth century Jewish intellectuals argued ever more strenuously for Jewish spiritual superiority. Thus the celebrated physician and philosopher David de Pomis composed a polemical treatise in Latin (*De Medico Hebreo*), in which he advanced the claim that the science of medicine was invented by Jews,[80] and Judah Moscato revived Judah Halevi's claim for Jewish ontological superiority over non-Jews in a commentary on the *Kuzari*, entitled *Qol Yehudah* (*The Voice of Judah*).[81] The intensification of Jewish "particularism" was yet another factor that would pave the way for the popularity of kabbalah among Italian Jewish thinkers by the end of the sixteenth century.

Humanism and Platonism

Notwithstanding the prominence of Aristotelianism in Italy, it was humanism which gave Renaissance culture its distinct character. In turn, the impact of humanism on Jewish philosophy accounts for its expansion and creativity.[82] To understand the impact of Renaissance humanism on Jewish culture we must distinguish between the phases of the humanist tradition in the Renaissance.[83] The first phase, known as either "Latin humanism" or "civic humanism," involved the recovery of ancient Latin texts and the civic ideals of Roman civilization. It began in the fourteenth century under the leadership of Petrarch and continued into the fifteenth century in the activity of the Florentine scholars and statesmen Leonardo Bruni, Caluccio Salutati, and Poggio Bracciolini, who revived the political ideals of Roman society, as depicted in Cicero's orations.

Rhetoric – the art of effective communication and ornamental speech – stood at the core of Latin humanism. Eloquence became an ideal for the way of life of the Renaissance gentleman. He was expected to be versatile, sociable, well-versed in classical letters, and ready to apply the lessons of the past to current problems. The early humanists were attracted to rhetoric because of its flexibility to address all human concerns in their ever-changing, infinite particularity. Rhetoric thus undermined the fixed hierarchies of medieval cosmology, replaced them with man as the center of the universe, and articulated a new view of man as a mysterious bundle of psychic energies – sensual, emotional, intellectual, and spiritual.[84] Because rhetoric lacked a fixed philosophical substance, it could be used to advance diverse ideological positions, to gloss over logical inconsistencies, and even to obfuscate shallowness of thought.

The second phase of humanism, by contrast, consisted of the recovery of Greek texts and the revival of Platonism, Neoplatonism, and Hermeticism. It began in the middle of the fifteenth century under the leadership of Marsilio Ficino and John Argyropolous in Florence and lasted throughout the sixteenth century not only in Italy but throughout Western and central Europe. Greek humanism shifted the focus from emphasis on rhetoric and good literary style to philosophy, theology, and science (in the form of magic). For the Florentine humanists, human dignity no longer meant casting off bad medieval Latin and the excesses of medieval monasticism, or the attempt to imitate the sophisticated noble Roman, but rather a pursuit of holiness in one's relation to God. In Trinkaus' succinct formulation, "there was a decided tendency to emphasize not only that human dignity rested in the fact that man was created in the image of God but that the perfection of humanity would be realized in equality with dignity."[85] Humanists such as Pico and Ficino envisioned man as the magus. Standing between the earthly and the heavenly realms, man was endowed with divine creative powers by virtue of the divine spark in him. The free human will determined whether he would rise to the level of angels and gain immortal life or sink to the level of beasts and disintegrate at death with all flesh.

Unlike the civic humanists who worshipped human eloquence, Ficino and his cohorts expressed a certain distrust toward human language, especially in its regard of the richness of divine truth. Along with the ancient poets, the humanists maintained that the infinite truths of God were manifest in many ways that could be approached only indirectly through riddles, allegories, and hints. The humanist's task was to recover all aspects of ancient wisdom in order to fathom the infinite richness of divine revelation, culminating in the spiritual truths of Christianity. Instead of rejecting scholastic philosophy, the Greek humanists built upon the teachings of scholastic masters (especially Aquinas), highlighted the Platonic and Neoplatonic aspects of medieval philosophy, and eclectically fused several intellectual traditions – Platonism, Neoplatonism, Hermeticism, Pythagoreanism, Zoroastrianism, and kabbalah – in their attempt to uncover *prisca theologia*. The seminal texts of these religio-philosophic traditions were now translated into Latin and edited with new attention to philological standards, inaugurated by the Latin humanists. Thus the humanists in the second half of the fifteenth century developed the doctrine of the unity of truth in which diverse intellectual traditions all participate to some extent.[86]

Jewish intellectuals in Italy were well disposed to absorb the humanist movement. The secularist tendencies of Latin humanism were not perceived as a religious challenge to Judaism precisely because the Jewish philosophers relegated this type of knowledge to the realm of nature. Indeed, how could natural human knowledge undermine Judaism, if the former is declared imperfect and incomplete from the outset? Whether human knowledge is proffered by a pagan or a Christian, by an ancient sage or a contemporary thinker, in principle it could not conflict with the infinite wisdom of the revealed Torah which completes and perfects nature. Thus Jews could absorb the aesthetic and educational sensibilities of the humanist movement without following the logic of civic humanism to its secular conclusions. Absorbing Greek humanism was even easier, given its religious and otherworldly orientation, as well as the fact that medieval Jewish philosophy itself was suffused with Neoplatonism. The ancient pagan sources recovered by

Renaissance humanists could be viewed as but one intellectual tradition that participates in the universal truth of which Judaism is the most perfect expression.

Judah Messer Leon's *Nofet Tzufim* (*The Book of the Honeycomb's Flow*) was the first Jewish response to Latin humanism.[87] This manual of Hebrew rhetoric, which Messer Leon printed in 1476, contained an inventory of linguistic forms derived from two rhetorical traditions: the Averroist-Aristotelian (which Judah Messer Leon knew through Todros Todrosi's Hebrew translation of Averroes' *Middle Commentary on Aristotle's Rhetoric*) and the Ciceronian-Quintilian which reflected the renewed interest of the Italian humanists in Latin rhetoric. With the Latin humanists Judah Messer Leon adopted the Ciceronian view that eloquence was beneficial only in so far as it complemented both the moral and intellectual perfection of the individual. A good orator, therefore, had to be a good man and a good philosopher in order to make the best use of his rhetorical skills.[88] Messer Leon's appropriation of humanist rhetoric, however, advanced the claim that Torah, rather than the writings of the pagan classical orators, exemplifies perfect speech. As a revelation of perfect, divine wisdom the Torah encompasses all human sciences, including rhetoric. Therefore, Judah Messer Leon encouraged contemporary Jews to immerse themselves in the study of rhetoric, while reminding them that the biblical text is the ideal.

Aware of Renaissance humanism, Jewish scholars expanded the scope of philosophy by grafting the *studia humanitatis* on to the medieval scholastic curriculum. The humanist penchant for historiography and the outburst of Renaissance artistic creativity inspired Jewish intellectuals to launch new literary genres in Hebrew such as biographies, historical narratives, comedies, and treatises on the performing arts, especially music and theater.[89] In continuity with the medieval past, trained philosophers also composed poetry in Hebrew and Italian, some of which made reference to philosophical themes, and cultivated the love of prose, not only in Hebrew but also in the vernacular.[90] Undoubtedly the return of conversos to the Jewish fold contributed to the expansion of philosophy and the literary efflorescence among Italian Jews. The returning conversos introduced their coreligionists not only to the seminal philosophical and scientific textbooks of European universities, but also to the masterpieces of Iberian and French literature written in some cases by authors of converso extraction. For example, the celebrated drama *La Celestina* by Fernando de Rojas was translated into Hebrew by Joseph Tzarfati – the physician of Pope Julius II (1503–13) and Leo X (1513–21), a philosopher and a poet – and enjoyed great popularity among Italian Jews.[91]

The most interesting work to illustrate the fluid boundaries between philosophy and belles lettres was the *Dialoghi d'Amore* (*The Dialogues on Love*) by Judah Abravanel, more commonly known as Leone Ebreo. Though the *Dialoghi's* date of composition, original language, intended audience, and philosophical meaning are still disputed among scholars,[92] all agree that it became a European bestseller. Its Italian version (1535) was translated into Spanish, French, Latin, and Hebrew and was published in twenty-eight editions. The fourth part of the *Dialoghi* and Ebreo's other philosophical work, *De Coeli Harmonia* (*The Harmony of the Heavens*) are now lost, although traces of the former could possibly be recovered in the writings of Giordano Bruno.[93]

Trained by his father, Isaac Abravanel, in the courts of Portugal and Castile, Leone culled his philosophy of love from a variety of intellectual traditions: classical and late Greek philosophy (especially Plato, Aristotle, and Proclus); medieval Jewish, Muslim, and Christian philosophers; the Provençal and Spanish courtly love tradition which flourished in fifteenth-century Castile; the theosophic and mystical doctrines of Spanish kabbalah; and Ficino's commentary on Plato's *Symposium*.[94] Leone Ebreo was not the first Jew to be acquainted with Ficino's revival of Plato's philosophy of love and to articulate a Jewish response to it. Yochanan Alemanno, with whom Leone Ebreo became acquainted soon after he settled in Italy, already composed a commentary on the Song of Songs, *Chesheq Shlomo* (*The Desire of Solomon*), which addressed many of the questions of interest to Ficino. Lesley insightfully suggested that "Alemanno's voluminous commentary on the Song of Songs stands in the same relation to the *Dialoghi* as Marsilio Ficino's commentary on the *Symposium* to his *Platonic Theology*: the commentary on the classical text prepares the way for the systematic study of some of the same questions."[95]

Leone Ebreo shared three major features with Ficino's philosophy, while articulating a Jewish counterpoint to Ficino's Christian "Platonic theology." First, Ebreo sought to integrate revealed religion with pagan ancient wisdom, which he defined very broadly to include the philosophy of the Presocratics, Plato, Aristotle and his late Greek commentators, Hermes Trismegistus, Plotinus, Proclus, and the Stoics. Ebreo could reconcile these philosophical texts and the rich medieval tradition because he postulated the "oneness" of truth, whatever its origins, in which the various intellectual traditions participated to some extent. But in response to Ficino, Ebreo considered revealed Judaism – and especially the esoteric teachings of the ancient kabbalah from which, according to Leone Ebreo, Plato derived his philosophy – as the most perfect expression of abstract truths about God and the universe.[96]

Second, for both Ficino and Leone Ebreo, the return to Platonism meant the recognition of the value of beauty, alongside truth and goodness. Ebreo's philosophy of love (like Ficino's) amounted to a religious aesthetics that connected the literary interests of the humanists with the aesthetic sensibilities of the visual artists. Following Plato, Ebreo held that particular things are beautiful (and concomitantly true and good) to the extent that they share or participate in the absolutely perfect form of beauty (and in the form of truth and goodness, respectively).[97] The recognition of beauty leads the lover of beauty to desire to unite with the beautiful as well as to reproduce beauty. Combining Platonic, Neoplatonic, and kabbalistic discourses, Ebreo expresses the love of the beautiful in genderized symbolism: the beloved beauty functions as the active male principle that "impregnates" the passive, receptive female lover by imparting the form of beauty on to it.[98] The copulation between the lover and the beloved gives birth to beauty. This process encompasses all levels of reality – divine, cosmic, and human – and accounts for the creation of the universe, its continued existence, and the constant desire of humans to unite with God – the unity of beauty, goodness, and truth.

Third, Ebreo agreed with Ficino that philosophical wisdom is best taught through the allegorical mode. Allegory (that is, the truth that hides itself in figurative speech) best corresponds to the metaphysical dualism of matter and form and to the dualism of body and soul in humans. The preference of the allegorical mode appears at first glance to repeat merely Maimonides' philosophical allegorism.[99] But, in fact, Ebreo differs greatly from Maimonides as regards the role of the imagination in the pursuit of philosophical wisdom.

Maimonides agreed with Aristotle that the "creative" power of the human imagination is the source of errors that lead the intellect away from knowledge of God. Maimonides held that a given religion is divine if it can be shown that its founder was the most perfect philosopher, whose teachings contain demonstrative truths rather than poetic inventions of the imagination. Maimonides asserted that the Torah of Moses is the most perfect religion because its founder, the prophet Moses, was the most perfect philosopher, whose prophecy was not sullied by the emotions and the imagination. Moses employed the imagination only to communicate his philosophic knowledge, in order to assure that all Israel would grasp it. According to Maimonides, then, the figurative speech of the philosophic Torah was a concession to the intellectual imperfection of the multitude. The perfect philosopher, however, must strip away the "silver lining" of metaphoric speech in order to grasp "the golden apples" of the Torah's philosophy.

Leone Ebreo, by contrast, maintained that human imagination is not a hindrance to truth but the very faculty that enables the mind to recognize the beautiful and to generate beautiful entities that imitate the beautiful. A given speech is beautiful to the extent that it imitates the beauty of objective reality and participates in the absolute beauty, God. The beauty of a given speech (and by extension all other artistic productions) signifies the degree of its participation in divine beauty. Ebreo suggested that the Torah of Moses is the most perfect speech because its words express the spiritual principles of the universe. In the Torah form and content fit in perfect harmony, thus indicating its divine origin. Greek and Roman philosophy approximate the truth, but in less perfect form. Ebreo's references to biblical verses, therefore, were not a sprinkling of Jewishness on a non-Jewish work, but a profound argument for the superiority of divinely revealed Judaism.

Leone Ebreo's reassessment of the imagination entailed a new vision of philosophy among Jews. The good philosopher is not the one who discards the figurative language of the Torah in order to capture its philosophical content, but rather the one who finds in the beautiful speech of the Torah the key to the mysteries of God and creation. By the same token, the good philosopher should not regard figurative language as antithetical to philosophy, but must create beautiful allegories whose interpretation would lead the reader to the true, the good, and the beautiful – to God. This is what Ebreo attempted to do when he composed his philosophical allegory about the two earthly Jewish courtiers, Philo and Sophia, whose love affair embodies the abstract principles of love. As a superb philosopher-artist – a Renaissance magus of words – Ebreo composed a fictitious philosophical allegory to teach that God's love is creative and that human intellectual love of God is a creative activity, an art of the highest order. To understand Ebreo's philosophy of love the reader has to trace the development of the plot, namely, the love affair between the two Jewish courtiers, as well as to pay close attention to the meaning of their philosophical discourse.[100] By composing an allegorical dialogue about the love affair between earthly lovers, Ebreo not only imitated the biblical Song of Songs but also ended the tradition of philosophic esotericism. Now all readers, even including women, and not only the philosophic elite could understand metaphysics, because it is conveyed in a beautiful dramatic narrative.[101]

Not surprisingly, the initial response to Leone Ebreo's philosophy of love was rather negative. The Aristotelian scholar Saul ha-Kohen Ashkenazi, the disciple of Elijah del Medigo, expressed his displeasure with Ebreo's syncretistic tendencies and departure from philosophic esotericism in a letter written to Isaac Abravanel.[102] But with the increasing popularity of both Platonism and kabbalah in sixteenth-century Italy, several Jewish philosophers – for example, Judah Moscato, Judah del Bene, Azariah de Rossi, and Gedaliah ibn Yachya – aspired to teach philosophy in aesthetically pleasing forms, studied Jewish sacred sources in the light of pagan poetry and mythology, and harmonized Aristotelian and Neoplatonic philosophies.[103] In 1568 Gedaliah ibn Yachya translated the *Dialoghi* into Spanish dedicating it to Emperor Philip II, and in this version it reached the Sephardi community in Salonica where it was studied by Jewish intellectuals, who debated whether the knowledge of God or the love of God constitutes the ultimate end of human life.

The greatest success of the *Dialoghi*, however, was outside the Jewish community. Harari plausibly argued that Giordano Bruno's *Eroici Furori* (*The Heroic Frenzies*) encompasses selections from the no longer extant fourth dialogue of the *Dialoghi*, and Dorman exposed the similarities between Baldassare Castiglione's *The Courtier* and Ebreo's *Dialoghi*.[104] Dorman has also showed that the *Dialoghi* was highly esteemed among converso philosophers (for example, Louis de Leon) and Jewish philosophers of converso descent (for example, Abraham Cohen Herrera and Spinoza) during the late sixteenth and the seventeenth centuries.[105] Undoubtedly, Leone Ebreo was a unique case of a Jew who became an eloquent spokesman of the regnant philosophy without converting to Christianity.

Philosophy, kabbalah, and the natural sciences

The revival of Platonism in fifteenth-century Italy facilitated the growing popularity of kabbalah among Renaissance intellectuals, Jews and non-Jews alike. From the very start of its dissemination in Italy, kabbalah was viewed as a speculative science whose mastery yields control of nature, on the one hand, and the attainment of a mystical union with God, on the other. The works of Abraham Abulafia, Menachem Recanati, and the anonymous *Ma'arekhet ha-'Elohut* (*Constellation of the Godhead*) with the commentary of Reuben Tzarfati were the major sources for knowledge of kabbalah in Italy from the late thirteenth century until the last quarter of the fifteenth century.[106] The *Zohar*, however, was relatively unknown in Italy until the end of the fifteenth century.[107] Viewed as a type of speculative lore, kabbalah was studied autodidactically from extant texts without the supervision of authoritative mentors. The absence of authoritative traditions, as Idel has shown, facilitated a degree of hermeneutical freedom which was not common in Spain. A scholar interested in kabbalah could rely on his own powers in the interpretation of kabbalistic texts and articulate his own peculiar reading of kabbalah on the basis of his philosophical knowledge. This, in turn, further enhanced the image of kabbalah as an ancient, theoretical science with a universal appeal, rather than as a set of practices for the proper observance of Jewish law. It is no surprise, therefore, that in Italy Christian humanists could view kabbalah as an integral part of universal, ancient wisdom and would desire to study it from Jewish masters.

Yochanan Alemanno played a major role in the revival of kabbalistic studies in Italy, the rise of Christian kabbalah, and the fusion of Jewish philosophy and kabbalah in the last quarter of the fifteenth century.[108] Even though he was trained as an Aristotelian philosopher and physician, Alemanno went beyond the bounds of scholastic Aristotelianism. Unlike his teacher, Judah Messer Leon, who restricted the study of nature to theories derived from bookish learning of Aristotle and his authoritative commentators, Alemanno desired to unite theoretical knowledge about nature with actual manipulation of nature. To this end Alemanno established contacts with practicing magicians in Italy (Jews and non-Jews) and studied alchemy, astrology, astral medicine, physiognomy, dream interpretation, and talismanic magic from a vast array of sources including the recently published Hermetic corpus, extant medieval Muslim and Jewish Neoplatonic texts, medieval magical manuals, and kabbalah. From these highly diverse sources Alemanno developed an organic view of nature in which there is no meaningful distinction between the animate and the inanimate and in which bodies exert influences on each other through sympathies and antipathies. Projecting mind into nature, Alemanno endowed all existing things with spirit, which served as the locus and carrier of active life and perception. In this organically unified universe the spiritual penetrates the physical or more precisely, a spiritual energy assumes material forms.

Alemanno's "proto-experimental" approach to nature was closely related to his conception of language. Along with other Renaissance Neoplatonic thinkers (for example, Cornelius Agrippa), Alemanno made a sharp distinction between natural, human languages, in which words signify things through the mediation of concepts, and divine languages, in which words express the essence of things.[109] The words of a divine language possess an innate creative power because they are composed from the elementary particles of nature – the sacred letters of the divine name. Needless to say, Alemanno regarded Hebrew as the one and only divine language whose letters are the "building blocks" of the created universe. This magical conception of the Hebrew language can be traced to ancient Jewish mystical and theurgic sources, to which Abraham Abulafia gave a philosophical reformulation.[110] For Alemanno (who was an ardent student of Abulafia's writings), the mastery of nature and the mystical union with God were thus possible through the manipulation of language. Whoever possesses the knowledge of the supernal exoteric Torah can "tap into" the spiritual energy of the Godhead and channel the divine efflux into the corporeal world, either into his or her own body or into material objects. Through self-

spiritualization, the magician-philosopher may control natural substances, prognosticate future events, heal the physically and mentally
afflicted, attain a temporary union with God in this life, and enjoy the
bliss of immortality in the afterlife.

Alemanno's syncretism and magical approach to the Torah made
him a favorite mentor of Renaissance humanists such as Pico, his
nephew Alberto Pio, and Yohannes Reuchlin, but it enraged the Aristotelian philosopher, Elijah del Medigo. Alemanno's philosophico-magical
interpretation of kabbalah also did not find favor in the eyes of Sephardi
kabbalists who began to settle in Italy during the last decade of the
fifteenth century. These kabbalists brought with them the authoritative
texts of the *Zohar* and its theosophico-theurgic outlook, which differed
markedly from the philosophical kabbalah of Alemanno. Already in
1490, the kabbalist Isaac Mor Chayim, who briefly sojourned in Italy
on his way to Israel, complained to Isaac da Pisa that Alemanno
misinterpreted the doctrines of *sefirot* because he regarded them as
instruments (*kelim*) of divine activity rather than as the essence (*atzmut*)
of God.[111] And in 1493 another Sephardi exile who settled in Italy,
Judah ben Jacob Chayat, went even further to specify which texts
constitute authentic and authoritative kabbalah and which texts should
not be studied as kabbalah.[112] The latter category included texts devoted
to the harmonization of philosophy and kabbalah by Abraham Abulafia, Isaac ibn Laṭīf, Samuel ibn Motot, and Yochanan Alemanno.

By the middle of the sixteenth century the *Zohar* had become
an authoritative, venerated text among Italian kabbalists, Jewish and
Christian. Half a decade after the Talmud was consigned to the flames
in 1553 and Jewish works were subject to severe censorship, the *Zohar*
was printed by two Christian publishing houses, an event surrounded
by a vehement controversy.[113] None the less, Alemanno's brand of
philosophical kabbalah did not disappear. His works were preserved
by scholars such as Mordechai Rosillo and Elijah ben Menachem Chalfon, and inspired other scholars in Italy to harmonize philosophy,
kabbalah, science, and magic.

In the sixteenth century a new philosophy of nature began to
emerge as a result of geographical discoveries, experimentation, mechanical and technological progress, and the appreciation for practical
experience. Though Jewish scholars played a very marginal role in the
development of early modern science, they were not ignorant of it.
Jewish physicians (many of whom trained at the University of Padua)
followed Alemanno's fascination with the patent and latent dimensions
of nature.[114] Going beyond the parameters of Aristotle's natural philosophy, Jewish scholars immersed themselves in the new scientific discoveries in astronomy, human physiology, botany, zoology, and
mineralogy, while seeking to capture the occult powers of nature

through the study of kabbalah, alchemy, astrology, and magic. These intertwined scientific pursuits were all part of one religious quest to find the hidden "signature" of God in the universe. Abraham Yagel, one of Alemanno's most ardent students, exemplified the close nexus between kabbalah, magic, and science. In Ruderman's succinct summary:

> Yagel was a practicing *magus* who assumed that the universe contained a network of correspondences and who placed great credence in the power of magical words and formulas to transform reality. But he was also an empiricist who sought to understand nature by observing it, constructing it, and by mastering it. And above all he was a masterful architect of an integrated view of reality that fused his religious identity with his medical-magical and scientific aspirations.[115]

The works of Yagel and his successors at the turn of the seventeenth century lead us to endorse Bonfil's claim that kabbalah (rather than philosophy) functioned as a modernizing agent.[116] The kabbalistic conception of God as *Ein Sof* (the Infinite) facilitated the shift "from the closed world" of Aristotle's "to the infinite universe" of modern science.[117] Crescas already anticipated that shift at the turn of the fifteenth century, but lacked the experimental proof for it. Furthermore, the kabbalists' attempt to tap divine energy inspired interest in the actual working of nature and made Jewish scholars responsive to the observational and experimental discoveries of the age. And, finally, the fact that kabbalah was simultaneously theocentric and anthropocentric[118] encouraged Jewish scholars to delve into their own inner life (the life of dreams, emotions, and passions) in order to come closer to God, in whose image humans are created. Thus, the inherent ambivalence of kabbalah facilitated the transition from one world view to another.

The transformation of Italian Jewish philosophy during the sixteenth century becomes clearer if we juxtapose two thinkers who were influenced by Yochanan Alemanno: Abraham Yagel (who flourished at the end of the century and in the first quarter of the seventeenth century) and David, the son of Judah Messer Leon (who was active at the beginning of the century).[119] David ben Judah Messer Leon was trained by his father, Judah Messer Leon, as an Aristotelian philosopher and physician but, like Alemanno, was genuinely interested in kabbalah. He considered kabbalah an authentic and authoritative interpretation of rabbinic Judaism and adopted Alemanno's philosophization of kabbalah, but without the interest in magic and theurgy. To reconcile Aristotelian philosophy and kabbalah, David ben Judah adopted the philosophy of Aquinas (especially his distinction between a mode of existence and a mode of signification) to explain how the *sefirot* can be both the essence of God and the attributes of divine action.[120] Kabbalah thus emerges as a distinctly Jewish version of the theory of divine perfections which exist in the divine mind in absolute unity and which serve as the paradigm for the creation of the universe.

David ben Judah was an important channel for the dissemination of Italian kabbalah outside the boundaries of the Apennine Peninsula. In 1495 David ben Judah fled Naples when it was conquered by the armies of Emperor Charles VIII. He found his way to the Ottoman Empire, settling first in Constantinople and later in Salonica and Valona. In the Ottoman Empire the incorporation of kabbalah into the conceptual framework of Jewish Aristotelianism would become quite common during the sixteenth century, as we shall soon see. Yet such fusion of intellectual trends did not engender kabbalistic creativity in the sixteenth century. Under the leadership of Isaac Luria in Safed, Sephardi kabbalists let their imagination run free, elaborating kabbalistic theosophy into an erotic fantasy of phantasmagoric proportions.[121] In the mythic universe of Lurianic theosophy and theurgy, Aristotelianism was irrelevant, though Lurianic ontology and psychology could be transposed in a "Platonic key," as Altmann aptly put it.[122] It was this platonization of Lurianic kabbalah that Israel Sarug disseminated in Italy at the end of the sixteenth century and which appealed to Jewish intellectuals such as Abraham Yagel and Abraham Cohen Herrera, who were deeply entrenched in Renaissance Platonism.[123]

❧ PHILOSOPHY AND THE PURSUIT OF ❧ HUMAN PERFECTION IN THE OTTOMAN EMPIRE[124]

Philosophy conserved and popularized

During the sixteenth century Lurianic kabbalah expressed the most creative aspect of Sephardi imagination and molded the rigorous rituals of a small religious elite. Yet until the end of the century it was philosophy rather than kabbalah that shaped the outlook of Jewish intellectuals in the Ottoman Empire, especially in the metropolitan centers of Salonica and Istanbul.[125] Within two decades after the expulsions from Iberia, Jewish philosophy flourished once again alongside an unprecedented creativity in biblical exegesis, halakhah, homiletics, and poetry. This cultural renewal, as Hacker has shown, took root in the exiles' determination to preserve and even enshrine the glorious past, be it real or imagined.[126] The exiles had brought from Iberia a strong aristocratic self-image, a sense of cultural superiority, a commitment to patronage of scholars and artists, a tradition of large-scale philanthropy for public and private education, a wistful nostalgia for the lost past, and a resolve to pass their legacy to their children. Sephardi culture blossomed in the Ottoman Empire, not in radical departure from pre-expulsion intellectual trends, but in conservation and embellishment of past achievements.

The culture that the Iberian exiles imported to their new haven was suffused with the rationalist approach to Judaism, from the incorporation of philosophy and its related arts and sciences into Jewish education, through the employment of human reason in the interpretation of the divinely revealed tradition, to the emphasis on knowledge of God as the purpose of Jewish religious worship. Precisely because religious rationalism was so deeply entrenched in Iberian Jewish culture, the exiles and their descendants did not, and indeed could not, excise philosophy from their endeavor to recreate the past. In the numerous Sephardi yeshivot of the Ottoman Empire, the most famous of which was that of Joseph Taitatzak in Salonica, the study of halakhah went hand in hand with the cultivation of the secular sciences.[127]

The Sephardi exiles did not arrive in a land devoid of philosophy. The local Romanyote community, concentrated mainly in Istanbul, could boast a flourishing intellectual life, which included the study of philosophy and the natural sciences (medicine in particular) in Greek, Arabic, Persian, and Turkish.[128] Rabbanite scholars such as Mordechai ben Eliezer Comtino (or Comatiano) and Karaite scholars such as Elijah Bashyatzi and his brother-in-law Kaleb Afendopolo were deeply anchored in medieval Aristotelianism and perpetuated Maimonidean intellectualism.[129] Romanyote scholars prepared abridged translations of Aristotle's works in logic and astronomy from the Greek originals for the benefit of Sephardi scholars who did not master Greek. In turn, local scholars such as Afendopolo were eager to absorb the philosophic learning that the émigrés brought with them.[130] Within a short period of time, however, the Sephardi emigrants dominated Ottoman culture, marginalizing the Romanyote community.

The primary concern of Jewish philosophers in the Ottoman Empire was to conserve, consolidate, and systematize the rich philosophical heritage of the past five centuries. Essential to this endeavor were digests that made the study of philosophy easier for the non-professional student. One example of such a philosophic encyclopedia was Solomon Almoli's *Me'asef le-Kol ha-Machanot*.[131] The extant introduction to the text indicates that the book was to summarize accumulated knowledge in the following disciplines: grammar, logic, mathematics, music, geometry, measurements and weights, optics, astronomy, physics, medicine, taslismanic magic and alchemy, ethics, and metaphysics.[132] Almoli insisted that mastery of these sciences was a necessary precondition to the correct understanding of the entire revealed tradition that for him included Hebrew language, the twenty-four books of the Bible, the dogmas of Judaism, kabbalah, and halakhah. Almoli was also convinced that the dissemination of philosophy would perfect the community at large and thereby hasten the messianic age.[133] For unknown reasons Almoli did not execute his ambitious plans, plans that fit into the compilatory tendencies of Ottoman scholars.

The technology of printing supported the upsurge of philosophical activity. The most popular philosophic works in print were Bachya ibn Paquda's *Chovot ha-Levavot* (*Duties of the Hearts*), Maimonides' *Guide of the Perplexed*, Yedaiah Bedersi's *Bechinat Olam*, Shem Tov ibn Shaprut's *Even Bochan* (*Discerning Stone*), and Joseph Albo's *Sefer ha-'Iqqarim* (*Book of Principles*).[134] These texts were popular because they perpetuated Sephardi religious rationalism, while arguing the superiority of Judaism over natural philosophy as well as over other religions purporting to be of divine origin. Not coincidentally, technical philosophical works by medieval Jewish authors (for example, the commentaries on Aristotle and Averroes) remained in manuscripts, thus reflecting a growing religious conservatism among the Sephardi exiles.

Printing, of course, compromised the old philosophical elitism of Maimonides. There was some hesitation about the publication of philosophical texts, not unlike the debate on the publication of kabbalistic books, especially the *Zohar*. In his introduction to *Sha'ar Adonai he-Chadash*, Solomon Almoli manifested apprehension about printing philosophical texts. Torn between a desire to raise the intellectual level of the many and a fear that philosophy would be harmful to those who are ill-equipped to study it, Almoli decided to print the introduction and to keep the body of the text only in manuscript. Thus the general public could read the chapter headings of philosophic wisdom, but only serious students would gain access to the core text (and hopefully pay handsomely for it).[135]

The students who wished to master philosophy continued to study the works of Aristotle with their medieval commentaries. For their needs, Moses Almosnino – the pre-eminent philosopher, communal leader of Salonican Jewry, and a close associate of Don Joseph Nasi and his circle of ex-conversos in Istanbul – composed new textbooks in philosophy.[136] Almosnino wrote a supercommentary on Averroes' long commentary to Aristotle's *Physics*, a commentary on the logical sections of al-Ghazālī's *Intentions of the Philosophers* (entitled *Migdal Oz*), the primary source for the study of Aristotelian logic,[137] and a commentary on Aristotle's *Ethics*.[138] Almosnino also encouraged Jewish students to master the logical treatises of ibn Bājja, Avicenna, and al-Ghazālī, Ptolemy's *Almagest*, and the commentaries of Averroes on

Aristotle's works in physics.[139] We can surmise that the works of these Muslim philosophers were readily available in the Ottoman Empire and that mastery of Arabic was easily gained in regions where it was a spoken language among Musta'arabi Jews and Muslims.

Almosnino derived his philosophic education from Aharon Afiya, a converso philosopher, astronomer, and physician who returned to Judaism in the Ottoman Empire. The two scholars collaborated on the translation of and commentary on two astronomical works – *Tractatus de Sphaera* by the thirteenth-century English astronomer John Sacrobosco and *Theoricae Novae Planetarum* by the fifteenth-century Austrian astronomer Georg Peurbach. It is very likely that the discovery of the Americas, to which Almosnino refers in the introduction to *Sha'ar ha-Shamayim* (*The Gate of Heaven*), inspired the two Jewish scholars to rethink and reaffirm the Aristotelian-Ptolemaic astronomy and cosmology.[140] That Almosnino still defended the validity of medieval cosmology, even though he was attuned to the new geographical sensibilities of his generation,[141] is yet another example of the transitional nature of this epoch: old models were perpetuated alongside the accumulation of new data that would eventually undermine the traditional outlook.

The conservative tendencies of Jewish philosophy in the Ottoman Empire were also evident in the reverence Sephardi philosophers in the Ottoman Empire accorded to Maimonides, the symbol of Jewish rationalism and *paideia*. They continued to treat Maimonides as the single most authoritative thinker, referring to him as the "master" and to his *Guide* as the "wondrous book" or "honorable book." They interpreted Maimonides in accordance with the trends charted by their predecessors in the fifteenth century, and like them felt the need to ascribe their own views to Maimonides, in order to give them greater weight. Not surprisingly, the allegiance to Maimonides rekindled yet another round of the Maimonidean controversy – the ideological context in which Jewish intellectuals have argued about the desired degree of interaction between Judaism and surrounding cultures.[142]

Philosophical hermeneutics

The consolidation of the philosophic legacy cannot obscure a major change in the orientation of Jewish philosophy in the Ottoman Empire. The most favored model of philosophical writing and the major vehicle for the dissemination of philosophy during the sixteenth century was not the digest or the commentary but philosophical hermeneutics and homily, both oral and written. In this traditional genre of Jewish hermeneutics Sephardi thinkers invested their creative powers, imaginatively weaving together philosophy with midrash and kabbalah. The philosophical exegesis of sacred texts reflected the theological posture that the exiles brought with them from Iberia, namely, that revealed religion perfects natural human reason and that the divinely revealed Torah contains all human wisdom because it is identical with the infinite wisdom of God.

The proliferation of philosophical hermeneutics captures the paradoxical status of philosophy. On the one hand, biblical commentaries and public preaching disseminated the knowledge of philosophy to a larger audience of lay intelligentsia. Merely to understand, let alone enjoy them, one had to be familiar with philosophical vocabulary and themes. The very inclusion of references to philosophical texts, authors, concepts, and theories made philosophy (albeit, a diluted version) a household commodity among the Jews of the Ottoman Empire. But on the other hand, more than ever before philosophy became the handmaiden of revealed theology. In the Ottoman Empire philosophy lost its autonomy and was employed primarily as a tool to penetrate the infinite meanings of divine revelation for the sake of attaining *devequt*, the mystical union of the soul with God.

This theological posture was manifested in the positive attitude of the philosophers toward kabbalah. Many Sephardi scholars who were trained in philosophy were sympathetic to Zoharic kabbalah even though they were not creative kabbalists. They accepted that Shimon bar Yochai wrote the *Zohar*. This led to the following chain of reasoning: midrash is an integral part of the revealed rabbinic tradition; the *Zohar* is rabbinic midrash; therefore, the *Zohar* is a sacred suprarational knowledge that is qualitatively superior to demonstrative philosophy.[143] Consequently, Ottoman philosophers attempted to harmonize the Maimonidean tradition with the *Zohar* by incorporating Platonic and Neoplatonic themes into the inherited Aristotelian tradition. This eclectic fusion of philosophy and kabbalah was not limited to Italy; it characterized Jewish thought throughout the sixteenth century.

The impact of kabbalah on philosophy was most evident in the philosophic conception of Torah. Following the kabbalists, the philosophers identified the Torah with God's essence (*atzmut*), and accordingly viewed the revealed Torah as the manifestation of a transcendent, supernal, perfect Torah that they then identified with the infinite wisdom of God.[144] With the kabbalists, philosophers such as Taitatzak, Aroyo, Aderbi, and Almosnino asserted that the Torah consists of the name of God.[145] Still loyal to an Aristotelian hierarchical cosmology, the philosophers located the supernal Torah "above time" ("*le-ma'alah me-ha-zeman*"), that is, in the realm of immaterial beings that are not governed by the laws of motion and change, whose measurement is time.[146] Identified with God's wisdom, the supernal Torah is the intelligible order of the universe (*defus ha-nimtza'ot*), the paradigm that God consulted when he brought the universe into existence. By cleaving to the revealed Torah (through Torah study and the performance of the mitzvot), the religious devotee could attain spiritual perfection, overcome the limits of human corporeality and particularity, and enjoy the spiritual rewards of the world to come, a mystical union with God.[147]

This conception of Torah had an important practical result that underscored the expansion of philosophical hermeneutics in the Ottoman Empire. Given that the wisdom of God is infinite and that the Torah is identified with it, then multiple, simultaneously correct readings of the same verse or rabbinic pericope are permissible, with no need for logical consistency. So even though the source material remained finite and limited, the philosopher-exegete could churn out new material with no bounds on its quantity or imaginativeness. He could thereby meet the demands of a market that featured increasing competition among suppliers and increasing rhetorical sophistication among consumers. It is no wonder that even a well-trained scholar such as Solomon ben Isaac Halevi was anxious about his ability to satisfy his audience's thirst for hermeneutic innovations[148] or that by the 1580s Abraham ibn Megash expressed exasperation with the wordiness of Jewish preachers in Salonica.[149]

An exegetical unveiling of the infinite meanings of Scripture required linguistic sophistication and rhetorical versatility. On the one hand, the explosion of philosophic hermeneutics was accomplished through a selective (and largely polemical) adaptation of the Renaissance cult of rhetoric discussed above. While Sephardi scholars in the Ottoman Empire could not boast direct contact with Renaissance humanists (as did some of their coreligionists in Italy), they could indirectly participate in the Renaissance recovery of the ancient civilization, because of their very presence on Greek soil. Though Sephardi scholars did not master the Greek language well enough to read ancient philosophy in the original, their domicile in the birthplace of philosophy concretized the ancient philosophical past.

Notwithstanding the interest of Jewish philosophers in classical philosophy and literature, their primary concern was not to recover the Greek and Roman past but to articulate a Jewish response to the challenge of the Renaissance. The Hebrew Bible anchored that response. Jewish scholars viewed the Bible not only as the record of the Jewish ancient past, but also as the repository of revealed, ancient Jewish wisdom. That wisdom, in turn, encompassed all human sciences, including those dear to the humanists – grammar, rhetoric, poetics, history, and moral philosophy. The very attempt to prove that the Bible included the aesthetic, moral, and intellectual achievements of the ancients necessitated a rereading of the Bible against a humanist background. As a result, King Solomon becomes the embodiment of the Renaissance *homo universalis* and the wisest of all ancient sages,[150] and the religious poetry of King David is favorably compared to Greek and Roman poetry.[151] So too the moral teachings of King David and King Solomon – recorded in Psalms, Proverbs, and Ecclesiastes, and interpreted by the rabbinic sages – surpass the moral wisdom of Aristotle, Cicero, and Seneca, and the other ancient moral philosophers.

A Jewish moral philosophy

The major contribution of Ottoman thinkers to the history of Jewish philosophy lies in moral philosophy. In their attempt to endow their traumatic experience with meaning, the exiles were obsessed with the pursuit of spiritual perfection whose ultimate reward is the salvation of the individual soul in the afterlife. For this purpose the Sephardi exiles instituted a very rigorous program of moral training which ritualized the study of the Psalms, Ecclesiastes, Proverbs, Song of Songs, and *Avot* by making it a part of synagogue service.[152] The habitual study of these texts was believed to cleanse one from the natural desire to sin, focus one's attention on the cultivation of the virtues, and orient one to the love of the supreme good, namely, God, who has revealed himself in the Torah.

The pursuit of perfection required a theoretical framework. It was provided by Aristotle's *Nicomachean Ethics* as interpreted by Maimonides and his followers during the fifteenth century. Maimonides was the first to fuse Aristotle's theory of happiness (*eudaimonia*) with the rabbinic ideal of human perfection, and his views dominated all subsequent reflections in moral philosophy.[153] Yet only during the fifteenth century, when the *Nicomachean Ethics* was translated anew from Latin into Hebrew,[154] did Jewish thinkers seriously confront the challenge of Aristotle's ethics to rabbinic Judaism. Like their Christian contemporaries, Jewish theologians (for example, Matitiahu ha-Yitzhari, Joseph ibn Shem Tov, Joel ibn Shu'aib, Joseph ben Abraham Chayyun, Isaac Abravanel, and Isaac Arama) addressed the Aristotelian challenge by distinguishing between true happiness in the afterlife (known only to the recipients of divine revelation) and imperfect happiness on earth (about which the *Ethics* speaks).[155] In their commentaries on *Avot*, Proverbs, Ecclesiastes, and Psalms, these scholars popularized Aristotelian terminology, while making very clear where Judaism differs. The interest of Jewish thinkers in the *Ethics* increased during the sixteenth century with the proliferation of new printed editions and commentaries of the *Ethics*, the rise of alternative ethical schemes (chiefly Platonic, Stoic, and Epicurean), and the critique of Aristotle by Protestant theologians.[156] Precisely because Jewish thinkers confined philosophy to earthly matters, they could freely consult Aristotle's *Ethics* (along with the works of other ancient moral philosophers), while insisting that his moral philosophy lacks salvific power.

Not surprisingly, the most important philosophical text to be produced in the Ottoman Empire was a new commentary on the *Nicomachean Ethics* by Moses Almosnino. Entitled *Penei Mosheh* (*The Countenance of Moses*), Moses Almosnino's commentary on the *Ethics* allows us a glimpse into the scope of philosophical knowledge among Jewish intellectuals in Salonica. In accord with the humanist climate of his generation, Almosnino attempted to uncover the original intent of Aristotle by paying close attention to philological problems. He compared the translations of ibn Shem Tov and ibn Ya'ish and tended to prefer the latter because it was based on Argyropolous' Latin translation of the Greek original. For philosophical purposes, Almosnino consulted scholastic commentaries on the *Ethics*, citing the commentaries of Eustratius of Nicaea, Albertus Magnus, Thomas Aquinas, Geraldus Odonis, John Buridan, Walter Burley, and Lefèvre d'Étaples.[157] On the basis of this array of philosophic sources, Almosnino formulated a moral philosophy that eclectically fused Aristotelian, Platonic, Stoic, and rabbinic ideals. Almosnino disseminated his moral philosophy to the public at large in his biblical commentaries, homilies, sermons, and a manual for good conduct.

Though Almosnino was by far the most outstanding philosopher of his generation, he was not alone. Many of his views were shared by contemporaries who had an intimate knowledge of the *Ethics* and who also reflected on the meaning of human happiness in their commentaries on the Torah, Proverbs, Ecclesiastes, Psalms, and *Avot*. By the same token, Almosnino's moral philosophy had many parallels in the writings of Italian thinkers such as Obadiah Sforno, Yechiel Nissim of Pisa, and Joseph ibn Yachya. The moral philosophy outlined below thus reflects a shared outlook among Jewish intellectuals during the sixteenth century. This discourse illustrates the shift from intellectualism to voluntarism, from philosophic universalism to religious particularism, from Aristotelianism to Neoplatonism and kabbalah.

The psychological premises

Aristotle's conception of happiness was rooted in a certain view of human nature, or more precisely, in a psychological theory that explained the relationship between the intellectual and the material aspects of the human species. Sixteenth-century Jewish philosophers in the Ottoman Empire fused Aristotelian and Platonic psychological theories. When they spoke about the human species at large, they employed Aristotelian theories: the soul is the form *of* the body, the organizational principle of the human organism.[158] But when these thinkers reflected on the soul-body nexus in the case of Jews, they adopted the Platonic two-substance theory: the soul is a form *in* a body. While this eclecticism is philosophically unsatisfactory, it reflects the realization that Platonic doctrines are more compatible with traditional Jewish beliefs in personal immortality and divine retribution than Aristotle's views.[159] By applying Platonic psychology exclusively to Jews, the Jewish philosophers grounded continued allegiance to Judaism: Jews alone can enjoy the bliss of immortality because their soul is by nature a pre-existent, eternal substance. The "platonization" of Aristotelian philosophy enabled Jewish philosophers to assimilate kabbalistic doctrines into their philosophic discourse.

In agreement with the kabbalists, thinkers such as Taitatzak, Aroyo, Almosnino, and Aderbi maintained that the souls of Jews are literally divine; they are a part of the divine essence, or a "particle of God" (*cheleq mimenu*).[160] Israel's soul "was carved from under the Throne of Glory" (*kise ha-kavod*) and was "infused" (*mushpa'at*) into the human body by God.[161] As a divine substance, the soul of Israel is pre-existent, holy, and eternal. Prior to its descent into the body, the soul resides in a special realm (*olam ha-neshamot*) to which it will return after the demise of the body, provided it has perfected itself on earth.[162] Precisely because the soul of Jews is a divine spark, Israel alone can be said to have been created in the image of God. Therefore, whenever Scripture uses the word "man" (*adam*), it refers exclusively to Israel, rather than to the human species at large.[163]

Whereas the soul of Israel is a pre-existent, holy substance, the human soul is but "an incorporeal substance with a propensity for intellection" (*etzem ruchani mukhan el ha-haskalah*).[164] The human soul is "generated" (*mithavah*) by the separate intelligences (*sekhalim nifradim*) and requires an association with the body in order to actualize its potential for intellection. By abstracting intelligibles from perception of sensible things, the human soul can perfect itself. It can acquire moral and intellectual virtues, culminating in philosophical wisdom, as Aristotle teaches. But precisely because Sephardi philosophers believed that the "way of investigation" (*derekh ha-chaqirah*) is inherently imperfect, they claimed that philosophic wisdom can at best constitute earthly happiness; it falls short of ensuring the survival of the individual soul that itself constitutes transcendent happiness.[165] Lacking a divine soul and benefit of the grace of divine revelation, gentiles are barred from the afterlife. By contrast, Jews who walk the "path of faith" have access to both true beliefs and just actions, necessary for earthly perfection as well as for the suprarational and supernatural knowledge necessary for transcendent happiness.[166]

Isaac Aroyo creatively employed Plato's theory of *anamnesis* (recollection) to explain the difference between Jews and non-Jews, as well as between the path of reason and the path of faith. The two paths differ from each other not only in terms of content and ultimate goal, but also in epistemological terms. Whereas the "path of reason" consists in abstracting intelligible universals from perception of sensible particulars, the "path of faith" consists of "recollection" (*hizakhrut*) of truths that the divine soul possessed prior to its descent into the body, precisely as Plato had taught.[167] For Moses Almosnino and Isaac Aroyo, for example, the absolute truth and certainty which attends the "path of faith" entail that a Jewish child who has just learned to read Torah and can understand its literal meaning is wiser and closer to the attainment of immortal life than a non-Jewish adult who has made a lifelong study of philosophy.[168]

Since the soul of Jews is literally a divine substance, Jews experience a very acute conflict between the (spiritual) soul and the (corporeal) body. The body naturally seeks sensuous pleasures (derived primarily from food and sex) and seduces the soul to pursue external goods such as wealth and honor. The sense appetite (*ha-koach ha-margish*) is the power of sensation and perception and the appetitive part (*ha-koach ha-mit'orer*) is the seat of all desires and passions that arise as a result of the information provided by the senses. Both powers are dependent upon the body, and as such are the source of the human tendency to sin. Therefore, the body and the body-related functions of the soul function as a "partition" or "dividing barrier" (*mechitzah*; *masakh mavdil*) between the spiritual soul and its divine origin, alienating the soul from God.[169] If left to satisfy its own desires, the body would hinder the return of the soul to the supernal world. The task of the soul, therefore, is to gain control over the body, "spiritualize" it through the acquisition of virtues, and direct it toward the attainment of the ultimate goal of life – the love of God.

Ideally, there should be "peace between the matter and the form" (*shelom ha-chomer ve-ha-tzurah*), as Moses Almosnino put it.[170] Such peace is indicative of mental health. Yet this inner balance is not the harmonious coexistence of two equal partners, but a hierarchical relationship in which the soul dominates the body. The virtuous man (*ha-shalem*), says Almosnino, "subdues and subordinates the corporeal part (*ha-cheleq ha-chomri*) to the rational part (*ha-cheleq ha-sikhli*). When one subdues (*yashpil*) the material [principle] and elevates (*yinase*) the formal [principle], one removes himself from all inequities (*pechituyot*) and ascends in the ladder of perfections."[171] A failure of the soul to control the body manifests a sickness that requires healing (*refuah*) no less than physical sickness.[172] As recipients of divine revelation, Israel already possesses the best and only true medication for the sickness of body and soul – the divine Torah.[173] Those who cling to the Torah through study and performance of its commandments attain the desired inner balance and experience happiness in this world and immortality in the next.

The intellect and the will

Whether or not one actually cleaves to the laws of the Torah depends on the perfection of the human will. Echoing the humanist emphasis on the dignity of man, Almosnino stated that human excellence (*ma'alat ha-adam*) is found in the freedom of the will to determine whether one will be as happy as God or as unhappy as beasts.[174] Almosnino, of course, did not forsake the philosophic premise that the ability to reason distinguishes humans from all other species. Drawing heavily on Buridan's commentary on the *Ethics*, Almosnino sought to define the relationship between the intellect and the will in human action.[175]

The human will, says Almosnino, is by nature rational and free. The will is rational because it acts in accordance with information provided by the intellect, but it is free because it can either will the known object, will against it, or not will it at all. The will is superior to the intellect not only because the known object cannot compel the will to act or not to act, but also because the will can freely choose to pursue evil. The human desire to sin is neither uncommon nor merely the result of a mistaken judgment by the intellect. Rather, it reflects the imperfection of the will, or the sickness of the soul. The freedom of the will is evident even within the act of cognition. The human intellect does not engage in cognitive activity at all times. It is the will that orders the intellect to cognize this or that object, and it is the will that can prevent the intellect from progressing from premises to conclusions through syllogistic reasoning. In short, the acquisition of knowledge is a voluntary activity rather than a compelled one. The intellect acts only as a "counsellor" (*yo'etz*) to the will, but the will is free either to accept or ignore the information provided by the intellect, exactly as a king can either accept or reject the advice of his ministers.[176]

The emphasis on the freedom of the will went together with a return to a personal conception of God, one that Maimonides and his followers attempted to explain away. Indeed, Jewish philosophers in the Ottoman Empire continued to talk about God as the first cause of the universe, the necessary being whose essence is identical with his existence. But instead of dwelling on the ontological "otherness" of God, sixteenth-century philosophers highlighted the goodness of the divine will. Thus Almosnino states that "the divine will is the good that is desired for its own sake and that is not subject to change."[177] As a supremely good, willing self, God possesses personal character traits (*middot*), traits which God revealed to Moses at Sinai. Whereas for Maimonides, the "ways" of God are the fixed laws of nature by which God governs the universe, for Almosnino they are the infinite, dynamic perfections of God that the kabbalists call *sefirot*.[178] By revealing his perfections to Israel, God enabled those who love him to imitate him and attain happiness in this world and immortal life in the next. Those who willingly cling to God's Torah and love God unconditionally – the love of the noble for its own sake – become like God and enjoy both earthly and transcendent happiness.[179]

As indicated above, the Sephardi philosophers endorsed the kabbalistic doctrine that the esoteric Torah is the essence of God, comprised of infinite permutations of the divine name. Since the soul of Israel is also "carved" from the essence of God, it follows that God, the supernal Torah, and the souls of Israel are one and the same, precisely as the *Zohar* teaches.[180] The study of the Torah and the acquisition of knowledge are two aspects of the same endeavor, two aspects of the process of self-knowledge. The pursuit of perfection consists of the two parallel moves of removing the veils of corporeality from the believer and from the Torah. In the human believer the veil of corporeality is the body; in the revealed Torah, the veils of corporeality are the figurative expressions that wrap the esoteric divine truth in metaphors, narratives, and laws. The attainment of union between the divine and the human requires that the believer spiritualize himself or herself through the study of Torah and performance of its laws. The better Jews understand themselves and purify themselves by doing what God demands, the deeper they can penetrate the infinite mysteries of the Torah which, paradoxically, conceal and reveal the divine self. Thus, the revealed Torah is not only the most perfect law, whose observance assures perfection of body and soul, as Maimonides had taught, but it is also a sacred medium through which the human self and the divine self can encounter each other. In Almosnino's words "the Torah is the intermediary" (*emtza'i*) through which Israel can communicate with God by doing God's will.[181] It is this convergence of psychology, ethics, moral training, rhetoric, and hermeneutics that accounts for the distinct character of Jewish philosophy in the sixteenth century.

The love of God and the primacy of praxis

Throughout the fifteenth and sixteenth centuries moral philosophers (both Jewish and non-Jewish) debated whether the ultimate end of human life consists in the contemplation of God or in the love of God.[182] For Jewish intellectuals, Maimonides was regarded as the exponent of the first view and Crescas of the second. In their moral philosophy Sephardi thinkers reconciled the views of Maimonides and Crescas by focusing on practical reason (*sekhel ma'asi*), the psychic capacity that links intellect and will, knowledge of God and love of God. Until the late fifteenth century Jewish philosophers paid little attention to practical reason. Maimonides adopted an Aristotelian ethic: the wise individual becomes virtuous by habitually practicing virtuous acts toward others, and, conversely, the virtue that is exhibited in the social sphere presupposes knowledge of the supreme good. Maimonides agreed that ethics is the cultivation of a virtuous character that functions intelligently by curbing desires and practicing virtuous acts toward others, governed by a worthwhile end, happiness. Yet Maimonides had little interest in Aristotelian practical wisdom (*phronesis*), precisely because he insisted that the moral life was only a means to the attainment of theoretical wisdom that culminates in the knowledge of God. Moreover, Maimonides' own analysis of halakhah (the praxis of Judaism) rendered the discussion of practical reason redundant. The one who lives by halakhah (as interpreted by Maimonides) attains perfection of body and soul.

By contrast, during the period under consideration Jewish philosophers in Spain, Italy, and the Ottoman Empire highlighted the importance of practical reason in the pursuit of human perfection precisely because their view of the moral life differed from Maimonides'. The cultivation of the moral virtues is not merely a means to a theoretical end – the contemplation of God – but the very core of religious life in this world. The moral life that is guided by practical reason is informed by the values of the religious tradition. By imitating the divine perfections as revealed in the Torah, the religious believer can acquire the moral virtues and attain the necessary "self-spiritualization" that leads to a mystical union with God in this world and eternal life after death. Moreover, the moral life of action is the arena where one manifests the perfection of the will and a total devotion to God. Hence, the highest virtue in this life is not the intellectual virtue of philosophical wisdom (*chokhmah*), but rather the virtue of prudence (*binah* or *tevunah*). Such an approach is closer to the Christian understanding of the moral life than to Maimonides'.

In the writings of Almosnino the virtue of practical wisdom, prudence, is placed at the center of moral discourse. Combining two schemes of human virtue – the Aristotelian and the Platonic-Stoic-Christian – Almosnino presented prudence as the most important of the four cardinal virtues, because it entails the acquisition of all moral virtues.[183] The prudent are the wise who are religiously perfect because they live by the divine commands of the Torah.[184] The prohibitions of the Torah (*mitzvot lo ta'aseh*) enable them to subdue the passions of the body and to avoid sin, while the positive commandments of the Torah (*mitzvot 'aseh*) facilitate the acquisition of moral virtues through habitual practice of good deeds. Those who acquire prudence know how to distinguish between real and apparent goods. They realize that bodily pleasures, wealth, honor, glory, and fame do not constitute true happiness, even though a certain modicum of external goods is necessary for the performance of good deeds toward others.[185]

The perfection of practical reason entails both knowledge of God and perfection of the will, that is, love of the good for its own sake. Since the supreme good is the divine will, the prudent one who knows "divine things" is also the one who unconditionally loves God. Maimonides was correct, says Almosnino, in teaching that the more one knows God the more one loves God. But Almosnino reinterprets the meaning of the love of God. Love is not the perfection of theoretical reason but rather the perfection of the will, the inner dimension of praxis (*ma'aseh penimi*).[186] The man of prudence is therefore the one who diligently performs the mitzvot, not because they are instrumental to (theoretical) knowledge of God, but because they have an intrinsic value as the expression of God's will. In short, the virtuous man (*ha-me'ushar*) who has acquired the virtue of prudence is the human ideal about whom King David sang in the Psalms, whom King Solomon praised in Ecclesiastes and Proverbs, and whom the *tannaim* portrayed in *Avot*. He is the one who is rewarded with happiness on earth and with immortal life in the world to come.

The man of practical wisdom who resists the passions of the body and cultivates the virtues is the true lover of God. In any virtue there is a love for honor and esteem that entails right reasoning and right choice and that connects it to the other virtues. With each "correct" choice the love of God is reinforced. Hence, it is through love of God that one attains the perfection of all the virtues in this world and for which one is rewarded with eternal life. The love of God is everlasting and inexhaustible because it is an unconditional love.[187] The love of God is indeed commensurate with one's knowledge of God, as Maimonides said. But, contra Maimonides, the love of God is understood not as the union of two perfect intellects but rather as the love between two perfect characters. Only a perfect will can discern the infinite variations of particulars and can unconditionally love God, the most perfect will, with the infinite "particulars of the beloved" (*pirtei ha-davar ha-ne'ehav*).[188] Therefore, those who unconditionally love the Torah, the manifestation of God's infinite love, love God and enjoy everlasting salvation.

God's self-revelation in the Torah assures the personal immortality of Israel. But the road toward salvation is painful, suffused with misery and anguish. Ottoman thinkers interpreted the temporary association of the soul with the body not only as a form of imprisonment (as Plato taught) but also as a dangerous exile.[189] Desperately the soul seeks to liberate itself from the body and regain its initial spirituality and holiness. No one understood the yearnings of the soul and its anguish better than King David, whose Psalms expressed the profound truths of the human condition in poetic language. Those who penetrate the meaning of the Psalms gain a deeper understanding of the ultimate end of human life and its attainment.[190] As noted above, the Sephardi exiles instituted the ritualized study of the Psalms, along with Proverbs, Ecclesiastes, and *Avot*, as part of a rigorous program for ethico-religious training. By virtue of that program, the soul of the believer could "polish and purify" (*le-zakekh u-le-mareq*) itself of the contaminating influences of the body,[191] preparing the believer to encounter God during the re-enactment of the Sinaitic theophany on the festival of Shavuot.

Pain and suffering were regarded by the philosophers as positive means for a cathartic self-purification. Adversity and pain cleanse the body of the natural inclination to enjoy physical pleasure and cleanse the soul of the polluting influences of the body.[192] Unlike the kabbalists of Safed,[193] however, philosophers such as Almosnino and Solomon ben Isaac Halevi were not ascetics. They did not recommend mortification of the body in order to gain a higher level of spirituality. As members of wealthy families, these philosophers enjoyed material comfort and endorsed Aristotle's claim that human perfection requires the presence of a modicum of external goods, as well as human association.[194] None the less, Almosnino repeatedly exhorted his audience to accept suffering (*be-sever panim yafot*), indeed with a positive attitude and even with joy (*simchah*).[195] This acceptance of suffering and pain reflects the impact of Stoic attitudes (derived primarily from the writings of Cicero and Seneca), at least as much as it reflects the influence of Bachya ibn Paquda's ascetic teachings or contemporary kabbalah. According to Almosnino, the acceptance of suffering indicates that the soul has already neutralized the passions of the body and has reached the desired control over the body, so that it is no longer perturbed by it.[196] Those who perfect themselves through clinging to the Torah can release their soul from its embodied condition while they are still alive. In other words, they can attain communion with God (*devequt*) in this world.[197]

The perfected soul that has removed from itself the vestiges of corporeality embraces God in a mystical union (*hitchabrut*; *hit'achadut*), in which the beloved, the lover, and the act of loving are one and the same, as Leone Ebreo taught in the *Dialoghi d'Amore*. Transcending time, nature, and evil, the separated soul of Israel becomes one with God and the supernal Torah, just as it was before the descent into the body. In an incomparable spiritual delight (ta'anug), the soul finds its final repose and completion in God, whose symbol is the ritual of the Sabbath.[198] Not unlike Abraham Abulafia, the Sephardi philosophers in Ottoman Turkey advocated a non-political, individualistic interpretation of the messianic ideal. The redemption (ge'ulah) to which the Jews aspire is not the ingathering of the exiles into the land of Israel, but the freedom (cherut) of the individual soul from its exile in the body.[199] This is the true freedom from the travails of time and from the determinism of natural causality (ma'arakhah).[200] Those Jews who devote themselves to God and his Torah experience the bliss of immortality, despite the continuation of political exile and the waiting for the messiah. Sephardi thinkers in the Ottoman Empire did not ignore the traditional hope for the coming of the messiah. They depoliticized it by "spiritualizing" its meaning. The messianic age is not an historical period of the ingathering of Jews into the land of Israel, but the total transformation of human existence from corporeality to spirituality. In the messianic age all Jews will see the "face of the shekhinah" during their lifetime because their body will no longer be a material entity.[201] By "psychologizing" the historical experience of exile, post-expulsion philosophers took the sting out of the bite of history and articulated a hopeful message: redemption is within the reach of each and every Jew in this life, despite the suffering of this world.

The bliss of personal immortality is reserved for perfect Jews. Surprisingly, the community of the perfect now includes both men and women. In a remarkable departure from the Maimonidean tradition, Ottoman philosophers stated that women can enter the world-to-come, even though their intellect is naturally imperfect.[202] Precisely because ultimate felicity does not depend on philosophical wisdom, but rather on faith, the perfection of the will, and the performance of mitzvot, women can enjoy the bliss of immortality.[203] Thus, although Ottoman thinkers continued to regard women as intellectually inferior to men, and their task was one of facilitating the perfection of their husbands, they asserted that as *religious* devotees women are equal to men.

In sum, the purpose of Jewish moral philosophy in the Ottoman Empire was not to solve meta-ethical problems but to guide the Jewish public toward the attainment of human perfection. In a society of immigrants ravaged by communal and interpersonal disputes and diverse interpretations of moral values, the philosophical commentaries filled an important civic function: they molded the inchoate Jewish masses into a genuine community seeking to attain spiritual perfection. Though their moral philosophy reflected a dialogue with non-Jewish systems of thought, its overall tenor was highly particularistic and ethnocentric. It was the dignity of Israel (rather than human dignity), the personal immortality of Jews (rather than the survival of non-Jews), and the divine perfection of Torah (rather than the claims of other religions) that concerned the Jewish philosophers in the Ottoman Empire. In the ancient Jewish sources the Jewish philosophers found the humanist emphasis on the dignity and worth of the human personality, the primacy of the human will, and the striving for personal immortality through the cultivation of moral virtues. As much as intense suffering made Iberian Jews receptive to the humanist emphasis on the human emotions and passions, so did the Bible provide them with evidence that the virtuous individual who lives by the Torah is able to transcend the vicissitudes of time and the determinism of nature.[204]

❧ CONCLUSIONS ❧

Eclecticism

On the eve of the modern era Jewish philosophy exhibited both conservative and innovative trends, characteristic of transitional epochs. On the one hand, Jewish philosophers preserved and consolidated the medieval Aristotelian tradition. They continued to study and comment on the authoritative texts of Aristotle and to view the world in the conceptual framework of medieval Aristotelianism. But, on the other hand, Jewish Aristotelianism was transformed from within. Averroes lost his status as the most authoritative commentator on Aristotle and, instead, Jewish philosophers consulted alternative readings of Aristotle by Hellenistic, Muslim, and Christian philosophers. While Aristotelianism became more variegated, the very need to reconcile the various readings of Aristotle perpetuated the loyalty to the Greek philosopher.

Though Aristotelianism remained the basis of philosophical training among Jews, Jewish philosophers did not ignore the emergence of alternative philosophies, particularly Platonism, Neoplatonism, and Stoicism, revived by the Renaissance humanists. In fact, the incorporation of Platonic themes into the framework of Jewish Aristotelianism characterizes Jewish philosophy in the period under consideration. Platonic philosophy was perceived to be more consonant with Jewish religious beliefs than was Aristotelianism, especially in regard to the vexed question of the origin of the universe and the nature of the human soul. But since Jewish philosophers did not renounce the Aristotelian tradition, the result was an eclectic fusion of philosophical positions, often at the expense of logical coherence.

The absorption of Renaissance Platonism into Jewish philosophy went together with the reception of humanism. Humanism deeply influenced the orientation of Jewish philosophy in the period under consideration. Under the influence of humanism, Jewish philosophers expanded the scope of philosophy to include the *studia humanitatis*, introduced new literary genres, paid close attention to textual and philological problems, and shifted the focus of philosophy from logic, physics, and metaphysics to rhetoric and moral philosophy. Like their non-Jewish counterparts, the Jewish humanists did not always possess rigorous philosophic training and keen analytic minds. Their contribution to the history of philosophy is found in the richness and subtlety of their rhetorical expression, especially in their philosophical exposition of religious texts.

Rhetoric enabled Jewish thinkers to reconcile the diverse, and often conflicting, intellectual currents. Eclecticism characterizes the intellectual universe of individual thinkers as well as the discipline as a whole. The particular manner in which a given thinker harmonized diverse philosophical positions varied greatly in accordance with his time, place, and intellectual orientation. The eclectic nature of Jewish philosophy of the period should be described not as shallow but rather as indicative of the transitional nature of this era, when old paradigms were not yet replaced by new ones. By virtue of its flexibility, rhetoric made this transition a gradual and smooth process.

Universalism and particularism

By definition, Jewish philosophy combines universalist and particularist tendencies. Qua philosophy, the discipline claims to possess universally true knowledge which transcends time, place, and the ethnic identity of its producers. Yet what makes Jewish philosophy Jewish is its subject matter, that is, the beliefs, canonic texts, and practices of the Jewish religious tradition. On the eve of modernity the tension between the universalist and particularist aspects of Jewish philosophy became more pronounced. On the one hand, Jewish philosophers were engaged in an intimate conversation with contemporary scholars and were better informed of current intellectual debates than ever before. This conversation was enhanced by the liminal status of the converso community, some of whose scholars returned to the Jewish fold, thus enhancing Jewish familiarity with the dominant philosophical currents. But, on the other hand, the deterioration of Jewish political status and the strong gentile missionizing pressure required the Jewish philosopher to defend Judaism against its detractors. Jewish philosophy now became a tool in the justification of Jewish religious beliefs.

The philosophic defense of Judaism developed in two directions.

First, the philosopher attempted to prove that Judaism is rationally superior to (pagan) philosophy, because it is grounded in a divine revelation. As a revealed religion, Judaism consists of truths which exceed the ken of human reason. Therefore, only a belief in Judaism can assure the attainment of the ultimate end of human life – the immortality of the soul. Concomitantly, the Jewish philosopher attempted to show that Judaism is superior to other religions purporting to be of divine origin, because Judaism is a *rational* religion. Employing his extensive philosophical knowledge, the Jewish philosopher proceeded to analyze the fundamental doctrines of Judaism in order to show that they do not contradict human reason.

The struggle to rebut Christian polemics led Jewish theologians to systematize Judaism as a set of dogmas, those foundational beliefs whose affirmation constitutes membership in the community of Jewish believers and assures individual salvation. Since the dogmas of Judaism are divinely revealed, they are necessarily true and could not contradict the truths of philosophy. The dogmas constituted the doctrinal infrastructure of the Jewish textual tradition, whose interpretation of sacred texts (both exegetical and homiletical) became the dominant preoccupation of Jewish philosophers, often at the expense of commenting on authoritative philosophical texts.

This hermeneutical endeavor had both theoretical and practical ramifications. On the level of theory, the sacred text was presumed to contain not only truths about the universe and its relationship to the creator, but also the revelation of the essence of God. And since humans are created in the image of God, the sacred text mirrored the recesses of the human personality. Through the act of interpretation the student of Torah understood not only the structure of the created universe, but also encountered God, who was, paradoxically, concealed and revealed in the text. Interpretation of texts was therefore not a mere intellectual exercise in which certain philosophic propositions were gleaned from the narratives and laws of the Torah, but a religious ritual of the highest order. It was an act that combined both theoria and praxis. Through the study of Torah (and by extension the observance of Jewish law as a whole) the religious philosopher purified body and soul, created the just social order, and became the good person whose perfected soul encountered the ultimate good – God. Thus, in the period under consideration the Jewish philosophers highlighted the intrinsic value of the *mitzvot*, viewing them as the exclusive path to salvation, both individual and collective.

Philosophy and kabbalah

By the end of the fifteenth century and even more so throughout the sixteenth century, philosophy incorporated kabbalistic themes and motifs. Notwithstanding the opposition of some Jewish Aristotelians to kabbalah, most thinkers trained in philosophy accepted kabbalah as an authentic interpretation of Judaism and sought to harmonize its mythical, theurgic, and mystical outlook with philosophy. Renaissance Platonism provided the theoretical framework for the harmonization of kabbalah and philosophy, but the particular manner in which these two modes of thought were harmonized varied considerably. Some thinkers viewed kabbalah as a body of metaphysical knowledge of a higher epistemic value because kabbalah was knowledge revealed by God. For others, kabbalah was a speculative knowledge whose mastery had practical results. The one who knows the mysteries of kabbalah could tap into the supernal world and consequently activate the occult forces of the created universe. And still others regarded kabbalah primarily as an esoteric interpretative tradition that unlocked the mysteries of the sacred text. By virtue of kabbalistic interpretation of the sacred text, the devotee could attain a mystical union with God.

Regardless of how a given scholar approached kabbalah, the end result was the same. If Maimonides "demythologized" Judaism, to use Seeskin's apt phrase,[205] early modern thinkers "remythologized" Jewish philosophy. By this I mean that they personalized the conception of God; endorsed the dualism of body and soul; paid greater attention to the non-cognitive dimensions of the human personality; highlighted the importance of the will in human conduct; recognized the religious value of moral action through the performance of *mitzvot*; diminished the importance of theoretical wisdom and focused instead on practical reason; and posited the love of God as the ultimate end of life, envisioning ultimate felicity as a mystical union with God.

Those scholars who studied philosophy also paved the way for the emergence of kabbalah as the dominant interpretation of Judaism. By the seventeenth century, Maimonideanism (especially in its radical, intellectualist, Averroist mode of the fourteenth century) became irrelevant to Jews, either because its Aristotelian premises were invalidated by new scientific discoveries or because it no longer addressed the existential needs of perplexed Jews. In a time when allegiance to Judaism was anything but rational, kabbalah justified the commitment to Judaism on the level of mythos rather than logos. Kabbalah reasserted the myth of rabbinic Judaism as an everlasting love affair between two persons – Israel and God. In its sacramental conception of the *mitzvot*, kabbalah (be it Zoharic, Cordoverianic, or Lurianic) empowered Jews to view themselves as co-partners with God, thereby attenuating the tension between the incipient anthropocentrism of modernity and the theocentrism of rabbinic theism.

With the renewed affirmation of the myth of Judaism, as elaborated by kabbalah, medieval philosophy reached its inevitable demise. The synthesis of religion and philosophy – the hallmark of the medieval outlook – was dissolved by the end of the sixteenth century. In the seventeenth century kabbalah became the dominant explanatory paradigm for the universe and the role of the Jews in it. Medieval philosophy did not disappear, but it became only one voice in the interpretation of God's infinite, multi-vocal, multi-valent, symbolic, verbal self-revelation. During the seventeenth and eighteenth centuries Jewish thinkers who cultivated philosophy can be divided into two groups. First, those who still affirmed the primacy of the human intellect in the discovery of truth – most notably Spinoza – had to challenge the validity of the Jewish myth. For them, the myth was not a divinely revealed truth but the construct of human imagination, which came into existence at a certain time and place to serve specific political purposes. Inevitably, Spinoza and like-minded thinkers were excommunicated from the Jewish community on a charge of heresy. And, second, those scholars (mostly physicians) who were faithful to the myth of Judaism, but refused to renounce philosophy, had to separate philosophy and religion. Natural philosophy, which in the Middle Ages was intrinsically connected to metaphysics and theology, was now absorbed into the natural, experimental sciences. While science could explain the processes of the created universe, it had little to say about the religious destiny of Israel. As religion was deemed superior to and impenetrable by scientific analysis, philosophy became increasingly irrelevant to the Jewish religion. How to bridge the gap between science and religion in order to salvage the enterprise of Jewish philosophy would become the primary concern of modern Jewish philosophers.

❧ NOTES ❧

1 I would like to thank J. Samuel Preus, Robert Bonfil, and Warren Harvey for reading an earlier draft of this chapter and making many helpful comments. The remaining mistakes are mine.

2 The fifteenth and sixteenth centuries constituted a "transition period" not only in the history of Jewish philosophy, but also in European history. An array of political, social, religious, and educational changes took place at that time, resulting in the gradual breakdown of medieval institutions and outlook and the emergence of new social arrangements and modes of thought, paving the way for the modern epoch. For a general summary of the period in European history, see Ferguson 1962.

3 In this chapter the term "Jewish philosophy" denotes an intellectual discipline

that consists of systematic reflections about Judaism by means of philosophical categories and in light of philosophical questions. Written exclusively by Jews but not only for Jews, Jewish philosophy is a self-conscious program expounding the religious beliefs, ethical ideals, and legal norms of rabbinic Judaism. The main concern of Jewish philosophy has been to articulate the desired relationship between the Jewish religious tradition (believed to be grounded in an historical divine revelation) and the secular, universal truth-claims of philosophy (grounded in the natural rational capacity of humans). Precisely because Jewish philosophy was the medium in which Judaism conversed with the surrounding civilizations, the nature of these philosophic reflections would evolve as the partners to the conversation changed over time.

4 Philosophy was cultivated not only in these three regions but also in North Africa, Yemen, Crete, and to a lesser extent in central Europe. However, this chapter focuses on Iberia, Italy, and the Ottoman Empire because they were the most creative philosophically and because their evolution best accounts for the transformation of Jewish philosophy in the period under consideration.

The order of the presentation (Iberia, Italy, Ottoman Empire) undoubtedly gives this chapter a Sephardi slant. By this I do not mean to suggest that Jewish history should be studied from the vantage point of Sephardi Jewry, but that Sephardi Jewry dominated the history of Jewish philosophy during the Middle Ages and the early modern period. The attempt to create a smooth narrative may also give the misleading impression of uninterrupted continuity over two centuries. Indeed, each of the three centers had a distinct character, reflecting specific historical circumstances. None the less, the centers should not be studied in isolation. Migration of scholars, family and business ties, and the invention of the printing press all contributed to the diffusion of ideas and shared intellectual concerns among the Jewish philosophers in Iberia, Italy, and the Ottoman Empire.

5 By definition, Jewish philosophy cannot be understood apart from the philosophical climate of a given generation. Therefore, this chapter has a comparative dimension even though it does not attempt to provide a systematic comparison between Jewish philosophy and European philosophy in the period under consideration. Rather, this essay seeks to understand Jewish philosophy on its own terms, as an expression of problematics unique to the Jewish experience itself.

6 Though a bit outdated, Baer 1978, 2: 95–174 is still the best general survey of these traumatic events. I use 1391 as a springboard for the story of Jewish philosophy, presented here in order to signal the emergence of the converso population that will have an important impact on the history of Jewish of philosophy in the following two centuries.

7 See Shlomo Al'ami, *Iggeret Musar* 1945. For a discussion of Al'ami's opposition, see Netanyahu 1966, pp. 103–6.

8 On Shem Tov ibn Shem Tov, the author of *Sefer ha-Emunot* (*The Book of Beliefs*), and his critique of philosophy, see Gottlieb 1976, pp. 347–56.

9 The status of kabbalah in fifteenth-century Spain is a complex subject that requires further research. On the one hand, as *Ma'aseh Efod* by Profiat Duran testifies, already by the beginning of the fifteenth century the distinction between talmudists, philosophers, and kabbalists was well in place. In certain

yeshivot in Castile, kabbalah was even integrated into halakhic training and studied as an exoteric subject; see Hacker 1983. But, on the other hand, philosophy remained the dominant and most creative mode of thought among Sephardi intellectuals throughout the fifteenth century. Most Jewish intellectuals in Spain were not creative kabbalists even if they regarded kabbalah as an authentic interpretation of Judaism and studied *Sefer ha-Zohar* as rabbinic midrash.

10 Crescas helped the immigration of Jews from Aragon and Castile and their resettlement in Comtat Venaissin, the Kingdom of Navarre, and perhaps even the land of Israel. On Crescas' diplomatic activities see Baer 1978, 2: 120–30 and Assis 1990.

11 On the impact of Halevi on Crescas, see Pines 1977, p. 213. On the role that kabbalah played in Crescas' enterprise, see Harvey 1982–3.

12 For an analysis of Crescas' conception of the universe, see Davidson 1987, pp. 365–6 and Sirat 1985, pp. 359–70. Crescas' critique of Aristotelian physics played some role in the dissolution of Aristotelianism in the West, when it was employed by Giordano Bruno and Gian Francesco Pico della Mirandola.

13 For a detailed analysis of Crescas' critique of Maimonides' political philosphy and its epistemological premises, see Harvey 1973, pp. 23–63 and idem 1977.

14 Crescas' critique of the doctrine of the acquired intellect must not be seen in isolation. Similar attacks against Averroes' and ibn Bājja's epistemology were articulated by Christian scholastics, most importantly by Aquinas. Though Crescas and Aquinas vary greatly in regard to the validity of Aristotelianism, they both agree that conjunction of the human intellect with the separate intelligence does not comprise ultimate human felicity.

15 *Or ha-Shem* 2.6.1.

16 *Or ha-Shem* 2.6.1; 3.2.1.

17 The text survived only in the Hebrew translation of Joseph ibn Shem Tov who entitled it *Sefer Bittul 'Iqqarei ha-Notzrim (Refutation of Christian Principles)*. However, neither the original title of the work nor its original language can be ascertained today. While it can be established that Crescas wrote the text in one of the local dialects of Aragon, it is impossible to determine whether it was Aragonese or Catalan; see Crescas 1990a, pp. 13–14 and idem 1992, pp. 2–4.

18 A full analysis of these themes goes beyond the scope of this chapter. On the reluctance of fifteenth-century Jewish thinkers to accept Crescas' views, see Feldman 1984, pp. 37–53 and Ravitzky 1988, p. 15.

19 On Isaac ibn Shem Tov's opposition to Crescas' critique of Aristotle, see Wolfson 1977, p. 490 and Rosenberg 1973, 1: 46.

20 Ravitzky 1988, p. 13.

21 See the excerpt in Hacker 1983, p. 55.

22 On the use of Aristotelian logic in the Sephardic method of *pilpul*, see Boyarin 1989, pp. 47–68. For a discussion of the curriculum and ambience of Sephardi yeshivot, see Gross 1987 and Hacker 1983, pp. 47–59.

23 The demonization of philosophy in *Sefer ha-Meshiv* was rooted in its highly mythical and theurgic kabbalah; see Idel 1983 and 1992c, pp. 129–30.

24 To date, the most comprehensive source of information on the Hebrew translations of Aristotle and Averroes is still Steinschneider 1893.

25 For information about the commentaries and supercommentaries of these authors, consult the following studies: Regev 1983; Davidson 1964; Lazaroff 1981; Nuriel 1975; Wolfson 1977.

26 Isaac ibn Shem Tov's commentary, entitled *Lechem ha-Panim* (MS London 912), is a typical example of this genre. For a summary of its main themes, see Schwartzmann 1991. For an overview of the genre of commentaries on the *Guide*, see Ravitzky 1986.

27 A typical example of such defense was offered by Abraham Shalom in his *Neveh Shalom* (*The Abode of Peace*). See Davidson 1964, pp. 9–11; Harvey 1973, pp. 180–232; and Tirosh-Rothschild 1990a.

28 This judgment was expressed already by Guttmann in 1933 (1964, pp. 256–7) and reiterated recently by Idel 1992c, p. 124.

29 The access of Jewish scholars to scholastic philosophy and theology must not be taken to be limited to the written medium. Oral communication was no less an important way of disseminating Christian theology among Jews, since they were subject to forced preaching and public debates. For an overview of this issue, see Lasker (forthcoming).

30 Isaac Arama, *Chazut Qashah* 1849, p. 8, excerpted in Heller Wilensky 1956, p. 69.

31 Steinschneider 1893, pp. 469–89.

32 Rosenberg 1973, 1: 37.

33 Joseph ibn Shem Tov, *Kevod Elohim* (*The Glory of God*) 1556, p. 3a. In the introduction to his *Commentary on Aristotle's Ethics*, MS Oxford Bodleian 1432 (= Michael 404), fol. 1b, ibn Shem Tov states that he often engaged in public discussions with "the greatest of Christian scholars" (*gedolei chakhmei ha-notzrim*) in the presence of "kings and counsellors" (*melakhim ve-yo'atzei aretz*), and that these scholars helped him to understand "the principles of this book and its mysteries" (*shorashav ve-ta'alumotav*). On the status of Aristotle's *Nicomachean Ethics* in Jewish philosophy of the fifteenth and sixteenth centuries, see below, note 154.

34 For the scholastic authors cited by Abraham Bibago, consult Nuriel 1975, pp. 3–36, and Lazaroff 1981, pp. 1–7.

35 See, for example, Abravanel's praise for Aquinas in *Mif'alot Elohim* (*The Deeds of God*) 6.2 and his reference to Christian arguments in favor of the doctrine of creation ex nihilo in 9.7. On the indebtedness of Abravanel to Aquinas, consult Netanyahu 1953, p. 295.

36 Abraham Bibago's *Derekh Emunah* (*The Path of Faith*) offered the most systematic analysis of the relationship between these two ways of approaching truth. His views were shared by Isaac Arama, Abraham Shalom, Isaac ibn Shem Tov, Joseph ibn Shem Tov, Joseph ben Abraham Chayyun, and Isaac Abravanel in the last decade of the fifteenth century. For a general discussion of this topic in fifteenth-century thought, consult Regev 1986b. For individual monographs, see Heller Wilensky 1956, pp. 58–77; Davidson 1964, pp. 92–101; Gross 1993, pp. 79–103; Lazaroff 1981, pp. 33–40.

37 The conception of prophecy as divine grace was articulated by Joseph Albo in his *Sefer ha-'Iqqarim* (*Book of Principles*); see Schweid 1976. Albo's views were adopted by other Sephardi thinkers, for example, Abraham Shalom's *Neveh Shalom*, pp. 33a; 36b.

38 Averroes' claims concerning the conjunction of the human intellect with the active intellect were used in the fifteenth century to prove the possibility of a prophetic knowledge which is qualitatively superior to natural knowledge. This trend is exemplified in Joseph ibn Shem Tov's long and short commentaries on Averroes' *Epistle on the Possibility of Conjunction* written in the 1450s. For a critical edition of ibn Shem Tov's short commentary, see ibn Shem Tov 1982; for an analysis of ibn Shem Tov's conception of prophecy, see Regev 1983, pp. 139–78.

39 The view that God is the ideal order of reality was held both by Averroes and by Aquinas and has parallels in kabbalistic thought, as will be discussed below. During the fifteenth and sixteenth centuries it was adopted by many Jewish philosophers, among them Abraham Shalom, Abraham Bibago, Joseph Taitatzak, Isaac Aderbi, David ben Judah Messer Leon, and Solomon Alqabetz. For a discussion of this motif, see Sack 1988.

40 Rosenberg 1984, p. 284.

41 Regev 1987, 1990a; Heller Wilensky 1956, pp. 121–36.

42 On Abravanel's use of astrology, see Regev 1987. On the status of astrology in medieval Jewish philosophy, see Barkai 1987.

43 For a reconstruction of Abravanel's philosophy of history as moments of human choice of God, see Regev 1990a.

44 Baer 1937 and Strauss 1937 noted the indebtedness of Abravanel to humanism and the peculiar blending of Augustinian and Stoic elements in his philosophy of history. The precise interplay of these intellectual trends in Abravanel's works still awaits a systematic analysis. The influence of humanism on Jewish scholars in pre-expulsion Spain also requires further attention. Humanism began to make headway into Spain after the House of Aragon conquered the Kingdom of Naples in the 1440s. In the 1480s, under the active patronage of Queen Isabella, Italian humanist scholars settled in Spain and Spanish scholars went to study in Italy. Since famous conversos (for example, Pablo de Santa Maria) played a central role in the dissemination of humanism in Spain, it is unlikely that Jewish scholars were oblivious to these cultural developments. On Pablo de Santa Maria's translations into Castilian of Leonardo Bruni's *De Militia* and several works by Seneca, see Esteban 1992, pp. 338–9.

45 On Abravanel's messianism, see Netanyahu 1953, pp. 195–247.

46 By "radical fideism" I mean an exclusive reliance upon faith, which disparages and denigrates reason. Such a position, which began to emerge in the late Middle Ages among the followers of William of Ockham and would flourish in Protestantism, was unacceptable to Jewish philosophers because it would undermine the claim that the Torah is a philosophic text whose esoteric meaning conforms to the structure of the universe.

47 For a survey of medieval Jewish philosophical refutations of Christianity, see Lasker 1977. For a specific focus on late-fifteenth-century philosophical polemics, see Lasker 1992.

48 For a systematic analysis of Jewish dogmatism, see Kellner 1986, esp. pp. 83–217. The following two paragraphs briefly summarize Kellner's detailed analysis.

49 On Abravanel's conception of Jewish dogmas, consult Kellner 1986, pp. 179–95

and his introduction to the critical edition and English translation of Abravanel's *Rosh Amanah* (1982).

50 On the demographic, social, and economic conditions of Italian Jewry during the fourteenth and fifteenth centuries, see Bonfil 1994, pp. 19–59.

51 For a reconstruction of Jewish education in Renaissance Italy, particularly among the upper classes, see Ruderman 1982; Tirosh-Rothschild 1991, pp. 16–19, 34–39; Bonfil 1994, pp. 125–44.

52 This point is elaborated with great sophistication by Bonfil 1994, esp. pp. 114–25. I have illustrated this line of argument in my study of David ben Judah Messer Leon (1991).

53 For an overview of the Aristotelian tradition in Italy, see Kristeller 1979, pp. 32–49.

54 For an overview of Jewish philosophy in Italy in the thirteenth century, consult Sirat 1985, pp. 266–72 and the bibliography cited there.

55 Sermoneta 1971–8, 1980, 1984 has shown conclusively that there was a distinct "Thomistic trend" among the Jewish philosophers of Italy in the late Middle Ages. That is to say, a group of Jewish scholars translated Aquinas' philosophical texts into Hebrew and adapted the logic of Aquinas' position to their own interpretation of Scripture and to their interpretation of Maimonides. Sermoneta's position has been further substantiated by Shechterman 1988 and Rigo 1989, 1993a, and 1993b. I thank W. Harvey for directing me to Rigo's work.

56 Interestingly, Hebrew was the first foreign language into which Dante was translated; see Pagis 1976, p. 258.

57 On the admission of Jews to the medical faculties in Italian universities, see Carpi 1989, pp. 96–130, and Ruderman 1992.

58 So far this philosophic text has received but cursory attention by historians of Italian Jewry – Roth 1964, p. 103, and Bonfil 1994, p. 155 – and by scholars of Jewish literature interested in the literary style of Italian Jewish poetry – Pagis 1976, pp. 258, 329–32.

59 On this poetic topos, see Pagis 1993, pp. 277–85.

60 See Cassuto 1967, p. 196; Melamed 1985b, esp. pp. 71–86, and 1986, pp. 56–7.

61 On the indebtedness of Albo to Aquinas' fourfold analysis of law and the differences between the Jewish and the Christian philosophers, see Lerner 1964 and Melamed 1985b and 1986.

62 For a succinct survey of Aristotelianism in Italian universities during the Renaissance and Baroque periods, see Schmitt 1983 and Kristeller 1990.

63 On the life and philosophical activity of this outstanding Jewish scholar, consult Tirosh-Rothschild 1991, pp. 24–33 and the bibliography cited there.

64 Rosenberg 1973, 1: 46–9.

65 Messer Leon's commentary to Maimonides, entitled *Moreh Tzedeq*, is no longer extant and his commentary on *Bechinat Olam*, which is extant in several manuscripts, still awaits a systematic analysis.

66 On Farissol's activities in disseminating Judah Messer Leon's logical works, see Ruderman 1981, pp. 17–18, 112–14.

67 For a discussion of del Medigo's life, works, contacts with Christian scholars, and philosophic outlook, see Geffen 1970 and 1973–4; and cf. del Medigo 1984, pp. 11–61; Ruderman 1988b, pp. 385–8.

68 See Geffen 1973–4, p. 72.

69 On del Medigo's translations of Averroes' epistemological treatises, see Geffen 1970, pp. 12–13. On the disputes concerning the immortality of the soul in Italian universities from the 1490s to the 1530s, see Pine 1986, pp. 124–234 and Schmitt (ed.) 1988, pp. 455–535.

70 The status of philosophy among Ashkenazi Jews during the late Middle Ages has been recently re-evaluated. For a summary of the discussion and a cogent argument that Maimonideanism was more widespread than previously thought, see Davis 1993.

71 Crete was an important center of Jewish philosophical activity during the late Middle Ages, especially after the persecution of 1391. With the fall of Constantinople in 1453, Byzantine scholars used Crete as a stop-off point on the way to Italy, making it a center for the study of philosophy. This survey excludes the discussion of Jewish philosophy in Crete and in Byzantium because of the relative paucity of modern research. For now consult Rosenberg 1973, passim, and Bowman 1985, pp. 129–70.

72 On Alemanno's association with Pico and a list of his works, see Lesley 1976, pp. 4–11. Alemanno's fusion of philosophy and kabbalah and its significance for the history of Jewish philosophy in Italy are discussed below.

73 Mithridates' translations, through which Pico became acquainted with kabbalah, were in fact a creative fabrication of Christian kabbalah by a Jewish author; see Wirszubski 1989, pp. 69–118.

74 This point is well taken in Bland 1991.

75 See Lasker 1977, pp. 36–7 and his index.

76 A detailed discussion of these translations is provided by Cranz 1976.

77 Bonfil was the first to present "eclecticism" as an expression of a new Jewish Weltanschauung in the fifteenth and sixteenth centuries; see Bonfil 1979, pp. 179–206; 1990, pp. 280–98.

78 See Bonfil 1976. The gist of Bonfil's analysis applies as well to *Minchat Qena'ot* by Yechiel ben Nissim da Pisa and to *Torah Or* by Joseph ibn Yachya. As we shall see below, the views of these authors were also shared by Sephardi thinkers in Salonica at that time.

79 These policies are discussed in detail in Stow 1977; Bonfil 1994, pp. 65–77.

80 See Ruderman 1992, p. 539.

81 Halevi's *Kuzari* was highly popular during the fifteenth and sixteenth centuries among Jewish intellectuals in Iberia and Italy because of its attempt to disengage philosophy and religion, on the one hand, and its unabashed assertion of Jewish particularism and spiritual superiority, on the other. The genre of philosophical commentaries on the *Kuzari* still awaits systematic analysis.

82 The degree to which humanism penetrated Judeo-Italian culture in general and Jewish philosophy in particular is a matter of heated dispute. The dispute arises from a lack of consensus on the nature of the Renaissance in general and humanism in particular, as well as on the status of the Jewish minority in Italian society. For an overview of this controversy and the assumptions of the various participants, see Tirosh-Rothschild 1990b. The following reconstruction presents my own view; it may not be shared by other scholars.

83 This distinction follows Yates 1964, pp. 159–66.

84 See Bouwsma 1976, p. 424.

85 Trinkaus 1983, p. 29.

86 This theme is analyzed in Kristeller 1979, pp. 196–210.

87 For an analysis of this text, its classical and medieval rhetorical sources, and its polemical import, see Rabinowitz 1983, pp. xv-lxx; Bonfil 1981 and 1992b.

88 See Melamed 1978.

89 These literary genres did not constitute "philosophy" in the strict sense of the term. Yet they must be mentioned in this context because they either illustrated general philosophical principles (as was the case with biographies) or were based on theoretical assumptions of other branches of philosophy (as was the case with treatises on music); see Lesley 1982 and Tirosh-Rothschild 1990b. For a different view that minimizes the significance between these literary interests and highlights the gulf between humanist and Jewish outlooks, consult Bonfil 1992d.

90 Hebrew prose literature (either in the original or in translation) was a source of entertainment and a popular guide to life for the lay intelligentsia in Italy. The most popular works were Judah al-Charīzī's *Takhkemoni*, Isaac ibn Sahula's *Meshal ha-Qadmoni*, Berachia ha-Naqdan's *Mishlei Shu'alim*, and Immanuel of Rome's *Machbarot Immanuel*. For an excellent analysis of Jewish literary interests in Renaissance Italy, based on the contents of the libraries of Mantovan Jews, see Baruchson 1993.

91 On the popularity in Europe of the *Celestina*, the biography of Joseph Tzarfati, and the poem that commenced the now lost Hebrew translation of that work, see Carpenter forthcoming.

92 For contrasting viewpoints on the *Dialoghi* and pertinent biographical information on Leone Ebreo, compare Lesley 1992 and Scrivano 1986. I join those scholars who regard 1502 as the year of composition, Hebrew as the original language, and Jewish intellectuals (native Italian and Sephardi émigrés) as the intended audience of this text. Therefore, I do not share Sirat's view that Ebreo's *Dialoghi* is "not a work of Jewish philosophy, but a book of philosophy written by a Jew" (Sirat 1985, p. 408), a view also shared by Melamed 1985a.

93 See note 106 below.

94 On the various philosophic, kabbalistic, and literary sources of the *Dialoghi*, see Pines 1983; Idel 1985; and Parker 1985.

95 Lesley 1992, p. 181.

96 On Ebreo's familiarity with kabbalah, see Idel 1985.

97 Ebreo's philosophy has had a peculiar history in scholarly literature. Until quite recently the *Dialoghi* was of interest primarily to Renaissance scholars and to historians of Spanish and Italian literatures. Historians of Jewish philosophy, however, paid relatively little attention to Ebreo precisely because he was a Platonic philosopher who diverged from the well-known parameters of medieval Jewish Aristotelianism. To my knowledge, Z. Levy (1985) is the first to have situated Ebreo's philosophy of love in the broader context of the history of aesthetics, a branch of philosophy to which Jews have contributed very little. However, to understand Ebreo's aesthetics fully, more attention should be given to the interplay between kabbalistic theosophy and Platonic philosophy.

98 For an analysis of the motif of androgyneity in the *Dialoghi*, see Yavneh 1991.

99 This is how Levy (1985, p. 32) understands Judah Abravanel's preference for allegory.

100 The best summary of the interplay between the development of the plot and the philosophical content of the discourse is provided by Perry 1980.

101 The portrayal of the female protagonist, Sophia, as an astute student of philosophy, who often advances the discourse by challenging her male counterpart, should be seen in the broader context of the contemporary literary debate on the merits of women, a debate that preoccupied Italian literati, both Jews and non-Jews. On that debate, see Pagis 1993, pp. 124–65.

102 See Lesley 1992, p. 185.

103 A comprehensive treatment of Jewish thought in sixteenth-century Italy is still a desideratum, notwithstanding the important contributions of Barzilay 1967; Bonfil 1979, 1992a; Idel 1992a, 1992d; and Ruderman 1988b.

104 See Harari 1988 and Dorman 1985.

105 Dorman 1983, pp. 156–71.

106 The dissemination of kabbalah in Italy is analyzed in Idel 1992a, 1992b, and 1992c and in Bonfil 1979, pp. 179–90, and 1990, pp. 280–98.

107 The importance of this fact is elaborated in great detail in Idel forthcoming.

108 Alemanno's idiosyncratic philosophy, in which Aristotelianism, Neoplatonism, Hermeticism, and kabbalah are ingeniously fused, still awaits a systematic monograph; for now consult the pioneering work of Idel 1992b and Lesley 1976.

109 Vickers 1984, pp. 105–9.

110 On Abualfia's conception of language, see Idel 1989, esp. pp. 1–28.

111 On the correspondence of Isaac Mor Chayim and Isaac of Pisa and the debate on the nature of *sefirot*, see Idel 1982.

112 What constitutes the "true kabbalah" (*qabbalah amittit*) was a subject of constant dispute among the kabbalists themselves, ever since kabbalah emerged in the late twelfth century. The debate was heated in fifteenth-century Italy because of the encounter between Sephardi and Italian kabbalists after the expulsion from Spain and the rise of Christian kabbalah. For an instructive list of definitions of "true kabbalah," see Penkower 1989.

113 The printing of *Sefer ha-Zohar* was surrounded by a heated controversy within the Jewish community; see Tishby 1982.

114 The involvement of Jewish university-trained physicians in the scientific discoveries of the sixteenth and seventeenth centuries is explained in great detail in Ruderman 1988a.

115 Ibid., p. 162.

116 See Bonfil 1994, pp. 169–72; 1992c.

117 See Koyré 1957.

118 The inherent ambivalence of kabbalah is especially clear in the works of Alemanno, who highlighted the status of man as an intermediary being. For a detailed analysis of Alemanno's anthropology, see Idel 1990.

119 See Tirosh-Rothschild 1991, pp. 47–9.

120 For a detailed analysis of this point, see Tirosh-Rothschild 1982–3.

121 The mythic and erotic dimensions of Lurianic kabbalah are best analyzed in Liebes 1992.

122 Altmann 1982. Herrera's case suggests that the shift from Maimonideanism to kabbalah in the history of Jewish philosophy was but another expression of the general shift from Aristotelianism to Neoplatonism in European philo-

sophy during the sixteenth century. For a recent analysis of Herrera's thought, see Yosha 1994. I thank R. Bonfil for bringing this work to my attention.

123 The "platonization" of kabbalah and its dissemination at the end of the sixteenth century goes beyond the scope of this chapter. On Herrera's fusion of Renaissance Platonism and kabbalah, see Scholem 1978 and Altmann 1982.

124 Modern scholarship on Jewish philosophy in the Ottoman Empire is still in its early stages. The following discussion is based on Tirosh-Rothschild forthcoming.

125 This point was first made in Hacker 1984, pp. 587–93; English translation 1987, pp. 116–23.

126 On the sociocultural context of Jewish philosophy in the Ottoman Empire, see Hacker 1987, 1992.

127 Recent scholarship has shed light on this interesting figure. For a general description of Taitatzak's academy in Salonica, see Benayahu 1984. Taitatzak's hermeneutical method was discussed in Shalem 1971–8 and Sack 1988, and Taitatzak's reliance on scholastic philosophy was explored in Sermoneta 1971–8.

128 On Jewish philosophy among Romanyote scholars during the late Byzantine and early Ottoman period, see Bowman 1985, pp. 147–52; Wust 1990; and Attias 1991.

129 On Karaite philosophy in the fifteenth century, see Lasker 1983–4.

130 He purchased a copy of Gersonides' *Milchamot ha-Shem* (*Wars of the Lord*) from David ben Judah Messer Leon; see David 1973.

131 The printed edition of Almoli's *Sefer Me'asef le-Kol ha-Machanot* (Constantinople, 1530) includes only the introduction. Selections from the introduction are published in Yalon 1960.

132 See Regev 1990b. Almoli's encyclopedic definition of scientifico-philosophic knowledge resembles the extensive list of Alemanno's in *The Song of Solomon's Ascent*, though it lacks Alemanno's internal order of the sciences; see Lesley 1976, pp. 82–3.

133 Almoli spelled out the messianic import of the study of philosophy in his introduction to *Sha'ar Adonai he-Chadash* (*The New Gate of God*), pp. 13a–17a. In this regard Almoli followed in the footsteps of Isaac Abravanel, who also saw a causal connection between the intellectual perfection of individuals and the collective redemption of the Jewish people.

134 For information on printed editions in the Ottoman Empire, consult Yaari 1967; Hacker 1972 and 1987, p. 113 n. 37.

135 *Sha'ar Adonai he-Chadash*, 2a-b. This text constituted the first section of *Shomer Emunim*, yet another text which Almoli did not complete.

136 For a description of this social circle and its philosophical interests, see Roth 1948, pp. 168–82.

137 Almosnino's commentary on the *Physics* is no longer extant. His commentary on al-Ghazālī's *Intentions of the Philosophers* is extant in several manuscripts. An excerpt from the introduction is published in Cantera-Burgos 1959. Al-Ghazālī's work was one of the major sources for the study of Aristotelian philosophy in the Ottoman Empire; see Hacker 1987, p. 105 n. 20.

138 This commentary is extant in a single manuscript (MS Oxford Bodleian 1435 (= Michael 409)). Unfortunately, it is incomplete, consisting of Almosnino's

commentary on books 1, 2, and 10 of the *Ethics*. Its significance for the history of Jewish philosophy is explored at length below.

139 The relevant excerpt from this text was published in Assaf 1954, 3: 13.

140 These texts are extant in several manuscripts. For *Beit Elohim*, I consulted MS Oxford Bodleian 2038 and for *Sha'ar ha-Shamayim*, I consulted Oxford Bodleian 2036/2.

141 In *Beit Elohim* fols. 35a–42b, Almosnino manifests a new geographical sensibility that is clearly the mark of his generation. He describes prominent ancient and medieval figures (for example, Alexander the Great, Galen, Pliny, Virgil, Cicero, Ptolemy, Alfasi, Maimonides, and Agostino Nifo) with their native cities. Similarly, he locates famous places in biblical, rabbinic, and Greek literature in their precise geographic environment. Almosnino's interest in geography is similar to the fascination of Italian Jews with the new discoveries; see Ruderman 1981, pp. 131–43.

142 On the renewal of the Maimonidean controversy in the Ottoman Empire, see Hacker 1986 and Tirosh-Rothschild 1991, pp. 85–98.

143 For example, in *Lev Avot*, p. 59b Solomon ben Isaac Halevi states that "*Sefer ha-Zohar* was composed one thousand and two hundred years ago." The emphasis on the antiquity of the *Zohar* reflects both Halevi's attempt to refute charges that the *Zohar* was a medieval innovation (a view expressed, for example, by Judah Messer Leon) as well as the impact of humanist historiography on him.

144 On the kabbalists' conception of the Torah as identical with God's infinite wisdom, see Idel 1986.

145 See, for example, Joseph Taitatzak, *Porat Yosef*, p. 28b; Isaac Aroyo, *Tanchumot El*, p. 4a; Almosnino, *Pirqei Mosheh*, p. 6. On the evolution of this view in Spanish kabbalah, see Scholem 1965, pp. 37–44.

146 See, for example, Aderbi, *Divrei Shalom*, p. 25b.

147 *Tefillah le-Mosheh*, p. 64a and consult also pp. 10b; 34b; 48a; 51b; 55a. The same position is reiterated in his *Yedei Mosheh*, pp. 79–109.

148 Solomon ben Isaac Halevi, *Lev Avot*, introduction, p. 2a.

149 Abraham ibn Megash, *Kevod Elohim*, p. 17a.

150 See, for example, Almosnino, *Yedei Mosheh*, p. 248. The image of King Solomon as an exemplary figure who combined scientific learning, royal magnificence, just government, and mystical speculation was articulated most fully by Alemanno in his *Song of Solomon's Ascent*; see Lesley 1976.

151 Beginning with Petrarch, Renaissance thinkers exalted the poetic excellence of King David as matching that of the Greek and Roman poets; see Kugel 1981, pp. 212–18. Thus, while the Jewish philosophers were interested in the Psalms for their ethical content, indirectly they also insisted on the "Jewishness" of the greatest poet.

152 See Hacker 1987, pp. 111–12, esp. n. 34.

153 For an analysis of Maimonides' conception of human perfection and the relevant secondary literature, consult Kellner 1990.

154 The first Hebrew translation of the *Ethics* was done only in the 1320s by the Provençal scholar Judah ben Samuel of Marseilles, who translated Averroes' *Middle Commentary on the Ethics* from the Arabic original; see Berman 1967. This translation, however, had relatively little impact on Jewish philosophy,

for reasons that cannot be explored here. In 1405 Meir Alguades translated the *Ethics* into Hebrew on the basis of the Latin translation of Robert Grosseteste, the Latin translation of Averroes' *Middle Commentary* by Hermann the German, and an anonymous commentary ascribed to Aquinas that included excerpts from al-Fārābī's now lost commentary on the *Ethics*; see Berman 1988. In 1452 Joseph ibn Shem Tov wrote a long commentary on the *Ethics*, which became the standard text for Jewish students of the *Ethics*, as well as two abridgements; see Regev 1983. Another translation of the *Ethics* was made by Baruch ibn Ya'ish in the 1480s either in Portugal or in Italy. This translation was based on two fifteenth-century Latin translations of the commentary – Leonardo Bruni's (1416) and John Argyropolous' (1457); see Tirosh-Rothschild forthcoming.

155 The analysis of Jewish moral philosophy in the fifteenth century is yet to be undertaken; for now consult Dan 1975, pp. 105–20. On the twofold nature of happiness in fifteenth-century moral philosophy, see Kraye 1988, p. 342.

156 For an excellent survey of the various trends in Renaissance moral philosophy, see Kraye 1988.

157 For full information about these sources in *Penei Mosheh*, consult Tirosh-Rothschild forthcoming. From a stylistic perspective Almosnino's commentary is closest to Lefevre d'Étaples' *Moralis in ethicen introductio*. Like the French humanist, Almosnino interspersed his exposition of Aristotle with biblical and literary exempla that were designed to stimulate the reader to practice the rules of ethics.

158 In accordance with the Aristotelian tradition, post-expulsion thinkers understood the duality of matter and form in genderized categories: form (*tzurah*) relates to matter (*chomer*) as the male relates to the female; see, for example, Moses Almosnino, *Tefillah le-Mosheh*, pp. 26a, 35a; Isaac Aroyo, *Tanchumot El*, p. 7a.

159 The same viewpoint was shared by Christian moral philosophers during the Renaissance. On the evolution of rabbinic psychological theories and their indebtedness to Platonism, see Rubin 1989.

160 Isaac Aroyo, *Tanchumot El*, pp. 42b, 92a.

161 See Joseph Taitatzak, *Porat Yosef*, p. 33a; Meir Arama, *Meir Tehillot*, p. 110a; Isaac Aderbi, *Divrei Shalom*, p. 36b; Moses Almosnino, *Tefillah le-Mosheh*, 10b; *Pirqei Mosheh*, p. 70; *Penei Mosheh*, fols. 47r, 96r. The notion that Israel's soul was carved from under the Throne of Glory is asserted in *Tiqqunei Zohar*, Tiqqun 22, p. 65b. Isaac Aroyo was more loyal to the dominant view of the *Zohar* that located the origin of the soul in *Sefirah Malkhut*; see Isaac Aroyo, *Tanchumot El*, p. 7a.

162 See Joseph Taitatzak, *Porat Joseph*, p. 7a; Isaac Aroyo, *Tanchumot El*, p. 6b; Moses Almosnino, *Tefillah le-Mosheh*, pp. 23b, 34b. All three scholars insist that the descent of the soul into the body serves a moral purpose: by performing good deeds and acquiring the knowledge of truths, the soul spiritualizes the body and cleanses itself of the negative impact of the body. The ultimate reward is commensurate with the degree of such "spiritualization."

163 Isaac Aroyo, *Tanchumot El*, pp. 3a, 6b, 8b; Moses Almosnino *Pirqei Mosheh*, p. 4; *Penei Mosheh*, fol. 47r. Aroyo (who apparently had rather strong kabbalistic inclinations) went further to claim that the souls of non-Jews are associated

with the realm of evil and the forces of impurity (*sitra achra; sitra mesa'ava*). As such, non-Jews are not only ontologically inferior to Jews, but are also fundamentally evil.

164 This was Crescas' definition of the soul in *Or ha-Shem* 3.2.1., one that pre-expulsion Sephardi scholars accepted. That the soul is an incorporeal substance was held by both Avicenna and Judah Halevi, Crescas' most obvious sources.

165 See, for example, Almosnino, *Ma'ametz Koach*, p. 51b. This position was almost universally shared by Jewish and Christian authors during the late fifteenth and sixteenth centuries.

166 See Isaac Aroyo, *Tanchumot El*, pp. 62b, 120b; Solomon ben Isaac Halevi, *Lev Avot*, p. 57b. The immediate source of these discussions was Abraham Bibago's *Derekh Emunah*, printed in Salonica in 1522.

167 Isaac Aroyo elaborates the Platonic doctrine of recollection (*anamnesis*) in *Tanchumot El*, p. 8b.

168 Almosnino, *Tefillah le-Mosheh*, p. 41b; Aroyo, *Tanchumot El*, p. 8b.

169 Almosnino, *Tefillah le-Mosheh*, p. 12a; Isaac Aroyo, *Tanchumot El*, p. 8b. Almosnino and Aroyo perpetuated the Maimonidean notion that the acquisition of moral and intellectual virtues removes the barriers that separate the human and the divine. But if Maimonides viewed the body as a barrier to intellection of abstract truths, Almosnino and Aroyo viewed the body as a barrier that prevents the mystical union with God.

170 Moses Almosnino, *Tefillah le-Mosheh*, p. 26b; *Pirqei Mosheh*, p. 22.

171 Almosnino, *Pirqei Mosheh*, p. 70.

172 Aristotle (*Nicomachean Ethics* 1138b30) already posited the analogy between ethics and medicine: ethics is the science for the healing of the soul as medicine is the science that heals the body. Maimonides "judaized" this view when he attempted to show that the Torah provides the best cure for physical as well as psychic illnesses, and his view was shared by all subsequent Jewish philosophers who countenanced the interdependence of physical and psychic health.

173 See Moses Almosnino, *Pirqei Mosheh*, pp. 4, 98.

174 *Penei Mosheh*, fol. 47r. Almosnino's portrayal of man as an intermediary being between angels and beasts bears very close resemblance to Pico della Mirandola's theme in his famous oration "On the Dignity of Man."

175 A detailed analysis of Almosnino's indebtedness to Buridan in *Penei Mosheh*, especially fols. 146–9, cannot be undertaken here; it will be published in a separate study.

176 Almosnino, *Penei Mosheh*, fol. 148r.

177 Almosnino, *Pirqei Mosheh*, p. 37.

178 See Almosnino, *Tefillah le-Mosheh*, p. 21b; *Penei Mosheh*, fol. 4v.

179 On this motif in Jewish philosophy of the fifteenth and sixteenth centuries, see Melamed 1985a.

180 Isaac Aroyo, *Tanchumot El*, p. 73b.

181 Almosnino, *Tefillah le-Mosheh*, pp. 48a, 51b.

182 See Kraye 1988, p. 351.

183 Almosnino was not the first to combine these two models. He took his cue from John Buridan's commentary on the *Ethics*, which was deeply indebted to the Stoic philosophy of Seneca. On Buridan's dependence on Seneca, see Walsh 1966.

184 Almosnino, *Tefillah le-Mosheh*, p. 56a; *Penei Mosheh*, fol. 149v; *Ma'ametz Koach*, p. 17b.

185 *Penei Mosheh*, fol. 120v. In his commentary on book 6 of the *Nicomachean Ethics*, which is no longer extant, Almosnino apparently provided a full philosophical analysis of prudence. We can reconstruct his views from the numerous references to prudence in his extant works.

186 Almosnino, *Pirqei Mosheh*, p. 154; cf. *Penei Mosheh*, fols. 149r-151r, where Almosnino offers a subtle analysis of love as perfection of the will and prudence.

187 See Moses Almosnino, *Tefillah le-Mosheh*, pp. 24a, 57a; *Penei Mosheh*, fol. 20v; Isaac Aderbi, *Divrei Shalom*, pp. 46a-48b.

188 Almosnino, *Penei Mosheh*, fol. 149r; *Pirqei Mosheh*, p. 45.

189 Moses Almosnino, *Tefillah le-Mosheh*, p. 9b. According to Aroyo, since the soul is a particle of God, God himself experiences the misery of Israel directly. Since God is himself in exile, the liberation of Israel (collectively and individually) is God's own liberation; see *Tanchumot El*, p. 42b.

190 Almosnino's interpretation of Psalms 42, in *Tefillah le-Mosheh*, pp. 11a-b, is a typical example of this "psychological" reading of the Psalms. In contrast to earlier "political" interpretations of this Psalm, Almosnino interprets its central verse ("As a hind longs for the running streams, so I long for you, my God") as a metaphor for the yearning of the soul to free itself from exile in the body.

191 Almosnino, *Pirqei Mosheh*, p. 114; *Tefillah le-Mosheh*, p. 7b; Solomon ben Isaac Halevi, *Lev Avot*, p. 22b.

192 See Almosnino, *Tefillah le-Mosheh*, p. 33a-b; 34a.

193 For an overview of kabbalistic asceticism in Safed and a translation of seminal texts, see Fine 1984.

194 Almosnino, *Penei Mosheh*, fol. 20v; Solomon ben Isaac Halevi, *Lev Avot*, p. 6a.

195 See, for example, *Tefillah le-Mosheh*, pp. 23b, 24a-b, 33a-b; *Pirqei Mosheh*, p. 235; *Penei Mosheh*, fol. 172v; Solomon ben Isaac Halevi, *Lev Avot*, p. 17b.

196 In *Tefillah le-Mosheh*, p. 23b, Almosnino holds the view that patience (*savlanut*) is one of the prerequisites for happiness, an idea not found in Aristotle, but quite close to Stoic teachings on equanimity. Equanimity was not, of course, the monopoly of the Stoics. It was commonly taught by the Sufis and entered Jewish philosophy and kabbalah through the influential teachings of al-Ghazālī; see Idel 1992b, pp. 107-69.

197 Aroyo, *Tanchumot El*, p. 19a; Almosnino, *Tefillah le-Mosheh*, p. 51b.

198 Almosnino, *Pirqei Mosheh*, pp. 67, 154.

199 Solomon ben Isaac Halevi, *Lev Avot*, pp. 5a-10b. The notion that reason is the source of human freedom was, of course, the hallmark of Greek philosophy, especially Stoicism.

200 See, for example, Isaac Aderbi, *Divrei Shalom*, p. 49a. While taking the science of astrology very seriously, Jewish scholars held that the affairs of Israel are not controlled by a natural determinism because Israel is governed directly by God; see, for example, Almosnino, *Tefillah le-Mosheh*, p. 54b; Abraham ibn Megash, *Kevod Elohim*, pp. 31a-b, pp. 40a-b.

201 Aroyo, *Tanchumot El*, p. 103a; Isaac Aderbi, *Divrei Shalom*, p. 118a; Almosnino, *Ma'ametz Koach*, p. 6b.

202 See, Almosnino, *Ma'ametz Koach*, p. 216a; Isaac Aderbi, *Divrei Shalom*, p. 105a; Isaac Aroyo, *Tanchumot El*, p. 57a.

203 The attitude of medieval and early modern Jewish philosophers toward women requires a separate study. To my knowledge, all Aristotelian Jewish philosophers agreed with Aristotle that women are (by nature) intellectually inferior to men and that, therefore, they could not attain intellectual perfection. Since the philosophers identified the world-to-come with intellectual perfection, they took it for granted that women would not be part of it. Yet, once the perfection of the *will* rather than the perfection of the intellect became the necessary condition for salvation, women could be deemed the religious equals of men. I suspect that the new valuation of women had a lot to do with the fact that wealthy women such as Doña Gracia Nasi were patronesses of Jewish learning. Almosnino's eulogies for Doña Gracia Nasi and for the wife of Meir Arama, printed in *Ma'ametz Koach*, bear witness to the new public respect accorded to women.

204 See Almosnino, *Penei Mosheh*, fol. 172b; *Yedei Mosheh*, p. 85.

205 Seeskin 1991, p. 74.

⚹ BIBLIOGRAPHY ⚹

Texts

Abravanel, I. (1970) [1574] *Perush le-Moreh Nevukhim* (Jerusalem; English trans. by A. Reiner in *Maimonides and Abravanel on Prophecy* (Cincinnati: Hebrew Union College Press)).

—— (1972) [1892] *Opera Minora* (Westmead: Gregg International).

—— (1979) [1579] *Perush 'al ha-Torah* (Jerusalem: Hotza'at Sefarim Abravanel).

—— (1982) [1505] *Principles of Faith (Rosh Amanah)*, translated with introduction and notes by M. M. Kellner (Rutherford: Fairleigh Dickinson University Press).

—— (1988) [1592] *Mif'alot Elohim*, edited by B. Genut-Daror (Jerusalem: Reuben Mass).

Aderbi, I. (1580) *Divrei Shalom* (Salonica).

Al'ami, S. (1945) *Iggeret Musar*, edited by A. Haberman (Jerusalem: Meqorot).

Albo, J. (1929) *Sefer ha-'Iqqarim*, edited and translated by I. Husik (Philadelphia: Jewish Publication Society).

Almoli, S. (1532) *Sha'ar Adonai he-Chadash* (Salonica).

—— (1530) *Sefer Me'asef le-Kol ha-Machanot* (Constantinople).

Almosnino, M. *Beit Elohim*. MS Oxford Bodleian 2038.

—— *Sha'ar ha-Shamayim*. MS Oxford Bodleian 2036/2.

—— (1563) *Tefillah le-Mosheh* (Salonica).

—— (1564) *Libro Intutilado Rigimiento de la Vida* (Salonica).

—— (1588) *Ma'ametz Koach* (Venice).

—— *Penei Mosheh*. MS Oxford Bodleian 1435 (= Michael 409).

—— (1970) [1563] *Pirqei Mosheh* (Jerusalem: Makhon Torah Shelemah).

—— (1986) [1597] *Yedei Mosheh* (Jerusalem: Makhon le-Cheqer Yahadut Saloniqi).

Arama, I. (1849) *Chazut Qashah*, edited by C. Falk (Pressburg).

Arama, M. (1898) [1590] *Meir Tehillot* (Warsaw).

Aroyo, I. (1578) *Tanchumot El* (Salonica).

Bibago, A. (1522) *Derekh Emunah* (Constantinople).

Crescas (1990a) *Sefer Bittul 'Iqqarei ha-Notzrim: Translation of Joseph ben Shem Tov* [Hebrew], edited by D. J. Lasker (Ramat Gan: Bar Ilan University Press; Beer Sheva: Ben Gurion University Press).

—— (1990b) *Or ha-Shem* (Jerusalem: Sifrei Ramot).

—— (1992) *The Refutation of the Christian Principles*, translated with introduction and notes by D. J. Lasker (Albany: State University of New York Press).

del Medigo, E. (1984) *Sefer Bechinat ha-Dat*, critical edition with introduction, notes, and commentary by J. J. Ross (Tel Aviv: Chaim Rosenberg School of Jewish Studies).

Ebreo, L. (1929) *Dialoghi d'Amore*, edited by S. Carmella (Bari: Guis, Laterza and Figli).

Halevi, Solomon ben Isaac (1565) *Lev Avot* (Salonica).

Hillel ben Samuel of Verona (1981) *Sefer Tagmulei ha-Nefesh* (*Book of the Rewards of the Soul*), edited by Joseph Sermoneta (Jerusalem: Israel Academy of Sciences and Humanities).

ibn Megash, A. (1585) *Kevod Elohim* (Salonica).

ibn Shem Tov, J. *Commentary on Aristotle's Nicomachean Ethics*. MS Oxford Bodleian 1432 (= Michael 404).

—— (1556) *Kevod Elohim* (Ferrara).

—— (1982) *Perush le-Iggeret Efsharut ha-Devequt*, edited by S. Regev, *Jerusalem Studies in Jewish Thought* 2: 38–93.

ibn Yachya, Joseph ben David (1538) *Torah Or* (Bologna).

Messer Leon, Judah (1983) *The Book of the Honeycomb's Flow: Sēpher Nōpheth Ṣuphīm*, edited and translated by I. Rabinowitz (Ithaca and London: Cornell University Press).

Moscato, J. (1894) [1594] *Qol Yehudah*, edited by Y. Goldman (Warsaw).

Pisa, Yechiel Nissim da (1898) *Minchat Qena'ot* (Berlin: Mekitze Niradamim).

Rieti, M. (1851) *Miqdash Me'at* (Vienna).

Taitatzak, J. (1608) *Lechem Setarim* (Venice).

—— (1599) *Porat Yosef* (Venice).

Studies

Altmann, A. (1982) "Lurianic Kabbala in a Platonic Key: Abraham Cohen Herrera's *Puerta del Cielo*," *Hebrew Union College Annual* 53: 317–55.

—— (1992) "Ars Rhetorica as Reflected in Some Jewish Figures of the Italian Renaissance," in *Essential Papers on Jewish Culture in Renaissance and Baroque Italy*, edited by D. B. Ruderman (New York: New York University Press), pp. 63–84.

Assaf, S. (1954) *Meqorot le-Toledot ha-Chinnukh be-Yisrael* (Tel Aviv: Dvir).

Assis, Y. T. (1990) "R. Hasdai Crescas' Endeavor to Rebuild Jewish Communities after the Persecution of 1391" [Hebrew], *Proceedings of the Tenth World Congress of Jewish Studies*, Division B (Jerusalem: World Union of Jewish Studies), 1: 145–8.

Attias J. C. (1991) *Le Commentaire biblique Mordekhai Comtino ou l'hermeneutique du dialogue* (Paris: Cerf).

Baer, Y. F. (1937) "Don Isaac Abrabanel and his Attitude to the Problems of History and Politics" [Hebrew], *Tarbitz* 8: 241–59.

—— (1978) *The History of the Jews in Christian Spain*, 2nd ed., translated by L. Schoffman, 2 vols. (Philadelphia: Jewish Publication Society of America).

Barkai, R. (1987) "L'Astrologie juive médiévale: aspects théorique et pratiques," *Le Moyen Age: Revue d'Histoire et de Philologie* 93: 319–48.

Baruchson, S. (1993) *Books and Readers: The Reading Interests of Italian Jews at the Close of the Renaissance* [Hebrew], (Ramat Gan: Bar Ilan University Press).

Barzilay, I. (1967) *Between Reason and Faith: Anti-Rationalism in Italian Jewish Thought 1250–1650* (The Hague and Paris: Mouton).

Benayahu, M. (1982) "The Sermons of R. Yosef b. Meir Garcon as a Source for the History of the Expulsion from Spain and Sephardi Diaspora," *Michael* 7: 42–205.

—— (1984) "Rabbi Joseph Taitatzak of Salonika – The Head of the Sephardi Diaspora" [Hebrew], in *Me'az Ve'ad Atah*, edited by Z. Ankori, 2: 21–34.

Berman, L. V. (1967) "Greek into Arabic: Samuel ben Judah Marseilles, Fourteenth Century Philosopher and Translator," in *Jewish Medieval and Renaissance Studies*, edited by A. Altmann (Cambridge MA: Harvard University Press), pp. 289–320.

—— (1978) "Ibn Rushd's *Middle Commentary on the Nicomachean Ethics* in Medieval Hebrew Literature," in *Multiple Averroes*, edited by J. Jolivet (Paris: Belles Lettres), pp. 287–311.

—— (1988) "The Latin to Hebrew Translation of the *Nicomachean Ethics*" [Hebrew], in *Shlomo Pines Jubilee Volume*, vol. 1, edited by M. Idel, E. Schweid, and W. Z. Harvey (= *Jerusalem Studies in Jewish Thought* 7), pp. 147–68.

Bland, K. P. (1991) "Elijah del Medigo's Averroist Response to the Kabbalahs of Fifteenth-Century Jewry and Pico della Mirandola," *The Journal of Jewish Thought and Philosophy* 1: 23–53.

Bonfil, R. (1975) "Expressions of Jewish Particularism in the Italian Renaissance" [Hebrew], *Sinai* 76: 36–46.

—— (1976) "The Doctrine of the Soul and Holiness in the Teachings of R. Obadia Sforno" [Hebrew], *Eshel Beer Sheva* 1: 200–57.

—— (1979) *The Rabbinate in Renaissance Italy* [Hebrew], (Jerusalem: Magnes).

—— (1981) "Introduction" [Hebrew] to the anastatic reproduction of the *editio princeps* of the *Nofet Zufim* (Mantua, 1475), pp. 7–69.

—— (1990) *Rabbis and Jewish Communities in Renaissance Italy*, translated by J. Chipman (Oxford: Oxford University Press).

—— (1992a) "Preaching as Mediation between Elite and Popular Culture: The Case of Judah del Bene," in *Preachers of the Italian Ghetto*, edited by D. B. Ruderman (Berkeley: University of California Press), pp. 67–88.

—— (1992b) "*The Book of the Honeycomb's Flow* by Judah Messer Leon: The Rhetoric Dimension of Jewish Humanism in Fifteenth-Century Italy," in *The Frank Talmage Memorial Volume*, edited by B. Walfish [= *Jewish History* 6. 1–2] (Haifa: Haifa University Press), 2: 21–33.

—— (1992c) "Change in the Cultural Patterns of a Jewish Society in Crisis: Italian Jewry at the Close of the Sixteenth Century," in *Essential Papers on Jewish Culture in Renaissance and Baroque Italy*, edited by D. B. Ruderman (New York: New York University Press), pp. 401–25.

—— (1992d) "How Golden was the Age of the Renaissance in Jewish Historiography?" in *Essential Papers on Jewish Culture in Renaissance and Baroque Italy*, edited by D. B. Ruderman (New York: New York University Press), pp. 219–51.

—— (1994) *Jewish Life in Renaissance Italy*, translated by A. Oldcorn (Berkeley: University of California Press).

Bouwsma, W. (1976) "Changing Assumptions in Later Renaissance Culture," *Viator* 7: 422–40.

Bowman, S. (1985) *The Jews in Byzantium: 1204–1453* (University, AL: University of Alabama Press).

Boyarin, D. (1989) *Sephardi Speculation: A Study in Methods of Talmudic Interpretation* [Hebrew], (Jerusalem: Yad Itzhak Ben Zvi and the Hebrew University of Jerusalem).

Cantera-Burgos, F. (1959) "Nueva serie de manuscritos hebreos de Madrid," *Sefarad* 19: 5–8.

Carpi, D. (1972) "R. Judah Messer Leon and His Activity as a Physician" [Hebrew], *Michael* 1: 277–301.

—— (1989) *Between Renaissance and Ghetto: Essays on the History of the Jews in Italy in the 14th and 17th Centuries* [Hebrew], (Tel Aviv: University Publishing Project).

Carpenter, D. (forthcoming) "A *Converso* Best-Seller: *Celestina* and Her Foreign Offsprings," in *Crisis and Renewal in Iberian Jewry 1391–1648*, edited by Y. H. Yerushalmi and B. Gampel.

Cassuto, M. D. (1967) *Gli Ebrei a Firenze nell'eta del Rinascimento*, translated [into Hebrew] by M. Artom (Jerusalem: Kiryat Sefer).

Cranz, F. E. (1976) "Editions of the Latin Aristotle Accompanied by the Commentaries of Averroes," in *Philosophy and Humanism: Renaissance Essays in Honor of Paul Oskar Kristeller*, edited by E. P. Mahoney (New York: Columbia University Press), pp. 116–28.

Dan, J. (1975) *Hebrew Ethical and Homiletical Literature* [Hebrew], (Jerusalem: Keter).

David, A. (1973) "New Information about Caleb Afendopolo" [Hebrew], *Kiryat Sefer* 48: 180.

Davidson, H. (1964) *The Philosophy of Abraham Shalom: A Fifteenth-Century Exposition and Defense of Maimonides* (Berkeley: University of California Press).

—— (1983) "Medieval Jewish Philosophy in the Sixteenth Century," in *Jewish Thought in the Sixteenth Century*, edited by B. D. Cooperman (Cambridge, MA and London: Harvard University Press), pp. 106–45.

—— (1987) *Proofs for the Eternity, Creation and the Existence of God in Medieval Islamic and Jewish Philosophy* (New York: Oxford University Press).

Davis, J. (1993) "Philosophy, Dogma, and Exegesis in Medieval Ashkenazic Judaism: The Evidence of *Sefer Hadrat Qodesh*," *AJS Review* 18.2: 195–222.

Dorman, M. (1983) "Judah Abrabanel, His Life and Work," in *Sichot 'al ha-Ahavah: Leone Ebreo (Guida Abrabanel), Dialoghi d'amore*, edited and translated by M. Dorman (Jerusalem: Mossad Bialik), pp. 13–182.

—— (1985) "Leone Ebreo and Baldassare Castiglione" [Hebrew], in *The Philosophy of Leone Ebreo: Four Lectures*, edited by M. Dorman and Z. Levy (Haifa: Ha-Kibbutz Hameuchad), pp. 43–6.

Esteban, F. D. (1992) "The Literary Activity of Jews in Spanish" [Hebrew], in *Moreshet Sepharad: The Sephardi Legacy*, edited by H. Beinart (Jerusalem: Magnes), pp. 330–64.

Feldman, S. (1984) "A Debate Concerning Determinism in Late Medieval Jewish Philosophy," *Proceedings of the American Academy for Jewish Research* 51: 15–54.

Ferguson, W. (1962) *Europe in Transition: 1300–1520* (Boston: Houghton Mifflin).

Fine, L. (1984) *Safed Spirituality* (New York: Paulist Press).

Geffen, D. (1970) *Faith and Reason in Elijah del Medigo's Bechinat ha-Dat*. Ph.D. dissertation, Columbia University.

—— (1973–4) "Insights into the Life and Thought of Elijah del Medigo based on his Published and Unpublished Works," *Proceedings of the American Academy for Jewish Research* 41–2: 69–86.

Gottlieb, E. (1976) *Studies in the Kabbalah Literature*, edited by J. Hacker (Tel Aviv: Chaim Rosenberg School for Jewish Studies).

Gross, A. (1987) "Toward a Portrait of the Jewish Academies in Castile in the Fifteenth Century" [Hebrew], *Pe'amim* 31: 3–21.

—— (1993) *Rabbi Joseph ben Abraham Hayyun: Leader of the Lisbon Jewish Community and His Literary Work* [Hebrew], (Ramat Gan: Bar Ilan University Press).

Guttmann, J. (1964) [1933] *The Philosophies of Judaism*, translated by D. Silverman (New York: Schocken).

Hacker, J. (1972) "The Place of Abraham Bibago in the Controversy on the Study and Status of Philosophy in Fifteenth Century Spain" [Hebrew], *Proceedings of the Fifth World Congress of Jewish Studies* (Jerusalem: World Union of Jewish Studies), 3: 151–8.

—— (1983) "On the Intellectual Character and Self Perception of Spanish Jewry in the Late Fifteenth Century" [Hebrew], *Sefunot* 17 (= n.s. 2): 21–95.

—— (1984) "The Intellectual Activity of the Jews of the Ottoman Empire during the Sixteenth and Seventeenth Centuries" [Hebrew], *Tarbitz* 53.4: 569–603; English translation in Hacker 1987.

—— (1986) "Agitation Against Philosophy in Istanbul in the 16th Century," in *Studies in Jewish Mysticism, Philosophy, and Ethical Literature Presented to Isaiah Tishby on his Seventy-Fifth Birthday*, edited by J. Dan and J. Hacker (Jerusalem: Magnes), pp. 507–36.

—— (1987) "The Intellectual Activity of the Jews of the Ottoman Empire during the Sixteenth and Seventeenth Centuries," in *Jewish Thought in the Seventeenth Century*, edited by I. Twersky and B. Septimus (Cambridge, MA: Harvard University Press), pp. 95–135.

—— (1989) "Pride and Depression – Polarity of the Spiritual and Social Experience of the Iberian Exiles in the Ottoman Empire" [Hebrew], in *Culture and Society in Medieval Jewry: Studies Dedicated to the Memory of Haim Hillel Ben-Sasson*, edited by R. Bonfil, M. Ben-Sasson, and J. Hacker (Jerusalem: Historical Society of Israel and Zalman Shazar Center), pp. 541–86.

—— (1992) "The Sephardi Exiles in the Ottoman Empire during the Sixteenth

Century – Community and Society" [Hebrew], in *Moreshet Sepharad: The Sephardi Legacy*, edited by H. Beinart (Jerusalem: Magnus), pp. 460–78.

Harari, D. (1988) "The Traces of the Fourth Dialogue on Love by Leone Ebreo in *Eroici Furori* by Giordano Bruno" [Hebrew], *Italia* 7.1–2: 93–155.

Harvey, W. Z. (1973) *Hasdai Crescas' Critique of the Theory of the Acquired Intellect*. Ph.D. dissertation, Columbia University.

——(1977) "R. Hasdai Crescas and His Critique of Philosophic Happiness" [Hebrew], *Proceedings of the Sixth World Congress of Jewish Studies* (Jerusalem: World Union of Jewish Studies), 3: 143–9.

——(1982–3) "Kabbalistic Elements in *Or Adonai* by R. Hasdai Crescas" [Hebrew], *Jerusalem Studies in Jewish Thought* 2.1: 75–109.

Heller Wilensky, S. (1956) *The Philosophy of Isaac Arama in the Framework of Philonic Philosophy* (Jerusalem: Mossad Bialik; Tel Aviv: Dvir).

Idel, M. (1982) "Between the Views of Sefirot as Essence and Instruments in the Renaissance Period" [Hebrew], *Italia* 3: 89–111.

——(1983) "Studies in the Thought of the Author of *Sefer ha-Meshiv*: A Chapter in the History of Spanish Kabbalah" [Hebrew], *Sefunot* 17 (= n.s. 2): 185–265.

——(1985) "Kabbalah and Philosophy in R. Isaac and Judah Abrabanel," in *The Philosophy of Leone Ebreo: Four Lectures*, edited by M. Dorman and Z. Levy (Haifa: Ha-Kibbutz Hameuchad), pp. 73–112.

——(1986) "Infinities of Torah in Kabbalah," in *Midrash and Literature*, edited by G. Hartman and S. Budick (New Haven: Yale University Press), pp. 141–57.

——(1989) *Language, Torah and Hermeneutics in Abraham Abulafia* (Albany: State University of New York Press).

——(1990) "The Anthropology of Yochanan Alemanno: Sources and Influences," *Annali di storia dell'esegesi* 7.1: 93–111.

——(1992a) [1986] "Major Currents in Italian Kabbalah between 1560–1660," in *Essential Papers on Jewish Culture in Renaissance and Baroque Italy*, edited by D. B. Ruderman (New York: New York University Press), pp. 345–72.

——(1992b) [1987] "The Magical and Neoplatonic Interpretations of the Kabbalah in the Renaissance," in *Essential Papers on Jewish Culture in Renaissance and Baroque Italy*, edited by D. B. Ruderman (New York: New York University Press), pp. 107–69.

——(1992c) "Religion, Thought and Attitudes: The Impact of the Expulsion on the Jews," in *Spain and the Jews: The Sephardi Experience 1492 and After*, edited by E. Kedourie (London: Thames & Hudson), pp. 123–39.

——(1992d) "Judah Moscato: A Late Renaissance Jewish Preacher," in *Preachers of the Italian Ghetto*, edited by D. B. Ruderman (Berkeley: University of California Press), pp. 41–66.

——(forthcoming) "Encounters between Spanish and Italian Kabbalists in the Generation of the Expulsion," in *Crisis and Creativity in the Sephardic World 1391–1648*, edited by Y. H. Yerushalmi and B. Gampel.

Ivry, A. (1983) "Remnants of Jewish Averroism in the Renaissance," in *Jewish Thought in the Sixteenth Century*, edited by B. D. Cooperman (Cambridge MA: Harvard University Press), pp. 243–65.

Kellner, M. (1986) *Dogma in Medieval Jewish Thought: From Maimonides to Abravanel* (Oxford: Oxford University Press).

——(1990) *Maimonides on Human Perfection* (Atlanta: Scholars Press).

Koyré, A. (1957) *From the Closed World to the Infinite Universe* (New York: Harper Torchbooks).

Kraye, J. (1988) "Moral Philosophy," in *The Cambridge History of Renaissance Philosophy*, edited by C. B. Schmitt, Q. Skinner, E. Kessler, and J. Kraye (Cambridge: Cambridge University Press), pp. 301–86.

Kristeller, P. O. (1979) *Renaissance Thought and Its Sources*, edited by M. Mooney (New York: Columbia University Press).

—— (1990) *Renaissance Thought and the Arts: Collected Essays* (Princeton: Princeton University Press).

Kugel. J. (1981) *The Idea of Biblical Poetry: Parallelism and Its History* (New Haven and London: Yale University Press).

Lasker, D. (1977) *Jewish Philosophical Polemics Against Christianity in the Middle Ages* (New York: B'nai B'rith Publications).

—— (1983–4) "Maimonides' Influence on the Philosophy of Elijah Bashyazzi," *Jerusalem Studies in Jewish Thought* 3.3: 405–25.

—— (1992) "Jewish-Christian Polemics in Light of the Expulsion from Spain," *Judaism* 41.2: 148–55.

—— (forthcoming) "The Impact of Christianity on Late Iberian Jewish Philosophy," in *Iberia and Beyond: Hispanic Jews Between Two Cultures*, edited by B. Cooperman and A. Seeff (Newark: University of Delaware Press).

Lazaroff, A. (1981) *The Theology of Abraham Bibago: A Defense of the Divine Will, Knowledge and Providence in Fifteenth Century Spanish-Jewish Philosophy* (University, AL: University of Alabama Press).

Lerner, R. (1964) "Natural Law in Albo's *Book of Roots*," in *Ancients and Moderns*, edited by J. Cropsey (New York: Basic Books), pp. 132–47.

Lesley, A. M. (1976) *"The Song of Solomon's Ascents" by Yochanan Alemanno: Love and Human Perfection according to a Jewish Colleague of Giovanni Pico*. Ph.D. dissertation, University of California, Berkeley.

—— (1982) "Hebrew Humanism in Italy: The Case of Biography," *Prooftexts* 2: 163–77.

—— (1988) "Jewish Adaptation of Humanist Concepts in Fifteenth- and Sixteenth-Century Italy," in *Renaissance Rereadings: Intertext and Context*, edited by M. C. Horowitz (Urbana and Chicago: University of Illinois Press), pp. 51–65.

—— (1992) "The Place of the *Dialoghi d'amore* in Contemporaneous Jewish Thought," in *Essential Papers on Jewish Culture in Renaissance and Baroque Italy*, edited by D. B. Ruderman (New York: New York University Press), pp. 170–88.

Levy, Z. (1985) "On the Concept of Beauty in the Philosophy of Judah Abrabanel," in *The Philosophy of Leone Ebreo: Four Lectures*, edited by M. Dorman and Z. Levy (Haifa: Ha-Kibbutz Hameuchad), pp. 27–42.

Liebes, Y. (1992) " 'Two Young Roes of a Doe': The Secret Sermon of Isaac Luria before his Death" [Hebrew], in *Proceedings of the Fourth International Conference on the History of Jewish Mysticism*, edited by R. Elior and Y. Liebes (= *Jerusalem Studies in Jewish Thought* 10), pp. 113–70.

Melamed, A. (1978) "Rhetoric and Philosophy in *Nofet Tzufim* by R. Judah Messer Leon" [Hebrew], *Italia* 1: 7–38.

—— (1985a) "The Transformation of the Love-of-the-Noble Motif in Albo, Alemanno, Judah Abrabanel, and Moscato" [Hebrew], in *The Philosophy of Leone*

Ebreo: Four Lectures, edited by M. Dorman and Z. Levy (Haifa: Ha-Kibbutz Hameuchad), pp. 57–72.

—— (1985b) "Natural, Human, Divine: Classification of the Law among Some Fifteenth and Sixteenth Century Italian Jewish Thinkers," *Italia* 4: 59–93.

—— (1986) "The Law of Nature in Medieval and Renaissance Jewish Thought" [Hebrew], *Da'at* 17: 49–66.

Motzkin, A. (1987) "Elia del Medigo, Averroes, and Averroism," *Italia* 6. 1–2: 7–19.

Netanyahu, B. Z. (1953) *Don Isaac Abravanel: Statesman and Philosopher* (Philadelphia: Jewish Publication Society).

—— (1966) *The Marranos of Spain from the Late XIVth to the Early XVIth Centuries According to Contemporary Hebrew Sources* (New York: American Academy for Jewish Research).

Nuriel, A. (1975) *The Philosophy of Abraham Bibago*. Ph.D dissertation, Hebrew University of Jerusalem.

Pagis, D. (1976) *Change and Tradition in the Secular Poetry: Spain and Italy* [Hebrew], (Jerusalem: Keter).

—— (1993) *Poetry Aptly Explained: Studies and Essays on Medieval Hebrew Poetry* [Hebrew], edited by E. Fleischer (Jerusalem: Magnes).

Parker, A. A. (1985) *The Philosophy of Love in Spanish Literature: 1480–1680* (Edinburgh: Edinburgh University Press).

Penkower, J. S. (1989) "New Considerations Concerning *Sefer Massoreth ha-Massoreth* by Elia Levita" [Hebrew], *Italia* 3: 7–73.

Perry, A. T. (1980) *Erotic Spirituality: The Integrative Tradition from Leone Ebreo to John Donne* (University, Al: University of Alabama Press).

Pine, M. L. (1986) *Pietro Pompanazzi: Radical Philosopher of the Renaissance* (Padua: Antenore).

Pines, S. (1977) "Scholasticism after Thomas Aquinas and the Thought of Hasdai Crescas and his Predecessors" [Hebrew], in *Studies in the History of Jewish Philosophy: The Transmission of Texts and Ideas* (Jerusalem: Mossad Bialik), pp. 178–252.

—— (1983) "Medieval Doctrines in Renaissance Garb? Some Jewish and Arabic Sources of Leone Ebreo's Doctrines," in *Jewish Thought in the Sixteenth Century*, edited by B. D. Cooperman (Cambridge, MA: Harvard University Press), pp. 365–98.

Rabinowitz, I. (1983) "Introduction," in *The Book of the Honeycomb's Flow: Sēpher Nōpheth Ṣūphīm by Judah Messer Leon* (Ithaca and London: Cornell University Press), pp. xv–lxx.

Ravitzky, A. (1986) "The Secrets of *The Guide of the Perplexed* between the Thirteenth and Twentieth Centuries" [Hebrew], *Jerusalem Studies in Jewish Thought* 5: 23–69.

—— (1988) *Crescas' Sermon on the Passover and Studies in his Philosophy* [Hebrew] (Jerusalem: Israel Academy of Sciences and the Humanities).

Regev, S. (1983) *Theology and Rational Mysticism in the Writings of R. Joseph ben Shem Tov*. Ph.D dissertation, Hebrew University of Jerusalem.

—— (1986a) "The Ratio-Mystical Thought in Jewish Philosophy of the Fifteenth Century" [Hebrew], *Jerusalem Studies in Jewish Thought* 5: 155–89.

—— (1986b) "On the Problem of the Study of Philosophy in 15th Century Thought: R. Joseph ibn Shem Tov and R. Abraham Bibago," *Da'at* 16: 57–86.

—— (1987) "Messianism and Astrology in the Thought of R. Isaac Abrabanel," *Asufot* 1: 169–87.

—— (1990a) "Collective Revelation and the Sinaitic Event in Maimonides and His Commentators: Narboni, Shem Tov, and Abrabanel," in *Shlomo Pines Jubilee Volume*, vol. 2, edited by M. Idel, E. Schweid, and W. Z. Harvey (= *Jerusalem Studies in Jewish Thought* 9), pp. 251–65.

—— (1990b) "Redemption and Intellection in the Thought of R. Solomon Almoli" [Hebrew], *Proceedings of the Tenth World Congress of Jewish Studies*, Division C (Jerusalem: World Union of Jewish Studies), 1: 345–52.

—— (1991) "Sermons on Repentance by Joseph ibn Shem Tov" [Hebrew], *Asufot* 5: 183–211.

Rigo, C. (1989) "Un passo sconosciuto di Alberto Magno nel *Sefer 'esem ha-shamayim* di Yehudah b. Mosheh," *Henoch* 11: 295–318.

—— (1993a) "Yehudah b. Mosheh Romano, traduttore di Alberto Magno Commento al *De Anima* III, II, 16," *Henoch* 15: 65–91.

—— (1993b) "Un'antologia filosofica di Yehudah b. Mosheh Romano," *Italia* 10: 73–104.

Rosenberg, S. (1973) *Logic and Ontology in Jewish Philosophy in the 14th Century*. Ph.D. dissertation, Hebrew University of Jerusalem.

—— (1984) "The Concept of *Emunah* in Post-Maimonidean Jewish Philosophy," in *Studies in Medieval Jewish History and Literature*, edited by I. Twersky (Cambridge, MA: Harvard University Press), 2: 273–308.

Roth, C. (1948) *The House of Nasi: The Duke of Naxos* (Philadelphia: Jewish Publication Society).

—— (1964) *The Jews in the Renaissance* (Philadelphia: Jewish Publication Society).

Rubin, N. (1989) "From Monism to Dualism: Relations between the Body and the Soul in Talmudic Thought," *Da'at* 23: 33–64.

Ruderman, D. B. (1981) *The World of a Renaissance Jew: The Life and Thought of Abraham ben Mordecai Farissol* (Cincinnati: Hebrew Union College Press).

—— (1982) "An Exemplary Sermon from the Classroom of a Jewish Teacher in Renaissance Italy," *Italia* 1: 7–38.

—— (1988a) *Kabbalah, Magic and Science: The Cultural Universe of a Sixteenth-Century Jewish Physician* (Cambridge, MA: Harvard University Press).

—— (1988b) "The Italian Renaissance and Jewish Thought," in *Renaissance Humanism: Foundations and Forms*, edited by A. Rabil, Jr., (Philadelphia: University of Pennsylvania Press), 1: 382–433.

—— (1992) "The Impact of Science on Jewish Culture and Society in Venice (With Special Reference to Jewish Graduates of Padua's Medical School)," in *Essential Papers on Jewish Culture in Renaissance and Baroque Italy*, edited by D. B. Ruderman (New York: New York University Press), pp. 519–53.

Sack, B. (1988) "R. Joseph Taitazak's Commentaries," in *Shlomo Pines Jubilee Volume*, vol. 1, edited by M. Idel, E. Schweid, and W. Z. Harvey (= *Jerusalem Studies in Jewish Thought* 7), pp. 341–55.

Schmitt, C. B. (1983) *Aristotle and the Renaissance* (Cambridge, MA: Harvard University Press).

—— (ed.) (1988) *The Cambridge History of Renaissance Philosophy* (Cambridge: Cambridge University Press).

Scholem, G. (1965) *On the Kabbalah and Its Symbolism* (New York: Schocken).

—— (1978) *Abraham Cohen Herrera: Leben, Werk, und Wirkung* [Hebrew], translated by H. Isaac (Jerusalem: Mossad Bialik).

Schwartzmann, J. (1991) "Isaac ibn Shem Tob's Commentary on *The Guide of the Perplexed*" [Hebrew], *Da'at* 26: 43–60.

Schweid, E. (1976) "Albo's Conception of Prophecy" [Hebrew], *Tarbitz* 35: 48–60.

Scrivano, R. (1986) "Platonic and Cabalistic Elements in the Hebrew Culture of Renaissance Italy: Leone Ebreo and his *Dialoghi d'amore*," in *Ficino and Renaissance Neoplatonism*, edited by K. Eisenbichler and O. Z. Pugliese, *University of Toronto Italian Studies* 1: 123–39.

Seeskin, K. (1991) *Maimonides: A Guide for Today's Perplexed* (West Orange, NJ: Behrman House).

Sermoneta, J. (1971–8) "Scholastic Philosophic Literature in Yosef Taitasak's *Porat Yosef*" [Hebrew], *Sefunot* 11 (= *Book of Greek Jewry* 1), pp. 137–85.

—— (1980) "Jehudah Ben Moshe Daniel Romano, Traducteur de Saint Thomas," in *Hommage à Georges Vajda*, edited by G. Nahon and C. Touati (Louvain: Peeters), pp. 231–62.

—— (1984) "Prophecy in the Writings of R. Yehuda Romano," in *Studies in Medieval Jewish History and Literature*, edited by I. Twersky (Cambridge MA: Harvard University Press), 2: 337–74.

Shalem, S. (1971–8) "The Exegetical Method of R. Yosef Taitatzak and his Circle: Its Nature and its Form of Inquiry" [Hebrew], *Sefunot* 11 (= *Book of Greek Jewry* 1), pp. 116–34.

Shechterman, D. (1988) "The Doctrine of Original Sin in Jewish Philosophy of the Thirteenth and Fourteenth Centuries" [Hebrew], *Da'at* 20: 65–90.

Sirat, C. (1985) *A History of Jewish Philosophy in the Middle Ages* (Cambridge: Cambridge University Press).

Steinschneider, M. (1893) *Die Hebräischen Übersetzungen des Mittlelalters* (Berlin; reprinted 1956, Graz: Akademische Druck– u. Verlagsanstalt).

Stow, K. (1977) *Catholic Thought and Papal Jewry Policy: 1555–1593* (New York: Jewish Theological Seminary).

Strauss, L. (1937) "On Abravanel's Philosophical Tendency and Political Teaching," in *Isaac Abravanel: Six Lectures*, edited by J. B. Trends and H. Loewe (Cambridge: Cambridge University Press), pp. 95–129.

Tirosh-Rothschild, H. (1982–3) "*Sefirot* as the Essence of God in the Writings of David Messer Leon," *AJS Review* 7–8: 409–25.

—— (1986) "Maimonides and Aquinas: The Interplay of Two Masters in Medieval Jewish Philosophy," *Conservative Judaism* 39: 54–66.

—— (1990a) "The Political Philosophy of Abraham Shalom – The Platonic Tradition" [Hebrew], in *Shlomo Pines Jubilee Volume*, vol. 2, edited by M. Idel, E. Schweid, and W. Z. Harvey (= *Jerusalem Studies in Jewish Thought* 7), pp. 409–40.

—— (1990b) "Jewish Culture in Renaissance Italy – A Methodological Survey," *Italia* 9.1–2: 63–96.

—— (1991) *Between Worlds: The Life and Thought of Rabbi David ben Judah Messer Leon* (Albany: State University of New York Press).

—— (forthcoming) "The Ultimate End of Human Life in Post-Expulsion Philosophic Literature," in *Crisis and Creativity in the Sephardic World 1391–1648*, edited by Y. H. Yerushalmi and B. Gampel.

Tishby, I. (1982) "The Controversy about *Sefer ha-Zohar* in Sixteenth-Century Italy" [Hebrew], in *Studies in Kabbalah and Its Branches: Researches and Sources* (Jerusalem: Magnes Press), 1: 79–130.

Trinkaus, C. (1965) *Adversity's Noblemen: The Italian Humanists on Happiness* (New York: Octagon).

—— (1983) *The Scope of Renaissance Humanism* (Ann Arbor: University of Michigan Press).

Vickers, B. (1984) "Analogy Versus Identity: The Rejection of Occult Symbolism, 1580–1680," in *Occult and Scientific Mentalities in the Renaissance*, edited by B. Vickers (Cambridge: Cambridge University Press), pp. 95–153.

Walsh, J. J. (1966) "Buridan and Seneca," *The Journal of the History of Ideas* 27: 23–40.

Wirszubski, C. (1989) *Pico della Mirandola's Encounter with Jewish Mysticism* (Cambridge, MA: Harvard University Press).

Wolfson, H. A. (1977) "Isaac ibn Shem-Tov's Unknown Commentaries on the *Physics* and His Other Unknown Works," in *Studies in the History of Philosophy and Religion*, edited by I. Twersky and G. H. Williams (Cambridge MA: Harvard University Press), 2: 479–90.

Wust, E. (1990) "Elisha the Greek – A Physician and Philosopher at the Beginning of the Ottoman Period," *Pe'amim* 41: 49–57.

Yaari, A. (1967) *Hebrew Printing in Constantinople: Its History and Bibliography* (Jerusalem: Magnes).

Yalon, H. (1960) "Chapters from R. Solomon Almoli's *Me'asef le-Kol ha-Machanot*" [Hebrew], *Areshet* 2: 96–108.

Yates, F. (1964) *Giordano Bruno and the Hermetic Tradition* (Chicago: University of Chicago Press).

Yavneh, N. (1991) "The Spiritual Eroticism of Leon's Hermaphrodite," in *Playing with Gender: A Renaissance Pursuit*, edited by J. R. Brink, M. C. Horowitz, and A. P. Coudert (Urbana: University of Illinois Press), pp. 85–98.

Yosha, N. (1994) *Myth and Metaphor: Abraham Cohen's Herrera's Philosophic Interpretation of Lurianic Kabbalah* [Hebrew], (Jerusalem: Ben Zvi Institute and Magnes).

III

Modern Jewish philosophy

CHAPTER 21

The nature of modern Jewish philosophy

Ze'ev Levy

Most of the attempts to define the essence of "Jewish philosophy" are of recent origin. In the past Jewish thinkers were not bothered at all by this question; but what seemed obvious at first glance is really fraught with a diversity of problems. This is reflected by the terminological distinctions which modern scholars make between "Jewish philosophy," "philosophy of Judaism,"[1] "Jewish thought," etc.[2] These concepts extend beyond the bounds of terminology or definition. Also, there has not yet been any satisfactory way of integrating Jewish philosophy within the teaching of general philosophy. Therefore, to define Jewish philosophy is *itself* an upshot of *modern* Jewish philosophy which raises two basic questions: how can a certain concept be really philosophical, and at the same time be Jewish in its essence? How can one reconcile the universal nature of philosophical discourse with the particularistic essence of Judaism? Isaac Husik, one of the most eminent scholars of medieval Jewish philosophy, ended his book with the questionable assertion: "There are Jews and there are philosophers, but there are no Jewish philosophers and there is no Jewish philosophy."[3] This, evidently, was an extreme and provocative formulation of a problem which had occupied Jewish thought from Mendelssohn to our times, and has given birth to many different answers. To investigate the nature of modern Jewish philosophy is therefore more or less congruent with exploring the nature of Jewish philosophy itself, which has been the topic of the first chapter of this book. However, a Jewish philosopher is entitled to be called a philosopher, if his or her thought contributes to philosophy. This characterization indeed holds for most of the Jews who have excelled in the field of philosophy from Philo, through Saadia, ibn Gabirol, Maimonides, and others in the Middle Ages, to Spinoza, Mendelssohn, H. Cohen, Rosenzweig, and Buber in modern times. All of them are of universal importance, some of them obviously better known than others. We are interested in them not merely because they are Jews but because we are confident that their philosophy has a Jewish dimension as well. In this chapter the inquiry will therefore take as its point of departure the working hypothesis that there exists something which can be defined as a "Jewish philosophy," and concentrate on the differences and changes which it has undergone in the modern era.

While medieval Jewish philosophy evolved simultaneously with Arabic philosophy that was its counterpart and source of inspiration on the general scene, this was not the case of modern Jewish philosophy in its beginnings. During the two-hundred-and-fifty-year transition period from the Middle Ages to the modern era Jews were forced to live in a physical as well as spiritual ghetto which, with very few exceptions, narrowed their spiritual horizons and put an end to the former fruitful encounter with general culture and philosophy, especially as it had flourished in the Islamic regions. With the demolition of the ghetto walls at the end of the eighteenth century, in the wake of Napoleon's armies, Jews found themselves culturally and spiritually lagging behind their non-Jewish contemporaries. M. Mendelssohn and S. Maimon were but two impressive exceptions that confirmed the rule. (B. Spinoza and the Jewish community in the Netherlands were a case apart.) Therefore, in Western Europe, from the period of the struggle for emancipation, Jewish intellectuals had to cope with many new problems of which their predecessors had been unaware, especially how to remain a Jew while taking part in the general spiritual and cultural life of their surroundings. For more than a century this was the chief enterprise of German Jewish philosophers. Only in the twentieth century, and a fortiori after the Second World War and the destruction of German Jewry, did Jewish philosophy begin to develop outside Germany – in America, Israel, Britain, and France.

But there is one more problem which did not exist in the Middle Ages. Except for a few famous converts, such as Abner of Burgos, who abandoned Judaism, the Jewishness of the Jewish philosophers and of their writings did not arouse any particular problem. But what about the greatest philosopher that the Jewish people has produced in the modern era, namely Baruch Spinoza? Does his work belong to Jewish philosophy? The answer of most scholars seems to be affirmative.[4] And what about S. Maimon,[5] K. Marx, H. Bergson, E. Bloch, and other thinkers?[6] Similarly, what about the general philosophical writings of thinkers such as M. Mendelssohn, H. Cohen, E. Levinas, etc.? Do they belong to Jewish philosophy? Or may one perhaps portray their authors as split personalities, dealing simultaneously with Jewish and general philosophy? (Levinas indeed tried to distinguish between his

"Hebrew" and "Greek" writings, both in French of course.) Although these are more methodological than theoretical questions, they cannot be ignored. They also are relevant in determining the nature of modern Jewish philosophy. But they will be of lesser concern to the ensuing inquiry which focuses on modern Jewish philosophy in its commonly accepted sense, namely philosophy of Jews in a Jewish context.

All these processes led also to the emergence of different religious streams inside Judaism that were fostered by certain philosophical outlooks. Modern Jewish philosophy is distinct from that of the Middle Ages by exhibiting a much more marked religio-philosophical pluralism. While the various medieval trends in Jewish philosophy, such as kalām, Neoplatonism, Aristotelianism, etc. did not substantially differ in their conception of Judaism – all of them were "orthodox" (the sole exception being the Karaites) – Judaism today is apprehended differently by Orthodox, Reform, Conservative, Reconstructionist, and secular Jews.

This entailed another major change. Medieval Jewish philosophy relied on two main sources of authority – on the one hand Aristotle's (and to a lesser degree Plato's) philosophy, and on the other hand the Bible and the thought of the Sages. Moreover, since the Torah and the Oral Law were believed to have been conferred by divine revelation, their teachings were not open to critical inquiry; they were interpreted by way of exegesis and commentary. Also independent philosophical thought was usually couched in the language of interpretation. This explains the preponderant role of *hermeneutics* in medieval thought; its purpose was to bridge the gap between philosophical inquiry and authoritative prophetic revelation. Although this did not diminish the importance of Jewish medieval philosophy which still occupies a paramount position in the history of Jewish philosophy, such procedures are no longer compatible with modern philosophical methods of inquiry. From Spinoza onwards Jewish thinkers emphasized and investigated the philosophical issues for their own sake; they resorted to interpretation of scriptural passages only for illustration or for didactic purposes. While in the Middle Ages the main road led from the sacred writings of Judaism to philosophy, the new point of departure was general philosophy. This came to its most striking expression in the writings of the two thinkers who stood on the threshold of modern Jewish philosophy – B. Spinoza and M. Mendelssohn. Both had grown up in the religious tradition of Judaism although Spinoza turned away from it and considered it inconsistent with rationalist philosophical discourse while Mendelssohn did not see any contradiction between his philosophical thought and his Jewish belief. One cannot get an appropriate understanding of their thought without searching for the Jewish origins and traces in their philosophies. This holds for Spinoza no less than for Mendelssohn.[7] However, their philosophical thought was not only shaped by outside influences, but it transgressed the limits of Jewish problematics. Their philosophical work (except Mendelssohn's *Jerusalem* which was expressly written for apologetical reasons) does not belong to Judaism although all later Jewish philosophers could not ignore it, and came to grips with it in various ways.

Most modern Jewish philosophers look upon Judaism as a spiritual creation of human thought which has evolved in history. This means that to criticize various elements of the Jewish religious tradition or to contest the veracity and authority of biblical and talmudic statements, stories, beliefs, and injunctions no longer constitutes an act of heresy. This was the chief implication of Spinoza's Bible criticism which still looked preposterous to the scholars of his time, Jews or Christians. It has meanwhile become a commonplace for modern Jewish philosophers that one ought to distinguish between the more permanent along with the more transient elements in the Jewish religious heritage. Consequently, modern Jewish philosophy is no longer a handmaiden of religion or theology but like philosophy in general.

Although most Jewish philosophers in the modern era were and are religious, their philosophical inquiries are not subjugated to religious authority nor motivated by Jewish religious goals. They engage in their philosophical studies as philosophers, not as rabbis or commentators. Independence of thought replaces subordination. They formulate their philosophies on an essentially secular basis, explicating the religious norms and beliefs of Judaism by cultural, social, ethical, and national aspects. Also, unlike medieval Jewish philosophy which exhibited more or less continuous trends – Aristotelian or Neoplatonic ones, etc. – modern Jewish philosophy manifests itself in the work of individual thinkers. It would be misleading to speak of a Kantian, Hegelian, or Schellingian school although one can trace the influence of these philosophers, and others, on the work of their Jewish acolytes. The quest for independent thought does not blur the impact of general philosophical trends, of Kant, Hegel, and Schelling, and of Marx, existentialism and phenomenology, and to a lesser degree British empiricism and American pragmatism. They represent sources of philosophical inspiration, but none of them acquired such authority as, for example, Aristotle in medieval Jewish philosophy. Despite the enormous imprint of Kant's philosophy on many nineteenth-century Jewish philosophers, foremost among them M. Lazarus and H. Cohen, or the influence of Herder on N. Krochmal, Hegel on S. Hirsch, Schelling on Sh. Formstecher, L. Steinheim, and F. Rosenzweig, Condillac's "sensualism" on S. D. Luzzatto, Spencer on Achad Ha'am, or Dewey on M. Kaplan, the Jewish philosophers always maintained an unmistakable critical stance in their regard.

These changes are sometimes indicated by new meanings given to certain traditional religious concepts. Revelation, for example, still occupies an important place in modern Jewish thought, among others in the philosophies of S. Steinheim and F. Rosenzweig.[8] But it is no longer conceived as an extrinsic occurrence but as an intrinsic belief, based on the presupposition of faith. While in medieval philosophy revelation was regarded as an objective event, a view which was still upheld by Mendelssohn, and formed the basis of his definition of the distinctiveness of Judaism, today most Jewish philosophers regard it as a subjective phenomenon.

The two main traditional arguments for revelation – prophecy and miracles – do not stand up to modern rationalist criticism. This was already demonstrated by Spinoza in the *Theologico-Political Treatise*.[9] Therefore, modern religious thinkers shifted the term "revelation" from the realm of philosophy to that of belief. This, however, gave rise to another difficulty of which they were perhaps not fully aware. It undermined, for example, the traditional objective historical basis of the covenant between God and Israel at Mount Sinai, as related in the Bible. Certain modern Jewish philosophers – Rosenzweig, Buber, Will Herberg – responded that revelation occurred to those men, who spoke about it in their writings. The Torah is the word of God, but at the same time it is a literary creation, written by man.[10]

Modern Jewish philosophy continues to explore most of the subjects investigated by medieval Jewish philosophy, such as God's reality, his essence and attributes, the reasons for the commandments, the relationship between reason and revelation, etc. But in addition it turns now to several new topics of philosophical interest – philosophy of history, political philosophy, ethics. The political, social, and legal status of Jews in their countries of residence pushed modern Jewish scholars to take up political philosophy, as demonstrated by Spinoza's *Theologico-Political Treatise* and Mendelssohn's *Jerusalem*. In the case of Spinoza's book the original incentive was a general political aim – to defend freedom of thought and expression – but this involved a thoroughgoing discussion of the political function of the ancient Hebrew state, and – at the end of the third chapter – of the political and historical status of the Jews in his time. Similarly, the uniqueness and continuity of the Jewish people in the Diaspora, without a homeland of their own, aroused interest in philosophy of history. It gave birth to the movement of the sciences of Judaism (*Chochmat Israel*) in the first decades of the nineteenth century, and found a stimulating expression in N. Krochmal's *Guide of the Perplexed of our Times*.[11] Also H. Graetz forewarded his great historiographical work with a historico-philosophical essay, in the Hegelian spirit, on "The construction of Jewish history."[12] In this field the turnabout in modern Jewish philosophy was indeed very dramatic. Almost all the Jewish philosophers interpreted Jewish existence on the basis of historical factors. While Spinoza tried to show that the history of the Jewish people in the diaspora was governed by the same laws that held for all other peoples,[13] Krochmal and Rosenzweig strove to demonstrate that the historical laws that are valid for all other nations are inapplicable to the Jewish people and its history.

But the mainstream of Jewish philosophy in the nineteenth century was engrossed in reconciling the particularism of the Jewish religious tradition with the universalism of philosophy. To this end Jewish philosophers devoted much thought to elaborating the concept of the "essence" or "spirit" of Judaism. In the past – and this still held for Mendelssohn – Judaism was identified with the observance of the "law." There was not felt to be any need to look for its essence, which was considered to be self-evident. This changed in the nineteenth century when many Jewish thinkers no longer observed all the religious commandments; they had therefore to search for another way of explaining their adherence to Judaism. This they did by leaning on the concept of "essence." The particular essence of Judaism consisted, as it were, in the universal message of "ethical monotheism." This idea became the key concept of the liberal trends of Judaism. So, rather paradoxically, the particular essence of Judaism was presented by removing its particularistic features and by stressing its universal content.[14] Simultaneously, most modern Jewish thinkers endeavored to interpret the values of Western culture and thought in the light of the ancient Jewish source. This trend culminated in H. Cohen's magisterial *Religion of Reason out of the Sources of Judaism*.[15] As a matter of fact, all these new interpretations were a dialectical outcome of the inevitable encounter with modern philosophical ideas. It was only after the Jewish philosophers had become acquainted with concepts such as social justice, equality, etc., that they perceived them to be implied already by the Torah, and availed themselves of the biblical terms in order to discuss modern issues. Similarly, only after confronting the philosophical problem of freedom and determinism was it possible to reach a proper understanding of the concept of (divine) providence or of the famous saying, ascribed to Rabbi Aqibah: "Haqol tzafui vehareshut netunah" ("Everything is foreseen but freedom of action is granted"). Likewise, only · the apprehension of Kant's categorical imperative opened up the implicit philosophical vistas of Hillel's admonition: "Do not do unto others what you do not want to be done unto you." All these philosophical problems which were latent in the Jewish scriptures acquired their explicit and adequate elaboration only in modern Jewish philosophy. Although external influences were never absent in medieval Jewish philosophy, they fulfilled an incomparably greater role in the modern era. Then the concept of Judaism was shaped to a far-reaching degree by the fruitful dialogue with philosophical concepts, drawn from outside trends. Seen from this angle, H. Cohen did not merely work out a "religion of reason out of the sources of Judaism," but rather interpreted those sources by the precepts of his neo-Kantian epistemology and ethics.

In the modern era, Jewish philosophy thus encountered new problems that until then had received but little attention. At the same time, various traditional concepts acquired new meaning. For instance, the traditional idea of Israel's chosenness was exchanged for that of Israel's mission. Modern Jewish philosophers were aware of the problematical nature of the traditional concept. Spinoza had already asserted that any claim of election, based on intellectual or moral superiority, is philosophically indefensible.[16] Mendelssohn and nineteenth-century Jewish philosophers, struggling for equality, also felt uncomfortable with the concept of chosenness. The latter introduced and emphasized the idea of the "mission of Israel," which is to propagate "ethical monotheism," that is, the moral teachings of the Bible, especially as expressed by the Prophets. However, does this change in terminology indicate a conceptual shift? The traditional belief in chosenness undoubtedly constituted some sort of ideological self-compensation for the inferior status of the Jewish people in the diaspora throughout the ages. It "enabled the Jews to defy the powers of destruction and to reverse the normal patterns of history."[17] From this angle it had fulfilled an important positive role in Jewish life in the past, but it now became metaphysically and ethically untenable in the light of modern philosophical thought; it contravened the humanistic view that every person and every nation embodies the values of one common humanity and one human spirit. None the less, several modern Jewish philosophers still upheld the notion of election, including even such an important secular thinker as Achad Ha'am; he vindicated the idea of the chosen people without believing in a choosing God. The people of Israel, as it were, excels by its essential "differentness" and by its unique ethics of absolute justice; the latter expresses its "mission."

If a secular thinker like Achad Ha'am approved of the concept of chosenness, despite its ethical difficulties, it comes as no surprise that various Jewish religious philosophers did so, although with great care and caution. Rosenzweig stated in his famous correspondence with Eugen Rosenstock:

> That is why even today, when the idea of being elected has been adopted by every nation, the election of the Jews is something unique, because it is the election of the "one people," and even today our peculiar pride or peculiar modesty, the world's hatred or the world's contempt, rejects an actual comparison with other

peoples. Though its content has now become something
universal, it has lost nothing of its metaphysical weight.[18]

However, for Rosenzweig, Jewish uniqueness and chosenness is
embodied in Israel's being *outside* of history while all other peoples
and religions fulfill their roles inside the historical orbit. Israel's chosenness had also been the focal point of Leo Baeck's Jewish religious
thought. He shared some of Rosenzweig's later ahistorical approach.
Baeck conceived of chosenness as a consequence of revelation, which
was Israel's unique experience; the more certain the act of revelation,
the more pronounced the sense of chosenness derived from it. But, for
Baeck, this was an article of faith and not an historical judgment.
It involves Israel's responsibility toward other peoples. This implies,
evidently, the concept of the mission of Israel again. The people of
Israel is chosen, according to Baeck, because it is part of humanity and
accomplishes the latter's task in the world. Baeck thus links together
the concepts of revelation, chosenness, and mission; they form the
theological expression of that Jewish particularity which was destined
to become universal. However, while for Rosenzweig this universal
mission implied the concept of Israel as a metahistorical people, Baeck
conceived it as the outcome of historical theology although at the same
time transcending historical definitions and limitations.

Already Abraham Geiger had insisted, in a more or less Hegelian
way, that doctrines of chosenness were characteristic features in the
development of almost all peoples, and not just peculiar to the Jewish
people. On the contrary, according to him, the uniqueness of Judaism
is embodied in the fact that more than any other people or religion it
has completely overwhelmed such particularist notions and developed
its universalist credo.

The concept of "chosenness," because of its significant role in
Jewish life and history, certainly must not be disparaged as scandalous;
but it is now utterly incompatible with a modern world view, based
on the ethical essentials of humanism and universalism. In this regard
Kaplan stated very clearly: "As a psychological defense to counteract
the humiliation to which the Jewish people was subjected, the doctrine
of 'election' had its value as an expression of the sense of spiritual
achievement in the past; it had some justification in fact."[19] But he
hastens to add that nowadays "from an ethical standpoint, it is deemed
inadvisable, to say the least."[20] After Spinoza, it was Kaplan who discarded the notion of chosenness more systematically than any other
Jewish thinker. He did not hesitate to name the chapter devoted to it:
"The chosen people idea an anachronism."[21] To hold on to the concept
of chosenness now is no more than "self-infatuation." This equally
applies, according to Kaplan, to the attempts to replace it by the

doctrine of "mission," which he characterized, using again a pejorative term, as "religious imperialism," clashing with "the ethical basis of democracy."[22] Both are not merely undesirable concepts but useless claims. The notion of chosenness occupies a relatively large place in this chapter because it is an instructive paradigm case of the treatment of traditional concepts by modern Jewish philosophers.

Similar changes took place with regard to the belief in the messiah. The personalistic version of the messiah gave way to messianism, that is, to the messianic idea as an essentially moral vision that will unite all humankind in a life of justice and righteousness. This conception occupied a central position in the thought of Jewish non-Orthodox philosophers; some of them tried to interpret it in terms of a universal ethical and social prophecy; others tended to identify it with the rise of emancipation. Still others converted the messianic idea into the idea of redemption, both on the personal and on the communal plane. This became one of the three focal notions of Rosenzweig's *Star of Redemption*, and traces of it can even be found in E. Bloch's Marxist-utopian philosophy of hope. The idea of messianism was perceived by secular Zionist thinkers as self-realization, opposed to passive waiting for the coming of the redeemer. It thus became a symbolic expression of the national redemption of the Jewish people.

There was, however, an important Jewish philosopher, the late Steven Schwarzschild, who vehemently attacked all these attempts to replace the messiah by messianiam. In his essay "The Personal Messiah – Toward the Restoration of a Discarded Doctrine,"[23] he was perhaps less concerned with reintroducing the traditional belief of the past than refuting modern versions of what he named "pseudo-Messianism." The great danger for modern humanity consists, as it were, in the illusion that the messianic idea has been accomplished, whether by the modern national movements, including Zionism, or in the so-called "socialist" states (history has indeed proved him right on this), or by the establishment of the state of Israel. The doctrine of a personal messiah does not necessarily lead to quietism or passive waiting. On the contrary, the fact that we are still waiting for him ought to make us more suspicious of those who claim that messianism is already a fait accompli, and especially of its secularized interpretation. But Schwarzschild's rather idiosyncratic view on this matter, although inspired by humanist and socialist ideals, is not characteristic of the general trend of modern Jewish philosophy with regard to the messianic idea.

Finally, a few remarks on the important place of ethics in modern Jewish philosophy. Modern and contemporary Jewish inquiries into ethics differ from the ethical teachings of Jewish philosophy in the past. There are multiple new problems, many of them engendered by the enormous changes that have occurred on the social plane and as a result of recent scientific and technological progress. This evidently is a problem which Jewish ethics shares with general ethics. The particularly Jewish aspect consists in there being not only many new issues which Jewish religious thinkers in the past, no less than non-Jewish ones, could not even have imagined but that they have provided nowadays a mutliplicity of answers. This is, of course, an inevitable outcome of the pluralism which has become the distinctive feature of modern Jewish philosophy. There is no longer a place for a "Jewish" position, if there ever was, but one must now usually ask: What do Orthodox, Conservative, Reform, Reconstructionist, or secular philosophers (and scholars) say about this or that specific ethical question? In this connection there is another point worth mentioning. When modern Jewish philosophers discuss ethical problems, they usually attempt to come to grips with halakhic positions on those ethical issues that preoccupy contemporary thought. All these problems acquired a new dimension with the rise of liberal religious currents inside Judaism that did not observe many or even most of the halakhic commandments, and a fortiori with the rise of secularism inside Judaism. Although for the majority of Jews today, whether religious or secular, halakhah is considered to represent only a part of the religious outlook of Judaism, one cannot shut one's eyes to the fact that in the Jewish religious tradition halakhah has played a predominant role. Therefore any modern inquiry into Jewish ethics must take halakhah into account too, whether one wishes to acknowledge its ongoing authority or to submit it to a critical scrutiny. From the philosophical viewpoint this can be reduced to one common denominator: does there exist a Jewish extra-halakhic ethics? This has become one of the most fascinating questions of contemporary Jewish philosophy.[24]

In conclusion, notwithstanding the shift of emphasis from election to mission, from the belief in a personal messiah to the messianic idea and other similar connotational changes, as well as the new approaches to ethics and halakhah, many issues of medieval Jewish philosophy have retained their vitality and relevance. Jewish philosophy resembles general philosophy in that both display intellectual continuity, although the hiatus between medievality and modernity was much more profound and conspicuous in Jewish than in general philosophy. However, as David Neumark has written in the introduction to his *History of Jewish Philosophy in the Middle Ages*: "The aim of any investigation into the history of philosophy is philosophy itself, philosophical awareness."[25]

❧❧ NOTES ❧❧

1 This was the title of Julius Guttmann's famous book on the history of Jewish philosophy. The title of the English edition accentuated this still more: *Philosophies of Judaism*.

2 These questions were treated extensively in the third part of my *Between Yafeth and Shem*, pp. 95–131.

3 Husik 1958, p. 432.

4 Only J. Guttmann expressed an ambivalent opinion. In his *Philosophies of Judaism* he defined it as "beyond Jewish philosophy" while in his important essay "Mendelssohn's *Jerusalem* and Spinoza's *Theologico-Political Treatise*," in Jospe 1981, pp. 361–86 he expressed a contrary view.

5 Apart from *Givat HaMoreh*, his Hebrew commentary to the first part of Maimonides' *Guide of the Perplexed*, all his work was in the field of general philosophy.

6 See Levy 1987, pp. 107–8; Jospe 1988, p. 9.

7 Levy 1989.

8 By the way, Rosenzweig's *Star of Redemption* exemplifies the profound changes in modern Jewish philosophy; notwithstanding its religious dimension and its salient Jewish elements, especially in the third part, the book was not motivated by Jewish aims, apologetic or others, but it was written out of general philosophical deliberations.

9 Spinoza 1951, chapters 1, 2, 6.

10 Herberg 1975, pp. 246–50.

11 Krochmal 1961.

12 Graetz 1936.

13 Spinoza 1951, p. 56.

14 Leo Baeck's *Das Wesen des Judentums* of 1905, responding to Adolf von Harnack's book on the essence of Christianity, contributed much to the popularity of the concept of "essence of Judaism."

15 Cohen 1972.

16 "In regard to intellect and true virtue, every nation is on a par with the rest, and God has not in these respects chosen one people rather than another." Spinoza 1951, p. 56.

17 Herberg 1970, p. 279.

18 Rosenstock-Huessy 1971, p. 131.

19 Kaplan 1934, p. 43.

20 Ibid.

21 Kaplan 1948, pp. 211–30.

22 Ibid., pp. 222, 224.

23 Schwarzschild 1970, pp. 519–37.

24 For example Lichtenstein 1978, pp. 102–23.

25 Neumark 1907–10, p. 5.

❧ BIBLIOGRAPHY ❧

Texts

Baeck, L. (1936) *The Essence of Judaism* (London: Macmillan).

Cohen, H. (1972) *The Religion of Reason out of the Sources of Judaism* (New York: Unger).

Herberg, W. (1975) *Judaism and Modern Man* (New York: Meridian).

Husik, I. (1958) *A History of Medieval Jewish Philosophy* (New York: Meridian).

Jospe, R. (1988) *What is Jewish Philosophy?* (Tel Aviv: Open University).

Kaplan, M. M. (1934) *Judaism as a Civilisation* (New York: Macmillan).

—— (1948) *The Future of the American Jew* (New York: Macmillan).

Krochmal, N. (1961) *More Nevukhee ha-zeman: The Writings of Nachman Krochmal*, edited with an introduction by S. Rawidowicz (Waltham, MA: Ararat).

Levy, Z. (1987) *Between Yafeth and Shem – On the Relationship between Jewish and General Philosophy* (New York and Berne: Lang).

Neumark, D. (1907–10) *Geschichte der jüdischen Philosophie des Mittelalters* (Berlin: Reimer).

Rosenstock-Huessy, E. (ed.) (1971) *Judaism despite Christianity – The "Letters on Christianity and Judaism" between Eugen Rosenstock-Huessy and Franz Rosenzweig* (New York: Schocken).

Spinoza, B. (1951) *Theologico-Political Treatise*, in *The Chief works of B. de Spinoza* (New York: Dover).

Studies

Graetz, H. (1936) *Die Konstruktion der jüdischen Geschichte* (Berlin: Schocken).

Guttmann, J. (1973) *Philosophies of Judaism*, translated by D. W. Silverman (New York: Schocken).

Herberg, W. (1970) "The 'Chosenness' of Israel and the Jew of today," in *Arguments and Doctrines*, edited by A. A. Cohen (New York: Harper & Row).

Jospe, A. (1981) *Studies in Jewish Thought* (Detroit: Wayne State University Press).

Levy, Z. (1989) *Baruch or Benedict: On Some Jewish Aspects of Spinoza's Philosophy* (New York and Berne: Lang).

Lichtenstein, A. (1978) "Does Jewish Tradition Recognize an Ethic independent of Halakhah?," in *Contemporary Jewish Ethics*, edited by M. M. Kellner (New York: Sanhedrin).

Schwarzschild, S. S. (1970) "The Personal Messiah: Toward the restoration of a Discarded Doctrine," in *Arguments and Doctrines*, edited by A. A. Cohen (New York), pp. 519–37.

CHAPTER 22

The social and cultural context: seventeenth-century Europe

Elisheva Carlebach

INTRODUCTION

Decisive historical breaks from the past led to the gradual emergence of new political and cultural forms in seventeenth-century Europe that would predominate through the nineteenth century. By the end of the sixteenth century, the Catholic Church had lost the exclusive hegemony it had enjoyed for so many centuries. Decades of religious wars weakened confessional loyalties as European states changed denominations. Political thinkers such as Jean Bodin and the jurist Hugo Grotius had begun to separate politics from theology. Christian Hebraists asserted a need for Jews as teachers of the sacred texts and a philo-semitic movement arose in some Protestant millenarian circles. States began to adopt the principle of raison d'état, of which mercantilism was the economic expression. European economic power began to shift from the Mediterranean basin toward the north Atlantic states. In the seventeenth century, Jewish spokesmen such as Menasseh ben Israel of Amsterdam and Simone Luzzatto of Venice could urge the resettlement of Jews by appealing to the economic self-interest of states. The economic success of the Protestant Netherlands, and later of England, led their rivals for economic power to emulate their success by ameliorating their posture toward Jewish settlement.

RESETTLEMENT

These changes paved the way for princes and states, particularly of the new sea-based powers, England and the Netherlands, to invite Jews to settle for the purposes of developing their economies. By the seventeenth century, Jews, often crypto-Jews (Marranos, see below) who initially concealed their true beliefs, had begun to resettle Western Europe. These new Jewish settlements reversed the centuries-long medieval process of expulsions of Jews which had emptied Western Europe of its Jewish communities by the late fifteenth and early sixteenth centuries.[1]

By the 1570s, Jews were readmitted to Bohemia, and greatly expanded their settlements in other parts of Germany and Austria. German Jews who had trickled into Metz were formally acknowledged by the French king in 1595. A nucleus of Portuguese crypto-Jews settled in Hamburg in the 1590s, to become the most important north European Jewish community through the seventeenth century. The Italian city-states defied papal preferences and encouraged settlement of more Jews in Venice, Livorno, Pisa, Mantua, Ferrara, and other cities. Portuguese crypto-Jews settled in Amsterdam in 1595. Their numbers greatly expanded in Bordeaux and Bayonne, and later in central France. The petition by Menasseh ben Israel, a Dutch rabbi, to Oliver Cromwell, to permit Jews to settle in England, sparked a fierce controversy in 1655. While the Jews were not formally admitted, they began to settle in London openly as Jews after that date. Many of these settlements followed a similar process of consolidation: they were granted first freedom from persecution and eventually, legal status as professing Jews.

❧ PATTERNS OF GOVERNANCE ❧

As the medieval model of a society comprised of corporate entities gave way to stronger centralized bureaucracies and absolute governments, the special status of the Jewish communities became more antithetical to the principles of central government. Yet after having admitted or retained a Jewish community which served their economic interests, European governments were not yet willing to remove the social and economic barriers to integration. In the end, Jewish communities maintained their distinctive framework, with the governments retaining the right to curtail aspects of Jewish autonomy as it suited them.

Most new communities, founded and populated by emigrants, consciously emulated the medieval model of judicial and cultural autonomy in which the Jewish community, the *kehillah*, functioned as a corporate entity.[2] Like its medieval predecessors, the constitutions of the communities granted power to elected boards of *parnasim*. These were often a narrow and powerful oligarchy composed of the most wealthy and influential members. While tension existed both within the leading class and between classes, the system was remarkably effective in maintaining social control and a full range of social services, and mediating between the Jewish community and the local and central governments.

The medieval paradigm in which each city contained one *kehillah* which embraced all the Jewish inhabitants of that locale was no longer valid by the seventeenth century. In addition to containing at least one Sephardic and one Ashkenazic community, many were further subdivided into additional *kehillot* based on city of origin. The Jewish population of Venice was divided into three nations, the Ponentine, Levantine, and German. In Rome, Italian, Spanish, Sicilian, and German congregations coexisted with varying degrees of harmony. Geographic and cultural particularism, embodied by the existence of parallel communities, contended with the impulse to consolidate. Portuguese Jews who began arriving in Amsterdam in the last decade of the sixteenth century established three separate congregations. In 1639, they had combined into one powerful *kehillah* whose leaders wielded great power over its members, an authority ratified by the municipal government. In 1703, the young congregation Sa'ar Asama'im (Gates of Heaven) in London issued a ban against establishment of additional Sephardic congregations.

Older communities with venerable traditions, particularly those in Italian cities – Venice was the pre-eminent exemplar – provided models for Jewish governance and organization to newer communities that were established in the seventeenth century, such as those in Amsterdam, London, and Hamburg. Marranos who fled Spain and Portugal arrived in fits and spurts through the eighteenth century and were united with the Sephardic communities.[3] The encounter between the exiles sparked unprecedented clashes over customs, liturgy, and educational ideals.

After 1648, refugees from Poland's decades-long tumult, the "Protop," initiated by the Cossack rebellion, brought to the western Jewish communities Judaic erudition, books, the Yiddish language, and a seemingly infinite neediness that strained the limited financial resources of the communities. The new layers of refugees were greeted with ambivalence. Ashkenazic *kehillot* soon came to outstrip their Sephardic counterparts in Western Europe in population, but not in prestige and influence. An exception to this was the rise of court Jews in central Europe, particularly during the Thirty Years War, 1618–48, when both sides of the ostensibly religious conflict turned to Jewish financiers and suppliers thereby creating a new class of courtiers. Many used their influence to become advocates for Jewish causes, founders of new communities, and patrons of Jewish learning.[4]

The medieval model in which communities had absolute authority to levy taxes continued into the early modern period. *Cherem*, the ban of excommunication, along with less potent variants, was one of the most powerful weapons of social control available to communal leaders. From an expression of censure to total ostracism, the mere threat of *cherem* generally kept deviance well checked. The power of *cherem* underpinned the constitution of every Jewish community, and it was invoked for a variety of infractions. While there had always been a delicate balance between lay and rabbinic power, in some new communities lay leaders were so powerful that the traditional balance of powers was decisively altered in their favor, a subtle prefiguration of the course of Jewish communal leadership in modern times. With the passage of time, the frequent use of *cherem* to resolve every dispute eroded its power; the loss of Jewish autonomy rendered it harmless.

Other means of control included the *haskamah*, approbation, required for all books before they could be published. From the time of the earliest Hebrew books printed during their authors' lifetime, rabbinic *haskamot* were required, placed first at the end of books and later after the title page. Ostensibly letters of recommendation to rabbinic colleagues, they also served as declarations of copyright and, more importantly, as a means of exercising Jewish self-censorship. In the seventeenth century, lay councils attempted to assert exclusive authority over *haskamot*, provoking rabbinic opposition.

The autonomous *kehillah* administered the formal religious, social, and judicial institutions necessary to the life of the community. Synagogues served the traditional functions of worship and study. They often served as social centers where news and information circulated together with official announcements. More important to the fabric of daily life than the formal communal structures, for most seventeenth-century Jews, was the network of overlapping voluntary societies, known as *chevrot*, which proliferated in this period. These associations had religious, educational, charitable, or social goals, such as study of holy texts, burial of the dead, dowering poor brides, or occupational association. The *chevrot* formed a social infrastructure parallel to the communal hierarchy – often cooperating with it, sometimes overlapping it, but completely independent of it.[5]

The small size and large number of the fraternities, twenty members on average, meant that every member could play an important role and that a significant proportion of the Jewish population looked to these fraternities for their primary social identity. Admittance to some *chevrot* was restricted on the basis of wealth, family, and scholarship; in these, membership was a coveted privilege; expulsion the equivalent of excommunication. In other cases, the associations served as alternatives for those who could not attain leadership positions within the communal structure, often maintaining separate prayer groups with their own scholarly leaders functioning as rabbi. The importance of these cells for the social, spiritual, and intellectual lives of many seventeenth-century Jews cannot be overestimated. Many of the most important unifying trends in the Jewish world spread by means of the *chevrot*. The dissemination of kabbalah, the maintenance of close links with the Holy Land, and efforts to hasten the redemption, were achieved through the fraternities. As the *chevrot* became sufficient sources of social consensus and spiritual sustenance for their members, they contributed to the forces that eroded central authority within the *kehillah*.

❧ SPIRITUAL AND INTELLECTUAL ❧ CURRENTS

For the Jews who entered Western Europe to form new communities, social and communal life could be modeled on the medieval forms, but their spiritual and intellectual content could not simply revert to the medieval mode. The vague but pervasive concept of "crisis of authority" that has been affixed to seventeenth-century Europe is useful as a framework for understanding the disparate and often paradoxical trends within seventeenth-century Western European Jewry.[6] Few seventeenth-century Jews were spared the pangs of dislocation that began with the Iberian expulsions, and their attendant multiple migrations and forced conversions.[7] The responses to these ruptures from the past and loss of security can be grouped into two essential patterns. Some idealized the institutions and values of the past and attempted to endow them with centrality and authority. This impulse was nourished by turning inward to Jewish spiritual and cultural traditions. The attempts to retrieve the worlds that were lost often led to innovative adaptations of traditional forms. For others, the profound sense of exile and alienation proved stronger than the pull of tradition. In this paradigm, Jews turned outward to the larger society in social, economic, and intellectual configurations that became pathways for breaking with the medieval model.

❧ MARRANISM ❧

Jewish converts to Christianity and their descendants emerged from the Iberian Peninsula and reverted to Judaism through the eighteenth century. Their contribution to the religious, social, and economic complexion of newly reconstituted Jewish communities was considerable. Those who emerged from the Marrano matrix carried with them or developed in their new abodes a broad range of attitudes and beliefs.

For some, the sacrifices made to maintain a secret Judaism at risk of great peril led to a wholehearted embrace of all things Jewish in their new communities. As the instances of the physicians Isaac Cardoso and Isaac Orobio de Castro demonstrate, some even became zealous polemicists for the Jewish faith.[8] At the other end of the spectrum were Marranos whose Jewish knowledge was so distorted and fragmentary that they could never become reconciled to the version of Judaism that was practiced by their contemporaries; they became outright skeptics, as the case of Uriel da Costa illustrates. Others fled persecution or pursued economic opportunities and lived at the margins of Jewish commitment. Marranos engendered reactions in the Jewish community, from great admiration for those who became defenders of the Jewish faith to rejection and condemnation of those who could not or would not adjust. The communities and their religious leaders strove to ease the reintegration of the Marranos by providing them with schools, teachers, and literature in their vernacular. Marranos contributed to every sphere of Jewish activity. Their ranks included philosophers, messianists, physicians, kabbalists, and rabbis. Some were world-class merchants, bankers, brokers, and diplomats whose entrepreneurial skills contributed to the mercantilist goals of their respective states and helped modernize the global economy with the development of capital, stock markets, and insurance. Their wealth and status enabled many of these figures to play leading roles within the Jewish communities.

❦ KABBALAH ❦

Until the sixteenth century, study of kabbalah, Jewish mystical doctrines whose canonical text was the *Zohar* (*The Book of Splendor*), had been the province of a small scholarly elite. During the sixteenth century, new emphases and new impulses were introduced into kabbalah in the circle of Isaac Luria in Safed. Toward the end of the sixteenth and the early decades of the seventeenth centuries, the esoteric doctrines were more widely disseminated. The *Zohar* was published in 1589, followed by other works. Kabbalistic terminology began to appear in sermons and popular ethical literature so that its basic vocabulary entered the public discourse. Among the most important concepts of Lurianic Kabbalah were that of a cosmic cataclysm, *shevirat ha-kelim* (shattering of the vessels), which occurred during creation when the divine essence overcame the vessels that were intended to contain it. The scattered and intermingled *kelippot*, shards, symbolized gross matter; the *nitzotzot*, sparks of divine matter. The most crucial element in the process is that of *tiqqun*, repair and restoration, which would result in wordly redemption and cosmic harmony in the divine spheres.

Humanity played a decisive role in the process, as each fulfillment of a religious obligation released the trapped sparks to return to their source.[9] Alongside the kabbalah there flourished, particularly in Italy, a sharply critical anti-kabbalist school which denied the authenticity of kabbalah and decried its irrational elements.[10]

THE SABBATIAN MESSIANIC MOVEMENT

Although centrally concerned with redemption, Lurianic kabbalah assigned no special role to a messiah figure. In an age so concerned with ending the travails of exile, this void would not last long. The messianic impulse in the post-exilic Sephardic world was manifested in a variety of ways. In sixteenth-century Safed, an attempt to revive *semikhah*, apostolic ordination of rabbis, as a prerequisite for the establishment of a Sanhedrin, was one expression of the desire for an end to the fragmented condition of Jewish authority. Many kabbalistic confraternities devoted their energies to programs of study and works intended to hasten the redemption. Authors wrote consolatory works announcing or implying that the redemption of Israel was imminent. Several messianic movements ignited the hopes of the exile-weary Jews. The most notable in the sixteenth century were the movements of Asher Lemlein in 1503 and David Reubeni and Solomon Molkho in 1530.

In the seventeenth century, several factors contributed to the immense scope and profound impact of the Sabbatai Zevi movement, which reached its apogee in 1665–6. The continued persecution of *conversos* in Iberia, the calamities which befell Polish Jewry after 1648, and an expectation of the millennium in the Christian world converged to make the Sabbatian messianic movement more widespread than any in medieval Jewish history. This messianic movement transcended every boundary of geography, class, and nationality. In her acclaimed memoir, Glückel of Hameln recalled the excitement of the Sabbatai Zevi's appearance:

> Throughout the world Thy servants and children rent themselves with repentance, prayer, and charity. . . . My good father-in-law left his home in Hameln, abandoned his house and lands and all his goodly furniture . . . sent . . . two enormous casks packed with linens and with peas, beans, and dried meats, shredded prunes . . . all manner of food that would keep. For the old man expected to sail any moment from Hamburg to the Holy Land.[11]

Spinoza's correspondent Henry Oldenberg reported the events to

Spinoza and asked for his impressions. "Everyone here is talking of a report that the Jews, after remaining scattered for more than two thousand years are about to return to their country. Few here believe it but many desire it."[12]

The impact of the Sabbatian messianic movement was more profound than any of its predecessors because its theologian and spokesman, Nathan Ashkenazi of Gaza, translated all the activities of the messiah into the vocabulary of Lurianic kabbalah, which had by then been disseminated throughout the Diaspora. The dénouement of the movement came in 1666, when Sabbatai converted to Islam under duress; he died ten years later. While most Jews sadly resigned themselves to the failure of the movement, some had been so profoundly convinced by their experience of a new era that they refused to relinquish their faith even in the face of the messiah's apostasy and death. Sabbatianism endured as a heretical sect in many varieties for several centuries. At its most extreme, Sabbatianism inspired its adherents to emulate the messiah's apostasy. In 1683, a group known as the Donmeh converted to Islam; in 1753, the Frankists in Poland converted to Catholicism. While some practiced ritual deviations from the normative tradition, more moderate varieties of Sabbatianism flourished throughout Europe in secret circles devoted to the study of Sabbatian kabbalah.

The Sabbatian movement, and the conflicts surrounding it, added to the sense of crisis both within the rabbinate and within the Jewish communities. After the failure of the movement, some Jews despaired and converted or developed a skeptical attitude toward religion. Many communities were driven by the suspicions that some members were secret Sabbatians. The rabbinic careers of Jacob Sasportas, at the height of the Sabbatian movement, Moses Hagiz and Chakham Zevi in the early eighteenth century, and Jacob Emden in the mid eighteenth century were energized by their zealous pursuit of Sabbatian adherents. Rabbinic reputations, such as those of Nechemiah Hayon, Moses Chayim Luzzatto, and Jonathan Eybeshuetz, were tainted by the suspicion that they harbored Sabbatian beliefs.[13] The lay leaders used their power to stifle any discordant notes sounded within the Jewish community, regardless of whether they were nourished by skeptical rationalism or zealous messianism. The founding fathers of the young Jewish communities in London, Amsterdam, and Hamburg were aware of the tenuous nature of their foothold. Communal leaders believed that the newly granted toleration by Christian society extended only to those who shared the belief system of normative (rabbinic) Judaism. They felt a civic duty to suppress any deviance that might reflect negatively on the ideological wholesomeness of the Jewish community. Although many were themselves victims or refugees from persecution, numerous parallels can be found to demonstrate that refugees from intolerance are not necessarily willing to extend the rights they have painfully gained to others. The rigid standards of conformity and limits of toleration demanded by the Jewish lay communal authorities of the seventeenth and eighteenth centuries were conditioned by their own experience of persecution. Those who had developed successful polemical mechanisms to parry the thrusts of their mortal religious foes easily adapted them to internal polemical battles.

❧ RABBINIC CULTURE ❧

While the seventeenth century was a golden age of talmudic scholarship in Poland, rabbinic emphasis in Western and central Europe reflected the compelling concerns of the day. Scholars produced an abundance of responsa literature; every contemporary concern was reflected within its pages. Leone Modena's *Responsa Ziqnei Yehudah* reveals the rich texture of Jewish life in an Italian ghetto, Zvi Ashkenazi's *Responsa Chakham Zvi*, Jacob Sasportas' *Ohel Jacob*, and Yair Chayim Bachrach's *Chavot Ya'ir* considered definitions of heresy and heterodoxy, the Jewish status of Marranos, delineations of rabbinic and communal authority, and the status of myriad disputed customs, among others. Rabbis wrote significant polemics against Christianity, often intended to disabuse former Marranos of Christian views, and many pedagogical manuals, aimed at the same audience, to aid the process of integration into contemporary Jewish life.

❧ SCIENCE ❧

The influence of new scientific developments within the thought of Jewish intellectuals was considerable. Marranos who had been educated as Christians in Iberia often brought knowledge of the most recent scientific and philosophical trends when they entered the Jewish community. Jewish authors considered every scientific subject from astronomy to zoology. Jews from every corner of Europe were admitted to the University of Padua to study medicine. Scientific, philosophical, and theological thought were not yet completely distinct disciplines; Jewish physicians such as Isaac Cardoso, Elijah Montalto, Samson Morpurgo were also religious polemicists and philosophers. Nowhere were the paradoxes of a transitional age demonstrated more vividly than in the Italian ghetto, where an indigenous Renaissance culture continued to exert its influence despite the restrictions of the counter-Reformation.

❧ NOTES ❧

1 For an excellent summary of the expulsion and resettlement period, see Israel 1991, pp. 5–69.
2 Baron 1942, pp. 208–82. On the historic contours of the *kehillah*'s autonomy, see recently Stolzenberg and Myers 1992, pp. 636–42, and the literature cited there.
3 On the integration of Marranos into the Jewish communities of Western Europe, see the masterful study of Yerushalmi 1971, esp. pp. 1–50.
4 Stern 1985, pp. 38–59; 177–226.
5 Baron 1942, pp. 348–72; Rivlin 1991, pp. 11–160.
6 For an influential account of this crisis in European intellectual history, see Hazard 1971, pp. 3–52; 119–97. On its application to European Jewry, see, inter alia, Abramsky 1979, pp. 13–28.
7 Baron 1967, pp. 236–83.
8 Yerushalmi 1971; Kaplan 1983.
9 Scholem 1987, pp. 135–44.
10 Idel 1987, pp. 137–200.
11 Glückel of Hameln 1978, pp. 46–7.
12 Spinoza 1951, p. 293.
13 On the aftermath of the Sabbatian movement, see Carlebach 1990.

❧ BIBLIOGRAPHY ❧

Texts

Glückel of Hameln (1978) [1932] *The Memoirs of Glückel of Hameln*, translated by M. Lowenthal (New York: Schocken).
Spinoza (1951) *Correspondence*, in *Works of Spinoza*, vol. 2, translated and edited by R. H. M. Elwes (New York: Dover).

Studies

Abramsky, C. (1979) "The Crisis of Authority Within European Jewry in the Eighteenth Century," in *Studies in Jewish Religious and Intellectual History Presented to Alexander Altmann*, edited by S. Stein and R. Loewe (University, Al: Alabama University Press), pp. 13–28.
Baron, S. (1942) *The Jewish Community*, 3 vols. (Philadelphia: Jewish Publication Society).
—— (1967) *A Social and Religious History of the Jews*, vol. 11 (New York and Philadephia: Columbia University Press and Jewish Publication Society).
Carlebach, E. (1990) *The Pursuit of Heresy: Rabbi Moses Hagiz and the Sabbatian Controversies* (New York: Columbia University Press).
Hazard, P. (1971) *The European Mind, 1680–1715*, translated by J. L. May (New York: Meridian).

Idel, M. (1987) "Differing Conceptions of Kabbalah in the Early 17th Century," in *Jewish Thought in the Seventeenth Century*, edited by I. Twersky (Cambridge MA: Harvard University Press), pp. 137–200.

Israel, J. (1991) [1985] *European Jewry in the Age of Mercantilism: 1550–1750* (Oxford: Clarendon Press).

Kaplan, Y. (1983) *From Christianity to Judaism* (Jerusalem: Magnes).

Rivlin, B. (1991) *Mutual Responsibility in the Italian Ghetto: Holy Societies 1516–1789* [Hebrew] (Jerusalem: Magnes).

Scholem, G. (1987) [1974] *Kabbalah* (New York: Dorset).

Stern, S. (1985) [1950] *The Court Jew: A Contribution to the History of Absolutism in Europe* (New Brunswick: Transaction).

Stolzenberg, N. and D. Myers (1992) "Community, Constitution, and Culture: The Case of the Jewish Kehilah," *University of Michigan Journal of Law Reform* 25: 633–70.

Yerushalmi, Y. (1971) *From Spanish Court to Italian Ghetto: Isaac Cardoso – A Study in Seventeenth-Century Marranism and Jewish Apologetics* (New York: Columbia University Press).

CHAPTER 23

The Jewish community of Amsterdam

Richard H. Popkin

The Jewish community of Amsterdam is usually portrayed as a rigid orthodox group because of its excommunication of Spinoza. It was, however, a unique intellectual group in modern Jewish history. Almost of all of its members were New Christians or Marranos, raised as Christians in Spain, Portugal, southern France, Belgium, or Italy, with little or no Jewish education. As the Netherlands gained its freedom from Spanish rule at the beginning of the seventeenth century, some New Christians came to Amsterdam and other Dutch cities. The supposed story of the founding of the Jewish community is that a group of these refugees from Iberia were found holding a religious service in the home of the Moroccan ambassador. The Dutch authorities were going to arrest them as enemy Spanish Catholics. When it was made clear that they were also victims of the Spanish enemy, and were Jews rather than Catholics, they were allowed to stay. The Dutch authorities sought to figure out what status these Jews should have. At the time there was no legal Jewish community in England, France, Spain, or Portugal. In Germany and Italy, the Jewish communities were highly regulated and restricted usually to ghettos. The legal expert Hugo Grotius was asked to formulate the conditions under which Jews could live in the Netherlands. His response, though tolerant for its day, still imposed many restrictions on Jewish activities, religious as well as social and economic. No decision was made, but an informal agreement developed under which the Jews could live freely in the Netherlands as long as they did not cause scandal to their Christian neighbors, and as long as no members of the group became public charges.

As a result, the first free Jewish community in modern Europe came into being. It was not confined to a ghetto, but existed without walls (until 1940 when Hitler sealed it off). Rembrandt lived on Joodenbreestraat (Jewish Broad Street, a block from the Great Synagogue). Jews could enter into the commercial world developing in Amsterdam, and some soon became important merchants in the vast overseas trade that poured through Amsterdam. The Jewish community was open to the outside world, and soon some Jews were conferring with Christians about points of Jewish lore, and about Hebrew studies. Many Christians attended services in the synagogue. The professor of Hebrew at Cambridge, Hugh Broughton, described attending the synagogue in its early days, and arguing there with members about the merits of Judaism and Christianity. Adam Boreel, the leader of the Dutch Collegiants, a creedless Christian group that later took Spinoza in, worked with leading rabbis on preparing an edition of the Mishnah in Hebrew with points, and a Spanish translation of the text. He financed the model of Solomon's Temple that was exhibited in Rabbi Judah Leon's garden next to the Synagogue. Pierre-Daniel Huet, the future bishop of Avranches, visited Menasseh in 1652 and went with him to the Synagogue. The Quaker Samuel Fisher attended services, and then discussed religious matters with members for hours afterwards in their homes. Later on Gilbert Burnet, the future bishop of Salisbury, studied Hebrew in the community, and attended services with an interpreter. Knorr von Rosenroth around the same time acquired from a rabbi in the community the collection of kabbalistic manuscripts that he translated in the *Kabbala Denudata* of 1677–8.

It was the first Jewish community that was accepted by the non-Jewish world, and allowed to defend its views publicly. It was able to interact with the Christian world in terms of common philosophical ideas. (Apparently enough of its members knew Latin and/or French to take part in current discussions.) The development of the Amsterdam Jewish community in an emergent secular society helped pave the way for modern pluralist, tolerant societies in Western Europe and America.

As the economic miracle of seventeenth-century Holland unfolded, more New Christians migrated to the Netherlands where they could throw off their Christian disguise and return to their ancestral faith. But many of them knew little of it. Hence, almost from the beginning the community had to set up schools for the young and old to prepare them for a Jewish life, and to give them a Jewish education. The most learned of the early members had been trained in Christian universities, some of them even holding theological degrees from those institutions.

Since there was no antecedent Jewish community to build upon, the Amsterdam one was self-created. Originally it had a Sephardic rabbi from North Africa, who soon left apparently because the congregation was so bizarre. A very early member was the very learned Abraham Cohen Herrera, who had been raised in Florence, and knew pagan, Christian, Jewish, and Arabic philosophy as well as the Lurianic kabbalah. He wrote a textbook in logic for Spanish-speaking students, and his masterpiece, *Puerto de Cielo*, in Amsterdam (the most philosophical interpretation of the kabbalah, which was published in Hebrew translation in 1655, and influenced Spinoza, and in Latin in 1677, and influenced Henry More, Isaac Newton, G. W. Leibniz, among others). Herrera lived in Amsterdam until his death, and seems to have played little role in the development of the community except that he passed on his immense kabbalistic learning to two young rabbis, Menasseh ben Israel and Isaac Aboab de Fonseca.

By 1617 or 1618, two figures who became very important in the group arrived, Saul Levi Morteira and Menasseh ben Israel. The former, who became the first chief rabbi, was an Ashkenazi Jew from Venice, who had been taken to Paris by Elijah de Montalto, the doctor of Queen Marie de Medici. Morteira was the doctor's secretary at the Louvre from 1610 to 1617. When Montalto died, Morteira transported his master's body to Ouderkerk near Amsterdam for burial since there was no legal functioning Jewish cemetery in France. He stayed and became a rabbi-teacher for the community. In 1617 a dissident member, David Farrar, who questioned various Jewish teachings, was causing problems. Morteira was sent as part of a delegation to Venice to find out what to do about the rebel. The delegation returned with the cherem statement to be used against Farrar, and the exact same later used against Spinoza. (Excommunication became the means by which the community regulated its members. Around 280 cases of excommunication are recorded during the seventeenth century, most for failing to pay dues, or to keep marriage contracts. Usually the excommunicatee apologized, was fined, and was reinstituted as a member in good standing.)

Morteira, unlike most of the other members, knew Hebrew and had had some Jewish training. In Paris he was involved with the Royal professor of Hebrew, Philip d'Aquin, a convert from Judaism. Recently around five hundred sermons in Hebrew by Morteira have been discovered, which were written in Hebrew but no doubt delivered in Portuguese, the language understood by the congregation. Morteira's writings, which will be discussed below, are in Portuguese, challenging Christian theological claims.

Menasseh was apparently born in Rochelle, France where his parents had fled from the Portuguese Inquisition. He was raised in Lisbon thereafter, and turned up in Amsterdam around 1618, and was quickly put to work as a teacher and a rabbi. He soon became a Hebrew teacher for Christian scholars, the first printer of Hebrew books in the Netherlands, and a renowned expositor of Jewish views. He wrote only one book in Hebrew, the rest in Spanish, sometimes followed by Latin translations. He was regarded as a great preacher. Christian scholars from various parts of Europe came to hear him, and to consult with him about various theological matters. He became known as *the* Jewish philosopher.

Menasseh and Isaac Aboab learned about Jewish mystical and kabbalistic thought from Herrera, and from del Medigo who was in Amsterdam in the 1620s. Aboab became the first rabbi in the Western hemisphere when he became the religious leader of the Jewish community in Brazil. He was there for a dozen years, and then returned to Amsterdam in 1654. With the support of one of the rich Jewish merchants, Abraham Peyrara, he established a school for the study of Jewish mysticism.

Another early intellectual figure was a Portuguese cleric, Uriel da Costa, who fled Portugal when the Inquisition was closing in on him. He had secretly reverted to Judaism in Portugal, by studying the religion described in the Old Testament. When he arrived in Amsterdam he found that the religion being practiced and taught there was very very different from his own. He challenged some of the basic practices, and wrote a work arguing that true ancient Judaism taught the *mortality* of the soul. His work was condemned by the community and it was thought all copies had been destroyed. Recently a copy has been found and is being prepared for publication. Da Costa was excommunicated, and for several years wandered around Holland and northern Germany. He finally asked for forgiveness, and after being whipped in the synagogue he was forced to lie in the doorway while the entire congregation walked over him. On being readmitted, he soon became contentious again, and before being expelled once more he committed suicide. His tragic story appears in his autobiography, which was published only in 1687 at least forty years after his death, printed by a Protestant, Philip van Limborch, to show how bad the Jewish community was. Pierre Bayle's article, "Acosta," based on this text, made Da Costa a famous martyr who has been seen as a precursor of Spinoza.

Da Costa's autobiography, *Exemplar*, indicates that he was a deist, perhaps one of the first, and had become a critic of all institutional religions. He proclaimed that one should not be a Jew or a Christian, but a man! His *Examen* has recently been published. The article describing the work by Herman Salomon suggests he was a rationalist thinker even before Descartes. But no matter how good or bad he may have been as a philosopher in his discussion of the mortality of the soul, the influence of the work as far as we can tell was nil since almost all of the copies were destroyed, and only a refutation by Samuel da Silva (also very rare) has survived.

The Amsterdam community kept up central features of Iberian education in philosophy and literature. Manuscripts in the Etz Chaim collection include courses in ethics and metaphysics corresponding to what was being taught in Spain and Portugal at the time. There are two logic texts by Abraham Cohen Herrera, printed in Spanish before his death in 1635. (The exact dates are not known.) One of these includes a chapter on "method," before Descartes' *Discours sur la méthode* had appeared, in which Herrera used the phrase "clear and distinct ideas." Since only one copy is known, the work was probably not influential at the time, but shows that Jewish thinkers were dealing with the same problems as gentile philosophers in the Netherlands. Some of Menasseh ben Israel's works were written to explain the Jewish point of view on philosophical-theological issues, to both Jewish and Christian audiences. Christian thinkers consulted Menasseh by letter and in person in Amsterdam. He published all except one work in Spanish or Latin. The one Hebrew work, *Nishmat Chaim*, contained a Latin summary in many of the copies, and a dedication to the Holy Roman Emperor. Copies are in the libraries of Queen Christina of Sweden and many important thinkers of the time.

The free situation of the Jewish community of Amsterdam allowed for open discussion of many issues in terms of the intellectual background of its members. In the 1650s, there seems to have been an explosion of radical new ideas, of messianic and mystical thought, and of intellectual rejection of Christianity and defenses of Judaism.

To begin with the radical views, they seem to have been brought to Amsterdam by Dr Juan de Prado and Isaac La Peyrère. Prado was born around 1612. He studied for nine years at the University of Alcalá, where he received degrees in medicine and theology. (He was a classmate of Orobio de Castro in the theology school.) Prado left Spain before the Inquisition could arrest him for secretly judaizing. He went in the entourage of a Spanish bishop to Rome, and then escaped to Hamburg, where he met Queen Christina immediately after her abdication, and greeted her, "Hail to the new Messiah. But who would have expected it to be a woman?" He then moved to Amsterdam, where he and young Baruch de Spinoza and one David Ribiera were all teaching elementary religious classes, and apparently were making critical comments about the Bible. Prado wrote, but did not publish, a work on why the law of nature takes precedence over the law of Moses.

Some of the criticism of the Bible seems to have come from the views expressed in Isaac La Peyrère's *Men before Adam*, which was published in Amsterdam in 1655 in four different editions, and was soon condemned by the states of Holland, and refuted by theologians all over Europe. La Peyrère was a New Christian from Bordeaux who was a secretary to the Prince of Condé. In 1654 he showed the work (originally written in 1641) to Queen Christina in Belgium, and she apparently offered to pay for having it printed in Amsterdam. La

Peyrère met Menasseh ben Israel when the latter came to call on the former Queen. Then he carried his manuscript to Amsterdam and stayed there until the book came out in the fall of 1655, dedicated to all the Jews and all the synagogues in the world, "by one who wishes to be one of you." The book challenges the authenticity of the biblical text, the Mosaic authorship of the Pentateuch, and the Bible's claim to portray the history of all humankind. La Peyrère claimed that there have been people in the world from all eternity, living a nasty brutish life. God created Adam and the Jewish people to save all humankind. The Bible is the history of the Jews, presented in somewhat garbled form because all that has come down to us is a "heap of copie of copie." The Jews were elected through Adam, rejected when they did not accept Jesus, and now were about to be recalled with the coming of the *Jewish* messiah.

The many heresies in the book led to a great furore, condemnations everywhere, and finally in late 1656 to the arrest of the author in Belgium, charged as a "heretic and a Jew," and to his formal recantation and apology to the Pope and his conversion to Catholicism. In 1655 while the book was being printed Menasseh ran into La Peyrère in Amsterdam and tried to arrange a public debate with him about his pre-Adamite theory. In Menasseh's list of works ready for publication which was appended to his last few writings, there is a refutation of the pre-Adamite theory in Latin. Unfortunately the work has not been located.

Apparently Prado, Ribiera, and Spinoza were charged with teaching false and heretical views. Only the cases of Prado and Ribiera survive, and show that they were accused of holding some of La Peyrère's radical views about the Bible and about human history. Spinoza owned the book and used it liberally in the *Tractatus*.

One of the rebels, Ribiera, left the community. Prado made a formal apology, and Spinoza was excommunicated. Spinoza's excommunication was probably a non-event as far as the community was concerned. It came during a time of great involvement with refugee problems, resettling thousands of Brazilian Jews, and dealing with thousands of Russian Jews fleeing from the Swedish invasion of Poland. Spinoza had already left the community, and the community's elders were preoccupied with immediate events and had no time for arguing about the Bible. The Spinoza case was never mentioned again in the community records.

Prado continued advancing his deistical views in letters to rabbi Morteira. He was formally excommunicated in 1658. In 1659 it is reported that he and Spinoza attended a theological discussion group, where rabbi, priest, and pastor got together, and that Prado and Spinoza advanced the view that God exists, but only philosophically. After this

Prado apparently moved to Belgium. His erstwhile classmate from Spain, Orobio de Castro, wrote two answers to his views, and Prado's son wrote a reply.

Counter to the rationalism and skepticism about religion that was developing, there was also a growing mystical and kabbalistic current. Rabbi Isaac Aboab had returned from Brazil in 1654. He and Abraham Peyrera set up a yeshivah for the study of mystical texts. In 1655, Aboab published in Hebrew Abraham Cohen Herrera's masterpiece, *Puerto del Cielo* (which Spinoza read and used in the *Ethics*). Aboab also read out the excommunication statement about Spinoza, probably just to a tiny audience.

Menasseh ben Israel offered a different kind of mysticism and messianism. In 1650 he published his best-known work, *The Hope of Israel*, in Spanish, Latin, English, Hebrew, and later in Dutch. The work set forth the Jewish view of the importance for messianic expectation of the reappearance of the lost tribes of Israel. Menasseh took the account of a Portuguese explorer in the Andes as evidence that at least part of a lost tribe had appeared. (The English Millenarians immediately expanded this news into the claim that the American Indians were Jews.) The book became a standard statement of the contention that the End of Days was at hand. English Millenarians rushed to press for the readmission of the Jews to England so that they could be converted as the penultimate step before the onset of the Millennium, the Second Coming of Jesus and his thousand-year reign on earth. The Millenarians were convinced that the Jews would be converted in 1655–6. A high-level delegation was sent to negotiate with Menasseh about the conditions of the Jews' return to England. The discussions dragged on until 1654 when Menasseh met La Peyrère in Belgium, and read his early and very rare work, *Du Rappel des Juifs* of 1643. Menasseh returned to Amsterdam and excitedly told a gathering of Protestant Millenarians that the coming of the messiah was imminent. This led to a work by one of the Protestants, *Good News for the Jews*, dedicated to Menasseh, and containing Menasseh's evidence that the Jewish messiah would soon arrive. Menasseh wrote his most mystical messianic work, *Piedra gloriosa*, interpreting Daniel's dream (illustrated by Rembrandt), and departed for England to present a petition to Cromwell. Menasseh was convinced that the return of the Jews to England would fulfill the last prophecy before the messiah's appearance. In England, where he was from 1655 to 1657, he met often with leading English thinkers such as Robert Boyle, Henry Oldenburg, Ralph Cudworth, and Henry More, and discussed theological and philosophical topics with them. He published one work in England (in English), *De Vindicatio Judeorum*, answering charges made against the Jews and advancing a view he took over from La Peyrère about how

Jewish and Christian expectations could be reconciled. They agreed basically on what was about to happen, and disagreed only about a historical question concerning what happened in the early first century. Since what was about to happen was all-important, the disagreement about the long past event could be overlooked. Menasseh's visit to England formally ended in failure, but informally it marked the beginning of the Jews' return to England. He returned to the Netherlands and died shortly thereafter.

A leading Millenarian, Peter Serrarius, who was also a patron of Spinoza's, met frequently with kabbalistic thinkers at the Synagogue and worked on Gematria with them, seeking to ascertain when the messiah would appear. As soon as news reached Amsterdam about Sabbatai Zevi, Serrarius was publishing pamphlets in English and Dutch telling everyone about the signs of the messianic age and that the king of the Jews had arrived. Serrarius, as well as almost all of the Amsterdam Jewish community, became followers of Sabbatai Zevi. Rabbi Aboab, by now chief rabbi, was a Sabbatian. The wealthy merchant Abraham Peyrera published his religious philosophical work, *La Certeza del Camino*, and then left for Palestine and set up a yeshivah in Hebron to teach Sabbatai Zevi's doctrines. Even the most rational thinker in the group, Orobio de Castro, was at first a believer. Only rabbi Sasportas struggled against the wild enthusiasm. After Sabbatai Zevi's conversion to Islam, many, including Orobio, gave up their belief in him, while others continued secretly being followers for the next decades.

The most philosophical member of the Amsterdam Jewish community, and the only one within the community who seriously contributed to general philosophical discussion of the time, was Isaac Orobio de Castro. He had been raised as a Christian in Spain, and was part of a secret judaizing group, which retained some Jewish practices and strong Jewish yearnings. He had studied medicine and theology, and became an important doctor. After being arrested and tortured by the Inquisition, he escaped to France, where he became professor of pharmacy at the University of Toulouse. He soon tired of being a fake Christian and went to Amsterdam, circumcized himself, and joined the community in the early 1660s. Like others raised in a Christian world, he had some difficulties in reconciling Judaism with his previous ideas. In Amsterdam, the rabbi who replaced Menasseh ben Israel, Moses d'Aguilar, a disciple of Saul Levi Morteira, was well versed in both Jewish matters and in general philosophy. Orobio wrote out some of his difficulties which Aguilar answered, especially concerning how to refute Pablo de Santa Maria, the famous Spanish convert. Orobio started out in Amsterdam with practically no Jewish learning. Aguilar supplied some of it, enabling Orobio to argue with Christian theologians in the

Lowlands. Orobio also quickly learned about the radical views of his classmate Prado, and in 1663 sent him a lengthy answer, followed by two answers to Prado's answers, defending Judaism against the budding naturalism of Prado. Orobio also wrote against a Belgian Lullist, Alonso de Zepeda, against various opponents of Judaism, defending the Jewish interpretation of Isaiah 53 and the validity of the law of Moses. Later on he wrote a very important apologetic answer to Christians who claimed that Judaism had been superseded by Christianity, the *Prevenciones divinas contra la vana idolatria de las gentes*. And Orobio wrote the only known answer to Spinoza by a member of the Jewish community of Amsterdam, the *Certamen Philosophicum, Propugnatae Veritatis Divinae ac Naturalis*, which was published and was included in Fénélon's collection of refutations of Spinoza. At the end of his life, he publicly debated with Locke's friend Philip van Limborch on the truth of the Christian religion. The debate was published by van Limborch and was important in its day. Orobio used a wide range of pagan, Christian, and Jewish sources in his writings. He was the best philosopher in the community and the best at answering Christians of the time. He was not a rationalist in the Maimonidean tradition. Rather he accepted strong limitations upon human abilities to *know* ultimate truths, or to *prove* the existence of God, and saw the need to accept certain fundamental beliefs on faith. His recent biographer, Yosef Kaplan, has suggested that he may have adopted the fideistic skepticism of Montaigne and Francisco Sanches when he was in Toulouse.

Orobio's most significant work, the *Prevenciones*, is part of a genre of anti-Christian polemics that developed in Amsterdam. Freed from immediate fear of persecution, Jewish thinkers began circulating critical answers to Christianity and defenses of Judaism in manuscript, sometimes elegant illuminated ones. (If they had been published this might have constituted "scandal" and brought down the wrath of the political authorities.) The earliest of these "clandestine" works in the Amsterdam collection is the *Chizzuk Emunah* of the Lithuanian Karaite rabbi Isaac Troki. This strong rationalist defense of Judaism, written probably in 1592, appealed to the Amsterdam group, since it used no rabbinical material. Manuscripts of it exist in Spanish, Portuguese, French, and Dutch. It apparently was still circulating well into the nineteenth century in Amsterdam. Next writings of Dr Elijah Montalto in answer to Christians were presented in manuscript form. Montalto had been Rabbi Morteira's employer in Paris, and his body was brought from there to the Netherlands for burial.

There are many different polemical works by various thinkers in the community, the two most important being those of Morteira, *Providencia de Dios con Israel*, and Orobio, who both sought to answer Christian claims about what was wrong with Judaism, and to show that philosophical, scriptural, and historical evidence prove that God was on the Jewish side. There are also dialogues and debates between Jews, Calvinists, and Catholics.

On the flyleaf of Orobio's holograph copy of *Prevenciones* the author explained that he did not publish the work for fear of causing scandal, but he sent it to the Jesuits in Brussels who liked it very much! We do not know the extent of the distribution of these anti-Christian writings at the time. Some are mentioned by Christian authors. Others were known but not obtainable. The diffusion of manuscripts all over Europe and in America suggests that they were sent, or were taken, to Sephardic Jewish communities and even sent to Marrano groups in Spanish and Portuguese territories. The first general diffusion occurred in 1715 when several of the manuscripts were included in an auction in The Hague. Thereafter they are cited by English deists, by Voltaire, by Baron d'Holbach, and other Enlightenment figures. A sales catalogue from 1811 reveals that there were still many of these manuscripts in circulation. Until very recently only a little was published. A German Christian orientalist had published Troki in the late seventeenth century in Hebrew, and it and a toned-down version of Orobio were printed in English in the 1840s. Recently Morteira's text had been published in the original Portuguese.

By the end of the seventeenth century, most of the intellectual energy had been worn out in Amsterdam. The community was established and did not feel the need to justify itself or to answer its Christian neighbors. A few continuations of the polemics occurred, but by and large the philosophical underpinnings of the journey back to Judaism had been worked out, and most of the members of the community were now from Dutch families rather than Iberian ones. The only major intellectual figure in the eighteenth century was an economist, Isaac de Pinto, who started out as the secretary of the Dutch Academy of Sciences. He gave two discourses there (in French rather than Spanish or Portuguese) on science and religion. Nothing Jewish appears in these papers. De Pinto became a leading figure in the Dutch West India Company. After its bankruptcy he left the Netherlands for Paris where he came to know various leading Enlightenment figures. De Pinto wrote an answer to Voltaire's nasty views about Jews, in which he defended the status of Sephardic Jewry but not the rest of the Jews. He came to know David Hume in Paris, and wrote an answer to Hume's economic views in his *Treatise on Circulation and Credit*, which was one of the first works to explain and advocate capitalism. This work was read by Adam Smith, Karl Marx, and many others. Lastly De Pinto became the leading European defender of colonialism and opponent of the American Revolution. Although he was the chairman of the board of the synagogue, he seems to have been a thoroughly secular figure who enjoyed the company of Diderot, Hume, and others.

The philosophy developed in the Amsterdam Jewish community has not been uniform, nor has it had the lasting importance of the philosophy developed by one of its ex-members, Spinoza, who derived some of his ideas and issues from thinkers in the community. He was even accused of plagiarizing from the kabbalists, and using the geometrical method to hide his theft! Except for occasional items such as Da Costa's autobiography, Orobio's answer to Spinoza, and De Pinto's explanation of capitalism, the works were not much known outside the Jewish community. Bits and pieces entered into the mainstream of the Enlightenment as further reasons for attacking Christian beliefs and practices.

The Amsterdam Jewish community was the first to confront modernity, and it also helped to create it. The community saw the importance of economic coexistence with its non-Jewish neighbors, tolerance, and intellectual acceptance of them. (The community has been called one of "reluctant cosmopolitans.") The ambience created by the Amsterdam Jewish community from the early seventeenth century to the late Enlightenment has been forgotten because of major confrontations between Jews and non-Jews that occurred during the French Revolution and in the Germany of Moses Mendelssohn's time, which directly led to the emancipatory world of nineteenth-century Europe. In fact the Amsterdam Jewish community had to be dragged kicking and screaming to accept the status of citizens in the French Revolutionary and Napoleonic worlds.

❧ BIBLIOGRAPHY ❧

Texts

Da Costa, U. (1993) *Examination of Pharasaic Traditions*, trans. and int. H. P. Salomon and I. Sassoon (Leiden: Brill).

Menasseh ben Israel (1987) *The Hope of Israel*, reprint of 1652 edition with introduction and notes by H. Méchoulan and G. Nahon (Oxford: Oxford University Press).

Salomon, H. P. (1988) *Saul Levi Morteira en zijn Traktaat betreffende de Waarheid van der wet van Mozes* (Braga: Tipografia Barbosa & Xavier).

—— (1990) "A Copy of Uriel da Costa's *Examen des tradicoes phariseas* located in the Royal Library of Copenhagen," *Studia Rosenthaliana* 24: 153–68.

Studies

Fuks, L. and R. Fuks-Mansfeld (1984) *Hebrew Typography in the Northern Netherlands, 1585–1815* (Leiden: Brill) [contains a catalogue of the manuscript writings by members of the Synagogue].

Israel, J. (1985) *European Jewry in the Age of Mercantilism 1550–1750* (Oxford: Clarendon Press).

Israel, J. and D. Katz (eds) (1990) *Sceptics, Millenarians and Jews* (Leiden: Brill).

Kaplan, Y. (1989) *From Christianity to Judaism: The Story of Isaac Orobio de Castro* (Oxford: Oxford University Press).

Kaplan, Y., H. Méchoulan and R. Popkin (1989) *Menasseh ben Israel and his World* (Leiden: Brill).

Méchoulan, H. (1991) *Être Juif à Amsterdam au temps de Spinoza* (Paris: Albin Michel).

Popkin, R. H. (1970) "Hume and Isaac de Pinto," *Texas Studies in Literature* 12: 417–30.

—— (1971) "The Historical Significance of Sephardic Judaism in the 17th Century," *The American Sephardi* 51: 18–27.

—— (1974) "Hume and Isaac de Pinto II. Five new letters," in *David Hume and the Enlightenment: Essays in Honor of Ernest C. Mossner*, edited by W. B. Todd (Edinburgh: Edinburgh University Press), pp. 99–127.

—— (1987) *Isaac La Peyrère: His Life, his Times, his Influence* (Leiden: Brill).

—— (1988) "Spinoza's Earliest Philosophical Years, 1655–61," *Studia Spinozana* 4: 37–54.

—— (1990) "Notes from the Underground," *New Republic* 21 May: 35–41.

—— (1992) "Jewish Anti-Christian Arguments as a Source of Irreligion from the Seventeenth to the Early Nineteenth Century," in *Atheism from the Reformation to the Enlightenment*, edited by M. Hunter and D. Wootton (Oxford: Clarendon Press), pp. 159–81.

Révah, I. (1959) *Spinoza et le Dr Juan de Prado* (Paris and The Hague: Mouton).

—— (1964) "Aux origines de la rupture Spinozienne: nouveaux documents sur l'incroyance dans la communauté Judéo-Portugaise à l'époque de l'excommunication de Spinoza," *Revue des Études Juives* 123: 359–431.

Saperstein, M. (1991) "Saul Levi Morteira's *Treatise on the Immortality of the Soul*," *Studia Rosenthaliana* 25: 131–48.

van den Berg, J. and E. G. E. van der Wall (1980) *Jewish Christian Relations in the Seventeenth Century: Studies and Documents* (Dordrecht: Kluwer).

CHAPTER 24

Spinoza

Seymour Feldman

In 1656 Baruch Spinoza was excommunicated from the Amsterdam Jewish community at the age of twenty-four. Henceforth, he was to have hardly any contact with Jews and Judaism. Why then is he included in an account of Jewish philosophy? According to Julius Guttmann, one of the greatest historians of Jewish philosophy, Spinoza's philosophy falls outside the domain of Jewish thought and belongs instead to general philosophy.[1] After all, Spinoza was excommunicated, made no effort to be reinstated and lived among non-Jews the rest of his life. This judgment has been shared by other Jewish thinkers, some of whom defend the original ban with great vigor. To some historians of Jewish thought, however, Spinoza does belong to Jewish philosophy, albeit in an unorthodox way. After all, Spinoza lived the first half of his life as a Jew; he received a Jewish education and knew the writings of some of the major medieval Jewish philosophers, such as Maimonides and Crescas. Although he will ultimately criticize and reject much of what his medieval predecessors had maintained, in his philosophy Spinoza seems to be conducting a debate with these thinkers. And so, as one of the greatest historians of medieval Jewish philosophy as well as interpreter of Spinoza has claimed, Spinoza was the last of the medievals and the first of the moderns.[2]

The attempt to include Spinoza within Jewish thought has been made more recently from a different angle. Instead of looking backwards to the Middle Ages, why not look forward? Let us see how and to what extent Spinoza influenced subsequent Jewish thought. Even though he remained apart from the Jewish community, his ideas eventually elicited responses, some negative to be sure, but others positive. From Mendelssohn to Buber, Jewish thinkers considered Spinoza as someone whom they needed to answer or agree with in their own attempt to develop a Jewish philosophy for modern times. In this sense the excommunication was a complete failure.

The circumstances and reasons for Spinoza's excommunication have been subjects of discussion for centuries. More recent research, especially by I. S. Revah,[3] R. Popkin, and others has clarified some of the issues concerning this intellectual tragedy; but not all the relevant questions have been resolved. What makes this particular fact of Spinoza's intellectual biography especially intriguing is that it affords us a glimpse not only into seventeenth-century Amsterdam Jewry but into the formative period of Spinoza's own thinking. Whatever ideas and influences led to his excommunication most probably played a part in the development of his mature philosophy. So what do we know about the events of the summer of 1656 in the Amsterdam ghetto?

In the first place, we know that Spinoza was not the only one excommunicated at that time. There are documents indicating that he was associated with a Marrano émigré, Juan de Prado, whose unorthodox ideas have been recorded in an exchange of letters between himself and Orobio de Castro, another Marrano, who arrived in Amsterdam after Spinoza's death. Along with some other reports emanating from several Spanish Catholic visitors to Amsterdam, these materials indicate that both Prado and Spinoza were suspected of "deviationist" tendencies that warranted severe remedies. Ultimately Spinoza was excommunicated in July 1656; Prado was expelled early in the following year after his efforts at reconciliation had failed. Why and how did this come about?

Until the summer of 1656, Spinoza had been occupied with his brother Gabriel as a merchant in the dried fruit and nut import business established by his father. Contrary to some well-entrenched myths, he was not trained for the rabbinate and was not even a student in the advanced school of rabbinic studies in Amsterdam. Perhaps he attended the adult education institute sponsored by the community, but he was not enrolled in any formal academic study of an advanced sort. Nor is it clear, even after considerable study of this issue, when Spinoza began to study Latin, which was still the scholarly language for philosophy and science. He certainly could have begun his study while still in good standing with the Jewish community; after all, two of the rabbis of the community were competent Latinists – Menasseh ben Israel and Saul Levi Morteira. So the study of Latin itself had nothing to do with Spinoza's heresies.

I. S. Revah and even earlier Carl Gebhardt emphasize the role of Prado in shaping and stimulating Spinoza's "exit from Judaism." Revah also appeals to the influence of the earlier "arch"-heretic Uriel da Costa. Although it is noteworthy that amongst the Amsterdam Marrano community there were some "marginal" Jews with whom Spinoza may have had some contact, it does not follow that the twenty-four-year-old Spinoza was suddenly let down the path of heresy by the recently arrived Prado, whose knowledge of Judaism was minimal and of Hebrew non-existent. As he was eventually to prove, Spinoza was a genius who did not need anybody to fill his mind with philosophical ideas. It is not improbable that Prado and Spinoza had conversations with each other before his *cherem*; after all, the Amsterdam Jewish community was small. But it is even more probable that, prior to his first meeting with Prado, Spinoza had begun to entertain heterodox thoughts. If Prado had any impact upon Spinoza, it was because Spinoza had been already receptive to such an "evil influence."[4] So the question now is, who or what prepared him?

Some recent scholars have tended to explain Spinoza's heterodoxies by bringing into the picture both the curious character Isaac La Peyrère,[5] a heterodox, unstable Christian, perhaps of Marrano background, and the circle of liberal Christians "without denomination"[6] with whom Spinoza was to be associated for the rest of his life after his excommunication. Indeed, according to some scholars, Spinoza came into contact with some of these heterodox Christians *before* his expulsion, since several of these Christians were importers of dried fruits and knew Spanish. Isaac La Peyrère, however, was an outsider who came to Amsterdam in 1655 where he had discussions with Menasseh ben Israel, one of Spinoza's teachers, and had one of his books printed, a book that Spinoza owned. In this book, La Peyrère argued, among other things, that the Pentateuch could not have been written by Moses and that the present text of the Bible is not accurate. These theses are defended vigorously by Spinoza in his *Theological-Political Treatise*. They are just the kind of ideas that could in 1655–6 lead an intelligent and inquiring mind to raise doubts about Judaism in particular and revealed religion in general. We do know from the several reports about Prado and Spinoza that they rejected the authority of the Mosaic law. Certainly this is an inference that one could plausibly draw from La Peyrère's critique of the Bible.

In several passages in Spinoza's works one finds approving allusions to Jesus, or "Christ." It is not unlikely that Spinoza was introduced to a more "liberal" form of Christianity through Christian business associates, some of whom became close friends after his excommunication. Although Spinoza never became a Christian, indeed, explicitly rejected and ridiculed several of the dogmas of orthodox Christianity (Letter 76), he was not averse to using Christian theological expressions, such as "the son of God" (*Short Treatise* I, chapter 9) or "the Spirit of Christ" (*Ethics* 4.68). Indeed, according to Richard Popkin, Spinoza either shortly before or shortly after his excommunication had established contacts with the Quakers.[7] At any rate, it is obviously true that after 1656 Spinoza lived amongst Christians and that all of his friends were Christians. It is not improbable then that even before his excommunication his mind was open to Christianity, at least in a less orthodox form. To a community of ex-Marranos, this was certainly suspicious.

Finally, some recent research has suggested that the person who has been traditionally considered to be Spinoza's chief teacher in Latin, the ex-Jesuit Franciscus van den Enden, taught him things besides just Latin.[8] Van den Enden was also a physician of Cartesian philosophical proclivities, and as such he may have been the conduit by means of which Spinoza became familiar with Cartesian philosophy and science. He was also the author of several treatises on political theory in which he advanced ideas that are remarkably similar to those presented in Spinoza's own political writings. In addition, several of Spinoza's philosophical doctrines as developed in his *Ethics* are also suggested by Van den Enden, according to W. Klever, who proposes that we "consider Van den Enden as the mastermind behind the young genius." This area in Spinoza studies is still underdeveloped, and we must await the publication of the Van den Enden materials before rendering a decisive judgment. It is also crucial to determine exactly when Spinoza studied with Van den Enden. But it is certainly plausible to hold that Spinoza's knowledge of the Cartesian system, which was for all practical purposes "modern" philosophy and science in the first half of the seventeenth century, was mediated or at least initiated by Van den Enden.

Although we are perhaps still not in the position where we can definitely answer the question why Spinoza was excommunicated, enough has been uncovered to enable us to see why the Amsterdam Jewish elders believed him to be dangerous. Given the tenuous status of the Jewish community and the explicit directives to make sure that unorthodox ideas would not surface amongst the Jews, the Amsterdam Jews had no choice but to expel Baruch from the community. Incipient heterodoxy is unpredictable: who would know where it would lead? And so on 27 July 1656 Baruch Spinoza was excommunicated.

The next few years in Spinoza's life are not clear. Evidently he remained in Amsterdam until 1660 and was still in contact with Prado. No doubt he continued his secular studies, especially in philosophy, mathematics, and science. As his writing shows, he was a fairly competent mathematician and quite informed in physics, especially optics, and anatomy. After Spinoza left Amsterdam and took up residence in several small towns nearby, he finally settled in the Hague, where he remained until he died in 1677. During this time he cemented his early friendships with several Christian thinkers and acquired new friends of a similar intellectual stripe. They constituted the "Spinoza circle." Tradition has it that Spinoza supported himself by grinding lenses. It is more likely that this activity was scientifically motivated. The Netherlands was the center for optical research, and Spinoza's reputation as an "optician" was more scientific than economic in character. There is some evidence that he was supported by subventions from several of his friends. His modest and frugal habits, as well as his having no family, made it relatively easy for him to pursue independently his philosophical and scientific studies, even to the point of refusing a professorship at the University of Heidelberg in 1673 (*Letters* 47–8).

What was Spinoza thinking during these years? The earliest written testimonies date from 1661. During 1661–3, Spinoza wrote several important letters as well as two treatises in which the seeds of his subsequent and mature philosophy are present. In these writings we see him breaking out of the Cartesian philosophical framework in which he had been nurtured. The language is that of René, but the thought is Baruch's, or should we say now, of Benedictus. For example, in the earliest letter we possess, dated September 1661 addressed to Henry Oldenberg, the future secretary of the London Royal Society, Spinoza responds to several philosophical queries that Oldenberg had raised concerning the nature of God and the errors committed by Descartes and Francis Bacon. This letter is especially significant since it begins by laying down several basic definitions and then specifying a few of the essential propositions of his metaphysics, which were to be expanded in his major work the *Ethics*. Of special interest is Spinoza's claim that extension is one of the attributes of God, a thesis that goes against the whole philosophical tradition from Plato through Descartes. Moreover, Spinoza explicitly states that the "geometric," or axiomatic, method is the best way to do philosophy. In replying to Oldenberg's request to specify the errors of Descartes and Bacon, Spinoza lists three. First, they failed to have an adequate knowledge of God – presumably because they excluded extension as a divine attribute; second, they did not know the true nature of the human mind – most likely because they were psychological dualists, believing that the mind and the body were radically distinct substances; and third, they did not understand the nature of error, believing that it comes about because of human free will, which for Spinoza does not exist. Accordingly, already in 1661, Spinoza had denied three fundamental dogmas of medieval and Cartesian philosophy: first, God is a wholly spiritual or intellectual being; second, the human soul or mind is a separable substance, and hence immortal; and, third, that human beings have free will. If he rejected any one of these in 1656, it would have been sufficient grounds for excommunication.

In the following spring (April 1662), Spinoza writes to Oldenberg again, commenting upon Oldenberg's report of some chemical experiments performed by Robert Boyle, and remarks in conclusion that he does "not separate God from nature as everyone known to me has done." Already in 1662 Spinoza's "atheistical" equation: God, or Nature (deus sive natura), is in place and awaits to be demonstrated in full in his subsequent works. With this formula, the dualistic cosmology of Plato, Aristotle, the medievals, and Descartes is replaced with a monistic metaphysics that has naturalized the divine and divinized nature. Again, here is an idea that would be sufficient grounds for suspicion, if not excommunication, if Spinoza had entertained it in 1656.

The two philosophical works that emanate from this period (1660–1) are the *Treatise on the Emendation of the Intellect* and the *Short Treatise on God, Man, and His Well-Being*. Although the traditional view has considered the latter work to be the earliest sustained piece in Spinoza's corpus, recent scholarship, especially that of F. Mignini,[9] has assigned the priority to the former essay. Both works are definitely anti-Cartesian, and the *Short Treatise* expounds a substantial part of the *Ethics* in a non-axiomatic form. By now virtually all vestiges of the traditional dualistic metaphysics and cosmology have been abandoned, although it may be that some traces of psychological dualism are still present. But not for long. Three years later Spinoza seems to have completed a preliminary version of a work that will later become known as the *Ethics* (Letter 28, June 1665). Like the earlier *Short Treatise*, it comprised three parts, whereas the final version will contain five parts. Spinoza continually revised the book for quite a while; by 1675 it was ready for publication. Nevertheless, Spinoza decided to defer its publication because of the rumblings of both "conspiring theologians" and "dull-witted Cartesians," who found his earlier *Theological-Political Treatise* (1670) to be "harmful" to religion and suspected his *Ethics* to be "atheistical" (Letter 68, September 1675). Spinoza died before its publication. But the uproar after its publication proved his fears to have been well founded. Indeed, Spinoza's philosophy was too much even for several of his friends, including Oldenberg.

Spinoza's mature philosophy is found in his *Ethics*, whose axiomatic style is reminiscent of Euclid's *Elements* and anticipates Newton's *Mathematical Principles of Natural Philosophy* (1686). Part I of the *Ethics* is subtitled *On God*. This is in itself a novelty: both the Aristotelian and Cartesian methods in metaphysics began a posteriori, starting with some empirical fact, motion or mind (Descartes' mind at least), and then asking for its cause. Spinoza rejected this approach and explicitly states that it is a fundamental mistake (*Ethics* 2.10, scholium). If it is truly the case that both nature in general and man in particular are effects of God, as the medieval Aristotelians and Cartesians believed, then why reason "backwards"? Let us start with the true beginning of things, that is, with God, for we do possess an adequate idea of God (*Ethics* 2.47). In part I Spinoza is concerned to prove two main metaphysical theses: first, that there is a one and only substance, which is identical with God, a being consisting of infinite attributes; second, that everything else in the universe follows necessarily from God in such a way that God is their immanent, not transcendent, cause. Two important corollaries of the first thesis are: extension is an attribute of God, and that God and nature are one and the same entity. The gap between an unextended God and an extended universe – a distinction insisted upon by both Maimonides and Descartes – is closed. Spinoza could have agreed with the rabbinic teaching that God is "the place of the universe" (ha-maqom); but he would go on to say that this is because God too is extended, as is the physical universe, and as such is the immanent cause of all extended things. Since the ontological gap between God and nature has been effaced, the question of creation has no point. Nature is eternal since it is God. If, as Maimonides stated, the belief in creation is the cornerstone of the Bible, then Spinoza's metaphysics clearly undermines biblical religion.

Spinoza's second main thesis of part 1 results in a new notion of divine freedom and in the rejection of the traditional doctrine of human free will. God is free precisely because literally every possible thing does exist and exists necessarily. That is, reality is maximally full. It contains everything that can exist; it is also subject to inexorable laws, the laws of nature which are identical with the divine decrees. Given Spinoza's definition of "free" (definition 6, part 1), God is the only free agent, since only God acts solely according to the laws of its own nature. Divine omnipotence, divine freedom, and divine causation turn out to be for Spinoza equivalent concepts, which entail strict determinism. One explicit consequence of this determinism is the rejection of the possibility of miracles, a consequence foreseen by Maimonides and now strictly inferred and adhered to by Spinoza.

But if God is the only free entity, humans are not; indeed, as we have seen, the belief in free will is a mistake. If free will means the capacity to have done other than what one has in fact done, then no one, including God, has such a capacity. Everything has a cause from which it necessarily follows (Ethics 1. axiom 3, propositions 26–9). There is a persistent concern throughout Spinoza's writings to disabuse us of the fiction of free will (see Letters 19, 21, 56, and 58). Indeed, there is no distinct psychological faculty or part of the mind as the will. All that exists are distinct volitions, or better appetites (Ethics 2.48; Ethics 3.9, scholium), all of which have definite causes. In so far as human beings are finite modes, or particular things, subject to the external, or transitive, causal power of other finite things, humans are not free agents. To be free is to be wholly self-determined, that is, to be God.

Parts 2–5 of the *Ethics* present Spinoza's psychology and moral philosophy. Like Aristotle Spinoza believed that ethics makes sense only if we understand human nature. There is no point in proposing moral principles if we can not live by them, if they are contrary to our nature. This was the mistake committed by those moralists who advised us to free ourselves entirely from passion. A more adequate psychology, Spinoza claims, will teach us that this is impossible. Nor does complaining about this situation help either. Instead, let us get a clear picture of what we are, and then see what moral rules are appropriate.

Spinoza begins by offering an account of the human mind that differs considerably from the Cartesian theory. According to this latter model a human being is a composite consisting of both mind, or soul, and body, each regarded as substantial entities. Moreover, although radically distinct from each other, mind and body interact. Something like this account is also found throughout many of the medieval philosophers and theologians, who inherited it from Plato. Both Plato and Descartes were very concerned to prove immortality of the soul. To do this they had to show the radical distinctness of the soul or mind, its separability from the body. Whereas the body is divisible and hence corruptible, the mind is not; indeed, for Descartes the mind is simple, that is, not composite, having no parts.

Almost immediately after publishing his *Meditations*, Descartes was attacked on all sides for his psychological dualism and interactionism. One astute reader, the Princess Elizabeth of Bohemia asked, how can two radically disparate things be united and interact with each other? Others proposed more simple solutions: why not consider the mind to be material, for example the brain? All so-called mental phenomena are just physical events or states. This was Hobbes' reply to Descartes. Berkeley proposed an alternative both to the Cartesian and materialist models: everything is mental, that is, all so-called physical states are just ideas; bodies are really collections of perceptions. Hobbesian materialism and Berkelian mentalism are monistic systems that admit only one of Descartes' two substances and exclude the other. In doing so they avoid Descartes' problems. But do they succeed in accommodating all the facts?

As we have seen, Spinoza was a monist: there is only one substance. But his one substance – God, or nature – has infinite attributes, including both thought and extension, each one of which "must be conceived through itself" (*Ethics* 1.10). In this sense we cannot eliminate or reduce thought to extension or conversely. Each attribute is a distinct and true way of understanding and describing the one substance. Accordingly, neither strict materialism nor strict mentalism is true; both leave out something from their pictures of the universe. Spinoza then is non-reductivist, or pluralist, with respect to attributes, although a monist concerning substance, whose essential infinity allows for, indeed entails, multiple ways of self-expression.

The same is true of the modes of substance, especially for human modes. Each mode is in theory equally a mode of extension and a mode of thought and a mode of every other attribute. Since we know only two attributes of substance, let us confine ourselves to them. A human being, then, is a finite mode under the attribute of thought in so far as "man thinks" (*Ethics* 2, second axiom). But as thinking beings "we feel a certain body to be affected in many ways" (*Ethics* 2, fourth axiom). That is, we feel our own body being affected by other bodies. For Spinoza these are basic truths. So a reductivist account of human nature, whether materialist or mentalist, cannot be right. On the other hand, these two basic propositions do not refer to two radically different sets of facts, as they do in Platonic and Cartesian dualism. Rather, there is *one* set of facts, events, or states of affairs – the infinite number of modes of nature – which can be described and explicated in terms of any of the attributes of substance. Human beings can be understood as thinking modes, as minds; but they can also be described as extended modes, as bodies. But whichever method of description we choose to employ, we are referring to one and the same mode.

Spinoza believed that this account of human nature solves the problems infecting Cartesian dualism. If there is only *one* thing, then there is no need to explain how mind and body are united nor how they interact: "mind and body are one and the same thing, conceived now under the attribute of Thought, now under the attribute of Extension" (*Ethics* 3.2, scholium). Princess Elizabeth's questions have been answered, not by reducing mind to body nor conversely, but by realizing that, if substance is only one, although exhibiting many attributes, so is a mode, especially a human being. Each attribute gives an adequate account in its terms of what this mode is. There is nothing wrong or superfluous in describing a human being as a "thinking thing;" there is, however, nothing wrong or redundant in describing it as an "extended thing;" and there is nothing incorrect in saying it is both – as Descartes did. But Berkeley and Hobbes were wrong in fastening upon one way of looking at us; Descartes was wrong in thinking that multiple attributes imply multiple substances.

Nevertheless, it must be noted that here and there in Spinoza there are hints, indeed expressions, of a latent materialism. Consider his definition of the mind: "the object of the idea constituting the human mind is the body, i.e. a definite mode of extension actually existing, and nothing else" (*Ethics* 2.13). The mind is, for Spinoza, its ideas; in turn, these ideas are ideas of one's own body, especially of one's body as it is affected by other bodies. In fact, "an idea that excludes the existence of our body cannot be in our mind" (*Ethics*

3.10). The whole Cartesian enterprise of isolating the mind, emptying it of all bodily associations and ties, and exalting it as independent substance is for Spinoza utterly misconceived. I can no more think of my mind separate from my body than I can think of a triangle not having three sides. One significant consequence of this quasi-materialistic approach is that for Spinoza psychology becomes a natural science, a branch of biology, devoid of moralistic connotations and sermonizing. One studies psychology in the same way as one studies physics (*Ethics* 3, preface). One important theological consequence of this thesis is that the doctrine of immortality of the soul no longer has a sense. If my soul, or mind, is no more than the idea of my body, then, with the death of my body, my mind dies too.

The remaining parts of the *Ethics* concern the twin themes of human bondage and salvation. Spinoza advances the claim that moral concepts and principles do not stem from abstract reasoning but from our desires. Our moral evaluations express our feelings and sentiments, which in turn are rooted in our basic drive (*conatus*) for self-preservation and pursuit of power (*virtus*). Spinoza is a psychological and moral hedonist who sees human beings striving to maximize their own pleasure and utility. At first our moral assessments are subjective, reflecting our own individual tastes; ultimately, however, we come to realize – if we are rational, and we can be rational – that our pleasure and utility will be optimally achieved within a social context in which cooperation and harmony are pursued. Here Spinoza's moral and social philosophy shows some affinities with that of Hobbes. But perhaps more than Hobbes he optimistically describes a society of *free* people under the guidance of reason mutually enjoying the benefits of the life of reason (*Ethics* 4.35–7, 46, 65–73).

The free person is someone who understands himself or herself. As the ancient Stoics realized, most people are slaves of their emotions. Some, however, the wise, can so completely dominate their emotions by means of self-discipline and renunciation that they become *apathetic*, that is, emotionless. Spinoza too sees us as creatures of passion; after all, we are finite modes within Nature. This is *human bondage*. Liberation is, however, attained not through asceticism, or emotional extirpation, but by means of knowledge. The key idea in Spinoza's moral philosophy is the thesis that cognition turns a bad emotion, or passion, into a good emotion, or action. Passions are bad because they literally cause pain; actions are good because they are pleasurable and express our self-determination, or autonomy, to the extent that we, as modes, are able to achieve this goal. Knowledge of our emotions, which involves knowing not only ourselves but also the world in which we live, "takes the sting out of them." We can understand the causal history of why we feel the way we do, what is causing us now to feel such emotions and, most important, what courses of action can alleviate, perhaps even remove, the cause of *binding* emotion, or passion. Spinoza's moral philosophy is really a form of cognitive therapy whereby an individual progressively comes to understand his or her present position and to recognize how this state can be changed for the better.

As Spinoza closes his *Ethics* he warns us that this moral education is difficult; for it involves a kind of knowledge that is both comprehensive and detailed – intuitive science. Indeed, this is knowledge that has as its starting point an adequate knowledge of God from which we proceed to a knowledge of particular things, especially ourselves (*Ethics* 5.24–7). On the other hand, this knowledge of God, which in part at least derives from our self-understanding, is either identical with or necessarily leads to the love of God (*Ethics* 5.15). This is the "amor Dei intellectualis:" the intellectual love of God, which is for Spinoza the salvation that we cannot just hope for but actually attain by our own efforts. Although the phrase and perhaps some of its meaning are rooted in some Jewish philosophers such as Maimonides and Judah Abravanel (Leone Ebreo), Spinoza's "amor Dei intellectualis" no longer has any supernatural connotations or implications. We liberate ourselves, and our salvation is within this world, which is the only one that exists. Indeed, Spinoza's God does not even love or, for that matter, hate us. It is beyond all emotion (*Ethics* 5.17). Yet, in our knowing and hence loving God we attain "the highest possible contentment of mind" (*Ethics* 5.27). For by means of this knowledge we come to understand *how things are and must be*. Indeed, we now see ourselves "under a form of eternity," an insight that affords us not only pleasure but also a kind of eternity (*Ethics* 5.29–33). This eternity is not to be confused with the false doctrine of individual immortality of the soul or intellect (*Ethics* 5.21). Our eternity is just the realization that we are and have been a necessary chapter in an eternal story in which we shall be recorded for ever. For Spinoza, this kind of eternity is sufficient for salvation. At any rate it is true, and that is what counts (Letter 76).

Although pieces and earlier drafts of the *Ethics* were in circulation amongst his friends, its final version was published posthumously in 1677. Not so with his second major work the *Theological-Political Treatise* (*TTP*), which was published in 1670, although only with his initials, indicating that Spinoza himself sensed the subversive character of this work. He was right: the book caused an immediate uproar. There is no mystery why this book had such a negative response. Spinoza does not wait even one page to announce his radical and revolutionary program: the separation of religion from both politics and philosophy (preface). But there is more: chapters 1–19 contain a detailed and penetrating critique of biblical religion. Some scholars have suggested that in the *TTP* we have a mature version of an earlier but lost *Apologia*. Whether or not this is so, this later treatise can help us understand why Spinoza should have been excommunicated had he held any of these views in 1656 or at any time for that matter. In several important respects the *TTP* is one of the more revolutionary books ever written. It undermines and uproots many of the basic pillars of traditional religion and politics.

Spinoza's announced purpose in writing the *TTP* was to present a proposal for political and religious peace. He was living in a period of considerable political turmoil caused or at least aggravated by religion. Political peace can, he argued, be achieved only when religion stays out of politics. Spinoza believed that, since contemporary political conflict was fueled by the conviction that the Bible supported religious intrusion into politics, the best way to defend the separation of Church and state was to undermine the conviction that the Bible should be the model for contemporary political life. He could not succeed in doing this by simply rejecting the Bible outright; he could gain an audience only if he could show that the Bible read *literally* does not support his opponents' views. Accordingly, the *TTP* is not only an essay in political theology but also a treatise in biblical hermeneutics and as such raises a question that is still of considerable interest: how does one read the Bible?

The basic error of those who want to turn the state into a theological-political battlefield is the belief that the Bible can provide authoritative political guidelines for modern society. Many of Spinoza's contemporaries believed that the biblical polity could be imported and transferred to Geneva or to the Netherlands, that the divine law of the Bible could be the basis of modern European political life. Spinoza concedes that the biblical polity during Moses' life was a theocracy in which there was no distinction between divine and civil law. This system had some advantages as well as disadvantages. But in either case it is no longer valid for us, since this system was designed and intended only for the Israelites when they were living in the land of Israel (*TTP*, chapters 5, 17–19). Mosaic law is not only obsolete for the Jews living in exile, it is irrelevant and inapplicable to any other society, especially those of the seventeenth-century. Theocracy may have made sense for a people just liberated from Egyptian slavery and living in a desert or underdeveloped rural economy. But it has no force or significance for modern times.

Throughout the treatise, Spinoza appeals to the biblical text itself to support his claims. Since his opponents too read the Bible, but draw different conclusions, he has to show that these conclusions are unwarranted. To do this, Spinoza lays down as his fundamental hermeneutical principle that we are not to read into or take out of the

Bible what is not there (*TTP*, preface). Spinoza singles out Maimonides in particular as a prime example of those who cannot read the biblical text honestly and simply. If Maimonides is taken, as he has been, as a paradigm of religious rationalism in Judaism, then Spinoza's critique of Maimonides is a critique not only of Maimonidean biblical hermeneutics but of the attempt to forge some kind of synthesis of biblical faith and philosophy. Spinoza's separation of religion from politics also involves the divorce of philosophy from religion. If religion has nothing at all to do with philosophy, and if a particular form of religious polity has only limited and restricted political relevance, then philosophy, religion, and politics are all distinct from each other. Each has a job to do in its particular sphere of activity. So long as each keeps to its proper role there is peace; when they do not there is conflict.

Spinoza begins his deconstruction of traditional biblical hermeneutics and theological-political theory by a frontal attack on several fundamental dogmas shared by both Jews and Christians: (1) that prophecy is a special mode of cognition that supplements and transcends human reason; (2) that the Jews are or were God's chosen people; (3) that the divine law consists of or includes ceremonial law; (4) that miracles are not only possible but prove the existence and providence of God; (5) that all of the Pentateuch was written by Moses; (6) that the Bible as we have it is an historically authentic and correct text; and (7) that scriptural religion sets the limits for philosophy, and hence is philosophy's mistress. As is obvious, to reject any of these theses is to reject the authority of the Bible, and hence Judaism and Christianity.

This is exactly what Spinoza does: (1) Prophecy is utterly non-cognitive – it teaches nothing philosophical or scientific; it has only moral significance. (2) The Jews were perhaps chosen by God, but that was a long time ago when they were a sovereign nation; now they are no longer chosen, unless they become a sovereign nation again. Indeed, any nation is chosen by God if it is sovereign. (3) The divine law is identical with the laws of nature, for God and nature are identical. Ritual law has nothing to do with divine law; at best it has only political or social utility. (4) Miracles are not only impossible, but to believe in them is to deny God, since a miracle is a violation of nature. (5) Moses was not the author of all of the Pentateuch, as the last verses of Deuteronomy, as well as others (noted by Abraham ibn Ezra, albeit cryptically) indicate. Indeed, more generally the question of authorship of other biblical books needs to be reconsidered. (6) The biblical text is not in the best shape; it needs to be studied scientifically with the best philological and historical tools to determine the correct version and especially its true meaning. When this is done, we shall see that it has little philosophical or scientific content. Finally (7), in showing that the Bible is not a philosophical book, that whatever philosophical or scientific ideas it embodies are either false or crudely formulated, we shall have liberated philosophy from theology. This does not necessarily result in dismissing the Bible altogether, however. For in emancipating philosophy from theology, we also free the Bible from foreign philosophical misreadings and we shall see it for what it really is: a book teaching morality and piety. As long as religion restricts itself to the teaching and cultivation of morals this is fine. But once religion oversteps its proper border and begins to make philosophical, scientific, or political claims, then we are in trouble. The *TTP* has then literally domesticated religion: it is primarily a private matter, having no *a priori* claims upon philosophy or politics.

Although the *TTP* is both brilliant and original, it also reveals Spinoza in a most uncharacteristic light: it is replete with bitter, cynical, indeed even hateful, emotions which he claimed in the *Ethics* are antithetical to the free person and for which he has always been praised as not exhibiting. These unseemly features are most evident in his discussions of Jews and Judaism, such that it is difficult to avoid the judgment that Spinoza was one of the original Jewish anti-semites, or self-hating Jews. Of course, in his case it is easy to understand why: he never really got over his excommunication from the synagogue. But whatever the cause, it is clear that the *TTP* does manifest a definite hostility toward the Jews and their religion. For example, Jesus, he claims, was superior to Moses, ironically for the very same reason that Moses is claimed by Maimonides to be superior to all other men: Jesus spoke to God mind to mind, whereas Moses spoke to God only "face to face." That is, whereas Moses communicated with God using language, Jesus communed with God "purely intellectually," without words (*TTP*, chapters 1 and 4). Although Spinoza explicitly states that he does not accept the Christian dogmas about Jesus, such as the incarnation and resurrection (see also Letters 73, 75, 76, and 78), he makes it clear that for him Jesus was a philosopher, whereas the Prophets, including Moses, were not. The one biblical figure Spinoza really admires is Solomon, who, like Jesus, is transformed into a philosopher. After all, in Ecclesiastes, ascribed to King Solomon, one finds determinism; in Proverbs, also attributed to Solomon, one can find the doctrine that intellect, or wisdom, is the first creation of God (Proverbs 8: 22–31). Spinoza agrees with both theses (*TTP*, chapter 4).

Spinoza's hostility is also evident in his frequent use of the term "Pharisee" to refer to Jews or to the rabbis. This was of course a commonly employed epithet used against the Jews ever since the New Testament. Indeed, Spinoza not only adopts this New Testament expression but attributes to the Jews ideas that were originally foisted upon them in the New Testament or by later Christian writers. For example, according to Spinoza, Mosaic law was imposed upon the

Israelites by compulsion and hence is bondage (*TTP*, chapters 2 and 5). To support this view he quotes Ezekiel's comment in 20: 25 that God gave the Israelites "statutes that were not good" (*TTP*, chapter 17). Here Spinoza appeals to the New Testament and Christian view that the law is a burden from which the Christian has been relieved by virtue of the belief in the redeeming death of Jesus. Of course, Spinoza does not believe in vicarious atonement; but he uses the New Testament view toward Mosaic law to show that it is no model for seventeenth-century Netherlands to follow.

Although Spinoza's negative attitude towards Jews and Judaism is quite evident in the *TTP*, it should be noted that in Letter 76 he expresses a more positive view. This letter is a response to a letter written to him by one of his former associates, Albert Burgh, a convert to Catholicism who tried to convert Spinoza (Letter 67). Spinoza clearly finds Burgh's conversion and missionary efforts repulsive. Besides ridiculing various Catholic dogmas and rituals, he criticizes several of Burgh's arguments in favor of Catholicism, one of which was the argument from martyrdom. To counter the Catholic's claim that Christian martyrs prove the truth of Christianity, Spinoza cites the example of the "Pharisees," who "number far more martyrs than any other nation" (Letter 76). Spinoza cites the case of someone about whom he has good information, Judah the Faithful, who willingly sacrificed himself to the flames of the Inquisition while singing Psalm 31, "To thee O God I commit my soul." Spinoza does not go on to compare explicitly this Judah with Jesus; but the informed reader cannot help make the comparison with Judah's citation of Psalm 31 with Jesus' invocation of Psalm 22: "My God, my God, why hast thou forsaken me . . .?" The former expresses absolute and complete trust in God, the latter despair and disappointment. In other words, Judah the Faithful is just as much a martyr as was Jesus. Whether or not Spinoza intended such comparisons, it is clear that in Letter 76 Spinoza puts Judaism in a far better light and even defends it, perhaps unintentionally, against Christianity.

In excommunicating Spinoza, the leaders of the Amsterdam community thought they were eradicating a poisonous plant that had to be nipped in the bud. History has shown, however, that they failed. Indeed, not only has Spinoza influenced much of modern European philosophy but he has also impacted upon Jewish thought as well. For despite the ban upon reading anything he wrote or was to write, Jews eventually began to read Spinoza and to respond to him. These reactions range from outright condemnation and refutation to explicit acceptance and rehabilitation. Spinoza's importance for modern Jewish thought is so pronounced that Eliezer Schweid can say, with considerable justification, that, although Spinoza is not the first chapter in the story of modern Jewish philosophy, he is the first modern thinker to whom modern Jewish philosophy responds: "the beginning [of modern Jewish thought] was the beginning of [its] confrontation with the doctrine of Spinoza."[10]

The first known explicit philosophical reaction to Spinoza was from the ex-Marrano physician Isaac Orobio de Castro, the critic of Juan de Prado. Orobio's response to Spinoza was, however, indirect: his *Certamen Philosophicum* was directed against a Dutch Christian amateur philosopher-theologian, Johann Bredenburg, who had attempted to formulate a Spinozistic form of Christianity. Throughout his critique of Bredenburg, however, Orobio mentions Spinoza by name, and it is clear that he is after bigger prey than the inconsequential Bredenburg. Yet, there is one *novella* of Bredenburg that is especially vexing to Orobio, and it is one that is particularly relevant to subsequent Jewish thought. Orobio vehemently opposes any attempt to make Spinoza religiously acceptable, from either a Christian or Jewish perspective. Spinoza's excommunication was, for Orobio, completely justified; his philosophy is atheistic, despite his protestations to the contrary. Spinoza's naturalistic and deterministic monism is just another form of ancient Stoic materialism, and this doctrine is inimical to biblical religion. The latter accentuates the metaphysical gap between creator and creature, a distance that allows the former to do anything to what he has made. In particular, miracles are possible for biblical religion; for Spinoza they are not. Orobio is also quite critical of Spinoza's denial of free will, a doctrine that Orobio makes central to Judaism. In short, Spinoza's philosophy, whatever its philosophical merits, is foreign to biblical religion, and any truly religious Jew or Christian must reject it completely.

Although Orobio's critique had some influence upon several Christian thinkers, it did not have much importance for Jewish thought. The first significant response to Spinoza from a major Jewish thinker came from Moses Mendelssohn, the German eighteenth-century philosopher usually credited with being the first modern Jewish philosopher. Mendelssohn's attitude toward Spinoza was ambivalent. On the one hand, he not only read his forerunner with sympathy but saw him as a tragic figure who had to do what he did yet was justly condemned for it. For Mendelssohn, Spinoza's metaphysics was a necessary prerequisite for Leibniz's metaphysics, which Mendelssohn took as his philosophical point of departure. Indeed, he attempted to purify Spinoza's philosophy of its errors and excesses by accommodating and assimilating it to Leibniz's metaphysics. Some Spinozistic doctrines are retained: Spinozism's strong determinism is softened by reformulating it in terms of

Leibniz's principle of sufficient reason; the eternity of nature is claimed to be logically possible and not incompatible with Judaism, a point admitted not only by Leibniz but by the late medieval Jewish theologian Chasdai Crescas. But Mendelssohn correctly and honestly recognizes the fundamental difference between Jewish dualistic supranaturalism and Spinoza's monistic naturalism, although he attempts to close the gap by pointing to the special role that Spinoza assigned to the attribute of thought, which for Mendelssohn is a departure from his strict naturalism and a turn toward classical Jewish philosophy.

Mendelssohn's more positive appreciation of Spinoza's thought is perhaps more revealed in his own political-theological treatise, *Jerusalem*. Although the second part of this essay is an explicit defense of Judaism and an attempt to formulate it as a religion of reason, its first part is in several important respects a concession to some of Spinoza's theses in the *TTP*. Mendelssohn accepts Spinoza's basic position that religion and politics must be kept separate. Religion is a private matter: it should not intrude into government, and the state should not interfere with religion. Of more relevance to Judaism, Mendelssohn also asserts that the Jewish community should not have any coercive powers over its members; in particular, excommunication is to be eliminated since it infringes religious liberty. Membership of the Jewish community is purely voluntary based upon religious conviction and practice. Jewish political identity is to be sought in the secular state, which will soon grant the Jews full citizenship (Mendelssohn hoped). Indeed, the traditional dream of returning to Zion and re-establishing a Jewish polity is for Mendelssohn obsolete. Although he retains, whereas Spinoza did not, Jewish religious identity in the Diaspora, Mendelssohn advocates the rejection of Jewish ethnic and corporate separatism. Cultural and social assimilation are not only acceptable but desirable; religious changes are not. Although Mendelssohn did not explicitly endeavor to forge a synthesis of Spinoza's political theology with Judaism, many of his ideas amount to such an attempt. This vision of a "modernized" Judaism will be a dominant theme throughout Jewish thought after Mendelssohn.

In his own days Mendelssohn's cautious and critical appreciation of Spinoza already bore fruit. His younger contemporary and friend Solomon Maimon expressed an even more receptive attitude towards Spinoza and tried to incorporate Spinozistic themes into his own philosophy. Since Maimon himself was a marginal Jew, albeit not quite excommunicated, this was easier than it would have been for Mendelssohn. Maimon made two observations about Spinoza's metaphysics that are of special interest. First, like a number of Christian scholars of his day, and even earlier, Maimon believed that Spinoza's philosophy evolved out of the kabbalah. Spinoza's system of modes, infinite and finite, corresponds to the kabbalistic doctrine of contraction (*tzimtzum*) of the infinite substance, or God. It is not without interest to note that Leibniz too saw a link between Spinoza and kabbalah, a view that has champions even amongst some contemporary Spinoza scholars (R. Popkin). Second, Maimon attempted to deflect the standard charge of atheism against Spinoza by claiming instead that Spinoza advocated acosmism. For, if God and nature are really one, and since for Spinoza our highest goal is to love and know God, then, Maimon concluded, nature, or the physical world, has no independent status.

Although Maimon's admiration of Spinozism would probably have caused Mendelssohn a great deal of distress, it was an attitude that was adopted and advanced by a number of East European Jewish intellectuals of the next generation. Trying to emancipate themselves from the yoke of both the halakhah and the ghetto, these *maskilim* (enlightened ones) saw in Spinoza a kindred spirit, who had accomplished what they wanted to achieve, except for one thing. Unlike Spinoza, they still desired to locate themselves within the Jewish community, albeit a community reformed by "enlightenment" and "emancipation." In several respects Spinoza was their model. Did he not show that one could be a believer in God without, however, subscribing to outmoded modes of religious worship? Did he not teach and practice a moral philosophy of considerable sublimity? Finally, did he not write a Hebrew grammar, indicating that he still believed in the worthiness of Hebrew? So, to people like Abraham Krochmal (the son of the great Galician historian and philosopher Nachman Krochmal), Meir Letteris (1800–71), Shlomo Rubin (1823–1910), and several others, Spinoza was the guide to salvation. Rubin himself translated the *Ethics* and the *Hebrew Grammar* into Hebrew and wrote his doctoral dissertation on Spinoza. He considered Spinoza to be "the new guide of the perplexed" who would lead the Jews out of their intellectual and social isolation to the new world of secular salvation.

Spinoza's "rehabilitation," expressed especially in Hebrew, was too much for more traditional Jewish thinkers, particularly the great Italian Bible scholar S. D. Luzzatto (1800–65), who reacted vehemently against the judaization of Spinoza attempted by Letteris and Rubin. Luzzatto's critique of Spinoza was far more negative than Mendelssohn's; there was very little in Baruch that Samuel David could accept or appreciate. Indeed, for Luzzatto the Amsterdam Jews were absolutely correct in expelling Spinoza. And Jews for ever after ought to avoid his philosophy like the plague. An ethicist as well as biblical scholar, Luzzatto was quite qualified to assume the role of Spinoza's critic. Whereas Mendelssohn had confined himself primarily to addressing certain ideas in Spinoza's metaphysics, Luzzatto focuses upon the latter's moral philosophy, which was for Spinoza the culminating point of his *Ethics*. Both in style and substance Spinoza's ethics is un-Jewish, Luzzatto charges. Just consider the literary form of the *Ethics*: its mathematical presentation is cold and dry, hardly of any use in encouraging or exhorting the reader to pursue its ethical program. More important its moral content is hedonistic and egocentric, tendencies that Jewish ethics suppress. We can see this in Spinoza's analyses of several specific moral values, especially prized in Jewish ethics, such as pity and humility. Pity for Spinoza is defined as the pain we feel when we observe someone else in pain (*Ethics* 3.22, scholium and definition of emotions, 18); hence, it is bad (*Ethics* 4.50). For, according to Spinoza, all pain is a diminution of one's own power, and as such is to be avoided. Humility for Spinoza is the pain we experience when we observe our own weakness (*Ethics* 3.55). Since this is a painful experience, it is not a virtue (*Ethics* 4.53). No wonder, Luzzatto comments, that Spinoza was excommunicated: in denying the value of pity and humility he was uprooting Jewish morality. Spinoza's secular morality based upon hedonism and utilitarianism is for Luzzatto utterly despicable and has nothing to do with Judaism or for that matter with humanity.[11]

Luzzatto's vitriolic critique of Spinoza had, however, limited circulation since it was written in Hebrew, and by the second half of the century most Jews in Western and central Europe could no longer read Hebrew, except for the Bible at best. By this time, for many Western-educated Jews Spinoza had become a model of what they wanted to be. This was especially true in Germany, where Spinoza had become the hero of Goethe, Heine, and other German poets and intellectuals. Germany was the original cradle of liberal Judaism, which advocated linguistic and cultural assimilation, religious reform and abandonment of Jewish nationalism in favor of German nationalism and citizenship. All of these goals are consistent with and indeed present in, Spinoza's *TTP*. For many German Liberal Jews, particularly those recently educated in the gymnasia and universities, Spinoza was their "passport to European culture," and they embraced Spinoza as a "role model" who would teach them how to be both a Jew and a German.

But the greatest German-Jewish philosopher of the late nineteenth and early twentieth centuries would have nothing of this. Like Luzzatto, Hermann Cohen saw Spinoza as the "most difficult obstacle and thus misfortune for modern Jewish history"; even worse he is "the true accuser of Judaism before the Christian world."[12] But, unlike Luzzatto, Cohen focused his *Spinoza-Kritik* upon the *TTP*, not the *Ethics*. In his essay devoted to Spinoza's critique of Judaism, Cohen tackles Spinoza directly. Amongst the many diverse criticisms Cohen makes against Spinoza, several are especially noteworthy.

The *TTP* began with a critique of biblical prophecy and of the biblical text itself. It is here, Cohen maintains, that Spinoza's hostility to Judaism was most glaring. Just consider the fact that, whereas he devoted ten chapters to the criticism of the Hebrew Bible, he discussed the New Testament only in one. True, he excused himself by saying that his knowledge of Greek was insufficient. But was this the real reason? For Cohen, the uneven biblical criticism Spinoza presented was symptomatic of an underlying animus against his former religion and a bias in favor of Christianity. Spinoza was the first Jew to offer a critique of Judaism and show a preference for Christianity *without* becoming a Christian.[13] Is it any wonder then that Spinoza was so admired by Goethe and Hegel, who both advocated Jewish assimilation?

In his *Bibelkritik* Spinoza continually, Cohen argues, attributes to Judaism views that are not only false but he either knew or should have known to be false. For example, in Matthew 5: 43 Jesus is reported to have said: "You have learned that they were told: 'Love your neighbor, hate your enemies'." Spinoza takes this statement at face value and uses it to support his general thesis that Mosaic law was purely political: hatred of the enemy was politically useful, perhaps necessary, and served to separate the Israelites from the "gentiles" (Spinoza, *TTP*, chapter 19). Indeed, for Spinoza, Jewish hatred of the gentiles is the main reason for anti-semitism (*TTP*, chapter 3)! Now all of this is, for Cohen, not only sheer nonsense but reveals Spinoza's bias and hatred for Judaism, features unbecoming for a scholar. Spinoza simply has ignored the many teachings in both the Bible and rabbinic literature that express love for the stranger, help toward one's enemies, and the conversion of enemies into friends through love. But, by selective quotation and use of the New Testament as the authoritative interpretation of the Hebrew Bible, Spinoza was able to prove to his readers and to himself that Judaism was not only obsolete but primitive as well. If not the first, Spinoza was then one of the early and more prominent propagators of the canard of Jewish particularism.[14] Did he fail to read the book of Jonah, a book that is read on the Day of Atonement? And where is it taught to hate one's enemies?[15] It is not uninteresting to note that in the Oxford edition of the English Bible the editor comments on Matthew 5: 43: "*Hate your enemy* is not found in the Old Testament or Pharisaic, Rabbinic Judaism." Surely, Spinoza knew this. But why did he accept Matthew's report? For Cohen, Spinoza's own theological-political agenda led him to falsify *intentionally* the Bible and the nature of Judaism, thus vitiating or diminishing much of the value of his "biblical science."

Cohen frequently singles out Spinoza's pantheism, or naturalism, as the cause of several of Spinoza's biases and errors. Spinoza's naturalism led him to deny any objective, or rational, basis for morality. Virtue is power (*Ethics* 4, definition 8). Or, as others have put it, might makes right. Cohen claims that Spinoza's moral and political doctrines are based upon this equation. Not only is nature morally neutral, or amoral, so is the state. Just as the former is in some sense the "sum total of all individuals," so is the state.[16] And just as the laws of nature are not themselves moral nor correspond to the diverse moral maxims that people frame for themselves, so the laws of the state may not coincide with those of private, or individual, morality. Like nature, the state is power. For a Kantian philosopher like Cohen, Spinoza's moral-political philosophy is just an apology for power politics.[17] Indeed, for Spinoza it turns out that religion is legitimate only so far as it is approved by the state! So what began as an attempt to separate Church and state ends in pure state absolutism. Spinoza's "original" philosophical sin was his rejection of rational morality in favor of naturalism, his advocacy of materialism against idealism; his original moral sin was his utter hatred of Judaism. To us, Cohen concludes, Spinoza remains an "enemy."[18]

One would have expected after the detailed and penetrating criticisms of Luzzatto and Cohen that any attempt to rehabilitate Spinoza would be quixotic. But this was not to be so. While Cohen was condemning Spinoza, a deep and radical change was beginning to surface in the Jewish world – Zionism. Joseph Klausner, the eminent Jewish historian, tells this story, which he had heard about Leo Pinsker, one of the founding and leading figures in the early Zionist movement. Pinsker had been an advocate of assimilation; but when a passage at the end of chapter 3 of the *TTP* had been brought to his attention, he made an about-face.[19] This is the passage:

> Indeed, if the fundamental principles of their religion have not emasculated their spirit, I should believe unhesitatingly that they will one day, given the opportunity since human affairs are changeable, re-establish their empire, and that God will again elect them.

This sentence became the "proof-text" for quite a number of Zionist thinkers and pioneers and allowed them to represent to themselves and to others a more positive picture of Spinoza: Spinoza the proto-Zionist.

An excellent example of this attitude is Klausner himself, who in several of his essays attempted to reclaim Spinoza and his philosophy not only for the Jewish people but for Jewish thought as well. This becomes possible, he argued, because, with the verification of Spinoza's biblical science, a more liberal and diverse Jewish religious culture is possible, one in which Spinoza, despite his "sins against the Jews," can be brought back into the fold. Klausner is quite aware of Spinoza's anti-Jewish side; but, unlike Cohen, he stresses those aspects of his thought that are Jewish in origin and in spirit. Fundamental to his rehabilitation of Spinoza is Klausner's capacious conception of Judaism and Jewish philosophy: throughout its history the Jewish religious and philosophical genius has assumed different expressions, some closer to the original biblical spirit, other more distant. Within a wider perspective, Spinoza's philosophical "deviations" are often not much more radical than those of ibn Gabirol, Maimonides, Gersonides or Crescas, or even some of the kabbalists. Nor is his biblical criticism, revolutionary in his own day, more radical than the Bible science taught today in Israeli universities and in some rabbinical seminaries throughout the world. It is of course a historical fiction to tell a story about how Spinoza and the Amsterdam congregation would have behaved in the twentieth century. Nevertheless, his ideas are hardly more "atheistical" than those entertained by the majority of Jews today. He was, to his misfortune, "ahead of his time." In his own day, there was probably no choice for the community of elders in banning Spinoza. But we live in a different world, one that embraces such diverse Jewish thinkers as Mordecai Kaplan, Martin Buber, the Lubavitcher Rabbi and J. B. Soloveitchik. In a way, Spinoza's excommunication was a tragedy in the Hegelian sense: a clash between two incompatible rights. Spinoza had the right to express his own conception of religion and philosophy; but the Jewish community had the right to do everything to preserve itself. At that time and place, these two rights could not coexist; now they can, indeed they do. In 1927 on Mount Scopus, the original campus of the Hebrew University, Klausner concluded one of his Spinoza lectures with the conciliatory words: "The ban has been lifted! The Jewish crime against you and your sin against Judaism have been both atoned for! You are our brother, you are our brother, you are our brother."[20]

A few years later David Ben-Gurion, who studied Spinoza all his adult life, seconded Klausner's proposal and acted as Spinoza's "defense attorney" in 1953 when he published a piece in the Israeli newspaper *Davar* entitled "Let us straighten out the crooked," proposing the end of the ban. Although the discussions about and efforts to annul the excommunication were inconclusive, the Zionist "in-gathering" of Spinoza succeeded; for since then virtually all of Spinoza's works have been translated into Hebrew and published in Israel. Moreover, Israel has become a major center for Spinoza studies, especially with the establishment of the Jerusalem Spinoza Institute, which sponsors biennial conferences on Spinoza's philosophy. Philosophers and their philosophies, as well as books, have their own fates, as Spinoza would have admitted. And perhaps the felicitous irony in contemporary Jewry's incorporation of Spinoza's legacy would have not been lost upon Spinoza himself; indeed it might have amused him.

❧ NOTES ❧

1 Guttmann 1973, p. 301.
2 Wolfson 1934.
3 Revah 1959.
4 Yovel 1989, 1: 213–15.
5 Strauss 1982, chapter 3; Popkin 1988, pp. 38–9.
6 Kolakowski 1969; Meinsma 1983.
7 Popkin 1988, pp. 38–9.
8 Klever 1990, pp. 282–9.
9 Mignini 1983, pp. 6–13; 1979, pp. 87–160.
10 Schweid 1975, p. 126; Levy 1983.
11 Luzzatto 1913, pp. 198–222.
12 Cohen 1924, 2: 371.
13 Ibid., pp. 359–60.
14 Ibid., p. 329.
15 Ibid., p. 358.
16 Ibid., p. 304.
17 Ibid., p. 309.
18 Ibid., p. 371.
19 Klausner 1955, pp. 295–6.
20 Ibid., p. 329.

❧ BIBLIOGRAPHY ❧

Texts

Spinoza (1951) *Theologico-Political Treatise, Political Treatise*, translated by R. Elwes (New York: Dover).
—— (1966) *The Correspondence of Spinoza*, translated by A. Wolf (New York: Russell & Russell).
—— (1992) *Ethics, Treatise on the Emendation of the Intellect and Selected Letters*, translated by S. Shirley and edited by S. Feldman (Indianapolis: Hackett).

Studies

Cohen, H. (1924) *Jüdische Schriften*, edited by B. Strauss, 3 vols (Berlin: Schwetschke).

Guttmann, J. (1973) *Philosophies of Judaism*, translated by D. W. Silverman (New York: Schocken).

Klausner, J. (1955) *From Plato to Spinoza; Philosophical Essays* [Hebrew] (Jerusalem: Mada).

Klever, W. (1990) "Proto-Spinoza: Franciscus van den Enden," *Studia Spinozana* 6: 281–9.

Kolakowski, L. (1969) *Chrétiens sans Église*, translated by A. Posner (Paris: Gallimard).

Levy, A. (1983) *Spinoza's Interpretation of Judaism* [Hebrew] (Tel Aviv: Sifriyat Poalim).

Luzzatto, S. (1913) "Against Spinoza" [Hebrew], in *Studies in Judaism* (Warsaw: Ha-Tzefirah) 1.2: 198–222.

Meinsma, K. (1983) *Spinoza et son circle*, translated by S. Rosenburg (Paris: Vrin).

Mignini, F. (1979) "Per la datazione e l'interpretazione del 'Tractatus de intellectus emendatione' di Spinoza," *La Cultura* 17: 87–160.

—— (1983) *Introduzione a Spinoza* (Rome: Laterza).

Popkin, R. (1988) "Spinoza's Earliest Philosophical Years: 1655–1661," *Studia Spinozana* 4: 37–54.

Revah, I. (1959) *Spinoza et Juan de Prado* (Paris: Mouton).

Schweid, E. (1975) *The Solitary Jew and Judaism* [Hebrew] (Tel Aviv: Am Oved), p. 126.

Strauss, L. (1982) *Spinoza's Critique of Religion* (New York: Schocken).

Wolfson, H. (1934) *The Philosophy of Spinoza* (Cambridge MA: Harvard University Press).

Yovel, Y. (1989) *Spinoza and Other Heretics*, 2 vols. (Princeton: Princeton University Press).

CHAPTER 25

The social and cultural context: eighteenth-century Enlightenment

Lois C. Dubin

❦ INTRODUCTION ❦

From approximately the 1680s to 1789, the Enlightenment popularized the new science and philosophy of Bacon, Descartes, Newton, and Locke, and brought their rationalist, empiricist, and naturalist premises to bear on every sphere of science and society. Reason, nature, experience, utility, and progress became the criteria according to which the institutions and traditions of old-regime Europe – a pre-industrial world of hierarchical orders and hereditary privilege, dominated by monarchs, aristocrats, and clergy – were evaluated, and often found wanting. The Enlightenment forged the anthropocentric and secular discourse of the last two centuries.

The Enlightenment's secular definition of civil society and the state was decisive for Jews and Judaism, for it made room for Jews as potential members of that realm by virtue of their possession of universal human rationality. Thus, the Enlightenment helped usher Jews into modern Europe, but it did so on problematic terms that often bore the burdensome weight of the past and generated new tensions.

The Enlightenment also spawned a new ideology and self-awareness among Jews themselves, the Haskalah or Jewish Enlightenment, that represented the intellectual effort to appraise and reconfigure Judaism according to Enlightenment rationalism and naturalism. The Haskalah reflected and helped guide the passage of Jews from the status of resident aliens to fellow subjects, thereby producing the ideological premises for a modern Judaism that would be an engaged yet distinctive participant in European culture and society.

636

For Jewish philosophy in particular, the Enlightenment and Haskalah led to intensive interaction of Jews with the dominant intellectual culture of the day, and hence for its third great efflorescence after the Hellenistic and medieval Islamic phases. From the late eighteenth to the early twentieth centuries, Jewish philosophy would bear the imprint of German philosophy.

This chapter will discuss first the eighteenth-century European Enlightenment, then the Enlightenment views of Jews and Judaism, and finally the Haskalah in its formative late eighteenth-century German phase.

⚬⚬ PERSPECTIVES ON THE ⚬⚬
ENLIGHTENMENT

What was the Enlightenment? Some years ago, it was easier to answer that question than it is now. Widespread were the appellations Age of Philosophy or Age of Reason that reflected the self-consciousness of the French *philosophes* and German *Aufklärer*; d'Alembert had called his the "century of philosophy" (Cassirer 1955, p. 3). The Enlightenment was understood to be a coherent set of ideas or attitudes, held by a relatively unified intellectual movement that fought for the triumph of reason over superstition, of light over darkness.

The unity of the Enlightenment was stressed by two of its most influential interpreters, Cassirer and Gay. Cassirer's *The Philosophy of the Enlightenment* (Cassirer 1955) remains unsurpassed for its penetrating analysis of the realm of philosophy and ideas. He found unity by seeing much of the Enlightenment as leading teleologically to Kant. Gay's *The Enlightenment: An Interpretation* (Gay 1966, 1969) focused on the practical experience of the *philosophes* in applying ideas to reality. Gay depicted the *philosophes* as modern pagans who broke free from both their Christian and the ancient classical inheritances, but who mostly used the latter to overthrow or neutralize the former. His portrait was of a unified anti-clerical movement headquartered in Paris.

Yet Age of Reason proved unsatisfactory. In his quirky but widely read essay, Becker considered it more an "age of faith" because of the *philosophes'* passionate utopian faith in their own outlook, which he claimed was closer to the medieval than they cared to acknowledge (Becker 1932). Others have noted that Enlightenment thinkers hardly relied on reason alone and showed increasing attention through the course of the eighteenth century to sensation, materialism, sentiment, and the irrational (Crocker 1959, 1963; Darnton 1970; Taylor 1989, pp. 282–301). Even Cassirer and Gay modified reason and transformed it into criticism, echoing Kant who had spoken of the "very age of criticism" (Kant, *Critique of Pure Reason*, in Gay (ed.) 1973, p. 17); both stressed the critical and dynamic functions of Enlightenment reason in contrast to earlier contemplative, metaphysical, and systematizing uses of reason. Gay argued that the *philosophes'* dislike of abstract metaphysics and their keen sense of the limits of reason actually made their movement a "Revolt against Rationalism" (Gay 1966, p. 141).

A less unified and more variegated picture of the Enlightenment is emerging as scholars take seriously its practical thrust of "realistic rationalism" (Anchor 1967, p. 7), of criticism aiming at real social reform in areas such as criminal law, education, and agriculture. In recent years scholars have left the realms of grand syntheses and definitions, of ideas and high culture, in order to examine the Enlightenment on the ground: in many different national and regional settings (Porter and Teich 1981); in its various social contexts and political functions (Koselleck 1988; Scott 1990; Venturi 1969–, 1971, 1972, 1989, 1991); in its dissemination, legal and clandestine, of critical texts of both high and low culture (Darnton 1971, 1979; Goodman 1989).

The effort to determine how Enlightenment ways of thinking were actually expressed, received, and acted upon has revealed that the Enlightenment message appealed to different social groups – to many nobles and clergy, government bureaucrats, and rulers, as well as to bourgeois with increasing wealth, education, leisure, and civic interest (Darton 1979; Scott 1990). Its spread was linked to the rise of a new kind of sociability centered in voluntary associations, reading and discussion groups, provincial academies, masonic lodges, and coffee houses (Dülmen 1992; Jacob 1991; Roche 1978), and the gradual development of a "public sphere" with new avenues for the expression and organization of civic opinion (Habermas 1989). The Enlightenment was certainly not a conspiracy to make revolution – it sought to reform, not destroy the ancien régime – but it was one sign of its decay and the emergence in its interstices of the habits and institutions of modern civil society. The precise connections between the intellectual-cultural Enlightenment and politics, both the existing political order and nascent modern political culture, is at the heart of bicentennial reconsiderations of the relation between the Enlightenment and the French Revolution; they need addressing in the many other national settings of the Enlightenment as well (Baker and Lucas 1987–8; Chartier 1991; Jacob 1991). On issues of power and politics, it should be noted that some scholars have focused attention on what they consider to be the negative – indeed totalitarian – implications of the Enlightenment' brand of reasoning and social engineering (Foucault 1984; Talmon 1952).

The newer pan-European perspective forces a re-examination of the Enlightenment and religion. Earlier emphasis on the French Enlightenment had skewed the picture, for it was decidedly more anti-clerical and anti-religious than its counterparts in many other places, for example Germany and Scotland. Denunciation of religious dogma and ecclesiastical institutions – signified in Voltaire's battle cry "Écrasez l'infâme!" – is well known, but the view from other countries, and even France itself, shows that the Enlightenment and religion were not always sworn enemies (Palmer 1939). A "religious enlightenment" has been detected among European Catholics, Protestants, and Jews (Sorkin 1991). Further study should be devoted to the appropriation of the Enlightenment by those who remained committed to their respective religious traditions, including also the Orthodox and Armenian.

Thus these many newer national, social, political, and religious configurations of Enlightenment press forward the old question of the one and the many in a new guise: dare we speak any longer of one Enlightenment, or only rather of many Enlightenments? For now, no elegant answer or new grand synthesis beckons.

❦ KNOWLEDGE, CRITICISM, AND ❦ AUTONOMY

But while the question "What *was* the Enlightenment?" has become more difficult, it may still be appropriate in a volume on Jewish philosophy to attempt some definition and to proceed by way of Kant and Hegel's answers to the late eighteenth-century formulation "What *is* Enlightenment?"

For Kant, the question was Enlightening rather than Enlightenment, a process rather than a result. Enlightening was the emergence of humanity from a self-imposed age of minority, "man's quitting the nonage occasioned by himself." The means were intellectual daring: "*Sapere audere*! Have courage to make use of thy own understanding!" (Kant, *Answer to the Question, What is Enlightening?* 1965, p. 34). We hear echoes of the *Encyclopédie*'s definition of the *philosophe* as one who "trampling on prejudice, tradition, universal consent, authority, in a word, all that enslaves most minds, dares to think for himself" (Porter 1990, pp. 3–4). For Hegel, the Enlightenment meant that "heaven is transplanted to earth below" (Hegel, *Phenomenology of Spirit* 1977, sec. 581: p. 355, as human understanding and self-will bring "ideas belonging to the world of sense, and ... finitude" to bear on "that heavenly world," and faith is "expelled from its kingdom" (Hegel, *Phenomenology*, 1977, sec. 572–3: pp. 348–9). In other words, Enlightening meant daring to know and valuing the finite.

The Enlightenment fostered a cast of mind that approached the natural and the social worlds as a finite order, without regard to the overall cosmos or ultimate purpose, in other words "that heavenly world." "The power of reason does not consist in enabling us to transcend the empirical world but rather in teaching us to feel at home in it" (Cassirer 1955, p. 13). Nature was understood to constitute a self-regulating and harmonious order whose laws, principles, and mechanisms of order could be observed and comprehended by the human mind, itself a part of the natural world. Through observing nature, the human mind could arrive at a proper sense of its own capacities and limits, and learn to combine reason and experience in order to understand both nature and humanity, and ultimately reshape human society. The work of Enlightenment was both theoretical and practical, involving observation and understanding, critique and action. "The true nature of Enlightenment thinking cannot be seen in its purest and clearest form where it is formulated into particular doctrines, axioms, and theorems; but rather where it is in process, where it is doubting and seeking, tearing down and building up" (ibid., p. ix). Tearing down: tradition – the given, the existing, the customary – was due not reverence but critique; it could not simply be accepted, but had to be subjected to the cold analytic light of reason, then justified, modified, or rejected. And it was human reason, daring to act autonomously and critically, that determined the reasonable. Building up: taking the results of rationalist critique and reshaping tradition and society in the image of nature, common sense, science, and utility.

Reason was thus process, tool, and ideological weapon. The prime function of knowledge was ultimately not to contemplate eternal truths or seek communication with a higher power. Its thrust was activist and pragmatic, and would still be "salvific" (Funkenstein 1993) if and only if it dealt realistically with the finite world. The job of enlightened philosophy was to overthrow old idols and construct an improved, more humane moral and social world. A *philosophe* was defined as a man of action whose superior intellect imposes on him the responsibility of enlightening his fellow men (Raynal, *Histoire des deux Indes*, in Yolton et al. (eds) 1991, p. 172). More critic than philosopher, a man of Enlightenment saw himself as a committed social actor engaged in the essentially practical work of enlightening, that is, of combating ignorance and prejudice by means of all-important critique and education. This was holy work towards the goal of secular salvation, progress towards this-worldly individual and societal happiness. The *philosophes* saw themselves called to this new vocation, and, in asserting their authority to speak on all intellectual, moral, and social matters, they set themselves up as an alternative lay authority to the clergy, indeed as the new "clerks" – as moral arbiters and interpreters of conscience. In fact, this secular intelligentsia did represent a new social type, not identifiable with any particular order in the old regime.

"A critique and a permanent creation of ourselves in our autonomy" was Foucault's description of the Enlightenment's self-consciousness (Foucault 1984, p. 44). It is perhaps strange to find convergence among the views of Kant, Hegel, Cassirer, Gay, and Foucault. Yet from all there emerges a sense of the dynamic, critical, autonomous, self-confident, creative, and pragmatic functioning of reason which was central to the work of Enlightening. Belief in the importance of human concerns, and in the efficacy of human rationality, responsibility, and agency – these attitudes, rooted in the seventeenth-century advances of natural science, became the hallmarks of the Enlightenment and its ongoing legacy.

‍ THE ENLIGHTENMENT AND ‍ RELIGION

Enlightenment views on religion ranged from rationalist belief in a particular religion through skepticism, deism, materialism, and atheism. But common to all was the tendency to submit the positive religious traditions to rationalist scrutiny and to measure them according to the theoretical construct of natural religion, which was considered consonant with nature and its norms of rationality and universality. To enlightened eyes, all existing religions necessarily suffered from being "positive," that is, composed of arbitrary convention and artifice. Rationalist scrutiny usually involved "tearing down" and "building up," in other words, destruction and construction, as enlightened thinkers proffered both aggressive critique of the existing religious order, and alternative formulations of an acceptable reasonable religion. Some expressed outright hostility to religion, on the one hand, while others attempted to modernize and purify it, on the other. Generally, savage assault was more part of the French repertoire, while reinterpretation was more part of the German.

For most Enlightenment considerations of religion, the starting point was a secular definition of civil society and the state. Faith was expelled not only from its kingdom, in Hegel's phrase, but also from the civil kingdom. Locke's *A Letter on Toleration* made the case for the state as a secular institution, and its separation from the powerful embrace of religion: the state was no longer to be seen as a Christian commonwealth, responsible for the eternal salvation of its members, but rather as an entity devoted to fostering temporal goods such as life, liberty, health, and property. A corollary of the secular state was a secular and utilitarian definition of the ideal person: one who contributed to temporal society by being useful. The move from a confessional to administrative state rested on two foundations: fallibilism – the human mind cannot know which religion is true – and individual autonomy – each person alone is responsible for his or her own soul and salvation. In a secular administrative state, crime would be synonymous no longer with sin, but rather with the violation of the civic rules or public order. These premises and the bitter experience of religious strife in early modern Europe led to but one conclusion: tolerance of religious diversity was a political necessity. These became Enlightenment maxims: intolerance begets civil strife, tolerance begets civil peace.

Locke's secular foundation for the modern state left two issues unresolved. First, though theoretically the state and religion were assigned separate spheres, respectively the temporal and spiritual, practically there was overlap in the realm of morality. Especially in Germany, the state continued to be seen as a tutelary entity responsible for the moral welfare of its denizens – a fact that conditioned the nature of the tolerance extended to religious minorities. The second unresolved issue was precisely the bounds of tolerance. According to Locke's criterion of civil harm, pagans, Muslims, and Jews were admissible, but Catholics (supposedly beholden to foreign papal power) and atheists (supposedly lacking all morality) were not. For many Enlightenment thinkers, a contradiction persisted between the theoretical principle of toleration as a good, and its practical limitation so as to exclude a particular religious group for one reason or another.

A secular definition of the state became the cornerstone of the enlightened critique of existing religions. In France in particular, the Catholic Church came in for devastating criticism as an institution that wielded too much political power. Moreover it was charged with promoting values and practices that clashed with civil and social utility. Thus, for example, its monasteries and Inquisition were ridiculed and harshly indicted, the first for the crime of social inutility and the second for intolerance, which, as the fomenter of civil strife, constituted both inutility and crime.

But the Enlightenment critique of religion not only leveled political and social charges, but, building upon the writings of the English Deists, proceeded also on rationalist and historical grounds. To put it simply, existing religion was all too often seen as irrational or unreasonable superstition – stemming from human fear and ignorance, manipulated by devious priestcraft, and nurtured by unfounded and unreliable human traditions. The *philosophes* had little patience for, or even understanding of, mysteries, ceremony and ritual, or subtle metaphysical dogma, all of which struck them as absurd, unnecessary, and particular. Many of these were based upon testimony about foundational miracles, testimony now deemed suspect because tradition and even its fount, the biblical scriptures, could no longer be trusted since they were seen as human documents, necessarily subject to self-interested and unreliable transmission. To a Voltaire, the contents of the entire Bible were full of absurdity and immorality, hardly mitigated by claims of divine revelation that rested on weak and faulty chains of tradition.

Thus the positive religions were suspect. Their differences made them all seem relative. And what they offered seemed contrary to what nature and reason demanded: a clear and distinct apprehension of the design of the universe based upon observation, and inner appreciation for its designer. One expression of this was the deistic scheme of a clockmaker creator-God who then retired from active duty to enjoy contemplating the mechanism he had created. Thus universal nature and reason – and not particular texts or traditions – were the proper sources for an enlightened and natural religion. As if to highlight the universal, Enlightenment literature was replete with exotic or uncorrupted Others – such as the travellers Usbek and Rica in Montesquieu's *The Persian Letters* – who criticize European Christianity and Judaism, and who represent an alternative religious model.

Universal, reasonable, natural religion would express its awareness of design and designer by some kind of interior response – intellectual assent to a few simple beliefs for Voltaire, conscience or "simplicity of heart" for Rousseau (Rousseau, *The Creed of a Priest of Savoy* 1990, p. 75) – and the performance of morally and socially useful actions. Above all, it would be simple in both belief and action, requiring, as Voltaire admonished, no more than "adoration of one God, justice, tolerance, and humanity" (Voltaire, "Religion" in *A Philosophical Dictionary* 1903, 13: 85), and "be just and not persecuting sophists" (Voltaire, "Just and Unjust," in ibid., 11: 29). According to Herder, "True religion therefore is a filial service of God, an imitation of the most high and beautiful represented in the human form, with the extreme of inward satisfaction, active goodness, and love of mankind" (Herder, *Ideen*, book 4, sec. 6.6 (Bollacher, p. 162; Churchill tr., p. 184)). In other words, the proof of one's inward religiosity was not dogmatic certainty, ceremony, or the imposing of religious conformity upon others, but rather moral action and humanitarian tolerance. In sum, an acceptable enlightened religion would be reasonable, socially useful, politically powerless, and non-authoritarian, that is, allowing individuals to make their own observations and come to their own conclusions. It would also entertain some skepticism deriving from a keen awareness of the limits of the human mind.

The thrust of natural religion was thus universal, rational, commonsensical, and moral. This construct functioned in two ways: first, it provided an ideal natural yardstick by which to measure the various positive religions; and second, it addressed the problem of diversity and relativism by purporting to represent a discernible core of basic universal religion common to all. As morality was stressed, it was in effect divorced from its previous base of revealed religion, and made the independent touchstone by which to evaluate existing religions. A specific positive religion would be deemed acceptable only if it was in keeping with the moral commandments of natural religion. As Lessing put it, "the best revealed or positive religion is that which contains the fewest conventional additions to natural religion, and least hinders the good effects of natural religion" (Lessing, "On the Origin of Revealed Religion" 1956, p. 105).

Not all Enlightenment thinkers found the concept of natural religion congenial (Hume for example thought it self-contradictory and French materialists such as Holbach rejected divine design altogether), but it was a way-station that could satisfy various temperaments. It could serve those who waged vigorous assault on the Church and its temporal power by offering an alternative minimalist and ethical core of religion. It could also serve those lay intellectuals or churchmen who started from a fundamentally more favorable view of religion. Among the French, Montesquieu and Rousseau especially recognized the social value of religion. Most Protestant *Aufklärer* did so as well, and primed themselves to salvage religion from the onslaught of materialism and atheism. In this respect Lessing was paradigmatic of the German Enlightenment when he asked: "Why are we not more willing to see in all positive religions simply the process by which alone human understanding in every place can develop and must still further develop, instead of either ridiculing or becoming angry with them?" (Lessing, *The Education of the Human Race* 1956, p. 82). By introducing history, Lessing was able to see religion as an important early, stage of human development – "what education is to the individual man, revelation is to the whole human race" – and its "revealed truths" as primitive "truths of reason" that would develop in time as more fully rational truths (ibid., pp. 82, 95). Thus, revealed religion could be seen as consonant with modern rationalist philosophy and reinterpreted in its terms.

Harmonization of the naturalist faith of the Enlightenment with commitment to an existing religion might be reached through different routes. One route was that of the advocates of Enlightenment who came to see something positive in existing religions after all. The other was that of the "religious Enlightenment," as seen in the devotees of a particular religion, clergy or lay, "who welcomed the new science and philosophy of the Enlightenment as a means to renew and reinvigorate faith . . . [who] attempt[ed] to put the Enlightenment in the service of revealed religion" (Sorkin 1994a, p. 130).

None the less, to summarize in broad terms, while many Enlightenment thinkers were seriously engaged with the problem of religion and came to some appreciation of its moral and social role, there was a pronounced tendency to see religion primarily in rationalist or reductionist psychological terms. Many tended to equate religion with a set of intellectual propositions or a response to fear and weakness. Generally, they failed to comprehend the nature and power of religious experience and expression (for example, in ritual and ceremony), and they were blind to its social-communal aspects, the ties of human solidarity that could be forged by religious communities.

❧ A CASE STUDY OF TOLERANCE: ❧ THE ENLIGHTENMENT AND THE JEWS

Tolerance of the religious Other was considered by Enlightenment thinkers to be the very essence of its enlightened, humanitarian, universalist ideals. The Other too belonged to the one species of humanity bound together by common rationality, despite the apparent welter of human diversity. Theoretically, the Enlightenment preached tolerance for all except those dangerous to civil peace, and ringingly denounced intolerance as a barbaric, secular sin, a crime against the secular state and humanity. The tolerated should enjoy the right to practice their religion and be granted civil, though not necessarily full political, rights.

How were the new universalist and rationalist ideals applied to the Jews? The dimensions of the issue were many: practical and theoretical, historical and contemporary, religious and political. We must consider both the practice of rulers and reformers – such as the Habsburg Emperor Joseph II and the Prussian bureaucrat Dohm – who, at least partly influenced by Enlightenment ideals, sought to improve Jewish civil status, as well as the representations of Jews, Judaism, and the Hebrew Bible in important Enlightenment writings. As is well known, the record is decidedly mixed.

Dohm's influential *Concerning the Amelioration of the Civil Status of the Jews* and the Toleration edicts issued by Joseph II through the 1780s advocated inclusion of Jews in the family of humanity and the civic realm, and amelioration of their civic and economic conditions in the hope of actualizing the potential "utility" of Jewish subjects. Montesquieu recognized Judaism as the "old tree trunk," the mistreated yet still proud mother that had produced Islam and Christianity (Montesquieu, *The Persian Letters* 1964, 60: 101), and he employed the voice of a Jewish victim of the Inquisition in eighteenth-century Lisbon to plead for humane tolerance (*The Spirit of the Laws* 1949, book 25:13 [Nugent 2:55]). In his dramas *The Jews* and *Nathan the Wise*, Lessing produced sympathetic Jewish figures – modeled on his friend and fellow *Aufklärer* Moses Mendelssohn – who embodied the humanity, morality, and natural religion of which he believed Jews capable. All urged that

Christians stop persecuting Jews; Voltaire suggested that Jews had been less intolerant than Christians (Gay 1964, p. 107).

Yet even those who spoke positively of Jews continued to ascribe negative characteristics to them, such as an association with money, superstition, and exclusiveness. Advocates such as Dohm and Lessing believed that contemporary Jews were for the most part benighted, hence useful and moral only in potential. Opting for environmental rather than innate factors as explanation, they ascribed Jewish defects to oppression. Therefore they called for two kinds of improvement: first, the removal of conditions oppressing the Jews, and, second, the changing of the Jews themselves, specifically of their spiritual, moral, and civic habits, so that Jews could earn and prove their place in the tutelary German state and among enlightened humanity. Dohm averred that "the Jew is even more man than Jew" (Dohm, *Concerning the Amelioration of the Civil Status of the Jews* (1980), p. 28). But while this statement and Lessing's rosy dramas asserted a common humanity between Jews and others, they really contained the implicit condition of improvement and the qualifier of potentiality: the Jews were human and moral only in potential and only if they divested themselves of their undesirable and noxious characteristics. Dohm and Lessing were confident that the requisite changes on all sides could be made, and that the potential would become actual. But it is important to recognize that inclusion – even by the most friendly advocates of the Jews – was not yet full, immediate, or unqualified.

The problem on the theoretical plane is illustrated most graphically by the case of Voltaire, the self-proclaimed grand champion of tolerance. For him, intolerance was barbaric and immoral, but so were the Jews and their religion, ancient and modern. As Hertzberg has exhaustively catalogued, Voltaire's writings are studded with charges of Jewish inferiority, irrationality, and immorality (Hertzberg 1968). He held the Hebrew Bible responsible for much of the evil in Christianity, and considered the Jewish character so constant through time as to be virtually unredeemable. No environmentalism for him when it came to the Jews. To him the Jews were "only an ignorant and barbarous people, who have long united the most sordid avarice with the most detestable superstition and the most invincible hatred for every people by whom they are tolerated and enriched. Still, we ought not to burn them" (Voltaire, "Jews," in *A Philosophical Dictionary* (1903), 10: 284). Even when he advocated tolerance for all, his advocacy of tolerance for Jews was grudging at best: his visceral disgust for Jews was evident as he worried about giving the Jew dinner because of the deeds of Ezekiel or Balaam's ass (Voltaire, "Tolerance," in ibid., 14: 112).

Voltaire's case begs explanation because of the virulence of his anti-Judaism and his prominence in the Enlightenment. The most important attempt to explain it away is Gay's claim that his anti-Judaism was primarily a mask for anti-Christianity, a necessary and safe tool for chipping away at the ground floor of the Christian edifice (Gay 1964). But, while partially true, this view is ultimately unconvincing. Hertzberg issued the major rejoinder to it by arguing that Voltaire's anti-Judaism should not be dismissed but rather placed in the chain of anti-Judaic tradition going back to pagan antiquity, which Voltaire was responsible for reviving in a modern, secular, post-Christian form (in this Hertzberg followed Gay's overall interpretation of the Enlightenment as a revival of paganism! (Hertzberg 1968; Popkin 1990)). Thus the champion of enlightened rationalism and tolerance is recast as the fountainhead of lethal racist modern anti-semitism, and a dark side of the Enlightenment emerges.

Leaving aside for the moment Hertzberg's broader claims about the Enlightenment as the source of modern racist anti-semitism, let us still consider Voltaire's case. How indeed can his undeniable anti-Judaism be explained? Does it tell us something specific about Voltaire, or something more generally about the Enlightenment and the Jews, or something about the Enlightenment in general of which the Jewish case is an example? I believe the answer is yes to all three questions. About Voltaire himself, it illustrates his static ethnographic and characterological approach to history which he saw peopled by groups possessing fixed unchanging essences (Katz 1980). While Voltaire's venom exceeded that of his fellow *philosophes*, it none the less shows a tendency prevalent among others, the "dialectic of rationalism" (ibid.): the genuine problem that many enlightened rationalists had with regard to the Jews. Even when they had intellectually rejected much of their Christian inheritance, they retained both intellectually and emotionally much of its anti-Jewish legacy. The distrust that had attended Jews extra ecclesiam continued to animate many who still saw Jews extra societatem. The call for conversion was replaced by a secular call for improvement or regeneration (Sorkin 1994b). The barriers to reconceptualizing the Jew not as perfidious Other but as loyal, trusted One of Us, member of humanity in actuality as well as potentially, were not only legal, but also psychological – and difficult to overcome.

Yet, as scholars have recently pointed out, the tolerance and inclusiveness of Enlightenment discourse fell short for groups other than Jews: the common people, women, and blacks (Chisick 1981; Hunt et al. 1984; Landes 1988; Popkin 1990). The full humanity and equality of Jews, women, and blacks were not taken as self-evident by Enlightenment intellectuals or by French revolutionaries acting in the name of Enlightenment humanitarianism.

But once the real limitations of the Enlightenment vision concerning religion, race, and gender are acknowledged, how then can we evaluate its legacy for the Jews? At best, was Enlightenment rationalism but a sham, and at worst, as Hertzberg claimed, the fount of secular racist anti-semitism? The real question is twofold: first, where to locate the sources and conduits of the most virulent anti-semitism of the last two centuries? and, second, how to evaluate the Enlightenment's mixture of inclusive universalist rationalism and exclusivist prejudice?

The murderous racist anti-semitism of the Nazis did not develop primarily on Enlightenment bases. This is not to absolve the Enlightenment of perpetuating anti-Jewish prejudices, but it is to note that the lead in destroying Jews was taken by ideologies and movements which proceeded – in reaction to the Enlightenment and French Revolution – to divide humanity into exclusive, mutually antagonistic closed groups based on blood, descent, and race. Those ideologies could postulate nothing in common between Jews and the superior race, or the rest of humanity. Recent scholarship has succeeded in showing the dark underside and inner contradictions of the Enlightenment, but it will hardly do to swing the pendulum so far in that direction as to ignore the crucial role of anti-universalist, anti-rationalist movements in modern anti-semitism.

Theoretical or potential inclusion of the Jews in a common rational humanity was better than no possibility of inclusion whatsoever. This was the new and significant step taken by the Enlightenment. Yet, as we have seen, the potentiality of it, its linkage to the demand for improvement of the Jews themselves, made the promise difficult to attain and somewhat self-defeating. The assertion of the Jews' potential humanity, that their humanity could be regenerated, meant essentially that the Jews were no longer read out of humanity altogether, but they were not fully read in yet either. Abbé Grégoire expressed the difficulty in his statement that the Jews had been for a long time hated and "considered in a manner as intermedial beings between us and the brutes" and had therefore "seldom [been] able to attain to the dignity of the rest of mankind" (Grégoire, *Essai*, chapter 25, p. 172: Eng. tr., pp. 213–14). Now, partially in, partially out, still outsiders but potentially insiders, the Jews were in a situation fraught with ambiguity.

Of the Masonic lodges, Jacob has written that we must "understand the lodges as embedded in their time and place and yet as practicing and speaking in new ways" (Jacob 1991, p. 8), and that "the old order was acutely mirrored while it was being transformed" (ibid., p. 219). The same can be said of the Enlightenment on the Jewish question: the old order of prejudice and distrust of Jews was acutely mirrored as adherents of the Enlightenment, embedded in those old ways, began to speak and practice the new language of universalist rationalism.

✒ THE HASKALAH (JEWISH ✒ ENLIGHTENMENT)

The Haskalah, the name of the Jewish movement of Enlightenment that lasted from the 1770s to the 1880s, comes from the Hebrew word *sekhel* meaning "reason" or "intellect" (on the term see Shavit 1990). Its formative German phase – producing works in both Hebrew and German – was intense but short, starting in Berlin and Königsberg in the 1770s among intellectuals in the orbit of Mendelssohn, and ending by the turn of the century. The Eastern European phase existed in Galicia and Russia through most of the nineteenth century, maintaining Hebrew as its primary language of expression. (The significant differences between the social and political contexts of Germany and Eastern Europe were crucial for the development of Haskalah, but the focus of this essay is the eighteenth-century German phase and its fundamentals, which became common property of all Jewish Enlighteners.) An adherent of Haskalah was a *maskil* (plural, *maskilim*), literally one who acquires or transmits knowledge through reason. The *maskilim* saw the task of Jewish Enlightening as twofold: first, to bring about Jewish cultural renewal (primarily through study of Hebrew language and Bible), and second, to equip Jews with the requisite linguistic and economic skills in order to integrate with gentile Europeans, that is, to enjoy the promise they saw inherent in Enlightenment ideals and realizable through enlightened absolutist policies. They read their times optimistically, believing that a new age was dawning for European Jews. They envisaged the Haskalah as the educational program that would enable Jews to quit the ghetto, imposed legally from without but now perpetuated culturally from within by insularity and parochialism.

The Haskalah was so closely bound up with efforts to attain a new legal status and new social standing for Jews that its thrust of Hebraic cultural renewal has often been overlooked (by historians though not by scholars of modern Hebrew literature), and the relation of that goal to Europeanization seldom satisfactorily explained. Moreover, the Haskalah has usually been conflated with the phenomena it accompanied, such as acculturation, assimilation, integration, and emancipation. Since the Haskalah has been considered as the "ideology of emancipation," views of it have necessarily been colored by attitudes towards that ending of corporate Jewish existence. Long praised by its spiritual heirs, and denounced by opponents as religious heresy or nationalist betrayal, the Haskalah has only in recent decades received scholarly attention that seeks to determine its precise role in modern Jewish history and culture.

It is generally agreed that Haskalah was a variant of Enlightenment critical rationalism and that as an ideology of modernization, it brought crisis to traditional Jewish society in Central and Eastern Europe (Katz 1973, 1993). But beyond that, no grand synthesis concerning Haskalah is yet on the horizon, for so much basic work remains to be done to advance its study – beyond the existing handful of biographies and major figures (e.g. Altmann 1973; Stanislawski 1988), the many articles on individual *maskilim* and texts (e.g. Eisenstein-Barzilay 1955, 1956a; Feiner 1987; Fishman 1987; Pelli 1979; Rezler-Bersohn 1980; Werses 1990), the few studies of Haskalah in specific settings (Etkes (ed.) 1993; Mahler 1985; Meyer 1967; Shochat 1960; Sorkin 1987; Stanislawski 1983; Zipperstein 1982, 1985). Recently some promising attempts have been made at more diversified national, social, and comparative study of Haskalah: the geographic lens has been broadened to bring places other than Germany and Russia into focus (Katz (ed.) 1987; Malino and Sorkin (eds) 1990); attention is being paid to the social and institutional bases of the Haskalah, and the means of its dissemination (Eliav 1960; Feiner 1987; Lowenstein 1982, 1994; Hertz 1988; Zalkin 1992; Zipperstein 1982, 1985); and the Haskalah has been compared to Protestant and Catholic forms of "religious Enlightenment" (Sorkin 1991, 1994a). Much work on the interplay of culture, society, and politics, and on secularization, remains to be done.

None the less let us attempt to distil and analyze the Haskalah message by employing the familiar Kantian and Hegelian maxims: what did daring to know and bringing heaven down to earth mean for the *maskilim*? How did the knowledge, criticism, and autonomy of Enlightenment rationalism translate into the Jewish context? In brief, *maskilim* dared to criticize their own culture, society, and religion, and they dared to construct a new view of the ideal Jew and of the Jewish relation to the surrounding non-Jewish world.

The new cultural ideal – a Jew possessing both Torah and worldly knowledge – was heralded in *Divrei Shalom ve-Emet* (*Words of Peace and Truth*), Hartwig Wessely's controversial manifesto in 1782. To support the Toleration edicts of Joseph II which called for teaching Jewish children German, mathematics, history, geography and the like in order to make Jews "more useful" to the state, Wessely urged that young Jews first be taught the "torah of man," and then the "torah of God." By the former, Wessely meant the kinds of knowledge concerning humanity and the world which are universally accessible through human reason and empirical observation, for example mathematical and natural sciences, civility, and ethics. By the "torah of God," he meant the divinely revealed teachings and laws pertaining to Jews alone. In Judaic studies, emphasis should be placed on Hebrew language and grammar, the Bible, the literal meaning of sacred texts, and morality. Thus students should emerge as practical, productive people who could earn a decent living, acquit themselves honorably in gentile company, and exemplify the broad cultural horizons and Hebraic ideals of the medieval rationalist Sephardic tradition. (Philosophy, one of the most important components of this ideal, was held somewhat at arm's length by Wessely, though it was certainly encouraged by other *maskilim*.) Enlightened Jews would accrue moral benefits from speaking both Hebrew and German well, and eschewing impure Yiddish. They would see themselves religiously as Jews, but otherwise, in consonance with universalist Enlightenment values, simply as human beings. Their model would be the renowned Jewish *Aufklärer* Moses Mendelssohn.

The educational maxims of the *maskilim* can be summarized thus: dare to know something beyond Talmud, dare to know something beyond Torah and Judaica, dare to learn to function in this finite practical and gentile world. "Return to the world of reality" from heaven: become acculturated and productive (Eisenstein-Barzilay 1956a, p. 14).

What was daring in Wessely's call for educational reform? Ipso facto, invoking Sephardic precedents could hardly be entirely novel. But it went against the grain of his Ashkenazic culture, in which study of Talmud and halakhah dominated the curriculum. The *maskilim* launched a Kulturkampf by pressing for an alternative ideal to the traditional Torah scholar (*talmid chakham*), and by criticizing – often harshly – scholars whose sole expertise was Talmud and rabbinics. It was not simply, as in the past, the supplementing of Torah with other intellectual disciplines, which according to many traditional Jewish thinkers were really included ultimately within the divine Torah anyway. Rather, for many *maskilim*, no matter their protestations, it was the effective supplanting of Torah by the emphasis and value accorded other bodies of knowledge shared universally with gentiles. The Haskalah called for a restructuring of knowledge in the name of new priorities, and indeed for a new function for knowledge itself. The function of knowledge was no longer to be explanatory of one's own tradition, or salvific religiously; it became a bridge to the outside world, and salvific in utilitarian, practical, worldly terms.

Wessely's "torah of man" represented the emergence of a new and autonomous sphere, that of culture distinct from religion. In Hegel's terms, it marked a separation of the "world of sense, and . . . finitude" from the "kingdom of faith" or the "heavenly world." Though its initial effect was to constrict Torah and Judaism from an all-encompassing way of life to religion alone, this separation was one of the beginnings of secularization within Judaism. The Haskalah originally gave rise to the notion of culture as cosmopolitan and universal, but it also spurred the nascent development of a secular as opposed to religious Jewish culture by its cultivation of Hebrew as a modern literary language, Hebrew belles-lettres and journalism.

Calling for a more this-worldly orientation necessarily involved the *maskilim* in criticism of their contemporary society, and the centrality within it of religion and religious leaders. They indicted traditional rabbis whose authority lay in their knowledge of halakhah for failing to live up to the new cultural ideal; according to the new Enlightenment standards, they were often depicted as narrow-minded, obscurantist, superstitious, boorish, and not very useful, even to their own Jewish society. They also impugned the rabbis on political grounds, claiming that they wielded too much power, especially when they used the ban of excommunication (they failed to notice that their right to pronounce the ban had already been severely curtailed in many German states). Some disputed the right of the Jewish community to live as an autonomous corporate body enforcing its own law upon its members. Various religious practices and customs, such as early burial of the dead, became targets of the rationalist ire of the *maskilim*. Galician *maskilim* in particular excoriated the Hasidic movement as the worst embodiment of unenlightened and superstitious folk religion – the very infâme that the Haskalah sought to combat and extirpate.

Among the *maskilim* in all three centers, Germany, Galicia, and Russia, there were both moderates and radicals on religious matters. Moderates such as Mendelssohn and Wessely well illustrate the category of "religious enlightenment," for they sought to fashion a reasonable Judaism, to rationalize and clarify Judaism with Enlightenment tools. Mendelssohn's definition of Judaism as an amalgam of natural religion and revealed law is a good example of the moderates' harmonizing tendency. It became paradigmatic for moderates of later generations not in its details but in its pattern of harmonizing Judaism or at least part of it with contemporary intellectual currents. Developing a reasonable Judaism usually involved translating difficult rabbinic discourse into contemporary, universal, and moral terms – often in the form of didactic catechisms or short formulations of the essentials of faith. Even those who upheld the necessity of halakhic observance labored more to define Judaism as a faith than to expound the details of halakhic practice.

The religious radicals such as Friedländer, Homberg, and Wolfsohn tended to dismiss halakhic observance as unnecessary and outmoded, indeed as detrimental to the full development of one's human potential. They thereby turned the Oral Law and the religious tradition itself into a problem. As good rationalists, they saw tradition not as a repository of wisdom but as a burdensome weight borne by unreliable transmission. They posited the need to separate the divine core of religion from the merely human and therefore variable customs. This indeed became one of the theoretical starting points of Reform Judaism in the nineteenth century. What is striking however in Haskalah writings on religion is the paucity of criticism of the possibility of divine revelation itself. *Maskilim* were hardly Spinozists: the faith they lost, if they did, tended to be in the rabbinic Oral Tradition, not in the Bible and divine revelation.

In which settings did *maskilim* dare to voice their manifold criticisms of Jewish culture, religion, and society? Mostly they were teachers in new Jewish schools, tutors in rich private homes, employees in the Hebrew printing trade, founders and contributors to new Jewish periodicals devoted to Haskalah such as *Ha-Measef*, members of new voluntary associations devoted to cultivating the Hebrew language or spreading enlightenment. They wrote manifestos and reform tracts, translated works of the European Enlightenment into Hebrew, and produced new editions of classic Jewish texts – mostly philosophy and ethics – with updated commentary (indeed Mendelssohn's biblical translation and commentary the *Biur* was one of the initial defining moments of the Haskalah). Though both producers and consumers of Haskalah culture were often the recipients of traditional Jewish education, *maskilim* based their right to speak on a new source of authority and knowledge. They spoke as those who could – like their model Mendelssohn – successfully navigate the passage to the ideal "neutral" or "semi-neutral" society (Katz 1973, 1993) in which belonging would be determined not by one's religious affiliation but rather by a person's simple humanity.

Essentially the *maskilim* sought to create a synthesis of the contemporary Enlightenment and Judaism. But, while they drew inspiration from the European Enlightenment in their efforts to modernize Judaism, the Haskalah was not synonymous with the Enlightenment. The Haskalah differed from the European Enlightenment in three significant ways. First, on religion and religious tradition, the Haskalah tended to be more moderate or conservative. *Maskilim* did not express materialist, atheist, or even deist views. In this respect, they reflected the moderate tenor of the German Enlightenment compared to the French. Second, this religious moderation of the Haskalah probably was due in part to its dynamic of internal cultural reform: the fact that its critique of Ashkenazic culture called for revival of the medieval Sephardic philosophic tradition (Funkenstein 1993). In Gay's view of the Enlightenment, the *philosophes* denigrated medieval Christianity in order to recover the ancient pagan classical past. *Maskilim* too leapt backwards into the past, valuing the original biblical Jewish past over the later accretions of rabbinic Judaism. But they also asserted continuity with, and the ongoing relevance of, at least one part of the medieval Jewish inheritance, the Sephardic, which to them represented Hebraism, rationalism, and worldliness. Certainly they tactically sought legitimizing precedents for their own activities, but it is significant that they found them among certain medieval Jewish forebears.

Third, the *maskilim* also differed from the *philosophes* and *Aufklärer* in that they were forced to wage a two-front war: as much as they dared to criticize and tried to reform their own Jewish culture and society, they had to defend Jews and Judaism against outside attack. The charges from gentile thinkers and publicists forced *maskilim* to engage in defensive apologetic, to prove the worth of Judaism before the bar of enlightened European opinion. The tension between criticism for internal purposes and apologetic for external consumption reflected the minority situation of the Jews, and has attended the adaptation of many minorities and peoples to the dominant Western model. Like all champions of the Enlightenment, *maskilim* dared to know and value the finite, but daring to see Judaism in relation to Enlightenment culture and its vision of universal rational humanity writ large meant for the *maskilim* a certain loss of intellectual self-sufficiency and autonomy. No longer speaking in a self-enclosed Jewish world, they could not merely determine what was reasonable about Judaism; they had also to answer for Jewish particularity.

❧ CONCLUSION ❧

"The Enlightenment thus decisively launched the secularisation of European thought. To say this is not to claim that the *philosophes* were all atheists or that people thereafter ceased to be religious ... But after the Enlightenment the Christian religion ceased, finally, to preoccupy public culture" (Porter 1990, p. 72). From the educated elites of the old regimes, there came forth the Enlightenment and the Haskalah, both offering rationalist and ultimately secularizing critiques of contemporary society and plans for reform. While not all *philosophes*, *Aufklärer*, and *maskilim* abandoned religion to adopt a fully secular world view, they did lay the groundwork for the modern secular discourse on science and society. And as bearers of the Enlightenment ideology, they represented the coming to influence of a new social group, the secular intelligentsia, playing a new public role. Yet the legacy of the Haskalah differed somewhat from the consequences of the European Enlightenment: while it created space for the emergence of a secular Jewish culture, it never made the Jewish religion an irrelevant factor in Jewish public culture. Religion had been too integral a part of Jewish identity for too long to be easily displaced. The Haskalah spurred the development of modern Hebraic culture, but Haskalah Hebraism, even when moving in secular directions, still had – often unwittingly – deep ties to religion. The decisive step of the Haskalah was that it put European thought and culture firmly on the Jewish public agenda.

❧ NOTE ❧

It is my pleasure to thank Benjamin Braude, David Myers, Aron Rodrigue, and David Sorkin for their helpful suggestions. I also wish to thank the Reference and Special Collection librarians of Smith College, Bowdoin College, and Wesleyan University for their assistance.

❧ BIBLIOGRAPHY ❧

Texts

Dohm, C. W. von (1980) *Concerning the Amelioration of the Civil Status of the Jews*, translated by H. Lederer, excerpts in P. R. Mendes-Flohr and J. Reinharz (eds), *The Jew in the Modern World: A Documentary History* (New York and Oxford: Oxford University Press), pp. 27–34.

Gay, P. (ed.) (1973) *The Enlightenment: A Comprehensive Anthology* (New York: Simon & Schuster).

Grégoire, H. (1789) *Essai sur la régénération physique, morale et politique des juifs* (Metz, 1789; reprinted Paris: Editions d'Histoire Sociale, 1968). English translation: *An Essay on the Physical, Moral, and Political Reformation of the Jews*, translator not given (London: n.d., c. 1790 or 1791).

Hegel, G. W. F. (1977) *Phenomenology of Spirit*, translated by A. V. Miller, edited by J. N. Findlay (Oxford: Clarendon Press).

Herder, J. G. von (1989) *Ideen zur Philosophie der Geschichte der Menschheit*, in vol. 6 of *Werke*, edited by M. Bollacher et al., 10 vols (Frankfurt am Main: Deutscher Klassiker Verlag). English translation: *Outlines of a Philosophy of the History of Man*, 2nd ed., translated by T. Churchill, 2 vols. (London: John Johnson, 1803).

Kant, I. (1965) *Answer to the Question, What is Enlightening?*, in F. E. Manuel, *The Age of Reason* (Englewood Cliffs: Prentice-Hall).

Lessing, G. E. (1956) *Lessing's Theological Writings*, translated by H. Chadwick (Stanford: Stanford University Press).

—— (1973) *The Jews*, translated by E. Bell, excerpts in Gay 1973, pp. 746–65.

—— (1983) *Nathan the Wise*, translated by B. Q. Morgan (New York: Continuum).

Locke, J. (1950) *A Letter Concerning Toleration* (Indianapolis: Bobbs-Merrill).

Montesquieu (1949) *The Spirit of the Laws*, translated by T. Nugent (New York: Hafner, Macmillan).

—— (1964) *The Persian Letters*, translated by G. R. Healy (Indianapolis: Bobbs-Merrill).

Rousseau, J. J. (1990) *The Creed of a Priest of Savoy*, translated by A. H. Beattie, 2nd rev. ed. (New York: Continuum).

Voltaire (1903) *The Works of Voltaire: A Contemporary Version*, translated by W. F. Fleming, edited by T. Smollett, 42 vols. (Akron: St Hubert Guild).

Wessely, N. H. (1980) *Words of Peace and Truth*, translated by S. Weinstein and S. Fischer, excerpts in P. R. Mendes-Flohr and J. Reinharz (eds), *The Jew in the Modern World: A Documentary History* (New York and Oxford: Oxford University Press), pp. 62–7.

Studies

Altmann, A. (1973) *Moses Mendelssohn: A Biographical Study* (Philadelphia and University, Al: Jewish Publication Society and University of Alabama).

Anchor, R. (1967) *The Enlightenment Tradition* (Berkeley, Los Angeles and London: University of California Press).

Baker, K. M. and C. Lucas (1987–8) *The French Revolution and the Creation of a Modern Political Culture*, 2 vols, 1: *The Political Culture of the Old Regime*, 2: *The Political Culture of the French Revolution* (Oxford: Pergamon).

Becker, C. L. (1932) *The Heavenly City of the Eighteenth-century Philosophers* (New Haven: Yale University Press).

Cassirer, E. (1955) *The Philosophy of the Enlightenment*, translated by F. C. A. Koelln and J. P. Pettegrove (Boston: Beacon).

Chartier, R. (1991) *The Cultural Origins of the French Revolution*, translated by L. G. Cochrane (Durham, NC and London: Duke University Press).

Chisick, H. (1981) *The Limits of Reform in the French Enlightenment: Attitudes toward the Education of the Lower Classes in Eighteenth-Century France* (Princeton: Princeton University Press).

Crocker, L. G. (1959) *An Age of Crisis: Man and World in Eighteenth Century Thought* (Baltimore: Johns Hopkins University Press).

—— (1963) *Nature and Culture: Ethical Thought in the French Enlightenment* (Baltimore: John Hopkins Press).

Darnton, R. (1970) *Mesmerism and the End of the Enlightenment in France* (New York: Schocken).

—— (1971) "The High Enlightenment and the Low-Life of Literature in Pre-Revolutionary France," *Past and Present: A Journal of Historical Studies* 51: 81–115.

—— (1979) *The Business of Enlightenment: A Publishing History of the Encyclopédie, 1775–1800* (Cambridge, MA: Belknap Press of Harvard University Press).

—— (1990) "The Social History of Ideas," in *The Kiss of Lamourette: Reflections in Cultural History* (New York and London: Norton), pp. 219–52 (originally in *The Journal of Modern History* 1971, 43: 113–32).

Dülmen, R. von (1992) *The Society of the Enlightenment: The Rise of the Middle Class and Enlightenment Culture in Germany*, translated by A. Williams (New York: St Martin's).

Eisenstein-Barzilay, I. (1955) "The Treatment of the Jewish Religion in the Literature of the Berlin Haskalah," *Proceedings of the American Academy for Jewish Research* 24: 39–68.

—— (1956a) "The Ideology of the Berlin Haskalah," *Proceedings of the American Academy for Jewish Research* 25: 1–37.

—— (1956b) "The Jew in the Literature of the Enlightenment," *Jewish Social Studies* 18: 216–43.

Eliav, M. (1960) *Jewish Education in Germany in the Period of Enlightenment and Emancipation* [Hebrew], (Jerusalem: Jewish Agency).

Etkes, E. (ed.) (1993) *The East European Jewish Enlightenment* [Hebrew], (Jerusalem: Zalman Shazar Center for Jewish History).

Feiner, S. (1987) "Isaac Euchel – 'Entrepreneur' of the Haskalah Movement in Germany" [Hebrew] *Zion: A Quarterly for Research in Jewish History* 52: 427–69.

Fishman, D. (1987) "A Polish Rabbi Meets the Berlin Haskalah: The Case of Baruch Schick," *AJS Review* 12: 95–121.

Foucault, M. (1984) *The Foucault Reader*, edited by P. Rabinow (New York: Pantheon).

Funkenstein, A. (1993) "Haskala, History, and the Medieval Tradition," in *Perceptions of Jewish History* (Berkeley, Los Angeles, and Oxford), pp. 234–47.

Gay, P. (1964) "Voltaire's Anti-Semitism," in *The Party of Humanity: Essays in the French Enlightenment* (New York: Knopf), pp. 97–108.

—— (1966) *The Enlightenment: An Interpretation*, 1: *The Rise of Modern Paganism* (New York: Knopf).

—— (1969) *The Enlightenment: An Interpretation*, 2: *The Science of Freedom* (New York: Knopf).

Goodman, D. (1989) *Criticism in Action: Enlightenment Experiments in Political Writing* (Ithaca and London: Cornell University Press).

Habermas, J. (1989) *The Structural Transformation of the Public Sphere: An Inquiry into a Category of Bourgeois Society*, translated by T. Burger with the assistance of F. Lawrence (Cambridge, MA: MIT Press).

Hertz, D. (1988) *Jewish High Society in Old Regime Berlin* (New Haven and London: Yale University Press).

Hertzberg, A. (1968) *The French Enlightenment and the Jews* (New York, London, and Philadelphia: Columbia University Press and Jewish Publication Society).

Hunt, M., M. Jacob, P. Jack, and R. Perry (1984) *Women and the Enlightenment* (New York: Institute for Research in History; Haworth Press).

Jacob, M. C. (1991) *Living the Enlightenment: Freemasonry and Politics in Eighteenth-Century Europe* (New York and Oxford: Oxford University Press).

Katz, J. (1970) *Jews and Freemasons in Europe 1723–1939*, translated by L. Oschry (Cambridge, MA: Harvard University Press).

—— (1973) *Out of the Ghetto: The Social Background of Jewish Emancipation 1770–1870* (Cambridge: Harvard University Press).

—— (1980) *From Prejudice to Destruction: Anti-Semitism, 1700–1933* (Cambridge: Harvard University Press).

—— (ed.) (1987) *Toward Modernity: The European Jewish Model* (New Brunswick and Oxford: Transaction).

—— (1993) *Tradition and Crisis: Jewish Society at the End of the Middle Ages*, translated and edited by B. D. Cooperman (New York: Schocken).

Koselleck, R. (1988) *Critique and Crisis: Enlightenment and the Pathogenesis of Modern Society* (Cambridge, MA: MIT Press).

Landes, J. B. (1988) *Women and the Public Sphere in the Age of the French Revolution* (Ithaca and London: Cornell University Press).

Lowenstein, S. (1982) "The Readership of Mendelssohn's Bible Translation," *Hebrew Union College Annual* 53: 179–213.

—— (1994) *The Berlin Jewish Community: Enlightenment, Family, and Crisis, 1770–1830* (New York and Oxford: Oxford University Press).

Mahler, R. (1985) *Hasidism and the Jewish Enlightenment: Their Confrontation in Galicia and Poland in the First Half of the Nineteenth Century*, translated by E. Orenstein, A. Klein, and J. M. Klein (Philadelphia: Jewish Publication Society).

Malino, F. and D. Sorkin (eds) (1990) *From East and West: Jews in a Changing Europe, 1750–1870* (Oxford: Blackwell).

Manuel, F. E. (1967) *The Eighteenth Century Confronts the Gods* (New York: Atheneum).

—— (1992) *The Broken Staff: Judaism through Christian Eyes* (Cambridge, MA: Harvard University Press).

Meyer, M. A. (1967) *The Origins of the Modern Jew: Jewish Identity and European Culture in Germany, 1749–1824* (Detroit: Wayne State University Press).

Meyer, P. H. (1963) "The Attitude of the Enlightenment towards the Jew," *Studies on Voltaire and the Eighteenth Century* 26: 1161–205.

Palmer, R. R. (1939) *Catholics and Unbelievers in Eighteenth-century France* (Princeton: Princeton University Press).

Pelli, M. (1979) *The Age of Haskalah: Studies in Hebrew Literature of the Enlightenment in Germany* (Leiden: Brill).

Popkin, R. (1990) "Medicine, Racism, Anti-Semitism: A Dimension of Enlightenment Culture," in *The Languages of Psyche: Mind and Body in Enlightenment Thought*, Clark Library Lectures 1985–6, edited by G. S. Rousseau (Berkeley, Los Angeles and Oxford: University of California Press), pp. 405–42.

Porter, R. (1990) *The Enlightenment* (Houndmills and London: Macmillan).

Porter, R. and M. Teich (1981) *The Enlightenment in National Context* (Cambridge: Cambridge University Press).

Rezler-Bersohn, N. (1980) "Isaac Satanow: An Epitome of an Era," *Yearbook of the Leo Baeck Institute* 25: 81–99.

Roche, D. (1978) *Le Siècle des Lumières en province: Académies et académiciens provinciaux, 1680–1789* (Paris: Mouton).

—— (1993) *La France des Lumières* (Paris: Fayard).

Scott, H. M. (1990) *Enlightened Absolutism: Reform and Reformers in Later Eighteenth-century Europe* (Ann Arbor: University of Michigan Press).

Shavit, U. (1990) "Haskalah mahi? Le-virur musag ha-haskalah be-sifrut ha-ivrit," *Mechkarei yerushalayim be-sifrut ivrit* 12: 51–83.

Shochat, A. (1960) *Beginnings of the Haskalah among German Jewry* [Hebrew] (Jerusalem: Bialik Institute).

Sorkin, D. (1987) *The Transformation of German Jewry, 1780–1840* (New York and Oxford: Oxford University Press).

—— (1991) "From Context to Comparison: The German Haskalah and Reform Catholicism," *Tel Aviver Jahrbuch für Deutsche Geschichte* 20: 23–58.

—— (1992) "Jews, the Enlightenment and Religious Toleration – Some Reflections," *Yearbook of the Leo Baeck Institute* 37: 3–16.

—— (1994a) "The Case for Comparison: Moses Mendelssohn and the Religious Enlightenment," *Modern Judaism* 14: 121–38.

—— (1994b) "The Jewish Question in Eighteenth-Century Germany," paper given at a Colloquium on Discourses of Tolerance and Intolerance in the Enlightenment, The Clark Library, University of California, Los Angeles, May.

Stanislawski, M. (1983) *Tsar Nicholas I and the Jews: The Transformation of Jewish Society in Russia 1825–1855* (Philadelphia: Jewish Publication Society).

—— (1988) *For Whom Do I Toil?: Judah Leib Gordon and the Crisis of Russian Jewry* (New York and Oxford: Oxford University Press).

Talmon, J. L. (1952) *The Origins of Totalitarian Democracy* (London: Secker & Warburg).

Taylor, C. (1989) *Sources of the Self: The Making of the Modern Identity* (Cambridge, MA: Harvard University Press).

Venturi, F. (1969–) *Settecento riformatore*, 5 vols. (Turin: Einaudi).

—— (1971) *Utopia and Reform in the Enlightenment* (Cambridge: Cambridge University Press).

—— (1972) *Italy and the Enlightenment: Studies in a Cosmopolitan Century*, edited by S. Woolf, translated by S. Corsi (New York: New York University Press).

—— (1989) *The End of the Old Regime in Europe, 1768–1776: The First Crisis*, translated from vol. 3 of *Settecento riformatore* by R. B. Litchfield (Princeton: Princeton University Press, 1969).

—— (1991) *The End of the Old Regime in Europe, 1776–1789*, 2 vols, 1: *The Great States of the West*, 2: *Republican Patriotism and the Empires of the East*, translated from vol. 4 of *Settecento riformatore* by R. B. Litchfield (Princeton: Princeton University Press, 1969).

Werses, S. (1990) *Trends and Forms in Haskalah Literature* [Hebrew] (Jerusalem: Magnes, Hebrew University).

Yolton, J. W., R. Porter, P. Rogers, and B. M. Stafford (1991) *The Blackwell Companion to the Enlightenment* (Oxford and Cambridge, MA: Blackwell).

Zalkin, M. (1992) *Haskalat Vilna (1835–1860): Kavim li-demutah*. M.A. thesis, Hebrew University of Jerusalem.

Zipperstein, S. J. (1982) "Jewish Enlightenment in Odessa: Cultural Characteristics 1794–1871," *Jewish Social Studies* 44: 19–36.

—— (1985) *The Jews of Odessa: A Cultural History 1794–1881* (Stanford: Stanford University Press).

CHAPTER 26

Mendelssohn

Michael L. Morgan

On Saturday 31 December 1785, Moses Mendelssohn walked to the home of his publisher and friend Christian Friedrich Voss and delivered the manuscript of *To Lessing's Friends*. For two years, Mendelssohn and Friedrich Jacobi had publicly debated the nature of Spinozism and Lessing's alleged pantheism. The new book was to be Mendelssohn's final contribution to the controversy. He died five days later on 4 January 1786; the book was published posthumously on 24 January.[1]

In *To Lessing's Friends* Mendelssohn makes it clear that in his view the controversy had been a conflict about faith, reason, and religion. Jacobi, in league with Mendelssohn's old nemesis Johann Caspar Lavater, represented the forces of anti-rationalism, one wing of those fideists aligned against the *Aufklärung*.[2] Mendelssohn was "obsessed," as Altmann puts it, "with the idea that Lavater was behind it all."[3] The controversy was not simply over Lessing's character; it was a full-scale battle between the *Aufklärung* and its enemies, between reason and unreason, the forces of light and those of darkness. Jacobi saw Lessing as hopelessly mired in sophistry and confusion; he "magnanimously resolved to cure him of his ills" by luring him deeper and deeper into the quagmire of Spinozism and then offering him the only way out, "to retreat to the shelter of faith."[4] Failing with Lessing, Jacobi sought to make him a lesson with others, an "edifying example" to others to make use of the palliative of faith before it is too late.[5]

In the course of his exposé in *To Lessing's Friends*, Mendelssohn stakes out his own territory and lays out his own convictions. He points out that Jacobi is not the first to try to redeem him from his errors, alluding to the earlier affair with Lavater. But such attempts are "doomed to failure," given who he is and his version of natural religion. This is how he describes his views:

> in respect of doctrines and eternal truths, I recognized no conviction save that grounded in reason. Judaism demands a faith in historical truths, in *facts* upon which the authority of our prescribed ritual law is founded. The existence and authority of the Supreme Law-giver, however, must be recognized by reason, and there is no room here for revelation or faith, neither according to the principles of Judaism nor my own. Further, Judaism is not revealed *religion* but revealed *law*. As a Jew, I said, I had even more reason to seek conviction through rational arguments.
>
> ... My assertion that Judaism in no wise presumes belief in eternal truths but simply historical belief, is clearly set forth in a more appropriate place to which I refer the reader. The Hebrew language has no proper word for what we class *religion*. Neither is Judaism a revelation of doctrinal statements and eternal truths, which demanded our belief. It consists exclusively of revealed laws of worship and presumes a natural and reasonable conviction as to religious truth; without which no divine law can be established.[6]

Judaism, for Mendelssohn, is both a rational religion and a particular religious life. It is grounded in a rational understanding of God and a historical relationship to that God. That relationship is established by revelation, but it is a revelation of law and not of doctrine. This is the kernel of Mendelssohn's version of *Aufklärung* and the heart of his conception of Judaism. Here, in his last work, he summarizes it; elsewhere, as he indicates explicitly, he develops it more fully.

The text to which Mendelssohn refers is of course his most mature and most systematic account of Judaism as a rational religion; that work, published in May 1783, is *Jerusalem, or, On Religious Power and Judaism*. It is the capstone of his career as a Jewish thinker and Jewish philosopher. No other work better exhibits his combined commitments to philosophy and Judaism. If we want to understand the summary of his Judaism and his rationalism that Mendelssohn gives in *To Lessing's Friends*, we must first understand its elaboration in his great earlier work.

The author of *Jerusalem* regularly referred to himself as Moshe mi-Dessau, Moses from Dessau. Born in Dessau on 6 September 1729, Mendelssohn began at ten to study with his brilliant young rabbi, David Fraenkel, and, when Fraenkel was called to Berlin in 1743, he followed him, remaining in Berlin for the remainder of his life. In 1759 he became a tutor in the household of Isaac Bernhard, a wealthy silk manufacturer. Eventually Mendelssohn became a book-keeper in Bernhard's factory and its manager in 1761. But his first love was philosophy. In later years he never tired of bemoaning the time and effort such work took away from philosophy.

Mendelssohn was self-taught.[7] In philosophy, he first read Locke, then Leibniz and Wolff, and he early became entranced with natural theology and the problem of reconciling reason and the non-rational features of human character. While he was impressed by the psychology of Locke and Shaftesbury, it was the systematic rationalism of the Leibnizian-Wolffian school that ultimately captured his heart. From his *Philosophical Dialogues* of 1755 to the *Morgenstunden* of 1785, Mendelssohn's works fall squarely in the tradition of this school and its inheritance, the Berlin *Aufklärung*. Even his reading of Spinoza, a life-long enterprise, attempted to mitigate Spinoza's radicalism and to situate him in the world of Leibniz and Wolff, to reinterpret the purported pantheism or atheism of this controversial philosopher into a domesticated deism.[8]

Mendelssohn's life had three venues. The one, his work in the silk factory, he endured and resented. The second, his life as a Jew, a family man, and a Jewish spokesperson, he relished in some ways and accepted reluctantly, with a sense of dedication, in others. His liberalism, philosophically grounded, led him to his own version of moral activism; he was, however, both a liberal and a Jew, so that this activism was married to a defense of Jewish dignity and efforts to enrich Jewish identity. He was eager to educate Jews in Hebrew, to strengthen moral conduct among Jews, to defend the cause of tolerance, to argue for the reasonableness and the worth of Judaism, and to support the cause of Jewish citizenship. Moreover, these were not occasional interests for him; in a deep sense, Mendelssohn devoted his entire adult life to these causes. In 1758, these interests led him to edit a Hebrew monthly, *Kohelet Musar*, with the express hope of teaching Jewish youth Hebrew and strengthening moral conduct. In the years after 1774, they nurtured his project of a new German translation of the Pentateuch, and in 1772 they grounded his statement on early burial.[9] And again and again, it was his sense of responsibility and devotion to a Judaism that was liberal, rational, and dignified that encouraged him to intercede, when asked, on behalf of Jewish civil rights.[10]

The third venue for Mendelssohn's life was intellectual, cultural, and philosophical. It was a venue filled with salons, publishers, artists, writers, correspondence, coffee houses, and especially with a circle of friends. Gotthold Lessing, whom he first met in 1754, was a lifelong and intimate friend; the *Philosophical Dialogues* of 1755 reflected conversations between the two about Shaftesbury and the role of the sentiments in human character. And it was Thomas Abbt, whom Mendelssohn met in 1761, who stimulated his defense of reason and especially his treatment of the role of morality in arguing for the soul's immortality in the third dialogue of the *Phaedon* of 1767.[11] In 1755 Mendelssohn first met Friedrich Nicolai, publisher, editor, and writer, who remained his friend for thirty years. And then there were his disciples and younger friends, from Marcus Herz, Kant's student, to Herz Homberg, August Hennings, and David Friedländer. These are only the central figures in a wide circle of colleagues and friends that provided Mendelssohn with continuous opportunities for discussion and debate; there was nothing abstract about his conviction that rationality was intimately associated with intellectual conversation.

❧❧ WORKS ❧❧

Mendelssohn wrote on a variety of subjects and in a variety of modes. By subject, they can be divided into philosophical essays, monographs, and dialogues, the most important being the *Philosophical Dialogues* (1755), the prize essay for the Royal Academy (1763),[12] the *Phaedon* (1767), and the *Morgenstunden* (1785); biblical commentary and translation; and writings on Judaism and Jewish issues, especially *Jerusalem* (1783). Mendelssohn also wrote on literature, art, and culture, including important essays in aesthetics and the philosophy of art. By period, his authorship has a break in 1771, when a neurological illness led him away from philosophy for several years. Although he had begun biblical translation and commentary prior to 1771, he became preoccupied with the Pentateuch translation and commentary only thereafter. Indeed, *Jerusalem* and his last works, contributions to the Lessing controversy, were in the order of reactions to external stimuli and not premeditated projects.

None the less, *Jerusalem* remains the single work most emblematic of Mendelssohn's life and thought. It contains his most articulated political philosophy and his fullest account of Judaism as a religion of reason, and it capitalizes on his philosophical views as these are developed in *Phaedon*, the prize essay, the later *Morgenstunden*, and elsewhere. If Mendelssohn's blending of Judaism and rationalism, liberalism, and the *Aufklärung* succeeds, it does so in *Jerusalem*. And if that work fails, so does his great project.

That project Mendelssohn inherited from the seventeenth century. It was the challenge to integrate the universality of reason, science, and morality with the particularity of positive religion, in his case with the historical and traditional distinctiveness of Judaism. The issue was an historical one. In the end, once history had been culminated, no religious particularity would remain. But during the historical process, religions were distinct. What, Mendelssohn was bound to ask, justified this distinctiveness? What obligated Jews to their special way? Why not expect the enlightened Jew, who recognized Judaism's rationality, to assimilate to a universal religion, to become, in Spinoza's words, a member of the universal faith of all humankind?[13] Why not abandon all those beliefs and practices that segregate Jews and that prevent their blending into the society around them?

To Mendelssohn, there were religious, moral, political, and even metaphysical issues at work here. Some were general and concerned natural theology, human perfection, tolerance, and human obligations. Others were particular, for they were intimately connected to the liberalism of the Berlin *Aufklärer* and to the special interests of Jews, as they aspired to citizenship and sought recognition of their civil rights. At the center of Mendelssohn's rationalism was morality, the primacy of the human aspiration, infinite though it is, to virtue and perfection, public and private, to happiness or eudaimonia as human well-being. No special revelation and hence no particular tradition was required to understand that goal and the means to attain it. This insight was given to all, through reason.[14] About these matters Mendelssohn was always convinced, as much when he wrote chapter 4 of his Royal Academy essay (1763) and the third dialogue of the *Phaedon* (1767) as he was when he wrote *Jerusalem* (1783).[15] Still, the revelation to the Jewish people and hence its historical and functional particularity were undeniable, grounded in divine will and shaped by a historical purpose. They too were rational, or at least Mendelssohn believed they were, so that in Judaism, the universality of morality and the particularity of Jewish life were married by reason. It is the task of *Jerusalem* to show why and how this marriage occurs.

If the roots of Mendelssohn's rational religion – his commitment to God's existence, his providence, the centrality of the desire for moral perfection, the soul's immortality, and much else – go back at least to the 1760s and the work that led to the prize essay and the *Phaedon*, his conception of Judaism as a religion of reason and revealed legislation goes back at least to the Lavater affair of 1769–70. Johann Caspar Lavater was an anti-rationalist and a Calvinist millenarian. In Mendelssohn's mind, he would later become the paradigmatic fideist and critic of *Aufklärung*. In 1769, when he published a translation of parts of Charles Bonnet's *Palingenesis*, a defense of Christianity, with a dedication challenging Mendelssohn to refute it or to do as Socrates would have done and accept its results, Mendelssohn saw him as brash but not inherently evil. His challenge to convert was misguided but perhaps not malicious; tolerance forbad such a challenge and the rational character of genuine religion made it unnecessary. The challenge elicited a flurry of letters, a brisk correspondence often marked by miscommunication and confusion. In addition, Mendelssohn responded by preparing a forty-page set of comments on Bonnet's arguments, "Counter-reflections on Bonnet's *Palingenesis*," which were never published but which served, a dozen years later, as a primary source for Mendelssohn's writing of the second part of *Jerusalem* and for his argument that Judaism, as a rational faith, none the less is bound to a revealed ceremonial law.[16]

In the spring of 1771, when the fury over the Lavater challenge had abated, Mendelssohn suffered a paralytic episode and was put on a restricted regimen, with reduced reading and no sustained philosophical work. Slowly he recovered, but only by 1778 did he feel healthy again. It was during this period that he decided to embark upon the Bible translation project, a new German translation of the Pentateuch with commentary as a vehicle for education and for teaching Hebrew to the younger generation. It was in the years when the project was nearing completion that events occurred that led to the return to these old notes on Bonnet, to new work on natural law, and to the writing of a monograph on the nature of Judaism and the relation between religion and politics.

When, in 1780, the Jews of Alsace invited Mendelssohn to write a memorial to the French government in support of their petition for lifting restrictions, he was hard at work on the commentary on Exodus. Mendelssohn sought the help of a young Berlin *Aufklärer*, a teacher, diplomat, and writer, Christian Wilhelm Dohm (1751–1820). Along with Mendelssohn and Christian Garve, Dohm was a premier Berlin *Aufklärer* and a staunch liberal. Mendelssohn's request provided him with an ideal opportunity to publicize his views on a major social issue, the emancipation of the Jews. In September 1781, Dohm published his treatise, "On the Civil Improvement of the Jews," in which he admitted the criticisms of Jews and their negative qualities but ascribed them to the hostility and oppression of the environment in which they lived. Hence his recommendation, that the Jews be made into better citizens by a policy that would improve their situation. Such a policy would involve giving Jews equal rights and obligations, encouraging their entrance into agriculture and craft production, eliminating housing restrictions, and recommending that Jewish schools include a general curriculum.[17] Broadly, Dohm advocated a tolerant, benevolent policy that assumed that the social and human development of the Jews, their "betterment," was possible.

Mendelssohn could agree with much of Dohm's argument, but on one point he was adamantly opposed. Dohm endorsed the integrity of the Jewish community as an ecclesiastical, quasi-political entity. In order to function, it would have to utilize coercive power, especially by sanctioning behavior through the use of the ban (cherem). Mendelssohn disagreed; Jews should have jurisdiction even over property rights but without coercive power. Religion should be open to all; it should operate by reason and persuasion, not by force. Hence, Mendelssohn needed an opportunity to clarify his relation to Dohm and his treatise. In order to achieve this goal, to stimulate further discussion about tolerance and the issue of emancipation, and to explore his conception of religion, Mendelssohn invited his friend Dr Marcus Herz to translate the 1656 treatise of the Dutch rabbi Manasseh ben Israel, *Vindiciae Judaeorum*, for which he prepared a preface that contained his views on these matters.[18] The book, which appeared in April 1782, caused quite a stir. Many readers saw Mendelssohn as moving toward a form of Judaism that seemed alienated from Jewish law and very close to Christianity; to some, Mendelssohn already *was* a Christian.[19] And indeed, was this not correct? Did full citizenship not require abandoning one's distinctiveness and becoming an unqualified participant in the state? What was a Judaism without law but Christianity?

In September 1782, there was published in Berlin an anonymous tract of forty-seven pages entitled "The Search for Light and Right in a Letter to Herr Moses Mendelssohn occasioned by his remarkable Preface to Manasseh Ben Israel."[20] It was signed "S*** – Vienna, June 12, 1782." Then and for some time Mendelssohn believed that this stark critique was the work of Josef von Sonnenfels, a convert to Catholicism from Judaism, a statesman, and a leader of the Viennese *Aufklärung*.[21] Had Mendelssohn, the Searcher argued, by rejecting force and compulsion for the Jewish community, dealt a "decisive blow" to the statutory system of Mosaic law?[22] Did Judaism not prevent full participation in the state? If citizenship required the renunciation of distinctiveness and exclusiveness, then how could it be achieved without abrogating the ceremonial law? And if ban or cherem can be cancelled, why not all the law, so that the goal of emancipation can be achieved?

JERUSALEM AND THE RATIONALITY OF RELIGION

By the summer of 1782 the manuscript of this tract was in Mendelssohn's hands, and by September he was at work on a response. It was completed by April 1783, and published in May, the same month as his translation of the book of Psalms. The book was called *Jerusalem, or, On Religious Power and Judaism*.

Jerusalem originally was to have three parts; it came to have two. In the first, Mendelssohn develops his version of a natural law theory, of a social contract doctrine, of religious and civil institutions, and of tolerance. In short, Part 1 contains the rudiments of a moral and political philosophy. Part 2 contains Mendelssohn's conception of Judaism. It is, he argues, a religion of reason but a distinct religion none the less. Jews are bound to a precise form of life, a legally defined round of conduct binding only upon them. This too is reasonable, as he tries to show. So, in the end, Judaism can take its place within the liberal state as a legitimate, wholly rational mode of life; it is authorized by reason, and at the same time it contributes to the state's ultimate goals, public and private moral perfection and well-being.

Part 1 of *Jerusalem* is indebted to Mendelssohn's work on natural law and the little tract of 1781 called "On Perfect and Imperfect Duties." It also derives from his reading of John Locke's *A Letter on Toleration*, Thomas Hobbes' *Leviathan*, Baruch Spinoza's *Tractatus Theologico-Politicus*, and his appreciation of the collegianist view of Church organization that goes back to Hugo Grotius and Samuel Pufendorf.[23] Mendelssohn sets out the problem of how religious and political institutions are to be related and gives his own solution to that problem. Part 1 then summarizes Mendelssohn's results and their implications. Let us begin with the problem.

The problem is the theoretical one of how to balance state and religion, secular and churchly authority, so that they enhance and do not burden social life.[24] Sometimes one, sometimes the other is thought to have dominance. Sometimes there is support for political despotism, sometimes for unqualified religious authority. And for some, liberty invades both, so that there is popular political sovereignty or widespread religious autonomy.

Hobbes and Locke offer two different solutions to the problem. To Hobbes, the English Revolution and the execution of Charles I were the result of too much freedom and religious diversity.[25] He was willing to sacrifice all to "tranquillity and safety ... as the greatest felicity."[26] These required investing unconditional power and authority in a unified, indivisible sovereign. Still, Hobbes allowed the fear of God to ground obligations of belief and worship, which was the philosopher's sole concern, what he called "inward religion." Furthermore, Hobbes' original contract could not be binding, Mendelssohn argued, without the moral obligation to obey one's contracts even in the state of nature. And the fear of God, which required the sovereign to act on behalf of their subjects' welfare, can also be seen as the ground of a natural law for all individuals in the state. Hence, Mendelssohn argues, Hobbes appears to subordinate religious to political authority but in the end shows us why the moral and religious must themselves be superior to the political. None the less, Hobbes was aware of the need for the state to be concerned with the individual's well-being and welfare.

Locke took a different approach in order to protect liberty of conscience. The state is concerned with people's "temporal welfare" and not with their eternal well-being. Hence, it must protect people against harm and injury, while tolerating religious differences. But if we allow this distinction between temporal and eternal welfare and if the former is subordinate in worth to the latter, then at points of conflict, the secular authority must give way to the religious. Mendelssohn points to the arguments of Cardinal Robert Bellarmine in his *De Romano Pontifice* along these lines; it is not surprising that the longest chapter of Hobbes' *Leviathan* is devoted to a critique of Bellarmine.[27] But, as Mendelssohn claims, the distinction between temporal and eternal welfare is faulty. There is continuity between this life and the soul's endless future; if the state is concerned with one, he implies, it must also be concerned with the other.[28] Politics is a part of religion and ethics; it is not exclusive of them.

Hence, Mendelssohn implies that the state cannot dominate nor be dominated by religion. Nor can the state ignore human well-being and simply protect people from each other. Like other conservatives of his day, Mendelssohn advocates the paternalistic state, like that of Frederick the Great, the purpose of which is to enhance human well-being. But it must do so cooperatively, together with religious institutions, and not by ruling them or being ruled by them. Mendelssohn, that is, believed that religion, morality, and politics were deeply continuous and not exclusive; in this regard he shared more with Hobbes than he did with Locke.

According to Mendelssohn, then, state and religion have the same goal, human well-being in this life and in the future life, a life of striving for human perfection.[29] This is the goal of human life formulated in terms that go back to Socrates, Plato, Aristotle, Epicurus, the Stoics, and others; it is the goal of eudaimonia, happiness, or well-being.[30] Both civil and religious institutions are means to this goal, which is an individual and a collective one. To attain human well-being, we must perform certain obligations, prohibitions, and positive prescriptions. That is, we must perform certain actions from pure motives, whereby we become more and more perfect as human beings. Human perfection involves both, doing the right things for the right reasons. The common good is a society of agents with the kind of perfection or character sufficient to act in this way regularly. Bildung is the process of cultivating this human character, of educating and shaping people in the direction of such perfection. "By the Bildung of man," Mendelssohn says, "I understand the effort to arrange both actions and convictions in such a way that they will be in accord with his felicity [viz. eudaimonia]; that they will *educate* and *govern* men."[31] Church and state are the "public institutions for the Bildung of man."[32] Both are concerned with *action* and with *conviction*, that which accomplishes duties and that which leads to such accomplishment, that is, the causes or motives of actions. Religion and the state, that is, "should direct the actions of its members toward the common good, and cause convictions which lead to these actions,"[33] by developing reasons that motivate the will and persuade the mind. One concerns reasons regarding humans and humans, the other reasons regarding humans and God.

Ideally the state should govern by Bildung alone, that is, simply by educating people's convictions. The best state, in other words, is one in which people act out of a deep and abiding commitment to justice and benevolence, without the need for laws or sanctions.[34] To persuade, reason, and to convince about moral principles – these are the primary functions of religion. Bildung is the Church's chief responsibility, and in an ideal world, such perfection would be sufficient.

> But if the character of a nation, the level of culture to which it has ascended, the increase of population which has accompanied the nation's prosperity, the greater complexity of relations and connections, excessive luxury, and other causes make it impossible to govern the nation by convictions alone, the state will have to resort to public measures, coercive laws, punishments of crime, and rewards of merit.[35]

If necessary, that is, coercion can be used to ensure "outward peace and security."[36] Mendelssohn calls these "mechanical deeds" or "works without spirit," and he ascribes them to the state but not to religion, whose domain is not power and coercion but rather teaching, persuasion, love, and beneficence.[37]

One might be tempted to think that for Mendelssohn the ideal is a stateless religious-moral society and that religion is solely concerned with convictions, the state with actions. Such conclusions, however, would be false. Both religious and civil institutions are necessary. The ideal state is still a state; it still governs its citizens, but it does so by Bildung alone, without coercion, internally, as it were, and not externally. With respect to convictions or moral beliefs, the state, like the Church, seeks to teach, exhort, persuade, and preach ideals that "will of themselves tend to produce actions conducive to the common weal."[38] With regard to actions, on the other hand, only the state can, when it is necessary, establish coercive mechanisms to shape conduct.[39] Religion, to be sure, is *interested* in action in so far as action is an important constituent of human well-being, but its only means of affecting action is through the agent's own reasons and motives.[40] So, for Mendelssohn, state and religion are complementary aspects of a social life aimed at human welfare and happiness.[41]

Mendelssohn draws a number of conclusions from this portrait of Church, state, and the moral life. One is that ministers and teachers of religion should not be paid by religious organizations but at most might be compensated by the state for their time.[42] Another is that both religious organizations and the state should tolerate differences of belief and principle, even public debate, and should decline any favors, bribes, or sanctions concerning commitment and allegiance.[43] The state must censor atheism, however, and fanaticism, for, like Locke, Mendelssohn fears their effects on society.[44] Furthermore, he argues against oaths of allegiance as prerequisites for office or vocation, and here he was speaking to an issue of contemporary interest and not in the abstract.[45]

Finally, Mendelssohn concludes that religious actions are less like public, civil actions than they are like convictions and beliefs. They "lead to convictions" and hence must be "performed voluntarily and with proper intent."[46] For religion, some acts lead to convictions, while others are "tokens of convictions," and in both cases coercion is ruled out. Religion can use only reason and persuasion to affect conduct, and it must eschew all sanctions. "Excommunication and the right to banish, which the state may occasionally permit itself to exercise, are diametrically opposed to the spirit of religion."[47] Here we arrive at the difference with Dohm and the core of the Searcher's challenge to Mendelssohn.[48] Coercion is incompatible with genuine religion, as it is conceived alongside the state. There is no such thing as authentic religious power, and this is a result secured by reason, by a theory of natural law, and by a political philosophy. Whether it is also a result that destroys Judaism, we shall have to see.

In Part 2 of *Jerusalem* Mendelssohn confronts several tasks. First, he must meet the Searcher's challenge by showing that a Judaism without coercive power is possible. Second, he must show that Judaism can exist in the state as a partner in the task of Bildung and the achievement of human well-being. Finally, Mendelssohn needs to show how Judaism is a religion of reason, and that means clarifying what makes Judaism rational and what makes it a distinctive way of life. By the end of *Jerusalem*, Mendelssohn has, in his own mind, achieved all of these goals.

Mendelssohn already hints at his solution in Part 1. There are three clues. First, in Part 1, Mendelssohn distinguishes actions that are political when coerced or moral when done from pure motives from *religious actions*, which must, he says, be "performed voluntarily" and hence cannot be coerced and which "lead to convictions."[49] Clearly, these latter are not moral or political actions; rather they are ritual ones, and it is Mendelssohn's view that they must be voluntary and that they play some role *akin to* persuasion. They in some way help to bring about conviction, the holding of moral principles that will lead to morally correct actions. In Part 2, Mendelssohn will say a good deal more about these religious or ceremonial actions and how they function.

Second, virtue and happiness cannot be achieved only by right actions performed for the right reasons; these are necessary but not sufficient for human well-being. More is needed, specifically belief in "fundamental principles on which all religions agree," namely "God, providence, and a future life."[50] That is, the three dogmas of natural or rational religion are necessary for the attainment of virtue and happiness. In Part 2, Mendelssohn will capitalize on this relationship; indeed, the way in which ritual conduct "leads to conviction" will be through this connection between these truths and moral perfection.

Third and finally, in Part 1 Mendelssohn makes empirical judgments about the state of society and culture in the eighteenth century, and these become relevant to the function of the Jewish ceremonial law in his own day. There was, he claims, decline in culture, population increase, and excessive luxury, all of which, he says, make it impossible for the nation to be grounded in education and governed by convictions alone. In this way Mendelssohn justifies the "public measures, coercive laws," rewards and punishments that come with a full-scale political apparatus. In a society in which morality has a weakened grip on people's souls, more than preaching and persuasion is needed to facilitate virtue and even to keep the peace. But these conditions might very well have other effects too that give rise to this need for political control. They might include, that is, the erosion of beliefs that would lead to moral conduct, among them the beliefs in God, providence, and immortality. In Part 2, Mendelssohn will utilize this further insight, as he seeks to identify the special function that Jewish ceremonial conduct is intended to perform in his own day.

In Part 2, Mendelssohn restates the Searcher's objection this way:[51] by Mendelssohn's own arguments, worship and ritual conduct cannot be coerced. But the whole system of Mosaic law is based on sanctions, fear of punishment and curses; it was a law "armed with power." How can Mendelssohn destroy the edifice and still choose to dwell in it? Moreover, the Searcher suggests, perhaps Mendelssohn's act of destruction is "a step toward the fulfillment of the wishes which Lavater formerly addressed" to him.[52] Perhaps, that is, Mendelssohn had thereby accepted the falsity of Judaism and the truth of Christianity.

No, Mendelssohn responds. His Judaism is a religion of reason and a moral faith. It serves the purposes of virtue and human perfection, and it can take its rightful place in a liberal state. Ritual conduct is not coerced, although it is revealed. Hence, Judaism is both distinctive and liberal, with a particular role in a universal project, the achievement of the well-being of all. "Judaism knows of no revealed religion . . . .

The Israelites possess a divine *legislation* – laws, commandments, ordinances, rules of life, instruction in the will of God as to how they should conduct themselves in order to attain temporal and eternal felicity."[53] Judaism involves no supernatural revelation of truths or rational principles; rather it involves a revelation of law or legislation. Metaphysical truths and moral principles are given to reason and hence to all; the particular shape of Jewish life, given through its laws and rules of conduct, must be grounded in an historical act of legislation, and that means in an act of revelation. Herein lies the solution to all Mendelssohn's problems. Judaism is distinctive as a revealed legislation and the way of life grounded in that legislation; it is also universal as a rational faith. The crucial point is to understand the connection between these two dimensions. What does Judaism share with all rational, moral religions? What is binding only upon Jews? And how are these two components of Judaism related to each other?

Mendelssohn repeats this solution seveal times in *Jerusalem*. Judaism is not a revealed religion, he says; it contains no eternal truths not comprehensible to reason and demonstrable by reason. But what makes Judaism distinctive is its divine, revealed legislation.[54] Later he puts it this way: "Judaism boasts of no *exclusive* revelation of eternal truths that are indispensable to salvation .... Revealed *religion* is one thing, revealed *legislation*, another."[55] Finally, in summarizing his conception of pristine, Mosaic Judaism, Mendelssohn includes "*eternal truths* about God and his government and providence without which man cannot be enlightened and happy" which are, he says, not revealed supernaturally but are given to "rational acknowledgment" through "*things* and *concepts*."[56] He adds to these truths "laws, precepts, commandments, and rules of life, which were to be peculiar to this nation," revealed by God and imposed "as an unalterable duty and obligation."[57]

Nor was this conception new in *Jerusalem*. In the manuscript reflections on Bonnet's *Palingenesis*, Mendelssohn had claimed that "all truths that are indispensable to mankind's salvation can be based upon rational insights" but that God revealed special laws to this particular people for quite specific reasons.[58] And in a letter of 1770, written during the Lavater controversy, Mendelssohn distinguishes between the internal worship of the Jew, based on the principles of natural religion, and the external worship, which consists of specific rules and prescriptions and is binding only on Jews.[59] Here, in these texts, the same conception is present as Mendelssohn later employs in *Jersualem*. Judaism is a combination of rational principles and revealed, particularly binding laws. The former are true and obligatory because rational, and hence they are given to all people. The latter are binding only upon the Jews.

But in order to make his case for this conception of Judaism,

Mendelssohn must show why and how it contains these laws and especially why they are still, in 1783, millennia after the demise of the original Mosaic constitution, still binding. This argument is the core of Part 2 of *Jerusalem*.[60]

❧ JUDAISM AS REVEALED LEGISLATION ❧

Once again, however, Mendelssohn's account is not new. The gist is already present in the notes on Bonnet. There Mendelssohn claimed that Judaism contains three central principles: God, providence, and legislation. All can be grasped rationally and verified by reason. "The laws of Moses are strictly binding upon us," he argued, "as long as God does not revoke them explicitly and with the same public solemnity with which He has given them."[61] They are binding whether or not we know their purpose[62] and "only upon the Jewish people."

> However, most peoples have deviated from the simplicity of this first religion and, to the detriment of truth, have evolved false notions of God and His sovereignty. Therefore, it seems that the ceremonial laws of the Jews *have, among other unfathomable reasons, the additional purpose* of making this people stand out from among all the nations and reminding it, through a variety of religious acts, perpetually of the sacred truths that none of us should forget. This is undoubtedly the *purpose of most religious customs* . . . These customs are to remind us that God is one; that He has created the world and reigns over it in wisdom; that He is the absolute Lord over all of nature; that He has liberated this people by extraordinary deeds from Egyptian oppression; that He has given them laws, etc. This is the purpose of all the customs that we observe.[63] [italics mine]

These are precisely the views that Mendelssohn will later, in *Jersualem*, repeat, elaborate, clarify, and defend. Originally, in the Mosaic constitution, the laws were binding, whatever their purposes. As time passed, beliefs and convictions eroded, giving rise to false notions of God and much else. These false notions, to which he refers, surely included, by Mendelssohn's own day, atheism and materialism, unwelcome by-products of industrial culture, naturalism, scientific advances, and much else.[64] In Part 1 of *Jerusalem*, he had, as we have seen, already alluded to these developments and to the eternal truths about God and divine providence, necessary for virtue and human perfection. In Part 2, the hints are taken up explicitly in order to develop this account of Judaism and the nature of the ceremonial law and especially to clarify how Jewish ceremonial practice serves to remind people of these eternal truths, thus serving the purposes of salvation, that is, human well-being.

The standard interpretation of Mendelssohn's argument in Part 2 that the ceremonial law is still obligatory in 1783 is this:[65] all rational agents understand the principles of morality; all desire human perfection and seek it. The eternal truths of God, providence, and the future life are necessary for the achievement of virtue and the attainment of happiness. But cultural and social conditions have eroded people's belief in these principles. The ceremonial practices of Judaism remind Jews and others of these truths, hence promoting and indeed facilitating the ultimate human and moral goal.

As it stands, however, this account, widely endorsed, has obvious flaws, three of which are particularly telling. The first concerns the obligation or duty associated with the ritual law. Where, indeed, does that obligation come from? Surely the obligation to seek a goal does not, under all circumstances, transfer to any means that might usefully facilitate its attainment. Second, why, if the ceremonial law is so useful, should only the Jews be obligated to it? Why should there not be a universal ceremonial law?[66] And finally, even if this function were to justify Jewish religious practice in 1783, it does not do so for pristine, Mosaic Judaism. For in his comments on Bonnet and in *Jerusalem* Mendelssohn is clear that false notions and corrupt conviction are manifest only once there has been decline, after the passing of that original Mosaic constitution.[67]

While the standard interpretation may be able to accommodate this last objection, it has little to say to the first two. We must look harder at the text and especially at Mendelssohn's precise formulation, which is the key to a correct account. Judaism, he says, is not a *revealed religion*, but it is a *revealed legislation*. Sometimes purposes for the ritual life will be manifest, sometimes not. Still the law is obligatory, for it is revealed and binding until the lawgiver revokes it. Jews may never, and probably will never, understand fully what God intended by the ceremonial law. What they will know, however, is that, through revelation, God established certain laws as binding. These laws are imperative, each with different content, yet each with a certain form, the form of a divine command, supernaturally revealed and grounded in divine status and divine power. Mendelssohn says this again and again: the legislation is revealed. If we distinguish, as I suggest, the law's form from its content and purpose, clearly its form – as an imperative based on authoritative command – derives from the *fact* that it was revealed. Mendelssohn's natural law theory here extends itself into a divine command theory of ritual obligation.[68] The content of a particular law depends on the law's function or purpose, and this latter is historically determined by changing circumstances and context. But the form is independent of purpose and of history, given by its character as a divine command, as revealed legislation. Only if that form and status were rescinded, would the law cease to be law and thereby cease to be binding.

If read carefully, *Jerusalem* says just this, and it is what Mendelssohn says elsewhere, earlier in the comments on Bonnet, also in his commentary on the Pentateuch, and in an important letter to his disciple Herz Homberg, written on 22 September 1783, only a few months after *Jerusalem* was published. In any given instance, Mendelssohn was willing to debate how the law should be understood; what he rejected consistently was denying its authority altogether.[69]

In *Jerusalem*, Mendelssohn elaborates and extends an idea already present in the Bonnet notes, that the ritual law today has a purpose connected with but not identical to its purpose in the original Mosaic constitution. Here, I think, Mendelssohn is responding to Spinoza's famous conception of the ceremonial law in the *Tractatus Theologico-Politicus*.[70] Similar to Spinoza's view in some ways, Mendelssohn's account is fundamentally different in another. Like Spinoza, Mendelssohn argues that the content and purpose of the ceremonial law may change historically; the law does have an historical dimension. But unlike Spinoza, Mendelssohn denies that the law is wholly historical and political. In fact, it is fundamentally not political at all, since the law and ceremonial practice are tied not to political loyalty but rather to grasping and understanding fundamental truths and moral principles. Moreover, and most importantly, the law is grounded, as obligations, not in the sovereign's will but rather in the divine will. It is the immortal God and not Hobbes' mortal God, the sovereign, that grounds Mendelssohn's ceremonial laws of Judaism and makes them imperatives.

Mendelssohn's understanding of Judaism's ritual law, then, has two sides. It is law grounded in divine command, and its content and purpose vary with historical circumstance. In Mendelssohn's day it served the purposes of maintaining the unity and distinctiveness of the Jewish people and of reminding people of the eternal truths necessary for human perfection. Mendelssohn discusses both of these dimensions in *Jerusalem*. He tells us that the ceremonial laws "refer to, or are based upon, eternal truths of reason, or *remind us* of them, and *rouse us* to ponder them."[71] He says that "the ceremonial law itself is a kind of living script, rousing the mind and heart, full of meaning, never ceasing to inspire contemplation and to provide the occasion and opportunity for oral instruction."[72] In original Judaism, that is, one learned the central doctrines of rational religion *naturally*, through a "living, spiritual instruction," the opportunity for which was given in the book of the law "and in the ceremonial acts which the adherent of Judaism had to observe incessantly."[73] Ritual, then, was the context for that kind of rational reflection and discussion aimed at teaching and under-standing the truths and principles of universal moral faith. However, once that original state was in decline and conditions eroded the knowl-edge of those truths and recognition of those principles, the ceremonial law served to remind people of them.[74] Originally a vehicle for instruc-tion, ritual became a vehicle for recollection, and, in Mendelssohn's day, a means for unifying monotheists against their opponents.[75] The purpose changed, but, as Mendelssohn firmly notes, the status as law remained, even after the original state no longer existed.

What made the law obligatory, originally, and what still does so is its divine status. In the original, Mosaic constitution, "the laws, precepts, commandments, and rules of life" were "peculiar to this nation" and given by God the lawgiver as "King and Head of the people." Moroever, they were given in a public, solemn ceremony and were thereby "imposed upon the nation and all their descendants as an unalterable duty and obligation."[76] But, as he immediately makes clear, it is not their content or interpretation that is "unalterable." Rather it is their obligatory status. As he puts it, the law may change in reason and content but not as law:

> We are permitted to reflect on the law, to inquire into its spirit,
> and here and there, where the lawgiver gave no reason, to
> surmise a reason which, *perhaps*, depended upon time, place, and
> circumstances, and which, *perhaps*, may be liable to change in
> accordance with time, place, and circumstances – if it pleases the
> Supreme Lawgiver to make known to us His will on this
> matter, to make it known in as clear a voice, in as public a
> manner, and as far beyond all doubt and ambiguity as He did
> when He gave the law itself. As long as this has not happened,
> as long as we can point to no such authentic exception from
> the law, no sophistry of ours can free us from the strict obedience
> we owe to the law.[77]

Mendelssohn calls this a "rabbinic principle;" "He who is not born into the law need not bind himself to the law; but he who is born into the law must live according to the law, and die according to the law."[78] The point is not merely one of scope; it is about the obligatory status of the law, its form as a divinely revealed imperative. This latter is what is "unalterable" about the law – until publicly, explicitly, and authoritatively revoked by the divine commander.

Mendelssohn's conception of Judaism as *revealed legislation* is part of his conception of Judaism, as a religion of reason. Pristine Judaism as a theocracy was a unity of rational truths and laws, ordi-nances, rules of life. Also, state and religion were one; God was king, and the community was a community of God. But this constitution exists no longer; there exists no such unity of interests.[79] In what sense, then, is it rational to remain a Jew? Why not become a citizen but eschew one's particular allegiance to Judaism? Is the ceremonial law a law of reason? The answer to these questions must lie with Mendelssohn's conception of providence. God's revelation to the Jewish people at Sinai was an act of divine providence; historically, it occurred, and reason shows that God exists and cares for His creation. However, we can only speculate about why God revealed Himself at Sinai and what the law is intended to accomplish. We can know *that* the law was revealed; we cannot know *why*.

This conclusion is precisely what Mendelssohn said it was when, in the course of writing *To Lessing's Friends*, he referred to the argument of *Jerusalem*. For there he summarizes his conception of Judaism in these terms: eternal truths and fundamental moral principles are rational, grasped by rational thought and verified by reason. Reason also proves the existence of God and his authority. In addition to these beliefs, however, Judaism admits "historical truths, . . . *facts* upon which the authority of our prescribed ritual law is founded."[80] The crucial one of these facts is the revelation at Sinai; the law is authoritative, that is, obligatory, because it was revealed by God and hence is divinely commanded. In Judaism, therefore, reason takes us so far and then history takes over.

In the end, then, there is a gap in human understanding between the possibility of revelation, proved by reason, and the actuality of Sinai, given to us by the authority of witnesses and texts. But there is no gap in Mendelssohn's rationalism. In the case of revelation, reason can defend both it and the conception of God and divine providence that grounds its reality. The gap between possibility and actuality may mark the limit of Mendelssohn's confidence in human understanding, but it is no obstacle to his rationalism.[81]

Mendelssohn's commitment to reason is comprehensive and deep. But it is not without problems. Already in the winter of 1785, when he personally delivered his last manuscript to his publisher, there were signs that Mendelssohn's confidence in reason might be unwarranted. But the signs were yet to explode into the most severe warfare over the fate of reason. These were battles Mendelssohn died too soon to wage.[82]

❧❧ NOTES ❧❧

1 For an account of Mendelssohn's final days, see Altmann 1973, pp. 729–41.

2 On the outlines of the general debate over reason and faith and for Lessing's and Mendelssohn's roles in it, see Beiser 1987, Vallée 1988, and Bell 1984.

3 Altmann 1973, p. 732.

4 Mendelssohn's *To Lessing's Friends*, in Vallée 1988, p. 135.

5 Ibid., p. 136.

6 Ibid., p. 137.

7 See the autobiographical letter to Johann Jacob Spiess of 1 March 1774: *Gesammelte Schriften* 5: 524–7, esp. 526–7 (translated by Eva Jospe in Mendelssohn 1975, pp. 52–3).

8 See Altmann 1973, pp. 50–5; also *Morgenstunden*, sections 13–15 (partially translated in Vallée 1988, pp. 65–77).

9 See the response to the Jewish community, Schwerin, translated in Mendelssohn 1975, pp. 102–4; Altmann 1973, pp. 288–93.

10 See Altmann 1973, passim; Mendelssohn 1975, pp. 79–106.

11 Mendelssohn, *Gesammelte Schriften Jubiläumsausgabe*, 3.1: 1–159.

12 Ibid., 2: 267–330.

13 Spinoza describes this universal faith in chapter 14 of the *Tractatus Theologico-Politicus*.

14 This theme, as Altmann points out, was central to Mendelssohn's position during the Lavater affair. See Altmann 1973, p. 200.

15 Altmann, 1973, pp. 118–30, 156.

16 See Mendelssohn, *Gesammelte Schriften Jubiläumsausgabe*, 7: 65–107, esp. 73ff. (translated by Eva Jospe in Mendelssohn 1975, pp. 112–14) and 7: pp. 95–9 (translated by Alfred Jospe 1969, pp. 154–6), and compare with *Jerusalem*, translated Arkush 1983, pp. 128–9.

17 Epstein 1966, pp. 221–3.

18 For an English translation of *Vindiciae Judaeorum* with Mendelssohn's preface, see Mendelssohn 1838, 1: 3–116.

19 Altmann 1973, pp. 490ff., especially the letters from August Hennings and Baron Friedrich Eberhard von Rochow.

20 For an English translation of this pamphlet, see Mendelssohn 1838, 1: 119–45.

21 It was not, as Mendelssohn eventually discovered. As Jacob Katz showed (*Zion* 1971, 36: 116–17), it was August Friedrich Cranz, a Berlin journalist.

22 Altmann 1973, p. 507.

23 See Altmann's notes in *Jerusalem*, esp. pp. 146–8, and his articles in *Die trostvolle Aufklärung*.

24 Mendelssohn states this problem in the first sentence of *Jerusalem*, p. 33: "State and religion – civil and ecclesiastical constitution – secular and churchly authority – how to oppose these pillars of social life to one another so that they are in balance and do not, instead, become burdens on social life, or weigh down its foundations more than they help to uphold it – this is one of the most difficult tasks of politics."

25 This was Hobbes' diagnosis in *Behemoth*. For discussion, see Martinich et al. His solution was Erastian.

26 *Jerusalem*, p. 35.

27 See Hobbes, *Leviathan*, chapter 45.

28 See *Phaedon* and the little tract "On the Soul," in *Gesammelte Schriften Jubiläumsausgabe*, 3.1: 201–33.

29 *Jerusalem*, p. 70.

30 For an excellent discussion of the Hellenistic dimension of this conception of ethics and human life, see Annas 1993 and Nussbaum 1994.
31 *Jerusalem*, p. 41.
32 Ibid.
33 Ibid., p. 40.
34 Ibid., pp. 41–3.
35 Ibid., p. 43.
36 Ibid., p. 44.
37 Ibid., p. 45; see also pp. 70–5.
38 Ibid., p. 41; see also p. 61: "Both must teach, instruct, encourage, and motivate."
39 Ibid., p. 72.
40 See also ibid., p. 57.
41 For Mendelssohn's sketch of a natural law theory of perfect and imperfect rights and duties that supports this portrait of the roles of state and religion and their interrelationship, see ibid., pp. 45–63. I have discussed this theory in some detail in Morgan 1992, chapter 3.
42 *Jerusalem*, pp. 60–1.
43 Ibid., pp. 61–2.
44 Ibid., p. 63.
45 Ibid., pp. 63–70.
46 Ibid., p. 72.
47 Ibid., p. 73.
48 Ibid., pp. 77–8.
49 Ibid., p. 72.
50 Ibid., p. 63; see also Altmann's commentary, 1973, pp. 191–2. Also, the letter to Thomas Abbt in Mendelssohn 1975, pp. 163–4.
51 *Jerusalem*, pp. 84–5.
52 Ibid., p. 86.
53 Ibid., pp. 89–90. Note the implicit criticism of Locke: like the state, Judaism is concerned with both temporal and eternal happiness, that is, human perfection as an infinite task.
54 Ibid., pp. 89–90.
55 Ibid., p. 97.
56 Ibid., p. 126.
57 Ibid., p. 127.
58 *Gesammelte Schriften Jubiläumsausgabe* 7: 65–107 (translated in Mendelssohn 1969, p. 128). See ibid., p. 156, also from the *Counter-reflections*.
59 *Gesammelte Schriften* 8: 500–4, esp. 503–4 (translated in Mendelssohn 1969, p. 134). See also *Gesammelte Schriften Jubiläumsausgabe* 7: 7–17 (partially translated in Mendelssohn 1969, p. 116 and Mendelssohn 1975, p. 135) and a letter to Elkan Herz of 22 July 1771 (partially translated in Mendelssohn 1969, p. 137 and Mendelssohn 1975, p. 121).
60 *Jerusalem*, pp. 90–135.
61 *Gesammelte Schriften Jubiläumsausgabe* 7: 97; this sentence is repeated almost verbatim in *Jerusalem*, pp. 133–4.
62 See Mendelssohn's commentary on Exodus 32: 19 in *Biur*, translated in Mendelssohn 1969, p. 149: "God has given us many commandments without revealing their purpose to us. However, it should be sufficient for us to know that they

were commanded by Him. Inasmuch as we have to take the yoke of His dominion upon us, we are obligated to do His will. Their value lies in their practice, not in the understanding of their origin or purpose."

63 From the *Counter-reflections*, in *Gesammelte Schriften Jubiläumsausgabe* 7: 95–9, esp. 98 (translated in Mendelssohn 1969, pp. 155–6 and Mendelssohn 1975, pp. 125–6).

64 See Buckley 1987 on the rise of modern atheism and Beiser 1987, on the role of Spinoza in Enlightenment debates in England over reason and atheism.

65 The interpretation is essentially Altmann's in Altmann 1973, pp. 546–7. It is also Meyer's in Meyer 1967 and my own in Morgan 1992, chapters 2–3. The following account is meant to supersede my own in these earlier essays.

66 Altmann 1973, p. 547. See also Morgan 1992.

67 This difference is clearest in the passage from the notes on Bonnet, quoted above.

68 In his interpretation of Hobbes' theory of obligation and the laws of nature in *Leviathan*, Martinich uses a similar strategy, distinguishing the form from the content of the laws of nature; see Martinich 1992.

69 A clear case of this is his role in the early burial case; see Altmann 1973, pp. 288–93.

70 See Altmann's notes in Mendelssohn 1983, pp. 236–7; Guttmann 1981; Morgan 1992, chapter 1.

71 *Jerusalem*, p. 99 (italics mine).

72 Ibid., pp. 102–3.

73 Ibid., p. 102; see also esp. pp. 117–20 and 127–8.

74 Ibid., pp. 132–3.

75 See *Gesammelte Schriften* 5: 668–70, esp. 669, a letter to Herz Homberg, 22 September 1783 (translated in Mendelssohn 1969, p. 148).

76 *Jerusalem*, p. 127.

77 Ibid., p. 133.

78 Ibid., p. 134.

79 Ibid., pp. 99, 128ff., 131.

80 Vallée 1988, p. 137.

81 This account is meant to supersede my earlier account of the limits of reason in *Jerusalem*; see Morgan 1992.

82 For an excellent account, see Beiser 1987.

❧ BIBLIOGRAPHY ❧

Texts

Mendelssohn, M. (1789) *Phaedon; or, the Death of Socrates* (London: Cooper; (reprinted New York: Arno, 1973).

—— (1838) *Jerusalem: A Treatise on Ecclesiastical Authority and Judaism*, translated by M. Samuels, 2 vols (London: Longman, Orme, Brown & Longmans).

—— (1843–4) *Gesammelte Schriften*, 7 vols (Leipzig: Brodhaus).

—— (1929–30) *Gesammelte Schriften Jubiläumsausgabe* (Berlin: Akademie).

—— (1969) *Jerusalem and Other Jewish Writings*, translated and edited by A. Jospe (New York: Schocken).

—— (1975) *Moses Mendelssohn: Selections from His Writings*, edited and translated by E. Jospe (New York: Viking).

—— (1983) [1783] *Jerusalem, or, On Religious Power and Judaism*, translated by A. Arkush (Hanover: University Press of New England).

Vallée, G. (1988) *The Spinoza Conversations between Lessing and Jacobi* (Lantham: University Press of America).

Studies

Altmann, A. (1973) *Moses Mendelssohn: A Biographical Study* (Philadelphia: Jewish Publication Society).

—— (1982) *Die trostvolle Aufklärung* (Stuttgart and Bad Cannstatt: Frommann-Holzboog).

Annas, J. (1993) *The Morality of Happiness* (Oxford: Oxford University Press).

Arkush, A. (1994) *Moses Mendelssohn and the Enlightenment* (Albany: State University of New York Press).

Beiser, F. (1987) *The Fate of Reason* (Cambridge, MA: Harvard University Press).

Bell, D. (1984) *Spinoza in Germany from 1670 to the Age of Goethe* (London: Institute of German Studies, University of London).

Buckley, M. J. (1987) *At the Origins of Modern Atheism* (New Haven: Yale University Press).

Eisen, A. (1990) "Divine Legislation as 'Ceremonial Script': Mendelssohn on the Commandments," *AJS Review* 15.2: 239–67.

Epstein, K. (1966) *The Genesis of German Conservatism* (Princeton: Princeton University Press).

Guttmann, J. (1981) "Mendelssohn's *Jerusalem* and Spinoza's *Theologico-Political Treatise*," in *Studies in Jewish Thought*, edited by A. Jospe (Detroit: Wayne State University Press).

Martinich, A. P. (1992) *The Two Gods of Leviathan* (Cambridge: Cambridge University Press).

Meyer, M. A. (1967) *The Origins of the Modern Jew* (Detroit: Wayne State University Press).

Morgan, M. L. (1992) *Dilemmas in Modern Jewish Thought* (Bloomington: Indiana University Press).

Nussbaum, M. (1994) *The Therapy of Desire* (Princeton: Princeton University Press).

Sorkin, D. (1996) *Moses Mendelssohn and the Religious Enlightenment* (Berkeley: University of California Press).

CHAPTER 27

Nineteenth-century German Reform philosophy

Mordecai Finley

INTRODUCTION

Reform Judaism begins in the late eighteenth century with lay people and, somewhat later, some rabbis tinkering with the traditional worship ceremony and other aspects of traditional practice, a tinkering which may seem insignificant in hindsight. As those minor reforms grew in scope, they led to a bitter and protracted halakhic controversy. Reform Judaism begins, in a formal sense, when the Reformers began to understand that they might no longer be governed by the traditional halakhah, not by its methods, rules, nor basic premises.

It would be fair to say that the philosophic basis of Reform Judaism grew through reflection, as a response to action and challenge. In other words, Reform philosophy can be understood as the legitimation of the reform of halakhah, itself perceived to be a pressing need for the survival of Judaism in Germany, a philosophizing which led to a truly radical break with traditional Jewish law, practice, and theology. The fact that Reform philosophy can be seen at its core to be a legitimation of the reform of law does not mean that it cannot be applied, interpreted, or have ramifications far beyond the focus suggested here. The history of Reform Judaism in Germany allows for a choice of views in assessing its philosophical character. Those assessments can range from, at one end, seeing Reform as most of all concerned with fitting into the emerging liberal society in Germany, an essentially assimilationist motivation, to, at the other end, seeing Reform as a messianism, a reworking of Judaism to open its doors to the expected droves of post-Christians who would be seeking rational faith. Both assessments certainly have their place in describing German Reform's self-understanding. The goal of this chapter, however, is not to describe that great range of self-understandings that motivated Reform in Germany but rather to describe a core philosophical self-understanding which accounts for the two mentioned above and the range between them.

The scope of this chapter is further narrowed in that, in this brief treatment of the philosophy of early German Reform, it is not my goal to give an account of the teachings of a series of philosophers who may be identified as Reform. Similarly, I do not intend simply to present the historical-philosophical context in which Reform arose. My intent here is more overtly hermeneutical and interpretative than historiographic. In other words, my intent is to describe the philosophic world view of Reform, the matrix within which Reform philosophers arose, the matrix which took form in dialogue with the contemporaneous philosophic context.[1] Reform as a movement begins as the reform of Jewish law, halakhah. Further philosophic developments of Reform ideology as expressed in the thought of its major exponents are to be seen here as resting on the prior philosophic problem of the criteriology for the reform of law.

By finally asserting that the traditional halakhah no longer had absolute authority over their lives or the way they understood and practiced Judaism, the Reformers were also asserting, consciously or not, that something else had replaced the halakhah as the authoritative criterion in religious life. This change in authority indicates a change in the normative universe, the nomos, which is the context of Reform Judaism's world view, and, for the purposes here, its view of law. The goal of this chapter is to describe that normative universe.

Methodological note – comparative normative hermeneutics

Once reform of traditional laws became Reform of Judaism itself, a transition in thinking that took place roughly between 1820 and 1840, one can properly speak of Reform philosophy. This philosophy begins with two core notions: first, that the traditional, halakhic understanding of Judaism has been superseded, and, second, that Reform is not a break with "authentic" Judaism but rather its discovery. Reform thinkers, generally speaking, are reading the same traditional texts that the halakhists read, but derive an entirely different definition of Judaism from them. In other words, Reform begins in a hermeneutical move, a difference in interpretation of an existing canon.

Before going further in this line of thought, it would be well to define briefly some essential terms, such as "canon" and "hermeneutics" as they are to be used here. The lexicon and method of study here may be defined as that of "normative hermeneutics."[2]

By "hermeneutics," I mean theory of understanding and interpretation, how we derive and establish the meaning of "texts," this latter term understood rather widely.[3] By "normative," I mean that the meaning of the text will have some impact on the moral life. The starting point of normative hermeneutics is the idea that some texts teach us, assert a moral claim over us, to act, believe, or live in certain ways. Normative hermeneutics addresses questions of how texts provide that normative guidance, especially in a community which holds a set of texts to be authority.

The issue of which texts teach or have authority over actions or beliefs entails the notion "canon." Torah, Talmud, Codes, etc., for example, comprise the core of the traditional Jewish canon. "Canon" refers to the boundary of what is considered to be a sacred text, but not what the texts mean or how they should be employed.

The issue of whom the canon properly addresses entails the notion "faith community." Jews typically construe the addressed faith community of the Jewish canon to be the people Israel.

The issue of which features or properties of the canon allows or licenses it to teach, and what kind of authority that license implies, entails the notion "Scripture." For example, is Torah Scripture because it is direct, divine revelation, or is it Scripture because it embodies the highest ethical ideals of ancient Israelite religion? These different notions of what warrants Torah to be canon lead to vastly different notions of how Torah functions as authority.

How the canon is understood as Scripture will inform the issue of how and to what ends the canon teaches, which entails notions of "construing and interpreting" the text. For example, to claim that Torah is Scripture because it is divine revelation does not necessarily entail the classical rabbinic midrashic construal of the text, a construal which allows for the type of discourse which typifies the Talmud. The rabbinic use of midrash when interpreting the Torah is evidence of a construal of the text that leads to interpretive moves peculiar to Judaism. The Christian hermeneutic of prefiguration, that events or figures in the Hebrew Bible prefigure christological themes, would be an example of a peculiarly Christian construal of the canon.

The issue of defining the normative world in which the interpretive action takes place entails the notion "nomos". This normative world is expressed and shaped by our myths or narratives about human nature, the function and point of law, our senses of history and destiny. Nomos refers to the structure of our spiritual existence, the moral analogue of "cosmos."

The issue of describing how the nomos is brought to bear directly on decisions in normative hermeneutics entails the notion "world view." One way to understand world view is to see it as a conscious, focused articulation of a nomos, through, for example, concepts and attitudes. In other words, a nomos is something which needs to be interpreted or inferred. A world view is a more or less conscious "image" of the world and its possibilities, an image which can determine moral conduct. Max Weber writes,

> [V]ery frequently the "world images" that have been created by "ideas" have, like switchmen, determined the tracks along which action has been pushed by the dynamic of interest. "From what" and "for what" one wished to be redeemed, depended on one's image of the world.[4]

A world view, then, functions as an articulation of the basic normative commitments in a nomos, one's normative universe, and this image can shape a course of behavior.

The goal of this chapter is to provide a description of the Reform nomos and philosophic world view, especially as it relates to Reform notions of the authority of halakhah. The Reform world view, especially as it relates to the reform of law, Reform's starting place, has been informed by particular notions of liberalism and history, which will be the topic of the second part of this chapter. Later on, I will present some of the relevant history and thought of early Reform, especially that of Abraham Geiger, as attitudes toward what replaces the authority of halakhah began to take shape. Some of the inherent conflicts in the nomos of Reform Judaism, especially regarding the authority of the tradition, will be discussed finally.

❧ THE AUTHORITY OF RIGHT AND ❧ HISTORY IN THE REFORM WORLD VIEW

The theories of liberalism and history proferred here are not meant to be exhaustive, but rather suggestive of a style of thinking which informed the world view of Reform Judaism since its inception. In another work, I argued that Reform Judaism can be seen as standing on a natural law critique of authority, which involved natural law understandings of right and history.[5] Though the detail of that argument is not necessary here, the main point is that the notions of right and history rest within the natural law/natural rights tradition of Western political and philosophic thought.

My own thought about Reform Judaism and natural law theory has been informed by the thought of Ronald Garet, cited above for his work in normative hermeneutics. Garet defines natural law in this way:

> By "natural law," I understand a human-nature naturalist theory

of law. Such a theory contends that there is a human nature, that this nature is knowable, and that it is the mission of law to realize this nature or to forestall the evil that inheres in it. . . . Natural law is a special form of ethical naturalism for two reasons. Its naturalism consists of claims about human nature; and those claims culminate in a thesis about the purpose and function of law.[6]

Garet connects natural law theory to Robert Cover's notion of nomos, the normative universe of which a world view is an articulation, in the following way:

Because *nomos* is a conception of both law and of human nature, it is plausible to think of it as providing the basis for a theory of natural law. Such a theory would seek the justification of laws in their fidelity to the human situation, and the lawful situation, that *nomos* names.[7]

Put simply, one would want to shape law in accord with how one understood the nature of the normative universe. In other words, law ought to accord with moral reality.[8] As Reform thinkers began to understand the normative world in ways different from the classic rabbinic way, they would necessarily, in Cover's and Garet's views, feel compelled to make changes in how they understood law as well.

In using the category of natural law to understand early Reform thought, I am emphasizing especially one idea: for the Reformers, the halakhah, as they experienced it, was "unnatural." The Reformers were trying to bring a Judaism into the world which was in accord with the normative world, as they understood it. It is a misunderstanding of Reform to see it as being philosophically antinomian simply because it posits itself against the traditional halakhah. I would maintain that many early Reformers saw themselves as loyal to higher law than the halakhah, law which mandated and legitimated their action. The general nature of these higher laws may be understood as natural law theories of right and history. First, natural law theory of the right will be considered, and then natural law theory of history.

An important caveat should be observed here: I am not claiming that Reform thinkers used these terms, "natural right" in their own thinking. I am claiming that, when we examine the thought of Reform thinkers, protocols of rabbinic conferences, prayerbooks, etc., we discover a strong affinity between the ideas expressed there and a concept such as "natural right." I am using this term hermeneutically and even heuristically to bring to light aspects of Reform thought which seem to me to be foundational in understanding Reform philosophy.

Natural right and liberalism

Our first task in this section is a discussion of natural right theory. Leo Strauss' *Natural Right and History* is invaluable, and perhaps definitive, in approaching this discussion. Strauss bases the origin of the notion of natural right in philosophy, which itself is marked by the discovery of nature. Once nature, physis, is conceived, its antithesis, nomos (not Cover's nomos, which is opposed to chaos, not nature), comes into being as well. Nomos, as Strauss uses the term, refers to social forms which are conventional and human made, and especially refers to socially created laws and customs. Evils, too, are described similarly: malum in se versus malum prohibitum, for example.

Strauss' nomos-as-convention, then, means not necessarily in accord with nature, and therefore, of lesser value than that which is in accord with nature, if the criterion for the good is the natural. This distinction has an impact on value – there are things which are good by nature, and those which are good by convention. Philosophy will naturally, as it were, take an interest in principles or laws of nature, that is, laws rooted in the nature of things. Knowing what is right by nature as opposed to what is right by convention is not a simple task, for what is natural is hidden by conventional authority. This task of finding what is right by nature implies both a critique of what is considered good ancestrally or communally, and *a transfer of authority from tradition to reason*, which discovers that which is naturally right.

The nature-versus-convention distinction is crucial for the entire natural right tradition. Nature is seen as having a deeper, more abiding character than convention, and is considered the ultimate criterion for the good. A thing is good inasmuch as it accords with its nature. Everything has a true nature, and we must determine that nature to know what its good is.

The move from classical natural right to modern natural right is a knotty one; the story is much too complex to be raised here.[9] Whatever its historical and intellectual origins are, modern natural right, or natural rights theory, begins with a notion of the pre-social person who is fully human. His or her main end is self-preservation, not necessarily intellectual or moral perfection. Human beings enter into society to secure their own ends, their own self-preservation. Human beings are motivated by desire, not virtues. Reason does not discover truth, but rather is put to the service of desire – how to effect self-preservation and maximize pleasure. Preservation, not perfection, brings us into civil society. According to modern natural right theory, we have no perfect duty vis-à-vis society, only perfect rights, originating in the right of self-preservation. Each individual is the best judge of the best way to effect personal self-preservation, so one person's wisdom is not necessarily better than another's. The state's coercive authority, then, is derived from individuals granting to it their right to violence.

Liberalism, then, as understood here, would not denote a specific content in respect to thinking about the moral world, but would rather involve a commitment that each individual could think the way he wanted. This notion may be understood in two different ways, reflected by two different streams of liberal thought. One stream, characterized by Hobbes and Hume, for example, would claim that there really is no morality; morality is reduced to a subjective sense of approbation for some act whose consequence ultimately redounds to the public good, which itself is understood in terms of the self-interest of the individual. Kant, on the other hand, would also hold that there is no intrinsically morally good act, but because he holds that the only truly good thing is the will. A person may act in a way conventionally thought to be moral, but the person's intent may be purely prudential or self-interested. Kant would hold that right reason really can accord with the truly right; for this reason, he may be understood to be a natural-right type of liberal, not one who would reduce notions of rights to public utility, and finally to self-interests. The type of liberalism which shaped Reform was the Kantian, natural-right variety.

Philosophically speaking, the differences between classical natural right and modern natural right are important. For the purposes of this chapter, however, the distinctions between the two philosophical approaches are not as important as the imprint they make together on the intellectual spirit of the times in which Reform arose. Conventions either occluded, or at best pointed back to, truths, essences, the real nature of things.

While I will present below an examination of how natural right thinking informs Reform philosophy, I will adumbrate here that discussion. The philosophical approach of the natural right tradition is devastating to a core halakhic principle such as, for example, "*hilkh'ta k'vatra'ei*," "the law is in accord with later decisors." "Later" comes to mean superconventional – truth is in origins, the core, canonically speaking, the Bible, or even just the Ten Commandments.

Canon itself can be seen as convention, once the text is historicized. Reason is so elevated in the time period under discussion that it becomes the criterion according to which the canon is assessed and interpreted. The idea of the authority of tradition, certainly a bulwark of halakhah, is thoroughly undermined by the evolving Reform world view, itself an image of a moral world where reason became the guiding star. Certainly, the canon stays roughly the same, although Reformers argue for its expansion (for example, including Philo and Josephus). Its license to teach, however, is derived from its being an historicized albeit constitutional expression of ethics, not a direct expression of divine will. If the truth of the canon is rationality and ethics, then the faith community perforce becomes all of humankind. Israel is the steward of rational faith held in store for all humanity.

While classical natural right undoes the grip of tradition in a philosophic sense, modern natural right does similar work in a political sense. Modern natural right conceives of persons who contract to create the state and thus become citizens – authority is derived from the consent of the governed. Philosophically speaking, a path is opened which allows both for the critique of tradition and for the sidestepping of traditional institutions of authority.

We see already, then, a certain tension between liberal thought on one hand, itself a mix of modern and classical natural right thinking, and halakhic thought on the other, itself seen here as a subset of traditional religious thought. Religion aims at certitude, a description of how the world is and what we must do – religions typically establish conventions which must be followed. Classical natural right tells us that tradition can actually obfuscate that which is naturally right, while liberalism tells us that the world is no special way, it has no essential character other than that of the individuals who associate with one another to make up society. No act is intrinsically moral; only the will may be characterized as such. Following the conventions of a religion would not necessarily be following right reason, which is the human being's avenue to apprehending that which is truly right. The essential terms of religion, canon and community, are incomprehensible without the notion of authority, an authority which at some point can transcend individual reasoning and interests. Liberalism is hard put to legitimate any authority which ultimately transcends individual interests or conscience; on the contrary, the natural rights of human beings trump any institution's understandings or dictates. Reform, which begins as a critique of halakhah, contains the seeds of the critique of religion in general.

A natural law theory of history

At first glance, the notion of a natural law theory of history is an oxymoron. Natural law refers to that which does not change, to that which is linked to the eternal. History, on the other hand, is constant flux, constant change. An examination of late eighteenth- and early nineteenth-century notions of history, however, shows us that the two terms, natural law and history, were not seen as contradictory. History, even as change and flux, was seen as able to command, that is, to determine the structure of thought and consequently behavior, according to the nature of the world.

The conception of history which I will describe has its foundations in a variety of thinkers, such as Vico, Herder, Leibniz, Hegel, and, later, Marx. The conception I will present is not reducible to any of them, but rather reflects a way of thinking that was widespread in the early nineteenth century. The Reform world view I am presenting here is not one which merely reflects the thought of one philosopher of history or another, but rather is a result of Reform thinkers participating in the discussion concerning a general and widely held conception of history. This general conception of history is best captured in the terms "progress" and "evolution."

The epigram of the French philosopher of history Turgot (1727–81) sums up the sentiment of progress well: "[T]he whole human race, through alternate periods of rest and unrest, of weal and woe, goes on advancing, although at a slow pace, towards greater perfection."[10] Ernst Breisach, in his *Historiography*, notes that

> [N]o one work proclaimed and explained the concept of progress. Rather progress was proposed, debated, and praised in many works, and belief in it became sustained less by an agreed-upon theory than by a broadly shared expectation.[11]

This idea of progress had several components. One central one was the idea of the emancipation of "mankind." Human history was the story of human progress, the "gradual liberation of rationality from bondage."[12] Breisach notes a teleology in this notion of history:

> The unity of mankind's destiny was no longer vouchsafed by the common descent from Adam and Eve but by the presence of reason in its every member and its development bore no longer the marks of Divine Providence but those of the emancipation of rationality from error and superstition.[13]

This notion of history devalued earlier stages in history. Instead of the past being the teacher, the "expectations for the future governed the life of the present and the evaluation of the past."[14]

The idea of progress contains the notion of struggle: reason and progress are hypostatized into entities which fight against darkness, oppression, and obscurantism. Reason had its own "liberating dynamics," and, although its march took place in a terrain of cultural environments with which it had to interact, the march was inexorably forward.

In the thought of Herder, for example, we see another variable factored into the notion of progress, the notion of the Volk, the people. Herder held, at times (according to Breisach, he was not always consistent), that each Volk went through different ages on its path toward maturity. Herder entertained teleological notions as well, such as divine providence educating humanity toward greater moral development.[15]

The notion of evolution reached its peak only in the mid nineteenth century, but its impact as an idea can clearly be seen on German Reform Judaism. The core idea of evolution is that life forms undergo change through time. Nature came to be seen not as reproducing eternally fixed forms of life, but rather producing new and improved forms. Darwin's language had a teleological character,[16] and it can be seen resonating in the thought of someone like Schopenhauer, who saw "the evolutionary process as the self-expression of the blind will, a creative and directive force."[17] The nature of the world was such, then, that historical forms gave way to new historical forms. The newer ones would be more highly valued than the older ones, as they were more natural, that is, more in accord with the nature of evolving reality.

The Reformers sought to discover natural, right "authentic" Judaism, which meant, in the context of this discussion, the Judaism which was right for that age. The "laws of history," the "fact" of historical progress and evolution helped shape new notions of canon and the construal of such. Jewish history became a text in and of itself and it taught of Judaism's changing forms. The literary/textual canon was now to be construed historically and interpreted in accord. Problems of hermeneutical distance, translating scripture across different ages, became an essential interpretative endeavor.

The two intellectual forces mentioned here, "right" and "history," form the two foundations of early Reform philosophy. The first taught that Judaism had a nature, an essence, discoverable through reason, occluded by convention. The second taught that that essence was expressed in changed forms, and newer forms were more highly evolved than former ones.

It is hardly possible to overemphasize a final point in this vein: the interpretive tool was science, Wissenschaft, the rational methods of the academy that would yield moral and historical truth. The epistemology of the age dictated that science yielded truth. The canon was construed so that the modern scholar, the scientist of Geisteswissenschaften, especially of history, literature, and language, was the authorized interpreter of the Scripture; the academic scholar-rabbi, not the halakhist, would determine Judaism's meaning.

❧❧ PHILOSOPHY OF EARLY REFORM ❧❧ JUDAISM IN THE MATRIX OF NATURAL RIGHT AND HISTORY

We now turn to the early history of Reform Judaism, where we will see affinities between early Reform thinkers and the types of thinking presented above.

First of all, Michael Meyer, in the widely accepted standard history of Reform Judaism, *Response to Modernity*, notes the importance of history and natural right, though not with the terminology used here. For example, Meyer notes that Lessing (1729–81) had a notion of history which held that revelation and reason "led upward as the human spirit progressed from stage to stage." Judaism was an anachronism, having spent its energies for internal religious development during the Second Commonwealth, at which time Christianity took the mantle, as it were. Meyer states that the "thrust of Lessing's approach soon became essential for the theological enterprise of the Reformers... adopt[ing] Lessing's notion of religious advance during the course of history," disagreeing, of course, with Lessing's rather negative understanding of Judaism in the universal process of religious development.[18]

The pillars of natural rights theory, as inherited and taught by Kant, such as the primacy of reason and morals, and the notion of the just, liberal state, became central in the Reform. In a sense, Kantianism provides an incipient criteriology for radical Reform. Michael Meyer states:

> Kant's influential idea that beyond all historical religions there was a "single, unchanging, pure religious faith" dwelling in the human conscience – in essence the religion of the future – made indifference to all specific elements of Judaism respectable. For if God required nothing more than steadfast diligence in leading a morally good life, in fulfilling one's duties to fellow human beings, then all ceremonial and symbolic expressions were ultimately superfluous.[19]

Meyer goes on to say that "[t]he idea that pure religious faith is essentially moral became the theoretical basis and the practical operative principle of the Reform movement."[20] Kant's notions of moral autonomy served to undermine the justification of rabbinic authority, and presented a critique against the authority of the canon. Kant saw the Bible as subject to the judgment of the reader, according to rational and moral criteria. In other words, there was a morality which transcended Scripture.

As we look to Reform thought, we turn first to Moses Mendelssohn (1729–86), who can be seen as an inceptive Reform thinker. While Mendelssohn was himself certainly not a Reformer, he is important for understanding early Reform thought. He took liberal philosophy very seriously. His magnum opus, *Jerusalem, or, On Religious Power and Judaism*, may be seen as a proposal for understanding how liberalism and Judaism might meet.

In *Jerusalem*, Mendelssohn conceives of two moral entities, the state and religion, both of which have a claim on persons as moral agents. Each entity has its own proper domain, its own trust; the state is to take care of the world of actions, religion is to take care of the world of convictions. Only civil society, that is, the liberal state, has the right of coercion, through the social contract. Religious society has no right to coercion, and the state has no right to forbid inquiry. It becomes clear that Mendelssohn is trying to set up a moral and political philosophy which will allow both for freedom for the Jewish religion and for the removal of disabilities against the Jews. He expresses this philosophy not in the language of modern natural rights but in the spirit of his contemporary, Kant. Mendelssohn claims that Judaism makes no claim to universal truths (including the moral truths concerning the liberal state), which are discernible only through reason and available to all, but rather to divine legislation, a legislation which was presented to the Jewish people at a specific historical moment. This legislation came to be known through the tradition, which is both credible and authoritative, though it does not have the status of reason. Mendelssohn states that there is the universal religion of mankind, which is based on reason, but that Judaism is based on divine legislation revealed in history.

Mendelssohn's neat typology exemplifies the weak position in which traditional Judaism found itself vis-à-vis European philosophy in the early nineteenth century. For Mendelssohn to write during the Age of Reason that there was a universal religion which one could appropriate through reason was to cast doubt on the very authority and legitimacy of Judaism, whose truths were only historical (that is, conventional). This doubt was a serious one given the circumstances in the early nineteenth century, when Kant's influence was at its apex. It should be noted here that Mendelssohn's thought is decidedly non-historicist and non-teleological. Judaism is eternal and unchanging. However, when we take Mendelssohn's natural right theory, that is, that reason is the path to universal religion and morality is the center of universal religious life, and introduce it to a natural law theory of history with its teleological focus, we have the material for the beginnings of the intellectual history of Reform Judaism.

We see notions of morality and justice, on one hand, and history and progress, on the other, in the thought of several early Reform thinkers. Michael Meyer instructively distinguishes among those early Reformers interested mostly in theological issues (Solomon Ludwig Steinheim (1789–1866), Solomon Formstecher (1808–89), and Samuel Hirsch (1815–89), the academicians Zunz (1794–1886) and Steinschneider (1816–1907), and the "practical ideologists" Samuel Holdheim (1806–60), Abraham Geiger (1810–74), and Zacharias Frankel (1801–75). We shall examine here only the most influential of the practical ideologists, at least for Reform Judaism, Abraham Geiger, because, as Meyer states, "[f]or a long time, and to some extent still, [Geiger's] views remained the common coin of the Reform movement."[21]

We shall examine Geiger's thought especially as it relates to the development of Reform notions of the authority of the canon in terms of right and history. Initially, we must note that to call Geiger a theologian is rather an imprecise appellation. We need to qualify this term "theologian" somewhat, for Geiger did not write a comprehensive Jewish theology, nor did he seem especially concerned with speculation into the nature of God. Geiger's theology underwent constant development from its beginning during the nebulous period of the intellectual interregnum of the 1830s, when Reform thought went from halakhic reform to philosophic self-consciousness as displayed at the German conferences of the 1840s, to his last years in the 1870s. Geiger's thought, at least the part in which we are most interested, may be characterized as being concerned with the philosophy and meaning of history and the meaning and authority of texts, interests certainly subsumable under the rubric of "hermeneutics." He felt that, by a study of both Jewish history and the authoritative holy texts embedded in that history, Reformers would know how to proceed. As an historian and philosopher of history, he wanted to grasp the religious spirit of each age in order to understand his own and bring it into the future. In other words, he studied history in order to know how history worked as holy history, and in order to know what was required of him in the present day, or, as Geiger himself puts it, to be an "organ" of history.[22] The rabbi/scholar would not cut himself off from history or let history overcome him; he would rather use history as a means for knowing how to work with the tradition handed down to him.

For example, Geiger says:

> We have devoted ourselves to and have acquired the culture
> which mankind has developed during the course of thousands
> of years; but Judaism has preserved its eternal divine content in
> forms, most of which were the outcome of temporal conditions;
> they have therefore lived their day. This exterior must be
> refashioned, this form must be changed if Judaism is to
> continue to influence the lives of its followers in accordance

with its purpose and its power, and if it is to persist among the world forces in a manner worthy of its high destiny.[23]

Judaism was to be refashioned according to its own principles, which would be discovered scientifically. The practical work of Reform would be joined with the theoretical work of the scholar:

> Judaism must receive its scientific foundation, its truths must be clearly expressed, its principles must be probed, purified, established, even though they be not finally defined; the investigation into the justification and the authority of its sources and the knowledge of these are the constant object of study. Dependent upon this theoretical work is the practical purpose which keeps in view the needs of the community ... from this union of the theoretical and the practical will flow the insight into what rules of life are necessary, and which institutions and religious practices will serve indeed to improve the religious life, and which are moribund.... This knowledge of the true significance of Jewish doctrine and of the present must arouse to united effort all such as are sincerely interested, so that a transformation of Jewish religious practices in harmony with the changed point of view of our time may result, and awaken true inner conviction and noble religious activity.[24]

Geiger felt that those in his age had become "organs of history," with the job of developing in history that which had grown in history, sometimes "following the wheel of time," at other times "putting our hands to its transformation."[25]

Geiger argued that Judaism's historical changes, variety, and vicissitudes needed to be shown and understood. His study of history revealed to him four great epochs in the evolution of Judaism. The first period was revelation, the biblical period, ending approximately the fifth century BCE, when the Jewish people enjoyed a heightened perceptual awareness which allowed for direct apprehension of religious and ethical truth. The second period was the period of tradition, a period ending with the closing of the Babylonian Talmud, in the sixth century. In this period, the rabbis adapted and erected methods for the adaption of biblical law to the vicissitudes of Jewish life. Geiger called the third stage "rigid legalism," certainly betraying a bias. While Geiger, as a master of rabbinics himself, appreciated the rabbinic period with its rich complexity and flexibility of Jewish law and custom, he saw the period which lasted from the sixth until the eighteenth century as one of rigid codification, where the flexibility of the law and the creativity of rabbis were severely circumscribed. All that was handed down was to be obeyed, and there was no room for further refreshments of the law. Geiger and other Reformers saw this period of legalism as a perhaps necessary cultural armor during the great distress of the "dark ages."[26]

Geiger felt himself to be living in a new age, one of liberation and criticism. This did not mean a break with the past, but rather evaluation of the past, and reintroduction of the historical process in Jewish law and tradition. Geiger's historical theology and his reformist tendency were both evolutionary and organic; there would be no revolutionary break with tradition, nor any cutting off from the soil of the Jewish past. Geiger certainly had his adversaries to his left who came to be known as the radical Reformers, who did favor a radical break with the past and most Jewish life forms. His critics to the right included those who objected to too active a role in reshaping Jewish forms for the new age.

Jewish texts, for Geiger, were embedded in their historical moment. Their authority and validity could not be taken for granted in later historical ages (meaning of course, his own). The texts revealed, however, an inner continuity, not of halakhic authority but rather of its own creative spirit, which produces principles and moral ideals, in addition to law. Geiger's understanding of the ceremonial law is understandably connected to his notion of the authority of the texts. Just as the sacred texts, which were a revelation of the religious consciousness of a specific age, had authority in the present only if the community considered them viable in its religious life, so ceremonial law was seen as instrumental. Ritual was not eternally binding, but rather had to be meaningful, and should be a "tangible representation of the spirit."[27]

His later notions concerning revelation are of importance to us. The different sacred texts of Jewish history were evidence of Israel's genius for revelation, for being a receptacle for acts of divine enlightenment. Meyer states the following concerning Geiger's notion of revelation:

> Israel's task in the world was to preserve and propogate that message whose basic content remained unchanging, though its elaboration evolved from age to age. The message was sustained by the ongoing working of God's spirit in and through Israel. It was that spirit, divine in origin but human in expression, Geiger argued, which assured the continuity of Judaism even as it destined it ultimately to become the religion of humanity.[28]

What it meant for Judaism to be a religion of humanity is partly revealed in the statement of principles adopted at the Leipzig Synod in 1869. While Geiger did not write these words (they were submitted by

Ludwig Philippson), he was one of the vice-presidents of the Synod, and concurred with them:

> The synod declared Judaism to be in agreement with the principles of modern society and of the state as these principles were announced in Mosaism and developed in the teaching of the prophets, viz., in agreement with the principles of the unity of mankind, the equality of all before the law, the equality of all as far as duties toward and rights from the fatherland and the state are concerned, as well as the complete freedom of the individual in his religious conviction and profession.
>
> The Synod recognizes in the development and realization of these principles the surest pledges for Judaism and its followers in the present and the future, and the most vital conditions for the unhampered existence and the highest development of Judaism.
>
> The Synod recognizes in the peace of all religions and confessions among one another, in their mutual respect and rights, as well as in the struggle for the truth – waged, however, only with spiritual weapons and along strictly moral lines – one of the greatest aims of humanity.
>
> The Synod recognizes, therefore, that it is one of the essential tasks of Judaism to acknowledge, to further, and to represent these principles and to strive and work for their realization.[29]

A clearer statement regarding the connection between Reform Judaism and political liberalism would be hard to find. Geiger concurred in the idea that Judaism, as discovered and taught by Reform, held rationality, ethics, and justice at its core.

We can see from this brief look at one major Reform theologian the affinity between his understanding of history and his construal of the sacred text. For while the link with the Jewish tradition was certainly not to be broken, the link with the halakhah, that complete and self-justifying authority of traditional Jewish law, had been severed, for him necessarily and ineluctably. A new period of history had been entered. The period of legalism had ended, and the period of tradition would not return. Some new criterion or authority had to be worked out if the scholar who was also a practical theologian, an active Reformer, would know what to do. His knowledge of the intellectual and spiritual past would empower him with knowledge of what to do in the present. While Geiger opposed a careless cutting away at Jewish ritual, he did hold that Jewish forms and the authority that rested behind them had come into history at a certain time. Reason could and should criticize the traditional textual canon, because of the nature of the new age with its new conditions. In fact, the canon, that to which Jews ought to refer for guidance in the life of the faith community, is expanded to include history and reason, but without a set of clear hermeneutical rules by which history and reason are to be interpreted. Canon was Scripture not because it was direct, divine inerrant revelation but because it was a deposit of Israel's literary testimony which preserved the rational and ethical essence as well the historical vessels that carried that essence forward. The canon was construed to be about ethics, about rational faith, and ought to be interpreted to those ends. Embarrassments to (nineteenth-century German Jewish) rationality and ethics abounded, but that was due to the text's provenance in less enlightened and developed ages. The essence and ideals were sublime, even divine; the vessel was necessarily defective, necessarily because of the nature of history and evolution.

The nomos, the normative universe, we can infer from the above, is one where religious truth unfolds. Law is not eternally binding – it is a child of its own age. But the feel of the nomos in which the early Reformers thought is not one of an age among ages, but an apex, something of a denouement in the history of religion seeking its purest form in rationality and ethics. Later Reform thinkers, in Germany and North America, held that view unabashedly. Reform Judaism, by the late nineteenth century, gave way among some thinkers to a not always subtle messianism, but overall to a sense that Reform Judaism was that religion of reason and ethics, that Reform Judaism was the fulfillment, or at least the surest means toward it, of the biblical ideal.

❧ ETHICS, HISTORY, AND THE NOMOS ❧
OF REFORM JUDAISM

We see from our survey that the Reformers had a strong notion of the conventional versus the eternal; they sought to find out what was essential for Reform, and what was essentially dispensable. Conventions were only right for a certain circumscribed period of time, and when the world changed, the forms had to change as well. The religion of reason was at hand, and Reformers felt that history required rational reforms, so that Judaism could take its rightful place as the religion of the future.

The myth of early Reform consisted largely of the notion that morality is at the center of the religious life, that Judaism's historical forms are unnatural for the age at hand, and that history requires change. The special genius of Judaism, revelation, or morality, was to be carried forth for all humankind, the expanded faith community whom the canon now addressed, as if Judaism had its special task in the universal religion. The "telos", or eschatology (depending on whom one reads), was a world in which the universal religion of reason reigned, civic justice in the liberal state flourished, and the brotherhood of "man" was triumphant.

We notice, in this very powerful myth and eschatology, a lack of a specific Jewish content. Jewish forms could be judged by universal criteria. Jewish genius was seen to be ultimately in the service of all humankind; Judaism was seen to be in fundamental agreement with the tenets of modern liberalism. Forms themselves, that is, religions in history, had only intermediate value. The nomos of early Reform placed universalism at the center, setting into place problems that have vexed Reform ever since.

"Paideic" and "imperial" patterns of law and Reform philosophy

What notions of law and authority are generated by this depiction of the normative universe? In addressing this problem, we refer again to Robert Cover's "Nomos and Narrative" for more interpretive help, but this time to a different part of his argument. One of Cover's premises in that article is that the creation of legal meaning in the normative universe takes place in a cultural medium. The liberal state does not necessarily create legal meaning, in fact, it may have a stake in quashing some nomic communities. In other words, the state enforces the law, and has a stake in suppressing theories of meaning which would overthrow or delegitimize the state. As a way of understanding these opposing tendencies, Cover introduces the dichotomy of the "paideic" and the "imperial" patterns of what law means, reflected in two mishnayot from *Pirqei Avot* (1: 2 and 1: 18) and elaborated by Joseph Karo in his commentary, *Beit Yosef*, to *Tur, Choshen Mishpat* 1.

The first pattern, the "paideic," that of legal meaning, is exemplified by the world's standing on pillars of Torah, 'Avodah and Gemilut Chasadim. Torah refers to a body of precept and narrative. Cover describes 'Avodah (divine service) in terms of "personal education" but it might better be understood as volitional participation in the linguistic or ritual world with a consequent shaping of consciousness. Gemilut Chasadim (acts of loving-kindness) Cover describes as the working out of the law, meaning here, apparently, at the moral, interpersonal level.

The second pattern, that of legal power, called the "imperial," is exemplified by the world's standing on three other pillars: truth, justice, and peace. Cover tells us that this pattern is essentially universalistic and system-maintaining, composed of "weak" virtues necessary for the coexistence of worlds of "strong" normative meaning, those based on the paideic model. The imperial pattern is universalistic in that it can countenance a variety of "meanings," as long as none directly threatens the state itself. The "strong" forces, Torah, 'Avodah, and Gemilut Chasadim, "create the normative worlds in which law is predominately a system of meaning rather than an imposition of force."[30]

Cover suggests that these two cultural patterns may be seen as corresponding to the two aphorisms from the Mishnah. The first, world-creating one is called "paideic," as its center is a moral, spiritual, and communal teaching, and the second, world-maintaining one is called "imperial," as it suggests an empire consisting of sub-units of juridical and cultural autonomy.[31] This second pattern is universalistic, identifiable with modern liberalism, for a variety of reasons. Liberalism does not advocate an interpretation of life, or necessarily hold forth on what the good is, but rather sets up the apparatus by which a citizenry can pursue various notions of the good without resorting to violence. The universalism may also be found in liberalism's focus on formal justice as opposed to some specific theory of substantive justice.

Cover stresses that these two patterns are ideal types: "N[o] normative world has ever been created or maintained wholly in either the paideic or imperial mode."[32] Cover says that "any *nomos* must be paideic to the extent that it contains within it the commonalities of meaning that make continued normative activity possible."[33] The question is, how is any kind of security or harmony assured in the polynomic society? – here we have the imperial, system-maintaining pattern of law. "Truth, justice and peace" ensure that competing paideic communities can exist alongside one another, as long as certain commitments are made to the imperial virtues. I will argue below that Cover's typology sheds important light on the crucial tensions inherent in Reform philosophy.

Inherent tensions in early Reform philosophy

Cover's ideal patterns help us understand some of the inherent conflicts found in the nomos of early Reform Judaism. We see that the center of paideic nomos, the normative corpus, common ritual, and strong interpersonal commitments are weakened as Reform takes to its center a natural right theory of morals and justice and a natural law theory of history with its notions of progress and evolution. To put it in Cover's terms, we would say that Reform took the imperial virtues as its core, displacing the supremacy of the paideic virtues. Theoretically speaking, the canon and the common ritual were to be criticized by history and reason. Israel's telos was universal religion and the "brotherhood of mankind;" at the threshold of the religion of the future, strong interpersonal bonds among Jews could be seen as a mere temporizing measure until universal brotherhood had been achieved.

The world view which saw Judaism standing at a moment in history when change was required, mandated by Judaism's telos and the nature of the epoch, led itself to long-lived spiritual and intellectual quandaries. The Reformers' commitment to their understanding of Judaism and the future resulted in their changing not just Jewish laws but the whole idea of law in Judaism, for the halakhah was not in accord with the new reality. What exactly is authoritative in Reform, from a Jewish point of view (that is, aside from universal ethics, rationality, etc.), is highly in question.

In this context, we notice a strange twist to Cover's original distinctions. If the universal religion of reason takes the high ground in the paideic world of meaning, the former center of the paideic community, its Torah, slips perforce into the realm of power. Mendelssohn's thought would be a case in point. For Mendelssohn, the moral law and reason were categories of meaning, while Torah was (simply) the divine legislation; divine positive law.

From the liberal point of view, however, positive law gains its legitimacy only from the consent of the governed. Once the traditional rabbinate finally loses its coercive power, it would seem that the governed may choose to be subject to this positive law or not. Ritual observance becomes a boundary issue of obedience and consent, not the "common ritual" by which the community is bonded to its understanding of the holy.

A related problem has to do with the liberal critique of religious authority which intellectually justified assimilation into secular society, a critique which remained a central pillar of Reform in theories of authority. The Reformers took into their understanding of religion the liberal notion that the state exists at the pleasure of the citizens. The purpose of the state, according to liberal thought, is to regulate society for the benefit of the citizens, and to protect the rights of the citizens. The state has no right to interfere in the religious lives of the citizens. This moral prohibition against state authority interfering in religious matters, combined with the notion that the individual is the locus of religious authority, creates the ambience for the political or moral legitimation of religious reform. Religion, too, loses its power to coerce in matters of conscience, and in religion itself. Put epigrammatically, Reform is not inherently antinomian; it is inherently anarchic. In other words, Reform has trouble justifying *any* authority in matters of religious practice.

In general, then, Reform Judaism is partly a result of the Jewish discovery of both the liberal concept of the person and the citizen, and the rejection of the notion of the "subject." According to liberalism, a person has inalienable rights, rights which the state neither grants nor may justly deny. The notion "citizen" suggests, from a liberal perspective, a voluntary contract with the state, whose primary function is to protect and regulate the rights of its citizens. The notion of a "subject" is one where the individual has only perfect duties to the lord, no perfect rights. Mendelssohn saw the Jew as a subject of the "Torah-state," as it were, with perfect duties but no perfect rights vis-à-vis the authority of Jewish law. Jews ought to be free to live out their religious identity unmolested by and without discrimination from the liberal state, of which they are citizens, in a secondary sense. Politically speaking, for Mendelssohn the Jew is first a subject vis-à-vis Torah, and then person/citizen vis-à-vis the liberal state.

Reform theory seems to deny that Jews are primarily subjects of the Torah-state, but rather are also persons and citizens in that religious polity. As such, religion has no absolute claim over the Jew as "subject." The jurisdiction then becomes anything but clear – over what things does religion have authority? The Reformers saw themselves as Jews as they saw themselves in the liberal state, as full persons and only then as citizens, whose obligation to obey (conventional, ritual, temporal) law is weak at best.

As citizens of the state and now as Jews, their deepest moral category and commitment is that of the rights-endowed person. As persons, they have rights which they may wield against authority, including even the authority of Jewish law, especially since Jewish law had been reduced to a humanly constructed and historically conditioned convention. Judaism can only be "authoritative," if that word can be used any more, and can establish jurisdiction only through a paideic claim of meaningfulness, personal meaningfulness. Judaism loses its coercive force, and Jewish observance becomes purely voluntary, in a philosophic, not just sociologically descriptive sense. As a true political notion of subjecthood is lost, and traditional Jewish jurisprudence, especially in areas of civil law, falls away as well, what is left of Jewish law retains its jurisdiction only in a voluntaristic way.

Reform, then, may be understood in two ways: as a critique of the authority of Jewish law, and as a struggle for meaning, to form a paideia, for this age in the Jewish religion. But we find that the liberal critique and the struggle to find meaning are at odds. To couch this understanding in Cover's terms, we might say that Reform, which begins as a movement to reform the halakhah, is finally interested in the reformulation and reconstitution of the Jewish paideia. That paideia, however, had been reconceived in terms of the imperial virtues, which may be seen as finally inimical to the creation of meaning. The essence of Judaism as formulated by the Reformers does not appear to have been essentially Jewish. Reform originally meant reforming the paideia into a vessel consonant with the age. The age, however, allows for no authoritative vessel.

At this point, we can see the critical nature of the question of authority of traditional law, where this chapter began. The liberal forces at the center of the intellectual Reform world seem to be inimical to "strong" notions of legal or religious authority. The work of nineteenth-century Reform was to break from the traditional, halakhic understanding of Judaism, and provide a philosophic basis for that break. That break cleared the stage for the critical questions for the religious life facing Reform: What is the scope of the canon? What does God want from the faith community? How is God's will present in the canon? How does the canon teach and to what end? What is the nature of its authority over the faith community? Who interprets – how, and by what authority? We have seen that Reform philosophy, the Reform world view, clearly provided answers to those questions, answers which, however, laid down an inheritance for much perplexity and intellectual gnashing of teeth.

Reform's own philosophy, as articulated by early and later teachers, does give some solace to the perplexed. Reform understands that there is a core truth to religion which finds expression through historical paradigms. This expression is not found in a few decades, nor does it achieve refined articulation in just a few generations. Nineteenth-century German Reform provided the threshhold into a new understanding of the eternal covenant between God and Israel; new understandings had been achieved before in history, and they would be achieved again. From a Reform perspective, fidelity to the covenant requires tolerance of ambiguity as Reform thinkers form that understanding.

❧ NOTES ❧

This chapter is adapted from sections of my unpublished thesis for rabbinic school, *Authority and Canon in the Thought of Three Reform Theologians*, Hebrew Union College-Jewish Institute of Religion (Cincinnati, Ohio), 1990; and my unpublished doctoral dissertation, *The Jurisprudence of Personal Status in Reform Judaism: An Essay in Normative Hermeneutics*, University of Southern California (Los Angeles, California), 1992.

I am most indebted to my friend, teacher, and doctoral dissertation chairperson Ronald Garet of the USC Law Center for his inspired, albeit close to the chest, introduction into natural law theory, studies which form the basis of the thoughts presented here. I thank as well my teachers Stephen Passamaneck and Barry Kogan of HUC-JIR for their meticulous readings of earlier versions of this chapter. Their critiques have been invaluable. The arguments presented here, however, especially any errors or excesses, are entirely my own. I especially thank my friend and teacher David Ellenson for his introduction to and guidance in the field of study.

I would like to dedicate these thoughts to those who study and davven with me here in Los Angeles. The ideas presented here ought to be pretty familiar to them.

1 An historiographic account of the philosophers and philosophic context of Reform have been lucidly and economically presented in Michael Meyer's by now standard *Response to Modernity*, 1988.

2 This term, "normative hermeneutics," was extensively developed by Ronald R. Garet in his 1985 article, "Comparative Normative Hermeneutics: Scripture, Literature, Constitution." Garet himself has been influenced by the work of the late Robert Cover, especially his 1982 article *"Nomos* and Narrative," a work which has been important in the preparation of this chapter, as well. Also important for this methodological section was David Kelsey, *The Uses of Scripture in Recent Theology*, 1975.

3 In hermeneutical studies, the word "text" can be understood widely – history can be a text, a dream can be a text, etc.

4 Max Weber, "The Social Psychology of World Religions," chapter in *From Max Weber: Essays in Sociology*, translated and edited by H. H. Gerth and C. Wright Mills (New York 1946, paperback reprint, 1981), p. 280, quoted in Garet 1985, p. 45 n. 14.

5 Finley 1990, chapter 2.

6 Garet 1987, p. 1802 n. 7.

7 Ibid. p. 1802.

8 For an assessment of how current natural law thinking might be expressed in adjudication, see Michael Moore, "A Natural Law Theory of Interpretation," *Southern California Law Review* 58: 2 (January 1985).

9 See chapters 5 and 6 in Strauss 1953.

10 Quoted in Breisach 1983, p. 205.

11 Ibid.

12 Ibid., p. 206.

13 Ibid.

14 Ibid.

15 For Breisach's comments on Herder, see ibid., p. 223.

16 Collingwood 1945, p. 135.

17 Ibid., p. 135.

18 Meyer 1988, p. 64.

19 Ibid., pp. 19, 65.

20 Ibid., p. 65.

21 Ibid., p. 99.

22 Ibid., p. 91.

23 Abraham Geiger, *Allegemeine Zeitung des Judentums*, 8 (1844) p. 87, cited in Philipson 1907, p. 62.

24 Geiger, in *Allegemeine Zeitung des Judentums*, 9 (1845), 340, cited in Philipson 1907, p. 67.

25 Philipson 1907, citing Geiger, p. 67.

26 For Geiger's periodization, see Wiener 1962, part 3.
27 Meyer 1988, p. 96.
28 Ibid., p. 99.
29 *Verhandlung der ersten israelitischen Synode zu Leipzig* (Berlin, 1869), p. 62, cited in Philipson 1907, pp. 412–13.
30 Cover 1983, p. 12.
31 Ibid., pp. 12–13
32 Ibid., p. 14.
33 Ibid.

❧ BIBLIOGRAPHY ❧

Texts

Breisach, E. (1983) *Historiography: Ancient, Medieval and Modern* (Chicago: University of Chicago Press).
Hume, D. (1969) *A Treatise on Human Nature*, in *British Moralists*, edited by D. D. Raphael (Oxford: Clarendon).
Kant, I. (1959) *Lectures on Ethics*, translated by L. W. Beck (Indianapolis: Library of the Liberal Arts).
Mendelssohn, M. (1983) *Jerusalem, or, On Religious Power and Judaism*, translated by A. Arkush (Hanover: Brandeis University Press and University Press of New England).
Philipson, D. (1907) *The Reform Movement in Judaism* (New York: Macmillan).

Studies

Collingwood, R. G. (1945) *The Idea of Nature* (London: Oxford University Press).
—— (1956) *The Idea of History* (London: Oxford University Press).
Cover, R. (1983) "The Supreme Court, 1982 Term – Forward: *Nomos* and Narrative," *Harvard Law Review* 97:4; 4–68.
Finley, M. (1990) *Authority and Canon in the Thought of Three Reform Theologians*. Unpublished rabbinic thesis, Hebrew Union College-Jewish Institute of Religion, Cincinnati.
Garet, R. R. (1985) "Comparative Normative Hermeneutics: Scripture, Literature, Constitution," *Southern California Law Review* 58:1; 35–134.
—— (1987) "Meaning and Ending," *Yale Law Journal* 96:8; 1801–24.
Kelsey, D. (1975) *The Uses of Scripture in Recent Theology* (Philadelphia: Fortress).
Meyer, M. A. (1988) *Response to Modernity: A History of the Reform Movement in Judaism* (New York and Oxford: Oxford University Press).
Strauss, L. (1953) *Natural Right and History* (Chicago: University of Chicago Press).
Wiener, M. (1962) *Abraham Geiger and Liberal Judaism: The Challenge of the Nineteenth-Century*, translated by E. Schlochauer (Philadelphia: Jewish Publication Society).

CHAPTER 28

The ideology of Wissenschaft des Judentums

David N. Myers

The first circle of university-trained professional historians, members of the Verein für Cultur und Wissenschaft der Juden, assembled at a most anxious moment in history. In the second decade of the nineteenth century, a strong conservative tide swept Prussia and other German states following the defeat of Napoleon and the Congress of Vienna; among the prominent targets of this backlash were Jews, who had been partly emancipated in 1812, and yet whose demand for total "liberation" engendered hostility and resentment in both popular and elite strata of society. Anti-Jewish fulminations issued from the mouths of well-known intellectuals and academics, some of whom instructed the young Jewish scholars in university lecture halls.[1] The sharp polemics of these figures served as backdrop to a more violent expression: the Hep! Hep! riots of 1819 which broke out against Jews first in Bavaria, and then spread throughout Germany.

The Hep! Hep! riots undermined the incipient sense of security and confidence which German Jews had begun to develop. But the anxiety felt by this generation of German Jews was not fueled only by the threat of physical violence or by impudent rhetoric. Perhaps more troubling was a deep existential concern: would Jews and Judaism have a meaningful function to play in the modern age? Indeed, in a post-Enlightenment world where religious difference need no longer act to distinguish one group from another, would Jews find a sufficiently compelling rationale to continue their ongoing existence as a discrete collectivity?

This question lay at the heart of the Verein für Cultur und Wissenschaft der Juden (Society for the Culture and Scientific Study of the Jews), which first assembled in Berlin in November 1819. One of the founding members of the Verein, J. A. List, asked with brutal candor: "Why a stubborn persistence in something which I do not respect and for which I suffer so much?" (Ucko 1967, p. 326). In fact, earlier generations of modern Jews had already begun to pose this question.[2] Debate over the utility and malleability of Jews animated German Enlightenment discourse and polemics in the latter half of the eighteenth century. This debate prompted the leading German Jewish intellectual personality of that century, Moses Mendelssohn, to produce his famous exposition and affirmation of Judaism, *Jerusalem*, in 1783. Subsequent generations found it difficult to match Mendelssohn's exemplary, though delicate, balance between Jewish allegiance and philosophic openness, ritual observance and counter-normative critique of rabbinic authority. His disciples in the Jewish Enlightenment circles of Berlin, as well as his own children, responded to the question of the viability of Judaism in a way quite different from his – for instance, by calling for the reform of Jewish religious ritual or, more radically, by converting to Christianity. With increasing clarity, the post-Mendelssohn generations apprehended the terms of the social contract of Enlightenment: in order to gain societal acceptance and rights as citizens, Jews had to dilute, at times even abandon, their communal and religious bonds. The problematic features of this exchange became all the more apparent in the post-Napoleonic era of reaction, when Jewish political rights and social aspirations were subjected to new and unfavorable scrutiny.

At this ominous juncture, the founding members of the Verein proposed an agenda whose direction and scale were quite different from that offered by other Jews of their day. Through the illuminating powers of critical scholarship, they hoped to produce a comprehensive literary and historical account of the Jewish past. This account would not only serve to clarify the contours of the Jewish past; it might also yield a sharper image of Judaism's function and relevance in the present.

Actually, the imperative to provide such an account was first articulated shortly before the founding of the Verein by a young Jewish scholar named Leopold Zunz. Born into a traditional Jewish family in Detmold, Zunz reflected the extraordinary pace of change which German Jewry was experiencing in the early nineteenth century. Before the age of ten, he had neither read nor possessed a book written in the German language. But, over the next decade, Zunz graduated from a Jewish primary school run by Enlightenment devotees, was admitted as the first Jew to his local high school, and moved to Berlin to pursue studies at the newly opened university there (Schorsch 1977, pp. 109ff.). It was in Berlin that he encountered a group of Jews engaged in intense intellectual explorations. Initially, this group, calling itself the Wissenschaftszirkel (Scientific Circle), did not devote itself specifically to Jewish matters. Some years later, however, the same group of individuals reorganized as the Verein für Cultur und Wissenschaft der Juden, with an explicit program to pursue Jewish scholarly themes.

The conceptual (and linguistic) thread linking the earlier and later groups was Wissenschaft, connoting both scientific study and an all-encompassing scope of inquiry. Even before the Verein was formed, Leopold Zunz set out to demonstrate how this ubiquitous concept in German intellectual life could be applied to the study of the Jewish past. In May 1818, he published "Etwas über die rabbinische Literatur" in which he outlined in considerable detail the mission of "unsere Wissenschaft" (our science). "Our science," Zunz explained in this essay, must entail a comprehensive survey of rabbinic literature (Zunz 1875, p. 1). But rabbinic literature, for Zunz, was not confined to the classical sources of rabbinic learning – Mishnah, Talmud, and halakhic codes and commentaries. It also included writings in history, theology, philosophy, rhetoric, jurisprudence, natural science, mathematics, poetry, and music – indeed, the full expanse of cultural expression in Hebrew from biblical to modern times.

Zunz believed that the time had arrived to undertake a systematic study of this vast Hebrew literary legacy. Jews in his native Germany no longer read Hebrew with ease nor faithfully turned to Hebrew sources for spiritual or intellectual inspiration. Their cultural frame of reference was less determined by talmudic virtuosity than by Bildung, embodying a quest for German culture and self-refinement. At this point of transition, Zunz observed with barely a wisp of sentimentality, Wissenschaft "steps in demanding an account of *what has already been sealed away.*" No "new significant development" in rabbinic (that is, Hebrew) literature was to be anticipated; the canon had been closed (Mendes-Flohr and Reinharz 1980, p. 197). A humorous episode from Zunz's later life seems to confirm this belief. Once, a prominent Russian Jew visiting Berlin called upon Zunz, and introduced himself as a Hebrew poet. Zunz drew back and was said to have asked with incredulity: "When did you live?" (Stanislawski 1988, p. 123).

If this anecdote accurately reflected Zunz's belief that Hebrew literature was essentially an historical relic, what might have been his motivation for pursuing scholarly research of it? Was it the archeologist's attempt to reconstruct an ancient, though fossilized, civilization? In his programmatic essay of 1818, Zunz often evinced an air of detachment and a concern for scientific rigor that would appear to preclude any present-day application of his research conclusions. But there are also moments in his essay when Zunz exhibits another sensibility. His tone becomes passionate, even agitated, when he discusses the neglect of Jewish literary and cultural history by various groups: first, by traditionally observant Jews who regard critical methods of scholarship as sacrilegious; second, by secular Jews and others who find no value whatever in scholarly investigations of the past; and, third, by Christian scholars who have studied and distorted classical Jewish sources in order to validate their own religious tradition (Mendes-Flohr and Reinharz 1980, pp. 197–201).

And yet, the impulse to reclaim the Jewish literary past from incompetent or hostile hands was but part of Zunz's motivation. Traces of a deeper inspiration reside in the very formulation "unsere Wissenschaft" which Zunz used to designate his labors. At first glance, the phrase appears oxymoronic, for Wissenschaft implies a standard of scientific validation which requires a clear demarcation between subject and object.

At second glance, however, this seemingly ironic phrase underscores the existence of a pervasive instrumental quality to Jewish scholarship in Germany from the early nineteenth century. In his important programmatic essay of 1818, Zunz observed with cautious optimism that "the complex problem of the fate of the Jews may derive a solution, if only in part, from this science" (Mendes-Flohr and Reinharz 1980, p. 197). In other words, Wissenschaft could help to ameliorate the status of the Jews in this age of anxiety. A far more ebullient characterization came thirty-five years later from the scholar Zacharias Frankel, who described Wissenschaft as "the heart of Judaism through which blood flows to all the veins" (Brann 1904, Appendix 1).[3] From Zunz's time to Frankel's in mid-century, scholarship had emerged as the arena of discourse in which Judaism was to be defined. Indeed, it was Wissenschaft, Zunz averred, that could "distinguish among the old and useful, the obsolete and harmful, and the new and desirable" (Mendes-Flohr and Reinharz 1980, p. 197).

From its inception, Wissenschaft des Judentums marked the intersection of competing impulses and influences. The explicit desire to seal the canon of Hebrew literature stood in tension with the implicit aim of revitalizing Judaism for the present. These competing impulses created a divided personality for the Verein, whose members belonged to a generation nervously approaching an intellectual and existential crossroad. The members of the Verein were, after all, children of the Enlightenment who faithfully believed that Judaism was – and must be acknowledged as – a vital constituent of European civilization (Ucko 1967, p. 320). But their Enlightenment-inspired ecumenism (and the resulting apologia) did not wholly consume the Verein scholars. Chronologically and temperamentally, they were situated in a decidedly Romanticist era. Non-Jewish contemporaries, inspired by the example of J. G. Herder and J. Fichte, strove to grasp the essence of the German Volksgeist. This quest for a unique national spirit acquired depth through historicism, a perspective which emphasized the dynamic development of an individual historical organism. Those "children of the Enlightenment" who founded the Verein came of intellectual age just as this Romanticist historicism was taking root. Reflecting the imprint of the broader milieu, some spoke of the need to define the unique inner spirit and cultural heritage of the Jewish nation (Ucko 1967, p. 328). That is not to say that they, or German Jews generally, were precocious proponents of an independent Jewish nation-state. Politically, they continued to profess loyalty to Germany. And intellectually, Verein members envisaged a Jewish culture which fitted seamlessly into European society (Meyer 1967, p. 165).

But the stamp of Romanticism was clearly visible. Even Gershom Scholem, a fierce critic of Wissenschaft des Judentums, noted with begrudging admiration that Leopold Zunz's programmatic statement of 1818 demonstrated "a new attitude to the past, a celebration of the splendor and glory of the past in and of itself, an evaluation of sources in a new light ... and above all – a turn to the study of the people and nation."[4]

Zunz was especially committed to studying the literary past of the Jewish nation, for that past could serve as a "gateway to a comprehensive knowledge of the course of its [i.e., the nation's] culture throughout the ages" (Mendes-Flohr and Reinharz 1980, p. 198). Notable here is the search for holism, for comprehensive knowledge of the historical-cultural organism. This search informed the very notion of Wissenschaft which reigned in Germany in the early nineteenth century. An encyclopedia article from 1820 defined Wissenschaft as "the embodiment of knowledge systematically united into a Whole, in contrast to a mere aggregate" (*Allgemeine deutsche Real-Encyclopaedie* 1820, p. 761).

In fact, the aspiration for holism has a rich pedigree in modern German thought, receiving an important early formulation in Immanuel Kant's *Critique of Judgment*. Later, in the writings of Herder and Fichte, the search for holism became closely associated with the Romanticist mission of identifying an organic Volksgeist. By the second decade of the nineteenth century, the idea of the whole, animated by an absolute spirit, had become the province of G. W. F. Hegel. In this period, Hegel's influence was rapidly spreading throughout the German academic world, reaching Jewish intellectual circles such as the Verein. Eduard Gans, an exceptional young legal historian and guiding force behind the Verein, sought to replicate in his work "the simple and grand architectonic of a deeply-rooted edifice" which anchored Hegel's notion of Wissenschaft.[5] As a confirmed disciple of Hegel, Gans also sought to apply the master's model of historical dialectics to recent Jewish history. Thus, for Gans, the Jewish Enlightenment (Haskalah) was an antithetical response to a traditional Judaism whose animating ideal had been lost. But in its own antithetical excess, the Haskalah offered up only "scorn and disdain for the traditional without taking pains to give that empty abstraction another content" (Meyer 1967, p. 167). Though he offered this criticism of the Haskalah antithesis, Gans failed to provide a synthetic response, in large measure because he seemed to share Hegel's own intuition that Judaism was incapable of spiritual vitality.

Curiously, Gans' most memorable epitaph for Judaism is also one of the most enigmatic prescriptions for Jewish existence in modern times. In an address to the Verein membership in 1822, Gans expressed the hope, through a bewildering metaphor, that Jews "live on as the river lives on in the ocean" (Mendes-Flohr and Reinharz 1980, p. 192). If his subsequent life path be seen as commentary, then this cryptic statement should be read as a call for full social and cultural integration. For only a few years after serving as president of the Verein für Cultur und Wissenschaft der Juden, Gans chose the ultimate path of integration. In 1825, he converted to Protestantism, thereby overcoming the chief obstacle to a regular professorial appointment in Germany.

A more affirmative Jewish adaptation of Hegel came from another Verein member, Immanuel Wolf, in his 1822 essay, "On the Concept of a *Wissenschaft des Judentums.*" Along with Zunz's 1818 manifesto, Wolf's essay provided an intellectual foundation for the incipient Wissenschaft des Judentums. Notwithstanding the fact that both extolled the virtues of Wissenschaft, the men who authored the two programmatic statements had little in common. Zunz was a careful and methodical scholar who came to be regarded as one of the founding fathers of modern Jewish scholarship. Though he briefly studied with Hegel at Berlin, he deliberately eschewed Hegelian teleology in favor of a more mundane empirical method. Indeed, his formative scholarly training came not in philosophy but rather in classical philology at Berlin under August Boeckh and F. A. Wolf.

By contrast, Immanuel Wolf was a man of limited training and skill, according to what little is known of him. His scholarly résumé effectively begins and ends with the 1822 essay. Still, the essay has importance beyond Wolf's career. First, it signals the absorption of an Hegelian framework and vocabulary into the Verein circle. The quest for holism, so ubiquitous in German intellectual circles of the day, was everywhere evident. Wissenschaft des Judentums, Wolf declared, must capture "the systematic unfolding and representation of its object in its whole sweep" (Wolf 1822, p. 17). The object to be represented was Judaism, whose controlling idea was the unity of God. Wolf borrowed the Hegelian dialectical apparatus to argue that this grand idea had struggled with, and ultimately transcended, the material form of a nation to persist as a vibrant spiritual force. It was now the task of Wissenschaft to comprehend this grand idea.

Apart from its absorption of Hegelian idealism, Wolf's essay is important for exposing the competing impulses mentioned earlier as constitutive of modern Jewish scholarship. On one hand, Wolf believed it imperative to develop a scholarship that "is alone above the partisanship, passions, and prejudices of the base life, for its aim is truth" (Wolf 1822, p. 23). On the other hand, he regarded Wissenschaft as the "characteristic attitude of our time," a method and language which Jews must acquire in order to render themselves fit for the modern age. Wissenschaft was both purely scientific and instrumental, both critical method and medium of self-definition. These overlapping sets of functions emanated from a larger pair of aspirations underlying modern Jewish existence: the desire to attain intellectual (and professional) validation through appeal to non-Jewish standards; and the desire to reshape, without altogether obliterating, the visage of traditional Judaism.

Although Immanuel Wolf's text is one of the earliest and clearest articulations of these dual values, it is hardly the only one. The poles of Wissenschaft, as science and as source of identity formation, served as boundary markers for the generation of Wolf and Zunz, and have continued to do so for every subsequent generation of Jewish scholars. In light of this, one is surprised to discover the steadfast unwillingness of Jewish scholars to mediate between the poles, to recognize the fundamental tension between them, to undermine the sacred claim to reine Wissenschaft. But so powerful has been the guiding rhetoric of scientific objectivity as to repress any acknowledgement of tension. Indeed, acknowledgement of tension might yield an acknowledgement of prejudice.[6] And, for Jewish scholars, the price of such an acknowledgement has been too high to pay.

Why has the price been perceived to be too high? Part of the answer surely lies in the question of institutional power. Unlike contemporaneous non-Jewish scholars, German Jewish researchers desperately craved, but never achieved, privileged positions in a state-sponsored university system. They were not offered professorial appointments nor was their field of study introduced in the university curriculum. Despite this lack of acceptance by the German university system, Jewish scholars rarely wavered in their adherence to the ultimate standard of German (and gentile) validation: Wissenschaft. For them, Wissenschaft was more than scholarly method; it was an instrument of power through which to achieve social and intellectual acceptance. To question the utility or composition of this instrument was to diminish the capacity to reshape Judaism and, hence, block full entrance to German society.

The relationship of German Jewish scholars to institutional power mirrored the position of the broader German Jewish community in the nineteenth century. Initially encouraged by the promise of Emancipation, German Jews soon encountered formal and informal obstacles in their path. Their response was not wholesale self-abnegation but rather the construction of an identity and communal structure parallel to those of the surrounding gentile society. As David Sorkin has persuasively argued, Jews from the late eighteenth century formed a Jewish "subculture" which served as the primary repository of their group identity. This subculture offered a circumscribed public sphere where Jews could engage in activities from which they were excluded in the surrounding non-Jewish society (Sorkin 1988, pp. 5–6).

The realm of scholarship offers an illuminating example of this structural and psychological mechanism. Trained in German universities, but prevented from teaching in them, Jewish scholars faced professional and intellectual marginalization. In the first stage of Wissenschaft des Judentums, commencing with the establishment of the Verein, Jewish scholars operated without institutional support for their research. Leopold Zunz, for example, led a peripatetic existence through his forties, unable to find stable and satisfying employment. The most secure job he was able to hold, for a period of some twelve years, was as director of a Jewish teachers' seminary in Berlin. Similarly, Zunz's childhood friend and classmate I. M. Jost supported himself as a teacher and director of various high schools in Frankfurt. Even without stable employment or subvention for research, Zunz and Jost undertook monumental scholarly labors in their early careers. Zunz produced a major study of the history of Jewish homiletics, *Die gottesdienstliche Vorträge der Juden*; Jost, meanwhile, published a nine-volume history of the Jews, *Geschichte der Israeliten*, from 1820 to 1828. These efforts went far toward fulfilling Zunz's programmatic call for "sundry and good preliminary works," expansive syntheses which "take upon themselves to describe the literature of hundreds, even thousands of years" (Mendes-Flohr and Reinharz 1980, pp. 197–8). But they did not rest upon nor hasten the prospects of financial or institutional support from German universities. Instead, Jewish scholars of this era were pushed, through benign neglect or malicious intent, to the periphery of the German academic culture.

What concluded this first, one might say heroic, phase of Wissenschaft des Judentums was the creation of a modern rabbinical seminary in Breslau in 1854. The opening of the Breslau seminary not only addressed the growing demands for a modern, professionalized rabbinate in Germany. It also inaugurated a new era of institutional support for Jewish scholarship. Several decades later, two other seminaries, the Hochschule für die Wissenschaft des Judentums and the Orthodox

Rabbinerseminar, were opened in Berlin. They too emerged as centers of Jewish scholarly research and teaching. Nevertheless, several ironies regarding this process of institutionalization warrant elaboration. First, though the seminaries did provide a new home for critical research, they could employ only a fraction of the pool of qualified, university-trained Jewish scholars. Moreover, some of the most prominent Jewish scholars of the time, such as Leopold Zunz and the bibliographer Moritz Steinschneider, refused to accept appointments to the seminaries. Their opposition stemmed from the fear, as Steinschneider put it, that the seminaries would become "the new ghetto for Jewish scholarship" (Baron 1950, pp. 101–2). But this fear related to an even larger irony. The relegation of Jewish scholarship to rabbinical seminaries confirmed the circumscription of Jewish identity to the private or domestic sphere of religion. In the post-Enlightenment world, there were strong social pressures on Jews to regard their religion as a private confession of faith rather than as an all-embracing guide to social conduct.

The expected benefits of this privatization of religion – rapid integration into the majority culture – did not materialize instantly. To compensate for the unfulfilled promise, German Jews developed institutions within their subculture which simulated those in the surrounding society. For example, the rabbinical seminaries became institutions of higher learning, quasi-universities, where Jewish scholars could pursue their research interests.[7] In this regard, the seminaries created and inhabited a kind of *Jewish* public sphere (Habermas 1989, p. 72). Simultaneously, they symbolized, in paradoxical fashion, the privatization of Jewish identity. For one of their primary missions was to train a new breed of rabbis to cater to the diminishing religious demands of German Jews and, at least in part, to facilitate the accommodation of Judaism to modern German culture.

Straddling public and private domains, vocational and more purely academic functions, the seminaries manifested some of the central tensions of Wissenschaft des Judentums and German Jewish identity in the nineteenth century. To be sure, the three did not do so in identical fashion. In fact, each was home to a competing interpretation of, and a different denominational strain in, German Judaism. The first seminary in Breslau arose as an attempt to lift Jews out of the "currently wretched inner condition of Judaism" (Brann 1904, Appendix 1: i/iii). Toward that end, the founders of this seminary felt it necessary to reconcile the extremes of Jewish religious expression in their day – on one hand, a narrow-minded traditionalism which countenanced no historical inquiry or developmental perspective of Judaism, and, on the other, an increasingly bold Reform movement which advocated large-scale changes in Jewish ritual practice, as well as a model of a dynamically-evolving Judaism. The Breslau founders attempted to forge a middle ground which preserved a reverential attitude to the tradition, and still integrated critical modes of historical analysis. The foremost adepts of this "positive-historical" approach were the seminary's first director, Zacharias Frankel, and its first professor of Jewish history, Heinrich Graetz, whose eleven-volume history of the Jews represents one of the great achievements in nineteenth-century Jewish historiography.

With Breslau as the center of the new positive-historical movement, two competing institutions were established in Berlin in the 1870s to propagate alternative religious-ideological visions. The Hochschule für die Wissenschaft des Judentums was an institution whose very name was intended to evoke the exalted standards of a German academic institution; however, it was also the home of a Reform rabbinical seminary. It is no coincidence that the Hochschule hired, in the last years of his life, Abraham Geiger, the most distinguished Reform rabbi and scholar of his day. Geiger's research generated the image of an historical Judaism which had passed through various phases of development, most recently from an age of "rigid legalism" to one of emancipation and enlightenment (Wiener 1962, p. 168). His unabashed willingness to expose Judaism to critical analysis bespoke a spirit of free inquiry which inspired the Hochschule, and animated Reform innovations in Jewish theology and ritual.

The balance between free inquiry and religious devotion was quite different at the third major rabbinical seminary in Germany, the Rabbinerseminar founded by Rabbi Esriel Hildesheimer. According to Hildesheimer, the primary objective of the seminary was not a critical appreciation of Judaism in its historical development, but rather the "advancement of religious life" based on "knowledge of Biblical and Talmudic literature" (*Jahresbericht* 1873-4, p. 59). Its faculty consisted of eminent Orthodox rabbi-scholars such as David Zvi Hoffmann, Abraham Berliner, and Jakob Barth who instructed a scrupulously observant, "Torah-true" student body.

Separated by their respective ideological visions, the three seminaries emerged as competitors in a struggle to define the contours of German Judaism in the late nineteenth century. Consequently, it can be concluded that the institutionalization of Wissenschaft des Judentums in the seminaries did not yield a monolithic definition of Judaism. And yet, there were common features among them. For instance, the curricula of the seminaries were remarkably similar, emphasizing Talmud and rabbinic codes, Bible and medieval commentaries, and Hebrew and Aramaic languages. But an even most pervasive commonality must be noted. While there may have been differences in the degree of appreciation, scholars at all three seminaries professed allegiance to Wissenschaft. Ismar Schorsch has observed that, even at the Orthodox

Rabbinerseminar, the critical historical approach which anchored wissenschaftlich method was applied "no less assiduously than at Breslau or the Hochschule" (Schorsch 1975, p. 11). And indeed Esriel Hildesheimer insisted that the seminary's students be well acquainted with this scientific method (Ellenson and Jacobs 1988, p. 27). Wissenschaft had become the ubiquitous language of exchange (and polemic) among German Jewish scholars – from the Reform to the Orthodox extremes. This ubiquity also attested to the global predicament of Jewish scholars vis-à-vis the German academic establishment. Though they occupied an academic world of their own, the Jewish scholars remained university professors manqués. Lacking formal institutional acceptance, they turned again and again to Wissenschaft in the hope of demonstrating their scholarly merit, and achieving ultimate social validation.

The reliance on Wissenschaft sustained a pervasive discourse of objectivity in nineteenth-century Jewish scholarship. At the same time, another connotation of Wissenschaft, as a disciplinary whole, underwent an important transformation. There can be little doubt that the work of figures such as Frankel, Graetz, Geiger, and Hoffmann reprised the monumental scope and erudition of the Verein generation. Yet, those whom they trained in the seminaries eschewed the holism of the earlier generation, a development which had strong parallels in broader German historiographical circles (Iggers 1983, p. 131). This younger generation devoted itself not to massive syntheses but to smaller projects such as critical editions of classical religious texts. In the words of one observer, Jewish scholarship by late century had become "Kleinarbeit", research of extremely modest scope and aim (Elbogen 1922, p. 17).

Closely related to this narrowing topical focus was a concerted effort by turn-of-the-century Jewish scholars to introduce new methodologies, to expand inquiry beyond the predominant interest in philological and literary analysis to the study of social, economic, urban, and legal history. The twin effects of a narrowed focus and methodological expansion point to a new professionalization (and fragmentation) in the institutional phase of Wissenschaft des Judentums.

It is curious that a new professional ethos developed in rabbinical seminaries. It is especially curious given that one effect of the new professionalism was to forswear any instrumental function for Jewish scholarly activity. Evidence of this effect comes from Sigmund Maybaum, a professor at the Hochschule für die Wissenschaft des Judentums in Berlin from the late nineteenth century. In 1907, Maybaum declared:

> Wissenschaft des Judentums is, above all, not a Jewish Wissenschaft. . . . The subject stands opposite the object with

so little consciousness of, or connection to, his Jewishness that
we can not speak of a Jewish Wissenschaft or Jewish art. On
the contrary, so much depends on the object that Wissenschaft
des Judentums can be cultivated and advanced by non-Jews.

Maybaum 1907, p. 643

These remarks reflect a new consciousness that the dual functions
of Wissenschaft, as science and as agent of Jewish self-definition, could
no longer coexist. Intuitively aware of the tension between these two
features, Maybaum sought to resolve it. In his view, scholarship, even in
a seminary, could not serve as the tool of denominational partisanship.
Wissenschaft des Judentums was to be a purely academic pursuit, as
legitimately the domain of the non-Jew as of the Jew.

The institutional phase of Wissenschaft des Judentums, commencing in
the mid nineteenth century, was marked by the growing specialization,
fragmentation, and methodological expansion of Jewish scholarship. By
the early twentieth century, some important Jewish thinkers had begun
to call attention to the deficiencies of these processes. The most distinguished among them were neither historians nor philologists but rather
philosophers with a deep concern over the use and abuse of historical
method: Hermann Cohen and Franz Rosenzweig. Both thinkers had
become disenchanted with the dispassionate and detached nature of
Wissenschaft des Judentums in their day. Cohen, for instance, took a
position in complete opposition to Sigmund Maybaum. The study of
Judaism, he maintained in 1907, could "only be treated scientifically
[wissenschaftlich] by one who belongs to it with inner piety" (Cohen
1907, p. 12). His aim was to encourage Jewish scholars to re-establish
an intimate bond between their scholarly and spiritual interests. Franz
Rosenzweig, Cohen's one-time student at the Berlin Hochschule, shared
this aspiration. In 1917, Rosenzweig wrote a long letter to Cohen in
which he called for the creation of an Academy for Jewish Scholarship
(Akademie für die Wissenschaft des Judentums) in Berlin. This institution would employ a cadre of one hundred and fifty teacher-scholars
who would divide their time between pure research and communal
service (Rosenzweig 1918, pp. 23–4).

Rosenzweig's proposal emanated from the same sense of dissatisfaction which Cohen earlier expressed toward Jewish scholarship. Both
men favored a conscious acknowledgement of the link between academic pursuits and spiritual concerns in Wissenschaft des Judentums.
Only through such an acknowledgement, they believed, could the full
constructive potential of Jewish scholarship, as a vitalizing force of
Judaism, be realized. Their call was for an unapologetic recognition
of the instrumental value of Jewish scholarship – a value which had

been present from the time of the Verein in the early nineteenth century, though only episodically articulated in explicit fashion.

The antidote which Cohen and Rosenzweig proposed for the malaise of Jewish scholarship was the Akademie für die Wissenschaft des Judentums, which was formally established in 1919. Very quickly, this institution assumed a direction quite different from that imagined by Cohen or Rosenzweig; it became an institution of pure scholarly research (Myers 1992, p. 121). Notwithstanding this paradoxical development (which, incidentally, attests to the staying power of Wissenschaft qua science), Cohen's and Rosenzweig's criticism serves as a fitting culmination to a century of Jewish scholarship. Like the Verein generation, they felt a certain anxiety over the fate of Judaism in their day, an anxiety which they hoped could be ameliorated through a vital, holistic Wissenschaft des Judentums. But, unlike the first generation of researchers, Cohen and Rosenzweig also felt antipathy toward an historical method which contextualized and, to their minds, atomized Judaism. It was precisely this historicization of Judaism which led another prominent Jewish scholar of this century, Salo Baron, to call Wissenschaft des Judentums "the richest Jewish movement of the nineteenth century" (Baron 1937, p. 218).

In a way, both of these opposing perspectives bear elements of truth. Both Cohen and Rosenzweig, on one hand, and Baron, on the other, apprehended that Jewish scholars in the nineteenth century held loyalties to different masters. Divided between a commitment to redefining and reviving Judaism and obedience to scientific discipline, these scholars took refuge in the realm of Wissenschaft. Their significance is not limited to the annals of arcane scholarship. For they embody the tensions between centrifugal and centripetal impulses, between inner spiritual fulfillment and external social validation, that shaped the complex historical experience of modern German Jewry at large.

❦ NOTES ❦

1 Leopold Zunz, a founder of Wissenschaft des Judentums, briefly studied history with a leading anti-Jewish publicist, Friedrich Rühs, at the University of Berlin. After one semester, Zunz decided to stop because Rühs "writes against the Jews." Zunz's recollections are quoted in Meyer 1967, p. 158.

2 Anxiety over Jewish survival, either physical or spiritual, was hardly a modern innovation. The shattering experience(s) of exile – following the demise of the First and Second Temples and the expulsion from Spain (a kind of double exile) – engendered deep anxiety over the prospects of a continued existence for the Jewish people. In each of these generations, anxiety yielded creative reformulations of Judaism (such as Babylonian Judaism, rabbinism, Lurianic kabbalah, etc.).

3 See Frankel's statement in Appendix 1 of Brann 1904, p. i.

4 While noting these exemplary Romanticist features, Scholem maintained in 1944 that Zunz's program ultimately failed; it was the product of an assimilationist and apologetic generation, and not sufficiently devoted to "the building of the Jewish nation." See Scholem 1979, p. 156.

5 Gans acknowledged this desire in his foreword to a volume of Hegel's writings. G. W. F. Hegel, *Grundlinien der Philosophie des Rechts, oder Naturrecht und Staatswissenschaft im Grundrisse* (Berlin, 1840), p. vi, quoted in Reissner 1965, p. 59. More generally on Hegel's influence, see Wallach 1959, pp. 10–16.

6 Hans-Georg Gadamer argues that "[w]e must raise to a conscious level the prejudices which govern understanding," especially historical understanding. Gadamer 1979, p. 156.

7 The three seminaries did insist that students undertake studies at a German university leading toward a doctorate. Thus, professional scholarly training, especially in critical historical method, was also acquired in the universities. However, it was only in the seminaries that a student received broad and deep exposure to the classical sources of Jewish literature and history.

❧ BIBLIOGRAPHY ❧

Texts

Allgemeine deutsche Real-Encyclopaedie für die gebildeten Stände (1820) (Leipzig, vol. 10).

Brann, M. (1904) *Geschichte des Jüdisch-Theologishes Seminar (Fraenckel'sche Stiftung)* (Breslau: Schatzky).

Cohen, H. (1907) "Zwei Vorschläge zur Sicherung unseres Fortbestands," *Bericht der Grossloge für Deutschland U.O.B.B.: Festgabe (1882–1907)* 2 (March): 9–12.

Elbogen, I. (1922) *Ein Jahrhundert Wissenschaft des Judentums* (Berlin: Philo).

Graetz, H. (1853–76) *Geschichte der Juden von dem ältesten Zeiten bis auf die Gegenwart* (Leipzig: Leinier).

Jahresbericht des Rabbiner-Seminars für das orthodoxe Judenthum pro 5634 (1873–4), 1.

Maybaum, S. (1907) "Die Wissenschaft des Judentums," *Monatsschrift für Geschichte und Wissenschaft des Judentums* 51: 654–8.

Rosenzweig, F. (1918) *Zeits ists: Gedanken über das jüdische Bildungsproblem des Augenblicks an Hermann Cohen* (Berlin: Neues jüdisches Monatsheft).

Wolf, I. (1822) "Über den Begriff einer Wissenschaft des Judenthums," *Zeitschrift für die Wissenschaft des Judenthums* 1: 1ff.

Zunz, L. (1875) "Etwas über die rabbinische Literatur," *Gesammelte Schriften*, vol. 1 (Berlin: L. Gerschel).

Studies

Baron, S. W. (1937) *A Social and Religious History of the Jews*, vol. 2 (New York: Columbia University Press).

—— (1950) "Moritz Steinschneider's Contributions to Jewish Historiography," in *Alexander Marx Jubilee Volume* (New York: Jewish Theological Seminary).

Ellenson, D. and R. Jacobs (1988) "Scholarship and Faith: Rabbi David Zvi Hoffmann and his Relationship to *Wissenschaft des Judentums*," *Modern Judaism* 8.1: 27–40.

Gadamer, H.-G. (1979) "The Problem of Historical Consciousness," in *Interpretive Social Science*, edited by P. Rabinow and W. M. Sullivan (Berkeley: University of California Press).

Habermas, J. (1989) *The Structural Transformation of the Public Sphere*, translated by T. Burger (Cambridge, MA: MIT Press).

Iggers, G. G. (1983) *The German Conception of History: The National Tradition of Historical Thought from Herder to the Present* (Middletown: Wesleyan University Press).

Mendes-Flohr, P. and J. Reinharz (eds) (1980) *The Jew in the Modern World* (New York: Oxford University Press).

Meyer, M. A. (1967) *The Origins of the Modern Jew* (Detroit: Wayne State University Press).

Myers, D. N. (1992) "The Fall and Rise of Jewish Historicism: The Evolution of the *Akademie für die Wissenschaft des Judentums* (1919–1934)," *Hebrew Union College Annual* 63: 107–44.

Reissner, H. G. (1965) *Eduard Gans: Ein Leben im Vormärz* (Tübingen: Mohr (Paul Siebeck)).

Scholem, G. (1979) "Mi-tokh hirhurim 'al Chokhmat Yisrael," in *Chokhmat Yisrael: heiybetim historiyim u-filosofim*, edited by P. Mendes-Flohr (Jerusalem: Shazar Center).

Schorsch, I. (1975) "Ideology and History in the Age of Emancipation," in *Heinrich Graetz: The Structure of Jewish History and Other Essays*, edited by I. Schorsch (New York: Jewish Theological Seminary).

—— (1977) "From Wolfenbüttel to Wissenschaft: The Divergent Paths of Isaak Marcus Jost and Leopold Zunz," *Leo Baeck Institute Year Book* 22: 109–28.

Sorkin, D. (1988) *The Transformation of German Jewry, 1780–1840* (New York: Oxford University Press).

Stanislawski, M. (1988) *For Whom Do I Toil?: Judah Leib Gordon and the Crisis of Russian Jewry* (New York: Oxford University Press).

Ucko, S. (1967) "Geistesgeschichtliche Grundlagen der Wissenschaft des Judentums," in *Wissenschaft des Judentums im deutschen Sprachbereich: Ein Querschnitt*, edited by K. Wilhelm, vol. 1 (Tübingen: Mohr (Paul Siebeck)).

Wallach, L. (1959) *Liberty and Letters: The Thoughts of Leopold Zunz* (London: East and West Library).

Wiener, M. (ed.) (1962) *Abraham Geiger and Liberal Judaism: The Challenge of the Nineteenth Century* (Philadelphia: Jewish Publication Society).

CHAPTER 29

Samson Raphael Hirsch

Harry Lesser

Blessed be God, who in His wisdom created Kant.

Isaac Breuer (grandson of Hirsch)[1]

Samson (ben) Raphael Hirsch (1808–88, chief rabbi of Oldenburg) was one of the main defenders of Orthodoxy in Germany in the nineteenth century. He took very seriously the critique provided by Reformers, and argued that on the contrary there was no need for a reform of religion, only of the Jews who constituted it. He opposed the separation of Orthodox and Reform Judaism, but came reluctantly to regard it as inevitable. Although he was a staunch defender of Orthodoxy he was by no means an enemy of secular subjects as part of the education of Jews, and also advocated the use of Hebrew as a means of communication between Jews in the Diaspora. In many ways he is the founder of that form of Orthodoxy which seeks to reconcile the letter of the law with the possibility of living a modern life, and as such he has been very influential.

The first question to be considered is whether it is appropriate to regard Hirsch as a philosopher. Certainly he was not a theologian: his concern was with Torah, with law and observance, and "nothing could be more senseless ... than to call the Torah 'theology'" (quoted in Grunfeld's introduction, 1962, p. xlix). Indeed, Hirsch has, either implicitly or explicitly, five arguments against either trying to do theology or regarding Torah study as theological. These are first, that theology as a systematic science is, like any other transcendent metaphysics, impossible; second, that human thoughts about God are necessarily vastly inferior to divinely revealed legislation; third, that theology, unlike Torah, has no relevance to our practical duty; fourth, that the way to come to know God is to study his thoughts, not human thoughts; fifth, that to call Torah "theology" would imply that it was the province of study of a special group of theologians, rather than being "the common property of every cottage and every palace in Israel" (ibid.).

Nor was Hirsch essentially a religious apologist. His principal work, *Horeb*, is an exposition of the commandments and the reasons for them, not a justification; and the divine origin of the written and oral Torah is presupposed, not argued for. It is true that one of Hirsch's main aims was to combat secularism and Reform Judaism, and that he thought that a proper exposition would convince any unprejudiced person that authentic Judaism without Torah was a contradiction in terms. It is also true, as we shall see, that, though he thought it senseless to try to produce evidence of the Torah's divine origin, he had nevertheless philosophical reasons for believing in it. But essentially, Hirsch's work is an explanation of what Judaism is, of what the duties of a Jew are, in the belief that anyone who properly understands this will inevitably at least try to perform them: and explanation, even with this intention, is still explanation rather than apologetics.

Again, Hirsch is not simply a moralist. His primary concern is practical; but then ethics has normally been regarded by philosophers as a practical subject – the contrary view can be found, and was popular with some mid-twentieth-century analytic philosophers, but it is a minority view. Moreover, he is concerned not just to give a systematic account of a Jew's duties and the reasons for them but also to explain the reasons by using not only all the resources of the biblical text and of Jewish tradition but also the resources of philosophy. And philosophy is used not, as a moralist might use it, as a source of arguments that sound convincing, but as a systematic understanding of the nature of law, ethics, and religious revelation.

This understanding derives very largely from Kant, though Hirsch disagrees with Kant at certain critical points. Essentially, Hirsch was convinced of the truth of two things, that the Torah is divine in origin and that the supreme end of ethics and politics should be the moral and intellectual development of the whole human race. Hence, unlike those orthodox thinkers who were disposed to damn the Enlightenment and all its works, he saw the values of Judaism and of the Enlightenment as being the same. Consequently, if Kant is taken to be the supreme Enlightenment philosopher, it is appropriate to expound Judaism within a Kantian framework. Hirsch had probably three reasons for thinking this: he believed that Kant's philosophy was largely true, he believed that it provided a way of making Judaism accessible to the thinking people of his day, and he believed that it could be used to combat some of the major intellectual and moral errors of the time. That he thought this about Kant's moral philosophy is not surprising. It may seem more remarkable that he valued the critical epistemology so highly. There were various reasons for this, some expressed by his grandson Breuer in the passage from which the opening quotation is taken (*Horeb*, pp. xxiv-xxv). First, while the shift from other-worldly to this-worldly preoccupations, which began with the Renaissance and continued with the Enlightenment, was seen by Hirsch and Breuer as being in itself thoroughly desirable, it contained the great danger of producing a quite unwarranted confidence in the power of the human intellect. Kant's demonstration of the limits to what we can know, of the impossibility of transcendent metaphysics and of having any knowledge of things-in-themselves, was seen as a healthy corrective to this intellectual pride.

More precisely, we may say that, if Kant is right, we can have no knowledge of anything beyond human experience. This has three important consequences. First, speculative theology, as we have noted already, is impossible. This was a welcome conclusion for Hirsch, since for him religion is about action, not speculation. Second, we can have no knowledge of what the natural world is like in itself, as opposed to how it appears to human experience: hence materialism, or the view that the world of nature and science is the only world, and the only reality is physical reality – one of the main challenges to any religious view – is as "metaphysical" and unprovable as anything in theology. Third, no religious or moral principles can be logically derived from the existence of the physical world or from the qualities it exhibits to our experience.

This all comes from Kant's critical philosophy. From his moral philosophy comes the conclusion that when reason is used practically, that is to discover and act on truths of morality, it can have a knowledge of things-in-themselves which is impossible when it operates purely theoretically. Hence we reach the interesting conclusion that the only possible religious revelation to beings such as us would be moral revelation, that is something like the giving of the Torah – so far from the moral and religious being different, and having to be brought together, as some have thought, the only intelligible kind of religious insight is a moral one. (Hirsch does not say this explicitly, but seems to presuppose it.)

But Kant's conception of moral revelation is very different from Hirsch's (supposing either were to use the expression). The difference relates both to the nature of morality and the nature of revelation. For Kant morality is essentially the fulfillment of duties to oneself and to other people, which is to be done from the motive of duty. The point of the moral life lies in the production, as far as is possible, of a combination of human perfection and happiness (Kant, Introduction to Part 2 of the *Metaphysics of Morals*). But the performance of a duty does not relate to this as means to an end, but rather as part to whole:

the carrying out of each of one's various moral duties is already part of the end itself, not something that leads to it.

As regards knowing what one's duties are, reason alone, according to Kant, is sufficient for this, if used properly. Hence a moral revelation could tell us only what we know already or at least were capable of knowing: it might be psychologically effective in making us more ready to do our duty but could not be strictly necessary. Indeed, the only way of knowing that it was a genuine revelation would be by checking its context against our existing moral knowledge – Kant says as much in the *Groundwork of the Metaphysics of Morals* 408, though as a Christian he speaks of the example of Jesus rather than the revelation of Sinai: "Even the Holy One of the Gospel must be compared with our ideal of moral perfection before He is recognized as such."

With much of this Hirsch was in sympathy. Kant's assertion (*Metaphysics of Morals* 386) that "Man has a duty of striving to raise himself from the crude state of his nature, from his animality, and to realize ever more fully in himself the humanity by which he alone is capable of setting ends" has many parallels in Hirsch's work: indeed he sees God's plan for humanity (humanity, not Israel alone) as the development from the physical and animal to the intellectual, moral, and spiritual, and the Torah as the way of bringing this about. But there are important differences. First, the distinction between duties to oneself and duties to others is not really present in Hirsch. There are certainly duties that concern what we owe to other people, whether those be duties of justice (mishpatim) or love (mitzvot), and other duties which essentially concern ourselves, such as the cultivation of the right thoughts and feelings about God, Torah, and our fellow creatures, the duties that Hirsch calls *Toroth* because of their fundamental importance. But all these are to be performed by a person, not simply as an individual, but as a Jew and a human being, a Mensch-Jisroel (*Horeb*, section 1, chapter 1, paragraph 4, and many other places).

For Hirsch morality and intellectual advance are essentially a communal enterprise. Any moral achievement, or morally right action, both furthers this end and is part of it. Moreover, the agent belongs to various communities, each part of a wider one. In his *Commentary on Exodus*, quoted by Grunfeld (1962, p. xlvi), Hirsch distinguishes between Judaism and religion as ordinarily understood. Ordinarily, one can distinguish between religious and secular communities: churches, etc. are formed by God, but nations and peoples are independent of Him. But, for Judaism, "God founds not a church but a nation; a whole national life is to form itself on Him." Connected with this is the concern of the Torah not only with the inward experience but equally, or more, with outward action: the Torah is addressed "to man in his totality," and "unlike 'religion,' the Torah is not the thought of man, but the thought of God" (Hirsch, "The Festival of Revelation and the Uniqueness of the Torah," 1962, p. xlvii).

Interestingly, Hirsch is here agreeing with Kant's view, expressed in *Religion within the Limits of Reason Alone*, that Judaism is not a religion (though Kant confined his comments to the Judaism of the Old Testament). He does so for the same reason as Kant: both take Protestant Christianity as the archetype of a religion, and both observe that Judaism, with its primary emphasis on communal action rather than individual experience, is something very different. But for Kant this makes it something inferior to "religion," for Hirsch something very much better.

Kant and Hirsch differ in their view both of morality and of the relation between God and humanity. For Kant both essentially involve the individual and their duties (which of course include duties to others), and religion involves, in essence, only the "inner" individual – outwardly, religion involves of necessity only moral duties, and anything else, whether worship, ritual, or observance, exists only to promote the right inner attitude, and is otherwise undesirable. For Hirsch both are addressed to the individual as a member of a community, as a member of the human race, and ultimately as part of the world-order: one might suggest, despite Hegel's ignorance of and contempt for Judaism, that Hirsch's approach is here Hegelian rather than Kantian. It may be noted that, though this approach of Hirsch's is essentially Jewish, and obviously derives from his Judaism, it is logically independent of it: a secular humanist could make an analogous criticism of Kant, and take a view of morality that is communitarian rather than individualist.

This conception of morality has the consequence that a number of distinctions made by philosophers and religious writers no longer apply, or else apply in a new way. I mentioned above that Hirsch does not really have a distinction, as Kant does, between duties to oneself and duties to other people, since all one's duties are performed as a Mensch and, if one is a Jew, as a Mensch-Jisroel. Hence there are no duties only to oneself: first, because anything one does may affect one's fellow Jews, one's fellow human beings, and the whole world-order, and second, and more strongly, because in any case anything done by part of the world-order is done by the whole. Thus in condemning revenge (*Horeb*, section 89), Hirsch quotes with approval the sages' comment "If your left hand wounds the right hand, shall the right hand out of revenge wound the left hand?" and adds "Are we not all members of one entity ... limbs of one body?" Also, on suicide he says (section 62), in contrast to Kant, "Is it not self-deception to think that suicide is a crime only against God and yourself, and not also a crime against your fellow-creatures? . . . do you not deprive the world of its justified demands when you destroy your existence here?"

We should also note that Hirsch has rejected Kant's view that, since God needs nothing from us, we have no duties towards him, so that religious duties are really duties to ourselves. For Hirsch God does need humanity, and this is explained in his *Commentary on Genesis* 9: 26–7: "At the moment that God made the fulfilment of His Will on earth dependent on the free decision of Man, He said to them . . . 'bless Me . . . bless my work, the achievement of which on earth I have laid in your hands'." If the world can be made as God wishes it to be only by human activity, that activity, when as it should be, actually benefits God: hence, Hirsch points out, we do not only promise and thank God but actively bless him. One could indeed say that, though the emphasis varies, all our duties are both to God, ourselves, our fellow humans, and the world as a whole.

In this respect, there is no fundamental difference between what is required from humans in general and what is required from Jews in particular. Different communities have different duties, but, since they all have the aim of promoting spiritual and ethical advance, one cannot say that some duties are moral and therefore universally binding and others merely the ritual requirements of one particular group. Rather, for Hirsch, there is an overall divine plan, involving not only humanity but also all of nature: human beings are special in that they can choose whether or not to obey, and Jews have a special task among human beings, but in all cases there is a divine law to be obeyed and a contribution to the overall plan: "the great purpose of God is only then fulfilled when each one joyfully and faithfully carries out the law and the calling that God has appointed for *him*, and in such fulfilment makes his contribution to the whole" (*Commentary on Genesis* 1: 11). Grunfeld amplifies the point, but is no doubt faithful to Hirsch, when he comments "each plant and each animal, every man and every nation, have their peculiar task, which is to bring to perfection . . . their particular kind of created entity" (Hirsch 1962, 2: 579).

From this follows Hirsch's insistence that the commandments of Torah cannot be divided into moral and ceremonial. It is true that he regards the purpose of some laws as obvious, and of others as harder to understand; and it is also true that he makes extensive and detailed use of symbolism in his explanation of the various laws. But his use of symbolism is very different from the way it was used by the non-Orthodox, and even from some of the ways it has been used by "Orthodox," thinkers. Admittedly, Hirsch shares with all mainstream Jewish thinkers the views that all theories of the purposes of the mitzvot are mere human speculation, which may be right or wrong, and that the mitzvot must in any case be obeyed whether one has found a good reason for them or not. But he differs both from the thoroughgoing rationalists and from the more radical mystics. He differs from the mystics in seeing nothing "sacramental" in the performance of mitzvot, nothing that has cosmic effects other than those on the minds of the participants and witnesses: admittedly, if Grunfeld is right (Hirsch 1962, p. lxxiv), this view of mitzvot as mystery rites was held, even among the mystics, only by a few essentially heretical groups. He differs from the rationalists, first, in regarding *all* the details of the mitzvot as being significant, so that his symbolism is much more thoroughgoing and worked out in detail. Second, the performance of a symbolic act does not only have a pedagogic effect, of reminding those who perform or watch of their duties or of events in Jewish history or of the relation between God and humanity: it is also in itself, if done in the proper frame of mind, a way of advancing spiritually and intellectually, valuable in itself as well as for its effects. One might say that, whereas for Kant the point of prayer lay in its production of moral improvement, for Hirsch to pray *is* to improve morally and spiritually. Hence – though Hirsch does not quite put it this way – *every* mitzvah is a moral duty.

One may summarize Hirsch's position so far as follows. He agrees with Kant that transcendent metaphysics and speculative theology are impossible, that knowledge of the physical world as it is in itself is impossible, that morality cannot be inferred from a study of the natural world, and that human reason is able in the practical, that is, moral, sphere, to obtain a knowledge of things-in-themselves that is otherwise impossible. He also agrees that morality can be expressed in imperatives, in instructions as to what to do and what not to do, that the aim of moral behavior is human happiness and human intellectual and spiritual advance, and that right actions performed for the right motive are valuable in themselves, as being part of the end, independent of their consequences.

But Kant viewed ethics as being addressed to people as individuals, as consisting of universal principles (with their application to specific circumstances), and as operating only with regard to human nature: cruelty to animals, for Kant, is wrong only because it leads to cruelty to people. In contrast, Hirsch sees ethics as addressed to people as members of a national community, members of the human race, and members of the cosmic order. Hence it must include instructions on how to treat non-human nature, both living and inanimate, and also, if necessary, special obligations for particular communities, to aid their particular development and contribution. One could say that, for Kant, only rational nature is of intrinsic value, and only the development of such nature is good in itself, whereas, for Hirsch, everything that exists is of value, should be helped to develop, and makes its own contribution to the whole. Moreover, when this is done by free human agency, this actually benefits God as well as the created universe, by furthering his purposes.

Even more importantly, whereas Kant saw ethics as requiring moral autonomy and "self-legislation," and the human mind as capable of working out for itself which principles can rationally be given in self-legislation, Hirsch sees us as needing a moral revelation from outside. For if we are imperfect morally, and need to develop – as Kant certainly holds – we must be incapable of working out an entire correct morality for ourselves. From all this three things follow, which are implicit throughout Hirsch's philosophy. First, any religious revelation would have to be a practical one, concerned essentially with how we should live: it could not be theological or metaphysical. Second, we need such a revelation in order to live properly, and cannot do this only through our own resources. Third, any such revelation would have to be addressed to a particular community, and to include laws specifically for that community, as well as more universal laws.

In other words, Hirsch has argued, by implication, that if God exists and if he has revealed himself, then the revelation would have to be something like the Torah as we have it: if Torah contains many things which are surprising and many things that relate to Jewish life rather than universal human life, that is exactly what one should expect. For only by developing as a distinctive community can a group contribute to the development of humanity as a whole: Jews do not need to throw off their distinctiveness and join the human race (as, at the time, many Germans and some Jews were maintaining), but contribute to human advance precisely by developing the distinctive Jewish life to the full. Hence, for a Jew the way to serve the Enlightenment, and the way to play a "world-historical" role, lies precisely in the study and practice of Jewish tradition.

But this argument could show only that Torah might be divinely inspired, not that it actually is. Indeed, Hirsch says in a passage quoted by Grunfeld (Hirsch 1962, p. 1) that the only ground for this belief is our trust in tradition; and he points out that Jewish oral tradition has to be self-validating: "it refuses any documentation by the written Torah, which, after all, is only handed down by the oral tradition and presupposes it everywhere." As to why we should accept tradition, Hirsch makes two points, one in this passage and one in the *Commentary on Exodus* 19: 4. In the Commentary he points out that tradition begins with two historical events, the Exodus from Egypt and the lawgiving on Sinai, which were "experienced simultaneously by so many hundreds of thousands of people," so that if one accepts the tradition one is accepting the direct experience, that is, the knowledge of, and not merely belief in, God and the revelation of his law. Second, he argues in effect that the survival of this tradition is at least strong evidence of its truth: the implication is that so many generations could hardly have continued being so totally convinced of the truth of something false.

It also has to be said that Hirsch was not an apologist, doing his best to *prove* to the unbeliever that they were wrong – an enterprise he thought in any case impossible. His philosophical aims would seem to have been, first, to show the plausibility of believing that Judaism was a divine revelation (presumably hoping that unbelievers could then convert themselves); second to show that Judaism was totally compatible with everything true in Kant and the Enlightenment, and indeed constituted the only way a Jew could properly put Enlightenment values into practice; third, to expound Torah in detail in a way that showed how *all* the mitzvot, and not only the ones obviously concerned with justice to fellow humans, promoted these values, and in this way simultaneously to promote commitment to Torah in theory and practice and understanding of it. The third of these occupies by far the largest part of *Horeb*.

This, interestingly, suggests another argument for the divine origin of Torah, which Hirsch might have used, and which may be there implicitly. Although he thinks we need a moral revelation, Hirsch was, it seems, enough of a Kantian to believe that we are capable, by the use of reason in its practical function, of recognizing such a revelation as being morally true, and therefore of divine rather than human origin. Hence to display the moral message of Torah in detail, and show how it goes beyond what we could think out for ourselves, is in fact to demonstrate its divine provenance. This might suggest that Hirsch's work has typically a double function: on the one hand, he assumes the validity of Jewish tradition, and works out the consequences of this; on the other, he is in effect constantly seeking to show us how the consequences, when worked out in detail, demonstrate the tradition's validity.

One might, indeed, rather surprisingly, see Hirsch as a particularly thoroughgoing religious philosopher, who is prepared to think philosophically all the time rather than using philosophy up to a point. He was able to do this, while holding emphatically that Jewish tradition must be interpreted entirely in its own terms and not subjected to any alien test, because he was thinking ethically rather than metaphysically, and because he found it possible to express the aims of Torah in terms derived from the moral philosophy of his time. Hence he could assume the truth of Torah as an ethical revelation, expound it in detail, and show how the detail confirmed the assumption. The philosophy he used for this was largely Kantian; but, while he accepted Kant's critical epistemology and most of his moral philosophy, he totally rejected the idea of "moral autonomy," and he added a conception of self-fulfillment in a community that has more in common with Aristotle and Hegel. Students of Hirsch will of course decide for themselves how successful he was; but there is no doubt that his influence on nineteenth- and twentieth-century Orthodox Judaism has been very great. It is hard to find a better example of religious humanism, of "enlightened" Orthodoxy, than Samson Raphael Hirsch.

❧ NOTES ❧

The philosophy of Hirsch is to be found in particular in *Horeb*, published in 1837, when he was already chief rabbi of Oldenburg, and subtitled "Essays on Israel's duties in the Diaspora, written mainly for Israel's thinking young men and women." (A two-volume edition in English, translated by Dayan Dr I. Grunfeld, was published by the Soncino Press in 1962: my debt to Dr Grunfeld's masterly introductory essay is very great.) Hirsch's philosophy is also to be found in *Nineteen Letters on Judaism* (1836) and in his *Commentary on the Pentateuch and Haftoroth* (1867, English translation in 7 vols, by Isaac Levy (New York: Judaica Press, 1967).
1 Quoted by I. Grunfeld in Hirsch 1962, p. xxiv.

❧ BIBLIOGRAPHY ❧

Texts

Hirsch, S. R. (1959a) *Judaism Eternal*, translated by I. Grunfeld (London: Soncino) [selected essays; also includes a complete bibliography].
—— (1959b) *Nineteen Letters on Judaism*, translated by B. Drachman, revised by J. Breuer (New York: Feldheim).
—— (1962) *Horeb*, translated by I. Grunfeld, vols 1 and 2 (London: Soncino).
—— (1967) *Commentary on the Pentateuch and Haftoroth*, translated by I. Levy (New York: Judaica).
Kant, I. (1956) *Groundwork of the Metaphysic of Morals*, translated by H. J. Paton as *The Moral Law*, 3rd ed. (London: Hutchinson).
—— (1960) *Religion Within the Limits of Reason Alone* (New York: Harper & Row).
—— (1964) *The Metaphysics of Morals*, part 2, translated by M. J. Gregor as *The Doctrine of Virtue* (New York: Harper & Row).
—— (1969) *Groundwork of the Metaphysics of Morals*, translated L. W. Beck, with critical essays edited by R. P. Wolff as *Foundations of the Metaphysics of Morals* (New York: Bobbs-Merrill).

Studies

Grunfeld, I. (1958) *Three Generations: The Influence of Samson Raphael Hirsch on Jewish Life and Thought* (London: no publisher).

—— (1962) Introduction to Hirsch 1962.

Rosenheim, J. (1951) *Samson Raphael Hirsch's Cultural Ideal and Our Own Times* (London: Shapiro, Vallentine).

CHAPTER 30

Traditional reactions to modern Jewish Reform: the paradigm of German Orthodoxy

David Ellenson

Leo Baeck, in his famous essay, "Does Traditional Judaism Possess Dogmas?," pointed out that "whether Judaism, in its form of belief, is a religion without dogmas is a question that has often been raised" (Baeck 1981, p. 41). At the outset of this article, Baeck recalled that Moses Mendelssohn, in *Jerusalem*, had maintained that "the Israelites have a divine legislation: commandments, statutes, rules of life . . . , but no dogmas." However, Baeck noted that a number of Jewish scholars disagreed with Mendelssohn's assertion and claimed that Judaism had a number of theological assertions and dogmas that provided the foundation for Jewish faith. Rabbi David Einhorn, for example, stated that "freedom from dogma is so little known to historical Judaism that the Talmud includes him who denies the divine revelation of even a single letter of the Torah in the category of *minim*." Einhorn's colleague Rabbi Samuel Holdheim asserted that Judaism promulgated "eternal religious truths," and Leopold Loew of Hungary contended that the liturgies of the synagogue "protest loudly and solemnly against the doctrine of the nonexistence of dogmas" (Baeck 1981, pp. 43–4).

Baeck himself, in approaching the subject, sided with Mendelssohn. In support of this position, he cited the stance of Abraham Geiger who, echoing Mendelssohn, asserted, "Judaism has no dogmas, that is . . . articles of faith . . . the denial or doubt of which would place him who negates them outside the fold of the ecclesiastical community" (Baeck 1981, pp. 41 and 44). Offering a definition of dogma as "a doctrine backed up by authoritative power," Baeck concluded that, in so far as "the exact formulation of creedal concepts" was unknown in classical rabbinic literature and that inasmuch as "the existence of an ecclesiastical authority empowered to formulate decrees" had been absent among Jews for over two millennia, "Judaism . . . has no dogmas" (Baeck 1981, pp. 46–50). He dismissed the contrary claims of Einhorn and Holdheim, proponents of what Baeck labeled "uncompromising Reform Judaism," as attempts to construct a "formulated credo" that would "secure a foundation for the religious community" (Baeck 1981, p. 42). These men, Baeck continued, "wanted to transform . . . Judaism into a Jewish *Konfession* which could have its place alongside the Christian denominations. And, therefore, they wanted to formulate Jewish articles of faith which . . . would distinguish their Jewish denomination from the others" (Baeck 1981, p. 50).

Whether Baeck or his opponents are correct is beyond the scope of this chapter. However, Baeck's last observation, that men such as Einhorn were driven "to formulate Jewish articles of faith" in order to distinguish Reform Judaism from other Jewish denominations, provides an appropriate starting point for this chapter, for it cautions the observer to pay attention to the role that religious dogma, as well as religious practice, have occupied in struggles that have divided Jewish denominations in the modern world. Traditionalist reactions to Reform, no less than classical Reform responses to Orthodoxy, hinged not only upon disputes over religious behaviors but upon disagreements over faith as well. The Orthodox, like many Reformers, were often moved by the conditions of the modern world to establish a "formulated credo" that would draw boundaries over against the Reformers and, in this way, "secure a [distinct] foundation for the [Orthodox] religious community" in the world of nineteenth-century Jewish religious denominationalism.

This chapter, in delineating the indictment Orthodoxy hurled against Reform in nineteenth-century Germany, will pay attention to both poles of the indictment. It will demonstrate that Orthodox charges against Reform did not only include attacks on what were seen as unwarranted Reform departures from traditional Jewish customs and practices. These charges also involved what were regarded as unforgivable Reform deviations from traditional Jewish religious ideology and belief. As Germany was the crucible in which both Reform and Orthodox Judaism were formed in the first half of the nineteenth century, a description and analysis of central European Orthodox polemics against Reform in that time and place will do more than illuminate the contours of the traditionalist case against Reform in Germany during the 1800s. The presentation and consideration of these charges will indicate that the parameters as well as substance of the Orthodox case against Reform in the contemporary world on the levels of both practice and belief had already been well established in Germany long before the onset of the twentieth century and that present-day traditionalist criticisms of liberal varieties of Judaism simply echo positions that were advanced by central European Jewish leaders over a century earlier.

〜 *ELLEH DIVREI HA-BERIT*: THE INITIAL 〜 ORTHODOX RESPONSE TO REFORM

With the rise of the Reform movement in Germany at the beginning of the nineteenth century, the ire of the traditional rabbinate was aroused. The Orthodox were particularly infuriated by innovations in prayer and ritual that the Reformers introduced in Hamburg during the second decade of the 1800s. As Rabbi David Zvi Hoffmann (1843–1921), head of the Orthodox Rabbinical Seminary in Berlin at the beginning of the twentieth century, later observed, '[It was there] in the city of Hamburg [between 1817 and 1819] that the evil [of Reform] first burst forth' (*Melammed Leho'il, Orach Chayyim*, pp. 11–13).

The transgressions of the Hamburg Reformers were many in the eyes of the Orthodox, and the traditional European rabbinate found the Reformers' care to legitimate their changes in Jewish ritual and custom on the basis of warrants drawn from halakhic precedent outrageously galling. In 1818, Eliezer Liebermann, a teacher and itinerant preacher, collected and issued two volumes of responsa – *Nogah ha-Tzedek* and *Or Nogah* – that provided Jewish legal justification for the innovations in liturgy and synagogue practice that Reformers in Berlin had made two years earlier. The subsequent reforms in Hamburg bestowed additional import upon these volumes, and the Orthodox were unable to ignore them. Their reaction found expression in an 1819 work published by the Orthodox Rabbinic Court of Hamburg under the title *Elleh Divrei ha-Berit*, a pamphlet which collected twenty-two opinions signed by forty Orthodox rabbis. This pamphlet not only constituted a response to *Nogah ha-Tzedek* and *Or Nogah* but attacked the innovations of the Reformers bitterly and in no uncertain terms as standing, in Michael Meyer's words, "outside the pale of Judaism" (Meyer 1988, p. 58). The rabbis of *Elleh Divrei ha-Berit* charged that the Reformers had improperly introduced prayer in the vernacular into formal Jewish worship, recklessly altered the content and order of the traditional liturgy, and wantonly permitted musical instruments to accompany synagogue services on both Sabbaths and holidays. In this sense, the pamphlet argued against what it regarded as unwarranted changes the Reformers had made in the liturgical practices of the synagogue.

The tone which marks *Elleh Divrei ha-Berit*, as well as the concerns that inform it, are evidenced at the outset of the volume. Rabbi Hirz Scheur of Mainz, in the work's second responsum, laments the dawn of an era "where the lawless among our people have publicly increased . . . and where many publicly profane the Sabbath." The rabbis of this generation, Scheur argued, must be as zealous in condemning the Reformers and innovations such as the employment of the organ during Jewish worship as authorities were in the generation of Elisha ben Abuyah when they stoned Elisha for riding his horse on the Sabbath. The necessity of "erecting a barrier" against Reform was the most pressing issue confronting the traditional rabbinate of this generation.

Other colleagues echoed Scheur's concerns and shared his sentiments. For example, Rabbis Eliezer Fleks, Samuel Segal Landau, and Leib Melish – members of the Orthodox Rabbinical Court in Prague – began their letter to the Hamburg rabbis by asserting that what was transpiring in Hamburg "sickens and pains the heart of the listener. Woe to the generation where such a thing has occurred." Moreover, these Prague rabbis went beyond excoriating the Reformers for their departures from the realm of traditional Jewish practice. Instead, they asserted that these deviations constituted, in effect, a rebellion against the authority of Tradition itself. Consequently, they charged that the Hamburg Reformers were persons of no religion, neither Jew nor gentile (*Elleh Divrei ha-Berit*, p. 17). In making such a charge, the Prague rabbis were implicitly issuing a theological claim against the Reformers. Reform changes in the realm of practice were accompanied by and signaled a concomitant abandonment of traditional Jewish faith. The nature of this initial Orthodox argument against Reform not only involved a protest against Reform departures from traditional Jewish practice, but, in a nascent though not yet fully developed fashion, indicted Reform for failing to acknowledge the proper parameters and foundations of Jewish faith. It was an argument that was to be more explicitly put forth by others, including Rabbi Moses Schreiber of Pressburg, the Chatam Sofer, who was destined to become the most influential architect of the Orthodox polemic against Reform.

In *Elleh Divrei ha-Berit*, as well as elsewhere in his writings, the Chatam Sofer fully crystallized the nature of this twofold Orthodox complaint against Reform, and his Orthodox contemporaries, as well as later generations of Orthodox leaders, echoed the structure and sentiments of this position. The Chatam Sofer savagely attacked the Reformers for the innovations they had introduced into Jewish religious life. The Reformers' omission of prayers calling for the coming of the messiah, the return of the Jewish people to the land of Israel, and the re-establishment of the Temple service as conducted in ancient days all drew his ire. In addition, Schreiber insisted that Jewish prayer be conducted only in Hebrew and he objected strenuously to the introduction of musical instruments into the synagogue. On the level of practice, his complaints against Reform were many (*Elleh Divrei ha-Berit*, pp. 6–11 and 30–45).[1] He condemned their deeds as "pernicious." However, Schreiber did not stop there. He, like the Prague rabbis, attacked the Reformers as persons of no religion. Moreover, he explicitly linked this position to the fact that the Reformers denied the validity of the Oral Law. The Reformers, the Chatam Sofer asserted, were "heretics – *apikorsim*" (*Elleh Divrei ha-Berit*, p. 9). They merited censure not simply because they failed to preserve Jewish traditions and practices. They deserved condemnation for their denial of classical Jewish religious doctrine. Belief in the eternality and divinity of the Oral Law established the foundation for the Chatam Sofer's denominational identity and it provided him with an Archimedean point from which he could attack Reform.

Schreiber's positions are echoed in the writings of other colleagues in *Elleh Divrei ha-Berit*. Representative of them are Mordechai Benet, rabbi of Nikolsburg and Akiba Eger, rabbi of Posen and Schreiber's father-in-law. Eger maintained that the fundamental Jewish belief in the divinity of the commandments – upon which Jewish observance depended – could be preserved only by a "faith in the [revealed nature] of the Written and Oral Law" and in the authority of the traditional rabbinate to interpret it. To neglect even a single dictum of the rabbis as prescribed in the Oral Law would result in the downfall of the entire Torah. Reform Jews who did not affirm a belief in the notion that all of the Torah was revealed "from the mouth of the Almighty to Moses" and passed on in a legitimate chain of tradition were guilty of denying the basic foundation of Jewish faith. The Reformers, who denied such beliefs, should be understood, like the Sadducees and Karaites before them, as sectarians who had separated themselves from the community of Israel (*Elleh Divrei ha-Berit*, p. 12). It was the Reformers' rejection of theological doctrine, and not just their deviations from what these Orthodox rabbis considered to be authentic Jewish practice, that formed the essential basis for the Orthodox rejection and condemnation of Reform. It is small wonder that the Chatam Sofer, on another occasion, wrote of the Reformers,

> Our daughters should not be given to their sons, and their sons to our daughters. Their community is like the community of the Sadducees and the Boethusians, the Karaites and the Christians. They to theirs and we to ours. And if they were subject to our jurisdiction, my view would be to push them beyond the boundaries [of our community].'
>
> *She'elot u'Teshuvot Chatam Sofer* 6:89

The Reformers, in these rabbis' opinions, were not simply "sinners." They were, in a fundamental sense, a separate sect apart from the community of Israel. Contemporary political conditions did not allow these rabbis to excommunicate the Reformers. However, these conditions did not prevent them from viewing, and condemning, Reform as embodying a religious ideology distinct from their own. An examination of *Elleh Divrei ha-Berit* indicates the emerging contours and content of the Orthodox polemic against Reform. It reveals that Orthodox dissatisfaction with Reform Judaism rested upon issues not only of practice but of belief as well. A principal basis for the Orthodox rejection of Reform was established by these early leaders of nineteenth-century central European Orthodoxy. How the next generation of Orthodox leaders dealt with their legacy and evolved a more complete policy in respect to Reform will be the focus of the next section.

❧ THE 1840s AND THE MATURATION OF ❧ THE ORTHODOX RESPONSE

As Steven Lowenstein has observed, "The 1840s were the crucial decade for the creation of a Jewish religious Reform Movement in Germany" (Lowenstein 1992, p. 85). While the Hamburg Temple, as we have seen, gave rise to great controversy, it was not until the late 1830s that a significant number of secularly trained and Reform-oriented rabbis began to introduce innovations into a number of German communities. In 1841 the first Reform prayerbook since the 1819 Hamburg Temple prayerbook was issued, and in 1843 the radical Frankfurt Reform Society of Friends of Reform, the Reformverein – organized by Theodor Creizenach and M. A. Stern – was formed. This Society rejected the ritual of circumcision for Jewish boys, advocated moving the Jewish Sabbath to Sunday, and opposed the authority of talmudic law in Jewish life. Though virtually all German Jews opposed the radicalism of the Society's proposals, the Society did "push the more moderate Reform rabbinical leadership to call the First [of what were to be three] Rabbinical Conference[s] in Braunschweig [Frankfurt, and Breslau in 1844, 1845, and 1846]" (Lowenstein 1992, pp. 85–6).[2] While Reform may not have come to dominate completely the communal-religious life of German Jewry by the end of the 1840s, Reform's ever-escalating influence was apparent.

The leadership of the Orthodox community was aware of the precariousness of the Orthodox position, and Orthodoxy's responses to Reform at this time were sharp and multifaceted. These attacks both drew upon and more fully crystallized the parameters of the Orthodox polemic against Reform found in *Elleh Divrei ha-Berit*. A number addressed the Hamburg Temple Reform prayerbook, which was reissued in 1841. Isaac Bernays, Orthodox rabbi of Hamburg, asserted that it was forbidden to pray from this work and said that people who did so had not fulfilled their obligations concerning prayer (*Theologische Gutachten*, p. 15).

His colleague in Altona, Jacob Ettlinger, issued a circular on the first night of Chanukkah, 8 December 1841, stating that the Reformers, in offering this revised edition of the original 1818 prayerbook, had solicited opinions from rabbis outside of Hamburg in support of their own. In so doing, the Reformers had transformed the struggle over Reform in Hamburg from a local debate to one of profound religious principles that had implications for Jews throughout Germany. As a "spiritual leader" of the Jewish people, Ettlinger felt compelled, as a matter of conscience, to respond to the Reformers' claims as well as constrained to offer his opinion on the prayerbook in support of Bernays. Citing the views of those rabbis whose opinions had been collected in *Elleh Divrei ha-Berit*, Ettlinger reiterated their contentions that Jewish communal prayer should be conducted only in Hebrew and that it was forbidden to change either the order or contents of the traditional service. Beyond this, Ettlinger was profoundly disturbed, as his predecessors had been two decades earlier, that the Hamburg Temple prayerbook rejected the classical Jewish belief in a personal messiah who would bring about redemption for the Jewish people and all of humanity. For all these reasons, Ettlinger, like Bernays, proscribed the employment of this prayerbook and concluded, "It is forbidden for any Jew to pray from this book" (*Binyan Tziyon ha-Shaleim*, p. 157).

The radical Frankfurt Reformverein also elicited passionate Orthodox commentary. Rabbi Ettlinger's comments upon the Reform-freunde are representative of Orthodox responses to the group's stances and activities. On 20 August 1843, Ettlinger described the group as a calamity and not only attacked their denial of traditional Jewish messianic doctrine but was infuriated by their insistence that the commandment of circumcision was given only to Abraham. These Reformers, Ettlinger pointed out, maintained that this commandment was not transmitted by Moses to the Jewish people. Consequently, it was no longer incumbent upon Jews to have their sons circumcised on the eighth day of their progeny's young lives as a sign of the covenant that obtains between God and the people Israel (*Binyan Tziyon ha-Shaleim*, p. 73).

Rabbi Zvi Hirsch Chajes of Zolkiew, one of the foremost rabbinic scholars of the nineteenth century, elaborated on this development in a blistering polemic, *Minchat Qena'ot*, which he issued in 1845 and to which he added an excursus in 1849. Like Ettlinger, Chajes was shocked that these Reformers advocated abandoning this central Judaic rite of passage. Past generations of Jews had willingly chosen martyrdom and death when confronted with the prospect of not maintaining this ritual. How could one attached to the Jewish people even consider such a possibility? (*Minchat Qena'ot*, pp. 1003–4). Chajes, like Ettlinger, noted that the Frankfurt Reformers defended their abrogation of the commandment of circumcision on the grounds that the commandment was given to Abraham alone. When their critics pointed out to them that in Leviticus 12:3 the commandment was also issued to Moses, Stern and Creizenach, as leaders of the Frankfurt Reform Association, defended their position by claiming that the Leviticus passage was a later addition to the biblical text. Chajes, in disgust, observed that faithful Jews had nothing in common with these people. "In their disgusting opinion, the Torah is not eternal." These Reformers, as "*kofrim* (heretics)," were persons who denied the fundamental religious beliefs upon which traditional Judaism rested. Their abrogation of the commandment of circumcision resulted from and reflected their rejection of traditional Jewish dogma (*Minchat Qena'ot*, p. 1004).

This linkage of faith and practice, and the causal relationship that obtained between them, is further evidenced in the remainder of Ettlinger's attack upon the Frankfurt Reformverein. Ettlinger observed that these Reformers, by rejecting the doctrine of biblical inerrancy, had not only gone beyond the parameters of Jewish faith. They had attacked the foundations of Christianity as well. Any Jew who concurred with their religious views was, "without a doubt, a *kofer be'ikkar* – one who denied the most fundamental tenet of Jewish faith." Indeed, echoing the rabbis of *Elleh Divrei ha-Berit*, Ettlinger concluded that "from a universal-religious perspective" it could well be maintained that these Reformers were persons "of no faith and no religion." The Torah, for these people, was simply a product of ancient Near Eastern civilization. The notion of a supernatural revelation at Sinai was, in effect, denied by these people, and the Reformers, in Ettlinger's opinion, reduced Judaism to a product of "human understanding" and invention. The Reformers should therefore be regarded as "a wolf of prey that seeks to destroy the holy sheep of the flock of Israel." They should be watched carefully and it was incumbent upon Orthodox Jewish leaders to protect and warn the people against their deceptions, denials, and lies (*Binyan Tziyon ha-Shaleim*, p. 74).

This obligation was felt most keenly by a whole host of Orthodox leaders as a result of the three Reform rabbinical conferences that were held between 1844 and 1846 in three German cities. As Reform, at this point, had begun to make significant inroads in the German Jewish community, the Orthodox rabbinate, immediately after the 1844 conference in Braunschweig, responded, as they had a quarter century earlier, by issuing spirited broadsides against the Reformers. The need for a concerted Orthodox response against the Braunschweig conference engendered more than one collective response. Rabbis Zevi Hirsch Lehren and Abraham Prins gathered together attacks from over forty Orthodox rabbis (including Samson Raphael Hirsch) against the work of the conference (Meyer 1988, pp. 134–5 and Hirsch, *Shemesh Marpei*, p. 188). Rabbi Ettlinger shared their convictions and, in a spirited response to the conference, noted that the participants in this conference unjustifiably claimed for themselves the title of "rabbi." Their words disgraced the Talmud and threatened authentic Jewish tradition. The Reformers' decision to publicize their resolutions compelled the Orthodox to respond so as "to awaken those who slumber." The people needed to be warned of "the approaching danger" Reform represented. Ettlinger circulated a petition protesting the conference among the Orthodox rabbis of central Europe. In introducing his protest to his correspondents, he expressed the hope that "the ambitions of Reform and the destruction [of their] party would not vanquish our holy Torah." God, Ettlinger was sure, would protect the contemporary faithful of Israel from the Reformers as God had protected the past faithful of Israel from the Sadducees and the Karaites. Nevertheless, God needed the Orthodox to act so that the Torah and its ways would be defended. One hundred and sixteen Orthodox rabbis from Germany and surrounding countries responded to Ettlinger's appeal and signed this petition which both protested the actions of the Reformers and called upon the traditionalists to remain strong in their faith. Among those who signed or supported the resolution were Samson Raphael Hirsch and the Ktav Sofer, Rabbi Abraham Samuel Benjamin Wolf, son of the Chatam Sofer and his father's successor as head of the Pressburg Yeshivah (*Binyan Tziyon ha-Shaleim*, pp. 148–56).

Individual rabbis responded as well. The work of Maharam Schick, Rabbi Moses Schick of Hungary, the outstanding student of the Chatam Sofer, is representative of these individual traditionalist critiques. Schick, like other Orthodox champions of the day, offered the oft-repeated claim that the Reformers should be seen as "Karaites." Like Ettlinger, he derisively noted that the members of the Braunschweig conference referred to themselves as "rabbis." "At night," Schick scoffed, "they went to bed with nothing and in the morning they opened their eyes and were rabbis." Rehearsing a standard litany of Orthodox charges against the Reformers, Schick contended that the Braunschweig Reformers had attacked the divinity of the Written Torah as well as the Oral Law, blasphemed God, and denied the coming of the messiah. Schick angrily asserted, "I am ready at any time to smash and break the molars of the sinners to the limits of my strength" (*She'elot u'Teshuvot Maharam Schick, Yoreh De'ah*, no. 331). Other Orthodox rabbis also questioned the Reformers' integrity and knowledge, and asserted that the Reformers were motivated primarily by the opportunity for material gain (Katz 1992, pp. 43–72). The sentiments as well as the substance of these attacks were akin to the tone and content of the Schick responsum.

Yet others engaged the Reformers in substantive disagreement. In looking at them, one appreciates the genuine divisions of belief and practice that distinguished Orthodoxy from Reform. Chajes' *Minchat Qena'ot*, cited previously, stands out among such works and was one of the most extensive Orthodox reactions elicited by the conferences. It bespeaks the nature of Orthodoxy's quarrels with Reform as well as the case Orthodoxy had developed against Reform by this time.

In *Minchat Qena'ot* Chajes labeled the Reformers as *madichim* (those who lead others astray) and *mumarim* (open opponents of Jewish law), terms, as Jakob Petuchowski has observed, reserved for apostates in medieval rabbinic literature (Petuchowski 1959, pp. 179–91). These "legislators of sin" haughtily transgressed the commandments and caused the community to violate the tradition. Chajes, in his brief against Reform, initially turned his attention to the Hamburg Temple Reformers of 1818. These men, by employing the vernacular as a vehicle for prayer, abandoned centuries of traditional Jewish practice. They changed the formula of the traditional *Shemoneh Esreh* by omitting prayers that called for the resurrection of the dead, the rebuilding of the Temple, and the restoration of the Davidic dynasty. Owing to the efforts of the rabbis who mounted their attack against Reform in *Elleh Divrei ha-Berit*, Reform remained an isolated Hamburg phenomenon for nearly two decades. However, through the criticisms they leveled at traditional Jewish religious practice and belief, the leaders of Reform were able to exploit emancipatory aspirations for equality and opportunity in the larger society that were then prevalent among masses of Jews. Reform could no longer be confined to Hamburg. It had begun to take root throughout Germany (*Minchat Qena'ot*, pp. 981–5).

Chajes, throughout his work, chastised the Reformers for their abandonment and alterations of traditional Jewish practices. Besides the liturgical changes mentioned above and the Reformverein's rejection of the commandment of circumcision, contemporary Reformers, Chajes pointed out, employed the organ on the Sabbath. In addition, they no longer read the entire lectionary on the Sabbath but opted for a triennial Torah reading in which only one-third of the assigned lectionary was read. In matters of personal status, the Reformers, Chajes charged, totally abandoned traditional Jewish standards. In violation of traditional Jewish law, the Reformers would allow an *agunah* to remarry without receiving a Jewish divorce[3] and they would permit a *kohen*, a man of priestly descent, to marry a divorcee. The Reformers also rejected the traditional stricture regarding levirate marriage and the practice of *halitzah* associated with it (*Minchat Qena'ot*, pp. 997–9 and 1004).[4]

In the course of this indictment against the deviations the Reformers had introduced into Jewish religious practice, Chajes went on to single out the activities of the most radical Reform rabbi in Germany, Rabbi Samuel Holdheim of Berlin, for special censure. Holdheim, Chajes charged, opposed, as the members of the Frankfurt Reform Association had, the ritual of circumcision as a required rite for entering baby boys into the covenant as well as all traditional Jewish laws of marriage and divorce. Holdheim also advocated that Sabbath services be moved from Saturday to Sunday in his Genossenschaft für Reform im Judenthum, the separatist Berlin Reform congregation Holdheim headed. Finally, Holdheim would neither allow the shofar to be blown on Rosh Hashanah nor would he countenance the recitation of the traditional musaf (additional morning) or minchah (afternoon) services on Yom Kippur. Indeed, he had these services removed from the prayerbook of the community. Chajes noted that even Abraham Geiger and Ludwig Philippson, the two other great rabbinic leaders of Reform in Germany, were more moderate than Holdheim. Philippson, Chajes observed, had attacked the Frankfurt Reformers for their stance on the matter of circumcision and both Philippson and Geiger had opposed Holdheim's plan to move the Sabbath from Saturday to Sunday. Chajes was thus able to distinguish among contemporary Reform leaders, and he did not lump the views and practices of a Philippson or a Geiger together with the stances of a Holdheim. Nevertheless, neither Philippson nor Geiger, despite their greater moderation, was able to avoid Chajes' ire. Neither of them, Chajes observed, was careful to observe the details of Jewish law and Geiger, Chajes charged, permitted traveling, writing, and smoking on the Sabbath despite the traditional Sabbath proscriptions forbidding these activities. Differences among these Reformers were therefore insignificant. All had traversed the boundary of acceptable Jewish practice (*Minchat Qena'ot*, pp. 999–1003 and 1006–8).

Chajes was particularly agitated by the debates concerning the issue of mixed marriage that took place at the Braunschweig conference of 1844. While the assembled rabbis rejected a motion which stated that "marriages between Jews and Christians, in fact, marriages with monotheists in general are not forbidden," they did agree to the following resolution: "Members of monotheistic religions in general are not forbidden to marry if the parents are permitted by the law of the state to bring up children from such wedlock in the Jewish religion" (Plaut 1963, p. 222).[5] To Chajes such a resolution was a serious and unforgivable breach of Jewish tradition. His fury over this interpretation of

Jewish custom and practice knew virtually no bounds (*Minchat Qena'ot*, pp. 996–7 and 1008–9).[6]

Most importantly, Chajes, as has been pointed out earlier, recognized that the Reformers' abandonment of traditional Jewish law and practices in so many areas resulted from their rejection of the classical rabbinic beliefs upon which authentic Judaism rested. He charged that the Reformers did not accept the doctrine of "torah min ha-Shamayim u'nitzchiteha," "the divinity and eternality of Jewish law." Instead, the Reformers maintained that the commandments of Judaism were embedded in culture and reflected the various times and places in which they were promulgated. As a result, the Reformers saw Jewish laws and practices, like woman's fashions, as going in and out of style and the Reformers, like fashion-conscious women, were all too anxious to discard the old in favor of the new (*Minchat Qena'ot*, pp. 978–81 and 985).

The Reformers claimed that Ezra himself wrote elements of the Torah and they contended that the Torah was not complete during the time of the First Temple. In making these claims and by accepting as true the assertions of biblical criticism, the Reformers of the 1840s revealed themselves to be more outrageous in their heresy than comparable sectarian groups in the Jewish past. After all, the Sadducees accepted the divinity of the Written Law and the Karaites, despite their rejection of the authority of the rabbis and the Oral Law, were punctilious in their observance of the Written Law and unshakable in their belief that the Written Law was divinely revealed. The Reformers, alone among all the sectarian groups in Jewish history, denied the very foundation upon which Judaism had rested for millennia (*Minchat Qena'ot*, pp. 979 and 985–6). There was a causal link, in Chajes' opinion, between the Reformers' rejection of classical Jewish belief and their failure to observe and maintain traditional Jewish standards of practice. It is small wonder, in light of all this, that Chajes queried, "What do we [Orthodox Jews] have in common with these people? . . . How are these people able to call themselves by the name of Israel?" They were heretics (*kofrim*) who, through their denial of traditional rabbinic doctrine, had abandoned the fundamental dogmas that served as the foundation of Jewish faith. In so doing, they placed themselves beyond the parameters of the faithful within the Jewish community (*Minchat Qena'ot*, pp. 1004 and 1008). For Chajes and many of his colleagues, as for Reformers such as Einhorn and Holdheim, religious dogma had come to occupy a central role in their assessment and presentation of Judaism.

The need to defend the integrity of traditional Jewish belief from the heresies of the Braunschweig Reformers compelled the Orthodox to confront the critical historical claims that undergirded Reform as well. The realm of modern academic scholarship, which the Reformers employed to defend their positions, could not be ignored, and the scholarship and commentaries of non-Orthodox Jews were increasingly subject to Orthodox onslaught at this time. Typical is the following remark found in the mishnaic commentary (*Tif'eret Yisrael*) of Rabbi Israel Lipschutz of Danzig, a signator to Ettlinger's circular protesting against the Braunschweig conference. Published in Danzig in 1845 one year after the Braunschweig conference, the *Tif'eret Yisrael*'s commentary upon the mishnaic order *Nezikin* ridiculed an element of Ludwig Philippson's comments upon the Bible as "words of double stupidity – *divrei burut kaful*" (*Tif'eret Yisrael, Baba Metzia*, p. 60a).

Meir Leibish Malbim, who was then serving as a rabbi in the Prussian town of Kempen, went far beyond such detailed strictures in his Commentary on Leviticus. He composed a conscious Orthodox intellectal response to the challenges the Braunschweig Reformers presented to traditional Jewish belief and dogma in the Preface to his Commentary on Leviticus, entitled *Ha-Torah ve-ha-Mitzvah*. Addressing the events of 1844 in Braunschweig, Malbim furiously asserted that "the Torah of God was crying bitterly, . . . as its friends had betrayed her." The Reformers, in gathering together and passing their resolutions, had "denied God." These "shepherds" of Israel had betrayed the community and devoured "the sheep under their care." As a result of these events, Malbim concluded that it was necessary for him to "construct a reinforced wall for both the Written and the Oral Law, [a wall] with locks and bolts surrounding its doors so that [the wall itself] cannot be breached." The Reformers, "an evil congregation," had equated the Written Torah with the myths of previous civilizations and they had viewed the wisdom of the Bible as parallel to the wisdom of other religions. The Oral Law, in their eyes, was reduced to the fanciful imaginations of the ancient rabbis. Indeed, the Reformers held the rabbis of the tannaitic and amoraic periods in contempt and arrogantly believed that the authors of the Talmud and ancient rabbinic midrash had no knowledge of either linguistic principles or grammar. The Reformers perceived the classical explanations of biblical passages these ancient rabbinic authorities offered as twisted, ignorant, and superstitious. Malbim felt constrained to respond to these charges. The intellectual integrity of traditional Judaism was at stake (*Ha-Torah ve-ha-Mitzvah*, p. 3).

Malbim constructed his response by insisting that the words of the ancient rabbis conformed to accepted "linguistic principles as well as to the laws of rhetoric and logic." Chazal, the ancient rabbis, "had in their hands vast treasures and storehouses full of wisdom and knowledge, overarching principles and fixed rules concerning grammar, linguistics, and knowledge." While the majority of these rules and principles had been lost by those who followed these earliest sages, Malbim claimed to have rediscovered them. His task, as he saw it, was restorative – to recover the pristine meaning of the text. This could be done, Malbim insisted, only through rabbinic commentary. As he asserted, "I have [in this work] shown and explained clearly that the exegesis of the ancient rabbis (*Ha-Derush*) in fact literally embodies the actual meaning (*Ha-Peshat*) [of the biblical text] and [the grammatical principles and usages employed by the ancient rabbis to establish such meaning] are fixed and stamped in the depths and principles of the Hebrew language" (*Ha-Torah ve-ha-Mitzvah*, p. 1). Malbim detailed these principles and usages in an introduction to the Commentary. The introduction, entitled *Ayelet ha-Shahar*, self-consciously defended the truth of Jewish tradition and law by enumerating 613 such principles and usages!

Malbim's novel defense of the Tradition – that d'rash embodied the plain meaning of the Bible and that classical rabbinic tradition had developed 613 grammatical and logical principles and usages to achieve such plain meaning – was obviously artificial and contrived. Nevertheless, in making these assertions, Malbim felt that he had composed a successful intellectual response to the heresies of the Reformers, "[those] Karaites who deny the traditions of *Chazal*." His argument and exposition defend the notion that the Written and Oral Laws were two parts of a seamless whole. Rabbinic exegesis, far from being fanciful, was coherent and consistent. Rabbinic interpretations, based as they were on rules of grammar and usage, were the keys to unlocking the meaning of God's revelations as they appeared in Scripture. The Reform attack upon the Oral Law was misguided and ignorant, for it failed to understand the logic inherent in rabbinic tradition. The Oral Law and rabbinic exegesis were essential if the meanings of God's revelation were to be made manifest in the contemporary world.

Malbim's defense of Jewish oral tradition ignored the challenges Reform had presented to the authority of written Scripture itself. He clearly felt that an intellectual defense of the Oral Law was sufficient to repel the claims of the Reformers. Indeed, his contention that the Oral tradition displayed an internal coherence informed by a fidelity to rules and principles of logic and grammar was propelled and informed by the intellectual context of his day. His was an argument self-consciously designed to respond to the challenges presented by Reform Judaism in the 1840s. Malbim's conclusion, that d'rash alone could provide for the plain meaning of a biblical text, was driven by the need to defend the traditional Jewish belief in the sanctity of the Oral Law from its Reform detractors.

Malbim's arguments indicate that an Orthodox defense of Jewish tradition was not confined to the realm of practice. That defense also addressed issues of religious belief. Orthodox polemics against Reform affirmed the classical rabbinic dogma which asserted that a twofold revelation – both Written and Oral – was vouchsafed Israel by God at Sinai. As Samson Raphael Hirsch phrased it, Orthodox Jews believed that "the law, both Written and Oral, was closed with Moses at Sinai" (*Horeb*, p. 20). To deny this, as Rabbi Ettlinger put it, "was to deny God" (*Binyan Tziyon ha-Shaleim*, p. 146). For these Orthodox leaders, dogma had come to occupy the same central role in defining Judaism as it had for men such as Einhorn and Holdheim.

∾ THE DEVELOPMENT OF AN ∾ ORTHODOX ATTITUDE AND POLICIES: FINAL PARAMETERS

In the pages of *Der Zionswächter*, a prominent journal of traditionalist thought edited by Rabbi Ettlinger, a number of Orthodox Jews offered their opinion as to what they felt a proper Orthodox policy toward Reform ought to be. One writer, typical of many others who expressed their views in the pages of this journal, claimed that the Reformers ought to be excluded from the Jewish community altogether. Echoing the sentiments of the Chatam Sofer, this author contended that it was permitted neither to eat in their homes nor to marry their daughters. "No common religious bond exists between us," he wrote. "They must be viewed as any other religious confession" (*Der Zionswächter* 1846, p. 50). Rabbi Mattathias Levian of Halberstadt issued a responsum enunciating the implications of this approach in 1847. Levian, responding to the first manifestations of Reform in his bailiwick, condemned as "apostates (*mumarim*) to the entire Torah" eight Jewish citizens of the community who had requested permission from secular city officials to leave the Orthodox-controlled Jewish community. Levian suspected that these men intended to convert to Christianity. However, even if they did not formally do so, these Reform men were, by virtue of their rejection of the Oral Law and traditional rabbinic authority, "akin to gentiles." They were not to be married in a Jewish wedding ceremony, be counted as Jews for purposes of a prayer quorum, or receive a Jewish burial. In addition, they were not to be called to a public reading of the Torah nor were they to be permitted to recite the mourner's prayer on behalf of deceased relatives (*She'elot u'Teshuvot Rabbi Esriel, Orach Chayyim*, no. 7). Levian's responsum gave practical expression to the words of Rabbi Solomon Eger of Posen who, at the same time, wrote to Ettlinger urging him to heed a decree issued by the rabbis of Posen to ban the Reformers from the community. The Orthodox were obligated, Eger wrote, "to separate them from Israel for they are not in any way to be considered as belonging to the people Israel" (*Iggerot Soferim*; 1; p. 84).

Ettlinger, despite the vociferous attacks he had issued against Reform, was not prepared to honor Eger's request. To have done so would have reduced Judaism to a confession of faith alone – and Ettlinger, like most other Orthodox leaders, refused to do this. Jacob Katz has explained why this is so. Katz writes, "As Orthodoxy adhered to Jewish tradition and especially to the Halakhah (religious law), it could hardly dismiss one of the law's basic principles: that being Jewish was a question of descent rather than of conviction" (Katz 1973, p. 210). A person born of a Jewish mother, irrespective of actions or beliefs, remained a Jew. The Orthodox were thus presented with a quandary. On the one hand, Orthodox polemics consistently and vehemently denounced the Reformers for their deviations from traditional Jewish thought and practice. On the other, the strictures of Jewish law proclaimed them Jews. The challenge remaining for the Orthodox was to articulate a policy concerning the Reformers that would take account of all these considerations.

One of the earliest proponents of what was to become the dominant Orthodox attitude toward Reform was the university-educated Rabbi Esriel Hildesheimer, holder of a doctorate from Halle and an ordinand of Rabbi Ettlinger. He was destined, in 1874, to establish and head the Orthodox Rabbinical Seminary of Berlin. An exposition of Hildesheimer's position concerning Reform will reveal the parameters and complexity of the Orthodox reaction to Reform. In 1847 Hildesheimer, like his senior colleague Levian, served the Halberstadt community. However, unlike Levian, Hildesheimer acknowledged that a decision to reject the traditional basis of Jewish faith need not be accompanied by a desire to convert to Christianity. These men's desire to secede was not tantamount to an effort "to destroy God's covenant with Israel at Sinai." These men were not "apostates to the entire Torah." Rather, they were persons "who separated themselves from the ways of the community," a lesser, albeit serious, offense. This caused Hildesheimer, like his senior colleague Levian, to issue several proscriptions against the Reformers. However, like his teacher Ettlinger, Hildesheimer insisted that these men remained Jews (*She'elot u'Teshuvot Rabbi Esriel, Orach Chayyim*, no. 7).

Hildesheimer's decision on this occasion does not mean that he ignored the significance of either dogma or practice in his approach to Reform. Nor does it indicate that he granted Reform any religious legitimacy. Indeed, an episode regarding an ordinand of the Breslau Jewish Theological Seminary reveals that neither he nor his colleague Samson Raphael Hirsch was prepared, on grounds of religious dogma and practice, to accord any religious legitimacy to the positive-historical, much less the Reform, trend in German Liberal Judaism. On 20 October 1879, Hildesheimer wrote the following to Wilhelm Karl von Rothschild:

> I do not know whether you are aware that three-quarters of a year ago some members of a community in Russia turned to Samson Raphael Hirsch ... and myself with the question as to whether one can put one's mind to rest with the appointment of a graduate of the Breslau [Jewish Theological] Seminary to the post of community rabbi.... Our judgment of course was negative."
>
> *Eliav 1965*, Letter 46

In reporting this, Hildesheimer was accurately reflecting the position of Hirsch who, in addressing this matter on 5 May 1879, had asserted that no Orthodox community could feel secure with a religious leader trained in Breslau (*Shemesh Marpei*, p. 206). The opposition of Hildesheimer and Hirsch to religious reform was intractable. An explication of their views will indicate why this was so and will illuminate the attitude and policy positions Orthodoxy ultimately came to hold concerning religious reform.

When, early in 1879, a group of men from the community of Trier asked Hildesheimer whether it was permissible for the community to select a graduate of Breslau as its rabbi, Hildesheimer's reply was an emphatic no. Hildesheimer delineated the reasons for this decision in a correspondence he carried on with Theodor Kroner, the ordinand of the Breslau Seminary who had applied for the post of community rabbi in Trier. Kroner considered himself a knowledgeable and observant Jew and rabbi, and he was upset with Hildesheimer's recommendation to the community. Hildesheimer responded by assuring Kroner that he bore him no personal animus. Rather, his opposition to Kroner's appointment was a principled one. The graduates of the Breslau Seminary could not be recognized as legitimate rabbis, Hildesheimer maintained, because both its students and faculty were not wholly committed "to the words of the Sages and their customs." Breslau graduates did not prohibit the purchase of milk produced under gentile supervision. Furthermore, their failure to forbid the buying of gentile wine constituted a major violation of Jewish law. Finally, these men allowed their wives to appear in public without a head covering. This was an extremely serious trespass of Jewish religious practice, and Hildesheimer insisted that no man could be considered a fit candidate for the rabbinate if he permitted such behavior. Hildesheimer thus initially posed his objections to the more religiously conservative positive-historical trend in German Liberal Judaism on the grounds of religious practice (Hildesheimer 1953, pp. 69 and 71).

However, Hildesheimer did not stop with these practical objections to the positive-historical school. Instead, he added that "there are important differences of [religious] opinion between us." These differences focused on matters of doctrine. In highlighting the significance these doctrinal differences held for distinguishing between Orthodox and non-Orthodox varieties of Judaism, Hildesheimer was not alone. Indeed, Hirsch shared Hildesheimer's views. Hirsch, years earlier, had assailed the religious views of both Zacharias Frankel and Heinrich Graetz, the leaders of the positive-historical school. Frankel served as head of the Breslau Seminary while Graetz, the most famous Jewish historian of his era, was the Seminary's most prominent faculty member. The research of both men, in Hirsch's opinion, denied the divinity and eternality of the Oral Law and emphasized, in its stead, the human and developmental nature of Jewish law. In 1860 and 1861, Hirsch, in his journal *Jeschurun*, published a series of articles by Rabbi Gottlieb Fischer attacking Frankel for his famous work, *Darkhei Ha-Mishnah*. This book, Fischer charged, maintained that elements of the Oral Law had evolved in history. Frankel had contended that talmudic laws subsumed under the category *halakhah le-Moshe mi-Sinai*, were not, as a literal translation would understand it, laws given orally by God to Moses at Sinai. Instead, these laws were of such great antiquity that it was *as if* they had been revealed to Moses. As Fischer and Hirsch understood it, Frankel had written that the authors of these laws were unknown and they were not given by God to Moses at Mount Sinai at all. Rather, they were the enactments of later generations. While Frankel cited a traditional rabbinic warrant – *Rosh* on *Hilkhot Mikvaot* – to indicate that his stance on this phrase did not deviate from that adopted by classical rabbinic tradition, Frankel's understanding of the *Rosh*, in the view of both Hirsch and Fischer, was incorrect. Fischer and Hirsch, who believed in the divinity and the immutability of the Oral Tradition, therefore accused Frankel of "*kefirah g'murah* – absolute heresy" (*Shemesh Marpei*, p. 205 and Hirsch 1988, pp. 229–30).

Hirsch, several years earlier, attacked Graetz in a similar vein. Graetz, in the fourth volume of his *History of the Jews*, which dealt with the talmudic period of Jewish history, had presented the rabbis of the Talmud – the tannaim and amoraim – as the creators, not the bearers, of Jewish tradition. This meant that Graetz, no less that Frankel, advanced a religiously inauthentic portrait of Judaism that was subversive of traditional Jewish dogma (Hirsch 1988, pp. 3–201). Doctrine was elevated to a position of such supreme importance by Hirsch that, in 1861, he wrote that it was unimportant whether a man such as Frankel was personally observant if his observance was unaccompanied by correct belief. Affirmation of the principle of *Torah min Ha-Shamayim* – that the Oral Law as well as the Written Law was revealed from the mouth of the Almighty to Moses at Sinai – was a prerequisite for an authentic Judaism (*Jeschurun* 1861, pp. 297–8).

Hildesheimer, who shared Hirsch's doctrinal views, therefore asserted that, before any Breslau graduate could be confirmed as a legitimate rabbi, the ordinand would have to repudiate the views of his teacher Frankel and declare that he believed that the phrase "halakhah le-Moshe mi-Sinai" referred directly and literally to Moses' receipt of certain laws while he was on Mount Sinai. Second, such a rabbi would also have to indicate his belief in the holiness and divinity of both the Written and the Oral Laws. Finally, the graduate would have to acknowledge publicly the erroneous conclusions of historical investigation about the development of the Oral Law as put forth by Frankel and, by extension, Graetz. Only if all these conditions were fulfilled did Hildesheimer indicate that he might accept such a person as a rabbi. However, he gave no assurances that he would do so even in the unlikely event that all these criteria were met (Hildesheimer 1953, p. 71). Jewish tradition, for the Orthodox, was clear. Judaism rested upon the notion, as Hirsch phrased it, "that the Written Law and the Oral Law were equal, as both were revealed to us from the mouth of the Holy One, Blessed be He" (*Shemesh Marpei*, p. 206). Liberal Jews – whether Reform or positive-historical – had, through their insistence that Jewish law was the product of historical development, rejected classical rabbinic doctrine and, in so doing, had gone beyond the pale of authentic Judaism. The case against the Reformers had been made. The issue which remained for the Orthodox was crucial. In light of this posture, what should be the nature of the Orthodox community's policy towards these Reformers? Here the Orthodox divided among themselves.

One group, as seen above, wanted to deny the "Jewishness" of the Reformers altogether. However, this was impossible. Jewish law clearly defined these people, born as they were of Jewish mothers, as Jews, regardless of their departures from the realms of traditional observance and authentic belief. Nevertheless, Orthodox Jews sympathetic to the direction indicated by this school of thought advanced a policy of separation from and non-cooperation with Reform Judaism as the policy best suited to the defense of traditional Judaism in the modern world. As Jacob Katz has worded it, "The only guarantee for pure Orthodoxy" lay in a refusal "to cooperate with those not absolutely traditional and observant" (Katz 1975, pp. 11–12). Orthodox rabbis such as Maharam Schick therefore routinely forbade Orthodox Jews to enter into Liberal synagogues. Nor would a rabbi like Schick permit his community to intermarry with non-Orthodox Jews (*She'elot u'Teshuvot Maharam Schick, Orach Chayyim*, no. 304). Indeed, Schick became a driving force among the Orthodox at the Hungarian Jewish

Congress of 1868–9 and was instrumental in constructing a policy which called for the creation of separate and distinct Orthodox and Liberal Jewish communities in Hungary. In this way the Orthodox could maintain legally sanctioned autonomous communities that could assure the integrity of an Orthodox way of life. The constraints a non-Orthodox Jewish population might impose as well as the temptations they might present could be avoided by this policy of strict separation. As Schick wrote, "The people who were a singular nation on earth have been divided, and now we are in two camps – one camp which clings to God's Torah . . . and a second which . . . in its haughtiness says that it is progressive when, in reality, it is regressive" (*She'elot u'Teshuvot Maharam Schick, Orach Chayyim*, no. 309 and Ellenson 1994, pp. 51–3).

In Germany it was Samson Raphael Hirsch who was the chief architect of this policy of separatism via-à–vis the Reform. In 1876, owing principally to the efforts of Hirsch, a bill was passed by the Prussian Parliament which modified the Prussian Jew Law of 1847. That law raised each Jewish community to the status of a "public body" and required each Jew "to become a member of the community in his place of domicile" (quoted in Baron 1938, p. 12). While the 1847 law guaranteed the legal unity of each Jewish community in Germany, it also prevented Orthodox Jews from seceding from a community dominated by Reformers. As far as Hirsch was concerned, such a law imposed an unwarranted constraint upon Orthodox Jews and denied them what should have been their legitimate right to exercise their freedom of conscience. Compulsion, Hirsch wrote, could not bring shared religious duty into existence. Only a sense of common religious purpose could do that. Hirsch concluded,

> The divergence between the religious beliefs of Reform and Orthodoxy is so profound that when an individual publicly secedes he is only giving formal expression to convictions which had long since matured and become perfectly clear to himself. All the institutions and establishments in the care of a community are religious in nature, and they are . . . intimately bound up with religious law [and belief].
>
> Quoted in Schwab 1950, pp. 68–9.

For Hirsch, no less than for Reformers like Einhorn or Holdheim, Judaism was viewed in religious-dogmatic terms.

Hildesheimer supported Hirsch in this struggle for Orthodox separatism from Reform in Germany and, in an 1875 letter written to the Prussian Chamber of Deputies urging the passage of legislation amending the 1847 law, he wrote, "The gulf between the adherents of traditional Judaism and its religious opponents is at least as deep and wide as in any other religious faith. In fact, it is greater than in most and much larger than what is permitted by law." Like Hirsch, Hildesheimer argued that a Jew's decision to participate in the life of a Jewish community ought to be a matter of conscience, not compulsion, and he declared that this entire matter was one "between man and God," not between an individual and the state (Eliav 1965, Letter 29). The efforts of Hirsch and Hildesheimer were rewarded. When the bill was passed on 28 July 1876, it stated, "Every Jew is entitled, without severing his religious affiliation, to secede, on account of his religious scruples, from the particular community to which he belongs by virtue of a law, custom, or administrative regulation" (quoted in Baron 1938, p. 15). Orthodox secession from the general Jewish community was now made possible and a policy of strict separatism could be effectuated by the Orthodox Jews of Germany who viewed this course of action as desirable.

Hirsch himself did more than see Orthodox separation from the religious institutions of a Reform-dominated community as desirable. Such separation, as he viewed it, was mandated by Jewish law (*Shemesh Marpei, Yoreh De'ah*, no. 46 and *Shemesh Marpei*, pp. 202–4). Furthermore, Hirsch believed that Orthodox Jews should not interact with non-Orthodox Jewish organizations at all – even when they were of a charitable or communal non-religious nature. For example, Hirsch proscribed Orthodox participation in the Alliance Israélite Universelle, a Paris-based international Jewish charitable and educational organization, and chided his colleague Hildesheimer for doing so on several occasions. Hirsch, in a letter to Hildesheimer, stated that non-Orthodox Jews, including graduates of the Breslau Seminary, were active members of the group and he noted that Adolphe Crémieux, the Paris head of the Alliance, was not only non-Orthodox but he had permitted his wife to have their children baptized! As a result, Hirsch wrote, "I have absolutely no connection with the Alliance . . . I fail to see how a man imbued with proper Jewish thought can attach himself to a group founded for the sake of a Jewish task when its founder and administration are completely removed from genuine religious Judaism." He concluded by stating that this was not the way of the pious men of old who dwelt in Jerusalem and separated themselves absolutely from the rest of the community for the sake of preserving Judaism. A total separatist, Hirsch contended that Orthodox Jews in nineteenth-century Germany needed to follow their example (*Shemesh Marpei*, pp. 201–2).

The consistency of the Hirsch position can be further viewed in an episode involving Hirsch's son-in-law Solomon Breuer in the 1890s. Breuer had succeeded Hirsch as the rabbi of the Orthodox separatist community in Frankfurt and was very upset that a number of Orthodox rabbis had joined with non-Orthodox rabbinic colleagues in signing a petition protesting anti-semitic attacks upon the Talmud. These Liberal rabbis were, in Breuer's opinion, *poshim* (sinners). To cooperate with them in any way implied, in Breuer's view, tacit recognition of their visions of Judaism. He therefore not only refused to join in general communal protests against anti-semitic attacks but condemned those Orthodox colleagues who did so (Ellenson 1990, pp. 102–3).

The absolutist posture adopted by Hirsch on the question of Orthodox separatism is most fully revealed in an episode involving Heinrich Graetz. In 1872, Graetz, along with two companions, went to Israel and toured the entire land. Upon their return, they reported that there were a number of Jewish orphans there and that Christian missionaries were luring these youngsters into the Christian fold by offering them physical sustenance in Christian homes and educational opportunities in Christian schools. These men, including Graetz, recommended that an orphanage under Jewish auspices be established to remedy the situation. Hirsch and a number of other Orthodox leaders in Europe objected to this recommendation for several reasons. Chief among them, as Hirsch put it, was that "the idea to establish an orphanage in Israel both to rescue the orphans from the hands of the missionaries and to raise the level of culture is the idea of Graetz" (Hildesheimer 1954, p. 45). Hirsch's commitment to a policy of Orthodox separatism, based as it was on a strict allegiance to the dogma of *Torah min Ha-Shamayim*, was so uncompromising that even in a matter such as this no cooperation with those deemed religiously heretical could be countenanced. Hirsch, Schick, and other Orthodox rabbis of this school recognized that such persons were Jewish. However, segregation from such Liberal Jews was a necessity if traditional Judaism was to maintain itself in the modern world. All joint activity with them had to be proscribed.

Other Orthodox leaders advanced a different position. While members of this group were no less concerned than Hirsch with Rechtgläubigkeit, correct belief, they did not feel that such concern demanded a policy of absolute separation on all matters from non-Orthodox Jews. Hildesheimer himself actually became the foremost proponent of this position. While he supported Hirsch in the 1876 struggle over Orthodox secession from the general Jewish community in Germany, Hildesheimer was anxious that Orthodox Jews not avail themselves of this right except in instances where Orthodox institutions and religious principles were compromised. Indeed, he wrote that "it is not only not forbidden" to strive for communal unity between Reform and Orthodox Jews in situations where the integrity of the Orthodox position could be assured, but to do so was, in fact, "a noble deed" (Eliav 1965, Letter 12). Hildesheimer's students often served as communal Orthodox rabbis in non-separatist Orthodox congregations and his own policy positions allowed for a clear distinction between religious and communal activities. While Hildesheimer proscribed Orthodox cooperation with Liberal Jews and Liberal Judaism in the religious domain, he simultaneously felt obligated to work together with non-Orthodox Jews on matters of charitable and communal concern. As Hildesheimer wrote, "I am of the... opinion that... one is obligated to act in concert with [Liberal Jews] as far as the conscience permits" (Eliav 1965, Letter 94).

The substance of the policy position advanced by Hildesheimer can be seen in contrasting his actions in several episodes to those of Hirsch. Hildesheimer, in contrast to Hirsch, enthusiastically supported the work of the Alliance Israélite Universelle. The charitable enterprises of the Alliance caused him to remark, "I feel myself obligated to promote the unity of various Jewish communities throughout the world [through the work of this group]." Crémieux, in Hildesheimer's opinion, was not a fit representative of religious Judaism. However, neither the active participation of Breslau Seminary graduates in the Alliance nor Crémieux's irreligiosity could obscure the positive functions the Alliance performed. It would be a grave mistake, Hildesheimer concluded, for Orthodox Judaism to adopt a separatist stance in regard to such organizations (Hildesheimer 1954, pp. 48–50).

Hildesheimer, in contrast to Hirsch and his circle, felt that concern for the religious purity of Judaism should not take priority over the threat posed by anti-semitism. In the face of this threat, Hildesheimer felt it obvious that Jewishness was a matter of fate, not choice. Consequently, Hildesheimer actively supported defense efforts organized by non-Orthodox elements of the Jewish community and participated actively in their endeavors (Ellenson 1990, pp. 101–2). The attitude Hildesheimer adopted in 1872 toward the orphanage in Israel that Graetz and his party proposed brings into sharp focus the distinctive nature of the policy position Hildesheimer and his followers adopted towards Reform. Hildesheimer asserted that no one had condemned Graetz as a "religious heretic" more than he. However, he was convinced that Graetz's report concerning the plight of Jewish orphans in Israel was accurate and felt that it ought to be relied upon to coordinate the active response of the European rabbinate. Hildesheimer therefore complained to Hirsch, "A grave situation has arisen... among circles who do not wish to distinguish between the heresies of Graetz and his reports concerning established facts in our times. There are great dangers bound up with this approach." To abstain from vital work that would enhance the lives of Jewish people throughout the world for these reasons was tantamount to "throwing the baby out with the bath water" (Hildesheimer 1954, pp. 44 and 51). As Hildesheimer phrased it elsewhere, "The truth is the truth even if it be on the side of our opponents" (Eliav 1965, Hebrew Letter 22).

As an Orthodox Jew, Hildesheimer was no more disposed than Schick or Hirsch to countenance any interpretation of Judaism that was not based upon the principle of *Torah min Ha-Shamayim*. He, like his other Orthodox colleagues, was determined not to grant any legitimacy to Jewish religious liberalism and he advocated complete separation from religious institutions and organizations tainted by Reform. However, this did not lead him to adopt a policy of complete separation from non-Orthodox Jews and non-Orthodox Judaism. Hildesheimer felt that the Orthodox were obligated to work in conjunction with their fellow Jews on matters of shared communal concern, even when the institutions which addressed these concerns were not only populated by Liberal Jews but were, in addition, under non-Orthodox auspices. His was a position that allowed for a moderation on this issue that Schick, Hirsch, and their supporters could not abide.

CONCLUSION

As this chapter has demonstrated, Orthodox polemics against Reform in Germany displayed a remarkable consistency throughout the nineteenth century. From the rabbis of *Elleh Divrei ha-Berit* at the beginning of the 1800s through rabbis such as Chajes, Ettlinger, Hirsch, Schick, and Hildesheimer in mid-century, Orthodox opposition to Liberal Judaism addressed and vehemently denounced Reform departures from traditional Jewish practice. However, Orthodox reaction to Reform was not confined to the realm of praxis alone. Rather, Orthodox opposition to Liberal Judaism centered upon the perceived deviance of Liberal ideologues in matters of doctrine and belief as well.

Every Orthodox leader surveyed in this chapter focused upon matters of dogma, as much as practice, in voicing their reaction to Reform. Indeed, for these Orthodox leaders, dogma was elevated to a position of such supreme importance that the positive-historical Judaism of a Frankel was attacked as strongly as the Reform of a Holdheim. The position of these Orthodox spokesmen appears to give the lie to Baeck's contention that Judaism possesses no "formulated credo." Or, to be more exact, this chapter indicates that the same conditions that led certain Reform leaders "to formulate Jewish articles of faith which ... would distinguish their Jewish denomination from the others" prompted these Orthodox rabbis as well. This focus upon dogma pushed Orthodox leaders such as Malbim and Hirsch to formulate intellectual positions defending traditional rabbinic doctrine. Simultaneously, this emphasis allowed the Orthodox to distinguish themselves from every variety of Liberal Judaism and provided them with a warrant for their refusal to cede even a modicum of legitimacy to religious Reform. This posture has remained the foundation for Orthodoxy's principled objection to religious Reform unto the present day (Ellenson 1986, pp. 23–6).

Orthodox reaction to the religious illegitimacy of Reform was unanimous. However, disagreement did arise among the champions of Orthodoxy as to whether there were any areas where Orthodox and Liberal Jews and Judaism could engage in joint endeavors. Here, two distinct Orthodox policy positions were put forth. According to one group, the integrity of Orthodoxy demanded complete separation from the Reform. To associate with the non-Orthodox in any way was seen as tantamount to granting Reform an absolutely unacceptable degree of religious legitimacy. The purity of Orthodoxy could be assured only through a policy of total non-association with Reform. Other Orthodox leaders disagreed. In the opinion of these men, Orthodox cooperation with the non-Orthodox in areas of common communal and charitable concern did not imply any act of Orthodox religious recognition of Reform. Instead, these persons simply regarded Orthodox participation in certain projects as desirable and advantageous to the Orthodox and Jewish cause. In advancing these distinctive attitudes, these central European Orthodox rabbis adumbrated two distinct policy positions vis-à-vis Liberal Jews and Judaism which continue to be operative within the world of contemporary Orthodoxy (Bulman 1993, p. 20–1). This chapter, in presenting the reaction of nineteenth-century German Orthodoxy to Reform, has illuminated a vital chapter in modern Jewish intellectual and religious history which remains instructive for an understanding of Orthodoxy and its attitudes toward liberal varieties of Judaism in the present.

❦ NOTES ❦

1 Schreiber's attacks against Reform on the level of practice in *Elleh Divrei ha-Berit* are paralleled in his legal writings as well. See, for example, *She'elot u'Teshuvot he-Chatam Sofer* 6: 84.

2 For a detailed account of Reform's growth in Germany at this time, see Meyer 1988, pp. 100–42, as well as Liberles 1985, pp. 23–86.

3 An *agunah* is literally "a chained woman." It refers to a woman whose marriage has been terminated de facto (for instance her husband is missing in war or has abandoned her for another reason), but not de jure. As husbands alone possess the right to initiate divorce in Jewish law, the *agunah* is prohibited from remarrying because she is still technically married to her previous husband.

4 When a woman's husband dies without male offspring, Jewish law requires the woman to marry her husband's brother in the hope that this union will produce

a surrogate son and heir to the dead brother, so that the dead brother's name "may not be blotted out in Israel" (Deuteronomy 25:6). Should the living brother reject his deceased brother's widow and opt not to fulfill his levirate duty, he is able to do so through the ritual of *halitzah*, "unshoeing," whereby he releases the levirate widow from her automatic marital tie to him. His sister-in-law is then free to remarry or not at will.

5 Also see Meyer 1988, pp. 134–5.

6 Indeed, Chajes' outrage on this point was paralleled by the anger other Orthodox rabbis expressed on this particular issue. Rabbi Samson Raphael Hirsch, whose response to the conference was written at the end of 1844 during the festival of Chanukkah, compared the efforts of the Orthodox to save Jewish faith in contemporary Germany to those exerted by the Maccabees twenty centuries before. Both were determined to save Jewish faith from those who would cause the teachings of God to be forgotten and transgressed among the people Israel. Hirsch singled out the Reformers' stance on intermarriage between Jews and monotheistic gentiles as a particularly glaring example of the Reformers' distortions of Jewish faith and practice (*Shemesh Marpei*, pp. 188–90).

⚭ BIBLIOGRAPHY ⚭

Texts

Chajes, Z. H. (1958) *Minchat Qena'ot*, vol. 2 (Jerusalem).

Elleh Divrei ha-Berit (1980) (Jerusalem).

Eliav, M. (ed.) (1965) *Rabbiner Esriel Hildesheimer Briefe* (Jerusalem: Verlag Rubin Mass).

Ettlinger, J. (1989) *Binyan Tziyon ha-Shaleim* (Jerusalem).

Hildesheimer, A. (ed.) (1953) "Ha-Rav Azriel Hildesheimer al Zechariah Frankel u-Veit ha-Midrash ba-Breslau," *Ha-Ma'ayan* 1: 65–73.

—— (ed.) (1954) "Hiluf mikhtavim bein ha-Rav Azriel Hildesheimer u-vein ha-Rav Shimshon Raphael Hirsch 'al 'inyanei eretz yisrael," *Ha-Ma'ayan* 2: 41–52.

Hildesheimer, E. (1969 and 1976) *She'elot u'Teshuvot Rabbi Esriel*, 2 vols (Tel Aviv: Chaim Gittler).

Hirsch, S. R. (1861) *Jeschurun* (Periodical) (1962) *Horeb*, translated by I. Grunfeld (New York and London: Soncino).

—— (1988) *The Collected Writings*, vol. 5 (New York: Feldheim).

—— (1992) *Shemesh Marpei* (New York).

Hoffmann, D. Z. (1954) *Melammed Leho'il* (New York).

Iggerot Soferim (1970) vol. 1, edited by S. Sofer (Tel Aviv).

Lipschutz, I. (1953) *Tiferet Yisrael* (New York).

Malbim, M. L. (1969) *Ha-Torah ve-ha-Mitzvah* (Jerusalem).

Nogah ha-Zedek and Or Nogah (1818) written and edited by E. Liebermann (Dessau).

Schick, M. (n.d.) *She'elot u'Teshuvot Maharam Schick* (Jerusalem).

Schreiber, M. (1972) *She'elot u'Teshuvot he Hatam Sofer* (Jerusalem).

Theologische Gutachten über das Gebetbuch nach dem Gebrauche des Neuen Israeli-tischen Tempelvereins in Hamburg (1842) (Hamburg).

Studies

Baeck, L. (1981) "Does Traditional Judaism Possess Dogmas?," in *Studies in Jewish Thought: An Anthology of German-Jewish Scholarship*, edited by A. Jospe (Detroit: Wayne State University Press), pp. 41–53.

Baron, S. (1938) "Freedom and Constraint in the Jewish Community," in *Essays and Studies in Memory of Linda R. Miller*, edited by I. Davidson (New York: Jewish Theological Seminary), pp. 9–24.

Bulman, N. (1993) "A Healing Sun," *The Jewish Observer* (February): 17–25.

Ellenson, D. (1986) "The Integrity of Reform Within *Kelal Yisra-el*," *The Yearbook of the Central Conference of American Rabbis*: 21–32.

—— (1990) *Rabbi Esriel Hildesheimer and the Creation of a Modern Jewish Ortho-doxy* (Tuscaloosa, Al: University of Alabama Press).

—— (1994) *Between Tradition and Culture: The Dialectics of Modern Jewish Religion and Identity* (Atlanta: Scholars Press).

Katz, J. (1973) *Out of the Ghetto* (Cambridge, MA: Harvard University Press).

—— (1975) "Religion as a Uniting and Dividing Force in Jewish History," in *The Role of Religion in Modern Jewish History*, edited by J. Katz (Cambridge, MA: Association for Jewish Studies), pp. 1–17.

—— (1992) *Ha-Halakhah ba-Meitzar* (Jerusalem: Magnes).

Liberles, R. (1985) *Religious Conflict in Social Context: The Resurgence of Religious Orthodoxy in Frankfurt am Main* (Westport: Greenwood).

Lowenstein, S. (1992) *The Mechanics of Change: Essays in the Social History of German Jewry* (Atlanta: Scholars Press).

Meyer, M. (1988) *Response to Modernity: A History of the Reform Movement in Judaism* (New York and Oxford: Oxford University Press).

Petuchowski, J. (1959) "The *Mumar* – A Study in Rabbinic Psychology," *Hebrew Union College Annual* 30: 179–91.

Plaut, G. (1963) *The Rise of Reform Judaism* (New York: World Union for Progressive Judaism).

Schwab, H. (1950) *The History of Orthodox Jewry in Germany* (London: Mitre).

IV

Contemporary Jewish philosophy

CHAPTER 31

Jewish nationalism

Ze'ev Levy

The rise of Jewish nationalism is a unique phenomenon of modernity, following the nationalist ideas and national movements in Western Europe during the nineteenth century. It expressed the transformation from mere awareness of ethnically distinctive features to consciousness of national identity and the willingness to fight for its recognition and realization. The concept of nationalism made its first appearance on the European scene in the wake of Napoleon's armies[1] and afterwards in the struggles for national liberation from 1848 onwards. Its causes and development obviously are a matter of historical research rather than of philosophical reflection. Judaism seemed to be better equipped for national consolidation than other groups, owing to its long history of religious and communal isolation and to the strong impact of messianism throughout the ages. But de facto there was nothing of the kind before, neither in medieval Jewish philosophy nor in Mendelssohn's concept of Judaism. Furthermore, since the struggle for emancipation had not succeeded in the 1860s, most Jewish thinkers were reluctant to defend the idea of Jewish nationalism. They feared that to represent Jews as a separate national entity would play into the hands of the opponents to emancipation. Therefore it should not come as a surprise that the notion of nationalism was first mentioned in modern Jewish thought by its adversaries, namely those Jewish philosophers who were opposed to it as an alleged obstacle to integration in European culture. They differentiated between religion and nationality in order to present Judaism as a religion, along with Protestantism and Catholicism, inside a common national environment. Jewish religion and Jewish nationhood were conceived as antagonistic and excluding each other. According to this view Jews share their national identity with other citizens, and are distinguished only on the denominational level. Therefore, in order to achieve national and cultural assimilation, Jews ought to get rid of their separate national traditions and eliminate all references to Zion and

Jerusalem. This came to a striking expression in the resolutions of the Assembly of Jewish Notables and the Sanhedrin, convened by Napoleon in 1806/7.[2] This negative view with regard to Jewish nationalism became more or less characteristic of the mainstream of Jewish philosophy during the nineteenth century and the first decades of the twentieth, until the rise of Nazism in Germany. One of its most famous and extreme philosophical spokesmen was Hermann Cohen.[3]

As against this mental outlook which distinguished Judaism from its surroundings solely on religious grounds, there evolved, principally in Eastern Europe, another viewpoint. It emphasized the notion of national association and belonging, and regarded the Jewish religious dimension as one of the constituents to be derived from it. Most of the protagonists of this conception, however, did not formulate it in any systematic philosophical manner. There was only one notable exception, Nachman Krochmal (see below). Although a few of these thinkers, such as Achad Ha'am, J. Klatzkin, and several others had some philosophical schooling or certain philosophical inclinations, most of them came from a different background. P. Smolenskin, M. Lilienblum, and M. J. Berdiczewski were Hebrew writers, L. Pinsker was a medical doctor, B. Borochov was a Marxist theoretician, Y. Kaufman was a biblical scholar. (Some of them will be discussed in the following chapter.) All of them, and many others, made important contributions to modern Jewish national thought; they certainly drew inspiration from the general and Jewish philosophical currents of their time, but their work does not belong to Jewish philosophy. It ought to be emphasized, however, that, unlike their immediate predecessors who considered the concept of a Jewish nation to be incompatible with emancipation, they regarded Jewish nationalism as the inevitable consequence of the struggle for emancipation. In what follows, we shall call attention to the underlying philosophical elements of their writings. In the twentieth century one encounters again Jewish philosophers who elaborate the essence of Jewish nationality and nationalism by explicit philosophical criteria, foremost among them A. D. Gordon, M. Buber, F. Rosenzweig, L. Baeck, F. Weltsch, M. Brod, M. M. Kaplan, and others. One might perhaps say schematically that in the nineteenth century Jews fought for the right of Jews to be equal citizens – the struggle for emancipation – while Jewish national consciousness in the twentieth century emphasizes the right to be recognized as different.

When one sets out to explore the philosophical roots of Jewish nationalism, one cannot not mention the greatest and at the same time most controversial Jewish philosopher of modern times – Baruch Spinoza. Despite his excommunication by and alienation from the Jewish community, Spinoza referred on various occasions to the Jewish nation, not only to the Jewish religion – first of all in the *Theologico-*

Political Treatise but also in his letters, and implicitly even in his *Hebrew Grammar*.[4] He certainly did not work out any theory of Jewish nationality, and personally he was indifferent to Jewish destiny, but there is one important passage in the *Treatise* which exerted a significant influence on the crystallization of national consciousness of later Jewish thinkers. It therefore contributed, though indirectly, to the shaping of their nationalist and Zionist ideas.

Spinoza asserted that the religious commandments, prescribed by the Bible, constituted the political laws of the Hebrew nation in its ancient state. Since this state has ceased to exist, its laws have become obsolete. So why do the Jews still cling to the laws of a state which has disappeared from the historical scene? Why has the Jewish people conserved its distinctiveness while this is no longer necessary? By Spinoza's definitive premise, which is obviously questionable, this distinction cannot be explained through internal reasons; therefore its cause must be external. Spinoza claims that it was "gentile hatred" which prevented the disappearance of Jewish national distinctiveness.[5] He even tried to corroborate his thesis by an "historical" example, a distinction between the converted Jews in Spain and Portugal. All these "renegades" (Spinoza's term) abandoned their Jewish distinctiveness but the converted Jews in Portugal, unlike those in Spain, remained victims to discrimination – ethnically though not religiously – and therefore preserved their ties to Judaism. The hatred of the gentiles which did not dissipate after the conversion of the Jews preserved their Jewishness. Whatever the truth or plausibility of Spinoza's historical argument, it explicates very clearly the role which he ascribed to the national-ethnic element in Judaism. To the negative aspect of Jew-hatred as conserving the Jewish people he added another, positive, aspect, namely circumcision which he described as a national characteristic, like the pigtail of the Chinese.[6] It "is so important . . . that it alone would preserve the nation for ever."[7]

Spinoza does not use the abstract concept of Judaism but speaks about the Jewish people – he also employs the concept of "nation" – and explains its separate national existence by two arguments that grow out of each other. On the one hand, gentile hatred separates the Jews from the surrounding world; on the other, this hatred sustains the alienation of the Jews and perpetuates their separate existence. The obvious flaw in Spinoza's argument was his disregard of the intrinsic spiritual elements of Judaism which played a preponderant role in the preservation of the Jewish people in the Diaspora. Yet, despite these shortcomings, Spinoza's attempt to offer a secular historical interpretation of Jewish nationhood, although he himself was indifferent to it, left its strong imprint on later Jewish thinkers. From this it follows, rather unexpectedly, that notwithstanding Spinoza's alienation from

Judaism, his concept of the Jewish people was more germane to future Jewish national aspirations than, for instance, the concept of Judaism put forward by Mendelssohn. The latter's starting-point was the same as Spinoza's (and perhaps influenced by him), namely that the religious commandments had been the political laws of the ancient Jewish state. But while according to Spinoza political laws without a political framework become anachronistic, Mendelssohn affirmed their abiding validity qua religious laws. According to his view they were divinely revealed (at Mount Sinai), and therefore cannot be discarded by humanity. They are still of a binding nature but only on the descendants of those upon whom they were imposed, that is, Jews. Jewish distinctiveness is limited by Mendelssohn to the observance of the "revealed law" while as human beings Jews are, or at least ought to be, part of their surrounding nations and participate in their spiritual and cultural life.[8] Although Mendelssohn uses on several occasions, more or less casually, the word "nation" with regard to Jews, his concept of Judaism leaves no place for any national definition.

It is therefore rather surprising again that Mendelssohn's contemporary Solomon Maimon who, like Spinoza, quit the Jewish religion (although he did not relinquish his personal and sentimental ties to Jewishness), opposed the latter on this point and emphasized the national traits of Judaism. Jewish religion after the destruction of the Jewish state has become the expression of national consolidation. Judaism represents a "theocratic state," and as such is entitled to enforce laws on its "citizens." All who acknowledge their membership in this "state" must obey its laws. Only Jews who, like himself, have given up their membership in this theocratic state, that is, have renounced their national identity, are exempt from its laws.[9] Moreoever, to Maimon it looks simply "unlawful" (*unrechtmässig*) to proclaim adherence to the Jewish religion (i.e. nation) out of family sentiments or other interests but at the same time to transgress its laws.[10] One has to either belong to the Jewish nation and obey all the laws of its state or drop out of it entirely. Reform Judaism would appear to him to be some kind of unacceptable hybridism. Maimon negated any distinction between Jewish religion and Jewish state. But while Spinoza limited their identity to the ancient Jewish state, and considered its laws to be invalid in the Diaspora, or while Mendelssohn emphasized their sole religious connotation, Maimon vindicated their religious and national identity in the Diaspora as well.[11]

These remarks on Spinoza's, Mendelssohn's, and Maimon's conceptions of Judaism and Jewishness highlight a significant turnabout in Jewish philosophy. In chapter 21 above attention was called to the growing interest of modern Jewish thinkers in political philosophy and philosophy of history. It reflected the increasing national awareness of

Jewish philosophy; Jewish philosophers tried to come to grips with the extraordinary political, social, and legal situation of Jews in their countries of residence, that is, their exceptional national status in the Diaspora. Already the Maharal in his *Be'er ha-Golah* and his disciple David Gans in his *Tzemah David*,[12] in the sixteenth century, sought to shed light on the continuing national existence of the Jews in the Diaspora although they had not yet at their disposal the philosophical tools which Spinoza used a century later. All of them – and that holds for the subsequent thinkers as well – endeavored to derive the anomalous national status of the Jews from the exceptional historical development of Judaism. All were in agreement that understanding Jewish history was an essential precondition for the conduct and planning of Jewish life in the present and the future.

The outstanding philosophical work in this respect was Nachman Krochmal's *Guide of the Perplexed of our Times* of 1844.[13] We are not concerned here with Krochmal's philosophical speculations on "absolute spirit" (*Ha-ruchani ha-muchlat*), etc., but with those parts of the book that elaborate a philosophy of history. This was based on the assumption that the decisive factor in history is spiritual perfection, and that each nation is endowed with a peculiar spiritual principle which determines its existence and contributes to the general spiritual treasure of humankind. "The substance of a nation does not lie in its being a nation, but in the substance of the spirit therein." Inspired by G. Vico, and in particular by J. G. Herder, Krochmal divided history into cycles of three periods – growth, flowering, and withering away (development, vigor, and decline) – that characterize the history of every nation. After having contributed its particular spiritual share to humankind, it vanishes from the historical scene. Although the Jewish people undergo the same threefold cycle as other nations, it differs from them through its eternity. After each period of decline it begins a new cycle. This exceptional national status results, as it were, from the special relation between the Jewish people and absolute spirit (God). According to this metaphysical speculation that blends together ideas of Herder and Hegel, the eternity of Israel manifests itself in a never-ending renewal of its national life. Later Zionist thinkers regarded Krochmal's historiographical scheme as anticipating their conception of Jewish-national revival although Krochmal never uttered any explicit proto-Zionist ideas. He was, however, one of the first modern Jewish thinkers to interpret Jewish nationhood through philosophical concepts.

Another very important Jewish thinker of the nineteenth century to vindicate the national essence of the Jewish people by resorting to modern philosophical ideas was Moses Hess, a precursor of socialism as well as of Zionism. Although his thought was not an outcome of pure philosophical reasoning or scientific research, he acquired extensive knowledge by his independent inquiries into Jewish life and history. The vagueness of his concepts, together with his predilection for sentimental and prophetic language, are balanced by the freshness and originality of his thought. Hess, who until the end of his life was deeply involved with the German workers' movement and who had in his early years collaborated closely with Marx and Engels, was reminded of his Jewish ties by two fateful external events – the notorious blood-libel of Damascus in 1840 and the so-called "Spring of the Nations," that is, the emergence of the national idea (especialy in the wake of the liberation struggles in Italy). Although he mentioned, in the fifth letter of *Rome and Jerusalem*, the shock that the Damascus affair and prior anti-Jewish outcries ("Hep! Hep!") in Germany had had on him, they did not leave any traces in his literary and public activities at the time. His explanation, twenty years later, that the greater misery of the European proletariat then stifled his Jewish patriotic feelings,[14] looks rather apologetic. It was not the "Jewish question" as an expression of *particular* Jewish issues that instigated Hess' rekindled Jewish national consciousness but the *general* cause of national liberation that ought to include the rights of the Jewish people together with those of the Greek, Italian, and other peoples. This led Hess to the conclusion that national liberation must go hand in hand with social emancipation. This idea he tried to buttress with Spinoza's philosophy which he glorified as the supreme spiritual manifestation of Judaism in modern times. Hess did not reach his Jewish-national outlook immediately. In his early writings he professed an exceedingly negative stance toward Judaism which did not refrain from quasi-anti-semitic locutions, for example a "fossilized mummy," etc.[15] After 1848, in exile in Switzerland, he began to evolve his monistic theory of cosmic, organic, and social life, aspiring toward perpetual harmony. Notwithstanding its scientific deficiencies and far-fetched analogies between biological and social evolution, these speculations ultimately drove him to a reassessment of the problem of nationalism on the general and Jewish plane. True to his biological analogies, he regarded national entities as members of a living organism; every one is destined to fulfill a particular definite role in the life and history of humanity. All the nations are but facts of nature whose distinctions are directed to one single purpose – to develop the appropriate qualities that conform to each particular environment. The final unfolding of the optimal qualities of the different nations will encourage their merger and assure a harmonious life of human society in the future. The universal social end inspired Hess' outlook on the functions of nations. This was the philosophico-ideological background of Hess' new conception of Jewish nationhood. If every nation fulfills its special function in the organism of humankind, this holds no less for the Jewish people. His interest in the latter's destiny he now tried to establish on a philosophical basis. After the national liberation of Greece and Italy there remains, as it were, one single "last nationality question" (this was the subtitle of *Rome and Jerusalem*) that awaits its solution. The national revival of the Jewish people is part of the general struggle for national emancipation. The impact of Romanticism and the rise of nationalism in Europe become clearly visible in his terminology; he writes about "national renaissance," the "creative genius of the nation," and so on. Like Spinoza's argument by analogy that the same historical laws govern the life of the Jews and the Chinese,[16] Hess elicits Jewish national revival from the Italian national liberation struggle, but he does so by resorting to a wide though sometimes rather dubious historiographical perspective.

All social institutions and spiritual outlooks reflect original racial creations. Hess' use of the term "race" has, of course, no racist connotation; it is synonymous with "nation." It simply reflects his tendency to derive his thought from natural science, in order to corroborate his monistic world view. "All history until now was moved by race and class struggles. Race-struggle is primary, class-struggle secondary."[17] Races, that is, nations, manifest the multifariousness of nature. Humankind is an organism of which the races are the members. Some of them, after having accomplished their purpose, die and wither away (Egypt, Greece, Rome, etc.) while the people of Israel belongs to those members that enrich humanity for ever anew. This may remind us of Krochmal although Hess probably did not know about him. The people of Israel is a member, endowed with unique predestined features that determine its particular role in human history – its "mission." While his Jewish contemporaries spoke about the Jewish "mission" of propagating the idea of "ethical monotheism" which implies the disintegration of Jewish nationhood, Hess extolled the "mission" of propagating the unity of cosmic, organic, and social life which necessitates the maintenance and revival of Jewish nationhood. Hess' close friend the historian H. Graetz expressed similar ideas in a small essay on *The Renewal of Youth of the Jewish Race*,[18] postulating some special *innate* features of the Jewish race which open up new roads for world history.[19] Hess defined his theory sometimes as a "genetic world view,"[20] exhibiting "innate" racial qualities of the Jewish people (both Graetz and Hess employed the Cartesian notion of "innate"), but denying any superiority of one race over another. These innate exceptional character traits make the Jewish people especially well chosen to accomplish its mission – to spread the above-mentioned monistic idea. All races (nations) possess different and unique features but they are of equal value; the eventual synthesis of their good qualities (and elimination of the bad ones) will inaugurate the ideal harmonious human society to come. (In the next chapter we shall see how Hess' conception of Jewish nationalism, and the idea of a "mission" derived from it, led him to his Zionist conclusions.)

Most later Jewish philosophers more or less identified Jewish nationalism with Zionism, and will be discussed mainly in the next chapter. The two most prominent among them were A. D. Gordon and M. Buber. Gordon, who was influenced by Tolstoy, elaborated a conception of nationality which was couched in religious language and reflected his personal encounter with Palestine and its social reality. The yearned-for end is redemption which will set up the individual inside an organic whole, progressing from the family to the nation, from the nation to humanity, and ultimately to the infinite cosmos. The nation is an organic whole, composed of individuals who draw their inspiration from all these spheres and contribute, by their activity, their own particular share to the harmonious integration of all cultures. (Some of these ideas show an astonishing similarity to those of Hess although Gordon was probably not aware of it.) In order to achieve this ultimate aim, the Jewish creative genius which was muti-lated in the Golah (Diaspora) will be resuscitated in a national Jewish frame in Palestine. There are multiple traditional religious elements in Gordon's conception of Jewish nationality, and according to some scho-lars (such as E. Schweid), even kabbalist influences.

Martin Buber's conception of Jewish nationality was strongly influenced by M. Hess whose fervent admirer he was (he wrote the introductions to the two volumes of Hess' writings, translated into Hebrew), and by A. D. Gordon. At the same time, however, he also absorbed certain ideas of such non-Zionist Jewish philosophers as H. Cohen and F. Rosenzweig. Buber conceived of Judaism not merely as a spiritual or cultural phenomenon, and certainly not as a religious denomination, but as a manifestation of certain particular biological roots. He yearned for an intellectual and social renaissance of Judaism "here and now," to be realized on a national basis. His thought thus reflects a fruitful encounter of modern Jewish philosophy with modern national thought. His aim was to create, or perhaps to renew, what he considered to represent the intrinsic relationship between Jewish religiosity (but not in its traditional Orthodox forms) and Jewish nationality. However, the national basis, that is, the political framework of a Jewish state, is not the ultimate quintessence but a necessary tool to assure genuine spiritual revival of Judaism as part of an all-encompassing spiritual and social redemption of humankind.

This does not exhaust the picture. There evolved also trends of Jewish nationalism that opposed or denounced the Zionist conclusions and sought to develop some kind of Jewish nationalism in the Diaspora. We shall limit our survey to those of them that tried to elaborate these viewpoints by certain philosophical arguments. The two most important representatives of this tendency were the historian Simon Dubnow and the philosopher Franz Rosenzweig. Dubnow proposed to create autonomous national and cultural Jewish institutions in their respective countries of residence, in order to overcome the anomalous situation of a Jewish minority. This was in line with his general historiographical conception that in the future all nations would or should no more depend on any particular territory but would be distinguished by their cultural and historical heritage alone. Dubnow believed that, by establishing national autonomy in the Diaspora, the Jews would become the forerunners and teachers of all other nations to realize this prophetic vision. There were also several more versions of Diaspora nationalism in Eastern Europe, for example those of Chaim Zhitlowski, and in particular the Jewish Socialist Bund. The latter was very influential until the Second World War, but had no philosophical foundations. It considered Yiddish to be the chief national distinctive feature of Jewishness but had no further significant Jewish-nationalist aspirations.

Very important attempts to elaborate a concept of Jewish nationalism on a philosophical basis are found in the work of Franz Rosenzweig. Rosenzweig rejected the view that Judaism is distinguishable only as a religion. Unlike the Christian who *becomes* a Christian, the Jew is *born* a Jew. Jewishness is a particular biological fact by which Jews form a nation. However, this nation differs from all other nations by its continuous existence. This reflects the fact that all other nations are subject to history while the people of Israel, on account of its unique proximity to God the Father, is not. Rosenzweig speaks of both Judaism and Christianity as "eternities," but, once again, Christianity – "the eternal way" – is plunged into history, while Judaism – "the eternal life" – is already, from the very beginning, beyond history. The Jewish people is different from the "worldly" nations by its particular spiritual essence. These speculative ideas come to their most striking expression in Rosenzweig's essay on "The Spirit and the Periods of Jewish History"[21] as well as in the third part of his *Star of Redemption*.

Rosenzweig's idea of the metahistorical status of the Jewish people was not entirely new. Already S. R. Hirsch, the founder of neo-Orthodoxy, had expressed similar ideas in the nineteenth century. According to Hirsch, the sources of truth are beyond history which is of no relevance to the people of Israel, already in possession of the true faith. History applies only to other peoples and cultures. Although in 1848 he had been active in the struggle for national liberation and Jewish emancipation, Hirsch, being an extremely Orthodox thinker, was more concerned with the religious nature of Judaism than the national aspect of the Jewish people that formed the subject matter of Rosenzweig's essay. Anyway, he expressly spoke about the Jewish people and even employed the concept of "national Jewish consciousness." His Jewish nationalism entailed an affirmative view of the Diaspora where it is Israel's mission to spread its ideas about God. But on the whole his religious outlook was more concerned with the duties of a Jew – Jisroel-Mensch – than with the role of the Jewish people.[22] Although Rosenzweig did not share his Orthodox beliefs, Hirsch's approach to Jewish nationalism anticipated certain of his views. (He mentioned S. R. Hirsch on several occasions in his letters.)

Rosenzweig stressed the spiritual essence of Jewish nationhood. This led him to the assertion that it was the talmudic period, distinguished by very intensive spiritual activity, which overthrew the dichotomy of homeland and Diaspora. It suspended the power of history over the Jewish people and released it from subordination to time and place. It became the basis of Jewish eternity which means to exist outside of "wordly" history and to become part of the sphere of the "spiritual." Therefore, all peoples are tied to the soil and subjugated to time, except the people of Israel. Following Hegel's logic that every finite thing will bring itself to extinction, Rosenzweig interprets non-temporality or infinity as implying the eternity of the Jewish people and applies it to the Diaspora as well. Hegel asserted that every nation contributes its special share to "world spirit" (*Weltgeist*) and exists from history. Rosenzweig, like Krochmal before him, ripostes that the Jewish people did not disappear because it exists outside history, in the sphere of eternity. According to this historiographical scheme, the Golah characterized Jewish existence from its very beginnings in Egypt, or even Mesopotamia (for example Abraham):

> Since its outset Jewish history wanders from one diaspora to another, because the spirit of Galut, estrangement from the land, strife for higher life, instead of succumbing to the rule of land and time, is entrenched in this history from its very beginning.[23]

The ties to a homeland are not essential; Palestine never was a homeland but the "holy land," a land of nostalgia (*Sehnsucht*). It was only a temporary spiritual center while Jewish history – namely the history of that people which is outside of history – is characterized by going from one Diaspora to another. This disdainful attitude toward real life on the land and in an historical reality distinguished Rosenzweig from the assimilationist thesis, on the one hand, and from the Zionist outlook, on the other. The former denied, according to him, the national identity of the Jewish people and viewed Judaism as only a religion. The latter considered the Jewish people as a nation, active in history like other nations, and yearned for a return to its historical homeland. However, the intent to reintroduce the Jewish people into history betrays its eternity. As against these two tendencies Rosenzweig endeavored to emphasize the national uniqueness of Judaism as based on a metahistorical conception. He took upon himself to demonstrate the reality of the Jewish nation, although it lacked the habitual characteristics of a nation. The anomaly which Zionism aspired to redress seemed to him to express the normal patterns of Jewish national existence. In the same vein he also characterized the Hebrew language as a "living" language, not a dead one like Latin, but at the same time as an eternal, "holy" language not to be soiled by profane use.[24] (This he proclaimed when Hebrew had already become again a colloquial language in Palestine.)

In the third part of the *Star of Redemption* Rosenzweig reiterates the same ideas. The land, the soil, is the human's enemy because it alienates one from one's true spiritual essence,[25] and ties one to worldly affairs. He represents extraterritoriality as the desirable ideal, and, as mentioned above, totally disregards the problem of normalization of Jewish life propounded by Zionist thinkers. Although there is a kernel of truth in his assertion that when the land or the state are regarded as the ultimate end instead of being mere means for assuring the life of the people, this endangers the true essence of the nation. He, however, also rejected their role as tools, since he proclaimed that to be an authentic Jew means to live in the Diaspora.[26] The Jew, as it were, is at home everywhere; this may include Palestine too. It was not Jewish life in Eretz Yisrael which aroused his scorn but the programmatic goal of the Zionist vision to revive the Jewish people on the historical plane and to cherish Palestine (Eretz Yisrael) as the national Jewish homeland. Judaism has not, and ought not to have, worldly ties; it is not moved by the will for a homeland but by "the will to be a people" ("der Wille zum Volk")[27] that can be accomplished only by the people itself.[28]

Mordecai M. Kaplan, the founder of Reconstructionism, was one of the latest Jewish thinkers to devote attention to Jewish nationalism using philosophical standards. In this chapter we are not concerned with his religious naturalism and its theological and humanist implications. Although Kaplan was a fervent Zionist, and spent some of the last years of his long life in Jerusalem, he considered Jewish life in the Diaspora to be no less creative and desirable than Zionist realization. From this point of view he made an interesting and original, though disputable, contribution to the philosophical foundations of modern Jewish nationalism. He defined Judaism as an "evolving religious civilization" or as a "religion of ethical nationhood." These concepts enabled him to stipulate both Eretz Israel and the Golah as forming the underlying structures of Jewish creative existence and activity. His outlook was in part inspired by Achad Ha'am's concept of "center and periphery" (see the following chapter). He dedicated his *Religion of Ethical Nationhood* to the memory of Achad Ha'am, among others; he characterized him there as one "who revealed to me the spiritual reality of the Jewish people."[29] The concept "civilization" is to a certain extent ambivalent and problematic because it transgresses national boundaries. Therefore, Kaplan's intertwining of national existence in Israel and creative existence in the Golah insinuates that Jewish nationality also includes some sort of a supranational element. While in his theological conception of the Jewish religion Kaplan rejects supranaturalism, in his philosophical conception of Jewish nationality he allows for some supranaturalism. By referring to Judaism as an "evolving" civilization, Kaplan endeavored to award priority to the concrete national character-istics of the Jewish people in changing historical situations rather than to its religio-metaphysical sources. Jewish life is concerned with the actual needs of the Jewish people in the present. Tradition, as derived from the ancient holy scriptures, must be subordinated to present-day tasks and requirements, in order to assure a meaningful existence for the Jewish people in the surrounding world. Under the influence of E. Durkheim, Kaplan considered any meaningful and collective entity as displaying religious features the task of which is to link the individual to the group and to underscore the importance of his or her identifi-cation with it. In line with this view, religion lies at the bottom of every culture and civilization; there does not exist any civilization without it. One can obviously ask whether by this quite arbitrary definition would a secular Frenchman, and a fortiori a secular Jew, be nationally defective? Kaplan probably thought so. On the other hand, from all this it also follows that there is no contradiction between religious and national-cultural components because both take part in the shaping of the all-encompassing spiritual reality of Jewish civiliz-ation. Hence "Judaism" and "Jewish religion" are not synonyms. The latter is part of the former although Kaplan considers it, as shown above, a most important part. There is no other nation where religion occupies such a focal position as in the Jewish nation. This view con-tinues, of course, a characteristic view of the nineteenth-century Jewish philosophers. Yet, in order to conserve Jewish life it is not enough to maintain the Jewish religion but it is imperative to preserve the unlike-ness, the otherness, of Judaism, that is, all those features by which a Jew differs from a non-Jew.

> Judaism as otherness is thus something far more comprehensive than the Jewish religion. It includes that nexus of a history, literature, language, social organization, folk sanctions, standards of conduct, social and spiritual ideals, aesthetic values, which in their totality form a civilization.[30]

Judaism represents an all-encompassing social-spiritual heritage; by defining it as a "civilization," Kaplan wishes to explain all that by which it is distinguished from others. There obviously are common elements, shared by different civilizations and transmitted from one to another, in the areas of science, etc., but they are unable to constitute a civilization by themselves. This is accomplished only by those elements that mold otherness and uniqueness and that cannot be transmitted elsewhere: language, literature, art, religion, and laws.

The concept of Judaism as a civilization thus sets before Jewish life in modernity three alternatives: first, life in Eretz Yisrael, that is, the Zionist solution which is indeed the most perfect, authentic, and ideal one. Second, life as an autonomous cultural minority. This possibility (formerly recommended by Dubnow, see above) does not exist after the Second World War. Third, communal life in a general civilization (such as Western culture), together with an affiliation to a Jewish sub-civilization. Since not all Jews will opt for the first alternative, the third one must be taken into consideration too. It means to define Judaism as "a new type of nation – an international nation with a national home."[31] This sounds prima facie like a contradiction but according to Kaplan it would give an adequate answer to the fact that Jewish dispersion is a permanent phenomenon. However, he admits himself that this definition would be accepted neither by non-Jews (the accusation of "double loyalty") nor by the Jews themselves. None the less he is firmly convinced that "the restoration of the Jews to national status will contribute, rather than detract from, international-mindedness."[32]

There was another trend of Jewish nationalism in the twentieth century, known as territorialism. It included several movements which had split off from the Zionist organization. They aimed at establishing some kind of Jewish settlement on a territory where Jews will then form the majority of the population. From the philosophical viewpoint they had no interesting and original ideas. They differed from Zionism (see the following chapter) in that they considered Palestine not to be the only territory where a Jewish homeland might be re-established. Their aim was "to procure a territory upon an autonomous basis for those Jews who cannot, or will not, remain in the lands in which they at present live."[33] Their chief spokesman was Israel Zangwill. In 1935, there was also founded the Freeland League, pursuing a similar aim, namely "to find and obtain large scale room in some sparsely populated area for the Jewish masses where they could live and develop according to their own views and culture and religion." The League emphasized that it wants to help "those Jews who seek a home and cannot or will not go to Palestine."[34]

The thinkers mentioned in this chapter, do not exhaust, of course, the list of modern and contemporary Jewish philosophers who dealt with the problem of Jewish nationalism. Some of them we shall encounter in the next chapter.

❦ NOTES ❦

1 For example, J. G. Fichte's famous *Reden an die deutsche Nation* of 1807/8 in Berlin.

2 To what degree these resolutions were forced on the delegates by Napoleon is a matter for historical research.

3 Hermann Cohen, *Deutschtum und Judentum* (Giessen: A. Topelmann 1915). This pamphlet, written during the First World War, aroused the unanimous indignation of all Jewish philosophers at the time, including F. Rosenzweig, who was Cohen's faithful disciple.

4 In his *Hebrew Grammar* Spinoza emphasized twice that his intention was to write a grammar of the *Hebrew* language while all former grammarians had dealt with the holy language. Spinoza 1962, pp. 36, 96.

5 Spinoza, 1951, p. 55.

6 Ibid., p. 56.

7 Ibid.

8 In his preface to the German translation of Menasseh ben Israel's *Vindiciae Judaeorum* Mendelssohn also emphasized the right of the Jews to become "citizens of the state."

9 Maimon 1911, p. 263.

10 Ibid., p. 264.

11 Personally Maimon was perhaps inconsistent because despite his declaration that he, as a 'freethinker," has joined the "philosophical religion," and no longer belongs to the Jewish state (nation), he remained attached to it sentimentally all his life.

12 On these two books see Neher 1991 [1966], 1974.

13 Krochmal 1961.

14 Hess 1935, p. 35.

15 The young Hess' anti-Jewish vituperations reached their climax in his article "Über das Geldwesen" of 1845.

16 Spinoza 1951, p. 56.

17 Hess 1935, p. 199. The title of the fifth paragraph (of the "Epilog") is: "Die letzte Rassenherrschaft," pp. 197–200.

18 Graetz 1969, pp. 103–9.

19 Ibid., p. 124.

20 The third paragraph in the epilogue of *Rom und Jerusalem* is called "Die genetische Weltanschauung." Hess 1935, pp. 180–7.

21 Rosenzweig 1984, pp. 527–38.

22 Hirsch 1962.

23 Rosenzweig 1984, p. 537.

24 Ibid., pp. 535–6. Also "Neuhebräisch," ibid., pp. 723–9.

25 Rosenzweig 1988, pp. 332–5.

26 "Jude sein *heisst* im 'Golus' sein." Rosenzweig 1979, p. 700.

27 Rosenzweig 1988, p. 333.

28 "Das Volk ist Volk nur durch das Volk," ibid.

29 Kaplan 1970, p. v.

30 Kaplan 1934, p. 178.

31 Ibid., p. 232.
32 Ibid., p. 241.
33 *Encyclopedia Judaica* 1971, 15: 1019.
34 Ibid., p. 1021.

❧ BIBLIOGRAPHY ❧

Texts

Hess, M. (1935) *Rom und Jerusalem – Die letzte Nationalitätenfrage* (Vienna and Jerusalem: Loewit).

Kaplan, M. M. (1934) *Judaism as a Civilization: Toward a Reconstruction of American-Jewish Life* (New York: Macmillan).

—— (1970) *The Religion of Ethical Nationhood: Judaism's Contribution to World Peace* (New York: Macmillan).

Krochmal, N. (1961) *More Nevuchej ha-Zeman*, in *The Writings of Nachman Krochmal*, edited by S. Rawidowicz (Waltham: Ararat).

Rosenzweig, F. (1979) *Gesammelte Schriften, I. Abteilung: Briefe und Tagebücher*, 2. Band (The Hague: Nijhoff).

—— (1984) "Geist und Perioden der jüdischen Geschichte," *Gesammelte Schriften, III. Abteilung: Zweistromland. Kleinere Schriften zu Glauben und Denken* (Dordrecht: Nijhoff), pp. 527–38.

—— (1988) *Stern der Erlösung* (Frankfurt am Main: Suhrkamp).

Spinoza (1951) *Theologico-Political Treatise*, vol. 1 in *The Chief Works of B. de Spinoza* (New York: Dover).

—— (1962) *Hebrew Grammar (Compendium Grammatices Linguae Hebraeae)*, translated by Rabbi M. Bloom (New York: Philosophical Library).

Studies

Graetz, H. (1969) *Essays – Memoirs – Letters* [Hebrew] (Jerusalem: Bialik Institute).

Hirsch, S. R. (1962) *Horeb – A Philosophy of Jewish Laws and Observances*, trans. I. Grunfeld, 2 vols. (London: Soncino).

—— (1969) *The Nineteen Letters on Judaism* (Jerusalem and New York: Feldheim).

Maimon, S. (1911) *Salomon Maimons Lebensgeschichte* (Munich: Müller).

Neher, A. (1974) *David Gans, disciple du Maharal de Prague, assistant de Tycho Brahe et de Jean Kepler* (Paris: Klincksieck).

—— (1991) [1966] *Le Puits de l'exil, tradition et modernité: La Pensée du Maharal de Prague* (Paris: Cerf).

CHAPTER 32

Zionism

Ze'ev Levy

The emergence of the idea of Jewish nationality in its modern form – Zionism – took place relatively late, long after the idea of nationalism had taken hold of other European peoples. At the same time as nation-states were already coming into actual existence in Europe, in Judaism there were only a very few precursors of the Jewish national – Zionist – idea. The most important among them from the philosophical view-point was M. Hess (1812–75) whose conception of Jewish nationalism was analyzed in the last chapter.

There were several other forerunners of Zionism at the time, foremost among them Rabbi Yehuda Alkalai and Rabbi Zvi Kalischer (with whom Hess corresponded), but they were mainly inspired by religious and messianic motives, without any philosophical background. They were, however, strongly impressed by the liberal and nationalist ideas, flourishing in Europe in the mid-century; these certainly served as a springboard for their messianic-flavored notions too. The rise of anti-semitism, on the other hand, did not play any significant role in their activities.

Hess' outlook on Jewish nationality was shaped by the concepts of Hegelian philosophy, and by his enthusiastic inspiration from and interpretation of Spinoza. His starting-point was philosophy; it determined his response to tradition. In this connection another important philosophical concept played a decisive role in steering his notion of Jewish nationality to its Zionist consequences, namely the Fichtian concept of Bestimmung. This ambiguous German word signifies "determination" as well as "destination;" at the same time it also arouses associations with the notion of "mission," so dear to Hess and Jewish thinkers of the nineteenth century. It indeed fits Hess's trend of thought extremely well; the destination – the mission – is determined by general objective laws. The concept of "mission" underwent several metamorphoses in Hess' thought; in his early writings its heralds were Jesus and Spinoza, later on he assigned it to certain nations, in particular France, and finally he ascribed it to Judaism.

But how did Hess reach his Zionist conclusions? How do mission and national revival converge in his philosophical world view? To accomplish its historical mission, the Jewish people must establish its own state. To diffuse the idea of universal human harmony which is incumbent upon the Jews as part of the global struggle for social and national liberation necessitates a normal national life. Without the precondition of a natural and independent life in one's own land the mission will be of no effect.

> Concerning the Jews, much more than those nations that are
> oppressed on their own soil, national independence must
> precede any political-social progress. The common soil of the
> homeland is for them the first condition of appropriate working
> relations. . . . Otherwise [man] will deteriorate to the level of a
> parasite that subsists only at the expense of alien production.[1]

His general socialist vision intermingles with his Zionist message. Like Marx, Hess firmly believed the establishment of a socialist society to be a forthcoming reality. "In the Exile Judaism cannot regenerate. . . . The masses of the Jewish people will take part in the great historical movement of humanity only when they will have a Jewish homeland."[2]

Although the theoretical layer of Hess' Zionist conviction was derived from a metaphysical conception of Israel's "mission" among the nations, he did not ignore the prevailing anomaly of Jewish life in the Golah. His conclusions with regard to a renewal and normalization of Jewish life in its homeland anticipated many ideas which the socialist–Zionist movement proclaimed half a century later, and which Borochov tried to explicate by means of a systematic Marxist method. Hess was not only the precursor of socialism and the precursor of Zionism but the precursor of socialist Zionism. He grasped by his intuitive vision many ideas that formed the ideological infrastructure of the Zionist labor movement in the twentieth century. At the same time he emphasized that Jewish patriotism ought not to prevent the participation of Jews (including himself) in the social and cultural life of their countries of residence in the Golah. Yet, emancipation does not solve the Jewish question; it is only a first step towards national freedom.

Although his book *Rome and Jerusalem* caused a sensation, it did not elicit any positive responses from Jews (except Graetz). Western Jews to whom Hess addressed his book already enjoyed a substantial repeal of former economic and social restrictions; liberal individualism reigned supreme and enabled Jews in the West to prosper as never before, and, despite growing anti-semitism, to integrate into their environment. The time was not yet ripe for Hess' Zionist message. Only about three decades later, with the founding of the Zionist organization, Hess' book was retrieved from oblivion, and became an integral part of Zionist ideology. Notwithstanding its philosophical weaknesses and mixture of theoretical analysis with intuition and sentimental speculation,[3] it has become an important keystone of the philosophical foundations of Zionism.

Pre-Herzlian Zionist ideas began to spread in Eastern Europe through the Hibbat-Zion movement, which drew its inspiration from Jewish tradition. Religious feelings of attachment to Eretz Yisrael, on the one hand, and difficulties in attaining true emancipation, on the other, outweighed by far any philosophical deliberations. The sole attempts to give a philosophical (or ideological) basis to Hibbat-Zion were undertaken by L. Pinsker and Achad Ha'am. In his *Autoemancipation* of 1882 Pinsker (1821–91) began with an analysis of anti-semitism, from which he went on to explicate Jewish existence, as did Hess before him, as a distinct ethnic organism that cannot be assimilated or integrated into its environment. The reason is not that Jews are unable to assimilate but that they are not tolerated. Like Spinoza, he postulated Jew-hatred as the chief cause of Jewish separateness. "Judophobia," the anti-semitic form of "xenophobia," is a persevering psychosocial phenomenon that prevents Jews everywhere from becoming a normal national entity. The nations dislike foreigners,[4] and, in order to overcome their perennial state as foreigners, Jews must become a proper nation with a state of their own. The only solution is to leave the places of residence where they are the object of hatred, and to regain a homeland where they can live in peace and dignity like any other normal nation. Pinsker attacked the Jewish Liberal idea that the Jews were dispersed in order to fulfill a "mission" in the world, as well as the Orthodox view that they ought to wait passively for the coming of the messiah. It is noteworthy that, according to Pinsker himself, Spinoza's remarks (at the end of the third chapter of the *Theologico-Political Treatise*) were one of the main reasons that instigated him to write his book.

> Oh yes, if Spinoza, the moderate and unbiased thinker, who considers everything very carefully, and does not show much sympathy to Judaism – if he could believe in the possibility that the Jews may, "if occasion offers ... raise up their empire afresh, and that God may a second time elect them," it proves that this is no mere dream or illusion.[5]

At the end of his life, however, Pinsker seemed to have adopted the view that Palestine will become only the spiritual center of Judaism, an idea which became famous through Achad Ha'am (see below).

Theodor Herzl, the founder of modern Zionism, expressed in his *Der Judenstaat* (Vienna, 1896) the same idea as Pinsker, namely that the Jewish problem can be solved only if the Jews cease to be a national anomaly. However, notwithstanding his paramount role in the history of Zionism, Herzl was a journalist, a prophetic visionary, and a great statesman, but he was not a philosopher. He is therefore of no concern to this inquiry.

It is different with Achad Ha'am (1856–1927). Although he was more of a first-rank publicist than a systematic philosopher, his thought was strongly influenced by the evolutionist conceptions of the nineteenth century, and especially by the philosophy of H. Spencer. Albeit his outlook never became the main road of Zionist ideology, it left a powerful impact on its philosophical and theoretical implications, and even more so since the establishment of the state of Israel. According to his principal presupposition, rational truths cannot explicate Jewish particularity. Jewish nationality, as every other nationality, is acquired naturally, in contradistinction to the concept of humanity which is derived by abstract reasoning. Jewish particularity is grounded in a spontaneous sentiment of national belonging, akin to family ties. A person's relation to his or her nation is in no need of theoretical proofs; it is prior to consciousness. The nation's "will to live" is an outcome of every individual's will to live. At the same time Achad Ha'am maintained an idea, expressed already by N. Krochmal (with whose philosophy he was very much impressed), namely that every nation is distinguished by some particular characteristic culture of its own which is based on some central spiritual principle. Under the influence of this idea, which also exhibits some infiltration of Hegelian concepts, Achad Ha'am awarded priority to spiritual determinants over the real political factors of actual statehood. There does not exist, as it were, any Jewish national problem, any more than there exists a French or English one. The peculiarity of the Jewish question derives from the fact that Jewish national reality engenders special problems which are much more complex than those of other nations. The most portentous of them is assimilation, to which Achad Ha'am devoted much of his thought.[6] He believed it to represent a danger to Jews only as individuals. A "spiritual center" in Palestine that will radiate to the Jewish "periphery" in the Golah will constitute an efficient barrier to assimilation, "will strengthen national consciousness in the Golah . . . and endow spiritual life with a true national content."[7] But do the Jews who are influenced by the center show any willingness to cooperate with those that desire to influence them? This question indeed highlights one of the cardinal issues of Zionist thought: to what extent does the Zionist solution of the Jewish question entail the consent and readiness of Jewish individuals to realize it or to identify with it?

Achad Ha'am thus distinguished between the problem of Judaism, to be solved by a spiritual center in Palestine, and the problem of Jews in the Golah whose identity will be assured by their relation to that center. The tragic error of his idealist philosophical conception was that he did not try to search for any deeper roots of these special Jewish national problems. He paid very little attention to the anomaly and extraterritoriality of Jewish life. He believed that his Zionist solution of the problem of Judaism would lead also to the desired solution of the problem of the Jews, without entailing the necessity for all of them to immigrate to Palestine. What was most important to him was to suggest a solution to the problem of Judaism. This distinguished him from other important Zionist thinkers of his time, such as J. Klatzkin, B. Borochov, and N. Syrkin.

Jacob Klatzkin (1882–1948) was a philosopher who devoted the bulk of his scholarly work to Jewish medieval philosophy as well as to Spinoza, whom he held in high esteem as a metaphysician but denounced from the Jewish national viewpoint. (He wrote a Hebrew book on Spinoza and translated the *Ethics* into Hebrew.) Yet, in addition to his scientific inquiries, he also elaborated some kind of a philosophical conception of Jewish nationalism. He strongly criticized the liberal tendency to transform Judaism into a spiritual idea; this he condemned as "Jude-sein ohne Jüdisch-sein", which paves the road to assimilation. To be an "assimilated Jew" is, as it were, a contradiction that reflects the Jewish anomaly. To speak about the "spirit" or "essence" of Judaism is incompatible with a national conception of Judaism. Both the Orthodox way of life as well as the Liberal aspiration to reduce Judaism to a spiritual mission manifest *subjective* criteria of Judaism while a national definition requires an *objective* standard. Jewishness is not merely a matter of religion or morality because to be a Jew does not any more entail a particular religious or spiritual mentality. On the other hand, the *objective* phenomenon of national belonging stems from the *subjective* historical will to belong to the Jewish people.[8] In the modern era voluntaristic elements – the *will* to be a Jew – determine the self-identification and belonging of Jewish nationality. Klatzkin does not deny the spiritual influence of Judaism on other religions and on Western culture; he does not even reject the notions of "spirit of Judaism" and "Jewish ethics," but he is bitterly opposed to employing them as national paradigms. The criteria of Jewish nationalism must be rooted in objective ground – land and language. "They are the forms of national existence."[9] His Jewish-national conception was part of his general philosophy which emphasized vitalistic and biological aspects rather than rational ones. In order to preserve Jewish life, the Jewish people ought to abandon the intellectualist and spiritualist trends that characterized Jewish life throughout the ages, and to resume national life in its own homeland and with its own language.

When Klatzkin wrote this, towards the end of the First World War, he defined land and language as "anticipations of national demand." If there exists already the subjective will for redemption, "for the revival of our land and language," the Jewish people can be regarded as a "nation" already in the Galut.[10] From the philosophical angle, however, his arguments were fraught with many theoretical short-comings. He defined land and language as national "forms," following his hypothesis that "only forms can serve as national criteria,"[11] and denied them value as contents. This arbitrary explication of "form" led him to quite idiosyncratic conclusions. Since contents become Jewish only as a result of national form, then literature, or philosophy, even if they deal with Jewish matters but are not written in Hebrew, do not belong to Jewish national property;[12] on the other hand, a detective novel, translated into Hebrew, does. These eccentric ideas do not diminish the importance of his conception that the will to settle on one's own land and to speak one's own language is one of the preconditions of Jewish nationalism. At the same time he did not underrate external factors. Like Spinoza, Klatzkin also stressed the role of Jew-hatred, persecutions, discrimination, etc. Therefore it is not enough to establish in Palestine a spiritual center à la Achad Ha'am; only a *national* center in Eretz Yisrael can solve the Jewish question.[13] The modern definition of being a Jew is secular. Only those whose homeland is Eretz Yisrael and whose language is Hebrew (or who aspire to achieve this) can be considered as Jews. This arbitrary definition of Judaism virtually excludes from the Jewish nation all Jews who continue to live outside Israel and do not intend to settle there. Prima facie Klatzkin's conception of Jewish nationalism and its Zionist conclusion look much more realistic than Achad Ha'am's spiritual one, but, viewed retrospectively, it may have been the other way round. Perhaps this was the reason why, unlike his important explorations in the field of Jewish philosophy that have become an integral part of modern Jewish scholarship, his philosophical reflections on Jewish nationhood played only a minor role in Zionist thought and left no significant traces.

We have already mentioned certain theories of Jewish nationalism and Zionism that derived their inspiration from socialist ideas, foremost among them those of M. Hess. From a philosophical perspective there are two more thinkers whose theories deserve closer attention – B. Borochov and N. Syrkin.

Ber Borochov (1881–1917) laid the foundations of a socialist-Zionist Weltanschauung that combined a Marxist outlook with an analysis of Jewish national needs, based on a synthesis of class struggle and nationalism. It was one of the first theoretical attempts to explicate the national question in general and the Jewish question in particular by Marxist concepts.[14] This became the starting-point of his search for the deeper covert causes of Jewish existence which underlie its overt spiritual and cultural manifestations. They consist in the separation of the Jewish people from its homeland, because without a country of its own, without normal economic relations, Jews remain a powerless national minority. This means that only in their own country will the Jewish workers be able to wage their class struggle against the bourgeoisie under normal conditions. The return to Palestine will put an end to the anomaly of Jewish life in the Diaspora where Jews are restricted to "unproductive" and peripheral pursuits, that is, to a life without a healthy and independent economic basis. Since in the anomalous situation of the Diaspora Jewish workers are confined to petty and secondary trades and have no access to modern heavy industry which represents "the axis of the historical wheel," they lack a "strategic basis" for a normal and influential class struggle. While orthodox Marxists emphasized the conflict between "forces of production" and "relations of production" as the chief agent of class struggle, Borochov emphasized the lesser-known Marxist concept of "conditions of production" that distinguish the Jewish from the non-Jewish workers. They prevent them from becoming true proletarians; "proletarianization" will be possible only when the "inverted pyramid" of Jewish economic life is put on its broad base. Although Borochov did not play down the threat of anti-semitism, it was the social and economic anomaly of Jewish life which held his attention and drove him to his Zionist conclusion. He condemned assimilation; it is not only objectively of no avail but introduces a morally faulty distinction between the individual rich Jews "who made it" and the multitude of the Jewish masses who continue their miserable alienated life. Furthermore, assimilation is a dangerous illusion because it turns Jews away from the main struggle for national emancipation and normalization.

Socialism and Zionism are mutually interlocked because both aim at making Jewish life normal and productive again. In order to achieve this end, the Jewish people should migrate not to other countries, because that will merely perpetuate the anomaly, but to its own territory, to Palestine. Borochov considered Palestine not only to be a strategic base for Jewish proletarian class struggle but as the homeland for the Jewish people as a whole. Various concepts of Borochov's Marxist interpretation of the Jewish question look obsolete now, but his contribution to socialist-Zionist thought was exceedingly influential. It made a powerful impact on the Zionist labor movement.

Another prominent ideologist of socialist Zionism was Nachman Syrkin (1868–1924). Like Borochov, though before him and independently of him, he developed at an early age a synthesis of socialism and Zionism (although for a short while he adhered to the trend of territorialism (see previous chapter). Already in 1898 he declared that "a classless society and national sovereignty are the only means of completely solving the Jewish problem."[15] He criticized the assimilationist tendencies of Jewish socialists and liberals as well as Achad Ha'am's spiritual conception of Judaism because all of them disregarded the actual social realities which constitute the main causes of the Jewish question – anti-semitism, mass migration, etc. The Jewish masses are the "proletariat of the proletariat," the "slave of slaves" – miserable peddlers, tailors, shoemakers, and so on – whose "sole redemption lies in Zionism" (1901).[16] Although he criticized Borochov's Marxist interpretation of the Jewish question, and gave class struggle only secondary importance in his Zionist outlook, he also considered the Jewish proletarian masses to be the true realizers of the Zionist idea.

There were also other non-Marxist socialist Zionists, such as A. D. Gordon or Berl Katznelson and their followers. For them Zionism was first of all a voluntary act of the individual who affirmed the dignity of physical labor and the ties to the soil. They aspired to create a new Jew instead of the alienated Jew of the Golah. Some others, like the writer J. H. Brenner, influenced by Nietzsche, also accentuated this outlook in a radical way. They not only denounced Golah mentality, but called for a total break with most of Jewish spiritual heritage. Their opposition to any solidarity with Judaism and Jews outside Israel attracted, however, only a tiny fraction of some later Jewish writers in Israel who called themselves Kana'anites, in order to distinguish themselves from Jews elsewhere.

Finally, M. Buber (discussed also in other chapters) played an important role in shaping the Zionist consciousness of young Jews in Western Europe at the beginning of the century, especially in the wake of his three famous *Addresses on Judaism* of 1909–11. But his Zionist thought was on the whole overshadowed by his dialogical philosophy, his studies of Chasidism and the Bible, and his general philosophico-sociological work. His Zionist outlook stressed certain ideas of utopian socialism, under the influence of A. D. Gordon and the anarchist G. Landauer (a close friend of Buber). It developed into what he described as "Hebrew humanism," emphasizing those idealist features by which Zionism differed from other national movements. Buber, guided by the humanist principles of his philosophy, was among the first and most important Zionist ideologists to devote much thought to the issue of Jewish–Arab relations. He stressed relentlessly the goal that the Jewish and Arab peoples should live together in peace and harmony in their common homeland. Regrettably these ideas of Buber aroused little response in the Zionist movement and thought at the time.

This chapter has dealt with the philosophical roots of Zionism, with its "founding fathers" on the philosophical plane. There were and are many more philosophers and historians who engaged in theoretical and ideological issues of Zionism. They included, among others, Yechezkel Kaufmann, Josef Klausner, Ben-Zion Dinur (Dinaburg), Fritz Baer, Felix Weltsch, Max Brod, Nathan Rotenstreich, Yeshayahu Leibowitz, and many others who realized their Zionist convictions by *Aliyah* and life in Israel. Also working on this issue were M. M. Kaplan, A. J. Heschel, A. Neher, E. Levinas, and many others. Contemporary Jewish thought, dealing with various problems of Zionist ideology, embraces a very impressive list of Jewish philosophers. Notwithstanding their important and original contributions, they belong, however, to a generation for which Zionism has become a fait accompli, a living and active reality. They were no longer concerned with its "roots" but – to continue the metaphor – with cultivating its different and multicolored "flowers."

❧ NOTES ❧

1 Hess 1935, pp. 128–9.
2 Ibid., p. 130.
3 Hess himself wrote in a letter to A. Herzen: "I am more of an apostle than a philosopher" (Hess 1959, p. 241).
4 We still are witness to this distressing state of affairs in present-day Europe with the ever-growing migration of refugees and "guest-workers" from East to West.
5 Klausner 1955, p. 296.
6 His famous essay "Imitation and Assimilation" became a classic signpost of Zionist literature.
7 Achad Ha'am 1930, p. 92.
8 Klatzkin 1918, p. 10.
9 Ibid., p. 23.
10 This also may have served him as an apologetical excuse for not putting into practice his national convictions by immigrating himself to Eretz Yisrael.
11 Klatzkin 1918, p. 27.
12 Ibid., p. 130.
13 Ibid., p. 70.
14 Borochov developed his theory most systematically in *Class Struggle and the National Question* and *Our Platform* (Borochov 1955, pp. 154–80, 193–310).
15 *Encyclopedia Judaica* 1971, 15: 653.
16 Ibid.

❧ BIBLIOGRAPHY ❧

Texts

Achad Ha'am (1930) *Al Parashat Derahim* (*On the Crossroads*) (Berlin: Jüdischer Verlag).

Borochov, B. (1955) *Works* [Hebrew], vol. 1 (Tel Aviv: Hakibbutz Hameuchad and Sifriat Poalim).

Hess, M. (1935) *Rom und Jerusalem – Die letzte Nationalitätenfrage* (Vienna and Jerusalem: Loewit).

—— (1959) *Briefwechsel* (The Hague: Mouton).

Klatzkin, J. (1918) *Probleme des modernen Judentums* (Berlin: Jüdischer Verlag).

Studies

Klausner, J. (1955) *From Plato to Spinoza* [Hebrew], (Jerusalem: Madda).

CHAPTER 33

Jewish neo-Kantianism: Hermann Cohen

Kenneth Seeskin

Although his published works indicate that he was not enamored of Judaism, no philosopher in modern times had as profound an effect on Jewish self-understanding as Immanuel Kant.[1] This is true not only for those who look at religion in Kantian terms but for those who do not. Love him or hate him, there is no getting around the fact that for the past two hundred years, a lot of Jewish philosophy has been a dialogue with the sage of Königsberg.

History books record that it was Kant who changed the orientation of philosophy from a study of things as they are in themselves to things as they are constituted by an experiencing subject. This shift led Kant to deny that we can have certain knowledge about God, the soul, or the origin of the universe. But lack of certainty about the truths of metaphysics does not mean we have to reject them altogether. In Kant's words, transcendental philosophy limits knowledge in order to make room for faith (*Glaube*).[2] This faith does not involve a leap in the sense intended by existentialists but a rational belief based on our awareness of and aspiration for the highest good.[3] According to Kant, God is not a necessary being or first cause that we infer from the world around us. To extrapolate from knowledge of the world to God, we would have to prove that this world is the best possible. To make such a judgment, we would have to compare this world to all other possible worlds – a feat that would require infinite intelligence.

Kant therefore concludes that the only content we can ascribe to our idea of God is moral: "It was the moral ideas that gave rise to that concept of the Divine Being which we now hold to be correct – and we so regard it not because speculative reason convinces us of its correctness, but because it completely harmonizes with the moral principles of reason."[4] The important point is not that the world has a creator but that, to fulfill our obligations under the moral law, we must assume that it does. In a word, all legitimate theology is moral theology.

It is easy to see why the practical dimension of Kant's philosophy appealed to Jewish audiences. The metaphysical speculation Kant decries is not indigenous to Judaism. Rather than a first cause, the Jewish understanding of God is that of a merciful agent ready to forgive iniquity (Exodus 34: 6–7), a protector of the disadvantaged (Deuteronomy 10: 18), a judge who insists on righteousness (Deuteronomy 16: 20), and a redeemer who will not be appeased by outward shows of piety (Amos 5: 21–4; Micah 6: 6–8; Isaiah 1: 11–17). As Emmanuel Levinas put it in an interview, the omni-predicates so familiar to students of medieval philosophy are inadequate to describe the Jewish conception of God; rather than look to the almighty first cause of creation, we should look to the persecuted God of the Prophets.[5]

On the issue of morality, Kant is often viewed as an opponent of traditional religion. It is well known that, in the *Groundwork*, he rejects the idea that morality can be derived from a system of divine commands, and, in *Religion Within the Limits of Reason Alone*, proclaims that everything we do to please God above and beyond morality is religious delusion and spurious worship.[6] Still, there is a respect in which the Kantian revolution in morality not only allows for participation in a religious tradition but encourages it. In the *Critique of Practical Reason*, he asks: "Who would want to introduce a new principle of morality and, as it were, be its inventor, as if the world had hitherto been ignorant of what duty is or had been thoroughly wrong about it?"[7] Kant's modesty is not accidental. If, as he insists, moral judgments are a priori, if every rational agent has the ability to act autonomously, legislating for himself or herself, it would be absurd for him to argue that *he* was the first person in history to understand the duties incumbent on a human being. Thus the purpose of Kantian moral theory is not to invent the idea of duty but to formulate a principle from which all existing duties can be derived.

In *Religion Within the Limits*, he enlarges on this idea by pointing out that:

> There exists meanwhile a practical knowledge which, while resting solely upon reason and requiring no historical doctrine, lies as close to every man, even the most simple, as though it were engraved upon his heart – a law, which we need but name to find ourselves at once in agreement with everyone else regarding its authority, and which carries with it in everyone's

consciousness *unconditioned* binding force, to wit, the law of morality.[8]

Although it is unclear whether the mention of a law *engraved upon the heart* is a deliberate reference to Deuteronomy 30: 14, where Moses uses the same metaphor in giving the Torah to Israel, it is clear that Kant has a real interest in showing that historical religion did not develop in ignorance of the moral law. He wants to claim that actual religions have in one way or another approached the ideal of a pure faith founded on a universal conception of humanity and a commitment to its moral improvement. Unless actual religions approached this ideal, it would be impossible for Kant to argue that it is engraved on each of our hearts.

The purpose of *Religion Within the Limits* is to present an idealized picture of Christianity, by which I mean a picture that emphasizes the moral necessity of its teachings. According to Kant, these teachings include the conviction that the disposition of our hearts is more important than obedience to statutory laws, the need to repair injuries done to our neighbor by going to the offended party himself or herself, and the hope that the natural propensity of the human heart to evil can be overcome. Kant believes that these teachings constitute valid principles whatever the historical record may show about their application. In this respect, he is and claims to be a Platonist. If the fact that there are no absolutely perfect circles or parallel lines in the physical world does not refute the ideas of circularity or parallelism, why should the fact that no historical religion has lived up to the ideal of a rational faith show that such a faith is illegitimate? As Kant puts it: "Nothing is more reprehensible than to derive the laws prescribing what *ought to be done* from what *is done*, or to impose upon them the limits by which the latter is circumscribed."[9]

There is always a danger in thinking that, because he offers an idealization of Christianity, his real purpose is to provide a glorification. Certainly there are passages where he falls prey to the latter, as when he argues that Jesus is the founder of the first true Church.[10] But despite occasional slips of parochialism, Kant's intention is to show that, amidst all the dogmas, rituals, statutes, and historical accidents that make up Christianity, there is a thread of moral truth. That the practices of Christian Churches may not always recognize this truth, and in some instances renounce it, Kant is the first to admit. His picture is a model to which historically specific examples may aspire but of which they invariably fall short.

The legacy of Kantian philosophy is therefore a gap between reality and ideality. Although it is instructive to see Hegel and Marx as attempting to close this gap, we can agree with Steven Schwarzchild that, from a Jewish perspective, the suggestion that the real world already embodies the ideal was bound to seem implausible.[11] In the first place, many Jews continued to live in conditions that were a long way from ideal. In the second place, Judaism holds that the messiah has not come and therefore the world, though redeemable, is not *yet* redeemed. Kant himself argued that morality presents us with an infinite task or puts us on an infinite future trajectory. In the *Critique of Practical Reason*, he maintains that: "The thesis of the moral destiny of our nature, viz., that it is ... only in an infinite progress toward complete fitness to the moral law, is of great use, not merely for the present purpose of supplementing the impotence of speculative reason, but also with respect to religion."[12]

Without doubt, the greatest thinker to take up the idea of the infinite task and "re-open" the gap between reality and ideality was Hermann Cohen. Cohen (1842–1918) was a prominent follower of Kant, and in some ways responsible for the revival of his thought. He founded the Marburg School of philosophy, which came to have considerable status in the German-speaking world, and which advocated a particular approach to Kant, one which emphasized his ethical principles. As he got older he became more interested in Judaism, and sought to use Kantianism to explore some of the main themes of religion. In a nutshell, Cohen tried to do for Judaism what Kant had done for Christianity. Although the title of Cohen's most famous work, *Religion of Reason Out of the Sources of Judaism*, is often taken to mean that Judaism is the religion of reason, this impression is highly misleading. By "religion of reason," Cohen meant an idealized, rational faith stressing the same principles Kant stressed. According to Cohen, this faith can be constructed out of Jewish sources, Christian sources, or others.[13] So while Judaism may not be *the* religion of reason, Kant was wrong to think it was not *a* religion of reason.

Like Kant's Christianity, Cohen's Judaism puts heavy emphasis on the idea of duty. Behind the development of monotheism, he sees the belief that all humanity has a common origin in God. Thus the biblical injunction (Leviticus 24: 22): "You shall have one law for the stranger and for the homeborn, for I am the Lord your God." Cohen argues that this sentiment permeates the whole Torah and substantial portions of rabbinic literature as well.[14] It can be found in the idea of the Noachide Covenant (Genesis 9: 11–16), a pact that God makes with all humanity to prohibit the shedding of innocent blood regardless of the nationality of the victim.[15] It can be found in the conviction that not just Jews but the righteous of every nation will share in salvation. Finally, it can be found in the repeated injunction (Deuteronomy 23: 8) that Israel cannot hate or take advantage of the stranger because it was once a stranger in a foreign land. Cohen concludes that the idea of universal humanity arose not in Plato or Aristotle but in the Hebrew Prophets.

For Kant, religion is the recognition that all duties can be seen as divine commands.[16] Cohen's effort to construct such a view from Jewish sources is long and detailed, with more textual references than most philosophers of religion would think possible. Rather than summarize the entire project, it would be better to take up a single idea: revelation. In the Torah, revelation is an historical event in which God descends on Mount Sinai and addresses a single person, Moses. In Cohen's hands, the historical dimension of revelation is transformed so that, instead of a miracle occurring in the desert, it becomes the discovery of reason in the broadest sense. Put otherwise, revelation is not an event but a principle: the awareness that moral reason is the highest human calling and the faculty that brings us into contact with the divine.

We can better understand Cohen's view of revelation by comparing it to a related idea: the social contract. As originally formulated, social contract theory was an account of the historical origin of society. Interpreted this way, the theory is not only implausible but in many ways irrelevant. Why should actions undertaken by a group of unnamed ancestors put moral restrictions on people living in the present? It is not until we free the social contract of its historical associations and regard it as a principle for explaining ideas like freedom or citizenship that its philosophic significance can be grasped. In Cohen's terms, the social contract does not become valid until we realize that it is not an actual occurrence forced on us by the historical record but a rational construction arising out of our idea of a just society.

To return to revelation, the mechanics of the process – "What sounds did God utter?" or "What exactly did the people hear?" – become unimportant when compared to the content: the call of duty engraved on each of our hearts. According to Cohen, God is the source of moral reason not in the way that Homer is the source of the *Iliad* but in the way that a generative principle is the source of the consequences that follow from it. There is simply no way for us to conceive of a perfect being except as a being who wills the moral law: that every rational agent must be treated as an end in himself or herself.

The moral law is therefore the crux of revelation. Anything other than the moral law would be unworthy of a perfect being and could not be part of the teaching that God gives to Israel. Like Maimonides, Cohen admits that there is more to religion than an abstract principle.[17] If the moral law is the supreme principle of human conduct, it is not necessarily the most immediate. In addition to the moral law, people require symbols to remind them of it, institutions to help them promote it, festivals to encourage them to follow it, and a host of statutory legislation to help them conceptualize it. His point is that the symbols, festivals, and statutory requirements are not heteronomous commands imposed by an arbitrary will but necessary prerequisites for obeying the commands of a rational one. Again, Cohen insists that divine commands not be understood in a historical fashion. From the recognition that all moral duties *can be seen as* divine commands, it does not follow that there was a specific moment in which God gave them to Israel *in fact*. This means that the discovery of moral reason leads to imperatives that are *worthy* of a perfect being, not that a perfect being shouted them from the mountain top.

The issue of commandment leads straight to the issue of autonomy. The standard criticism of Kantian morality is that autonomy makes the individual supreme and undermines respect for authority. If the only commands that have moral authority are those that I impose on myself, autonomy is synonymous with independence.[18] But here, too, we must make a distinction between legislation in principle and legislation in fact. It is noteworthy that, in his best-known formulation of the principle of autonomy, Kant does not say what generations of philosophy students have been told that he says: I am subject only to those laws of which I am the author. This principle, if true, would make me the supreme moral legislator for myself and take away any obligation to obey commands that originate with God, the state, the family, or anything else. What Kant actually says is that I am subject only to those laws of which *I can regard myself* as author.[19] Surely the fact that I can regard myself as the author of a law is compatible with saying that I am not the author in fact. Although I did not write the Fifth Amendment to the US Constitution, which claims that a person cannot be forced to testify against himself or herself, I have no trouble regarding myself as if I did. So, even though I learned about the law by reading a history book, I can appropriate it in an autonomous fashion.

According to Cohen, there is no possibility of a conflict between God's law and the law our moral reason imposes on itself.[20] The imperative to treat all of humanity as an end in itself is valid for all times and all places. We can view it either as a law worthy of a perfect being or as something we could write ourselves, as God's attempt to educate us about our highest calling or our attempt to discover how God is to be served. In the end, the issue is not who wrote the law but its moral necessity.

Another way to see this point is to recognize that, when we talk about self-legislation, we are referring not to the empirical self but to the noumenal one, the self that responds to the causality of reason. Cohen is one of a long line of neo-Kantian thinkers who emphasize that the noumenal self is not a "given" of experience.[21] It is not something we can reach out and touch or discover by introspection. Like God or revelation, the self is a rational construction, something we come to on the basis of argument, historical experience, literary analysis, and every other research tool at our disposal. A rational construction is therefore a task we must strive to fulfill. In virtually all of his writing, Cohen emphasizes that the task is infinite in the sense that it can never be fulfilled completely but must be approached as a mathematical function approaches its limit. Though one generation may be closer to the limit than its predecessor, the gap between reality and ideality remains open for all time.

The result is that contrary to popular misconceptions, autonomy need not imply that I am a rational monad, acting in isolation from everyone else around me. To learn about laws of which I can regard myself as the author, I need a family, friends, religious and secular institutions, and, if Cohen is right, a conviction that, in discovering the demands of moral reason, I am coming to know the will of God. In religious terms this means that revelation is not a one-time event but an ongoing process. In Cohen's view, we are as much a part of the process as Moses and the generation of the Exodus.

A typical criticism of Cohen is that his account of revelation is so abstract that it is not really a *Jewish* theory at all. But oddly enough, the text of Torah is more amenable to idealization than one might think. Although the story of revelation occurs in the book of Exodus, it is re-enacted in the book of Deuteronomy, hence the title *deuteros-nomos* (second law) which is a Greek rendering of the Hebrew *mishneh Torah* (repetition of the law). Immediately before the re-enactment of the giving of the Ten Commandments (Deuteronomy 5: 3), Moses claims: "It is not with our fathers that the Lord made this covenant but with us, all of us who are alive here this day." Why would Moses say "it is not with our fathers" when any reader of the Torah knows that it was? The people addressed in Deuteronomy are the children of the people who stood at Sinai. Long before Cohen, commentators argued that the passage should be taken to mean "it was not with our fathers *alone*" and went on to say that the covenant extended not only to the generation of the Exodus but to that of Deuteronomy and *to all future generations as well.*[22]

Further support can be found in the fact that throughout Deuteronomy (11: 13, 11: 32, 27: 9), Moses claims that God is entering into a covenant with Israel "this day" even though the actual agreement was struck forty years before with the generation of the Exodus. Again, the traditional commentators took "this day" to refer not to a particular point in history but to *any* day; in other words, they understood revelation to be an eternally renewable process. In Cohen's words, the historical thread was broken, and the process of idealization was under way.[23]

Another noteworthy feature of Deuteronomy is that the law revealed to Israel is described as a body of wisdom that must be taught and learned (Deuteronomy 4: 6–8). Instead of a herald who communicates marching orders from the commanding officer, Moses is portrayed as a teacher whose job is to awaken the people's understanding. This theme reaches its climax at Deuteronomy 30: 14, when Moses claims the law is no longer in heaven but in our mouths and written on our hearts. According to Cohen, the fact that the law is no longer in heaven, no longer shrouded by mystery, indicates that even in the Torah there is an attempt to demystify revelation and internalize the law. Rather than an arbitrary command that comes to us with a bolt of lightning and a blast of thunder, the law is so close to us that we can regard it as the product of our own will.

It is clear, as Cohen himself remarks, that it is lucky for him that the book of Deuteronomy was written, for, once we accept Deuteronomy as part of God's revelation to Israel, we have grounds for saying that idealization is not just a neo-Kantian obsession but part of the way the Jewish people understood itself. In his own mind, Cohen embarked on a path that had its origins at Sinai. Like Kant, he claims he is not really an innovator but someone trying to illuminate the sources of an already existing morality.[24] It would be fair to say, then, that both Kant and Cohen see idealization as a hermeneutic exercise. Both are convinced that if we get past the mythical level of religion, replacing temporal relations with logical ones, we will see how the sacred texts of Judaism and Christianity express the unconditioned necessity of the moral law.

Cohen's influence can be seen in such diverse thinkers as Ernst Cassirer, Julius Guttmann, Yechezkel Kaufmann, Leo Baeck, J. B. Soloveitchik, and Steven S. Schwarzschild.[25] The fact is, however, that for a long time Cohen's critics received more attention than his followers. We have seen that Kantian philosophy rejects any attempt to investigate the nature of a mind-independent reality. According to Hilary Putnam, any reference to "things in themselves" or "facts independent of conceptual choices" is incoherent.[26] That is why Cohen does not discuss God but our idea of a perfect being, not my personality but our idea of a finite moral agent. It is also why revelation is not an historical event but an abstraction: the connection *between* a perfect being and a finite agent. In Cohen's words: "Man, not the people, and not Moses: man, as rational being, is the correlate to the God of revelation."[27] Thus all of Cohen's discourse takes place in the realm of ideas.

By the 1920s, two of Cohen's most famous disciples, Martin Buber and Franz Rosenzweig, began to protest that idealized religion was too abstract and that philosophy had to break through the circle of ideas by returning to the concrete reality of everyday life. For Rosenzweig this meant recognition of the ineluctable fact of death, for Buber reaching out to the living God of antiquity rather than a philosophic conception of divinity. By the time Heidegger and Cassirer had their infamous meeting at Davos in 1929, Jewish neo-Kantianism was regarded as an historical relic.

There is some evidence that, in today's world, neo-Kantianism has regained some of its former glory. With the demise of logical positivism, Kantian themes have been rediscovered by people like Thomas Kuhn, Hilary Putnam, John Rawls, and Jürgen Habermas. In the Jewish world, the universalist/particularist debate, not to mention the ongoing discussion of freedom and autonomy, revolves around the *Groundwork* and *Second Critique*. And while many of Kant's critics take issue with claims of transcendental necessity, there remains a widespread conviction that Kant is right on at least one point: the gap between reality and ideality. One of the central ideas of Judaism is that the world was created in an incomplete state so that God and humans must work together to finish the job. Thus the fundamental human task is that of mending the created order (*tiqqun olam*). As long as the gap remains open, the task requires renewed effort.

The question is: will the gap remain open for ever? Will ideal justice always be beyond the reach of imperfect beings or will there be a time when the striving of imperfect beings reaches fulfillment and the moral law is realized on earth? The orthodox Kantian answer is that the gap will never be closed. Thus Cohen is fond of quoting Ecclesiastes 7: 20: "For there is not a righteous man upon earth, that doeth good, and sinneth not." Looking back on a lifetime of philosophic activity, Schwarzschild expressed deep sympathies with Rav, who argued that all the messiahs have come and gone, and, from now on, everything turns on repentance and good deeds.[28] Can there be enough repentance and good deeds to usher in a new age? On this point, Schwarzschild demurred, arguing, with Cohen, that the task is infinite in individual human life, in history, beyond history, and into the world to come.[29] No matter how much progress is made, there will never be a time when the human race achieves complete coincidence between what is and what ought to be. In religious terms, the messianic age will never come but always be in the *process* of coming.[30]

The problem is that, if perfection is always ahead of us, and an infinite gap can never be closed by a finite being, perfection will always be beyond our reach. Ought, as Kant never tires of pointing out, implies can. To say that I ought to strive for something implies that I am capable of achieving it. How, then, can I be obliged to strive for an ideal that is infinitely far away, for no matter how much *finite* progress I make, the distance between me and the end I seek will remain infinite?

The way out of the puzzle is to see that repentance and good deeds are ongoing tasks in the sense that our obligations under the moral law never end. Doing one's duty is not like winning a race or being elected to the Hall of Fame. Even if we act for the purest of motives today, we will be under an obligation to do the same thing tomorrow. So it is fair to say that there is no limit to the effort I am required to put forth. As Kant puts it, morality is always in progress and yet always starts from the beginning.[31] But does it follow that because the demands of morality never end they are infinite in the sense that no finite agent can ever fulfill them? I suggest it does not. I can be obliged to do only what, in the present circumstances, my nature allows me to do. If I am obliged to treat every rational agent as an end in himself or herself, it must be possible for me to do so without assuming infinite moral progress or another life.[32] The moral law may require me to act like a saint or sage, but it cannot require me to act like an angel.

Let us return to the critical text for the Kantian account of revelation: Deuteronomy 30: 11–14:

> For this commandment which I command thee this day, it is not too hard for thee, neither is it far off.
> It is not in heaven, that thou shouldest say: "Who shall go up for us to heaven, and bring it unto us, and make us to hear it, that we may do it?"
> Neither is it beyond the sea, that thou shouldest say: "Who shall go over the sea for us, and bring it unto us, and make us hear it, that we may do it?"
> But the word is very nigh unto thee, in thy mouth, and in thy heart, that thou mayest do it.

This is the passage that supports Kant's claim that the moral law is engraved on our hearts and Cohen's contention that the Torah itself begins the process of demystification. Surely the passage implies that the law is not intended for angels or people of superhuman strength. Contrary to Paul's contention (Romans 7: 13–25) that the law is unfulfillable, the passage seems to say that, in principle, it could be fulfilled by anyone, for it is nothing but the dictates of our own heart. This does not mean that the law is likely to be fulfilled tomorrow or anyday in the foreseeable future. We can agree with Cohen and Schwarzschild that the human condition leaves much to be desired. All we have to admit is that we do not need infinite time or infinite power to perfect it.

Eschatology is, of course, a difficult subject. Even a cursory look at Jewish history will show that the tradition is full of false messiahs, false proclamations about the messianic age, and foolish speculation about what the age will be like. But here, as elsewhere, it is difficult to discuss eschatology without distinguishing between reality and ideality, the is and the ought. Once the distinction is made, it is difficult to say anything important without coming to grips with Kant.

❧ NOTES ❧

1 See for example, *Religion Within the Limits of Reason Alone* 2.2, 3.2, 4.2; 74, 116–18, 154 (Greene and Hudson).
2 *Critique of Pure Reason*, Bxxx: 29 (Kemp Smith). For the connection between Kant's view of the limit of human knowledge and Maimonides', see Fox 1990, pp. 83–4.
3 *Critique of Practical Reason*, 138–9: 143–5 (Beck).
4 *Critique of Pure Reason* A818/B846: 643 (Kemp Smith).
5 "Dialogue with Emmanuel Levinas," in Levinas 1986, pp. 31–2. Also see Baeck 1961, pp. 34–41 (Howe).
6 *Foundations*, 443: 61–2 (Beck); *Religion Within the Limits* 4.2: 158 (Greene and Hudson).
7 *Critique of Practical Reason*, 8: 8 (Beck).
8 *Religion Within the Limits* 4.2: 169 (Greene and Hudson).
9 *Critique of Pure Reason*, A319/B375: 313 (Kemp Smith). Favorable references to Plato occur in the preceding three pages.
10 *Religion Within the Limits* 3.2: 118 (Greene and Hudson).
11 Schwarzschild, "Modern Jewish Philosophy," in Schwarzschild 1990, p. 230.
12 *Critique of Practical Reason*, 122: 127 (Beck).
13 *Religion of Reason*, chapter 16, p. 364 (Kaplan).
14 *Religion of Reason*, chapter 8, pp. 113–43 (Kaplan).
15 On the Noachide covenant, see *Sanhedrin* 56a. The best recent commentary on this aspect of Jewish law is Novak 1983.
16 *Critique of Practical Reason*, 129: 132 (Beck). I say "can be seen as" because, according to Kant, God's existence is a postulate of moral reason and cannot be known for certain.
17 *Religion of Reason* 16: p. 346 (Kaplan), cf. Maimonides, *Guide* 3.32.
18 Cf. Novak 1992, pp. 46–8.
19 *Groundwork*, 431: 49 (Beck).
20 Cohen 1971, p. 81 (Jospe).
21 For Cohen's view of the construction of the self, see Schwarzschild 1975; cf. Allison 1990, pp. 3–5, 141–3.
22 See Rashi's commentary on Deuteronomy 5: 3, 11: 13, and 27: 9.
23 *Religion of Reason*, chapter 4: p. 76 (Kaplan).
24 *Religion of Reason*, Introduction: pp. 24–34 (Kaplan).
25 See, for example Cassirer 1981; Guttmann 1973; Kaufmann 1972; Baeck 1961; and Schwarzschild 1990. For Cohen's influence on Soloveitchik, see Ravitzky 1986; for his influence on later Kant scholarship, see Martin 1955, p. v. For a modern attempt to defend Jewish neo-Kantianism, see Seeskin 1990.
26 Putnam 1987, pp. 33–6.
27 *Religion of Reason*, chapter 4, p. 79 (Kaplan).

28 "Afterword," in Schwarzschild 1990, p. 254. The reference to Rav is taken from *Sanhedrin* 97a.

29 "On Jewish Eschatology," in Schwarzschild 1990, p. 225.

30 Ibid., p. 211.

31 *The Metaphysics of Morals*, 409: 209 (Gregor).

32 Both Kant and Cohen believe that there *is* infinite moral progress in the next world. See *Critique of Practical Reason*, 122–3; 126–8 (Beck) and *Religion of Reason*, chapter 15, pp. 307ff. But how can moral progress be made in a disembodied state? We are never told; cf. Allison 1990, pp. 171–9.

❧ BIBLIOGRAPHY ❧

Texts

Cohen, H. (1971) "Affinities Between the Philosophy of Kant and Judaism," in *Reason and Hope*, translated by E. Jospe (New York: Norton).

—— (1972) *Religion of Reason out of the Sources of Judaism*, translated by S. Kaplan (New York: Ungar).

Kant, I. (1958) *Critique of Practical Reason*, translated by L. W. Beck (Indianapolis: Bobbs-Merrill).

—— (1959) *Foundations of the Metaphysics of Morals*, translated by L. W. Beck (Indianapolis: Bobbs-Merrill).

—— (1960) *Religion Within the Limits of Reason Alone*, translated by T. M. Greene and H. H. Hudson (New York: Harper & Row).

—— (1965) *The Critique of Pure Reason*, translated by N. Kemp Smith (New York: St Martin's).

—— (1991) *The Metaphysics of Morals*, translated by M. Gregor (Cambridge: Cambridge University Press).

Studies

Allison, H. (1990) *Kant's Theory of Freedom* (Cambridge: Cambridge University Press).

Baeck, L. (1961) *The Essence of Judaism*, edited by I. Howe (New York: Schocken).

Cassirer, E. (1981) *Kant's Life and Thought*, translated by J. Haden (New Haven: Yale University Press).

Fox, M. (1990) *Interpreting Maimonides* (Chicago: University of Chicago Press).

Guttmann, J. (1973) *Philosophies of Judaism*, translated by D. W. Silverman (New York: Schocken).

Kaufmann, Y. (1972) *The Religion of Ancient Israel*, translated by M. Greenberg (New York: Schocken).

Levinas, E. (1986) "Dialogue with Emmanuel Levinas," in *Face to Face with Levinas*, edited by R. Cohen (Albany: State University of New York Press).

Martin, G. (1955) *Kant's Metaphysics and Theory of Science*, translated by P. G. Lucas (Manchester: Manchester University Press).

Novak, D. (1983) *The Image of the Non-Jew in Judaism* (Toronto: Edwin Mellen).
—— (1992) *Jewish Social Ethics* (New York: Oxford University Press).
Putnam, H. (1987) *The Many Faces of Realism* (LaSalle: Open Court).
Ravitzky, A. (1986) "Rabbi J. B. Soloveitchik on Human Knowledge: Between Maimonidean and Neo-Kantian Philosophies," *Modern Judaism* 6: 157–88.
Schwarzschild, S. (1975) "The Tenability of H. Cohen's Construction of the Self," *Journal of the History of Philosophy* 13: 378–9.
—— (1990) *The Pursuit of the Ideal* (Albany: State University of New York Press).
Seeskin, K. (1990) *Jewish Philosophy in a Secular Age* (Albany: State University of New York Press).

CHAPTER 34

Jewish existentialism: Rosenzweig, Buber, and Soloveitchik

Oliver Leaman

It is always difficult to group philosophers together under labels, and defining thinkers as "existentialists" is perhaps the most difficult label to apply appropriately. Existentialists seem to have an aversion to being labeled in any way at all, which has the merit of being consistent with their existentialism but which also makes it difficult to know which thinkers should be grouped together.[1] But there are good arguments for considering these three thinkers together, as representative of what might be called Jewish existentialism, although it must not be thought that they share a party line. It will be argued here that considering them together is a useful way of highlighting a number of difficult but interrelated philosophical issues which have come to have great prominence in the twentieth century, and which form part of the curriculum of Jewish philosophy itself. After introducing some basic aspects of their general thought, their contrasting views and arguments on the attitude which Jews should adopt to halakhah, to Jewish law, will be described in order to see how their philosophical views actually work when they are trained on a particular issue.

FRANZ ROSENZWEIG

Many would argue that the greatest philosopher of the three is Franz Rosenzweig (1886–1929), and his *Star of Redemption* is undoubtedly a masterpiece. Born in Kassel in Germany, he grew up within an environment which regarded itself as Jewish in a social rather than religious sense. As he approached adulthood he experienced the familiar forces

799

of assimilation which came to characterize so much of the Jewish experience of his times. He was particularly marked by his relationship with a lecturer in philosophy in Leipzig, Eugen Rosenstock-Huessy, who converted to Christianity from Judaism. Rosenzweig's own cousin, Hans Ehrenberg, had also abandoned his religion and become a Christian, and this struck Rosenzweig as a profoundly correct move. As he often points out, the sort of society in which the Jews of Germany lived was thoroughly Christian, and the "Jewish" culture which they experienced was so strongly marked by Christianity that it seemed more honest to become a Christian and throw off the pretense of maintaining a nominal Judaism. This led to Rosenzweig's own desire to convert, but he felt, typically of the seriousness with which he acted, that, before he became a Christian, he ought to become a Jew in a real sense, since that would give the act of conversion an aspect of authenticity which otherwise it might well lack. His participation in Jewish religiosity disabused him of his desire to convert. He came to think that it was possible to come close to God without the mediation of Jesus Christ as a result of his new awareness that many of his contemporary Jews had no difficulty in finding a deep spirituality and meaning in their religion.

He came to this decision when he was twenty-seven years old, and decided to spend the rest of his life working on Judaism. In Berlin he joined the classes which Hermann Cohen gave which emphasized the significance of philosophy for the understanding of what Judaism means. His interest was far from entirely academic, though, and he came to create and organize a very important institution of Jewish learning in Germany, when he set up the Lehrhaus, which sought to communicate all aspects of Jewish learning to the community at large, and in particular to those who trained there to work in that community. This took place after the First World War, during which he spent much of his time on the front. Sadly, in 1921, he became very unwell with a growing paralysis, and over the next few years rapidly declined in health, dying in 1929. His last eight years were very rich intellectually, and he played a very full academic and pedagogical life with the assistance of his wife and other assistants who helped him work around his ever-increasing disabilities. His ability to continue working despite his sufferings, and the poignancy of such a fluent writer becoming trapped in a body which stopped working, has done a lot to increase his romantic aura.

Rosenzweig's philosophy should originally be seen as in opposition to philosophies which he first of all accepted and then rejected. His first target was Hegelianism, which he rejected on account of what he saw as the reification of entirely general concepts such as "humanity" and its inability to make sense of the life of the individual. He also rejected the sort of approach to Judaism promoted by Hermann Cohen, which regards it as a religion of reason and so as a representation of entirely general universal truths. It is worth noting that both of these approaches are in line with assimilation as a personal decision by the Jewish philosopher. After all, if Judaism is just a stage along the progress of the idea in history, then there is nothing much to be said for adhering to it once that period of history has passed. Similarly, if Judaism is just a particular version of entirely general ethical truths, all that one needs to do when abandoning religion is to ensure that wherever one goes one maintains the same ethical principles. This could be adherence to a new religion, or to no religion at all but to some principle like socialism. Rosenzweig wanted to reject philosophical approaches which represented a justification for assimilation, not just because he came to disapprove of that as a strategy but largely because he came to see that Judaism could not be reduced to anything else.

The "new thinking" which Rosenzweig called for was not in itself very new, since it owed a lot to Nietzsche and Kierkegaard, but it was certainly quite new when applied to Jewish philosophy.[2] It is based on the principle that being is prior to thought, in the sense that the place to start philosophically is with the experiences of the individual, and then to expand from these experiences to more complex and abstract concepts. Rosenzweig's analysis maintains its existentialist flavor throughout, in that when he discusses religious and philosophical concepts he emphasizes the significance of how they relate to our experiences and situation in the world. Reality is a matter of the dynamic interaction of God, world, and humanity, and what is of crucial significance here is this notion of interaction. Judaism manages to bring these diverse ideas together in such a way that they form a picture of the way things are in mutual relationships. It is that which creates and establishes a form of reality which allows human beings to find meaning in their lives.

The notion of God in Judaism is not of a distant creator, someone whose contribution to the world was merely to create it, like an irresponsible parent. On the contrary, he represents the notion of interaction with his creatures, and this is represented through revelation. Although particular revelations occur at certain times and places, this is merely symbolic of the deeper notion of revelation, according to which human beings establish a notion of their own selfhood through their consciousness of the fact that they are created and loved by God. The important thing about this love is that it is not just a passive emotion in which to indulge, but it has serious practical consequences. It provides the emotional juice which keeps the fact of revelation from becoming just a dead symbol, a past event of little present force. It is true that creation took place in the past, and revelation brings out its implications for us in the present, but these would be incomplete without redemption which points to the future. Redemption is seen as something which takes place in our world and time, not in some distant abstract future, not something brought about by divine fiat. Redemption is brought about by ourselves, although perhaps not entirely by ourselves, and represents our power to experience eternity within finitude. How can this be done? For Rosenzweig, the route to this feeling of redemption lies through the religious practices of Judaism, through the rituals and roles of religion. We respond to God by responding to other human creatures, and in so doing we set upon a path which can end in the construction of a messianic state of affairs, and it should be noted yet again that this is not to be seen as something which comes about because of the arrival of the messiah, as a sort of messiah ex machina, but we ourselves, through our actions and attitudes, can bring the messiah about ourselves. Judaism is a call to action, to the creation of meaning and love in our world.

Rosenzweig's insistence that we make the rituals of religion a living part of our lives is based on his theory that we have to recognize that the main events of Jewish history are not just historical events. In a sense we are still participating in those events, and it is incumbent on us to bring those events to life in our activities. He discusses at length the nature of the Jewish year, and in particular the cycle of religious festivals and the daily order of service, arguing that they are based on the idea of eternity in time; they give us some idea in their very repetitiveness of what it would be like to live eternally. The Sabbath in particular brings to our mind every week the fact of the creation, not just as an event which occurred in the past but in a sense as an event which occurs every week in our lives, an event which is represented and celebrated in terms of the rituals surrounding the Sabbath.

Why not use Christianity to find meaning in the world? As we have seen, this was far from just an abstract question for Rosenzweig, who for a period actively considered becoming a Christian. The answer is that, for all its merits, Christianity lacks the "rootedness" of Judaism as a religion of which one is a part for entirely natural reasons. That is, Jews are born Jews, and they are therefore members of a community which over the centuries has adopted, and been consigned to, a set number of roles, chief among which has been a concentration not on the practical affairs of the world but rather on religious duties and spirituality. Hence his distrust of Zionism, which often was based on the idea that the Jews should be like everyone else, citizens of a state which thus makes them "normal." This goes against what Rosenzweig saw as the special role of the Jews, as the representatives of an other-worldliness which results in a deeper commitment to acknowledging

God's links with the world than can be found in other groups of people. I think it has to be said that Rosenzweig's critical approach towards Zionism was based on what he saw as its secular background, and he would probably have found little to complain about had he contemplated the possibility of a religious Zionism. The latter, after all, would provide a viable route for the successful commitment of at least some people to what it is to live a Jewish life. It is clear, though, from his writings, that he shrewdly acknowledged the danger of Zionism replacing Judaism in the lives of many Jews, a danger which exists in the very notion of a Jewish nationality which is in principle unconnected with spirituality. We see today many Jewish communities in the Diaspora maintaining their sole links with their religion through their commitment to Israel, in effect hiding from themselves their practical rejection of religion through their adherence to a nationalistic political movement. Were Rosenzweig able to see the present situation in the Diaspora, he would probably feel that his criticisms of Zionism were solidly based.

∾ MARTIN BUBER ∾

It is interesting to compare Rosenzweig with Martin Buber (1878–1965), and not only because they constantly saw their work through each other's eyes. Buber was born in Vienna, but spent much of his early youth in Galicia, within a family with a far more explicit commitment to religious Judaism than the Rosenzweigs. Whereas Rosenzweig came to religious Judaism from the life of the secular Jew, Buber followed precisely the opposite route, and in his early teens stopped practising Orthodox Judaism. For both of them the philosophy of Nietzsche was very important, in particular his turn from Hegel and the abstract towards the situation of individuals trying to make sense of what is happening to them. Buber became very interested in promoting two aspects of Judaism for which Rosenzweig felt no enthusiasm, Chasidism and Zionism. The latter seemed to Buber to be a movement capable of genuinely reflecting the demands for a Jewish life in the twentieth century. Certainly it seems to have played an important part in bringing him back to a form of adherence to Judaism and to life within the Jewish community from which initially he felt excluded. He became immersed in the political activities of the Zionists, but obviously still felt unsatisfied that he had really found an entirely fulfilling form of life. When he came across a saying of the Baal Shem Tov, the creator of Chasidism, he suddenly felt that here was a way of living and thinking which was entirely in tune with his needs. One can easily imagine how someone who had spent much of his early life concentrating on entirely intellectual and political activities would be impressed by the piety and the natural religiosity of a movement such as Chasidism, and Buber spent several years immersing himself in the study of their writings.

It has to be said at the beginning that Buber had a highly romantic notion of Chasidism which bore little relationship to its reality. But that is surely of no significance. What is important is how he used his understanding of that religious movement to explore some of the basic concepts of Judaism. Chasidism represents for Buber the freshness and creativity of religious experience, and also the ability to combine the life of the mind and the body in a satisfying whole. The idea that everything in life is holy, that it is possible to imitate the love of God in our relationships with our fellow creatures, and the mysticism of the Chasidic movement all attracted Buber. He was not so interested in actually living the life of the Chasid as in using their writings, and in particular the highly evocative stories which the movement produced, to show how it is possible to live a natural religious life. One of the aspects of the stories which impressed him was their ability to represent just such a life, where the individuals felt that they belonged to a community which celebrated its links with God in an entirely natural and unselfconscious way. This lifestyle was impossible for someone with Buber's background, since it was no longer open to him to accept as natural a form of life to which he came, as it were, from outside. But the principles of Chasidism could still be used to enliven a concept of Judaism which might otherwise become unduly nomocentric and formal.

Buber was far more than an abstract philosopher. He went on to run the Lehrhaus on the death of Rosenzweig, set on the enormous task with him of translating the Hebrew Bible into German, and was an important part of the spiritual leadership of German Jewry up to the Holocaust. But his main achievement is undoubtedly his short but pellucid *I and Thou*, a rather pretentious translation of the original title *Ich und Du*. This book was intended to be part of the "New Thinking" movement, in that it stressed the significance of dialogue between persons as a route to authenticity. According to Buber, there are two types of relationship. The I–Thou is a direct and reciprocal relationship with another person, and through it the I is created. By contrast, the I–It relationship is abstract and impersonal, and is not genuinely reciprocal. What is interesting about Buber's account of this contrast is that he sees the nature of the dialogue as not just characterizing a relationship but as actually creating the participants of that relationship.[3] That is, in real dialogue each of the participants has to do something which is quite difficult. The other has to be regarded as an other, and yet as a person with whom one can relate. He or she must be regarded not as an object, nor as a subject, since either of these alternatives misrepresents the nature of the other in genuine dialogue. An object is more appropriately a part of an I–It relationship, in that one sees the other as essentially separate from oneself to be acted toward for some purpose which one has. On the other hand, the other is not a pure subject either, since one is aware throughout the interaction that he or she is a different person from oneself. The I–Thou relationship is constantly on a metaphysical knife-edge, as it were, between plunging into objectivity or subjectivity, yet it is worth trying to achieve none the less. Moral behavior is not a matter of responding to others entirely subjectively or in terms of an objective ethical code, but is rather an attempt to meet the needs and deserts of the other by recognizing their status as a genuine person.

The best way to understand this relationship is through its existence in relationships such as friendship and love. These relationships are authentic, Buber argues, if they represent genuine reciprocity between persons. That is, one should not confuse love with setting out to use someone for one's own purpose, nor even to try to mold that person into someone more appropriate as an object of one's affection. One has to accept the other as he or she is, and care for them for their own sake. As a result of that relationship it may well be that both participants in the relationship will change, but one cannot go out from the beginning to try to bring about that change, since that would condemn the relationship to inauthenticity. That is not to say that we have to spend all our time trying to establish I–Thou links with other people, since there are obviously many occasions on which these would be entirely inappropriate. Often our only links with other people are quite cursory, and there is no need to regret this. My milkman is not entitled to expect me to love him, nor am I entitled to expect him to be concerned with me as anything more than the person who pays him every week. That is not to say that we are entitled to treat each other with contempt but rather that it is appropriate for us to have an impersonal relationship.

One of the main difficulties of establishing a genuine I–Thou relationship is that one tends to slip into an I–It relationship without even realizing it. That is, one might start off by appreciating the genuine otherness of the other person and celebrating that otherness in the relationship, and yet over time there is a tendency for us to try to change the other, to make him or her more like ourselves, and so to treat him or her as an object to be manipulated. The important thing to notice here is that if we fail to respect the otherness of the other, if we do not allow them to be different, then not only do we not help them realize themselves, but we also limit our own ability to achieve our own potentiality. The relationship here is genuinely mutual in that, if one part suffers, so does the other.

How does this affect our relationship with God through religion? According to Buber, the main achievement of Judaism is to establish the possibility of dialogue with God, and this is what monotheism is really about. Like Maimonides, he denies the possibility of knowing God's attributes, but he insists that God is the "Eternal Thou" whom we can meet through our dialogue with the world. God is always there, but it is we who are unwilling to enter into dialogue with him, and our route to dialogue is through our relationships not with him as a person but rather through our relations with other people, with the events of the world and nature. In so far as we see the rest of creation as something we should love, we are open to and aware of the present-ness of God. This leads to Buber adopting a rather critical approach to the practices of Orthodoxy, and also to those of the Reform move-ment in Judaism. The former regards the Bible as literally true, and halakhah to be followed rigorously, while the latter would tend to interpret the events of the Bible as being symbols of the truth rather than the literal truth, and halakhah as a system of law to be followed selectively and critically. Buber tries to insert a wedge between these two positions, and suggests that we can see the events of the Bible as both true and symbolic, since they represent aspects of lived experience which in themselves were unique events in which attempts at establish-ing dialogue between humanity and God took place, and such events have a character which is both objective and subjective. When an event is experienced by a person or the community it may have a significance for them which no natural or supernatural explanation may diminish, and it is such events which often figure in the Bible. The trouble with the conflict between the traditionalists and the modernists is that they emphasize unduly one side only of dialogue. The traditionalists stress the impact of God on the world, and so they insist on the literal truth of the miracles and the historical events represented in the text. Yet what is also important about those events, according to Buber, is how they were received and intepreted by the Jews, the object of the com-munication. The modernists see the Bible as not literally true, but the representative of a message which it is trying to get across. This overemphasizes the role of the audience, and downplays the significance of the agent, and both participants in dialogue are vital for dialogue itself to be possible.

Buber shared Rosenzweig's suspicion of Zionism as paradigmatic-ally a national movement, yet the former had a far fonder attitude to the idea of the Jews becoming a holy people in their own land than did his friend. Buber tended to be critical of much of the exclusivity of Zionism, though, and became quite unpopular in Israel for his insistence on the mutual respect of the rights of the Arabs in the country. He adopted a similarly unusual attitude to halakhah also. Rosenzweig came to adopt a strict adherence to religious law and ritual, yet Buber's approach was very different. He saw strict observance of the law as potentially dangerous, in that it made Jews concentrate not upon their dialogue with God but rather on an objective system of legislation. In his controversy with Rosenzweig on this issue, Buber argues that he is happy to accept that a law is a mitzvah if it is really addressed to him by God. That is, he cannot obey all the laws blindly, but has to enter into a dialogue with the giver of the law before he can genuinely accept it as something which really stems from God. Buber is very critical of those who see the Jewish revelation as a one-off event, since that gives them a sense of security in their faith and in their ability to carry out their religious obligations which is entirely misplaced. In his interpretation of Jewish history Buber sees a constant struggle against the tendency to objectify the law and in favor of the reassertion of a living and dynamic relationship with God. Hence the critique of sacrifices without the right attitudes by the Prophets, leading up to the Chasidic movement, with its insistence that it is only the specific intention to see every action as that of the person turning to God which really makes a mitzvah a mitzvah.

JOSEPH SOLOVEITCHIK

It is difficult to know how precisely to classify Joseph Soloveitchik (1903–1993) as a philosopher, since he does not immediately strike one as a philosopher. A talmudist, without doubt, and a theologian of considerable stature, his works also provide evidence of interesting and pervasive philosophical ideas. He was brought up in a rabbinical family in Poland and received a traditional education in halakhah and the Talmud while young. He later on went to study philosophy at Berlin University before moving in 1932 to the United States, where he became chief rabbi of Boston. Soloveitchik took charge of the training of many of the new Orthodox rabbis in the United States through his teaching in New York, and through his sermons and other writings came to have great importance in stimulating the intellectual life of American Orthodoxy.

It has to be said right from the beginning that Soloveitchik actually wrote rather little, but from what we have it is possible to build up a fairly accurate view of his thought, since in addition to his writings we have reports on his addresses from audiences. Like Buber and Rosenzweig, he concentrates on constructing a picture of human beings which emphasizes the concept of the self. Human beings experience the sensation of being alone, and out of that feeling we establish some notion of our distinctness from what is around us, of our self. But becoming a self is a task which has to be actively accomplished, and it is quite easy for us to refuse to perform this task and to become objects instead. Religion is a matter of self-realization, self-awareness, and self-creation, and it enables us to escape from assimilation into the mass. When we seek to approach God, we also transform our own selves, and the idea of the covenant is of a relationship between persons in which both sides of the agreement help the other to establish their selves. How do we come near to God? According to Soloveitchik, we need to dedicate ourselves to the carrying out of God's will, and this is possible for us through following halakhah and basing our lives on the Torah.

Jewish life rests on a number of basic principles. There is the acknowledgement that God exists and is the sole and unique cause of everything. All other values and aims are necessarily secondary to the absolute good represented by the deity. It follows that our total commitment must be to working for God, since there can be nothing more important than having this as one's aim. Finally, the truth of the Torah and the halakhah has been revealed in Judaism, and it is incumbent upon Jews to believe totally in the former, and behave rigorously in line with the latter. Halakhah should not be seen as a rigid set of rules, but rather as a form of life which is capable of giving meaning to the life of the Jew, assisting in the creation of a spiritual self which is constructed in accordance with the laws of God and which has as a result a divine nature. Halakhah is both spiritual and practical, since it is capable of organizing our lives whatever we do in society, and at the same time it presents us with an ideal model of how we ought to live, thus appealing to our spiritual needs and reconciling them with material necessities. One of the excellences of this system of law is that it recognizes the dual nature of human beings, that we are capable of being both material and spiritual, objects and subjects, and it provides us with rules and advice which enable us to balance in our lives these different parts of ourselves, to the end that not only do we live acceptable material lives but we also leave open the possibility of following the divine purpose as specified in Judaism.

It is important for Soloveitchik that we do not follow the law blindly, merely out of habit or tradition, but we have to use our intellect to work out how we are to act, and what purpose there is in such action. We have been given an intellect by God, and he expects us to use it. Excellent and complete though the Torah is, it cannot be expected to state explicitly what we ought to do in every possible situation, and we need to think rationally based on what the Torah does tell us to work out where our duty lies. What he has in mind here are the discussions in halakhah of how we should act in situations which are slightly different from those specified in the Torah, problems around which a huge literature has grown in Jewish law. Is not all this effort to specify the halakhic solution to these very minor difficulties misplaced? For example, does having a handkerchief in one's pocket constitute carrying, and so constitute work, and thus is forbidden on Sabbath? Naturally, the Torah does not comment explicitly on this point, but later rabbis certainly have done. It might be put to Soloveitchik that having rules on matters as minor as this in one's religion is an exercise in triviality. The answer would be, though, that God insists that we explore the nature of every area of our lives, even the most petty and seemingly unimportant. If we think of every aspect of our lives as part of the service of God, then we have to work out how he wants us to live throughout our existence, and this gives us a sense of the divine purpose which is implicit in the world.

One of the advantages of Soloveitchik's view is that it accurately represents the nature of Judaism as a religion which relates far more to the everyday activities of the Jew as compared to public rituals in synagogues. The idea that the halakhah is a comprehensive system which sanctifies the whole of life, which in fact replaces the secularity of the everyday with the transcendental character of religion, implies that the attitude which one should adopt to the legal regulations is more than purely formal. It is not enough just to carry out the laws, but one must also carry them out in the right way, with the attitude that they represent the route to achieving heaven on earth, not through some extra-terrestrial decree but rather by incorporating the infinite into the finite. The comprehensiveness of the law is not a burden placed on Jews, but is rather a way of escaping from the dualism of wondering which rules to obey and which to ignore, which is surely the appropriate attitude for the Jew who accepts some of halakhah but not everything. For Soloveitchik, nothing in life is really secular, and the all-encompassing nature of halakhah constantly reminds the observant Jew of this.

What is it that makes halakhah sacred? One is tempted to say that it is the fact that it has been prescribed by God, and of course this is certainly part of the answer for Soloveitchik. But an even more important part of the answer lies with us, with the ability of human beings to regard certain practices and beliefs as obligatory and holy. Soloveitchik contrasts Mount Sinai and Mount Moriah in this regard. The former, which saw God come down to humanity to deliver the Torah, is after the event of no especial significance. By contrast, Mount Moriah, on which Abraham set out to sacrifice Isaac and where the Temple stood, is regarded in Jewish law as holy, and will always be so. It was the manner in which Abraham approached God, trusting him completely in being prepared to sacrifice his child when commanded to do so, and also the ceremonies of the Temple that represent the ways in which the Jewish people recognized the sanctity of God and his law, that make Mount Moriah special. In a sense, the Jewish people discover themselves in their approach to God, and they create for God a self and persona which reflects back on themselves, and the creative activity of the individual and the community is a vitally significant aspect of meaning-making in both religion and life. Of course, for Soloveitchik, one cannot really distinguish between these categories at all.

Religion and life can be very distinct, of course, in that one may sink into a sort of spiritual lassitude in which one thinks that religion is of no significance, or where one fails to maintain the laws of Judaism. Yet those laws represent a perfect way for us to regulate our personal, emotional, and religious life, since they point us toward the mean in action, which is where we ought to be. There is little doubt but that Soloveitchik is faithfully representing his early interest in Maimonides on this point, since his language here is highly Maimonidean. There is nothing to be said for the empty following of ritual, yet it is often better to follow a ritual without thinking much about it than not to follow anything at all, since the ritual at least represents the fact that one has put oneself one step above the entirely secular. As Soloveitchik points out, many regulations of the halakhah anyway require only performance, not any particular motivation. It is wrong to stop at obedience to ritual in one's commitment to religion, but perhaps better than nothing, and certainly it is capable of leading the individual in the right direction more surely than any other form of behavior.

One of the useful features of Soloveitchik's style is his constant production of oppositions, between different types of personalities, and his arguments that they are capable of being reconciled in religion. As with Buber, these personalities create and recreate themselves by coming into contact with each other, by trying to attain certain sorts of relationships with others and at the same time trying to keep something of themselves to themselves. This is the essentially unstable nature of the dialogic relation, the dialectic which is constantly in motion working to relate changing theses and antitheses as it becomes more and more sophisticated and ambitious in its aims. As our understanding of this dialectic progresses, we achieve more satisfactory relationships with each other and with God, since we ought continually to seek to transcend duality in our lives. Of course, many people do not do much to reduce what they experience as the tremendous gap between themselves and others, and especially God, and they see the gap as natural and inevitable. Even if they become practicing and believing Jews, or have always been so, they do not manage to work out how to get away from the forms of inauthentic duality which characterize their lives.

It may be that one of the problems which they experience is their inability to get away from the idea that they can know exactly what God expects of them, since they know what the law is and they set out to obey it. They believe that God has revealed himself in the Torah, and they study and follow the Torah to bring their lives into alignment with what God has ordered and recommended. Yet for Soloveitchik God conceals a lot of himself even from believers. It is not enough for them to wait for God to reveal himself, but they have to participate in the act of revelation itself. How are they to do this? By living in accordance with halakhah and by studying Torah, since in this way they have the opportunity to share in the process of creativity which essentially stems from God but which we can also experience through the exercise of our intellect and our free choice as to how we are to behave. There is no doubt that the passionate love which Soloveitchik advocates as the best sort of relationship we can have with God is in tune with the tradition of Jewish mysticism, and yet throughout his writings there is a theme of respect for reason and for the demand that the grounds on which adherence to Judaism can be put must be rationally defensible. That is, we should be able to examine rationally the arguments for halakhah, and assess the claims of halakhah to be a way of ending the duality of human life in a way which appeals to reason. It is not surprising that Soloveitchik had an early interest in science and mathematics, since his works are replete with claims for support on general and rational grounds which would not be out of place in a scientific context. It is also not surprising that many of his interpreters have stressed his role as the Orthodox antagonist of the demands of modernity. He certainly tries to beat modernity at its own game, by arguing that it can be used to defend the structure of Judaism, if not the central revelation on which it is based.

Was Soloveitchik really a philosopher? He was primarily a talmudist, and his more philosophical thoughts are often expressed within a theological context where the theology almost submerges the philosophy. But the question as to whether he was a philosopher is in some ways a strange one, since it is not possible to segregate the Talmud or even the Torah from philosophy, as though these were entirely discrete areas of inquiry. As a thinker Soloveitchik certainly went through some intellectual changes, ranging from a fascination with neo-Kantianism to some sort of commitment to forms of existentialism, and yet his work appears to be quite unified. The central issues which concerned him were essentially those of Buber and Rosenzweig, namely, what are the constituents of an authentic relationship. Not, it should be noted, an authentic relationship to God, since that is just a particular form of authentic relationship in general, and for all of them it turns out that getting the right relationship with God established implies getting the right relationship with other people going also.

❧ THE DISPUTE OVER RELIGIOUS LAW ❧ (HALAKHAH)

How should we go about evaluating the thought of the Jewish existentialists? First of all, they emphasize certain aspects of Judaism, in particular love, and the importance of understanding the nature of the relationship which we have with God in terms of relationships with each other, and these are positive features of the theory. Also, the amount of time they spend analyzing what it is to be a subject and an object is not misplaced, since they certainly add conceptual depth to these terms. If one puts Buber and Rosenzweig in their cultural context, as coming after neo-Kantianism and Hermann Cohen, it can be seen that they take the debate at least a few steps further along the way. In a sense, all three are addressing precisely the same issues which were early on signposted by Moses Mendelssohn, in particular how the Jewish people should react to modernity. It is far from trivial that Buber and Rosenzweig set out to translate the Hebrew Bible into German, a task which had already been performed quite exceptionally well by Mendelssohn. But of course the sort of translation which the latter provided was written in the language of his own times, bearing on its face all the assumptions of the Enlightenment. A new translation was needed, they thought, because the old one no longer spoke to its Jewish readers in a way capable of rousing their excitement and commitment. They suspected, quite accurately, that the way in which Mendelssohn saw his translation being used was very different from what they regarded as appropriate. Mendelssohn wanted to show both the Jews and the German people how elegantly the Bible spoke to the Jews in its representation of past events. Buber and Rosenzweig wanted to bring the freshness and relevance of the Bible to the attention of the Jewish community in the German-speaking world (which we should remember extended far beyond the boundaries of the German state). When we look at their correspondence on the project we can see that they certainly were not lacking in pride in their ability to use the German language with grace and precision, but this was not high up the list of desiderata. The point was to show how the Bible demands a response from the Jews, who are not allowed to regard it as just an account of past events. It is ironic that the translation project came to an end only long after the death of Rosenzweig, when Buber produced the last few volumes, but not very long after the complete extirpation of the German-speaking Jewish cultural world.

One of the problems of existentialism has always been that the glorification of subjectivity leads to what might appear to be an arbitrary drawing of conclusions. Let us take as an example here the contrasting positions of Buber and Rosenzweig on how Jews should relate to halakhah. As we have seen, Buber is suspicious of the ways in which the religious authorities in Judaism lay out as necessary a whole system of law to be obeyed. He argued that one should only obey what one can authentically obey, and that consists of those laws which one feels have been addressed to one personally as a Thou. In fact, he implies, there are great dangers in Jews feeling that they need to adhere to a whole realm of law, since they may use that adherence to think that they have done their duty and need not seriously examine their relationship with God, and, even more importantly, it gives Jews the impression that their duty lies in observing a set of objective standards, whereas in fact what we should be doing is investigating how God addresses us personally and responding as to a person on the basis of those present and pressing contacts.

Rosenzweig criticized this sort of approach. He points out quite rightly in his essay "The Builders" that Buber had come over the years to appreciate more readily a much wider breadth of theoretical work in Judaism than at the start of his writings on the subject (when he tended to prioritize the work of those Jewish thinkers on the margins, such as mystics, prophets, and so on), and yet his rather critical attitude to halakhah persisted throughout. Rosenzweig suggested that Buber might see halakhah as a possible realm of responsiveness to God. That is, he claims that it seems arbitrary to deny that this aspect, one might say this extraordinarily important aspect of Jewish culture, is alone excluded from the gamut of possible institutions that may be employed to relate in a direct way to the deity. Many halakhists write of performing a mitzvah in precisely the sort of way of which one might expect Buber to approve. That is, they are conscious that they are responding to the word of God, and they are aware of the presence of God while carrying out the task. They feel that God is addressing them personally and asking them to perform that act, and they freely accept that obligation and do their best to act in accordance with the divine request.

In his response to Rosenzweig Buber makes clear that his main objection to halakhah is his insistence that revelation cannot be embodied in law. This is to deny the immediacy of revelation, the way in which revelation affects the individual as though his life was suddenly illuminated, and this sort of experience, and the personal growth which stems from it, cannot be a reaction to a law. Rosenzweig wonders why not. After all, both he and Buber are agreed that a page of the Bible is just a page, and the words can be mechanically recited and repeated in a fairly meaningless sort of way from their point of view. On the other hand, those words may be seen as constituting the moment of encounter between God and his creatures, transforming us and guiding us on our route through life. Why cannot Jewish law operate in precisely the same way? Buber responds that it can, but it has to be viewed as a commandment addressed directly to him by God, and Buber suggests that we cannot see the whole corpus of law like that. We can certainly recognize some in this way, but not the whole of the law. Rosenzweig wonders why not, since the only way to discover which laws are personally addressed to us is to try them all out, and if one then comes across a law for which one feels no personal compulsion, then at least there are prima facie grounds for rejecting it as a commandment. Until we try, though, we shall not know where we stand in this respect, and the only way to try is through embedding one's life in the system of law as a whole.

This is an interesting debate, and it is one which continued in the writings of Buber for many decades after his friend's death. In a sense it is a typical existentialist debate. Buber reports on his own experience, and says that he can make no sense of the idea that the whole of Jewish law is God addressing him as a Thou. Rosenzweig, on the contrary, seems to suggest that there is no difficulty in using halakhah to sanctify the whole of his life, and he argues at some length that the structure of Judaism with its rituals and holidays is precisely in line with such a project of sanctification. The important existentialist move for them both is the emphasis upon freedom and the necessity to choose without sliding into doing what is traditional or habitual. Rosenzweig did not, it should be remembered, become a halakhic observer through following what was for him a natural lifestyle. On the contrary, he came from outside of halakhah, in a sense, and saw it as the route to communion with God *for him*. Buber, coming from within the tradition, rejected it as just such a route *for him*. Now, is this just a matter of different people having different attitudes to something, like someone just liking carrots and someone else not liking them? If so, then the argument is trivial, and of very little interest. It would just go to show how poor and arbitrary much of the discussion which takes place in existentialism is, which is perhaps not surprising given the emphasis upon subjectivity within that philosophical method.

We do not have to leave it at this, though. Both Buber and Rosenzweig have good arguments for their conclusions. As Buber says, it is very difficult to see a body of law as constituting a personal address from the deity. The law may be experienced as a complicated system of rules and regulations which has to be understood and mastered throughout one's life, thus getting in the way of the sort of spontaneity which Buber thought was so important in relationships. It may dominate one's life, and give one the false impression that one had lived entirely as one ought. In any case, although we can certainly see the point of many laws, there are plenty which have no obvious justification, and obeying the whole system implies acting in obedience to principles which one has not considered and arguments which one has not heard. The law stands rather as an obstacle between God and the person. It certainly cannot be used by the person who is always trying to be a subject and who is trying to treat many significant others as subjects. Halakhah produces uniformity of treatment and result which deadens our relations with each other, and with God. We need to pick and choose which laws we are going to obey, on the simple criterion of which laws appear to us to be personal commandments from God. The law as a whole, as a vast system of impersonal rules, certainly cannot stand as such a personal commandment.

Rosenzweig would argue that this argument was invalid. It is certainly true that no one should accept halakhah uncritically, and nor should anyone feel that, if they have carried out their legal requirements, then they have done everything required of them. On the other hand, one cannot see the system of law as like an à la carte meal. One cannot just obey what appeals to one as being a direct commandment and ignore the rest, perhaps only for a while. The whole system has a divine basis and it allows us to bring holiness into every area of our lives. The arguments which Soloveitchik produces would provide useful support for this view here, in that he goes into great detail into how this can work. But even Rosenzweig uses the main religious symbols of Judaism to explore the notion of using ritual to import infinity into the finite, and this has to be all of the system of ritual, not just what one fancies on a particular occasion. As Soloveitchik points out, basing one's life on halakhah does have the advantage that it frees one's thinking from concerns about how one should behave in everyday terms, and allows us to concentrate on higher things, such as our relationship with God and with other creatures.

We are left here with something of a dilemma. Who is right? Is Rosenzweig justified in thinking that it is possible to interpret the whole of halakhah as a personal commandment, as a personal address which has to be freely accepted? Is Buber right in arguing that he does not recognize all the laws and rituals of halakhah as just such a commandment, and so chooses not to follow them? One might be tempted to say that they could easily both be right, in that they are both reporting on what seems valid for them, and, given the high respect given to subjectivity in both philosophers' thought, this seems to be as far as one can go. But this would surely diminish the interest of their arguments a good deal, since if arguments stop at the point where individuals recount what their personal opinion is on an issue, the whole process of argument seems nugatory. Fortunately it is not quite like this here. What Buber is saying is something stronger than just that he cannot see the whole of the law as a personal commandment. He is implying that no one can really do this, since the system of law is not the sort of concept which can be seen as a personal commandment. It is too abstract, too complex, and far too mechanical to constitute an appropriate address. There are certainly aspects of it which are possible commandments, but not the whole system.

Rosenzweig denies this, since he argues that once we accept the chosenness of the Jewish people we have also to accept the whole of the law as part of that chosenness, since it supports the distinctiveness of a lifestyle consequent upon election. We need to distinguish here between an institution and that which the institution makes possible. The institution of halakhah makes possible a particular way of living within which it is possible to experience aspects of law as personal addresses from God, yet there may well be difficulties in accepting the institution itself as a personal address, since it is an institution. It is difficult to see an institution as something personal since it is nothing more than a set of rules, and what makes a set of rules valuable or otherwise is its application to practice, not what it is in itself. Any value it may have in itself is based on its value in practice. So Buber is quite right in arguing that there are problems in seeing a system of law as a personal commandment. Rosenzweig is also right to argue that, if we are going to be able to see the law as just such a commandment, we have to try it out first in its entirety and then reflect on how successfully it fits the bill as something which God could address to us personally. This contrast of views brings out nicely how much more of an existentialist Buber is as compared with Rosenzweig. The former is not prepared to allow human freedom to be limited by the imposition of law, even law which is freely chosen, on the basis that that law is God-given. It is incumbent on us as free agents to consider each and every law and instruction we are given before we accept it, since otherwise our behavior falls short of authenticity. For Rosenzweig and Soloveitchik, the fact of human finitude and frailty as compared with the power and authority of God compel certain forms of initial acceptance. Yet once those forms and structures are established, it is possible, and indeed necessary, to regard the links with God as personal, and for us to choose freely within that context.

So the contrast between Buber and Rosenzweig on this issue is far from arbitrary, but is based upon very different views of what it is to operate authentically within a religious tradition. Rosenzweig and Soloveitchik argue that Jews have to accept certain principles and practices as given, and then can work and live within those constraints.

One might argue that freedom makes sense only within a particular structure, since only then can one tell what one is free from. Buber, on the other hand, is not prepared to accept that he must adhere to a system of law as a whole before he can recognize personal commandments in that law. This strikes him as a radical constraint on his freedom. To look at another example, suppose someone were to wonder whether he would like playing soccer, but is not prepared to obey the rules and try the game out. Would this be a rational decision? It could be, since he might in observing others play to the rules conclude that this is not the game for him, because, perhaps, it does not give the sort of scope for creativity and spontaneity which he looks for in a game. When Buber looks at the whole corpus of Jewish law, he sees an objective and impersonal system which he could not possibly regard in any other way. There is no reason in principle why someone else, someone like Rosenzweig or Soloveitchik, might not be able to see that system differently, but Buber implies it would take some doing. Bodies of law are just of their very nature objective and impersonal, and they are not the sort of thing which we can feel personally addressed by.

Since Buber hovers between arguing that we cannot feel thus addressed, or that we are unlikely to be able to feel thus addressed, it is not entirely clear how strong his thesis is. But there is no unclarity at all about the very real problem which he highlights here, and from the point of view of existentialism it would be extraordinary to see law as our route to divine contact. On the other hand, one of the impressive aspects of the thought of Rosenzweig and Soloveitchik on this issue is that they make the idea of the subject realizing himself as a subject through following religious law almost plausible.

Is there any one central contribution which these three thinkers made to Jewish philosophy? Notwithstanding their many significant differences, they all emphasized the crucial role of the subject in making Judasim the religion it is. Judaism is a faith with a justifiable claim for adherence despite the urgings of modernity which would abandon it altogether, or translate it into something less particular and more universal. They sought to reassert what they took to be the central principles of Judaism in the notion of the individual subject, since it is that which creates meaning in the world, and, if anything is to revive and make religion vital, it can be nothing other than human subjectivity.

⤞ NOTES ⤝

1 This is excellently discussed in M. Warnock, *Existentialism* (Oxford: Oxford University Press, 1970).

2 For a discussion of this way of doing philosophy, see O. Leaman, *Evil and Suffering in Jewish Philosophy* (Cambridge: Cambridge University Press, 1995).
3 This is discussed slightly differently in chapter 9, "Buber," in ibid., pp. 165–84. In this chapter there is an extended discussion of how Buber, and to a certain extent Rosenzweig, deal with the phenomena of evil and suffering in their philosophies.

❧ BIBLIOGRAPHY ❧

Rosenzweig

Texts

Rosenzweig, F. (1970) *The Star of Redemption* (New York: Holt, Rinehart, & Winston).
—— (1976–84) *Gesammelte Schriften* (Dordrecht: Nijhoff).

Studies

Borowitz, E. (1983) *Choices in Modern Jewish Thought* (New York: Behrman).
Cohen, A. (1979) *The Natural and the Supernatural Jew* (New York: Behrman).
Guttmann, J. (1964) *Philosophies of Judaism: The History of Jewish Philosophy from Biblical Times to Franz Rosenzweig* (New York: Holt, Rinehart, & Winston).
Rosenstock-Huessy, E. (ed.) (1969) *Judaism despite Christianity* (New York: Schocken).
Rotenstreich, N. (1968) *Jewish Philosophy in Modern Times* (New York: Holt, Rinehart & Winston).
Schmied-Kowarzik, W. (ed.) (1988) *Das neue Denken und seine Dimensionen* (Freiburg: Alber).

Buber

Texts

Buber, M. (1937) *I and Thou* (Edinburgh: T. & T. Clark).
—— (1948) *Between Man and Man* (New York: Macmillan).
—— (1953) *Good and Evil, Two Interpretations* (New York: Charles Scribner's Sons).
—— (1955a) *The Legend of the Baal Shem* (New York: Harper).
—— (1955b) *Tales of the Hasidim: The Early Masters* (London: Thames & Hudson).
—— (1955c) *Tales of the Hasidim: The Later Master* (London: Thames & Hudson).
—— (1967) *On Judaism* (New York: Schocken).

Studies

Diamond, M. (1960) *Martin Buber: Jewish Existentialist* (New York: Oxford University Press).

Friedman, M. (1981–5) *Martin Buber's Life and Work* (New York: Dutton).

Katz, S. (1983) *Post Holocaust Dialogues: Critical Studies in Contemporary Jewish Thought* (New York: New York University Press).

Niehoff, M. (1993) "The Buber-Rosenzweig Translation of the Bible within German-Jewish Tradition," *Journal of Jewish Studies* 44.2: 258–79.

Rosenthal, E. (1980) "Die Wissenschaft des Judentums: Vortrag," in *Martin Buber: Leben, Werk, Wirkung* (Heilbronn: Heilbronner Vortrage), pp. 52–80.

Schilpp, P. and M. Friedman (eds) (1967) *The Philosophy of Martin Buber* (La Salle: Open Court).

Vermes, P. (1980) *Buber on God and the Perfect Man* (Atlanta: Brown Judaic Studies).

Soloveitchik

Texts

Soloveitchik, J. B. (1974) *Shiurei Harav* (*Sermons of the Rabbi*) (New York: Yeshiva University Press).

—— (1965) "The Lonely Man of Faith," *Tradition* 7.2: 5–67.

—— (1980) *On Repentance*, translated by P. Peli (Jerusalem: Oroth).

—— (1984) *Halachic Man*, translated by L. Kaplan (Philadelphia: Jewish Publication Society).

Studies

Besdin, A. (ed.) (1980) *Reflections of the Rav* (Jerusalem: World Zionist Organization).

Borowitz, E. (1983) *Choices in Modern Jewish Thought* (New York: Behrman).

Hartman, D. (1985) *A Living Covenant* (New York: Free Press).

Kaplan, L. (1973) "The Religious Philosophy of Rabbi Joseph Soloveitchik," *Tradition* 15.3: 43–64.

—— (1988) "Rabbi Joseph B. Soloveitchik's Philosophy of Halakhah," *Jewish Law Annual* 7: 139–97.

Ravitsky, A. (1986) "Rabbi J. B. Soloveitchik on Human Knowledge: Between Maimonidean and Neo-Kantian Philosophy," *Modern Judaism* 6.2: 157–88.

Singer, D. (1986) *Joseph B. Soloveitchik* (New York: New York University Press).

CHAPTER 35

Leo Strauss

Kenneth Hart Green

•~ INTRODUCTION ~•

It has often been thought that Leo Strauss (1899–1973) is one of the leading political thinkers of the twentieth century. In recent years, however, another side of Leo Strauss has been discovered that may be of equal, if not greater, significance: his contribution as a Jewish scholar, and as a major Jewish thinker in his own right.

Strauss began his career as a Jewish philosophical thinker by initiating a critique of contemporary philosophy and its subsequent influence on modern Jewish thought. In this critique, Strauss judged contemporary philosophy to be morally and intellectually bankrupt owing to its surrender to radical historicism. As a result, Strauss began to explore and reconsider the wisdom of the medieval and ancient philosophers.

This culminated in Strauss' focus on Maimonides, whom he viewed as an exemplary Jewish philosophical thinker, able to achieve a perfect balance between philosophy, morality, politics, and religion. Strauss saw the enduring basis of Maimonides' position as grounded in his adherence to the idea of the eternal truth, in whose light a defense of both revelation and reason is made possible. Indeed, Strauss' own Jewish thought may be characterized as a "return to Maimonides": he made a modern effort to revive Maimonideanism as a corrective to the contemporary dilemmas and defects of modern Jewish thought. In doing so, Strauss also recovered the notion of philosophical "esotericism," or of "writing between the lines." He brought to light the forgotten reasons why thinkers like Maimonides considered it imperative to express what they truly thought in a concealed and diversionary manner.

The following account begins by offering a short overview of the life of Leo Strauss, while also noting the appearance in print of his chief Jewish philosophical writings. Second, it makes a presentation of Strauss' basic position as a Jewish thinker vis-à–vis his contemporaries and his predecessors, seen in light of the contemporary "theological-political" crisis. Third, it discusses in some detail Strauss' original and critical understanding of the three Jewish philosophical thinkers to whom he devoted most of his intellectual efforts as a Jewish scholar – Hermann Cohen, Benedict (Baruch) Spinoza, and Moses Maimonides. Strauss' unconventional views of these three Jewish thinkers are presented in reverse chronological order so as to reflect the course of Strauss' own progress in thought.[1]

❧ LIFE AND WORK ❧

Leo Strauss was born 20 September 1899 in Kirchhain, Hesse, Germany to a traditionally Orthodox Jewish family. He completed his doctoral dissertation at the University of Hamburg in 1921, supervised by Ernst Cassirer, on "The Problem of Knowledge in F. H. Jacobi's Philosophical Teaching."[2] Recruited by Franz Rosenzweig, Strauss taught for two years at the Free Jewish House of Learning in Frankfurt (1923–5). Brought to the attention of Julius Guttmann by a study of "Cohen's Analysis of Spinoza's Bible Science," published by Martin Buber in *Der Jude* (1924), Strauss was appointed to the Academy for the Science of Judaism in Berlin as a research fellow in Jewish philosophy, which appointment he held from 1925 to 1932.[3] It was during this period of his life that Strauss published *Spinoza's Critique of Religion* (1930), as well as volumes 2 and 3 (part 1) of the *Jubilee Edition of the Complete Works of Moses Mendelssohn* (1931 and 1932).

Strauss was able to leave Germany in 1932 just prior to Hitler's accession to power, having been awarded a Rockefeller Grant with the help of recommendations from Ernst Cassirer, Julius Guttmann, and Carl Schmitt.[4] While an itinerant scholar in France and England from 1932 to 1938, he published *Philosophy and Law: Contributions to the Understanding of Maimonides and His Predecessors* (1935), and worked on volume 3 (part 2) of *Moses Mendelssohn's Works*, which appeared in print only posthumously (1974), since the publication project had been halted by Nazi Germany. During those years Strauss married Miriam Bernson Petri. (He and his wife raised two children, a son, Thomas, and a daughter, Jenny Ann.)[5]

In 1938, Strauss secured both a permanent home in the United States as a naturalized citizen and his first true academic position as a lecturer in philosophy at the New School for Social Research in New York. During the next eleven years (1938–49) he rose to the rank of full professor. He was also appointed a fellow of the American Academy for

Jewish Research, and he served as a member of the Executive Committee of the Leo Baeck Institute in New York.[6]

In 1949, Strauss was persuaded by Robert Maynard Hutchins to relocate to the University of Chicago, where he taught in the Department of Political Science for the next nineteen years (1949–68). During those years Strauss became renowned for his excellence as a teacher and his influence as a thinker. In 1960 he was named Robert Maynard Hutchins Distinguished Service Professor. It was also in this period of his life that he published *Persecution and the Art of Writing* (1952), wrote the introductory essay, "How to Begin to Study *The Guide of the Perplexed*," to the English translation by Shlomo Pines of Maimonides' *Guide* (1963), and delivered The First Frank Cohen Public Lecture in Judaic Affairs at the City College of New York, which was published as *Jerusalem and Athens: Some Preliminary Reflections* (1967).

Strauss spent a year in Israel, teaching at the Hebrew University of Jerusalem (1954–5), while also delivering there its Judah L. Magnes Lectures.[7]

When Strauss retired from the University of Chicago in 1968, he taught briefly at Claremont College, California, and then in 1969 removed to St John's College in Annapolis, Maryland, which named him its first Scott Buchanan Scholar in Residence. During these last years of his life, he contributed the "Introductory Essay" to the English translation of Hermann Cohen's *Religion of Reason out of the Sources of Judaism* (1972). He died 18 October 1973 in Annapolis, leaving as a legacy an array of remarkable students who carry on his teaching to the present day.[8]

❧ JEWISH PHILOSOPHY AND THE CRISIS ❧ OF MODERNITY

Leo Strauss' perspective on the essential condition of modern Jewish philosophic thought can be understood properly only by beginning with Strauss' conviction that this is an era of grave crisis for modern Judaism, which he called the "theological-political crisis." This crisis was in great measure brought to light by the historical events of the twentieth century, such as Communism in Russia and Nazism in Germany, which administered a traumatic shock to modern Jewish thought, since they called into question the ideas of human rationality and liberalism.[9] This made problematic the related belief of the Enlightenment that in the progress of history not only was the triumph of liberalism guaranteed, but also the Jews and Judaism would flourish in freedom through its triumph.[10] The erosion of these beliefs, on which the political hopes of modern Jews rested, suggested that the ground on which modern Judaism had been built was about to collapse.[11]

But the apparent overturning of liberal politics was not the only cause of the contemporary crisis for modern Jews. The decline of rational philosophy posed a threat of perhaps even greater profundity to the viability of modern Judaism. The "theological-political crisis" first manifested itself to Strauss in his youth by the observation that most Jewish philosophical responses to the challenges of modernity were in a state of critical disintegration. For Strauss, this applied to *all* of the leading theological positions representing modern Jewish thought from Spinoza to Buber. Especially by 1933, Strauss recognized that the leading positions in modern Jewish thought were faced with a fundamental dilemma: they could no longer adequately defend their spiritual integrity. This spiritual integrity had been based on previously authoritative philosophical positions (such as those of Spinoza, Locke, Rousseau, Kant, and Hegel) which were no longer persuasive or had lost their value to most modern thinkers. In other words, modern Jewish thinkers had been able to establish their own well-fortified positions only because they were authentic Jewish responses to serious philosophical challenges. Once the seriousness of the challenges were removed, how crucial were the responses?[12]

In Strauss' view, the modern rationalist philosophy to which most Jewish thinkers adhered was faced with a gradual devastation due to the wave of thought which was conquering every sphere of traditional moral authority and vital philosophical life.[13] Specifically, the thought of Nietzsche and especially Heidegger, whose thought Strauss calls "radical historicism," was responsible for bringing about the triumph of such notions as: the priority of will to reason in human beings; the radical doubts about a fixed human nature; history as true but not rational; atheism and the fundamental abyss; human beings as creator of their own meanings and values; eternal truth as a defunct, if not a pious fraud; the challenge of nihilism; the will to power, resoluteness, and authenticity. In Strauss' estimation, this thought in both its subtle and crude forms has exercised an enormous, if not *the* decisive, influence on philosophical, religious, moral, and political thought in the last hundred years, so much so that it has been the major cause of the "theological-political" crisis in Western civilization and in modern Judaism, the proportions of which are difficult to measure because it is still unfolding. Thus, modern Jewish thought (along with modern rationalist philosophy) was challenged by the same need to justify and account for itself according to the categories of the "new thinking" enunciated by those two thinkers, and certainly could not hope to return to the "naive" state it assumed prior to their appearance.

Ironically, Strauss accepted much of the critique of the modern philosophical positions made by the new thinking, because he believed that this thought did accurately highlight the serious flaws contained in the modern rationalist tradition of philosophy which has been dominant since the Enlightenment. But unlike Nietzsche and Heidegger, Strauss was not attracted to the types of irrationalism which they preached. He sought a philosophy based on reason, that is, on rational inquiry and rational principles, though not of the sort presented in the dominant forms of modern reason, if only because it proved susceptible to such a devastating critique. He then asked whether there might still be found a rational philosophy of a different sort, one which would still be able to claim confidently to teach *the* truth. This is what led him to reconsider and ultimately "return" to the position of the medieval Jewish rational theologian Maimonides; it was that same concern which also led him to reflect on the ancient philosophical thought of Plato and Aristotle, in the tradition of whose philosophy Maimonides' own thought was itself grounded. In other words, Strauss began to search in premodern sources of philosophical thought in order to help guide modern Judaism toward an adequate resolution of its contemporary crisis.

❧ THE IMPORTANCE OF HERMANN ❧ COHEN

Prior to turning to the premodern Jewish thinkers, however, Strauss needed to assess the claims of contemporary Jewish thinkers, since they had already been able to exercise a substantial influence on him. During Strauss' youth, the most powerful spokesman for the vitality of modern Jewish philosophic thought was Hermann Cohen. Strauss encountered a Jewish thinker who had been a major figure in German academic philosophy, and who also claimed audaciously to apply his neo-Kantian philosophic teaching to Judaism so as to enable it to resolve its fundamental modern dilemmas. As Strauss interpreted modern Judaism, and as he experienced its vicissitudes in his own life, Hermann Cohen emerged as perhaps the most appealing and yet somehow also the least persuasive modern figure.[14] Essentially, Cohen was appealing to Strauss as "a passionate philosopher and a Jew passionately devoted to Judaism."[15] In point of fact, Cohen exercised a formative influence on Strauss' intellectual development: in his youth, Strauss was persuaded by Cohen's Marburg neo-Kantianism, and he affirmatively viewed Cohen as one who was able to blend happily a strict devotion to philosophy with a passionate commitment to Judaism. Strauss was also impressed with how much Cohen had been determined to wrestle with the conflict between Judaism and philosophy, produced by their fundamental differences, in the hope of yielding a decisive resolution to their conflict.[16] Cohen remained for Strauss until the very end the image of the proud and self-respecting modern Jew who engages in philosophical activity; he served as a kind of exemplar, standing for the virtues which he hoped to imitate in the sphere of modern Jewish thought.[17]

Yet Cohen was also not persuasive to Strauss precisely because of his vaunted modern synthesis, constructed on the basis of his neo-Kantian system of philosophy, with Judaism (represented by its classical and medieval texts) playing a leading role. Strauss concluded even in his youth that in so far as Cohen's "idealizing" method of interpreting Jewish texts presupposed the truth of the neo-Kantian philosophical system, it could not do simple philosophical justice to the religious thought of the sources of Judaism.[18] This is because, as Strauss started to believe, the neo-Kantian philosophic system of Cohen was itself deeply flawed, especially in its supplementing of Kant with the Hegelian premise of a necessary dialectical progress in history. Thus, it was Strauss' view that Cohen's philosophical teaching about humanity and history aroused exaggerated hopes about the modern liberal order, because it was not grounded in a sober assessment of the true modern human achievements in politics and in science.

Alert to the growing philosophical critique of Cohen (in the form of Husserl and phenomenology), Strauss calls himself already in 1922 "a doubting and dubious adherent of the Marburg school of neo-Kantianism."[19] From a purely Jewish perspective, it also seemed evident to Strauss that none of his fundamental doubt about Cohen's philo-sophico-historical synthesis of modernity as it was applied to modern Judaism could be dispelled by Cohen's resort to the ancient Jewish sources in order to secure and bolster the ground beneath his philo-sophical teaching. Thus, Strauss was critical of Cohen for approaching the ancient Jewish sources by his peculiar style of "idealization" in order to make his historical arguments. This method of interpretation assumed that Cohen could uncover in the classical Jewish texts their "highest possibility." However, as Strauss perceived, this amounted to the explication of the texts so that neo-Kantian wisdom, only fully made available in the present, was the single true "highest possibility" of those ancient sources. In so far as Cohen claimed to make an historical argument, he does not do justice to the historical truth about those texts; in so far as he claimed to make a philosophical argument, he did not provide modern Jews with any autonomous Jewish standard by which to criticize the defective present and its thought. According to Strauss, by doing so Cohen made this ancient tradition and its classical texts of an even greater irrelevance than that to which they had been consigned by modern Judaism hitherto.

Of course, what also seemed so faulty to Strauss, in commonsense terms, was Cohen's firm belief in modern Germany as the chief ground of hope for modern Jews. For him that hopeful teaching did not express a view of modernity which corresponded to his own experience of actual political reality as a Jew in post-First-World-War Germany, which scarcely seemed on the verge of the triumph of liberalism and the rejection of anti-semitism. As Strauss observed, how could Cohen be right if the most powerful voices at work in modern Germany, which seemed to him determinative of the immediate historical reality, had not actually been inspired by Kant or even by Hegel, but by Nietzsche and especially Heidegger.[20]

Consequently Strauss began to drift away from Cohen both because of gnawing doubts about his neo-Kantian philosophical system, and because of massive political forces not discussed or predicted by Cohen by which Strauss was threatened and with which he, unlike Cohen, had to deal. Perhaps because of these doubts about Cohen provoked by historical events, and perhaps also in anticipation of not yet fully articulated philosophical doubts, Strauss was not able to discover in Cohen the resources to deal with his immediate perplexities. As a solution to the Jewish political problem, Strauss had been moved to embrace political Zionism at the youthful age of seventeen, and he continued to accept the force of its essential argument, although one might think that this would have been put in doubt by Cohen's strictures. Responding to deeper spiritual needs, he also grew attracted to Rosenzweig's return to a revised Orthodox theology, although certainly it too was not in basic accord with the spirit of Cohen, since Rosenzweig stressed the individual's experience of revelation in an encounter with God, a notion contradicting Cohen's emphasis on the primacy of human autonomy, which excluded any such encounter.[21]

Disregarding for the moment the precarious Jewish political situation of Strauss' youth, to which he was so alert in his thinking, and which forced a Zionist political direction and neo-Orthodox theological orientation on it, let us investigate in somewhat greater detail what Cohen's grand modern philosophical synthesis entailed, and try to explain why would it not provide enough philosophical or theological sustenance for Strauss as a young Jewish thinker. In Cohen's synthesis, it was argued that the modern West was constituted by the bringing together of the Hebrew prophetic idea of ethical monotheism with the Platonic idea of philosophy as science, especially as the two have been raised to modern systematic perfection by the critical philosophy of Kant, in which the essential ideas of both are taken into account and given their highest possible rational articulation, culminating in the moral idea and messianic task of humanity. Strauss was in a definite sense impressed with the bold uniqueness of Cohen's enterprise. As a philosophical thinker who was also a Jewish thinker, Cohen tried to defend the integrity of the Jewish tradition – with all "necessary" qualifications, such as the divestment of its mysticism – as compatible with the modern requirement, defined by neo-Kantianism, that religion not detract from the absolute moral autonomy and pure rational creativity of man. Thus, Cohen showed in his synthesis how Jewish thought was sufficient to the task of responding with a true seriousness to the enormous challenges of Kantian ethics and epistemology, while seemingly not surrendering or reducing the Jewish religious view of humanity and the world.

Strauss, however, could not help but observe that in this synthesis classical Jewish theology was ultimately required to surrender or reduce its own religious view, especially in regard to its claim to genuine knowledge of things, and in its expression of moral principles. This is because Kantian (or neo-Kantian) philosophy conceived of religion in terms of postulated belief rather than as a source of knowledge, and also viewed morality as in its very nature defined as a consequence of human autonomy, and not as a revealed (that is, heteronomous) set of fundamental principles. Hence, Cohen allowed the Jewish religious view to stand only inasmuch as it was transferable from a claim of knowledge to a claim of belief, and only in so far as it could be interpreted as consistent with human autonomy of reason and freedom of will, as such notions were conceived in Cohen's neo-Kantian epistemology and moral philosophy. Moreover, Strauss saw that Cohen needed the sources of Judaism clearly to ratify his modern synthesis, and hence in this light he reworked them as needed to suit his preordained end. But Cohen did not perceive that the elements of this synthesis, as well as this synthesis itself, were entirely creatures of his own construction. For him it was apparently a simple historical fact that purely rational ethics had been manifested originally, though unconsciously, by the Hebrew prophets. This historical fact he believed to be confirmed by his study of the ancient sources of Judaism.

In Strauss' view, Cohen could achieve such full evidence often only by reading those Jewish sources with the utmost selectiveness, and hence by seeing them in a distorting light. As Cohen chose to interpret the sources of Judaism, the "highest possibility" of the ancient Jewish religious view was its promise of Kantian (or neo-Kantian) ethics, in the sense that this modern philosophy supposedly represents its first completely rational articulation. In Cohen's reading, the ancient Jewish religious view could be reconstructed as a postulated belief necessary to support and fulfill a correctly rational morality, and it was this that had been developed unsystematically by ancient Jewish religious thinkers.[22] Though not neo-Kantian philosophers, they acted on "primitive" or unconscious impulses yielded in an historical dialectic:

they carried through and expressed imaginatively the logical consequences, or the moral implications, of the rational idea of the one God
as creator, which they discovered in their own native tradition.

Strauss also discerned that Cohen's synthesis was a defense of
modernity, in the face of the massive critique of the modern project
which emerged in Nietzsche. On the positive side of the scale, it seemed
to Strauss to have been rooted in a rare modern seriousness about both
reason and revelation, that had somehow been revived by Cohen in
recognizing a deep need of the modern sensibility which had been made
visible in the critique of modernity. Strauss was certainly impressed with
Cohen's historical justification of Jewish sources on the very highest
philosophic plane, which in his system were praised for their once
decisive contribution to modern Western civilization. However, on the
negative side of the scale, Strauss noticed that, while for Cohen this
idea of ethical monotheism had originally been contributed to Western
civilization by the Jews, it puts a high value on the Jewish tradition in
an *ultimately* philosophic translation and as *primarily* an historical
artifact. Even if Jews must persist as the teachers of "the pure monotheism," Judaism is reduced to an idea.[23] Even if an historical future is
preserved for the Jews, as adherents of "the pure monotheism" in their
relation to the fulfillment of the messianic task to build one humanity
in the *idea* of the future, it is no longer as a vital and self-creative
people. And as should also be mentioned, both of the two original
elements of the final modern synthesis, Platonism and Judaism, do not
possess in themselves the same vitality or dynamic which the synthesis
itself possesses as it unfolds, since by the unadmitted Hegelian logic of
Cohen's historical synthesis, they have been perforce "sublated" by it.
It is not evident from Cohen's argument, then, whether, once the truth
of the ethical monotheistic idea has been done justice in modern Kantian or neo-Kantian philosophy, there is any further *essential* need for
the Jewish religion, or anything genuinely new for the Jews to do but
proclaim the old teaching while working for the victory of European
liberalism in the form of democratic socialism.

Moreover, as mentioned previously, Strauss also grew to doubt
the neo-Kantian philosophic system as this had been devised by Cohen,
both because of the influence of Husserl's phenomenological critique
of Cohen's idea of modern scientific reason, and because of the exposure
to neo-Orthodox theology in the 1920s, offered by Franz Rosenzweig
and Karl Barth, which put in doubt the adequacy of Cohen's historically
progressive notion of revelation. Strauss was never able to restore his
faith in Cohen's system because of these criticisms, which suggested it
was not able to meet the type of challenge issued by radical historicism
to its view of modern scientific reason – a view which indeed verged
on, if it did not merge with, positivism, and hence is itself only a step

away from historicism.[24] In one respect only, then, was there a role of fundamental importance for Cohen to play in Strauss' mature Jewish thought: Strauss revered Cohen ultimately neither for the supposedly final modern synthesis of his philosophical system, nor for the acknowledged philosophical depth evident in his thought, but for the general attempt at such a synthesis, however misguided and unfulfilled Cohen's specific effort. He showed not just the possibility of a modern Jewish philosophy which resembled and even imitated its medieval ancestor, but also an unavoidable modern Jewish need. Cohen was the model for Strauss himself of the modern Jewish philosopher: an undoubtedly original philosophical thinker, who is immersed in the Western tradition of philosophy and science, and yet who still remains devoted to Judaism in the highest sense, trying by an exacting scholarly consideration, on the ground of intellectual honesty and consistency, to reconcile his two commitments.

Consequently, Strauss defends Cohen against the charges laid against him by Isaac Husik, a leading historian of medieval Jewish philosophy, who thought that the integrity of Cohen as a modern Jewish philosopher was diminished, if not nullified, by the dubiousness of Cohen's scholarly efforts in the history of Jewish thought.[25] In this context, Strauss carries through a true "vindication" of Hermann Cohen against Husik's sharp criticisms.[26] In doing so, Strauss was compelled to defend also the very idea of a modern Jewish philosophy, since it was Husik's view that there could not be such a thing. This is because, as Husik believed, Jewish philosophy means, and can only mean, *medieval* Jewish philosophy; in his view, this entity called "Jewish philosophy" made sense only in terms of the fixed coordinates which once made it possible, things now known to be noble medieval delusions which have been irrevocably dispelled: belief in the literal truth of the Torah as a once only historical revelation, and belief in a comprehensive, rigorous, and completed (Aristotelian) science. But as Strauss counters here quite simply, the lack in modern Jewish philosophy of the identical fixed coordinates which perhaps once "historically" defined medieval Jewish philosophy *cannot* be the last word, since these fixed coordinates do not define, in the most basic sense, what Judaism is or what philosophy is. This leads Strauss to the trenchant observation that "the fundamental problem," which aroused the need for Jewish philosophy during the medieval period and beyond, remains the same. If this is so, then ultimately Husik's and Cohen's approaches coalesce, for they both recognize that this still "fundamental problem" is most evident in the vital need to wrestle with and to reconcile "the relation of the spirit of science and of the spirit of the Bible."[27]

However, in spite of Strauss' admiration for Cohen as a model of the modern Jewish philosophical thinker, and for his revival of Jewish

philosophy pursued with exemplary passion, Strauss was not able to
revive his interest in Cohen's actual philosophical thought, since Cohen
remained beholden to the very modern philosophy to which Strauss
was searching for a rational alternative.[28] Strauss relegated the intellectual faults and moral vices of Cohen's thought to the effects and limits
of his historical experience. Such awareness of subsequent events did
not permit Strauss to consider trying to revive Cohen's thought.[29] Thus,
Strauss rests his case against the adequacy of Cohen's thought on its
pre-First-World-War character: "The worst things that he experienced
were the Dreyfus scandal and the pogroms instigated by Czarist Russia:
he did not experience Communist Russia and Hitler Germany."[30] For
Strauss these historical experiences make the "naive" belief in historical
progress and in the rationality of the historical process impossible. As
a result, Strauss was convinced that we must reconsider and rethink as
radically as possible all of our modern premises which have brought
us to this pass – indeed, he insisted on it already by 1935. However,
that conviction did not lead him either to call for an embrace of
irrationalism in its "ultramodern" forms, or to argue for a supposedly
simple "rejection" of reason in favor of revelation, as this is known in
the modern Jewish tradition, but it did arouse in him the notion of a
reassessment of the theological value and rational truth possibly still
contained in a premodern Jewish philosophical tradition of rational
theology, whose wisdom may not have been entirely surpassed by
modern Jewish thinkers like Cohen.

In other words, a reconsideration or rethinking of the modern
tradition of philosophy and theology, however radical, never entailed
for Strauss a simple rejection of modern reason, which he did not
regard as a sober option worth entertaining. Thus, Strauss did resemble
Cohen in one highly important regard: he was like him in maintaining
an adherence to modern liberal democracy, not to mention to modern
science and to biblical criticism, that is, for all practical purposes, to
the unavoidable legacy of Spinoza judiciously appropriated.[31] And
Strauss also stood with Cohen, although put in his own terms, on the
need for modern Jewish thinkers to wrestle with the deepest conflicts
between reason and revelation, which have not been resolved by
modern man, in light of the pressing moral concerns, powerful historical
experiences, and most serious intellectual difficulties and impasses of
modern man.

At the same time, in contradistinction to Cohen, Strauss was
growing attracted to the form of premodern rational thought which he
discovered in Maimonides, and the move toward it required a much
greater radical turn of thought and critical reassessment of the modern
than was available to him in Cohen's system. Responding to the extreme
terms and unprecedented light in which modernity was placed by

Nietzsche and Heidegger, Strauss would come to doubt in theory the entire modern project which Cohen could not think beyond, and did not see any reason to think beyond. Strauss goes to the point of connecting the origins of modernity with Machiavelli, and hence he views it as rooted in what would be regarded in traditional terms as an amoral philosophic thought, contrary to Cohen's Kantian idealization of the primacy of a traditional moral impulse in the move to modernity and Enlightenment. The shock of recognition of this ambiguous origin and impulse in which the idea of the modern arose is for Strauss a sobering realization that seemed to help him account for the repeated collapse in our century of liberal morality, politics, and religion as bulwarks against tyranny as well as against subtler forms of evil. In addition, Strauss was fully aware that the challenge presented by Nietzsche to the ideas of traditional morality, of reason in human nature, and of the rationality of history was greater than Cohen imagined, who was virtually a Hegelian in his faith in the march of modern progress toward rationality and morality.[32]

It was Cohen's views on Judaism, however, that were ultimately unsatisfactory to Strauss. In particular, Strauss assessed the position of Cohen on divine revelation as defective,[33] concluding that the unique elements in the Jewish teaching on revelation are not adequately comprehended by Cohen's notion of the greater "originalness" of Judaism as a cultural or historical source (such as is brought to light by his difficulties with "God as a reality").[34] Strauss also did not believe Cohen's position did justice to revelation's claim to universal truth, especially in so far as this truth may contradict modern ideas, such as human rational and moral autonomy. Although Cohen's system admits that in the divine revelation of Judaism there is displayed a primitive form of Kantian moral reasoning and human autonomy, revelation still remains on the most basic level a relic or artifact of the past, however impressive, rather than a vital teaching of the present, or even a teaching which may be needed to instruct the present. In Strauss' judgment, if this is all there is to the truth of Judaism as a divinely revealed teaching, as a magnificent anticipation of modern (neo-Kantian) ideas, then Cohen does not provide a fully compelling reason why we must preserve and give priority to the *unchanged* sources and traditions of Judaism, which had been the essence of the debate between Spinoza and Jewish orthodoxy. This leads Strauss to stress that Cohen does not believe in "revealed truths or revealed laws in the precise or traditional sense of the terms." Strauss would perhaps admit that Cohen provides us with a motive for maintaining a liberal Jewish religion, as a perfectly acceptable and even in some respects superior version of the religion of reason.[35] But then over and above everything else, Strauss seems to doubt whether this rationale is likely to provide a motive for devotion to the sources of Judaism, if they are no longer a teaching of revealed truths separate from, and claiming superiority to, the truths of reason.

✦ SPINOZA RECONSIDERED ✦

Strauss' critique of Hermann Cohen's notions of Judaism led him to the conclusion that modern reason contains serious flaws, flaws which also manifested themselves in the leading positions of modern Judaism, and hence which had been allowed gradually to compromise its integrity. In order to grasp how this compromise of modern Judaism had been allowed to occur, Strauss began with the beginning: he started with Spinoza. Indeed, in Strauss' view, modern Judaism can be defined as "a synthesis between rabbinical Judaism and Spinoza."[36] Not daunted by Spinoza's reputation as a modern saint, a canonization promoted by Moses Mendelssohn and confirmed by German Romanticism, Strauss quickly advanced to the heart of Spinoza's originality: his critique of religious orthodoxy, both Jewish and Christian. Strauss focused on Spinoza's relatively obscure *Theological-Political Treatise* rather than on his well-known *Ethics* as the proper introduction to his philosophy. This was unconventional but highly fortuitous since, as Strauss observed, in the former work Spinoza had to give reasons and arguments for his critique of orthodoxy, while in the latter work most of these reasons and arguments are simply taken for granted. He became aware that in Spinoza, because of his famous boldness, one may readily detect the fundamentally "anti-theological" premises of modern philosophy, and hence one may also see the most dubious grounds of those premises, in a clearer light than in any of his predecessors or even successors. As such, Strauss reached the following conclusion: Spinoza wrote his *Treatise* essentially in order to refute religious orthodoxy in so far as it is based on the Bible. As Strauss discovered, this explains why Spinoza needed to invent biblical criticism – in order to subvert, if not to refute, the belief in the orthodox religious teachings.

As Strauss conceived it, Spinoza was neither revolutionary nor saint, but rather the heir of the modern revolt against the premodern Western tradition both philosophic and religious, a revolt which is known as the Enlightenment. He applied to Judaism the critique of religion initiated by Machiavelli, and executed by Bodin, Bacon, Descartes, and Hobbes. Spinoza attacked (as well as mocked) not only the orthodox religious teachings embraced by the multitude of simple Jewish believers, but also the chief medieval philosophical defense and reform of Judaism which was elaborated by Maimonides.

What Strauss was not deceived by was Spinoza's artful rhetoric. To most unsuspecting readers of his *Treatise*, he appears in the guise of a modern religious reformer attempting to correct what he viewed as erroneous methods of reading the Bible. As Spinoza presents himself, he is a man who still believes in the Bible as the genuine word of God, however far removed he may be from a fanatical orthodoxy. But as Strauss discovered, this is certainly not Spinoza's genuine belief; he was able to trace Spinoza's philosophic thought to its true source in the *Treatise* only by avoiding such rhetorical traps set by Spinoza for the unwary reader. Hence Strauss listens very carefully to Spinoza's seemingly random denials of the cognitive value of every crucial biblical teaching, and his apparently incidental expressions of fundamental doubt about every important religious belief.[37] Strauss also rejects the notion that Spinoza was some sort of martyr for the cause of the eternal truth because, as Strauss discerned, Spinoza never entertained the possibility that the Bible might contain something of this highest truth. Since this possibility was never even taken seriously by Spinoza, it was doubtful to Strauss if he is the model, as he has been mythically presented by modern philosophy, of the genuinely open-minded thinker who sacrifices himself for the truth which he discovered and maintained with the greatest difficulty. Indeed, Spinoza advocates modern philosophy from the start, which means he presupposes both the notion of truth developed in modern science by his predecessors Bacon, Descartes, and Hobbes, as well as "his belief in the final character of his [own] philosophy as *the* clear and distinct and, therefore, *the* true account of the whole."[38] If Spinoza can show the biblical teachings to be self-contradictory, immature, confused, and hence absurd, then the logical conclusion to be drawn from this absurdity is that the Bible offers nothing to the genuine searcher for the truth. For Spinoza, truth by definition, as it were, cannot be given by God, and thus the entire notion of divine revelation is *impossible* pure and simple.

The doubt that animated Strauss is whether Spinoza has ever been able to show this. If Spinoza can only demonstrate that there are contradictions and other such difficulties in the text and the teachings of the Bible, this is still certainly compatible with belief in the truth of the biblical God:

> But what is Spinoza actually proving? In fact, nothing more than that it is not *humanly* possible that Moses wrote the Pentateuch.... This is not denied by the opponents.... [This is because,] on the assumption that Scripture is revealed, it is more apposite to assume an unfathomable mystery, rather than corruption of the text, as the reason for obscurity.[39]

In Strauss' view, Spinoza could meet his claim to "refute" the Bible only if the biblical God has already been proved to be false, if the mysterious God – the one omnipotent and transcendent God whose will is unfathomable – is somehow an "absurd" notion. But does Spinoza prove this?

According to Strauss' assessment, Spinoza's critique of religion is rooted in a single genuinely cogent argument, an argument which pertains to all revealed religion.[40] Strauss recognized that in order to dispose of both the Bible as the basis for all revealed religion, and its claim to teach the suprarational truth, Spinoza must disprove or refute philosophically the notion of revelation per se. But Strauss argues that revelation can occur only in a certain kind of universe: one in which the human mind can naturally achieve perfect knowledge only to a certain degree, and in which God, who is all-powerful and who "acts with unfathomable freedom,"[41] can satisfy human yearning for such perfect knowledge in so far as he chooses to let human beings know. As Strauss discerned, the unequalled cogency of Spinoza's critique of the notion of revelation (especially as this was philosophically defended by Maimonides) lies in his awareness that the possibility of such revelation can be refuted only if the universe and the human mind are so constructed as to disallow it unconditionally. Strauss considers Spinoza's entire position, his attempt at unfolding *the* completed philosophic system, as an uncompromising attempt to do just that: to think it through as far as possible and, as a result, to construct the universe and the human mind so as to prevent the possibility of any revelation from ever occurring in them.

Although Spinoza already attempts to achieve this goal in the *Theological-Political Treatise*, Strauss proves by paying careful and critical attention to Spinoza's actual arguments that he is not in fact able to construct the universe and the human mind in this fashion. As Strauss observes, this claim about the superiority of the completed system of Spinoza does not even succeed in retrospective terms against the medieval Maimonides. Maimonides was perhaps Spinoza's toughest-minded philosophical opponent. Spinoza attacks his hermeneutical method, his Aristotelianism and "scholastic" attitude to science, his view of man and of Jewish society and faith, his prophetology and attitude toward miracles. However, inasmuch as these attacks do not fall into logical fallacies or meet with other rational limitations, they all still assume the refutation of revelation as a human or natural possibility. If, as directed by Strauss, we finally turn to the *Ethics* in anticipation of discovering the truly systematic refutation, our hopes will be disappointed: this completed system, rather than being a refutation of revelation, presupposes its falsity from the very first page of the *Ethics*. Thus Spinoza never refutes it *in* the system since its falsity is presupposed *by* the system.

But why is it necessary for Spinoza to presuppose such falsity? What premise is so difficult to refute or even to face directly? According to Strauss, the difficulty lies in the following concept: God as unfathomable will. If God is unfathomable will because he is omnipotent, who reveals himself as he wills, revelation is possible. It could be refuted only if human beings could attain the clear and distinct knowledge of the whole, the knowledge which Spinoza strives to contain in the *Ethics*, the knowledge which in principle makes all causes explicable and hence renders all things intelligible. In a completely comprehensible universe, the mysterious God would be a superfluous hypothesis. Since, according to Strauss, Spinoza never adequately demonstrates his view,[42] the system presented in the *Ethics*, "the clear and distinct account of everything . . . , remains fundamentally hypothetical. As a consequence, its cognitive status is not different from that of the orthodox account." For this reason, Spinoza cannot refute, or even "legitimately deny," the *possibility* of the theological view presented in the Bible; there is then no justification whatever for his not considering the revealing God and revelation *per se* as possibly the truth.[43]

Not only in matters of theological argument, but also in purely "personal" terms, Strauss was certainly not impressed with the attitude or behavior of Spinoza as a Jew in the *Treatise*. In so far as Spinoza might be styled the hidden "lawgiver" of modern Judaism, Strauss asked whether his consistently hostile attitude to traditional Judaism reflects an essential flaw in modern Judaism itself, which learned so much from him. Can it be relegated to a mere idiosyncrasy of Spinoza's character, a regrettably skewed emphasis resulting from his unhappy personal experience with the Amsterdam Jewish community? Or rather, does this hostile attitude not detract from the honorableness of the intention of mounting "true" criticisms of traditional Judaism, as a result of which any possible honest conclusion about their truth has been seriously compromised? Strauss had undoubtedly been taught by Hermann Cohen not to be deceived by the aura surrounding Spinoza as a modern saint so as to miss the "anti-theological ire" which moved his criticisms of Judaism, an aura which had been acquired in some measure by the ban pronounced against him by the Amsterdam rabbis, not to mention by his support for Dutch liberal republicanism, and perhaps also by his family's persecuted Marrano origins. The mystique of Spinoza's life combined to issue in an even greater aura entirely unrelated to a sober assessment of his philosophic thought and its Jewish implications. Strauss acknowledged that this aura was somehow allowed to vindicate Spinoza's words and actions as a plainly unjust accuser against Judaism, since his supposedly "pure" intentions are used to serve as an exoneration.

At the same time, Strauss detected that Spinoza's disloyalty as a Jew may not just be evidence of moral depravity, but may also be derived from a much bigger political exigency which he was involved in meeting – the need to destroy the "medieval" order. Strauss knew that Spinoza followed with full conviction the modern project first suggested by Machiavelli, to build a wall of separation between the political and the religious realms. This modern project aimed to subordinate the religious realm in order to ensure the supremacy and autonomy of the political realm, which would be commanded by statesmen liberated from religion and devoted to glory, guided by benevolent scientists free to pursue unhampered knowledge, and supported by an enlightened people disenchanted with supernatural religion, busy with commerce, and moved by patriotism.[44] Although some of these beliefs were clearly antithetical, in whole or in part, to traditional Judaism, they supported a greater aim with which Jews certainly could, and mostly did, sympathize. Jews were distinctly unfriendly to the survival of the medieval Christian order which the Enlightenment aimed to destroy, since for them its meaning was clear, as Strauss put it so well: "The action most characteristic of the Middle Ages is the Crusades; it may be said to have culminated not accidentally in the murder of whole Jewish communities."[45] If only for this reason, Strauss recognized that it is difficult for modern non-Orthodox Jews to stand in a critical relation to Spinoza, as "the first philosopher who was both a democrat and a liberal," and hence as the thinker who is responsible for some of the greatest blessings of modernity in his commanding argument for liberal democracy, as the only modern regime which has been more or less consistently friendly to the Jews.[46] It is only in this regime that they have been allotted an honorable settlement, though one not always free of contradictions, that is, as individual human beings with natural rights.

Strauss thus uncovers the Machiavellian political considerations which permitted Spinoza to attack the Jewish people and faith if it helped him strategically win his battle to separate Christian religious faith and European political life.[47] Spinoza's Machiavellian moral calculus may be stated as follows: he needed to make a direct attack on the Jews both in order to make surreptitiously a greater attack on the Christians, and in order to protect his own safety as a lone attacker against a powerful and oppressive order. As Strauss further perceived, Spinoza could make an argument against Christianity acceptable to Christians via an argument against Judaism and the Jewish Bible, because his attack was put in the disguised form of an attack on the Jews who were despised by his Christian readers, and hence they would be receptive to it. Spinoza could meanwhile vindicate himself by claiming to liberate the Jews both from their own oppressive religion and from the oppressive medieval Christian order. Eventually, once the war has been victorious, once the common enemy has been demolished and liberal democracy has been established, the Jews will be grateful to him.[48]

This led to Strauss' mature conclusion that Spinoza was not entirely a bad Jew, despite his amoral Machiavellian tactics and strategy. Strauss thus moved to a greater appreciation for Spinoza's contribution to modern Judaism. Strauss' earlier view of Spinoza as entirely unconcerned with the Jews and Judaism seems to have been qualified decisively, for in his later essays Strauss recognized in Spinoza's suggestions for reforming the Jews, so as to make possible their accommodation to this projected liberal democracy, a vital and even deep remaining "sympathy with his people." Although he may have been definitely set against Judaism, he was not set against the Jews, especially once they had been freed by him from any ultimate ties to what he regarded as their "effeminating" traditional religion.[49] Strauss refers directly to perhaps the most important "solution to the Jewish problem" which Spinoza first suggested, namely, "liberal assimilationism," which enables the Jews as secular individual citizens to fit in with a liberal democracy so as to derive the decent benefits and protections of their "natural rights."

In fact, Strauss credits Spinoza not only with the idea of liberal assimilationism, but also with the quite different possibility of a "solution to the Jewish problem" on the basis of a restored Jewish political autonomy in their ancestral homeland. Although it is Strauss' view that this option sketched by Spinoza is atheistic in its origins and impulses, and derives from liberalism while pointing correctly to the limits of liberalism,[50] it nevertheless restores to the Jews a fighting spirit, teaches them to resist by arms the evils which befall them, and forces them to control their own political destiny. Spinoza, witness to the Shabbatai Zvi messianic episode which illustrated to him how theology led the Jews astray, made this "Zionist" suggestion as a logical deduction from his liberalism. He envisioned that, once the Jews have been liberated from the "debilitating" aspects of their religion, this will enable them to choose either individual or collective freedom in the modern age. Although both of these political suggestions are in full conformity with what Strauss calls "Spinoza's egoistic morality," a morality which in his analysis is not compatible with Judaism, they do prove to Strauss that Spinoza was not unmoved by the political plight and suffering of the Jews.[51]

In the subtle and dialectical approach of Leo Strauss, Spinoza is presented as a highly complex, original, and yet questionable figure. He was a keen student of Machiavelli and his "disciples" Bacon, Descartes, and Hobbes, and was animated by the "anti-theological ire" of the modern project, and yet he advocated its aim to dismantle the medieval Christian order so as to establish the humane liberal democracy devised originally in his philosophy. He was a philosophical system builder, and a defender of the open-minded pursuit of modern science and philosophy in complete freedom, yet he was also a closed-minded antagonist of revelation, especially in its claim to knowledge, and he even attempted to "refute" it by a brilliant but unavailing argument. He was a hostile critic of orthodox Judaism, an unjust attacker of the basis of its faith, and the consequent author of biblical criticism, and yet he was also the originator of the powerful modern Jewish ideas of political Zionism and liberal Jewish religion. For Strauss, this leads to the unassailable conclusion that modern Judaism simply cannot be separated from the dubious figure of Spinoza, in whom such troublesome contradictions coincide. In Strauss' search for the causes of the contemporary crisis of modern Judaism and for a way toward its possible resolution, he tried to comprehend Spinoza in his full complexity: as a bold and original modern philosopher in his own right, as a Jewish thinker compared against the standard of Maimonides, and as the benefactor of modern Judaism in the light of whose legacy his modern Jewish heirs were viewed and measured. By this means Strauss hoped to attain a solid ground beyond the present predicament, a ground that somehow encompasses both the true importance, and the problematic nature, of Spinoza.

❧ STRAUSS' MAIMONIDEANISM ❧

Strauss attempted to achieve this wholeness of thought that for him was lacking in Spinoza by rooting his own unique position as a modern Jewish thinker in the medieval Jewish thought of Maimonides. The Maimonides whom Strauss rediscovered, and whose essential thought he claimed to penetrate by the careful explication of the texts, inspired him with the possibility of doing justice to the truths of both reason and revelation. In proceeding so, Strauss also showed it is possible to cross the great divide between modern and premodern philosophic thought in order to reappropriate the fundamental truth of the premodern thinkers. In particular, Strauss believed that Maimonides' theological and political approach is possessed of an enduring and universal validity, and is actually as relevant for us in our modern dilemmas as it was for the medieval Jewish community for whom it was written.

What is Strauss' "Maimonideanism," and why does he claim so much for it? First, if we recall Strauss' criticism of Spinoza, perhaps the main point in contention for Strauss was that modern philosophy (following Spinoza's lead) never proved its own highest speculative premises to be true, but just acted as if they were, and so proceeded on this faulty basis to attack revealed religion. But if, as Strauss counters, these premises are not true, as rationally knowable or demonstrable, the entire refutation, defeat, and dismissal of revelation as "irrational" is not sound. Modern philosophy has thus been misled by its own *hubris*, that is, by a mere assertion of knowledge of things which is not in its power. Thus, according to Strauss, if modern reason does not seem to possess such knowledge, it also does not know what is good, pure, and simple for man. To prove his case, Strauss allows modern (especially twentieth-century) history to be brought to light as evidence against the faulty assumptions of modern reason.

There is, then, according to Strauss, a need to recover the original meaning of what philosophy is, and of what reason is, which paradoxically should also lead us to recover an original awareness of what revelation is as well, since reason and revelation are the true natural rivals, whose opposition cannot be done away with, despite the pretensions of modern reason. In Strauss' perception, this dispute is not only the source of the modern view of morality (although the modern view claims to reject both premodern sources as well as their dispute), but it remains the only sound basis from which the Western philosophic thinker is able to derive his knowledge of what is good for man. Does modern reason deserve to be victorious, that is, can it demonstrate that divine revelation is implausible, not to mention refutable? If it cannot do this, should all wisdom from the past, like the "medieval" or orthodox legacy of Jewish thought, have been rejected as benighted?

Following careful study of the medieval Jewish texts, Strauss reached the conclusion that the medieval thinkers, such as Maimonides, were actually wiser about the very things on which the moderns claimed proud and decisive superiority, such as on the fundamental relations between philosophy, religion, and politics. In his monumental work *Philosophy and Law*, Strauss oriented his "return to Maimonides" toward this very point: he stressed that what distinguishes Maimonides' position as a Jewish thinker is his defense of divine law. Belief is not the key notion for revealed religion, as the moderns maintained it was, since such a notion artificially detaches belief from law or commandment which is in actuality primary. In other words, revelation counted for Maimonides as a philosopher in so far as it appears in the form of a divinely revealed law, which (as Strauss' research on Spinoza showed) has never been refuted by reason.

Strauss discerned that law received such a high estimation for Maimonides in great measure because he was a Jewish philosophic thinker in the tradition of Plato. In this tradition, originally cultivated by some of the great Islamic philosophers who preceded Maimonides, it was recognized that the freedom of philosophy, as this means absolutely free reflection on God, humanity, and the world, is not the natural beginning point of its own activity. It is not self-evident why such free philosophizing should be permitted to arise in the context of a revealed religion, grasped as revealed not in the modern sense of religion as belief but as a polity-forming comprehensive divine law which defines what actions are commanded by God as lawgiver. It is law that constitutes and defines the religious community. But, as Strauss further perceived, philosophy poses a potential threat to the religious community, since one might reach conclusions other than those prescribed by the divine law. As an activity which arises in the polity guided by divine law, free philosophic thought (as a form of action in theological-political life) rightly needs to be considered by the law, which is the highest authority of the religious community. Hence, such free reflection needs to be justified in terms of the law, and limited according to the law.

Strauss also comprehended that for Maimonides, as for Plato and Aristotle, the human being is naturally a political animal; because of this view, Maimonides was in a philosophical sense fully able to justify the great authority of law in Judaism. Law is the natural expression of civilized political life, and is the proper instrument for the fulfillment of the imperatives of human nature. What distinguishes divine law, according to Maimonides, is its concern with the full perfection of human nature, that is, in terms of both body and soul. But the divine law's teaching which bears on the perfection of the human soul is presented in a form which is not always clear, and hence this teaching (or the text on which it is based) is in need of interpretation. In Maimonides' view, the required explication of the text of the divine law is the basis for the free reflection which is permitted, and even commanded to the philosophical believer, in order to know rationally the true meaning of this revealed teaching, so long as the believer does not use his or her rational freedom to subvert or circumvent the law.

If Maimonides was so much concerned with philosophical pursuits, as Strauss seems to have been convinced, why was it so important *philosophically* to him to defend the Jewish law, and to make himself a legal authority? As a loyal citizen of the Jewish polity, Maimonides obviously believed it to be essential to remain devoted to its imperatives in the highest sense. By contrast with Maimonides, Spinoza did not regard himself as bound by such considerations; indeed, he made it a point of honor to stand free of such considerations. This is because Spinoza believed that a better (if humanly devised) law could be constructed by modern reason. Around this point their fundamental argument revolves, with regard to what best constitutes a good and truly binding law: Maimonides was persuaded that only a prophet, as stringently defined by him, could bring a "perfect" and hence divine law. Further, Maimonides acknowledged that it was this law which made possible his activity as a Jewish philosopher; he must remain attached and obedient to the polity which created him, as Socrates argued in the *Crito*, lest philosophy itself be discredited by the liberties which the philosopher allows himself with the commitments he makes, and with the debts he owes. Spinoza in contrast believed in the philosopher who can lead a life remote from the crowd; as a cosmopolitan citizen of the world, the philosopher or scientist possesses a political freedom from any undue attachment to specific polities which serve the ignorant multitude. But Maimonides denied that such a world posited by Spinoza existed in any essential sense other than in the mind or imagination of the philosopher or the scientist, who does not lead his life detached from his body, and whose soul does not produce or educate itself.

The political wisdom of Maimonides,[52] which Strauss was very much influenced by, did not, however, exhaust his interest in Maimonides. Strauss was further impressed with how this political acuity allowed Maimonides to unfold a rational defense of the Jewish tradition as laws and ritual life in a highly elaborate, even "scientific," fashion which did not aim to diminish the importance of those laws. Maimonides ordered the laws so as to bring to light their purpose with regard to enlightenment, and so as to reflect the proper order of the soul, since according to him, the laws are able to educate human beings by acting as imaginative or poetic expressions of rational truths. The theological and moral teaching of the divine law is not compromised by its complex and dialectical political aims, but rather it is connected with and dependent on them; in order to enhance the rationality of human beings in society, it is imperative to ensure decent relations between human beings, and to convey true notions about God. But according to Strauss' reading of Maimonides, this would not have been possible on any other basis than by a prophet, who is the most perfect man – a philosopher-lawgiver. Strauss perceived that by taking seriously the key political role played by the prophet, that is, in the bringing of a good and binding law, and by combining it with a defense of the Jewish philosophical life as an attempted imitation of the prophet, Maimonides was even able to give a plausible philosophical account of the seemingly "obsolete" laws of the ancient Temple sacrifices in purely anthropological and historical terms. Maimonides was able to achieve this while not detracting from the sense of permanent obligation to obey the laws, since these laws (and others like them) are the fundamental support of Jewish political life, and fidelity to them is required of every loyal citizen. Further, he safeguarded the duty to obey the law by his teaching the philosophizing Jews who learned from him to respect the perennial wisdom about human nature and human need that is contained in even the most "ritualistic" laws: that is, he taught that the law is divine because it is guided by one highest aim – to serve the cause of knowing the truth. This "explanation" of the laws is not, as with Spinoza, moved by the intention of philosophical refutation or historical debunking, but to provide a theological understanding and political overview whose aim is to deepen the reasons for "philosophical" obedience.[53]

But Strauss recognized that this rationalistic justification for Judaism was not sufficient for a defense of Judaism in its uniqueness even according to the Jewish thought of Maimonides himself. On the matter of the highest truth taught by Judaism, to what is Maimonides ultimately loyal: to revelation or to reason? Does Maimonides' interpretation of Judaism acknowledge nothing beyond what unaided reason can achieve on its own, hence claiming only to accord with rational philosophical truth?[54] Or, does Maimonides acknowledge that Judaism, even if this religion is called "the most rational," still teaches a suprarational theological truth which surpasses what unaided reason can achieve on its own, and which needs some faith, commitment, or act of will in order to "know" its highest truth? According to Strauss, Maimonides did not accede to that simple either/or alternative, since he did not believe the fundamental choice is between radical human rational autonomy versus irrational or blind religious commitment. Most illustrative is Maimonides' view on the matter of creation versus eternity; with regard to this matter, he argues for the creation of the world on the ground that this teaching is not of any greater irrationality than the eternity of the world, if the true rationality of the Aristotelian philosophical arguments for eternity are critically scrutinized and honestly assessed.

Proceeding from this argument for creation, Strauss perceived that all of the theological issues treated in Maimonides' *Guide* may be reduced to a fundamental issue at stake, which separates between philosophy and Judaism: the philosophical belief in the autonomous, all-comprehensive, and self-encompassing principle of "nature" ruled by divine mind and knowable by the human mind versus the theological belief in unqualified divine omnipotence mitigated by an absolutely moral will which has been revealed to humanity in history by the supreme prophet. In the first place, it seems that Maimonides himself adhered with full awareness of the difficulties yet with much greater consistency than is usually the case, to the Jewish doctrine of an absolute divine omnipotence which is yet morally and naturally self-limiting in opposition to philosophy which relies on "nature." At the same time, he did not surrender or compromise his commitment to rationality, and even to "the supremacy of reason," on any point.[55] As this implies, he did not accept any "irrational" religious dogmas; he accepted only such religious dogmas as could be made at least cognitively consistent with rationally knowable, or demonstrated, truth. He achieved this feat of balance between divine omnipotence and "nature" by maintaining that human intellect, which knows as much as we can know about "nature," is the chief expression of the divine image in us.

Thus, over and above everything else, as Strauss seems to have been persuaded, Maimonides' fruitful adherence to the notion of divine omnipotence (as passing beyond but not denying "nature") was based on the belief that only on this religious ground is a "genuine" moral code made possible, that is, a moral code which is both rationally true and absolutely binding.[56] Morality is revealed, however, not by some spectacular miracle (as divine omnipotence might suggest), but through the prophet as the most perfect man, whose supreme excellence of the moral and the rational-intellectual in one human being makes him most suitable to receive the truth of these moral and speculative command-ments in what he calls a divine "overflow." What apparently guides divine law, and what accounts for its appeal to all human beings, is the depth of comprehension by the prophet of the full range of needs, high and low, of the human soul, and of how best to satisfy and harmonize those needs. The prophet as philosopher-lawgiver conveys this harmon-izing wisdom in the form of a law which, for those who want to learn, is a wisdom of prudence about how a measured accommodation of the law to those needs helps to produce well-ordered souls in a well-ordered society – the supreme aim of a divine law.[57] Indeed, what defines the highest type of prophet is he who is able to enshrine virtue, piety, and wisdom in a law; this law alone is divine because it perfectly balances those various and sundry conflicting human needs, while never forgetting the requirements of morality. If political and theological history may serve as a roundabout proof for its moral and religious excellence, the law of Moses has been the inspiration for two great "imitators," as Maimonides would put it, by whose teaching Western civilization has been guided for several millennia; apparently for Mai-monides this is no accident but a function of the superior spirituality that emanates from the original model, the Torah of Moses.

At the same time, however, Strauss suggested surreptitiously that perhaps Maimonides himself did not fully embrace this vision of perfec-tion in prophecy, and that he did not remain completely satisfied with traditional religion as a comprehensive or self-contained mode of thought. Strauss perceived that Maimonides subtly leaves room for doubt in the very heart of his own theology, and he reserves a lawful place for doubt for a very specific reason: this is because Maimonides, like every philosopher, was aware of the problematic character and even questionability of every final resolution, and hence even of his own seemingly "perfect" one, to the perplexities of the Torah. Indeed, according to Strauss' mature reading of Maimonides, the crucial element of fundamental or radical doubt, essential to the philosophic experience, led Strauss to perceive a hidden dimension in the writings of Maimonides: his use of esotericism, so that his true philosophical defense of medieval Judaism could be comprehended only by the Jewish spiritual elite, who would be able to handle philosophical doubt in his resolute encounter with the tough questions of theology, and in his subtle uncoverings of the problems of the law.

How did Strauss comprehend the theological logic which animated Maimonides' use of such esotericism? He maintained that this logic could be grasped only if seen in the light of Maimonides' philosophical view of the perfection of the prophet. The true prophet, according to Maimonides, possesses the unique or superhuman ability to communicate on two levels simultaneously, the imaginative and the intellectual, which are expressions of separate teachings dialectically or pedagogically intertwined. While the Torah is a ladder of ascent to the truth with numerous rungs, still in the decisive respect it remains a three-tiered system, as it represents human nature: it trains all human beings to religious piety and moral goodness; it prepares the life of the better and most decent person, and it does so through leading a noble life dedicated to fulfilling God's law and educating to the highest belief possible about him; it guides the philosopher (or the potential prophet), since the Torah makes allowance for the search for wisdom, with a promise to culminate in knowledge of *the* truth. The Torah, it would seem, tries especially to harmonize the two higher human types of the three: the moral-religious person and the philosophical person. But this suggests that the life of search for wisdom and the life of elevated or moral piety are not in harmony but in conflict; between the two higher types, a higher disaccord emerges.[58] According to Strauss, this fundamental conflict was taken most seriously by Maimonides, who believed it needed to be resolved, and it was that need which gave rise to Maimonidean esotericism.

Maimonidean esotericism, as Strauss rediscovered it, was a method employed to both conceal and reveal the conflict between the two most basic and permanent classes of human beings, the philosophical few and the non-philosophical many, in the life of Judaism. The study of the religious texts is used as a common ground for these opposed types to be able to encounter one another on a high plane, and especially as a common ground on which the few can learn vital truths about the many. To be sure, such a "textual encounter" could potentially lead to a clash, in that the Jewish philosophical student could be brought to attack the religious texts as philosophically "primitive," and to reject them unthinkingly as sources of knowledge or wisdom. But in the subtle method of Maimonides, this textual encounter emerges as the basis for harmony, in that by studying these texts the Jewish philosophical student learns fundamental lessons about religion, prophecy, and wisdom, and especially vital truths about how precarious the life of thought is in any society, but especially in a religious society based on revelation. Thus, in order to avoid this clash, and to ensure that the Jewish philosophical student is taught a prudent and wise respect for the religion, and especially revealed texts, which had been perplexing to him or her, Maimonides needs to conceal with numerous artful literary devices his most radical arguments and conclusions which might be a threat both to the piety of the simple faithful and, in a preliminary stage, to the proper moral and cognitive development of the Jewish philosophical student. However, this concern for the proper order in the uncovering of truth is balanced in creative tension, as Strauss recognized, with a contrary aim in the pedagogical regimen of Maimonides: it is also true that to recognize these same radical truths, even to learn how to think them through for himself, is essential to the very production of the elite of Jewish philosophical students which he aimed to educate and hence to create. Indeed, this learning is not in any sense intended to diminish respect for a religious society based on revelation, but just the opposite is true. Thus, it is meant to raise respect for its unique excellence, because as has already been observed, divine revelation by the one omnipotent God is for Maimonides the only ground on which a "genuine" morality can be established.

Strauss made his name in Jewish scholarly circles by his careful study and detailed reiteration of the subtle method used by Maimonides in writing the *Guide* as peculiarly as he did. But a mere scholarly discovery, however prodigious, was scarcely Strauss' main contribution to modern Jewish thought. Rather, it is the examination of Maimonides' thought concealed beneath the discovery which reveals Strauss' deeper insight. This can be discerned in Strauss' analysis of why Maimonides entertained such a passion for the life of the mind in his approach to Judaism. In Strauss' reading, Maimonides regarded the production of the highest intellectual excellence or virtue in an elite class of Jewish philosophical students as the most difficult task, one fraught with risks, but he also regarded no other task as so imperative for the well-being and future survival of the Jewish people. Maimonides saw that from the days of the patriarchs and prophets, the distinguishing mark of the Jews, what has been the key to their ability to discern and receive the highest religious truths, has been their devotion to the life of the mind, to pursuit of knowledge in the philosophical and scientific sense, and to human perfection in the form of comprehensive wisdom about God. It was this notion of the history of Judaism that guided Maimonides in his efforts as a great teacher, a notion which Strauss found highly appealing, and which he sought to stress in his reading of the philosophical argument concealed beneath esotericism. Although the elite of Jewish philosophical students receive the same moral education as everyone else, and are held to the same if not higher moral standards, their intellectual excellence is the guarantee of the health of their souls and of the soul of the people: the moral excellence of humanity is a prerequisite of its intellectual perfection, and, once such perfection is achieved, it overflows to an even higher moral excellence informed by intellectual truth. Strauss, with his concern for defending both political morality and the moral integrity of philosophy, was further drawn to the depth of wisdom he uncovered in Maimonides. For Maimonides it would seem, as for Socrates, proper knowledge is true virtue.

In this light, Strauss learned from Maimonides that religion is essential to any healthy political society, and certainly for the moral life of human beings. Over and above this, Maimonides convinced Strauss that Jewish religion, based on the Hebrew Bible, is most essential to ground a "genuine" morality for almost every human being. As Strauss would seem to concede, it is possible some rare philosophers may reach the same moral truths on the basis of their own rational speculation, but this possibility is certainly no guarantee that they will reach them or be guided by them in their life, and hence most if not all philosophers are also still in need of the morality and religion taught by the Hebrew Bible. Moreover, Strauss was convinced that philosophy not only cannot dispute the usefulness of religion, but also (and indeed of much greater importance) has not been able to disprove or refute the truth claims of revealed or monotheistic religion. Together with this, however, Strauss did not forget the previously mentioned truth about philosophy: it must be free to doubt. Indeed, the philosopher must, in the search for knowledge, doubt some of the most fundamental beliefs and dearly held opinions of the moral and religious tradition. But most people cannot live with such excruciating doubts about the universe and the meaning and value of life, which are most interesting and essential to the life of philosophers, whatever decent or defective final conclusions they may reach. As a result, Strauss followed Maimonides in defending the view that such speculations must be confined to an elite who need this activity of doubt, and they must be hidden as much as possible from society, that is, preferably confined to thought or communicated only to trustworthy friends. If they publish their speculations, they must communicate them esoterically, "write between the lines," in order to mask their doubts about the generally accepted or traditional truths. This means that even they must be guided by a higher authority, and, in the case of Judaism, by the law brought by Moses, the highest prophet, whose law harmonizes the conflict of the human types in society. To Strauss, this Maimonidean wisdom permits philosophy to flourish in freedom while the moral life of society is preserved and shielded from the doubts that the philosophers must ever bring to bear against it.

⚇ CONCLUSION ⚇

Although Strauss did not go so far as to regard Maimonides' teaching as a prescription to solve all modern Jewish theological or political problems, his deep reflection on Maimonides did lead him to maintain that this teaching is a vital source of wisdom which modern Judaism needs in order to help it resolve its contemporary crisis. If Strauss himself was not as traditionally pious as it is suggested a "true" Maimonidean would be, this was perhaps because for him the Maimonidean inspiration resided in the general approach and not in the specific details of Maimonides' medieval philosophical theology.[59] In other words, Strauss remained a modern Jew, committed to learning from the past while not attempting to revive it.

This apparent acceptance of the condition of the modern Jew, however, did not lead Strauss to believe that things could continue as previously constituted. Strauss argued that Jewish thought needs to rethink the entire range of modern positions to discover what has been rendered obsolete, and what can endure. In consequence of this need, together with careful study of Maimonides' writings, Strauss was undoubtedly persuaded that it would be better for future Jewish theology to adapt or embrace some of the most essential arguments (and even structures) of Maimonides' teaching as a model for Jewish life and thought. In Strauss' view, Maimonides' theology is superior in its theoretical reasoning and practical wisdom on fundamental points as compared with almost every modern Jewish thinker, even though such wisdom and reasoning is usually dismissed as distressingly "medieval." Strauss pointed to such fundamental theological points as: the belief in creation, and the powerful arguments which can be made for it; the need for the law, and its rational-moral character; the prophets as searchers for knowledge and bearers of truth; the proper relations of the theological sphere to the political sphere; and his metaphysical-moral notion of human perfection.

As for those contemporary Jews who are driven to despair of reason, or to despise it, because of the "catastrophes and horrors" that have occurred in the modern West during the present century, Strauss would caution against too quickly saying "farewell to reason," even if it is said in the name of revelation.[60] Neither intellectual honesty nor love of truth impels one to a simple rejection of all things modern and Western, such as science and philosophy, liberal democracy, or even modern individualism, because of the evident deficiencies which have been displayed by them. Certainly one is entitled, based on sound Jewish and even Maimonidean principles, to respond with revulsion to contemporary moral relativism and philosophical nihilism. But the question stands, whether Judaism is not at its origin closer to genuine philosophical rationalism than it is to any fideistic orthodoxy whether religious or secular. In the face of the retreat from both reason and revelation in the contemporary era, Strauss points to the wisdom of Maimonides to serve as a guide for meeting the true challenges of Western philosophical thought, while simultaneously showing how to defend honestly what is most essential in Judaism. As an important task for contemporary Jewish thought, this would require thinking through with greater critical awareness the relations between Judaism and Western civilization, especially Western philosophy, in light of our modern historical experience and modern intellectual legacy. Indeed, we must still face the difficult questions put to Judaism by premodern Western philosophy which are perennial – just as is Judaism's basic questioning of it. We must also rethink the historical doubts raised by modern Western philosophy about the entire premodern tradition, that is, about the original texts and revelations of Judaism, in order to know which doubts are still valid or true.

As has been shown, Strauss came to maintain that the search for wisdom in the midst of our contemporary crisis seems to require us to return to the original sources of our wisdom. Over and above everything else, this meant in Strauss' mind that we need especially to turn to the Hebrew Bible, the most fundamental Jewish source, in order to consider whether this book contains a unity of forgotten knowledge that had provided us with our first light, and with an unrefuted truth that we can still recover. Just as Maimonides focused on the Hebrew Bible in order to meet the medieval philosophical challenge and the crisis it provoked, Strauss believed that modern Jews should return to studying the Hebrew Bible as one book with one teaching about God, humanity, and the world. As this suggests, Strauss thought that we are in need of its essential teaching – blurred by tradition and obscured by modern critique – which we must try to grasp afresh. This is because, to Strauss, it is only in the original sources of our wisdom that true wisdom may reside and can best be rediscovered.

❧ NOTES ❧

1 See Green 1993a, which deals elaborately (chapters 3 through 6) with the stages in the development of Strauss' thought, especially as they relate to his views on Maimonides.

2 In Strauss 1970, p. 2, he refers to it as "a disgraceful performance." To be fairer to him than he was to himself, Strauss was only twenty-two on its completion.

3 Fradkin 1993, p. 343.

4 Lerner 1976, pp. 91–2.

5 Fradkin 1993, p. 344.

6 Altmann 1975, p. xxxiv.

7 The 1954–5 Magnes Lectures were published in Hebrew translation as *What Is Political Philosophy?*, and first appeared in the English original in Strauss 1959, pp. 9–55.

8 Lerner 1976, p. 93.

9 See, e.g., Strauss 1989a, pp. 24–6, 28–31; Strauss 1965, pp. 29–31; Strauss 1959, pp. 17–27, 54–5. See also Green 1993a, p. xii.

10 See Strauss 1965, pp. 1–7.

11 See, e.g., Strauss 1983, pp. 167–8.

12 See, e.g., Strauss 1983, p. 168; Strauss 1965, pp. 28–31; Strauss 1935, p. 28; Strauss 1995, p. 38; Strauss 1971, pp. 1–8; Strauss 1958, p. 173.

13 See Strauss 1989b, pp. 81–98; Strauss 1959, pp. 54–5. See also Strauss' letter to Karl Löwith of 23 June 1935, Strauss 1988, p. 183.

14 See Strauss 1983, pp. 30–1, 34–7, 233; Strauss 1959, p. 242; Strauss 1970, pp. 2–3; Strauss 1989a, pp. 28–35; Strauss 1988, pp. 189–90.

15 See Strauss 1970, p. 2; Strauss 1983, p. 233, 167–8; Strauss 1959, p. 242.

16 See Strauss 1970, pp. 2–3; Strauss 1983, pp. 31, 233, 167–8; Strauss 1959, p. 242.

17 See Strauss 1935, pp. 120–2, and Strauss 1995, pp. 131–3; Strauss 1983, pp. 246–7. See also Altmann 1975, p. xxxvi; Udoff 1991, note 3, pp. 22–3; Pangle 1983, p. 26.

18 See Strauss 1979–80, p. 1; Strauss 1970, p. 2. Cf. also Strauss 1924.

19 See Strauss 1970, pp. 2–3; Strauss 1983, p. 31.

20 See Strauss 1965, pp. 1–2. See also Strauss forthcoming: "Why We Remain Jews."

21 See Strauss 1965, pp. 7–9, 22–5.

22 See ibid., pp. 24–5.

23 See Strauss 1983, pp. 233–4.

24 See Strauss 1959, pp. 25–7; Strauss 1989a, pp. 20–4, and 8–10; Strauss 1971, pp. 1–6. Cf. also Gildin 1989, pp. xiv-xvii. See also Schwarzschild 1987, pp. 168–9. It seems to me that this attempted defense unwittingly illustrates about as well as could have been done Strauss' point about the positivist as well as neo-Kantian idealist slide toward historicism: the purely regulative function of reason, which is filled by the content of the current historical state of scientific knowledge, is saved from the positivism of infinite pursuit, regulated by "method," only by the moral addition of the infinite "messianic task" of reason. Hence, it is only a step away from the positivist surrender to historicism, once doubts about the moral and cognitive value of science and its "method" enter the purview of the thinker. Schwarzschild seems willing to jettison the wall which protected Kant from such a slide toward positivism, because he seems to doubt the truth of what is "frequently alleged" about Kant's "metaphysical commitment to Euclidean geometry and Newtonian science;" instead, for Cohen and Marburg neo-Kantianism, Schwarzschild puts beyond "legitimate dispute" the fact that this school accepts the "historical character of the cognitive (and other) categories."

25 See Strauss 1952a, pp. xxi-xxxii. See also his critique of Julius Guttmann (Strauss 1935 and 1995, beginning of chapter 2) for Strauss' dictum: "There is no inquiry

into the history of philosophy that is not at the same time a *philosophical* inquiry."

26 See Strauss 1952a, pp. xxvi, xxx-xxxii.

27 See ibid., p. xxviii, as well as pp. xxx-xxxii. Strauss quotes the words of Husik himself: " 'All will not be well in Judaism until the position of the Bible as a Jewish authority is dealt with in an adequate manner by Jewish scholars who are competent to do it . . . the scholar who is going to undertake it . . . must be a philosopher and thinker of eminent abilities. And he must have a love of his people and sympathy with its aspirations.' That is to say, what is needed is a modern Jewish philosopher. . . . For the fundamental problem for the modern Jewish philosopher – the relation of the spirit of science and of the spirit of the Bible – was also the fundamental problem for the medieval Jewish philosopher. The modern Jewish philosopher will naturally try to learn as much as possible for his own task from his illustrious predecessors. Since he has achieved greater clarity at least about certain aspects of the fundamental issue than the medieval thinkers had, he will not be exclusively concerned with what the medieval thinkers explicitly or actually intended in elaborating their doctrines. He will be much more concerned with what these doctrines mean in the light of the fundamental issue regardless of whether the medieval thinkers were aware of that meaning or not."

28 See Strauss 1965, pp. 21–2.

29 Strauss 1983, pp. 167–8, 233–5, 246–7.

30 See ibid., p. 168.

31 See Strauss 1965, p. 15–16, 28–31.

32 See ibid., p. 25.

33 See Strauss 1983, pp. 233–4, 237–9.

34 See Strauss 1935, pp. 33, 38–9; Strauss 1995, pp. 44–5, 49–51.

35 See Strauss 1983, pp. 233–4.

36 See Strauss 1965, p. 27, and pp. 15–30 passim.

37 See Strauss 1952b, p. 184: "To exaggerate for purposes of clarification, we may say that each chapter of the *Treatise* serves the function of refuting one particular orthodox dogma while leaving untouched all other orthodox dogmas."

38 Ibid., p. 154.

39 Strauss 1965, pp. 143, 157: "In principle, no critique of Scripture can touch Maimonides' position, since such critique is capable of no more than establishing what is *humanly* possible or impossible, whereas his opponent assumes the divine origin of Scripture."

40 Ibid., pp. 159–60.

41 Ibid., p. 155.

42 Strauss briefly summarizes his own doubts about Spinoza's *Ethics* as follows: "But is Spinoza's account of the whole clear and distinct? Those of you who have ever tried their hands, for example, at his analysis of the emotions, would not be so certain of that. But more than that, even if it is clear and distinct, is it necessarily true? Is its clarity and distinctness not due to the fact that Spinoza abstracts from those elements of the whole which are not clear and distinct and which can never be rendered clear and distinct?" (Strauss 1989b, pp. 307–8). Strauss also remarks: "Spinoza and his like owed such successes as they had in their fight against orthodoxy to laughter and mockery," and he was thus also

"tempted to say": "mockery does not succeed in the refutation of the orthodox tenets but is itself the refutation" (Strauss 1965, pp. 28–9); see also Strauss 1935, pp. 18–19; Strauss 1995, pp. 29–30.

43 See Strauss 1965, pp. 28–9, 42, 144–6, 204–14.

44 This also meant that the "Machiavellian" modern project wanted to ensure the control and diminution of the religious realm, which will be allowed by the political realm to play only a pedagogical role once it has been duly "reformed," and hence solely in the sphere of liberal moral training; it will be banished both from the sphere of the claim to know the truth, and from the sphere of ambition for political power. This is because it is the view of Spinoza and the Enlightenment that religion, if it is not otherwise kept to the function of teaching a liberal morality, is one of the chief causes, if not *the* chief cause by itself alone, of evil, wickedness, and suffering in human life. This controlling aim of the modern project, to subordinate if not also to refute the truth claims made by biblical religion, and hence to prevent it from exercising any serious political influence on statesmen or on the people, resulted eventually in the full articulation by Spinoza of the beliefs in liberalism, progress, science, natural morality and religion, the secular state, and popular enlightenment, as both the necessary and the sufficient beliefs of modern humanity.

45 See Strauss 1965, p. 3.

46 Ibid., p. 16.

47 "Our case against Spinoza is in some respects even stronger than Cohen thought." See ibid., p. 19. (But cf. also pp. 25–28.) See Strauss 1924, p. 314. Strauss also viewed Spinoza's "Jewish motives" as follows: "However bad a Jew he may have been in all other respects, he thought of the liberation of the Jews in the only way in which he could think of it, given his philosophy" (Strauss 1965, pp. 20–1, 26–7).

48 See Strauss 1965, pp. 6–7.

49 See ibid., pp. 5, 20–1, and also 23–5, 27. For Spinoza's view of the Jews and Judaism, see his *Theological-Political Treatise*, and for these points, especially chapter 3, toward the end. Spinoza regarded the Mosaic law as binding only so long as the Jews possessed their own state, and hence he viewed himself as no longer obligated to obey it; for him it was, in any case, primarily a political, not a religious, law. By way of contrast, he also believed that the Jews could reconstitute their state – "so ultimately changeable are human affairs" – and, as this suggests, they might perhaps need the Mosaic law again: is it only the rabbinic law of the exile which "emasculates," precisely because it does not inculcate virtues which would constantly drive them to attempt to reconquer their state? See also Strauss forthcoming, "Why We Remain Jews;" Strauss 1991, pp. 183–4; Strauss 1959, pp. 102–3. (Cf. also the same pages in the "Restatement" for Strauss' prior discussion of Machiavelli's remark on "the 'unarmed heaven' and 'the effeminacy of the world' which, according to him, are due to Christianity.") See also Strauss 1983, p. 207; Strauss 1937, pp. 106–7.

50 See, e.g., Strauss 1965, pp. 4–7.

51 See Yaffe 1991, pp. 38–40.

52 See Strauss 1983, p. 207; Strauss 1991, pp. 184, 206. See Green 1993a.

53 Strauss 1983, pp. 198–203.

54 See Green 1993a, pp. 127–38, and Strauss 1989b, pp. 269–73.

55 Strauss 1963, pp. xiv, xx, xxiii-xxiv, xxxix, xliv, li; Strauss 1937, p. 100.

56 See Green 1993b.

57 See Maimonides, *Introduction to the Talmud*, chapter 8, for his answer to the question: why do the several essential types of human beings need to exist?

58 Strauss makes the following statement: "Now I do not deny that a man can believe in God without believing in creation, and particularly without believing in creation out of nothing. After all, the Bible itself does not explicitly teach creation out of nothing, as one might see. But still Judaism contains the whole notion of man's responsibility and of a final redemption" (Strauss forthcoming, "Why We Remain Jews").

59 Strauss 1983, pp. 150–1.

60 Ibid., p. 168; Strauss 1965, p. 31.

❧ BIBLIOGRAPHY ❧

Texts

Strauss, L. (1924) "Cohens Analyse der Bibel-Wissenschaft Spinozas," *Der Jude* 8: 295–314.

—— (1935) *Philosophie und Gesetz: Beiträge zum Verständnis Maimunis und seiner Vorläufer* (Berlin: Schocken).

—— (1937) "On Abravanel's Philosophical Tendency and Political Teaching," in *Isaac Abravanel*, edited by J. B. Trend and H. Loewe (Cambridge: Cambridge University Press), pp. 93–129.

—— (1952a) "Preface," in *Isaac Husik's Philosophical Essays*, edited by M. Nahm and L. Strauss (Oxford: Blackwell), pp. vii-xli.

—— (1952b) *Persecution and the Art of Writing* (Glencoe: Free Press).

—— (1956) "Social Science and Humanism," in *The State of the Social Sciences*, edited by L. D. White (Chicago: University of Chicago Press), pp. 415–25.

—— (1958) *Thoughts on Machiavelli* (Glencoe: Free Press).

—— (1959) *What is Political Philosophy?* (New York: Free Press).

—— (1961) "Relativism," in *Relativism and the Study of Man*, edited by H. Schoeck and J. W. Wiggins (Princeton: Van Nostrand), pp. 135–57.

—— (1963) "How to Begin to Study *The Guide of the Perplexed*," in *The Guide of the Perplexed*, by Moses Maimonides, translated by S. Pines (Chicago: University of Chicago Press), pp. xi-lvi.

—— (1965) *Spinoza's Critique of Religion*, translated by E. Sinclair (New York: Schocken).

—— (1970) "A Giving of Accounts," *The College* 22: 1–5.

—— (1971) *Natural Right and History*, 7th ed. (Chicago: University of Chicago Press).

—— (1979–80) "Preface to *Hobbes Politische Wissenschaft*," translated by Donald L. Maletz, *Interpretation* 8: 1–3.

—— (1983) *Studies in Platonic Political Philosophy* (Chicago: University of Chicago Press).

—— (1988) "Correspondence between Karl Löwith and Leo Strauss," *Independent Journal of Philosophy* 5–6: 177–92.

—— (1989a) *The Rebirth of Classical Political Rationalism*, edited by T. L. Pangle (Chicago: University of Chicago Press).

—— (1989b) *An Introduction to Political Philosophy: Ten Essays*, edited by H. Gildin (Detroit: Wayne State University Press).

—— (1991) *On Tyranny*, rev. ed., edited by V. Gourevitch and M. S. Roth (New York: Free Press).

—— (1995) *Philosophy and Law: Contributions to the Understanding of Maimonides and his Predecessors*, translated by E. Adler (Albany: State University of New York Press).

—— (forthcoming) *Jewish Philosophy and the Crisis of Modernity: Essays and Lectures*, edited by K. H. Green (Albany: State University of New York Press).

Studies

Altmann, A. (1975) "Leo Strauss: 1899–1973," *Proceedings of the American Academy for Jewish Research* 41–2: xxxiii-xxxvi.

Fradkin, H. (1993) "Leo Strauss," in *Interpreters of Judaism in the Late Twentieth Century*, edited by S. T. Katz (Washington, DC: B'nai B'rith), pp. 343–67.

Gildin, H. (1989) "Introduction" to L. Strauss, *An Introduction to Political Philosophy: Ten Essays*, edited by H. Gildin (Detroit: Wayne State University Press), pp. vii-xxiv.

Green, K. H. (1993a) *Jew and Philosopher: The Return to Maimonides in the Jewish Thought of Leo Strauss* (Albany: State University of New York Press).

—— (1993b) "Religion, Philosophy, and Morality: How Leo Strauss Read Judah Halevi's *Kuzari*," *Journal of the American Academy of Religion* 61: 225–73.

Lerner, R. (1976) "Leo Strauss (1899–1973)," *American Jewish Year Book* 76: 91–7.

Pangle, T. L. (1983) "Introduction" to L. Strauss, *Studies in Platonic Political Philosophy* (Chicago: University of Chicago Press), pp. 1–26.

Schwarzschild, S. S. (1987) "Authority and Reason Contra Gadamer," in *Studies in Jewish Philosophy*, edited by N. M. Samuelson (Lanham: University Press of America), pp. 161–90.

Udoff, A. (1991) "On Leo Strauss: An Introductory Account," in *Leo Strauss's Thought: Toward a Critical Engagement*, edited by A. Udoff (Boulder: Rienner), pp. 1–29.

Yaffe, M. D. (1991) "Leo Strauss as Judaic Thinker: Some First Notions," *Religious Studies Review* 17.1: 33–41.

CHAPTER 36

The Shoah

Steven T. Katz

•• INTRODUCTION ••

It is not surprising that no event has impacted on contemporary Jewish
thought as has the Shoah. The majority of original works in the area
of Jewish thought in the past quarter century have grown out of and
have been a response to the annihilation of European Jewry. Since the
deaths of Buber in 1966 and of Heschel in 1972, little Jewish existentialist work (except that of Levinas) has been produced. In Israel, the
history of Jewish philosophy in all its phases has flourished – one
thinks here immediately of Nathan Rotenstreich's *Jewish Thought in
Modern Times*, published in Hebrew in 1945 and updated in an English
version in 1968; of Eli Schweid's various important studies; of Fleischer's analysis on Rosenzweig – and more recently, of Paul Mendes-
Flohr's work on Buber, and Stephan Moses' study of Rosenzweig –
but one is hard pressed to find a single, original philosophical work of
major standing in the narrow area of Jewish philosophy. In this context
I specifically and explicitly acknowledge Gershom Scholem's genius,
while denying that he was a philosopher, despite the claims of some of
his admirers. Surprisingly, even Zionism has been nearly wholly absent
as a subject of original philosophical work. Yeshayahu Leibowitz
deserves mention here – but only that. America, too, has produced
significant historical studies – I think at once and most prominently of
the scholarship of the late Alexander Altmann on Mendelssohn, and
of a host of able younger scholars, such as Kenneth Seeskin, Norbert
Samuelson, Elliot Dorff, David Novak, David Blumenthal, Robert
Gibbs, and Mel Scult, but lasting, fundamental, conceptual work, with
the exception of Michael Wyschograd's *Body of Faith* (1983) and some
of Eugene Borowitz's work on autonomy, such as *Renewing the Covenant* (1991), is hard to find.

In contrast, the Holocaust has evoked a large number of interesting and provocative conceptual responses. These range from the radical pagan naturalism of Richard Rubenstein's *After Auschwitz* (1966, new edition 1992), through the dialectical theism of Emil Fackenheim and Irving (Yitz) Greenberg, to the dipolar theology of Arthur A. Cohen, and the classical "orthodox" response of Eliezer Berkovits. In addition, reflection on the Shoah has also generated less systematic, but at times highly suggestive – and sometimes even true – comment from thinkers as disparate as Rav Hutner, Jacob Neusner, Rav Soloveitchik, the Lubavitcher Rebbe (R. Schneerson), Ignaz Maybaum, and Harold Schulweis. (And no event in Jewish history since the Crucifixion has caused as much Christian theological and philosophical rethinking as Auschwitz. Here one thinks immediately of, for example, the work of Paul Van Buren, Franklin Littell, John Pawlikowski, and A. Roy Eckardt, among others.) Which is to say that, in both quantity and interest, wrestling with, as Arthur Cohen called it, the tremendum has been at the very center of contemporary Jewish thought, and I believe this circumstance will continue into the next century.

It will do so because the Shoah has challenged all inherited truths and widely shared assumptions. Old truths might still be defensible, but they must be defended anew. And this applies not only in the narrowly theological domain but also as regards all the elemental issues that relate to a consideration of modern Jewish thought. For example, first, the meaning of modernity, and now the meaning of the so-called "postmodern" explored by such influential thinkers as Derrida, has again to be analyzed in light of what modernity has wrought in the death camps; second, the entire relationship between Jews and Judaism and the larger social order has to be re-evaluated after the failure of modern politics in the Europe of the 1930s and 1940s; third, the implications of secularism and scientific culture, of technology, bureaucracy and ideology, not only for Jews but also for the future of humankind is open for reconsideration given this culture's creation of Auschwitz; fourth, the meaning and character of Zionism and anti-semitism remains an unsettled issue; and, last but not least, a host of historiographical and historiosophical issues about the writing and meaning of history, such as the current debates about the value of historical narrative that stretch from the revisionism of Hayden White to Lyotard's *Heidegger and the "Jews"* all require deep and careful reconsideration.

In sum, the contemporary conversation about the implications of the Shoah touches almost every essential Jewish philosophical concern while at the same time far transcending narrowly Jewish concerns and constituting the very core of any truly serious conversation about the project of modernity itself.

❧❧ INTERPRETATION ❧❧

I would like to illustrate the broad significance of this post-Holocaust debate by taking a closer, very critical, look at the analysis of three issues – God, history, and Zion – in the work of three contemporary thinkers: Richard Rubenstein, Irving (Yitz) Greenberg, and Arthur A. Cohen. I choose both the topics and the thinkers as examples of a larger problematic, hoping to illuminate the more general topoi of concern through a somewhat detailed consideration of these specific, very different, subjects and thinkers.

Untypical of Jewish thinkers of the past, post-Holocaust think-ers have had a great deal to say – however one estimates what has been said – about God and, in turn, about God's relation to history and Zion. Consider the following three proposals, beginning with the work of Richard Rubenstein. Rubenstein has argued that God is dead. The logic that has led him to this conclusion can be put directly in the following syllogism:

1 God, as he is conceived of in the Jewish tradition, could not have allowed the Holocaust to happen.
2 The Holocaust did happen. Therefore,
3 God, as he is conceived of in the Jewish tradition, does not exist.

Yet, interestingly, despite this negative theological conclusion, the "death of God" for Rubenstein does not destroy Judaism and the Jewish people but rather forces their reinterpretation in pagan, naturalistic terms. Rubenstein waxes eloquent on the virtues of this paganism, urging the Jew to return to the harmonious patterns of nature. His statement of this reconstruction is so extraordinary that I quote it at length:

> In the religion of history, only man and God are alive. Nature is dead and serves only as the material of tool-making man's obsessive projects. Nature does not exist to be enjoyed and communed with; it exists to be changed and subordinated to man's wants – the fulfillment of which brings neither happiness nor satisfaction. In the religion of nature, a historical, cyclical religion, man is once more at home with nature and its divinities, sharing their life, their limits, and their joys. The devitalization of nature, no matter how imposing, has its inevitable concomitant the dehumanization of man with its total loss of eros. Herbert Marcuse states the issue extremely well when he speaks of the subordination of the logic of gratification to the logic of domination. Only in man at one with nature is eros rather than eroticism possible. Historical man knows guilt, inhibition,

acquisition, and synthetic fantasy, but no eros. The return to the soil of Israel promises a people bereft of art, nature, and expansive passion, a return to eros and the ethos of eros. In place of the Lord of history, punishing man for attempting to be what he was created to be, the divinities of nature will celebrate with mankind their "bacchanalian revel of spirits in whom no member is drunk."[1]

Rubenstein argues that Jews must now reinterpret their traditional, normative categories in naturalistic rather than linear and historical terms. They must recognize that both salvation in the here and now, as well as the future and final redemption, will not be, as traditionally conceived, the conquest of nature by history but rather the reverse. As a consequence of this inversion of the priority and relation of nature and history, Jews have to rediscover the sanctity of natural life. They have to learn to enjoy their bodies, rather than follow the classical, but now recognized as self-destructive, paths of sublimation and transformation. Above all, they have to reject the futile transcendentalizing (and historicizing) of these phenomena.

Rubenstein sees in the renewal of Zion and the rebuilding of the land of Israel, with its return to the soil by the Jew, a harbinger of this movement. This regression to the earth points toward the Jews' final escape from the negativity of history to the vitality of self-liberation through the rediscovery of primal being.

Second, let us consider the extreme post-Shoah theological recommendations of Irving (Yitz) Greenberg. Greenberg has argued the provocative thesis that the Shoah marks a new era in Jewish history – what Greenberg labels "the Third Era" – in which the Sinaitic covenant has been shattered. Therefore, if there is to be any covenantal relationship at all today, it must assume new and unprecendent forms.[2] In this context Greenberg insists that Israel's covenant with God always implied further human development. The natural outcome of the covenant is full responsibility. "In retrospect," he argues, paraphrasing A. Roy Eckardt,

> It is now clear that the divine assignment to the Jews was untenable. In the Covenant, Jews were called to witness to the world for God and for a final perfection. After the Holocaust, it is obvious that this role opened the Jews to a total murderous fury from which there was no escape. Yet the divine could not or would not save them from this fate.
>
> Therefore, morally speaking, God must repent of the Covenant, i.e., do *Teshuvah* for having given this chosen people a task that was unbearably cruel and dangerous without having

provided for their protection. Morally speaking, then, God can have no claims on the Jews by dint of the Covenant.[3]

What this means is that the covenant

> can no longer be commanded and subject to a serious external enforcement. It cannot be commanded because morally speaking – covenantally speaking – one cannot order another to step forward to die. One can give an order like this to an enemy, but in a moral relationship, I cannot demand giving up one's life. I can ask for it – but I cannot order it. To put it again in Wiesel's words: when God gave us a mission, that was all right. But God failed to tell us that it was a suicide mission.[4]

Moreover, for a witness of the horrors of the Endlösung, nothing God could threaten for breach of the covenant would be frightening, thus the covenant can no longer be enforced by the threat of punishment.[5]

As a consequence of this complex of considerations, Greenberg asserts that the covenant is now voluntary! And this "voluntariness" altogether transforms the existing covenantal order. First, Greenberg tells us, Israel was a junior partner in its relationship with the Almighty (in the biblical era), then an equal partner (in the rabbinic era), and now after Auschwitz it becomes "the senior partner in action. In effect, God was saying to humans: you stop the Holocaust. You bring the redemption. You act to ensure: never again. I will be with you totally in whatever you do, wherever you go, whatever happens but you must do it."[6]

And to this suggestive theo-historical analysis Greenberg adds his understanding of the meaning of the creation of the State of Israel, which he describes as: "the Revelation in the Redemption of Israel."[7] Greenberg is here willing, as a corollary of his basic and deepest belief that Judaism is a religion of and in history, to posit direct theological weight to the recreation of a Jewish state. He wisely proposes that "if the experience of Auschwitz symbolizes that we are cut off from God and hope, and the covenant may be destroyed, then the experience of Jerusalem symbolizes that God's promises are faithful and His people live on."[8]

Our third thinker, Arthur A. Cohen, has offered the still more radical contention that:

> Any constructive theology after the *tremendum* must be marked by the following characteristics: first, the God who is affirmed must abide in a universe whose human history is scarred by genuine evil without making the evil empty or illusory nor disallowing the real presence of God before, even if not within, history; second, the relation of God to creation and its

creatures, including, as both now include, demonic structure and unredeemable events, must be seen, nonetheless, as meaningful and valuable despite the fact that the justification that God's presence renders to the worthwhileness of life and struggle is now intensified and anguished by the contrast and opposition that evil supplies; third, the reality of God in his selfhood and person can no longer be isolated, other than as a strategy of clarification, from God's real involvement with the life of creation. Were any of these characteristics to be denied or, worse, proved untrue and unneeded, as strict and unyielding orthodox theism appears to require, creation disappears as fact into mere metaphor or, in the face of an obdurate and ineffaceable reality such as the *tremendum*, God ceases to be more than a metaphor for the inexplicable.[9]

What these three theological requirements entail for Cohen is the bringing together of two seemingly opposite traditional theological strategies. One of these is what Cohen labels "the kabbalistic counter history of Judaism"[10] by reference to which he intends to call attention to the kabbalistic doctrine of the Ein Sof and the related doctrine of creation in which:

> God, in the immensity of his being, was trapped by both its absoluteness and necessity into a constriction of utter passivity which would have excluded both the means in will and the reality in act of the creation. Only by the spark of nonbeing (the interior apposition of being, the contradiction of being, the premise of otherhood, the void that is not vacuous) was the being of God enlivened and vivified.[11]

And this cosmogonic speculation has now to be linked to a second cosmological tradition, that associated with Schelling and Rosenzweig. This Cohen describes as follows:

> "What is necessary in God," Schelling argues, "is God's nature," his "own-ness." Love – that antithetic energy of the universe – negates "own-ness" for love cannot exist without the other, indeed, according to its nature as love, it must deny itself that the other might be (contracting itself that the other might be, setting limits to itself). However, since the divine nature as *esse* cannot have personality without the outpouring, the self-giving of love to define those limits, it must be postulated that within God are two directions (not principles, as Schelling says): one which is necessary selfhood, interiority, self-containment and another, vital, electric, spontaneous that is divine *posse*, the abundant and overflowing. There arises from all this the

dialectic of necessity and freedom, the enmeshment of divine egoity and person, divine self-love and free love, divine narcissism and the created image, the sufficient nothing of the world and the creation of being. The human affect is toward the overflowing, the loving in God; his containment, however, the abyss of his nature, is as crucial as is his abundance and plenitude. These are the fundamental antitheses of the divine essence without which the abyss would be unknown or all else would be regarded as plenitude ... the quiet God is as indispensable as the revealing God, the abyss as much as the plenitude, the constrained, self-contained, deep divinity as the plenteous and generous.[12]

What the synthesis of these kabbalistic and Schellingian vectors entails for Cohen is that, first, there is an elemental side of God that is necessarily hidden, but still necessary, in the process of creation and relation; second, conversely, reciprocally, creation, which is continuous and ongoing, is a necessary outcome of God's loving nature; third, God's nature requires our freedom; and, lastly, we require a "dipolar"[13] theological vision which admits that things and events look different from God's perspective and to God as he is in himself than they do from our vantage point and vis-à-vis our relation to the transcendent.

Cohen argues that in the context of the analysis of the Shoah this means that we require a new understanding of God's work in the world that insistently differs elementally from that taught by traditional theism. The understanding of the traditionalists issues forth in the putatively "unanswerable" question: "How could it be that God witnessed the holocaust and remained silent?"[14] Alternatively, Cohen's recommendation would free us of this causal understanding of the need for direct divine intervention and allow us to see: "that which is taken as God's speech is really always man's hearing, that God is not the strategist of our particularities or of our historical condition, but rather the mystery of our futurity, always our *posse*, never our acts."[15]

If we can acquire this alternative understanding of what divine action allows – as well as of what it does not allow – we will "have won a sense of God whom we may love and honour, but whom we no longer fear and from whom we no longer demand."[16] This argument, with its redefinition of God and its emphasis on human freedom, emerges as the centerpiece of Cohen's revisionist "response" to the tremendum.

Exegesis of Cohen's position, however, would not be complete without brief comment on one further aspect of his argument, his critique of Zionism. Whereas most of the other major thinkers[17] who have discussed the Shoah in theological terms have embraced the recreation of the State of Israel as a positive event, even while under-standing its value in a variety of ways, for example in terms of Richard Rubenstein's naturalism or Yitzchak Greenberg's incipient messianism, Cohen remains wedded to a non-Zionist (which must be scrupulously distinguished from an anti-Zionist) theological outlook. Cohen's reser-vation stems from his continuing understanding, indebted as it is to Rosenzweig, of the Jewish people's "peculiar" role in history, or rather, as Cohen describes it "to the side of history."[18]

> It may well be the case that the full entrance of the Jewish people into the lists of the historical is more threatening even than genocide has been, for in no way is the Jew allowed any longer to retire to the wings of history, to repeat his exile amid the nations, to disperse himself once again in order to survive. One perceives that when history endangers it cannot be mitigated. This we know certainly from the *tremendum*, but we know it no less from the auguries of nationhood, that every structure of history in which an eternal people takes refuge is ominous.[19]

❧ CRITIQUE ❧

In response to these intriguing philosophical and theological proposals the following needs to be said. First, in reply to Rubenstein, I would argue that the "Death of God," putatively grounded in the Holocaust experience, is not as easily defended as he believes, not least because it concerns nothing less than how one views Jewish history, its continuit-ies and discontinuities, its "causal connectedness" and interdependen-cies. By raising the issue of how one evaluates Jewish history and what hermeneutic of historic meaning one need adopt, I mean to bring into focus the fact – and it is a fact – that radical theologians see Jewish history too narrowly, that is focused solely in and through the Holo-caust. They take the decisive event of Jewish history to be the death camps. But this is a distorted image of Jewish experience, for there is a pre-Holocaust and post-Holocaust Jewish reality that must be con-sidered in dealing with the questions raised by the Nazi epoch. These questions extend beyond 1933–45 and touch the present Jewish situ-ation as well as the whole of the Jewish past. One cannot make the events of 1933–45 intelligible in isolation. To think, moreover, that one can excise this block of time from the flow of Jewish history, and then by concentrating on it extract the "meaning" of all Jewish existence, is more than uncertain,[20] no matter how momentous or demonic this time may have been.

This recognition of a pre-Holocaust and post-Holocaust Israel forces two considerations upon us. The first is the very survival of the Jewish people despite their "sojourn among the nations." As Karl Barth once said, "the best proof of God's existence is the continued existence of the Jewish people." Without entering into a discussion of the metaphysics of history, let this point just stand for further reflection, that the Jews survived Hitler and Jewish history did not end at Auschwitz. Second, and equally if not more directly significant, is the recreation after Auschwitz of a Jewish state.[21] This event, too, is remarkable in the course of Jewish existence. Logic and conceptual adequacy require that if in our discussion of the relation of God and history we want to give theological weight to the Holocaust then we must also be willing to attribute theological significance to the State of Israel. Just what weight one assigns to each of these events, and then again to events in general, in constructing a theological reading of history is an extraordinarily complex theoretical issue, about which there is the need for much discussion, and which allows for much difference of view. However, it is clear that any final rendering of the "meaning of Jewish history" that values in its equation only the negative factors of the Nazi Holocaust is, at best, arbitrary.

History is too variegated to be understood only as good and evil; the alternating rhythms of actual life reveal the two forces as interlocked and inseparable. For our present concerns, the hermeneutical value of this recognition is that one comes to see that Jewish history is neither conclusive proof for the existence of God (because of the possible counter-evidence of Auschwitz), nor conversely, for the non-existence of God (because of the possible counter-evidence of the State of Israel as well as the whole three-thousand-year historical Jewish experience). Rubenstein's narrow focus on Auschwitz reflects an already determined theological choice based on certain normative presuppositions and a compelling desire to justify, without real warrant, certain conclusions. It is not a value-free phenomenological description of Jewish history.

Second, with respect to Rubenstein's use of A. J. Ayer's positivist principle of empirical falsification, while this challenge is an important one that is often too lightly dismissed by theologians, and respecting Rubenstein's employment of it as an authentic existential response to an overwhelming reality, it none the less needs to be recognized that the empirical falsifiability challenge is not definitive one way or the other in theological matters and therefore cannot provide Rubenstein (or others) with an unimpeachable criterion for making the negative theological judgments that he seeks to advance regarding the non-existence of God. The "falsifiability" thesis neither allows one decisively to affirm nor disaffirm God's presence in history, for history provides evidence both for and against the non-existence of God on empirical-verificationist grounds. Moreover, the very value of the "empirical falsification criteria" rests, on the one hand, on what one considers to be empirical-verificationist evidence, that is, on what one counts as empirical or experiential, and on the other, on whether the empirical-verificationist principle is, in itself, philosophically coherent, which it is not. Again, here too, the State of Israel is a crucial "datum" (and solidly empirical).

Space prevents extended analysis of Rubenstein's advocacy of pagan naturalism and his reinterpretation of Zionism in its light, but four theses require comment in the context of the Holocaust. The first is that Rubenstein misunderstands the innermost character of Zionism. Certainly the Jew, through this decisive Zionist act, breaks out of the narrow parameters of his exilic existence and "break[s] with bourgeois existence as the characteristic form of Jewish social organization,"[22] (though to a more limited extent). But to equate these Zionist realities with the "resurrection of the divinities of Israel's earth"[23] is sheer mythography.

Second, what is the "cash-value" of this return to nature à la Rubenstein? After one reads through it all there is no actual program on which to build a life either for the individual or for the national community. The point seems to be that in some Freudian sense (as represented in Norman Brown's writings, for example, which Rubenstein specifically commends) humans will be "happy" (that is, not neurotic). But there is no clear sense of what this "happiness" really consists of either in Freud or in Brown – or in Rubenstein. Does Rubenstein, who, in his long opening essay in *After Auschwitz* entitled "Religion and the Origin of the Death Camps," concentrates on anality as the key to decoding the Holocaust, really want to suggest that three thousand years of Jewish history – or even that of 1933–45 – can be explained primarily by reference to anal satisfaction and that all Israel's suffering now leads it to the "promised land" of sexual gratification above all else?

Third, this late in the history of philosophy, it is odd to find someone extolling the values of nature per se. Nature is morally neutral; it will not provide the basis for any new comradeship. The return to nature, its deification and worship, is a blind idolatry without recompense. Out of nature can emerge no overcoming of the contradictoriness of existence, no lessening of the "absurdity" which surrounds us, rather it portends what it has always portended: the cruel, amoral, "meaningless" drudgery of natural selection and survival.

In this connection let me say too that Rubenstein's forceful naturalistic imagery carries one along primarily because of its illicit anthropomorphizing and spiritualizing of blind forces. Only thus is nature equated with spirit, or again with demonic. However, this anthropomorphizing rests on philosophical improprieties rather than on phenomenological astuteness. This is not to deny the evocative power of Rubenstein's mystification of nature, but rather it is to assert that for all its appeal the mystical seductiveness attributed to nature is chimerical.

Fourth, and perhaps most important, is an issue already hinted at: was it not precisely a mystical pagan naturalism that Nazism extolled? Was it not in the name of the pagan deities of primal origins that Europe was enjoined to shed the yoke of the Jewish God – "conscience is a Jewish invention," Himmler reminded the SS – and thereby liberate itself to do all that had heretofore been "forbidden"? Was it not the rejection of the taboos of good and evil associated with the God of the covenant, a rejection now made possible by his "death," which made real the kingdom of night? Was it not that very romanticism of blood and land so deeply ingrained in German culture that Hitler appealed to when he spoke of the extermination of the Jew? Was it not in the name of "self-liberation" and "self-discovery" that six million Jews, and upwards of thirty million others, died? After Auschwitz, the very title of Rubenstein's most well-known work, is it not time to be afraid of naturalism and paganism and skeptical in the extreme about the purported health-restoring, life-authenticating, creative, organic, and salvific qualities claimed for them?

Passing now to Irving Greenberg's not uninteresting proposals, one must offer at least the following demurrals. To begin, the structure of Greenberg's three covenantal eras, his many assertions about a "saving God," his talk of revelation and redemption, and his radical contention that the Almighty is increasingly a "silent partner" in Jewish and world history, cannot be advanced without pondering the consequences of these ideas for the "God of Abraham, Isaac, and Jacob."

To put it directly, what happens to the God of Judaism in Greenberg's theology? Prima facie the God of all the traditional omnipredicates does not fit easily with a "God" who is a "silent partner." This may not be a telling criticism, though I think it is, because Greenberg is free to redefine "God" for the purposes of theological reflection. But, having redefined "God" however he feels it appropriate, Greenberg must attend to the myriad metaphysical and theological consequences of such an action. On the one hand, this means that the ontological entailments of treating God as a "silent partner" have to be spelled out. On the other hand, the implication of such a metaphysical principle (God as a "silent partner") for such traditional and essential Jewish concerns as covenant, reward and punishment, morality, Torah, mitzvot, redemption, and other eschatological matters, have to be attended to. For example, is a God who is a "silent partner" capable of being the author and guarantor of moral value both in human relations as well as in history and nature more generally? Or is the axiological role traditionally occupied by God largely evacuated?[24] Likewise, is there a possibility of sin, in a substantive and not merely a metaphorical sense, in this perspective? Again, is God as a "silent partner" capable of being the God of salvation both personal and historic? And, lastly, is God as a "silent partner" the God to whom we pray on Yom Kippur and to whom we confess our sins and ask forgiveness? If my skepticism regarding the ability of Greenberg's "God-idea" to answer these challenges is misplaced, this has to be demonstrated. For it would appear that while this revised "God-idea" allows him to unfold the logic of the "Third Era" as he desires, it in turn generates more theological problems than it solves.

These critical considerations in turn bring us to the most dramatic, most consequential, of Greenberg's affirmations – his espousal, in our post-Holocaust era, of a "voluntary covenant." According to Greenberg, as already explicated above, the Sinaitic covenant was shattered in the Shoah. As a consequence he pronounces the fateful judgment: *the covenant is now voluntary*! Jews have, quite miraculously, chosen after Auschwitz to continue to live Jewish lives and collectively to build a Jewish state, the ultimate symbol of Jewish continuity, but these acts are, post-Shoah, the result of the free choice of the Jewish people.

Logically and theologically the key issue that arises at this central juncture, given Greenberg's reconstruction, is this: if there was ever a valid covenant,[25] that is, if there is a God who entered into such a relationship with Israel – then can this covenant be "shattered" by a Hitler? Or put the other way round, if Hitler can be said to have "shattered" the covenant, was there ever such a covenant, despite traditional Jewish pieties, in the first place? The reasons for raising these questions are metaphysical in kind and are related to the nature of the biblical God and the meaning of his attributes and activities, including his revelations and promises, which are immune, by definition, from destruction by the likes of a Hitler. If Hitler could break God's covenantal promises, God would not be God and Hitler would indeed be central to Jewish belief.

Finally, passing on to Arthur Cohen's radical theological suggestions, the following philosophical consideration needs to be noted. The subtle intention that lies behind Cohen's transformative redescription of God is twofold. On the one hand it seeks to assure the reality of human freedom and hence to facilitate a simultaneous re-employment of a sophisticated version of a "free-will" theodicy. On the other hand, and reciprocally, it redefines the transcendent nature of God's being such that he is not directly responsible for the discrete events of human history and hence cannot be held responsible for the Shoah or other acts of human evil. This is a very intriguing two-sided ontological strategy. Our question therefore must be: does Cohen defend it adequately?

Let us begin to explore this question by deciphering Cohen's second thesis as to God's redefined role in history. The clearest statement of Cohen's revised God-idea in respect of divine accountability for the Shoah comes in his discussion of God's putative silence and what Cohen takes to be the mistaken tradition-based expectation of miraculous intervention.

> The most penetrating of post-*tremendum* assaults upon God has been the attack upon divine silence. Silence is surely in such a usage a metaphor for inaction: passivity, affectlessness, indeed, at its worst and most extreme, indifference and ultimate malignity. Only a malign God would be silent when speech would terrify and stay the fall of the uplifted arm. And if God spoke once (or many times as scripture avers), why has he not spoken since? What is it with a God who speaks only to the ears of the earliest and the oldest and for millennia thereafter keeps silence and speaks not? In all this there is concealed a variety of assumptions about the nature and efficacy of divine speech that needs to be examined. The first is that the divine speech of old is to be construed literally, that is, God actually spoke in the language of man, adapting speech to the styles of the Patriarchs and the Prophets, and was heard speaking and was transmitted as having spoken. God's speech was accompanied by the racket of the heavens so that even if the speech was not heard by more than the prophetic ear, the marks and signals of divine immensity were observed. As well, there is the interpretive conviction that God's speech is action, that God's words act. Lastly, and most relevantly to the matter before us, God's speech enacts and therefore confutes the projects of murderers and tyrants – he saves Israel, he ransoms Jews, he is forbearing and loving. God's speech is thus consequential to the historical cause of justice and mercy. Evidently, then, divine silence is reproof and punishment, the reversal of his works of speech, and hence God's silence is divine acquiescence in the work of murder and destruction.

> Can it not be argued no less persuasively that what is taken as God's speech is really always man's hearing, that God is not the strategist of our particularities or of our historical condition, but rather the mystery of our futurity, always our *posse*, never our acts? If we can begin to see God less as the interferer whose insertion is welcome (when it accords with our needs) and more as the immensity whose reality is our prefiguration, whose

speech and silence are metaphors for our language and distortion, whose plenitude and unfolding are the hope of our futurity, we shall have won a sense of God whom we may love and honor, but whom we no longer fear and from whom we no longer demand.

The Tremendum, p. 97

In response to this reconstruction of the God-idea, some critical observations are in order. First, it need not be belabored that there is truth in the proposition that "what is taken as God's speech is really always man's hearing."[28] But at the same time, it is only a half-truth as stated. For our hearing the word of revelation does not create "God's speech" – this would be illusion and self-projection. Certainly we can *mis*hear God, or not hear what there is to hear at all – but these qualifications do not erase the dialogical nature of divine speech, that is, the requirement that there be a Speaker as well as a Hearer. And if revelation requires this two-sidedness then we have to reject Cohen's revisionism because it fails to address the full circumstance of the reality of revelation and God's role in it. Alternatively, if Cohen's description is taken at face value, revelation, in any meaningful sense, disappears, for what content can we ultimately give to "man's hearing" as revelation? Moreover, from a specifically Jewish point of view, anything recognizable as Torah and mitzvot would be negated altogether.

Second, this transformation of classical theism and its replacement by theological dipolarity fails to deal, as did Greenberg's revisionism, with the problem of divine attributes. Is God still God if he is no longer the providential agency in history? Is God still God if he lacks the power to enter history vertically to perform the miraculous? Is such a dipolar absolute still the God to whom one prays, the God of salvation? Put the other way round, Cohen's divinity is certainly not the God of the covenant,[29] nor again the God of Exodus-Sinai, nor yet again the God of the Prophets and the Churban Bayit Rishon (Destruction of the First Temple) and the Churban Bayit Sheni (Destruction of the Second Temple). Now, none of these objections, the failure to account for the very building blocks of Jewish theology, counts *logically* against Cohen's theism as an independent speculative exercise. However, they do suggest that Cohen's God is *not* the God of the Bible and Jewish tradition and that if Cohen is right, indeed, particularly if Cohen is right, there is no real meaning left to Judaism and to the God-idea of Jewish tradition. Cohen's deconstruction in this particular area is so radical that it sweeps away the biblical and rabbinic ground of Jewish faith and allows the biblical and other classical evidence to count not at all against his own speculative metaphysical hypotheses.

867

The dipolar ontological schema is certainly logically neater and sharper than its "normative" biblical and rabbinic predecessor but one questions whether this precision has not been purchased at the price of adequacy, that is, an inadequate grappling with the multiple evidences and variegated problems that need to be addressed in any attempt, however bold, to fashion a defensible definition and description of God and his relations to humanity. Logical precision must not be achieved here too easily, nor given too high a priority, in the sifting and sorting, the phenomenological decipherment and rearranging, of God's reality and our own.

Third, is the dipolar, non-interfering God "whom we no longer fear and from whom we no longer demand" yet worthy of our "love and honor?"[30] This God seems closer, say, to Plato's Demiurgos or perhaps closer still to the innocuous and irrelevant God of the Deists. Such a God does not count in how we act, nor in how history devolves or transpires. After all "God is not," Cohen asserts, "the strategist of our particularities or of our historical condition." But if this is so, if God is indeed so absent from our life and the historical record, what difference for us between this God and no God at all? Again, is such a God who remains uninvolved while Auschwitz is generating its corpses any more worthy of being called a "God whom we may love," especially if this is his metaphysical essence, than the God of tradition?[31] A God whom we can see only as the "immensity whose reality is our prefiguration," while rhetorically provocative, will not advance the theological discussion for it provides negations and evasions just where substantive analysis is required.

Cohen recognizes that his programmatic reconstruction impacts upon the fundamental question of God's relation to history. In explicating his understanding of this vexing relationship he writes:

> God and the life of God exist neither in conjunction with nor disjunction from the historical, but rather in continuous community and nexus. God is neither a function nor a cause of the historical nor wholly other and indifferent to the historical.[32]

If God then is unrelated to the historical in any of these more usual ways, as "neither a function nor a cause," how then is he present, that is, not "wholly other and indifferent," and what difference does he make in this redefined and not wholly unambiguous role? "I understand divine life," Cohen tells us:

> to be rather a filament within the historical, but never the filament that we can identify and ignite according to our requirements, for in this and all other respects God remains

God. As filament, the divine element of the historical is a precarious conductor always intimately linked to the historical – its presence securing the implicative and exponential significance of the historical – and always separate from it, since the historical is the domain of human freedom.[33]

But this advocacy of an "implicit" but non-causal nexus is hardly sufficient.

In the final reckoning, this impressionistic articulation of the problem must collapse in upon itself for at some level of analysis the reciprocal notions of "causality" and "function" cannot be avoided. One can talk lyrically of God as a "filament" and a "conductor" in history as if these were not causal or connective concepts but upon deeper probing it will be revealed that they are. For talk of God as "filament" and "conductor" to retain its coherence, for it not to evaporate into empty metaphor, we have to know what it means to refer to God as a "filament," as a "conductor," no matter how precarious. To rescue these instrumental concepts from complete intellectual dissolution we need also to know something of how God is present in the world in these ways – what evidence we can point to in defense of these images.[34] For example, and deserving of a concrete answer, is the question: What of God is conducted? His love? Grace? Salvation? And if so, how? Wherein, against the darkness of the tremendum, do we experience his love, his grace, his salvation? To anticipate this objection as well as to attempt to deflect it by arguing that God is a "filament" but "never the filament that we can identify"[35] is a recourse to "mystery"[36] in the obfuscatory rather than the explanatory sense. For as explanation it means simply: "I claim God is somehow present or related to history but don't ask me how." Alternatively, to come at this thesis from the other side, the analogies of "filament" and "conductor" are disquieting as analogs of the relation of God and history because they so strongly suggest passivity and inertness. If they are the proper analogs for God's activity or presence in history, all our earlier concrete concerns about maintaining the integral vitality of Judaism resurface. For the God of creation, covenants, Sinai, and redemption is altogether different, qualitatively, metaphysically, and morally other, from a "conductor" or "filament."

Given the dispassionate, disinterested, amoral nature of Cohen's deity, it is not surprising that the conclusion drawn from this descriptive recasting of God's role in "community and nexus" is, vis-à-vis the Shoah, finally trivial (in the technical sense).

That the Holocaust makes no difference to God's relation to himself we can grant *in principle* for the purposes of this analysis. And, logically and structurally, that is, ontologically, we can allow for the purposes of argument Cohen's conclusion that "the *tremendum* does not alter the relation in which God exists to the historical." But, having granted both these premises it is necessary to conclude, contra Cohen, that the tremendum is not, and *in principle* could not be, a theological problem. It is, on its own premises, irrelevant to God's existence, irrelevant to God's relation to history and, on these criteria, irrelevant to God's relation to humankind – whatever humankind's relation to God.

The a-Zionism[37] which is the complement of this ontology is logically consistent. If God is not the causal agent of Auschwitz, he is not the causal agent of the return to the land. Hence Zionism becomes, if not theologically problematic, then certainly theologically irrelevant. Cohen, in effect, falls back on a Rosenzweigian-like vocabulary and ideology to describe and interpret the state of Israel. But this is inadequate because it clearly does not dare enough, from a Jewish theological perspective, where the State of Israel is concerned. And this not least because after Auschwitz, and after more than forty years of the existence of the State of Israel, one cannot so easily dissociate the nature and face of the Jewish people from that of the Jewish state in which about thirty per cent of the Jewish people now live, an ever increasing percentage, and in which more than forty per cent of Jewish infants worldwide are born. A theology in which this does not matter, as the Shoah does not matter theologically, cannot speak meaningfully to the Jewish condition after Auschwitz.[38]

❧ LARGER CONSIDERATIONS ❧

What is most important about this brief dialogue with Rubenstein, Greenberg, and Cohen is not, in the present context, the details of their argument and the particulars of my critique but rather the enormous range of absolutely fundamental questions that their work, in its alternating diversity, raises for all contemporary reflection. That is, their imaginative investigations, along with the contributions of other Holocaust thinkers, raise elemental and inescapable topoi for further exploration. Among these elemental subjects are:

(1) The status of history in Jewish thought, that is, is Judaism an historical religion? Can historical events "disconfirm" Judaism's basic theological affirmations?

(2) How does one weigh, evaluate, good and evil as historical phenomena vis-à-vis theological judgments?

(3) How does one divide up and evaluate the meaning of Jewish history?

(4) Is Jewish history in any way singular?

(5) Is the Shoah unique? And, if it is, does it matter philosophically and theologically?

(6) What is the status of empirical disconfirmation as a procedure in Jewish thought?

(7) What does it mean to speak of providence, and God's intervention into human affairs?

(8) What is "revelation"? What is "covenant"? Here I note that the essential need for precision in the use of such technical terms is widely ignored by contemporary thinkers, even though the meaning of such terms is decisive in relation to claims made for the putative revelatory character of the Shoah and the reborn State of Israel.

(9) What is the relationship between anthropological and theological judgments?

(10) Recognizing the existence of a long tradition of reflection on this matter, what limits, if any, are we bound by in interpreting God's attributes?

(11) What traditional and contemporary sources, if any, have an authoritative status in this discussion? Here, in addition to the proposals advanced by the three thinkers considered in detail above, think of Emil Fackenheim's questionable appeal to midrash as the key mode and resource for responding to Auschwitz.

(12) Then, last but not least, the colloquy in which we are engaged raises a host of conceptual questions relating to the philosophical and theological meaning of the land of Israel, Zionism and the State of Israel, and for some, also to matters pertaining to messianism.

This is to ask, how are we to decide between Rubenstein's denial of the existence of God, Greenberg's reduction of God to a "junior partner," and Cohen's advocacy of a Hartshorneian type of God – not to speak of Buber's *Eternal Thou* who Buber tells us is "eclipsed" by the Shoah, or Maybaum's God who uses Hitler as he had used Nebuchadnezzar, or Berkovits' God who must be silent in the face of Auschwitz so man can be free, or the Lubavitcher Rebbe's God for whom the Holocaust is a tiqqun. And again, what meaning are we to give to the State of Israel? That of Rubenstein's earth-bound paganism, Greenberg's "revelation of redemption," Cohen's metahistoric neutrality – or, again, Maybaum's classical Reform denial of its theological valence, Fackenheim's linkage of the state with his "614th Commandment," Rav Kook the younger's intense messianic identification, or the Satmar Rebbe's rejection of the state as an illicit and premature pseudo-messianic initiative? Now these are not easy questions, but they are questions that cannot be avoided by contemporary Jewish thinkers. That is to say, as a consequence of thinking about the kingdom of night we come to realize that we need to consider with increased methodological and hermeneutical sophistication the primal conditions, the elemental possibilities, of Jewish thought. Certainly it is not only the thinking through of the philosophical and theological implications of the Shoah that raises these foundational questions, but it has been primarily in connection with the Shoah that these issues have been raised most forcefully and urgently in our time. This, more than the substantive positions so far staked out, has been the real contribution of post-Holocaust thought to contemporary Jewish philosophy.

❧ NOTES ❧

1 Rubenstein 1966, pp. 136–7.
2 Greenburg recognizes that we must even take seriously the possibility that the covenant is at an end. See Greenberg 1981, p. 23.
3 Ibid. There may be some final difference of meaning between Eckardt's and Greenberg's understanding of this seminal issue.
4 Ibid.
5 Ibid., pp. 23–4.
6 Ibid., p. 27.
7 Greenberg 1977, p. 32.
8 Ibid.
9 Cohen 1981, p. 86.
10 Ibid.
11 Ibid., pp. 86f.
12 Ibid., pp. 89f.
13 This is Cohen's term, ibid., p. 91.
14 Ibid., pp. 95f.
15 Ibid., p. 97.
16 Ibid., p. 101.
17 A notable exception here is Ignaz Maybaum. For more on Maybaum's theological position see Maybaum 1965. I have analyzed and criticized Maybaum's views in my essays "Jewish Faith After the Holocaust: Four Approaches," and "The Crucifixion of the Jews: Ignaz Maybaum's Theology of the Holocaust," both reprinted in Katz 1983, pp. 155–63 and 248–67.
18 Ibid., p. 103. This is Cohen's phrase.
19 Ibid., p. 101.
20 Those who would deal with the Holocaust need to master not only Holocaust materials but also the whole of Jewish history.
21 On Rubenstein's appreciation of the State of Israel see, for example, his essay on "The Rebirth of the State of Israel in Jewish Philosophy," in Rubenstein 1966, pp. 131–42.
22 Ibid., p. 138.
23 Ibid., p. 142.
24 Here a further nuance must be noted. Greenberg insists that though God is intentionally more self-limited in the "Third Era," this should not be misunderstood as positing either God's absence or weakness. God is still active, though he is more hidden. In a private correspondence Greenberg argued that in his

view God is still seen as possessing, at least, the following four classical attributes of "calling," "accompanying," "judging," and "sustaining" men and women, as well as the world as a whole. Whether Greenberg has a right to maintain these attributes for his "God-idea," given the other characteristics of his theology, is open to question.

25 An open question on independent philosophical and theological grounds.

26 Cohen 1981, pp. 96f.

27 Ibid., pp. 96–7.

28 Ibid., p. 97.

29 Note my parallel comments on Greenberg above.

30 Cohen 1981, p. 97.

31 It is worth comparing Cohen's present description and understanding of the divine as dipolar with his comments made in conversation with Mordecai Kaplan over the idea of God in Kaplan's reconstruction and printed in M. M. Kaplan and A. A. Cohen, *If Not Now, When?* (New York: Schocken, 1973). Also of interest is a comparison of his present views as to the nature of God with those voiced in his earlier, *The Natural and the Supernatural Jew* (New York: Pantheon Books, 1962).

32 Cohen 1981, p. 97.

33 Ibid., pp. 97–8.

34 Here, that is, we raise issues as to meaning and related, but separate, questions as to verification, that is, not conflating the two but asking about both.

35 Cohen 1981, pp. 97f.

36 See my paper on "The Logic and Language of Mystery," in S. Sykes and J. Clayton (eds), *Christ, Faith and History* (London: Cambridge University Press, 1972), pp. 239–62, for a fuller criticism of this common theological gambit.

37 Described in Cohen 1981, pp. 101ff.

38 The single exception to this generalization is to be found in right-wing ultra-Orthodox circles, for example Satmar Chasidism and among the Naturei Karta of Jerusalem, who can carry on a meaningful Jewish existence because of their profound commitment to traditional Torah observance and study. Outside of these very small, very specially constituted groups, however, my judgment stands.

∾ BIBLIOGRAPHY ∾

Berkovits, E. (1973) *Faith after the Holocaust* (New York: Ktav).
—— (1976) *Crisis and Faith* (New York: Sanhedrin).
—— (1979) *With God in Hell* (New York: Sanhedrin).
Biale, D. (1980) Review of Emil Fackenheim's *The Jewish Return into History*, *Association for Jewish Studies Newsletter* (October) 11–12, 16.
Cain, S. (1971) "The Question and the Answers after Auschwitz," *Judaism* 20: 263–78.
Cohen, A. A. (1970) (comp.) *Arguments and Doctrines: A Reader of Jewish Thinking in the Aftermath of the Holocaust* (New York: Harper & Row).
—— (1981) *The Tremendum* (New York: Crossroad).

Fackenheim, E. L. (1967) *The Religious Dimension in Hegel's Thought* (Bloomington: Indiana University Press).

—— (1968) *Quest for Past and Future* (Bloomington: Indiana University Press).

—— (1970) *God's Presence in History* (New York: New York University Press).

—— (1973) *Encounters between Judaism and Modern Philosophy* (New York: Basic Books).

—— (1978) *The Jewish Return into History* (New York: Schocken).

—— (1982) *To Mend the World* (New York: Schocken).

Greenberg, I. (1968) "Judaism and History: Historical Events and Religious Change," in *Ancient Roots and Modern Meanings*, edited by J. V. Diller (New York: Bloch), pp. 139–62.

—— (1977) "Cloud of Smoke, Pillar of Fire: Judaism, Christianity and Modernity after the Holocaust," in *Auschwitz: Beginning of a New Era?*, edited by E. Fleischner (New York: Ktav), pp. 7–55.

—— (1979) "New Revelations and New Patterns in the Relationship of Judaism and Christianity," *Journal of Ecumenical Studies* 16: 249–67.

—— (1981) *The Third Great Cycle in Jewish History* (New York: CLAL Resource Center).

Katz, S. T. (1983) *Post-Holocaust Dialogues: Critical Studies in Modern Jewish Thought* (New York: New York University Press).

—— (1992) *Historicism, the Holocaust and Zionism* (New York: New York University Press).

—— (1994) *The Holocaust in Historical Context*, vol. 1 (New York: Oxford University Press).

Maybaum, I. (1965) *The Face of God after Auschwitz* (Amsterdam: Polak & van Gennep).

Meyer, M. A. (1972) "Judaism after Auschwitz," *Commentary* 53 (June): 55–62.

Neher, A. (1981) *The Exile of the Word: From the Silence of the Bible to the Silence of Auschwitz* (Philadelphia: Jewish Publication Society).

Rubenstein, R. L. (1966) *After Auschwitz: Radical Theology and Contemporary Judaism* (New York: Bobbs-Merrill).

—— (1968) *The Religious Imagination* (Boston: Beacon).

—— (1970) *Morality and Eros* (New York: McGraw-Hill).

—— (1978) *The Cunning of History* (New York: Harper & Row).

—— (1983) *The Age of Triage* (Boston: Beacon).

Tiefel, H. O. (1976) "Holocaust Interpretations and Religious Assumptions," *Judaism* 25 (Spring): 135–49.

Wyschogrod, M. (1971) "Faith and the Holocaust," *Judaism* 20 (Summer): 286–94.

CHAPTER 37

Postmodern Jewish philosophy

Richard A. Cohen

Assuming that what Jewish philosophy or Jewish thought is has been made clear enough, then the distinctiveness of this chapter hinges on clarifying the meaning of the term "postmodern." The meaning of postmodern, however, is notoriously slippery. It appears to be no more than a label, rubric, or family name. It may be no less than a pseudonym, a *nom de plume*, a mask concealing a much older name. In any event, much of what passes for postmodern writing is sufficiently novel, or rather sufficiently different, to elude facile submission to prior standards of validity, or even canons of sense.

Not only are definition and hence also evaluation difficult, but postmodern writers appear to delight in exacerbating precisely these two difficulties. At the same time they seem also to delight in striving to overcome these difficulties, writing endless articles and books about the meaning of postmodernism, instead of simply doing whatever it is postmodernism does. It so happens, too, that to engage in both of these efforts, one no less obscurantist than the other, is one of the marks of "successful" postmodernism.

It is safe to say that the postmodern is a kind of avant-gardism. It is avant-gardism without limit, ad absurdum, rebellion without cause. Its discourse is deliberately strange and self-estranged, not a metaphysics but a writing indeterminate and unsettled, like a stream of consciousness neither fully awake nor fully asleep. Always in media res, it attempts to articulate a submergence in history without origin or goal. It is a discourse never univocal, indeed it vigilantly seeks and destroys all claims and vestiges of stability, permanence, autochthony, hence it is Israelite in this sense rather than Canaanite, but even more aptly it is Visigoth, or, more aptly still, cannibal.

Clearly it is a topic resistant to frontal approach. Another approach is called for. The name postmodern literally means "after the modern." Presumably, then, in some important sense the postmodern is *beyond* the modern. To clarify exactly what it is that the postmodern is beyond, what it comes after, that is, the modern, should bring us closer to grasping the essentially elusive meaning of the postmodern. But although the postmodern that concerns us in this chapter is philosophical and Jewish, by birth it is the child of literary criticism. This is important because what is modern for philosophy is not the same as what is modern for literary criticism. Thus two paths lie before us. I will begin with the modern in philosophy. Let us note from the outset, none the less, that the most characteristic symptom of postmodernism is a blurring of boundaries, especially those which separate philosophy, literary criticism, and literature.

Broadly defined, philosophy is science, rational knowledge of such dimensions of meaning as nature, art, ethics, and metaphysics. Chronologically, the modern period of philosophy begins with Descartes' methodological reflections on constructive geometry and ends with Kant's critical philosophy of nature, ethics, and aesthetics. It is preceded by two periods: the ancient, which begins with Thales and ends with Plotinus, and the medieval, which comprises everything after Plotinus and before Descartes. Rational knowing for the ancients meant ontology, cognizing being; for the medievals it meant theology, cognizing God; and for the moderns it has meant epistemology, cognizing knowing itself, with mathematical knowing taken as the ideal type.

To do *post*modern philosophy, then, would mean philosophizing beyond the bounds defining ontology, theology, and epistemology, with special emphasis on the latter since its attractions are most recent and ascendent. And indeed one finds that trashing Cartesianism and all its multifarious vestiges, both subtle and crude, is a sine qua non of postmodernist writing. The corrosive forces of the social, historical, economic, and psychological suspicions unleashed by Marx, Freud, and Nietzsche are deployed to undermine and expose the false posturing, the ersatz "grounds" of scientific subjectivity and objectivity. All the positive spiritual efforts of ancient paganism, medieval religion, and modern secular humanism, are rejected as empty optimism, simple-minded naivety.

There is a second more radical strain of postmodern philosophy. Here it is not enough to offer the latest philosophical breakthrough beyond ontology, theology, and epistemology, a new knowledge beyond these obsolete forms. Rather one must break with rational knowledge altogether. The postmodern thus would be a rejection of philosophy qua science, that is, a rejection of philosophy per se, philosophy itself, a rejection of the "per se," the "itself" of philosophy. What is postmodern would not simply resist definition provisionally, then, as would its less radical strain, it would resist definition in principle, attacking all such tasks as ruses of the philosophy it would deflect or infect absolutely. In actual usage the term "postmodern" vacillates between its more and its less radically deconstructive senses, further muddying already murky waters.

A final complication. Until recently philosophizing after the modern period has been called "contemporary philosophy." Figures as diverse in place, time, and meaning as Kierkegaard, Feuerbach, Bergson, Dewey, Nietzsche, Heidegger, Russell, Wittgenstein, Sartre, and Merleau-Ponty are in this sense all contemporary philosophers. "Postmodern" is a late twentieth-century designation, icing on the contemporary cake. It refers to a bolder awareness, a more deliberate acceleration of certain self-destructive tendencies inherent in almost all contemporary philosophies. Its bravado and pace, the wit from which postmodernism lives, though based on prefigured tendencies, have largely been awakened and spurred on by developments in contemporary literary criticism, to which I now turn.

Modernism in literary criticism took the earlier Romantic revolt against classicism and turns it against the latent optimism it uncovers in Romanticism itself. In other words, modernism raises the Romantic ante. Thus it is a writing permeated by the sense of loss, disappointment, failure, disillusion, resignation, even ennui. Lionel Trilling has defined it as "the disenchantement of our culture with culture itself."

Literary *post*modernism, then, would raise the ante yet again. It would extend the modernist extension of the Romantic revolt against classicism to modernism itself. It would be modernism sans nostalgia, a thoroughly modern modernism, right up to embracing nihilist consequences. Classicism would be so utterly destroyed that such basic distinctions as that between plagiary and originality, for example, or copying and creating, would be obliterated. Culture and lack of culture would be indistinguishable. Brillo boxes, laundry lists, chance remarks, Shakespeare's plays would be the equal of one another, and of everything else, and would all be unequal to one another too. The only certainty would be that through all transformations and obliterations of genre, no one and nothing would have the authority to legitimize or to delegitimize meanings, much less rules of the game. Gone would be modern malaise and ill humor. There would be no disappointment because there would be no hope. The center would no longer hold, but no one would care or notice. Beyond deicide, regicide, and patricide . . . joyful suicide, or maybe only oblivious suicide.

What do these preliminary considerations teach us about postmodern Jewish philosophy? They serve, I hope, as warnings. Beware of the latest jargon. To stick the label "postmodern" on to a self-destructive discourse in no way minimizes its negativity, or justifies it.

Quite simply, postmodernism cuts itself off from *everything that has hitherto counted as philosophy and Jewish thought*. Its old and true name is sophism, notwithstanding all the refinements of its tomfoolery, its theatrics, whining, bravado, self-advertisement, ideology, tyranny, and all the other shenanigans, verbal and otherwise, which may be seductive in the short run, or just plain silly, but can and do prove dangerous. Postmodernism lacks, and indeed scorns, not only the straightforwardness and decency of plain common sense, and not only the dignity, universality, and seriousness of philosophy, but above all the profound and hard–won wisdom and the deep community bonds of the Jewish tradition. Precisely where one hears the most noise about transcending self, author, soul, tradition, law, God, etc., there and precisely there one finds the least humility, indeed the most outrageous self-assertiveness, linked to the most rigid and exclusive ideology.

It is time, then, to move on to better and more important matters. But before doing so, let us take one last tack. Instead of trying and failing to define an essentially indefinable postmodernism, let us ask more simply who is "doing" postmodern Jewish philosophy? One name invariably suggests itself. Jacques Derrida (b. 1930), in Paris, is without question the outstanding postmodern. It so happens, too, that he is born Jewish. Furthermore, as Susan Handelman has shown in *The Slayers of Moses* (1982), subtitled "The Emergence of Rabbinic Interpretation in Modern Literary Theory," there are similarities between key maneuvers employed by Derrida to deflate texts and techniques used by the rabbis in traditional talmudic reasoning. Still, neither genealogy nor similarities in technique add up to make Derrida's postmodernism either Jewish (a point which I take to be incontestable) or philosophy (an assessment which I admit is debatable). Derrida himself has certainly never noted or cultivated these connections.

Perhaps postmodern Jewish philosophy is being "done" in recent Jewish feminist writings, those, say, of Susannah Heschel, Paula Hyman, Judith Plaskow, or Chava Weissler? The attack on tradition and any form of foundationalism which are cornerstones of the postmodern is in the hands of feminists, generally, license to challenge all gender differentiations whatsoever, and in the hand of Jewish feminists, more particularly, license to challenge what is taken to be a completely distorted because male chauvinist Jewish tradition. Liberated, Judaism would be completely egalitarian, all vestiges of male privilege excised, from God's masculine attributes to male rabbis and minyans, from the paternalism of rabbinics to the no less pernicious paternalism of the science of Judaism, unto Judaism's fundamental division between public and private, that is, between work and synagogue and home and family. One is left to wonder, however, what remains that is Jewish.

Total and permanent revolution is not only the price of postmodernism, it is also its "nature."

Caution is required on this point. My advice regarding the tenuous Jewishness and philosophical character of so called "postmodern Jewish philosophy" is to keep in mind the reply of Moses Mendelssohn, in *Jerusalem* (1783), when he was, as he puts it, accused of "the scandalous design of subverting the religion which I confess, and of renouncing it, if not expressly, but as it were, in an underhand manner." He wrote: "This practice of wresting meanings should be forever discarded from the conversation of the learned." Most of what passes under the label "postmodern Jewish philosophy" is no more and no less than wresting of meanings. More honest would be simply to attack Judaism outright, and let the chips fall where they will.

So much for artifice and vanity. Let us now turn to what is genuinely new and profound in contemporary Jewish thought. First I will turn to the ethical metaphysics of Emmanuel Levinas (1906–96), which ranks, as I see it, at the forefront of contemporary Jewish thought. Then I will turn to other bright but as yet still dimmer lights.

Levinas wrote voluminously both in philosophy and in Jewish thought from the late 1920s. His philosophy, in addition to being found in several collections of original and secondary articles, appears in four main books (all of which have been translated into English): *Existence and Existents* (1947), *Time and the Other* (1947), *Totality and Infinity* (1961), and *Otherwise than Being or Beyond Essence* (1974). The last two works represent the mature expression of Levinas' ethical metaphysics. His Jewish thought, which is by no means sharply distinguished from his philosophy, has appeared in articles which can be found in the following collections (most of which have been translated into English): *Difficult Freedom* (1990a), *Nine Talmudic Readings* (1990b), *From the Sacred to the Holy* (1977), *Beyond the Verse* (1994a), *In the Time of the Nations* (1994b).

Levinas overturns long-standing priorities in philosophy. His most basic move is to anchor meaning in the good (morality, social justice) rather than in the true (knowledge, science, opinion). But instead of dispensing with the true, or reducing it to an epiphenomenon, like many contemporary philosophical critics, he shows how it is conditioned by goodness. So instead of the priorities expressed in the Socratic dictum that "to do the good one must know the good," Levinas' position echoes the order of the famous biblical response said by the Jewish people at Mount Sinai: "we will hearken and we will understand." The philosophical, phenomenological basis for this revolution in thought is the primacy Levinas sees in the moral transcendence which originally constitutes social life, the primacy, that is to say, of inter-subjectivity as moral encounter. Morality and justice, beginning with the other person one encounters face to face in everyday life, precede philosophical justification, and "justify" it.

Levinas is thus concerned to preserve a moral sense of otherness irreducible to the categories of classical philosophy. Rather than find such otherness in the endless play of absent and present signifiers, where all language is reduced to textuality, Levinas is concerned to account for the origin of the seriousness which constitutes moral relations, to account for the urgency and exigency which constitute the responsibility one person has for another. Indeed, responsibility to respond to the other is, for Levinas, the ultimate starting point, the ground zero, of all signification. Hence first philosophy must be an ethics rather than epistemology, theology, or ontology. From the primary obligation one person has for another, moral obligation, Levinas discovers the obligation each person has for all others, the call to justice, for those not present as well as those present.

Levinas thus links transcendence, sociality, morality, and social justice. One thus recognizes in Levinas' thought, as well as in his references, examples, and phrases, the deepest themes of Jewish ethics and spirituality, the grand gestures and minute details of prophetic and rabbinic morality, defining a redemptive history not only for Jews but for all humankind. In his metaphysical ethics Levinas weaves the specifics of the moral and holy language of Judaism into a compelling and critical web with the most advanced issues and idioms of contemporary continental philosophy. He thus reawakens the unification of Hellenic and Judaic thought inaugurated by (Wolfson's) Philo, not, however, by binding philosophy's commitment to logic with Judaism's commitment to scriptural revelation, as did Philo and his heirs, in a reconciliation finally undone by Spinoza's naturalism, but rather outflanking the primacy which both Philo and Spinoza gave to epistemology, on the side of philosophy, by uncovering and binding philosophy's no less profound and no less constitutive commitment to ethics, to the "good beyond being," with Judaism's commitment to personal transcendence, goodness, and social justice. The brilliance of Levinas' achievement is to have made of precisely this shift, the troubling of the true by the good, the uplifting movement which defines the ethical. He persuades not by citing proof-texts, which would have no force in philosophical discourse in any event, but by giving voice to the prior and discordant claims of morality, to the very priority of its claim, as exerted by the one who faces, the other person to whom the morally elected self is obligated, the "orphan, widow, and stranger," for whom and to whom one is responsible unto death.

Levinas' thought has influenced and inspired many other thinkers, Jewish, Christian, and non-religious. In France, Jean-Luc Marion, in *Idol and Distance* (1977) and *God Without Being* (1982), has produced a reading of Christianity pivoted on reconceiving God's mystery in terms of the radical otherness beyond being which, as we have seen, moves Levinas' thought. In Argentina, Enrique Dussel has articulated a liberation theology, in *Philosophy of Liberation* (1980), for example, where the entire Third World is thought in Levinasian terms of ethical otherness, though adapted to a more thoroughly Christian and New Testament idiom.

In a non-religious context, Derrida, who has always acknowledged a certain technical debt to Levinas, has recently come around also to the ethical dimension which is central to Levinas' entire project. In an address to the American Philosophical Association (1988), published as an article entitled "On the Politics of Friendship," for example, one finds Derrida borrowing not only from Levinas' ethical sensibility but from his precise and distinctive phraseology. Also in Paris, Jacques Rolland, who edited several of Levinas' later publications, in *Dostoyevsky: The Question of the Other* (1983) gives a Levinasian ethical reading to Dostoyevsky, and elsewhere does the same with some of Kafka's shorter writings.

In the Jewish intellectual world, Edith Wyschogrod, author of the first book in English on Levinas, *The Problem of Ethical Metaphysics* (1974), has more recently, in *Spirit in Ashes: Hegel, Heidegger, and Man-Made Mass Death* (1985), and more recently still in *Saints and Postmodernism* (1990), subtitled "Revisioning Moral Philosophy," brought Levinas' social ethics to bear on contemporary continental philosophy, on Holocaust studies, and on the image of the saint. In view of this chapter's heading and the title of her latest book, it should be emphasized that Wyschogrod, almost alone, must be credited with a "postmodernism" where ethics is taken more seriously than aesthetic play. Catherine Chalier, in Paris, in a series of books on a variety of Jewish themes, including Jewish themes in Levinas – *Judaism and Alterity* (1982), *Feminine Figures* (1982), *The Matriarchs* (1985), *The Perseverance of Evil* (1987), *The Alliance with Nature* (1989), *Thoughts on Eternity* (1993), and *Levinas: The Utopia of Humanness* (1993) – has shed new light by giving a Levinasian ethical reading to them. The influence of Levinas' ethical metaphysics is also visible, and acknowledged, in the masterful exposition of Franz Rosenzweig's magnum opus that Stephane Moses has presented in *System and Revelation* (1982), just as it permeates the reading Annette Aronowicz gives to the writings of the French Catholic thinker Charles Péguy (1873–1914).

Moving on from Levinas and his wide influence, but still under the banner of new and profound contemporary Jewish thought, several other fine thinkers have produced and are in the process of producing works of a high caliber which merit mention. With apologies to many, however, in the following I have chosen to single out two thinkers, David Novak and Eugene Borowitz.

David Novak, who was for many years a synagogue rabbi and from 1997 a Professor of Judaic Studies at the University of Toronto, does not claim the dubious honor of postmodernity. His thought is rather a development in the positive-historical school of modern Judaism, committed both to halakhic Judaism and to changing times. Novak's thought maintains a careful balance between the dual dangers of a Liberal capitulation to modernity on the one side, and an Orthodox rejection of modernity on the other. Against the assimilation tendencies of the former, Novak adheres to halakhah, and against the isolationist tendencies of the latter, he calls for a more imaginative theology and a greater social and political responsibility, especially in the light of the modern State of Israel.

A prolific writer, Novak's main work thus far is *Jewish Social Ethics* (1992). Centered on social ethics, Novak provides a philosophical grounding of social good in the truth of a natural law ontology, for which in turn he provides a religious ground in theonomy, a theology of creation. But taking his place in a venerable tradition of Jewish thinkers, Novak is not satisfied with mere deep thinking, with philosophical speculation, however secure. His thinking is equally committed to the realm of the practical. The law must not only be conceived in relation to its ground, principles of social good, and thus also in relation to ontology and theonomy, but its very formulation must be tempered and must proceed with the flexibility, specificity, and humaneness which are characteristic of the rabbinic talmudic tradition, attuned as that tradition is to concrete instances, to judicious application of law.

Eugene Borowitz, who is rabbi and professor of Jewish thought at the Hebrew Union College in New York, rejects halakhah and accepts the postmodern label. Pursuing Reform Judaism's commitment to Enlightenment thought, for Borowitz halakhah and individual autonomy contradict one another, and it is with the latter, with individual autonomy, that he sides. Such is his modernity. But Borowitz's recent and central work, *Renewing the Covenant* (1991), is subtitled "A Theology for the Postmodern Jew." His postmodernity lies in two theses. First, attempting to stake out a middle path, he rejects the "naivety" of both premodern theologism and modern humanism. Borowitz reconceives religion as neither God-centered nor human-centered but as an exchange between the two, between God and human and human and God. Second, again finding a middle way, he rejects the particularist communion of the premodern conception of revelation and the abstract universalism of the modern humanist conception. Instead, Borowitz defends the worth and hence the continued existence of the Jewish people, but does so in response to both the imposed devastation of the Holocaust, on the one hand, and in opposition to the voluntary dissolution of the Jewish people through assimilation and intermarriage, on the other.

In an interesting reversal, whose strength remains to be tested, Borowitz believes he can temper his modernity, his unshakable belief in the ultimacy of individual autonomy, precisely by his postmodernity, where reliance on human freedom must be "reformed by being in a God-grounded, particular context."

～ BIBLIOGRAPHY ～

Texts

Borowitz, E. (1990) *Exploring Jewish Ethics: Papers on Covenant Responsibility* (Detroit: Wayne State University Press).

—— (1991) *Renewing the Covenant: A Theology for the Postmodern Jew* (Philadelphia: Jewish Publication Society).

Fackenheim, E. (1970) *Quest for Past and Future: Essays in Jewish Theology* (Boston: Beacon).

—— (1980) *Encounters Between Judaism and Modern Philosophy* (New York: Schocken).

—— (1982) *To Mend the World: Foundations of Future Jewish Thought* (New York: Schocken).

Levinas, E. (1969) *Totality and Infinity*, translated by A. Lingis (Pittsburgh: Duquesne University Press).

—— (1978) *Existence and Existents*, translated by A. Lingis (The Hague: Nijhoff).

—— (1981) *Otherwise than Being or Beyond Essence*, translated by A. Lingis (The Hague: Nijhoff).

—— (1985) *Ethics and Infinity*, translated by R. Cohen (Pittsburgh: Duquesne University Press).

—— (1987) *Time and the Other*, translated by R. Cohen (Pittsburgh: Duquesne University Press).

—— (1990a) *Difficult Freedom: Essays on Judaism*, translated by Sean Hand (Baltimore: Johns Hopkins University Press).

—— (1990b) *Nine Talmudic Readings*, translated by A. Aranowicz (Bloomington: Indiana University Press).

—— (1993) *Outside the Subject*, translated by M. Smith (Stanford: Stanford University Press).

—— (1994a) *Beyond the Verse: Talmudic Readings and Lectures*, translated by G. Mole (London: Athlone).

—— (1994b) *In the Time of the Nations*, translated by M. Smith (London: Athlone).

Levy, B.-H. (1979) *Barbarism with a Human Face*, translated by G. Holoch (New York: Harper & Row).

—— (1980) *The Testament of God*, translated by G. Holoch (New York: Harper & Row).

Novak, D. (1989) *Jewish-Christian Dialogue: A Jewish Justification* (New York: Oxford University Press).

—— (1992) *Jewish Social Ethics* (New York: Oxford University Press).

—— (1995) *The Election of Israel: The Idea of the Chosen People* (Cambridge: Cambridge University Press).

Wyschogrod, E. (1985) *Spirit in Ashes: Hegel, Heidegger, and Man-Made Mass Death* (New Haven: Yale University Press).

—— (1990) *Saints and Postmodernism* (Chicago: Chicago University Press).

Studies

Cohen, R. (ed.) (1986) *Face to Face with Emmanuel Levinas* (Albany: State University of New York Press).

—— (1994) *Elevations: The Height of the Good in Rosenzweig and Levinas* (Chicago: University of Chicago Press).

Handelman, S. (1982) *The Slayers of Moses: The Emergence of Rabbinic Interpretation in Modern Literary Theory* (Albany: State University of New York Press).

—— (1991) *Fragments of Redemption: Jewish Thought and Literary Theory in Benjamin, Scholem, and Levinas* (Bloomington: Indiana University Press).

Mosès, S. (1992) *System and Revelation: The Philosophy of Franz Rosenzweig*, translated by C. Tihanyi (Detroit: Wayne State University Press).

Rose, G. (1993) *Judaism and Modernity: Philosophical Essays* (Oxford: Blackwell).

CHAPTER 38

Jewish feminist thought
Judith Plaskow

Jewish feminist thought is praxis-oriented. Its goal is not simply the formulation of a meaningful philosophy of Judaism, but the transformation of Jewish history and law, religious practice, and communal institutions in the direction of the full inclusion of women. Because of its activist bent, feminist thought finds expression in many modes of writing – from prayers to novels, and from rituals to historical research. Seeking to imagine and create a Judaism that reflects women's experience, feminists often embody their philosophy and visions in forms that are immediately usable by Jewish communities and individual Jews. While, for the purposes of this essay, I will limit myself to Jewish feminist theoretical reflection on the nature of Judaism, in actuality, such reflection always nourishes and is nourished by non-discursive modes of expression.

❧ DIAGNOSING THE PROBLEM ❧

Individual Jewish feminist voices can be identified from the beginning of the modern era (Umansky and Ashton 1992). As a movement, however, Jewish feminist thought emerged in the early 1970s as an attempt to describe and protest the subordination of women within the Jewish tradition. The first feminist works generally agreed on the contours of women's subordination – exclusion from the minyan, exemption from study, women's inability to function as witnesses or to initiate divorce – but different Jewish feminists understood the causes of women's marginalization in different ways. Rachel Adler, in her classic piece "The Jew Who Wasn't There," argued that women are "viewed in Jewish law and practice as peripheral Jews" (1971; reprinted 1983, p. 13).[1] Paula Hyman contended that "the position of women in Judaism rests upon... patriarchal sex-role differentiation and the concomitant disparagement of women" (1972; reprinted 1976, p. 106). Cynthia Ozick, exploring the "woman question" from a variety of angles, insisted that the status of women in Judaism is a sociological and not a theological problem (1979; reprinted 1983). Blu Greenberg essentially agreed, arguing that women's disabilities result from the tradition's unwillingness to apply its "revolutionary ethical teachings" to women (1981, p. 3). I argued that women's specific disabilities are symptoms of a far more basic problem in that the Otherness of women is embedded in the central categories of Jewish thought (1983a).

Although some of these understandings of women's position were complementary, they did not all represent alternative ways of describing the same set of problems. On the contrary, they reflected deep – and continuing – disagreements about just how fundamental women's subordination is to Judaism, and thus how easy or difficult it is to dislodge. Thus, while Paula Hyman wanted to see an end to the sex-role differentiation that is central to Jewish life, Blu Greenberg was willing to accept different roles for men and women so long as those roles were equal (pp. 36f.). While Ozick and Greenberg saw the achievement of equality as essentially a practical problem of getting the tradition to live up to its own best ideals, I saw it as requiring the profound transformation of every area of Jewish thought and practice.

In part, these disagreements reflected denominational divisions, with Orthodox women more sanguine about the possibilities of reform within a traditional framework. But time also brought changes in focus. As, over the last twenty years, women have gained increasing access to public religious roles, they have been brought face to face with the *content* of the tradition and the ways in which it contradicts or is simply irrelevant to women's religious participation (Plaskow 1990b). This has led many Jewish feminists to shift their emphasis from criticizing the legal disabilities of women to examining the exclusion of women's experience from the creation and formulation of tradition. Rachel Adler's work nicely illustrates this change. In "The Jew Who Wasn't There," she implied that empathetic and open legal scholars can find ways to foster women's religious self-actualization within the context of halakhah (1971). But, in an article published twelve years later, she argued that attempts at halakhic change come up against the fact that many of women's deepest concerns are simply non-data for a tradition that has obliterated women's experience (1983, p. 23).

The claim that women's experience is largely invisible in Judaism is echoed in different forms by many feminist thinkers. Feminists have argued that since all (or virtually all) the sources for Jewish theology were composed by and for men, Torah as we have it represents only half the Jewish religious experience (e.g., Umansky 1984; reprinted 1989, p. 194; Plaskow 1990a, p. 1 and passim). Drorah Setel contends that the real conflict between Judaism and feminism does not lie on the plane of specific legal and historical issues but on the deeper level of a "conflict between the feminist value of relationship and the Jewish concept of holiness as separation" (1986, p. 114). Rita Gross, Marcia Falk, and I have pointed out the ways in which the Jewish understanding of God recapitulates and supports women's subordination (Gross 1979; Falk 1987; Plaskow 1983b).

✒ RETHINKING TRADITION ✒

If one accepts this more thoroughgoing critique of tradition, the challenges to Jewish thought are profound. Indeed, feminists are calling for nothing less than the reconceptualization of every aspect of the Jewish religious experience. My book *Standing Again at Sinai* (1990a) is the only work to spell out the challenge of feminism for Jewish thought in a semi-systematic way, but it emerges out of twenty years of communal discussion and writing dealing with many central categories of Jewish religious thinking.

Halakhah

Of the halakhic problems that first drew feminist attention, all remain unsolved within Orthodox Judaism, while the non-Orthodox movements have either resolved or dissolved virtually all of them. This dual reality – on the one hand, the intransigence of the Orthodox rabbinate, on the other, the emergence of new contradictions generated by women's access to religious participation – has led to a deeper analysis of the patriarchal character of halakhah. Rachel Adler's shift from a straightforward call for more sensitive legal decision-making to an examination of the presuppositions of the halakhic system exemplifies this turn to "meta-halachic issues" (1983, p. 24). If Jewish religious life, she asks, rests on the continuing interpretation of a received body of knowledge that excludes the perceptions and concerns of women, on what can women ground their Jewish self-understanding and behavior? (1983, p. 26; 1992, p. 5). The fact that the Mishnah's Order of Women, for example, centers on "the orderly transfer of women and property from one patriarchal domain to another" means that large numbers of questions women might raise about how to function as autonomous religious agents lie completely outside the realm and imagination of normative Jewish sources (1983, p. 24). *This* problem cannot be resolved through a more sensitive application of the rules of halakhah; it requires a new moment of jurisgenesis, a transformation of "the normative universe Jews inhabit" (1992, p. 1). Moreover, since halakhic interpretation as a mode of religious discourse and experience has rested solely in the hands of a male elite, it is not clear whether, given the choice, women would turn to halakhah as a dominant form of religious expression. To presume that the solution to women's subordination will come within the framework of halakhah is to foreclose the question of women's experience before it has begun to be fully explored (Plaskow 1990a, pp. 60–74).

Torah

Such criticisms of halakhah raise powerful questions about the authority of Jewish sources and classical modes of thinking. In this area, as in others, feminism focuses and intensifies the problems for Judaism raised by modernity, especially the attack on traditional forms of authority (Heschel 1983, pp. xxiii-xxv). To the extent that normative texts are silent about women's experience, how can they function as authoritative for contemporary Jewish women?

While no Jewish feminist simply turns her back on Jewish sources, non-Orthodox feminists often characterize normative texts as partial and incomplete. From a feminist perspective, only a portion of the record of the Jewish encounter with God has been passed down through the generations. Jews know how an elite group of men named God, human beings, and the world, but they have yet to recover and imagine women's perceptions of Jewish reality. Before Jewish feminists can transform and transmit Jewish teaching, they must first hear their own voices within the tradition and discover the contours of their own religious experiences (Plaskow 1990a, pp. 25–36; Umansky 1984, p. 194).

The recovery of women's experience is a difficult process that takes place on many levels simultaneously. In part, it is a historiographical task requiring bold new readings of traditional texts, supplemented by studies of archeological evidence and non-normative sources. But it also assumes a process of continuing revelation through which women, in interaction with both traditional sources and each other, "receive" new understandings of themselves and of Jewish stories, practices, and concepts (Umansky 1984, pp. 194–5). Midrash and ritual, because they allow for the interface of tradition and contemporary experience, are important vehicles for Jewish feminist expression. What is important theoretically, however, is that Jewish feminists are defining and accepting the new material emerging from these avenues of exploration as

Torah. Torah in its traditional sense is decentered and placed in a larger context in which the experience of the *whole* Jewish people becomes a basis for legal decision-making and spiritual and theological reflection (Plaskow 1990a, pp. 32–60).

Hierarchy and connection

This expansion of the meaning of Torah poses a challenge to the content of Torah in many different areas. Drorah Setel points out, for example, that the Hebrew word for "holy," *kadosh*, means "separate" or "set apart," with separateness often being understood in dualistic, oppositional, and hierarchical terms (Setel 1986). Thus men and women are not simply distinct from each other, but women are *Other* than men; Israelite worship is not simply different from Canaanite worship, it is "set apart" from Canaanite "whoring after false gods." Feminist thought, on the other hand, has been sharply critical of hierarchical dualisms, particularly the association of groups of human beings – men/women, whites/blacks, Christians/Jews – with oppositional categories such as spiritual/material or sacred/profane.[2] Jewish feminist thought, in seeking to reconcile Jewish and feminist world views, has sought ways to speak about the distinctiveness of Jewish identity, belief, and practice that are not invidious or hierarchical. Thus in terms of Jewish practice, the havdalah ceremony's "paradigmatic statement of hierarchical dualism" has been rewritten by feminists to affirm both distinction and connection (Setel 1986, p. 117; Falk 1986, p. 125). In terms of Jewish theology, I have tried to rethink the central concept of chosenness using a part/whole rather than a hierarchical model. While the notion of chosenness cannot be separated from some claim, however weak, about the privileged nature of Israel's relationship to God, the less dramatic term "distinctness" acknowledges the uniqueness of the Jewish experience but without the connotation of superiority. Rather than locating Jews as the "favored child" in relation to the rest of the human community, it points to the specialness of all human groups as parts of a much larger association of self-differentiated communities (Plaskow 1990a, pp. 96–107).

God

The paradigm of hierarchical dualism within Judaism is the traditional concept of God. Especially as depicted in the liturgy, God is a power outside of and above the world, a king robed in majesty whose sovereignty is absolute and infinite, a merciful but probing father who knows all hearts and judges all souls. Since this God is also consistently imagined as male, male/female hierarchical dualism is correlated with and supported by the overarching dualism of God/world (Plaskow 1990a, pp. 123–34).

Feminist attempts to dislodge this conception of God initially focused on issues of gender. Rita Gross suggested in the 1970s that every quality appropriately attributed to God imaged as male could also be attributed to God imaged as female (1979, p. 173).[3] The pervasiveness of male God-language, she claimed, tells us nothing about the reality of God, but it says a great deal about a Jewish community that perceives men as the normative human beings. Referring to God as "she," she argued, would enable Jews to overcome the idolatrous equation of God and maleness, to speak to God in new ways, and to acknowledge the "becoming of women" as full members of the Jewish community (pp. 171–2). Feminist experiments with God-language that have given concreteness to this plea for new imagery have not simply altered the *gender* of God, however, but have *reconceptualized* God's nature and power in more far-reaching terms. Feminists have emphasized the metaphorical nature of God-language. Calling for the freeing of our symbolic imaginations, they have offered a plethora of new images for God from the female (*shekhinah*, mother, queen), to the conceptual (flow of life), to the natural and gender-neutral (lover, friend, fountain, unseen spark). They have emphasized the immanence of God over transcendence, and God as empowerer rather than as majestic and distant power (Gross 1979, p. 169; Plaskow 1983b and 1990a, chapter 4; Falk 1987).

Underlying this explosion of new images and concepts is a new understanding of monotheism. The dominant Jewish conception of God has identified God's oneness with the worship of a single image of God. For those who hold this view, thinking of God as female seems to threaten monotheism. But feminists have offered an alternative conception, arguing, in Marcia Falk's words, that an "authentic" monotheism is not "a singularity of image but an embracing *unity* of a *multiplicity of images*" (1987, p. 41). Monotheism is not the worship of a finite being projected as infinite but the capacity to find the One in and through the changing forms of the many. It requires us to discover the divine unity in images rich and plentiful enough to reflect the diversity of the human and cosmic communities (Falk 1987, p. 41; Falk 1990; Plaskow 1990a, pp. 150–2).

❧ NEW DIRECTIONS ❧

Since Jewish feminist thought began with a critique of the patriarchal character of Judaism, it chose as its initial constructive topics areas where there seemed to be the greatest conflict between feminism and traditional Jewish thinking. As feminism has developed in depth and scope, however, it offers fresh approaches to many Jewish philosophical and theological issues. When one considers the range of subjects that feminists have addressed, it becomes clear that Jewish feminist thought is not simply thinking about women but *a perspective on the world* (Setel 1985, p. 35) that begins from a commitment to the full humanity of women. As issues of equal access become less pressing, and feminists develop a longer history of reflecting on the content of tradition, the scope of themes receiving feminist attention will only widen further.

Covenant

Up until now, for example, the central Jewish concept of covenant has received relatively little feminist attention, but at least two thinkers have put the topic on the feminist agenda. Heidi Ravven suggests that women's experiences in the family may provide models of covenantal relationship different from those offered by men (1986, pp. 97–8). Since the Bible and the tradition conceptualize the covenant in erotic as well as political terms, women need to find a spiritual-erotic imagery that reflects "female experiences of love and passion." Ravven thinks that Carol Gilligan's delineation of a female ethic of caring in contrast to a male ethic of "rights and obligations" might provide an interesting starting point for a new model of covenant (p. 98). In contrast to Ravven, Laura Levitt uses the feminist critique of patriarchal marriage as a starting point for *criticizing* erotic images of covenant. Given the understanding of marriage in the Jewish tradition as male acquisition and possession of female sexuality, Levitt questions whether the erotic understanding of covenant is salvageable from a feminist perspective – that is, whether it can be disconnected from traditional models of marriage. She argues that while liberal theologians tend to prefer a marital to a contractual model of covenant because the former seems more egalitarian, in fact the liberal marriage contract still supports the subordination of women, and the same inequalities and potential for abuse are built into the Sinaitic covenant (1992).

The problem of evil

Another classical theological problem just beginning to be addressed in feminist work is the problem of evil. While feminist discussions of God-language initially focused on finding images that reflect women's experiences as women, the human problem of evil and suffering demands attention as part of any adequate understanding of the sacred. In line with the emphasis on an inclusive monotheism that I discussed above, Jewish feminists seem to prefer a conception of God that makes room for, and reflects, the ambiguities of reality to one that imagines God as perfectly good and locates evil outside the divine realm (Umansky 1982, pp. 116, 118; Madsen 1989; Plaskow 1990a, pp. 167–8 and 1991). The passage from Isaiah, "I form light and create darkness / I make weal and create woe" (45: 7) is a model for a holistic understanding of God that incorporates both femaleness and maleness and good and evil. Moreover, the Jewish tradition of protest against God that began with Abraham and moves through Elie Wiesel is also attractive to feminists who would rather struggle with and against an ambiguous deity than worship a God who cannot contain the complexities of human existence.

Feminist thought, then, struggles to transform Judaism by incorporating the missing voices of women into all aspects of the Jewish tradition. In doing so, it addresses key issues in Jewish philosophy and theology, seeking to reframe them in ways that both foster women's full incorporation into Jewish life and create a meaningful Judaism for the modern world.

❧ NOTES ❧

1 A number of early feminist articles have been anthologized in books that are much more readily available than the original publications. In such cases, I have given page references to the anthology, while preserving the original date to give a sense of historical development.
2 Christian feminist Rosemary Ruether has articulated this critique clearly in all her work. Jewish feminists have learned it from her and other theorists.
3 The essay was first published in 1979 but was circulating from the beginning of the decade.

❧ BIBLIOGRAPHY ❧

Texts and Studies

Adler, R. (1971) "The Jew Who Wasn't There: *Halakhah* and the Jewish Woman," in *On Being a Jewish Feminist: A Reader*, edited by S. Heschel (New York: Schocken, 1983), pp. 12–18.

—— (1983) " 'I've Had Nothing Yet so I Can't Take More,' " *Moment* 8: 22–6.

—— (1993) "Feminist Folktales of Justice: Robert Cover as a Resource for the Renewal of *Halakha*," *Conservative Judaism* 45: 40–55.

Falk, M. (1986) Respondent to "Feminist Reflections on Separation and Unity in Jewish Theology," *Journal of Feminist Studies in Religion* 2.1: 121–5.

—— (1987) "Notes on Composing New Blessings: Toward a Feminist-Jewish Reconstruction of Prayer," *Journal of Feminist Studies in Religion* 3.1: 39–53.

—— (1990) "Toward a Feminist Jewish Reconstruction of Monotheism," *Tikkun* 4.4: 53–6.

Greenberg, B. (1981) *On Women and Judaism: A View From Tradition* (Philadelphia: Jewish Publication Society).

Gross, R. (1979) "Female God Language in a Jewish Context," in *Womanspirit Rising: A Feminist Reader in Religion*, edited by C. P. Christ and J. Plaskow (San Francisco: Harper & Row), pp. 167–73.

Heschel, S. (1983) "Introduction," in *On Being a Jewish Feminist: A Reader* (New York: Schocken), pp. xiii-xxxvi.

Hyman, P. (1972) "The Other Half: Women in the Jewish Tradition," in *The Jewish Woman: New Perspectives*, edited by E. Koltun (New York: Schocken, 1976), pp. 105–13.

Levitt, L. (1992) "Covenantal Relationships and the Problem of Marriage: Toward a Post-Liberal Jewish Feminist Theology," unpublished paper delivered at the Annual Meeting of the American Academy of Religion, November.

Madsen, C. (1989) " 'If God is God She is Not Nice,' " *Journal of Feminist Studies in Religion* 5.1: 103–5.

Ozick, C. (1979) "Notes toward Finding the Right Question," in *On Being a Feminist: A Reader*, edited by S. Heschel (New York: Schocken, 1983), pp. 120–51.

Plaskow, J. (1983a) "The Right Question is Theological," in *On Being a Jewish Feminist: A Reader*, edited by S. Heschel (New York: Schocken), pp. 223–33.

—— (1983b) "Language, God and Liturgy: A Feminist Perspective," *Response* 44: 3–14.

—— (1990a) *Standing Again at Sinai: Judaism from a Feminist Perspective* (San Francisco: Harper & Row).

—— (1990b) "Beyond Egalitarianism," *Tikkun* 5.6: 79–81.

—— (1991) "Facing the Ambiguity of God," *Tikkun* 6.5: 70–1.

Ravven, H. (1986) "Creating a Jewish Feminist Philosophy," *Anima* 12.2: 96–105.

Setel, D. (1985) "Feminist Insights and the Question of Method," in *Feminist*

Perspectives on Biblical Scholarship, edited by A. Y. Collins (Atlanta: Scholars Press), pp. 35–42.

—— (1986) "Feminist Reflections on Separation and Unity in Jewish Theology," *Journal of Feminist Studies in Religion* 2.1: 113–18.

Umansky, E. (1982) "(Re)Imaging the Divine," *Response* 41–2: 110–19.

—— (1984) "Creating a Jewish Feminist Theology," in *Weaving the Visions: New Patterns in Feminist Spirituality*, edited by J. Plaskow and C. P. Christ (San Francisco: Harper & Row, 1989), pp. 187–98.

Umansky, E. and D. Ashton (eds) (1992) *Four Centuries of Jewish Women's Spirituality: A Sourcebook* (Boston: Beacon).

CHAPTER 39

The future of Jewish philosophy

Oliver Leaman

It is difficult to make any sensible predictions about the future of anything, let alone philosophy, but the fact that something is difficult should not mean that it is not undertaken. It is worth speculating on the future of a subject, since that makes possible reflection on its present state, and how that existing condition might develop in particular directions. Philosophy is perhaps the most obstinate cultural phenomenon to relate to the material conditions of its production, although this may not be such a problem when we are looking at a particular tradition in philosophy. Jewish philosophy essentially uses the ways of working philosophically which are current in its time, and adapts those techniques to a range of specific problems which have a Jewish interest. So in a sense speculating on the future of Jewish philosophy is a subsidiary activity to speculating on the future of philosophy itself, and that would certainly take us a long way from this particular topic. Is it not possible, though, to look at the main lines of work in the recent past, and work out what the leading issues and approaches will be in the future?

One reason why it is difficult to predict the future is that there is no accounting for the appearance of great and creative thinkers who revolutionize the subject. It is very much part of the nature of creativity that it is difficult to work out what is going to happen in the future, since the creative thinker transforms the subject and creates entirely new ways of working. It is certainly true that this is done on the basis of the existing tradition, and it makes sense to talk of creativity only when compared with an existing tradition, yet one cannot use the tradition as a source for prediction of the next creative leap. If one could, this would not be a leap, but very much of a step. When we consider the nature of Jewish philosophy we need to take seriously the impact of modernity on the Jewish world, which results in many philosophers of Jewish origin ignoring what might be called specifically Jewish philosophy. Two of the major thinkers of the twentieth century, Ludwig Wittgenstein and Jacques Derrida, albeit working within very different traditions, are of Jewish origin, yet they did not work within what might be called Jewish philosophy. A good example of the contrast between philosophy and Jewish philosophy is provided in the case of Emmanuel Levinas, whose early work was entirely within what might be called pure philosophy, and whose later work is determinedly and self-consciously part of Jewish philosophy.

If there can be said to be a central issue which occurs in the Jewish philosophy of the twentieth century it is precisely this discussion of how Jewish philosophers are to react to modernity, to the relationship of Jews with the wider cultural and social community of which they are a part. This issue has arisen over the last few centuries, as Jews have progressively become more and more integrated within their local societies. Here we need to make some distinctions between different Jewish communities, and it is worth acknowledging that there are significant numbers of Jews living in non-Jewish communities yet doing all they can to ignore their surroundings. They pursue the traditional ways of learning and study, and maintain religious practices which seek to preserve past forms of worship. For them there is no need to change their ways of understanding the theoretical bases of what they are doing, since the existing forms of theoretical inquiry are acceptable. That is not to suggest that they do not incorporate within those forms new ways of operating. We have seen how quite recently a figure like Rav Soloveitchik manages to combine Orthodoxy with ideas from secular philosophy, and this is not in itself a new development. Jews intent on pursuing a traditional lifestyle have continued throughout history to use the contemporary culture of the gentile world to help reconstruct that sort of lifestyle.

One might expect that Orthodox communities would do all in their power to reject modernity, and to reject the theoretical systems which go along with it. Of course, some do try, yet in a sense even they fail, since in turning their back on a system of thought, one is irretrievably influenced by it, even just through adopting a strategy to try to avoid it. So even those Jews who are not prepared to question the idea of *Torah min Ha-Shamayim* are obliged to explain how that idea fits in with secular understandings of the world, since those understandings are all around them in their everyday lives. This point becomes far more clear when we look at Jewish communities which live very much as parts of the gentile world, wearing the same clothes, speaking the same language, doing the same work and having similar aspirations. Rosenzweig described this situation nicely at the start of the twentieth century when considering conversion to Christianity. He points out that Jews are already really part of Christian society, so that in a sense they are already Christians in all but name. They seem to persist stubbornly in a distinctness which their lifestyle denies. Would it not be more authentic, he suggests, to throw in the towel and take the step of assimilating completely with the sort of society of which one is so surely a part?

We know now, as he did not, that gentile society was shortly to throw off its Jews in Germany and Europe generally, and that assimilation was no escape for Jews seeking to avoid destruction. Yet the questions raised by assimilation at the end of the twentieth century are the same as they were at the beginning, and the experience of the Holocaust does not appear to have changed the nature of the problem. In many parts of the world Jews live valued and satisfying lives as parts of the general community, while within the State of Israel they live as normal citizens of a specifically Jewish state. Indeed, some would argue that in the State of Israel the normal state of affairs has been inverted, so that it is the non-Jewish minorities who have problems of identity in pursuing their sense of who they are by contrast with the dominance of Jewish culture and the Hebrew language! If Israel comes to live in relative peace with its neighbors, the question of assimilation will arise yet again, since there will be a small Jewish state in the middle of a large Arab and Persian world. The creators of Zionism saw Israel as far more than just another Levantine state, yet this is a status which might appear to be very desirable by comparison with the constant history of strife which has existed in the Middle East in the twentieth century.

So the question of whether to assimilate might arise both nationally (in Israel) and in the Diaspora. In an increasingly secular world, it is only the embattled nature of the State of Israel which provides a distinctive status to many Jews in the Diaspora, for whom Zionism has replaced Judaism as the main source of their cultural and ethnic identity. Peace would raise important issues of identity both for Israelis and for Jews worldwide. Of course, this would not be an issue for those Jews with a strong commitment to their religion, but it may be that there will be a growing proportion of Jews who find their religion an anachronism, who wonder what it means when they can find no personal faith to cohere with the ethnic differentiation that separates them from the rest of the population of their countries. When being Jewish is an affiliation with no clear advantages or no obvious point to it, the question as to whether it has any meaning at all will arise in the future, as it has arisen throughout the recent past and arises today.

It might be argued that in the absence of any strong religious faith, there *is* no point in raising the issue of whether one should remain Jewish. It is like finding oneself a member of a tennis club, yet without any interest in tennis. Of course, there could be good reasons for staying in the tennis club apart from the tennis. It might be a good social community, it might have other attractions, but these features might be acquired in better and more direct ways by joining a different sort of club. If one is a non-player in a tennis club, it looks as though one is pretending to a status which one does not really deserve. This is why Rosenzweig criticized, for a period, the distinctiveness of Jewish life in a Christian society. If one is not Jewish in anything but a nominal sense, then it seems more honest to abandon the cultural affiliation just as one has abandoned the religious commitment. If he is right that a decision either way has to be taken here, that one has to decide to be a Jew or not, it is interesting to speculate what sorts of arguments could be produced to settle the issue, given stronger pressures for assimilation. Of course, the question might not arise, since as Sartre suggested, one is a Jew often as a result of being regarded as a Jew by others, and this ethnic label might be harder to discard than one imagines, but the assumption here is that a level of assimilation may occur which makes being Jewish for many Jews a puzzling and vacuous description.

Another important issue could well be the nature of Jewish philosophy itself. As readers of this volume will by now no doubt have discovered, if they did not already know it, the nature of Jewish philosophy is itself a controversial issue in Jewish philosophy. Is Jewish philosophy merely the application of general philosophical techniques to specifically Jewish issues? Or is it a separate type of philosophy which operates in tandem with those general techniques, offering a unique way of settling philosophical issues on the basis of its own rules? There are problems with accepting either proposal. This is not an issue which affects only Jewish philosophy, but has been much discussed in relationship to Christian and Islamic philosophy. How will this discussion move into the future? One development which is certainly called for is a clarification of the nature of Jewish philosophy. At the moment a lot of what goes under this description is rather vague in structure. There is no clear differentiation between the religious and the philosophical parts of the discussion. Why is this a problem? It is a problem because it is very unclear what the nature of the discussion actually is when there is a constant mingling of different theoretical approaches. Philosophical argument works to different rules as compared, say, with theology, and theology works to different rules as compared with Midrash, or Jewish history. Yet a good deal of what is called Jewish philosophy mixes up these different techniques, so that one is confronted with a conceptual mixture which provides far too rich a fuel for the engine of argument.

This might seem a surprising suggestion, since is it not precisely the combination of philosophy with aspects of Jewish culture which one would expect to find in Jewish philosophy? Otherwise in what sense is it Jewish? It is certainly true that it would be very surprising if Jewish philosophers did not discuss aspects of specifically Jewish culture in their work, but what is important is how they do it. In some ways the subject has declined in depth since the Middle Ages, since then there was a clear differentiation of the different forms of expression, so that it was clear that Talmud had a different purpose and rules from, say, a type of logical analysis. This did not mean that one could not use logic to explicate Talmud – certainly this was done, and there is no reason why it should not be done – but there was an attempt to be clear about the different rules of thought which are exemplified by the different forms of theory as represented by, say, Talmud and logic. There was a general theory which explained how these different forms of thought fitted in with each other, and it was argued that it is very important that we are clear on what is going on in an example of analysis before we compare it with an example from a different form of analysis. Thinkers like Maimonides and Abraham ibn Ezra, for example, spend a good deal of time in their writings explaining how the various forms of theory in Judaism relate to each other, and how they all relate to philosophy. This has the advantage of explaining to the reader precisely what is going on, or what is supposed to be going on, in their arguments. Much of contemporary Jewish philosophy has abandoned this tradition of seeking clarification of the methodology which is presupposed by the activity itself, and it shows.

In what ways does this disinclination to examine the form of analysis which one is using become evident? Let us take as an example much of the writing on the Holocaust, which takes the form of what an Aristotelian would call rhetoric. How does this form of writing go on? There is often a bit of description of the horrors of the Holocaust, one or two biblical passages slung in, a little talmudic or midrashic commentary, some references perhaps to more recent events, and a conclusion which often involves adopting some emotional attitude to suffering, and recommending that attitude as the conclusion of a process of reasoning in Jewish philosophy. What is confusing about this form of expression is that it is far from clear how one derives the conclusion, in the sense that the logical processes which are in operation are mysterious. They often bear more relationship to a sermon in a synagogue than they do to a piece of argumentation. There is nothing wrong with this, of course, since there is an important role for the sort of discourse which ministers produce in synagogues. Much of this discourse is designed to get the congregation to act in particular ways, and the skillful speaker will know how to address the congregation in ways which will be effective. This form of expression is hardly appropriate for anything which goes under the description of philosophy, though, since its argumentative value may be rather slight.

We do need to make a sharp distinction between the emotional value of a discourse, and the validity of an argument. The trouble with a lot of what goes on as though it were Jewish philosophy is that it has far too much rhetorical resonance in it, and this works often in opposition to its logical force. There are problems even when discussing topics which have a weaker emotional force, perhaps those which relate to general theoretical approaches to issues such as justice or equality within the Jewish tradition. Writers are often highly selective in their use of particular halakhic passages, which enables them to defend a certain view of halakhah as *the* Jewish halakhic view, whereas in fact it is only one of several. When one discusses halakhah it is certainly appropriate to consider a range of solutions to a particular problem, and then argue that despite a disparity of view, a certain conclusion may be plausibly taken to be the majority view, or the view which has the strongest arguments on its side. Within halakhah, and within a particular halakhic tradition, there are clear rules as to how to go on here, since the names and types of authorities are clear, and the ways in which one can adjudicate between different approaches is laid down within the tradition. This is not to suggest that only one such conclusion will be acceptable as a result of such a process of argument, since this is far from the case. But there are secure ways of reaching consensus on how to approach such issues, and although disputants may disagree on which conclusion represents the best view, within the context of the tradition, they can all agree on the sources to be examined and the techniques to be used in such a process. Jewish philosophers, by contrast, will often take a highly selective range of quotations from relevant texts which they will then argue are representative of the tradition as a whole, and which they then use in combination with their selection of philosophical techniques to argue to a conclusion which is *the* Jewish conclusion, and this introduces a looseness and implausibility in the analysis which reduces its value considerably.

Does this mean that it is never appropriate to take a religious text, say a talmudic passage, and then examine it using a particular philosophical technique? This would be an extraordinary claim to make, and is far from the point here. What is methodologically suspect is taking such a text, examining it philosophically, and then producing some conclusion which claims to represent *the* Jewish position on the topic at issue. Jewish philosophers should demonstrate at least as great respect for the variety of interpretations of religious texts as do halakhists, talmudists, historians, and so on. There is a particular danger in pursuing philosophy in that philosophers think, quite rightly, that they are using the most abstract forms of argument which are capable of producing absolutely valid conclusions, provided that their premises are appropriately organized. But this proviso is important, and one should beware of using a few religious premises and then deriving a conclusion which is representative of the religion as a whole. That conclusion may well be representative of an aspect of the religion, but cannot be taken to be generally representative of the religion as a whole without forcing a complex and indeterminate set of ideas into a conceptual straitjacket from which it will always struggle to escape.

This is not only a problem for Jewish philosophy, nor even for religious philosophy, but is a problem for any form of philosophy which is going to set out to analyze a wide range of statements from an entirely different form of expression. It is a problem for any sort of applied philosophy which has to cope with new facts and problems, and which then tries to fit them within some theoretical perspective. One of the reasons why the normally sober processes of Jewish philosophy have become somewhat derailed in the twentieth century is the emotional impact of major events such as the Holocaust and the creation of the State of Israel. It is very difficult to step back from such events and examine them dispassionately, since we are still too close to them for this to be possible. Besides, they exist within a political context which surely influences what we say about them philosophically. For example, a lot of effort is expended by some Jewish philosophers in arguing that the Holocaust is a unique event, and not just an evil event which differs from others solely in its scale. These philosophers give the Holocaust a metaphysical status which, they say, distinguishes it from what happened to the Jewish people in the past and from disasters which destroyed other ethnic communities in the past and present. Now, it is difficult to understand this as an argument unless one is aware of the fact that there are political groups at large which deny the fact and size of the Holocaust, and which seek to diminish the significance of Jewish suffering during that period. The Holocaust also plays a role in the justification for the creation of the State of Israel and the consequent displacement of the Arabs from the state, so it is felt to be important that its uniqueness is emphasized in order to provide a rationale for actions of which one might otherwise be expected to disapprove. It is very difficult for Jewish philosophers to stand back from these major events and disregard the political atmosphere which surrounds them, since those philosophers are themselves breathing the atmosphere and react emotionally to those events. None the less, it must be admitted that this is unlikely to be a fruitful context for the production of clear and analytical thought which really throws light on the nature of these events. Much of the work on the Holocaust brings this out nicely. What we find here is not so much Jewish philosophy, but varied reflections on Jewish experience which is still too shocked by the disaster to be able to come to terms with it philosophically. This is understandable, but it does not make for very valuable philosophy.

This is certainly not to suggest that the philosopher has to be abstracted from the situation which he or she is discussing. On the contrary, it is important to be able to relate emotionally to many issues and problems in order to understand them. That is, unless one can grasp from an experiential point of view what it would be like to be in a particular situation, one does not understand what that situation is, and so one's analysis of it is essentially limited and restricted. This is not true of all issues, of course, but there are some where it is. We might look here at the Passover festival, where Jews are told that they should think of themselves as though they themselves had left Egypt, so that the celebration is not just a commemoration of something which happened to other people in a distant past. Jews who could not do this, who just could not carry out the exercise in empathy here would be able to think rationally about aspects of the festival, and they would be able, for example, to explore the notion of liberation. Yet part of what it means to be free is to experience freedom, to contrast one's present position with that of the past, and one of the reasons why freedom is important for human beings lies in the fact that its possession can be a wonderful experience. The detached observer can only understand this from observing people's behavior, not through his or her own experience, and as a result would miss something of the significance of the concept of freedom. On the other hand, it would probably be difficult to carry out a philosophical analysis of the concept of freedom while its experience is still fresh in the mind. It would be difficult to become sufficiently detached to relate it to other concepts and experiences, and place it within some sort of wider context. This is very much the position today of people writing about the Holocaust and the State of Israel. They are often responding to an emotional agenda which precludes the sort of detachment such philosophical analysis requires, whereas in the future it should be possible both to carry out such analysis and also think back to the experiences which are so important a part of those events.

How will the history of Jewish philosophy be understood in the future? It is possible that thinkers will be more ambitious about what Jewish philosophy can achieve. Different Jewish philosophers often think that their views on how to resolve particular philosophical difficulties are better than opposing views, and they tend to think that there exists such a thing as progress in philosophy, in the sense that our concepts become progressively more refined and we approach nearer to the truth. On the other hand, there are plenty of thinkers in this area who take a more guarded attitude to the idea of progress in philosophy, and they see their task as essentially historical, as one of explaining and discussing the various solutions which have been produced at different times to persisting philosophical problems, while not necessarily making any value-judgment as to which solution is preferable to another. It has to be said that this sort of attitude is not uncommon given the positioning of most Jewish philosophy not in philosophy departments, but in departments primarily concerned with Semitic studies, Near Eastern languages and cultures, religious studies, and, of course, Jewish studies. This means that there is often a scholarly concern with the editing of texts, the translation and collection of relevant materials, and the relating of particular texts to their antecedents. All this work is very important and valuable, and the study of Jewish philosophy would be impossible without it, yet it is worth noting that it gives the subject the flavor more of the history of ideas or the history of philosophy than of philosophy itself.

Will writers in the future be happy to continue along the same path? Some certainly will, and it is not unlikely that very similar work will take place in the future as has gone on in the past, and is going on today. On the other hand, it is also not unlikely that the very real issue of assimilation will induce writers on Jewish philosophy to take a more personal interest in their subject, and they will ask themselves questions about the relevance of what they are doing for their lives as Jews. It will not be enough to conclude that they are analyzing key concepts of Jewish thought, even though objectively this is indeed what they are doing. The issue will be how far these concepts become progressively refined and better understood as a result of their investigations. A dilemma will arise as a result of such a question, and the dilemma is that it often looks as though despite the efforts of writers on Jewish philosophy, there is not much in the way of progress here. Do we really today understand more what it means to regulate our lives in accordance with halakhah than, say, Maimonides did? Do we know more about how to reconcile a good and omnipotent God with innocent suffering than Job did? How far has our understanding of the links between our world and God improved on the model produced by Philo? Is our understanding of what it means to be a good person superior to that outlined in the Torah?

We need to distinguish here between a variety of theoretical treatments which takes place over time, and which brings out more and different features of familiar problems, and a progression in understanding the problem. We certainly tend to see problems in Jewish philosophy somewhat differently from our predecessors, since we are operating in a very different conceptual world, yet they might still wonder whether there was much difference in our treatment of the issue apart from a changed way of reproducing it. Perhaps this is unduly pessimistic, but there does not seem to have been much progress in the treatment of the sorts of problems which constitute the main content of Jewish philosophy. One might expect that over a period of time prolonged investigation of a particular topic would result in ever-increasing conceptual clarification, yet this does not seem to have come about. On the other hand, it could be that this view of how concepts becomes clarified as a result of sustained investigation relies too much on a comparison with natural science, where one expects that prolonged investigation of a problem will result, eventually, in its solution. There is no reason to think that philosophy is like that, and there probably is little reason to think that natural science is like that either. Yet this leaves us with the apparent paradox that Jewish philosophers are involved in an enterprise which does not come to any final result.

If this is true now, then it is likely to be true in the future. There is no reason to think that there will suddenly be a vast conceptual breakthrough which will allow us to solve philosophical problems which have defied resolution for thousands of years. Does this not mean that the whole enterprise is meaningless? If there is no clear criterion of progress here, then what is the point of the whole enter-prise? It may have an extrinsic point, of course, to give some people jobs and other people something interesting to read, but these seem rather weak as aims of the project of Jewish philosophy as a whole. We can certainly appreciate why an aesthetic enterprise need not come to an end, since we have here a variety of ways of representing feelings and facts which can be expected to change over time to reflect changing historical and cultural factors, and which are by no means any worse for that. It would be difficult to argue that there is no longer any point in writing poems about roses, since there have been lots of such poems over the years, and they do not seem to be getting anywhere. Jewish philosophy cannot be compared with poetry, though, since it is not the aim of Jewish philosophy to present gracefully constructed arguments and skillful collections of bons mots as an end in itself, although Jewish philosophy may on occasion contain these literary forms. The point of Jewish philosophy is to get close to the truth concerning the persistent conceptual problems which have been discussed within the subject since the time that the Torah was given to the Jewish people. If it has to limit itself to recounting a history of possible solutions, none of which is compelling, we shall inevitably have to conclude that we are not really dealing here with philosophy but just with the history of ideas.

If the argument here is successful, then is it not just too successful, in that it implies that *all* philosophy, and not just Jewish philosophy, is an interminable representation of unsatisfactory solutions which vary over time only by virtue of the different ways in which a number of points are made? This would be a pessimistic conclusion to be forced to adopt, and there is no necessity to go along with it. We have to remember that Jewish philosophy is limited only to certain areas of philosophy, primarily ethics, political philosophy, metaphysics, philosophy of religion and jurisprudence, whereas philosophy as a whole contains subdivisions such as epistemology and logic, for example, where it may be more sensible to talk of progress being made over time. What will be required if there is to be progress in Jewish philosophy is a systematic study of Judaism as a whole, and the linking of that study to philosophy. At the moment this is rarely undertaken, since it is such a major task. And once one thinks about it, it is quite evident that there is no prospect of any final and complete success, since the most important question which has yet to be resolved concerns the nature of Judaism itself.

There is not just one notion of Judaism, in just the same way that there is not just one definition of who is a Jew. Given this fact, it is hardly surprising that there is never going to be an all-encompassing Jewish philosophy. What we have to acknowledge, and respect, is that different Jews have different attitudes to their religion, and to the forms of Judaism which make sense to them. This is far from being an entirely logical issue, but is often affected by one's emotional relationship to the sort of religion which resonates with one's personality. This accounts for the varying nature of the subject, since it is obvious that in different contexts different forms of religion will be felt to be appropriate by different thinkers. In the future we might expect that greater significance will be applied to this notion of what it is in religion which accords with what we expect to find, what we think we need, in other words, a reassertion of the significance of subjectivity. There is a tendency to think of philosophy as primarily an objective and logical form of inquiry, and this is certainly appropriate, yet it is also true that when philosophy starts to examine that which forms a part of the emotional and personal life of individuals, it has to respond to those aspects of human life. It can seek to reject them as not proper objects of philosophical study, but it does so at its peril, since the result is a denuded analysis of religion, a description which often omits the flavor of the activity while trying to preserve its essence. Yet the flavor is part of the essence, and often the most significant part of the essence for practitioners.

One of the main novel developments in the last two centuries has been a reassertion of subjectivity as a significant philosophical concept. This change was signaled by Nietzsche and Kierkegaard, and strongly taken up by Rosenzweig and Buber. It plays an important role as a corrective to the long tradition of philosophy which emphasizes the objective. It is vital to have some grasp of the role of subjectivity in philosophy if one is going to examine religion, since the nexus of ideas connected to faith and the religious lifestyle are strongly bound together by the felt experience of the believer.

We might expect that in the future the analysis of the subjective will proceed rapidly until it achieves some sort of balance with the existing work on the objective aspects of Judaism, and out of the synthesis of these two crucial categories a new and valuable perspective on the religion will result. It may be that this is not really going to take place. After all, when a millennium comes to an end there tends to be an increase of interest in the spiritual and emotional aspects of human life, and, although the millennium is an entirely Christian date, there is little doubt that most Jews will be affected by the general cultural interests of the communities in which they live. It is easy to laugh at the confused and confusing claims of those interested in personal growth, mysticism, and Eastern religion, yet their claims are a reaction to what they see, quite rightly, as an absence of spirituality in everyday life. Once this interest in spirituality is connected to the tradition of analytical Jewish philosophy, one might with some confidence expect some very fruitful results.

So there is an exciting prospect for the future of Jewish philosophy. Increasing pressures for assimilation will lead thinkers to reassess constantly their precise relationship with Judaism, what it means for them both emotionally and rationally to be Jewish. Now that philosophers are discussing seriously what the significance of subjectivity is, it will be possible to discuss in some depth how we are to assess the notion of subjectivity, and how to differentiate between a variety of emotional and personal attitudes to one's faith. Combined with this debate will be the tradition of Jewish philosophy as it has reached us today, dealing as it does with the analyses of the main concepts which arise from a logical approach to Judaism. This all constitutes very rich material which could well result in a future development of Jewish philosophy which will take it in a novel and satisfying direction.

✀ BIBLIOGRAPHY ✀

Akhtar, S. (1995) "The Possibility of a Philosophy of Islam," in *The History of Islamic Philosophy* edited by S. H. Nasr and O. Leaman (London: Routledge), pp. 1162–9.

Leaman, O. (1995a) "The Future of Philosophy," *Futures* 27.1: 81–90.

——(1995b) "Introduction" and "Back to the Bible," in *Evil and Suffering in Jewish Philosophy* (Cambridge: Cambridge University Press), pp. 1–18, 220–50.

—— (1995c) "Introduction," in *The History of Islamic Philosophy*, edited by S. H. Nasr and O. Leaman (London: Routledge), pp. 1–10.

—— (1995d) "Is a Jewish Practical Philosophy Possible?," in *Commandment and Community: New Essays in Jewish Legal and Political Philosophy*, edited by D. Frank (Albany: State University of New York Press), pp. 55–68.

Index of names

Index of terms

active intellect 208, 213, 263, 480
adam (man) 537
'*adl* (divine justice) 118
aggadah (speculative commentaries) 64, 73, 212, 296
ahl al-'adl wa-'l-tawḥīd (the people of justice and unity) 118
ajal (predetermined span of life) 133
alchemy 211, 530
allegory/allegorical method 532–4; in Ebreo and Maimonides 523; in Philo 50; in Plato 217, 275, 278
alul (effect) 506
amānāt (beliefs) 130
'*āmma* (masses) 121, 130
amoraic period, *amoraim* (rabbinic authorities) 40, 234, 457
'*amr* (divine word) 215
angels 213, 215, 233, 249, 255–6, 265, 392; and mysticism 460–1
anthropology 30, 450
anthropomorphism 118, 131, 269, 405, 466; and conception of God 473–4
anti-rationalists 207
anti-semitism 625, 648, 753, 766, 777–8
anti-Zionism 6
Aqedah (binding of Isaac) 17–18, 387–8
Arabic 96, 97, 98, 116, 124, 126, 127, 130, 150, 151, 159, 163, 164, 167, 350; and logic 505; and Maimonides 250, 277, 297, 300, 303, 305; and philosophy 578; rhyme and meter 189, 229; and science 530; song and rhetoric 188; in Spain 313, 420, 422–3

'*arayot* (illicit sexual relationships) 456
archai (first principles) 62
arithmetic 160
asceticism 208, 274
aṣlaḥ (absolute benevolence) 119
asman (gross) 206
assimilation 4, 837, 897
astrology 307, 368, 371, 508
astronomy 160, 164, 233; and Aristotle 231, 233, 532; and Gersonides 379f.; and Marranos 597; Ptolemaic 532; and Renaissance 527–8
'*atarah* (crown) 470
atheism 662
atomism 90, 119, 124, 126, 128, 130–2, 228, 231, 239
'*atzmut* (essence) 477, 527, 533
'*avodah* (work) 699–700

ba'alei ha-elohut (theologians) 164
baḥth (inquiry/search) 121
bara' (to create) 261
bareku (praise) 194
bāri' (creator) 277
bāṭin (esoteric) 194
bechirah (choice) 235, 366
bi-lā kayf (without (asking) how) 123–4
Bildung (culture) 668–9
binah/tevunah (prudence) 541
binyan 'elohi (divine edifice) 473
bitz'ua (arbitration) 75
blasphemy 21, 23, 79

Canaanite discourse 875, 889
canonical tradition 123

matter 153, 158; and God 171; *see also* *chomer ha-olam*

mechitzah/masakh mavdil (partition or dividing barrier) 538

medicine 296, 530, 597, 607

medieval philosophy 83–91, 149–73; Aristotle's influence on 228–39; Maimonides' influence on 504–15; and politics 102–5

medinah mekubbetzet (associated state) 429

medini (political) 429

mefursamot (self-evident truths) 168, 426

mequbalot (tradition) 168

merkavah (chariot) 455f., 481; and mysticism 458, 459, 464, 466

messiah 171, 544

messianism 551, 585

metaphysics 13, 151, 264, 272, 353, 358, 530; of Aristotle 14; and Halevi 213; and identification with theology 505; and Maimonides 249; and transcendence over ethics 72

metriopatheia (moderation of emotions) 49

microcosm/macrocosm 158, 167

Middle Ages 578; *see* chapter 5

middot (character traits) 540

miracles 14, 120–1, 268, 338–40, 343–4, 392–5

mishpat (justice) 75, 724

mistabra (rational) 78

mithavah (generated) 537

mitpalsefim (extremists) 312

mitzvah (commandment) 75, 395–6, 542, 548, 724, 727, 807, 864, 867

modernism 8

monasticism 519

money-lending 296, 307, 512

monism 150, 198; and determinism 627; and Spinoza 619

monotheism 4, 15, 94, 98, 198, 200, 582, 828, 890

Mosaic laws 7, 41, 47, 133, 340, 614, 623, 631, 671, 676

motion 257

murgashot (sense perceptions) 168

mushpa'at (infused) 537

music 160; and Zunz 708

musqalot (first principles/axioms) 168

mutakallimūn (theologians) 115, 121, 228, 335–6, 340

Mu'tazilite theology 117–23, 126–8, 228, 270

muwashshah (literary form) 190

mysticism 5–6, 53–4, 100, 450–83; and Christianity 483; and Moses Cordovero 477, 479, 482; and Shabbetai Donnolo 466, 467; and Judah Halevi 418, 423, 426, 428; and Abraham ibn Ezra 351, 466, 467; Islamic 458, 483; in Philo 53–4; and Gershom Scholem 452–3, 455, 459, 460, 470, 482; and Sufism 199; *see also* Avicenna; kabbalah; Philo; and chapter 19

mythology 524

nasi (prince) 164, 310; *see also* Bar Chiyya

nationalism 761–73, 780–3; *see* chapters 31 and 32

natural law 687–98; and Hobbes 688; and Hume 688; and Kant 688; and Stoics 423

natural sciences 44, 530; and Zunz 708

nature (*teva'*) 42, 45, 52, 62, 119, 163, 165, 343, 364, 640, 691, 842–3; and law of 393; as morally neutral 863; and Spinoza 616–17

naw'iyya (specificity) 153

nazar (rationalistic speculation) 121

Nazism 762, 822, 860, 864

nefesh (life/soul) 465

nefesh chokhmah (rational soul) 169

nefesh klallit (universal soul) 163

neo-Kantianism 637–9, 641, 786–96, 824–8, 831; *see* chapter 33

neo-Orthodox theology 828

Neoplatonism 5, 88, 90, 91, 100, 116, 198, 199–200, 213, 215, 216, 228, 252, 453, 466, 515, 516, 533, 579, 580; and Aristotelianism 117, 125, 197, 214, 524–5; and Crescas 171; and Gersonides 171; and Abraham ibn